The colour photographs of the Holy Land reproduced in
this Bible were specially taken by Alister Duncan.

JERUSALEM FROM MT. OF OLIVES

THE BIBLE READER'S
ENCYCLOPAEDIA
AND
CONCORDANCE

BASED ON
THE BIBLE READER'S MANUAL
BY
REV. C. H. WRIGHT, D.D.

UNDER ONE ALPHABETICAL ARRANGEMENT

COMPRISING

A COMPLETE CONCORDANCE TO THE BIBLE: AN INDEX TO PERSONS, PLACES, AND SUBJECTS; CHRONOLOGY OF THE BIBLE; A GEOGRAPHICAL DICTIONARY OF THE BIBLE; A DICTIONARY OF BIBLICAL CUSTOMS, ANTIQUITIES, ANIMALS AND PLANTS; THE GEOLOGY AND MINERALOGY OF THE BIBLE; A GLOSSARY OF ARCHAIC, OBSOLETE AND OBSCURE WORDS, A SUMMARY OF THE BOOKS OF THE BIBLE; HARMONY OF THE GOSPELS; MIRACLES AND PARABLES OF THE BIBLE; HEBREW FESTIVALS, AND MANY OTHER IMPORTANT AIDS TO THE STUDY OF THE BIBLE.

REVISED EDITION
1977

LONDON AND NEW YORK
COLLINS' CLEAR-TYPE PRESS
GLASGOW TORONTO SYDNEY AUCKLAND

TABLE OF SIGNS USED IN THIS BOOK

Every effort has been made that the signs used in this book should be as few and simple as possible.

The words of which the pronunciation is marked are divided into syllables by short hyphens (-). The syllable on which most stress is to be laid in reading is marked ('). In compound names two accents are often introduced. The longer hyphen (–) indicates the division into parts of compound names so far as it is noted in the Authorized Version.

ä	*as in*	ah, arm, father.
ă	„	abet, hat, dilemma.
ā	„	tame.
â	„	fare.
ạ	„	call.
ĕ	„	met, her, second.
ē	„	mete.
ĕ	=	a *in* tame.
ī	*as in*	fine.
ĭ	„	him, fir, plentiful.
î	„	machine.
ị	„	peculiar.
ō	„	alone.
ŏ	„	on, protect.
ô	„	nor.
ọ	„	son.
ū	„	tune.
û	„	rude.
ŭ	„	us.
ù	„	turner.
ȳ	„	lyre.

ў	*as in*	typical, fully.
āā	=	a *of* am.
âậ	=	a *of* fare.
ǣ / āē	} *as in*	mediæval.
âı	„	aisle.
aị	„	hail.
āō	=	o *of* alone.
aû	*as in*	maul.
ēĕ	„	heed.
êı	=	i *of* fine.
êû	*as in*	neuter.
c̄w̄	„	lewd.
ôı	„	oil.
ç	„	celestial.
ch	„	character.
c̄ı	„	delicious.
g̃	„	giant.
ṡ	„	his.
s̄ı	„	adhesion.
Th	„	Thomas.
t̄ı	„	attraction.

H. A. REDPATH, M.A.

Printed in Great Britain

PREFACE

BY THE

Rev. W. M. CLOW, D.D.

Principal-Emeritus of the United Free Church College, Glasgow.

A vast literature has been created because of the deeply-felt necessity of inter-preting the message, and understanding the spirit, of the Bible. This has involved inquiry into the character of its writers, the sources of their knowledge and the conditions under which they lived and, as important, has been the value of an understanding of their environment, and of the influences at work upon their personalities. Of even greater service has been explanations of the terms they used, and of their references to the customs, rites and observances of their social and religious life. There has been therefore, an urgent demand for explana-tory and enlightening notes on the Bible's distinctive terms, its traditions, its dynamic movements and its historic personages. The scholars who have devoted their lives to these studies on the Scriptures have enriched the moral and intellectual wealth of humanity.

But there are needs which these masters of learning have not kept in mind. Their intent regard for the issues which allure the critic and the grammarian and the use of academic language has sealed their writings to many earnest readers. This Bible Encyclopædia has been prepared to meet the needs of such readers. It will be a guide and interpreter to the devout reader of the Bible, to the members of that great company who give eager service in the teaching of the young, and to the preacher whose hours are filled with the exacting duties of his ministry. It will fulfil the purpose of a Bible Dictionary, with this vital difference, that while the Dictionary yields its stores of knowledge after only an assiduous reading, this volume will set it, in a wisely condensed statement, on a single page. Above all, there has been a regard for simplicity and explicitness in all references, and a watchful attention to accuracy in citations, expressed in language drawn from the well of undefiled English.

This Bible Encyclopædia has been compiled by students of theology who have also given full proof of their attainments in its various departments. A most practical feature is to be found in the order and arrangement, which is entirely alphabetical. There is required, therefore, only a single reference to the word, or the name, or the observance, to find that the requisite information has been included on a single page. Another noteworthy feature is the care in verifying citations, and historical allusions, with a constant attention to the chronology of the events of both the Old and the New Testaments. An endeavour has been made to be brief in regard to the less important topics, with a larger liberty towards those of supreme interest and of greater difficulty. There will be found a much fuller reference together with the inclusion of a larger number of subjects, than in similar publications.

Our knowledge of the Holy Land and its surrounding races has been greatly increased in recent years. There has been a more definite and detailed study of the customs and ideals of their peoples, and there has been given to the world many books of travel containing appreciative descriptions of life in Bible lands. As a consequence this volume has been enriched with a wealth of pictures and portraits which yield their message at a single glance. The abundant maps will be found to be clear, fully detailed, and inclusive of the lands alluded to in the Scriptures.

THE BIBLE READER'S
ENCYCLOPAEDIA AND CONCORDANCE

A

Aaron (ā-rŏn) [enlightened], brother of Moses, the first High Priest.
appointed to assist Moses, Ex. 4 : 14, 16, 27.
with Moses before Pharaoh, Ex. 5 : 1.
his rod becomes a serpent, Ex. 7 : 10.
changes the waters into blood, Ex. 7 : 20.
causes the plagues of frogs, lice, flies, Ex. 8 : 5, 17, 24; of boils, Ex. 9 : 10.
along with Hur holds up Moses' hands, Ex. 17 : 12.
set apart for the priest's office, Ex. 28.
his sin in making the golden calf, Ex. 32.
spared at Moses' intercession, Deut. 9 : 20.
consecration, Ex. 29; Lev. 8.
his duties, to offer sacrifice, Ex. 30 : 7; Lev. 9.
his sons (Nadab and Abihu) offer strange fire and die, Lev. 10 : 1; Num. 3 : 4.
not to drink wine when going into the tabernacle, Lev. 10 : 9.
his sons (Eleazar and Ithamar) censured by Moses, Lev. 10 : 16.
his sedition against Moses, Num. 12.
spoken against by Korah, Num. 16 : 3.
makes atonement, and the plague is stayed, Num. 16 : 46-48.
his rod buds, Num. 17 : 8.
excluded from the promised land, Num. 20:12.
dies on Mount Hor, Num. 20 : 28.
his descendants, 1 Chr. 6 : 49.
chosen by God, Ps. 105 : 26; Heb. 5 : 4.
his priesthood inferior to Christ's, Heb. 5 : 7.
See Ps. 77 : 20; 99 : 6; 106 : 16; Acts 7 : 40; Heb. 9 : 4.
Ab (ăb), the fifth Hebrew month (July-August). See Months.
Abaddon (ă-băd-dŏn) [destruction], **Apollyon** (ă-pŏl-lў-on) [angel of the bottomless pit], Job 28 : 22; 26 : 6 (R.V.); Rev. 9 : 11.
Abagtha (ă-băg-thă), a Persian name, probably identical with Bigtha, Bigthan [God's gift, i.q. Theodore], Esther 1 : 10; 2 : 21. One of the seven chamberlains sent by Ahasuerus (Xerxes) to fetch Queen Vashti to his banquet.
Abana (ăb-ă-nă), see **Amana** and **Pharpar** (phär-pär), rivers of Damascus, flow eastwards from the Anti-Lebanon and from Hermon respectively (2 Ki. 5 : 12); the former rises in a deep pool, and is a very rapid stream, passing by Abila of Lysanias (Luke 3 : 1), and through Damascus itself, and being lost, about twenty miles to the east, in the swampy lake (Bahret el Ateibeh) at the edge of the desert (it is now called

Nahr Barada, " cold river "); the Pharpar is less certainly identified, but appears to have been the parallel stream on the south, which flows from the eastern slopes of Hermon to a group of two lakes in the desert (Baheiret el Hijaneh), south of the preceding lake (it is now called Nahr el 'Auwaj, " crooked river ").
Abarah (ăb-ă-rā), Ford of the Jordan. See Beth-abarah, John 1 : 28.
Abarim (ăb-ă-rīm) [regions beyond], mountains of, including Nebo, Pisgah, Hor, Num. 27 : 12; 33 : 47, 48; Deut. 32 : 49; 34 : 1. The mountains of the **Abarim**, or " places beyond " Jordan, are those on the edge of the Moabite plateau, north of which is the higher chain of **Mount Gilead**.
Abase, Job 40 : 11, behold proud, and a. him.
Isa. 31 : 4, lion will not a. himself.
Ezek. 21: 26, and a. him that is high.
Dan. 4 : 37, walk in pride, he is able to a.
Matt. 23 : 12; Luke 14 : 11; 18 : 14, exalt himself shall be a.
Phil. 4 : 12, I know how to be a.
2 Cor. 11 : 7, offence in a. myself.
Abated, Gen. 8 : 3, 11, waters were a.
Lev. 27 : 18, be a. from thy estimation.
Deut. 34 : 7, nor was Moses' force a.
Judg. 8 : 3, then their anger was a.
Abba [Father], Mark 14 : 36; Rom. 8 : 15; Gal. 4 : 6.
Abda (ăb-dă) [servant], 1 Ki. 4 : 6; Neh. 11 : 17.
Abdeel (ăb-dēel) [servant of God], Jer. 36 : 26.
Abdi (ăb-dī) [my servant, or servant of Jah], 1 Chr. 6 : 44; 2 Chr. 29 : 12.
Abdiel (ăb-dĭ-ĕl) [servant of God], 1 Chr. 5 : 15; also written Abdeel.
Abdon (ăb-dŏn) [servile], Judg. 12 : 13, a judge of Israel.
A town of Asher, Josh. 21 : 30; 1 Chr. 6 : 74.
the Benjamite, 1 Chr. 8 : 23, 30; 9 : 36.
Abednego (ă-bĕd-nĕ-gō) [servant or worshipper of Nego, Nebo, a Babylonian God], one of three Hebrew captives, Dan. 1 : 7.
saved in the fiery furnace, Dan. 3 : 12.
Abel (Engl. ā-bĕl, Heb. Hebel) [breath, vapour], it has also been connected with Assyrian ablu, meaning son, Gen. 4 : 2.
the second son of Adam, his occupation, his offering, his murder, Gen. 4.
righteous, Matt. 23 : 35; 1 John 3 : 12.
blood of, Luke 11 : 51; Heb. 12 : 24.
his faith, Heb. 11 : 4.
Abel (ā-bĕl, Heb. ä-bĕl) [meadow], 2 Sam. 20:14.
Abel-beth-Maachah (ā-bĕl-bĕth-mā-ă-chäh) [meadow by Beth-Maachah], 1 Ki. 15 : 20.

7

Abel-Maim (ā-bĕl-mā-ĭm) [meadow of the waters], 2 Chr. 16 : 4.

Abel-Meholah (ā-bĕl-mĕ-hō-läh) [dance meadow], 1 Ki. 4 : 12, north part of Jordan valley.
Birthplace of Elisha, 1 Ki. 19 : 16.

Abel-Mizraim (ā-bĕl-mĭz-rā-ĭm) [meadow of Egypt], Gen. 50 : 11, mourning of the Egyptians.

Abel-Shittim (ā-bĕl-shĭt-tĭm) [acacia meadow], Num. 33 : 49.

Abez (ā-bĕz)—more correctly, Ebez—[gleam (?)], Josh. 19 : 20.

Abhor, Lev. 26 : 11, my soul shall not a. you.
1 Sam. 27 : 12, made his people to a. him.
Job 42 : 6, I a. myself and repent.
Ps. 5 : 6, Lord will a. bloody man.
Ps. 119 : 163, I hate and a. lying.
Prov. 24 : 24, nations shall a. him.
Jer. 14 : 21, do not a. us for thy name's sake.
Amos 6 : 8, I a. the excellency of Jacob.
Rom. 12 : 9, a. that which is evil.
Ex. 5 : 21, made savour to be a.
Job 19 : 19, my inward friends a. me.
Ps. 89 : 38, thou hast cast off and a.
Prov. 22 : 14, a. of the Lord shall fall therein.
Ezek. 16 : 25, made thy beauty to be a.
Isa. 66 : 24, an a. to all flesh.

Abi (ā-bī) [my father], or, perhaps, identical with Abiah, 1 Chr. 7 : 8 [Jah is a father], or Abivah, 2 Ki. 18 : 2.

Abi-albon (ā-bī-ăl-bŏn) [father of power (?)], 2 Sam. 23 : 31.

Abi-asaph (ā-bī-ă-săph) [my father has collected], Ex. 6 : 24.

Abiathar (ā-bī-ă-thär) [excellent father], the priest, 1 Sam. 23 : 9.
escapes Saul's vengeance, 1 Sam. 22 : 20.
faithful to David, 1 Sam. 23 : 6; 30 : 7; 2 Sam. 15 : 24.
follows Adonijah, 1 Ki. 1 : 7.
deposed by Solomon, 1 Ki. 2 : 26.

Abib (ā-bĭb) [ears of corn], name of the first Hebrew month, the passover month, Ex. 13 : 4; 23 : 15; 34 : 18.
See Months.

Abida (ā-bī-dä) [my father knows], Gen. 25 : 4; 1 Chr. 1 : 33.

Abidan (ā-bī-dăn) [my father is judge], Num. 1 : 11; 2 : 22; 7 : 60; 10 : 24.

Abide, Gen. 44 : 33, let servant a. instead.
Ex. 16 : 29, a. every man in his place.
Num. 24 : 2, he saw Israel a.
Num. 31 : 19, a. without camp seven days.
35 : 25, a. in city of refuge.
1 Sam. 5 : 7, ark shall not a. with us.
Job 24 : 13, nor a. in paths of light.
Ps. 15 : 1, who shall a. in tabernacle.
91 : 1, shall a. under the shadow.
Prov. 15 : 31, ear that heareth reproof a.
Eccl. 1 : 4, the earth a. for ever.
8 : 15, eat, drink, merry, a. with him of his labour.
Jer. 42 : 10, if ye will still a. in this land.
49 : 18, 33; 50 : 40, no man a.
Hos. 3 : 3, shalt a. many days.
Joel 2 : 11, day terrible, who can a. it?
Matt. 10 : 11; Mark 6 : 10; Luke 9 : 4, there a.

Luke 2 : 8, shepherds a. in the field.
19 : 5, I must a. at thy house.
24 : 29, a. with us.
John 3 : 36, wrath of God a. on him.
5 : 38, have not his word a. in you.
14 : 16, another Comforter, that he may a.
15 : 6, if a man a. not in me.
Acts 16 : 15, to my house and a.
1 Cor. 3 : 14, if any man's work a.
13 : 13, now a. faith, hope, charity.
2 Tim. 2 : 13, yet he a. faithful.
1 John 3 : 6, whosoever a. in him, sinneth not.
1 John 3 : 15, no murderer hath eternal life a. in him.
cf. befall, Acts 20 : 22.

Abiel (ă-bī-ĕl) [God is my father].
1 Sam. 9 : 11, grandfather of Saul.
14 : 51, grandfather of Abner.
1 Chr. 11 : 32, A. the Arbathite, one of David's thirty men.

Abiezer (ā-bī-ĕ-zĕr) [father of help], ancestor of Gideon, Josh. 17 : 2; Judg. 6.
Name of clan of tribe of Manasseh, Judg. 6 : 11.
Name of district, Judg. 6 : 34; 8 : 2.
the Anetholhite of David's men, 2 Sam. 23:27; 1 Chr. 11 : 28; 27 : 12.
son of Hammoleketh of tribe of Manasseh, 1 Chr. 7 : 18.

Abigail (ăb-ĭ-gail) [father of joy].
wife of Nabal, her character, 1 Sam. 25 : 3.
becomes David's wife, 1 Sam. 25 : 39.
daughter of Nahash, 2 Sam. 17 : 25.
and mother of Amasa, 2 Sam. 17 : 25.
sister of David, 1 Chr. 2 : 16.

Abihail (ăb-ĭ-hail) [father of strength], a Levite, father of Zuriel the chief of the Merarites in Moses' time, Num. 3 : 35.
wife of Abishur, 1 Chr. 2 : 29.
head of family in tribe of Gad, 1 Chr. 5 : 14.
niece of David and wife of Jeroboam, 2 Chr. 11 : 18.
father of Esther, Esther 2 : 15; 9 : 29.

Abihu (ă-bī-hū) [my father is He], son of Aaron, offers strange fire, and dies, Lev. 10 : 2.
son of Aaron, Ex. 6 : 23; Num. 3 : 2; 1 Chr. 24 : 2.
appointed with his father Aaron and with his brothers to priest's office, Ex. 28 : 1.
offers strange fire before Lord, Lev. 10 : 1.
consumed by fire with Nadab, Lev. 10 : 2; Num. 3 : 4; 26 : 61; 1 Chr. 24 : 2.

Abihud (ă-bī-hŭd) [father of majesty], son of Bela son of Benjamin, 1 Chr. 8 : 3.

Abijah (Engl. ă-bī-jäh) [Jah is father]. Or Abijam.
son of Jeroboam who died in youth, 1 Ki. 14 : 1-17.
a priest in time of David, 1 Chr. 24 : 10; 26 : 20.
son of Rehoboam, 2 Chr. 11 : 20; 11 : 22.
King of Judah, his evil reign, 1 Ki. 15 : 1; 2 Chr. 12 : 16.
his wars with Jeroboam, 2 Chr. 13.
mother of Hezekiah, 2 Chr. 29 : 1.
a priest in time of Nehemiah, Neh. 10 : 7.
a priest with Zerubbabel, Neh. 12 : 4; 12 : 17.

Abijam (Engl. ă-bī-jăm) [my father is day (light)]. See Abijah, son of Rehoboam.

Abila or Abela (now Abil), a town situated about twenty miles N.W. of Damascus toward Baalbek or Heliopolis, lying among the mountains of Antilibanus.

Abilene (ăb-ĭ-lē-nē), the region belonging to Abila, Luke 3 : 1.

Ability, Lev. 27 : 8, according to his **a.**
Ezra 2 : 69, they gave after their **a.**
Neh. 5 : 8, we after our **a.**
Dan. 1 : 4, had **a.** to stand in the palace.
Matt. 25 : 15, to every man according to **a.**
Acts 11 : 29, according to **a.** to send.
1 Pet. 4 : 11, as of the **a.** God giveth.

Abimael (ă-bĭm-āl) [father of Mael], an Arabian tribe.
son of Joktan of family of Shem, Gen. 10 : 28; 1 Chr. 1 : 22.

Abimelech (ă-bĭm-ĕ-lĕch, Heb. ă-bē-me-lek) [father of the king], Gen. 20 : 2.
king of Gerar, reproved by God about Abraham's wife, Gen. 20 : 3; restores her, Gen. 20 : 14.
(another), Isaac rebuked by, and makes a covenant with, Gen. 26.
son of Gideon, Judg. 8 : 31; slays his brethren, and is made king, Judg. 9 : 5, 6.
his cruelty, Judg. 9 : 48; his death, Judg. 9 : 54.
priest in time of David, 1 Chr. 18 : 16.

Abinadab (ă-bĭn-ă-dăb, Heb. ă-bē-na-dăb) [noble father], 1 Sam. 7 : 1; 16 : 8.
receives the ark from the Phillistines, 1 Sam. 7 : 1; 2 Sam. 6 : 3.
second son of Jesse, father of David, 1 Sam. 16 : 18; 1 Chr. 2 : 13.
a son of Saul, slain at Gilboa, 1 Sam. 31 : 2; 1 Chr. 8 : 33; 9 : 39; 10 : 2.
father of officer of Solomon, 1 Ki. 4 : 11.

Abinoam (ă-bĭn-ō-am) [father of graciousness], Judg. 4 : 6.

Abiram (ă-bĭ-răm) [high father], rebels against Moses, Num. 16.
his punishment, Num. 16 : 31; 26 : 10.
firstborn of Hiel the Bethelite who began to rebuild Jericho, 1 Ki. 16 : 34.

Abishag (ăb-ĭ-shăg) [father of wandering (?)], the Shunammite, ministers to David, 1 Ki. 1 : 3; Adonijah slain on her account, 1 Ki. 2 : 25.

Abishai (ăb-ĭ-shāi) compounded of Ab and Ishai (Jesse) [father of being, living], 1 Chr. 2 : 16.
brother of Joab, 1 Chr. 2 : 16.
prevented from slaying Saul, 1 Sam. 26 : 9.
and Shimei, 2 Sam. 16 : 9; 19 : 21.
his valiant deeds, 2 Sam. 21 : 17; 23 : 18; 1 Chr. 11 : 20; 18 : 12.

Abishalom (ă-bĭ-shă-lŏm) [my father is peace, or father of peace], identical with the name Absalom.
father-in-law of Jeroboam, 1 Ki. 15 : 2.
called Absalom, 2 Chr. 11 : 20, 21.

Abishua (ă-bĭ-shû-ă) [father of fortune].
a Levite, son of Phinehas, 1 Chr. 6 : 4, 5, 50.
a Benjamite, son of Bela, 1 Chr. 8 : 4.

Abishur (ă-bĭ-shŭr) [father of song], 1 Chr. 2 : 28, son of Shammai of tribe of Judah.

Abital (ă-bĭ-tăl) [father of dew], wife of David, 2 Sam. 3 : 4; 1 Chr. 3 : 3.

Abitub (ă-bĭ-tŭb) [father of goodness], a Benjamite, son of Shaharaim, 1 Chr. 8 : 11.

Abiud (a-bĭ-ŭd), Matt. 1 : 13; i.q. **Abihud** (ă-bĭ-hŭd) [father of glory], 1 Chr. 8 : 3.
son of Zerubbabel omitted, 1 Chr. 3 : 19.

Abjects or Slanderers, Ps. 35 : 15.

Able, Ex. 18 : 21, provide out of people **a.** men.
18 : 25, Moses chose **a.** men.
Deut. 16 : 17, every man give as he is **a.**
Josh. 23 : 9, no man been **a.** to stand.
1 Sam. 6 : 20, who is **a.** to stand before God?
1 Ki. 3 : 9, who is **a.** to judge?
2 Chr. 2 : 6, who is **a.** to build?
Prov. 27 : 4, who is **a.** to stand before envy?
Dan. 3 : 17; 6 : 20, God is **a.** to deliver.
Amos 7 : 10, land not **a.** to bear his words.
Matt. 3 : 9, God is **a.** of these stones.
9 : 28, believe ye that I am **a.**?
20 : 22, are ye **a.** to drink of cup?
Matt. 22 : 46, no man was **a.** to answer.
Luke 12 : 26, not **a.** to do least.
John 10 : 29, none is **a.** to pluck.
Acts 6 : 10, not **a.** to resist wisdom.
Rom. 8 : 39, **a.** to separate us from love of God.
1 Cor. 10 : 13, tempted above that ye are **a.**
2 Cor. 3 : 6, **a.** ministers of New Testament.
Eph. 3 : 18, **a.** to comprehend with all saints.
Phil. 3 : 21, **a.** to subdue all things.
Heb. 2 : 18, **a.** to succour them that are tempted.
Heb. 7 : 25, **a.** to save to the uttermost.
Jas. 4 : 12, **a.** to save and destroy.
Jude 24, **a.** to keep you from falling.
Rev. 5 : 3, no man **a.** to open book.
6 : 17, who shall be **a.** to stand?

Abner (ăb-nēr) [father of light], 1 Sam. 14 : 51; spelled Abiner in margin, 1 Sam. 14 : 50.
cousin of Saul, commander of his army, 1 Sam. 14 : 50.
taunted by David, 1 Sam. 26 : 5, 14.
makes Ish-bosheth king, 2 Sam. 2 : 8.
goes over to David, 2 Sam. 3 : 8.
treacherously slain by Joab, 2 Sam. 3 : 27.
lamented by David, 2 Sam. 3 : 31.

Aboard—to go, Acts 21 : 2, finding a ship we went **a.**

Abode, 2 Ki. 19 : 27; Isa. 37 : 28, I know thy **a.**
Num. 20 : 1, the people **a.** in Kadesh.
25 : 1, Israel **a.** in Shittim.
John 14 : 23, we will come, and make our **a.**
Gen. 49 : 24, his bow **a.** in strength.
Ex. 24 : 16, glory of the Lord **a.** on Sinai.
Judg. 21 : 2, people **a.** there before God.
1 Sam. 7 : 2, ark **a.** in Kirjath-jearim.
Ezra 8 : 15, we **a.** in tents three days.
John 1 : 32, Spirit, and it **a.** with him.
1 : 39, they came and **a.** with him.
John 8 : 44, a murderer, and **a.** not in truth.
Acts 14 : 3, long time **a.** speaking boldly.
18 : 3, Paul **a.** with them, and wrought.
Luke 1 : 56, Mary **a.** with her.

Abolish, Isa. 2 : 18, idols he shall utterly **a.**
Isa. 51 : 6, my righteousness shall not be **a.**
Ezek. 6 : 6, your works may be **a.**
2 Cor. 3 : 13, end of that which is **a.**
Eph. 2 : 15, **a.** in his flesh the enmity.
2 Tim. 1 : 10, Christ who hath **a.** death.

Abominable, Lev. 11 : 43, not make yourselves a. with.

Deut. 14 : 3, shalt not eat any a. thing.

Job 15 : 16, how much more a. is man?

Ps. 14 : 1; 53 : 1, they have done a. works.

Isa. 14 : 19, cast out like an a. branch.

  65 : 4, froth of a. things.

Jer. 44 : 4, this a. thing that I hate.

  16 : 18, filled land with carcases of detestable and a. things.

Mic. 6 : 10, scant measure that is a.

Titus 1 : 16, in works they deny him being a.

1 Pet. 4 : 3, walked in a. idolatries.

Rev. 21 : 8, unbelieving and the a. and murderers.

Abominably, 1 Ki. 21 : 26, Ahab did very a. in following idols.

Abomination of desolation, Matt. 24 : 15; Mark 13 : 14, probably a reference by our Lord to Daniel 9 : 27; 11 : 31; 12 : 11—passages which describe the profanation of the Temple at Jerusalem on December 15, 168 B.C., at the hands of Antiochus Epiphanes by the setting up, on the site of the altar of burnt offering, of a heathen altar to the honour of the pagan god, Zeus, followed by the sacrifice upon it of swine, the unclean animal.

The prophetic use of the phrase abomination of desolation (Heb., The abominable thing which maketh desolate) is variously interpreted. Some see in it merely an indication of the approaching laying waste of Jerusalem and destruction of the Temple, which occurred in A.D. 70. Some refer it to the profanities and internecine strife of the Zealots or Patriotic Jewish party which preceded that destruction. Others refer it to the introduction of the Roman Standards which, having an image carved upon them, violated the commandment. Generally now, however, the words are taken in connection with the murder of our Lord's brother, James, in the Temple Courts in the days before the siege, a desecration which fulfilled the prophecy and, completing the breach between Jews and Christians, led the latter to retire from Jerusalem to Pella beyond Jordan.

Abomination of offerings, Lev. 7 : 18; Deut. 17 : 1; 23 : 18; Prov. 15 : 8; Isa. 1 : 13; 41 : 24.

defilement, Deut. 24 : 4; Prov. 16 : 12; Isa. 66 : 17; Ezek. 16; Rev. 21 : 27.

idolatry, Deut. 7 : 25, 26; 27 : 15; 1 Ki. 11 : 5; 2 Ki. 23 : 13; Ezek. 18 : 12; Mal. 2 : 11.

pride and falsity, Prov. 3 : 32; 6 : 16; 11 : 1, 20; 16 : 5; 17 : 15; 20 : 10, 23.

of the heathen censured, Lev. 18 : 26; Deut. 18 : 9; 1 Ki. 14 : 24; Rom. 1 : 18; Col. 5 : 3.

of Jerusalem described, Isa. 1; 3; Jer. 2; Ezek. 5 : 11; 7; 8; 11; 16; 23; Hos. 1.

prayer of the wicked, Prov. 28 : 9.

of desolation foretold, Dan. 11 : 31; 12 : 11; Matt. 24 : 15; Mark 13 : 14.

Gen. 43 : 32; 46 : 34, a. to Egyptians.

Lev. 11 : 10, be an a. to you.

Deut. 7 : 25, it is a. to the Lord.

25 : 16, all that do unrighteously are a.

Prov. 3 : 32; 11 : 20, the froward a. to the Lord.

Prov. 8 : 7, wickedness on a. to my lips.

  15 : 8, 9, 26, sacrifice, etc., of wicked a.

  28 : 9, even his prayer shall be a.

Isa. 44 : 19, the residue thereof an a.

Ezek. 33 : 29, land desolate because of a.

Dan. 11 : 31; Matt. 24 : 15; Mark 13 : 14, a. of desolation.

Luke 16 : 15, esteemed among men, a. in sight of God.

Rev. 21 : 27, not enter that worketh a.

Abound, Prov. 28 : 20, faithful shall a. with blessings.

Matt. 24 : 12, because iniquity shall a.

Rom. 5 : 20, that the offence might a.

  15 : 13, that ye may a. in hope.

1 Cor. 15 : 58, always a. in work of the Lord.

2 Cor. 1 : 5, as sufferings a., so consolation a.

Phil. 4 : 12, I know how to a.

2 Pet. 1 : 8, these things be in you, and a.

Rom. 5 : 15, grace by Jesus Christ hath a. to many.

Above, Ex. 20 : 4; Deut. 5 : 8, thing that in heaven a.

Deut. 4 : 39, God in heaven a.

Deut. 28 : 13, a. only and not beneath.

1 Ki. 8 : 23, no God like thee in heaven a.

Job 31 : 28, have denied the God a.

Ps. 138 : 2, magnified thy word a.

Prov. 8 : 28, established the clouds that a.

  15 : 24, way of life a. to the wise.

Matt. 10 : 24; Luke 6 : 40, disciple not a. master.

John 3 : 31, He that cometh from a. is a. all.

  8 : 23, I am from a.

  19 : 11, power given thee from a.

Gal. 4 : 26, Jerusalem a. is free.

Eph. 4 : 6, one God who is a. all.

Col. 3 : 2, set your affection on things a.

Jas. 1 : 17, every perfect gift is from a.

Abraham (āb-ră-hăm) [father of a multitude] (Abram) born, Gen. 11 : 27, called by God, and sent to Canaan, Gen. 12 : 1-5.

goes down to Egypt, Gen. 12 : 10.

makes his wife pass for his sister, Gen. 12 : 13; 20 : 2.

dispute with and separation from Lot, Gen. 13 : 7-11.

receives the promise, Gen. 13 : 14; 15 : 5.

rescues Lot from captivity, Gen. 14 : 14.

blessed by Melchizedek, king of Salem, Gen. 14 : 19; Heb. 7 : 1.

his faith counted for righteousness, Gen. 15:6.

God's covenant with him, Gen. 15 : 18; 17; Ps. 105 : 9.

he and his household circumcised, Gen. 17.

entertains angels, Gen. 18.

pleads for Sodom, Gen. 18 : 23.

dismisses Hagar and Ishmael, Gen. 21 : 14.

his faith in offering Isaac, Gen. 22.

purchases Machpelah for a buryingplace, Gen. 23.

sends for a wife for his son, Gen. 24.

invests Isaac with all his goods, Gen. 25 : 5.

death, Gen. 25 : 8.

his posterity, Gen. 25 : 1.

testimonies to his faith and works, Isa. 41 : 8;

51 : 2; John 8 : 31; Acts 7 : 2; Rom. 4; Gal. 3 : 6; Heb. 11 : 8; Jas. 2 : 21-24.

Abram (Engl. ăb-ˈrăm, Heb. ăbh-ˈrăm) [high father], Gen. 11 : 27.

Absalom (ăb-ˈsă-lǫm) or **Abishalom** (ă-bĭ-ˈshă-lǒm) [father of peace], 2 Sam. 3 : 3; 1 Ki. 15 : 2.

son of David, 2 Sam. 3 : 3.

slays Amnon, 2 Sam. 13 : 28.

conspires against David, 2 Sam. 15.

David flies from, 2 Sam. 15 : 17.

caught by hair in an oak, 2 Sam. 18 : 9.

slain by Joab, 2 Sam. 18 : 14.

lamented by David, 2 Sam. 18 : 33; 19 : 1.

Absalom's Pillar, or **Place,** a monument or tomb set up by Absalom during his lifetime in the King's Dale (cf. Gen. 14 : 17) as a memorial to himself. Possibly this may have been something in the nature of a sanctuary where funeral rites were performed. As, however, such rites were celebrated by sons or descendants, it is strange that his action should be explained by the fact that he had no son, 2 Sam. 18 : 18. But see 2 Sam. 14 : 27 for his three sons. Probably the monument was erected at a later date and became through process of time associated with the name of Absalom. The King's Dale is in the valley of the Kedron, at the foot of Mount Olivet, near Jerusalem.

Absent, Gen. 31 : 49, when we are a. one from another.

1 Cor. 5 : 3, as a. in body.

2 Cor. 5 : 8, willing to be a. from body.

10 : 1, being a. am bold towards you.

5 : 6, a. from the Lord.

Col. 2 : 5, a. in body.

Abstain, Acts 15 : 20, a. from pollutions of idols.

1 Thess. 5 : 22, a. from all appearance of evil.

I Tim. 4 : 3, commanding to a. from meats.

1 Pet. 2 : 11, a. from fleshly lusts.

Abstinence, Acts 27 : 21, after long a. Paul stood forth.

Abundance. Deut. 33 : 19, suck of the a, of the seas.

1 Sam. 1 : 16, out of a. of my complaint.

1 Ki. 18 : 41, sound of a. of rain.

Ps. 72 : 7, a. of peace.

Eccl. 5 : 10, loveth a. with increase.

5 : 12, a. of rich not suffer to sleep.

Isa. 60 : 5, the a. of the sea shall be.

66 : 11, with the a. of her glory.

Matt. 12 : 34; Luke 6 : 45, out of a. of heart.

Matt. 13 : 12; 25 : 29, he shall have more a.

Luke 12 : 15, life consisteth not in a.

2 Cor. 8 : 2, a. of their joy abounded.

12 : 7, through a. of revelations.

Abundant, Ex. 34 : 6, Lord God a. in goodness.

Isa. 56 : 12, as this day and more a.

1 Tim. 1 : 14, grace was exceeding a.

1 Pet. 1 : 3, according to his a. mercy.

Abundantly, Gen. 1 : 20, let waters bring forth a.

Job 36 : 28, clouds drop and distil a.

Ps. 36 : 8, a. satisfied with fatness.

145 : 7, a. utter the memory.

Isa. 55 : 7, he will a. pardon.

John 10 : 10, might have life more a.

1 Cor. 15 : 10, I laboured more a. than.

Eph. 3 : 20, able to do exceeding **a.**

Titus 3 : 6, shed a. through Jesus Christ.

2 Pet. 1 : 11, entrance ministered **a.**

Abuse, 1 Sam. 31 : 4, lest uncircumcised **a. me.**

1 Cor. 7 : 31, use world as not **a.**

9 : 18, that I **a.** not my power.

Accad (ăc-ˈcăd) probably high-land, North Babylonia, Gen. 10 : 10.

a city in Shinar built by Nimrod.

Accept, Gen. 4 : 7, shalt thou not be a. ?

Ex. 28 : 38, a. before the Lord.

Deut. 33 : 11, a. the work of his hands.

2 Sam. 24 : 23, the Lord thy God a. thee.

Job 13 : 8; 32 : 21, will ye a. his person?

Ps. 19 : 14, let the meditation of my heart be **a.**

Ps. 20 : 3, and a. thy burnt sacrifice.

Isa. 61 : 2; Luke 4 : 19, to proclaim the **a.** year of the Lord.

Jer. 42 : 2, let our supplication be **a.**

Mal. 1 : 13, should I a. this?

Luke 4 : 24, no prophet is **a.**

Acts 10 : 35, he that worketh righteousness is **a.**

Rom. 12 : 1, sacrifice, holy, a. to God.

2 Cor. 5 : 9, present or absent, we may be **a.**

Eph. 1 : 6, made us a. in the beloved.

1 Tim. 1 : 15, worthy of all **a.**

Heb. 12 : 28, serve God a. with fear.

Access to God by faith, Rom. 5 : 2; Eph. 2 : 18; 3 : 12; Heb. 7 : 19; 10 : 19.

See Isa. 55 : 6; Hos. 14 : 2; Joel 2 : 12; John 14 : 6; Jas. 4 : 8.

its blessedness, Ps. 65 : 4; 73 : 28; Isa. 2 : 3; Jer. 31 : 6.

See **Prayer.**

Accho (ăc-ˈchō) [curve], so called from the shape of the bay, Judg. 1 : 31.

or **Akka,** a seaport town of Canaan, now called Acre.

Accomplish, Job 14 : 6, a. as an hireling.

Ps. 64 : 6, they a. a diligent search.

Prov. 13 : 19, desire a. is sweet.

Isa. 40 : 2, her warfare is a.

Isa. 55 : 11, it shall a. that I please.

Luke 9 : 31, decease he should a. at Jerusalem.

Luke 12 : 50, how am I straitened till it be **a.**?

1 Pet. 5 : 9, afflictions are a. in brethren.

Accord, Acts 1 : 14, with one a. in prayer.

Acts 2 : 46, daily with one a. in temple.

Acts 4 : 24, their voice to God with one **a.**

Phil. 2 : 2, being of one a. of one mind.

According, Ex. 12 : 25, a. as he hath promised.

Ps. 33 : 22, a. as we hope in thee.

62 : 12, to every man a. to his work.

103 : 10, nor rewarded us a. to iniquities.

Rom. 8 : 28, the called a. to his purpose.

12 : 6, gifts differing a. to grace.

2 Cor. 8 : 12, a. to that a man hath.

Account, Ps. 144 : 3, man, that thou makest a. of him.

Matt. 12 : 36, give a. in the day of judgment.

Luke 16 : 2, give a. of thy stewardship.

Rom. 14 : 12, every one give a. to God.

Gal. 3 : 6, a. to him for righteousness.

1 Pet. 4 : 5, give a. to him ready to judge quick and dead.

Accursed, what so called, Deut. 21 : 23; Josh.

6 : 17; 7 : 1; 1 Chr. 2 : 7; Isa. 65 : 20;
Gal. 1 : 8.
Deut. 21 : 23, hanged is a. of God.
Josh. 6 : 18, keep yourselves from the a. thing.
Rom. 9 : 3, wish myself a. from Christ.
1 Cor. 12 : 3, no man by Spirit calleth Jesus a.
Gal. 1 : 8, 9, preach other Gospel, be a.
Accusation, Ezra 4 : 6, an a. against Judah.
Luke 19 : 8, anything by false a.
Matt. 27 : 37; Mark 15 : 26, over his head his a.
1 Tim. 5 : 19, against elder, receive not a.
2 Pet. 2 : 11; Jude 9, railing a.
Accuse, Prov. 30 : 10, a. not servant to master.
Luke 3 : 14, neither a. any falsely.
John 5 : 45, think not that I will a. you to the Father.
Titus 1 : 6, not a. of riot.
Rom. 2 : 15, thoughts a. or excusing.
1 Pet. 3 : 16, that falsely a. your good conversation.
Aceldama (ă-çĕl-ʹdă-mă) [field of blood] (R.V. Akeldama), Matt. 27 : 8; Acts 1 : 19.
In Jerusalem there was a field used for the burial of strangers, or more probably criminals. Possibly it may originally have been a potter's field or clay-pit, but with the new use it acquired the unenviable name of " field of blood." The two accounts differ as to the purchase. In Matt. 27 : 8, it is the priests who buy the field with the returned, " defiled " money; in Acts 1 : 19, Judas buys it. Probably the name itself is historical. The story supplies the Christian explanation for the name. The supposed site of the " field of blood " is nowadays shown on the steep, southern slope of the ravine or Valley of Hinnom.
Achaia (ă-chāʹ-ă) [Greece], a Roman province in Greece, of which Corinth was the capital, and which included the Peloponnesus.
Paul in, Acts 18 : 12.
contribution for poor made by those of, Rom. 15 : 26; 2 Cor. 9 : 2.
See 1 Cor. 16 : 15; 2 Cor. 11 : 10.
Achaicus (ă-chā-ĭ-cŭs) [native of Achaia], 1 Cor. 16 : 17.
Achan (āʹchăn) or **Achar** (ăʹchär) [he that troubleth], Josh. 7 : 18-26; 1 Chr. 2 : 7.
his trespass and punishment, Josh. 7 : 22-26; 1 Chr. 2 : 7.
Achaz (āʹchăz) [R.V. Ahaz], Matt. 1 : 9, Jotham begat A.
Achbor (ăchʹbôr) [field-mouse], Gen. 36 : 38.
Achim (āʹchim) Matt. 1 : 14, not mentioned in Old Test. genealogy, Sadoc begat A.
Achish (āʹchish) [serpent (?)], king of Gath, succours David, 1 Sam. 21 : 10; 27 : 2; 28 : 1; 29 : 6.
See 1 Ki. 2 : 39.
Achmetha (ăchʹmē-thă) [Egbatana], capital of Media, where was re-discovered the decree of Cyrus regarding the rebuilding of the temple of Jerusalem, Ezra 6 : 2.
Achor (āʹchôr) [causing trouble], valley of, Achan slain there, Josh. 7 : 26. See Hos. 2 : 15.
Achsah (ăchʹsăh) [anklet], Josh. 15 : 16. Caleb's daughter, 1 Chr. 2 : 49; Judg. 1 : 13-15.

Achshaph (ăchʹshăph) [enchantment], Josh. 11 : 1; 12 : 20.
Achzib (ăchʹzīb) [deception], Josh. 19 : 29; Mic. 1 : 14; Josh. 15 : 44, a city of the tribe of Asher, on the shore of the Mediterranean Sea.
Acknowledge, Ps. 32 : 5; 51 : 3, I a. my sin.
Prov. 3 : 6, in all thy ways a. him.
Isa. 63 : 16, though Israel a. us not.
Jer. 14 : 20, we a. our wickedness.
Hos. 5 : 15, till they a. their offence.
1 John 2 : 23, he that a. the son.
Col. 2 : 2, to the a. of the mystery of God.
Acquaint, Job 22 : 21, a. thyself with him.
Ps. 139 : 3, a. with my ways.
Isa. 53 : 3, a. with grief.
Acquit, Job 10 : 14, not a. me from mine iniquity.
Nah. 1 : 3, Lord will not at all a. wicked.
Acre, Bay of, see Accho.
of land, 1 Sam. 14 : 14; Isa. 5 : 10.
Actions, 1 Sam. 2 : 3, by the Lord a. are weighed.
Activity, Gen. 47 : 6, if thou knowest men of a.
Acts, Judg. 5 : 11, rehearse righteous a. of the Lord.
Ps. 145 : 4, 6, speak of thy mighty a.
150 : 2, praise him for his mighty a.
Isa. 28 : 21, his a. his strange a.
Acts of the Apostles, The.
Author and Title.—It is certain that the author of the Third Gospel was the author of the Acts, and companion of St. Paul. It is practically certain that this companion was St. Luke. Christian tradition on this point is early, full, and unanimous. And it is twofold. There is separate testimony to Luke as the author of the Third Gospel and to Luke as the author of Acts; and each enormously strengthens the other. No conjecture as to what is possible, seeing that Paul had various companions, ought to weigh against such strong evidence as to what is the fact. Luke is the author of all but the title of the book. The earliest form of it seems to have been " Acts of Apostles," which was shortened to " Acts " or " The Acts," and lengthened to " The Acts of the Apostles." The book is rather the Acts of Peter and Paul. A little is told about the two sons of Zebedee; but most of the Twelve are mere names. In the work of Peter among the Jews and Paul among the Gentiles the author joyously sketches the triumphant progress of the faith from Jerusalem, the centre of Judaism, to Rome, the centre of paganism and the capital of the civilised world.
Date.—Two events are mentioned, of which the dates are fixed by secular history:—the death of Herod Agrippa I. (12 : 23), A.D. 44; and the accession of Festus (25 : 1), A.D. 60. The date of the treatise itself cannot be determined. It may have been published in any year between 62 and 70, but probably not long after 62. There is no hint of the Neronian persecution, or of the death of Peter or of Paul, or of the destruction of Jerusalem.

Sources.—In his Gospel St. Luke is never an eye-witness, but obtains his information from eye-witnesses. In the Acts he has both sources of knowledge: in the first half he is mainly dependent upon others; but in the second half records a great deal that he himself witnessed. Without mentioning his own name he slips from the third person into the first, and thus indicates his own presence (16 : 10-17; 20 : 5–21 : 18; 27 : 1 -28 : 16). These are the famous " we " sections, which every one admits to be contemporary evidence. Even those who deny that the book as a whole is by Luke allow that the compiler has here inserted material which is by an eye-witness. This theory is untenable for two reasons—(1) The writer, a person of great literary ability, who could design and execute with such skill, could hardly, in three long sections, forget to change the first person into the third. (2) The very marked characteristics of the style which distinguishes the writer of the Third Gospel and the Acts are as frequent in the " we " sections as in the rest of the book. These sections are probably extracts from a diary kept by Luke, which, like all diaries, is very much more full at some times than at others. Where he was not present himself, he may have used notes taken by others, e.g., in the report of Stephen's speech. In various ways he had excellent opportunities of obtaining first-hand testimony of the events which he records. Philip, with whom he spent many days at Cæsarea (21 : 8-10), could tell him most of the contents of 7 and 8. At Cæsarea he would also hear all about Cornelius (10). The three not quite harmonious accounts of St. Paul's conversion very possibly came from three different sources, which St. Luke gives just as he received them. The excellence of his information and his fidelity in using it have been abundantly proved. Wherever we can test him, by secular writers, by inscriptions, by excavations, and the like, he is found to be accurate.

Characteristics.—Luke evidently regards the book as a continuation of his Gospel (1 : 1-8), and as such perhaps gave it no title. " The former treatise " gives us the ministry of Christ in His own person; the latter gives us His ministry through the Spirit acting upon His Apostles. It has been called " the Gospel of the Holy Spirit," and forms a link between the Gospels and the Epistles.

Summary.—He himself indicates the main divisions of his treatise, in the last words of Christ before the Ascension (1 : 8)—" Ye shall be My witnesses both in Jerusalem (1 : 15–8 : 3), and in all Judea and Samaria (8 : 4-11 : 8), and unto the uttermost part of the earth " (11 : 19–28 : 31). Of the opening verses, 1–5 are Preface and 6–14 are Introduction, which overlaps the Gospel.

Acts, Apocryphal. See Apocrypha of the New Testament.

Adad (ā-dăd), a city west of the Dead Sea.
Adadah (ă-dā-dăh) [festival (?)], Josh. 15 : 22.
Adah (ā-dăh) [ornament], Gen. 4 : 23.
Adaiah (ă-dā-ăh) [adorned by Jah], 2 Ki. 22 : 1.
Adaliah (ă-dā-lī-ă), a Persian name, Esther 9 : 8.
Adam (ă-dăm) [red, man], created, Gen. 1, and blessed, Gen. 1 : 28.
placed in Eden, Gen. 2 : 8.
creatures named by, Gen. 2 : 20.
his disobedience and punishment, Gen. 3.
hides from God, Gen. 3 : 8.
his death, Gen. 5 : 5.
his transgression referred to, Job 31 : 33; Rom. 5 : 14.
first Adam, 1 Cor. 15 : 45; I Tim. 2 : 13.
in, all die, 1 Cor. 15 : 22.
the last, 1 Cor. 15 : 45.
a city, Josh. 3 : 16.
Adamah (ăd-ă-măh) [red, earth], Josh. 19 : 36.
Adamant (Heb. Shāmīr; Adamantus—Jer. 17 : 1; Ezek. 3 : 9; Zech. 7 : 12).—Originally the adamas (ἀδάμας) of the ancients appears to have been a hard metal (viz., Indian steel—see Iron). Subsequently it was applied to a very hard stone (shamir), possibly corundum; ultimately in the time of Pliny the adamas included the diamond (see Diamond). According to some, shamir signified merely the point of a diamond, the stone itself being called yahalom.
Adami (ăd-ă-mī)—more correctly, Adami-Nekeb (ăd-ă-mī-nē-kĕb)—[the pass of Adami (?)], Josh. 19 : 33.
Adana, a town near Tarsus.
Adar (ā-dăr) [glory], the twelfth month of the Hebrews, so called from the beauty of the flowers, Ezra 6 : 15; Esther 3 : 7. See Months.
Adbeel (ăd-bĕel) [meaning doubtful]. Fried. Delitzsch compares the Assyrian Idib-a-il, Gen. 25 : 13.
Addan (ăd-dăn) [humble (?)], a place in Babylon, Ezra 2 : 59.
Adder, Gen. 49 : 17, Dan shall be an a.
Ps. 58 : 4, like the deaf a. that stops.
91 : 13, thou shalt tread on the a.
140 : 3, a. poison is under their lips.
Prov. 23 : 32, wine stingeth like an a.
Addi (ăd-dī) [meaning doubtful], Luke 3 : 28.
Addicted, 1 Cor. 16 : 15, a. themselves to the ministry.
Additions, 1 Ki. 7 : 29, 30, 36.
Addon (ăd-dŏn), Neh. 7 : 61. See Addan.
Ader (ā-dĕr) [a flock], 1 Chr. 8 : 15, a Benjamite, son of Berah.
Adiel (ăd-ī-ĕl) [ornament of God], 1 Chr. 4 : 36.
Adin (ā-dīn) [voluptuous], Ezra 2 : 15.
Adina (ăd-ī-nă) [slender], 1 Chr. 11 : 42.
Adino (ăd-ī-nō) [ornament], one of David's valiant men.
2 Sam. 23 : 8, The Tachmonite . . . the same was A.
Adithaim (ăd-ī-thā-īm) [double ornament (?)], Josh. 15 : 36.
Adjure, Josh. 6 : 26, Joshua a. them at that time.
1 Sam. 14 : 24, Saul had a. the people.
1 Ki. 22 : 16, how many times shall I a. thee.
2 Chr. 18 : 15, how many times shall I a. thee.
Matt. 26 : 63, I a. thee by the living God.

Mark 5 : 7, I a. thee by God, torment not.

Acts 19 : 13, we a. you by Jesus.

Adlai (ăd-lā-ī) [righteousness of Jah (?)], 1 Chr. 27 : 29.

Adlun, a village, famous for its caves and tombs.

Admah (ăd-mäh) [earthy (?)], Gen. 10 : 19, city of the plain, destroyed, Gen. 19; Deut. 29 : 23; Hos. 11 : 8.

Admatha (ăd-mā-thă), a Persian name [probably indomitable], Esther 1 : 14.

Administered, 2 Cor. 8 : 19, which is a. by us to the glory.

8 : 20, this abundance which is a.

Administration, 1 Cor. 12 : 5, there are differences of a.

2 Cor. 9 : 12, for the a. of this service.

8 : 19, a. by us to the glory.

Admiration, Jude 16, having men's persons in a.

Rev. 17 : 6, I wondered with great a.

2 Thess. 1 : 10, to be a. in all them.

Admonish, Eccl. 4 : 13, who will no more be a.

Jer. 42 : 19, know certainly that I have admonished.

Eccl. 12 : 12, by these, be a.

Acts 27 : 9, Paul a. them.

Rom. 15 : 14; Col. 3 : 16, a. one another.

1 Thess. 5 : 12, over you in Lord, and a. you.

2 Thess. 3 : 15, a. him as a brother.

Heb. 8 : 5, Moses was a. of God.

Admonition, 1 Cor. 10 : 11, are written for our a.

Eph. 6 : 4, bring them up in the a.

Titus 3 : 10, after first and second a.

Adna (ăd-nă) [pleasure], Ezra 10 : 30; 2 Chr. 17 : 14.

Ado, Mark 5 : 39, why make ye this a.

Adoni-bezek (ăd-ō-nī-bē-zĕk) [Lord of Bezek], Judg. 1 : 5.

Adonijah (ăd-ō-nī-jäh) [my Lord is Jah], fourth son of David, usurps the kingdom, 1 Ki. 1 : 5.

is pardoned by Solomon, 1 Ki. 1 : 53.

requesting Abishag in marriage, is slain, 1 Ki. 2 : 17-25.

Adonikam (ăd-ö-nī-kăm) [my Lord rises], Ezra 2 : 13.

Adoniram (ăd-ō-nī-răm) [Lord of height], contracted into Adoram, 1 Ki. 4 : 6.

Adoni-zedek (ăd-ō-nī-zē-dĕk) [Lord of righteousness], king of Jerusalem, resists Joshua, Josh. 10 : 1.

his death, Josh. 10 : 26.

Adoption of the children of God described, John 1 : 12; 20 : 17; Rom. 8 : 14; 2 Cor. 6 : 18; Gal. 4; Eph. 1 : 5; Heb. 2 : 10; 12 : 5; Jas. 1 : 18; 1 John 3.

of the Gentiles, Isa. 66 : 19; Hos. 2 : 23; Acts 15 : 3; Rom. 8 : 15; 9 : 24; Gal. 4 : 5; Eph. 1 : 5; 2; 3; Col. 1 : 27.

Rom. 8 : 15, received the spirit of a.

Rom. 8 : 23, waiting for the a.

9 : 4, to whom pertaineth the a.

Gal. 4 : 5, might receive a. of sons.

Eph. 1 : 5, predestinated us to the a.

Adoraim (ăd-ō-rā-īm) [the two heights (?)], one of the fortified cities built in Judah by Rehoboam, 2 Chr. 11 : 9.

Adoram (ăd-ō-răm), probably the same as Adoniram and Hadoram, 2 Sam. 20 : 24; 2 Chr. 11 : 9.

Adorn, Isa. 61 : 10; Rev. 21 : 2, as a bride a. herself.

Luke 21 : 5, temple a. with goodly stones.

1 Tim. 2 : 9; 1 Pet. 3 : 3, 5, women a.

Titus 2 : 10, a. the doctrine of God.

Adrammelech (ă-drăm-mĕ-lĕch) [Adar (the Assyrian bull-god) is king], Isa. 37 : 38; 2 Ki. 17 : 31; 19 : 37.

the name of an idol introduced into Samaria by the colonists whom Shalmaneser brought to people the cities of Israel after carrying their inhabitants captive to Assyria. The rites in this worship, as with that of Moloch, included the sacrifice by fire of children.

2 Ki. 17 : 31, Sepharvites burnt their children to a. This god, probably representative of the male power of the Sun, has, perhaps, as his female consort, the goddess Anammelech (q.v.).

a son of Sennacherib, king of Assyria, 2 Ki. 19 : 37; Isa. 37 : 38.

Adramyttium (ăd-ră-mỹt-tï-ŭm), Acts 27 : 2, a town on the coast of Mysia.

Adria (ā-drī-ă), the Adriatic Sea, between Greece and Italy, Acts 27 : 27.

Adriel (ā-drī-ĕl) [flock of God], 1 Sam. 18 : 19; 2 Sam. 21 : 8.

Adullam (ă-dŭl-lăm) [righteousness of the people (?)], 1 Sam. 22 : 1; 1 Chr. 11 : 15, an ancient city of Judah; in a cave near it David hid from Saul.

Adultery forbidden, Ex. 20 : 14; Deut. 5 : 18; Matt. 5 : 27; 19 : 18; Rom. 13 : 9; Gal. 5 : 19; Heb. 13 : 4.

penalty of, Lev. 20 : 10; 1 Cor. 6 : 9.

instances of, 2 Sam. 11 : 2; Mark 6 : 18; John 8 : 3.

in what it consists, Matt. 5 : 28; 15 : 19; 19 : 9; Mark 7 : 21; 10 : 11.

spiritual, Jer. 3; 13 : 27; Ezek. 16; 23; Hos. 2; Rev. 2 : 22.

Jude 16, in admiration because of a.

Adummim (ă-dŭm-mïm) [red], plur., in the compound phrase, " the going up to Adummim," or, the ascent to Adummim, Josh. 15 : 7; 18 : 17, where it probably means " the red country."

range of hills west of Gilgal, between Judah and Benjamin.

Advance, advanced him, Esther 3 : 1; 5 : 11; 10 : 2.

1 Sam. 12 : 6, Lord that a. Moses.

Advantage, Job 35 : 3, what a. will it be ?

Luke 9 : 25, what is a man a. ?

Rom. 3 : 1, what a. hath the Jew ?

1 Cor. 15 : 32, what a. if the dead ?

2 Cor. 2 : 11, lest Satan get a. of us.

Jude 16, in admiration because of a.

Adventure, Deut. 28 : 56, would not a. to set her.

Judg. 9 : 17, fought for you, and a.

Acts 19 : 31, not a. himself into the theatre.

Adversary, Ex. 23 : 22. I will be a. to thy a.

Num. 22 : 22, angel stood for a.

Job 31 : 35, that mine a. had written a book.

Ps. 74 : 10, how long shall a. reproach ?

Isa. 50 : 8, who is mine a. ?

Matt. 5 : 25, a. quickly lest a. deliver.

Luke 18 : 3, saying, avenge me of mine a.

1 Cor. 16 : 9, there are many a.

14

Phil. 1 : 28, nothing terrified by your **a.**
1 Tim. 5 : 14, give no occasion to **a.**
1 Pet. 5 : 8, your **a.** the devil.
Heb. 10 : 27, shall devour the **a.**
Adversity, 1 Sam. 10 : 19, saved you out of all **a.**
2 Sam. 4 : 9, my soul out of all **a.**
Ps. 10 : 6, I shall never be in **a.**
   31 : 7, known my soul in **a.**
   94 : 13, give rest from days of **a.**
Prov. 17 : 17, brother is born for **a.**
Eccl. 7 : 14, in the day of **a.** consider.
Isa. 30 : 20, bread of **a.**
Heb. 13 : 3, remember them which suffer **a.**
Advertise, Num. 24 : 14, Ruth 4 : 4, I will **a.**
   (counsel) thee.
Advice, Judg. 20 : 7, give your **a.** and counsel.
1 Sam. 25 : 33, blessed be thy **a.**
2 Sam. 19 : 43, our **a.** not be first.
Prov. 20 : 18, with good **a.** make war.
2 Cor. 8 : 10, herein I give my **a.**
Advise, 2 Sam. 24 : 13; 1 Chr. 21 : 12, **a.** and
   see.
1 Ki. 12 : 6, how do ye **a.** that I ?
Prov. 13 : 10, with well **a.** is wisdom.
Acts 27 : 12, the more part **a.** to depart.
Advocate (Christ) of the Church, 1 John 2 : 1.
Æneas (æ-nē-ăs).
   healing of, Acts 9 : 33.
Ænon (æ-nŏn).
   a brook, John baptizes there, John 3 : 23.
Æolian Islets, off coast of Sicily.
Afar off, Gen. 22 : 4, Abraham saw the place **a.**
Ps. 139 : 2, thou understandest my thoughts
   a.
Jer. 23 : 23, at hand, not a God **a.**
Acts 2 : 39, promise to all **a.**
Eph. 2 : 17, preached peace to you **a.**
Heb. 11 : 13, seen promises **a.**
Rev. 18 : 10, 15, 17, stand **a.**
Affairs, Ps. 112 : 5, guide **a.** with discretion.
1 Chr. 26 : 32, **a.** of the king.
Dan. 3 : 12, thou hast set over the **a.**
Phil. 1 : 27, I may hear of your **a.**
Eph. 6 : 21, now my **a.**
2 Tim. 2 : 4, entangleth himself with **a.**
Affect, Lam. 3 : 51, mine eye **a.** mine heart.
Gal. 4 : 17, they zealously **a.** you.
   4 : 18, good to be zealously **a.**
Acts 14 : 2, minds evil **a.** against brethren.
Affection to God's house, 1 Chr. 29 : 3; Ps.
   26 : 8; 84.
to God, Ps. 42 : 1; 73 : 25; 91 : 14; 119.
set on things above, Col. 3 : 2.
worldly affections to be mortified, Rom. 8 : 13;
   13 : 14; 1 Cor. 9 : 27; Gal. 5 : 16, 24;
   2 Pet. 2 : 10.
1 Chr. 29 : 3, set **a.** to house of God.
Rom. 1 : 31; 2 Tim. 3 : 3, without natural **a.**
Rom. 12 : 10, be kindly **a.** one to another.
2 Cor. 7 : 15, his inward **a.**
Afflict, Ex. 1 : 11, taskmasters to **a.** them.
Ruth 1 : 21, Almighty have **a.** me.
1 Ki. 11 : 39, I will **a.** seed of David.
Ps. 44 : 2, how thou didst **a.** the people.
   82 : 3, do justice to the **a.**
   90 : 15, the days wherein thou hast **a.**
   116 : 10, I was greatly **a.**
   140 : 12, Lord will maintain cause of **a.**
Prov. 22 : 22, neither oppress the **a.**

Isa. 53 : 4, smitten of God and **a.**
   63 : 9, in all their **a.** he was **a.**
Nah. 1 : 12, I will **a.** thee no more.
2 Cor. 1 : 6, whether we be **a.** it is.
1 Tim. 5 : 10, if she have relieved the **a.**
Heb. 11 : 37, destitute **a.** tormented.
Jas. 4 : 9, be **a.** and mourn.
   5 : 13, is any among you **a.** ?
Afflicted, our duty towards the, Job 6 : 14; Ps.
   82 : 3; Prov. 22 : 22; I Tim. 5 : 10; Jas.
   1 : 27; 5 : 13.
Affliction, the consequence of sin, 2 Sam. 12 : 14;
   Job 4 : 8; Ps. 90 : 7; Prov. 1 : 31; Ezek.
   6 : 13; Rom. 5 : 12.
man born to, Job 5 : 6, 7; 14 : 1.
foretold, Gen. 15 : 13; Isa. 10 : 12; Jer.
   29 : 17; 42 : 16; Ezek. 20 : 37.
sent from God, Num. 14 : 33; 2 Ki. 6 : 33;
   Job 10 : 15; Ps. 66 : 11; Isa. 9 : 1.
sent in mercy, Gen. 50 : 20; Ex. 1 : 12;
   Deut. 8 : 16; Ps. 30 : 5; 106 : 43, 44;
   119 : 75; Isa. 54 : 7; Ezek. 20 : 37; Nah.
   1 : 12; Matt. 24 : 9; John 16 : 20, 33;
   Acts 20 : 23; Rom. 8 : 18; 2 Cor. 4 : 17;
   Heb. 12 : 6; Jas. 5 : 10; 1 Pet. 1 : 6; 4 : 13;
   Rev. 3 : 19; 7 : 14.
promises of support under, Ps. 27 : 5; 46 : 5;
   Isa. 25 : 4; 43 : 2; 49 : 13; 63 : 9; Jer.
   16 : 19; 39 : 17; Nah. 1 : 7; Matt. 11 : 28;
   John 14; 2 Cor. 1 : 4; Heb. 2 : 18; 12 :
   Rev. 3 : 10.
comfort under, Isa. 61 : 2; Jer. 31 : 13; Matt.
   5 : 4; Luke 7 : 13; 2 Cor. 7 : 6.
object of, 1 Cor. 11 : 32; 1 Pet. 5 : 10.
behaviour under, 1 Sam. 1 : 11; 3 : 18; 2
   Sam. 12 : 16; 2 Ki. 20 : 1; Neh. 9 : 3;
   Job 1 : 21; 2 : 10; 5 : 17; 13 : 15; 34 : 31;
   Ps. 18 : 6; 27 : 4; 39 : 9; 50 : 15; 55 : 16,
   22; 56 : 3; 66 : 13; 71 : 14; Prov. 3 : 11,
   12; Jer. 50 : 4; Lam. 3 : 39; Hos. 6 : 1;
   Mic. 7 : 9; Luke 15 : 17; 21 : 19; Rom.
   12 : 12; 2 Cor. 1 : 9; 1 Thess. 4 : 13;
   2 Thess. 1 : 4; Heb. 12 : 1; Jas. 1 : 4;
   5 : 11; 1 Pet. 2 : 20.
supplication under, Judg. 4 : 3; 1 Sam. 1 : 10;
   2 Sam. 24 : 10; 2 Ki. 19 : 16; 2 Chr. 14 : 11;
   20 : 6; Ezra 9 : 6; Neh. 9 : 32; Job 10 : 2;
   13 : 23; 33 : 26; Ps. 66 : 13; Jer. 17 : 13;
   31 : 18; Lam. 5 : 1; Dan. 9; Hab. 3 : 2;
   Matt. 26 : 39; 2 Cor. 12 : 8; Jas. 5 : 13.
deliverance from, Ps. 34 : 4, 19; 40 : 2;
   Prov. 12 : 13; Isa. 63 : 9; Jonah 2 : 1, 2;
   2 Tim. 3 : 11; 4 : 17, 18.
benefits of, Job 23 : 10; 36 : 8; Ps. 66 : 10;
   119 : 67, 71; Eccl. 7 : 2; Isa. 26 : 9; 48 :
   10; Lam. 3 : 19, 27, 39; Ezek. 14 : 11;
   Hos. 5 : 15; Mic. 6 : 9; Zech. 13 : 9; John
   15 : 2; Acts 14 : 22; Rom. 5 : 3; Phil.
   1 : 12; Heb. 1 : 3, 12; 12 : 10; 1 Pet. 1 : 7.
Ex. 3 : 7; Acts 7 : 34, seen **a.** of my people.
Deut. 16 : 3; 1 Ki. 22 : 27; 2 Chr. 18 : 26,
   bread of **a.**
2 Chr. 20 : 9, cry to thee in **a.**
Job 5 : 6, **a.** cometh not forth of the dust.
   30 : 16, 27, days of **a.**
   36 : 8, cords of **a.**
Ps. 34 : 19, many are **a.** of righteous.
   119 : 50, this is my comfort in **a.**
Isa. 30 : 20, water of **a.**

48 : 10, furnace of a.
Jer. 16 : 19, refuge in day of a.
Hos. 5 : 15, in a. will seek me early.
Mark 4 : 17, a. ariseth for the word's sake.
2 Cor. 2 : 4, out of much a. I wrote.
8 : 2, great trial of a.
Phil. 1 : 16, add a. to my bonds.
1 Thess. 1 : 6, received word in much a.
Heb. 10 : 32, great fight of a.
11 : 25, suffer a. with people of God.
Jas. 1 : 27, visit fatherless in a.
Affright, Deut. 7 : 21, thou shalt not be a.
2 Chr. 32 : 18, to a. and to trouble.
Job 39 : 22, mocketh at fear and is not a.
18 : 20, that went before were a.
Isa. 21 : 4, fearfulness a. me.
Mark 16 : 5; Luke 24 : 37, they were a.
Rev. 11 : 13, remnant were a.
Afoot, Mark 6 : 33, ran a. thither out of all cities.
Acts 20 : 13, minding himself to go a.
Aforehand, Mark 14 : 8, she is come a. to anoint my body.
Aforetime, Jer. 30 : 20, children also shall be as a.
Dan. 6 : 10, gave thanks before his God as a.
John 9 : 13, brought him that a. was.
Rom. 15 : 4, things written a.
Afraid, Lev. 26 : 6; Job 11 : 9; Isa. 17 : 2, none make a.
Deut. 1 : 17, not be a. of face of man.
1 Sam. 18 : 29, Saul yet the more a.
Job 3 : 25, that I was a. of is come.
9 : 28, I am a. of sorrows.
Ps. 27 : 1, of whom shall I be a. ?
56 : 3, what time I am a.
65 : 8, a. at thy tokens.
77 : 16, waters saw thee and were a.
91 : 5, not be a. for terror by night.
112 : 7, a. of evil tidings.
Isa. 41 : 5, ends of the earth were a.
Matt. 14 : 27; Mark 5 : 36; 6 : 50; John 6 : 20, be not a.
Mark 9 : 6; Luke 2 : 9, sore a.
Gal. 4 : 11, I am a. of you.
1 Pet. 3 : 6, not a. with any amazement.
2 Pet. 2 : 10, not a. to speak evil.
Afresh, Heb. 6 : 6, they crucify son of God a.
Afternoon, Judg. 19 : 8, they tarried until a.
Afterwards, Ps. 73 : 24, a. receive me to glory.
Prov. 20 : 17, deceit sweet, but a.
29 : 11, wise keepeth till a.
Matt. 4 : 2, he was a. an hungred.
John 5 : 14, a. Jesus findeth him.
13 : 36, thou shalt follow me a.
1 Cor. 15 : 23, a. they that are Christ's.
15 : 46, that which is natural; and a.
Gal. 3 : 23, faith a. revealed.
Heb. 12 : 11, a. yieldeth fruit of righteousness.
Agabus (ăg-á-bŭs) [a locust], Greek form of Hagah (Ezra 2 : 46). A prophet from Jerusalem who went to Paul at Antioch foretells a famine, Acts 11 : 28.
and Paul's suffering at Jerusalem, Acts 21 : 10.
Agag (ă-́găg), king of Amalek, spared by Saul, but slain by Samuel, 1 Sam. 15.
spoken of by Balaam, Num. 24 : 7.
Agagite (ăg-́ăg-īte), a descendant of Agag, Esther 3 : 1.

Against, Gen. 16 : 12, hand a. every man.
Matt. 10 : 35, man a. his father.
12 : 30, he not with me, is a. me.
Luke 2 : 34, for a sign spoken a.
Acts 28 : 22, sect everywhere spoken a.
Agar (ā-́găr). See Hagar.
Agate, Ex. 28 : 19; Isa. 54 : 12. This English word translates two different words i n Hebrew. In the one instance (Ex. 28: 19; 39 : 12) it refers to a precious stone, such as some form of quartz, in the third row of stones in the high priest's breastplate. In the other (Isa. 54 : 12; Ezek. 27 : 16), a reference appears to be intended to a more translucent form of silica, cf. " windows of agate," and possibly here mica is the substance.
Age, Job 5 : 26, come to grave in a full a.
Ps. 39 : 5, my a. is as nothing before thee.
Eph. 2 : 7, a. to come he might shew.
Col. 1 : 26, mystery hid from a.
Aged, 2 Sam. 19 : 32, Barzillai very a. man.
Titus 2 : 2, that the a. men be sober.
Philem. 9, such an one as Paul the a.
Agee (ā-́gée) [fugitive], 2 Sam. 23 : 11, father o Shammah, one of David's valiant men.
Ages, Eph. 2 : 7, a. to come.
Eph. 3 : 5, in other a. not made known.
3 : 21, throughout all a.
Col. 1 : 26, mystery . . . hid from a.
Agines or Ahwaz, a city of Susiana.
Agone [gone by, past] (cf. Latin vb. " ago ").
1 Sam. 30 : 13, three days a. I fell sick.
See Matt. 11 : 21; Acts 10 : 30; 2 Cor. 12 : 2.
Agony of Christ in the garden, Matt. 26 : 36.
Luke 22 : 44, being in an a. he prayed.
Agree, Amos 3 : 3, two walk except they be a.
Matt. 5 : 25, a. with adversary quickly.
18 : 19, if two shall a. on earth.
Acts 23 : 20, Jews have a. to desire thee.
1 John 5 : 8, these three a. in one.
2 Cor. 6 : 16, what a. hath temple ?
Agrippa (ă-grĭp-́pă), Acts 25; 26, great-grandson of Herod the Great. In A.D. 53 became tetrarch of Abilene, Galilee, Iturea, and Trachontis.
Paul's defence before, Acts 25 : 22; 26.
his respective decisions, Acts 26 : 28, 32.
See Herodian Family.
Aground, Acts 27 : 41, they ran the ship a.
Agur (ā-́gŭr) [a collector], his confession and instructions, Prov. 30.
Aha ! exclamation of malicious joy, Ps. 35 : 21, a., a., our eye hath seen it.
Ps. 40 : 15, desolate, that say unto me a.
70 : 3, be turned back that say a. a.
Isa. 44 : 16, a. I am warm.
Ezek. 25 : 3, thou saidst a. against my.
26 : 2, a. she is broken.
36 : 2, a. even the ancient high places.
Ahab (ā-́hăb) [father's brother], king of Israel, 1 Ki. 16 : 29.
marries Jezebel, his idolatry, 1 Ki. 16 : 31.
meets Elijah, 1 Ki. 18 : 17.
defeats the Syrians, 1 Ki. 20 : 13.
condemned for sparing Ben-hadad, 1 Ki. 20 : 42.
takes Naboth's vineyard, 1 Ki. 21.
his repentance, 1 Ki. 21 : 27.

seduced by false prophets, 1 Ki. 22 : 6.

mortally wounded at Ramoth-gilead, 1 Ki. 22 : 34; 2 Chr. 18 : 34.

a false prophet, Jer. 29 : 21.

Aharah (ă-hâr-ăh) [probably born behind a fort], 1 Chr. 8 : 1. The same as the following.

Aharhel (ă-här-hĕl) [behind the breast-work], 1 Chr. 4 : 8. See above.

Ahasai (ă-hā-sâî), rather Āh-sâî, shortened from Ahaziah [Jah holds], Neh. 11 : 13.

Ahasuerus (ă-hăs-ū-ē-rŭs) [Persian, probably protector of the land], king of Persia, Esther 1 : 1.

divorces Vashti, Esther 1 : 21.

makes Esther queen, Esther 2 : 17.

advances Haman, Esther 3.

his decree to destroy the Jews, Esther 3 : 12.

rewards Mordecai for his loyalty, Esther 6.

hangs Haman, Esther 7 : 9.

advances Mordecai, Esther 9 : 4; 10.

Ahava (ă-hā-vă) or **Ivah,** name of a canal or river, Ezra 8 : 15.

Ahaz (ā-hăz) [possessor], probably shortened from Jehoahaz [Jehovah possesses], or from Ahaziah [Jah preserves or seizes], king of Judah, his wicked reign, 2 Ki. 16.

profanes the temple, 2 Ki. 16 : 17.

afflicted by Pekah, king of Israel, 2 Chr. 28.

comforted by Isaiah, Isa. 7.

refuses to ask a sign, Isa. 7 : 12.

Ahaziah (ā-hă-zī-ăh) [Jah preserves, or seizes], king of Judah, his wicked reign, 2 Ki. 8 : 25.

slain by Jehu, 2 Ki. 9 : 27; 2 Chr. 22 : 9.

king of Israel, 1 Ki. 22 : 40, 49.

his sickness and idolatry, 2 Ki. 1.

his death denounced by Elijah, 2 Ki. 1.

Ahban (ăh-băn) [brother of the intelligent], 1 Chr. 2 : 29.

Ahi (ā-hī), shortened form of Ahiah, 1 Chr. 5 : 15.

Ahiah (ă-hī-ăh) [Jah is my brother], 1 Sam. 14 : 18.

Ahiezer (ă-hī-ē-zēr) [brother of help]. Num. 1 : 12.

Ahihud (ă-hī-hŭd) [brother of majesty], Num. 34 : 27.

Ahijah (ă-hī-jäh), prophesies against Solomon, 1 Ki. 11 : 31.

prophesies against Jeroboam, and foretells his son's death, 1 Ki. 14 : 7.

Ahikam (ă-hī-kăm) [my brother raises himself], 2 Ki. 22 : 12.

protects Jeremiah, Jer. 26 : 24.

Ahilud (ă-hī-lŭd), 2 Sam. 8 : 16.

Ahimaaz (ă-hī-mă-ăz) [brother of anger], son of Zadok, serves David, 2 Sam. 15 : 27; 17 : 17; 18 : 19.

Ahiman (ă-hī-măn) [my brother is a gift], 1 Chr. 9 : 17.

Ahimelech (ă-hīm-ĕ-lĕch) [my brother is king], 1 Sam. 21 : 1; 22 : 9.

high priest, slain by Saul's order for assisting David, 1 Sam. 22 : 18.

Ahimoth (ă-hī-mōth) [brother of death], 1 Chr. 6 : 25.

Ahinadab (ă-hīn-ă-dăb) [noble brother], 1 Ki. 4 : 14.

Ahinoam (ă-hīn-ō-ăm) [brother of pleasantness], 1 Sam. 14 : 50.

Ahio (a-hī-ō, but properly āh-yō), contraction for āh-yōn [brotherly], 2 Sam. 6 : 3.

Ahira (ă-hī-ra) [possibly Ra (the Egyptian sun-god) is a brother (Cheyne)], Num. 1 : 15.

Ahiram (ă-hī-răm) [high brother], Num. 26 : 38.

Ahiramite [a descendant of Ahiram], Num. 36 : 38.

Ahisamach (ă-hīs-ă-măch) [my brother helps], Ex. 31 : 6.

Ahishahar (ă-hī-shā-här) [brother of the morning], 1 Chr. 7 : 10.

Ahishar (ă-hī-shär) [my brother sings(?)], 1 Ki. 4 : 6.

Ahithophel (ă-hīth-ō-phĕl) [brother of folly(?)], his treachery, 2 Sam. 15 : 31; 16 : 20.

disgrace and suicide, 2 Sam. 17 : 1-23.

See Ps. 41 : 9; 55 : 12; 109.

Ahitub (ă-hī-tŭb) [brother of goodness], 1 Sam. 14 : 3.

Ahlab (äh-lăb) [fat, fruitful], Judg. 1 : 31.

Ahlai (äh-lā-ī) [oh that!], 1 Chr. 2 : 31.

Ahmed, a valley and brook near Jerusalem.

Aholah (ă-hō-lăh, more correctly ŏ-hŏ-lăh) [her tent], i.e. she who has her tent or sanctuary, and

Aholibah (ă-hŏl-ī-băh, more correctly spelled with initial O) [my tent is in her], their abominations figurative of Samaria and Jerusalem, Ezek. 23 : 4.

Aholiab (ă-hō-lī-ăb, properly ŏ-hŏ-lē-ăb) [tent of the father], inspired to construct Tabernacle, Ex. 35 : 34, 36.

Aholibamah (ă-hŏl-ī-bă-măh, more correctly with O) [tent of the high place], Gen. 36 : 2; 1 Chr. 1 : 52.

Ahumai (ă-hū-mâî) [brother of (i.e., dweller near) water, or possibly sufficiently having a heart like water], 1 Chr. 4 : 2.

Ahuzam (ă-hū-zăm) [possessor], 1 Chr. 4 : 6.

Ahuzzath (ă-hŭz-zăth) [possession], Gen. 26 : 26.

Ai or **Hai** (ā-ī) [heap (of stones)], a royal city of the Canaanites near Beth-el, Jer. 49 : 3.

men of, defeat Israel, Josh. 7.

but are subdued, Josh. 8.

Aiah (â-ăh) or **Ajah** [a hawk], Gen. 36 : 24; 2 Sam. 3 : 7.

Aiath (â-ăth), same as Ai, but feminine, Neh. 11 : 31.

Aija (ay-ya), same as Ai, Neh. 11 : 31.

Aijeleth Shahar (â-jĕ-lĕth shā-här) [morning hind], Ps. 22, title; (more correctly ăy-yĕ-leth hăsh-shā-här)—probably the name of a song, to the tune of which this psalm was sung. Not a proper name.

Aileth, Gen. 21 : 17, what a. thee, Hagar ?

Judg. 18 : 23, Micah, what a. thee ?

1 Sam. 11 : 5, what a. the people ?

Ps. 114 : 5, what a. thee, O sea ?

Isa. 22 : 1, what a. thee now ?

Ain (ā-īn) [fountain], Num. 34 : 11.

Ain Shems, the modern name for Beth-Shemesh.

Air, 2 Sam. 21 : 10, birds of the a. to rest.

Job 41 : 16, no a. can come between.

Eccl. 10 : 20, bird of the a. carry voice.

Matt. 8 : 20, birds of the a. have nests.

1 Cor. 9 : 26, not as one that beateth the a.

Eph. 2 : 2, prince of power of the a.

1 Thess. 4 : 17, to meet the Lord in the **a.**
Rev. 9 : 2, sun and **a.** were darkened.
Ajalan, ancient Eglon.

Valley of Ajalon

Ajalon (ăi-jă-lŏn, properly ay-yâ-lŏn) [place of stags], a city of the tribe of Dan, Judg. 1 : 35.
Near by was valley notable for Joshua's miracle, Josh. 10 : 12, 13.
Akaba, Gulf of, an arm of the Red Sea.
Akan (ă-kăn), Gen. 36 : 27. Spelled " Jakan " in the margin.
Akkub (ăk-kŭb) [insidious]. The name Jacob comes from the same root, 1 Chr. 3 : 24; Ezra 2 : 42.
Akir, the modern name for Ekron.
Akka, a division of modern Palestine.
Akra, a summit in Jerusalem.
Akrabbim (ăk-răb-bĭm) [scorpions], Num. 34 : 4.
Akrabeh, a city in Nablus.
Alabaster (Alabastrum), Matt. 26 : 7; Mark 14 : 3; Luke 7 : 37. It is a variety of gypsum largely used in Egypt in early times for carving into boxes and vases for holding ointment and perfumes. " Breaking the box " meant breaking the seal only.
Alameth (ăl-ă-měth), son of Becher and grandson of Benjamin, 1 Chr. 7 : 8.
Alammelech (ă-lăm-mě-lĕch) [king's oak (?)], Josh. 19 : 26.
Alamoth (ăl-ă-mŏth) [virgins], Ps. 46, title. Not a proper name, therefore usually explained as meaning " for sopranos or trebles."
Alarm, how to be sounded, Num. 10 : 5.
Jer. 4 : 19; 49 : 2, **a.** of war.
Joel 2 : 1, sound a. in holy mountain.
Zeph. 1 : 16, **a.** against the fenced cities.
Alas, 2 Ki. 6 : 5, 15, **a.** my master.
Ezek. 6 : 11, stamp, and say **a.**
Joel 1 : 15, **a.** for the day of the Lord.
Amos 5 : 16, say in highways **a. a.**
Rev. 18 : 10, **a. a.** that great city.
Albeit, Ezek. 13 : 7, **a.** I have not spoken.
Philem. 19, **a.** I do not say.
Alemeth (ăl-ĕ-měth) [hiding], or **Almon,** a city of the tribe of Benjamin, Josh. 21 : 18; 1 Chr. 6 : 60.
Alexander (ăl-ĕx-ăn-dĕr) [assister of men], and Rufus, Mark 15 : 21.
a member of the council, Acts 4 : 6.
an Ephesian Jew, Acts 19 : 33.
the coppersmith, I Tim. 1 : 20; 2 Tim. 4 : 14.
Alexandria (ăl-ĕx-ăn-drĭ-ă), from Alexander,

Acts 18 : 24; 6 : 9; 27 : 6; 28 : 11, a city in Egypt of which it was the Hellenic, Roman and Christian capital.
Situation.—On the Mediterranean Sea opposite the island of Pharos, 12 miles west of the Canopic branch of the Nile, and 125 miles north of the city of Cairo. The modern city of the name is built on the ruins of the ancient one.
Description.—Founded circa 332 B.C. by Alexander the Great, who is said himself to have traced the ground plan of the city, it became one of the most important commercial centres of the Mediterranean. Its population and wealth were enormous, while its importance as one of the chief grainports for Rome secured to it the general favour of the first emperors. From the first its population was mixed. According to Josephus, Alexander himself assigned to the Jews a place in his new city. Philo, born 25 B.C. estimated the number of Jews in Alexandria in his day at little less than a million.
Algum, trees, 2 Chr. 2 : 8; 9 : 10, 11. See **Almug.**
Aliah (ăl-ĭ-ăh) [unrighteous (?)], or **Alvah** in margin, 1 Chr. 1 : 51.
Alian (ăl-ĭ-ăn) [unrighteous], or **Alvan,** 1 Chr. 1 : 40.
Alien, Deut. 14 : 21, sell it to an **a.**
Ex. 18 : 3, I have been an **a.**
Job 19 : 15, I am an **a.** in their sight.
Isa. 61 : 5, sons of the **a.** your plowmen.
Ps. 69 : 8, an **a.** unto my mother's children.
Eph. 2 : 12, **a.** from commonwealth.
Heb. 11 : 34, armies of the **a.**
Alienated, Ezek. 23 : 17, 18, 22, 28, mind was **a.**
Eph. 4 : 18, **a.** from life of God.
Col. 1 : 21, that were sometime **a.**
Alike, Job 21 : 26, lie down **a.** in dust.
Ps. 33 : 15, fashioneth their hearts **a.**
139 : 12, darkness and light both **a.**
Eccl. 9 : 2, all things come **a.** to all.
Rom. 14 : 5, esteemeth every day **a.**
Alive, Deut. 4 : 4, **a.** every one this day.
1 Sam. 2 : 6, killeth and maketh **a.**
15 : 8, he took Agag **a.**
Ezek. 18 : 27, save soul **a.**
Luke 15 : 24, 32, son was dead, and is **a.**
24 : 23, angels who said he was **a.**
Acts 1 : 3, shewed himself **a.**
Rom. 6 : 11, 13, **a.** unto God.
1 Cor. 15 : 22, in Christ all be made **a.**
I Thess. 4 : 15, **a.** and remain.
Rev. 1 : 18, I am **a.** for evermore.
2 : 8, which was dead, and is **a.**
All to brake, broke all to bits; shattered, Judg. 9 : 53, an archaic form omitted by the R.V. The particle " to," attaching to the word it precedes, means " asunder "; thus " tobreak " means to break in two pieces.
Alleging, Acts 17 : 3, opening and **a.** that Christ must.
Allegory (of Hagar), Gal. 4 : 24.
Alleluia (ăl-lĕ-lū-ya), Greek form for Hallelujah [praise ye Jah], Rev. 19 : 1, 3, 4, 6. See **Hallelujah.**
Allied, Neh. 13 : 4, house of our God **a.**

Allon (ăl-lŏn) [an oak], Josh. 19 : 33.

Allon-bachuth (ăl-lŏn-bā-chûth) [oak of weeping], Gen. 35 : 8; 1 Ki. 13 : 4.

Allow, Luke 11 : 48, that ye a. the deeds.
Rom. 7 : 15, that which I do, I a. not.
1 Thess. 2 : 4, as we were a. of God.

Allure, Hos. 2 : 14, a. her into the wilderness.
2 Pet. 2 : 18, they a. through lusts.

Almighty, Gen. 17 : 1, I am the a. God.
Ex. 6 : 3, by the name of God a.
Job 11 : 7, find out the a. to perfection.
32 : 8, inspiration of the a.
Ps. 91 : 1, under shadow of the a.
Rev. 1 : 8, was and is to come, the a.
4 : 8. Lord God a. which was.
God, Num. 24 : 4; Ruth 1 : 20; Job 5 : 17;
Isa. 13 : 6; Ezek. 1 : 24. See **God.**

Almodad (ăl-mō-dăd) [the Modad], an Arab tribe, Gen. 10 : 26.

Almon (ăl-mŏn) [concealment], Josh. 21 : 18.
Spelled Alemeth in margin.

Almond (Heb. shaked; Amygdalus communis).
—This well-known tree blossoms early, before its leaves are expanded. Native to Asia and North Africa, it is also cultivated in the milder parts of Europe. In form, blossom and fruit it resembles the peach, being, indeed, another species of the same genus. In height it reaches 12 or 14 feet. Its chief value is in its nuts. In Jer. 1 : 11, 12 there is a play on the name (see Revised Version), and in Eccl. 12 : 5, " the almond tree shall blossom," is supposed by many to be an allusion to the hoary head.

Almonds, produced by the rod of Aaron, Num. 17 : 8.
See Jer. 1 : 11.

Almon-diblathaim (ăl-mŏn-dĭb-lă-thā-ĭm), Num. 33 : 46.
See under **Beth-diblathaim.**

Almost, Ps. 73 : 2, my feet were a. gone. Acts 26 : 28, 29, a. thou persuadest.

Alms, Matt. 6 : 1, do not your a. before men.
Luke 11 : 41, give a. of such things.
Acts 3 · 3, seeing Peter and John, asked a.
10 : 2, Cornelius gave much a.
24 : 17, to bring a. to my nation.

Almsgiving, Matt. 6 : 1; Luke 11 : 41; 12 : 33.
examples of, Acts 3 : 2; 10 : 2; 24 : 17.

Almug Trees or **Algum Trees.** The Hebrew word is left untranslated. They were brought from Ophir (1 Ki. 10 : 11), and were used for pillars or railing for the Temple, and for harps and psalteries, probably as inlayings. Solomon asked Huram, King of Tyre, to send him algum trees out of Lebanon (2 Chr. 2 : 8), and afterwards we find (2 Chr. 9 : 10) that these trees were brought by the servants of Huram from Ophir, and were used not only for the purposes mentioned above, but for the terraces of the House of the Lord. Most probably the Red Sandalwood was the almug. A native of India and Ceylon this Red Sandalwood is very heavy, hard and fine-grained, and of a beautiful garnet colour.

Aloes, or **Lign Aloes.** The aloes, mentioned four times in the Bible in connection with myrrh, would seem to have been a perfume, or a perfumed wood, not known in the early days of the Jews, and probably brought from the East. Ps. 45 : 8; Cant. 4 : 14; John 19 : 39; Num. 24 : 6; Prov. 7 : 17.

Alone, Gen. 2 : 18, not good man should be a.
Num. 11 : 14; Deut. 1 : 9, bear all these people a.
Deut. 32 : 12, Lord a. did lead him.
Ps. 136 : 4, who a. doeth great wonders.
Hos. 4 : 17, Ephraim joined to idols let him a.
Matt. 4 : 4; Luke 4 : 4, not live by bread a.
Matt. 14 : 23; Luke 9 : 18, Jesus was a.
John 8 : 16; 16 : 32, I am not a.
Heb. 9 : 7, went high priest a. once.
Jas. 2 : 17, faith is dead, being a.

Aloth (ā-lŏth), in 1 Ki. 4 : 16, is a mistake of our A.V. for Bealoth (R.V.).

Alpha (ăl-phă), the first letter of the Greek alphabet; Omega is the last letter, Rev. 1 : 8, 11; 21 : 6; 22 : 13.

Alphæus (ăl-phæ-ŭs) [deputy], probably i.q. Cleopas, Matt. 10 : 3; Mark 2 : 14.

Altar, the place of meeting with God who, in the sacrifice, was approached with a gift. Generally erected for the offering of sacrifices, altars in some instances appear to have been merely memorials. Though probably originally made of earth the law of Moses allowed, as an alternative, the use of unhewn stone.
Erected by Noah, Gen. 8 : 20. Abram, Gen. 12 : 7, 8; 13 : 4, 18; 22 : 9. Isaac, Gen. 26 : 25. Jacob, Gen. 33 : 20; 35 : 7. Moses, Ex. 17 : 15. Balaam, Num. 23 : 1. Reubenites, Josh. 22 : 10. Saul, 1 Sam. 14 : 35. Elijah, 1 Ki. 18 : 30-32. Solomon, 2 Chr. 4 : 1; of Damascus, 2 Ki. 16 : 10.
Jacob commanded to make, Gen. 35 : 1.
how built, of earth, Ex. 20 : 24.
how built, of stone, Ex. 20 : 25.
how built, of wood, Ex. 27 : 1.
of incense, Ex. 30 : 1; 37 : 25.
in the temple, 2 Chr. 4 : 1.
golden, Rev. 8 : 3; 9 : 13.
gift brought to, Matt. 5 : 23.
we have an, Heb. 13 : 10.
Ps. 26 : 6, so will I compass thine a.
43 : 4, then will I go to a. of God.
Matt. 5 : 23, bring thy gift to a.
1 Cor. 9 : 13; 10 : 18, partakers with a.
Heb. 7 : 13, gave attendance at the a.
13 : 10, we have an a.

Altar of Burnt Offering. In construction this varied at different times. (1) In the Mosaic tabernacle where portability was necessary the dimensions were small. Square in shape, five cubits in length and breadth and with a height of three cubits (Ex. 27 : 1-8) it was made of planks of shittim or acacia wood, covered with brass, the interior being left hollow (Ex. 27 : 8). At the four corners were brazen horns to which, at least occasionally (Ps. 118 : 27), the victims were bound. It was covered with a grating of network of brass, through which the ashes fell; and this grating was lifted by four brazen rings in the corners. Staves of wood overlaid with brass, passing through brazen rings on two sides, provided an easy mode of transport. The situation of the altar of burnt offering was " by the door of the tent of the tabernacle of the congregation " (Ex. 40 : 29) in the outer court which was accessible to all Israelites. (2) In Solomon's temple, where a more stable structure was possible, the dimensions were considerably increased, while the material used was now wholly brass (1 Ki. 8 : 64; 2 Chr. 7 : 7). The grating disappeared and, in place of the single gradual ascent to the altar level, there was substituted probably a succession of three platforms mounted by stairs. (3) In Herod's temple the dimensions were still further altered, giving a square fifty cubits in length and breadth, and fifteen cubits in height. That on this altar a fire which should never die out must be kept burning, appears to be implied by Lev. 6 : 13.

Altar of Incense. See **Tabernacle.**

Al-taschith (ăl-tăs-chîth) [destroy not or corrupt not], in titles of Pss. 57, 58, 59, 75, probably the opening words of some song to the tune of which these psalms were sung.

Alter, Ps. 89 : 34, not a. thing gone out.
Dan. 6 : 8, law of Medes and Persians, which a. not.
Luke 9 : 29, fashion of countenance a.

Altogether, Ps. 14 : 3; 53 : 3, a. become filthy.
50 : 21, a. such an one as thyself.
Cant. 5 : 16, he is a. lovely.
Acts 26 : 29, almost and a. such as I.

Alush (ā-lŭsh) [crowd], according to the Talmud, Num. 33 : 13, a place in the neighbourhood of Red Sea.

Alvah (ăl-văh) or **Aliah,** descendant of Esau, Gen. 36 : 40; 1 Chr. 1 : 51.
See **Aliah.**

Alvan (ăl-văn) or **Alian,** son of Shobal, a descendant of Seir, Gen. 36 : 23; 1 Chr. 1 : 40.
See **Alian.**

Always, Job 7 : 16, I would not live a.
Ps. 103 : 9, not a. chide.
Matt. 28 : 20, I am with you a.
Mark 14 : 7; John 12 : 8, me ye have not a.
Luke 18 : 1, men ought a. to pray.
2 Cor. 6 : 10, yet a. rejoicing.
Phil. 4 : 4, rejoice in the Lord a.

Am, Gen. 4 : 9, a. I my brother's keeper?
Gen. 30 : 2, a. I in God's stead.
2 Ki. 5 : 7, a. I God to kill and to make alive.
2 Ki. 18 : 25, a. I now come up without the Lord.
Jer. 23 : 23, a. I a God at hand.
Matt. 18 : 20, there a. I in the midst.
John 7 : 33, a little while a. I with you.
1 Cor. 9 : 1, a. I not an apostle ? a. I not free ?
2 Cor. 12 : 10, when I a. weak, then a. I strong.

Amad (ā-măd) [people of duration], Josh. 19 : 26.
Amal (ā-măl) [labour, sorrow], 1 Chr. 7 : 35.
Amalek (ă-măl-ĕk) [dwelling in the valley], Gen. 36 : 12.
fights with Israel in Rephidim, and is discomfited, Ex. 17 : 8-13.

perpetual war declared against, Ex. 17 : 16; Deut. 25 : 17.
smitten by Gideon, Judg. 7 : 12.
smitten by Saul, 1 Sam. 14 : 48; 15 : 7, 8.
smitten by David, 1 Sam. 27 : 9; 30 : 17.
Amalekite (ă-măl-ĕk-īte), self-accused of killing Saul, is slain, 2 Sam. 1.
land of. See **Palestine,** early inhabitants of.

Amam (ā-măm) [congregated], Josh. 15 : 26.
Amana (ă-mā-nă) [security], Song of Solomon 4 : 8.
Amardus, a river of Media.
Amariah (ăm-ă-rī-ăh) [Jah hath said], 1 Chr. 6 : 52; 24 : 23.
Amasa (ă-mā-să) [burden], 2 Sam. 17 : 25.
captain of the host of Absalom, 2 Sam. 17 : 25.
treacherously slain by Joab, 2 Sam. 20 : 9, 10; 1 Ki. 2 : 5.
See 1 Chr. 12 : 18.
an Ephraimite, 2 Chr. 28 : 12.
Amasai (ă-mā-sâi) [burden-bearer], a descendant of Kohath, son of Levi, 1 Chr. 6 : 25, 35; 2 Chr. 29 : 12.
a captain who joined David at Ziklag, 1 Chr. 12 : 18.
a priest, 1 Chr. 15 : 24.
Amashai (R.V. Amashsai) [carrying spoil], a priest dwelling at Jerusalem, Neh. 11 : 13.
Amasia, a town in Pontus.
Amasiah (ăm-ă-sī-ăh) [burden of Jehovah], 2 Chr. 17 : 16, chief captain of the army of Jehoshaphat.
Amastris, a town in Bithynia.
Amanthus, a city east of the Jordan, now called Amatch.
Amazed, Matt. 19 : 25, disciples exceedingly a.
Mark 2 : 12; Luke 5 : 26, a. and glorified God.
Mark 14 : 33, he began to be sore a.
Luke 9 : 43, a. at mighty power of God.
Acts 9 : 21, all that heard Saul were a.
1 Pet. 3 : 6, not afraid with any a.
Acts 3 : 10, filled with wonder and a.
Amaziah (ăm-ă-zī-ăh) [Jah is strong], 2 Ki. 14 : 1.
king of Judah, 2 Ki. 14 : 1; 2 Chr. 25 : 1.
defeats Edom, 2 Ki. 14 : 7; 2 Chr. 25 : 11.
defeated by Joash, king of Israel; 2 Ki. 14 : 12; 2 Chr. 25 : 21.
slain at Lachish, 2 Ki. 14 : 19.
priest of Bethel, Amos 7 : 10.
Ambassadors, sent to Hezekiah, 2 Chr. 32 : 31; Isa. 39.
apostles so called, 2 Cor. 5 : 20.
Josh. 9 : 4, made as if they had been a.
2 Chr. 32 : 31, a. of the princes of Babylon.
35 : 21, he sent a. to him saying.
Isa. 30 : 4, a. came to Hanes.
33 : 7, a. of peace shall weep.
Jer. 49 : 14, a. to the heathen.
Ezek. 17 : 15, sending his a.
2 Cor. 5 : 20, a. for Christ.
Eph. 6 : 20, an a. in bonds.
Amber (Heb. Chashmal; ἤλεχτρον; Electrum), Ezek. 1 : 4, 27, and 8 : 2. Four substances were known to the ancients by the name of electrum. (1) An alloy of four parts of gold to one of silver. (2) Glass. (3) Amber. (4) Shellac. It is probable that the substance mentioned in Ezekiel, if not the alloy

above referred to, was one of baser metals; the former, according to Pliny, was more brilliant than pure silver.
See **Copper** and **Brass**.
Ambition reproved, Gen. 11 : 4; Matt. 18 : 1; 10 : 25; 23 : 8; Luke 22 : 24.
punishment of, Prov. 17 : 19; Isa. 14 : 12; Ezek. 31 : 10.
of Aaron and Miriam, Num. 12.
Korah, Dathan, and Abiram, Num. 16 : 3.
Absalom, 2 Sam. 15–18.
Adonijah, 1 Ki. 1 : 5.
Babylon, Jer. 51 : 53.
James and John, Matt. 20 : 21.
man of sin, 2 Thess. 2 : 4.
Diotrephes, 3 John 9.
Ambush, Josh. 8 : 4; Judg. 20 : 29; 2 Chr. 13 : 13; 20 : 22.
Ambushment, 2 Chr. 20 : 22, Lord set a.
2 Chr. 13 : 13, Jeroboam caused an a. . . . and the a. was.
Amen, true, form of assent, Num. 5 : 22; Deut. 27 : 15, etc.; 1 Cor. 14 : 16; 2 Cor. 1 : 20.
Christ so called, Rev. 3 : 14.
An archaic word used in Hebrew and Greek. (1) At the conclusion of a prayer to signify " so let it be." (2) After a statement in token of its confirmation and truth.
Amend, Jer. 7 : 3; 26 : 13; 35 : 15, a. your ways.
John 4 : 52, hour when he began to a.
Amerce, to impose a fine upon; Deut. 22 : 19, a. him in . . . silver.
Amethyst, (Heb. achlāmāh; Αμέθυστος ; Amethystus), Ex. 28 : 19; 39 : 12; Rev. 21 : 20. The common amethyst of the ancients was identical with the stone now known by that name. It is a purple variety of quartz. The Greeks believed it to be an antidote to drunkenness, an idea which may have originated in the fact that vessels of this material or colour, when containing only water, appeared as if they held wine. The Jews supposed the stone procured pleasant dreams, and from that notion the Hebrew name is supposed to have been assigned.
Amhaaretz (ăm-hă-ă-rĕtz), the common people of the land; equivalent to the hoi polloi of the Greek.
Ami (ā-mī), servant of Solomon, Ezra 2 : 57; or **Almon** [steadfast], Neh. 7 : 59.
Amiable, Ps. 84 : 1, how a. are thy tabernacles.
Amianthus = **Asbestos** (Incontaminatus), 1 Pet. 1 : 3, 4. This word is used in the figurative sense for imperishable, indestructible, referring to the well-known property of this mineral which enables it to resist the action of fire.
Aminadab (ă-mĭn-ă-dăb) [my people is willing], son of Aram, son of Esrom, Matt. 1 : 4; Luke 3 : 33.
Aminon (ă-mī-nŏn) and **Amnon** (ăm-nŏn) [faithful, true], 2 Sam. 3 : 2; 13 : 20.
Amiss, 2 Chr. 6 : 37, we have done a.
Dan. 3 : 29, speak anything a.
Luke 23 : 41, hath done nothing a.
Jas. 4 : 3, because ye ask a.
Amittai (ă-mĭt-tāī) [true], 2 Ki. 14 : 25.
Ammah (ăm-măh) [mother], 2 Sam. 2 : 24.

Amman (ăm-măn), modern name for Rabbath Ammon.
Ammi (ăm-mī) [my people], Hos. 2 : 1. Not a proper name.
Ammiel (ăm-mĭ-ĕl) [people of God], Num. 13 : 12.
Ammihud (ăm-mĭ-hŭd) [people of praise], Num. 1 : 10.
Ammihur (ăm-mĭ-hŭr) [id.], 2 Sam. 13 : 37. (Heb. text.)
Amminadab (ăm-mĭn-ă-dăb) [my people are noble], Ex. 6 : 23.
Ammishaddai (ăm-mĭ-shăd-dāī) [people of the Almighty], Num. 1 : 12.
Ammizabad (ăm-mĭ-ză-băd) [my people have given, or gift of my people], 1 Chr. 27 : 6.
Ammon (ăm-mŏn) [belonging to the people], Gen. 19 : 38.
Ammonites (ăm-ŏn-ītes), a tribe descended from Ammon, Deut. 2 : 20.
children of, Gen. 19 : 38.
their possessions to remain inviolate, Deut. 2 : 19.
not to enter the congregation, Deut. 23 : 3.
subdued by Jephthah, Judg. 11.
slain by Saul, 1 Sam. 11 : 11.
insult David's servants, 2 Sam. 20.
chastised by David, 2 Sam. 12 : 26.
prophecies concerning, Jer. 25 : 21; 49 : 1; Ezek. 21 : 28; 25; Amos 1 : 13; Zeph. 2 : 8.
See **Palestine,** early inhabitants of.
Amnon (ăm-nŏn) [faithful], son of David, 2 Sam. 3 : 2.
his wickedness and death, 2 Sam. 13.
Amok (ā-mŏk) [deep], Neh. 12 : 7.
Amon (ā-mŏn), the Egyptian god Amon, 2 Ki. 21 : 19.
king of Judah, his wicked reign, 2 Ki. 21 : 21, 2 Chr. 33 : 22.
killed by his servants, 2 Ki. 21 : 23.
Amorite (ăm-ŏr-īte) [highlander], Gen. 10 : 16.
Amorites, dispossessed for their iniquities, Gen. 15 : 16; Deut. 20 : 17; Josh. 3 : 10.
See **Palestine,** early inhabitants of.
Amos (ā-mŏs) [loaded, one with a burden], Amos 1 : 1; Luke 3 : 25.
Amos, Book of.
Author.—Amos, was a herdsman of Tekoa (about nine miles south of Jerusalem), who also (7 : 14) was employed in the cultivation of sycamore trees. He disclaims being a prophet by profession or education (7 : 14). Though apparently a native of Judah, he was commissioned by Jehovah to go and prophesy unto Israel. His prophetic ministry belongs to the reigns of Uzziah and Jeroboam II. He was therefore somewhat earlier than Isaiah, and an elder contemporary of Hosea.
Place.—In accordance with the Divine commission, he came to the kingdom of Israel, Beth-el being the chief scene of his prophetic activity. His sojourn at Beth-el lasted probably no longer than a year, when, having incurred the hostility of Amaziah, the priest of Beth-el, by prophesying disaster to King Jeroboam II. in the midst of his victories, he returned to Judea, where we

may infer he committed his prophecy to writing.

Contents.—Ch. 1 and 2 are introductory, announcing that God's judgment will come upon Damascus, Gaza, Tyre, Edom, Ammon, Moab, and Judah, but will fall most heavily upon Israel. Ch. 3–6 contain three discourses, commencing with the emphatic words, " Hear ye," in which the indictment and sentence of ch. 1 and 2 are further justified and expanded. Ch. 7–9, 10 describe in five visions the judgments that are coming upon Israel, the book concluding (10 : 10 to end) with a promise that the kingdom of God (" the tabernacle of David that is fallen ") shall again be restored.

Amoz (ā-mŏz) [strong, vigorous], Isa. 1 : 1.

Amphipolis (ăm-phĭp-ŏ-lĭs), named from the river Strymon flowing round the city, Acts 17 : 1, a city of Macedonia.

Amplias (ăm-plĭ-ăs), for Ampliatus, a Latin name [enlarged], Rom. 16 : 8.

Amram (ăm-răm) [exalted people], Ex. 6 : 20.

Amraphel (ăm-rā-phĕl) [the son is ruler], king of Shinar or Babylon, Gen. 14 : 1.

Amwas, thought by some to be Emmæus, but most improbable.

Amzi (ăm-zî) [Jah strengthens], shortened form of Amaziah, 1 Chr. 6 : 46.

Anab (ă-năb) [place of grapes], Josh. 11 : 21.

a town of Judah, Josh. 15 : 50.

Anah (ā-näh) [answering], Gen. 36 : 2, 20.

Anaharath (ăn-nā-hă-răth), Josh. 19 : 19.

Anaiah (ă-nā-äh) [Jah answers], Neh. 8 : 4.

Anak (ă-năk) [neck-collar, or long-necked], Num. 13 : 22, 28.

Anakim (ă-nă-kîm), a tribe called after Anak, Deut. 1 : 28.

(giants), Num. 13 : 33; Deut. 9 : 2.

cut off by Joshua, Josh. 11 : 21.

Anammelech (ă-năm-mĕ-lĕch) [Ana (an Assyrian god) is king], 2 Ki. 17 : 31.

Anan (ā-năn) [a cloud], Neh. 10 : 26.

Anani, Ananiah (ă-nā-nî) [Jah covers (protects)], 1 Chr. 3 : 24; Neh. 3 : 23.

a Benjamite city, Neh. 11 : 32.

Ananias (ăn-ă-nî-ăs), Greek form of the preceding.

(and Sapphira), their sin and death, Acts 5.

(disciple), sent to Paul at Damascus, Acts 9 : 10; 22 : 12.

(high priest), Paul brought before, Acts 22 : 30.

smitten by order of, and rebuked by Paul, Acts 23 : 2, 3.

Anata, the ancient Anathoth.

Anath (ā-năth) [answering], supposed by some to be the name of a goddess, Anath, Judg. 3 : 31.

Anathema Maranatha (ă-năth-ĕ-mă măr-ăn-ä-thă), 1 Cor. 16 : 22.

The Greek word Anathema renders the Hebrew term " cherem " or " put under the ban " *i.e.*, devoted to God for destruction and therefore unable to be redeemed, cf. Achan and his plunder, Josh. 6 : 17, and Lev. 27 : 28. Maranatha is an expression in Aramaic, of the dialect of Jerusalem, which is found also in the Didache and the Apostolic Constitutions. How the word

should be divided is a disputed point. Maran atha means " Our Lord is come." This division with its reference to the past is improbable in an early church whose interest was centred on Christ's Second Coming. Many scholars, therefore, have tried to make the tense a prophetic perfect, " Our Lord cometh "; this is grammatically questionable. Probably it should be read Marana tha, " Our Lord, come " as in Rev. 22 : 20. The reading then is " If any man . . . let him be accursed, our Lord, come."

Anatho, a town in Syria.

Anathoth (ăn-ă-thōth) [answers], or supposed by some to be images of Anath, Jer. 11 : 21.

a city of Benjamin, the birthplace of Jeremiah, Jer. 1 : 1.

men of, condemned for persecuting Jeremiah, Jer. 11 : 21.

See 1 Ki. 2 : 26; Isa. 10 : 30.

Anchor of the soul, Heb. 6 : 19.

Anchors, Acts 27 : 29, 30, 40.

Ancient of Days, Dan. 7 : 22.

Ancients, elderly, aged persons; seniors, Ps. 119 : 100; Isa. 3 : 14; 47 : 6; Ezek. 8 : 11; 27 : 9; Job 12 : 12; Ezra 3 : 12.

places or times, Prov. 22 : 28; Jer. 18 : 15; Ezek. 36 : 2; 2 Ki. 19 : 15; Isa. 23 : 7; 45 : 21; 46 : 10; 51 : 9.

Ancle, Ezek. 47 : 3.

Ancle bone, Acts 3 : 7.

Ancyra, a town in Galatia.

And if, Matt. 24 : 48, preceding " and " or " an " for emphasis on " if " in A.V. R.V. omits the " and."

Andrew (ăn-drū), a Greek name, or **Andreas,** Luke 6 : 14.

the apostle, Matt. 4 : 18; Mark 13 : 3; John 1 : 40; 6 : 8; 12 : 22; Acts 1 : 13.

Andrew, Acts and Martyrdom of. See Apocrypha of New Testament.

Andrew and Matthias, Acts of. See Apocrypha of New Testament.

Andronicus (ăn-drō-nî-cŭs), a Greek name, Rom. 16 : 7, disciple at Rome.

Anem (ă-nĕm) [the two springs], 1 Chr. 6 : 73.

Aner (ā-nĕr) [meaning unknown], Gen. 14 : 24.

Anethothite (ăn-ĕ-thō-thîte), a native of Anathoth, 2 Sam. 23 : 27; 1 Chr. 27 : 12.

Angel [Greek ἄγγελος, messenger]. A race of beings of a spiritual nature above that of man, yet infinitely below that of God. Messengers of God whose task is to do God's service in Heaven, or to aid and succour men on earth.

Angel of the Lord, a special form of manifestation of Himself by God to man. By some this is associated with the doctrine of the Pre-Incarnate Christ.

appears to Hagar, Gen. 16 : 7; 21 : 17. Abraham, Gen. 18, etc. Lot, Gen. 19. Balaam, Num. 22 : 23. Israelites, Judg. 2. Gideon, Judg. 6 : 11. Manoah's wife, Judg. 13 : 3. David, 2 Sam. 24 : 16; 1 Chr. 21 : 16. Elijah, 1 Ki. 19 : 7. Daniel, Dan. 8 : 16; 9 : 21; 10 : 11; 12. Joseph, Matt. 1 : 20. Two women, Matt. 28 : 2-5; Mark 16. Zacharias, Luke 1 : 11. Mary, Luke

1 : 26. The shepherds, Luke 2 : 8-12. The apostles, Acts 5 : 19. Peter, Acts 12 : 7. Philip, Acts 8 : 26. Cornelius, Acts 10 : 3. Paul, Acts 27 : 23.
See Ps. 34 : 7; 35 : 5; Zech. 1 : 11.
Angels, their nature, office, and characteristics, 2 Sam. 14 : 20; 1 Ki. 19 : 5; Neh. 9 : 6; Job 25 : 3; 38 : 7; Ps. 68 : 17; 91 : 11; 103 : 20; 104 : 4; 148 : 2; Isa. 6 : 2; Dan. 6 : 22; Matt. 13 : 39; 16 : 27; 18 : 10; 24 : 31; 25 : 31; Mark 8 : 38; Luke 15 : 7; 16 : 22; Acts 7 : 53; 12 : 7; 27 : 23; Eph. 1 : 21; Phil. 2 : 9; Col. 1 : 16; 2 : 10; 1 Thess. 4 : 16; 2 Thess. 1 : 7; 1 Tim. 3 : 16; 5 : 21; Heb. 1 : 6; 2 : 2; 12 : 22; 1 Pet. 1 : 12; 3 : 22; 2 Pet. 2 : 11; Jude 9; Rev. 5 : 2; 7; 11; 12 : 7; 14 : 6; 16; 17.
announce the nativity, Luke 2 : 13.
minister to Christ, Matt. 4 : 11; 26 : 53; Luke 22 : 43; John 1 : 51.
saints shall judge, 1 Cor. 6 : 3.
not to be worshipped, Col. 2 : 18; Rev. 19 : 10; 22 : 9.
rebellious, 2 Pet. 2 : 4; Jude 6.
of the churches, Rev. 1 : 20; 2; 3, etc.
Gen. 48 : 16, the a. who redeemed me.
Ex. 23 : 23, my a. shall go before thee.
Ps. 34 : 7, a. of Lord encampeth.
Isa. 63 : 9, a. of his presence saved them.
Hos. 12 : 4, he had power over the a.
Matt. 13 : 39, the reapers are the a.
Mark 12 : 25; Luke 20 : 36, as a. in heaven.
John 5 : 4, a. went down at a certain season.
Acts 6 : 15, saw as face of an a.
1 Cor. 6 : 3, we shall judge a.
2 Thess. 1 : 7, with his mighty a.
Heb. 2 : 16, took not nature of a.
13 : 2, entertained a. unawares.
1 Pet. 1 : 12, a. desire to look into.
Rev. 5 : 11, voice of many a. about throne.
Anger (human), nature and effects of, Gen. 27 : 45; 44 : 18; 49 : 7; Ex. 32 : 19; Ps. 37 : 8; 69 : 24; Prov. 15 : 18; 16 : 32; 19 : 11; 21 : 19; 29 : 22; Eccl. 7 : 9; Matt. 5 : 22; Titus 1 : 7.
See **Wrath.**
cure for, Prov. 15 : 1; 21 : 14.
to be put away, Eph. 4 : 26, 31; Col. 3 : 8.
instances of, Gen. 4 : 5; 31 : 36; Ex. 11 : 8; Lev. 10 : 16; Num. 22 : 27; 1 Sam. 20 : 30; 2 Ki. 5 : 11; Jonah 4 : 1; Matt. 2 : 16.
(divine), Gen. 3 : 14; 4; Deut. 29 : 20; 32 : 19; Josh. 23 : 16; 2 Ki. 22 : 13; Ezra 8 : 22; Job 9 : 13; Ps. 7 : 11; 21 : 9; 78 : 21, 58; 89 : 30; 90 : 7; 99 : 8; 106 : 40; Prov. 1 : 30; Isa. 1; 3 : 8; 9 : 13; 13 : 9; 47 : 6; Jer. 3 : 5; 7 : 19; 44 : 3; Nah. 1 : 2; Mark 3 : 5; 10 : 14; John 3 : 36; Rom. 1 : 18; 2 : 5; 3 : 5; 1 Cor. 10 : 22; Eph. 5 : 6; Col. 3 : 6; I Thess. 2 : 16; Heb. 3 : 18; 10 : 26; Rev. 21 : 8; 22.
kindled, Ex. 4 : 14; Num. 11 : 1; 12 : 9; Josh. 7 : 1; 2 Sam. 6 : 7; 24 : 1; 2 Ki. 13 : 3; Jer. 17 : 4; Hos. 8 : 5; Zech. 10 : 3.
is slow, Ps. 103 : 8; Isa. 48 : 9; Jonah 4 : 2; Neh. 1 : 3.
deferred, Ps. 103 : 9; Isa. 48 : 9; Jer. 2 : 35; 3 : 12; Hos. 14 : 4; Jonah 3 : 9, 10.
instances of, Gen. 19; Ex. 14 : 24; Job 9 : 13;

14 : 13; Ps. 76 : 6; 78 : 49; 90 : 7; Isa. 9 : 19; Jer. 7 : 20; 10 : 10; Lam. 1; Ezek. 7; 9; Nah. 1.
reserved for the day of judgment, Rom. 2 : 5; 2 Thess. 1 : 8; 2 Pet. 3; Rev. 6 : 17; 11 : 18; 19 : 15.
to be dreaded, deprecated, and endured, Ex. 32 : 11; 2 Sam. 24 : 17; Ps. 2 : 12; 6; 27 : 9; 30 : 5; 38; 39 : 10; 74; 76 : 7; 79 : 5; 80 : 4; 85 : 4; 90 : 11; Isa. 64 : 9; Jer. 4 : 8; Lam. 3 : 39; Dan. 9 : 16; Mic. 7 : 9; Hab. 3 : 2; Zeph. 2 : 2; 3 : 8; Matt. 10 : 28; Luke 18 : 13.
propitiation of, by Christ, Rom. 3 : 25; 5 : 9; 2 Cor. 5 : 18; Eph. 2 : 14; Col. 1 : 20; 1 Thess. 1 : 10; 1 John 2 : 2.
turned away by repentance, 1 Ki. 21 : 29; Job 33 : 27, 28; Ps. 106 : 43; 107 : 13, 19; Jer. 3 : 12; 18 : 7, 8; 31 : 18; Joel 2 : 14; Luke 15 : 18.
Ex. 4 : 14, a. of Lord kindled against Moses.
Deut. 13 : 17, fierceness of his a.
Ps. 30 : 5, his a. endureth but a moment.
37 : 8, cease from a.
90 : 7, we are consumed by thine a.
Isa. 5 : 25, his a. is not turned away.
Hos. 14 : 4, mine a. is turned away.
Col. 3 : 8, put off a.
Angle, a rod with line and hook for fishing, archaic form, Isa. 19 : 8; Hab. 1 : 15.
Angry, Gen. 18 : 30, let not Lord be a.
Ps. 2 : 12, kiss the son, lest he be a.
7 : 11, God is a. with the wicked.
Eccl. 7 : 9, be not hasty to be a.
Isa. 12 : 1, though thou wast a. with me.
Jonah 4 : 9, I do well to be a.
Matt. 5 : 22, whoso is a. with brother.
Eph. 4 : 26, be a. and sin not.
Rev. 11 : 18, the nations were a.
Anguish, Ex. 6 : 9, hearkened not for a.
Job 7 : 11, I will speak in a. of spirit.
Ps. 119 : 143, trouble and a. take hold.
John 16 : 21, remember not a. for joy.
Rom. 2 : 9, tribulation and a. upon every soul.
Aniam (ă-nī-ăm), a Manassehite, 1 Chr. 7 : 19.
Anim (a-nĭm), fountains, Josh. 15 : 30.
Anise, or dill, a species of parsley (Anethum graveolens). Allied to the caraway; it was cultivated for its aromatic seed-like fruits (Matt. 23 : 23).
Anna (ăn-nă), Græcised form of Hannah, a prophetess, Luke 2 : 36.
Annas (ăn-năs), Græcised form of Hanan; in Josephus, Ananas.
high priest, Luke 3 : 2.
Christ brought to, John 18 : 13, 24.
Peter and John before, Acts 4 : 6.
Anoint, Ex. 28 : 41, shalt a. them.
1 Sam. 15 : 1, the Lord sent me to a. thee king.
2 Sam. 14 : 2, a. not thyself with oil.
Isa. 21 : 5, arise and a. shield.
Mark 14 : 8, a. my body to burying.
Luke 7 : 46, my head thou didst not a.
John 9 : 6, a. eyes of blind man.
12 : 3, Mary a. feet of Jesus.
2 Cor. 1 : 21, hath a. us is God.
1 John 2 : 27, the same a. teacheth.
Jas. 5 : 14, a. with oil in name of the Lord.
Rev. 3 : 18, a. thine eyes with eye salve.

Anointed, the (Christ), Isa. 61 : 1; Luke 4 : 18; Acts 4 : 27; 10 : 38.
the Lord's, 1 Sam. 24 : 10; 26 : 9.
mine, 1 Sam. 2 : 35; 1 Chr. 16 : 22; Ps. 132 : 17.

Anointing of Aaron and his sons as priests, Lev. 6 : 20; 8 : 10; 10 : 7.
Saul as king, 1 Sam. 10 : 1. David, 1 Sam. 16 : 13.
Solomon, 1 Ki. 1 : 39. Elisha, 1 Ki. 19 : 16.
Jehu, 2 Ki. 9. Joash, 2 Ki. 11 : 12.
Christ by Mary, Matt. 26 : 6; Mark 14 : 3; John 12 : 3.
Christ by a woman that was a sinner, Luke 7 : 37.
of the sick, Jas. 5 : 14.
of the Holy Spirit, 2 Cor. 1 : 21; 1 John 2 : 20.

Anointing Oil, directions for making, Ex. 30 : 22; 37 : 29.

Anon [straightway, directly, at once], Matt. 13 : 20; Mark 1 : 30.

Another, Gen. 4 : 25, a. seed.
Ruth 2 : 8, glean in a. field.
Prov. 27 : 2, let a. praise thee.
Isa. 42 : 8; 48 : 11, my glory not give to a.
2 Cor. 11 : 4; Gal. 1 : 6, 7, a. gospel.
Gal. 6 : 2, bear one a. burdens.
Jas. 5 : 16, pray one for a.
Rev. 20 : 12, a. book.
See 1 Sam. 10 : 6; Job 19 : 27; Esther 9 : 19, 22; Mal. 3 : 16.

Answer, Gen. 41 : 16, Pharaoh an a. of peace.
Job 19 : 16, he gave me no a.
Prov. 15 : 1, a soft a. turneth away wrath.
Cant. 5 : 6, I called him, he gave no a.
John 1 : 22, that we may give a.
19 : 9, Jesus gave him no a.
1 Pet. 3 : 15, be ready to give an a.
3 : 21, a. of good conscience.
Job 13 : 22, call thou, and I will a.
Ps. 65 : 5, by terrible things wilt thou a.
Eccl. 10 : 19, money a. all things.
Luke 21 : 14, not to meditate what ye a.
2 Cor. 5 : 12, somewhat to a.
Col. 4 : 6, how ye ought to a.

Ant, an insect of a species abundant in Palestine. It has become proverbial for that foresight which lays in stores against the time of need. In instinct and industry it surpasses most other insects. Prov. 6 : 6; 30 : 25.

Antichrist (ăn-′tĭ-chrīst) [adversary to Christ], only found in 1 John 2 : 18, 22; 4 : 3; 2 John 7; in the three latter passages it is used with the article.
See 2 Thess. 2 : 9; 1 Tim. 4 : 1.

Anti-Libanus, eastern range of Lebanon.

Antimony [Heb. Pŭk; Στίμμι; Stibium], 2 Ki. 9 : 30; Jer. 4 : 30. Used in Biblical times, as it still is in Oriental countries (where it is called surma), as a paint to give lustre to the eyes of women.

Antioch (ăn-tĭ-ŏch). From Antiochus.
(1) Antioch in Syria—founded by Seleucus Nicator, 300 B.C., who named it after his father. It remained the capital city of the Greek dynasty of kings of Syria till it was captured by Pompey, 64 B.C. It then became the residence of the Roman gover-

nors of the province which bore the same name. This province included Palestine, the procurators and tetrarchs in which were under the rule of the legate at Antioch. Situated 300 miles north of Jerusalem, it was the scene of the founding of the Gentile Christian Church, Acts 11 : 20, 21. Here also the name Christian was applied to the disciples of Jesus Christ, Acts 11 : 26. It was from here that St. Paul started out on his three missionary journeys, Acts 13 : 1, while in Antioch took place the great controversy between Paul and Peter, which was to have as its result the freeing of Christianity from the shackles of Judaism, Gal. 2 : 11.

Antioch

(2) Antioch in Pisidia, on the borders of Phrygia, Asia Minor. West of Iconium, it is situated about six miles distant across the mountains from Ak-sher. Like the Syrian Antioch, this city also was founded by Seleucus Nicator. Its modern name is "Yalowatch." Acts 13 : 14; 14 : 19, 21; 2 Tim. 3 : 11.

Antipas (ăn-′tĭ-păs), Greek name; contracted form of Antipatros or Antipater, a Christian martyr, Rev. 2 : 13.

Antipatris (ăn-tĭp-′a-trĭs), a city between Joppa and Cæsarea, called after Antipater, Acts 23 : 31.

Antiquity, whose a. is of ancient days, Isa. 23 : 7.

Antonia, a castle in Jerusalem.

Antothijah (ăn-tŏ-thī-jăh), a Benjamite, 1 Chr. 8 : 24.

Antothite (ăn-′tŏth-īte), also written Anethothite [belonging to Anathoth], 1 Chr. 11 : 28; 12 : 3.

Anub (ă-nŭb) [bound together], 1 Chr. 4 : 8.

Anvil, Isa. 41 : 7, with hammer him that smote the a.

Apace, swiftly, 2 Sam. 18 : 25; Jer. 46 : 5.

Apart, Ps. 4 : 3, Lord hath set a. godly.
Matt. 14 : 13, desert place a.
Mark 6 : 31, come ye yourselves a.

Ape, brought to Solomon in ships of Tarshish, 1 Ki. 10 : 22; 2 Chr. 9 : 21.

Apelles (ă-pĕl-′lēs), a Greek name, Rom. 16 : 10, saluted by Paul.

Apharsathchites (ă-phär-′săth-chītes), Ezra 4 : 9, or **Apharsachites** (ă-phär-′să-chītes), Ezra

5 : 6, people belonging to the Assyrian empire, perhaps identical with the Paractaceni of Herodotus.

Apharsites (ă-phär-ṣites), possibly Persians, Ezra 4 : 9.

Aphek (ā-phĕk) [probably fortress], the name is given to several different places, Josh. 12 : 18; 13 : 4.

defeat of Saul at, 1 Sam. 29 : 1.

See Josh. 13 : 4; 19 : 30; 1 Sam. 4 : 1; 1 Ki. 20 : 26.

Aphiah (ă-phī-ăh) [Heb. Aphiach; derivation unknown], 1 Sam. 9 : 1.

Aphrah (ăph-ṛăh), so written in Mic. 1 : 10, as if the feminine form of a word meaning dust, but probably identical with Ophrah.

Aphses (ăph-ṣĕs), a Levite chief, 1 Chr. 24 : 15.

Apocalypse, the Greek name for the Book of Revelation.

Apocrypha, The.

The Old Testament Apocrypha.—The exact technical meaning of the word Apocrypha (lit. hidden or concealed) is a matter of dispute among scholars. From the time of the Reformation, however, it has been the title employed by the Protestant Church to designate those books which are appended to the ancient Greek and Latin versions of the Bible, but which were not admitted into the Hebrew Canon by the Jews. This latter point is clear from the evidence of Josephus, and from other considerations; and Jerome expressly distinguishes between the canonical writings as works of authority, and the non-canonical, which he considered useful for private perusal, and " for example of life and instruction of manners," but which ought not to be used to " establish any doctrine." The Church of England adopted Jerome's view (which, however, was current before his time), and expressed a similar opinion in Art. VI.; but the Roman Church, in accordance with the decision of the so-called Council of Trent, regards the books as canonical. The importance of the study of the Apocrypha is obvious, when we consider that it serves in a great measure to fill up the interval (of about 400 years) between the writings of the Old and New Testaments. It is composed partly of independent works, and partly of additions to canonical works, and was, with the exception of Ecclesiasticus, 1 Maccabees, Judith, and perhaps Baruch and Tobit, originally written in Greek. Some of the books are of great historical value, while others are important as exhibiting various moral and doctrinal views.

1. The third book of Esdras is variously entitled the first book of Esdras (Auth. Version, so LXX. and Syriac), and the third book of Esdras (Vulgate). The book is for the most part compiled from other books of the Bible, chiefly from the canonical book of Ezra, but chaps. 3, 4, 5 : 1-6, seem to be an independent work, of no historical value, derived from unknown sources. The object of the compiler is to urge his compatriots to a more zealous observance of the Law, and to obtain for them the favour of some foreign ruler, perhaps one of the Ptolemies. Its author is unknown, and the date of its composition uncertain. Josephus made use of the book in compiling his history.

2. The fourth book of Esdras, otherwise called the Apocalypse of Ezra, and in the Auth. Version the second book of Esdras, was originally written in Greek, but is now extant only in translations, the oldest and best preserved form of the book being found in the Latin Version. The main portion of the work (ch. 3–14) consists of seven Visions, alleged to have been seen by Ezra, in Babylon, in the 30th year of the Captivity (cf. 3 : 1), which are in some respects similar to the Book of Daniel, and may have been modelled on that work. This part is generally assigned to the end of the first century, A.D. The remaining chapters—1, 2, 15, and 16—are probably of later date about A.D. 260–270. The contents of the book possesses no historical value.

3. The book of Tobit.—The work is now only extant in several translations, viz., Greek, Latin, Hebrew, and Aramaic. The date of composition cannot be fixed, but the book ought perhaps to be assigned to the 2nd or 1st century B.C., rather than to a later period. The book is probably to be regarded as a romance, resting on a certain historical basis. Its demonology and angelology exhibit much that is curious and interesting (cf. 3 : 17; 5 : 4 fol., 6 : 1 f., 7 : 2 f., etc.). The writer's object in composing his work has been supposed to be, to promote kindness and the giving of alms, to inculcate the duty of burying the bodies of those slain by tyrants, and to encourage marriages within the family circle, rather than with strangers.

4. The book of Judith relates how Holofernes, the chief captain of Nebuchadnezzar, King of Assyria, was commissioned to set out and take vengeance on the nations who had refused that king assistance in his campaign against Arphaxad, King of the Medes. Holofernes proceeds to execute his master's commands, and in due course lays siege to Bethulia, a fortress on the way to Jerusalem. Judith, a Jewish widow, by means of a stratagem, obtains access to Holofernes, and slays him; this daring act so encouraged the defenders of Bethulia, that they easily routed the demoralised Assyrian hosts. The original of the book is not known, but it was probably written in Hebrew or Aramaic. It is probable that the book dates from the Maccabean period, and may have been written when Antiochus VII. (Sidetes) was besieging Hyrcanus in Jerusalem (cf. the numerous parallels with the books of the Maccabees). This is the view generally adopted. This book is an historical fiction composed with a moral purpose.

5. The rest of the book of Esther, containing chaps. 10 : 4—16, is separated in the English

Bible from the canonical book, forming a kind of appendix to it, and placed among the Apocrypha. In the Vulgate the additions are appended to the book of Esther, the Roman Church holding them to be canonical. In the LXX. they are scattered over the whole book. These additions were doubtless originally written in Greek, and were known to, and used by, Josephus. They are later than the canonical book of Esther, and were not composed by the author of that work. A marked characteristic of the additions is the religious tone that pervades them (cf. 10 : 9; 11 : 10; 13 : 18; 14 : 3).

6. The book of Wisdom is also entitled the Wisdom of Solomon. The name of Solomon was used because it had become " a sort of collective name for all sapiential Hebrew literature " (Farrar). The book falls into two parts. (1) chap 1–9, Wisdom is praised as the guide to a blessed immortality, and as the source of all blessings. (2) chap. 9–19, contains historical illustrations of the power of Wisdom in human history. The work was perhaps composed between 150 and 50 B.C., and is not a translation.

7. The Wisdom of Jesus the Son of Sirach, otherwise called Ecclesiasticus, the latter title being due to the fact that the book was much used in the early church as an ecclesiastical reading book. The work was originally composed in Hebrew and was probably edited and translated into Greek, in Egypt, about 132 B.C. by the author's grandson Jesus, the Son of Sirach. Nothing certain is known about the author himself. The book is mainly (ch. 1–43) a collection of proverbs and sayings touching matters of morality and doctrine together with a section in praise of the wise man (44–50 : 26), a short epilogue (50 : 27-29), and a final chapter (51) containing the prayer of Jesus the Son of Sirach.

8, 9. The book of Baruch consists of two distinct sections, the work of different authors, to which, in the English version of the Apocrypha (and also in the Vulgate), a third is appended, entitled the Epistle of Jeremy, an independent work, proceeding from another author. (1) was probably composed in Hebrew, not by Baruch (as the historical errors in this part preclude the idea that he wrote the book), but by an unknown author, perhaps in the first half of the third century. (2) may have been written in Hebrew, though more probably in Greek. It is of later date, and may possibly have been composed a short time before the Roman supremacy. Some scholars, however, considered that (1) and (2) should be assigned to a date subsequent to A.D. 70. (3) was doubtless written in Greek, probably by a Hellenistic Jew of Alexandria, about 100 B.C.

10, 11, 12. The additions to Daniel. (1) The Prayer of Azariah, and the Song of the three children, in the LXX. and Vulgate

ch. 3 : 24-90, was probably written in Hebrew or Aramaic. (2) The Story of Susannah, or the Judgment of Daniel. In the LXX. this is a separate work, placed after the book of Daniel, but in the Vulgate is Dan. 13. The original was probably composed in Greek. The form of the story varies in the different versions. (3) The story of Bel and the Dragon, a separate book in the LXX., curiously entitled, from " the prophecy of Habakkuk, son of Joshua, of the tribe of Levi." These " additions " in language and style are very similar to the Greek version of the canonical Daniel. Though interesting as legends, they possess no historical value.

13. The prayer of Manasses is only found in some MSS. of the LXX. It was probably composed by a pious Jew, who based his work on the narrative in 2 Chr. 33 : 11-13, and may be assigned to pre-Christian times (perhaps to the Maccabean period) rather than to a date after the Christian era. The original was probably Greek.

14. The first book of the Maccabees is a work of great historical value. It contains an account of the history of the Jews in Palestine, from 175 to 135 B.C., beginning with Antiochus Epiphanes' attempt to abolish the Jewish religion, narrating the heroic exploits of the Maccabean brothers, and concluding with the death of Simon the high priest. The work was probably composed by an unknown author about 105 B.C. There is no reason to doubt the authenticity of the work; but in the portions relating to the history of foreign nations, and of times remote from the writer's own day, some inaccuracies are to be found.

15. The second book of the Maccabees is of inferior historical value to the first, and of later date. The author was probably a Jew of Alexandria, who composed his work in Egypt. The date of 2 Maccabees may have been some time between 140 and 50 B.C.

16. The third book of the Maccabees is generally held to be fictitious, but it may have had some historical basis. Its canonicity is maintained by none.

17. The fourth book of the Maccabees, more correctly entitled the Triumph of Reason, was probably composed before the destruction of Jerusalem, by an Alexandrian Jew, acquainted with Stoic philosophy. It attempts to prove, from the story of the Martyrdom of Eleazar, and the seven brethren, described in 2 Macc. 6, 7, that " religious reasoning is absolute master of the passions." The writer's object in this appears to be to encourage the observance of the law and a life of piety.

18. Among the other apocryphal writings of the Old Testament may be enumerated : (1) The book of Jubilees or the little Genesis. (2) The book of Enoch. (3) The Assumption of Moses. (4) The Ascension of Isaiah. (5) The Apocalypse of Baruch. (6) The Sibylline Oracles. (7) The Psalter of Solo-

mon; and (8) The Testament of the twelve Patriarchs. Not one of all these, though each important from various points of view, has been recognised as canonical, with the single exception of the book of Enoch, which is received by the Abyssinian Church, but by no other.

The New Testament Apocrypha.—A number of writings professing to supplement the New Testament, and which may be styled for convenience " New Testament Apocrypha," were known in the early ages of the Church. These writings, which were always carefully excluded from the Canon, may be arranged in four divisions—I. Gospels; II. Acts; III. Apocalypses; and IV. Epistles.

I. Gospels.—According to the unanimous opinion of all critics, these are mostly forgeries of little value, of no literary merit, and abounding in inaccuracies. They throw some light upon early Christian thought, are useful in tracing the growth of legends, and of value in the defence of the canonicity of the genuine writings of the New Testament. Some of them were very early condemned as heretical, while all betray more or less unhealthy tendencies. Some contain the germs of false doctrines, which afterwards prevailed in the Christian Church. The Apocryphal Gospels presuppose the existence of the canonical, as is apparent, not only from their quotations from the Evangelists, but also from their silence in reference to many events in the life of Jesus.

1. The most important of the Apocryphal Gospels is the Protevangelium of James, extant in some fifty MSS., written in Greek, and containing twenty-five chapters. It gives particulars respecting the birth of the Virgin Mary.

2. The Gospel of the Pseudo-Matthew consists of forty-two chapters. The date of this work is about the fifth century; its contents are based upon the Protevangelium. An ox and an ass are here related to have adored the infant Jesus in the manger, in fulfilment of Isa. 1 : 3, this being declared (ch. 14) an accomplishment of Hab. 3 : 2, where the LXX. has " between two animals thou art made known."

3. The Gospel of the Nativity of Mary is a short book of ten chapters, in Latin. Its use of the Vulgate proves the book to be later than Jerome, probably about the sixth century. The book shows the growing veneration for the Virgin.

4. The History of Joseph the Carpenter was originally written in Coptic, but was also translated into Arabic. This book contains thirty-two chapters, and is variously assigned by critics to the fourth, fifth, and sixth centuries. The book was written with the object of giving Joseph a share in the honour then accorded to the Virgin.

5. The Gospel of Thomas is contained in Greek MSS. This Gospel is probably almost as old as the Protevangelium. It records the " infant acts of the Lord,"

which are sometimes puerile, sometimes vindictive.

6. The Arabic Gospel of the Infancy also contains legends of our Lord's childhood. It consists of fifty-five chapters, is oriental in style, and abounds in miracles. It is probably not older than the eighth century.

7. The Gospel of Nicodemus is divided into two portions, treating of different subjects. The first division, or " the Acts of Pilate," gives many new details concerning our Lord's trial. The second part of the book relates Christ's descent into the under world.

8. The Gospel of Peter, discovered in a tomb in Egypt in 1886, and published in 1892, was probably the Docetic Gospel, and is most important witness to the story of the crucifixion and resurrection, though disfigured by alterations in favour of that heresy. A few brief documents may be conveniently mentioned here, viz. :—

(a) The Assumption of Mary, is a glorification of the Virgin.

(b) The Correspondence between Abgar, King of Edessa, and Jesus. Abgar, afflicted with incurable disease, beseeches Christ by letter to visit and heal him. The letter is conveyed to Jerusalem by one Ananias. Jesus, in reply, promises to send a disciple after his ascension to cure him. Thaddæus, who executes this commission, heals and instructs the king. It is a forgery of perhaps the third century.

(c) The Epistle of Lentulus is a forgery of a later date. The object of the writer was to satisfy a craving for a minute description of the features of Christ and His personal characteristics.

(d) The Story of Veronica is associated with a number of legends of early date. Some identify her with the woman of Matt. 9 : 20. The story generally current about Veronica is that which represents her as offering a cloth to Christ to wipe His face on His way to Golgotha, and receiving the same back impressed with His features.

(e) There are several other documents relating to Pilate. One is a letter addressed by him to the emperor about Christ. Another purports to be the official report of the trial of Jesus. " The Giving up of Pilate," narrates the story of his condemnation and conversion prior to execution. " The Death of Pilate " relates a different story. Pilate is said to have died by his own hand while awaiting execution. " The Narrative of Joseph of Arimathea " contains a romantic history of the Penitent Thief (Dysmas). " The Saviour's Revenge" is another version of the legend of Veronica.

II. The Acts, though abounding in extravagances, are superior to the Apocryphal Gospels. They are romantic in character, and tinged with an oriental colouring.

1. Acts of Peter and Paul. It contains the famous " Domine quo vadis ? " story of Peter's flight from Rome, to avoid the approaching persecution, and his return

after meeting Christ outside the gate. Peter was crucified with his head downward, while Paul was beheaded.

2. The Acts of Paul and Thecla is of high antiquity. The work is a romance, in which Thecla, a virgin, plays the chief part.

3. The Acts of Barnabas relates how Barnabas was burned to death by the Jews.

4. The Acts of Philip is written in Greek, and is extravagant throughout.

5. The Acts and Martyrdom of Andrew records Andrew's death by crucifixion.

6. The Acts of Andrew and Matthias. Another document, bearing the title " Acts of Peter and Andrew," forms an appendix to this book.

7. Acts and Martyrdom of Matthew. Christ is described as appearing to the Apostles in the form of " one of the infants who sing in Paradise."

8. Acts of Thomas is a lengthy book full of the wildest romance, detailing the Apostle's doings in India. The Martyrdom of Thomas records how Thomas was speared to death by Misdeus, King of India.

9. The Martyrdom of Bartholomew makes India the scene of the Apostle's labours and death.

10. The Acts of Thaddæus is perhaps of the sixth or following century.

11. The Acts of John recounts John's exile to Patmos, his return during the reign of Trajan, and lastly, his translation to heaven.

III. Apocalypses.—Clement of Alexandria, in the third century, and other writers, have preserved fragments of the so-called Apocalypse of Peter. The Apocalypse of Paul is a description of what the Apostle saw and heard when caught up into the third heaven (2 Cor. 12). Tischendorf assigns its date to the end of the fourth century.

IV. Epistles.—These are not properly New Testament Apocrypha. They may, however, conveniently be given here.

1. The Epistle of Barnabas was probably written during the reign of Vespasian (A.D. 70–79). Clement of Alexandria, Origen, and Eusebius consider the author to be the Barnabas of Acts 4 : 36. The evidence afforded by the Epistle is adverse to such an identification. The author was probably a Gentile Christian, poorly acquainted with the Old Testament, who occupied the position of a teacher in the Church of Alexandria, to which the letter is addressed.

2. The Epistle of Clement.—The genuineness of this Epistle is admitted by all. The writer is often reckoned fourth bishop of Rome. The Epistle originated as follows :— The Church at Corinth, distracted by dissensions culminating in the dismissal of certain presbyters, appealed for advice to the Church at Rome. The counsel thus solicited came after some delay, caused by " calamities sudden and repeated." These calamities were probably entailed by the persecution under Domitian, which would

fix the date of the letter near the close of the first century. The Epistle contains an earnest exhortation to humility and "godly peace," enforced by examples and precepts culled from the Old and New Testaments. The style approaches most nearly that of the Apostolic Epistles. The writer incidentally alludes to the martyrdom of Paul at Rome, and also of Peter, though where the latter suffered is not stated.

3. The Second Epistle of Clement is admitted to be spurious. The writer was probably a Gentile, and wrote about the middle of the second century.

4. The Shepherd of Hermas occupies a unique position among the writings of the sub-Apostolic age. The writer speaks of himself as a contemporary of Clement of Rome, which city was the scene of his Visions. The first part of the book contains four Visions, in which the Church is depicted under various forms. The second part contains Twelve Commandments, given to Hermas by an angel in the guise of a shepherd, whence the title. The last portion of the book contains Similitudes, in which the Church and Christian virtues are represented under symbolic forms. The writer alludes to prophets endowed with spiritual gifts as at Corinth (see 1 Cor. 14). Great pains are taken to discriminate between the true and the false prophet. Hermas mentions Apostles, Teachers, and Presbyters.

5. The Didache or Teaching of the Twelve Apostles was practically unknown until its discovery by Bryennios in the MS. at Constantinople. The first part consists of a number of precepts arranged after the order of the Ten Commandments, and as comments on them.

The accepted date of the Didache is the close of the first or the beginning of the second century. Its antiquity gives great importance to its contents. Apostles, Prophets, Bishops, Teachers, and Deacons, are spoken of as Church officers; the chief place being assigned to the two former. The Apostle of the Didache appears to have been an itinerating minister moving from place to place. Directions are laid down in reference to the conduct of Apostles and Prophets, and the respect due to them. There are features of resemblance between the Didache and Hermas. The Sacraments of Baptism and the Lord's Supper receive peculiar treatment. The book concludes with the announcement of our Lord's Second Advent.

Apollonia (ăp-ŏl-lō-nī-ă), a city of Macedonia, Acts 17 : 1.

a seaport town of Samaria.

Apollos (ă-pŏl-lŏs), a Greek name, an eloquent disciple, Acts 18 : 24; 19 : 1; 1 Cor. 1 : 12; 3 : 4.

Apollyon (ă-pŏl-lў-ŏn) [destroyer], Rev. 9 : 11.

Apostates described, Deut. 13 : 13; Matt. 24 :10; Luke 8 : 13; John 6 : 66; Heb. 3 : 12; 6 : 4; 2 Pet. 3 : 17; 1 John 2 : 19.

their punishment, Zeph. 1 : 4; 2 Thess. 2 : 8; 1 Tim. 4 : 1; Heb. 10 : 26; 2 Pet. 2 : 17.

Apostle. One sent forth, that is, to act for and on the authority of the sender. The title is applied (1) to Jesus, as sent forth from God to redeem and save mankind (Heb. 3 : 2); (2) to the Twelve whom Jesus sent forth (Matt. 10 : 2); (3) to persons of eminence in apostolic fellowship and service (Rom. 16 : 7); (4) to other workers, 2 Cor. 8 : 23, so Greek, though in Authorised Version, messengers; also in 1 Cor. 15 : 8; compare ver. 5.

Apostles, calling of the, Matt. 4 : 18, 21; 9 : 9; Mark 1 : 16; Luke 5 : 10; John 1 : 38.

their appointment and powers, Matt. 10; 16 : 19; 18 : 18; 28 : 19; Mark 3 : 13; 16 : 15; Luke 6 : 13; 9; 12 : 11; 24 : 47; John 20 : 23; Acts 9 : 15, 27; 20 : 24; 1 Cor. 5 : 3; 2 Thess. 3 : 6; 2 Tim. 1 : 11.

witnesses of Christ, Luke 1 : 2; 24 : 33, 48; Acts 1 : 2, 22; 10 : 41; 1 Cor. 9 : 1; 15 : 5; 2 Pet. 1 : 16; 1 John 1 : 1.

their sufferings, Matt. 10 : 16; Luke 21 : 16; John 15 : 20; 16 : 2, 33; Acts 4, etc.; 1 Cor. 4 : 9; 2 Cor. 1 : 4; 4 : 8; 11 : 23, etc.; Rev. 1 : 9, etc.

their names written in heaven, Luke 10 : 20; Rev. 21 : 14.

false, condemned, 2 Cor. 11 : 13.

Apothecary [R.V., perfumer]. See **Handicraft.**
Ex. 30 : 25, 35, art of the a.
Ex. 37 : 29, work of the a.
Eccl. 10 : 1, ointment of the a.

Appaim (ăp-pā-ĭm) [the nostrils, anger], 1 Chr. 2 : 30.
son of Nadab, 1 Chr. 2 : 30, 31.

Apparel, exhortations concerning, Deut. 22 : 5; 1 Tim. 2 : 9; 1 Pet. 3 : 3.
of the Jewish women described, Isa. 3 : 16.

Apparently [openly], Num. 12 : 8.

Appeal of Paul to Cæsar, Acts 25 : 11.

Appear, Gen. 1 : 9, let the dry land a.
Ex. 23 : 15, none a. before me empty.
Ps. 42 : 2, when shall I come, and a.
90 : 16, let thy work a.
Cant. 2 : 12, flowers a. on earth.
Isa. 1 : 12, ye come to a. before me.
Matt. 6 : 16, a. unto men to fast.
23 : 28, outwardly a. righteous.
Rom. 7 : 13, that it might a. sin.
2 Cor. 5 : 10, all a. before judgment seat.
Col. 3 : 4, Christ our life shall a.

Appearance, 1 Sam. 16 : 7, man looketh on outward a.
John 7 : 24, judge not according to outward a.
See Num. 9 : 15; 2 Cor. 5 : 12.
1 Thess. 5 : 22, abstain from all a. of evil.

Appearing, Titus 2 : 13, looking for glorious a.
2 Tim. 4 : 1, quick and dead at his a.
See 1 Tim. 6 : 14; 1 Pet. 1 : 7.

Appearances of Christ. See **Harmony of the Gospels.**

Appease, Gen. 32 : 20, a. him with a present.
Prov. 15 : 18, slow to anger a. strife.
Acts 19 : 35, town-clerk had a. people.
Esther 2 : 1, wrath of king Ahasuerus a.

Appertain, Num. 16 : 30, all that a. unto them.
Jer. 10 : 7, O King . . . to thee doth it a.

Appetite, Job 38 : 39, a. of the young lions.
Prov. 23 : 2, man given to a.
Eccl. 6 : 7, the a. is not filled.
Isa. 29 : 8, his soul hath a.

Apphia (ăpph-ĭ-ă), a Greek female name, Philem. 2.

Appii Forum (ăp-pĭ-ĭ fô-rŭm), or market-place of Appius, where Paul, on his way a prisoner to Rome, met company of Christians, Acts 28 : 15.

Apple [Heb. tappuach]. Though mentioned only six times, the fruit so translated has been very graphically described. It was a tree of the field, like the vine, fig, and pomegranate (Joel 1 : 12), whose fruit was sweet-perfumed and sweet-flavoured (Cant. 2 : 3; 7 : 8). A word fitly spoken is like " apples of gold in filagree work of silver " (Prov. 25 : 11, Revised Version). Such descriptions cannot apply to the apple as known to us, which produces but a poor fruit in hot countries, but they fairly apply to the Apricot, a delicious and common fruit in Palestine.

Apple of the eye, Deut. 32 : 10; Ps. 17 : 8; Prov. 7 : 2; Lam. 2 : 18; Zech. 2 : 8.

Apply, Ps. 90 : 12, a. hearts unto wisdom.
Prov. 2 : 2, a. thine heart to understanding.
Prov. 22 : 17, a. thine heart unto my knowledge.
Prov. 23 : 12, a. thine heart unto instruction.
Eccl. 7 : 25; 8 : 9, 16, a. my heart.

Appoint, Job 14 : 5, thou hast a. his bounds.
14 : 4, days of my a. time.
30 : 23, house a. for all living.
Ps. 79 : 11; 102 : 20, preserve those a. to die.
Isa. 1 : 14, a. feasts.
Matt. 24 : 51; Luke 12 : 46, a. him his portion.
Acts 1 : 23, they a. two.
6 : 3, seven men whom we may a.
17 : 31, hath a. a day.
1 Thess. 5 : 9, God hath not a. to wrath.
Heb. 9 : 27, a. to men once to die.
See Heb. 3 : 2; 1 Pet. 2 : 8.

Appointment, Job 2 : 11, they had an a. together.

Apprehend, Acts 12 : 4, when he a. Peter.
2 Cor. 11 : 32, garrison desirous to a.
Philem. 3 : 12, I may a. that for which.

Approach, Num. 4 : 19, they a. unto the most holy.
Deut. 31 : 41, days a. that thou must die.
Job 40 : 19, his sword to a. unto him.
Ps. 65 : 4, blessed whom thou causest to a.
Isa. 58 : 2, take delight in a. God.
Luke 12 : 33, where no thief a.
1 Tim. 6 : 16, light no man can a.
Heb. 10 : 25, as ye see the day a.

Approve, Ps. 49 : 13, their posterity a. their sayings.
Acts 2 : 22, a man a. of God.
Rom. 16 : 10, a. in Christ.
Phil. 1 : 10, a. things that are excellent.
2 Tim. 2 : 15, show thyself a.

Apron, Gen. 3 : 7; Acts 19 : 12.

Apt, 2 Ki. 24 : 16, a. for war.
1 Tim. 3 : 2; 2 Tim. 2 : 24, a. to teach.

Aquila (ă-quĭl-ă) [Latinised form of the Greek Akulas], Acts 18 : 2.

and Priscilla accompany Paul, Acts 18 : 2.
instruct Apollos, Acts 18 : 26.
their constancy commended, Rom. 16 : 3; 1 Cor. 16 : 19.
Ar (ăr) [city], Num. 21 : 15, 28; Deut. 2: 9, 18, 29.
Ar Moab, the capital of Moab, Num. 21 : 28; Isa. 15 : 1.
Ara (âr-ă) [strong], son of Jether, 1 Chr. 7 : 28.
Arab (ă-răb), not identical in spelling with the name of the country of Arabia (see below) [ambush], Josh. 15 : 52.

Arab Encampment

Arabah (ăr-ă-băh) [the plain], Josh. 18 : 18.
Arabia [Heb. Arab, probably wilderness, desert, barren], a table-land which slopes gently downward from the mountainous south-west, where it overlooks the Red Sea and the Gulf of Oman. Thence it extends north-eastward to the Syrian Desert, and the low-lying plains of the Tigris and Euphrates and across to the Persian Gulf. One-third of this enormous table-land is irredeemable desert. Hence it comes that two apparently dissimilar places can be referred to in the Old Testament by this name.

(1) The east country—corresponding to the modern Trans-Jordania—variously known as the East or East country, Gen. 10 : 30; 25 : 6; Num. 23 : 7; Isa. 22 : 13; the land of the Sons of the East, Gen. 21 : 1; while its inhabitants were called Sons of the East, Judg. 6 : 3; 7 : 12; 1 Ki. 4 : 30; Job 1 : 3; Isa. 11 : 14; Jer. 49 : 28; Ezek. 25 : 4. These passages point to the land east of Palestine, and inhabited by the descendants of Ishmael and Keturah, possibly the ancestors of the modern Bedawin. From this restricted sense the name may have been extended to include

(2) The Arabian Peninsula which lies between the Mediterranean and Red Seas, the Indian Ocean and Persian Gulf, 2 Chr. 9 : 14; Isa. 21 : 13; Jer. 25 : 24; Ezek. 27 : 21.

See also **Arabia**, Ps. 72 : 10, 15.
kings of, pay tribute, 1 Ki. 10 : 15; 2 Chr. 9 : 14; 17 : 11; 26 : 7; Gal. 1 : 17; 4 : 25.
Arabians, Isa. 13 : 20; 21 : 13; Jer. 25 : 24; Acts 2 : 11.
Arabian Sea, or Red Sea, part of the Indian Ocean situated between India on the east and Arabia on the west.

Arad (âr-ăd) [wild ass], Num. 21 : 1, a royal city of the Canaanites.
Arair, modern name for Aroer on the Arnon.
Aral Sea, an inland sea in Tartary.
Aram (âr-ăm) [height], Gen. 10 : 22; 22 : 21, country north-east of Palestine, usually called Syria.
Aramitess (ăr-ăm-ĭ-těss), a woman of Aram, 1 Chr. 7 : 14.
Aram-Maacah (R.V.) (â-răm-mā-ă-cäh), 1 Chr. 19 : 6.
Aram-Naharaim (â-răm-nā-hă-rā-ĭm), district between the rivers Tigris and Euphrates, usually called Mesopotamia, Ps. 60, title.
Aram-rehob, an Aramean state.
Aram-zobah (â-răm-zō-băh), the land between the Orontes and Euphrates rivers, N.E. of Damascus and S. of Hamath, Ps. 60, title.
Aran (âr-ăn) [wild goat], son of Seir, Gen. 36 : 28; 1 Chr. 1 : 42.
Ararah, modern name for Aroer.
Ararat (ăr-ă-răt) [Armenia], which, according to Schrader, is called in Assyrian, A-ra-ar-ti. mountainous region in Armenia, resting place of the ark, Gen. 8 : 4; Jer. 51 : 27.

Mount Ararat

Araunah (ă-raû-năh), identical with Ornan [meaning uncertain, possibly Jah is firm], Jebusite, sells to David a site for the temple, 2 Sam. 24 : 16; 1 Chr. 21 : 15, 18; 22 : 1.
Araxes or **Gihon**, a river in Armenia, Gen. 2 : 13.
Arba (är-bă) [four], Gen. 35 : 27; Josh. 14 : 15; 21 : 11.
Arbathite (är-băth-īte), native of Arabah, 2 Sam. 23 : 31; 1 Chr. 11 : 32.
Arbela, a town in Assyria.
Arbite (är-bīte) [man of Arab], 2 Sam. 23 : 35.
Arch, Ezek. 40 : 16, 22, 26, 29.
Archangel, 1 Thess. 4 : 16, with the voice of the a. Jude 9, Michael the a.
Archelais, a city in Asia Minor, east of Antioch.
Archelaus (är-chĕ-lā-ŭs), Greek name [commanding the people]. See **Herodian Family**.
king of Judea, feared by Joseph, Matt. 2 : 22.
Archers, Gen. 21 : 20; 49 : 23; 1 Sam. 31 : 3; Job 16 : 13, etc.
Ahab and Josiah killed by, 1 Ki. 22 : 34; 2 Chr. 35 : 22.

Archevites (är-chĕ-vītes), inhabitants of Orchæ in Chaldea, Ezra 4 : 9.

Archi (är-chī), a city on the border of Ephraim, Josh. 16 : 2.

Archippus (är-chip-pŭs) [Greek name], exhorted by Paul, Col. 4 : 17; Philem. 2.

Archite (är-chīte), 2 Sam. 5 : 32; 16 : 16; 17 : 5, 14; 1 Chr. 27 : 33, Hushai the A.

Arcturus (ärc-tū-rŭs), the Latin name of the constellation; in Hebrew it is 'Ash, the Bear, Job 9 : 9; 38 : 32.

Ard (ärd) [fugitive], Gen. 46 : 21; Num. 26 : 40.

Ardite (är-dīte), member of the family of Ard, Num. 26 : 40.

Ardon (är-dŏn), son of Caleb, 1 Chr. 2 : 18.

Areli (ä-rē-lī) [heroic], from a word meaning " lion of God," Gen. 46 : 16; Num. 26 : 17.

Areopagite (är-ĕ-ŏp-ä-gīte), belonging to the council of the Areopagus, Acts 17 : 34.

Areopagus (är-ĕ-ŏp-ä-gŭs), the hill of Ares (or Mars). Here were held the sittings of the old, aristocratic court of Athens, which controlled the laws, education and religion. It may, perhaps, have been this court which inquired into Paul's teaching. Acts 17 : 19, 22.

Aretas (är-ĕ-tăs), Græcised name of many kings of Arabia; his deputy sought to apprehend Paul, 2 Cor. 11 : 32.

Argob (är-gŏb) [stony], Deut. 3 : 13; 2 Ki. 15 : 25.

Arguing, Job 6 : 25.

Arguments, Job 23 : 4.

Aridai (ä-rĭd-āī), Esther 9 : 9.

Aridatha (ä-rĭd-ā-thä), Esther 9 : 8.

Arieh (är-ī-ēh), 2 Ki. 15 : 25.

Ariel (är-ī-ĕl) [hearth of God], in reference to the altar, or [lion of God], Isa. 29 : 1, 7; Ezra 8 : 16; 2 Sam. 23 : 20.

Aright, Ps. 50 : 23, ordereth his conversation a.
78 : 8, set not their heart a.
Prov. 15 : 2, useth knowledge a.
23 : 31, wine, when it moveth itself a.
Jer. 8 : 6, they spake not a.

Arimathæa (är-ĭm-ä-thǣ-ä), or Arimathaim [the two Ramahs], home of Joseph, who buried Jesus in his own tomb, Matt. 27 : 57-60; Luke 23 : 51; John 19 : 38.

Arioch (är-ī-ŏch) [probably Accadian eri-aku, servant of the moon-god], Gen. 14 : 1, 9.

Arisai (är-ī-sāi), Esther 9 : 9.

Arise, Josh. 1 : 2, a., go over this Jordan.
1 Ki. 18 : 44, there a. a little cloud.
Ps. 68 : 1, let God a.
88 : 10, shall the dead a. and praise thee ?
102 : 13, a. and have mercy on Zion.
112 : 4, to upright a. light.
Isa. 60 : 1, a., shine, thy light is come.
Mal. 4 : 2, Sun of righteousness a.
Mark 5 : 41; Luke 8 : 54, damsel, a.
Luke 7 : 14, young man, a.
15 : 18, I will a. and go to my father.
Eph. 5 : 14, a. from the dead, and Christ.
2 Pet. 1 : 19, till the day a.

Aristarchus (är-ĭs-tär-chŭs) [Greek name, best-ruling], fellow-prisoner of Paul, Acts 19 : 29; 20 : 4; 27 : 2; Col. 4 : 10; Philem. 24.

Aristobulus (är-ĭs-tö-bū-lŭs) [Greek name, best

Ark of the Covenant

advising], his household greeted by Paul, Rom. 16 : 10.

Ark, of Noah, described, Gen. 6 : 14.
Noah's faith in making, Heb. 11 : 7; 1 Pet. 3 : 20.
of bulrushes, Ex. 2 : 3.
of God, an oblong chest which constituted the sole furniture of the Holy of Holies. Made of acacia wood it was overlaid, within and without, with gold. Its dimensions were two and a half cubits long by one and a half in breadth and depth.
its construction, Ex. 25 : 10; 37 : 1.
passes over Jordan, Josh. 3 : 15; 4 : 11.
compasses Jericho, Josh. 6 : 11.
captured by the Philistines, 1 Sam. 4 : 5.
their plagues in consequence, 1 Sam. 5.
restored, 1 Sam. 6.
carried to Jerusalem, 2 Sam. 6; 15 : 24; 1 Chr. 13; 15; 16.
ark of the covenant brought into the temple, 1 Ki. 8 : 3; 2 Chr. 5.
in heaven, Rev. 11 : 19.
See Heb. 9 : 4.

Arkite (är-kīte), Gen. 10 : 17; 1 Chr. 1 : 15.

Arm of God, Ex. 15 : 16; Deut. 33 : 27; Job 40 : 9; Ps. 77 : 15; 89 : 13; 98 : 1; Isa. 33 : 2; 51 : 5; 52 : 10; 53 : 1; Jer. 27 : 5; Luke 1 : 51; Acts 13 : 17.
Ex. 15 : 16, by greatness of thine a.
Job 40 : 9, hast thou an a. like God?
Ps. 89 : 13, thou hast a mighty a.
Isa. 53 : 1; John 12 : 38, to whom is the a. of the Lord revealed.

Arms, the everlasting, Deut. 33 : 27.

Armageddon (är-mä-gĕd-dŏn), more correctly Har-Magedon, or " The mountains of Megiddo." The reference of Rev. 16 : 16 is probably to the Plain of Esdraelon, " the classic battleground of Scripture," but the writer may have been influenced, owing to the proximity of mountainous country, by Ezek. 38 : 8, 21; 39 : 2, 4, where the prophet pictures the destruction of the forces of Gog " upon the mountains of Israel." See also Isa. 14 : 25.

For the Valley of Megiddon or Megiddo see 2 Ki. 23 : 29; Zech. 12 : 11.

Armenia (är-mē-́nĭ-ă), a mountainous country to the north-east of Babylonia, 2 Ki. 19 : 37; Isa. 37 : 38. In Hebrew Ararat.

Armholes, Jer. 38 : 12; Ezek. 13 : 8.

Armoni (är-mō-́nĭ) [of the palace], 2 Sam. 21 : 8.

Egyptian Archer

Armour. Of this both offensive and defensive forms are mentioned in Scripture. An army consisted of two classes of soldiers; light-armed, or skirmishers, and heavy-armed, who bore the brunt of the battle at close quarters. These were distinguished by their arms. Chief of the light-armed was the archer, who, on ancient monuments is seen with bow and arrow, and accompanied by a shield-bearer, a quiver-bearer and, when in a chariot, by a driver of horses. In this class also were included the slingers and throwers of darts.

The heavy-armed soldier carried such weapons as battle-axe, javelin, lance, sword and scimitar. Shields, cuirasses and helmets of various types were in use, while the feet were covered by sandals or shoes.

Swords and daggers were carried by both parties. The defensive armour worn by Goliath consisted of a " helmet of brass " (or copper rather, for brass was not then known); " a coat of mail," *i.e.*, a corslet of metal scales sewn on cloth and reaching down to the knees; " greaves of brass," *i.e.*, a covering of copper scales on the legs from the knees down.

Rom. 13 : 12, a. of light.

2 Cor. 6 : 7, by a. of righteousness.

Eph. 6 : 11, put on whole a. of God.

Armourbearer, an attendant on a warrior of superior rank, to carry the heavier arms,

Judg. 9 : 54; 1 Sam. 14 : 7; 16 : 21; 2 Sam. 23 : 37.

Armoury, Neh. 3 : 19; Jer. 50 : 25.

Army, Gen. 26 : 26, chief captain of his a.

Ex. 12 : 17, brought your a. out of Egypt.

1 Sam. 4 : 16, he that came out of the a.

1 Ki. 20 : 19, the a. which followed them.

2 Ki. 25 : 5, the a. of the Chaldees.

2 Chr. 25 : 9, given to the a. of Israel.

Ps. 44 : 9, goest not forth with our a.

Dan. 3 : 20, that were in his a.

Matt. 22 : 7, sent forth his a.

Acts 23 : 27, then came I with an a.

Heb. 11 : 34, turned to flight the a.

Rev. 19 : 14, a. which were in heaven.

19 : 19, against his a.

Arnan (är-năn) [nimble], 1 Chr. 3 : 21.

Arni, R.V., Luke 3 : 33. A.V. " Aram."

Arnon (är-́nŏn) [rushing], a river which was in early times the north border of Moab, while in later books of the Old Testament Moab extends to Heshbon. It is the largest of the perennial streams which enter the Dead Sea on the east, and the descent through a very deep gorge is very rapid, but like the other streams in this part of the desert, it is shallow, with a rocky bed, and only at times swollen to a dangerous torrent (Wady el Mojeb). Num. 21 : 13; Josh. 13 : 16; Deut. 3 : 12; 4 : 48. The name is applied to both river and valley.

Arod (ă-́rōd) [perhaps " wild ass "], also **Arodi** (ă-rō-́dī) [of the family of Arod], Gen. 46 : 16; Num. 26 : 17.

Aroer (ă-rō-́ẽr) [naked, bare], a city of the Amorites on the river Arnon, Josh. 13 : 16; Judg. 11 : 26.

a city in the south of Judah, 1 Sam. 30 : 28.

built by Children of Gad, Num. 32 : 34.

Aroerite (ă-rō-́ẽr-īte), 1 Chr. 11 : 44.

Arpad (är-́păd), camp, city and neighbourhood in Syria.

a fortified city near Hamath, 2 Ki. 18 : 34; 19 : 13; Isa. 10 : 9; 37 : 13.

Arphaxad (är-phăx-́ăd) [derivation doubtful], a tribe east of Tigris in North Assyria, Gen. 10 : 22; 1 Chr. 1 : 17.

son of Shem, Luke 3 : 36.

Arrabe or **Arraby**, a village in the mountains of Nablus.

Array (of order or arrangement), 2 Sam. 10 : 9, put them in a.

Job 6 : 4, terrors of God set in a.

(of dress or garb), Matt. 6 : 29; Luke 12 : 27, not a. like one of these.

1 Tim. 2 : 9, not with costly a.

Rev. 7 : 13, a. in white robes.

Arrived, Luke 8 : 26; Acts 20 : 15.

Arrogancy, 1 Sam. 2 : 3, a. come out of your mouth.

Prov. 8 : 13, pride and a.

Isa. 13 : 11, a. of the proud to cease.

Jer. 48 : 29, his a. and his pride.

Arrow, 2 Ki. 13 : 17, the a. of the Lord's deliverance.

Ps. 91 : 5, a. that flieth by day.

38 : 2, thine a. stick fast.

45 : 5, a. sharp in heart of enemies.

Ezek. 5 : 16, evil a. of famine.

CAESAREA — SUNKEN PORT

VIA DOLOROSA

Job 41 : 28, a. cannot make him flee.

Zech. 9 : 14, a. (of Lord) go forth as lightning.

Arrow-snake, R.V., Isa. 34 : 15; A.V., " great owl."

Arsuf, possibly Apollonia.

Art, 2 Chr. 16 : 14, apothecaries' a.
Acts 19 : 19, used curious a.

Artaxerxes (är-tă-xĕrx-ĕs), Græcised form of an old Persian compound, probably meaning having an exalted kingdom; the Hebrew form is somewhat different, Ezra 4 : 7.

king of Persia, his decree to prevent the building of the walls of Jerusalem, Ezra 4 : 17.

(Longimanus), permits Nehemiah to rebuild Jerusalem, Neh. 2.

(II.), permits Ezra to restore the temple, Ezra 7.

Artemas (är-tĕ-măs), Greek shortened form of Artemidorus [given by Artemis (or Diana)], Titus 3 : 12.

Artificer, Tubal-Cain the first, Gen. 4 : 22.

Artillery [bows and arrows], 1 Sam. 20 : 40, Jonathan gave his a. to the lad.

Arumah (ă-rû-măh), Judg. 9 : 41.

Arvad (är-văd), a city of Phœnicia, situated on a small island, Gen. 10 : 18; Ezek. 27 : 8.

Arvadite (är-văd-īte), inhabitants of Arvad, 1 Chr. 1 : 16.

Arza (är-ză), 1 Ki. 16 : 9.

As or Assarion, a copper penny equivalent to eight mites or lepta. In modern money the as is equal to a halfpenny or cent.

Asa (ā-sä) [physician, or contracted form of " Jah is healer "], his good reign, 1 Ki. 15 : 8.

his prayer against the Ethiopians, 2 Chr. 14 : 11.

his zeal, 2 Chr. 15.

wars with Baasha, 1 Ki. 15 : 16; 2 Chr. 16.

seeks aid from the Syrians, 2 Chr. 16 : 2.

rebuked by Hanani the seer, 2 Chr. 16 : 7.

his long reign and death, 2 Chr. 16 : 12.

Asahel (ă-să-hĕl) [God hath made], his rashness, slain by Abner, 2 Sam. 2 : 18-23; 3 : 27; 23 : 24; 1 Chr. 11 : 26.

Asahiah (ă-să-hī-ăh) or Asiah (ă-saī-ah) [Jah hath made], 2 Ki. 22 : 12.

Asaph (ā-săph) [a collector, or (God) collects], 1 Chr. 6 : 39.

a Levite, musical composer, his part in the temple service, 1 Chr. 6 : 39; 2 Chr. 5 : 12; 29 : 30; 35 : 15; Neh. 12 : 46. Psalms 50 and 73 to 83 are ascribed to him. And see 2 Ki. 18 : 18; Neh. 2 : 8.

Asareel (ăs-ă-réel), 1 Chr. 4 : 16.

Asarelah (ăs-ă-rē-lăh), 1 Chr. 25 : 2.

Asbestos, see Amianthus.

Ascend, Ps. 24 : 3, who shall a. into the hill of the Lord ?

Ps. 68 : 18; Eph. 4 : 8, a. on high.

Ps. 139 : 8; John 6 : 62; 20 : 17, if I a. up into heaven.

John 1 : 51, angels of God a.
3 : 13, no man hath a. to heaven.

Rev. 8 : 4, smoke of incense a.

Ascension of Christ (from Olivet), Luke 24 : 51; Acts 1 : 9; Rom. 8 : 34; Eph. 4 : 8; 1 Pet. 3 : 22.

prophecies concerning, Ps. 24 : 7-10; 68 : 18; John 6 : 62; 14 : 2, 28; 16 : 5; 20 : 17.

Ascent, 2 Sam. 15 : 30; 1 Ki. 10 : 5.

Ascribe, Deut. 32 : 3, a. greatness to God.

1 Sam. 18 : 8, a. unto David.

Job 36 : 3, a. righteousness to my Maker.

Ps. 68 : 34, a. ye strength to God.

Asenath (ăs-ĕ-năth) [meaning doubtful, compounded with the name of Neith, an Egyptian Goddess], wife of Joseph, Gen. 41 : 45; 46 : 20.

Aser (ā-sĕr), Luke 2 : 36; Rev. 7 : 6.

Ash [Heb. oren]. The word translated ash, in Isa. 44 : 14, in the Authorised Version, is translated fir in the Revised Version.

Ashamed, Gen. 2 : 25, and were not a.

Job 11 : 3, shall no man make thee a.

Ps. 25 : 3, let none that wait on thee be a.

31 : 1, let me never be a.

34 : 5, their faces were not a.

Isa. 45 : 17, not be a. world without end.

Jer. 6 : 15; 8 : 12, were they a.?

Mark 8 : 38, a. of me and my words.

Rom. 1 : 16, not a. of gospel.

5 : 5, hope not a.

2 Tim. 2 : 15, workman not needing to be a.

Heb. 11 : 16, not a. to be called their God.

1 Pet. 4 : 16, suffer as Christians, not to be a.

1 John 2 : 28, a. before him at his coming.

Ashan (ă-shăn), Josh. 15 : 42; 19 : 7; 1 Chr. 4 : 32; 6 : 59.

Ashbea (ăsh-bē-ă), 1 Chr. 4 : 21.

Ashbel (ăsh-bĕl), Gen. 46 : 21; 1 Chr. 8 : 1.

Ashchenaz (ăsh-chĕ-năz), 1 Chr. 1 : 6; Jer. 51 : 27.

Ashdod (ăsh-dŏd) [stronghold], a fortified town in plain of Philistia; now a mud village with cactus hedges, beside a red sandhill.

the ark carried there, 1 Sam. 5 : 1.

men of, smitten, 1 Sam. 5.

subdued by Uzziah, 2 Chr. 26 : 6.

prophecies concerning, Jer. 25 : 20; Amos 1 : 8; Zeph. 2 : 4; 9 : 6.

Ashdoth-pisgah (ăsh-dŏth-pīs-găh), [springs of Pisgah], Deut. 3 : 17.

Asher (ăsh-ĕr) [happy], son of Jacob, Gen. 30 : 13.

blessed by Jacob, Gen. 49 : 20.

blessed by Moses, Deut. 33 : 24.

his descendants, Num. 1 : 40; 26 : 44; 1 Chr. 7 : 30; Luke 2 : 36.

their inheritance, Josh. 19 : 24; Judg. 5 : 17.

See Ezek. 48 : 34; Rev. 7 : 6.

Asherah (ă-shē-răh) [A.V., grove], a sacred wooden post, possibly originally connected with tree worship, associated with the worship of Ashtoreth (Astarte), the Phœnician goddess of love, the moon (female) counterpart of Baal, the sun god. The asherah was set up near the altar of Baal. Judg. 3 : 7, and cf. 2 : 3; 6 : 25; 1 Ki. 18 : 19; 2 Ki. 23 : 14.

Asherites (ăsh-ĕr-ites), Judg. 1 : 32.

Asheroth (ăsh-ĕr-ōth), R.V., Judg. 3 : 7; A.V., groves.

Ashes, man likened to, Gen. 18 : 27; Job 30 : 19.

used in mourning, 2 Sam. 13 : 19; Esther 4 : 1; Job 2 : 8; 42 : 6; Isa. 58 : 5; Jonah 3 : 6, etc.; Matt. 11 : 21.

See Isa. 44 : 20; Heb. 9 : 13.

Ashima (ă-shī-̇mă), name of a Hamathite deity, derivation uncertain, 2 Ki. 17 : 30.

Ashkelon (ăsh-̇kĕ-lŏn), **Askelon**, or **Ascalon**, one of the five chief Philistine cities; derivation uncertain. Situated by the sea, though without a harbour, it was beautified by Herod, who was born there. A large Roman statue and other remains have been found here, and the walls, built by Richard Lion Heart, are still traceable. taken, Judg. 1 : 18; 14 : 19; 1 Sam. 6 : 17; 2 Sam. 1 : 20. prophecies concerning, Jer. 25 : 20; 47 : 5; Amos 1 : 8; Zeph. 2 : 4; Zech. 9 : 5.

Ashkenaz (ăsh-̇kĕ-năz), a north-Asiatic people; the modern Jews explain it as Germany, Ascania (?), and employ the word still in that sense, Gen. 10 : 3.
Sea, inland sea now called Black Sea.

Ashnah (ăsh-̇năh), Josh. 15 : 33.

Ashpenaz (ăsh-̇pĕ-năz) [uncertain derivation; possibly old Persian, horse-nosed], Dan. 1 : 3.

Ashtaroth (ăsh-̇tă-rŏth) [images of Ashtoreth, or of Astarte], goddess of Zidon, worshipped by Israel, Judg. 2 : 13; 1 Sam. 12 : 10; Solomon, 1 Ki. 11 : 5, 33.

Ashteroth Karnaim (ăsh-̇tĕ-rŏth kär-nā-̇ĭm), a ruined mound, now called Tell Ashtara, Gen. 14 : 5.

Ashtoreth (ăsh-tō-̇rĕth), **Astarte**, or **Ishtar**, the Asiatic moon-goddess [probably light-bringing], 1 Ki. 11 : 5.

Ashur (ă-̇shŭr) or **Asshur** (ăs-̇shŭr) [God of Assyria], Gen. 10 : 11, 22.
land of Assyria, Hos. 14 : 3.

Ashurites (ăsh-̇ūr-ītes), 2 Sam. 2 : 9; Ezek. 27 : 6.

Ashvath (ăsh-̇văth), son of Japhet, 1 Chr. 7 : 33.

Asia (ā-̇sĭa), Roman province within which the seven churches were situated.

Asia Minor, a province comprising the part of Asia between the Mediterranean and Black Seas.

Aside, Ex. 3 : 3, now turn a. and see this.
2 Ki. 4 : 4, thou shalt set a.
Mark 7 : 8, 33, a. from the multitude.
Heb. 12 : 1, let us lay a. every weight.
1 Pet. 2 : 1, wherefore laying a.

Asiel (ā-̇sĭ-ĕl), 1 Chr. 4 : 35.

Ask, 1 Sam. 12 : 17, in a. you a king.
1 Ki. 3 : 11, thou hast a.
Ps. 2 : 8, a. of me, and I shall give.
Jer. 6 : 16, a. for the old paths.
50 : 5, they shall a. way to Zion.
Matt. 5 : 42, give him that a.
Matt. 7 : 7; Luke 11 : 9, a. and it shall be given.
Mark 10 : 38, know not what ye a.
Mark 15 : 2, Pilate a. him.
Luke 11 : 10, every one that a.
John 14 : 13; 15 : 16, a. in my name.
1 Cor. 10 : 25, a. no questions.
Eph. 3 : 20, above all we a.
Jas. 1 : 5, lack wisdom, let him a. of God.
4 : 2, have not, because ye a. not.
1 Pet. 3 : 15, a. reason of hope.
1 John 3 : 22; 5 : 14, whatsoever we a.

Askelon (ăs-̇kĕ-lŏn). See **Ashkelon**.

Asleep, Judg. 4 : 21, he was fast a.
Matt. 8 : 24; Mark 4 : 38, but he was a.
Matt. 26 : 40; Mark 14 : 40, disciples a.
Luke 8 : 23, as they sailed he fell a.
(dead), 1 Cor. 15 : 6, some are fallen a.
I Thess. 4 : 13, them that are a.
2 Pet. 3 : 4, since fathers fell a.

Asnah (ăs-̇năh), Ezra 2 : 50.

Asnapper (ăs-năp-̇pĕr), probably corrupt form of Assur-bani-pal, king of Assyria, 667 B.C., Ezra 4 : 10.

Asp [Heb. pethen]. " The sucking child shall play on the hole of the asp " (Isa. 11 : 8). The venomous snake alluded to is most probably the cobra, Deut. 32 : 33; Job 20 : 14; Isa. 11 : 8; Rom. 3 : 13.

Aspatha (ăs-pā-̇thă), Esther 9 : 7.

Asriel (ăs-̇rĭ-ĕl) [God (is) prosperity (?)], Num. 26 : 31; similar are the names **Asariel**, 1 Chr. 4 : 16, and **Asarelah**, 1 Chr. 25 : 2.

Ass. This was in the Old Testament times the most important beast of burden of the East. It was strong, swift, and enduring. When first domesticated is unknown, but it was in use in Egypt thousands of years before the Christian era. Its importance was such that the " firstling of an ass might be redeemed with a lamb " (Ex. 14 : 13). It was not allowed to be yoked with an ox at the plough. Its flesh was unclean. In the dire extremity of famine in Samaria it was, however, sold for food (2 Ki. 6 : 23). White asses were in great esteem and of a high value.
(wild), the Hebrew word perè occurs frequently in Job and the Prophets, and probably refers to the Syrian wild ass (Asinus hemippus), as this ass is figured on the Ninevite sculptures; it was once apparently common in the countries around Palestine. Another form, arod, mentioned in Job 39 : 5 and in Dan. 5 : 21, was possibly the origin of the domesticated ass (A. onager), and still roams in flocks over the deserts of North Africa.
Num. 22 : 30, am not I thine a. ?
Prov. 26 : 3, bridle for a.
Isa. 1 : 3, a. his master's crib.
Zech. 9 : 9; Matt. 21 : 5, riding on an a.
Luke 13 : 15, each loose his a. on Sabbath.
14 : 5, a. fallen into pit.
John 12 : 14, had found a young a.
2 Pet. 2 : 16, the dumb a. speaking.
See Ex. 13 : 13; 23 : 4; Deut. 22 : 10; Job 39 : 5; Hos. 8 : 9.

Assarion or **As**, copper penny.

Assault, Esther 8 : 11, that would a. them.
Acts 14 : 5, there was an a. made.
17 : 5, a. the house of Jason.

Assay [attempt, try]. Job 4 : 2, if we a. to commune with thee.
Acts 9 : 26, Saul a. to join disciples.
16 : 7, they a. to go into Bithynia.
Heb. 11 : 29, Egyptians a. to do.

Assemble, Num. 10 : 3, shall a. themselves to them.
Joel 2 : 16, a. the elders.
Zeph. 3 : 8, that J may a. the kingdoms.

See Isa. 1 : 13; 4 : 5; Ezek. 44 : 24.
Assembling for public worship, Lev. 23; Deut. 16 : 8; Heb. 10 : 25.
David's love for, Ps. 27 : 4; 42; 43; 65; 84; 87; 118 : 26; 122; 134; 135.
instances of, 1 Ki. 8; 2 Chr. 6; 29; 30; Neh. 8; Luke 4 : 16; John 20 : 19; Acts 1 : 13; 2 : 1; 3 : 1; 13 : 2; 16 : 13; 20 : 7.
See Isa. 4 : 5; Mal. 3 : 16; Matt. 18 : 20.
Assembly, Ps. 22 : 16, **a.** of wicked.
Ps. 89 : 7, God feared in **a.** of his saints.
Eccl. 12 : 11, nails fastened by masters of **a.**
Heb. 10 : 25, forsake not the **a.**
Assent, 2 Chr. 18 : 12, with one **a.**
Acts 24 : 9, the Jews also **a.**
Asshur (ăssh-ùr), the original city which gradually gathered beneath its rule the surrounding country and cities to form the nucleus of what was to become the Assyrian Empire. Named after its god, Gen. 10 : 11, it gave its name to the whole region which it incorporated, Hos. 14 : 3. See **Ashur.**
Assigned, Gen. 47 : 22, had a portion **a.** them.
Josh. 20 : 8, **a.** Bezer in the wilderness.
2 Sam. 11 : 16, **a.** Uriah unto a place.
Assir (ăs-sĭr) [prisoner], Ex. 6 : 24.
Assist, Rom. 16 : 2.
Associate, Isa. 8 : 9.
Assos (ăs-sŏs), a maritime city of Asia Minor, Acts 20 : 13.
Assur (ăs-sùr), **Asshur** or **Ashur,** Assyria, Ezra 4 : 2; Ps. 83 : 8.
Assurance, Isa. 32 : 17, effect of righteousness **a.**

Assyrian Warrior

Acts 17 : 31, whereof he hath given **a.**
Col. 2 : 2, full **a.** of understanding.
1 Thess. 1 : 5, gospel came in much **a.**
Heb. 6 : 11, full **a.** of hope.
10 : 22, draw near in full **a.** of faith.
See 1 John 3 : 19.
Assure, Lev. 27 : 19, it shall be **a.** to him.
Jer. 32 : 41, **a.** with my whole heart.
Acts 2 : 36, house of Israel know **a.**
16 : 10, **a.** gathering that the Lord had.
1 John 3 : 19, shall **a.** our hearts before him.
Asswage, Gen. 8 : 1, and the waters **a.**
Job 16 : 5, my lips should **a.** your grief.
16 : 6, my grief is not **a.**
Assyria (ăs-sỹr-ĭ-ă) or **Asshur** (ăs-shùr), a country lying to the north of Babylon and centred on the Tigris. The name, derived from the national god, Ashir, was originally that of its earliest capital city, but later was extended to include the whole country. In 1300 B.C. the seat of government was transferred from Asshur (now Kalah Shergat) by Shalmaneser I. to Nineveh.
Extent.—From a narrow tract of country, bounded to the east and north by the mountains of Kurdistan and Armenia, to the west by Mesopotamia, and the south by Babylon, Assyria grew until in the heyday of its power its arms stretched from the Euphrates to the Nile. With the fall of Nineveh in 612 B.C., however, its power disappeared.
Population.—This was predominantly Semitic, probably a result of the migration of Semites which took place from Arabia in the fourth millennium B.C. Into this migratory invasion the original inhabitants would be absorbed.
Foundation of the Kingdom.—Tradition has it that this was the work of Belbani, at some date in the third millennium B.C. Nothing is at all certain, however, till the time of Khammurabi, about 1950 B.C.

Assyrian King

History.—While earlier kings had been consolidating their portion, it was not till the time of Shalmaneser II., a contemporary of Ahab and Jehu, about 860 B.C., that the westward movement of Assyrian Empire began. By him the countries round the east coast of the Mediterranean were ravaged, while Jehu, king of Israel, paid tribute. Rimmon-Nirari, grandson of Shalmaneser was next to appear, reducing Damascus to subjection. Afterwards came a usurper, Pul (Tiglath Pileser II.), 2 Ki. 15 : 19; 16 : 10, one of the greatest of eastern monarchs, in the times of Azariah, Menahem and their successors. He was succeeded by Shalmaneser IV., who, having captured Samaria, " carried Israel away into Assyria," 2 Ki. 17, and repopulated the country with the hybrid stock which was to become the Samaritan race of later days. Sargon, his successor, carried his wars to the gates of Egypt, though it was not till the reign of Sennacherib, his son, that Judah, under Hezekiah, 2 Ki. 18–19, again received Assyrian attention. Esarhaddon, who succeeded him, reigned from Euphrates to Nile, while Assur-bani-pal, his successor in 668 B.C., ravaged even Thebes in Upper Egypt. With his death in 630 B.C., the glory of Assyria began to decline, until finally it disappeared before the combined forces of Medes and Babylonians.

Character of the Empire.—This partook of the nature of a confederacy of states with the Assyrian as chief. Subject to " the great king " were his petty tributaries, holding their thrones at his behest and paying homage and tribute to him.

Religion.—This was polytheistic to an involved degree with Asshur or Ashir as chief and national deity.

Israel carried captive to, 2 Ki. 15 : 29; 17.

army of, miraculously destroyed, 2 Ki. 19 : 35; Isa. 37 : 36.

prophecies concerning, Isa. 8; 10 : 5; 14 : 24; 30 : 31; 31 : 8; Mic. 5 : 6; Zeph. 2 : 13.

its glory, Ezek. 31 : 3.

Astonied [astounded, stunned]. Ezra 9 : 3; Ezek. 4 : 17; Dan. 3 : 24, sat down a.

Astonished, Job 26 : 11, pillars of heaven are a.

Isa. 52 : 14, as many were a. at thee.

Jer. 2 : 12, be a. O ye heavens.

Dan. 8 : 27, was a. at the vision.

Matt. 7 : 28; 22 : 33; Mark 1 : 22; 11 : 18; Luke 4 : 32, a. at his doctrine.

Luke 2 : 47, a. at his understanding and answers.

5 : 9, a. at draught of fishes.

24 : 22, women made us a.

Acts 9 : 6, Saul trembling and a.

12 : 16, saw Peter, they were a.

13 : 12, deputy believed, being a.

Astonishment, Deut. 28 : 37, become an a. and a proverb.

Ps. 60 : 3, drink wine of a.

Jer. 8 : 21, a. hath taken hold.

Ezek. 23 : 33, filled with cup of a.

Astray, Ps. 58 : 3, they go a.

Prov. 28 : 10, causeth the righteous to go a.

Isa. 53 : 6, like sheep have gone a.

Matt. 18 : 12, one of them be gone a.

2 Pet. 2 : 15, gone a. following the way.

Astrologers, followers of, and believers in, the pseudo-science of astrology, a product of the ancient worship of the " host of heaven," according to which people believed men's destinies to be written in the movements of the stars.

(Chaldean), their inability, Isa. 47 : 13-15; Dan. 2; 4 : 7; 5 : 7.

Asuppim (ă-sŭp-̸pĭm) [stores], incorrectly rendered by the earlier authorities as a proper name, and so found in the A.V., 1 Chr. 26 : 15.

Asyncritus (ā-sўn-̸crĭ-tŭs), a Greek name [incomparable], a disciple, Rom. 16 : 14.

At one [in a state of friendship, reconciled]. " Would have set them at one again," Acts 7 : 26. From at one has come atone, " to set at one," to reconcile; and atonement (at-one-ment), reconciliation. So alone = all one. The numeral one was formerly pronounced own, as in alone, atone. " Atonement " was coined by Tyndale.

Atad (ā-̸tăd) [buck thorn], Gen. 50 : 10, 11.

Atarah (ăt-̸ă-răh), 1 Chr. 2 : 26.

Ataroth (ăt-̸ă-rŏth), Num. 32 : 3, 34; 1 Chr. 2 : 54.

Ataroth-adar (ăt-̸ă-rŏth-ă-̸där), Josh. 16 : 5; 18 : 13.

Ater (ā-̸tĕr), Ezra 2 : 16; Neh. 7 : 21; 10 : 17.

Athach (ā-̸thăch), 1 Sam. 30 : 30.

Athaiah (ă-thā-̸äh), Neh. 11 : 4.

Athaliah (ăth-ă-lī-̸äh) [Jehovah is strong], mother of Ahaziah, 2 Ki. 8 : 26.

slays the seed royal, 2 Ki. 11 : 1; 2 Chr. 22 : 10.

slain by order of Jehoiada, 2 Ki. 11 : 15; 2 Chr. 23 : 14.

Atharim [spies], Num. 21 : 1; caravan road, R.V.

The Parthenon, Athens

Athens (ăth-̸ĕns), the capital city of Attica in Greece. Once the intellectual centre of the world, and the chief school of philosophy, by Paul's time Athens was on the road to decay and living on its past reputation. This, however, was still sufficient to draw many to it, and a visit to Athens was still regarded as putting the finishing-touch to the education of a Roman. But the spirit of earnest inquiry was gone. Novelty alone could attract men's minds.

visited by Paul, Acts 17 : 15; 1 Thess. 3 : 1.

men of, described, Acts 17 : 21.
Athirst, Judg. 15 : 18, he was sore **a.**
Ruth 2 : 9, thou art **a.**
Matt. 25 : 44, when saw we thee **a. ?**
Rev. 21 : 6, I will give to him that is **a.**
22 : 17, let him that is **a.** come.
Athlai (ăth-lā-ī), Ezra 10 : 28.
Atonement, under the law, Ex. 29 : 29; 30;
Lev. 1 ff.
made by Aaron for the plague, Num. 16 : 46.
made by Christ, Rom. 3 : 24; 5 : 6; 2 Cor.
5 : 18; Gal. 1 : 4; 3 : 13; Titus 2 : 14;
Heb. 9 : 28; Pet. 1 : 19; 2 : 24; 3 : 18;
1 John 2 : 2; Rev. 1 : 5; 13 : 8 ff.
prophecies concerning, Isa. 53; Dan. 9 : 24;
Zech. 13 : 1, 7; John 11 : 50.
commemorated in the Lord's Supper, Matt.
26 : 26; 1 Cor. 11 : 23.
Lev. 23 : 28; 25 : 9, day of **a.**
2 Sam. 21 : 3, wherewith shall I make **a. ?**
Rom. 5 : 11, by whom we have received **a.**
Atonement, Day of. This was a fast of peculiar
solemnity, hence called in Acts 27 : 9, " the
fast." It was, moreover, a day on which no
work could be done. This day was called
a " high Sabbath " as well as a day of
" holy convocation," Lev. 16. It lasted
from the evening of the 9th Tishri till that
of the 10th. The ritual acts were performed
by the high priest, of which the most
important was his entering into the holy of
holies, which took place only on this day.
Atroth (ăt-rŏth), Num. 32 : 35.
Attai (ă-tā-ī), 1 Chr. 2 : 36; 12 : 11; 2 Chr.
11 : 20.
Attain, Ps. 139 : 6, high, I cannot **a.** to it.
Rom. 9 : 30, Gentiles **a.** to righteousness.
Phil. 3 : 11, if I might **a.** to resurrection of
dead.
1 Tim. 4 : 6, doctrine, whereunto thou hast **a.**
Attalia (ăt-tā-lĭ-ă), a city of Pamphylia in Asia
Minor, lying on the sea-coast, Acts 14 : 25.
Attend, 1 Tim. 1 : 1; 61 : 1; 142 : 6, **a.** to my cry.
Prov. 4 : 1, **a.** to know understanding.
4 · 20, **a.** to my words.
5 : 1, **a.** to my wisdom.
Acts 16 : 14, **a.** to the things spoken.
Rom. 13 : 6, ministers **a.** continually.
Attendance, 1 Ki. 10 : 5, **a.** of his ministers.
1 Tim. 4 : 13, give **a.** to reading.
Heb. 7 : 13, no man gave **a.** at altar.
Attent, 2 Chr. 6 : 40; 7 : 15, ears be **a.** unto
prayer.
Attentive, Neh. 1 : 6; Ps. 130 : 2, let thine ears
be **a.**
Job 37 : 2, hear **a.** the noise.
Luke 19 : 48, people were very **a.**
Attire, Prov. 7 : 10, the **a.** of an harlot.
Jer. 2 : 32, or a bride her **a.**
Ezek. 23 : 15, in dyed **a.**
Lev. 16 : 4, linen mitre shall he be **a.**
Audience, 1 Chr. 28 : 8, in **a.** of our God.
Luke 7 : 1; 20 : 45, in **a.** of people.
Acts 13 : 16, ye that fear God, give **a.**
22 : 22, they gave him **a.** to this word.
Augment, Num. 32 : 14.
Augustus (aŭ-gŭs-tŭs) **Cæsar** (çæ-śăr), the first
Roman Emperor, and nephew of Julius
Cæsar, was born 63 B.C., and died A.D. 14.

The title Augustus (English, august or
venerable), was conferred on him, 27 B.C.,
by the Roman Senate. After his death it
was continued as one of the titles applied
to his successors. Luke 2 : 1; Acts 25 : 25.
Aul, or **Awl,** Ex. 21 : 6; Deut. 15 : 17.
Aunt, Lev. 18 : 14.
Aureus, Imperial, a Roman gold coin equal in
value to about the old-time guinea or a
little over five dollars.
Austere, severe or rigid, Luke 19 : 21, 22.
Author, 1 Cor. 14 : 33, God is not **a.** of con-
fusion.
Heb. 5 : 9, he became **a.** of salvation.
12 : 2, Jesus, the **a.** and finisher.
Authority, Matt. 7 : 29; Mark 1 : 22, as one
having **a.**
Matt. 8 : 9; Luke 7 : 8, I am a man under **a.**
Matt. 21 : 23, by what **a. ?**
Mark 1 : 27; Luke 4 : 36, with **a.** he com-
mandeth unclean spirits.
Mark 13 : 34, gave **a.** to his servants.
Luke 9 : 1, power and **a.** over all devils.
19 : 17, have **a.** over ten cities.
22 : 25, exercise **a.** called benefactors.
John 5 : 27, **a.** to execute judgment.
Acts 8 : 27, eunuch of great **a.**
1 Cor. 15 : 24, put down all **a.**
1 Tim. 2 : 2, kings, and all in **a.**
2 : 12, suffer not a woman to usurp **a.**
Titus 2 : 15, rebuke with all **a.**
1 Pet. 3 : 22, angels and **a.** made subject to.
Rev. 13 : 2, dragon gave him great **a.**
Ava (ä-vă), probably identical with " Ivah,"
2 Ki. 17 : 24; 18 : 34.
Availeth, Esther 5 : 13, all this **a.** me nothing.
Gal. 5 : 6, in Christ, circumcision **a.** not.
Jas. 5 : 16, prayer of righteous man **a.** much.
Aven (ă-věn) [iniquity], Ezek. 30 : 17; Hos.
10 : 8.
Avenge, Lev. 19 : 18, thou shalt not **a.**
Deut. 32 : 43, **a.** blood of his servants.
Josh. 10 : 13, sun stood still till people **a.**
1 Sam. 24 : 12, the Lord judge, and **a.**
2 Sam. 22 : 48; Ps. 18 : 47, God **a.** me.
Isa. 1 : 24, I will **a.** me of mine enemies.
Luke 18 : 3, **a.** me of mine adversary.
Rom. 12 : 19, **a.** not yourselves.
Rev. 19 : 2, God hath **a.** blood of his servants.
See Gen. 4 : 24; Judg. 15 : 7; 1 Sam. 25 : 26.
Avenger, the " avenger of blood " (Josh. 20 : 3)
was the next of kin to a slain person, upon
whom, as the nearest relation, the obliga-
tion lay to execute the law of natural justice
—" Whoso sheddeth man's blood, by man
shall his blood be shed." To stay this
vengeance in cases of accident or justifiable
homicide, " cities of refuge " were instituted, to which the manslayer might flee,
and in which, if innocent, he should find
asylum so long as he kept within their gates.
The provision of " cities of refuge " did not
abolish the law; it only mitigated, or
stopped its execution where murder was not
wilful (Num. 35 : 12).
Num. 35 : 12, refuge from the **a.**
Deut. 19 : 6, lest **a.** pursue slayer.
Ps. 8 : 2, mightest still the **a.**
Ps. 44 : 16, enemy and **a.**

1 Thess. 4 : 6, Lord the a.

Avenging, in Judg. 5 : 2 avenging stands for leaders. " The avenging of Israel " means " leading the leaders of Israel."

Averse, men a. from war, Mic. 2 : 8.

Avim (ā-'vĭm), dwellers in ruins, Josh. 18 : 23; 2 Ki. 17 : 31.

Avith (ā-'vĭth), Gen. 36 : 35; 1 Chr. 1 : 46.

Avoid [to get out of the way of, retreat], 1 Sam. 18 : 11.
David a. out of his presence.
Prov. 4 : 15, a. it, pass not by it.
Rom. 16 : 17, divisions, a. them.
1 Tim. 6 : 20, a. profane babblings.
2 Tim. 2 : 23, unlearned questions a.
Titus 3 : 9, a. foolish questions.

Avouch [to avow, declare openly], Deut. 26 : 17.
Thou hast a. the Lord this day to be thy God.

Awake, Ps. 17 : 15, satisfied, when I a., with thy likeness.
Ps. 57 : 8; 108 : 2, a., psaltery and harp, I will a.
Prov. 23 : 35, when shall I a.
Isa. 51 : 9; 52 : 1, a., a., put on strength.
Dan. 12 : 2, sleep in the dust shall a.
Joel 1 : 5, a. ye drunkards, weep.
Zech. 13 : 7, a. O sword.
Mark 4 : 38, asleep, and they a. him.
Luke 9 : 32, when a. they saw his glory.
Rom. 13 : 11, high time to a.
1 Cor. 15 : 34, a. to righteousness.
Eph. 5 : 14, a. thou that sleepest.

Aware, Jer. 50 : 24, and thou wast not a. R.V., " expecteth."
Matt. 24 : 50, hour he is not a. of.
Luke 12 : 46, at an hour when he is not a.

Away with, is short for " go away with," meaning accompany, and, as a consequence, " put up with," tolerate. " The calling of assemblies I cannot away with " (Isa. 1 : 13), that is, I cannot bear or endure.

Awe, Ps. 4 : 4, stand in a., and sin not.
33 : 8, inhabitants of world stand in a. of.
119 : 161, my heart standeth in a.

Awl, Ex. 21 : 6; Deut. 15 : 17.

A work [at work or to work]. " To set the people a work," 2 Chr. 2 : 18.

Axe, 1 Ki. 6 : 7, hammer nor a. was heard.
2 Ki. 6 : 5, a. head fell into water.
Ps. 74 : 5, famous as he had lifted up a.
Isa. 10 : 15, shall the a. boast ?
Matt. 3 : 10; Luke 3 : 9, the a. is laid to root.

Axletrees, 1 Ki. 7 : 32, 33.

Azal (ā-'zăl), Zech. 14 : 5.

Azaliah (ăz-a-lī-'ăh), 2 Ki. 22 : 3; 2 Chr. 34 : 8.

Azaniah (ăz-a-nī-'ăh), Neh. 10 : 9.

Azareel, Neh. 12 : 36; 1 Chr. 12 : 6.

Azariah (ăz-a-rī-'ăh) (Heb. ă-zar-'ya) [Jah helps] (Uzziah), king of Judah, his good reign, 2 Ki. 14 : 21; 2 Chr. 26.
invades the priest's office, 2 Chr. 26 : 16.
struck with leprosy, 2 Ki. 15 : 5; 2 Chr. 26 : 20.
See also 1 Chr. 2 : 8; 6 : 9; 9 : 11; 2 Chr. 15 : 1; 26 : 17; 31 : 10; Neh. 3 : 23; Dan. 1 : 7.

Azaz (ā-'zăz), 1 Chr. 5 : 8.

Azazel (ă-zā-'zĕl), R.V., on the Day of Atonement the High Priest came forth from his annual entry into the Holy of Holies. Laying his hands upon a goat chosen by lot, he confessed over it all the iniquities of the Children of Israel for the preceding year. The goat, thus devoted to Azazel or destruction, was then consigned to the care of an appointed person who, carrying it off to some lonely untrodden spot, set it free to carry away into the desert its burden of sin. Lev. 16 : 8, 10, 26.

Azaziah (ăz-a-zī-'ah), 1 Chr. 15 : 21; 27 : 20; 2 Chr. 31 : 13.

Azbuk (ăz-'bŭk), Neh. 3 : 16.

Azekah (ă-zē-'kăh) [plowed], a town of Judah, Josh. 10 : 10, 11.

Azel (ā-'zĕl) 1 Chr. 8 : 38; 9 : 44.

Azem (ā-'zĕm), Josh. 15 : 29; 19 : 3.

Azgad (ăz-'găd) [strong is fortune], Ezra 8 : 12; Neh. 7 : 17.

Aziel (ā-'zĭ-ĕl), 1 Chr. 15 : 20.

Aziza (ă-zī-'ză), Ezra 10 : 27.

Azmaveth (ăz-mā-'vĕth), a village near Jerusalem, Neh. 12 : 29.
David's treasurer, 1 Chr. 27 : 25.
one of David's mighty men, 2 Sam. 23 : 31.

Azmon (ăz-'mŏn), Num. 34 : 4, 5; Josh. 15 : 4.

Aznoth-tabor (ăz-nōth-tā-'bôr) [ears of Tabor], Josh. 19 : 34.

Azor (ā-'zôr), Matt. 1 : 13, 14.

Azotus (ă-zō-'tŭs), Greek name of Ashdod, city on the borders of the Mediterranean, Acts 8 : 40.

Azriel (ăz-'rĭ-ĕl), 1 Chr. 5 : 24; Jer. 36 : 26.

Azrikam (ăz-rĭ-'kăm), 1 Chr. 3 : 23.

Azubah (ă-zū-'băh), 1 Chr. 2 : 18; 1 Ki. 22 : 42.

Azur (ā-'zŭr) [helper], Neh. 10 : 17; Jer. 28 : 1; Ezek. 11 : 1.

Azzah (ăz-'zăh), form of " Gaza," Deut. 2 : 23.

Azzan (ăz-'zăn), Num. 34 : 26.

B

Baal (bā-'ăl) [Eng. Lord], originally the Ballim or Baals were local deities connected with agricultural operations, gods of the soil or fertility. In course of time the localised attributes became centred in a common worship of Baal, the sun-god or chief agent in the production of plenteous crops. His female counterpart was Ashtoreth, the moon-goddess.
As with all religions connected with the soil, the worship partook of a gross and sensual nature calculated to attract the hot-passioned Eastern peoples. This element, it was, which so often led astray the Israelites from the sterner worship of the God of Righteousness.
worshipped, Num. 22 : 41; Judg. 2 : 13; 8 : 33; 1 Ki. 16 : 32; 18 : 26; 2 Ki. 17 : 16; 19 : 18; 21 : 3; Jer. 2 : 8; 7 : 9; 12 : 16; 19 : 5; 23 : 13; Hos. 2 : 8; 13 : 1; etc.
his altars and priests destroyed by Gideon, Judg. 6 : 25; by Elijah, 1 Ki. 18 : 40; by Jehu, 2 Ki. 10 : 18; by Jehoiada, 2 Ki. 11 : 18; by Josiah, 2 Ki. 23 : 4; 2 Chr. 34 : 4.

Phoenician and Carthaginian Figures of Baal

Baalah (bā-ʹă-läh) [lady], city in the south of Judah, Josh. 15 : 29.

Baalath (bā-ʹăl-ăth), Josh. 19 : 44.

Baalath-beer (bā-ʹă-lath-bēʹer) [lady of the well], Josh. 19 : 8.

Baalbek (bāalʹbĕk), a Syrian town north of Damascus now noted for the ruins of a great Greek temple.

Baal-berith (bā-ʹăl-bē-ʹrĭth) [lord of the covenant], Judg. 8 : 33.

Baal-gad (bā-ʹăl-găd) [lord of fortune or felicity], Josh. 11 : 17.

Baal-hamon (bā-ʹăl-hā-ʹmŏn) [lord of riches], Song of Songs, 8 : 11.

Baal-hanan (bā-ʹăl-hā-ʹnăn) [Baal is gracious], Gen. 36 : 38, 39.

Baal-hazor (bā-ʹăl-hā-ʹzŏr) [Baal of Hazor]. Hazor means castle, court, 2 Sam. 13 : 23. See under Baal.

Baal-hermon (bā-ʹăl-hĕr-ʹmon) [lord of Hermon], Judg. 3 : 3. See under Baal.

Baali (bā-ʹă-lī) [my lord, my husband], Hos. 2 : 16.

Baalim, see under Baal, Judg. 2 : 11; 2 Chr. 28 : 2; Jer. 2 : 23.

Baalis (bā-ʹăl-ĭs) [son of rejoicing], an Ammonite king, Jer. 40 : 14.

Baal-meon (bā-ʹăl-mē-ʹon) [Baal of the house (or dwelling)], Num. 32 : 38; more fully, Beth-baal-meon, Josh. 13 : 17.

Baal-peor (bā-ʹăl-pē-ʹôr) [lord of Peor], a mountain in Moab. The older scholars are probably correct in considering the name contains an allusion to obscene rites. the trespass of Israel concerning, Num. 25; Deut. 4 : 3; Ps. 106 : 28; Hos. 9 : 10.

Baal-perazim (bā-ʹăl-pĕ-rā-ʹzĭm) [lord of breaches, i.e. defeats], David's victory over Philistines at, 2 Sam. 5 : 20.

Baal-shalisha (bā-ʹăl-shăl-ʹĭ-shă) [lord of Shalishah], a district mentioned in 1 Sam. 9 :4, probably from some triple division, 2 Ki. 4 : 42.

Baal-tamar (bā-ʹăl-tā-ʹmär) [lord of the palm-tree], Judg. 20 : 33.

Baal-zebub (bā-ʹăl-zē-ʹbŭb) [lord of flies], false God of Ekron. Ahaziah rebuked for sending to inquire of,

2 Ki. 1 : 2.

Baal-zebul (bā-ʹăl-zē-ʹbŭl) [lord of the (heavenly) height].

Baal-zephon (bā-ʹăl-zē-ʹphŏn) [lord of the north, or of darkness], Ex. 14 : 2, 9.

Baana (bā-ʹă-nă) and **Baanah,** [probably son of sorrow], 2 Sam. 4 : 2; 1 Ki. 4 : 12. and Rachab, for murdering Ish-bosheth, slain by David, 2 Sam. 4 : 2. See also 1 Ki. 4 : 12, 16; 2 Sam. 23 : 29.

Baasha (bā-ăsh-ʹă) [derivation doubtful], king of Israel, destroys the house of Jeroboam, 1 Ki. 15 : 16, 27. Jehu's prophecy against, 1 Ki. 16 : 1.

Babbler, Eccl. 10 : 11; Acts 17 : 18.

Babbling, Prov. 23 : 29; 1 Tim. 6 : 20; 2 Tim. 2 : 16.

Babe, Ex. 2 : 6, behold the b. wept. Ps. 8 : 2; Matt. 21 : 16, out of mouth of b. Ps. 17 : 14, leave their substance to b. Isa. 3 : 4, b. shall rule over them. Matt. 11 : 25, Luke 10 : 21, revealed to b. Luke 2 : 12, the b. wrapped in swaddling clothes. Rom. 2 : 20, teacher of b. 1 Cor. 3 : 1, b. in Christ. 1 Pet. 2 : 2, as newborn b.

Babel (bā-ʹbĕl) [gate of El (or of God), or confusion]. Nimrod, king of, Gen. 10 : 10. confusion of tongues at the building of, Gen. 11.

Babes (as newborn), 1 Pet. 2 : 2. the humble and teachable so called by Jesus, Matt. 11 : 25; Luke 10 : 21.

Babylon (băb-ʹў-lŏn) [Greek form of Babel], chief city of the Empire of Babylonia. Gen. 10 : 10; 2 Ki. 17 : 30. ambassadors from, come to Hezekiah, 2 Ki. 20 : 12; 2 Chr. 32 : 31; Isa. 39. Jews carried captive there, 2 Ki. 25; 2 Chr. 36; Jer. 39 : 52. their return from, Ezra 1; Neh. 2. its greatness, Dan. 4 : 30. taken by the Medes, Dan. 5 : 30.

Walls of Babylon
(From an ancient coin)

its fall, Isa. 13 : 14; 21 : 2; 47; 48; Jer. 25 : 12; 50; 51.

church in, 1 Pet. 5 : 13.

the Great, Rev. 14 : 8; 16 : 19; 17; 18.

Babylonia. Situated between the rivers Tigris and Euphrates lay the two states of Sumer and Accad which later were to become parts of the Empire of Babylonia. In the chief city of Accad, Sipar or Sippara ruled, about 3800 B.C. Sargani or Sargon of Agade, the first king of whom anything definite is known. His campaigns, at the head of a Babylonian confederacy, carried him as far as the Mediterranean Sea. His son, Naram-Sin, extended his father's conquest. Later these were followed by Chedor-laomer (Kudur-lagamar), king of Elam, supported by his vassals Arioch of Ellasar, Amraphel of Shinar (Sumer), and Tidal, king of nations, who came in contact with Abraham, Gen. 14. It was not, however, till about 2300 B.C. that this loosely-gathered confederacy took more definite form and became consolidated, with Babylon as its chief city into the kingdom of Babylonia.

Winged Human Figures from Babylon

Thereafter information becomes less definite, invasion and repulsion followed one another till with the revolt of Assyria in the sixteenth century B.C. Babylonian power began to wane. The seat of power now shifted back and forward between these two contending states, Babylonia ever growing weaker, until at last Babylon itself, the capital city, was destroyed by Sennacherib, 689 B.C. Esarhaddon who succeeded him (2 Ki. 19 : 37) rebuilt Babylon and used it as a centre whence to set out on his career of conquest and thither his captives were brought, 2 Chr. 33 : 11. The

fall of Assyria, 612 B.C., saw the resurrection of Babylon under Nabapolassar. His son Nebuchadrezzar, having defeated the forces of Egypt at Carchemish, 604 B.C., soon made himself master of the west. Under him Babylonia reached the summit of its glory. A succession of weak kings followed, and in 538 B.C. it fell, for the last time, before the victorious arms of Cyrus, the Persian.

Babylonish (băb-ȳ-lō̄-nĭsh), Josh. 7 : 21.

Baca (bā̄-că) [valley of misery], Ps. 84 : 6.

Back, Ps. 21 : 12, shalt make them turn their **b.**

Ps. 129 : 3, plowers plowed on my **b.**

Prov. 26 : 3, rod for the fool's **b.**

Isa. 38 : 17, cast my sins behind my **b.**

50 : 6, I gave my **b.** to the smiters.

Jer. 2 : 27; 32 : 33, turned their **b.** unto me.

Matt. 28 : 2, rolled **b.** the stone.

Luke 9 : 62, looking **b.** is fit for the kingdom.

Rom. 11 : 10, bow down their **b.** alway.

Heb. 10 : 39, not of them who draw **b.**

Backside [rear], Ex. 3 : 1, to the **b.** of the desert.

Ex. 26 : 12, over the **b.** of the tabernacle.

Rev. 5 : 1, within and on the **b.**

Backbite, Ps. 15 : 3, that **b.** not with his tongue.

Prov. 25 : 23, a **b.** tongue.

Rom. 1 : 30, **b.**, haters of God.

2 Cor. 12 : 20, lest there be debates, **b.**

Backsliding [turning from God], 1 Ki. 11 : 9; 2 Cor. 11 : 3; Gal. 3 : 1; 5 : 4; Rev. 2 : 4.

of Israel, Ex. 32; Jer. 3 : 6, 11; Hos. 11 : 7.

of Saul, 1 Sam. 15 : 11.

of Solomon, 1 Ki. 11 : 3, 4.

of Peter, Matt. 26 : 70-74; Gal. 2 : 14.

God's displeasure at, Ps. 78 : 57-59.

punishment of, Deut. 11 : 28; Prov. 14 : 14; Jer. 2 : 19.

pardon for, promised, 2 Chr. 7 : 14; Jer. 3 : 12; 31 : 20; 36 : 3.

return from, Ps. 80 : 3; 85 : 4; Jer. 3 : 22; Lam. 5 : 21; Hos. 6 : 1.

Jer. 2 : 19, thy **b.** shall reprove thee.

3 : 12, return, thou **b.** Israel, saith the Lord.

14 : 7, our **b.** are many.

Hos. 4 : 16, Israel slideth back as **b.** heifer.

14 : 4, I will heal their **b.**

Backward, 2 Ki. 20 : 10; Isa. 38 : 8, shadow return **b.**

Job 23 : 8, **b.** I cannot perceive.

Ps. 40 : 14; 70 : 2, driven **b.**

Isa. 59 : 14, judgment is returned **b.**

Jer. 7 : 24, they went **b.** and not forward.

John 18 : 6, they went **b.** and fell to the ground.

Bad, Gen. 24 : 50, cannot speak **b.** or good.

2 Sam. 13 : 22, Absalom spake neither good nor **b.**

1 Ki. 3 : 9, discern between good and **b.**

Matt. 13 : 48, good, but cast the **b.** away.

2 Cor. 5 : 10, done, whether good or **b.**

Badger [Heb. tachash; Meles taxus].—The badger is found in Palestine, but the skins used as coverings for the Tabernacle were probably the skins of the sea-cow or dugong, common in the Red Sea. The Hebrew word may be a general term for all such like marine mammals as the dugong, seals, or porpoises. The R.V. in Ex.

25 : 6 and Ezek. 16 : 10 translates the word by "seal skins," or in the margin, "porpoise skins."

Badgers' skins used in the tabernacle, Ex. 25 : 5; 26 : 14.

Bag, Deut. 25 : 13, in thy b. divers weights.
1 Sam. 17 : 40, smooth stones in a b.
Job. 14 : 17, transgression sealed in a b.
Prov. 7 : 20, taken a b. of money.
Isa. 46 : 6, lavish gold out of b.
Mic. 6 : 11, b. of deceitful weights.
Hag. 1 : 6, b. with holes.
Luke 12 : 33, b. that wax not old.
John 12 : 6; 13 : 29, Judas a thief, and had the b.

Bajith (bā-jĭth) [house, temple], Isa. 15 : 2.
Bake, Ex. 16 : 23, b. that you will b. to day.
Lev. 26 : 26, ten women shall b.
1 Sam. 28 : 24, women at Endor did b.
Isa. 44 : 15, he b. bread.

Bakemeats, Gen. 40 : 17.

Baker, Gen. 40 : 1, b. had offended the king.
41 : 10, put in ward both chief b.
1 Sam. 8 : 13, your daughters to be b.
Jer. 37 : 21, bread out of b. street.
Hos. 7 : 4, as oven heated by the b.

Balaam (bā-lāam), Greek transliteration of Hebrew Bil-am; probably connected with Bela, a thing swallowed, ruin, with formative am at the end; therefore signifies destruction. By the older scholars incorrectly supposed to be composed of two words, swallower-up of people, Num 22 : 5.
requested by Balak to curse Israel, is forbidden, Num. 22 : 13.
his anger, Num. 22 : 27.
blesses Israel, Num. 23 : 19; 24 ; 1.
his prophecies, Num. 23 : 7, 18; 24 : 17.
his wicked counsel, Num. 31 : 16; Deut. 23 : 4.
See Josh. 24 : 9; Judg. 11 : 25; Mic. 6 : 5; 2 Pet. 2 : 15; Jude 11; Rev. 2 : 14.
slain, Num. 31 : 8; Josh. 13 : 22.

Balak (bā-lăk) [he tears open, destroys], king of Moab, Num. 22 : 2.

Balances and measures to be just, Lev. 19 : 35; Prov. 16 : 11.
false, condemned, Prov. 11 : 1; Hos. 12 : 7; Amos 8 : 5; Mic. 6 : 11.
Lev. 19 : 36; Ezek. 45 : 10, just b.
Job 31 : 6, weighed in even b.
Ps. 62 : 9, laid, in b. are vanity.
Prov. 11 : 1; 20 : 23, a false b. is abomination.
16 : 11, just weight and b. are Lord's.
Isa. 40 : 12, weighed hills in b.
46 : 6, weigh silver in the b.
Dan. 5 : 27, weighed in the b. and found wanting.
Hos. 12 : 7, b. of deceit in his hand.
Rev. 6 : 5, a pair of b.

Bald, 2 Ki. 2 : 23, go up, thou b. head.
Jer. 48 : 37; Ezek. 29 : 18, every head b.

Baldness, 1 Sam. 21 : 5, not make b. on their head.
Deut. 14 : 1, any b. between your eyes.
Isa. 3 : 24, instead of well set hair b.
22 : 12, the Lord did call to b.
Mic. 1 : 16, enlarge thy b. as eagle.

Ball, Isa. 22 : 18, he will toss thee like a b.

Balm [Heb. Tzori].—Several trees and plants in Palestine yield fragrant gums or resins, and such were used as medicines or for external application to wounds. Of these the Mastick, the modern Balm of Gilead, and the True Balm of Gilead, may be mentioned. The most precious of these is the last. It was at one time cultivated in Judea.
Gen. 37 : 25, Ishmaelites bearing b.
Jer. 8 : 22, is there no b. in Gilead ?

Bamah (bā-măh) [a high place or sanctuary], Ezek. 20 : 29.

Bamoth-Baal (bā-mŏth-bā-ăl) [high places, or sanctuaries of Baal], Num. 22 : 41.

Band.—A "band of soldiers" (John 18 : 3) was the tenth part of a legion, and numbered from five to six hundred. The band was divided into centuria or companies of a hundred each, with an officer over each hundred called a centurion. The "Italian Band" (Acts 10 : 1) was a body of strictly Roman soldiers from Italy. "Augustus' band" (Acts 17 : 1) was one of the five cohorts stationed at Cæsarea.
Ps. 2 : 3; 107 : 14, break their b. asunder.
73 : 4, there are no b. in their death.
Isa. 58 : 6, to loose the b. of wickedness.
Hos. 11 : 4, drew them with b. of love.
Zech. 11 : 7, two staves, beauty and b.
Luke 8 : 29, he brake b. and was driven.
Acts 16 : 26, every one's b. were loosed.
Col. 2 : 19, all the body by b.
Matt. 27 : 27; Mark 15 : 16, gathered to him whole b.
Acts 10 : 1, b. called the Italian b.
23 : 12, certain of the Jews b.

Banished, 2 Sam. 14 : 13, fetch home his b.
2 Sam. 14 : 14, that his b. be not expelled.

Banishment, Ezra 7 : 26, unto death or b.
Lam. 2 : 14, false burdens and causes of b

Bank, 2 Sam. 20 : 15, cast up a b. against.
Ezek. 47 : 7, at b. of river many trees.
Dan. 8 : 16, man's voice between the b.
Luke 19 : 23, my money into the b.

Banner, Ps. 20 : 5, in name of God set up b.
S. of S. 6 : 4, terrible as an army with b.
2 : 4, his b. over me was love.
Isa. 13 : 2, lift ye up a b. on mountains.

Banquet, Esther 5 : 4, let Haman come to b. cf. 7 : 2.
Job 41 : 6, companions make a b. of him ?
S. of S. 2 : 4, brought me to the b. house.
Amos 6 : 7, b. of them that stretched.
1 Pet. 4 : 3, we walked in lusts, b.

Baptism, i.e., cleansing or washing by the application of water. It was one of the rites of the Jewish religion (Num. 19 : 7; Heb. 9 : 10), although converts were never baptized until after the Captivity. At the time of John the Baptist, proselytes from the Gentile faiths were baptized as a symbol of renunciation of pagan errors and of their becoming pure for the service of Jehovah now that they were cleansed from sin. John took the ceremony and adapted it to the new dispensation which he was proclaiming, a purifying for the reign of Messiah. Though Jesus never baptized, His disciples did; and the sacrament has been given a

central place in the Church, though, of course, it has been differently interpreted.
of John, Matt. 3 : 6; Mark 1 : 4; Luke 3; John 1 : 19; Acts 19 : 4.
Pharisees' answer concerning, Matt. 21 : 25; Mark 11 : 29; Luke 20 : 4.
appointed by Christ, Matt. 28 : 19; Mark 16 : 15; John 3 : 22; 4 : 1.
its signification, Acts 2 : 38; 19 : 3; 22 : 16; Rom. 6 : 3; 1 Cor. 10 : 2; 12 : 13; 15 : 29; Gal. 3 : 27; Col. 2 : 12; Titus 3 : 5; 1 Pet. 3 : 21.
instances of, Acts 8 : 12, 38; 9 : 18; 10 : 48; 16 : 15, 33; 1 Cor. 1 : 14, 16.
one baptism, Eph. 4 : 5.
Matt. 20 : 22; Mark 10 : 38; Luke 12 : 50; baptized with b.
Matt. 21 : 25; Mark 11 : 30; Luke 20 : 4, b. of John.
Mark 1 : 4; Luke 3 : 3; Acts 13 : 24, b. of repentance.
Rom. 6 : 4; Col. 2 : 12, buried with him by b.
Eph. 4 : 5, one Lord, one faith, one b.
Heb. 6 : 2, doctrine of b.
1 Pet. 3 : 21, whereunto even b.
Baptize, Matt. 3 : 11; Mark 1 : 8; Luke 3 : 16, b. with Holy Ghost.
Mark 10 : 39, the baptism I am b. withal.
16 : 16, he that believeth and is b.
Luke 3 : 7, multitude came to be b.
7 : 30, Pharisees and lawyers being not b.
John 1 : 33, he that sent me to b.
4 : 1, 2, Jesus made and b. more.
Acts 2 : 38, repent and be b.
8 : 12, were b. both men and women.
8 : 36, what doth hinder me to be b. ?
9 : 18, Saul arose, and was b.
10 : 47, that these should not be b. ?
18 : 8, many believed, and were b.
22 : 16, be b. and wash away thy sins.
Rom. 6 : 3; Gal. 3 : 27, b. into Jesus Christ.
1 Cor. 1 : 13, b. in name of Paul.
10 : 2, were all b. in cloud.
12 : 13, all b. into one body.
15 : 29, b. for the dead.
Bar, Ex. 26 : 28; 36 : 33, the middle b.
Deut. 3 : 5, high walls, gates, and b.
Job 17 : 16, go down to the b. of the pit.
40 : 18, his bones are like b. of iron.
Jonah 2 : 6, the earth with her b.
Barabbas (bär-ăb-bäs) [son of the father], Matt. 27 : 20; Mark 15 : 7; Luke 23 : 18; John 18 : 40.
Barachel (bă-rā-chĕl) [El (God) blesses], Job 32 : 2, 6.
Barachias (băr-ă-chi-äs) [Jah blesses], Greek form of Berechiah, 1 Chr. 3 : 20; Matt. 23 : 35.
Barak (băr-ăk) [lightning], delivers Israel from Sisera, Judg. 4 : 5; Heb. 11 : 32.
Barbarian [a foreigner, one not a Greek].
Acts 28 : 4, b. saw venomous beast.
Rom. 1 : 14, debtor both to Greeks and b.
1 Cor. 14 : 11, to him a b., and he a b.
Col. 3 : 11, neither Greek nor Jew, b.
Barber, Ezek. 5 : 1, take thee a b. razor.
Bare, Ex. 19 : 4, I b. you on eagles' wings.
Deut. 1 : 31, thy God b. thee as.
Isa. 53 : 12, he b. the sin of many.

63 : 9, he b. them all the days of old.
Matt. 8 : 17, himself b. our sicknesses.
1 Pet. 2 : 24, his own self b. our sins.
Rev. 22 : 2, the tree of life b. twelve.
Isa. 52 : 10, the Lord hath made b.
1 Cor. 15 : 37, that shall be but b. grain.
Barefoot, 2 Sam. 15 : 30; Isa. 20 : 2, 3.
Bariah (bă-rī-äh), 1 Chr. 3 : 22.
Bar-jesus [son of Jesus, or of Jeshua] (Elymas), smitten with blindness, Acts 13 : 6.
Bar-jona [son of Jonah, or of Johanan], sometimes so written in the LXX., Matt. 16 : 17.
Bark, Isa. 56 : 10; Joel 1 : 7.
Barkos (băr-kŏs), Ezra 2 : 53.
Barley [Heb. seorah].—Barley and wheat were the two staple cereal crops of Egypt and the Holy Land. While both were sown about the same time the barley arrived earlier at maturity, and was the less costly of the two. Barley was most extensively used as a food for cattle, though also by itself, or mixed with wheat and other substances, for man (Ezek. 4 : 9). Sown in November or December, it ripens in favourable seasons in March or April. When the barley was in the ear the wheat was not grown up (Ex. 9 : 31, 32). The cultivation of this crop was on a very extensive scale. The manner of sowing is detailed in Isa. 28 : 24.
Ex. 9 : 31, flax and the b.
Deut. 8 : 8, wheat and b.
Ruth. 1 : 22, b. harvest.
John 6 : 9, five b. loaves.
Rev. 6 : 6, three measures of b. for a penny.
Barnabas (băr-nă-băs) [son of consolation].
Levite of Cyprus, sells his possessions, Acts 4 : 36.
preaches at Antioch, Acts 11 : 22.
accompanies Paul, Acts 11 : 30; 12 : 25; 13; 14; 15; 1 Cor. 9 : 6.
their contention, Acts 15 : 36.
his error, Gal. 2 : 13.
Barns were caves, natural or artificial, in the limestone rocks. These primitive storehouses were used not only for grain, but all kinds of produce. Buildings were in use as barns in the time of Jesus (Luke 12 : 18).
Job 39 : 12, gather thy seed into b.
Matt. 6 : 26; Luke 12 : 24, nor gather into b.
13 : 30, gather wheat into b.
Luke 12 : 18, pull down my b.
Barrel, 1 Ki. 17 : 14, the b. of meal shall not.
1 Ki. 18 : 33, fill four b. with water.
Barren, 2 Ki. 2 : 19, water naught, and ground b.
Ps. 107 : 34, turneth fruitful land into b.
113 : 9, the b. woman to keep house.
Isa. 54 : 1, sing, O b., thou that didst not bear.
Luke 23 : 29, blessed are the b. and.
2 Pet. 1 : 8, be neither b. nor unfruitful.
Barrenness of Sarah, Gen. 11 : 30; 16 : 1; 18 : 9; 21.
of Rebekah, Gen. 25 : 21.
of Rachel, Gen. 29 : 31; 30 : 1.
of Manoah's wife, Judg. 13.
of Hannah, 1 Sam. 1.
of the Shunammite, 2 Ki. 4 : 14.
of Elizabeth, Luke 1.

See Gal. 4 : 27.

Barsabas (bär-′să-băs) [son of the sabbath], Acts 1 : 23.

Bartholomew (bär-thŏl-′ŏ-mew) [son of Tolmai, or Talmai, brotherly (?)], one of the Twelve, Matt. 10 : 3; Mark 3 : 18; Luke 6 : 14; Acts 1 : 13.

Bartimæus (bär-tĭ-mæ-′ŭs) [son of Timæus], Mark 10 : 46.

Baruch (bâr-′ŭch) [blessed], takes Jeremiah's evidence, Jer. 32 : 13; 36.
carried into Egypt, Jer. 43 : 6.
comforted, Jer. 45.

Barzillai (bär-zĭl-lā-′ī) [iron-like], his kindness to David, 2 Sam. 17 : 27.
David's gratitude, 2 Sam. 19 : 31; 1 Ki. 2 : 7.

Base [baser sort = the rabble], of humble rank.
Job 30 : 8, children of b. men.
Ezek. 17 : 14, kingdom might be b.
Zech. 5 : 11, set there upon her own b.
Mal. 2 : 9, I have made you b.
Acts 17 : 5, fellows of b. sort.
1 Cor. 1 : 28, b. things of the world.
2 Cor. 10 : 1, who in presence am b.

Bashan

Bashan (bā-′shăn) [fruitful], large fertile region east of the Jordan, conquered, Num. 21 : 33; Deut. 3 : 1; Ps. 68 : 15, 22; 135 : 11; 136 : 20.

Bashan-havoth-jair (bā-′shăn-hā-′vŏth-jā-′īr), Deut. 3 : 14.

Bashemath (băsh-′ĕ-măth) [sweet-smelling], Gen. 26 : 34; 36 : 3; 1 Ki. 4 : 15.

Basilisk [Heb. tzephâ].—In the R.V. this word is so translated in Jer. 8 : 17; in the A.V. it is cockatrice. It evidently refers to some venomous snake, and from the fact that it " will not be charmed," was probably the cobra.

Basket.—Three kinds of baskets are mentioned in the New Testament—(1) a " hand-basket," usually carried in the hand or on the arm. It was into this basket the broken pieces were put at the miracle of the five thousand (Matt. 14 : 20). (2) A " store-basket " of a larger size than the arm-basket. It was the store-basket which was used at the miracle of the four thousand (Matt. 15 : 37). (3) A twisted or " rope-basket," called also a fish-basket. One of this kind was used for Paul's escape (2 Cor. 11 : 33). The basket which Pharaoh's baker carried on his head is the Egyptian " bread-basket."

Deut. 28 : 5, blessed shall be thy b.

Amos 8 : 1, b. of summer fruit.
Matt. 14 : 20; Mark 6 : 43; Luke 9 : 17; John 6 : 13, twelve b.
Matt. 15 : 37; Mark 8 : 8, seven b.
Matt. 16 : 9; Mark 8 : 19, how many b. ?

Bason, Ezra 1 : 10, b. of gold.
John 13 : 5, water into a b.

Basra (băs-′râ), a city on the Tigris.

Bastards, not to enter the congregation, Deut. 23 : 2.
See Heb. 12 : 8.

Bat [Heb. átalleph].—Named among the birds in Lev. 11 : 18 and Deut. 14 : 10, as not to be eaten. The allusion in Lev. 11 : 20 to "fowls that creep going upon all fours," may refer to bats. Although flying mammals (suckling their young) they were commonly included among birds on account of their wing-like anterior extremities. There are many forms of bats in Egypt and Palestine. Among ruins and in caverns they often swarm.

Bath, a measure of capacity, 1 Ki. 7 : 26; 2 Chr. 2 : 10; Ezra 7 : 22; Isa. 5 : 10; Ezek. 45 : 14.

Egyptian Basin and Ewer

Bathing or Washing.—Frequent purification of the person as symbolical of spiritual cleansing obtained under the Mosaic law. Washing of hands and feet was an ever recurring thing among the Jews. The six water-pots or large earthenware jars in the house at Cana, where the water was made wine (John 2 : 6), were for this purpose—" after the manner of the purifying of the Jews." By Pharisaic and Rabbinical formality the spiritual signification of the Mosaic precepts was caused to run altogether to the surface, and become a substitute for, rather than an aid to, purity of thought and habit (Mark 7 : 1-5).

Lev. 15 : 5, 21, b. himself.

Bathsheba (băth-shĕ-bă) [daughter of the oath], 2 Sam. 11 : 3.
her sin with David, 2 Sam. 11 : 12.
her request for Solomon, 1 Ki. 1 : 15.
her request for Adonijah, 1 Ki. 2 : 19.

Battered, 2 Sam. 20 : 15, b. the wall.

Battering-ram, Ezek. 4 : 2; 21 : 22, set b. against it.

Battle, laws concerning, Deut. 20.
of great day of God, Rev. 16 : 14.
of Israelites, etc., described, Gen. 14; Ex. 17; Num. 31; Josh. 8 : 10; Judg. 4; 7; 8; 11; 20; 1 Sam. 4; 11; 14; 17; 31; 2 Sam. 2; 10; 18; 21 : 15; 1 Ki. 20; 22; 2 Ki. 3; 1 Chr. 18-20; 2 Chr. 13; 14 : 9; 20; 25.
1 Sam. 17 : 47; 2 Chr. 20 : 15, b. is the Lord's.
2 Sam. 11 : 1; 1 Chr. 20 : 1, when kings go forth to b.
1 Chr. 5 : 20, they cried to God in the b.
Job 39 : 25, war horse smelleth b. afar off.
Ps. 18 : 39, girded with strength to b.
24 : 8, the Lord mighty in b.
55 : 18, delivered my soul from the b.
Eccl. 9 : 11, not b. to strong.
Jer. 50 : 22, sound of b. in land.
1 Cor. 14 : 8, who shall prepare to b. ?
Rev. 16 : 14, b. of that great day.

Battle axe, Jer. 51 : 20.

Battle bow, Zech. 9 : 10; 10 : 4.

Battlements, Deut. 22 : 8; Jer. 5 : 10.

Bay, Josh. 15 : 2, b. that looketh southward.
Josh. 18 : 19, north b. of the south sea.

Bay Tree [Heb. ĕzrach].—While it must remain uncertain what the tree mentioned by the Psalmist is (Ps. 27 : 35), yet it may have been the sweet bay (Laurus nobilis), a native of Palestine, and often growing very luxuriantly.

Bdellium [Heb. bdolach].—Mentioned in Gen. 2 : 12 in connection with gold and onyx stone, and in Num. 11 : 7, where the appearance of the manna is said to have the appearance of bdellium. Some think it a precious stone; some that it was an odoriferous gum. The bdellium of India is a fragrant gum.

Beacon, Isa. 30 : 17.

Bealiah (bē-ă-lī-ăh) [Jehovah is Lord], 1 Chr. 12 : 5.

Bealoth (bĕ-ā-lŏth), Josh. 15 : 24.

Beam, 1 Sam. 17 : 7, spear like a weaver's b.
2 Ki. 6 : 5, one was felling a b.
Ps. 104 : 3, who layeth b. in waters.
Matt. 7 : 5; Luke 6 : 42, cast out b.

Beans [Heb. pol; Vicia faba].—A much cultivated vegetable. Beans formed part of the provision brought to David by Barzillai and others when he fled from Absalom (2 Sam. 17 : 28), and were mixed with barley and other substances to form barley cakes (Ezra 4 : 9).

Bear, Gen. 4 : 13, punishment greater than I can b.

Ex. 20 : 16; Luke 11 : 48; John 1 : 7; 8 : 18; Acts 23 : 11; 1 John 1 : 2; 5 : 8; b. witness.
Lev. 24 : 15; Heb. 9 : 28, b. sin.
Num. 11 : 14; Deut. 1 : 9, not able to b. people.
Esther 1 : 22; Jer. 5 : 31, b. rule.
Ps. 75 : 3, I b. pillars of the earth.
91 : 12; Matt. 4 : 6; Luke 4 : 11, they shall b. thee up.
Prov. 18 : 14, wounded spirit who can b. ?
Isa. 52 : 11, clean that b. vessels of Lord.
Jer. 31 : 19, b. reproach of youth.
Lam. 3 : 27, b. yoke in youth.
Matt. 3 : 11, shoes not worthy to b.
27 : 32; Mark 15 : 21; Luke 23 : 26, b. cross.
John 16 : 12, cannot b. them now.
Acts 9 : 15, chosen vessel to b. my name.
Rom. 15 : 1, b. infirmities of the weak.
1 Cor. 13 : 7, charity b. all things.
15 : 49, shall b. image of the heavenly.
Gal. 6 : 2, b. one another's burdens.
Jas. 3 : 12, can fig tree b. olive berries.

Bear [Heb. dob; Ursus syriacus].—At one time this animal must have been very common in the Holy Land, where in certain wooded districts it still is met with. Its peculiar plantigrade feet (walking on its soles not on its toes) are referred to in Rev. 13 : 2. Its state of rage and agitation, when robbed of its young, is specially mentioned in 2 Sam. 17 : 8 and Prov. 17 : 12. The deep growling of the bear is alluded to in Isa. 59 : 11.
Isa. 11 : 7, cow and b. shall feed.
Isa. 59 : 11, we roar all like b.
Hos. 13 : 8, as a b. bereaved.
Amos 5 : 19, as if a man did flee from a lion, and a b.

Beard, laws concerning, Lev. 19 : 27; 21 : 5.
See 2 Sam. 10 : 4; Jer. 41 : 5; Ezek. 5 : 1.
2 Sam. 10 : 5; 1 Chr. 19 : 5, till b. be grown.
Ps. 133 : 2, even Aaron's b.
Ezek. 5 : 1, cause razor to pass on b.

Bearing, Gen. 1 : 29, every herb b. seed.
Ps. 126 : 6, b. precious seed.
John 19 : 17, b. cross.
Rom. 2 : 15; 9 : 1, conscience b. witness.
2 Cor. 4 : 10, b. about in body dying of Jesus.
Heb. 13 : 13, b. his reproach.

Beasts, creation of, Gen. 1 : 24.
dominion over, given to man, Gen. 1 : 26, 28; Ps. 8 : 7.
named by Adam, Gen. 2 : 20.
preserved, Gen. 7 : 2; Ps. 36 : 6; 104; 147 : 9.
what clean and unclean, Lev. 11; Deut. 14 : 4; Acts 10 : 12.
laws concerning, Ex. 13 : 12; 20 : 10; 22; 23 : 4; Lev. 27 : 9; Deut. 5 : 14; Prov. 12 : 10.
Daniel's vision of, Dan. 7.
John's vision of, Rev. 4 : 7; 13, etc.
Gen. 3 : 1, serpent more subtil than any b.
Ps. 49 : 12, like b. that perish.
73 : 22, as a b. before thee.
Prov. 12 : 10, regardeth life of b.
1 Cor. 15 : 32, fought with b.
Jas. 3 : 7, every kind of b. is tamed.
2 Pet. 2 : 12, as natural brute b.

Beat, Isa. 2 : 4; Mic. 4 : 3, b. swords into.
Luke 12 : 47, b. with many stripes.
1 Cor. 9 : 26, not as one that b. the air.
2 Cor. 11 : 25, thrice was I b. with rods.
Beauty, vanity of, Ps. 39 : 11; 49 : 14; Prov.
  6 : 25; 31 : 30; Isa. 3 : 24.
instances of its danger, Gen. 12 : 11; 26 : 7;
  34; 2 Sam. 11; 13, etc.
1 Chr. 16 : 29; 2 Chr. 20 : 21; Ps. 29 : 2;
  96 : 9, b. of holiness.
Ps. 27 : 4, behold b. of the Lord.
  48 : 2, b. for situation.
  50 : 2, perfection of b.
Isa. 33 : 17, see the king in his b.
  53 : 2, no b. that we should desire him.
  52 : 7; Rom. 10 : 15, how b. are the feet.
and Bands, the two staves so called, Zech.
  11 : 7.
of Holiness, 1 Chr. 16 : 29; 2 Chr. 20 : 21;
  Ps. 110 : 3.
Bed.—This word is used throughout Scripture
  for the mattress only, which among the
  lower classes was mostly a mat or course
  rug. Such a " bed " could easily be rolled
  up and carried away (Luke 5 : 25).
Job 7 : 13, when I say, my b. shall comfort.
  33 : 15, in slumberings upon the b.
Ps. 41 : 3, make all his b. in his sickness.
  63 : 6, when I remember thee upon my b.
Isa. 28 : 20, b. is shorter than a man.
Matt. 9 : 6; Mark 2 : 9; John 5 : 11, take up
  thy b.
Bedad (bē-dăd) [solitary (?)], Gen. 36 : 35.
Bedan (bē-dăn), possibly the same as Abdon
  (Judg. 12 : 13), or probably to be read
  Barak (with LXX. and Syriac) in 1 Sam.
  12 : 11; the name occurs also in 1 Chr.
  7 · 17
Bedeiah (bĕ-dē͏i-äh), Ezra 10 : 35.
Bedstead of Og, king of Bashan, Deut. 3 : 11.
Bee [Heb. debōrah].—Although the promised
  land is described as a land of olive oil and
  honey, and honey is very frequently mentioned in the Bible, yet bees are referred to
  but four times. In Deut. 1 : 44 and Ps.
  118 : 12 their attacking in swarms is alluded
  to; in Judg. 14 : 8 they are described as
  building in the dried up carcase of a lion;
  while in Isa. 7 : 18 the Assyrian bee is
  referred to metaphorically. The wild bee
  of Palestine makes its nest (comb) in the
  hollows of rocks, and in hollow trunks of
  trees. Honey was among the choice things
  sent as a present by Jacob to Joseph in
  Egypt (Gen. 43 : 11).
Beelzebub (bē-ĕl͏-zĕ-bŭb), Baalzebub or Beel-
  zebul (bē-ĕl͏-zĕ-bŭl), the last of these is the
  correct reading in Matt. 10 : 25 and other
  New Testament passages.
prince of devils, Matt. 10 : 25; 12 : 24; Mark
  3 : 22; Luke 11 : 15.
Christ's miracles ascribed to, Matt. 9 : 34;
  12 : 24, etc.
Beer (bēĕr) [a well], Num. 21 : 16.
Beer-elim (bēĕr-ē͏-lĭm) [well of trees], Isa. 15 : 8.
Beer-lahai-roi (bēĕr-lā-hâi-rô͏i) [the well of the
  Living One who sees me], Gen. 16 : 14.
Beeroth (bēĕr͏-ōth), a city near Bethel now called
  Bireh, Josh. 9 : 17.

Beeroth-bene-jaakan (bēĕr͏-ōth-bĕ-nē-jā-ă-kăn),
  R.V., Deut. 10 : 6.
Beer-sheba (bēĕr-shē͏-bă) [well of the oath], city
  and site of a well in the south of Canaan.
  It is now called Bir-es-Seba.
Abraham dwells there, Gen. 21 : 31; 22 : 19;
  28 : 10.
Hagar relieved there, Gen. 21 : 14.
Jacob comforted there, Gen. 46 : 1.
Elijah flees to, 1 Ki. 19 : 3.
Beetle [Heb. chargol].—This word so translated
  (Lev. 11 : 22) in the Authorised Version is
  rendered in the Revised Version cricket,
  which more correctly answers to the
  description in the text. The sacred beetle
  of the Egyptians (Scarabeus) is not noticed
  in the Bible.
Beeves [oxen, cows (plural of beef)], Lev. 22 : 21,
  a freewill offering in b. or sheep.
Befall, Gen. 42 : 4; 44 : 29, mischief b. him.
Gen. 49 : 1; Deut. 31 : 29; Dan. 10 : 14, b.
  in last days.
Judg. 6 : 13, why is all this b. us ?
Ps. 91 : 10, no evil b. thee.
Eccl. 3 : 19, b. men b. beasts.
Acts 20 : 22, things that shall b. me.
Beg, Ps. 109 : 10, let his children b.
Matt. 27 : 58; Luke 23 : 52, b. body of Jesus.
Luke 16 : 3, to b. I am ashamed.
John 9 : 8, he that sat and b.
Gal. 4 : 9, the b. elements.
Begin, Ezek. 9 : 6, b. at my sanctuary.
2 Cor. 3 : 1, do we b. to commend ?
1 Pet. 4 : 17, judgment b. at house of God.
Beginning, the, a name of Christ, Rev. 1 : 8;
  3 : 14.
of time, Gen. 1 : 1; John 1 : 1.
of miracles, John 2 : 11.
Ps. 111 : 10; Prov. 9 : 10, b. of wisdom.
Eccl. 7 : 8, better end of a thing than b.
Matt. 24 : 8; Mark 13 : 8, b. of sorrows.
Col. 1 : 18, who is the b., the firstborn.
Heb. 3 : 14, the b. of our confidence.
Begotten, Ps. 2 : 7; Acts 13 : 33; Heb. 1 : 5;
  5 : 5, this day have I b. thee.
John 1 : 14, as of the only b. of the Father.
  3 : 16, God gave only b. son.
1 Pet. 1 : 3, b. us again to a lively hope.
Heb. 1 : 6, when he bringeth in first b.
Beguile, Gen. 3 : 13, serpent b. me.
  29 : 25, wherefore hast thou b. me ?
Josh. 9 : 22, wherefore have ye b. us ?
2 Cor. 11 : 3, lest as the serpent b. Eve.
2 Pet. 2 : 14, b. unstable souls.
Begun, Gal. 3 : 3, having b. in the spirit.
Phil. 1 : 6, hath b. good work.
Behalf [in respect of, on account of], Job 36 : 2,
  speak on God's b.
Rom. 16 : 19, I am glad on your b.
Phil. 1 : 29, in b. of Christ.
Behave, 1 Chr. 19 : 13, let us b. valiantly.
Ps. 101 : 2, I will b. wisely.
Isa. 3 : 5, child shall b. proudly.
1 Cor. 13 : 5, charity not b. unseemly.
1 Thess. 2 : 10, how unblameably we b.
1 Tim. 3 : 15, b. in the house of God.
Behemoth.—This Hebrew word (which in form
  is the plural of the common word for beast,
  possibly signifying gigantic beasts) is left

untranslated in Job 40 : 15. It is apparently a transliteration of the Egyptian p. ehe, mau, water-ox or hippopotamus, and the description given of its food and habits tallies well with what is known of that animal. The R.V. gives hippopotamus in the margin. In other places the word is translated great beast.

Behistun, a city of Elam.

Behind, Isa. 38 : 17, all my sins b. thy back.
1 Cor. 1 : 7, ye come b. in no gift.
Phil. 3 : 13, forgetting things b.
Col. 1 : 24, fill up that which is b.

Behold, Job 19 : 27, my eyes shall b. and not another.
Ps. 27 : 4, to b. beauty of Lord.
37 : 37, b. the upright man.
Hab. 1 : 13, of purer eyes than to b.
Matt. 18 : 10, their angels b. face.
John 17 : 24, they may b. my glory.
19 : 5, b. the man.
2 Cor. 3 : 18, b. as in a glass.
Jas. 1 : 23, like man b. natural face.

Beirut, a division of modern Palestine.

Beisan, identical with Beth-shan.

Beit Jenn, village close to Mount Hermon.

Beit Jibrin, site of ancient Eleutheropolis.

Beit Rima, the ancient Beth Rimmon.

Bekah (bĕ-käh), a measure of weight equal to half a shekel, Ex. 38 : 26.

Bel (bĕl), contracted from Baal, Assyrian-Babylonian god Bel, Isa. 46 : 1; Jer. 50 : 2.

Bela (bē-lă), a town of Reuben, Gen. 14 : 8.

Belial (bē-lĭ-ăl) [worthlessness, wickedness], not a proper name in Old Testament; although in New Testament, under the forms of Belial and Beliar, it is regarded as a name of Satan, Deut. 13 : 13; 2 Cor. 6 : 15.
men of, wicked men so called, Deut. 13 : 13; Judg. 19 : 22.
children of, 1 Sam. 10 : 27.

Believe, Num. 14 : 11, how long ere they b. me ?
2 Chr. 20 : 20, b. in Lord, b. his prophets.
Ps. 78 : 22, they b. not in God.
Prov. 14 : 15, simple b. every word.
Isa. 28 : 16, that b. not make haste.
53 : 1; John 12 : 38; Rom. 10 : 16, who hath b. our report ?
Matt. 8 : 13, as thou hast b., so be it.
9 : 28, ye that I am able ?
18 : 6; Mark 9 : 42, little ones which b.
Matt. 27 : 42, come down from cross, and we will b.
Mark 1 : 15, repent and b. Gospel.
5 : 36; Luke 8 : 50, be not afraid, only b.
Mark 9 : 23, if thou canst b., all things possible.
11 : 24, b. that ye receive them.
Luke 1 : 1, things most surely b.
8 : 13, which for a while b.
24 : 25, slow of heart to b.
John 1 : 7, all men through him might b.
3 : 12, b. heavenly things.
5 : 47, how shall ye b. my words ?
6 : 36, seen me and b. not.
7 : 48, have any of the rulers b. ?
10 : 38, b. the works.
11 : 15, to intent ye may b.
12 : 36, b. in the light.

14 : 1, ye b. in God, b. also in me.
16 : 30, we b. thou camest from God.
17 : 21, world may b.
20 : 31, written that ye might b.
Acts 8 : 37, I b. Jesus Christ is Son of God.
13 : 39, all that b. are justified.
16 : 34, b. with all his house.
27 : 25, I b. God that it shall be as.
Rom. 1 : 16, power of God to every one that b.
3 : 22, on all them that b.
4 : 11 father of all that b.
Rom. 9 : 33, b. on him shall not be ashamed.
10 : 14, how shall they b. ?
1 Cor. 1 : 21, by preaching to save them that b.
2 Cor. 4 : 13, we b., therefore speak.
Gal. 3 : 22, promise to them that b.
1 Thess. 1 : 7, ensamples to all that b.
2 Thess. 1 : 10, admired in all that b.
Heb. 10 : 39, b. to saving of soul.
11 : 6, must b. that he is.
Jas. 2 : 19, devils b., and tremble.
1 Pet. 2 : 7, to you which b. he is precious.
1 John 4 : 1, b. not every spirit.
5 : 1, whoso b. Jesus is the Christ.

Bells upon the priest's ephod, Ex. 28 : 33; 39 : 25.
See Zech. 14 : 20.

Belly, Gen. 3 : 14, upon thy b. shalt thou go.
Job 15 : 2, b. with east wind.
Ps. 22 : 10, my God from my mother's b.
Jonah 1 : 17; Matt. 12 : 40, in b. of fish.
Matt. 15 : 17; Mark 7 : 19, into b. and is cast out.
John 7 : 38, out of his b. flow rivers.
Rom. 16 : 18, serve their own b.
1 Cor. 6 : 13, meats for b., and b. for meats.
Phil. 3 : 19, whose God is their b.
Titus 1 : 12, Cretians slow b.
Rev. 10 : 9, it shall make thy b. bitter.

Belong, Gen. 40 : 8, interpretations b. to God.
Deut. 29 : 29, secret things b. to Lord.
Ps. 68 : 20, to God b. issues from death.
94 : 1, God, to whom vengeance b.
Dan. 9 : 7, righteousness b. to thee.
Mark 9 : 41, because ye b. to Christ.
Luke 19 : 42, things that b. to thy peace.
Heb. 5 : 14, strong meat b. to them.

Beloved, Deut. 33 : 12, b. of Lord dwell in safety.
Neh. 13 : 26, Solomon b. of his God.
Ps. 60 : 5; 108 : 6, thy b. may be delivered.
127 : 2, so he giveth his b. sleep.
Cant. 5 : 1, drink abundantly, O b.
Dan. 5 : 23; 10 : 11, 19, greatly b.
Matt. 3 : 17; 17 : 5, b. son.
Rom. 9 : 25, b. which was not b.
11 : 28, b. for the fathers' sakes.
Eph. 1 : 6, accepted in the b.
Col. 3 : 12, elect of God, holy and b.
4 : 9; Philem. 16, b. brother.
Rev. 20 : 9, compassed b. city.

Belshazzar (bĕl-shăz-zär). The Babylonian form is Bel-sharra-usur [Bel protect the king], Dan. 5 : 1; 8 : 1.
his profane feast, warning, and death, Dan. 5.

Belteshazzar (bĕl-tĕ-shăz-zär). The probable Babylonian form is Balatsu-usur [preserve his life], name given to Daniel in Babylon, Dan. 1 : 7, etc.

Ben (bĕn), a son, 1 Chr. 15 : 18.
Benaiah (bĕ-nâi-ăh) [Jah builds, or gives prosperity], 2 Sam. 8 : 18.
valiant acts of, 2 Sam. 23 : 20; 1 Chr. 11 : 22; 27 : 5.
proclaims Solomon king, 1 Ki. 1 : 32.
slays Adonijah, Joab, and Shimei, 1 Ki. 2 : 25-46.
Ben-ammi (bĕn-ăm-mī) [son of my people], Gen. 19 : 38.
Benches, Ezek. 27 : 6.
Bend, Ps. 11 : 2, the wicked b. their bow.
Ps. 58 : 7, he b. his bow.
Isa. 60 : 14, afflicted thee, come b. to thee.
Jer. 46 : 9, Lydians, that b. the bow.
Ezek. 17 : 7, vine did b. her root.
Beneath, Deut. 4 : 39, earth b.
Isa. 14 : 9, hell from b. is moved.
Amos 2 : 9, and his roots from b.
Mark 14 : 66, as Peter was b. in the palace.
John 8 : 23, ye are from b.
Bene-berak (bĕn-ĕ-bē-răk), Josh. 19 : 45.
Benefactors, Luke 22 : 25.
Benefit, Ps. 68 : 19, daily loadeth us with b.
Ps. 103 : 2, forget not all his b.
116 : 12, what render for all his b. ?
Jer. 18 : 10, I would b. them.
1 Tim. 6 : 2, partakers of the b.
Philem. 14, that thy b. should not be.
Benevolence, 1 Cor. 7 : 3.
Ben-hadad (bĕn-hā-dăd) [son of Hadad], shortened for Ben-hadad-hidri. There was a Syrian god Ben hadad, 1 Ki. 15 : 18.
king of Syria, his league with Asa, 1 Ki. 15 : 18.
war with Ahab, 1 Ki. 20.
baffled by Elisha, 2 Ki. 6 : 8.
besieges Samaria, 2 Ki. 6 : 24; 7,
slain by Hazael, 2 Ki. 8 : 7.
son of Hazael, wars with Israel, 2 Ki. 13 : 3, 25.
See Jer. 49 : 27; Amos 1 : 4.
Ben-hail (bĕn-hail), 2 Chr. 17 : 7.
Ben-hanan (bĕn-hā-năn), 1 Chr. 4 : 20.
Benjamin [son of the right hand] (Ben-oni), youngest son of Jacob, his birth, Gen. 35 : 18.
sent into Egypt, Gen. 43 : 15.
Joseph's stratagem to detain, Gen. 44.
his descendants, Gen. 46 : 21; 1 Chr. 7 : 6.
Jacob's prophecy concerning, Gen. 49 : 27.
twice numbered, Num. 1 : 36; 26 : 38.
blessed by Moses, Deut. 33 : 12.
their wickedness chastised, Judg. 20 : 21.
the first king chosen from, 1 Sam. 9 : 16.
support the house of Saul, 2 Sam. 2; afterwards adhere to that of David, 1 Ki. 12 : 20, 21; 1 Chr. 11.
their inheritance, Josh. 18 : 11.
See Ps. 68 : 27; Ezek. 48 : 32; Rev. 7 : 8.
the tribe of Paul, Phil. 3 : 5.
Ben-oni (bĕn-ō-nī) [son of my sorrow], Gen. 35 : 18.
Ben-zoheth (bĕn-zō-hĕth), 1 Chr. 4 : 20.
Beor (bē-ôr) [a torch], father of Balaam, Num. 22 : 5; Deut. 23 : 4; two of name.
Bera (bē-ră), Gen. 14 : 2.
Berachah (bē-rā-chăh) [blessing], 1 Chr. 12 : 3; 2 Chr. 20 : 26; person and valley.

Berachiah (bĕr-ă-chī-ăh), 1 Chr. 6 : 39.
Beraiah (bĕ-râi-ăh) [Jehovah created], 1 Chr. 8 : 21.
Berea (bĕ-rē-ă), a city of Macedonia.
Paul preaches at, Acts 17 : 10.
people of, commended, Acts 17 : 11.
Bereave, Eccl. 4 : 8, b. my soul of good.
Jer. 15 : 7; 18 : 21, b. them of children.
Lam. 1 : 20, abroad the sword b.
Ezek. 36 : 14, neither b. thy nations.
Hos. 13 : 8, as a b. bear.
Berechiah (bĕr-ē-chī-ăh) [the Lord hath blessed], 1 Chr. 9 : 16.
Bered (bĕ-rĕd), Gen. 16 : 14; 1 Chr. 7 : 20.
Beri (bē-rī), 1 Chr. 7 : 36.
Beriah (bĕ-rī-ah), Gen. 46 : 17; Num. 26 : 44; three of name.
Beriites (bĕ-rī-ītes), the descendants of Beriah, Num. 26 : 44.
Berith (bĕ-rīth) [covenant], Judg. 9 : 46.
Bernice (bĕr-nī-çē), Greek for Pherenice [victory-bringing], daughter of Herod Agrippa, Acts 25 : 13.
Berodach-baladan (bĕr-ō-dăch-băl-ă-dăn), 2 Ki. 20 : 12.
Berothah (bĕ-rō-thăh), or Beirut, seaport on the Mediterranean.
Berothai (bĕ-rō-thâi), 2 Sam. 8 : 8.
Beryl [Heb. Tarshish—Ex. 28 : 20; Ezek. 28 : 13; Rev. 21 : 20]. There is some uncertainty about this stone. The ordinary Greek Version and the A.V. identify tarshish with the beryl, while the Vulgate appears to translate yāshepēh thus, making tarshish to be chrysolite (meaning topaz thereby). On the other hand, shoham is by the LXX. given as meaning beryl. It has been suggested that the beryl came from Tartessus in Spain, but known sources of it existed in Egypt and India in early times.
Besai (bē-sâi), Ezra 2 : 49.
Beseech, Ex. 32 : 11; Deut. 3 : 23; 1 Ki. 13 : 6; Jer. 26 : 19, b. the Lord.
Ex. 33 : 18, I b. show me thy glory.
Ps. 80 : 14, return, we b., O God.
Mal. 1 : 9, b. God, he be gracious.
Matt. 8 : 5, centurion, b. him.
8 : 31; Luke 8 : 31, devils b. him.
Luke 5 : 12, fell on his face and b.
7 : 3, b. him that he would come.
8 : 37, b. him to depart from them.
John 4 : 40, b. that he would tarry.
Acts 27 : 33, Paul b. them all.
Rom. 12 : 1, b. you by the mercies of God.
1 Cor. 1 : 10, wherefore I b. you.
2 Cor. 5 : 20, as though God did b. you.
12 : 8, b. the Lord thrice.
Gal. 4 : 12, I b., be as I am.
Philem. 9, for love's sake b. thee.
1 Tim. 1 : 3, as I b. thee.
Beset, Ps. 139 : 5, b. me behind and before.
Hos. 7 : 2, own doings have b. them.
Heb. 12 : 1, sin which doth so easily b. us.
Beside, Mark 3 : 21, he is b. himself.
Acts 26 : 24, Paul, thou art b. thyself.
2 Cor. 5 : 13, whether we b. ourselves.
Besiege, Deut. 20 : 12, then thou shalt b. it.
Ezek. 6 : 12, remaineth and is b.
See Deut. 28 : 52; Jer. 52 : 5.

Besodeiah (bĕs-ō-dêî-ăh) [in the secret of the Lord], Neh. 3 : 6.

Besom, a broom or brush, Isa. 14 : 23.

Besor (bē-ʹsôr) [rich in grass], 1 Sam. 30 : 10.

Best, Gen. 47 : 6, b. of the land.
2 Sam. 18 : 4, what seemeth you b.
Ps. 39 : 5, man at his b. state is vanity.
Luke 15 : 22, b. r obe.
1 Cor. 12 : 31, covet b. gifts.

Bestead [placed, circumstanced], "Hardly bestead" (Isa. 8 : 21), means, involved in or beset with hardships.

Bestir, 2 Sam. 5 : 24.

Bestow, Ex. 32 : 29, b. upon you a blessing.
Isa. 63 : 7, the Lord hath b. on us.
Luke 12 : 17, no room to b. my fruits.
1 Cor. 13 : 3, though I b. all my goods.
15 : 10, grace b. on me not in vain.
Gal. 4 : 11, lest I have b. labour in vain.
1 John 3 : 1, manner of love the Father hath b.

Betah (bē-ʹtăh) [confidence], 2 Sam. 8 : 8.

Beten (bē-ʹtĕn) [belly, valley], Josh. 19 : 25.

Bethabara (bĕth-ăb-ʹă-ră) [house of the ford], one of the principal fords of the Jordan at which John the Baptist baptized those who came to him, John 1 : 28.

Bethany (bĕth-ʹă-nŷ) [house of dates], a village near Jerusalem, the home of Lazarus and his sisters.
visited by Christ, Matt. 21 : 17; 26 : 6; Mark 11 : 1; Luke 19 : 29; John 12 : 1.
raising of Lazarus at, John 11 : 18-44.
ascension of Christ at, Luke 24 : 50, 51.

Beth-arbel (bĕth-är-ʹbel) [house of Arbel], explained by some, "house of God's ambush," by others, "house of the four gods."
a town of Zebulon, Hos. 10 : 14.

Beth-aven (bĕth-ā-ʹvĕn) [house of vanity (idolatry)], Josh. 7 : 2.

Beth-barah (bĕth-băr-ʹăh), Judg. 7 : 24. See Bethabara.

Beth-birei (bĕth-bĭr-ʹĕ-ī) [house of my making], 1 Chr. 4 : 31, called in Josh. 19 : 6, Beth-lebaoth [house of lionesses].

Beth-car [house of the lamb, or pasture-house], 1 Sam. 7 : 11.

Beth-dagon [house of Dagon], Josh. 19 : 27, a city of Judah now called Beit Dejan, Josh. 15 : 41.

Beth-diblathaim (bĕth-dĭb-lă-thā-ʹim) [house of the two fig cakes], Jer. 48 : 22. The name is mentioned on King Mesha's stone. See Moabite Stone.

Beth-el (bĕth-ʹel) [house of God], a village twelve miles north of Jerusalem.
Jacob's vision there, Gen. 28 : 19; 31 : 13; he builds an altar, Gen. 35 : 1.
occupied by the house of Joseph, Judg. 1 : 22.
idolatry of Jeroboam at, 1 Ki. 12 : 28; 13 : 1.
prophets dwell there, 2 Ki. 2 : 2, 3 ; 17 : 28.
reformation by Josiah at, 2 Ki. 23 : 15.
See Amos 3 : 14; 4 : 4; 5 : 5; 7 : 10.

Beth-elite (bĕth-ʹel-īte), inhabitant of Bethel, 1 Ki. 16 : 34.

Bethesda (bĕth-ĕs-ʹdă) [house of mercy or house of the stream], a pool at Jerusalem which is remarkable for the sudden, intermittent flow of its waters, in the cave which now communicates, by an aqueduct, with the pool of Siloam. It is visited by the Jews for the healing of disease.
miracles wrought at, John 5 : 2.

Beth-horon (bĕth-hô-ʹrŏn) [house of caves], two towns of Ephraim—upper and nether, Josh. 10 : 10, 11, battle of.

Bethink, 1 Ki. 8 : 47; 2 Chr. 6 : 37, b. themselves.

Beth-jeshimoth (bĕth-jĕsh-ʹī-mŏth), a city of the Reubenites, Josh. 13 : 20.

Beth-lehem (bĕth-ʹlĕ-hĕm) [house of bread], Gen. 35 : 19.
birth-place of our Lord, cf. Mic. 5 : 2; Matt. 2 : 1, 5, 6, and the site of the so-called Church of the Nativity.
Naomi and Ruth returned to, Ruth 1–4.
David anointed at, 1 Sam. 16 : 13; 20 : 6.
well of, mentioned, 2 Sam. 23 : 15; 1 Chr. 11 : 17.
Christ's birth predicted, Mic. 5 : 2; Ps. 132 : 5, 6.
Christ's birth at, Matt. 2 : 1; Luke 2 : 4; John 7 : 42.
children of, slain, Matt. 2 : 16.

Beth-lehemite (bĕth-ʹlĕ-hĕm-īte), man of Bethlehem, 1 Sam. 16 : 18; 2 Sam. 21 : 19.

Beth-maachah (bĕth-mā-ă-chăh) [house of oppression], 2 Sam. 20 : 14, 15.

Beth-peor (bĕth-pē-ʹôr) [house of Peor] (Baal-peor), Deut. 3 : 29.

Bethphage (bĕth-ʹphă-ġē) [house of figs], Matt. 21 : 1.

Bethsaida (bĕth-sā-ʹī-dă) [house of fishing], north of Sea of Galilee.
blind man cured at, Mark 8 : 22.
condemned for unbelief, Matt. 11 : 21.
Christ feeds the five thousand at, Luke 9 : 10-17.
of Galilee, native place of Philip, Peter, and Andrew, Mark 6 : 45; John 1 : 44; 12 : 21.

Beth-shan (bĕth-ʹshăn), or Beth-shean (bĕth-ʹshē-an) [house of rest], a city west of the Jordan, Josh. 17 : 11; 1 Sam. 31 : 10.

Beth-shemesh (bĕth-shē-ʹmĕsh) [house of the sun], a city of Judah.
men of, punished for profanity, 1 Sam. 6 : 19.
great battle at, 2 Ki. 14 : 11.
two other cities, Josh. 19 : 22, 38; Judg. 1 : 33.

Beth-shemite (bĕth-shē-ʹmīte), native of Beth-shemesh, 1 Sam. 6 : 14, 18.

Bethuel (bĕ-thū-ʹĕl) [house of God], Gen. 22 : 22, 23.

Beth-zur (bĕth-ʹzúr) [house of rock], a city of Judah now called Beit Sur, Josh. 15 : 58.

Betimes [early], Gen. 26 : 31, they rose up b.
Job 8 : 5, seek unto God b.
Prov. 13 : 24, chasteneth him b.
See 2 Chr. 36 : 15; Job 24 : 5.

Betray, Matt. 24 : 10, shall b. one another.
Matt. 26 : 16; Mark 14 : 11; Luke 22 : 6, opportunity to b.
Matt. 26 : 21, 23, 46, b. me.
27 : 4, b. innocent blood.
Mark 14 : 42, he that b. me is at hand.
Luke 22 : 48, b. thou the Son of man ?
Acts 7 : 52, ye have been now the b.
1 Cor. 11 : 23, same night he was b.

Betroth, Hos. 2 : 19, 20.

Betrothal, Laws concerning, Ex. 21 : 9; Lev. 19 : 20; Deut. 20 : 7.

Better, 1 Sam. 15 : 22, to obey b. than sacrifice.
1 Ki. 19 : 4, I am no b. than my fathers.
Ps. 63 : 3, lovingkindness b. than life.
Prov. 16 : 16, b. to get wisdom than gold.
Eccl. 4 : 9, two are b. than one.
   7 : 1, b. a good name than.
   7 : 10, former days b. than these.
Matt. 6 : 26, are ye not much b. than they ?
   12 : 12, man b. than a sheep ?
Mark 5 : 26, nothing b., but rather grew worse.
Luke 5 : 39, old wine b.
Phil. 1 : 23, with Christ far b.
   2 : 3, esteem other b. than themselves.
Heb. 1 : 4, b. than the angels.
   8 : 6, the Mediator of a b. covenant.
   12 : 24, speaketh b. things than that of Abel.
2 Pet. 2 : 21, b. not have known the way.
Between, Ex. 31 : 13, a sign b. me and you.
Luke 16 : 26, b. us and you a great gulf.
1 Tim. 2 : 5, one God and one mediator b.
Betwixt, Jer. 39 : 4; Phil. 1 : 23.
Beulah (bĕū-lăh) [married], Isa. 62 : 4.
Bewail, Isa. 16 : 9, will b. with the weeping.
2 Cor. 12 : 21, shall b. many.
Rev. 18 : 9, shall b. her.
See Luke 8 : 52; Jer. 4 : 31.
Beware, Judg. 13 : 4, b. and drink not wine.
Job 36 : 18, b. lest he take thee away.
Matt. 7 : 15, b. of false prophets.
   16 : 6; Mark 8 : 15; Luke 12 : 1, b. of the leaven.
Mark 12 : 38; Luke 20 : 46, b. of scribes.
Luke 12 : 15, b. of covetousness.
Phil. 3 : 2, b. of dogs, b. of evil workers.
Col. 2 : 8, b. lest any man spoil you.
Bewitched, Acts 8 : 9, Simon b. the people.
Gal. 3 : 1, who hath b. you?
Bewray [reveal, betray], Prov. 27 : 16, ointment of his right hand b. itself.
Prov. 29 : 24, cursing, and b. it not.
Isa. 16 : 3, b. not him that wandereth.
Matt. 26 : 73, thy speech b. thee.
Beyond, Num. 22 : 18, b. the word of the Lord.
Mark 6 : 51; 7 : 37, amazed b. measure.
2 Cor. 8 : 3, b. their power.
Gal. 1 : 13, b. measure I persecuted.
1 Thess. 4 : 6, that no man go b.
Bichri (bĭch-rī) [youthful], 2 Sam. 20 : 1, 22.
Bid, 1 Sam. 22 : 14; 2 John 11.
   (invite), Matt. 22 : 9.
Bier, 2 Sam. 3 : 31, followed the b.
Luke 7 : 14, touched the b.
Bigtha (bĭg-thă) [gift of fortune], Esther 1 : 10.
Bigthan (bĭg-thăn) [given by God], and Teresh, conspiracy discovered by Mordecai, Esther 2 : 21; 6 : 2.
Bildad (bĭl-dăd) [son of contention], Job 2 : 11.
Bilgah (bĭl-găh), or **Bilgai** [cheerfulness], 1 Chr. 24 : 14; Neh. 12 : 5.
Bill, Deut. 24 : 1; Mark 10 : 4; Luke 16 : 6.
Billows, Ps. 42 : 7; Jonah 2 : 3.
Bimhal (bĭm-hăl), 1 Chr. 7 : 33.
Bind, Job 38 : 31, canst b. influences of Pleiades?
Ps. 118 : 27, b. the sacrifice with cords.
Prov. 6 : 21, b. them upon thine heart.
   26 : 8, he that b. a stone.
Isa. 61 : 1, to b. up brokenhearted.
Hos. 6 : 1, smitten and will b. us up.

Matt. 12 : 29; Mark 3 : 27; first b. the strong man.
Matt. 16 : 19; 18 : 18, b. on earth.
   23 : 4, b. heavy burdens grievous.
Acts 9 : 14, authority to b. all that.
   22 : 4, b. and delivering men.
Birds, created and preserved, Gen. 1 : 20; 7 : 3; Ps. 104 : 17; 148 : 10.
used in sacrifices, Gen. 15 : 9; Lev. 14 : 4; Luke 2 : 24.
what may not be eaten, Lev. 11 : 13; Deut. 14 : 12.
nests of, Deut. 22 : 6.
mentioned figuratively, Prov. 1 : 17; 6 : 5; Jer. 12 : 9; Amos 3 : 5; Rev. 18 : 2.
Ps. 11 : 1, flee as a b. to your mountain.
   124 : 7, our soul is escaped as a b.
Prov. 1 : 17, net spread in sight of any b.
   6 : 5, as a b. from the fowler.
Eccl. 10 : 20, b. shall tell the matter.
Song of Sol. 2 : 12, time of singing of b.
Matt. 8 : 20; Luke 9 : 58, b. of air have nests.
Birsha (bĭr-shă) [son of wickedness], Gen. 14 : 2.
Birth, foretold.
of Ishmael, Gen. 16 : 11.
of Isaac, Gen. 18 : 10.
of Samson, Judg. 13 : 3.
of Samuel, 1 Sam. 1 : 11, 17.
of Josiah, 1 Ki. 13 : 2.
of Messias, Gen. 3 : 15; Isa. 7 : 14; Mic. 5; Luke 1 : 31.
of John the Baptist, Luke 1 : 13.
Eccl. 7 : 1, better than the day of one's b.
Matt. 1 : 18, the b. of Jesus Christ.
John 9 : 1, blind from b.
Gal. 4 : 19, of whom I travail in b.
Birthday, Gen. 40 : 20, which was Pharaoh's b.
Matt. 14 : 6; Mark 6 : 21, Herod on his b.
Birthright, law concerning, Deut. 21 : 15.
despised of Esau, Gen. 25 : 31; Heb. 12 : 16.
lost by Reuben, 1 Chr. 5 : 1.
Gen. 25 : 31, sell me this day thy b.
   25 : 33, he sold his b.
1 Chr. 5 : 2, but the b. was Joseph's.
Heb. 12 : 16, for one morsel sold his b.
Bishop, qualifications of, 1 Tim. 3.
See Phil. 1 : 1.
of souls (Christ), 1 Pet. 2 : 25.
1 Tim. 3 : 1, if a man desire office of b.
Titus 1 : 7, b. must be blameless.
1 Pet. 2 : 25, the b. of your souls.
Bit, Ps. 32 : 9, must be held in with b.
Jas. 3 : 3, we put b. in horses' mouths.
Bite, Prov. 23 : 32, at last it b. like a serpent.
Eccl. 10 : 8, a serpent shall b. him.
Mic. 3 : 5, prophets that b. with teeth.
Gal. 5 : 15, if ye b. and devour one another.
Bithiah (bĭth-ī-ăh) [daughter of Jah], 1 Chr. 4 : 18.
Bithron (bĭth-rŏn) [mountain-cleft], 2 Sam. 2 : 29.
Bitter, Gen. 27 : 34, exceeding b. cry.
Ex. 12 : 8; Num. 9 : 11, with b. herbs.
Ex. 15 : 23, waters were b.
Deut. 32 : 24, devoured with b. destruction.
Job 13 : 26, writest b. things.
Isa. 5 : 20, that put b. for sweet.
   22 : 4, I will weep b.
Jer. 2 : 19, an evil thing and b.

Matt. 26 : 75; Luke 22 : 62, Peter wept **b.**

Col. 3 : 19, be not **b.** against them.

Jas. 3 : 14, if ye have **b.** envying.

Bitter herbs, eaten with the paschal lamb, probably small plants belonging to the Compositæ and Cruciferæ eaten as salad. The Rabbis give a long list of them.

eaten with the passover, Ex. 12 : 8.

water healed, Ex. 15 : 23.

Bittern [Heb. qippod], referred to in Isa. 14 : 23 and 34 : 11 as inhabiting damp and waste places; in Zeph. 2 : 14 the cormorant and bittern are said to frequent the ruins of Nineveh, and to lodge in the upper lintels (knops or chapiters) thereof. In all these passages the Revised Version translates the word as porcupine.

Bitterness, 1 Sam. 15 : 32, surely the **b.** of death is past.

Job 10 : 1; 21 : 25; Isa. 38 : 15, in **b.** of soul.

Prov. 14 : 10, heart knoweth own **b.**

Zech. 12 : 10, be in **b.** for him as one that is in **b.**

Acts 8 : 23, in the gall of **b.**

Eph. 4 : 31, let all **b.** be put away.

Heb. 12 : 15, lest any root of **b.**

Bitumen [Heb. Zepheth and Chêmar; Ασφαλτος; Bitumen], Gen. 11 : 3; Ex. 2 : 3; Isa. 34 : 9. The substance called pitch and slime in the A.V. was apparently a kind of asphalt obtained floating on the Dead Sea. It was used as a cement for building, etc.

Black, Song of Sol. 1 : 5, I am **b.** but comely.

Matt. 5 : 36, one hair white or **b.**

Heb. 12 : 18, ye are not come to **b.**

Jude 13, to whom is reserved **b.**

See Job 6 : 16; Lam. 4 : 8.

Blade, Judg. 3 : 22, haft also went in after the **b.**

Matt. 13 : 26, when the **b.** was sprung up.

Mark 4 : 28, first the **b.**, then the ear.

See Job 31 : 22.

Blain [a boil or tumour], Ex. 9 : 9, 10, **b.** upon man and beast.

Blame, 2 Cor. 6 : 3, that ministry be no **b.**

Gal. 2 : 11, because he was to be **b.**

Eph. 1 : 4, holy and without **b.**

Blameless, Luke 1 : 6, in ordinances of the Lord **b.**

1 Cor. 1 : 8, **b.** in the day of our Lord.

Phil. 2 : 15, **b.** and harmless.

3 : 6, touching righteousness in the law **b.**

2 Pet. 3 : 14, ye may be found **b.**

Blaspheme, 2 Sam. 12 : 14, occasion to enemies to **b.**

Ps. 74 : 10, enemy **b.** thy name.

Isa. 52 : 5, my name continually is **b.**

Matt. 9 : 3, this man **b.**

Mark 3 : 29, **b.** against the Holy Ghost.

John 10 : 36, thou **b.** because I said.

Acts 19 : 37, not yet **b.** of your.

26 : 11, I compelled them to **b.**

Rom. 2 : 24, name of God is **b.**

Jas. 2 : 7, they **b.** that worthy name.

1 Tim. 1 : 13, who was before a **b.**

1 : 20, learn not to **b.**

Blasphemous, Luke 22 : 65; Acts 6 : 11, 13.

Blasphemy, its punishment, death, Lev. 24 : 16; 1 Ki. 21 : 10.

occasion for, given by David, 2 Sam. 12 : 14.

Naboth, 1 Ki. 21 : 13, and Stephen, Acts 6 : 13; 7 : 54, unjustly stoned for.

Christ accused of, Matt. 9 : 3; 26 : 65; Mark 2 : 7; Luke 5 : 21; John 10 : 33.

against the Holy Ghost, Matt. 12 : 31; Mark 3 : 28; Luke 12 : 10; 1 John 5 : 16.

Matt. 12 : 31, all manner of **b.**

26 : 65; Mark 14 : 64, he hath spoken **b.**

Mark 2 : 7, why doth this man thus speak **b. ?**

John 10 : 33, stone thee not, but for **b.**

Col. 3 : 8, now ye also put off **b.**

See Ex. 20 : 7; Ps. 74 : 18; Isa. 52 : 5; Ezek. 20 : 27; Matt. 15 : 19; Col. 3 : 8; 1 Tim. 6 : 1; Rev. 2 : 9; 13 : 5, 6; 16 : 9.

Blast, Josh. 6 : 5, when they make a long **b.**

Blasted, Gen. 41 : 23, withered, thin, and **b.**

Blasting, Amos 4 : 9, I have smitten you with **b.**

Blaze abroad [proclaim far and near], Mark 1 : 45, **b. a.** the matter.

Bleating, Judg. 5 : 16; 1 Sam. 15 : 14.

Blemish, offerings must be free from, Ex. 12 : 5, etc.; Lev. 1 : 3, etc.; Deut. 17 : 1, etc.

priests to be without, Lev. 21 : 16.

the church to be without, Eph. 5 : 27.

lamb without, Christ compared to, 1 Pet. 1 : 19.

Bless, Gen. 12 : 3, **b.** them that **b.** thee.

Gen. 22 : 17, in blessing I will **b.** thee.

27 : 29, b. be he that **b.** thee.

32 : 26, not let thee go except thou **b.**

Num. 6 : 24, Lord **b.** and keep thee.

1 Chr. 4 : 10, oh that thou wouldest **b. me.**

Ps. 65 : 10, thou **b.** the springing thereof.

67 : 1, be merciful to us, and **b.** us.

132 : 15, I will abundantly **b.** her provision.

Isa. 65 : 16, who **b.** himself shall **b.** himself in God of truth.

Matt. 5 : 44; Luke 6 : 28; Rom. 12 : 14, **b.** them that curse.

Blessed, Gen. 12 : 3; Ps. 1 : 1; 65 : 4; 84 : 4, 5; 112 : 1; Isa. 30 : 18; Matt. 5 : 3-11; 25 : 34; Luke 6 : 21; 12 : 37; 14 : 15.

who are chosen and called by God, Ps. 65 : 4; Isa. 51 : 2; Eph. 1 : 3, 4; Rev. 19 : 9.

who trust and delight in God, Ps. 2 : 12; 34 : 8; 40 : 4; 84 : 12; 112 : 1; Jer. 17 : 7.

who hear and obey, Ps. 119 : 2; Matt. 13 : 16; Luke 11 : 28; Jas. 1 : 25; Rev. 1 : 3; 22 : 7, 14.

who endures chastisement, Ps. 94 : 12.

who endures temptation, Jas. 1 : 12.

who fears the Lord, Ps. 128.

who believe and suffer for Christ, Matt. 16 : 16, 17; 11 : 6; Luke 6 : 22; Gal. 3 : 9.

who die in the Lord, Rev. 14 : 13.

whose sins are forgiven, Ps. 32 : 1, 2; Rom. 4 : 7.

others pronounced blessed, Deut. 15 : 10; Ps. 5 : 12; 41 : 1; 106 : 3; 112 : 2; 119 : 1; Prov. 20 : 7; 22 : 9; Luke 14 : 13, 14; Rev. 16 : 15.

persons blessed : Jacob by Isaac, Gen. 27 : 27; Jacob by God, Gen. 48 : 3; Joseph and his sons by Jacob, Gen. 48 : 9, 15; the twelve tribes by Moses, Deut. 33.

Prov. 10 : 7, memory of just is **b.**

Acts 20 : 35, more **b.** to give than to receive.

2 Cor. 11 : 31, **b.** for evermore.

1 Tim. 1 : 11, glorious gospel of **b.** God.

Titus 2 : 13, looking for that **b.** hope.
Jas. 1 : 12, **b.** is the man that endureth temptation.
Blessedness, Rom. 4 : 6, 9; Gal. 4 : 15.
Blessing, form of, Num. 6 : 22-26.
Gen. 27 : 35, thy brother hath taken thy **b.**
Deut. 11 : 26, a **b.** and a curse.
23 : 5; Neh. 13 : 2, Lord turned curse into **b.**
Job 29 : 13, **b.** of him ready to perish.
Ps. 129 : 8, **b.** of the Lord be on you.
Prov. 10 : 22, **b.** of the Lord maketh rich.
Isa. 65 : 8, destroy it not, a **b.** is in it.
Mal. 3 : 10, pour you out a **b.**
Rom. 15 : 29, fulness of **b.** of Gospel.
1 Cor. 10 : 16, cup of **b.** which we bless.
Eph. 1 : 3, blessed us with all spiritual **b.**
Heb. 6 : 7, earth receiveth **b.** from God.
Jas. 3 : 10, proceedeth **b.** and cursing.
Rev. 5 : 12, worthy to receive honour and **b.**
5 : 13; 7 : 12, **b.** and glory.
Blind, laws concerning the, Lev. 19 : 14; Deut. 27 : 18.
Ex. 23 : 8, the gift **b.** the wise.
Job 29 : 15, I was eyes to the **b.**
Matt. 11 : 5; Luke 7 : 21, the **b.** receive sight.
2 Pet. 1 : 9, he that lacketh these things is **b.**
John 12 : 40, he hath **b.** their eyes.
2 Cor. 3 : 14, their minds were **b.**
1 John 2 : 11, darkness hath **b.**
Blindfolded, Luke 22 : 64.
Blindness, inflicted on the men of Sodom, Gen. 19 : 11.
inflicted on the Syrian army, 2 Ki. 6 : 18.
inflicted on Saul of Tarsus, Acts 9 : 8.
inflicted on Elymas, Acts 13 : 11.
healed by Christ, Matt. 9 : 27-30; 12 : 22; 20 : 30; Mark 8 : 22; 10 : 46; Luke 7 : 21; John 9 : 30.
spiritual, Ps. 82 : 5; Isa. 56 : 10; 59 : 9; Matt. 6 : 23; 15 : 14; 23 : 16; John 1 : 5; 3 : 19; 9 : 39; 1 Cor. 2 : 14; 2 Pet. 1 : 9; 1 John 2 : 9; Rev. 3 : 17.
judicially inflicted, Ps. 69 : 23; Isa. 6 : 9; 44 : 18; Matt. 13 : 13; John 12 : 40; Acts 28 : 26; Rom. 11 : 7; 2 Cor. 4 : 4.
prayer for deliverance from, Ps. 13 : 3; 119 : 18.
to be removed by Christ, Isa. 9 : 2; 42 : 7; Luke 4 : 18; John 8 : 12; 9 : 39; 2 Cor. 3 : 14; 4 : 6; Eph. 5 : 8; Col. 1 : 13; 1 Thess. 5 : 5; 1 Pet. 2 : 9.
Rom. 11 : 25, **b.** in part has happened.
Eph. 4 : 18, because of **b.** of their heart.
See Ps. 146 : 8; Isa. 29 : 18; 35 : 5; 42 : 7.
Blood, eating of, forbidden to man after the flood, Gen. 9 : 4.
eating of, forbidden to the Israelites under the law, Lev. 3 : 17; 7 : 26; 17 : 10; 19 : 26; Deut. 12 : 16; 1 Sam. 14 : 32, 33; Ezek. 33 : 25.
eating of, forbidden to the Gentile Christians, Acts 15 : 20, 29.
water changed into, Ex. 4 : 9, 30; 7 : 17; Rev. 8 : 8; 11 : 6.
shedding of human, forbidden, Deut. 21 : 1-9; Ps. 106 : 38; Prov. 6 : 16, 17; Isa. 59 : 3; Jer. 22 : 17; Ezek. 22 : 4; Matt. 27 : 6.
of legal sacrifices, Ex. 23 : 18; 29 : 12;

30 : 10; 34 : 25; Lev. 4 : 7; 17 : 11; Heb. 9 : 13, 19-22; 10 : 4.
of the covenant, Ex. 24 : 8; Zech. 9 : 11; Heb. 10 : 29.
of Christ, 1 Cor. 10 : 16; Eph. 2 : 13; Heb. 9 : 14; 1 Pet. 1 : 19.
in the Lord's Supper, Matt. 26 : 28; Luke 22 : 20; 1 Cor. 11 : 25.
redemption by, Col. 1 : 20; Heb. 9 : 12, 22; 10 : 19; 12 : 24; 13 : 12; 1 Pet. 1 : 2; Rev. 1 : 5; 5 : 9; 12 : 11.
typified under the law, Ex. 12 : 13; 29 : 16; 30 : 10; Lev. 1 : 5; 4; 16 : 15; Heb. 9 : 7 ff.
Gen. 9 : 6, whoso sheddeth man's **b.**
Deut. 32 : 43, avenge **b.** of his servants.
2 Sam. 1 : 16, thy **b.** be on thy head.
Ps. 30 : 9, what profit in my **b.** ?
72 : 14, precious shall **b.** be in his sight.
Isa. 1 : 15, your hands are full of **b.**
9 : 5, garments rolled in **b.**
Ezek. 9 : 9, land is full of **b.**
Zeph. 1 : 17, their **b.** poured out as dust.
Matt. 9 : 20; Mark 5 : 25; Luke 8 : 43, woman with issue of **b.**
Matt. 16 : 17, flesh and **b.** hath not revealed.
27 : 25, his **b.** be on us and our children.
Mark 14 : 24, new testament in my **b.**
John 1 : 13, born not of **b.**
6 : 54, who drinketh my **b.**
19 : 34, came thereout **b.**
Acts 17 : 26, made of one **b.**
20 : 28, purchased with his **b.**
Rom. 3 : 25, through faith in his **b.**
5 : 9, justified by his **b.**
1 Cor. 11 : 27, guilty of body and **b.** of the Lord.
15 : 50, flesh and **b** cannot inherit.
Eph. 1 : 7; Col. 1 : 14, redemption through his **b.**
Heb. 9 : 22, without shedding of **b.**
13 : 20, **b.** of the covenant.
1 John 1 : 7, **b.** of Jesus Christ cleanseth us.
5 : 8, the spirit, water, and **b.**
Rev. 7 : 14; 12 : 11, **b.** of the Lamb.
See Ps. 55 : 23; Ezek. 22 : 2; Acts 28 : 8.
Bloodguiltiness, Ps. 51 : 14.
Bloodthirsty, Prov. 29 : 10.
Blossom, Num. 17 : 5, the man's rod shall **b.**
Num. 17 : 8, bloomed, **b.** and yielded.
Isa. 35 : 1, desert shall **b.** as the rose.
Ezek. 7 : 10, rod hath **b.**
Hab. 3 : 17, fig tree shall not **b.**
Blot, Ex. 32 : 32; Ps. 69 : 28, **b.** out of book.
Deut. 29 : 20, **b.** out his name.
Isa. 43 : 25, **b.** out thy transgressions.
44 : 22, **b.** out, as a thick cloud.
Jer. 18 : 23, neither **b.** out their sins.
Acts 3 : 19, that your sins be **b.** out.
Col. 2 : 14, **b.** out the handwriting.
Blow, Num. 10 : 5, 6, **b.** an alarm.
Josh. 6 : 9, 13, and **b.** with the trumpets.
Ps. 147 : 18, causeth his wind to **b.**
Isa. 27 : 13, the great trumpet shall be **b.**
Luke 12 : 55, see the south wind **b.**
Rev. 7 : 1, wind shall not **b.** on the earth.
Blue, Ex. 25 : 4; 35 : 23; Esther 8 : 15; Prov. 20 : 30.
Blunt, Eccl. 10 : 10.

Blush, Ezra 9 : 6; Jer. 6 : 15; 8 : 12.

Boanerges (bō-ăn-ĕr-ʹgēṡ) [sons of thunder], James and John so called, Mark 3 : 17.

Boar [Sus scrofa], only mentioned in Ps. 80 : 13, " the boar out of the wood doth ravage." Though unclean to the Jews, the wild boar had to be constantly destroyed on account of its destructiveness to the crops. It still abounds in many parts of Palestine.

Boards, Ex. 26 : 15; 1 Ki. 6 : 9; Ezek. 27 : 5; Acts 27 : 44.

Boast, 1 Ki. 20 : 11, not **b.** as he that putteth it off.

Ps. 44 : 8, in God we **b.** all the day.

49 : 6, **b.** themselves in their riches.

Prov. 27 : 1, **b.** not of to morrow.

Eph. 2 : 9, not of works, lest any man should **b.**

Jas. 3 : 5, tongue **b.** great things.

Ps. 34 : 2, my soul shall make her **b.**

Rom. 2 : 17, makest thy **b.** of God.

Boasting, reproved, 1 Ki. 20 : 11; Ps. 52 : 1; 94 : 4; Prov. 20 : 14; 25 : 14; Isa. 10 : 15; Rom. 1 : 30; 11 : 18; 2 Cor. 10 : 13; Jas. 4 : 16.

excluded under the gospel, Rom. 3 : 27; Eph. 2 : 9.

of Paul, 2 Cor. 7 : 14; 8 : 24; 9 : 3, 4; 11 : 10.

Boat, 2 Sam. 19 : 18; John 6 : 22, 23; Acts 27 : 16.

Boaz (bō-ʹăz) [cheerfulness], Ruth 2 : 1. In Matt. 1 : 5, Booz (A.V.) Greek Boēs.

his kindness towards Ruth, Ruth 2; 3; 4.

ancestor of David and Christ, Ruth 4 : 17 22; Matt. 1 : 5; Luke 3 : 23, 32.

and Jachin [strength and stability], pillars of the temple, 2 Cor. 3 : 17.

Body (human) not to be disfigured, Lev. 19 : 28; 21 : 5; Deut. 14 : 1.

to be kept pure, Rom. 12 : 1; 1 Cor. 6 : 13; 1 Thess. 4 : 4.

of Christians, the temple of the Holy Ghost, 1 Cor. 3 : 16; 6 : 19; 2 Cor. 6 : 16.

dead, laws concerning, Lev. 21 : 11; Num. 5 : 2; 9 : 6; 19 : 11; Deut. 21 : 23; Hag. 2 : 13.

to be raised again, Matt. 22 : 30; 1 Cor. 15 : 12; Phil. 3 : 21.

See Resurrection.

of Christ (Heb. 10 : 5); Luke 2 : 35; John 19 : 34.

of Christ buried by Joseph, Matt. 27 : 58; Mark 15 : 42; Luke 23 : 50; John 19 : 38.

the Church so called, Rom. 12 : 4; 1 Cor. 10 : 17; 12 : 12; Eph. 1 : 22; 4 : 13; 5 : 23; Col. 1 : 18; 2 : 19; 3 : 15.

Job 19 : 26, worms destroy this **b.**

Prov. 5 : 11, flesh and **b.** are consumed.

Matt. 5 : 29, **b.** cast into hell.

6 : 22; Luke 11 : 34, **b.** full of light.

Mark 5 : 29, felt in **b.** that she was healed.

John 2 : 21, the temple of his **b.**

Acts 19 : 12, from his **b.** were brought.

Rom. 6 : 6, **b.** of sin destroyed.

7 : 24, **b.** of this death.

8 : 23, the redemption of our **b.**

1 Cor. 6 : 19, **b.** is the temple of the Holy Ghost.

13 : 3, though I give my **b.** to be burned.

2 Cor. 5 : 8, absent from the **b.**

12 : 2, whether in **b.,** or out of the **b.**

Gal. 6 : 17, I bear in **b.** marks.

Phil. 3 : 21, who shall change our vile **b.**

Col. 1 : 18, head of the **b.** the church.

Heb. 10 : 5, a **b.** hast thou prepared me.

Jas. 3 : 6, tongue defileth the whole **b.**

1 Pet. 2 : 24, in his own **b.** on tree.

Bodily, Luke 3 : 22, Holy Ghost descended in a **b.** shape.

2 Cor. 10 : 10, his **b.** presence is weak.

Col. 2 : 9, fulness of the Godhead **b.**

1 Tim. 4 : 8, **b.** exercise profiteth little.

Boil, Job 41 : 31; Isa. 64 : 2.

Boils and blains, the plague of, Ex. 9 : 10; Rev. 16 : 2.

See 2 Ki. 20 : 7; Job 2 : 7.

Bold, Prov. 28 : 1, righteous are **b.** as a lion.

John 7 : 26, he speaketh **b.**

Rom. 15 : 15, have written more **b.**

2 Cor. 7 : 4, great is my **b.** of speech.

Eph. 3 : 12, we have **b.** and access.

Heb. 4 : 16, let us come **b.** to throne.

10 : 19, **b.** to enter into holiest.

1 John 4 : 17, have **b.** in day of judgment.

Boldness through faith, Prov. 28 : 1; Isa. 50 : 7; Acts 5 : 29; Eph. 3 : 12; Heb. 10 : 19; 1 John 4 : 17.

exhortations to, Josh. 1 : 7; 2 Chr. 19 : 11; Jer. 1 : 8; Ezek. 3 : 9; Heb. 4 : 16.

of Peter and John, Acts 4 : 13; 5 : 29. Stephen, Acts 7 : 51. Paul, Acts 9 : 27; 19 : 8; 2 Cor. 7 : 4; Gal. 2 : 11. Apollos, Acts 18 : 26.

Bolled [having the seed-vessel formed], Ex. 29 : 9, the flax was **b.**

Bond (or vow), law of, Num. 30.

of peace, Eph. 4 : 3.

Acts 8 : 23, in **b.** of iniquity.

Eph. 4 : 3, **b.** of peace.

Col. 3 : 14, **b.** of perfectness.

Ps. 116 : 16, thou hast loosed my **b.**

Acts 20 : 23, **b.** abide me.

23 : 29; 26 : 31, worthy of death or **b.**

Heb. 11 : 36, others had trial of **b.**

Bondage of Israel in Egypt, Ex. 1–12; Ps. 105 : 25; Acts 7 : 6.

of Israel in Babylon, 2 Ki. 25; Ezra 1 : 9, 7; Neh. 1; Esther 3; Dan. 1.

spiritual, John 8 : 34; Acts 8 : 23; Rom. 6 : 16; 7 : 23; 8 : 2; Gal. 2 : 4; 4 : 3; 1 Tim. 3 : 7; 2 Tim. 2 : 26; Heb. 2 : 14; 2 Pet. 2 : 19.

deliverance by Christ, Isa. 61 : 1; Luke 4 : 18; John 8 : 36; Rom. 8 : 2; Gal. 3 : 13.

Ex. 1 : 14, lives bitter with hard **b.**

John 8 : 33, never in **b.** to any man.

Rom. 8 : 15, not received spirit of **b.**

Gal. 5 : 1, not entangled with yoke of **b.**

Heb. 2 : 15, lifetime subject to **b.**

Bondmaid, laws concerning, Lev. 19 : 20; 25 : 44.

Bondmen, laws concerning, Lev. 25 : 39; Deut. 15 : 12.

Bondwoman cast out, Gen. 21 : 10; Gal. 4 : 23.

Bones, Joseph's, Gen. 50 : 25; Ex. 13 : 19; Heb. 11 : 22.

scattered as a judgment, 2 Ki. 23 : 14; Ps. 53 : 5; 141 : 7; Jer. 8 : 1; Ezek. 6 : 5.

Gen. 2 : 23, this is **b.** of my **b.**
Ex. 12 : 46; Num. 9 : 12, neither shall ye break a **b.** thereof.
Job 19 : 20, my **b.** cleaveth to my skin.
Ps. 51 : 8, **b.** thou hast broken may rejoice.
Prov. 14 : 30, envy the rottenness of the **b.**
Ezek. 37 : 1, valley full of **b.**
Matt. 23 : 27, full of dead men's **b.**
Luke 24 : 39, spirit hath not flesh and **b.**
John 19 : 36, a **b.** of him shall not be broken.
Eph. 5 : 30, we are members of his **b.**
Bonnet [a man's head-dress], of the priests, directions for making, Ex. 28 : 40; 29 : 9; 39 : 28; Ezek. 44 : 18.
Ex. 29 : 9, Aaron and his sons, and put the **b.** on them.
Book. Among the Hebrews such were rolls of dressed skins or parchments. Sometimes they were of thin leather. Several skins stitched together and attached to a roller of wood formed " a roll of a book " (Jer. 36 : 2). The writing was in columns parallel to the rollers. The " great roll " (Isa. 8 : 1) was a large tablet coated with wax, written on with a pen, and then hung up to view. Writing with ink, on paper made from the papyrus, was in use in the Apostles' days (2 John 12). Our word volume (that which is rolled up, from volvere to roll) has its early sense of roll, in " the volume of the book it is written of me " (Heb. 10 : 7).
of Life, Ex. 32 : 32; Ps. 69 : 28; Dan. 12 : 1; Phil. 4 : 3; Rev. 3 : 5; 13 : 8; 17 : 8; 21 : 27; 22 : 19.
opened, Rev. 20 : 12.
of the Law, Deut. 28 : 61; 29 : 27, etc.; Gal. 3 : 10.
found and read, 2 Ki. 22 : 8; 23 : 2; Neh. 8 : 8.
of Jasher, Josh. 10 : 13; 2 Sam. 1 : 18.
Job 19 : 23, printed in a **b.**
31 : 35, adversary had written a **b.**
Ps. 40 : 7; Heb. 10 : 7, volume of the **b.**
Ps. 69 : 28, let them be blotted out of **b.**
139 : 16, in thy **b.** all my members.
Isa. 34 : 16, seek ye out of the **b.** of the Lord.
Mal. 3 : 16, **b.** of remembrance.
Luke 4 : 17, when he opened the **b.**
John 21 : 25, world could not contain **b.**
Phil. 4 : 3; Rev. 3 : 5; 13 : 8; 17 : 8; 20 : 12; 21 : 27, **b.** of life.
Rev. 22 : 19, take away from words of **b.**
Books, Eccl. 12 : 12; Dan. 9 : 2; John 21 : 25; 2 Tim. 4 : 13.
of various persons, 1 Chr. 29 : 29; 2 Chr. 9 : 29; 12 : 15; 20 : 34.
of Samuel, 1 Sam. 10 : 25.
of Solomon, 1 Ki. 4 : 32; 11 : 41.
of judgment, Dan. 7 : 10; Rev. 20 : 12.
burned at Ephesus, Acts 19 : 19.
Booth, used at the feast of tabernacles, Lev. 23 : 42; Neh. 8 : 14.
Lev. 23 : 42, dwell in **b.** seven days.
Job 27 : 18, as a **b.** the keeper maketh.
Jonah 4 : 5, Jonah made him a **b.**
Booths, Festival of, or Tabernacles, corresponds to the Autumnal feast of " Ingathering " mentioned in Ex. 23 : 16; 34 : 22, as taking

place at the end of the year. See Tabernacles.
Booty [plunder], Num. 31 : 32; Hab. 2 : 7; Zeph. 1 : 13.
Borders of the land determined, Num. 34; Josh. 1 : 4; Ezek. 47 : 13.
Boring of the ear, Ex. 21 : 6.
See Ps. 40 : 6.
Born of God, John 1 : 13; 3 : 3; 1 Pet. 1 : 23; 1 John 3 : 9; 5 : 1.
Job 5 : 7, man **b.** to trouble.
Ps. 22 : 31, a people that shall be **b.**
87 : 4, this man was **b.** there.
Prov. 17 : 17, a brother is **b.** for adversity.
Eccl. 3 : 2, a time to be **b.**
Isa. 9 : 6, unto us a child is **b.**
66 : 8, shall a nation be **b.** at once ?
Matt. 2 : 4, where Christ should be **b.**
Luke 2 : 11, to you is **b.** this day.
John 1 : 13; 1 John 3 : 9; 4 : 7; 5 : 1, 4, 18, **b.** of God.
John 3 : 3; 1 Pet. 1 : 23, **b.** again.
1 Cor. 15 : 8, as one **b.** out of due time.
1 Pet. 2 : 2, as new-**b.** babes.
Borne, Ps. 55 : 12, then I could have **b.** it.
Isa. 53 : 4, **b.** our griefs.
Matt. 20 : 12, **b.** burden and heat of day.
23 : 4, Luke 11 : 46, grievous to be **b.**
Acts 21 : 35, he was **b.** of the soldiers.
1 Cor. 15 : 49, have **b.** the image.
Borrow, Deut. 15 : 6; 28 : 12, shalt lend, but not **b.**
2 Ki. 4 : 3, **b.** thee vessels abroad.
Neh. 5 : 4, we have **b.** money for.
Ps. 37 : 21, wicked **b.** and payeth not.
Prov. 22 : 7, the **b.** is servant to the lender.
Matt. 5 : 42, from him that would **b.** of thee.
Borrowing, law concerning, Ex. 22 : 14; Deut. 15 : 2-6, etc.
its consequences, 2 Ki. 6 : 5; Prov. 22 : 7.
of Israel from the Egyptians, Ex. 3 : 22; 12 : 35.
Bosom, Job 31 : 33, iniquity in my **b.**
Ps. 35 : 13, prayer returned into mine own **b.**
Prov. 6 : 27, take fire into his **b.**
Eccl. 7 : 9, anger resteth in the **b.**
Isa. 40 : 11, carry lambs in **b.**
Luke 16 : 22, carried into Abraham's **b.**
John 1 : 18, in the **b.** of the Father.
13 : 23, leaning on Jesus' **b.**
Bosses, studs or knobs, of metal or some other hard substance, with which the face of a shield was covered.
Job 15 : 26, thick **b.** of his bucklers.
Botch [a swelling, a boil], Deut. 28 : 27, smite thee with the **b.** of Egypt.
Bottle. The bottles mentioned in the Bible are of two kinds—(1) an earthenware vessel, as in " get a potter's earthen bottle " (Jer. 19 : 1); (2) the skin-bottle, which is obtained from the goat. The skin is drawn off the body without splitting it. The hide is then tanned with aromatic bark, and when intended for wine, is hung by the fire to dry.
Gen. 21 : 14, **b.** of water.
Judg. 4 : 19, a **b.** of milk.
1 Sam. 1 : 24; 10 : 3; 16 : 20; 2 Sam. 16 : 1, a **b.** of wine.

Ps. 56 : 8, put tears into b.
119 : 83, like b. in smoke.
Hab. 2 : 15, puttest thy b. to him.
Matt. 9 : 17; Mark 2 : 22; Luke 5 : 37, new wine into old b.
Bottles of wine, Josh. 9 : 4, 13; 1 Sam. 25 : 18; Hos. 7 : 5.
old and new, Job 32 : 19; Matt. 9 : 17; Mark 2 : 22; Luke 5 : 37, 38.
Bottomless pit, Rev. 9 : 1; 11 : 7; 17 : 8.
Satan bound there, Rev. 20 : 1, 2.
Bough, Gen. 49 : 22, Joseph is a fruitful b.
Judg. 9 : 49, cut down every man his b.
Job 14 : 9, bring forth b. like a plant.
Ps. 80 : 10, b. like goodly cedars.
Ezek. 31 : 3, 14, top among thick b.
Bought, Luke 14 : 18, I have b. a piece of ground.
1 Cor. 6 : 20; 7 : 23, ye are b. with a price.
2 Pet. 2 : 1, denying Lord that b. them.
Bound, Deut. 32 : 8, he set the b. of the people.
Job 36 : 8, if they be b. in fetters.
Ps. 107 : 10, being b. in affliction.
Prov. 22 : 15, foolishness is b. in heart of child.
Isa. 61 : 1, opening of prison to them that are b.
Acts 20 : 22, I go b. in spirit.
2 Tim. 2 : 9, word of God is not b.
Heb. 13 : 3, in bonds, as b. with them.
Bountiful, Ps. 13 : 6, Lord hath dealt b.
Ps. 119 : 17, deal b. with thy servant.
Prov. 22 : 9, a b. eye shall be blessed.
Isa. 32 : 5, nor churl said to be b.
2 Cor. 9 : 6, he that soweth b. shall reap b.
9 : 11, enrich to all b.
Bounty, 1 Ki. 10 : 13, gave her of his royal b.
2 Cor. 9 : 5, as a matter of b.
Bow, in the cloud, sign of God's mercy, Gen. 9 : 13; Ezek. 1 : 28.
weapon, Gen. 48 : 22; Josh. 24 : 12; 1 Sam. 18 : 4; 2 Sam. 1 : 18, 22; 2 Ki. 9 : 24; Ps. 44 : 6; 78 : 57; Jer. 49 : 35; Hos. 7 : 16; Rev. 6 : 2.
Ex. 12 : 27, b. the head and worshipped.
20 : 5, thou shalt not b. down thyself.
Judg. 7 : 5, every one that b. down.
Prov. 22 : 17, b. down thine ear and hear.
Isa. 45 : 23, unto me every knee shall b.
Mark 15 : 19, b. their knees.
Eph. 3 : 14, I b. my knees unto the Father.
Bowels of mercy, Gen. 43 : 30; Ps. 25 : 6; Isa. 63 : 15; Luke 1 : 78; Phil. 1 : 8; 2 : 1; Col. 3 : 12, etc.
2 Cor. 6 : 12, straitened in your own b.
Phil. 1 : 8, long after you in b. of Christ.
2 : 1, if there be any b. and mercies.
1 John 3 : 17, b. of compassion.
Bowls, etc., offered by the princes, Num. 7.
See Zech. 4 : 2.
Bowmen, Jer. 4 : 29.
Bowshot, Gen. 21 : 16.
Box, 2 Ki. 9 : 1, b. of oil.
Matt. 26 : 7; Mark 14 : 3, alabaster b.
Box wood [Heb. teasshur], is twice mentioned in the A.V., and three times in the R.V. In the two passages in Isaiah it is enumerated with the fir tree and the pine (Isa. 41 : 19; 60 : 13). In Ezekiel we read " of the oaks of Bashan have they made thine oars; they have made thy benches of ivory inlaid in

box wood, from the isles of Chittim " (Ezek. 27 : 6, R.V.). The hardness of box wood is well known, and it is well adapted for the art of inlaying.
Boys, Gen. 25 : 27; Zech. 8 : 5.
Bozez (bō-ʹzĕz) [shining, or boggy], 1 Sam. 14 : 4.
Bozrah (bŏzʹ-răh) [fortified place], a city of Moab.
prophecies concerning, Isa. 34 : 6; 63 : 1; Jer. 48 : 24; 49 : 13; Amos 1 : 12; Mic. 2 : 12.

Ancient Egyptian Bracelets

Bracelet, Gen. 24 : 22, 30; Num. 31 : 50; 2 Sam· 1 : 10.
Brake, Ex. 32 : 19; Deut. 9 : 17, tables and b. them.
2 Ki. 23 : 14; 2 Chr. 34 : 4, Josiah b. the images.
Ps. 76 : 3, b. the arrows of the bow.
107 : 14, b. their bands in sunder.
Matt. 14 : 19; 15 : 36; 26 : 26; Mark 6 : 41; 14 : 22; Luke 9 : 16; 22 : 19; 1 Cor. 11 : 24, blessed and b.
See Ex. 34 : 1; Ezek. 29 : 7.
Bramble, Briers. References to briers, brambles, and thorns are very numerous, and several different words in the original are thus translated. It is possible to refer some of these with great probability to known plants. In other cases the term must be taken as applied in a general sense. Thus, the bramble in Jotham's parable, Tristram thinks, may be the box-thorn. The thistles and brambles, which choke the ground, and come up through deserted altars, may be some of the many thistles found in Palestine. Some of them have such a formidable armature of prickles, that it is impossible to make way through a field in which they grow. Zizyphus spinachristi is a large tree, with the branches ending in sharp spines : from these the crown of thorns is said to have been made.
Bramble, chosen to reign over the trees, Judg. 9 : 14.
Branch (of the Lord), prophecies concerning, Isa. 4 : 2; Jer. 23 : 5; Zech. 3 : 8; 6 : 12; John 15 : 5; Rom. 11 : 16.

Job 14 : 7, tender **b.** will not cease.
Ps. 80 : 15, **b.** thou madest strong.
Prov. 11 : 28, righteous flourish as **b.**
Isa. 60 : 21, the **b.** of my planting.
Jer. 23 : 5, raise a righteous **b.**
Matt. 13 : 32; Luke 13 : 19, birds lodge in **b.**
Matt. 21 : 8; Mark 11 : 8; John 12 : 13; cut down **b.**
John 15 : 5, I am the vine, ye are the **b.**
Rom. 11 : 16, if root be holy, so **b.**
Brand, as a, plucked from the fire, Amos 4 : 11; Zech. 3 : 2; Jude 23.
Judg. 15 : 5, he had set the **b.** on fire.
Zech. 3 : 2, **b.** plucked out of the fire.
Brandish, Ezek. 32 : 10.
Brass [Heb. Nĕchōsheth; Χαλκος ; Aereus (bronze)], Ex. 38 : 8; 2 Ki. 25 : 13.
used in construction of the tabernacle and temple, Ex. 25 : 3; 26 : 11; 1 Ki. 7 : 14.
for fetters, Judg. 16 : 21; 2 Ki. 25 : 7.
armour, 1 Sam. 17 : 5, 6.
musical instruments, 1 Chr. 15 : 19; 1 Cor. 13 : 1.
money, Matt. 10 : 9.
altar of, Ex. 39 : 39; 2 Ki. 16 : 14.
mentioned figuratively, Lev. 26 : 19; Job 6 : 12; Rev. 1 : 15.
Num. 21 : 9, serpent of **b.**
Deut. 8 : 9, out of whose hills mayest dig **b.**
28 : 23, the heaven shall be **b.**
Ps. 107 : 16, broken the gates of **b.**
1 Cor. 13 : 1, as sounding **b.**
Bravery [showy appearance, fine dress], Isa. 3 : 18, take away their **b.**
Brawler, Prov. 25 : 24, **b.** woman.
1 Tim. 3 : 3, a bishop must be no **b.**
Titus 3 : 2, to be no **b.**
Bray [to break or bruise small], Prov. 27 : 22; Job 6 : 5; 30 : 7, **b.** a fool in a mortar.
Brazen, Ex. 27 : 4, four **b.** rings.
Ex. 39 : 39; 1 Ki. 8 : 64; 2 Ki. 16 : 15, **b.** altar.
2 Ki. 18 : 4, **b.** serpent.
Mark 7 : 4, **b.** vessels.
Breach, Lev. 24 : 20, **b.** for **b.**, eye for eye.
Ps. 106 : 23, Moses stood in the **b.**
Isa. 58 : 12, the repairer of the **b.**
Lam. 2 : 13, thy **b.** is great like the sea.
Breaches [creeks, bays, havens], Judg. 5 : 17, Asher abode in his **b.**
Bread, man appointed to labour for, Gen. 3 : 19.
given from heaven (manna), Ex. 16 : 4.
miraculously supplied, 2 Ki. 4 : 42; John 6, etc.
a type of Christ, John 6 : 31; 1 Cor. 10 : 16.
offered before the Lord, Ex. 25 : 30; Lev. 8 : 26; 24 : 5.
hallowed, David obtains from Ahimelech, 1 Sam. 21 : 4.
used in the Lord's Supper, Luke 22 : 19; 24 : 30; Acts 2 : 42; 20 : 7; 1 Cor. 10 : 16; 11 : 23.
unleavened, Gen. 19 : 3; Ex. 12 : 8; 1 Sam. 28 : 24; 2 Ki. 23 : 9.
figuratively used, 1 Cor. 5 : 8.
Deut. 8 : 3; Matt. 4 : 4; Luke 4 : 4, man not live by **b.** alone.
Ruth 1 : 6, visited people in giving them **b.**
1 Sam. 21 : 4, hallowed **b.**
1 Ki. 17 : 6, ravens brought **b.** and flesh.

Job 22 : 7, withholden **b.** from hungry.
33 : 20, life abhorreth **b.** and soul.
Ps. 132 : 15, satisfy poor with **b.**
Prov. 9 : 17, **b.** eaten in secret.
12 : 11; 20 : 13; (28 : 19), satisfied with **b.**
Eccl. 11 : 1, cast **b.** on waters.
Isa. 33 : 16, **b.** given, and waters sure.
55 : 2, money for that which is not **b.**
Matt. 4 : 3; Luke 4 : 3, stones be made **b.**
Matt. 6 : 11; Luke 11 : 3, give us our daily **b.**
Matt. 15 : 26; Mark 7 : 27, not meet to take children's **b.**
Luke 24 : 35, known in breaking **b.**
John 6 : 35, 48, I am **b.** of life.
Acts 2 : 46, breaking **b.** from house to house.
1 Cor. 11 : 23, night he was betrayed, took **b.**
2 Thess. 3 : 8, did we eat **b.** for nought ?
Breadth, 1 Ki. 7 : 27; Job 37 : 10; Hab. 1 : 6; Eph. 3 : 18; Rev. 21 : 16.
Break, Cant. 2 : 17; 4 : 6, day **b.** and shadows flee.
Isa. 42 : 3; Matt. 12 : 20, bruised reed shall he not **b.**
Jer. 4 : 3; Hos. 10 : 12, **b.** up your fallow ground.
Matt. 5 : 19, **b.** one of these least commandments.
Acts 21 : 13, to weep and **b.** my heart.
1 Cor. 10 : 16, bread which we **b.**
Breaker, Mic. 2 : 13, the **b.** is come up.
Rom. 2 : 25, a **b.** of the law.
Breast, Lev. 7 : 30, the **b.** may be waved.
Dan. 2 : 32, **b.** and arms of silver.
Luke 18 : 13, smote upon his **b.**
John 13 : 25, lying on Jesus' **b.**
Rev. 15 : 6, girded with golden girdles.
Breastplate, The, of the high priest was one of the most important articles of his attire. This " breastplate of judgment," described in Ex. 28 : 17-30, was ornamented with twelve precious stones on which were engraven the names of the twelve tribes. See **Precious Stones.**
of the high priest described, Ex. 28 : 15; 39 : 8,
of righteousness, Eph. 6 : 14.
of faith and love, 1 Thess. 5 : 8.
Breath (life) dependent upon God, Gen. 2 : 7; 6 : 17; Job 12 : 10; 33 : 4; Ps. 104 : 29; Ezek. 37 : 5; Dan. 5 : 23; Acts 17 : 25.
of God, its power, 2 Sam. 22 : 16; Job 4 : 9; Ps. 33 : 6; Isa. 11 : 4; 30 : 28.
Gen. 2 : 7; 6 : 17; 7 : 15; **b.** of life.
Job 12 : 10, in whose hand is **b.** of all.
Ps. 146 : 4, his **b.** goeth forth, he returneth.
150 : 6, that hath **b.** praise the Lord.
Isa. 2 : 22, cease from man, whose **b.**
Lam. 4 : 20, the **b.** of our nostrils.
Dan. 5 : 23, in whose hand thy **b.** is.
Acts 17 : 25, he giveth to all life and **b.**
Breathe, Ps. 27 : 12, such as **b.** out cruelty.
Ezek. 37 : 9, O breath, **b.** on these.
John 20 : 22, he **b.** on them, and said.
Acts 9 : 1, Saul **b.** out threatenings.
Breeches, Ex. 28 : 42; Lev. 6 : 10; Ezek. 44 : 18.
Breed, Gen. 8 : 17; Deut. 32 : 14; Zeph. 2 : 9.
Brethren, duty of, towards each other, Gen. 13 : 8; Deut. 15 : 7; 24 : 14; Ps. 133; Matt.

5 : 22; 18 : 15, 21; 25 : 40; John 13 : 34;
15 : 12, etc.; Rom. 12 : 10; 1 Cor. 6;
8 : 13; Gal. 6 : 1; 1 Thess. 4 : 9; 2 Thess.
3 : 15; Heb. 13 : 1; 1 Pet. 1 : 22; 3 : 8;
2 Pet. 1 : 7; 1 John 2 : 9; 3 : 17.
Gen. 13 : 8, no strife, for we be b.
Ps. 122 : 8, for my b. and companions' sakes.
133 : 1, for b. to dwell together in unity.
Matt. 23 : 8, all ye are b.
Mark 10 : 29; Luke 18 : 29, no man left house or b.
Rom. 8 : 29, firstborn among many b.
Heb. 2 : 11, not ashamed to call them b.
1 Pet. 1 : 22, unfeigned love of the b.
1 John 3 : 14, because we love the b.
Bribe, 1 Sam. 12 : 3, have I received any b. ?
Ps. 26 : 10, right hand is full of b.
Isa. 33 : 15, hands from holding b.
Job 15 : 34, tabernacles of b.
Bribery forbidden, Ex. 23 : 2, 6; Deut. 16 : 19; Job 15 : 24.
denounced, Prov. 17 : 23; 29 : 4; Eccl. 7 : 7; Isa. 5 : 23; 33 : 15; Ezek. 13 : 19; Amos 2 : 6.
of Delilah, Judg. 16 : 5; of Samuel's sons, 1 Sam. 8 : 3; of Judas, Matt. 26 : 14; of the soldiers, Matt. 28 : 12.
Brick. To the present day houses in Palestine are built of sun-dried brick as being the cheapest material. These are generally about a foot square and with a depth of three or four inches, thus partaking more of the shape of tiles. On occasion, as a means of cementing together the mixture of which they are made, straw is intermingled with the mud.
made by Israelites, Ex. 1 : 14; 5 : 7.
Gen. 11 : 3, make b., had b. for stone.
Ex. 5 : 7, straw to make b.
Isa. 9 : 10, the b. are fallen down.
65 : 3, incense on altars of b.
Brickkiln, 2 Sam. 12 : 31; Jer. 43 : 9; Nah. 3 : 14.
Bride of Christ, the Church, John 3 : 29; Rev. 21 : 2; 22 : 17.
Isa. 61 : 10, as a b. adorneth with jewels.
Jer. 2 : 32, can a b. forget her attire ?
Rev. 18 : 23, voice of b. heard no more.
21 : 2, as a b. adorned for her husband.
22 : 17, Spirit and the b. say, come.
Bridechamber, Matt. 9 : 15; Mark 2 : 19; Luke 5 : 34.
Bridegroom, Christ the heavenly, Matt. 9 : 15; 25 : 1; John 3 : 29.
See Ps. 19 : 5; Isa. 61 : 10; 62 : 5.
Ps. 19 : 5, as a b. coming out of chamber.
Matt. 9 : 15; Mark 2 : 19; Luke 5 : 34, while the b. is with them.
Matt. 25 : 1, to meet the b.
John 3 : 29, because of b. voice.
Bridle, 2 Ki. 19 : 28; Isa. 37 : 29, my b. in thy lips.
Ps. 39 : 1, keep my mouth with a b.
Prov. 26 : 3, a b. for the ass.
Isa. 30 : 28, a b. in jaws of the people.
Jas. 1 : 26, b. not his tongue.
3 : 2, able to b. whole body.
Briefly, Rom. 13 : 9; 1 Pet. 5 : 12.
Brier, Isa. 5 : 6, there shall come up b.

Isa. 55 : 13, instead of the b. shall come.
Ezek. 2 : 6, b. and thorns be with thee.
Heb. 6 : 8, beareth thorns and b.
See **Brambles**.
Brigandine, scale armour formerly worn by a brigand, or light-armed foot-soldier.
Jer. 46 : 4; 51 : 3, put on the b.
Bright, Job 37 : 11, scattereth his b. cloud.
Matt. 17 : 5, b. cloud overshadowed.
Rev. 22 : 16, the b. and morning star.
Brightness, Isa. 60 : 3, to b. of thy rising.
Isa. 62 : 1, righteousness go forth as b.
Dan. 12 : 3, wise shine as b. of firmament.
Hab. 3 : 4, his b. was as the light.
Acts 26 : 13, a light above b. of sun.
2 Thess. 2 : 8, b. of his coming.
Heb. 1 : 3, the b. of his glory.
Brim, 1 Ki. 7 : 23, ten cubits from the one b.
1 Ki. 7 : 26, like the b. of a cup.
2 Chr. 4 : 2, from b. to b.
John 2 : 7, filled them up to the b.
Brimstone [Heb. Gophrīth; θεῖον; Sulphur], Gen. 19 : 24; Deut. 29 : 23, etc. Sulphur, often used figuratively in the Bible.
and fire, Sodom destroyed by, Gen. 19 : 24.
figurative of torment, Isa. 30 : 33; Rev. 9 : 17; 14 : 10; 19 : 20; 21 : 8.
Job 18 : 15, b. shall be scattered.
Ezek. 38 : 22, fire and b.
Luke 17 : 29, fire and b. from heaven.
Bring, Gen. 1 : 11, let the earth b. forth.
Ps. 126 : 6, rejoicing, b. his sheaves with him.
Prov. 27 : 1, knowest not what a day may b.
Nah. 1 : 15, feet of him that b. good tidings.
John 12 : 24; 15 : 5; Col. 1 : 6, b. forth fruit.
1 Thess. 4 : 14, will God b. with him.
1 Tim. 6 : 7, b. nothing into this world.
Heb. 7 : 19, the b. in of a better hope.
Brink, Ex. 2 : 3, by the river's b.
Josh. 3 : 8, when ye are come to the b.
Ezek. 47 : 6, return to the b.
Broad, Ps. 119 : 96, thy commandment is exceeding b.
Isa. 33 : 21, a place of b. rivers.
Matt. 7 : 13, b. way to destruction.
23 : 5, make b. their phylacteries.
Broidered work, Ezek. 16 : 10.
Broiled, Luke 24 : 42, b. fish.
Broken, Ps. 34 : 18; 51 : 17, b. heart.
Matt. 21 : 44, shall fall on stone, shall be b.
John 10 : 35, scripture cannot be b.
19 : 36, bone shall not be b.
Eph. 2 : 14, b. down middle wall.
Brokenfooted, Lev. 21 : 19.
Brokenhanded, Lev. 21 : 19.
Brokenhearted, Isa. 61 : 1; Luke 4 : 18.
Brood, Luke 13 : 34.
Brook, 1 Sam. 17 : 40, five stones out of the b.
Ps. 42 : 1, as hart panteth after b.
110 : 7, drink of the b. in way.
John 18 : 1, went over b. Cedron.
Broth, Judg. 6 : 19, Gideon put the b. in a pot.
Isa. 65 : 4, b. of abominable things.
Brother, Prov. 17 : 17, a b. is born for adversity.
18 : 19, a b. offended is harder to be won.
18 : 24, friend closer than b.
Eccl. 4 : 8, neither child nor b.
Matt. 10 : 21; Mark 13 : 12, b. deliver up b.
1 Cor. 6 : 6, b. goeth to law with b.

2 Thess. 3 : 15, admonish as a **b.**
1 John 2 : 10, loveth his **b.** abideth in light.
Brother's widow, law concerning, Deut. 25 : 5; Matt. 22 : 24.
Brotherly, Rom. 12 : 10, affectioned with **b.** love.
1 Thess. 4 : 9, as touching **b.** love.
Heb. 13 : 1, let **b.** love continue.
2 Pet. 1 : 7, to godliness, **b.** kindness.
Brow, Isa. 48 : 4; Luke 4 : 29.
Brown, Gen. 30 : 32, 33, 35, 40.
Bruise, Gen. 3 : 15, **b.** thy head, **b.** his heel.
Isa. 1 : 6, but wounds and **b.**
53 : 10, pleased the Lord to **b.** him.
Luke 9 : 39, the Spirit **b.** him.
Rom. 16 : 20, God of peace shall **b.** Satan.
Bruised (Christ) for us, Isa. 53 : 5.
reed, Isa. 42 : 3; Matt. 12 : 20; Egypt so called, 2 Ki. 18 : 21; Ezek. 29 : 6, 7.
Bruit [rumour, noise or report], Jer. 10 : 22; Nah. 3 : 19.
Brutish, Ps. 92 : 6, a **b.** man knoweth not.
Prov. 30 : 2, I am more **b.** than any.
Jer. 10 : 21, pastors are become **b.**
Buckler [a shield or protection], the Divine, 2 Sam. 22 : 31; Ps. 18 : 2; 91 : 4; Prov. 2 : 7.
2 Sam. 22 : 31; Ps. 18 : 30, a **b.** to all that trust.
Ps. 18 : 2, Lord is my God, my **b.**
91 : 4, his truth shall be thy **b.**
Prov. 2 : 7, **b.** to them that walk uprightly.
Budded, Gen. 40 : 10; Ezek. 7 : 10; Heb. 9 : 4.
Budding of Aaron's rod, Num. 17.
Buffet, Matt. 26 : 67; Mark 14 : 65, and **b.** him.
1 Cor. 4 : 11, to present hour **b.**
2 Cor. 12 : 7, messenger of Satan to **b.** me.
1 Pet. 2 : 20, when **b.** for your faults.
Build, Gen. 11 : 4, go to, let us **b.** a city.
Ps. 51 : 18, **b.** walls of Jerusalem.
127 : 1, except the Lord **b.** the house.
Eccl. 3 : 3, a time to **b.** up.
Isa. 58 : 12; 61 : 4, **b.** old waste places.
Matt. 7 : 24; Luke 6 : 48, wise man **b.** on rock.
Luke 14 : 30, began to **b.**, not able to finish,
Acts 20 : 32, able to **b.** you up.
Rom. 15 : 20, **b.** on another man's foundation.
1 Cor. 3 : 12, if any **b.** on this foundation.
Eph. 2 : 22, in whom ye are **b.** together.
Heb. 3 : 4, every house is **b.** by some man.
Builder, Ps. 118 : 22; Matt. 21 : 42; Mark 12 : 10; Luke 20 : 17; Acts 4 : 11; 1 Pet. 2 : 7, stone which **b.** refused.
1 Cor. 3 : 10, as a wise master-**b.**
Heb. 11 : 10, whose **b.** and maker is God.
Building, the Church compared to, 1 Cor. 3 : 9; Eph. 2 : 21; Col. 2 : 7.
1 Cor. 3 : 9, ye are God's **b.**
2 Cor. 5 : 1, we have a **b.** of God.
Eph. 2 : 21, in whom **b.** fitly framed.
Bul (bŭl) [Heb. teo], the eighth month (October-November) of the Hebrew Calendar, later called Marchesvan, 1 Ki. 6 : 38.
Bull, wild [Heb. teo]. This word occurs in Isa. 51 : 20 and in Deut. 14 : 5, where it is translated wild ox. In both these places the R.V. translates the word as antelope. There have been great differences of opinion as to what this animal may have been,

which was among those allowed for food, but it seems likely to have been the wild cow of the Arabs.
Bulrush. Flag, reed, paper reed, rush, weeds. These represent, in the A.V., six different words, and all refer to plants growing in or near the water. The bulrush was without doubt the Papyrus antiquorum, the fibrous portions of the leaf stalk of which were used when prepared as a writing material. Of this the ark in which Moses was hid was made, and the word is translated papyrus in Isa. 18 : 2, " vessels of papyrus," R.V. It grows in Palestine, and was common in Lower Egypt, from whence it has now disappeared. The demand for it was far in excess of the supply a few centuries after Christ. It was used in Egypt for writing material and for mummies. The reeds and flags were apparently some species of rush.
Ex. 2 : 3, an ark of **b.**
Isa. 18 : 2, send ambassadors in vessels of **b.**
58 : 5, bow his head like a **b.**
Bulwark, Deut. 20 : 20, **b.** against the city.
Ps. 48 : 13, mark well her **b.**
Isa. 26 : 1, salvation for walls and **b.**
Bunah (bŭ-năh), 1 Chr. 2 : 25.
Bunch, Ex. 12 : 22; 2 Sam. 16 : 1; 1 Chr. 12 : 40; Isa. 30 : 6, a camel's hump.
Bundle, of life, 1 Sam. 25 : 29.
Gen. 42 : 35, every man's **b.** of money.
1 Sam. 25 : 29, soul bound in **b.** of life.
Cant. 1 : 13, a **b.** of myrrh.
Matt. 13 : 30, bind the tares in **b.**
Acts 28 : 3, Paul gathered a **b.** of sticks.
Burden [meaning prophecy], 2 Ki. 9 : 25; Isa. 13; 15; 17; 19; 21; 22; 23; Nah. 1 : 1.
cast on the Lord, Ps. 55 : 22.
of affliction, Isa. 58 : 6; 2 Cor. 5 : 4.
of iniquities, Ps. 38 : 4.
of Christ, light, Matt. 11 : 30; Acts 15 : 28; Rev. 2 : 24.
bear one another's, Gal. 6 : 2.
Ps. 55 : 22, cast thy **b.** on the Lord.
Eccl. 12 : 5, grasshopper shall be a **b.**
Matt. 11 : 30, my **b.** is light.
20 : 12, borne **b.** and heat of day.
23 : 4; Luke 11 : 46, heavy **b.**
2 Cor. 12 : 16, I did not **b.** you.
Gal. 6 : 5, every man bear his own **b.**
2 Cor. 12 : 13, I was not **b.** to you.
Burdensome, 2 Cor. 12 : 13, I was not **b.** to you.
Burial. It was the usage of the Hebrew people to put their dead in tombs. They interred in the earth only when entombment was too costly or difficult. A natural cave, such as Machpelah, was their usual burial place. They also embalmed their deceased.
deprivation of, a calamity, Deut. 28 : 26; Ps. 79 : 2; Eccl. 6 : 3; Isa. 14 : 19; Jer. 7 : 33; 16 : 4; 25 : 33; 34 : 20.
of Sarah, Gen. 23 : 19. Abraham, Gen. 25 : 9. Isaac, Gen. 35 : 29. Jacob, Gen. 50. Abner, 2 Sam. 3 : 31, 32. Christ, Matt. 27 : 57; Luke 23 : 50. Stephen, Acts 8 : 2.
Eccl. 6 : 3, that he have no **b.**
Jer. 22 : 19, with the **b.** of an ass.
Matt. 26 : 12, she did it for my **b.**
Acts 8 : 2, carried Stephen to his **b.**

Buriers, Ezek. 39 : 15.
Burn, Gen. 44 : 18, let not thine anger **b.**
Isa. 27 : 4, I would **b.** them together.
Ps. 39 : 3, while musing the fire **b.**
89 : 46, shall thy wrath **b.** like fire ?
Prov. 26 : 23, **b.** lips and wicked heart.
Isa. 9 : 18, wickedness **b.** as the fire.
33 : 14, dwell with everlasting **b.**
Mal. 4 : 1, day that shall **b.** as oven.
Matt. 13 : 30, bind tares to **b.** them.
Luke 3 : 17, chaff he will **b.**
12 : 35, loins girded and lights **b.**
24 : 32, did not our heart **b.** ?
John 5 : 35, he was a **b.** and shining light.
1 Cor. 13 : 3, give body to be **b.**
Heb. 6 : 8, whose end is to be **b.**
12 : 18, not come to mount that **b.**
Rev. 19 : 20, cast into a lake **b.**
Burning bush, by some this is thought to be the thorn-bush, Acacia Nilotica.
the Lord appears to Moses in, Ex. 3 : 2; Mark 12 : 26; Luke 20 : 37; Acts 7 : 35.
Burnished, Ezek. 1 : 7.
Burnt offerings, law concerning, Lev. 1 : 1; 6 : 8.
illustrations of, Gen. 8 : 20; 22 : 13; Ex. 18 : 12; 1 Sam. 7 : 9; Ezra 3 : 4; Job 1 : 5.
See Ps. 40 : 6; 51 : 19; Isa. 40 : 16; Heb. 10.
the continual, Ex. 29 : 38; Num. 28 : 3; 1 Chr. 16 : 40; 2 Chr. 13 : 11.
Ps. 40 : 6, **b.** thou hast not required.
51 : 16, thou delightest not in **b.**
Isa. 61 : 8, I hate robbery for **b.**
Jer. 6 : 20, your **b.** not acceptable.
Hos. 6 : 6, knowledge of God more than **b.**
Mark 12 : 33, to love neighbour is more than **b.**
Heb. 10 : 6, in **b.** for sin no pleasure.
Burnt sacrifice, Lev. 1 : 13; 3 : 5; 2 Chr. 13 : 11.
Burst, Prov. 3 : 10, presses shall **b.** out.
Isa. 30 : 14, not be found in the **b.**
Jer. 30 : 8; Nah. 1 : 13, will **b.** thy bonds.
Mark 2 : 22; Luke 5 : 37, doth **b.** the bottles.
Acts 1 : 18, **b.** asunder in the midst.
Bury, Matt. 8 : 21; Luke 9 : 59, suffer me to **b.** my father.
Matt. 27 : 7, field to **b.** strangers.
Luke 9 : 60, let the dead **b.**
John 19 : 40, manner of Jews is to **b.**
Rom. 6 : 4; Col. 2 : 12, **b.** with him by baptism.
1 Cor. 15 : 4, he was **b.** and rose.
Buryingplace, Gen. 23 : 4; 47 : 30; Judg. 16 : 31.
Bushel [a measure], Matt. 5 : 15; Mark 4 : 21; Luke 11 : 33, a candle, and put it under a **b.**
Bushy, Song of Sol. 5 : 11.
Business, 1 Sam. 21 : 8, king's **b.** requireth haste.
Ps. 107 : 23, do **b.** in great waters.
Prov. 22 : 29, man diligent in **b.**
Eccl. 5 : 3, dream through multitude of **b.**
Luke 2 : 49, about my Father's **b.**
Rom. 12 : 11, not slothful in **b.**
1 Thess. 4 : 11, study to do your own **b.**
Busy, 1 Ki. 20 : 40.
Busybodies censured, Prov. 20 : 3; 26 : 17; 1 Thess. 4 : 11; 2 Thess. 3 : 11; 1 Tim. 5 : 13; 1 Pet. 4 : 15.

Butchers, 1 Cor. 10 : 25.
Butler, Gen. 40 : 1.
Butter, Gen. 18 : 8, Abraham took **b.** and milk.
Judg. 5 : 25, she brought **b.** in lordly dish.
Ps. 55 : 21, words smoother than **b.**
Isa. 7 : 15, 22, **b.** shall he eat.
Buy, Lev. 22 : 11, **b.** any soul with money.
Deut. 2 : 6, **b.** meat for money.
Prov. 23 : 23, **b.** the truth.
Isa. 55 : 1, **b.** and eat, **b.** wine and milk.
Matt. 14 : 15; Mark 6 : 36, **b.** victuals.
Matt. 25 : 9, go to them that sell, and **b.**
John 4 : 8, disciples were gone to **b.** meat.
6 : 5, whence shall we **b.** bread.
13 : 29, **b.** things we have need of.
1 Cor. 7 : 30, **b.** as though they possessed not.
Jas. 4 : 13, **b.** and sell, and get gain.
Rev. 3 : 18, **b.** of me gold tried.
13 : 17, no man might **b.** or sell.
18 : 11, no man **b.** their merchandise.
Buyer characterised, Prov. 20 : 14, it is naught, saith **b.**
Isa. 24 : 2, as with the **b.** so the seller.
Ezek. 7 : 12, let not **b.** rejoice.
Buzi (bū-‡zī) [my contempt], Ezek. 1 : 3.
Buzite (bū-‡zīte), Job 32 : 2, 6.
By [against], I know nothing **b.** myself. 1 Cor. 4 : 4.
By and by [instantly, at once]. " Give me by and by in a charger the head of John the Baptist " (Mark 6 : 25). " By and by " occurs four times in the Gospels, and in every instance signifies immediately, Matt. 13 : 21; Luke 17 : 7; 21 : 9.
Byword, Deut. 28 : 37, a **b.** among all nations.
Job 17 : 6; 30 : 9, a **b.** of the people.
Ps. 44 : 14, a **b.** among the heathen.

C

Cab, a liquid measure equal to about three and a half pints, 2 Ki. 6 : 25.
Cæsar (çæ-‡săr), a title of the Roman Emperor taken from Augustus Cæsar.
Augustus, Luke 2 : 1. Tiberius, Luke 3 : 1.
Claudius, time of dearth, Acts 11 : 28.
Nero, Paul appeals to, Acts 25 : 11.

Ruins of Cæsarea

Cæsarea (çæ-să-rē-‡ă), Peter sent there, Acts 10.
Paul visits, Acts 21 : 8.
Paul sent to Felix there, Acts 23 : 23.
Cæsarea Philippi (çæ-să-rē-‡ă phī-līp-‡pī),

visited by Christ, Matt. 16 : 13; Mark 8 : 27.

Cage, Jer. 5 : 27, as a c. is full of birds.

Rev. 18 : 2, Babylon, c. of every unclean bird.

Caiaphas (câi-â-phăs) [probably identical with Cephas, rock], Luke 3 : 2.

high priest, prophesies concerning Christ, John 11 : 49.

his counsel, Matt. 26 : 3.

he condemns Him, Matt. 26 : 65; Mark 14 : 63; Luke 22 : 71.

Cain (Engl. pronunciation is cain, the Heb. is ka-yin) [spear], the sound of the word would remind one of possession, Gen. 4 : 1.

kills Abel, Gen. 4 : 8.

his punishment, Gen. 4 : 11.

See Heb. 11 : 4; 1 John 3 : 12; Jude 11.

Cake, Judg. 7 : 13, a c. tumbled into host.

2 Sam. 6 : 19, to every man a c.

1 Ki. 17 : 12, I have not a c.

19 : 6, a c. baken on coals.

Hos. 7 : 8, Ephraim is a c. not turned.

Calamity, Deut. 32 : 35, day of their c. is at hand.

2 Sam. 22 : 19; Ps. 18 : 18, prevented me in day of c.

Ps. 57 : 1, until these c. be overpast.

Prov. 1 : 26, I will laugh at your c.

17 : 5, he that is glad at c.

19 : 13, foolish son is c. of father.

27 : 10, brother's house in day of c.

Calamus, Sweet [Heb. kaneh], or **Sweet Cane,** was used in the preparation of the anointing oil (Ex. 30 : 23). It was an aromatic cane brought from a far country (Jer. 6 : 20), and would seem to have been imported with wrought iron and cassia (Ezek. 27 : 19).

Caldron, Job 41 : 20, a seething pot or c.

Jer. 52 : 19, the c. and the candlesticks.

Ezek. 11 : 3, city is the c. and we.

Caleb (câ-lĕb) [dog], faith of, Num. 13 : 30; 14 : 6.

permitted to enter Canaan, Num. 26 : 65; 32 : 12; Deut. 1 : 36.

his request, Joshua 14 : 6 ff.

his possessions, Joshua 15 : 13.

gives his daughter to Othniel to wife, Judg. 1 : 13.

Calf. The calf made in Horeb had probably to do with Baal-worship (Ex. 32 : 4).

golden, Aaron's transgression in making, Ex. 32; Acts 7 : 40, 41.

of Samaria, Hos. 8 : 5, 6.

calves made by Jeroboam, 1 Ki. 12 : 28.

Ex. 32 : 4; Deut. 9 : 16; Neh. 9 : 18; Ps. 106 : 19, made a molten c.

Isa. 11 : 6, c. and young lion together.

Luke 15 : 23, bring fatted c.

Calkers, seamen who stop the chinks of ships with tow, Ezek. 27 : 9-27.

Call of God to repentance and salvation, Ps. 49 : 50, etc.; Prov. 1 : 20; 2–8; Isa. 1; 45 : 20; 55; Jer. 35 : 15; Hos. 6; 14; Joel 2; Jonah 3; Matt. 3; 11 : 28; John 7 : 37; 12 : 44; Rom. 8 : 28; 9; 10; 11; 2 Cor. 5 : 20; Rev. 2 : 5; 3 : 3, 19; 22 : 17.

danger of rejecting, Ps. 50 : 17; Prov. 1 : 24; 29 : 1; Isa. 6 : 9; 66 : 4; Jer. 6 : 9; 26 : 4; 35 : 17; Matt. 22 : 3; John 12 : 48; Acts 13 : 46; 18 : 6; 28 : 24; Rom. 11 : 8;

2 Thess. 2 : 10; Heb. 2 : 1; 12 : 25; Rev. 2 : 5.

of Noah, Gen. 6 : 13. Abraham, Gen. 12. Jacob, Gen. 28 : 12. Moses, Ex. 3. Gideon, Judg. 6 : 11. Samuel, 1 Sam. 3. Elijah, 1 Ki. 17. Elisha, 1 Ki. 19 : 16, 19. Isaiah, Isa. 6. Jeremiah, Jer. 1. Ezekiel, Ezek. 1. Hosea, Hos. 1. Amos, Amos 1; 7 : 14. See Mic. 1 : 1; Zeph. 1 : 1; Hag. 1 : 1; Zech. 1 : 1.

of Jonah, Jonah 1.

of Peter, etc., Matt. 4 : 18; Mark 1 : 16; Luke 5; John 1 : 39.

of Paul, Acts 9; Rom. 1 : 1; Gal. 1 : 1, 11; 1 Tim. 1.

or vocation of the Gospel, Rom. 11 : 29; 1 Cor. 1 : 26; Eph. 1 : 18; 4 : 1; Phil. 3 : 14; 2 Thess. 1 : 11; 2 Tim. 1 : 9; Heb. 3 : 1; 1 Pet. 2 : 9; 2 Pet. 1 : 10; Rev. 19 : 9.

Rom. 11 : 29, c. of God without repentance.

1 Cor. 7 : 20, abide in same c.

Eph. 1 : 18, the hope of his c.

Phil. 3 : 14, prize of high c. of God.

2 Thess. 1 : 11, worthy of this c.

2 Tim. 1 : 9, called us with holy c.

Heb. 3 : 1, partakers of heavenly c.

2 Pet. 1 : 10, make c. and election sure.

Calm, Ps. 107 : 29, maketh storm a c.

Jonah 1 : 11, sea may be c. unto us.

Matt. 8 : 26; Mark 4 : 39; Luke 8 : 24; great c.

Calvary [of a skull], Luke 23 : 33. Calvaria is the Latin word, which has come in here from the Vulgate; the original Greek has κρανίον. The Heb. name was Golgotha. This site of the Crucifixion of Jesus has been located in many different spots from the popular one within the walls of the Church of the Holy Sepulchre, fixed upon by Constantine in the fourth century, which is certainly incorrect, to Gordon's Calvary to the north of the city. All such identifications, however, must remain uncertain.

Calves, Hos. 14 : 2, render the c. of our lips.

Mic. 6 : 6, c. of a year old.

Heb. 9 : 19, blood of c. and sprinkled.

Camel [Heb. gamal]. Among the earliest records of man in the East the camel was reckoned among one of the important sources of wealth. When first mentioned as occurring in Egypt, Arabia, or Canaan, they were numerous, and are reckoned with sheep, oxen, and asses. The one-humped camel is the species referred to; it was not allowed as food, though camel's milk was largely consumed (Gen. 32 : 15). Camels were kept in immense herds; thus we read that those possessed by the Midianites and Amalekites were, as it were, without number (Judg. 7 : 27).

mentioned, Gen. 12 : 16; 24 : 19; Ex. 9 : 3; 1 Chr. 5 : 21; Job 1 : 3; Matt. 19 : 24.

their flesh unclean, Lev. 11 : 4; Deut. 14 : 7.

Camel's Hair. Clothing made of the hair of the camel was worn by persons of ascetic and self-denying habits. It did not retain

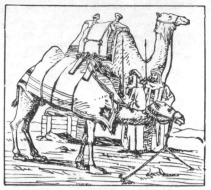

Camels caparisoned for a journey

perspiration, did not harbour vermin, was easily kept clean, and was very durable.

Camon (cā-mŏn) [firmness], Judg. 10 : 5.

Camp of Israelites, Ex. 14 : 19; Num. 1 : 52; 2; 24 : 5.

to be kept holy, Lev. 6 : 11; 13 : 4, 6; Num. 5 : 2; Deut. 23 : 10; Heb. 13 : 11.

Ex. 14 : 19, angel, which went before **c.**

Num. 11 : 26, they prophesied in **c.**

Deut. 23 : 14, Lord walketh in midst of **c.**

Heb. 13 : 13, go forth to him without the **c.**

Isa. 29 : 3, I will **c.** against thee round about.

Camphire, an old English form of the word camphor. The Hebrew word kopher, so translated in the A.V. at Cant. 1 : 14 and 4 : 13, is more correctly rendered henna. This is the " Lawsonia alba " of the botanist. A paste made of the pounded leaves is used to stain the finger nails.

Cana (cā-nă) [reeds], a town of Galilee.

Christ's first miracle at, John 2.

nobleman visits Christ at, John 4 : 47.

Canaan (cā-nāān) [low land], land of, Ex. 23 : 31; Josh. 1 : 4; Zeph. 2 : 5.

promised to Abraham, Gen. 12 : 7; 13 : 14; 17 : 8.

inhabitants of, Ex. 15 : 15.

their wickedness at Sodom and Gomorrah, Gen. 13 : 13; 19.

Israelites not to walk in their ways, Lev. 18 : 3, 24, 30; 20 : 23.

See Gen. 28 : 1, 6, 8; Judg. 3 : 1; 4 : 2, 23, 24; 5 : 19; Ps. 135 : 11; Isa. 19 : 18.

patriarchs dwell in, Gen. 12 : 6; 28; 36; 37.

the spies' visit, and their report, Num. 13.

the murmurers forbidden to enter, Num. 14 : 22.

also Moses and Aaron, Num. 20 : 12; Deut. 3 : 23; 32 : 48.

Moses sees from Pisgah, Num. 27 : 12; Deut. 3 : 27; 34 : 1.

allotted to children of Israel, Num. 26 : 52; Josh. 14.

a son of Ham, cursed on account of his father's mockery of Noah, Gen. 9 : 25.

Candace (căn-dă-çē), queen of Ethiopia, Acts 8 : 27.

Candle. Not a tallow rod with a wick, but an earthen vessel with a handle, and a nozzle through which a wick protruded. It was a species of oil lamp (Matt. 5 : 15).

figurative, Job 18 : 6; 21 : 17; Ps. 18 : 28; Prov. 20 : 27.

parable, Matt. 5 : 15; Luke 8 : 16.

Job 29 : 3, his **c.** shined on my head.

Ps. 18 : 28, the Lord will light my **c.**

Prov. 20 : 27, spirit of man is **c.** of Lord.

24 : 20, **c.** of wicked be put out.

Matt. 5 : 15; Mark 4 : 21; Luke 8 : 16, light a **c.**

Rev. 18 : 23, **c.** shine no more in thee.

22 : 5, need no **c.** nor light of sun.

Candlestick in the tabernacle, Ex. 25 : 31; 37 : 17; Lev. 24 : 4; Num. 8 : 2-4.

The candlestick was of pure gold of beaten work. It had seven arms, the centre one being the shaft, formed on each side of three cups of almond blossoms, their knops and flowers (Ex. 25 : 31-40). The base is not described. The lamps, which were placed on the tops of the seven branches, were separate from the candlestick itself, and were supplied with oil from oil vessels which are not specially described. The height of the candlestick is not mentioned. Its lamps were lighted and trimmed daily by the priests, and kept constantly burning (Ex. 27 : 20, 21).

in visions, Zech. 4 : 2; Rev. 1 : 12.

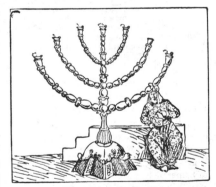

The Golden Candlestick

Cane, Sweet [Heb. kaneh], or **Calamus,** oils.

Isa. 43 : 24, bought no sweet **c.** with money.

Jer. 6 : 20, sweet **c.** from a far country.

See Ex. 30 : 23.

Canker, 2 Tim. 2 : 17, their word will eat as **c.**

Jas. 5 : 3, your gold and silver is **c.**

Cankerworm. This probably indicates the larval or caterpillar stage in the development of the locust, the insect plague of the East, Joel 1 : 4; 2 : 25; Nah. 3 : 15, 16.

Canon, The, of Scripture. By the Canon of Scripture, or the Canon of the Scriptures, is meant the measure of the contents of the Bible. " Canon " is a rod which has been measured and tested, and which then becomes a standard for measuring and testing other things. The word is easily applied in a figurative sense to any kind of standard. In the case of Scripture those books are called canonical which have been tested and admitted by rule, and then have themselves become a rule or standard by which to test doctrine and practice.

Capernaum (că-pĕr-‹nă-ŭm) [village of comfort], Christ preaches at, Matt. 4 : 17; Mark 1 : 21.
miracles at, Matt. 8 : 5; 17 : 24; John 4 : 46; 6 : 17.
parables at, Matt. 13 : 18, 24; Mark 4.
condemned for unbelief, Matt. 11 : 23; Luke 10 : 15.

Captain, Josh. 5 : 14, c. of the Lord's host.
2 Chr. 13 : 12, God himself is our c.
Heb. 2 : 10, c. of their salvation.
Rev. 19 : 18, eat the flesh of c.

Captive, Ex. 12 : 29, firstborn of c.
Isa. 52 : 2, loose thyself, O c. daughter of Zion.
61 : 1, proclaim liberty to the c.
Luke 4 : 18, preach deliverance to the c.
Eph. 4 : 8, he led captivity c.
2 Tim. 2 : 26, taken c. by him at will.
3 : 6, lead c. silly women.

Captivity, of the Israelites, foretold, Lev. 26 : 33; Deut. 28 : 36.
of the ten tribes, foretold, Amos 6 : 7; 7 : 11; fulfilled, 2 Ki. 17; 1 Chr. 5 : 26.
of Judah, foretold, Isa. 39 : 6; Jer. 13 : 19; 20 : 4; 25 : 11; 32 : 28; fulfilled, 2 Ki. 25; 2 Chr. 36; Esther 2; Ps. 137; Jer. 39; 52; Dan. 1.
return of the Israelites from, Ezra 1; 2; Neh. 2-7; Ps. 126.
Ps. 68 : 18; Eph. 4 : 8, led c. captive.
Rom. 7 : 23, into c. to law of sin.
2 Chr. 10 : 5, bringing into c. every thought.

Carbuncle [Heb. Nophek; **Emerald** of A.V.; Ανθραξ; Carbunculus], Ex. 28 : 18; Ezek. 28 : 13. The word so translated in the A.V. should have been rendered emerald and emerald by carbuncle. The mistake appears to have originated in the transposition of the two terms in the LXX. version of the passage in Ezekiel. Nophek [a glowing red stone] = Ανθραξ not σμάζαγδος. The term carbuncle, as understood by the ancients, included the ruby with several varieties of garnet.

Carcase, Matt. 24 : 28, c. is there will eagles be.
Heb. 3 : 17, whose c. fell in wilderness.

Care, worldly, forbidden, Matt. 6 : 25; Luke 8 : 14; 12 : 22; John 6 : 27; 1 Cor. 7 : 32; Phil. 4 : 6; 1 Tim. 6 : 8; 2 Tim. 2 : 4; Heb. 13 : 5.
Martha reproved for, Luke 10 : 41.
(loving) of the Samaritan, Luke 10 : 34.
of Christ for his mother, John 19 : 26.
of Paul for the Corinthians, 2 Cor. 7 : 12; 11 : 28.
of Titus for the Corinthians, 2 Cor. 8 : 16.
for Paul by Philippians, Phil. 4 : 10.
to be cast on God, 1 Pet. 5 : 7.
of thoughts, Ps. 39 : 1.
Ps. 142 : 4, no man c. for my soul.

Matt. 13 : 22; Mark 4 : 19; Luke 8 : 14, c. of this world.
John 12 : 6, not that he c. for the poor.
Acts 18 : 17, Gallio c. for none of these things.
1 Cor. 9 : 9, doth God take c. for oxen ?
12 : 25, have the same c. one for another.
2 Cor. 11 : 28, c. of all the churches.
Phil. 2 : 20, naturally c. for your state.
1 Pet. 5 : 7, casting all your c. on him.

Careful [over-anxious, fretfully concerned].
Jer. 17 : 8, not be c. in year of drought.
Dan. 3 : 16, not c. to answer thee.
Luke 10 : 41, c. about many things.
Phil. 4 : 6, be c. for nothing.
Heb. 12 : 17, he sought it c. with tears.

Carefulness [painful anxiety], 1 Cor. 7 : 32, I would have you without c.

Careless, Judg. 18 : 7; Isa. 32 : 9.

Carmel (cär-‹mĕl) [garden land].
mount, Elijah and the prophets of Baal, 1 Ki. 18.
Shunammite woman meets Elisha at, 2 Ki. 4 : 25.
her child restored to life, 2 Ki. 4 : 34.
Nabal's conduct to David at, 1 Sam. 25.
See also Josh. 15 : 55; Isa. 33 : 9; 35 : 2; Jer. 50 : 19; Amos 1 : 2; 1 Sam. 15 : 12.

Carmel

Carnal mind condemned, Rom. 8 : 7; 1 Cor. 3 : 1; Col. 2 : 18.
Rom. 7 : 14, c. sold under sin.
8 : 7, c. mind is enmity against God.
2 Cor. 10 : 4, weapons of warfare not c.
Heb. 7 : 16, law of a c. commandment.

Carpenters, vision of four, Zech. 1 : 20.
sent to David by Hiram, 2 Sam. 5 : 11.

Carpenter's Son, Christ reproached as, Matt. 13 : 55; Mark 6 : 3.

Carriage [what is carried, baggage], 1 Sam. 17 : 22, David left his c. in the hands of the keeper of the c.
Judg. 18 : 21, cattle and c. before them.
Isa. 46 : 1, your c. were heavy laden.
Acts 21 : 15, we took up our c.

Carry, Ex. 33 : 15, c. us not up hence.
Isa. 40 : 11, c. lambs in his bosom.
53 : 4, our sorrows.
63 : 9, c. them all days of old.
Mark 6 : 55, began to c. in beds.
Luke 10 : 4, c. neither purse nor scrip.
John 5 : 10, not lawful to c. thy bed.
21 : 18, c. thee whither wouldst not.
1 Tim. 6 : 7, can c. nothing out of world.

Eph. 4 : 14, c. about with every wind.
Heb. 13 : 9, c. about with divers doctrines.
Jude 12, clouds c. about of winds.
Cart, 2 Sam. 6 : 3, set ark on a new c.
Isa. 5 : 18, draw sin as with a c. rope.
Amos 2 : 13, c. full of sheaves.

Egyptian Agricultural Cart

Carved, 1 Ki. 6 : 18.
Case, Ps. 144 : 15, happy people in such a c.
Matt. 5 : 20, in no c. enter heaven.
John 5 : 6, long time in that c.
Casement, Prov. 7 : 6.
Cassia. Two Hebrew words are thus translated. The first, kiddah (Ex. 30 : 24), has been supposed to represent Cinnamomum cassia, of India, which formed part of the merchandise of Tyre (Ezek. 27 : 19). The inner bark of the twigs and stem of the tree yield the aromatic spice. The other, ketziah, referred to in Ps. 45 : 8, was also a spice-bearing tree.
Cast, Ps. 22 : 10, I was c. on thee from womb.
Prov. 16 : 33, the lot is c. into lap.
Isa. 25 : 7, covering c. over all people.
Matt. 5 : 29; Mark 9 : 45, whole body c. into hell.
Matt. 21 : 21, say to mountain, be c. into sea.
Mark 9 : 38; Luke 9 : 49, one c. out devils.
Luke 21 : 1, c. gifts into treasury.
2 Cor. 10 : 5, c. down imaginations.
1 Pet. 5 : 7, c. all care upon him.
1 John 4 : 18, love c. out fear.
Cast about [turned round], Jer. 41 : 14, c. about and returned.
Castaway, 1 Cor. 9 : 27, lest I be a c.
Castle, Gen. 25 : 16; 1 Chr. 27 : 25; 2 Chr. 17 : 12.
Castor and Pollux, ship so called, Acts 28 : 11.
Catch, Ps. 10 : 9, to c. the poor.
Matt. 13 : 19, devil c. away that which was sown.
Mark 12 : 13, to c. him in his words.
Luke 5 : 10, c. men.
John 10 : 12, wolf c. and scattereth sheep.
Caterpiller, possibly the larval stage of the locust or the moth, Job 27 : 18; Isa. 51 : 8.
Cattle of Jacob increased, Gen. 30; 43.
of Israelites preserved, Ex. 9 : 4.
regulations concerning, Ex. 20 : 1; 21 : 28; 22 : 1; 23 : 4; Deut. 5 : 14; 22 : 1; 25 : 4 (1 Cor. 9 : 9; 1 Tim. 5 : 18).
referred to by Christ, Matt. 12 : 11; Luke 13 : 15; 14 : 5.
an example of obedience, Isa. 1 : 3.
Gen. 46 : 32, their trade to feed c.

Deut. 2 : 35; 3 : 7; Josh. 8 : 2, the c. take for prey.
Ps. 50 : 10, c. on a thousand hills.
Caught, Gen. 22 : 13, ram c. by horns.
Mark 12 : 3, they c. the servant.
John 21 : 3, that night they c. nothing.
Acts 8 : 39, the Spirit c. away Philip.
2 Cor. 12 : 2, a man c. up to third heaven.
1 Thess. 4 : 17, be c. up together with them.
Caul. (1) a net-work covering for the head (Isa. 3 : 18). (2) the pericardium, or membrane around the heart (Hos. 13 : 8).
Cause, Ps. 140 : 12, Lord will maintain the c.
Eccl. 7 : 10, what is c. that former days.
Isa. 51 : 22, pleadeth c. of his people.
Matt. 19 : 5; Mark 10 : 7; Eph. 5 : 31, for this c. shall.
1 Cor. 11 : 30, for this c. many are sickly.
2 Cor. 4 : 16, for which c. we faint not.
1 Tim. 1 : 16, for this c. I obtained mercy.
Ps. 67 : 1; 80 : 3, God c. his face to shine.
Matt. 10 : 21; Mark 13 : 12, c. parents to be put to death.
Rom. 16 : 17, mark them who c. divisions.
Causeless, 1 Sam. 25 : 31; Prov. 26 : 2.
Causeway, 1 Chr. 26 : 16.
Caves of refuge, 1 Sam. 13 : 6; Heb. 11 : 38.
prophets concealed in, by Obadiah, 1 Ki. 18 : 4.
Elijah lodges in, 1 Ki. 19 : 9.
Cease, Deut. 15 : 11, poor never c. out of land.
Job 3 : 17, wicked c. from troubling.
Ps. 37 : 8, c. from anger.
46 : 9, he maketh wars to c.
Prov. 19 : 27, c. to hear the instruction.
23 : 4, c. from thine own wisdom.
Eccl. 12 : 3, grinders c. because few.
Isa. 1 : 16, c. to do evil.
Acts 20 : 31, I c. not to warn.
1 Cor. 13 : 8, tongues, they shall c.
1 Thess. 5 : 17, pray without c.
1 Pet. 4 : 1, hath c. from sin.
Cedar [Heb. erez]. Especially applied to the Cedrus libani, Cedar of Lebanon, but the cedar wood found in the wilderness and used in the purification of lepers (Lev. 14 : 4-6), was not this tree, but some other fragrant conifer.
temple built of, 1 Ki. 5 : 6; 6 : 15.
Behemoth compared to, Job 40 : 17.
2 Sam. 7 : 2, I dwell in a house of c.
2 Ki. 14 : 9, thistle sent to c.
Ps. 92 : 12, grow like a c. in Lebanon.

Cedars of Lebanon

Cedars of Lebanon, Judg. 9 : 15; Ps. 92 : 12; 104 : 16; 148 : 9; Cant. 5 : 15; Isa. 2 : 13; Ezek. 17 : 3.

Celebrate, Lev. 23 : 32; Isa. 38 : 18.

Celestial, 1 Cor. 15 : 40, there are c. bodies.

Cellars, 1 Chr. 27 : 27.

Censer, a small portable dish in which, coals from the altar having been placed, the incense was burned.
of brass, Lev. 10 : 1; 16 : 12.
of gold, 1 Ki. 7 : 50; Heb. 9 : 4; Rev. 8 : 3.
of Korah, reserved for holy use, Num. 16 : 36.

Centurion [the commander of a hundred men], servant of, healed, Matt. 8 : 5; Luke 7.
at crucifixion acknowledges Christ, Matt. 27 : 54; Mark 15 : 39; Luke 23 : 47.
Cornelius, Acts 10 : 1.
in charge of Paul, Acts 27 : 43.

Roman Centurion

Cephas (çē-̱phăs) [rock or stone].
(Peter) a stone, John 1 : 42; 1 Cor. 1 : 12; 3 : 22; 9 : 5; 15 : 5; Gal. 2 : 9.

Ceremonies, Num. 9 : 3.

Certain, Ex. 3 : 12, c. I will be with thee.
Luke 23 : 47, c. this was a righteous man.
1 Cor. 4 : 11, no c. dwellingplace.
1 Tim. 6 : 7, it is c. we can carry nothing.

Heb. 10 : 27, a c. looking for of judgment.

Certainty, Josh. 23 : 13, know for a c. that the Lord.
Acts 22 : 30, would have known the c.

Certify, Ezra 4 : 14, 16; Gal. 1 : 11.

Cesar or Cæsar, Matt. 22 : 17.

Chafed [fretted, irritated], 2 Sam. 17 : 8, they be c. in their minds.

Chaff, Ps. 35 : 5, let them be as c. before wind.
Jer. 23 : 28, what is c. to the wheat ?
Matt. 3 : 12; Luke 3 : 17, burn up c. with fire.

Chain, Gen. 41 : 42; Dan. 5 : 7, put a gold c. about his neck.
Mark 5 : 3, bind him, no, not with c.
Acts 12 : 7, Peter's c. fell off.
2 Tim. 1 : 16, not ashamed of my c.
2 Pet. 2 : 4, into c. of darkness.
Jude 6, everlasting c.

Chalcedony [Χαλκηδων; Chalcedonius]. Supposed to refer figuratively to a green variety of chalcedony, found at Chalcedon.
foundation of the Holy City, Rev. 21 : 19.

Chaldeans afflict Job, Job 1 : 17.
besiege Jerusalem, 2 Ki. 24 : 2; 25 : 4; Jer. 37–39.
wise men of, preserved by Daniel, Dan. 2 : 24.
prophecies concerning, Isa. 23 : 13; 43 : 14; 47 : 1; 48 : 14; Hab. 1 : 5.

Chalkstones, Isa. 27 : 9.

Challenge [to claim as one's due], Ex. 22 : 9, which another c. to be his.

Chamber, 2 Ki. 4 : 10, little c. on wall.
Ps. 19 : 5, as bridegroom coming out of c.
104 : 3, beams of c. in the waters.
Isa. 26 : 20, enter into thy c.
Ezek. 8 : 12, c. of imagery.
Matt. 24 : 26, in secret c.
Acts 9 : 37; 20 : 8, in upper c.

Chamberlain, 2 Ki. 23 : 11; Esther 1 : 10; 6 : 2.

Chameleon [Heb. tinshemeth], in Lev. 11 : 30, is translated in the R.V., land crocodile; and the word rendered mole in the same text, is in the R.V. given as chameleon. Tinshemeth probably refers to some of the numerous land lizards found in Palestine.

Chamois [Heb. zemer], occurs in Deut. 14 : 5. One of the animals fit for food, certainly not the European chamois, but possibly the wild mountain sheep, which probably was, in early times, found in numbers in Palestine.

Champaign [a level country], Deut. 11 : 30, the c. over against Gilgal.

Champion, 1 Sam. 17 : 4, 51.

Chance, 1 Sam. 6 : 9, it was a c. that happened.
2 Sam. 1 : 6, happened by c.
1 Cor. 15 : 37, it may c. of wheat.
See Deut. 22 : 6; Eccl. 9 : 11.

Chancellor, Ezra 4 : 8, 9, 17.

Change, Job 14 : 14, till my c. come.
Job 14 : 20, thou c. his countenance.
Ps. 15 : 4, sweareth, and c. not.
102 : 26, as a vesture shalt thou c. them.
Mal. 3 : 6, I am the Lord, I c. not.
Rom. 1 : 23, c. glory of uncorruptible God.
1 Cor. 15 : 51, we shall all be c.
2 Cor. 3 : 18, c. from glory to glory.
Phil. 3 : 21, c. our vile body.

Heb. 7 : 12, of necessity a c. of law.
Changeable, Isa. 3 : 22.
Changers, John 2 : 14, 15.
Changes, Gen. 45 : 22; Job 10 : 17; Ps. 55 : 19.
Channel, Ps. 18 : 15; Isa. 27 : 12.
Chant, Amos 6 : 5.
Chapel, the king's, Amos 7 : 13.
Chapiter [cornice crowning a pillar], 1 Ki. 7 : 17, the c. which were upon the top of the pillars.
Chapman [a market man, a trader; from the Ang. Sax. ceap, meaning trade], 2 Chr. 9 : 14, that which c. and merchants brought.
Chapt, cracked, Jer. 14 : 4.
Charge of God to Moses and Aaron, Ex. 6 : 13.
of Moses to Joshua, Deut. 31 : 7.
of David to Solomon, 1 Ki. 2 : 1; 1 Chr. 22 : 6.
of Jehoshaphat to the judges, 2 Chr. 19 : 6.
of Paul to the elders of Ephesus, Acts 20 : 17.
of Paul to Timothy, 1 Tim. 5 : 21; 2 Tim. 4.
of Peter to the elders, 1 Pet. 5.
Job 1 : 22, nor c. God foolishly.
Ps. 91 : 11; Matt. 4 : 6; Luke 4 : 10, give angels c.
Acts 7 : 60, lay not sin to their c.
Rom. 8 : 33, who shall lay anything to c. ?
1 Cor. 9 : 18, gospel without c.
1 Tim. 1 : 18, this c. I commit to thee.
6 : 17, c. them that are rich.
Chargeable [causing outlay or expense], 1 Thess. 2 : 9, not be c. unto any of you.
2 Cor. 11 : 9, I was c. to no man.
Charger [a large dish], Matt. 14 : 8, give me here John Baptist's head in a c.
Chariot of fire, Elijah ascends to heaven in, 2 Ki. 2 : 11.
Chariots of war, Ex. 14 : 7; 1 Sam. 13 : 5; 2 Sam. 10 : 18; Ps. 20 : 7; Nah. 3 : 2.
sent by the king of Syria to take Elisha, 2 Ki. 6 : 14.
of fire sent to defend Elisha, 2 Ki. 6 : 17.
of God, Ps. 68 : 17.
Charity [love], whether of God or man, cherished and practised, 1 Cor. 13.
love to our neighbour, Matt. 22 : 39; Mark 12 : 33; Rom. 13 : 8-10; 1 Cor. 13; 1 Thess. 1 : 3; 3 : 6; 4 : 9; 1 Tim. 1 : 5; 4 : 12; 2 Tim. 3 : 10; Heb. 6 : 10; Jas. 2 : 8; 1 Pet. 1 : 22; 1 John 2 : 10; 3 : 14; 4 : 11; Rev. 2 : 19.
almsgiving, Prov. 19 : 17; Matt. 19 : 21; Luke 11 : 41; 12 : 33; 18 : 22; Acts 10 : 2, 4; 2 Cor. 9; 3 John 6.
exhortations to, Lev. 19 : 18; Deut. 10 : 19; Matt. 5 : 44; Gal. 5 : 14; 6 : 10; Eph. 4 : 2; 1 John 3 : 23; 4 : 7, 21; 2 John 5.
commended, 1 Cor. 8 : 1; 13; Gal. 5 : 6, 22; Eph. 3 : 17; 4 : 16; 5 : 2; Col. 3 : 14.
how to be manifested, Lev. 19 : 17; 25 : 35; Isa. 58 : 7; Matt. 18 : 15; 25 : 35; John 13 : 35; Rom. 12 : 15; 1 Cor. 12 : 26; Gal. 5 : 13; Eph. 4 : 32; 1 Thess. 5 : 14; Heb. 6 : 10; 1 Pet. 4 : 8; 1 John 3 : 10, 17.
exemplified by Christ, John 13 : 34; 15 : 12; Eph. 5 : 2, 25; Rev. 1 : 5.
1 Cor. 8 : 1, c. edifieth.
13 : 4, c. suffereth long.

Col. 3 : 14, above all, put on c.
1 Tim. 1 : 5, end of commandment is c.
2 Tim. 2 : 22, follow faith, c.
1 Pet. 4 : 8, c. shall cover the multitude of sins.
2 Pet. 1 : 7, to brotherly kindness c.
Jude 12, spots in your feasts of c.
Charmer, Deut. 18 : 11; Ps. 58 : 5; Isa. 19 : 3.
Chase, Lev. 26 : 7, ye shall c. your enemies.
Josh. 23 : 10, one man of you shall c. a thousand.
1 Sam. 17 : 53, Israel returned from c.
Prov. 19 : 26, c. away his mother.
Isa. 17 : 13, shall be c. as the chaff.
Chaste, 2 Cor. 11 : 2, present you as c. virgin.
1 Pet. 3 : 2, your c. conversation.
Chasten, Ps. 6 : 1; 38 : 1, nor c. me in displeasure.
Ps. 94 : 12, blessed is man whom thou c.
Prov. 19 : 18, c. thy son while there is hope.
2 Cor. 6 : 9, as c., and not killed.
Heb. 12 : 5, despise not thou the c.
12 : 6; Rev. 3 : 19, whom the Lord loveth he c.
Heb. 12 : 11, no c. for the present.
Chastise, 1 Ki. 12 : 11, 14, c. you with scorpions.
Jer. 31 : 18, thou hast c. me.
Luke 23 : 22, c. him, and let him go.
Chastisement, Job 34 : 31, I have borne c.
Isa. 53 : 5, c. of our peace was upon him.
Heb. 12 : 8, if ye be without c.
Chatter, Isa. 38 : 14.
Check, Job 20 : 3.
Checker, 1 Ki. 7 : 17.
Cheek, Matt. 5 : 39; Luke 6 : 29, smiteth on right c.
See Ps. 3 : 7; Lam. 1 : 2; Joel 1 : 6.
Cheer, Eccl. 11 : 9, thy heart c. thee.
John 16 : 33; Acts 23 : 11, be of good c.
Cheerful, Prov. 15 : 13, merry heart maketh a c. countenance.
Zech. 9 : 17, corn shall make young men c.
Acts 24 : 10, more c. answer for myself.
2 Cor. 9 : 7, God loveth a c. giver.
Cheerfulness, Rom. 12 : 8, he that showeth mercy, with c.
Cheese, 2 Sam. 17 : 29; Job 10 : 10.
Chemosh (chē-mŏsh), national god of the Moabites and Ammonites, Num. 21 : 29; Judg. 11 : 24; Jer. 48 : 7.
worshipped by Solomon, 1 Ki. 11 : 7.
Cherethem (chē-rĕ-thĕm), Ezek. 25 : 16, or Cherethites [executioners (?)]; or perhaps rather so called from Crete, from which island a portion of the Philistines came, 2 Sam. 8 : 18.
Cherethites (and Pelethites), David's guard, 2 Sam. 15 : 18.
Cherish, Eph. 5 : 29, c. flesh, as Lord the church.
1 Thess. 2 : 7, as a nurse c. children.
Cherith (chē-rĭth) [cutting], 1 Ki. 17 : 3.
Cherub (chē-rŭb) [cherub], a place in Babylon, Ezra 2 : 59; Neh. 7 : 51. The word is the singular of the well-known cherubim.
Cherubim in garden of Eden, Gen. 3 : 24.
for the mercy seat and the temple, Ex. 25 : 18; 37 : 7; 1 Ki. 6 : 23; 2 Chr. 3 : 10; Ps. 80 : 1; Ezek. 41 : 18.
Ezekiel's visions of, Ezek. 1; 10.

Chesed (chĕs-ĕd) [derivation uncertain], name of ancestor of the Chaldeans, Gen. 22 : 22.

Chest [Heb., âron'], 2 Chr. 24 : 8, 10, 11; Ezek. 27 : 24.

Chestnut Tree. The Hebrew word Armon thus translated in the A.V., occurs twice; (1) in Gen. 30 : 37, where Jacob took and peeled some of its twigs; and (2) in Ezek. 31 : 8, where is the fine description of the cedar of Lebanon. The chestnut trees are said not to be like its branches. In both places the R.V. translates plane trees, which is the correct rendering.

Chew, Lev. 11 : 4; Num. 11 : 33; Deut. 14 : 7.

Chickens, Matt. 23 : 37, as a hen gathereth her c.

Chide, Ex. 17 : 2, the people did c.
Ps. 103 : 9, he will not always c.

Chief, Matt. 20 : 27, whosoever will be c. among you.
Luke 22 : 26, he that is c., as he that serveth.
Eph. 2 : 20, Jesus Christ being c. corner stone.

Chief Priests. These were (1) the high priest; (2) those who had held the office of high priest; (3) the seniors of the twenty-four courses (1 Chr. 24).
consulted by Herod, Matt. 2 : 4.
their persecution of Christ, Matt. 16 : 21; Mark 14 : 1; 15 : 31; John 7 : 32.

Chiefest, Cant. 5 : 10, c. among ten thousand.
Mark 10 : 44, be c., shall be servant.
2 Cor. 11 : 5, behind c. apostles.

Child, Gen. 37 : 30, c. is not; and I, whither.
42 : 22, do not sin against the c.
Ps. 131 : 2, quieted myself as a weaned c.
Prov. 20 : 11, even a c. is known by his doings.
22 : 6, train up a c. in way.
Isa. 9 : 6, unto us a c. is born.
65 : 20, c. shall die an hundred years old.
Jer. 1 : 6, I cannot speak, for I am a c.
Mark 9 : 36, Jesus took a c. and set him in the midst.
10 : 15, receive kingdom of God as little c.
Luke 1 : 66, what manner of c.
John 4 : 49, come down ere c. die.
Acts 4 : 27, against thy holy c. Jesus.
1 Cor. 13 : 11, when I was a c.
Gal. 4 : 1, heir as long as he is a c.
2 Tim. 3 : 15, from a c. hast known the Scriptures.

Childhood, 1 Sam. 12 : 2; Eccl. 11 : 10.

Childless, Lev. 20 : 20; Jer. 22 : 30.

Children, the gift of God, Gen. 33 : 5; Ps. 127; 128.
a blessing, Prov. 10 : 1; 15 : 20; 17 : 6; 23 : 24; 27 : 11; 29 : 3.
duty of, Ex. 20 : 12; Lev. 19 : 3, 32; Deut. 5 : 16; 30 : 2; Prov. 1 : 8; 6 : 20; 13 : 1; 15 : 5; 19 : 27; 23 : 22; 24 : 21; 28 : 7, 24; Eccl. 12 : 1; Eph. 6 : 1; Col. 3 : 20; 1 Tim. 5 : 4; Heb. 12 : 9; 1 Pet. 5 : 5.
of Bethlehem slain by Herod, Matt. 2 : 16; (Jer. 31 : 15).
blessed by Christ, Matt. 19 : 13; Mark 10 : 13; Luke 18 : 15.
of light, Luke 16 : 8; John 12 : 36; Eph. 5 : 8; 1 Thess. 5 : 5.
of God, Eph. 5 : 1; Heb. 12 : 5; 1 Pet. 1 : 14; 1 John 3 : 10.

Examples of obedient children—Christ, Luke 2 : 51. Isaac, Gen. 22 : 6. Joseph, Gen. 45 : 9. Jephthah's daughter, Judg. 11 : 36. Samuel, 1 Sam. 2 : 26.
Wicked children characterised—1 Sam. 2 : 12, 25; Prov. 15 : 5; 17 : 21; 19 : 13, 26; 28 : 7, 24; 30 : 11; Isa. 3 : 5; Ezek. 22 : 7.
their punishment, Ex. 21 : 15; Deut. 21 : 18; 27 : 16; 2 Ki. 2 : 23; Prov. 30 : 17; Mark 7 : 10.
(child) of the devil, Acts 13 : 10; 1 John 3 : 10.
Ps. 34 : 11, come ye c., hearken to me.
45 : 16, instead of fathers shall be c.
128 : 3, thy c. like olive plants.
Isa. 8 : 18; Heb. 2 : 13, I and c. given me.
Isa. 63 : 8, c. that will not lie.
Ezek. 18 : 2, c. teeth are set on edge.
Matt. 15 : 26; Mark 7 : 27, not take c. bread.
Matt. 19 : 14; Mark 10 : 14; Luke 18 : 16, suffer little c.
Luke 16 : 8, c. of this world wiser than c. of light.
John 12 : 36; Eph. 5 : 8; 1 Thess. 5 : 5, c. of light.
Rom. 8 : 16; Gal. 3 : 26; 1 John 3 : 10, c. of God.
Eph. 5 : 6; Col. 3 : 6, c. of disobedience.
Eph. 6 : 1; Col. 3 : 20, c., obey your parents.

Children of the East, or Men of the East, a title often applied in the Old Testament to the tribes dwelling in Arabia Petræa, Gen. 29 : 1; 1 Ki. 4 : 30; Ezek. 25 : 4, 10; Job 1 : 3.

Chileab (chī-lē-ăb) [probably same meaning as Caleb], 2 Sam. 3 : 3, second son of David.

Chimney, Hos. 13 : 3.

Chisleu (chĭs-lĕu), rather **Kislev** [Assyrian Ki-si-li-vu, month of December], the ninth month in the Hebrew Calendar, Neh 1 : 1.

Chittim (chĭt-tĭm), the island of Cyprus, so called from the city Kition, now Chiethi, Num. 24 : 24.
prophecies concerning, Num. 24 : 24; Isa. 23 : 1, 12; Jer. 2 : 10; Ezek. 27 : 6; Dan. 11 : 30.

Choice, 2 Ki. 3 : 19; Jer. 22 : 7; Acts 15 : 7.

Choke, Matt. 13 : 22; Mark 4 : 19, deceitfulness of riches c. the word.
Mark 5 : 13; Luke 8 : 33, c. in sea.
Luke 8 : 14, are c. with cares.

Choler [hot temper], Dan. 8 : 7; 11 : 11, moved with c. against him.

Choose, Ps. 65 : 4, blessed is man thou c.
Prov. 1 : 29, did not c. fear of Lord.
Heb. 11 : 25, c. to suffer affliction.

Chop, Mic. 3 : 3.

Chose, Gen. 13 : 11; Judg. 5 : 8; Isa. 66 : 4; Acts 13 : 17; 15 : 40.
Luke 14 : 7, how they c. chief rooms.

Chosen, Ps. 119 : 30, have c. the way of truth.
Prov. 16 : 16, rather to be c.
22 : 1, good name rather to be c.
Jer. 8 : 3, death rather be c. rather than life.
Matt. 20 : 16; 22 : 14, many called but few c.
Luke 10 : 42, Mary hath c. good part.
John 15 : 16, ye have not c. me.
15 : 19, have c. you out of the world.
Acts 9 : 15, a c. vessel unto me.

10 : 41, witnesses c. before God.
Rom. 16 : 13, c. in the Lord.
1 Cor. 1 : 27, God hath c. the foolish things.
Eph. 1 : 4, according as he hath c. us.
1 Pet. 2 : 4, c. of God, and precious.
Christ, Lord Jesus, Matt. 1 : 21; Luke 2 : 11;
   John 1 : 41; 4 : 42; Acts 11 : 17; 13 : 23;
   15 : 11; 16 : 31; 20 : 21; Rom. 5 : 1, 11;
   6 : 23; 7 : 25; 13 : 14; 15 : 6, 30; 16 : 13;
   1 Cor. 1 : 2, 3, 7, 10; 5 : 4; Eph. 5 : 23;
   Phil. 3 : 20; 1 Tim. 1 : 1, 12; 3 : 13; 4 : 6;
   5 : 21; 2 Tim. 1 : 10; Titus 1 : 4; 2 : 13;
   3 : 6; Philem. 3, 5, 25; Heb. 13 : 8, 21;
   Jas. 1 : 1; 1 Pet. 1 : 3; 2 Pet. 1 : 1, 11;
   2 : 20; 3 : 18; Jude 1, 4, 17, 21; Rev.
   22 : 21.
Son of God, Matt. 2 : 15; 3 : 17; 4 : 3, 6;
   Luke 1 : 32, 35; 3 : 22; 4 : 3, 9; 4 : 34,
   41; John 1 : 34; 3 : 16, 18; 5 : 22, 23;
   6 : 69; 13 : 3; 16 : 27, 30; 17 : 1; 19 : 7;
   Rom. 1 : 9; 5 : 10; 8 : 3, 32; 1 Cor. 1 : 9;
   Gal. 1 : 16; 4 : 4; Col. 1 : 13; 1 Thess.
   1 : 10; Heb. 1 : 2, 5, 8; 3 : 6; 4 : 14;
   5 : 5; 6 : 6; 1 John 1 : 7; 3 : 23; 4 : 9, 10;
   5 : 9.
Son of Man, Matt. 8 : 20; 10 : 23; 11 : 19;
   12 : 8, 32, 40; 13 : 37, 41; 16 : 13; 17 : 9,
   22; 24 : 27, 30, 44 ; 25 : 31; 26 : 2, 24, 45;
   Mark 8 : 38; 9 : 12, 31; Luke 5 : 24;
   6 : 22; 9 : 22, 56; 11 : 30; 12 : 8; 17 : 22;
   18 : 8; 19 : 10; 21 : 36; 22 : 48; John
   1 : 51; 3 : 13; 5 : 27; 6 : 27, 53, 62;
   8 : 28; 12 : 23, 34; 13 : 31; Acts 7 : 56;
   Rev. 1 : 13.
Prophet, Deut. 18 : 15; Nah. 1 : 15; Luke
   4 : 18, 24; Acts 3 : 22.
Priest, Heb. 2 : 17; 3 : 1; 5 : 6; 6 : 20; 7 : 8.
   See Ps. 110 : 4.
King, Matt. 2 : 2; 21 : 5; 25 : 34; John
   1 : 49; 18 : 36; Heb. 1 : 8; Rev. 1 : 5;
   11 : 15; 17 : 14; 19 : 16.
Life and Work on Earth :
his miraculous conception and birth predicted, Isa. 7 : 14; 11 : 1; Mic. 5 : 2.
accomplished at Bethlehem, Matt. 1 : 18;
   Luke 1 : 31; 2 : 6.
announced to shepherds by angels, Luke
   2 : 9-14.
wise men of the East do homage to, Matt.
   2 : 1.
circumcision of, and presentation in the
   temple, Luke 2 : 21.
carried into Egypt, Matt. 2 : 13.
first public appearance (doctors in temple),
   Luke 2 : 46.
baptized by John, Matt. 3 : 13; Mark 1 : 9;
   Luke 3 : 21; John 1 : 32; 3 : 24.
his temptation, Matt. 4; Mark 1 : 12; Luke 4.
begins to preach and heal, Matt. 4 : 12; Mark
   1 : 14; Luke 4 : 16.
his selection of disciples, Matt. 4 : 18; Mark
   1 : 16; Luke 4 : 31; 5 : 10; John 1 : 38.
his sermon on the mount, Matt. 5; 6; 7.
cleanses the temple, John 2 : 14; Ps. 69 : 9.
his conversation with Nicodemus, John 3.
and with a woman of Samaria, John 4.
refuses to be made king, John 6 : 15.
taunted by his kinsmen, John 7 : 4.
sufferings and death predicted, Matt. 16 : 21;

17 : 22; 20 : 17; Mark 8 : 31; 9 : 31;
   10 : 32; Luke 9 : 22, 44; 18 : 31.
transfiguration on the mount, Matt. 17; Mark
   9; Luke 9 : 28.
the people's testimony, Matt. 16 : 13; Mark
   8 : 27; Luke 9 : 18; John 7 : 12.
message to John the Baptist, Luke 7 : 22.
anointed at Simon the Pharisee's house, Luke
   7 : 36.
pays tribute at Capernaum, Matt. 17 : 24.
inculcates humility on apostles, Matt. 18;
   Mark 9 : 33; Luke 9 : 46; 22 : 24.
goes into Judea, Matt. 19 : 1; John 7 : 10.
teaches respecting divorce, Matt. 19 : 3; Luke
   16 : 18.
reproves Herod and Jerusalem, Luke 13 : 32,
   34.
pardons woman taken in adultery, John 8 : 3.
compares Martha and Mary, Luke 10 : 38-42.
blesses little children, Matt. 19 : 13; Mark
   10 : 13; Luke 18 : 15.
Zaccheus the publican called by, Luke 19 : 2.
anointed by Mary at Bethany, Matt. 26 : 6;
   Mark 14 : 3; John 12 : 3.
rides into Jerusalem, Matt. 21; Mark 11;
   Luke 19 : 29; John 12 : 12.
drives money changers out of temple, Matt.
   21 : 12; Mark 11 : 15; Luke 19 : 45.
curses the barren fig tree, Matt. 21 : 19; Mark
   11 : 12.
Greeks desire to see him, John 12 : 20.
his reply, John 12 : 23.
glorified by the Father, John 12 : 28.
his reply to the chief priests, Luke 20 : 3.
his reply to the Pharisees, Matt. 22 : 15.
his reply to the Sadducees, Mark 12 : 18.
chief priests conspire to kill, Matt. 26 : 3;
   Mark 14 : 1.
covenant with Judas to betray, Matt. 26 : 14;
   Mark 14 : 10; Luke 22 : 3; John 13 : 18.
gives directions for the passover, Matt.
   26 : 17; Mark 14 : 12; Luke 22 : 7.
foretells Peter's denial, Matt. 26 : 34; Mark
   14 : 29; Luke 22 : 31.
washes disciples' feet, John 13 : 5.
comforts and exhorts his disciples, John 14;
   15.
promises the Holy Spirit, John 16.
prays for disciples, John 17.
institutes the Lord's Supper, Matt. 26 : 26;
   Mark 14 : 22; Luke 22 : 19 (1 Cor. 11 : 23).
his agony, Matt. 26 : 36; Mark 14 : 32; Luke
   22 : 39.
betrayed by Judas, Matt. 26 : 47; Mark
   14 : 43; Luke 22 : 47; John 18 : 3.
forbids use of sword, Matt. 26 : 52; John
   18 : 11.
deserted by disciples, Matt. 26 : 31, 56; John
   18 : 15.
taken before Annas and Caiaphas, Matt.
   26 : 57; Mark 14 : 54; John 18 : 13.
and Pilate and Herod, Matt. 27 : 2; Mark
   15 : 1; Luke 23; John 18 : 28.
acquitted by Pilate, Matt. 27 : 23; Mark
   15 : 14; Luke 23 : 13; John 18 : 38; 19.
yet delivered to be crucified, Matt. 27 : 26;
   Mark 15 : 15; Luke 23 : 24; John 19 : 16.
his crucifixion, Matt. 27 : 33; Mark 15 : 21;
   Luke 23 : 33; John 19 : 17.

his legs not broken, John 19 : 33.

his side pierced, John 19 : 34.

his garments divided amongst soldiers, Matt. 27 : 35; Mark 15 : 24; Luke 23 : 34; John 19 : 24.

yields up the ghost, Matt. 27 : 50; Mark 15 : 37; John 19 : 30.

acknowledged by centurion to be the Son of God, Matt. 27 : 54; Mark 15 : 39; to be righteous, Luke 23 : 47.

buried by Joseph and Nicodemus, Matt. 27 : 57; Mark 15 : 42; Luke 23 : 50; John 19 : 38.

the sepulchre sealed and watched, Matt. 27 : 66.

his resurrection, Matt. 28 : Mark 16; Luke 24; John 20 : 21.

appears first to Mary Magdalene, Matt. 28 : 1; Mark 16 : 1; Luke 24 : 1; John 20 : 1; to his disciples at various times, Matt. 28 : 16; Mark 16 : 12; Luke 24 : 13, 26; John 20 : 21; 1 Cor. 15.

shews Thomas his hands and feet, John 20 : 27.

charges Peter to feed his lambs, John 21 : 15.

ascends into heaven, Mark 16 : 19; Luke 24 : 51; Acts 1 : 9, 10.

appears after his ascension, to Stephen, Acts 7 : 55. To Paul, Acts 9 : 4; 18 : 9; 22 : 6. To John, Rev. 1 : 13.

His Teaching :

preaches repentance at Galilee, Matt. 4 : 17.

preaches at Nazareth, Luke 4 : 16.

the gospel of the kingdom, Matt. 4 : 23; Mark 1 : 14.

testimony concerning John the Baptist, Matt. 11 : 7; Luke 7 : 24; 20 : 4.

upbraids Chorazin, Bethsaida, Capernaum, Matt. 11 : 20; Luke 10 : 13.

concerning his mission, John 5 : 17; 7 : 16; 8 : 12; 10; 12 : 30.

on the bread of life, John 6 : 26.

traditions of the elders, Matt. 15 : 1; Mark 7 : 1.

to Pharisees asking a sign, Matt. 12 : 38; 16 : 1; Mark 8 : 11; Luke 11 : 16; 12 : 54; John 2 : 18.

on humility, John 13 : 14.

concerning the Scribes and Pharisees, Matt. 23; Mark 12 : 38; Luke 11 : 37; 20 : 45.

prophesies the destruction of Jerusalem, and the last times, Matt. 24; Mark 13; Luke 13 : 34; 17 : 20; 19 : 41; 21 : 5.

his invitation to the weary and heavy laden, Matt. 11 : 28.

concerning the Galileans killed by Pilate, Luke 13 : 1.

on suffering for the Gospel's sake, Luke 14 : 26 (Matt. 10 : 37).

on marriage, Matt. 19; Mark 10.

on riches, Matt. 19 : 16; Mark 10 : 17; Luke 12 : 13; 18 : 18.

paying tribute, Matt. 22 : 15; Mark 12 : 13; Luke 20 : 20.

the resurrection, Matt. 22 : 23; Mark 12 : 18.

the two great commandments, Matt. 22 : 35; Mark 12 : 28.

the son of David, Matt. 22 : 41; Mark 12 : 35; Luke 20 : 41.

the widow's mite, Mark 12 : 41; Luke 21 : 1.

on watchfulness, Matt. 24 : 42; Mark 13 : 33; Luke 21 : 34; 12 : 35.

the last judgment, Matt. 25 : 31.

Sermon of the Mount, Matt. 5; 6; 7. See Luke 6 : 20-46.

Lord's prayer, Matt. 6 : 9-13; Luke 11 : 2-4.

hearers and doers, Matt. 7 : 24; Luke 6 : 46.

epistles to the seven churches in Asia, Rev. 1; 2; 3.

His Discourses :

on faith, the centurion's, Matt. 8 : 8.

to those who would follow him, Matt. 8 : 19; Luke 9 : 23, 57.

on fasting, Matt. 9 : 14; Mark 2 : 18; Luke 5 : 33.

on blasphemy, Matt. 12 : 31; Mark 3 : 28; Luke 11 : 15.

who are his brethren, Matt. 12 : 46; Mark 3 : 31; Luke 8 : 19.

His Parables :

the wise and foolish builders, Matt. 7 : 24-27.

children of the bridechamber, Matt. 9 : 15; Luke 5 : 34, 35.

new cloth and old garment, Matt. 9 : 16; Luke 5 : 36.

new wine and old bottles, Matt. 9 : 17.

the unclean spirit, Matt. 12 : 43.

the sower, Matt. 13 : 3, 18; Mark 4 : 3; Luke 8 : 5, 11.

the tares, Matt. 13 : 24, 36.

mustard seed, Matt. 13 : 31, 32; Luke 13 : 19.

leaven, Matt. 13 : 33.

treasure hid in a field, Matt. 13 : 44.

pearl of great price, Matt. 13 : 45, 46.

net cast into the sea, Matt. 13 : 47-50.

meats not defiling, Matt. 15 : 10-15.

the unmerciful servant, Matt. 18 : 23-35.

the labourers, Matt. 20 : 1-16.

the two sons, Matt. 21 : 28-32.

the wicked husbandmen, Matt. 21 : 33-45; Mark 12 : 1; Luke 20 : 9.

the marriage feast, Matt. 22 : 2; Luke 14 : 16.

fig tree leafing, Matt. 24 : 32-34.

man of the house watching, etc., Matt. 24 : 43-51.

ten virgins, Matt. 25 : 1.

the talents, Matt. 25 : 14-30; Luke 9 : 12.

kingdom and house divided against themselves, Mark 3 : 24, 25.

strong man armed, Mark 3 : 27; Luke 11 : 21.

seed growing secretly, Mark 4 : 26-29.

lighted candle, Mark 4 : 21; Luke 11 : 33-36.

man going on a long journey, Mark 13 : 34-37.

the creditor and two debtors, Luke 7 : 41-47.

the good Samaritan, Luke 10 : 30-37.

the importunate friend, Luke 11 : 5-9.

the rich fool, Luke 12 : 16-21.

cloud and wind, Luke 12 : 54-57.

the barren fig tree, Luke 13 : 6-9.

chief seats at a feast, Luke 14 : 7-11.

builder of a tower, Luke 14 : 28-30, 33.

king going to war, Luke 14 : 31-33.

savour of salt, Luke 14 : 34, 35.

lost sheep, Luke 15 : 3-7.

lost piece of silver, Luke 15 : 8-10.

prodigal son, Luke 15 : 11-32.

the unjust steward, Luke 16 : 1-8.

rich man and Lazarus, Luke 16 : 19-31.

unprofitable servant, Luke 17 : 7.
the importunate widow, Luke 18 : 1-8.
Pharisee and publican, Luke 18 : 9-14.
the good shepherd, John 10 : 1.
vine and branches, John 15 : 1.
His Miracles :
water turned into wine, John 2 : 6-10.
nobleman's son healed, John 4 : 46-53.
centurion's servant healed, Matt. 8 : 5-13.
draught of fishes, Luke 5 : 4-6; John 21 : 6.
devils cast out, Matt. 8 : 28-32; 9 : 32, 33; 15 : 22-28; 17 : 14-18; Mark 1 : 23-27.
Peter's wife's mother healed, Matt. 8 : 14, 15.
lepers cleansed, Matt. 8 : 3; Luke 17 : 14.
paralytic healed, Mark 2 : 3-12.
withered hand restored, Matt. 12 : 10-13.
impotent man healed, John 5 : 5-9.
the dead raised to life, Matt. 9 : 18, 19, 23-25; Luke 7 : 12-15; John 11 : 11-44.
issue of blood stopped, Matt. 9 : 20-22.
the blind restored to sight, Matt. 9 : 27-30; Mark 8 : 22-25; John 9 : 1-7.
the deaf and dumb cured, Mark 7 : 32-35.
the multitude fed, Matt. 14 : 15-21; 15 : 32-38.
his walking on the sea, Matt. 14 : 25-27.
with the tribute money, Matt. 17 : 27.
tempest stilled, Matt. 8 : 23-26; Mark 4 : 37; Luke 8 : 23.
woman healed of infirmity, Luke 13 : 11-13.
dropsy cured, Luke 14 : 2-4.
blighting of the fig tree, Matt. 21 : 19.
miracles performed in presence of the messengers of John, Luke 7 : 21, 22.
many and divers diseases healed, Matt. 4 : 23, 24; 14 : 14; 15 : 30; Mark 1 : 34; Luke 6 : 17-19.
Malchus healed, Luke 22 : 50, 51 (John 18 : 10).
his transfiguration, Matt. 17 : 1-8; Mark 9 : 2; Luke 9 : 29.
his resurrection, Luke 24 : 6; John 10 : 18.
his appearance to his disciples when the doors were shut, John 20 : 19.
his ascension, Acts 1 : 9.
His Character :
holy, Luke 1 : 35; Acts 4 : 27; Rev. 3 : 7.
righteous, Isa. 53 : 11; Heb. 1 : 9.
good, Matt. 19 : 16.
faithful, Isa. 11 : 5; 1 Thess. 5 : 24.
true, John 1 : 14; 7 : 18; 1 John 5 : 20.
just, Zech. 9 : 9; John 5 : 30; Acts 22 : 14.
guileless, Isa. 53 : 9; 1 Pet. 2 : 22.
sinless, John 8 : 46; 2 Cor. 5 : 21.
spotless, 1 Pet. 1 : 19.
harmless, Heb. 7 : 26.
obedient to God the Father, Ps. 40 : 8; John 4 : 34; 15 : 10.
subject to his parents, Luke 2 : 51.
zealous, Luke 2 : 49; John 2 : 17; 8 : 29.
meek, Isa. 53 : 7; Matt. 11 : 29.
lowly in heart, Matt. 11 : 29.
merciful, Heb. 2 : 17.
longsuffering, 1 Tim. 1 : 16.
compassionate, Isa. 40 : 11; Matt. 15 : 32; Luke 7 : 13; 19 : 41.
benevolent, Matt. 4 : 23, 24; 9 : 35; Acts 10 : 38.
loving, John 13 : 1; 15 : 13.

self-denying, Matt. 8 : 20; 2 Cor. 8 : 9.
humble, Luke 22 : 27; Phil. 2 : 8.
forgiving, Luke 23 : 34.
His Compassion :
for the weary and heavy laden, Matt. 11 : 28-30.
towards the afflicted, Luke 7 : 13; John 11 : 33.
towards the diseased, Matt. 14 : 14; Mark 1 : 41.
for perishing sinners, Matt. 9 : 36; Luke 19 : 41; John 3 : 16.
towards the tempted, Heb. 2 : 18.
necessary to his priestly office, Heb. 5 : 2-10.
an encouragement to prayer, Heb. 4 : 15, 16.
His Divine Nature :
the eternal God and Creator, John 1 : 1-5; Col. 1 : 16, 17; 2 : 9; Heb. 1 : 2, 3.
equality with God, John 5 : 17-23; 10 : 30, 38; 16 : 15; Phil. 2 : 6; 1 Thess. 3 : 11; 2 Thess. 2 : 16.
Son of God, Matt. 3 : 17; 26 : 63, 64; John 1 : 14, 18; 3 : 16, 18; 14 : 7-10; 1 John 4 : 9.
one with the Father, John 12 : 45; 17 : 10.
sending the Spirit equally with the Father, John 14 : 16; 15 : 26.
image of God and firstborn, Col. 1 : 15; Heb. 1 : 3.
the Lord of glory, 1 Cor. 2 : 8; Jas. 2 : 1.
the Lord of all, Acts 10 : 36.
Lord of the Sabbath, Matt. 12 : 8.
the Lord from heaven, 1 Cor. 15 : 47.
King of kings and Lord of lords, Rev. 19 : 16.
the Judge of men, Matt. 16 : 27; 25 : 31; 2 Cor. 5 : 10.
the true Light, Luke 1 : 78, 79; John 1 : 4, 9.
the way, John 14 : 6; Heb. 10 : 19, 20.
the Truth, 1 John 5 : 20; Rev. 3 : 7.
the Life, John 11 : 25; Col. 3 : 4; 1 John 5 : 11.
manifest in the flesh, John 1 : 14; 1 Tim. 3 : 16.
head of the Church, Eph. 1 : 22.
manifested in his works, Luke 4 : 22; John 7 : 46.
manifested in his words, Matt. 13 : 54; John 2 : 11; 5 : 21; 6 : 40.
acknowledged by his disciples, Matt. 16 : 16; John 1 : 49; 20 : 28.
object of Divine worship, Acts 7 : 59; Heb. 1 : 6; Rev. 5 : 12.
his omnipresence, omnipotence, and omniscience, Matt. 18 : 20; 28 : 20; John 3 : 13; 16 : 30; 21 : 17; Phil. 3 : 21; Col. 1 : 17; Heb. 1 : 8-10.
the Mediator, Gal. 3 : 19; Heb. 8 : 6; 12 : 24.
His Human Nature :
born of a woman, Matt. 1 : 18; Luke 1 : 31; Gal. 4 : 4.
partaking of our flesh and blood, John 1 : 14; Heb. 2 : 14.
having a human soul, Matt. 26 : 38; Luke 23 : 46; Acts 2 : 31.
increasing in wisdom and stature, Luke 2 : 52.
feeling hunger, Matt. 4 : 2; 21 : 18.
feeling thirst, John 4 : 7; 19 : 28.
feeling weariness, John 4 : 6.
sleeping, Matt. 8 : 24; Mark 4 : 38.

weeping, Luke 19 : 41; John 11 : 35.
Man of Sorrows, Isa. 53 : 3, 4; Luke 22 : 44; John 11 : 33; 12 : 27.
enduring indignities, Matt. 26 : 67; Luke 22 : 64; 23 : 11.
scourged, Matt. 27 : 26; John 19 : 1.
nailed to the cross, Luke 23 : 33; John 19 : 18.
buried, Matt. 27 : 59, 60; Mark 15 : 46.
like us in all things, Acts 3 : 22; Phil. 2 : 7, 8; Heb. 2 : 17; but without sin, John 8 : 46; 18 : 38; Heb. 4 : 15; 7 : 26, 28; 1 Pet. 2 : 22; 1 John 3 : 5.
asserted by men, Mark 6 : 3; John 7 : 27; 19 : 5; Acts 2 : 22.
denied by antichrist, 1 John 4 : 3; 2 John 7.
evidenced by the senses, John 20 : 27; 1 John 1 : 1, 2.
attested by himself, Matt. 8 : 20; 16 : 13.
called Son of David, Matt. 22 : 42; Mark 10 : 47; Acts 2 : 30; 13 : 23; Rom. 1 : 3.
the seed of Abraham, Gal. 3 : 16; Heb. 2 : 16.
one Mediator, the man Christ Jesus, 1 Tim. 2 : 5; Heb. 2 : 17.
His Different Titles :
Adam, the second, 1 Cor. 15 : 45.
Advocate, 1 John 2 : 1.
Alpha and Omega, Rev. 1 : 8; 22 : 13.
Amen, Rev. 3 : 14.
Apostle of our Profession, Heb. 3 : 1.
Author and Finisher of our faith, Heb. 12 : 2.
Beginning of the Creation of God, Rev. 3 : 14.
Blessed and only Potentate, 1 Tim. 6 : 15.
Captain of Salvation, Heb. 2 : 10.
Chief Corner Stone, Eph. 2 : 20; 1 Pet. 2 : 6.
Chief Shepherd, 1 Pet. 5 : 4.
Dayspring, Luke 1 : 78
Desire of all Nations, Hag. 2 : 7.
Emmanuel, Isa. 7 : 14; 8 : 8; Matt. 1 : 23.
Everlasting Father, Isa. 9 : 6.
Faithful Witness, Rev. 1 : 5; 3 : 14.
First and Last, Rev. 1 : 17; 2 : 8.
Good Shepherd, John 10 : 14.
Governor, Matt. 2 : 6.
Great High Priest, Heb. 3 : 1; 4 : 14.
Head of the Church, Eph. 5 : 23; Col. 1 : 18.
Heir of all Things, Heb. 1 : 2.
Holy One, Mark 1 : 24; Acts 2 : 27.
Horn of Salvation, Luke 1 : 69.
I Am, John 8 : 58. See Ex. 3 : 14.
Just One, Acts 7 : 52.
Lamb (of God), John 1 : 29, 36; Rev. 5 : 6, 12; 13 : 8; 21 : 22; 22 : 3.
Lion of Tribe of Judah, Rev. 5 : 5.
Lord God Almighty, Rev. 15 : 3; 22 : 6.
Lord our righteousness, Jer. 23 : 6.
Messenger of the Covenant, Mal. 3 : 1.
Messiah, Dan. 9 : 25; John 1 : 41.
Morning Star, Rev. 22 : 16.
Prince of Life, Acts 3 : 15.
Prince of Peace, Isa. 9 : 6.
Prince of the Kings of the Earth, Rev. 1 : 5.
Resurrection and Life, John 11 : 25.
Root of David, Rev. 22 : 16.
Saviour, 2 Pet. 2 : 20; 3 : 18.
Shepherd and Bishop of souls, 1 Pet. 2 : 25.
Son of the Blessed, Mark 14 : 61.
Son of the Highest, Luke 1 : 32.

Son of Righteousness, Mal. 4 : 2.
Wonderful, Counseller, Mighty God, Isa. 9 : 6.
Word of God, Rev. 19 : 13.
Word of Life, 1 John 1 : 1.
The Head of the Church :
declared by himself to be head of the corner, Matt. 21 : 42.
declared by St. Paul, Eph. 4 : 12, 15; 5 : 23.
as such, has pre-eminence in all things, 1 Cor. 11 : 3; Eph. 1 : 22; Col. 1 : 18.
saints complete in, Col. 2 : 10.
Types of :
Aaron, Ex. 28 : 1; Lev. 16 : 15; Heb. 4 : 15; 12 : 24.
Abel, Gen. 4 : 8, 10; Heb. 12 : 24.
Adam, Rom. 5 : 14; 1 Cor. 15 : 45.
David, 2 Sam. 8 : 15; Ps. 89 : 19; Ezek. 37 : 24; Phil. 2 : 9.
Eliakim, Isa. 22 : 20. See Rev. 3 : 7.
Isaac, Gen. 22 : 2; Heb. 11 : 17.
Jacob, Gen. 32 : 28; John 11 : 42; Heb. 7 : 25.
Jonah, Jonah 1 : 17; Matt. 12 : 40.
Joshua, Josh. 1 : 5; 11 : 23; Acts 20 : 32; Heb. 4 : 8.
Melchizedek, Gen. 14 : 18, 20; Heb. 7 : 1.
Moses, Num. 12 : 7; Deut. 18 : 15; Acts 3 : 22; 7 : 37; Heb. 3 : 2.
Noah, Gen. 5 : 29; 2 Cor. 1 : 5.
Solomon, 2 Sam. 7 : 12; Luke 1 : 32.
Zerubbabel, Zech. 4 : 7, 9; Heb. 12 : 2, 3.
the ark, Gen. 7 : 16; Ex. 25 : 16; Ps. 40 : 8; Isa. 42 : 6; 1 Pet. 3 : 20, 21.
Jacob's ladder, Gen. 28 : 12; John 1 : 51.
passover, Ex. 12; 1 Cor. 5 : 7.
lamb, Ex. 12 : 3; Isa. 53 : 7; John 1 : 29; Acts 8 : 32; 1 Pet 1 : 19; Rev 5 : 6; 6 : 1; 7 : 9; 12 : 11; 13 : 8; 14 : 1; 15 : 3; 17 : 14; 19 : 7; 21 : 9; 22 : 1.
manna, Ex. 16 : 11; John 6 : 32; Rev. 2 : 17.
rock, Ex. 17 : 6; 1 Cor. 10 : 4.
firstfruits, Ex. 22 : 29; 1 Cor. 15 : 20.
brazen altar, Ex. 27 : 1, 2; Heb. 13 : 10.
laver, Ex. 30 : 18; Zech. 13 : 1; Eph. 5 : 26.
burnt offering, Lev. 1 : 2; Heb. 10 : 10.
peace offering, Lev. 3; Eph. 2 : 14.
sin offering, Lev. 4 : 2; Heb. 13 : 11.
atonement, sacrifices upon day of, Lev. 16 : 15; Heb. 9 : 12.
scapegoat, Lev. 16 : 20; Isa. 53 : 6; Heb. 9 : 28.
brazen serpent, Num. 21 : 9; John 3 : 14.
cities of refuge, Num. 35 : 6; Heb. 6 : 18.
tabernacle, Heb. 9 : 8, 11.
temple, 1 Ki. 6 : 1, 38; John 2 : 21.
veil, Ex. 40 : 21; Heb. 10 : 20.
branch, Isa. 4 : 2; Jer. 23 : 5; Zech. 3 : 8.
Matt. 16 : 16, thou art the C.
24 : 5, many shall come, saying I am C.
Mark 9 : 41, because ye belong to C.
Luke 24 : 46, it behoved C. to suffer.
John 4 : 25, Messias, which is called C.
6 : 69, we are sure that thou art that C.
Acts 8 : 5, preached C. to them.
Rom. 5 : 8, while yet sinners, C. died for us.
1 Cor. 1 : 24, C. the power of God.
3 : 23, ye are C.'s, and C. is God's.
Gal. 3 : 13, C. hath redeemed us from.

Eph. 3 : 17, that C. may dwell in your hearts.
Eph. 5 : 14, C. shall give thee light.
Phil. 1 : 21, to me to live is C.
3 : 8, that I may win C.
Heb. 13 : 8, C. the same, yesterday and to day.
1 Pet. 1 : 11, the spirit of C. did signify.
1 John 2 : 22, denieth that Jesus is the C.
Rev. 20 : 4, they reigned with C. a thousand years.

Christian, Acts 26 : 28, almost persuadest me to be a C.
1 Pet. 4 : 16, if any suffer as a C.

Christians, disciples first called, at Antioch, Acts 11 : 26.

Christs, false, warnings against, Matt. 24 : 4, 5, 24; Mark 13 : 22.

Chronicles, The Books of.
Name.—In Hebrew manuscripts the books are regarded as one. The present division into two books is adopted from the LXX. and Vulgate. The Hebrew title, " Acts of the days," is a general term indicating the historical character of the work. In the LXX. (and similarly in the Vulgate) the books are called Paraleipomena, " things omitted," since the translators viewed the Chronicles as a supplement to the other historical books.
Author.—According to Jewish tradition Ezra was the author; but this seems inconsistent with the genealogy in 1 Chr. 3 : 19-24 (see below). The work may have been written by a Levite connected with the musical services of the second Temple, as the writer takes a great interest in all that appertains to the Temple and public worship, especially as regards the Levitical singers and the musical part of the service, but is probably of a comparatively late date.
Object.—The author's object appears to be, not merely to write a supplement to the already existing historical books, but to compose an independent work, from a Levitical and religious standpoint. He omitted much that was not connected with the object in view, such as the period of the Judges, and the history of Saul, and that of the northern kingdom, which is only related in as far as it is connected with that of the southern.
Contents.—The two books may be divided into four parts :—(1) 1 Chr. 1–10 contains an outline of the history from Adam to David, mainly consisting of genealogical lists; (2) 1 Chr. 11–31, the reign of David; (3) 2 Chr. 1–9, the reign of Solomon; (4) 2 Chr. 10–36, the history of the southern kingdom down to the Babylonian captivity.

Chronology of the Bible. About 1650 a careful scheme of Biblical chronology, based upon data from the Bible itself, was prepared by Archbishop Ussher. These dates may often still be found in reference Bibles. Later archæological investigation, however, has proved them to be worthless, and by scholars they are now discarded in favour of the revised scheme which is appended here.

Chronological Conspectus of New Testament History.

B.C.
4 Probable date of our Lord's birth. Herod's death. Archelaus becomes ethnarch of Judæa, Samaria and Idumæa.

A.D.
8 Jesus visits Jerusalem at the age of twelve, and converses with the rabbis in the Temple.
26 Ministry of John the Baptist.
27 Baptism of Jesus Christ at the age of thirty. His temptation, and inauguration of his ministry (Matt. 3 : 1-6, 13-17; Mark 1 : 1-11; Luke 3 : 15-18, 21, 22). First miracle at Cana in Galilee (John 2 : 1-11). First Passover (April 9). Discourse with Nicodemus (John 3 : 1-21). John the Baptist is imprisoned by Herod, the Tetrarch of Galilee (Luke 3 : 18-20). Christ leaves Judæa for Galilee, and on the way visits Sychar. His discourse with the Samaritan

A.D.
woman; visits Cana, and heals the nobleman's son (Matt. 4 : 12; Mark 1 : 14; John 4 : 46-54). Revisits Nazareth; address at the Synagogue, and escapes with his life (Luke 4 : 14-30). Gathers four disciples—Andrew, Simon, James and John (Matt. 4 : 18-22; Mark 1 : 16-20). First Galilean Circuit with the disciples (Matt. 4 : 23-25; Mark 1 : 35-39; Luke 4 : 42-44).

27–28 Sermon on the Mount (probably not one, but separate discourses and sayings collected). Subsequent miracles. Call of Levi or Matthew to be a disciple (Matt. 5–9 : 9; Mark 1 : 40; 2 : 14; Luke 5 : 1-28).

28 March 29. Christ's Second Passover (John 5). Discussions with the Pharisees. Heals the man with a withered hand (Matt. 12 : 1-13; Mark 2 : 23; 3 : 6; Luke 6 : 1-11). Returns to Galilee and chooses the Apostles (Matt. 10 : 2-4; Mark 3 : 13-19; Luke 6 : 12-16).

A.D.
Further miracles. Message from John the Baptist (Matt. 8 : 5-13; 11 : 2-30; Luke 7 : 1-35).
Second Galilean Circuit (Luke 8 : 1-3). Christ's Parabolic teaching (Matt. 13 : 1-53; Mark 4 : 1-34; Luke 8 : 4-18). (These parables were delivered on separate occasions at intervals which cannot be determined.) Quelling of the Storm. Heals the Gadarene demoniac and performs other miracles (Matt. 8 : 18-34; 9 : 18-34; Mark 5 : 1-43; Luke 8 : 22-56).

29 Third Galilean Circuit (Matt. 9 : 35 foll.; 10 : 1; Mark 6 : 7-13; Luke 9 : 1-6). Feeding of the five thousand (Matt. 14 : 13-23; Mark 6 : 30-46; Luke 9 : 10-17; John 6 : 1-14). Jesus walks on the sea and quells the storm, afterwards returns to Capernaum and performs many acts of healing (Matt. 14 : 24-36; Mark 6 : 47-56; John 6 : 16-24). Dis-

BIBLICAL CHRONOLOGY.   **SYNCHRONISM WITH BIBLICAL CHRONOLOGY.**

		Babylonia and Assyria.	Egypt. 2190-1680, c.	Syria.

B.C. 2250-2000 Approximate date for Abraham.
1750 Israel's entrance into, and settlement in, Egypt.
1320 The Exodus.

REGAL PERIOD.
Saul, 1037-1018.
David, 1018-1011 (Judah), 1011-978 (Israel and Judah).
Solomon, 978-938. Erection of the Temple 975.

Judah.	*Israel* (Ephraim).

Babylonia and Assyria.
Hammurabi, 2200 ?

Pudilu, *c.* 1350.

Ramman-nirari I., *c.* 1325.

Shalmaneser I., *c.* 1300.

Asshur-rish-ishi, *c.* 1150.

Tiglath - Pileser I., 1100.

Ramman-nirari II., 911-890.

Tiglath-Adar II., 890-884.

Asshur - nazir - abal, 884-860.

Egypt.
Hyksos period.
Dynasties xiii., xiv., xv., and xvi.

xix. dynasty, beginning with Rameses I.

Seti I., *c.* 1450-1445.

Rameses II., *c.* 1392-1326.

Menephtah, *c.* 1326-1306.
xxii. dynasty.

Sheshenk (Shishak) aids Jeroboam and besieges and captures Jerusalem, *c.* 935 B.C.

Syria.

Benhadad II. of Damascus, defeated by Shalmaneser.

Rehoboam, 938-921
Siege and capture of Jerusalem by *Shishak.*

Abijam, 921-918

Asa, 918-877
Defeats Zerah, the Cushite (Osarkon) Alliance with Syria.

Jeroboam I., 938-916

Nadab, 916-914

Baasha, 914-901

Elah, 901-900

Zimri, 900

Omri, 900-875
Builds and fortifies Samaria.

Jehoshaphat, 877-852
Alliance with Ahab, and battle of Ramoth-Gilead (853).

Ahab, 875-853
Elijah prophesies, and *Micaiah,* son of Imlah.

Ahaziah, 853-852

Jehoram. 852-843

Jehoram, 852-842
Career of *Elisha* as prophet.
Revolution and overthrow of the dynasty of Omri.

Ahaziah, 843-842

Athaliah, 842-837

Jehu, 842-815
Hazael, King of Syria, takes the East-Jordan country.

Shalmaneser II. 860-825.
Battle of Karkar, 854, in which Ahab's troops shared in the defeat.

Shamshi - Ramman, 825-812.

Ramman-nirari III., 812-78.
Total defeat of Syria and capture of Damascus, 803.

sarkon (Zerah of the Bible) invades Palestine and is repulsed by Asa, according to 2 Chr. 14 : 9; 16 : 8.

Hazael murders Benhadad and ascends the throne. Succcesses against Israel.

Benhadad III. of Damascus defeated by Ramman-nirari III.

Dynasty of Omri.

Joash, 837-797
Reformation and repair of *Temple.*

Amaziah, 797-777

Azariah or Uzziah, 777-736
Consecration - vision of *Isaiah,* 736.
Prosperity and military strength of Judah.
Jotham, as regent, 750-736

Jotham, as king, 736-735

Ahaz, 735-726
Syro-Ephraimite war, begun in Jotham's reign, is continued (Isa. 7).
Alliance with Tiglath-Pileser III.
Foreign innovations—an altar of new pattern set up in the Temple.

Jehoahaz, 815-798

Jehoash, 798-782

Death of Elisha—victories over Syria.

Jeroboam II., 782-741
Victories over Syria, Moab, and Ammon :—extension of the frontiers of Israel.
Amos and *Hosea* prophesy.

Zechariah, 741—end of Jehu's dynasty.

Shallum, 741

Menahem, 741-738
Pays tribute to Tiglath-Pileser, 738

Pekahiah, 738-736

Pekah 736-734
Alliance with Rezin, King of Syria, and invasion of Judah.
Invasion of the Northern kingdom by Tiglath-Pileser, 734—Defeat and the death of Pekah.

783-773 Shalmaneser III.

773-755 Asshur-dan III.

755-745 Asshur-nirari.

745-727 Tiglath - Pileser III., called Pulu or Pul.

738 war against Azariah (Uzziah); receives tribute from Menahem.

734 expedition to Palestine.

733-2 campaign against Rezin of Damascus.

727-722 Shalmaneser IV.
Siege of Samaria.

730 xxiv. dynasty, Saites—Egypt falls into the hands of Ethiopia.

Greece and Rome.

776 First Olympiad.

753 Foundation of Rome.

747 Pheidon, tyrant of Argos.

734 Syracuse founded by Archias of Corinth.

Judah.	Israel.	Assyria and Babylonia.	Egypt.	Greece and Rome.
			730 xxv. dynasty.	
Hezekiah 726-697 Isaiah continues his prophetic activity. Ministry of the prophet Micah. Embassy of Merodach Baladan, King of Babylon, and illness of Hezekiah, 712 ? Campaign of Sennacherib against Judah—Loss of towns—Siege of Jerusalem—Destruction of Sennacherib's army by pestilence, 701.	**Hoshea** 734 (730)-722 Revolt of Israel against Assyria—Siege and capture of Samaria after a three years' siege, and deportation of the inhabitants—Vain is the appeal to So (Sabaka), King of Egypt. End of the Northern or Ephraimite kingdom.	722-705 **Sargon.** Captures Samaria, 722. Battle of Raphia. Defeat of Sabaka (called Sabi), 720. Capture of Ashdod, 711 (Isa. 20). 705-681 **Sennacherib.** Expedition against Eygpt and Judah. Siege of Jerusalem, 701. Installs Asshur-nadin-shum as king of Babylon, 700.	**Sabaka** (So of Scripture, 2 Ki. 17 : 4) conquers Nubia and Upper Egypt. Defeated by Sargon at Raphia. **Taharka** (=Tirhaka of the Bible), Tarku of Assyrians, confronts the latter at Altaku (Eltekeh), and thus delivers Hezekiah.	710 Croton founded. 708 Tarentum founded.

Judah.

Manasseh, 697-641. Carried prisoner by Asshur-bani-pal to Babylon (2 Chr. 33 : 11). Manasseh's repentance and restoration.	688 Destruction of Babylon by Sennacherib. 681-668 **Esarhaddon.** Overthrow of Sidon, 678. Royal palace built at Nineveh. Restoration of Babylon. 677. Conquest of Egypt, 671. **Asshur-bani-pal,** 668-626. Advances against Egypt and captures Thebes — Overthrow and death of Tirhaka —668-663.	xxv. dynasty. **Taharka's** reign. Tirhaka = Assyrian Tarku. Recapture of Memphis from Assyrians. Defeated by the troops of Asshur-bani-pal. Death. **Urdamani** or **Rud - Amon** succeeds his father, and is overthrown by the Assyrians. A fresh rebellion of twelve vassal princes against the Assyrian rule is led by Psamtik, son of **Necho.** It succeeds mainly by the help of the Greeks of Asia-Minor.	
Amon, 641-639. Josiah, 639-608. **Nahum** prophesies. Prophetic activity of Jeremiah, and probably also of Obadiah (at a later date), and Zephaniah.	These events are referred to in Nahum 3 : 8-11. Rebellion of Shamash - shum - ukin crushed, 647. Manasseh, King of Israel, mentioned in a list of tributary vassals.		
627-6 Thirteenth year of **Josiah,** king of Judah. Beginning of Jeremiah's prophetic ministry (Jer. 1 : 2 ; 25 : 3). 622-1 Eighteenth year of Josiah. Discovery of the book of the law—Deuteronomy (2 Ki. 22, 3 foll.).		xxvi. dynasty.	
The Great Reformation.		650-610 **Psamtik I.** (Psammetichus) [Wiedemann, 660 ?-610].	
609-8 Thirty-first year of Josiah (comp. 2 Ki. 22 : 1). Josiah falls at the battle of Megiddo in conflict with Pharaoh Necho (2 Ki. 23 : 29). 608 **Jehoahaz** reigns three months. 608-7 First year of **Jehoiakim.** 605-4 Fourth year of Jehoiakim. First year of **Nebuchadrezzar (Nebuchadnezzar)** (Jer. 25 : 1). Battle of Carchemish (Jer. 46 : 2; comp. also Jer. 26 : 1 and 45 : 1). 598-7 Eleventh year of Jehoiakim : in which he died (2 Ki. 24 : 1). 597 **Jehoiachin** reigns three months, and is carried away by Nebuchadnezzar, with 10,000 of the Jewish population, to Babylon. Among these captives is the prophet Ezekiel (2 Ki. 24 : 12). This was the 8th year of Nebuchadrezzar. Jer. 24 : 1 ; 29 : 1, 2. 597-6 First year of **Zedekiah** and first of the deportation or exile of Jehoiachin. This is the event from which Ezekiel continually dates his events (2 Ki. 24 : 17; comp. Jer. 37 : 1 and 49 : 34). 594-3 Fourth year of Zedekiah (Jer. 28 : 1 ; 51 : 59). 593-2 Fifth year of Zedekiah and of the Exile—thirtieth year mentioned in Ezekiel 1 : 1 (according to Targum " thirtieth year " dates from the discovery of the book of Deuteronomy, but this is doubtful). 592-1 Sixth year of Zedekiah and of the Exile (Ezek. 8 : 1).	625-605 **Nabo-pa-lassar** King of Babylonia. Destruction of Nineveh, 607. DOWNFALL OF ASSYRIA and foundation of the NEW BABYLONIAN EMPIRE. 605-562 **Nebuchadrezzar** (=Nebuchadnezzar). All the Assyrian possessions west of the Euphrates and south of the Amanus subject to Babylonia — Nebuchadrezzar rules as far as the river of Egypt (Wady el Arish), 600.	610-600 **Necho I.** (Neku). Defeats Josiah of Judah and other allies of Assyria at Megiddo ; but is himself defeated by Nebuchadrezzar at the battle of Carchemish, 605. 600-590 **Psamtik II.**	Greek mercenaries settled in and near Bubastis. 625 Periander of Corinth. 624 Legislation of Draco. 612 Cylon's attempt to seize the Government of Athens. 610 Sappho Alcæus and Stesichorus. 600 Foundation of Massilia (Marseilles). 594 **Legislation of Solon.**

Judah.

591-0 Seventh year of Zedekiah and of the Exile (Ezck. 20 : 1).

589-8 Ninth year of Zedekiah and of the Exile ; 10th Tebeth, *i.e.*, near the end of December 589, beginning of the siege of Jerusalem (2 Ki. 25 : 1; Jer. 52 : 4 and 39 : 1; also Ezek. 24 : 1 foll.).

588-7 Tenth year of Zedekiah, eighteenth of Nebuchadrezzar (Jer. 32 : 1) ; the Babylonian army encamped before Jerusalem. Ezekiel's prophecy against Egypt (Ezek. 29 : 1) on 12th Tebeth.

587-6 Eleventh year of Zedekiah ; (9th Tammuz) capture of Jerusalem. Flight and capture of Zedekiah (2 Ki. 25 : 3 = Jer. 52 : 6; Jer. 39 : 2).

7th Ab, or July, 587 = Nineteenth year of Nebuchadrezzar, Jerusalem destroyed (2 Ki. 25 : 8; Jer. 52 : 12), with the precise date, 10th Ab.

5th Tebeth (end of December), Ezekiel hears the news of the fall of Jerusalem (Ezek. 33 : 21).

1st Nisan (?), prophecy against Tyre after the fall of Jerusalem, Ezek. 26 : 1, 2 (fall of Jerusalem referred to), etc.

7th Nisan (end of March, 586), new prophecy against Egypt (Ezek. 30 : 20).

1st Sivan (end of May), new prophecy against Egypt (Ezek. 31 : 1).

586-5 Twelfth year of the Exile—1st Adar (middle of Feb. 585), new prophecy against Egypt (Ezek. 32 : 1).

15th Adar (beginning of March, 585), lamentation over the defeat of Egypt (Ezek. 32 : 17).

573-2 Twenty-fifth year of Exile—10th Nisan (end of March, 572) = fourteenth year from the capture of Jerusalem (Ezek. 40 : 1).

571-70 Twenty-seventh year of Exile—1st Nisan (March 21, 570), prophecy on Tyre and Egypt (Ezek. 29 : 27).

561-60 Thirty-seventh year of Exile = first official year of Evil-Merodach—27th Adar (middle of March, 560). Jeholachin released from prison (2 Ki. 25 : 27).

550-536 The prophecies of Isaiah 40-66 mainly refer to the circumstances, events, and anticipations of this interval, and herald the coming restoration of the Jews by Cyrus II.

536 Cyrus' edict for the restoration of the Jews. First caravan journey of returning exiles under Zerubbabel and Joshua.

535 Rebuilding of the Temple commenced. It is opposed by the Samaritans.

529 A letter is sent to the Persian king in opposition to the rebuilding of the Temple.

522 The building is arrested by decree of the Persian king.

521 Edict of Cyrus to the Jews is reaffirmed by Darius, son of Hystaspes.

Assyria and Babylonia.

Tyre, besieged by the Babylonians, holds out successfully for thirteen years under Ethbaal II.

Comp. Ezek. 26:1 foll. ; 28 : 16-19.

568 Nebuchadnezzar invades Egypt in the thirty-seventh year of his reign (comp. Ezek. 29:17; 30 : 19).

562 Evil-Merodach *Amil (Avil) Maruduk* succeeds his illustrious father. Decline of Babylonia under his successors, viz. (560) Nergal sharezer and (556) Nabunaid (*Nabonidus*).

550 Cyrus II., son of Cambyses, conquers Media, Lydia, and subsequently Babylonia.

630 Capture of Babylon by Cyrus, and **Downfall of Babylonian Empire,** and establishment of the **Persian Dominion.**

538-529 Cyrus.

529 - 521 Cambyses advances against Egypt, the only power that remained in opposition to the supremacy of Persia. Conquers Memphis, and captures Psamtik and puts him to death.

Dies on the march of his army to suppress the rebellion of the Magian, who had given himself out to be Bartja (Smerdis), the king's brother, who had been put to death some years previously.

Egypt.

590-570 **Uaphris** or **Apries** (Egypt. *Uahabra, the Hophra* of the Bible) rendered uneasy by the victorious inroads of the Babylonians in Palestine, makes a descent on Sidon and captures it, defeats the Cyprians and Tyrians in a naval battle, and urges Zedekiah to conclude an alliance (Jer. 37 : 3-10).

When Jerusalem, after a second siege, had been captured by Nebuchadrezzar, the king of Egypt opens the frontiers of his realm to receive the exiled inhabitants.

570-526 **Amasis** (Manetho = *Amosis*) or **Aahmes** makes alliances with the Greek despot Polycrates of Samos.

Foreign colonists settle in Egypt. Prosperity of the Greek Naucratis.

Invasion by the Babylonians (568).

526-525 **Psamtik III.** captured and slain by Cambyses. xxvii. dynasty (Persians).

55-521 **Cambyses.**

Greece and Rome

	Persia.	Greece.	Rome.
520 Prophetic ministry of **Haggai** and **Zechariah** commences. Resumption of the building (Hag. 1). 515 Dedication of the Temple.	521-485 **Darius,** son of Hystaspes, an enlightened ruler—improves the commerce of his kingdom—completes a canal from the Nile to the Red Sea. His invasion of Scythia, and disastrous retreat.	510 Legislation of Cleisthenes.	510 Expulsion the Tarquins.
		500 Ionic revolt. Sardis burnt. 495 Battle of Lade. 490 Defeat of Datis and Artaphernes at the battle of Marathon. 480 Battle of Salamis. 479 Battle of Platæa. Final defeat of the host of Xerxes. 478 Confederacy	
	485-465 **Xerxes I.**		
Artaxerxes. 444 Commission to **Nehemiah,** the royal cup-bearer, who obtains leave of absence with letters to the governors west of the Euphrates. In spite of the opposition, plots, and accusations of Sanballat the Horonite, Tobiah the Ammonite, and Geshem (Gashmu) the Arabian, the walls are rebuilt. The Book of the Law is read for seven days, and Festival of rejoicing held (Feast of Tabernacles), followed by a fast of humiliation and repentance. 433 Nehemiah returns to the Persian court and again obtains permission to return to Jerusalem to reform the abuses which had sprung up in his absence. He abolishes the Sabbath trading, and checks the habit of mixed marriages. Prophetic ministry of **Malachi.**	465-425 **Artaxerxes I.** (Longimanus).	of Delos, and rise of Athenian power. **Herodotus.**	
424 **Joida,** High Priest.	424-404 **Darius Nothus.**	431 Outbreak of the Peloponnesian war. Career of Pericles.	
	404-359 **Artaxerxes II.**		
398 **Artaxerxes II.** commissions **Ezra** to go to Judea on a journey of inquiry, accompanied by seven royal counsellors and Israelites, priests and Levites (Ezra 7). The work of reformation and reorganisation begins, and continues during the following year. Foreign wives are put away (Ezra 9).			

Chronology of the Period Intervening between the Age of Malachi (450 B.C.) and the Birth of Christ

History of the Jews.	Persia.	Greece.	Egypt.	Syria.
B.C. 382 **Johanan** (or *Jonathan*), High Priest. 367 Murder of Joshua in the temple by his brother Johanan, the High Priest. 350 **Jaddua,** High Priest. 332 Alexander besieges Tyre, demands submission of the Jews, and marches on Jerusalem. 331 Settlement of Jews at Alexandria. 330 **Onias I.,** High Priest. 320 **Ptolemy I. Soter** takes Jerusalem. Jews are settled at Alexandria, Egypt, and Cyrene. 314 Antigonus, ruler over Palestine. 312-311 **Seleucus I. Nicator** conquers Babylon.—*Seleucid Era.* 301 War of the *Diadochi* or successors of Alexander brought to an issue by the battle of *Ipsus* in Phrygia. 301 Death of **Onias I Simon I., the Just,** High Priest. According to Jewish tradition, he was greatest of the later line of priests, last survivor of the "Great Synagogue" of 120, who returned with Ezra from the Babylonian captivity. The "New Synagogue" succeeded, whose office was, according to tradition, to interpret the Old Testament Scriptures. 292 **Eleazar,** High Priest.	335 **Arses.** Darius Codomanus.	356 Philip. 338 Battle of Chæronea. 336 Alexander. 322 Alexander dies.	322 Ptolemy Soter.	312 Seleucus. I.

History of the Jews—Continued.	Persia.	Greece.	Egypt.	Syria.

B.C.

285 Ptolemy II. Philadelphus. According to a tradition preserved by Aristeas, Ptolemy, with the co-operation of Eleazar, ordains the execution of the LXX. translation of the Old Testament. This marks the *epoch of Hellenism.*

N.B.—The dates of the High Priests down to Onias III. are not trustworthy.

251 Manasseh, High Priest.

240 Onias II., High Priest. He refuses to pay tribute to Ptolemy III. Euergetes. Joseph, son of Tobias, High Priest's nephew, contrives to appease Ptolemy.

226 Simon II., High Priest.

219 Antiochus III., of Syria, overpowers Palestine, which is shortly afterwards recovered by Ptolemy IV., of Egypt (Philopator), 217 B.C.

205 Ptolemy V. Epiphanes succeeds Pt. Philopator as ruler of Egypt at the age of five. Antiochus III. (the Great), of Syria, makes war upon him, and conquers Coelesyria and Palestine (198). Antiochus grants the Jews an annual subsidy for offerings, and Gentiles are forbidden to enter the Temple.

Egypt (right col top):
285 Ptolemy Philadelphus.
247 Euergetes.
222 Philopater.
205 Epiphanes.

Syria (right col):
279 Antiochus I.
261 Antiochus II.
246 Seleucus II.
226 Seleucus III.
223 Antiochus III.

	Rome.		Egypt.		Syria.
B.C.		B.C.		B.C.	

198 Death of the High Priest Simon II. **Onias III.,** High Priest. *Ecclesiasticus* written by Jesus Sirachides about 180 B.C.

175 Accession of **Antiochus IV.,** surnamed **Epiphanes** (but with the epithet *epimanes,* " mad "). Onias III. visits Antioch to clear himself from the charges of Simon, treasurer of the Temple. Through bribes and promises of tribute Joshua (or Jason), brother of Onias, representing the Hellenising party at Antioch, obtains the High Priesthood. Onias III. deposed. Temple worship neglected. Gymnasium erected for young Jews. Deputies sent with gifts to quinquennial games of Tyrian Hercules.

172 Menelaus outbids Jason in bribes, and supplants him. Summoned to Antioch, he sells the Temple vessels to the Tyrians in order to bribe Andronicus, governor at Antioch. He is accused by Onias, and the latter is murdered.

168 Deposition of Menelaus by Jason, who assaults Jerusalem with 1000 men. Antiochus invades Judæa, takes Jerusalem by storm, and slaughters without distinction of age or sex ; profanes the Temple altar by sacrifice of swine. Apollonius, by orders of Antiochus, commits frightful massacres on Sabbath. Antiochus promulgates his *Edict of Uniformity in Religion.* Temple on Mount Gerizim dedicated to Zeus Xenios, and at Jerusalem to Zeus Olympios. The courts of the latter polluted by licentious orgies and idolatrous offerings made on its altars.

Glorious resistance of the aged priest **Mattathias** and his sons, who gather *Chasidim* (Assidæans) around them and retire to mountain fastnesses, whence they issue and slaughter the idolatrous worshippers.

167 *Battle of Beth-horon.* Army of Apollonius routed by **Judas,** surnamed **Maccabæus** (the " Hammerer "), son of Mattathias.

Nicanor and Gorgias ordered by Antiochus to extirpate the Jewish people. *Battle of Ashdod.* Gorgias, attempting to surprise the Jewish camp, is utterly routed, with immense loss of booty.

166 *Battle of Bethsura,* Lysias, with 65,000 troops, defeated by Judas with much inferior force. Jerusalem retaken.

Judas cleanses the Temple and replaces the sacred vessels from the captured booty. Sanctuary is *re-dedicated,* and *Feast of Dedication* instituted.

164 Death of Antiochus at Tabæ. Succeeded by **Antiochus V. Eupator.**

163 Siege of Bethsura by Lysias with 100,000 troops.

162 Alcimus appointed High Priest by Antiochus, and head of the Hellenising party ; is supported by **Demetrius Soter.** Nicanor, despatched to restore him to the High Priesthood, defeated by Judas at Capharsalama.

161 *Battle of Adasa* (near Beth-horon), Nicanor defeated and slain. Bacchides sent by Demetrius to avenge Nicanor's death.

Battle of Eleasa. Judas attempts to fight against overwhelming numbers with a body of 800 men, and, after defeating the right wing of the Syrians, is himself slain. He is buried in

Rome column:
197 Battle of *Cynocephalæ.*
Macedonian War.
168 Defeat of Perseus by L. Æmilius Paullus in the *Battle of Pydna.*
Conquest of Macedonia.

Egypt column:
181 Accession of Ptolemy **VI. Philometor.**
171 Antiochus Epiphanes invades Egypt, but is compelled to withdraw by the Romans.
168 Ptolemy and Pyrsicon reign together.
167 Onias **IV.** takes refuge in Egypt, and founds a new temple at Leontopolis.

Syria column:
187 Seleucus IV. Philopator ascends the throne. Demetrius sent to Rome, and his succession usurped by
175 Antiochus **IV. Epiphanes** (Epimanes).
164 Antiochus V. Eupator. Demetrius returns from Rome overthrows Antiochus and reigns over Syria as
162 Demetrius I. Soter.

History of the Jews—Continued. B.C.	Rome. B.C.	Egypt. B.C.	Syria. B.C.
his father's sepulchre at Modin. **Jonathan,** surnamed **Apphus,** youngest son of Mattathias, is chosen leader.			
158 Bacchides makes peace with Jonathan, who governs the people from the stronghold of Michmash.			
153 Jonathan's favour is sought by Demetrius against his rival Alexander Balas. The latter nominates Jonathan High Priest, and sends him a purple robe and golden crown. Jonathan wears these at the Feast of Tabernacles, and *inaugurates the line of Asmonæan priest-princes.*		150 Marriage of Alexander Balas to Cleopatra, daughter of Ptolemy. Ptolemy supports Demetrius against his rival, Alexander.	150 **Alexander Balas** usurps authority.
The Jews support Alexander Balas in spite of the lavish promises of Demetrius.			
147 *Apollonius,* governor of Coelesyria, adherent of Demetrius, defeated by Jonathan at *Azotus.* The latter is established in his position as High Priest by Demetrius.	146 Destruction of Carthage by Scipio, and capture of Corinth by Mummius.	145 **Ptolemy VII.** Physcon or Euergetes.	146 **Demetrius II.** Nicator.
144 Jonathan confirmed in his authority by **Antiochus VI. Theos.** Simon appointed governor of the country from Tyre to Egyptian border. The followers of Demetrius overthrown by Jonathan near Gennesareth and Hamath. Simon takes Ascalon and Joppa. Towns of Judæa fortified, and walls of Jerusalem heightened. Jonathan is slain through the plots and treachery of Tryphon.			145 **Antiochus VI.,** supported by Tryphon, overpowers Demetrius.
143 **Simon,** surnamed **Thassi,** last of the five sons of Mattathias, becomes High Priest.			143 Tryphon puts Antiochus to death and usurps authority.
142-1 Tower of Jerusalem purified and entered. Prosperity and peace enjoyed by Jews (1 Macc. 13 : 43-53 ; 14 : 4 foll.). *First year of the freedom* of the Jews (141).			137 **Antiochus VII. Sidetes,** second son of Demetrius I., and brother of captive Demetrius II., defeats Tryphon and besieges him in Dora.
137 **Antiochus VII.** refuses the aid of Simon against the usurper Tryphon. War ensues with Syria. In the battle of *Jamnia,* Cendebeus, the Syrian general, is completely defeated by Simon's sons, Judas and John.			
135 Simon and his sons, Judas and Mattathias, treacherously assassinated by Ptolemy.			
133 **John Hyrcanus,** second son of Simon, becomes High Priest. He is compelled by famine to surrender Jerusalem and become tributary to **Antiochus Eusebes.**			
132 Prologue to Ecclesiasticus written by the grandson of Jesus Sirachides.	132-128 Career of Tiberius Gracchus.		
128 Judæa recovers independence with the death of Antiochus.			128 Is slain in Parthia. Release of Demetrius II.
125 Hyrcanus conquers the east of the Jordan,	123-1 Caius Gracchus *Leges Semproniæ* (agrarian reforms).	117 **Ptolemy VIII.** Lathyrus.	More than ten rulers follow in rapid succession till
109 destroys the temple on Mount Gerizim, and builds the tower of Baris north-west of the Jerusalem Temple enclosure (Antonia). In consequence of a quarrel with Eleazar, he turns Sadducee.	111 War with Jugurtha.	107 He is banished to Cyprus through his mother, Cleopatra.	
106 Death of Hyrcanus. **Aristobulus I.** seizes the High Priesthood, murders in jealousy his brother Antigonus ; dies of illness and remorse.	106 Birth of Cicero.	106 **Ptolemy IX.**	
105-4 **Alexander Jannæus.** The Pharisees instigate a rebellion against him (92). He is expelled, but returns to Jerusalem in triumph.	102-1 Cimbri and Teutones defeated by Marius. 100 Birth of Julius Cæsar. 90 First Mithridatic War. 86 Death of Marius.		
78 Alexander becomes reconciled to the Pharisees ; dies at the siege of Ragaba. His wife, **Alexandra,** succeeds him ; encourages Aristobulus, her son, to resist the Pharisees : makes her eldest son, Hyrcanus, High Priest.	80 Second Mithridatic War—Sulla dictator.	81 **Ptolemy X.** 80 **Ptolemy XI.** Auletes. 59 By bribes obtains recognition from Cæsar.	83 **Tigranes,** king of Armenia, becomes ruler of Syria.
70 **Hyrcanus II.** succeeds, on the death of Alexandra, and is supported by *Pharisees.* Both are defeated by **Aristobulus,** who captures Jerusalem.			
69 **Aristobulus II.,** High Priest and ruler. Antipater supports Hyrcanus. The latter appeal for help to Aretas, king of the Nabatheans, who, with 50,000 men, defeats Aristobulus, and besieges him in the Temple.	67 Pompey's successful war against the pirates *Lex Manilia.* 66 He defeats Mithridates.		69 **Tigranes** conquered by the Roman general Lucullus. **Antiochus XIII.** set up by the Romans as king.
65 *Scaurus,* Pompey's lieutenant, deposes Antiochus XIII., and annexes Syria to the Roman dominions. Receives ambassadors from Hyrcanus and Aristobulus, and decides in favour of the claims of Aristobulus. But this decision is afterwards reversed.			
64 **Pompey** holds a court at Damascus. Antipater bribes more than 1000 Jews to support Hyrcanus. Pompey decides in favour of Hyrcanus.			
63 Resistance of Aristobulus. He surrenders Jerusalem, and is himself taken prisoner. The Temple still resists, and after three months is captured and 12,000 Jews slain. Pompey enters the Holy of Holies.	63 Consulship of Cicero, and conspiracy of Catiline. 60 *First Triumvirate* of Julius Cæsar, Pompey, and Crassus.	58 Ptolemy Auletes is banished, and goes to Rome. Reign of Berenice and Tryphæna.	57 **Gabinius,** proconsul.
Hyrcanus II. restored to authority. Judæa ruled by Rome through Antipater.			

History of the Jews—Continued.

B.C.

54 Crassus receives Syria as his province, and is overthrown by the Parthians (53).

49 Aristobulus, released by Cæsar, is murdered by Pompeian adherents.

48 **Antipater** aids Julius Cæsar in the Egyptian War, and is appointed First Procurator of Judæa, with Hyrcanus as Ethnarch.

46 He appoints his sons **Phasael** and **Herod** governors of Jerusalem and Galilee respectively.

42 Herod is betrothed to Mariamne, granddaughter of Hyrcanus, and daughter of Alexander.

40 **Antigonus**, last of the Asmonæans.
Herod secures the favour of Octavian, and also of Antony, and a *decree from the Senate appointing him king of Judæa.*

37 Jerusalem is besieged for six months, and taken after fearful carnage. Antigonus sent in chains to Antony, who puts him to death by Herod's wish.

36 Herod appoints Aristobolus High Priest.

32 Herod is defeated by Malchus.

30 Is established by Octavian in his kingdom.

29 Puts Mariamne to death.

26 Builds a theatre at Jerusalem and an amphitheatre at Jericho. Games are appointed in honour of Augustus.

22 Simon appointed High Priest, whose daughter Mariamne is married to Herod.

18 Rebuilding of the Temple. Herod visits Rome and brings back with him his two sons, Alexander and Aristobulus, who had been sent there in 24 B.C.

16 Visits Agrippa, whom he invites to Judæa.

11 Accuses Aristobulus and Alexander before Augustus, who reconciles them.

6 Aristobulus and Alexander condemned to death by the Council and strangled. Antipater plots against Herod and goes to Rome.

5 Simon deposed and **Matthias** made High Priest,

4 who is himself deposed in favour of Joazar. Two chief rabbis burnt alive for resisting the innovation of a golden eagle placed over the Temple gate.
Herod orders the execution of Antipater, and dies of a painful internal disease. **Archelaus** succeeds.

Rome.

B.C.

58-51 Cæsar's campaigns in Gaul.

49 Civil war between Pompey and Cæsar.

48 Battle of Pharsalia.

44 Assassination of Cæsar.

43 *Second Triumvirate* of Octavian, Antony, and Lepidus.

42 Battle of *Philippi.* Defeat of Brutus and Cassius.

40 Antony and Octavian reconciled at Brundisium.

37-36 War against Sextus Pompey.

31 *Battle of Actium.* Defeat of Antony.

30 Octavian advances into Egypt. Death of Antony and Cleopatra.

29 Closing of the Temple of Janus.

27 Octavian assumes the name *Augustus.*

21 Augustus winters in Samos.

20 Passes into Syria. Standards taken from Crassus restored by Phraates.

8 Census of Roman citizens instituted.

Egypt.

B.C.

55 Gabinius restores Ptolemy Auletes.

51 **Cleopatra** and **Ptolemy XII.**, and **Ptolemy XIII.**

48-47 *Alexandrine War.*

36-31 Antony and Cleopatra.

27 Egypt made an imperial province.

Syria.

B.C.

54 **Crassus**, proconsul, is overthrown by the Parthians.

43 **C. Cassius Longinus**, proconsul.
After this Syria is ruled by *legati.*

27 Syria is made an imperial province, ruled by a prefect as *legatus Cæsaris.*

23 **M. Vipsanius Agrippa**, legatus of Syria.

20 Augustus visits Syria and meets Herod.

16 Agrippa once more legatus.

9-8 **C. Sentius Saturninus** *legatus.*

7 Census of Palestine.

---

course in the Synagogue of Capernaum on the bread of life (John 6 : 25-71).
Third Passover (April 16). Jesus stays in Galilee (John 7 : 1). Controversy with Scribes and Pharisees sent from Jerusalem. Jesus heals the demoniac daughter of the Syrophœnician woman and a dumb man (Matt. 15 : 1-30; Mark 7 : 1-37). Feeding of the four thousand and voyage to Magdala (Matt. 15 : 31-39; Mark 8 : 1-9). Jesus prophesies his coming death and resurrection, and subsequent persecution of his disciples. The transfiguration. Healing of a dumb demoniac (Matt. 16 : 21-23; 17 : 23; Mark 8 : 27; 9 : 31; Luke 9 : 18-45). Seventy evangelists sent forth (Luke 10 : 1-20).
Feast of Tabernacles (October), John 7 : 2 foll. Jesus goes to the feast privately.
Feast of Dedication (December), John 10 : 22. Christ again visits Jerusalem.

30 Raising of Lazarus (John 11 : 6-54).
March 30. Arrival in Bathany six days before the Passover (John 12 : 1-9).
Christ anointed by Mary (Matt. 26 : 6-13; Mark 14 : 3-9; Luke 7 : 36-50).
Plot against Jesus and Lazarus (John 12 : 10, 11).
Christ enters Jerusalem and cleanses the Temple (Matt. 21 : 1-16; Mark 11 : 1-18; Luke 19 : 29-48).

30 Parables and Discourses (Matt. 21–25; Mark 11–13; Luke 20–21).
Last Passover (April 5). (Matt. 26 : 1-5; Mark 14 : 1, 2; Luke 22 : 1, 2).
Conspiracy of the Jews. Paschal Supper (Matt. 26 : 1-35; Mark 14 : 1-31; Luke 22 : 1-39; John 13 : 1-38).

A.D. Discourses in John 14-17.
Gethsemane, Betrayal, Trial, Crucifixion, Resurrection and Ascension (Matt. 26 : 36–28; Mark 14 : 32–16; Luke 22 : 40–24; John 18-21).

Ascension of Jesus Christ. Matthias appointed by lot to fill Judas' place (Acts 1).

Day of Pentecost and Descent of the Holy Spirit (Acts 2).

Imprisonment of Peter and John by order of Sanhedrin (Acts 4).

31 Growth of the Christian community. Death of Ananias and Sapphira. Increasing activity and influence of the Christians awaken the hostility of the Sanhedrin. Imprisonment of the Apostles. They are miraculously liberated, and are ultimately allowed to depart by the Sanhedrin on the advice of Gamaliel.

36 Trial and martyrdom of Stephen (Acts 6 : 9–7).

Rapid growth in numbers of the Christians. They are persecuted by their Jewish brethren, in which persecution Saul takes an active part. Philip the deacon preaches in Samaria, whither St. Peter and St. John follow. Philip converts the Ethiopan eunuch (Acts 8).

37 Conversion of Saul. He spends three years in Arabia.

40 Paul returns to Jerusalem. The Jews plot to take away his life. He departs for Tarsus (Acts 9).

Cessation of persecution and increase of Christian believers.

Peter visits and baptizes Cornelius, a Roman centurion. Christianity extended to the Gentiles (Acts 10–11 : 18).

41 Growth in numbers of the Gentile Christians in Antioch. They are visited by Barnabas. They are now first called Christians.

43 Paul brought by Barnabas from Tarsus, and they labour together at Antioch. Severe famine prophesied by Agabus (Acts 11 : 21-30).

44 Herod Agrippa puts James, brother of John, to death, and imprisons Peter. He dies at Cæsarea (Acts 12).

45 Paul and Barnabas set apart to preach to the Gentiles.

Their first missionary journey (Acts 13, 14).

48 Dissensions awakened by the Judaisers at Antioch. Paul and Barnabas sent as representatives to Jerusalem. Decree in favour of Gentile liberty.

49–50 St. Paul's second missionary journey with Silas (Acts 15–17).

51 After preaching in Phrygia, Galatia, Mysia, and Troas, he is joined by Luke, and crosses over into Macedonia and visits Philippi, Thessalonica, and Berea, whence Jewish opposition drives him to Athens.

52 Paul at Corinth with Aquila and Priscilla. Epistles to Thessalonians.

A.D. 53 Proconsulship of Gallio in Achaia. Paul Paul quits Corinth for Ephesus (Acts 18 : 1-22).

54-55 Paul at Jerusalem. Third missionary journey.

56-57 Sets out from Antioch for Galatia and Phrygia. Paul at Ephesus for two years.

Writes perhaps First Epistle to Corinthians, and perhaps also Epistle to Galatians (see below).

Compelled by a tumult at Ephesus to leave for Macedonia (Acts 18 : 23-19).

Writes Second Epistle to Corinthians (and about this time perhaps the Epistle to Galatians). Paul reaches Corinth probably at the end of the year.

58 Stays three months at Corinth. Epistle to the Romans. He quits Corinth in the early part of the year, returns to Macedonia, revisits Philippi in company with Luke, and departs after Passover (Acts 20 : 1-6). Leaves Troas, bids farewell to Ephesian elders at Miletus (Acts 20 : 7-38).

Visits Tyre, then Cæsarea, and arrives at Jerusalem before Pentecost. Violent outburst of feeling against Paul. He is rescued by Claudius Lysias at the head of his troops. Defends himself before the Jews; is sent to Cæsarea. Defends himself before Felix (Acts 21–24).

60 Paul still prisoner at Cæsarea. Defends himself before Festus and Agrippa (25, 26). He is delivered with other prisoners to the centurion Julius. Voyage to Rome. Shipwreck at Melita, where he winters.

61 Sails for Rome. Visits Syracuse, Rhegium, Puteoli. At length he reaches Rome, and is placed under custody of the Pretorian prefect, Burrus. Lives two years in his hired house (Acts 27, 28).

62-63 Writes Epistles to the Ephesians and Colossians, to Philemon, and to Philippians.

64 Neronian Persecution.

The martyrdom of St. Paul is placed by most authorities somewhere between A.D. 64 and 66.

Chrysolite [Heb. Pitdah; Τοπαζιον; **Topaz** of A.V., Topazius], Ex. 28 : 17; Ezek. 28 : 13; Rev. 21 : 20. The chrysolite of the ancients was called topaz and vice versa, and so they are rendered in the A.V. and R.V. Chrysolite, a precious variety of Peridot, furnishes a rather soft gem of various shades of olive green.

Chrysoprase [Χρυσόπρχσος; Chrysoprasus], Rev. 21 : 20. It may be doubted whether this should be identified with the beautiful lustrous leek-green variety of chalcedonic quartz now called chrysoprase. Pliny classed it with the beryls. It never has, however, the transparency of the beryl, nor does it occur as a crystal. It is sometimes found in large masses.

Church of God, Acts 20 : 28; 1 Cor. 1 : 2; 10 : 32; 11 : 22; 15 : 9; Gal. 1 : 13; 1 Tim. 3 : 5.

foundation of, Matt. 16 : 18; Col. 1 : 18.

increase of, Acts 2 : 47; 14 : 23.

authority of, Matt. 18 : 17; 1 Cor. 5 : 4.

teaching of, Acts 11 : 26; 1 Cor. 12 : 28; 14 : 4, 5.

persecuted, Acts 8 : 3; 12 : 1; Gal. 1 : 13; Phil. 3 : 6.

saluted, Acts 18 : 22; Rom. 16 : 5; 1 Cor. 16 : 19.

loved of Christ, Eph. 5 : 25, 29.

Matt. 16 : 18, on this rock I will build my c.

18 : 17, tell it to the c.

Acts 2 : 47, Lord added to c. daily.

7 : 38, the c. in the wilderness.

14 : 23, ordained elders in every c.

16 : 5, c. established in faith.

19 : 37, robbers of c.

20 : 28, feed the c. of God.

Rom. 16 : 5; 1 Cor. 16 : 19; Philem. 2, c. in house.

Eph. 1 : 22, head over all things to c.

5 : 25, as Christ loved the c.

Col. 1 : 18, head of the body the c.

Heb. 12 : 23, the c. of the firstborn.

Churches, the seven, in Asia, Rev. 1 : 4, 11, 20; 2 : 7, 11, 17, 29; 3 : 6, 13, 22.

Churlish, Nabal so designated, 1 Sam. 25 : 3.

Churn, Prov. 30 : 33.

Ciel [to cover with boards, wainscot], same as ceil, 2 Chr. 3 : 5; 1 Ki. 6 : 15; Hag. 1 : 4, greater house he c. with fir tree.

Cilicia, disciples there, Acts 15 : 23, 41.

the country of Paul, Acts 21 : 39; 22 : 3; Gal. 1 : 21.

Cinnamon, the inner bark of Cinnamomum zeylanicum, was used in the preparation of the precious ointment of the Tabernacle (Ex. 30 : 23). It was also used, with other aromatic substances, for sprinkling bed tapestry (Prov. 7 : 16, 17). It is also mentioned in the Revelation, among the merchandise of Babylon (Rev. 18 : 13). It is not a native of Syria, but was imported from the East.

Circle, Isa. 40 : 42.

Circuit, 1 Sam. 7 : 16, from year to year in c.

Job 22 : 14, walketh in c. of heaven.

Ps. 19 : 6, his c. unto the ends of it.

Eccl. 1 : 6, returneth according to his c.

Circumcise, Gen. 17 : 11, ye shall c. foreskin.

Luke 1 : 59, they came to c. the child.

John 7 : 22, ye on sabbath c. a man.

Acts 15 : 1, except ye be c. ye.

Gal. 5 : 2, if ye be c., Christ shall profit nothing.

Phil. 3 : 5, c. the eighth day.

Circumcision, the covenant of, Gen. 17 : 10.

performed, Gen. 34 : 24; Ex. 4 : 25; 12 : 48, etc.

renewed by Joshua, Josh. 5 : 2.

of John, Luke 1 : 59; of Jesus, Luke 2 : 21; of Timothy, Acts 16 : 3.

superseded by the Gospel, Acts 15; Gal. 5 : 2.

of heart, Deut. 10 : 16; 30 : 6.

spiritual, Phil. 3 : 3; Col. 2 : 11.

how far profitable, Rom. 2 : 25; 4 : 9; 1 Cor. 7 : 19; Gal. 5 : 6; 6 : 15.

Rom. 3 : 1, what profit is there of c. ?

15 : 8, Jesus Christ minister of c.

Gal. 5 : 6; 6 : 15, in Christ neither c. availeth.

Eph. 2 : 11, by that called c. in flesh.

Phil. 3 : 3, the c., which worship God.

Col. 2 : 11, c. without hands.

3 : 11, neither c. nor uncircumcision.

Circumspect, Ex. 23 : 23, in all things, be c.

Eph. 5 : 15, see that ye walk c.

Cistern, 2 Ki. 18 : 31; Isa. 36 : 26, drink every one of his c.

Eccl. 12 : 6, wheel broken at the c.

Jer. 2 : 13, hewed out c., broken c.

Cities, what to be spared, Deut. 20 : 10.

what to be destroyed, Deut. 20 : 16.

of refuge, Num. 35 : 6; Deut. 19; Josh. 20.

Citizen, Luke 15 : 15; 19 : 14; Acts 21 : 39.

City, Gen. 4 : 17, Cain builded a c.

Num. 35 : 6; Josh. 15 : 59, c. of refuge.

2 Sam. 19 : 37, I may die in mine own c.

Ps. 46 : 4, make glad c. of God.

107 : 4, found no c. to dwell in.

127 : 1, except Lord keep c.

Prov. 8 : 3, wisdom crieth in c.

16 : 32, than he that taketh a c.

Eccl. 9 : 14, a little c., and few men.

Isa. 22 : 2, a tumultuous c., a joyous c.

26 : 1, we have a strong c.

33 : 20, c. of our solemnities.

Zech. 8 : 3, a c. of truth.

Matt. 5 : 14, c. set on a hill.

21 : 10, all the c. was moved.

23 : 34, persecute them from c. to c.

Luke 10 : 8, into whatsoever c. ye enter.

19 : 41, he beheld c. and wept.

Acts 8 : 8, great joy in that c.

Heb. 11 : 10, a c. that hath foundations.

12 : 22, the c. of living God.

13 : 14, no continuing c.

Rev. 3 : 12, name of the c. of my God.

20 : 9, compassed beloved c.

Clad, 1 Ki. 11 : 29; Isa. 59 : 17.

Clamour, Prov. 9 : 13; Eph. 4 : 31.

Clap, Ps. 47 . 1, c. your hands, all ye people.

98 : 8, let the floods c. their hands.

Isa. 55 : 12, the trees shall c. their hands.

Lam. 2 : 15, all that pass by c. their hands.

Claudius Cæsar (claū-dĭ-ŭs), Acts 11 : 28.

Claudius Lysias (claū-dĭ-ăs lȳs-ĭ-ăs), chief captain, rescues Paul, Acts 21 : 31; 22 : 24; 23 : 10.

sends him to Felix, Acts 23 : 26.

Clave, Gen. 22 : 3, Abraham c. wood for burnt offering.

Ruth 1 : 14, Ruth c. to her mother in law.

2 Sam. 23 : 10, his hand c. to the sword.

Neh. 10 : 29, they c. to their brethren.

Acts 17 : 34, certain men c. to Paul.

Claws, Deut. 14 : 6; Dan. 4 : 33; Zech. 11 : 16.

Clay, Job 4 : 19, that dwell in houses of c.

10 : 9, thou hast made me as c.

13 : 12, bodies like to bodies of c.

33 : 6, I am formed out of c.

Ps. 40 : 2, out of the miry c.

Isa. 64 : 8, we the c., thou our potter.

Jer. 18 : 6, as c. is in the potter's hand.

Dan. 2 : 33, part of iron, part of c.

John 9 : 6, made c., and anointed.

Clay, Rom. 9 : 21, potter power over c.

Clean, 2 Ki. 5 : 12, wash and be c.

Job 14 : 4, c. thing out of an unclean ?

15 : 15, heavens not c. in his sight.

Ps. 19 : 9, fear of the Lord is c.

24 : 4, he that hath c. hands.

51 : 10, create in me a c. heart.

77 : 8, is his mercy c. gone for ever ?
Prov. 16 : 2, ways c. in his own eyes.
Isa. 1 : 16, wash you, make you c.
52 : 11, be c. that bear vessels of the Lord.
Ezek. 36 : 25, then will I sprinkle c. water on you.
Matt. 8 : 2; Mark 1 : 40; Luke 5 : 12, thou canst make me c.
Matt. 23 : 25; Luke 11 : 39, make c. the outside.
Luke 11 : 41, all things c. unto you.
John 13 : 11, ye are not all c.
15 : 3, c. through the word.
Acts 18 : 6, I am c.
Rev. 19 : 8, arrayed in fine linen c. and white.
Cleanness, 2 Sam. 22 : 21, 25; Ps. 18 : 20; Amos 4 : 6.
Cleanse, Ps. 19 : 12, c. from secret faults.
73 : 13, I have c. my heart in vain.
119 : 9, a young man c. his way.
Matt. 8 : 3, his leprosy was c.
10 : 8, 11 : 5; Luke 7 : 22, c. lepers.
Matt. 23 : 26, c. first that which is within.
Luke 4 : 27, none was c. saving Naaman.
17 : 17, were not ten c. ?
Acts 10 : 15; 11 : 9, what God hath c.
2 Cor. 7 : 1, let us c. ourselves.
Eph. 5 : 26, might c. it with washing.
Jas. 4 : 8, c. your hands, ye sinners.
1 John 1 : 7, c. us from all sin.
Clear, Gen. 44 : 16, how shall we c. ourselves?
Ex. 34 : 7, by no means c. the guilty.
2 Sam. 23 : 4, c. shining after rain.
Job 11 : 17, thine age be c. than noonday.
Ps. 51 : 4, c. when thou judgest.
Cant. 6 : 10, c. as the sun.
Zech. 14 : 6, light shall not be c.
Matt. 7 : 5; Luke 6 : 42, see c. to pull out mote.
Mark 8 : 25, saw every man c.
Rom. 1 : 20, things from creation c. seen.
2 Cor. 7 : 11, approved yourselves to be c.
Rev. 21 : 11; 22 : 1, c. as crystal.
Clearness, Ex. 24 : 10, heaven is his c.
Cleave, Josh. 23 : 8, c. to the Lord your God.
Job 29 : 10; Ps. 137 : 6; Ezek. 3 : 26, tongue c. to roof of mouth.
Job 31 : 7, hath c. to my hands.
Ps. 119 : 25, my soul c. to dust.
Acts 11 : 23, with purpose of heart c.
Rom. 12 : 9, c. to that which is good.
Clefts, Song of Sol. 2 : 14, dove in c. of the rock.
Isa. 2 : 21, to go into c. for fear.
Jer. 49 : 16; Obad. 3, dwellest in the c.
Clemency, Acts 24 : 4.
Clement (clĕm-ĕnt), Phil. 4 : 3.
Cleopas (clē-ŏ-păs), in the A.V. stands for two names, one probably identical with Alphæus, John 19 : 25; the other a contraction of Cleopatros, Luke 24 : 18.
Clerk, Acts 19 : 35, town c. had appeased.
Climb, Amos 9 : 2, though they c. up to heaven.
Luke 19 : 4, c. up a tree.
John 10 : 1, c. up some other way.
Cloak. The cloak was the outer garment or robe worn by day as a mantle over the other clothing, and used to sleep in at night, for which reason it was not lawful to retain it as a pledge after sunset (Ex. 22 : 26).

Alluding to this exemption Jesus said, " If any man sue thee at the law, and take thy coat, let him have thy cloke also " (Matt. 5 : 40), that is, " meet your liabilities by giving toward their satisfaction even that which by law your creditor cannot take."
Isa. 59 : 17, clad with zeal as a c.
Matt. 5 : 40; Luke 6 : 29, let him have thy c. also.
John 15 : 22, no c. for their sin.
1 Thess. 2 : 5, c. of covetousness.
1 Pet. 2 : 16, c. of maliciousness.
Clods, Job 21 : 33, c. of valley be sweet.
Isa. 28 : 24, ploughman break the c.
Joel 1 : 17, seed rotten under c.
Close, Num. 16 : 33, earth c. upon them.
Isa. 29 : 10, Lord hath c. your eyes.
Prov. 18 : 24, friend sticketh c. than a brother.
Luke 9 : 36, they kept it c.
Closet, Joel 2 : 16; Matt. 6 : 6; Luke 12 : 3.
Cloth, Deut. 22 : 17, spread c. before the elders.
Mark 2 : 21, new c. on old garment.
14 : 51, 52, linen c.
Clothe, Ps. 65 : 13, pasture c. with flocks.
Ps. 93 : 1, Lord is c. with majesty.
132 : 9, priests be c. with righteousness.
132 : 16, c. with salvation.
132 : 18, enemies will I c. with shame.
Prov. 31 : 21, household c. with scarlet.
Isa. 50 : 3, heavens with blackness.
61 : 10, c. with garments of salvation.
Matt. 6 : 30; Luke 12 : 28, c. grass of the field.
Matt. 11 : 8; Luke 7 : 25, a man c. in soft raiment ?
Matt. 25 : 36, 43, naked, and ye c. me.
Mark 1 : 6, c. with camel's hair.
5 : 15; Luke 8 : 35, c., and in right mind.
Mark 15 : 17, c. Jesus with purple.
Luke 16 : 19, c. in purple and fine linen.
2 Cor. 5 : 2, desiring to be c. upon.
1 Pet. 5 : 5, be c. with humility.
Rev. 3 : 18, that thou mayest be c.
7 : 9, c. with white robes, and palms.
19 : 13, c. with a vesture dipped in blood.
Clothes, Gen. 44 : 13; Josh. 7 : 6; Esther 4 : 1; Mark 14 : 63, rent his c.
Deut. 29 : 5; Neh. 9 : 21, c. not waxen old.
Matt. 24 : 18, not return to take c.
Mark 5 : 28, if I touch but his c.
Luke 2 : 7, in swaddling c.
19 : 36, spread c. in the way.
24 : 12; John 20 : 5, linen c. laid.
John 11 : 44, bound with grave-c.
Acts 7 : 58, laid down c. at Saul's feet.
22 : 23, cried out, and cast off c.
Clothing, the first, Gen. 3 : 21.
rending, a mark of grief, Gen. 37 : 29, 34; Num. 14 : 6; Judg. 11 : 35; Acts 14 : 14.
laws concerning washing, Ex. 19 : 10; Lev. 11 : 25; Num. 19 : 7.
Job 31 : 19, perish for want of c.
Ps. 45 : 13, c. of wrought gold.
Prov. 31 : 22, c. is silk and purple.
Isa. 59 : 17, garments of vengeance for c.
Matt. 7 : 15, in sheep's c.
11 : 8, wear soft c. are in kings' houses.
Mark 12 : 38, love to go in long c.
Acts 10 : 30, a man in bright c.

Jas. 2 : 3, to him that weareth gay c.
Cloud, pillar of, children of Israel guided by,
Ex. 13 : 21; 14 : 19; Neh. 9 : 19; Ps.
78 : 14; 105 : 39; 1 Cor. 10 : 1.
appearance of the Lord in, Ex. 24 : 15;
34 : 5; Lev. 16 : 2; Num. 11 : 25; 12 : 5;
1 Ki. 8 : 10; Ezek. 10 : 4; Matt. 17 : 5;
Luke 21 : 27; Rev. 14 : 14.
Gen. 9 : 13, I set my bow in the c.
Ex. 13 : 21; 14 : 24; Neh. 9 : 19, pillar of c.
1 Ki. 18 : 44, a little c.
Ps. 36 : 5, faithfulness reacheth to c.
97 : 2, c. and darkness round about him.
104 : 3, maketh c. his chariot.
Prov. 3 : 20, c. drop down dew.
Eccl. 12 : 2, nor c. return after rain.
Isa. 5 : 6, the c. that they rain not.
44 : 22, blotted out as thick c.
60 : 8, fly as a c.
Dan. 7 : 13; Luke 21 : 27, Son of man with c.
Hos. 6 : 4; 13 : 3, goodness as morning c.
Matt. 17 : 5; Mark 9 : 7; Luke 9 : 34, c.
overshadowed.
Matt. 24 : 30; 26 : 64; Mark 13 : 26; 14 : 62,
in c. with power.
1 Cor. 10 : 1, fathers under c.
1 Thess. 4 : 17, caught up in c.
2 Pet. 2 : 17, c. carried with tempest.
Jude 12, c. without water.
Rev. 1 : 7, he cometh with c.
Cloudy, Ex. 33 : 9, c. pillar descended.
Ps. 99 : 7, spake in the c. pillar.
Ezek. 30 : 3, near a c. day.
Clouted [patched with clouts or old rags], Josh.
9 : 5, old shoes and c. upon their feet.
Clouts [old rags], Jer. 38 : 11.
Cloven, Lev. 11 : 3, c. footed, that eat.
Acts 2 : 3, c. tongues.
Cluster, Num. 13 : 23; 1 Sam. 30 : 12; Rev.
14 : 18.
Coal. In the English Bible " coal " represents
five different words in the original, not one
of which means mineral coal. A " fire of
coals " (John 21 : 9) means a charcoal fire.
" Thou shalt heap coals of fire on his head "
(Rom. 12 . 20) means, that showing kindness to an enemy, such as feeding him when
he is hungry, will awaken in him such a
glowing consciousness of his wrong, and
cover him with such a sense of burning
shame, that he will feel as though coals
of fire were heaped on his head. In 1
Ki. 19 : 6 and Isa. 6 : 6, hot stones are
meant.
Prov. 6 : 28, hot c., and not be burned.
25 : 22; Rom. 12 : 20, heap c. of fire.
Isa. 6 : 6, seraphim having live c. in hand.
John 18 : 18; 21 : 9, fire of c.
Coast, 1 Sam. 7 : 13; 1 Ki. 1 : 3, c. of Israel.
Zeph. 2 : 5; Matt. 4 : 13, sea c.
See Matt. 16 : 13; Mark 7 : 31; 10 : 1; Acts
27 : 2.
Coat. This was the inner garment or shirt,
usually having sleeves, and reaching down
to the knees. It was often the only clothing
worn. Corresponding to this coat was the
" vesture " of Jesus, which, like the robes
of the priests, was all of one piece, woven
without a seam (John 19 : 23).

Matt. 5 : 40, take away thy c.
10 : 10; Mark 6 : 9, neither provide two c.
Luke 6 : 29, to take c. also.
John 19 : 23, c. without seam.
21 : 7, fisher's c.
Acts 9 : 39, the c. which Dorcas made.
Cock.—Hen. Domestic poultry are not mentioned in the Old Testament, but were well
and universally known in our Lord's time.
The " fatted fowl " that were daily supplied
to King Solomon's table may have been
geese, domesticated so as to secure the
needed supply.
Matt. 26 : 34; Mark 14 : 30; Luke 22 : 34,
c. crow, deny me.
Mark 13 : 35, cometh at c. crowing.
Cockatrice. A.V. at Jer. 8 : 17. R.V. has
basilisk. It may possibly have been the
cobra.
Cockle [Heb. bo'shah] occurs but twice, in
Job 31 : 40, " cockle instead of barley,"
where the word is rendered in the margin,
" noisome weeds." It also occurs in Isa.
5 : 2, 4, where it has been translated " wild
grapes " growing up where good grapes
had been planted.
Coffer, I Sam. 6 : 8.
Coffin, Gen. 50 : 26, Joseph was put in a c.
Cold, Prov. 20 : 4, by reason of c.
25 : 13, c. of snow in harvest.
Prov. 25 : 25, c. waters to thirsty soul.
Matt. 10 : 42, cup of c. water.
24 : 12, love of many wax c.
2 Cor. 11 : 27, in c. and nakedness.
Rev. 3 : 15, neither c. nor hot.
Collection, 2 Chr. 24 : 6, to bring in c.
1 Cor. 16 : 1, concerning c. for saints.
Rom. 15 : 26; Acts 11 : 29.
College [the second ward]. Huldah dwelt " in
the college," 2 Ki. 22 : 14.
Collops [flakes of flesh], Job 15 : 27, c. of fat on
his flanks.
Colony, a corporation in possession of Roman
citizenship, viz.: A colony was a body of
Roman citizens occupying a city or town
of importance, and enjoying therein the
same rights and privileges as in Rome itself
(Acts 16 : 12).
Colossians, The Epistle to.
Position.—This Epistle, written at Rome
during Paul's imprisonment, occupies an
intermediate position between Ephesians
and Philemon. The letters to the Ephesians
and the Colossians were both entrusted to
Tychicus, and they have a great deal of
common material. Those to the Colossians
and to Philemon mention almost exactly
the same group of persons.
Date.—This was probably A.D. 63, shortly
before the martyrdom of the Apostle.
The Church of Colossæ.—Colossæ had been
a great city, but it had very much declined,
and was now the smallest of the three
neighbour cities in the valley of the Lycus;
for Laodicea and Hierapolis were still
prosperous. It was the most insignificant
of the churches which have been honoured
by receiving a letter from St. Paul, and it is
scarcely mentioned in later times. Neither

in this Epistle nor in the Acts is there any evidence that the Apostle ever visited the Colossians. He has "heard of their faith" (1 : 4, 9), and implies that they "have not seen his face in the flesh" (2 : 1).

Theme.—"Christ is all, and in all," is the main theme of the Epistle, which is written with less finish than most of St. Paul's letters, but with all his characteristic force. After the customary Salutation and Thanksgiving (1 : 1-8) he protests his intense Interest in the Colossians (1 : 9-29), which leads on to Warning against Errors (2 : 1–3 : 4), and Exhortation to Christian duties (3 : 5–4 : 6). Personal Explanations and Salutations bring the letter to a close (4 : 7-18).

Colour [pretext, semblance], Acts 27 : 30, under c. as though they would.
Gen. 37 : 3, coat of many c.
Prov. 23 : 31, giveth his c. in the cup.
Isa. 54 : 11, stone with fair c.
Colt, Matt. 21 : 2; Luke 19 : 35; John 12 : 15.
Come, Gen. 37 : 27, c. and let us sell him.
Ex. 1 : 10, c. on, let us deal wisely.
Job 14 : 2, c. forth like a flower.
Ps. 30 : 5, joy c. in the morning.
Matt. 3 : 11, he that c. after me.
11 : 3, he that should c.
11 : 28, c. unto me, all ye.
Mark 1 : 7, c. one mightier than I.
10 : 14, suffer little children to c.
Luke 7 : 8, to another, c., and he c.
12 : 40, Son of man c.
John 14 : 6, c. unto the Father.
17 : 1, Father, the hour is c.
1 Cor. 15 : 24, then c. the end.
Gal. 4 : 4, fulness of time was c.
1 Thess. 5 : 2, so c. as a thief.
Heb. 4 : 16, let us c. boldly.
Jas. 1 : 17, c. down from Father of lights.
Rev. 22 : 17, Spirit and bride say, c.
22 : 20, even so, c., Lord Jesus.
Come by [acquire, gain possession], Acts 27 : 16.
Comeliness, Isa. 53 : 2; Ezek. 27 : 10; 1 Cor. 12 : 23.
Comely, Ps. 33 : 1; 147 : 1, praise is c.
Song of Sol. 1 : 5, I am black but c.
1 Cor. 7 : 35, for that which is c.
Comers, Heb. 10 : 1.
Comfort, Ps. 23 : 4, rod and staff c. me.
77 : 2, refused to be c.
119 : 50, c. in affliction.
Isa. 12 : 1, thou c. me.
40 : 1, c. ye, c. ye my people.
61 : 2, c. all that mourn.
66 : 13, as one whom his mother c.
Matt. 2 : 18, would not be c.
5 : 4, that mourn, they shall be c.
Matt. 9 : 22; Mark 10 : 49; Luke 8 : 48; 2 Cor. 13 : 11, be of good c.
Luke 16 : 25, he is c. and thou art tormented.
John 11 : 19, to c. them.
Acts 9 : 31, c. of Holy Ghost.
Rom. 1 : 12, I may be c. with you.
15 : 4, patience and c. of Scriptures.
2 Cor. 1 : 3, God of all c.
1 : 4, able to c. them.
7 : 6, c. those that are cast down.

7: 13, were comforted in your c.
Phil. 2 : 1, if any c. of love.
1 Thess. 4 : 18, c. one another with these words.
2 Thess. 2 : 17, c. your hearts.
Comfortable, Isa. 40 : 2, speak ye c. to Jerusalem.
Hos. 2 : 14, I will speak c. to her.
Zech. 1 : 13, Lord answered with c. words.
Comforter, the Spirit of Truth, John 14 : 26; 15 : 26; 16 : 7.
Job 16 : 2, miserable c. are ye all.
Ps. 69 : 20, looked for c., but found none.
John 14 : 16; 15 : 26; 16 : 7, the Holy Ghost the c.
Comfortless, John 14 : 18, will not leave you c.
Coming, Mal. 3 : 2, abide the day of his c. ?
Matt. 24 : 30, see the Son of man c.
Luke 19 : 23, at my c. I might have.
1 Cor. 1 : 7, waiting for the c. of our Lord.
15 : 23, Christ at his c.
Jas. 5 : 8, c. of the Lord draweth nigh.
Command, of God to Adam, Gen. 2 : 16; to Moses, Ex. 3 : 14; to Joshua, Josh. 1 : 9.
of Moses to the sons of Levi, Deut. 31 : 10.
of Christ to the Twelve, Matt. 10 : 5; Mark 16 : 15; to Peter, John 21 : 15.
Gen. 18 : 19, he will c. his children.
Deut. 28 : 8, Lord shall c. the blessing.
Josh. 1 : 16, all that thou c. us.
Ps. 33 : 9, he c. and it stood fast.
42 : 8, Lord will c. his lovingkindness.
Luke 8 : 25, he c. even the winds.
9 : 4, c. fire from heaven.
John 15 : 14, if ye do whatsoever I c.
Acts 17 : 30, c. all men every where.
1 Tim. 4 : 3, c. to abstain from meats.
Heb. 12 : 20, could not endure that c.
Commander, Isa. 55 : 4.
Commandments (ten) delivered, Ex. 20; 31 : 18; Deut. 5 : 6.
on tables of stone broken, Ex. 32 : 19.
renewed, Ex. 34 : 1; Deut. 10 : 1.
fulfilled by Christ, Matt. 5 : 17; 19 : 17; 22 : 35; Mark 10 : 17; Luke 10 : 25; 18 : 18.
Ps. 119 : 86, c. are faithful.
119 : 96, c. exceeding broad.
119 : 127, I love thy c.
119 : 143, thy c. are my delight.
Matt. 15 : 9; Mark 7 : 7; Col. 2 : 22, the c. of men.
John 13 : 34; 1 John 2 : 7; 2 John 5, a new c.
Rom. 7 : 12, c. is holy, just, and good.
1 Cor. 7 : 6; 2 Cor. 8 : 8, not by c.
Eph. 6 : 2, first c. with promise.
1 Tim. 1 : 5, end of the c. is charity.
Commend, Luke 16 : 8, Lord c. unjust steward.
Luke 23 : 46, into thy hands I c. my spirit.
Acts 20 : 32, I c. you to God.
Rom. 3 : 5, our unrighteousness c. righteousness of God.
5 : 8, God c. his love toward us.
2 Cor. 3 : 1; 5 : 12, c. ourselves.
4 : 2, c. to every man's conscience.
10 : 18, not he that c. himself is approved.
Commendation, 2 Cor. 3 : 1.
Commission, Ezra 3 : 36; Acts 26 : 12.
Commit, Ps. 37 : 5, c. thy way to the Lord.
Ezek. 33 : 15, without c. iniquity.

John 2 : 24, Jesus did not c. himself.
John 5 : 22, hath c. judgment to Son.
8 : 34, c. sin is the servant of sin.
Rom. 3 : 2, c. oracles of God.
2 Cor. 5 : 19, c. to us word of reconciliation.
1 Tim. 1 : 18, charge I c. unto thee.
6 : 20, keep that which is c. to thee.
1 Pet. 2 : 23, c. himself to him that judgeth.
1 John 3 : 4, whosoever c. sin.
Commodious, Acts 27 : 12.
Common, Lev. 4 : 27, c. people sin through ignorance.
Eccl. 6 : 1, evil, and it is c. among men.
Matt. 28 : 15, is c. reported.
Mark 12 : 37, he c. people heard him gladly.
Acts 2 : 44; 4 : 32, all things c.
5 : 18, in the c. prison.
10: 14; 11 : 8, never eaten anything c.
1 Cor. 10 : 13, temptation c. to men.
Jude 3, write of c. salvation.
Commonwealth, Eph. 2 : 12.
Commotion, Jer. 10 : 22; Luke 21 : 9.
Commune, Gen. 23 : 8, he c. with them.
Job 4 : 2, if we c. with thee.
Ps. 4 : 4; 77 : 6, c. with own heart.
Luke 6 : 11, c. one with another.
24 : 15, c. together and reasoned.
Communicate, Gal. 2 : 2, c. unto them that gospel.
Gal. 6 : 6, let him that is taught c.
Phil. 4 : 15, church c. with me.
1 Tim. 6 : 18, be willing to c.
Heb. 13 : 16, do good and c.
Communication, Matt. 5 : 37, let your c. be, Yea.
Luke 24 : 17, what manner of c.
1 Cor. 15 : 33, evil c. corrupt good manners.
Eph. 4 : 29, let no corrupt c. proceed.
Col. 3 : 8, filthy c. out of your mouth.
Philem. 6, c. of thy faith.
Communion of the body and blood of Christ, 1 Cor. 10 : 16.
Lord's Supper, instituted, Matt. 26 : 26; Mark 14 : 22; Luke 22 : 19; 1 Cor. 11 : 23.
self-examination and preparation for, Acts 2 : 42; 20 : 7; 1 Cor. 10 : 21; 11 : 28.
unworthily partaken of, 1 Cor. 11 : 27.
1 Cor. 10 : 16, c. of blood of body.,
2 Cor. 6 : 14, what c. hath light with darkness.
13 : 14, c. of Holy Ghost be with you.
Communion, or fellowship, of Saints, Acts 2 : 42; 2 Cor. 8 : 4; Gal. 2 : 9; Phil. 1 : 5; 1 John 1 : 3.
See Eph. 2 : 19.
Compact, Ps. 122 : 3, Jerusalem is a city c.
Eph. 4 : 16, the whole body c.
Companies, 1 Sam. 11 : 11; Mark 6 : 39.
Companion, Ps. 119 : 63, c. of all them that fear.
Ps. 122 : 8, brethren and c. sakes.
Prov. 13 : 20, c. of fools shall be destroyed.
Isa. 1 : 23, c. of thieves.
Acts 19 : 29, Paul's c. in travel.
Phil. 2 : 25, c. in labour.
Heb. 10 : 33, ye became c. of them.
Rev. 1 : 9, c. in tribulation.
Company, evil, to be avoided, Ps. 1 : 1; 26 : 4; Prov. 1 : 10; 2 : 12; 4 : 14; 12 : 11; 14 : 7; 22 : 14; 24 : 19; 29 : 2, 24; Rom. 1 : 32; 1 Cor. 5 : 9; 15 : 33; Eph. 5 : 7.
Gen. 50 : 9, very great c.

1 Sam. 19 : 20, c. of prophets.
Ps. 55 : 14, walked to house of God in c.
68 : 11, great was the c. of those.
Luke 9 : 14, sit down by c.
Acts 13 : 13, Paul and his c. loosed.
2 Thess. 3 : 14, have no c. with him.
Heb. 12 : 22, innumerable c. of angels.
Rev. 18 : 17, all the c. in ships.
Compare, Ps. 89 : 6, who in heaven c. to Lord ?
Prov. 3 : 15; 8 : 11, not to be c. to wisdom.
Isa. 40 : 18, what likeness will ye c. unto him ?
46 : 5, to whom will ye c. me ?
Lam. 4 : 2, c. to fine gold.
Rom. 8 : 18, not worthy to be c. with the glory.
1 Cor. 2 : 13, c. spiritual things with spiritual.
Comparison, Judg. 8 : 2, I done in c. of you ?
Hag. 2 : 3, in your eyes in c. of it.
Mark 4 : 30, with what c. shall we.
Compass [spread endeavours all over].
2 Sam. 22 : 5, waves of death c. me.
2 Ki. 3 : 9; Acts 28 : 13, fetched a c.
Ps. 18 : 4; 116 : 3, sorrows of death c. me.
26 : 6, c. thine altar.
32 : 7, c. with songs of deliverance.
Prov. 8 : 27, c. on face of the deep.
Isa. 50 : 11, c. yourselves with sparks.
Matt. 23 : 15, c. sea and land.
Luke 21 : 20, Jerusalem c. with armies.
Heb. 5 : 2, himself c. with infirmity.
12 : 1, c. about with cloud of witnesses.
Compassion to be shown to the afflicted, etc., Job 6 : 14; Ps. 35 : 13; Prov. 14 : 21; 19 : 17; 28 : 8; Zech. 7 : 9; Rom. 12 : 15; 2 Cor. 11 : 29; Gal. 6 : 2; Col. 3 : 12; Heb. 13 : 3; Jas. 1 : 27; 1 Pet. 3 : 8.
Christ's, Matt. 15 : 32; 20 : 34; Luke 7 : 13, 21; Heb. 2 : 18; 4 : 15; 5 : 2.
Isa. 49 : 15, that she should not have c.
Lam. 3 : 22, his c. fail not.
Matt. 9 : 36; 14 : 14; Mark 1 : 41; 6 : 34; Jesus moved with c.
Matt. 18 : 33, c. on thy fellowservant.
20 : 34, had c. on them, and touched.
Mark 5 : 19, the Lord hath had c.
9 : 22, have c. and help us.
Luke 7 : 13, Lord saw her, he had c.
10 : 33, Samaritan had c.
15 : 20, father had c. and ran.
Rom. 9 : 15, I will have c. on whom I will.
Heb. 5 : 2, have c. on ignorant.
1 John 3 : 17, shutteth up bowels of c.
Jude 22, of some have c.
Compel, Matt. 5 : 41, c. thee to go a mile.
27 : 32; Mark 15 : 21, c. to bear cross.
Luke 14 : 23, c. to come in.
Acts 26 : 11, I c. them to blaspheme.
Gal. 2 : 3, was c. to be circumcised.
Complain, Job 7 : 11, I will c. in bitterness of soul.
Ps. 77 : 3, I c. and my spirit was overwhelmed.
144 : 14, no c. in our streets.
Lam. 3 : 39, wherefore doth a living man c. ?
Jude 16, these are murmurers, c.
Complaint, 1 Sam. 1 : 16, out of abundance of my c.
Job 23 : 2, to day is my c. bitter.
Ps. 142 : 2, I poured out my c. before him.

Complete, Col. 2 : 10, ye are c. in him.
  4 : 12, stand c. in all.
Comprehend, Isa. 40 : 12, c. dust of the earth.
  John 1 : 5, the darkness c. it not.
  Eph. 3 : 18, able to c. with all saints.
Conceal, Ps. 40 : 10, not c. thy lovingkindness.
  Prov. 12 : 23, prudent c. knowledge.
  25 : 2, glory of God to c. a thing.
  Jer. 50 : 2, publish and c. not.
Conceit (pride) reproved, Prov. 3 : 7; 12 : 15;
  18 : 11; 26 : 5; 28 : 11; Isa. 5 : 21; Rom.
  11 : 25; 12 : 16.
  Prov. 18 : 11, as high wall in own c.
  26 : 12, a man wise in his own c.
  Rom. 11 : 25, lest wise in your own c.
  12 : 16, be not wise in own c.
Conceive, Job 15 : 35; Isa. 59 : 4, c. mischief.
  Ps. 51 : 5, in sin did mother c. me.
  Isa. 7 : 14, a virgin shall c.
  Acts 5 : 4, c. this in thine heart ?
  Jas. 1 : 15, when lust hath c.
Concern, Ps. 138 : 8, Lord perfect that c. me.
  Acts 28 : 31, things which c. Christ.
Concerning, Luke 24 : 27, things c. himself.
  Rom. 9 : 5, as c. the flesh Christ came.
  16 : 19, simple c. evil.
  Phil. 4 : 15, c. giving and receiving.
  1 Thess. 5 : 18, will of God c. you.
  1 Pet. 4 : 12, c. fiery trial.
Conclude, Rom. 3 : 28, we c. a man is justified.
  11 : 32, c. them all in unbelief.
  Gal. 3 : 22, hath c. all under sin.
Conclusion, Ex. 12 : 13.
Concord, 2 Cor. 6 : 15.
Concourse, Prov. 1 : 21; Acts 19 : 40.
Concubine, 2 Sam. 3 : 7; 5 : 13; 1 Ki. 11 : 3;
  Dan. 5 : 2, 3.
Concupiscence [sinful desire], Rom. 7 : 8,
  wrought in me all manner of c.
  to be mortified, Col. 3 : 5; 1 Thess. 4 : 5.
Condemn, Job 9 : 20, my mouth shall c. me.
  10 : 2, I will say to God, do not c. me.
  Isa. 50 : 9, who is he shall c. me ?
  Matt. 12 : 7, not have c. guiltless.
  12 : 42; Luke 11 : 31, rise in judgment and c.
  Mark 14 : 64, all c. him to be guilty.
  Luke 6 : 37, c. not, and ye shall not be c.
  John 3 : 17, God sent not his Son to c. the
  world.
  Rom. 8 : 3, c. sin in the flesh.
  8 : 34, who is he that c. ?
  Jas. 5 : 6, ye c. and killed the just.
  1 John 3 : 21, if our heart c. us not.
Condemnation for sin, universal, Ps. 14 : 3;
  53 : 3; Rom. 3 : 12, 19; 5 : 12; 6 : 23.
  for unbelief, etc., Matt. 11 : 20; 23 : 14;
  John 3 : 18.
  by the law, 2 Cor. 3 : 6, 9.
  of false teachers, 2 Pet. 2 : 1; Jude 4.
  deliverance from, by Christ, John 3 : 18;
  5 : 24; Rom. 8 : 1, 33.
  final, Matt. 25 : 46; Rev. 20 : 15.
  John 3 : 19, this is the c., that light.
  Rom. 5 : 16, judgment by one to c.
  8 : 1, there is no c. to them in Christ.
  2 Cor. 3 : 9, ministration of c.
  1 Tim. 3 : 6, the c. of the devil.
  Jas. 5 : 12, lest ye fall into c.

Condescend, Rom. 12 : 16, c. to men of low
  estate.
Condition, 1 Sam. 11 : 2; Luke 14 : 32.
Conduct, 2 Sam. 19 : 15, to c. the king over the
  Jordan.
  Acts 17 : 15, c. Paul brought him unto Athens.
  1 Cor. 16 : 11, c. him forth in peace.
Conduit. " The conduit of the upper pool "
  (2 Ki. 18 : 17) was a subterranean water-
  course to Jerusalem from the elevated
  ground beyond the Damascus gate. Solomon built aqueducts which conveyed water
  from the Judæan hills to the pools of
  Gihon on Mount Zion. Pilate reconstruc-
  ted the work, a large part of which still
  exists.
Coney [Heb. shaphan]. Enumerated among the
  unclean animals in Lev. 11 : 5. Its timid,
  cautious habits and defenceless character
  are referred to in Scripture. It inhabits
  mountains and rocks (Prov. 30 : 26), is a
  soft furred and hare-like animal, with the
  toes joined together by skin, and does not
  chew the cud. There can be little doubt of
  its being the hyrax.
  Lev. 11 : 5, c. unclean unto you.
  Ps. 104 : 18, rocks a refuge for the c.
  Prov. 30 : 26, c. a feeble folk.
Confection, Ex. 30 : 35, make a c. after art.
  1 Sam. 8 : 13, your daughters to be c.
Confederate, Gen. 14 : 13; Ps. 83 : 5; Isa. 7 : 2.
Conference, Gal. 2 : 6.
Conferred, 1 Ki. 1 : 7, he c. with Joab.
  Acts 4 : 15, c. among themselves.
  Gal. 1 : 16, c. not with flesh and blood.
Confess, Lev. 26 : 40, if they c. their iniquity.
  Ps. 32 : 5, I said, I will c. my transgression.
  Prov. 28 : 13, who so c. and forsaketh.
  Matt. 10 : 32; Luke 12 : 8, c. me before men.
  John 9 : 22, if any man did c.
  12 : 42, did not c. him lest.
  Acts 23 : 8, Pharisees c. both.
  Rom. 14 : 11; Phil. 2 : 11, every tongue c.
  Heb. 11 : 13, c. they were strangers.
  Jas. 5 : 16, c. your faults one to another.
  1 John 1 : 9, if we c. our sins.
  4 : 2, every spirit that c. Christ.
  Rev. 3 : 5, I will c. his name before my
  Father.
Confession of Christ unto salvation, Matt.
  10 : 32; Mark 8 : 35; John 12 : 42; Rom.
  10 : 9; 2 Tim. 2 : 12; 1 John 2 : 23; 4 : 2.
  of sin, Lev. 5 : 5; Josh. 7 : 19; Hos. 5 : 15;
  1 John 1 : 9.
  examples of, Num. 12 : 11; 21 : 7; Josh.
  7 : 20; 1 Sam. 7; 15 : 24; Ezra 9 : 6; Neh.
  1 : 6; 9; Ps. 51; Dan. 9 : 4; Luke 23 : 41.
  at the offering of firstfruits, Deut. 26 : 1.
  " one to another," Jas. 5 : 16.
Confidence, through faith, Prov. 3 : 26; 14 : 26;
  Eph. 3 : 12; Heb. 3 : 6; 10 : 35; 1 John
  2 : 28; 3 : 21; 5 : 14.
  none in the flesh, Phil. 3 : 3.
  Ps. 65 : 5, the c. of all the ends of the earth.
  118 : 8, than put c. in man.
  Prov. 14 : 26, in fear of Lord is strong c.
  Isa. 30 : 15, in c. shall be your strength.
  Eph. 3 : 12, access with c. by faith.
  Phil. 3 : 3, no c. in the flesh.

Heb. 3 : 6, hold fast c.
10 : 35, cast not away c.
1 John 3 : 21, we have c. toward God.
5 : 14, this is the c. we have in him.
Confident, Ps. 27 : 3, in this will I be c.
Luke 22 : 59, another c. affirmed.
2 Cor. 9 : 4, same c. boasting.
Phil. 1 : 14, waxing c. by my bonds.
Confirm, Isa. 35 : 3, c. the feeble knees.
Mark 16 : 20, c. the word with signs.
Acts 14 : 22, c. souls of disciples.
Rom. 15 : 8, c. promises made.
Confirmation, Phil. 1 : 7, in the c. of the Gospel.
Heb. 6 : 16, an oath for c.
Conflict, Phil. 1 : 30, same c. ye saw in me.
Col. 2 : 1, what c. I have for you.
Conform, Rom. 8 : 29, c. to image of his Son.
12 : 2, not c. to this world.
Phil. 3 : 10, made c. to his death.
Confound, Gen. 11 : 7, c. their language.
Ps. 22 : 5, fathers trusted, and were not c.
40 : 14; 70 : 2, ashamed and c.
Acts 2 : 6, multitude were c.
1 Pet. 2 : 6, believeth shall not be c.
Confused, Isa. 9 : 5, battle is with c. noise.
Acts 19 : 32, the assembly was c.
Confusion, Dan. 9 : 7, to us belongeth c. of faces.
Acts 19 : 29, city was filled with c.
1 Cor. 14 : 33, God not author of c.
Congregation (of Israel), all to keep the passover, Ex. 12, etc.
sin offering for, Lev. 4 : 13; 16 : 17.
to stone offenders, Lev. 24 : 14; Num. 14 : 10; 15 : 35.
who not to enter, Deut. 23 : 1.
Lev. 16 : 33, atonement for all the c.
Num. 14 : 10, all the c. bade stone them.
Neh. 5 : 13, all the c. said, Amen.
Ps. 1 : 5, nor sinners in c. of the righteous.
22 : 22, in midst of c. will I praise.
Prov. 21 : 16, in the c. of the dead.
Joel 2 : 16, sanctify the c.
Acts 13 : 43, when c. was broken up.
Conquerors, Rom. 8 : 37, we are more than c.
Rev. 6 : 2, c. and to conquer.
Conscience [consciousness], Heb. 10 : 2, no more c. of sin, convicts of sin, Gen. 3 : 10; 4 : 13; 42 : 21; 1 Sam. 24 : 5; Prov. 20 : 27; Matt. 27 : 3; Luke 9 : 7; John 8 : 9; Rom. 2 : 15.
purified by faith, 1 Tim. 1 : 19; 3 : 9; 2 Tim. 1 : 3.
purified by blood of Christ, Heb. 9 : 14; 10 : 2, 22.
a good, Heb. 13 : 18; 1 Pet. 3 : 16.
effects of a good, Acts 24 : 16; Rom. 13 : 5; 14 : 22; 2 Cor. 1 : 12; 1 Pet. 2 : 19.
of others to be respected, Rom. 14 : 21; 1 Cor. 8; 10 : 28.
seared, 1 Tim. 4 : 2; defiled, Titus 1 : 15.
ignorant, Acts 26 : 9; Rom. 10 : 2.
Acts 24 : 16, c. void of offence.
Rom. 2 : 15; 9 : 1; 2 Cor. 1 : 12, c. bearing witness.
1 Tim. 1 : 5, 19; Heb. 13 : 18; 1 Pet. 3 : 16, a good c.
Heb. 9 : 14, purge c. from dead works.
10 : 22, hearts sprinkled from evil c.

Consecrate, 1 Chr. 29 : 5, to c. his service to the Lord.
Mic. 4 : 13, I will c. their gain to Lord.
Heb. 7 : 28, Son, who is c. for evermore.
10 : 20, living way, which he hath c.
Consecration, of priests, Ex. 29; Lev. 8.
of the Levites, Num. 8 : 5.
of Christ, Heb. 7; 8; 10 : 20.
Consent, Ps. 50 : 18, a thief, thou c. with him.
Prov. 1 : 10, if sinners entice thee, c. not.
Zeph. 3 : 9, to serve with one c.
Luke 14 : 18, with one c. began to make excuse.
Consider, Deut. 32 : 29, wise to c. latter end.
Ps. 8 : 3, when I c. thy heavens.
41 : 1, blessed is he that c. the poor.
48 : 13, c. her palaces.
50 : 22, c. this, ye that forget God.
119 : 153, c. mine affliction.
Prov. 6 : 6, go to ant, c. her ways.
23 : 1, c. diligently what is before thee.
Eccl. 5 : 1, they c. not that they do evil.
7 : 14, in days of adversity c.
Isa. 1 : 3, my people doth not c.
Jer. 23 : 20; 30 : 24, in latter days ye shall c.
Ezek. 12 : 3, it may be they will c.
Hag. 1 : 5, 7, c. your ways.
Matt. 6 : 28; Luke 12 : 27, c. the lilies.
Matt. 7 : 3, c. not the beam.
Luke 12 : 24, c. the ravens.
John 11 : 50, nor c. it is expedient.
Gal. 6 : 1, c. thyself, lest thou also be tempted.
Heb. 3 : 1, c. the Apostle and High Priest.
7 : 4, c. how great this man was.
12 : 3, c. him that endured.
13 : 7, c. the end of their conversation.
Consideration, exhortations to, Deut. 4 : 39; 32 : 29; Job 23 : 15; 37 : 14; Ps. 8 : 3; 50 : 22; Prov. 6 : 6; Eccl. 4 : 1; 5 : 1; 7 : 13; Hag. 1 : 5; Matt. 6 : 28; 2 Tim. 2 : 7; Heb. 3 : 1; 7 : 4; 10 : 24; 12 : 3.
Consist, Luke 12 : 15, life c. not in the abundance.
Col. 1 : 17, by him all things c.
Consolation under affliction, Deut. 33 : 27; Job 19 : 25; Ps. 10 : 14; 23; 34 : 6; 41 : 3; 42 : 5; 51 : 17; 55 : 22; 69 : 29; 71 : 9; 18; 73 : 26; 94 : 19; 119 : 50; 126; Eccl. 7 : 3; Isa. 1 : 18; 12 : 1; Lam. 3 : 22; Ezek. 14 : 22; Hos. 2 : 14; Mic. 7 : 18; Zech. 1 : 17; Matt. 11 : 28; Luke 4 : 18; 15; John 14; 15; 16; Rom. 15 : 4; 16 : 20; 1 Cor. 10 : 13; 14 : 3; 2 Cor. 1 : 3; 5 : 1; 7 : 6; 12 : 9; Col. 1 : 11; 1 Thess. 4 : 14; 5 : 11; 2 Thess. 2 : 16; Heb. 4 : 9; 6 : 18; 12; Jas. 1 : 12; 4 : 7; 2 Pet. 2 : 9; Rev. 2 : 10; 7 : 14; 14 : 13.
Job 15 : 11, are the c. of God small ?
Luke 6 : 24, ye have received your c.
Rom. 15 : 5, the God of c.
Phil. 2 : 1, if there be any c. in Christ.
2 Thess. 2 : 16, everlasting c.
Heb. 6 : 18, strong c.
Consorted [cast their lot together], Acts 17 : 4.
Conspiracy against Christ, Matt. 26 : 3; Mark 3 : 6; 14 : 1; Luke 22 : 2; John 11 : 55; 13 : 18.
against Paul, Acts 23 : 12.
2 Ki. 12 : 20, arose and made a c.

Ezek. 22 : 25, **c.** of her prophets.
Conspirators, 2 Sam. 15 : 31.
Conspired, Gen. 37 : 18; 2 Chr. 24 : 25; Amos 7 : 10.
Constancy of Ruth, Ruth 1 : 14.
of Priscilla and Aquila, Rom. 16 : 3, 4.
Constant, 1 Chr. 28 : 7; Prov. 21 : 28; Acts 12 : 15; Titus 3 : 8.
Constellations, Isa. 13 : 10.
Constrain, Job 32 : 18, the spirit in me **c.** me.
Matt. 14 : 22; Mark 6 : 45, Jesus **c.** disciples.
Luke 24 : 29, **c.** him, saying, abide.
2 Cor. 5 : 14, love of Christ **c.** us.
1 Pet. 5 : 2, the oversight, not by **c.**
Consult, Ps. 62 : 4, only **c.** to cast him down.
Matt. 26 : 4, **c.** that they might take Jesus.
Mark 15 : 1, chief priests held a **c.**
John 12 : 10, **c.** to put Lazarus to death.
Consume, Ex. 3 : 2, bush was not **c.**
Deut. 4 : 24; 9 : 3; Heb. 12 : 29, a **c.** fire.
Judg. 6 : 21, fire out of rock **c.** flesh.
1 Ki. 18 : 38; 2 Chr. 7 : 1, fire fell, and **c.** the sacrifice.
Job 4 : 9, by breath of his nostrils **c.**
20 : 26, fire not blown shall **c.** him.
Ps. 39 : 11, his beauty to **c.** away.
Mal. 3 : 6, therefore ye are not **c.**
Luke 9 : 54, fire to **c.** them, as Elias did.
Gal. 5 : 15, take heed that ye be not **c.**
Jas. 4 : 3, may **c.** it on your lusts.
Contain, 1 Ki. 8 : 27; 2 Chr. 2 : 6; 6 : 18, heaven of heavens cannot **c.** thee.
John 21 : 25, world not **c.** the books.
1 Pet. 2 : 6, it is **c.** in scripture.
Contemn, Ps. 10 : 13, wicked **c.** God.
15 : 4, in whose eyes a vile person is **c.**
107 : 11, **c.** counsel of Most High.
Ezek. 21 : 10, it **c.** rod of my son.
Contempt, Job 12 : 21; Ps. 107 : 40, **c.** on princes.
Ps. 123 : 3, exceedingly filled with **c.**
Prov. 18 : 3, wicked cometh, then cometh **c.**
Dan. 12 : 2, awake to everlasting **c.**
Contemptible, Mal. 2 : 9, I made you **c.**
2 Cor. 10 : 10, his speech **c.**
Contend, Isa. 49 : 25, I will **c.** with him that **c.**
50 : 8, who will **c.** with me?
Jer. 12 : 5, how canst thou **c.** with horses ?
Jude 3, earnestly **c.** for the faith.
Content, Job 6 : 28, now therefore be **c.**
Mark 15 : 15, willing to **c.** the people.
Luke 3 : 14, be **c.** with your wages.
Phil. 4 : 11, I have learned to be **c.**
1 Tim. 6 : 6, godliness with **c.** is great gain.
Heb. 13 : 5, be **c.** with such things as ye have.
Contention, Prov. 13 : 10, by pride cometh **c.**
18 : 18, lot causeth **c.** to cease.
23 : 29, who hath **c.** ?
Acts 15 : 39, the **c.** was sharp.
1 Cor. 1 : 11, there are **c.** among you.
Phil. 1 : 16, preach Christ of **c.**
Titus 3 : 9, avoid **c.** and strivings.
Contentious, Prov. 27 : 15, rainy day and a **c.** woman.
Rom. 2 : 8, unto them that are **c.**
1 Cor. 11 : 16, any man seem to be **c.**
See Prov. 21 : 19; 26 : 21.
Contentment, with godliness, great gain, Ps. 37 : 10; Prov. 30 : 8; 1 Tim. 6 : 6.

exhortations to, Ps. 37 : 1; Luke 3 : 14; 1 Cor. 7 : 20; 1 Tim. 6 : 8; Heb. 13 : 5.
of Paul, 1 Cor. 4 : 11; Phil. 4 : 11.
Continual, Gen. 6 : 5, imagination evil **c.**
Ps. 34 : 1; 71 : 6, praise **c.** in my mouth.
40 : 11, truth **c.** preserve me.
73 : 23, I am **c.** with thee.
Prov. 6 : 21, bind them **c.** on thine heart.
Isa. 14 : 6, smote with a **c.** stroke.
52 : 5, my name is **c.** blasphemed.
Luke 18 : 5, lest by her **c.** coming.
24 : 53, were **c.** in the temple.
Acts 6 : 4, give ourselves **c.** to prayer.
Rom. 9 : 2, I have **c.** sorrow in my heart.
Heb. 7 : 3, abideth a priest **c.**
Continue, Ps. 36 : 10, **c.** thy lovingkindness.
72 : 17, name shall **c.** as long as the sun.
Isa. 5 : 11, **c.** till wine inflame them.
Luke 6 : 12, he **c.** all night in prayer.
John 8 : 31, if ye **c.** in my word.
15 : 9, **c.** ye in my love.
Acts 1 : 14; 2 : 46, **c.** with one accord.
14 : 22, exhorting them to **c.** in faith.
Rom. 6 : 1, shall we **c.** in sin ?
12 : 12; Col. 4 : 2, **c.** in prayer.
Gal. 3 : 10, that **c.** not in all things.
Col. 1 : 23; 1 Tim. 2 : 15, if ye **c.** in faith.
Heb. 7 : 23, not suffered to **c.** by reason.
Heb. 13 : 14, here have we no **c.** city.
Jas. 4 : 13, **c.** there a year, and buy.
2 Pet. 3 : 4, all things **c.** as they were.
1 John 2 : 19, no doubt have **c.** with us.
Contradiction, Heb. 7 : 7, without **c.** less is blessed.
12 : 3, endured such **c.** of sinners.
Acts 13 : 45, with envy, **c.** and blasphem. ing.
Contrary, Matt. 15 : 24, wind was **c.**
Acts 18 : 13, **c.** to the law.
26 : 9, **c.** to name of Jesus.
Gal. 5 : 17, **c.** the one to the other.
Col. 2 : 14, handwriting **c.** to us.
1 Thess. 2 : 15, **c.** to all men.
1 Tim. 1 : 10, **c.** to sound doctrine.
1 Pet. 3 : 9, railing, but **c.** blessing.
Contribution for saints, Acts 20 : 35; Rom. 15 : 26; 2 Cor. 8.
Contrite heart not despised by God, Ps. 34 : 18; 51 : 17; Isa. 57 : 15; 66 : 2.
Ps. 34 : 18, such as be of **c.** spirit.
51 : 17, **c.** heart, wilt not despise.
Isa. 57 : 15, that is of a **c.** spirit, to revive heart of **c.** ones.
66 : 2, of **c.** spirit and trembleth.
Controversies, how to be decided, Deut. 17 : 8; 19 : 16; 21 : 5.
Jer. 25 : 31, a **c.** with the nations.
Mic. 6 : 2, Lord hath a **c.** with his people.
1 Tim. 3 : 16, without **c.** great is the mystery.
Convenient, Prov. 30 : 8, feed me with food **c.**
Mark 6 : 21, a **c.** day was come.
Acts 24 : 25, when I have a **c.** season.
Rom. 1 : 28, things which are not **c.**
Eph. 5 : 4, foolish talking, jesting, not **c.**
Conversant, Josh. 8 : 35; 1 Sam. 25 : 15.
Conversation (conduct), upright, Ps. 37 : 14; 50 : 23; Phil. 3 : 20; 1 Tim. 4 : 12; Heb. 13 : 5; Jas. 3 : 13; 1 Pet. 2 : 12; 2 Pet. 3 : 11.

as becometh the Gospel, 2 Cor. 1 : 12; (Gal. 1 : 13); Eph. 4 : 1; Phil. 1 : 27; 1 Pet. 1 : 15.

(speech) of the Lord with Moses, Ex. 33 : 9.

of Jesus with Nicodemus, John 3.

of Jesus with woman of Samaria, John 4 : 7-27.

on the walk to Emmaus, Luke 24 : 13.

of Peter with Cornelius, Acts 10 : 27.

of Festus and Agrippa, Acts 26 : 31.

Ps. 37 : 14, such as be of upright c.

50 : 23, ordereth his c. aright.

Eph. 2 : 3, had our c. in times past.

Phil. 1 : 27, c. as becometh the Gospel.

3 : 20, our c. is in heaven.

Heb. 13 : 5, c. without covetousness.

1 Pet. 1 : 15; 2 Pet. 3 : 11, holy c.

1 Pet. 2 : 12, your c. honest among Gentiles.

Conversion of sinners proceeds from God, 1 Ki. 18 : 37; Ps. 19 : 7; 78 : 34; Prov. 1 : 23; Jer. 31 : 18; John 6 : 44; Acts 3 : 26; 11 : 21.

See Ps. 51 : 13; Isa. 1 : 16; 6 : 10; Ezek. 18 : 23; 36 : 25; Joel 2 : 13; 2 Cor. 5 : 17; 1 Thess. 1 : 9.

call to, Isa. 1 : 16; Matt. 3 : 2; 4 : 17; 10 : 7; Acts 2 : 38; 17 : 30; Jas. 4 : 8.

prayer for, Ps. 80 : 7; 85 : 4; Lam. 5 : 21.

instruments of, blessed, Dan. 12 : 3; 1 Tim. 4 : 16; Jas. 5 : 19.

of the Jews, Acts 2 : 41; 4 : 32; 6 : 7.

of Paul, Acts 9; 22; 26.

of the Gentiles foretold, Isa. 2 : 2; 11 : 10; 60 : 5; 66 : 12.

of the Gentiles fulfilled, Acts 8 : 26; 10; 15 : 3; Rom. 10; 11; 1 Cor. 1; Eph. 2; 3; 1 Thess. 1.

Convert, Ps. 19 : 7, law of Lord perfect, c. soul. 51 : 13, sinners be c. unto thee.

Isa. 6 : 10; Matt. 13 : 15; Mark 4 : 12; John 12 : 40; Acts 28 : 27, lest they c.

Matt. 18 : 3, except ye be c.

Luke 22 : 32, when c., strengthen thy brethren.

Acts 3 : 19, repent and be c.

Jas. 5 : 19, do err, and one c. him.

Convey, 1 Ki. 5 : 9; Neh. 2 : 7; John 5 : 13.

Convicted, John 8 : 9.

Convince, John 8 : 46, which of you c. me of sin?

1 Cor. 14 : 24, he is c. of all.

Titus 1 : 9, able to c. gainsayers.

Convocation, Ex. 12 : 16; Lev. 23 : 2, 4.

Cook, 1 Sam. 8 : 13, daughters to be c.

1 Sam. 9 : 23, Samuel said to the c., Bring.

Cool, Gen. 3 : 8, walking in c. of the day.

Luke 16 : 24, and c. my tongue.

Copper [Heb. Něchŏsheth; Χαλκός; Aereus; Brass (bronze)], Ex. 38 : 3; 2 Ki. 25 : 13. Where our translators use the term brass, copper should often be understood. At the same time it is to be remembered that the alloy of copper and tin, known as bronze, has been in use since very early times, and in the countries of the west of Europe at least, its use preceded that of iron. The brazen serpent, the sacrificial forks, the mirrors of the Hebrew women, etc., were probably made of bronze.

Ezra 8 : 27, two vessels of fine c.

2 Tim. 4 : 14, Alexander the c. smith.

Copy of the law to be written by the king, Deut. 17 : 18.

Deut. 17 : 18, write a c. of law.

Josh. 8 : 32, on stones c. of law of Moses.

Ezra 4 : 11; 5 : 6, c. of letter sent.

Coral [Heb. ramoth; Corallium rubrum]. The precious coral is, in Job 28 : 18, associated with pearls, drawn up from the depths of the sea. This coral is a product of both the Red and Mediterranean Seas.

Corban. Mark 7 : 11. Jews sometimes rid themselves of their obligations by the present of a gift (Corban) to the Temple. The text is best rendered in the R.V.

Corcyra, an island in the Adriatic Sea.

Cord, Josh. 2 : 15, let spies down by a c.

Ps. 2 : 3, let us cast away their c.

118 : 27, bind the sacrifice with c.

Prov. 5 : 22, holden with the c. of sins.

Eccl. 4 : 12, a threefold c.

12 : 6, silver c. loosed.

Isa. 5 : 18, draw iniquity with c.

54 : 2, lengthen thy c.

Hos. 11 : 4, c. of a man.

John 2 : 15, scourge of small c.

Coriander [Heb. gad] is a well known umbel-bearing plant (Coriandrum sativum). The fruits have an aromatic flavour, and are used to season confectionery. It is only referred to in the Bible as indicating the size of the manna (Ex. 16 : 31 and Num. 11 : 7).

Coin of Corinth, shewing the wreaths worn by victors in the Isthmian games.

Corinth (cŏr-ĭnth), the capital of Achaia, 1 Cor. 1 : 2; 2 Tim. 4 : 20.

Paul and Apollos at, Acts 18; 19 : 1.

Corinthians, their divisions, etc., censured, 1 Cor. 1; 5; 11 : 18; 2 Cor. 13.

their gifts and graces, 2 Cor. 3.

instructed concerning spiritual gifts, 1 Cor. 14; and the resurrection, 1 Cor. 15.

exhorted to charity, etc., 1 Cor. 13; 14 : 1; 2 Cor. 8; 9.

their false teachers exposed, 2 Cor. 11 : 3, 4, 13.

Paul commends himself to, 2 Cor. 11; 12.

Corinthians, First Epistle to.

Place and Date.—The Epistle was written at or near Ephesus, before Pentecost (16 :8), and probably in A.D. 57. It was written near the end of St. Paul's second and long visit to Ephesus on his third missionary journey (Acts 19 : 1, 10; 20 : 31), shortly before his departure for Greece (19 : 21).

Church of Corinth.—Corinth, destroyed by Mummius (146 B.C.), was restored by Julius Cæsar (46 B.C.); and in a century it had become the political and commercial capital of Greece. As such it was the abode of the proconsul Gallio (Acts 18 : 12). With its luxury and its worship of Aphrodite, it became a byword for licentiousness. The Corinthian Christians had been rescued from this (1 Cor. 6 : 10, 11); but the evil influence was always there (5). The planting of the Gospel in this corrupt centre was the work of St. Paul (3 : 6, 10; 4 : 15; 16 : 15; 1 : 16). He was probably the first Christian to enter Corinth (c. A.D. 52).

The Occasion.—Five years after Paul's departure he was moved by three things to write our First Epistle—the news of the monstrous case of incest, perhaps brought by Stephanas and others (16 : 17); the news of the factions and kindred evils, brought by some of the household of Chloe (1 : 11); and the letter from the Corinthians (7 : 1).

Contents.—The contents of the Epistle are determined by the evils reported and the questions asked, and these involve a considerable number of disconnected topics. After the usual Salutation and Thanksgiving (1 : 1-9), he deals with the Factions (1 : 10–4 : 20) and Impurity (4 : 21–6 : 20). He then answers their questions about Marriage (7), Heathen Feasts (8 : 1–9 : 1), Public Worship and Spiritual Gifts (11 : 2–14 : 40), and expounds the doctrine of the Resurrection (15). He ends with Charges and Salutations (16). These contents are more varied than those of any other Epistle. They form a series of Tracts for the Times, and give us our first and fullest information about the institutions and ideas of the Apostolic age, e.g., Baptism (1 : 13-17); the Eucharist, which is evidently united with the Agape or Love-Feast (10 : 15-22; 11 : 23-34); the Ministry (12 : 28, 29); Public Worship (14 : 14-39); a Creed (15 : 3, 4); Belief in a Future State (15 : 12-34); the Observance of Sunday (16 : 2); the Holy Kiss (16 : 20).

Corinthians, Second Epistle to.

Place and Date.—Written in Macedonia, in the autumn of A.D. 57, but perhaps not all at one time or place. Apparently he was suffering from his chronic malady (1 : 9; 4 : 10-12, 16); certainly he was much depressed (1 : 6; 4 : 8, 9; 5 : 2; 7 : 4). The bearers of the letter were Titus and two others, who are not named, and about whom there have been many futile conjectures.

The Occasion.—The motive for writing it was news brought from Corinth by Titus (7 : 5, 6), especially as to the way in which the First Epistle had been received, and the success of the Judaising party, who had been intriguing in Corinth, as elsewhere, against the authority of St. Paul.

Contents.—The contents are less varied than those of the First Epistle, but the changes from one subject to another are very abrupt. After the usual Salutation and Thanksgiving (1 : 1-11), he discusses the News brought by Titus (1 : 12–7 : 16), the Collection for the Churches in Judea (8 : 1—9 : 15), and his own Apostolic Authority (10 : 1–12 : 13). He ends with Warning and Blessing (12 : 14–13 : 13).

Cormorant [Heb. shalak]. Enumerated among the unclean birds in Lev. 11 : 17 and Deut. 14 : 17. This bird is still common on the coasts and rivers of Palestine.

Corn. The ordinary cereals of Palestine, wheat and barley, and to some extent, millet and spelt, are embraced in this word. There was corn in general, as in corn and wine, the standing crop of corn, the ears of corn, and parched corn. Corn was much grown in Palestine, and in some parts of Egypt corn was the principal crop. The wheat of Minnith was traded in by the Phœnicians. Several Hebrew words are used to denote the different sorts and stages in the growth of this cereal.

" The treading out of." The mode was this : a large area of beaten and hardened earth having been made, the sheaves of corn were placed on it, and over these oxen were driven (Deut. 25 : 4) to crush out the grain. The law of Moses prohibited the Israelites from muzzling the ox when so occupied. St. Paul appeals to the natural justice of this precept (1 Cor. 9 : 9) to show the right of Christian workers to support in and from their work.

Gen. 42 : 2; Acts 7 : 12, c. in Egypt.
Deut. 25 : 4; 1 Cor. 9 : 9; I Tim. 5 : 18, ox treadeth c.
Judg. 15 : 5, let foxes go into standing c.
Job 5 : 26, like as a shock of c.
Ps. 65 : 9, thou preparest them c.
    72 : 16, handful of c. in the earth.
Prov. 11 : 26, he that withholdeth c.
Zech. 9 : 17, c. shall make men cheerful.
Matt. 12 : 1; Mark 2 : 23; Luke 6 : 1, pluck ears of c.
Mark 4 : 28, full c. in the ear.
John 12 : 24, a c. of wheat fall into ground.

Cornelius (cŏr-nē-lĭ-ŭs), devout centurion, his prayer answered, Acts 10 : 3.
sends for Peter, Acts 10 : 9.
baptized, Acts 10 : 48.

Corner, Ps. 118 : 22; Eph. 2 : 20, head stone of c.
    144 : 12, daughters as c. stones.
Isa. 28 : 16; 1 Pet. 2 : 6, a precious c. stone.
Isa. 30 : 20, teachers removed into c.
Matt. 6 : 5, pray in c. of the streets.
Rev. 7 : 1, four c. of the earth.

Cornet, 1 Chr. 15 : 28; Ps. 98 : 6, with sound of the c.
Dan. 3 : 5; Hos. 5 : 8.

Cornfloor, Hos. 9 : 1, reward upon every c.

Corpse, Mark 6 : 29.

Correct, Ps. 39 : 11, dost c. man.
Prov. 3 : 12, whom Lord loveth he c.

Jer. 30 : 11; 46 : 28 , I will c. thee in measure.

Heb. 12 : 9, fathers which c. us.

Correction, Prov. 3 : 11, neither be weary of his c.

Jer. 2 : 30; 5 : 3; 7 : 28; Zeph. 3 : 2, receive c.

2 Tim. 3 : 16, Scripture profitable for c.

Corrupt, Gen. 6 : 11, the earth was c.

Matt. 6 : 19 Luke 12 : 33, moth c.

Matt. 7 : 17; 12 : 33; Luke 6 : 43, a c. tree.

1 Cor. 15 : 33, evil communications c.

Eph. 4 : 22, put off old man, which is c.

1 Tim. 6 : 5; 2 Tim. 3 : 8, men of c. minds.

Jas. 5 : 2, your riches are c.

Corrupters, Isa. 1 : 4 ; Jer. 6 : 28.

Corruptible, Rom. 1 : 23, image like to c. man.

1 Cor. 9 : 25, a c. crown.

15 : 53, c. must put on incorruption.

1 Pet. 1 : 18, not redeemed with c. things.

Corruption, Ps. 16 : 10; 49 : 9; Acts 2 : 27; 13 : 35, not see c.

Jonah 2 : 6, brought up life from c.

Acts 2 : 31, neither his flesh did see c.

Rom. 8 : 21, bondage of c.

1 Cor. 15 : 42, sown in c.

Gal. 6 : 8, of flesh reap c.

2 Pet. 1 : 4, the c. that is in world.

2 : 12, perish in their own c.

Cost, 2 Sam. 24 : 24; 1 Chr. 21 : 24, offer of that which c. nothing.

Luke 14 : 28, sitteth not down and counteth c.

Costliness, Rev. 18 : 19, made rich by her c.

Costly, John 12 : 3, spikenard, c.

1 Tim. 2 : 9, c. array.

Couch, Luke 5 : 19, let him down with c.

Acts 5 : 15, laid sick on c.

Council of the Jews, Matt. 26 : 3, 59; Mark 15 : 1.

the apostles arraigned before, Acts 4, 5 . 29.

Paul's discourse before, Acts 23.

Matt. 5 : 22, in danger of c.

Luke 22 : 66, led Jesus into their c.

Acts 5 : 27, set them before c.

6 : 12, brought Stephen to c.

Counsel, advantage of good, Prov. 12 : 15; 13 : 10; 20 : 18; 27 : 9.

of God, asked by Israel, Judg. 20 : 18; by Saul, 1 Sam. 14 : 37; by David, 1 Sam. 23 : 2, 11; 30 : 8; 1 Chr. 14 : 10.

See Ps. 16 : 7; 33 : 11; 73 : 24; Prov. 8 : 14; Eccl. 8 : 2; Rev. 3 : 18.

danger of rejecting, 2 Chr. 25 : 16; Prov. 1 : 25, 26; Jer. 23 : 18-22; Luke 7 : 30.

of the wicked condemned, Job 5 : 13; 10 : 3; 21 : 16; Ps. 1 : 1; 5 : 10; 33 : 10; 64 : 2; 81 : 12; 106 : 43; Isa. 7 : 5; Hos. 11 : 6; Mic. 6 : 16.

Neh. 4 : 15, brought c. to nought.

Job 38 : 2; 42 : 3, darkeneth c. by words.

Ps. 1 : 1, c. of the ungodly.

33 : 11; Prov. 19 : 21, c. of Lord standeth.

Ps. 55 : 14, took sweet c. together.

73 : 24, guide me with thy c.

Prov. 1 : 25, set at nought all my c.

Isa. 28 : 29, wonderful in c.

40 : 14, with whom took he c. ?

Jer. 32 : 19, great in c., mighty in working.

Mark 3 : 6; John 11 : 53, took c. against Jesus.

Acts 2 : 23, determinate c. of God.

5 : 38, if this c. be of men.

Acts 20 : 27, declare all the c. of God.

1 Cor. 4 : 5, make manifest c. of the heart.

Eph. 1 : 11, after the c. of his own will.

Heb. 6 : 17, the immutability of his c.

Rev. 3 : 18, I c. thee to buy gold tried in fire.

Counsellers, safety in multitude of, Prov. 11 : 14; 15 : 22; 24 : 6.

Ps. 119 : 24, thy testimonies my c.

Prov. 11 : 14; 15 : 22; 24 : 6, in multitude of c.

Mark 15 : 43; Luke 23 : 50, an honourable c.

Rom. 11 : 34, who hath been his c. ?

Count, Gen. 15 : 6; Ps. 106 : 31; Rom. 4 : 3; Gal. 3 : 6, c. for righteousness.

Ps. 44 : 22, c. as sheep for the slaughter.

Isa. 32 : 15, field be c. for a forest.

Matt. 14 : 5; Mark 11 : 32, c. him as a prophet.

Luke 21 : 36; Acts 5 : 41; 1 Tim. 5 : 17, c. worthy.

Acts 20 : 24, neither c. I my life dear.

Phil. 3 : 8, I c. loss for Christ.

3 : 13, c. not myself to have apprehended.

Heb. 10 : 29, c. blood an unholy thing.

Jas. 1 : 2, c. it all joy.

2 Pet. 3 : 9, as some men c. slackness.

Countenance, Num. 6 : 26, Lord lift up his c. on thee.

1 Sam. 16 : 7, look not on his c.

Neh. 2 : 2, why is thy c. sad.

Job 14 : 20, thou changest his c.

Ps. 4 : 6; 44 : 3; 89 : 15; 90 : 8, light of thy c.

Prov. 15 : 13, merry heart maketh cheerful c.

Eccl. 7 : 3, by sadness of c., heart made better.

Isa. 3 : 9, c. doth witness against them.

Matt. 6 . 16, hypocrites, of a sad c.

28 : 3; Luke 9 : 29, c. like lightning.

Rev. 1 : 16, his c. as the sun shineth.

Country, Josh. 7 : 2, go up and view c.

Prov. 25 : 25, good news from a far c.

Matt. 13 : 57; Mark 6 : 4; Luke 4 : 24; John 4 : 44, in his own c.

Matt. 21 : 33; 25 : 14; Mark 12 : 1, went to far c.

Luke 4 : 23, do here in thy c.

Acts 12 : 20, their c. nourished by king's c.

Heb. 11 : 9, sojourned as in strange c.

Countrymen, 2 Cor. 11 : 26; 1 Thess. 2 : 14.

Couple, join, Ex. 26 : 6, c. the curtains.

39 : 4, two edges was it c.

1 Pet. 3 : 2, conversation c. with fear.

a pair, 2 Sam. 13 : 6, c. of cakes.

Isa. 21 : 7, c. of horsemen.

Courage, exhortations to, Num. 13 : 20; Deut. 31 : 6; Josh. 1 : 6; 10 : 25; 2 Sam. 10 : 12; 2 Chr. 19 : 11; Ezra 10 : 4; Ps. 27 : 14; 31 : 24; Isa. 41 : 6; 1 Cor. 16 : 13; Eph. 6 : 10.

through faith: Abraham, Heb. 11 : 8, 17. Moses, Heb. 11 : 25. Israelites, Heb. 11 : 29. Barak, Judg. 4 : 16. Gideon, Judg. 7 : 1. Jephthah, Judg. 11 : 29. Samson, Judg. 16 : 28. Jonathan, 1 Sam. 14 : 6. Daniel, Dan. 6 : 10, 23.

Deut. 31 : 6; Josh. 10 : 25; Ps. 27 : 14; 31 : 24, be of good c.

Acts 28 : 15, thanked God, and took c.
Course, Acts 20 : 24; 2 Tim. 4 : 7, finished my c.
2 Thess. 3 : 1, word may have free c.
Jas. 3 : 6, the c. of nature.
Courses, of the Levites, established by David, 1 Chr. 23 : 24.
of the singers, 1 Chr. 25.
of the porters, 1 Chr. 26.
of the captains, 1 Chr. 27.
Court, of the tabernacle described, Ex. 27 : 9; 38 : 9.
Ps. 65 : 4, that he may dwell in thy c.
84 : 2, soul fainteth for the c. of the Lord.
84 : 10, a day in thy c. is better.
92 : 13, flourish in the c. of our God.
100 : 4, enter into his c. with praise.
Isa. 1 : 12, to tread my c.
Luke 7 : 25, live delicately are in kings' c.
Courtesy, exhortation to, Col. 4 : 6; Jas. 3 : 17; 1 Pet. 3 : 8.
examples of, Acts 27 : 3; 28 : 7.
Cousin [kinsman or kinswoman], Luke 1 : 58, her neighbours and her c.
Covenant of God—
with Noah, Gen. 6 : 18; 9 : 8.
with Abraham, Gen. 15 : 7, 18; 17 : 2; (Luke 1 : 72; Acts 3 : 25; Gal. 3 : 16, 17).
with Isaac, Gen. 17 : 19; 26 : 3.
with Jacob, Gen. 28 : 13; (Ex. 2 : 24; 6 : 4; 1 Chr. 16 : 16).
with the Israelites, Ex. 6 : 4; 19 : 5; 24; 34 : 27; Lev. 26 : 9; Deut. 5 : 2; 9 : 9; 26 : 16; 29; Judg. 2 : 1; Jer. 11; 31 : 33; Acts 3 : 25.
with Phinehas, Num. 25 : 13.
with David, 2 Sam. 23 : 5; Ps. 89 : 3.
See Ps. 25 : 14.
God mindful of, Deut. 7 : 9; 1 Ki. 8 : 23; Ps. 105 : 8; 111 : 5, etc.
danger of despising, Deut. 28 : 15; Jer. 11 : 2; Heb. 10 : 29.
signs of: salt, Lev. 2 : 13; Num. 18 : 19; 2 Chr. 13 : 5. The Sabbath, Ex. 31 : 12.
book of the, Ex. 24 : 7; 2 Ki. 23 : 2; Heb. 9 : 19.
between Abraham and Abimelech, Gen. 21 : 27.
between Joshua and Israelites, Josh. 24 : 25.
between David and Jonathan, 1 Sam. 18 : 3; 20 : 16; 23 : 18.
new, Jer. 31 : 31; Rom. 11 : 27; Heb. 8 : 8.
ratified by Christ (Mal. 3 : 1), Luke 1 : 68-80; Gal. 3 : 17; Heb. 8 : 6; 9 : 15; 12 : 24.
of peace, Isa. 54 : 10; Ezek. 34 : 25; 37 : 26.
unchangeable, Ps. 89 : 34; Isa. 54 : 10; 59 : 21.
everlasting, Gen. 9 : 16; 17 : 13; Lev. 24 : 8; Isa. 55 : 3; 61 : 8; Ezek. 16 : 60; 37 : 26; Heb. 13 : 20.
Gen. 17 : 11, a token of the c. betwixt.
Ex. 31 : 16, Sabbath for a perpetual c.
Num. 18 : 19; 2 Chr. 13 : 5, c. of salt.
Ps. 105 : 8; 106 : 45, he remembereth his c. for ever.
Isa. 28 : 18, your c. with death disannulled.
Matt. 26 : 15; Luke 22 : 5, they c. with him.
Acts 3 : 25, children of the c.
Rom. 9 : 4, to whom pertaineth the c.
Eph. 2 : 12, strangers from c. of promise.

Heb. 8 : 6, mediator of a better c.
13 : 20, blood of the everlasting c.
Cover, Ex. 15 : 5, depths c. them.
33 : 22, I will c. thee.
1 Sam. 28 : 14, old man c. with a mantle.
Ps. 32 : 1; Rom. 4 : 7, blessed whose sin is c.
Ps. 73 : 6, violence c. as garment.
147 : 8, c. heaven with clouds.
Prov. 28 : 13, he that c. sins shall not prosper.
Isa. 26 : 21, earth no more c. her slain.
30 : 1, c. with a covering.
Matt. 8 : 24, ship c. with waves.
10 : 26; Luke 12 : 2, there is nothing c.
1 Cor. 11 : 7, a man not to c. head.
1 Pet. 4 : 8, charity c. multitude of sins.
Covering, Job 22 : 14, thick clouds are a c. to him.
26 : 6, destruction hath no c.
Isa. 28 : 20, c. narrower than he can wrap.
Covert, Ps. 61 : 4, trust in c. of thy wings.
Isa. 4 : 6, a tabernacle for a c.
32 : 2, a man be c. from tempest.
Covet, Ex. 20 : 17; Deut. 5 : 21; Rom. 7 : 7, thou shalt not c.
Prov. 21 : 26, he c. greedily all the day.
Hab. 2 : 9, c. an evil covetousness.
Acts 20 : 33, I have c. no man's silver.
1 Cor. 12 : 31; c. earnestly the best gifts.
Covetous, Ezek. 33 : 31, their heart goeth after c.
Mark 7 : 22, out of heart proceedeth c.
Rom. 1 : 29, filled with all c.
1 Cor. 6 : 10; Eph. 5 : 5, nor c. inherit kingdom.
2 Tim. 3 : 2, men shall be c.
Heb. 13 : 5, conversation without c.
2 Pet. 2 : 3, through c. make merchandise.
Covetousness described, Ps. 10 : 3; Prov. 21 : 26; Eccl. 4 : 8; 5 : 10; Ezek. 33 : 31; Hab. 2; Mark 7 : 22; Eph. 5 : 5; 1 Tim. 6 : 10; 2 Pet. 2 : 14.
forbidden, Ex. 20 : 17; Luke 12 : 15; Rom. 13 : 9.
its evil consequences, Prov. 1 : 18; 15 : 27; 28 : 20; Ezek. 22 : 13; 1 Tim. 6 : 9.
its punishment, Job 20 : 15; Isa. 5 : 8; 57 : 17; Jer. 6 : 12; 22 : 17; Mic. 2 : 1; Hab. 2 : 9; 1 Cor. 5 : 10; 6 : 10; Eph. 5 : 5; Col. 3 : 5.
of Laban, Gen. 31 : 41.
of Balaam, Num. 22 : 21 (2 Pet. 2 : 15; Jude 11).
of Achan, Josh. 7 : 21.
of Saul, 1 Sam. 15 : 9.
of Ahab, 1 Ki. 21.
of Gehazi, 2 Ki. 5 : 20.
of Judas, Matt. 26 : 14.
of Ananias and Sapphira, Acts 5.
of Felix, Acts 24 : 26.
Cow, Job 21 : 10, their c. casteth not.
Isa. 11 : 7, c. and the bear shall feed.
Craft, Mark 14 : 1, take him by c.
Acts 18 : 3, because he was of same c.
19 : 27, our c. is in danger.
Rev. 18 : 22, no c. be found any more.
Craftiness, Job 5 : 13; 1 Cor. 3 : 19, wise in their c.
Luke 20 : 23, he perceived their c.
2 Cor. 4 : 2, not walking in c.
Eph. 4 : 14, carried by cunning c.
Craftsman, 2 Ki. 24 : 14, all the c. and smiths.
Acts 19 : 24, gain unto the c.

Rev. 18 : 22, no c. of whatsoever.
Crafty, Ps. 83 : 3, taken c. counsel.
2 Cor. 12 : 16, being c., I caught.
Crag, Job 39 : 18.
Crane [Heb. agur]. This bird is associated, in the two references made to it in Isa. 38 : 14, and Jer. 8 : 7, with the turtle dove and the swallow, as observing the time of their coming. The crane is, according to Tristram, a regular, though for the most part a passing migrant in Palestine. In the A.V. our translators interchanged the words crane and swallow, but this has been rectified in the R.V.
Create, Ps. 51 : 10, c. in me a clean heart.
Isa. 40 : 26, who hath c. these things.
65 : 17, I c. new heavens and new earth.
Jer. 31 : 22, the Lord hath c. a new thing.
Mal. 2 : 10, hath not one God c. us ?
1 Cor. 11 :·9, neither man c. for woman.
Eph. 2 : 10, c. in Christ Jesus.
4 : 24, after God is c. in righteousness.
Col. 1 : 16, by him were all things c.
Rev. 4 : 11, hast c. all things, for thy pleasure they are and were c.
Creation of the world, Gen. 1; 2.
See Rom. 1 : 20; 8 : 22; Rev. 4 : 11.
the new, Rev. 22.
Mark 10 : 6, from c. male and female.
13 : 19, as was not from the c.
Rom. 1 : 20, from c. are clearly seen.
8 : 22, whole c. groaneth.
2 Pet. 3 : 4 continue as from the c.
Rev. 3 : 14, beginning of c. of God.
Creator, Eccl. 12 : 1, remember c. in youth.
Isa. 40 : 28, c. of ends of the earth.
Rom. 1 : 25, creature more than c.
1 Pet. 4 . 19, as to a faithful c.
Creature, a new, 2 Cor. 5 : 17; Gal. 6 : 15; Eph. 2 : 10; 4 : 24. See Rom. 8 : 19.
Mark 16 : 15; Col. 1 : 23, preach Gospel to every c.
Rom. 8 : 19, expectation of the c.
2 Cor. 5 : 17; Gal. 6 : 15, a new c.
Col. 1 : 15, firstborn of every c.
1 Tim. 4 : 4, every c. of God is good.
Heb. 4 : 13, any c. not manifest.
Creatures, the four living, vision of, Ezek. 1 : 5.
Creditor, parable of the, Luke 7 : 41.
of two creditors, Matt. 18 : 23.
Deut. 15 : 2, c. that lendeth shall.
2 Ki. 4 : 1, c. to take my two sons.
Luke 7 : 41, c. had two debtors.
Creep, Lev. 11 : 31, unclean all that c.
Ps. 104 : 20, beasts of the forest c. forth.
148 : 10, all c. things praise the Lord.
Ezek. 8 : 10, form of c. things pourtrayed.
Acts 10 : 12; 11 : 6, Peter saw c. things.
Jude 4, certain men c. in unawares.
Cretians, inhabitants of Crete, their character, Titus 1 : 12.
Crew, Matt. 26 : 74; Luke 22 : 60.
Crib, Job 39 : 9; Prov. 14 : 4; Isa. 1 : 3.
Cried, Ps. 3 : 4; 120 : 1, c. unto the Lord.
Ps. 72 : 12, needy when he c.
Prov. 1 : 20, wisdom c. without.
2 : 3, c. after knowledge.
Mark 15 : 34, 37, Jesus c. with loud voice.
Crime, Job 31 : 11; Acts 25 : 16.

Crimson [Heb. tole ah and tola ath]. The Hebrew word meaning crimson worm is translated either (as in Isa. 1 : 18) as crimson, or as often elsewhere, by scarlet, the dye obtained from the insect being the colour intended.
2 Chr. 2 : 7, cunning to work in c.
Isa. 1 : 18, though your sins be like c.
Jer. 4 : 30, though thou clothest with c.
Cripple healed at Lystra, Acts 14 : 8.
Crispus (cris-pŭs) baptized by Paul, Acts 18 : 8; 1 Cor. 1 : 14.
Crocodile. This is probably the same animal as the one called Leviathan. In Job 41 the description is too graphic and true to be mistaken. This reptile is only to be found in fresh water.
Lev. 11 : 29.
Crooked, Ps. 125 : 5, aside to their c. ways.
Eccl. 1 : 15; 7 : 13, c. cannot be made straight.
Isa. 40 : 4; 42 : 16; Luke 3 : 5, c. shall be made straight.
Isa. 45 : 2, make the c. places straight.
59 : 8; Lam. 3 : 9, c. paths.
Phil. 2 : 15, in midst of a c. nation.
Cross, Christ dies upon the, Matt. 27 : 32; Phil. 2 : 8; Heb. 12 : 2.
the preaching of, 1 Cor. 1 : 18.
to be taken up, self-denial, Matt. 10 : 38; 16 : 24.
offence of the, Gal. 5 : 11.
persecution for, Gal. 6 : 12.
Matt. 16 : 24; Mark 8 : 34; 10 : 21; Luke 9 : 23, take up c.
Matt. 27 : 32; Mark 15 : 21; Luke 23 : 26, compelled to bear c.
John 19 : 25, there stood by c.
1 Cor. 1 : 17; Gal. 6 : 12; Phil. 3 : 18, c. of Christ.
1 Cor. 1 : 18, preaching of the c.
Gal. 5 : 11, offence of the c.
6 : 14, glory save in the c.
Eph. 2 : 16, reconcile both by the c.
Phil. 2 : 8, the death of the c.
Col. 1 : 20, peace through blood of the c.
2 : 14, nailing it to his c.
Heb. 12 : 2, for joy endured the c.
Crown (and mitre) of the high priest, Ex. 29 : 6; 39 : 30; Lev. 8 : 9.
of thorns, John 19 : 5.
of righteousness, 2 Tim. 4 : 8.
of life, Jas. 1 : 12; Rev. 2 : 10.
of glory, 1 Pet. 5 : 4.
incorruptible, 1 Cor. 9 : 25.
See Rev. 4 : 4; 9 : 7; 12 : 3; 13 : 1; 19 : 12.
Job 19 : 9, taken the c. from my head.
31 : 36, bind it as a c. to me.
Ps. 65 : 11, thou c. the year.
103 : 4, c. thee with lovingkindness.
Prov. 4 : 9, c. of glory deliver to thee.
12 : 4, virtuous woman is a c.
16 : 31, hoary head a c. of glory.
Isa. 28 : 1, woe to the c. of pride.
Matt. 27 : 29; Mark 15 : 17; John 19 : 2, a c. of thorns.
1 Cor. 9 : 25, to obtain a corruptible c.
Phil. 4 : 1, my joy and c.
1 Thess. 2 : 19, c. of rejoicing.

2 Tim. 4 : 8, a **c.** of righteousness.
Jas. 1 : 12; Rev. 2 : 10, **c.** of life.
1 Pet. 5 : 4, a **c.** of glory.
Rev. 3 : 11, that no man take thy **c.**
19 : 12, on his head were many **c.**

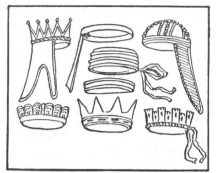

Eastern Crowns.

Crucify, Matt. 20 : 19, to Gentiles to **c.** him.
27 : 31; Mark 15 : 20, led away to **c.** him.
John 19 : 20, 41, where Jesus was **c.**
Acts 2 : 23, by wicked hands ye have **c.**
Rom. 6 : 6, old man is **c.** with him.
1 Cor. 1 : 23, we preach Christ **c.**
2 : 2, save Jesus Christ and him **c.**
2 Cor. 13 : 4, though he was **c.** through weakness.
Gal. 2 : 20, I am **c.** with Christ.
3 : 1, Christ set forth **c.**
5 : 24, have **c.** the flesh.
Heb. 6 : 6, **c.** to themselves afresh.
Cruel, Ps. 25 : 19, hath me with **c.** hatred.
27 : 12, breathe out **c.**
71 : 4, deliver out of hand of **c.**
Prov. 11 : 17, **c.** troubleth his own flesh.
12 : 10, tender mercies of wicked are **c.**
27 : 4, wrath is **c.**
Cant. 8 : 6, jealousy is **c.**
Heb. 11 : 36, trial of **c.** mockings.
Cruelty condemned, Ex. 23 : 5; Ps. 27 : 12;
Prov. 11 : 17; 12 : 10; Ezek. 18 : 18.
of Simeon and Levi, Gen. 34 : 25; 49 : 5.
of Pharaoh, Ex. 1 : 8.
of Adoni-bezek, Judg. 1 : 7.
of Herod, Matt. 2 : 16.
See Judg. 9 : 5; 2 Ki. 3 : 27; 10; 15 : 16.
Crumbs. Knives and forks were not in use in
Old or New Testament times. The Orientals
used their fingers at table, which they
cleaned by rubbing them with pieces of
bread. These pieces were sometimes
thrown out of the window, and sometimes
dropped on the floor. Such were " the
crumbs which fell from the rich man's
table," that Lazarus hungered for (Luke
16 : 21).
Matt. 15 : 27; Mark 7 : 28, dogs eat of **c.**
Luke 16 : 21, to be fed with the **c.**
Cruse. The cruse was an earthenware vessel
having a bulb about nine inches in diameter

and a neck three inches long; it had a
handle below the neck, and a spout on the
side opposite the handle, with an opening
about the width of a straw, through which
the contents were drunk by suction. This
was the vessel which held the widow's oil
(1 Ki. 17 : 12), and Elijah's water (1 Ki.
19 : 12).
Cry, Ex. 3 : 7, I have heard their **c.**
1 Sam. 5 : 12, **c.** of the city went up to heaven.
Job 34 : 28, he heareth the **c.** of the afflicted.
Ps. 9 : 12, forgetteth not **c.** of humble.
34 : 15, his ears open to their **c.**
88 : 2, incline thine ear to my **c.**
Prov. 21 : 13, stoppeth his ears at **c.** of the
poor.
Matt. 25 : 6, at midnight there was a **c.** made.
Ex. 14 : 15, wherefore **c.** thou unto me ?
Job 29 : 12, I delivered the poor that **c.**
Ps. 34 : 17, righteous **c.,** Lord heareth.
147 : 9, food to young ravens which **c.**
Prov. 8 : 1, doth not wisdom **c.** ?
Isa. 58 : 1, **c.** aloud, spare not.
65 : 14, shall **c.** for sorrow of heart.
Matt. 12 : 19, he shall not strive nor **c.**
20 : 31; Mark 10 : 48; Luke 18 : 39, **c.** the
more.
Luke 18 : 7, elect, who **c.** day and night.
John 7 : 37, Jesus **c.,** if any man thirst.
Acts 19 : 32; 21 : 34, some **c.** one thing, and
some another.
Rom. 8 : 15, whereby we **c.,** Abba, Father.
Jas. 5 : 4, hire of labourers **c.**
Crying, Prov. 19 : 18, soul spare for his **c.**
Isa. 65 : 19, voice of **c.**
Matt. 3 : 3; Mark 1 : 3; Luke 3 : 4; John
1 : 23, one **c.** in wilderness.
Heb. 5 : 7, prayers, with strong **c.**
Rev. 21 : 4, no more death, nor **c.**
Crystal, Job 28 : 17, **c.** cannot equal it.
Ezek. 1 : 22, as colour of terrible **c.**
Rev. 4 : 6, a sea of glass, like **c.**
21 : 11, light of city clear as **c.**
22 : 1, a pure river, clear as **c.**
Cubit, a measure of length. Deut. 3 : 11, after
the **c.** of a man.
Matt. 6 : 27; Luke 12 : 25, one **c.** to stature.
Cuckoo [Heb. shachaph]. One of the unclean
birds of Lev. 11 : 16 and Deut. 14 : 15.
The European cuckoo visits Palestine, but
some think the bird referred to was a sea
bird, and the Revised Version translates it
as sea-mew.
Cucumbers [Heb. kishu'im] are referred to
twice. In the wilderness the Israelites called
to mind the fish which cost them nought in
Egypt—the cucumbers and the melons
(Num. 11 : 5). Fresh vegetable food enters
so largely into the ordinary diet of the
people of a warm country that its loss is
soon felt. For protection's sake, then as
now, booths were constructed in the fields
of melons and cucumbers, in which the
person who watched the fields lay sheltered
from the heat of the sun (Isa. 1 : 8.).
Cumber [occupy injuriously], Luke 10 : 40, **c.**
about much serving; Luke 13 : 7, why **c.** it
the ground ?

Cumi (cū-mĭ), Mark 5 : 41.

Cummin. The fruit of Cuminum sativum, which is aromatic, and one of the umbel-bearers. It is a small plant, and the separation of the fruit from the stalks was done by beating with rods. " Neither is a cart wheel turned about upon the cummin " (Isa. 28 : 25, 27). Matt. 23 : 23.

Cunning, Gen. 25 : 27. Esau was a c. hunter.
Ex. 31 : 4, to devise c. works in gold.
Ps. 137 : 5, let my hand forget her c.
Isa. 40 : 20, he seeketh a c. workman.
Jer. 9 : 17, send for c. women.
Dan. 1 : 4, children c. in knowledge.
Eph. 4 : 14, carried about by c. craftiness.
2 Pet. 1 : 16, not followed c. devised fables.

Cup, Ps. 23 : 5, my c. runneth over.
116 : 13, I will take c. of salvation.
Matt. 10 : 42; Mark 9 : 41, c. of cold water.
Matt. 20 : 22; Mark 10 : 39, drink of my c.
Matt. 23 : 25, make clean outside of c.
26 : 27; Mark 14 : 23; Luke 22 : 17; 1 Cor. 11 : 25, took the c.
Matt. 26 : 39; Mark 14 : 36; Luke 22 : 42, let this c. pass.
Luke 22 : 20; 1 Cor. 11 : 25, this c. is New Testament.
John 18 : 11, c. which my Father hath given.
1 Cor. 10 : 16, c. of blessing we bless.
11 : 26, as often as ye drink this c.

Cupbearers, 2 Chr. 9 : 4; Neh. 1 : 11.

Curdle, Job 10 : 10.

Cure, Jer. 33 : 6, I will c. them.
Matt. 17 : 18, child c. that very hour.
Luke 7 : 21, in that hour he c. many.
9 : 1, power to c. diseases.
13 : 32, I do c. to day.

Curious, Ex. 28 : 8; 35 : 32; Ps. 139 : 15; Acts 19 : 19.

Current, Gen. 23 : 16.

Curse upon the earth in consequence of the fall, Gen. 3 : 17.
upon Cain, Gen. 4 : 11.
on Canaan, Gen. 9 : 25.
upon the breakers of the law, Lev. 26 : 14; Deut. 11 : 26; 27 : 13; 28 : 15; 29 : 19; Josh. 8 : 34; Prov. 3 : 33.
uttered by Job on his birth, Job 3 : 1.
also by Jeremiah, Jer. 20 : 14.
Christ redeems from, Rom. 3; Gal. 3 : 13; Rev. 22 : 3.
Gen. 8 : 21, I will not c. ground.
Ex. 22 : 28, not c. ruler of thy people.
Lev. 19 : 14, not c. the deaf.
Num. 23 : 8, how shall I c. whom God hath not ?
Deut. 11 : 26, I set before you blessing and c.
23 : 5, turn c. into blessing.
Judg. 5 : 23, c. ye Meroz, c. ye bitterly.
Job 2 : 9, c. God and die.
Ps. 62 : 4, they bless, but c. inwardly.
Isa. 8 : 21, c. their king, and God.
Mal. 2 : 2, I will c. your blessings.
3 : 9, ye are cursed with a c.
Matt. 5 : 44; Luke 6 : 28; Rom. 12 : 14, bless them that c. you.
Matt. 26 : 74; Mark 14 : 71, he began to c.
Mark 11 : 21, fig tree thou c.
John 7 : 49, who knoweth not the law are c.

Gal. 3 : 10, are under the c.
3 : 10, c. every one that continueth not.
Jas. 3 : 9, therewith c. we men.
Rev. 22 : 3, no more c.

Cursed, who so called, Deut. 27 : 15; Ps. 37 : 22; Prov. 11 : 26; 27 : 14; Jer. 11 : 3; 17 : 5; Lam. 3 : 65; Zech. 5 : 3; Mal. 1 : 14; Matt. 25 : 41; Gal. 3 : 10; 2 Pet. 2 : 14.

Cursing forbidden, Ex. 21 : 17; Lev. 24 : 15; Ps. 109 : 17; Prov. 30 : 11; Jas. 3 : 10.
to return blessing for, Matt. 5 : 44; Rom. 12 : 14.

Curtains of the tabernacle described, Ex. 26; 36.

Custody, Num. 3 : 36; Esther 2 : 3.

Custom [tariff, toll, legal duty], Matt. 9 : 9, sitting at the receipt of c. Compare Custom-House.
Matt. 17 : 25, of whom do kings take c. ?
Mark 2 : 14; Luke 5 : 27, receipt of c.
Luke 1 : 9, according to c. of priest's office.
4 : 16, as Jesus' c. was.
John 18 : 39, ye have a c.
Acts 16 : 21, teach c. which are not lawful.
Rom. 13 : 7, c. to whom c.
1 Cor. 11 : 16, we have no such c.

Cutting the flesh forbidden, Lev. 19 : 28; Deut. 14 : 1.
practised by prophets of Baal, 1 Ki. 18 : 28.

Cymbals used in worship, 2 Sam. 6 : 5; 1 Chr. 15 : 16; 16 : 5; Ps. 150 : 5.
tinkling, 1 Cor. 13 : 1.

Cypress, Isa. 44 : 14, he taketh the c.

Coin of Cyprus, of age of Sergius Paulus

Cyprus (cȳ-prŭs), a large island in the Mediterranean, disciples there, Acts 11 : 19.
Paul and Barnabas preach there, Acts 13 : 4.
Barnabas and Mark go there, Acts 15 : 39.

Cyrene (cȳ-rē-nē), disciples of, Acts 11 : 20; 13 : 1.
Simon of, Mark 15 : 21.

Cyrenius (cȳ-rē-nĭ-ŭs), Greek form of Quirinus, a Latin name, Governor of Syria, Luke 2 : 2.

Cyrus (cȳ-rŭs), probably identical with the name of the river Kur, 2 Chr. 36 : 22 and Isa. 44 : 28.
king of Persia, prophecies concerning, Isa. 44 : 28; 45 : 1.
See Dan. 6 : 28; 10 : 1.
his proclamation for rebuilding the temple, 2 Chr. 36 : 22; Ezra 1.

Statue of Cyrus.

D

Dagon (dā-gŏn) [fish], national idol-god of the Philistines, sacrificed to, Judg. 16 : 23.
smitten down in temple at Ashdod, 1 Sam. 5 : 3, 4.
Saul's head fastened in house of, 1 Chr. 10 : 10.
Daily, Ps. 13 : 2, sorrow in my heart **d.**
42 : 10, **d.** to me, where is thy God ?
68 : 19, **d.** loadeth us.
Prov. 8 : 30, I was **d.** his delight.
Dan. 8 : 11; 11 : 31; 12 : 11, **d.** sacrifice taken away.
Matt. 6 : 11; Luke 11 : 3, our **d.** bread.
Luke 9 : 23, take up cross **d.**
Acts 2 : 47, added to church **d.**
Acts 6 : 1, the **d.** ministration.
16 : 5, churches increased **d.**
17 : 11, searched the Scriptures **d.**
1 Cor. 15 : 31, I die **d.**
Heb. 3 : 13, exhort **d.**
7 : 27, needeth not **d.** to offer.
Jas. 2 : 15, destitute of **d.** food.
Dainty, Job 33 : 20, his soul abhorreth **d.** meat.

Ps. 141 : 4, let me not eat of their **d.**
Prov. 23 : 3, be not desirous of **d.**
Dale, Gen. 14 : 17, which is in the king's **d.**
2 Sam. 18 : 18, which is the king's **d.**
Dam, Ex. 22 : 30; Deut. 22 : 6, 7.
Damage, Prov. 26 : 6, drinketh **d.**
Dan. 6 : 2, king should have no **d.**
Acts 27 : 10, voyage will be with **d.**
2 Cor. 7 : 9, **d.** by us in nothing.
Damascus, subjugated by David, 2 Sam. 8 : 6; 1 Chr. 18 : 6.
Rezon reigns there, 1 Ki. 11 : 24.
Elisha's prophecy there, 2 Ki. 8 : 7.
taken by Tiglath-pileser, king of Assyria, 2 Ki. 16 : 9.
recaptured by Jeroboam, 2 Ki. 14 : 28.
king Ahaz copies an altar there, 2 Ki. 16 : 10.
Paul's journey to, Acts 9; 22 : 6.
prophecies concerning, Isa. 7 : 8; 8 : 4; 17 : 1; Jer. 49 : 23; Ezek. 27 : 18; Amos 1 : 3.
Damnation, denounced upon unbelievers, etc., Matt. 23 : 14; Mark 16 : 16; John 5 : 29; Rom. 3 : 8; 13 : 2; 2 Thess. 2 : 12; 1 Tim. 5 : 12; 2 Pet. 2 : 3.
Matt. 23 : 14; Mark 12 : 40; Luke 20 : 47, ye shall receive greater **d.**
Mark 3 : 29, in danger of eternal **d.**
John 5 : 29, to the resurrection of **d.**
Damned, Mark 16 : 16, believeth not be **d.**
Rom. 14 : 23, doubteth is **d.** if he eat.
2 Thess. 2 : 12, be **d.** who believed not.
2 Pet. 2 : 1, bring in **d.** heresies.
Damsel, Matt. 14 : 11; Mark 6 : 28, head given to **d.**
Mark 5 : 39, **d.** is not dead.
Acts 12 : 13, a **d.** came to hearken.
16 : 16, **d.** possessed with a spirit.
Dan [judge], son of Jacob, Gen. 30 : 6.
tribe of, numbered, Num. 1 : 38; 26 : 42.
their inheritance, Josh. 19 : 40.
blessed by Jacob, Gen. 49 : 16.
blessed by Moses, Deut. 33 : 22.
take Laish, Judg. 18 : 27, 28.
set up idolatry, Judg. 18 : 30; 1 Ki. 12 : 29.

Babylonian representation of Dagon and Derketo.

Dance, 1 Sam. 18 : 6, came out singing and **d.**
2 Sam. 6 : 14, David **d.** before the Lord.
Ps. 149 : 3; 150 : 4, praise him in the **d.**
Isa. 13 : 21, satyrs shall **d.** there.
Matt. 11 : 17; Luke 7 : 32, piped, and ye have not **d.**

House on wall at Damascus.

Mark 6 : 22, daughter of Herodias **d.**

Dancing, as a mark of rejoicing, Ex. 15 : 20; Judg. 11 ; 34; 1 Sam. 21 ; 11; Eccl. 3 : 4
of Herodias' daughter, Matt. 14 : 6.
Ex. 32 : 19, he saw calf and **d.**
Ps. 30 : 11, my mourning into **d.**

Dandled, Isa. 66 : 12.

Danger, Matt. 5 : 21, in **d.** of judgment.
Mark 3 : 29, **d.** of eternal damnation.
Acts 19 : 27, not only craft is in **d.**

Dangerous, Acts 27 : 9.

Daniel (dăn-ĭ-ĕl) [God is my judge] (Belteshazzar), one of the captives in Babylon, Dan. 1 : 3.
refuses to take the king's meat or drink, Dan. 1 : 8.
has understanding in dreams, Dan. 1 : 17.
interprets the royal dreams, Dan. 2; 4; and the handwriting on the wall, Dan. 5 : 17.
promoted by Darius, Dan. 6 : 2.
conspired against by the princes, Dan. 6 : 4.
disregards the idolatrous decree, Dan. 6 : 10.
cast into the lions' den, Dan. 6 : 16.
his preservation in, Dan. 6 : 22.
his vision of the four beasts, Dan. 7.
his vision of the ram and he goat, Dan. 8.
his prayer, Dan. 9 : 3.
promise given of return from captivity, Dan. 9 : 20; 10 : 10; 12 : 13.
his name mentioned, Ezek. 14 : 14, 20; 28 : 3.

Daniel, The Book of.
The Book.—It narrates the story of Daniel and his associates who were taken to Babylon in the third year of Jehoiakim (605 B.C.). Daniel is brought into the favour of Nebuchadnezzar, his captor, by the interpretation of the King's dreams. The language of the book is Hebrew, except for the portion 2 : 4 to 7, which is Aramaic. Though the material is largely historical, it contains much of the apocalyptic, and the book is reckoned among the Major Prophets.

Author.—Conservative critics have never doubted that Daniel was the author, and the many recent findings of archæology have verified the historicity of the book and confirmed the assurance that Daniel wrote it.

Contents.—The first part of the book, which is mainly historical, consists of chaps. 1–6. (1) Ch. 1 records the captivity of Daniel and his companions in the third year of Jehoiakim, and their subsequent training for civil service at the court of Nebuchadnezzar, king of Babylon. (2) Ch. 2 contains the account of Nebuchadnezzar's dream of the great image interpreted by Daniel, which fact led to the promotion of Daniel and his three companions in the province of Babylon. The vision of Nebuchadnezzar depicted the four great world-empires which were to come in contact with the people of Israel before the setting up of the Messianic kingdom and up to the time of its final victory. Ch. 3 gives the account of Nebuchadnezzar's erection of a golden image in the plain of Dura (probably with some reference to his vision), and the deliverance of Daniel's three companions from the fiery furnace, into which they were cast for refusing to worship that image. Chap. 4 records Nebuchadnezzar's dream of the

Daniel's Tomb.

great tree, and the fulfilment of that vision by his being afflicted with a seven years' madness because of pride. Ch. 5 records one of the grandest episodes in Israel's captivity—Belshazzar's feast and its tragic close. Ch. 6 records Daniel's deliverance from the den of lions.

The second portion of the book consists of Daniel's own visions. These are contained in the six last chapters (ch. 7–12). The first vision (ch. 7) is that of the four great wild beasts, which represent, though under somewhat different aspects, the four kingdoms portrayed in Nebuchadnezzar's dream. Ch. 8 contains the vision of " the ram and the he goat," which describes the contest between the Persian and the Grecian empires, and the overthrow of the latter by Alexander the Great (the notable horn of the he goat), with the division of the Macedonian kingdom into four. " The little horn," on the head of the Grecian he goat, which waxed great in the pleasant land, the land of Palestine, and there mightily oppressed the children of Israel, was the Greek power in the person of Antiochus Epiphanes, whose attempts to stamp out Judaism are described in 1 and 2 Maccabees. Ch. 9 describes Daniel's prayer and confession of sin at the end of the 70 years' captivity predicted by Jeremiah, and the answer to that prayer by the promise of Messiah's atoning work at the close of " the seventy weeks." Ch. 10 describes the vision of the mighty angel to Daniel, introductory to the description of the prophecy " noted in the scripture of truth " (ch. 10 : 21). This is given in chs. 11 and 12, in which chapters the wars between Syria (the kingdom of the north) and Egypt (the kingdom of the south) are depicted. The Jews were deeply concerned in those wars. The whole prophecy culminates in the description of Antiochus Epiphanes' attempt to uproot the Jewish religion, the struggle of the Maccabees, and their final victory.

Dare, Rom. 5 : 7, some would even d. to die.
15 : 18, d. to speak of anything.
1 Cor. 6 : 1, d. any of you go to law ?
2 Cor. 10 : 12, d. not make ourselves of number.

Darius (dă-rī-ŭs) [preserver ?] (the Median), takes Babylon, Dan. 5 : 31.
his decree to fear the God of Daniel, Dan. 6 : 25.
(another) his decree concerning the rebuilding of the temple, Ezra 6.

Dark, Job 12 : 25, they grope in the d.
Job 22 : 13, can he judge through d. clouds.
38 : 2, that d. counsel by words.
Ps. 49 : 4; Prov. 1 : 6, d. sayings.
Ps. 69 : 23; Rom. 11 : 10, let eyes be d.
Ps. 88 : 12, wonders be known in the d.
Eccl. 12 : 2, stars be not d.
12 : 3, look out of windows be d.
Amos 8 : 9, will d. the earth.
Zech. 14 : 6, light not clear nor d.
Matt. 24 : 29; Mark 13 : 24, sun be d.

Luke 23 : 45, sun d., and veil rent.
John 20 : 1, when it was yet d.
Rom. 1 : 21, foolish heart was d.
1 Cor. 13 : 12, see through a glass d.
Eph. 4 : 18, understanding d.
2 Pet. 1 : 19, shineth in a d. place.
Rev. 9 : 2, sun and the air were d.

Darkness, divided from light, Gen. 1 : 18.
created by God, Isa. 45 : 7.
instances of supernatural, Gen. 15 : 12; Ex. 10 : 21; 14 : 20; Josh. 24 : 7; Rev. 8 : 12; 16 : 10.
at the crucifixion, Matt. 27 : 45; Mark 15 : 33; Luke 23 : 44.
figurative of punishment, Matt. 22 : 13; 2 Pet. 2 : 4, 17; Jude 6.
of the mind, Job 37 : 19; Prov. 2 : 13; Eccl. 2 : 14; Isa. 9 : 2; 42 : 7; John 8 : 12; 12 : 35; Rom. 13 : 12; 1 Cor. 4 : 5; 2 Cor. 6 : 14; 1 Thess. 5 : 4; 1 John 2 : 9.
powers of, Luke 22 : 53; Col. 1 : 13.
Gen. 1 : 2, d. was upon the deep.
Deut. 5 : 22, spake out of thick d.
28 : 29, grope as the blind in d.
1 Sam. 2 : 9, wicked be silent in d.
2 Sam. 22 : 10; Ps. 18 : 9, d. under his feet.
1 Ki. 8 : 12; 2 Chr. 6 : 1, dwell in thick d.
Job 3 : 5, d. and shadow of death.
30 : 26, waited for light, there came d.
Ps. 91 : 6, pestilence that walketh in d.
97 : 2, clouds and d. are round about him.
112 : 4, to upright ariseth light in d.
139 : 12, d. and light alike to thee.
Prov. 20 : 20, lamp put out in d.
Eccl. 2 : 13, as far as light excelleth d.
Isa. 58 : 10, thy d. as noonday.
60 : 2, d. shall cover the earth, gross d.
Joel 2 : 2, day of clouds and thick d.
Matt. 6 : 23; Luke 11 : 34, body full of d.
Matt. 8 : 12; 25 : 30, outer d.
10 : 27; Luke 12 : 3, what I tell in d., that speak.
Luke 1 : 79; Rom. 2 : 19, light to them that sit in d.
John 1 : 5, d. comprehended it not.
3 : 19, loved d., rather than light.
Acts 26 : 18, turn from d. to light.
2 Cor. 4 : 6, light to shine out of d.
6 : 14, what communion hath light with d. ?
Eph. 5 : 11, works of d.
6 : 12, rulers of the d. of this world.
Col. 1 : 13, the power of d.
1 Thess. 5 : 5, not of the night, nor of d.
Heb. 12 : 18, ye are not come to d.
1 Pet. 2 : 9, out of d. into marvellous light.
1 John 1 : 5, in him is no d. at all.
2 : 8, the darkness is past.

Dart, Job 41 : 26, nor the d. cannot hold.
Prov. 7 : 23, till d. strike.
Eph. 6 : 16, to quench fiery d.
Heb. 12 : 20, thrust through with a d.

Dash, Ps. 2 : 9; Isa. 13 : 16; Hos. 13 : 16, d. in pieces.
Ps. 91 : 12; Matt. 4 : 6; Luke 4 : 11, d. thy foot.
Ps. 137 : 9, d. little ones against stones.

Daub, Ezek. 13 : 10.

Daughters, their inheritance determined, Num. 27 : 6; 36.

RUINS OF ANCIENT TYRE

GARDEN IN JERUSALEM

Gen. 24 : 23, 47, whose **d.** art thou ?
Deut. 28 : 53, eat flesh of sons and **d.**
Judg. 11 : 35, Jephthah said, Alas, my **d.!**
2 Sam. 12 : 3, lamb was unto him as a **d.**
Ps. 45 : 9, king's **d.** among honourable women.
    144 : 12, our **d.** as corner stones.
Prov. 30 : 15, horseleech hath two **d.**
    31 : 29, many **d.** have done virtuously.
Eccl. 12 : 4, the **d.** of music.
Isa. 22 : 4; Jer. 9 : 1; Lam. 2 : 11; 3 : 48,
    d. of my people.
Jer. 6 : 14, healed hurt of **d.**
Mic. 7 : 6; Matt. 10 : 35; Luke 12 : 53, **d.**
    riseth against mother.
Matt. 15 : 28, her **d.** was made whole.
Luke 8 : 42, one only **d.**
    13 : 16, this woman, **d.** of Abraham.
John 12 : 15, fear not, **d.** of Zion.
Heb. 11 : 24, refused to be called son o
    Pharaoh's **d.**
1 Pet. 3 : 6, whose **d.** ye are.
David [beloved], king, son of Jesse, Ruth 4 : 22;
    1 Chr. 2; Matt. 1.
anointed by Samuel, 1 Sam. 16 : 11.
plays the harp before Saul, 1 Sam. 16 : 19.
his zeal and faith, 1 Sam. 17 : 26, 34.
kills Goliath of Gath, 1 Sam. 17 : 49.
at first honoured by Saul, 1 Sam. 18.
Saul afterwards jealous of, 1 Sam. 18 : 8, 12.
tries to kill him, 1 Sam. 18 : 10.
persecuted by Saul, 1 Sam. 19; 20.
loved by Jonathan, 1 Sam. 18 : 1; 19 : 2; 20;
    23 : 16.
and by Michal, 1 Sam. 18 : 28; 19 : 11.
overcomes the Philistines, 1 Sam. 18 : 27;
    19 : 8.
flees to Naioth, 1 Sam. 19 : 18.
eats of the shewbread, 1 Sam. 21; Ps. 52;
    Matt. 12 : 4.
flees to Gath, and feigns madness, 1 Sam.
    21 : 10, 13; Ps. 34 : 56.
dwells in the cave of Adullam, 1 Sam. 22 : 1;
    Ps. 63 : 142.
escapes Saul's pursuit; 1 Sam. 23; Ps. 57; 59.
twice spares Saul's life, 1 Sam. 24 : 4; 26 :
    5.
his wrath against Nabal appeased by Abigail,
    1 Sam. 25 : 23.
dwells at Ziklag, 1 Sam. 27.
dismissed from the army by Achish, 1 Sam.
    29 : 9.
chastises the Amalekites, 1 Sam. 30 : 16.
kills messenger who brings news of Saul's
    death, 2 Sam. 1 : 15.
laments the death of Saul and Jonathan, 2
    Sam. 1 : 17.
becomes king of Judah, 2 Sam. 2 : 4.
forms a league with Abner, 2 Sam. 3 : 13.
laments his death, 2 Sam. 3 : 31.
avenges the murder of Ish-bosheth, 2 Sam.
    4 : 9.
becomes king of all Israel, 2 Sam. 5 : 3;
    1 Chr. 11.
his victories, 2 Sam. 5; 6; 8; 10; 12 : 29;
    21 : 15; 1 Chr. 18–20; Ps. 60.
brings the ark to Zion, 2 Sam. 6; 1 Chr.
    13; 15.
his psalms of thanksgiving, 2 Sam. 22; 1 Chr.
    16 : 7; Ps. 18; 103; 105.

reproves Michal for despising his religious
    joy, 2 Sam. 6 : 21.
desires to build God a house, 2 Sam. 7 : 2.
and is forbidden by Nathan, 2 Sam. 7 : 4;
    1 Chr. 17 : 4.
God's promises to him, 2 Sam. 7 : 11; 1 Chr.
    17 : 10.
his prayer and thanksgiving, 2 Sam. 7 : 18;
    1 Chr. 17 : 16.
his kindness to Mephibosheth, 2 Sam. 9.
his sin concerning Bath-sheba and Uriah,
    2 Sam. 11; 12.
his repentance at Nathan's parable, 2 Sam.
    12; Ps. 51.
troubles in his family, 2 Sam. 13; 14.
Absalom's conspiracy against him, 2 Sam. 15;
    Ps. 3.
Ahithophel's treachery against, 2 Sam. 15 : 31;
    16; 17.
cursed by Shimei, 2 Sam. 16 : 5; Ps. 7.
Barzillai's kindness to, 2 Sam. 17 : 27.
his grief at Absalom's death, 2 Sam. 18 : 33;
    19 : 1.
returns to Jerusalem, 2 Sam. 19 : 15.
pardons Shimei, 2 Sam. 19 : 16.
Sheba's conspiracy against, 2 Sam. 20.
renders justice to the Gibeonites, 2 Sam. 21.
his mighty men, 2 Sam. 23 : 8; 1 Chr.
    11 : 10.
his offence in numbering the people, 2 Sam.
    24; 1 Chr. 21.
regulates the service of the tabernacle, 1 Chr.
    23–26.
exhorts the people to fear God, 1 Chr. 28.
appoints Solomon his successor, 1 Ki. 1;
    Ps. 72.
his charge to Solomon, 1 Ki. 2; 1 Chr. 28 : 9;
    to build a house for the sanctuary, 1 Chr.
    22 . 6, 28 . 10.
his last words, 2 Sam. 23.
his death, 1 Ki. 2; 1 Chr. 29 : 26.
the progenitor of Christ, Matt. 1 : 1; 9 : 27;
    21 : 9; comp. Ps. 110 with Matt. 22 : 41;
    Luke 1 : 32; John 7 : 42; Acts 2 : 25;
    13 : 22; 15 : 15; Rom. 1 : 3; 2 Tim. 2 : 8;
    Rev. 5 : 5; 22 : 16.
prophecies connected with, Ps. 89; 132; Isa.
    9 : 7; 22 : 22; 55 : 3; Jer. 30 : 9; Hos.
    3 : 5; Amos 9 : 11.
Tomb of, in Jerusalem, Acts 2 : 29.
Dawn, Ps. 119 : 147, I prevented the **d.** of the
    morning.
Matt. 28 : 1, as it began to **d.**
2 Pet. 1 : 19, till the day **d.**
Day, the last, foretold, Job 19 : 25; Joel 2 : 11;
    Zeph. 1 : 14; John 6 : 39; 11 : 24; 12 : 48;
    Rom. 2 : 5; 1 Cor. 3 : 13; Rev. 6 : 17;
    16 : 14; 20.
last, mentioned, Isa. 2 : 2; Mic. 4 : 1; Acts
    2 : 17; 2 Tim. 3 : 1; Heb. 1 : 2; Jas. 5 : 3;
    2 Pet. 3 : 3.
Gen. 1 : 5, God called the light **d.**
    32 : 26, let me go, **d.** breaketh.
Deut. 4 : 10, **d.** thou stoodest before Lord.
    4 : 32, ask of **d.** that are past.
2 Ki. 7 : 9, this **d.** is a **d.** of good tidings.
1 Chr. 23 : 1; 2 Chr. 24 : 15, full of **d.**
1 Chr. 29 : 15; Job 8 : 9, our **d.** as a shadow.
Job 19 : 25, stand at latter **d.** upon the earth.

21 : 30, reserved to **d.** of destruction.
32 : 7, I said, **d.** should speak.
Ps. 2 : 7; Acts 13 : 33; Heb. 1 : 5, this **d.** have
    I begotten thee.
Ps. 19 : 2, **d.** unto **d.** uttereth speech.
84 : 10, a **d.** in thy courts.
Prov. 4 : 18, more and more to perfect **d.**
27 : 1, what a **d.** may bring forth.
Eccl. 7 : 1, **d.** of death better than **d.** of birth.
Eccl. 12 : 1, while the evil **d.** come not.
Cant. 2 : 17; 4 : 6, till the **d.** break.
Isa. 10 : 3, in the **d.** of visitation.
27 : 3, Lord will keep it night and **d.**
65 : 20, an infant of **d.**
Ezek. 30 : 2, woe worth the **d.**!
Zech. 4 : 10, **d.** of small things.
Mal. 3 : 2, who may abide **d.** of his coming ?
Matt. 7 : 22, many will say in that **d.**
24 : 36; Mark 13 : 32, that **d.** knoweth no
    man.
Matt. 25 : 13, ye know not the **d.** nor the
    hour.
Luke 18 : 7, elect, which cry **d.** and night.
21 : 34, that **d.** come upon you unawares.
23 : 43, to **d.** shalt thou be with me.
John 6 : 39, raise it again at last **d.**
8 : 56, Abraham rejoiced to see my **d.**
9 : 4, I must work while it is **d.**
Acts 17 : 31, he hath appointed a **d.**
Rom. 2 : 5, wrath against **d.** of wrath.
14 : 6, regardeth **a.** to the Lord.
1 Cor. 3 : 13, the **d.** shall declare it.
2 Cor. 6 : 2, the **d.** of salvation.
Eph. 4 : 30, sealed to **d.** of redemption.
Phil. 1 : 6, perform it until **d.** of Christ.
1 Thess. 5 : 2; 2 Pet. 3 : 10, **d.** cometh as a
    thief.
1 Thess. 5 : 5, children of the **d.**
Heb. 10 : 25, as ye see the **d.** approaching.
13 : 8, Jesus Christ same to **d.** and for ever.
2 Pet. 1 : 19, till the **d.** dawn.
3 : 8, one **d.** as a thousand years.
Rev. 6 : 17, great **d.** of his wrath is come.
Daysman [an umpire or arbiter], Job 9 : 33.
Dayspring, from on high, Luke 1 : 78.
Day star, arising in the heart, 2 Pet. 1 : 19.
Deacons appointed, Acts 6; Phil. 1 : 1.
    their qualifications, Acts 6 : 3; 1 Tim. 3 : 8.
Dead, the, Job 3 : 18; 14 : 12; Ps. 6 : 5; 88 : 10;
    115 : 17; 146 : 4; Eccl. 9 : 5; 12 : 7; Isa.
    38 : 18.
    resurrection of, Job 19 : 26; Ps. 49 : 15; Isa.
    26 : 19; Dan. 12 : 2, 13; John 5 : 25;
    1 Cor. 15 : 12; 1 Thess. 4 : 13.
    raised by Elijah, 1 Ki. 17 : 17; by Elisha,
    2 Ki. 4 : 32; 13 : 21; by Christ, Matt.
    9 : 24; Mark 5 : 41; Luke 7 : 12; 8 : 54;
    John 11; by Peter, Acts 9 : 40; by Paul,
    Acts 20 : 10.
Lev. 19 : 28, cuttings for the **d.**
1 Sam. 24 : 14; 2 Sam. 9 : 8; 16 : 9, **d.** dog.
Ps. 31 : 12, forgotten as a **d.** man.
88 : 5, free among the **d.**
115 : 17, the **d.** praise not the Lord.
Prov. 21 : 16, congregation of the **d.**
Eccl. 9 : 5, **d.** know not any thing.
10 : 1, **d.** flies cause ointment.
Isa. 26 : 19, thy **d.** men shall live.
Jer. 22 : 10, weep not for the **d.**

Matt. 8 : 22, let the **d.** bury their **d.**
9 : 24; Mark 5 : 39; Luke 8 : 52, maid not
    d., but.
Matt. 11 : 5; Luke 7 : 22, deaf hear, **d.** raised.
Matt. 22 : 31; Mark 12 : 26, touching resur-
    rection of **d.**
Matt. 23 : 27, full of **d.** men's bones.
28 : 4, keepers became as **d.** men.
Mark 9 : 10, rising from the **d.** should mean.
Luke 15 : 24, 32, was **d.**, and is alive again.
16 : 31, though one rose from the **d.**
John 5 : 25, **d.** shall hear.
6 : 49, did eat manna, and are **d.**
11 : 25, though **d.**, yet shall he live.
Acts 10 : 42; 2 Tim. 4 : 1, judge of quick
    and **d.**
Rom. 6 : 2, 11; 1 Pet. 2 : 24, **d.** to sin.
Rom. 7 : 4; Gal. 2 : 19, **d.** to the law.
Rom. 14 : 9, Lord both of **d.** and living.
1 Cor. 15 : 15, if the **d.** rise not.
2 Cor. 5 : 14, then were all **d.**
Eph. 2 : 1; Col. 2 : 13, **d.** in trespasses and
    sins.
Eph. 5 : 14, arise from the **d.**
Col. 1 : 18, firstborn from the **d.**
1 Thess. 4 : 16, **d.** in Christ shall rise first.
1 Tim. 5 : 6, **d.** while she liveth.
Heb. 6 : 1; 9 : 14, from **d.** works.
11 : 4, being **d.** yet speaketh.
Jas. 2 : 17, 20, 26, faith **d.**
1 Pet. 4 : 6, preached to them that are **d.**
Jude 12, twice **d.**
Rev. 1 : 5, first begotten of the **d.**
3 : 1, a name that thou livest, and art **d.**
14 : 13, blessed are the **d.**
20 : 12, the **d.** small and great.
20 : 13, sea gave up **d.**
Deadly, Ps. 17 : 9, from my **d.** enemies.
Mark 16 : 18, drink any **d.** thing.
Jas. 3 : 8, tongue full of **d.** poison.
Deaf, Lev. 19 : 14, shalt not curse the **d.**
Ps. 38 : 13, I as a **d.** man, heard not.
58 : 4, like **d.** adder that stoppeth.
Isa. 29 : 18, in that day **d.** hear words.
35 : 5, ears of the **d.** be unstopped.
Matt. 11 : 5; Luke 7 : 22, the **d.** hear.
Mark 7 : 32, brought to him one **d.**
9 : 25, thou **d.** spirit, come out.
Deal [a portion or part]. " A tenth deal of
    flour," Ex. 29 : 40. To act, as " deal
    truly," Gen. 24 : 49; " deal well," Gen.
    32 : 9; " deal worse," Gen. 19 : 9.
Lev. 19 : 11, nor **d.** falsely.
Job 42 : 8, **d.** with you after folly.
Ps. 75 : 4, **d.** not foolishly.
119 : 17; 142 : 7, **d.** bountifully with.
Prov. 12 : 22, they that **d.** truly are his delight.
Isa. 21 : 2; 24 : 16, treacherous dealer **d.**
    treacherously.
26 : 10, in land of uprightness **d.** unjustly.
Jer. 6 : 13; 8 : 10, every one **d.** falsely.
Hos. 5 : 7, have **d.** treacherously against Lord.
Mark 10 : 48, the more a great **d.**
Luke 2 : 48, why hast thou thus **d.** with us ?
John 4 : 9, no **d.** with Samaritans.
Acts 7 : 19, **d.** subtilly with kindred.
Rom. 12 : 3, as God hath **d.** to every man.
Dear, Jer. 31 : 20, is Ephraim my **d.** son ?
Acts 20 : 24, neither count I my life **d.**

Eph. 5 : 1, followers of God, as **d.** children.
Col. 1 : 13, into kingdom of his **d.** son.
Dearth, Gen. 41 : 54, **d.** was in all lands.
2 Ki. 4 : 38; Acts 7 : 11, was a **d.** in the land.
Neh. 5 : 3, buy corn because of **d.**
Acts 11 : 28, there should be great **d.**
Death, the consequence of Adam's sin, Gen. 2 : 17; 3 : 19; Rom. 5 : 12; 6 : 23; 1 Cor. 15 : 21.
universal, Job 1 : 21; 3 : 17; 14 : 1; 21 : 13; Ps. 49 : 19; 89 : 48; Eccl. 5 : 15; 8 : 8; 9 : 5, 10; 11 : 8; Heb. 9 : 27.
characterised, Gen. 3 : 19; Deut. 31 : 16 (John 11 : 11); Job 1 : 21; 3 : 13; 10 : 21; 12 : 22; 14 : 2; 16 : 22; 24 : 17; Ps. 16 : 10; 23 : 4; 104 : 29; Eccl. 9 : 10; Hab. 2 : 5; Luke 12 : 20; 2 Cor. 5 : 1, 8; Phil. 1 : 23; 1 Tim. 6 : 7; 2 Pet. 1 : 14.
inflicted as a punishment, Gen. 9 : 6; Ex. 21 : 12; 22 : 18; 31 : 14; 35 : 2; Lev. 20 : 2; 21 : 9; 1 Ki. 21 : 10; Matt. 15 : 4.
vanquished by Christ, Rom. 6 : 9; 1 Cor. 15 : 26; (Hos. 13 : 14); 2 Tim. 1 : 10; Heb. 2 : 15; Rev. 1 : 18.
prayers and exhortations concerning, 2 Ki. 20 : 1; Ps. 39; 90; Eccl. 9 : 10; John 9 : 4; 1 Pet. 1 : 24.
excluded from heaven, Luke 20 : 36; Rev. 21 : 4.
persons exempted from: Enoch, Gen. 5 : 24; Heb. 11 : 5; Elijah, 2 Ki. 2 : 11.
See 1 Cor. 15 : 51; 1 Thess. 4 : 17.
spiritual, Isa. 9 : 2; Matt. 4 : 16; 8 : 22; Luke 1 : 79; John 6 : 53; Rom. 5 : 15; 6 : 13; 8 : 6; Eph. 2 : 1; 4 : 18; Col. 2 : 13; 1 Tim. 5 : 6; Heb. 6 : 1; 9 : 14; 1 John 3 : 14; Rev. 3 : 1.
deliverance from, by Christ, John 5 : 24; Rom. 6 : 11; Eph. 2 : 5; 5 : 14; 1 John 5 : 12.
Eternal, Prov. 14 : 12; Dan. 12 : 2; Matt. 7 : 13; 10 : 28; 23 : 33; 25 : 30, 41; Mark 9 : 44; John 5 : 29; Rom. 1 : 32; 2 : 8; 6 : 23; 9 : 22; 2 Thess. 1 : 7; Jas. 4 : 12; 2 Pet. 2 : 17
(the second death), Rev. 2 : 11; 19 : 20; 20 : 14; 21 : 8.
salvation from, by Christ, John 3 : 16; 8 : 51; Jas. 5 : 20.
of Christ foretold, Isa. 53; Dan. 9 : 26; Zech. 13 : 7.
See Matt. 27 : 29 (Deut. 21 : 23; Gal. 3 : 13); Heb. 2 : 9; 12 : 2; 1 Pet. 1 : 11.
voluntary, Luke 12 : 50; John 10 : 11, 18; Heb. 10 : 7.
its object, Isa. 53; Dan. 9 : 26; Matt. 20 : 28; 1 Cor. 5 : 7; 1 Tim. 2 : 6; Titus 2 : 14; Heb. 9 : 26; 1 Pet. 1 : 18; Rev. 1 : 5.
of saints, Num. 23 : 10; 2 Ki. 22 : 20; Ps. 23 : 4; 48 : 14; 116 : 15; Dan. 12 : 2; Luke 16 : 25; John 11 : 11; Prov. 14 : 32; Isa. 26 : 19; 57 : 1; 2 Cor. 5 : 8; Phil. 1 : 21; 2 Tim. 4 : 8; Heb. 11 : 13; Rev. 2 : 10.
of Abraham, Gen. 25 : 8; Isaac, Gen. 35 : 29; Jacob, Gen. 49; Aaron, Num. 20 : 23; Moses, Deut. 34 : 5; Joshua, Josh. 24 : 29; David, 1 Ki. 2; Elisha, 2 Ki. 13 : 14; Stephen, Acts 7 : 54; Dorcas, Acts 9 : 37.

of the wicked, Job 18 : 11; 21 : 13; 27 : 19; Ps. 34 : 16; 49 : 14; 73 : 19; Prov. 10 : 7; 11 : 7; 14 : 32; 29 : 1; Isa. 14 : 9; Ezek. 3 : 19; 18 : 23; Dan. 12 : 2; Luke 12 : 20; 16 : 22; John 8 : 21; Acts 1 : 25.
of Korah, etc., Num. 16 : 32.
of Hophni and Phinehas, 1 Sam. 4 : 11.
of Absalom, 2 Sam. 18 : 9; Ahab, 1 Ki. 22 : 34.
of Jezebel, 2 Ki. 9 : 33; Athaliah, 2 Chr. 23 : 15.
of Haman, Esther 7 : 10; Judas, Matt. 27 : 5; Acts 1 : 18; Ananias, etc., Acts 5 : 5; Herod, Acts 12 : 23.
Num. 23 : 10, let me die **d.** of righteous.
Judg. 5 : 18, jeoparded lives to the **d.**
Ruth 1 : 17, if ought but **d.** part thee and me.
1 Sam. 15 : 32, the bitterness of **d.** past.
20 : 3, but a step between me and **d.**
2 Sam. 1 : 23, in **d.** not divided.
22 : 5; Ps. 18 : 4; 116 : 3, waves of **d.** compassed.
Job 3 : 21, long for **d.**, but it cometh not.
7 : 15, my soul chooseth **d.**
Ps. 6 : 5, in **d.** no remembrance.
13 : 3, lest I sleep the sleep of **d.**
23 : 4, valley of shadow of **d.**
48 : 14, our guide even unto **d.**
68 : 20, unto God belong issues from **d.**
73 : 4, no bands in their **d.**
89 : 48, what man shall not see **d.** ?
102 : 20, loose those appointed to **d.**
116 : 15, precious is **d.** of his saints.
Prov. 7 : 27, chambers of **d.**
8 : 36, they that hate me love **d.**
Cant. 8 : 6, love is strong as **d.**
Isa. 9 : 2; Jer. 2 : 6, land of the shadow of **d.**
Isa. 25 : 8; 1 Cor. 15 : 56, swallow up **d.** in victory.
Jer. 8 : 3, **d.** chosen rather than life.
Ezek. 18 : 32; 33 : 11, no pleasure in **d.**
Hos. 13 : 14, O **d.**, I will be thy plagues.
Matt. 15 : 4; Mark 7 : 10, let him die the **d.**
Matt. 16 : 28; Mark 9 : 1; Luke 9 : 27, not taste of **d.**
Matt. 26 : 38; Mark 14 : 34, my soul is sorrowful to **d.**
Mark 5 : 23; John 4 : 47, at point of **d.**
Luke 2 : 26, should not see **d.** before.
23 : 22, found no cause of **d.**
John 5 : 24; 1 John 3 : 14, passed from **d.** to life.
John 8 : 51, 52, keep my saying, shall never see **d.**
11 : 4, sickness not unto **d.**
12 : 33; 18 : 32; 21 : 19, signifying what **d.**
Acts 2 : 24, having loosed the pains of **d.**
Rom. 5 : 10; Col. 1 : 22, reconciled by the **d.**
Rom. 6 : 5, planted in likeness of his **d.**
6 : 23, wages of sin is **d.**
8 : 2, law of sin and **d.**
1 Cor. 3 : 22, life or **d.**, all are yours.
11 : 26, show the Lord's **d.** till he come.
15 : 21, by man came **d.**
15 : 55, O **d.**, where is thy sting ?
2 Cor. 2 : 16, savour of **d.** unto **d.**
Phil. 2 : 8, **d.**, even **d.** of the cross.
Heb. 2 : 9, taste **d.** for every man.
Jas. 1 : 15, sin bringeth forth **d.**

Rev. 1 : 18, keys of hell and of **d.**
2 : 10, be faithful unto **d.**
21 : 4, no more **d.**
Debate, Prov. 25 : 9, **d.** cause with neighbour.
Isa. 58 : 4, ye fast for strife and **d.**
Rom. 1 : 29, full of envy, **d.**
2 Cor. 12 : 20, I fear lest there be **d.**
Deborah (dĕb-ŏ-răh) [a bee], the prophetess, judges and delivers Israel, Judg. 4; her song, Judg. 5.
Debt censured, Ps. 37 : 21; Prov. 3 : 27; Luke 16 : 5; Rom. 13 : 8.
2 Ki. 4 : 7, pay thy **d.,** and live.
Neh. 10 : 31, leave exaction of every **d.**
Prov. 22 : 26, be not sureties for **d.**
Matt. 6 : 12, forgive us our **d.**
18 : 27, forgave him the **d.**
Rom. 4 : 4, reward reckoned of **d.**
Debtors, parables of, Matt. 18 : 21; Luke 7 : 41; 16. See Matt. 6 : 12.
Matt. 23 : 16, swear by gold, is a **d.**
Rom. 1 : 14, I am **d.** to the Greeks.
8 : 12, we are **d.,** not to the flesh.
Gal. 5 : 3, **d.** to do the whole law.
Decapolis (dĕ-căp-ŏ-lĭs).   The Decapolis, or "ten city" region (Matt. 4 : 25; Mark 5 : 20; Pliny, H. Nat. 5 : 18), was a sort of confederation of cities, similar to those which existed in other parts of the Roman Empire.
Decay, Lev. 25 : 35; Isa. 44 : 26; Heb. 8 : 13.
Decease, Isa. 26 : 14, **d.,** they shall not rise.
Luke 9 : 31, spake of his **d.**
2 Pet. 1 : 15, after my **d.** in remembrance.
Deceit, proceeds from the heart, Jer. 17 : 9.
and lying, work of the devil, John 8 : 44; Acts 5 : 3.
instances of :—
the serpent and Eve, Gen. 3.
Abram and his wife, Gen. 12 : 14.
Isaac and his wife, Gen. 26 : 10.
Rebekah and Jacob, Gen. 27.
the sons of Jacob, Gen. 37 : 31.
Rahab and spies at Jericho, Josh. 2 : 1, 4, 5.
Jael and Sisera, Judg. 4 : 20.
the old prophet, 1 Ki. 13 : 18.
Gehazi, 2 Ki. 5 : 25.
Herod and the wise men, Matt. 2 : 16.
Ananias and Sapphira, Acts 5 : 1.
Ps. 10 : 7, mouth full of **d.**
36 : 3, words of his mouth are **d.**
Ps. 38 : 12, imagine **d.** all the day.
50 : 19, tongue frameth **d.**
72 : 14, redeem their soul from **d.**
Prov. 12 : 5, counsels of wicked are **d.**
20 : 17, bread of **d.** is sweet.
Jer. 14 : 14; 23 : 26, prophesy the **d.** of their heart.
Hos. 11 : 12, compasseth me with **d.**
Amos 8 : 5, falsifying balances by **d.** ?
Zeph. 1 : 9, fill masters' houses with **d.**
Mark 7 : 22, out of heart proceed **d.**
Rom. 3 : 13, they have used **d.**
Col. 2 : 8, vain of **d.** after tradition.
Deceitful, Prov. 31 : 30, favour is **d.**
2 Cor. 11 : 13, false apostles, **d.** workers.
Eph. 4 : 22, according to **d.** lusts.
Deceitfully, 2 Cor. 4 : 2, not handling the word of God **d.**

Deceitfulness, Matt. 13 : 22; Mark 4 : 19, the **d.** of riches.
Deceive, Deut. 11 : 16, take heed that your heart be not **d.**
2 Ki. 19 : 10; Isa. 37 : 10, let not thy God **d.** thee.
Jer. 20 : 7, O Lord, thou hast **d.** me, and I was **d.**
37 : 9, **d.** not yourselves.
Obad. 3, pride of heart **d.** thee.
Matt. 24 : 4; Mark 13 : 5, no man **d.** you.
Matt. 24 : 24, **d.** the very elect.
John 7 : 12, nay, but he **d.** the people.
1 Cor. 6 : 9; 15 : 33; Gal. 6 : 7, be not **d.**
2 Cor. 6 : 8, as **d.,** and yet true.
Eph. 4 : 14, they lie in wait to **d.**
5 : 6; 2 Thess. 2 : 3; 1 John 3 : 7, let no man **d.** you.
2 Tim. 3 : 13, worse and worse, **d.,** and being **d.**
1 John 1 : 8, no sin, we **d.** ourselves.
Decision, how manifested, Ex. 32 : 26; Num. 14 : 24; Deut. 6 : 5; Josh. 1 : 7; 24 : 15; 1 Ki. 18 : 21; 2 Chr. 15 : 12; Isa. 56 : 6; Luke 9 : 62; 1 Cor. 15 : 58; Heb. 3 : 6, 14; Jas. 1 : 8; 4 : 7.
opposed to wavering, Deut. 5 : 32; 1 Ki. 18 : 21; Ps. 78 : 8; Matt. 6 : 24; Jas. 1 : 8.
of Moses, Ex. 32 : 26.
of Caleb, Num. 13 : 30.
of Joshua, Josh. 24 : 15.
of Ruth, Ruth 1 : 16.
of Paul, Acts 21 : 13; Gal. 1 : 16.
Deck, Job 40 : 10, **d.** thyself with majesty.
Isa. 61 : 10, as a bridegroom **d.** himself.
Jer. 4 : 30, though thou **d.** with gold.
Rev. 18 : 16, city that was **d.**
Declare, 1 Chr. 16 : 24; Ps. 96 : 3, **d.** glory among heathen.
Job 21 : 31, **d.** his way to his face.
38 : 4, **d.** if thou hast understanding.
Ps. 2 : 7, I will **d.** decree.
9 : 11, **d.** among the people his doings.
19 : 1, heavens **d.** glory of God.
40 : 10, I have **d.** thy faithfulness.
66 : 16, I will **d.** what he hath done.
118 : 17, live, and **d.** the works of the Lord.
145 : 4, shall **d.** thy mighty acts.
Isa. 12 : 4, **d.** his doings among people.
41 : 26; 45 : 21, who hath **d.** from beginning?
Isa. 45 : 19, I **d.** things that are right.
53 : 8; Acts 8 : 33, who shall **d.** his generation ?
Isa. 66 : 19, **d.** my glory among Gentiles.
John 17 : 26, have **d.** thy name, and will **d.** it.
Acts 13 : 32, we **d.** glad tidings.
20 : 27, **d.** the counsel of God.
Rom. 1 : 4, **d.** to be Son of God with power.
1 Cor. 3 : 13, the day shall **d.** it.
1 John 1 : 3, have seen, **d.** we to you.
Decline, Deut. 17 : 11, thou shalt not **d.** from sentence.
2 Chr. 34 : 2, **d.** neither to right nor left.
Ps. 102 : 11; 109 : 23, days like a shadow that **d.**
119 : 51, not **d.** from thy law.
Prov. 4 : 5, neither **d.** from words of my mouth.

Decrease, Gen. 8 : 5, the waters **d.** continually.
Ps. 107 : 38, suffereth not their cattle to **d.**
John 3 : 30, he must increase, **I d.**
Decree, Job 22 : 28, thou shalt **d.** a thing, and it shall be.
    28 : 26, made a **d.** for the rain.
Ps. 148 : 6, a **d.** which shall not pass.
Prov. 8 : 15, princes **d.** justice.
Isa. 10 : 1, that **d.** unrighteous **d.**
Acts 16 : 4, delivered the **d.** to keep.
Dedanim (dē-dăn-ĭm), descendants of Dedan, Isa. 21 : 13.
Dedicate, Deut. 20 : 5, a new house not **d.** it.
1 Ki. 7 : 51; 1 Chr. 18 : 11, which David had **d.**
1 Chr. 26 : 27, of spoil they did **d.**
Ezek. 44 : 29, every **d.** thing shall be theirs.
Dedication of tabernacle, Ex. 40; Lev. 8; 9; Num. 7.
of temple, 1 Ki. 8; 2 Chr. 5 : 6.
of wall of Jerusalem, Neh. 12 : 27.
Dedication, Feast of the. This festival, mentioned only once in Canonical Scripture (Τα εγκαίνια, John 10 : 22), was instituted by Judas Maccabæus to commemorate the purification of the Temple on the 25th Chisleu (about December), 164 B.C., three years after it had been polluted by Antiochus Epiphanes. Like the Feast of Tabernacles, it had a duration of eight days. It likewise resembled that Feast in the mode of celebration. Branches of trees were carried and songs sung while mourning and sorrow were forbidden.
Deeds of the body mortified, Rom. 8 : 13; 13 : 14; 1 Cor. 9 : 27; (2 Pet. 2 : 10).
Ex. 9 : 16, in very **d.** for this cause.
2 Sam. 12 : 14, by this **d.** hast given occasion.
Ezra 9 . 13, come upon us for our evil **d.**
Neh. 13 : 14, wipe not out my good **d.**
Ps. 28 : 4; Isa. 59 : 18; Jer. 25 : 14, according to their **d.**
Luke 11 : 48, ye allow the **d.** of your fathers.
    23 : 41, due reward of our **d.**
    24 : 19, a prophet mighty in **d.**
John 3 : 19, because their **d.** were evil.
    8 : 41, ye do the **d.** of your father.
Rom. 2 : 6, render to every man according to his **d.**
Acts 7 : 22, Moses, mighty in word and **d.**
Rom. 3 : 20, by **d.** of law no flesh justified.
Col. 3 : 9, put off old man with his **d.**
Jas. 1 : 25, shall be blessed in his **d.**
2 Pet. 2 : 8, vexed with unlawful **d.**
1 John 3 : 18, not love in word, but in **d.**
Deep, Gen. 1 : 2, darkness on face of **d.**
    7 : 11; 8 : 2, fountains of **d.**
Deut. 33 : 13, the **d.** that coucheth beneath.
Job 38 : 30, face of **d.** is frozen.
Ps. 36 : 6, thy judgments are a great **d.**
    42 : 7, **d.** calleth to **d.**
    107 : 24, see his wonders in the **d.**
Isa. 63 : 13, led them through **d.**
Matt. 13 : 5, no **d.** of earth.
Luke 5 : 4, launch out into **d.**
    6 : 48, digged **d.**, and laid foundation.
    8 : 31, command to go into the **d.**
John 4 : 11, the well is **d.**
1 Cor. 2 : 10, searcheth **d.** things of God.

Deer. See **Fallow Deer.**
Defence, God is, to His people, Job 22 : 25; Ps. 5 : 11; 7 : 10; 31 : 2; 59 : 9; 89 : 18.
of Paul before the Jews, the council, Felix, Festus, and Agrippa, Acts 22–26.
Num. 14 : 9, their **d.** is departed.
Job 22 : 25, the Almighty shall be thy **d.**
Ps. 7 : 10, my **d.** is of God.
    59 : 9; 62 : 2, God is my **d.**
    89 : 18; 94 : 22, Lord is **d.**
Eccl. 7 : 12, wisdom a **d.**, money a **d.**
Isa. 33 : 16, place of **d.** the munitions of rocks.
Acts 19 : 33, would have made his **d.**
Phil. 1 : 7, in **d.** of the Gospel.
Defend, Ps. 5 : 11, shout for joy, because thou **d.** them.
    59 : 1, **d.** me from them that rise up.
    82 : 3, **d.** the poor and fatherless.
Zech. 9 : 15, Lord of hosts shall **d.** them.
Acts 7 : 24, **d.** him, and avenged.
Defile, Ex. 31 : 14, that **d.** Sabbath be put to death.
Num. 35 : 33, blood **d.** the land.
Isa. 59 : 3, your hands are **d.** with blood.
Jer. 2 : 7; 16 : 18, **d.** my land.
Ezek. 23 : 38, they have **d.** my sanctuary.
Dan. 1 : 8, would not **d.** himself with meat.
Matt. 15 : 11; Mark 7 : 15, **d.** a man.
John 18 : 28, lest they should be **d.**
1 Cor. 3 : 17, if any **d.** temple of God.
Heb. 12 : 15, thereby many be **d.**
Jude 8, filthy dreamers **d.** the flesh.
Rev. 3 : 4, few which have not **d.** their garments.
Defraud, Lev. 19 : 13, shalt not **d.** neighbour.
1 Sam. 12 : 3, whom have I **d.** ?
Mark 10 : 19; 1 Cor. 7 : 5, **d.** not.
1 Cor. 6 : 7, rather suffer yourselves to be **d.**
2 Cor. 7 : 2, we have **d.** no man.
1 Thess. 4 : 6, no man **d.** his brother.
Degree, Ps. 62 : 9, men of low **d.**, of high **d.**
Luke 1 : 52, exalted them of low **d.**
1 Tim. 3 : 13, purchase a good **d.**
Jas. 1 : 9, brother of low **d.** rejoice.
Delay, Ps. 119 : 60, **d.** not to keep commandments.
Matt. 24 : 48; Luke 12 : 45, lord **d.** his coming.
Acts 9 : 38, not **d.** to come to them.
Delectable [delightful], Isa. 44 : 9, their **d.** things shall not profit.
Delicate [dainty]. " With my delicates," Jer. 51 : 34.
Prov. 29 : 21, he that **d.** bringeth up his servant.
Isa. 47 : 1, no more called tender and **d.**
Lam. 4 : 5, that did feed **d.** are desolate.
Luke 7 : 25, that live **d.** are in king's courts.
Delicately [cheerfully], 1 Sam. 15 : 32, Agag came unto him **d.**
Delight, Deut. 10 : 15, Lord had a **d.** in thy fathers.
1 Sam. 15 : 22, hath Lord as great **d.** in offerings.
2 Sam. 15 : 26, I have no **d.** in thee.
Job 22 : 26, have **d.** in Almighty.
    27 : 10, will he **d.** himself in the Almighty ?
Ps. 1 : 2, his **d.** is in law of Lord.

16 : 3, the excellent, in whom is my **d.**
37 : 4, **d.** thyself also in Lord.
40 : 8, I **d.** to do thy will, O God.
51 : 16, **d.** not in burnt offering.
94 : 19, thy comforts **d.** my soul.
119 : 24, thy testimonies are my **d.**
119 : 77, 174, thy law is my **d.**
Prov. 8 : 30, I was daily his **d.**
11 : 1, just weight is Lord's **d.**
12 : 22, that deal truly are his **d.**
18 : 2, fool hath no **d.** in understanding.
Cant. 2 : 3, under his shadow with great **d.**
Isa. 1 : 11, I **d.** not in blood of bullocks.
42 : 1, elect, in whom my soul **d.**
55 : 2, soul **d.** itself in fatness.
58 : 13, call Sabbath a **d.**
Jer. 6 : 10, no **d.** in word of Lord.
Mic. 7 : 18, he **d.** in mercy.
Mal. 3 : 1, messenger of covenant ye **d.** in.
Rom. 7 : 22, I **d.** in law after inward man.
Delilah (dē-lī-lăh) [weak], betrays Samson, Judg. 16.
Deliver, Ex. 3 : 8; Acts 7 : 34, come down to **d.** them.
Deut. 32 : 39; Isa. 43 : 13, any **d.** out of my hand.
Josh. 2 : 13, **d.** our lives from death.
1 Sam. 12 : 21, which cannot profit nor **d.**
2 Chr. 32 : 13, were gods able to **d.** their lands?
Job 5 : 19, **d.** thee in six troubles.
36 : 18, great ransom cannot **d.**
Ps. 33 : 19, to **d.** their soul from death.
Ps. 56 : 13, **d.** my feet from falling.
91 : 3, **d.** thee from snare of fowler.
Prov. 24 : 11, forbear to **d.** them.
Eccl. 8 : 8, shall wickedness **d.** those.
Isa. 50 : 2, have I no power to **d.** ?
Jer. 1 : 8, I am with thee to **d.** thee.
43 : 11, **d.** such as are for death to death.
Dan. 3 : 17, God is able to **d.,** and will **d.**
Amos 2 : 14, neither mighty **d.** himself.
Matt. 6 : 13; Luke 11 : 4, **d.** us from evil.
Matt. 11 : 27; Luke 10 : 22, all things **d.** to me of my Father.
Matt. 27 : 43, let him **d.** now.
Acts 2 : 23, being **d.,** by counsel of God.
Rom. 4 : 25, was **d.** for our offences.
2 Cor. 4 : 11, **d.** to death for Jesus' sake.
1 Thess. 1 : 10, **d.** us from the wrath to come.
Jude 3, faith once **d.** to the saints.
Deliverances—Lot, Gen. 14; 19; Moses; Ex. 2; Israel, Ex. 14; Judg. 4; 7; 15; 1 Sam. 7; 14; 17; 2 Ki. 19; 2 Chr. 14 : 20; Daniel and his companions, Dan. 3 : 19; 6 : 22; The apostles, Acts 5 : 19; 12 : 7; 16 : 26; 28 : 1; 2 Tim. 4 : 17.
Gen. 45 : 7, to save by a great **d.**
2 Ki. 5 : 1, Lord had given **d.** to Syria.
1 Chr. 11 : 14, Lord saved by great **d.**
Ps. 32 : 7, compass me with songs of **d.**
Luke 4 : 18, preach **d.** to the captives.
Heb. 11 : 35, not accepting **d.**
Deliverer, Judg. 3 : 9, 15, raised up a **d.**
2 Sam. 22 : 2, my fortress, and my **d.**
Ps. 18 : 2; 40 : 17; 70 : 5; 144 : 2, my **d.**
Acts 7 : 35, a ruler and a **d.**
Rom. 11 : 26, out of Sion the **D.**
Delusion, Isa. 66 : 4, I will choose their **d.**
2 Thess. 2 : 11, send them strong **d.**

Demand, Job 38 : 3; 40 : 7; 42 : 4, I will **d.** of thee.
Dan. 4 : 17, **d.** by the word.
Matt. 2 : 4, **d.** where Christ should be born.
Luke 17 : 20, **d.** of the Pharisees.
Acts 21 : 33, **d.** who he was.
Demetrius (dē-mē-trĭ-ŭs) [belonging to Demeter (or Ceres)], a disciple, 3 John 12.
a silversmith, Acts 19 : 24.
Demonstration, 1 Cor. 2 : 4, in **d.** of the Spirit.
Den, Judg. 6 : 2, Israel made them **d.**
Job 37 : 8, then the beasts go into **d.**
Isa. 11 : 8, put hand on cockatrice' **d.**
Jer. 7 : 11, is this house a **d.** of robbers ?
Matt. 21 : 13; Mark 11 : 17, a **d.** of thieves.
Heb. 11 : 38, they wandered in **d.**
Denial of Christ, deprecated, 2 Tim. 1 : 8; Titus 1 : 16; 2 Pet. 2 : 1; Jude 4.
its punishment, Matt. 10 : 33; 2 Tim. 2 : 12; 2 Pet. 2 : 1; Jude 4-15.
by Peter, Matt. 26 : 69.
by the Jews, John 18 : 40; 19 : 15; Acts 3 : 13.
Deny, Josh. 24 : 27, lest ye **d.** your God.
Prov. 30 : 9, lest I be full, and **d.** thee.
Matt. 10 : 33, shall **d.** me before men.
16 : 24, let him **d.** himself and take.
Luke 20 : 27, which **d.** resurrection.
2 Tim. 2 : 13, he cannot **d.** himself.
Titus 1 : 16, in works they **d.** him.
Depart, Gen. 49 : 10, sceptre shalt not **d.** from Judah.
2 Sam. 22 : 22; Ps. 18 : 21, have not **d.** from my God.
Job 21 : 14; 22 : 17, they say to God, **d.**
28 : 28, to **d.** from evil is understanding.
Ps. 34 : 14; 37 : 27, **d.** from evil, and do good.
Prov. 22 : 6, when old, he will not **d.** from it.
Matt. 14 : 16, they need not **d.**
25 : 41, **d.** from me, ye cursed.
Luke 2 : 29, lettest thy servant **d.** in peace.
4 : 13, devil **d.** for a season.
5 : 8, **d.** from me, I am a sinful man, O Lord.
John 13 : 1, when Jesus knew he should **d.**
2 Cor. 12 : 8, besought that it might **d.** from me.
Phil. 1 : 23, having a desire to **d.**
1 Tim. 4 : 1, some shall **d.** from faith.
2 Tim. 2 : 19, nameth Christ, **d.** from iniquity.
Departure, Ezek. 26 : 18, troubled at thy **d.**
2 Tim. 4 : 6, time of my **d.** is at hand.
Deposed, Dan. 5 : 20.
Deprived, Gen. 27 : 45; Job 39 : 17; Isa. 38 : 10.
Depth, Job 28 : 14, **d.** saith, it is not in me.
Ps. 33 : 7, he layeth up **d.** in storehouses.
77 : 16, the **d.** were troubled.
106 : 9, led through **d.** as through wilderness.
130 : 1, out of the **d.** have I cried.
Prov. 8 : 24, when no **d.** I was brought forth.
Prov. 25 : 3, heaven for height, earth for **d.**
Matt. 18 : 6, better drowned in **d.** of sea.
Mark 4 : 5, no **d.** of earth.
Rom. 8 : 39, nor height nor **d.** separate.
11 : 33, O the **d.** of the riches.
Deputy [one deputed to rule, a proconsul], 1Ki. 21 : 47, a **d.** was King.
Acts 13 : 8, to turn **d.** from the faith.
19 : 38, are **d.** let them implead.
Derision, Job 30 : 1, younger than I have me in **d.**

Ps. 2 : 4, the Lord shall have them in **d.**
44 : 13; 79 : 4, a **d.** to them round us.
59 : 8, have heathen in **d.**
Jer. 20 : 7, 8, in **d.** daily.
Lam. 3 : 14, I was a **d.** to my people.
See Luke 16 : 14; 23 : 35.
Descend, Ps. 49 : 17, glory not **d.** after him.
Ezek. 26 : 20; 31 : 16, them that **d.** into pit.
Matt. 7 : 25, 27, rains **d.**, and floods came.
Mark 1 : 10; John 1 : 32, Spirit **d.**
Mark 15 : 32, let Christ **d.** now from cross.
Rom. 10 : 7, who shall **d.** into deep ?
Eph. 4 : 10, he that **d.** is same that ascended.
Jas. 3 : 15, this wisdom **d.** not.
Rev. 21 : 10, city **d.** out of heaven.
Descent, Luke 19 : 37, the **d.** of Mount of Olives.
Heb. 7 : 6, he whose **d.** is not counted.
Describe, Josh. 18 : 4, go through land, and **d.** it.
Rom. 4 : 6, as David **d.** the blessedness.
10 : 5, Moses **d.** righteousness of the law.
Desert, Ps. 78 : 40, oft did they grieve him in **d.**
102 : 6, like an owl of the **d.**
Isa. 13 : 21; 34 : 14; Jer. 50 : 39, wild beasts of **d.** shall lie there.
Isa. 35 : 1, the **d.** shall rejoice.
35 : 6; 43 : 19, scream in the **d.**
40 : 3, in **d.** a highway for our God.
Jer. 17 : 6, like the heath in the **d.**
25 : 24, people that dwell in **d.** shall drink.
Matt. 24 : 26, say, behold, he is in the **d.**
Luke 9 : 10, aside privately into a **d.** place.
John 6 : 31, did eat manna in the **d.**
Heb. 11 : 38, they wandered in **d.**
Desire, Job 14 : 15, **d.** to work of thine hands.
Ps. 10 : 3; 21 : 2; Rom. 10 : 1, heart's **d.**
Ps. 38 : 9, all my **d.** is before thee.
54 : 7; 59 : 10; 92 : 11; 112 : 8, **d.** on enemies.
92 : 11; 112 : 10, **d.** of the wicked.
145 : 16, the **d.** of every living thing.
Prov. 10 : 24; 11 : 23, the **d.** of righteous.
13 : 19, **d.** accomplished is sweet.
21 : 25, the **d.** of slothful killeth him.
Eccl. 12 : 5, **d.** shall fail.
Ezek. 24 : 16, 21, 25, the **d.** of thine eyes.
Mic. 7 : 3, great man uttereth mischievous **d.**
Hab. 2 : 5, enlargeth **d.** as hell.
Hag. 2 : 7, the **d.** of all nations.
Luke 22 : 15, with **d.** I have **d.** to eat.
Rom. 10 : 1, my heart's **d.** for Israel.
Eph. 2 : 3, fulfilling **d.** of flesh and mind.
Phil. 1 : 23, having a **d.** to depart.
Desired, 1 Ki. 2 : 20, I **d.** one small petition.
Job 13 : 3, I **d.** to reason with God.
Ps. 19 : 10, more to be **d.** than gold.
27 : 4, one thing I **d.** of the Lord.
40 : 6, sacrifice and offering thou didst not **d.**
Ps. 45 : 11, king greatly **d.** thy beauty.
73 : 25, none on earth I **d.** beside thee.
Prov. 3 : 15, all thou canst **d.** not to be compared.
13 : 4, soul of sluggard **d.** and hath not.
Isa. 53 : 2, no beauty that we should **d.** him.
Hos. 6 : 6, I **d.** mercy and not sacrifice.
Matt. 13 : 17, have **d.** to see those things.
20 : 20, **d.** a certain thing of him.

Mark 9 : 35, if any **d.** to be first.
10 : 35, do for us whatsoever we **d.**
11 : 24, what things ye **d.**, when ye pray.
Luke 10 : 24, kings have **d.** to see.
16 : 21, **d.** to be fed with crumbs.
22 : 15, have **d.** to eat this passover.
Acts 3 : 14, **d.** a murderer to be granted.
1 Cor. 14 : 1, **d.** spiritual gifts.
Gal. 4 : 9, ye **d.** again to be in bondage.
Phil. 4 : 17, not because I **d.** a gift.
Heb. 11 : 16, they **d.** a better country.
Jas. 4 : 2, ye **d.** to have, and cannot obtain.
1 Pet. 1 : 12, the angels **d.** to look into.
2 : 2, as babes, **d.** sincere milk of the word.
Desirous, Prov. 23 : 3, be not **d.** of his dainties.
Luke 23 : 8, Herod was **d.** to see him.
2 Cor. 11 : 32, **d.** to apprehend me.
Gal. 5 : 26, not be **d.** of vain glory.
Desolate, Ps. 25 : 16, have mercy, for I am **d.**
40 : 15, let them be **d.** for a reward.
Ps. 69 : 25; Acts 1 : 20, let their habitation be **d.**
Ps. 143 : 4, my heart within me is **d.**
Isa. 54 : 1; Gal. 4 : 27, more are children of **d.**
Jer. 2 : 12, be ye very **d.**, saith the Lord.
32 : 43; 33 : 12, **d.** without man or beast.
Dan. 11 : 31; 12 : 11, abomination that maketh **d.**
Mal. 1 : 4, return and build the **d.** places.
Matt. 23 : 38; Luke 13 : 35, house left to you **d.**
Rev. 18 : 19, in one hour is she made **d.**
Desolation, 2 Ki. 22 : 19, they should become a **d.**
Ps. 46 : 8, what **d.** he hath made in the earth.
74 : 3; Jer. 25 : 9; Ezek. 35 : 9, perpetual **d.**
Prov. 1 : 27, when your fear cometh as **d.**
3 : 25, the **d.** of the wicked.
Isa. 47 : 11, **d.** come on thee suddenly.
61 : 4, raise up former **d.**, the **d.** of many generations.
Zeph. 1 : 15, a day of wasteness and **d.**
Matt. 12 : 25; Luke 11 : 17, kingdom divided brought to **d.**
Luke 21 : 20, know **d.** thereof is nigh.
Despair, deprecated, Deut. 20 : 3; Ps. 27 : 13; 31 : 24; 37 : 1; 42 : 11; Prov. 24 : 10; Isa. 40 : 30; Luke 18 : 1; 2 Cor. 4 : 8; Gal. 6 : 9; 2 Thess. 3 : 13; Heb. 12 : 3.
1 Sam. 27 : 1, Saul shall **d.** of me, to seek me.
Eccl. 2 : 20, to cause my heart to **d.**
2 Cor. 4 : 8, perplexed, not in **d.**
Desperate, Job 6 : 26, speeches of one that is **d.**
Isa. 17 : 11, grief and **d.** sorrow.
Jer. 17 : 9, **d.** wicked.
Despise, Lev. 26 : 15, if ye **d.** my statutes.
1 Sam. 2 : 30, that **d.** me shall be lightly esteemed.
Job 5 : 17; Prov. 3 : 11; Heb. 12 : 5, **d.** not chastening.
Ps. 51 : 17, contrite heart thou wilt not **d.**
73 : 20, thou shalt **d.** their image.
102 : 17, he will not **d.** their prayer.
Prov. 1 : 7, fools **d.** wisdom.
6 : 30, men do not **d.** a thief.
15 : 5, fool **d.** father's instruction.
Prov. 23 : 22, **d.** not mother when old.
Isa. 33 : 15, he that **d.** gain of oppressions.
53 : 3, he is **d.**, and rejected.

Ezek. 20 : 13, 16, they **d.** my judgments.
Amos 2 : 4, they **d.** the law of the Lord.
Zech. 4 : 10, who hath **d.** day of small things ?
Mal. 1 : 6, wherein have we **d.** thy name ?
Matt. 6 : 24; Luke 16 : 13, hold to one, **d.** the other.
Luke 10 : 16, **d.** you, **d.** me, **d.** him that sent me.
Rom. 2 : 4, **d.** thou the riches of his goodness.
1 Cor. 11 : 22, **d.** ye the church of God.
1 Thess. 4 : 8, **d.** not man, but God.
5 : 20, **d.** not prophesyings.
Titus 2 : 15, let no man **d.** thee.
Heb. 12 : 2, endured cross, **d.** the shame.
Jas. 2 : 6, ye have **d.** the poor.
Despisers, Acts 13 : 41, behold, ye **d.** wonder.
2 Tim. 3 : 3, fierce **d.** of those good.
Despite, Ezek. 25 : 6, with thy **d.** against the land of Israel.
Heb. 10 : 29, done **d.** to spirit of grace.
Despitefully, Matt. 5 : 44; Luke 6 : 28, that **d.** use you.
Acts 14 : 5, assault to use them **d.**
Rom. 1 : 30, haters of God **d.**
Destitute, Ps. 102 : 17, will regard prayer of **d.**
Prov. 15 : 21, folly is joy to him that is **d.** of wisdom.
1 Tim. 6 : 5, men **d.** of the truth.
Heb. 11 : 37, being **d.**, afflicted, tormented.
Jas. 2 : 15, if a brother or sister be **d.**
Destroy, Gen. 18 : 23, **d.** righteous with the wicked.
2 Sam. 1 : 14, **d.** Lord's anointed.
Job 19 : 10, he hath **d.** me on every side.
19 : 26, though worms **d.** this body.
Ps. 40 : 14; 63 : 9, seek my soul to **d.** it.
101 : 8, I will **d.** all wicked of the land.
Prov. 1 : 32, prosperity of fools shall **d.** them.
Eccl. 9 : 18, one sinner **d.** much good.
Isa. 11 : 9; 65 : 25, not **d.** in all my holy mountain.
Jer. 17 : 18, **d.** them with double destruction.
Hos. 13 : 9, thou hast **d.** thyself.
Matt. 5 : 17, not come to **d.** but to fulfil.
10 : 28, fear him that is able to **d.**
12 : 14; Mark 3 : 6; 11 : 18, they might **d.** him.
Matt. 21 : 41, miserably **d.** those wicked men.
Mark 1 : 24; Luke 4 : 34, art thou come to **d.** us ?
Mark 12 : 9; Luke 20 : 16, **d.** the husbandmen.
Mark 14 : 58, say, I will **d.** this temple.
Luke 6 : 9, is it lawful to save life, or to **d.** it ?
Luke 9 : 56, not come to **d.** men's lives.
17 : 27, flood came, and **d.** them all.
John 2 : 19, **d.** this temple, and I will raise.
Rom. 14 : 15, **d.** not him with thy meat.
Gal. 1 : 23, preacheth the faith he once **d.**
2 Thess. 2 : 8, **d.** with brightness of His coming.
Jas. 4 : 12, able to save and to **d.**
1 John 3 : 8, **d.** the works of the devil.
Destroyer, Ex. 12 : 23, suffer **d.** to come.
Judg. 16 : 24, **d.** of our country.
Job 15 : 21, **d.** shall come upon him.
Ps. 17 : 4, from paths of **d.**
Prov. 28 : 24, companion of a **d.**

Jer. 22 : 7, prepared **d.** against thee.
50 : 11, **d.** of mine heritage.
1 Cor. 10 : 10, destroyed of the **d.**
Destruction, Deut. 32 : 24, be devoured with bitter **d.**
2 Chr. 22 : 4, his counsellers to his **d.**
26 : 16, heart lifted up to his **d.**
Esther 8 : 6, endure to see **d.** of my kindred.
Job 5 : 21, neither be afraid of **d.**
18 : 12, **d.** is ready at his side.
26 : 6, **d.** hath no covering.
31 : 23, **d.** from God was a terror to me.
Ps. 90 : 3, thou turnest man to **d.**
91 : 6, the **d.** that wasteth at noonday.
103 : 4, redeemeth thy life from **d.**
Prov. 1 : 27, your **d.** cometh as a whirlwind.
10 : 29; 21 : 15, **d.** shall be to workers of iniquity.
16 : 18, pride goeth before **d.**
18 : 7, a fool's mouth is his **d.**
27 : 20, hell and **d.** are never full.
Isa. 14 : 23, the besom of **d.**
59 : 7, wasting and **d.** in their paths.
Jer. 17 : 18, destroy them with double **d.**
Lam. 2 : 11; 3 : 48; 4 : 10, **d.** of the daughter of my people.
Hos. 13 : 14, O grave, I will be thy **d.**
Matt. 7 : 13, broad is way that leadeth to **d.**
Rom. 3 : 16, **d.** and misery are in their ways.
9 : 22, vessels of wrath fitted to **d.**
Phil. 3 : 19, many walk, whose end is **d.**
1 Thess. 5 : 3, then sudden **d.** cometh.
2 Thess. 1 : 9, punished with everlasting **d.**
2 Pet. 2 : 1, bring on themselves swift **d.**
3 : 16, wrest Scriptures to their own **d.**
Determine, Ex. 21 : 22, pay as the judges **d.**
1 Sam. 20 : 7, be sure evil is **d.** by him.
Job 14 : 5, seeing his days are **d.**
Dan. 11 : 36, that that is **d.** shall be done.
Luke 22 : 22, Son of man goeth, as it was **d.**
Acts 3 : 13, Pilate was **d.** to let him go.
17 : 26, hath **d.** the times appointed.
1 Cor. 2 : 2, I **d.** not to know anything save Christ, and him crucified.
See Acts 2 : 23.
Detestable, Jer. 16 : 18; Ezek. 5 : 11; 7 : 20; 11 : 18; 37 : 23, **d.** things.
Deuteronomy, The Book of.
The giving of the Law is not recorded in this book, but here a second time Moses rehearses the Law in the ears of the people. Hence the name, which signifies " second " and " law." A new generation had grown up in the 38 years since the Law was received at Sinai. It was necessary that this generation should be instructed in the Law and trained to obedience to it. The command, " Begin to possess," had gone out, and the peoples east of the Jordan were already trembling before Israel. Moses expounds the Law of Jehovah and explains its application to the new circumstances the nation is about to encounter. He writes the Law and directs that every seven years at the Feast of Tabernacles it shall be read to the people. At the command of Jehovah, Moses writes the song (ch. 32) in which the shortcomings of the people and the faithfulness of God are stressed. This song was

to be sung by coming generations as a memorial.

Contents.—The book is almost entirely made up of addresses delivered by Moses to the people. It may be divided into five parts—(1) Chaps. 1–4 : 43, a *résumé* of the history of Israel during the journey through the wilderness, to which is attached an impressive admonition to obey the law, and an account of the appointment of cities of refuge on the eastern side of Jordan. (2) Chaps. 4 : 44–26 contain the second address, partly delivered by Moses (*i.e.*, 5–11) and partly added to at a later date in writing (*i.e.*, 12–26 : 15). This speech commences with a recitation of the Decalogue, with various warnings and exhortations based on this, and concludes with several special directions. (3) Comprises chaps. 27 and 28, concluding speech, containing directions as to the writing down of the law after the crossing of the Jordan, and the delivery of blessings and cursings from Mount Gerizim and Mount Ebal, respectively. (4) Chaps. 29–31, Moses' farewell speech and warning to the people, and his charge to Joshua. (5) Chaps. 32–34, the song of Moses and the announcement of his death; the blessing of Moses and his death and burial.

Device, Esther 9 : 25, d. return on his own head.

Ps. 21 : 11, imagined mischievous d.

33 : 10, maketh d. of the people of none effect.

140 : 8, further not his wicked d.

Prov. 1 : 31, be filled with their own d.

19 : 21, many d. in a man's heart.

Eccl. 9 : 10, no work nor d. in grave.

Jer. 18 : 12, walk after our own d.

Acts 17 : 29, stone graven by man's d.

2 Cor. 2 : 11, not ignorant of his d.

Devil, the adversary of God and man, 1 Pet. 5 : 8.

prince of the devils, Matt. 12 : 24.

prince of the power of the air, Eph. 2 : 2.

prince of this world, John 14 : 30.

sinner from the beginning, 1 John 3 : 8.

cast out of heaven, Luke 10 : 18.

cast down to hell, 2 Pet. 2 : 4; Jude 6.

as serpent causes the fall of man, Gen. 3 : 1.

cursed by God, Gen. 3 : 14.

appears before God, Job 1 : 6; 2 : 1.

called Beelzebub, Matt. 12 : 24.

called Satan, Luke 10 : 18.

called Belial, 2 Cor. 6 : 15.

called Abaddon and Apollyon, Rev. 9 : 11.

tempter of Christ, Matt. 4 : 3-10; Mark 1 : 13; Luke 4 : 2.

tempter of Eve, Gen. 3.

tempter of David, 1 Chr. 21 : 1.

tempter of Job, Job 2 : 7.

resisting Joshua, rebuked, Zech. 3.

desired to have Simon, Luke 22 : 31.

enters into Judas Iscariot, Luke 22 : 3; John 13 : 3.

enters into Ananias, Acts 5 : 3.

as Prince and God of this world, he hinders the Gospel, Matt. 13 : 19; 2 Cor. 4 : 4; 1 Thess. 2 : 18.

works lying wonders, 2 Thess. 2 : 9; Rev. 16 : 14.

appears as an angel of light, 2 Cor. 11 : 14.

is the father of lies, John 8 : 44; 1 Ki. 22 : 22.

vanquished by Christ, Matt. 4 : 11; who destroys his works, 1 John 3 : 8; by His death, Col. 2 : 15; Heb. 2 : 14.

to be resisted by believers, Rom. 16 : 20; 2 Cor. 2 : 11; 11 : 3; Eph. 4 : 27; 6 : 16; 2 Tim. 2 : 26; Jas. 4 : 7; 1 Pet. 5 : 9; 1 John 2 : 13; Rev. 12 : 11.

characterised as proud, 1 Tim. 3 : 6.

as powerful, Eph. 2 : 2; 6 : 12.

as wicked, 1 John 2 : 13.

as subtle, Gen. 3 : 1; 2 Cor. 11 : 3.

as deceitful, 2 Cor. 11 : 14; Eph. 6 : 11.

as fierce and cruel, Luke 8 : 29; 9 : 39, 42; 1 Pet. 5 : 8.

shows himself malignant, Job 1 : 9; 2 : 4.

everlasting fire prepared for, Matt. 25 : 41.

to be condemned at the judgment, Jude 6; Rev. 20 : 10.

compared to a fowler, Ps. 91 : 3.

to a sower of tares, Matt. 13 . 25, 28.

to a wolf, John 10 : 12.

to a roaring lion, 1 Pet. 5 : 8.

called that old serpent, Rev. 12 : 9; 20 : 2.

the wicked called children of, Matt. 13 : 38; Acts 13 : 10; 1 John 3 : 10.

the wicked do lusts of, John 8 : 44.

the wicked ensnared by, 1 Tim. 3 : 7; 2 Tim. 2 : 26.

Matt. 4 : 1, Jesus was led to be tempted of the d.

9 : 32; 12 : 22, dumb man possessed with d.

11 : 18; Luke 7 : 33, they say he hath a d.

Matt. 13 : 39, enemy that sowed is the d.

25 : 41, fire prepared for the d. and his angels.

Mark 7 : 29, d. is gone out of thy daughter.

Luke 4 : 33, had a spirit of an unclean d.

John 6 : 70, and one of you is a d.

7 : 20; 8 : 48, thou hast a d.

10 : 20, many said, he hath a d.

13 : 2, d. having put into heart of Judas.

Acts 13 : 10, thou child of the d.

Eph. 4 : 27, neither give place to the d.

6 : 11, able to stand against wiles of the d.

1 Tim. 3 : 6, fall into condemnation of the d.

2 Tim. 2 : 26, recover out of the snare of the d.

Heb. 2 : 14, had power of death, that is the d.

Jas. 4 : 7, resist d. and he will flee.

1 Pet. 5 : 8, your adversary the d.

1 John 3 : 8, to destroy works of d.

See Jas. 3 : 15.

Devils, sacrifices offered to, Lev. 17 : 7; Deut. 32 : 17; 2 Chr. 11 : 15; Ps. 106 : 37; 1 Cor. 10 : 20; Rev. 9 : 20.

cast out by Christ, Matt. 4 : 24; 8 : 31; Mark 1 : 23; 5 : 2; Luke 9 : 42.

cast out by his apostles, Luke 9 : 1; Acts 16 : 16; 19 : 12.

confess Jesus to be Christ, Matt. 8 : 29; Mark 1 : 24; 3 : 11; 5 : 7; Luke 4 : 34; Acts 19 : 15.

believe and tremble, Jas. 2 : 19.

Devise, Ps. 36 : 4, he d. mischief on his bed

Prov. 3 : 29, d. not evil against thy neighbour.

14 : 22, do they not err that d. evil ?

16 : 9, a man's heart d. his way.

Isa. 32 : 8, the liberal **d.** liberal things.
2 Pet. 1 : 16, cunningly **d.** fables.
Devoted, Lev. 27 : 28; Num. 18 : 14, every **d.** thing.
  Ps. 119 : 38, servant who is **d.** to thy fear.
Devotions [images, idols]. " As I passed by and beheld your devotions," that is, " the objects of your worship," Acts 17 : 23. The same Greek word is rendered " that is worshipped " in 2 Thess. 2 : 4.
Devour, Gen. 49 : 27, in morning **d.** prey.
  Ex. 24 : 17; Isa. 29 : 6; 33 : 14, **d.** fire.
  Lev. 10 : 2, fire from Lord **d.** them.
  2 Sam. 11 : 25, sword **d.** one as well as another.
  22 : 9; Ps. 18 : 8, fire out of his mouth **d.**
  Ps. 80 : 13, beasts of field **d.** it.
  Isa. 1 : 20, ye shall be **d.** with sword.
  Jer. 3 : 24, shame hath **d.** the labour.
  Ezek. 23 : 37, pass through fire to **d.** them.
  Hos. 8 : 14; Amos 1 : 14; 2 : 2, it shall **d.** palaces.
  Joel 2 : 3, a fire **d.** before them.
  Amos 4 : 9, fig trees and olive trees, palmerworm **d.** them.
  Zeph. 1 : 18; 3 : 8, **d.** by fire of jealousy.
  Matt. 13 : 4; Mark 4 : 4; Luke 8 : 5, fowls **d.** them.
  Matt. 23 : 14; Mark 12 : 40; Luke 20 : 47, **d.** widows' houses.
  Luke 15 : 30, this thy son hath **d.** thy living.
  2 Cor. 11 : 20, if a man **d.** you.
  Gal. 5 : 15, ye bite and **d.** one another.
  Heb. 10 : 27, which shall **d.** the adversaries.
Devout, persons so called : Simeon, Luke 2 : 25; Cornelius, Acts 10 : 2; Ananias, Acts 22 : 12.
  Luke 2 : 25, Simeon was just and **d.**
  Acts 2 : 5; 8 : 2, **d.** men.
  13 : 50, **d.** women.
Dew, a blessing, Gen. 27 : 28; Deut. 33 : 13, a sign, Judg. 6 : 37.
  figurative, Deut. 32 : 2; Ps. 110 : 3; 133 : 3; Prov. 19 : 12; Isa. 26 : 19, etc.
  Gen. 27 : 28, God give thee of the **d.**
  Deut. 32 : 2, my speech distil as the **d.**
  Judg. 6 : 37, if **d.** on fleece only.
  2 Sam. 1 : 21, let there be no **d.**
  17 : 12, light on him as **d.** falleth.
  1 Ki. 17 : 1, there shall not be **d.** nor rain.
  Job 38 : 28, who hath begotten the drops of **d.** ?
  Ps. 110 : 3, hast the **d.** of thy youth.
  Prov. 3 : 20, clouds drop down **d.**
  Isa. 18 : 4, like **d.** in heat of harvest.
  Dan. 4 : 33, body wet with **d.**
  Hos. 6 : 4; 13 : 3, as the early **d.** it passeth away.
  Hag. 1 : 10, heaven is stayed from **d.**
  Zech. 8 : 12, heavens give their **d.**
Diadem, Job 29 : 14, my judgment as a **d.**
  Isa. 28 : 5, for a **d.** of beauty to.
  62 : 3, a royal **d.** in hand of God.
  Ezek. 21 : 26, remove the **d.**
Diamond [Heb. Yăhălōm; Αδαμας ; Iaspis], Ex. 28 : 18, and 39 : 11; Ezek. 28 : 13. That the adamas of Pliny was, in part at least, the true diamond, cannot be doubted; but its extreme rarity, even in his time, and its omission from the list of gems by Theo-

phrastus, justify the conclusion that it was unknown in the Mosaic period. To some form of corundum, as the then hardest known stone, capable of engraving all others, the Hebrew epithet " The Smiter " may have applied, but the LXX. and Vulgate (and possibly Josephus, though, if so, it is misplaced in the order of the stones as given by him) identify yăhălōm with the jasper.

Diana (dī-ăn-ă) [Latin name of the Greek Artemis], chief goddess of the Ephesians, Acts 19 : 24, 27, 34.

Figure of Artemis, the Diana of Ephesus.

Dibon (dī-bŏn), or **Dhiban,** or **Diban.** See Moabite Stone.
Didymus (dĭd-ў-mŭs) [a twin], John 11 : 16.
Die, Gen. 2 : 17; 20 : 7; 1 Sam. 14 : 44; 22 : 16; 1 Ki. 2 : 37, 42; Jer. 26 : 8; Ezek. 3 : 18; 33 : 8, 14, thou shalt surely **d.**
  Gen. 3 : 3; Lev. 10 : 6; Num. 18 : 32, lest ye **d.**
  Gen. 27 : 4; 45 : 28; Prov. 30 : 7, before I **d.**
  Gen. 46 : 30, now let me **d.**
  Ex. 10 : 28, seest my face shall **d.**
  21 : 12, smiteth a man that he **d.**
  Lev. 7 : 24; 22 : 8; Deut. 14 : 21; Ezek. 4 : 14, that **d.** of itself.
  Num. 23 : 10, let me **d.** death of righteous.
  Ruth 1 : 17, where thou **d.** will I **d.**
  2 Sam. 12 : 18, the child **d.**
  2 Ki. 20 : 1; Isa. 38 : 1, shalt **d.**, and not live.
  Job 2 : 9, curse God, and **d.**
  14 : 14, if a man **d.**, shall he live again ?
  Ps. 49 : 17, when he **d.** he shall carry nothing away.
  82 : 7, ye shall **d.** like men.

Prov. 5 : 23, he shall d. without instruction.
Eccl 2 : 16, how d. the wise man ?
9 : 5, living know they shall d.
Isa. 66 : 24; Mark 9 : 44, worm shall not d.
Jer. 27 : 13; Ezek. 18 : 31; 33 : 11, why will ye d. ?
Ezek. 18 : 4, soul that sinneth shall d.
Jonah 4 : 3 it is better for me to d. than to live.
Matt. 15 : 4; Mark 7 : 10, let him d. the death.
Matt. 26 : 35; Mark 14 : 31, though I should d. with thee.
Luke 16 : 22, beggar d., the rich man d. also.
20 : 36, neither can they d. any more.
John 4 : 49, come down ere my child d.
11 : 21, 32, my brother had not d.
12 : 24, except a corn of wheat d.
19 : 7, by our law he ought to d.
Acts 25 : 11, I refuse not to d.
Rom. 5 : 7, scarcely for a righteous man will one d.
7 : 9, sin revived, and I d.
1 Cor. 15 : 3, Christ d. for our sins.
2 Cor. 5 : 14, if one d. for all.
Phil. 1 : 21, to d. is gain.
1 Thess. 4 : 14, if we believe that Jesus d.
Heb. 9 : 27, appointed unto men once to d.
Rev. 3 : 2, things that are ready to d.
14 : 13, blessed are the dead which d. in the Lord.
Diet, Jer. 52 : 34.
Differ, Rom. 12 : 6, gifts d. according to grace.
1 Cor. 4 : 7, who maketh thee to d. ?
15 : 41, one star d. from another.
Gal. 4 : 1, heir d. nothing.
Difference, Lev. 10 : 10, d. between holy and unholy.
Ezek. 22 : 26, put no d. between.
Acts 15 : 9, put no d. between us.
Rom. 3 : 22; 10 : 12, for there is no d.
1 Cor. 12 : 5, of administrations.
Jude 22, of some have compassion, making a d.
Dig, Deut. 6 : 11; Neh. 9 : 25; wells d., which thou d. not.
Deut. 8 : 9, out of hills mayest d. brass.
Ps. 7 : 15; 57 : 6, d. a pit and is fallen.
Matt. 21 : 33, d. a winepress.
25 : 18, d. in the earth, and hid his lord's money.
Luke 13 : 8, let it alone, till I d. about it.
16 : 3, I cannot d., to beg I am ashamed.
Rom. 11 : 3, and d. down thine altars.
Dignity, Eccl. 10 : 6, folly is set in great d.
2 Pet. 2 : 10; Jude 8, these speak evil of d.
Diligence, exhortations to, in the service of God, etc., Ex. 15 : 26; Deut. 4 : 9; 6 : 7; 13 : 14; 24 : 8; Josh. 1 : 7; Ezra 7 : 23; Ps. 37 : 10; 112 : 1; Prov. 2; 3; 4; 7; 8; Isa. 55 : 2; Jer. 12 : 16; Zech. 6 : 15; 2 Cor. 8 : 7; 1 Tim. 5 : 10; Heb. 6 : 11; 11 : 6; 12 : 15; 1 Pet. 1 : 5, 10; 2 Pet. 3 : 14.
in worldly business, Prov. 10 : 4; 12 : 24; 13 : 4; 21 : 5; 27 : 23; Rom. 12 : 11; 2 Thess. 3 : 11.
Prov. 4 : 23, keep heart with all d.
Luke 12 : 58, art in way, give d.
Rom. 12 : 8, he that ruleth, with d.

2 Tim. 4 : 9, do thy d. to come.
2 Pet. 1 : 10, give d. to make your calling sure.
Diligent, Josh. 22 : 5, take d. heed to do the commandments.
Ps. 64 : 6, accomplish a d. search.
Prov. 10 : 4, hand of d. maketh rich.
22 : 29, man d. in his business.
Luke 15 : 8, seek d. till she find it.
Acts 18 : 25, taught d. the things of the Lord.
Heb. 12 : 15, looking d. lest any man fail.
Dim, Deut. 34 : 7, eye not d., nor natural force abated.
Job 17 : 7, mine eye is d. by sorrow.
Isa. 32 : 3, eyes of them that see shall not be d.
Lam. 4 : 1, how is gold become d.
Diminish, Ex. 5 : 8; Deut. 4 : 2; 12 : 32, not d. ought.
Prov. 13 : 11, wealth gotten by vanity shall be d.
Rom. 11 : 12, d. of them the riches of the Gentiles.
Dinah (dī-nǎh) [judged], Jacob's daughter, Gen. 30 : 21.
outraged by Shechem, Gen. 34 : 2.
avenged by Simeon and Levi, Gen. 34 : 25.
Dine, Gen. 43 : 16, d. with me at noon.
Luke 11 : 37, Pharisee besought him to d.
John 21 : 12, Jesus saith, Come and d.
Dinner, Prov. 15 : 17, better is a d. of herbs.
Matt. 22 : 4, I have prepared my d.
Luke 14 : 12, when thou makest a d.
Dionysius (dī-ō-nўs-ĭ-ŭs), the Areopagite believes, Acts 17 : 34.
Diotrephes (dī-ŏt-rě-phěs) [Jove-nourished], loves pre-eminence, 3 John 9.
Dip, Gen. 37 : 31, d. coat in the blood.
Lev. 4 : 6, 17 ; 9 : 9, d. his finger in the blood.
2 Ki. 5 : 14, Naaman d. in Jordan.
Matt. 26 : 23; Mark 14 : 20, d. hand in dish.
John 13 : 26, when he had d. the sop.
Rev. 19 : 13, a vesture d. in blood.
Direct, Ps. 5 : 3, in morning will I d. my prayer.
Prov. 3 : 6, he shall d. thy paths.
11 : 5; Isa. 45 : 13, d. all his ways.
Prov. 16 : 9, Lord d. his steps.
Eccl. 10 : 10, wisdom is profitable to d.
Isa. 40 : 13, who hath d. the Spirit of the Lord ?
61 : 8, will d. their work in truth.
Jer. 10 : 23, not in man to d. his steps.
2 Thess. 3 : 5, d. your hearts into love of God.
Num. 21 : 18; Ezek. 42 : 12.
Dirt, Ps. 18 : 42; Isa. 57 : 20.
Disallow, Num. 30 : 5; 1 Pet. 2 : 4, 7.
Disannul, Isa. 14 : 27, the Lord hath purposed who shall d. it ?
Gal. 3 : 15, no man d., or addeth thereto.
3 : 17, this covenant the law cannot d.
Heb. 7 : 18, there is a d. of commandment.
Disappoint, Job 5 : 12, d. the devices of the crafty.
Ps. 17 : 13, d. him, cast him.
Prov. 15 : 22, purposes are d.
Discern, 2 Sam. 19 : 35, can I d. between good and evil ?
1 Ki. 3 : 9, that I may d. between good and bad.
3 : 11, understanding to d. judgment.

Prov. 7 : 7, I **d.** among the youths.
Eccl. 8 : 5, wise **d.** time and judgment.
Jonah 4 : 11, not **d.** between right and left.
Mal. 3 : 18, **d.** between righteous and wicked.
Matt. 16 : 3; Luke 12 : 56, ɑ. face of sky.
1 Cor. 2 : 14, because they are spiritually **d.**
    11 : 29, not **d.** the Lord's body.
Discerner, Heb. 4 : 12, word of God is a **d.** of the thoughts.
Discerning, 1 Cor. 12 : 10, to another **d.** of spirits.
Discharge, 1 Ki. 5 : 9, cause them to be **d.**
Eccl. 8 : 8, there is no **d.** in that war.
Disciples, of Christ, seventy sent out, Luke 10.
three thousand added to the church, Acts 2 : 41.
five thousand believers, Acts 4 : 4.
first called Christians at Antioch, Acts 11 : 26.
of John, inquire of Christ, Matt. 9 : 14; 11 : 2.
follow Christ, John 1 : 37.
dispute about purifying, John 3 : 25.
baptized by Paul, and receive the Holy Ghost, Acts 19 : 1.
Matt. 10 : 1; Luke 6 : 13, Jesus called his twelve **d.**
Matt. 10 : 24; Luke 6 : 40, **d.** not above his master.
Matt. 10 : 42, give cup of water in the name of a **d.**
    19 : 13, **d.** rebuked them.
    20 : 17, Jesus took **d.** apart.
    22 : 16, Pharisees sent their **d.**
    26 : 56, all the **d.** forsook him, and fled.
    28 : 7; Mark 16 : 7, go, tell his **d.** he is risen.
Mark 2 : 18; Luke 5 : 33, why do **d.** of John fast ?
Luke 19 : 37, **d.** began to rejoice and praise God.
John 1 : 35, John stood, and two of his **d.**
    2 : 11, **d.** believed on him.
    6 : 66, many of his **d.** went back.
    8 : 31; 13 : 35, then are ye my **d.**
    9 : 27, will ye also be his **d.** ?
    13 : 5, wash the **d.** feet.
    13 : 23; 19 : 26; 20 : 2, **d.** whom Jesus loved.
    21 : 24, this is the **d.** which testifieth.
Acts 9 : 1, breathing out slaughter against **d.**
    20 : 7, **d.** came together to break bread.
    21 : 16, an old **d.**
Discipline, Job 36 : 10, he openeth their ear to **d.**
Disclose, Isa. 26 : 21.
Discomfited, Josh. 10 : 10, Lord **d.** them before Israel.
Judg. 4 : 15, Lord **d.** Sisera.
    8 : 12, Gideon **d.** all the host.
2 Sam. 22 : 15; Ps. 18 : 14, lightnings, and **d.** them.
Isa. 31 : 8, his young men shall be **d.**
Discomfiture, 1 Sam. 14 : 20.
Discontented, 1 Sam. 22 : 2.
Discontinue, Jer. 17 : 4.
Discord, censured, Prov. 6 : 14, 19; 16 : 28; 17 : 9; 18 : 8; 26 : 20; Rom. 1 : 29; 2 Cor. 12 : 20.
Discourage, Num. 21 : 4, soul of the people was much **d.**
Num. 32 : 7, wherefore **d.** ye the heart ?

Deut. 1 : 21, fear not, neither be **d.**
    1 : 28, brethren have **d.** our hearts.
Isa. 42 : 4, he shall not fail nor be **d.**
Col. 3 : 21, children, lest they be **d.**
Discover, 1 Sam. 14 : 8, we will **d.** ourselves to them.
2 Sam. 22 : 16; Ps. 18 : 15, the foundations of the world were **d.**
Job 12 : 22, he **d.** deep things.
Ps. 29 : 9, and **d.** the forests.
Prov. 25 : 9, **d.** not a secret to another.
Ezek. 21 : 24, your transgressions are **d.**
Hab. 3 : 13, **d.** the foundation.
Acts 27 : 39, **d.** a certain creek.
Discreet, Gen. 41 : 33, a man **d.** and wise.
Mark 12 : 34, he answered **d.**
Titus 2 : 5, to be **d.**, chaste.
Discretion, commended, Ps. 34 : 13; Prov. 1 : 4; 3 : 21; 5 : 2.
Ps. 112 : 5, guide affairs with **d.**
Prov. 2 : 11, **d.** shall preserve thee.
    19 : 11, the **d.** of a man deferreth his anger.
Isa. 28 : 26, his God doth instruct him to **d.**
Jer. 10 : 12, stretched heavens by **d.**
Disdained, 1 Sam. 17 : 42; Job 30 : 1.
Disease, inflicted by God, Ex. 9; 15 : 26; Num. 12 : 10; 2 Ki. 1 : 4; 5 : 27; 2 Chr. 21 : 18; 26 : 21; Job 2 : 6, 7.
cured by Christ, Matt. 4 : 23; 9 : 20-22; John 5 : 8.
power given to his disciples to cure, Luke 9 : 1; Acts 28 : 8; exercised, Acts 3 : 1; 9 : 34.
Deut. 7 : 15, none of these **d.** on you.
    28 : 60, bring on thee all the **d.** of Egypt.
Ps. 103 : 3, who healeth all thy **d.**
Eccl. 6 : 2, vanity, and it is an evil **d.**
Matt. 4 : 24; Mark 1 : 34; Luke 4 : 40, all taken with divers **d.**
Disfigure, Matt. 6 : 16.
Disgrace, Jer. 14 : 21.
Disguise, resorted to, 1 Sam. 28 : 8; 1 Ki. 22 : 30; 2 Chr. 35 : 22.
disfiguring of face for the dead forbidden, Lev. 19 : 28; Deut. 14 : 1.
1 Ki. 14 : 2, Jeroboam said, Arise, and **d.** thyself.
    20 : 38, one of the prophets **d.** himself.
2 Chr. 18 : 29, I will **d.** myself.
Job 24 : 15, **d.** his face.
Dish, Judg. 5 : 25, butter in a lordly **d.**
2 Ki. 21 : 13, as a man wipeth a **d.**
Matt. 26 : 23; Mark 14 : 20, that dippeth with me in the **d.**
Dishonour, Ps. 35 : 26; 71 : 13, clothed with shame and **d.**
Prov. 6 : 33, and **d.** shall he get.
Mic. 7 : 6, son **d.** father.
John 8 : 49, I honour my Father, ye do **d.** me.
Rom. 1 : 24, to **d.** their own bodies.
    2 : 23, **d.** thou God ?
    9 : 21, one vessel to honour, another to **d.**
1 Cor. 15 : 43, it is sown in **d.**
2 Cor. 6 : 8, by honour and **d.**
2 Tim. 2 : 20, are vessels, some to honour, some to **d.**
See 1 Cor. 11 : 4, 5.
Disinherit, Num. 14 : 12.

Dismayed, Deut. 31 : 8;   Josh. 1 : 9;   8 : 1;
10 : 25;   1 Chr. 22 : 13;   28 : 20;   2 Chr.
20 : 15;   32 : 7, fear not, nor be **d.**
Isa. 41 : 10;   Jer. 1 : 17;   10 : 2;   23 : 4;
30 : 10;   46 : 27;   Ezek. 2 : 6;   3 : 9, be
not **d.**
Jer. 8 : 9;   10 : 2, the wise men are **d.**
17 : 18, let them be **d.**, let not me be **d.**
Obad. 9, thy mighty men shall be **d.**
Dismaying, Jer. 48 : 39, a derision and a **d.**
Dismissed, Acts 15 : 30;   19 : 41.
Disobedience, and its results, Lev. 26 : 14 ff.;
Deut. 8 : 11;   27;   28 : 15-68;   Josh. 5 : 6;
1 Sam. 2 : 30;   12 : 15;   Ps. 78;   Isa. 3 : 8;
42 : 24;   Jer. 9 : 13-16;   18 : 10;   22 : 21;
35 : 14;   Titus 1 : 16;   3 : 3.
of Adam and Eve, Gen. 3.
of Pharaoh, Ex. 5 : 2.
of Achan, Josh. 7.
of Saul, 1 Sam. 13 : 9–14;   15.
of man of God, 1 Ki. 13 : 21.
of Jonah, Jonah 1 : 2.
Rom. 5 : 19, by one man's **d.** many were made
sinners.
Eph. 2 : 2, worketh in children of **d.**
5 : 6;   Col. 3 : 6, wrath on children of **d.**
Heb. 2 : 2, every **d.** received just recompense
of reward.
Disobedient, Luke 1 : 17, turn **d.** to wisdom of
just.
Acts 26 : 19, not **d.** to heavenly vision.
Rom. 1 : 30;   2 Tim. 3 : 2, **d.** to parents.
1 Tim. 1 : 9, law is made for lawless and **d.**
Titus 3 : 3, we ourselves were sometimes **d.**
1 Pet. 2 : 7, to them which be **d.**
3 : 20, spirits which sometime were **d.**
Disorderly, 2 Thess. 3 : 6, withdraw from brother
that walketh **d.**
2 Thess. 3 : 7, behaved not ourselves **d.**
3 : 11, some walk among you **d.**
Dispensation, of the gospel, 1 Cor. 9 : 17;   Eph.
1 : 10;   3 : 2;   Col. 1 : 25.
Disperse, Ps. 112 : 9;   2 Cor. 9 : 9, he hath **d.**
Prov. 15 : 7, lips of wise **d.** knowledge.
Dispersed, of Israel, Esther 3 : 8;   Isa. 11 : 12;
John 7 : 35.
prophecies concerning, Jer. 25 : 34;   Ezek.
36 : 19;   Zeph. 3 : 10.
Displayed, Ps. 60 : 4.
Displease, Num. 11 : 1, it **d.** the Lord.
22 : 34, if it **d.** thee, I will get me back.
2 Sam. 11 : 27, thing David had done **d.** the
Lord.
1 Ki. 1 : 6, father had not **d.** him at any time.
Ps. 60 : 1, thou hast been **d.**
Prov. 24 : 18, lest the Lord see it, and it **d.**
him.
Isa. 59 : 15, it **d.** him that there was no judg-
ment.
Dan. 6 : 14, king **d.** with himself.
Jonah 4 : 1, it **d.** Jonah exceedingly.
Hab. 3 : 8, was the Lord **d.** against the rivers ?
Matt. 21 : 15, scribes saw it, they were **d.**
Mark 10 : 14, Jesus was much **d.**
Acts 12 : 20, Herod was highly **d.**
Displeasure, Deut. 9 : 19, I was afraid of hot **d.**
Judg. 15 : 3, though I do them a **d.**
Ps. 2 : 5, vex them in his sore **d.**
6 : 1;   38 : 1, neither chasten me in hot **d.**

Disposed, Job 34 : 13;   Prov. 16 : 33;   Acts
18 : 27;   1 Cor. 10 : 27.
Disposition [ordering of, appointment], Acts
7 : 53, received the law by the **d.** of angels.
Dispossess, Num. 33 : 53;   Deut. 7 : 17;   Judg.
11 : 23.
Disputation, Acts 15 : 2, dissension and **d.**
Rom. 14 : 1, not to doubtful **d.**
Dispute, Job 23 : 7, the righteous might **d.** with
him.
Mark 9 : 34, **d.** who should be greatest.
Acts 17 : 17, Paul **d.** in the synagogue.
Disputer, 1 Cor. 1 : 20, where is the **d.** of this
world ?
Disputing, with God, forbidden, Rom. 9 : 20.
with men, Mark 9 : 33;   Rom. 14 : 1;   Phil.
2 : 14;   1 Tim. 1 : 3, 4;   4 : 7;   6 : 20;   2 Tim.
2 : 14;   Titus 3 : 9.
1 Tim. 6 : 5, perverse **d.**
Disquiet, 1 Sam. 28 : 15, why hast thou **d.** me to
bring me up ?
Ps. 42 : 5, 11;   43 : 5, why art thou **d.** within
me ?
Jer. 50 : 34, and **d.** the inhabitants.
Dissemble, Josh. 7 : 11, they have stolen and **d.**
Ps. 26 : 4, nor will I go in with **d.**
Prov. 26 : 4, he that hateth **d.**
Gal. 2 : 13, the other Jews **d.**
Dissension concerning circumcision, Acts 15 : 1.
Acts 15 : 2, had no small **d.**
23 : 7, arose a **d.** between Pharisees.
Dissolve [solve, explain], Dan. 5 : 16, thou canst
d. doubts.
2 Pet. 3 : 11, all these things shall be **d.**
Ps. 75 : 3, inhabitants thereof are **d.**
Isa. 24 : 19, the earth is clean **d.**
2 Cor. 5 : 1, house of this tabernacle be **d.**
Distaff, Prov. 31 : 19, her hands hold **d.**
Distil, Deut. 32 : 2, my speech **d.** as dew.
Job 36 : 28, the clouds **d.** on man.
Distract, Ps. 88 : 15, I suffer thy terrors, I am **d.**
1 Cor. 7 : 35, attend without **d.**
Distress, Gen. 35 : 3, answered in day of my **d.**
42 : 21, therefore is this **d.** come upon us.
Judg. 11 : 7, why are ye come when in **d.** ?
2 Sam. 22 : 7;   Ps. 18 : 6;   118 : 5;   120 : 1, in
my **d.**, I called on the Lord.
1 Ki. 1 : 29, redeemed my soul out of all **d.**
Neh. 2 : 17, ye see the **d.** we are in.
Ps. 4 : 1, enlarged me in **d.**
25 : 17;   107 : 6, 13, 19, 28, out of **d.**
Prov. 1 : 27, I will mock when **d.** cometh.
Isa. 25 : 4, a strength to needy in **d.**
Luke 21 : 25, on earth **d.** of nations.
Rom. 8 : 35, shall **d.** separate us ?
2 Cor. 12 : 10, take pleasure in **d.**
Distribute, Neh. 13 : 13, their office was to **d.**
Luke 18 : 22, sell and **d.** to poor.
John 6 : 11, when Jesus had given thanks, he **d.**
Rom. 12 : 13, **d.** to necessity of saints.
1 Cor. 7 : 17, as God hath **d.** to every man.
2 Cor. 9 : 13, your liberal **d.**
Ditch, 2 Ki. 3 : 16, make valley full of **d.**
Ps. 7 : 15, made **d.** is fallen into **d.**
Matt. 15 : 14;   Luke 6 : 39, both fall into **d.**
Divers, Deut. 22 : 9, not sow with **d.** seeds.
22 : 11, not wear garment of **d.** sorts.
25 : 13, not have in bag **d.** weights.
25 : 14, **d.** measures, great and small.

Prov. 20 : 10, 23, **d.** weights and measures abomination.
Matt. 4 : 24; Mark 1 : 34; Luke 4 : 40, sick with **d.** diseases.
Matt. 24 : 7; Mark 13 : 8; Luke 21 : 11, earthquakes in **d.** places.
Mark 8 : 3, **d.** of them came from far.
1 Cor. 12 : 10, **d.** kinds of tongues.
2 Tim. 3 : 6; Titus 3 : 3, **d.** lusts.
Heb. 1 : 1, God, who in **d.** manners, spake.
Jas. 1 : 2, joy when ye fall into **d.** temptations.
Diversities, 1 Cor. 12 : 6, **d.** of operations, but same God.
  12 : 28, **d.** of tongues.
Divide, Gen. 1 : 18, to **d.** light from darkness.
  Ex. 14 : 16, stretch hand over the sea, and **d.** it.
  Lev. 11 : 4; Deut. 14 : 7, that **d.** the hoof.
  1 Ki. 3 : 25, **d.** living child in two.
  Ps. 68 : 12; Prov. 16 : 19; Isa. 9 : 3; 53 : 12, **d.** spoil.
  Matt. 12 : 25; Mark 3 : 24; Luke 11 : 17, kingdom or house **d.**
  Luke 12 : 13, that he **d.** inheritance with me.
  15 : 12, he **d.** unto them his living.
  Acts 14 : 4; 23 : 7, the multitude was **d.**
  1 Cor. 1 : 13, is Christ **d.** ?
  2 Tim. 2 : 15, rightly **d.** word of truth.
  Heb. 4 : 12, piercing to **d.** asunder.
Divination, Lev. 19 : 26; Deut. 18 : 10; 1 Sam. 28 : 7; 2 Ki. 17 : 17; Jer. 27 : 9; 29 : 8; Ezek. 21 : 21.
  Num. 22 : 7, rewards of **d.** in hand.
  Acts 16 : 16, damsel with a spirit of **d.**
Divine, Gen. 44 : 15, wot ye not that I can **d.** ?
  Ezek. 13 : 9, prophets that **d.** lies.
  Mic. 3 : 11, prophets **d.** for money.
  Heb. 9 : 1, ordinances of **d.** service.
  2 Pet. 1 : 4, partakers of **d.** nature.
Diviner, Deut. 18 : 14, nations hearkened to **d.**
  Isa. 44 : 25, that maketh **d.** mad.
  Jer. 27 : 9, hearken not to your **d.**
  29 : 8, let not your **d.** deceive you.
Division, kingdom and house, Matt. 12 : 25.
  in the Church forbidden, Rom. 16 : 17; 1 Cor. 1 : 10; 3 : 3; 11 : 18; 12 : 20.
  Christ's prayer against, John 17 : 21.
  Ex. 8 : 23, put a **d.** between my people.
  Judg. 5 : 15, for **d.** of Reuben great thoughts of heart.
  Luke 12 : 51, I tell you nay, but rather **d.**
  John 7 : 43; 9 : 16; 10 : 19, a **d.** because of him.
  Rom. 16 : 17, mark them which cause **d.**
Divorce, when permitted, Deut. 24 : 1; Matt. 5 : 32.
  condemned by Christ, Mark 10 : 4.
Do, Gen. 18 : 25, shall not Judge of all **d.** right.
  Deut. 27 : 26, words of law, to **d.** them.
  Eccl. 9 : 10, what thy hand findeth to **d., d.** it with might.
  Isa. 45 : 7, I the Lord **d.** all these things.
  Matt. 7 : 12, that men should **d.** to you, **d.** ye even so.
  Luke 10 : 28, this **d.,** and thou shalt live.
  22 : 19; 1 Cor. 11 : 24, this **d.** in remembrance of me.
  John 15 : 5, without me ye can **d.** nothing.

Acts 1 : 1, all Jesus began to **d.**
  9 : 6, Lord, what wilt thou have me to **d.** ?
  Rom. 7 : 15, what I would, that **d.** I not.
  1 Cor. 10 : 31, ye **d., d.** all to glory of God.
  Gal. 5 : 17, ye cannot **d.** the things ye would.
  Phil. 4 : 13, I can **d.** all things through Christ.
  Heb. 4 : 13, God with whom we have to **d.**
  Jas. 1 : 22, be ye **d.** of the word.
Do to wit [give or cause to know]. "We do you to wit," 2 Cor. 8 : 1.
Doctors, Christ questions, Luke 2 : 46.
  of the law, Luke 5 : 17; Gamaliel, Acts 5 : 34.
Doctrine of Christ, Matt. 7 : 28, 29; Mark 4 : 2; John 7 : 16; Acts 2 : 42; 1 Tim. 3 : 16; 6 : 3; 2 Tim. 3 : 16; Titus 1 : 1; Heb. 6 : 1; 2 John 9.
  adorned by obedience, Rom. 6 : 17; 1 Tim. 6 : 1; Titus 2 : 7, 10.
  no other to be taught, 1 Tim. 1 : 3; 4 : 6, 13.
  those opposed to, to be avoided, Rom. 16 : 17; 2 John 10.
  false, Jer. 10 : 8; Matt. 15 : 9; 16 : 12; Eph. 4 : 14; 2 Thess. 2 : 11; 1 Tim. 4 : 1; 2 Tim. 4 : 3; Heb. 13 : 9; Rev. 2 : 14.
  to be avoided, Jer. 23 : 16; 29 : 8; Col. 2 : 8; 1 Tim. 1 : 4; 6 : 20.
  Deut. 32 : 2, my **d.** shall drop as the rain.
  Jer. 10 : 8, the stock is a **d.** of vanities.
  Matt. 7 : 28; 22 : 33; Mark 1 : 22; 11 : 18; Luke 4 : 32, astonished at his **d.**
  Matt. 15 : 9; Mark 7 : 7, teaching for **d.** commandments of men.
  Matt. 16 : 12, the **d.** of the Pharisees.
  Mark 1 : 27; Acts 17 : 19, what new **d.** is this ?
  John 7 : 17, do his will, he shall know of the **d.**
  Acts 2 : 42, continued in apostles' **d.**
  Rom. 6 : 17, obeyed that form of **d.**
  16 : 17, contrary to the **d.**
  Eph. 4 : 14, every wind of **d.**
  1 Tim. 1 : 10, contrary to sound **d.**
  5 : 17, labour in word and **d.**
  2 Tim. 3 : 16, scripture profitable for **d.**
  Titus 2 : 1, things which become sound **d.**
  2 : 10, adorn the **d.** of God our Saviour.
  Heb. 6 : 1, principles of the **d.** of Christ.
  6 : 2, the **d.** of baptisms.
  13 : 9, not carried about with strange **d.**
Doeg (dṓ-ĕg) [fearful], the Edomite, slays the priests, 1 Sam. 22 : 9.
Dog [Heb. keleb]. The Jews do not seem to have in any true sense domesticated the dog. They did not, like the Egyptians, train it for hunting, though they seem to have employed it as a guard over their flocks (Job 30 : 1). Dogs, hunting in packs, were then, as now in eastern cities, useful as scavengers, and thus among the Jews they came to be regarded always with disgust and loathing.
  law concerning, Deut. 23 : 18.
  a term of reproach, 2 Sam. 9 : 8; Rev. 22 : 15.
  figurative of enemies, Ps. 22 : 16.
  figurative of impenitence, Prov. 26 : 11; 2 Pet. 2 : 22.
  false teachers so called, Isa. 56 : 10.
  beware of, Phil. 3 : 2.
  Ex. 11 : 7, against Israel shall not a **d.** move.

Deut. 23 : 18, not bring price of a **d**. into house.
Judg. 7 : 5, that lappeth as a **d**. lappeth.
1 Sam. 17 : 43; 2 Ki. 8 : 13, am I a **d**. ?
2 Sam. 9 : 8, upon such a dead **d**. as I am.
Ps. 22 : 20, darling from power of the **d**.
  59 : 6, make a noise like a **d**.
Prov. 26 : 11; 2 Pet. 2 : 22, as a **d**. returneth.
Eccl. 9 : 4, living **d**. better than dead lion.
Isa. 56 : 10, they are all dumb **d**.
Matt. 7 : 6, give not that which is holy to **d**.
  15 : 27; Mark 7 : 28, the **d**. eat of crumbs.
Luke 16 : 21, the **d**. licked his sores.
Phil. 3 : 2, beware of **d**.
Rev. 22 : 15, without are **d**.
Doing, Ex. 15 : 11, fearful in praises, **d**. wonders.
Judg. 2 : 19, ceased not from their own **d**.
Ps. 9 : 11; Isa. 12 : 4, declare his **d**.
  66 : 5, he is terrible in his **d**.
  77 : 12, I will talk of thy **d**.
  118 : 23; Matt. 21 : 42; Mark 12 : 11, the Lord's **d**.
Acts 10 : 38, went about **d**. good.
Rom. 2 : 7, patient continuance in well-**d**.
2 Cor. 8 : 11, perform the **d**. of it.
Gal. 6 : 9; 2 Thess. 3 : 13, weary in well-**d**.
Eph. 6 : 6, **d**. the will of God.
1 Pet. 2 : 15, with well-**d**. put to silence.
  3 : 17, better suffer for well-**d**.
  4 : 19, commit souls in well-**d**.
Dominion of God, Ps. 103 : 22; 145 : 13; Dan. 4 : 3, 34; 7 : 27; Col. 1 : 16; 1 Pet. 4 : 11; Jude 25.
Gen. 27 : 40, when thou shalt have the **d**.
  37 : 8, shalt thou have **d**. over us ?
Num. 24 : 19, he that shall have **d**.
Neh. 9 : 27, have **d**. over our bodies.
Job 25 : 2, **d**. and fear are with him.
Ps. 8 : 6, have **d**. over the works of thy hands.
  19 : 13; 119 : 133, let not sins have **d**. over me.
  72 : 8, have **d**. from sea to sea.
  103 : 22, bless the Lord in all places of his **d**.
Isa. 26 : 13, other lords have had **d**. over us.
Dan. 4 : 34; 7 : 14, **d**. is an everlasting **d**.
Matt. 20 : 25, princes of Gentiles exercise **d**.
Rom. 6 : 9, death hath no more **d**.
  6 : 14, sin shall not have **d**.
2 Cor. 1 : 24, not have **d**. over your faith.
Eph. 1 : 21, far above might and **d**.
Col. 1 : 16, whether they be thrones or **d**.
1 Pet. 4 : 11; 5 : 11; Rev. 1 : 6, to whom be praise, glory, and **d**. for ever.
Door of the sheep, Christ the, John 10 : 9.
Gen. 4 : 7, sin lieth at the **d**.
Ex. 12 : 7, strike blood on **d**. post.
Num. 12 : 5; 16 : 8, stood in **d**. of tabernacle.
Job 38 : 17, the **d**. of the shadow of death.
Ps. 24 : 7, ye everlasting **d**.
  141 : 3, keep the **d**. of my lips.
Prov. 8 : 3, wisdom crieth at the **d**.
  26 : 14, as **d**. turneth on hinges.
Isa. 26 : 20, enter, and shut thy **d**. about thee.
Hos. 2 : 15, for a **d**. of hope.
Matt. 6 : 6, when thou hast shut thy **d**.
  24 : 33; Mark 13 : 29, near, even at the **d**.
Matt. 25 : 10, and the **d**. was shut.
  27 : 60; 28 : 2; Mark 15 : 46, **d**. of sepulchre.

Mark 2 : 2, no room, not so much as about the **d**.
John 10 : 1, that entereth not by the **d**.
  18 : 16, Peter stood at the **d**. without.
Acts 14 : 27, opened **d**. of faith.
1 Cor. 16 : 9, great **d**. and effectual.
2 Cor. 2 : 12, **d**. opened to me of the Lord.
Col. 4 : 3, God would open a **d**. of utterance.
Jas. 5 : 9, judge standeth before the **d**.
Rev. 3 : 8, I set before thee an open **d**.
  3 : 20, I stand at the **d**. and knock.
Doorkeeper, Ps. 84 : 10, a **d**. in the house of my God.
1 Chr. 15 : 23, 24, **d**. for the ark.
Dorcas (dôr'-căs) [gazelle], Greek for Tabitha, see **Tabitha**.
raised from death by Peter, Acts 9 : 40.
Dote, Jer. 50 : 36, and they shall **d**.
1 Tim. 6 : 4, **d**. about questions.
Double, Gen. 43 : 12, take **d**. money.
Ex. 22 : 4, theft be found, restore **d**.
Deut. 15 : 18, worth a **d**. hired servant.
2 Ki. 2 : 9, a **d**. portion of thy spirit.
1 Chr. 12 : 33, not of **d**. heart.
Job 11 : 6, secrets of wisdom are **d**. to that which is.
Ps. 12 : 2, with a **d**. heart do they speak.
Isa. 40 : 2, received **d**. for all her sins.
Jer. 16 : 18, recompense their sin **d**.
Jer. 17 : 18, with **d**. destruction.
1 Tim. 3 : 8, deacons not **d**. tongued.
  5 : 17, elders worthy of **d**. honour.
Jas. 1 : 8, a **d**.-minded man is unstable.
  4 : 8, purify your hearts, ye **d**.-minded.
Doubt, Deut. 28 : 66, thy life shall hang in **d**.
Dan. 5 : 12, dissolving of **d**.
Matt. 14 : 31, wherefore didst thou **d**. ?
  21 : 21, if ye have faith, and **d**. not.
Mark 11 : 23, and shall not **d**. in his heart.
John 10 : 24, how long dost thou make us to **d**. ?
Acts 5 : 24, they **d**. whereunto this would grow.
Rom. 14 : 23, he that **d**. is damned if he eat.
Gal. 4 : 20, I stand in **d**. of you.
1 Tim. 2 : 8, pray without wrath and **d**.
See Luke 12 : 29; Rom. 14 : 1.
Doubtfulness rebuked, Matt. 14 : 31; 21 : 21; Luke 12 : 29; Acts 10 : 20; 1 Tim. 2 : 8.
Doubtless, Ps. 126 : 6, **d**. come again with rejoicing.
Isa. 63 : 16, **d**. thou art our Father.
Phil. 3 : 8, yea **d**. I count all but loss.
Dough, offering of, Num. 15 : 20; Neh. 10 : 37; Ezek. 44 : 30.
Dove [Heb. yonah]. The Jews distinguished, at least generally, between the pigeon (yonah) and the turtle dove (tor) (Gen. 15 : 9). The dove, or pigeon, was from an early date kept in a state of half domestication; the very poorest were able to have their dovecots, and they were, with the turtle doves, among the few birds allowed to be offered as a sacrifice under the law of Moses.
sent out from the ark, Gen. 8 : 8.
sacrificial, Gen. 15 : 9; Lev. 12 : 6; 14 : 22.
figuratively mentioned, Ps. 68 : 13; 74 : 19; Cant. 1 : 15; 2 : 14.

Holy Spirit in form of, Matt. 3 : 16; Mark 1 : 10; Luke 3 : 22; John 1 : 32.

Gen. 8 : 9, the **d.** found no rest.

Ps. 55 : 6, that I had wings like a **d.**

74 : 19, the soul of thy turtle **d.**

Cant. 5 : 12, his eyes are as eyes of **d.**

Isa. 59 : 11, we mourn sore like **d.**

60 : 8, flee as **d.** to their windows.

Matt. 3 : 16; Mark 1 : 10; Luke 3 : 22; John 1 : 32, descending like a **d.**

Matt. 10 : 16, be harmless as **d.**

21 : 12; Mark 11 : 15; John 2 : 14, that sold **d.**

Down, 2 Ki. 19 : 30; Isa. 37 : 31, take root **d.**

Ps. 59 : 15, let them wander up and **d.**

109 : 23, I am tossed up and **d.**

139 : 2, thou knowest my **d.** sitting.

Eccl. 3 : 21, spirit of the beast that goeth **d.**

Zech. 10 : 12, walk up and **d.** in his name.

Acts 27 : 27, were driven up and **d.**

Dowry, Gen. 30 : 20, endued me with good **d.**

34 : 12, ask me never so much **d.**

Ex. 22 : 17, pay according to the **d.**

1 Sam. 18 : 25, king desireth not **d.**

Dragon [Heb. tan, tannin, once tannim], Ezek. 29 : 3. The former word seems to describe a land animal, as in Mal. 1 : 3; the latter seems to refer to an animal living both on land and in water (Ezek. 29 : 3, and 32 : 2). Some think that the tan cannot refer to any snake-like form, but that the jackal prowling about at night is meant (Job 30 : 29; Mic. 1 : 8). For tannin see **Leviathan.**

Job 30 : 29; Ps. 74 : 13; Isa. 13 : 22; 27 : 1; Rev. 12 : 3; 13 : 2; 16 : 13. See Ezek. 29 : 3.

Deut. 32 : 33, their wine is the poison of **d.**

Job 30 : 29, I am a brother to **d.**

Ps. 74 : 13, breakest the heads of the **d.**

91 : 13, the **d.** shalt thou trample.

148 : 7, praise the Lord, ye **d.**

Isa. 34 : 13; 35 : 7, be habitation of **d.**

43 : 20, **d.** and owls shall honour me.

Jer. 9 : 11, make Jerusalem a den of **d.**

Rev. 20 : 2, laid hold on the **d.**, that old serpent.

Drank, Gen. 9 : 21, Noah **d.** of the wine.

1 Sam. 30 : 12, nor **d.** water three days and nights.

1 Ki. 17 : 6, he **d.** of the brook.

Dan. 5 : 4, they **d.**, and praised the gods of gold.

Mark 14 : 23, and they all **d.** of it.

John 4 : 12, our father Jacob **d.** thereof.

1 Cor. 10 : 4, they **d.** of that spiritual rock.

Draught [drain, " water-closet "], Matt. 15 : 17; Mark 7 : 19, cast out into **d.**

of fishes, miraculous, Luke 5 : 4-6; John 21 : 6, 11.

Luke 5 : 4, let down nets for a **d.**

5 : 9, astonished at **d.** of fishes.

Draw, Job 21 : 33, every man shall **d.** after him.

Ps. 28 : 3, **d.** me not away with the wicked.

73 : 28, it is good to **d.** near to God.

Eccl. 12 : 1, nor years **d.** nigh when.

Cant. 1 : 4, **d.** me, we will run after thee.

Isa. 5 : 18, **d.** iniquity with cords.

12 : 3, **d.** water from wells of salvation.

Jer. 31 : 3, with lovingkindness have I **d.** thee.

Matt. 15 : 8, people **d.** nigh with their mouth.

Luke 21 : 28, your redemption **d.** nigh.

John 4 : 11, thou hast nothing to **d.** with.

6 : 44, except the Father **d.** him.

12 : 32, I will **d.** all men unto me.

Heb. 7 : 19, by which we **d.** nigh to God.

10 : 22, let us **d.** near with a true heart.

Jas. 4 : 8, **d.** nigh to God, he will **d.** nigh.

Dread, Ex. 15 : 16, **d.** shall fall upon them.

Deut. 1 : 29, **d.** not, nor be afraid.

2 : 25; 11 : 25, begin to put **d.** of thee.

Isa. 8 : 13, let him be your fear and **d.**

Dreadful, Gen. 28 : 17, how **d.** is this place!

Dan. 9 : 4, the great and **d.** God.

Mal. 4 : 5, the great and **d.** day of the Lord.

Dreamer, Gen. 37 : 19; Deut. 13 : 1, 3, 5; Jer. 27 : 9; Jude 8.

Dreams, vanity of, Job 20 : 8; Ps. 73 : 20; Eccl. 5 : 3; Isa. 29 : 8; Jer. 23 : 28; 27 : 9; Zech. 10 : 2; Jude 8.

sent by God, Job 33 : 15; Joel 2 : 28.

of Abimelech, Gen. 20 : 3; Jacob, Gen. 28 : 12; 31 : 10; Laban, Gen. 31 : 24; Joseph, Gen. 37 : 5; Pharaoh's servants, Gen. 40 : 5; Pharaoh, Gen. 41; Midianite. Judg. 7 : 13; Solomon, 1 Ki. 3 : 5; Nebuchadrezzar, Dan. 2 : 4; Joseph, Matt. 1 : 20; 2 : 13; Wise men, Matt. 2 : 12; Pilate's wife, Matt. 27 : 19.

Gen. 31 : 11, angel spake to Jacob in a **d.**

1 Ki. 3 : 5, Lord appeared to Solomon in a **d.**

Job 33 : 15, in a **d.**, in a vision of the night.

Ps. 73 : 20, as a **d.** when one awaketh.

Eccl. 5 : 3, a **d.** cometh through the multitude of business.

Joel 2 : 28; Acts 2 : 17, old men **d. d.**

Matt. 1 : 20, angel of the Lord appeared in a **d.**

Dregs, Ps. 75 : 8, the **d.** . . . . the wicked of the earth shall wring out.

Isa. 51 : 17, the **d.** of the cup of trembling.

Isa. 51 : 22, **d.** of the cup of my fury.

Dress, Gen. 2 : 15, put man in garden to **d.** it.

Deut. 28 : 39, plant vineyards, and **d.** them.

2 Sam. 12 : 4, **d.** poor man's lamb.

Heb. 6 : 7, for them by whom it is **d.**

Dresser, 2 Chr. 26 : 10, vine-**d.** in the mountains.

Luke 13 : 7, said to **d.** of vineyard.

Drew, Gen. 47 : 29, time **d.** nigh that Israel must die.

Ex. 2 : 10, because I **d.** him out of the water.

Josh. 8 : 26, Joshua **d.** not his hand back.

Ruth 4 : 8, **d.** off his shoe.

1 Ki. 22 : 34; 2 Chr. 18 : 33, man **d.** a bow.

2 Ki. 9 : 24, Jehu **d.** bow with full strength.

Jer. 38 : 13, **d.** up with cords.

Hos. 11 : 4, **d.** them with cords of a man.

Zeph. 3 : 2, she **d.** not near to her God.

Matt. 21 : 34, when time of fruit **d.** near.

Luke 15 : 25, elder son **d.** nigh to house.

24 : 15, Jesus himself **d.** near.

Acts 5 : 37, **d.** away much people.

7 : 17, time of the promise **d.** near.

Drink, strong, forbidden, Lev. 10 : 9; Num. 6 : 3; Judg. 13 : 14; Luke 1 : 15.

use of, Prov. 31 : 6; 1 Tim. 5 : 23.

abuse of, Isa. 5 : 11, 22.

strong, raging, Prov. 20 : 1.

Lev. 10 : 9, do not drink strong **d.** when ye go.

Num. 6 : 3, Nazarite separate from strong d.
20 : 8, give congregation d.
Deut. 14 : 26, bestow money for strong d.
29 : 6, nor drunk strong d. forty years.
Prov. 20 : 1, strong d. is raging.
Isa. 5 : 11, may follow strong d.
28 : 7, erred through strong d.
Mic. 2 : 11, I will prophesy of strong d.
Hab. 2 : 15, that giveth his neighbour d.
Matt. 25 : 35, thirsty, and ye gave me d.
John 4 : 9, a Jew, askest d. of me.
6 : 55, my blood is d. indeed.
Rom. 12 : 20, if thine enemy thirst give him d.
14 : 17, the kingdom of God is not meat
and d.
1 Cor. 10 : 4, drink same spiritual d.
Col. 2 : 16, judge you in meat or d.
Ex. 15 : 24, what shall we d. ?
17 : 1, no water for people to d.
Num. 5 : 24, d. bitter water.
Judg. 4 : 19, water to d., for I am thirsty.
2 Ki. 18 : 31; Isa. 36 : 16; Prov. 5 : 15, d.
every one water of his cistern.
Ps. 36 : 8, d. of the river of thy pleasures.
60 : 3, d. the wine of astonishment.
80 : 5, givest them tears to d.
110 : 7, he shall d. of the brook in the way.
Prov. 31 : 4, it is not for kings to d. wine.
Cant. 5 : 1, d., yea d. abundantly.
Isa. 22 : 13; 1 Cor. 15 : 32, let us eat and d.
Isa. 65 : 13, my servants shall d., but ye shall
be thirsty.
Jer. 35 : 6, we will d. no wine.
Zech. 9 : 15, they shall d., and make a noise.
Matt. 10 : 42, whosoever shall give to d.
20 : 22; Mark 10 : 38, are ye able to d. ?
Matt. 26 : 27, saying, d. ye all of it.
26 : 29; Mark 14 : 25; Luke 22 : 18, when
I d. it new.
Matt. 26 : 42, may not pass except I d. it.
Mark 9 : 41, shall give you cup of water to d.
16 : 18, if they d. any deadly thing.
John 7 : 37, let him come to me and d.
Rom. 14 : 21, not good to d. wine.
1 Cor. 11 : 25, as oft as ye d. it.
Drink Offerings, law concerning, Ex. 29 : 40;
Lev. 23 : 13; Num. 6 : 17; 15 : 5 (Gen.
35 : 14).
to idols, Isa. 57 : 6; Jer. 7 : 18; 44 : 17; Ezek.
20 : 28.
Drive, Gen. 4 : 14, thou hast d. me out.
Ex. 6 : 1, with a strong hand d. out.
Deut. 4 : 38; Josh. 3 : 10, to d. out nations
from before thee.
Job 30 : 5, they were d. forth from among men.
Ps. 44 : 2, didst d. out the heathen.
68 : 2, as smoke, so d. them away.
Prov. 22 : 15, rod shall d. it away.
25 : 23, north wind d. away rain.
Dan. 4 : 25; 5 : 21, they shall d. thee from
men.
Hos. 13 : 3, as chaff d. with whirlwind.
Luke 8 : 29, he was d. of the devil.
Jas. 1 : 6, like wave d. with wind.
Dromedary [Heb. beker, bikrah] is a swift, well-
bred camel, and as such is referred to in
Isa. 60 : 6, " the dromedaries of Midian
and Ephah." The Heb. rekesh is translated
in the Authorised Version dromedary in

1 Ki. 4 : 28, and in Esther 8 : 10, and mule
in Esther 8 : 14.
Dromedaries, 1 Ki. 4 : 28; Esther 8 : 10; Isa.
60 : 6; Jer. 2 : 23.
Drop, Deut. 32 : 2, my doctrine d. as the rain.
33 : 28; Prov. 3 : 20, heavens d. dew.
Job 36 : 28, which the clouds do d.
Ps. 65 : 11, thy paths d. fatness.
68 : 8, heavens d. at presence of God.
Isa. 40 : 15, as a d. of a bucket.
45 : 8, d. down, ye heavens.
Joel 3 : 18; Amos 9 : 13, the mountains shall
d. down new wine.
Luke 22 : 44, sweat as it were great d. of blood.
Dropsy, cured by Christ, Luke 14 : 2.
Dross, wicked compared to, Ps. 119 : 119; Isa.
1 : 25; Ezek. 22 : 18.
Ps. 119 : 119, the wicked like d.
Prov. 25 : 4, take d. from silver.
Isa. 1 : 22, thy silver is become d.
Ezek. 22 : 18, house of Israel d.
Drought, Gen. 31 : 40, in day d. consumed me.
Ps. 32 : 4, my moisture into the d. of summer.
Isa. 58 : 11, Lord shall satisfy thy soul in d.
Jer. 17 : 8, not be careful in year of d.
Hos. 13 : 5, know thee in land of d.
Hag. 1 : 11, and I called for a d.
Deut. 28 : 24; 1 Ki. 17.
Drown, Cant. 8 : 7, neither can floods d. it.
1 Tim. 6 : 9, which d. men in perdition.
Drunk, 1 Sam. 1 : 15, I have d. neither wine nor.
2 Sam. 11 : 13, David made Uriah d.
1 Ki. 20 : 16, was drinking himself d.
Job 12 : 25; Ps. 107 : 27, stagger like a d. man.
Jer. 23 : 9, I am like a d. man.
Lam. 5 : 4, we have d. water for money.
Matt. 24 : 49; Luke 12 : 45, drink with the d.
Acts 2 : 15, not d. as ye suppose,
1 Cor. 11 : 21, one is hungry, and another d.
Eph. 5 : 18, d. with wine wherein is excess.
1 Thess. 5 : 7, they that be d., are d. in the
night.
Drunkard, Deut. 21 : 20, our son is a glutton
and a d.
Ps. 69 : 12, I was the song of the d.
Prov. 23 : 21, d. shall come to poverty.
Isa. 24 : 20, the earth shall reel like a d.
1 Cor. 6 : 10, nor d. inherit kingdom of God.
Drunkenness censured, Isa. 5 : 11; 28 : 1; Joel
1 : 5; Luke 21 : 34; Rom. 13 : 13; 1 Cor.
5 : 11; Gal. 5 : 21; Eph. 5 : 18; 1 Thess.
5 : 7; 1 Pet. 4 : 3.
its punishment, Deut. 21 : 20; Amos 6 : 7;
Nah. 1 : 10; Matt. 24 : 49; Luke 12 : 45;
1 Cor. 6 : 10; Gal. 5 : 21.
of Noah, Gen. 9 : 21; Lot, Gen. 19 : 33;
Nabal, 1 Sam. 25 : 36; Elah, 1 Ki. 16 : 9;
Benhadad, 1 Ki. 20 : 16; Belshazzar, Dan.
5 : 4; The Corinthians, 1 Cor. 11 : 21.
Deut. 29 : 19, to add d. to thirst.
Eccl. 10 : 17, eat for strength, not for d.
Ezek. 23 : 33, filled with d.
Luke 21 : 34, overcharged with d.
Rom. 13 : 13, not in rioting and d.
Drusilla (dru-sĭl-lă), Acts 24 : 24.
Dry, Gen. 8 : 13, face of ground was d.
Josh. 3 : 17, priests stood firm on d. ground.
Judg. 6 : 37, it be d. on all the earth.
Ps. 107 : 33, water springs into d. ground.

Prov. 17 : 22, a broken spirit **d.** the bones.
Isa. 32 : 2, as rivers in a **d.** place.
44 : 3, pour floods on **d.** ground.
53 : 2, as a root out of a **d.** ground.
Hos. 9 : 16, their root is **d.** up.
Matt. 12 : 43; Luke 11 : 24, through **d.** places.
Mark 5 : 29, fountain of blood **d.** up.
11 : 20, saw the fig tree **d.** up.
Due, Lev. 10 : 13, 14, it is thy **d.**, and thy sons' **d.**
Lev. 26 : 4; Deut. 11 : 14, rain in **d.** season.
Ps. 104 : 27; 145 : 15; Matt. 24 : 45; Luke
12 : 42, meat in **d.** season.
Prov. 15 : 23, word spoken in **d.** season.
Matt. 18 : 34, pay all that was **d.**
Luke 23 : 41, the **d.** reward of our deeds.
Rom. 5 : 6, in **d.** time Christ died for the
ungodly.
1 Cor. 15 : 8, as of one born out of **d.** time.
Gal. 6 : 9, in **d.** season we shall reap.
1 Pet. 5 : 6, he may exalt you in **d.** time.
Dulcimer, The, in its earliest form consisted of
flat boards (afterwards a box) of four sides,
two of them converging, the strings, which
were stretched over it, being struck with
small hammers. It is the ancestor of the
pianoforte, Dan. 3 : 5, 10, 15.
Dull, Matt. 13 : 15; Acts 28 : 27, ears are **d.**
Heb. 5 : 11, seeing ye are **d.** of hearing.
Dumb healed by Christ, Matt. 9 : 32; 12 : 22.
not to be oppressed, Prov. 31 : 8.
Ex. 4 : 11, who maketh the **d.** ?
Ps. 38 : 13, I was as a **d.** man.
Prov. 31 : 8, open thy mouth for the **d.**
Isa. 35 : 6, the tongue of the **d.** shall sing.
53 : 7; Acts 8 : 32, as sheep before shearers
is **d.**
Hab. 2 : 19, woe to him that saith to **d.** stone.
Matt. 9 : 32; 12 : 22; Mark 9 : 17, **d.** man.
1 Cor. 12 : 2, carried away to **d.** idols.
2 Pet. 2 : 16, the **d.** ass speaking.
Dumbness of Zacharias, Luke 1 : 20.
Dung, Luke 13 : 8, till I dig about it, and **d.** it.
Phil. 3 : 8, count all things but **d.**
Dungeon, Joseph cast into, Gen. 39; 40 : 15;
also, Jeremiah, Jer. 37 : 16; 38 : 6.
Dunghill, 1 Sam. 2 : 8, Ps. 113 : 7, lifteth beggar
from **d.**
Luke 14 : 35, neither fit for land, nor **d.**
Durable, Prov. 8 : 18, **d.** riches are with me.
Isa. 23 : 18, be for **d.** clothing.
See Matt. 13 : 21.
Dust of the earth, man formed of, Gen. 2 : 7;
3 : 19; 18 : 27; Job 10 : 9; 34 : 15; Ps.
103 : 14; 104 : 29; Eccl. 12 : 7.
mark of grief, Josh. 7 : 6; Job 2 : 12; Lam.
2 : 10.
Gen. 2 : 7, Lord God formed man of **d.**
3 : 14, **d.** shalt thou eat.
3 : 19, **d.** thou art, and unto **d.**
18 : 27, who am but **d.** and ashes.
Job 2 : 12, sprinkled **d.** upon heads.
34 : 15, man shall turn again to **d.**
42 : 6, I repent in **d.** and ashes.
Ps. 22 : 15, brought me into **d.** of death.
30 : 9, shall the **d.** praise thee ?
102 : 14, servants favour **d.** thereof.
103 : 14, remembereth that we are **d.**
119 : 25, my soul cleaveth to the **d.**
Eccl. 12 : 7, then shall **d.** return to the earth.

Isa. 40 : 12, comprehended **d.** of the earth.
Dan. 12 : 2, many that sleep in **d.** shall awake.
Matt. 10 : 14; Mark 6 : 11; Luke 9 : 5, shake
off **d.** from feet.
Acts 13 : 51, they shook off the **d.**
22 : 23, they threw **d.** into the air.
Duty of man, the whole, Eccl. 12 : 13; Luke
17 : 10.
Eccl. 12 : 13, the whole **d.** of man.
Luke 17 : 10, done that which was our **d.** to
do.
Rom. 15 : 27, their **d.** is to minister in carna
things.
Dwarfs not to minister, Lev. 21 : 20.
Dwell, Deut. 12 : 11, cause his name to **d.** there.
2 Ki. 19 : 15; Ps. 80 : 1; Isa. 37 : 16, which
d. between cherubims.
Ps. 23 : 6, will **d.** in house of the Lord.
Ps. 84 : 10, than to **d.** in tents of wickedness.
132 : 14, here will I **d.**
133 : 1, good for brethren to **d.** together.
Isa. 33 : 14, who shall **d.** with devouring fire.
57 : 15, I **d.** in the high and holy place.
John 6 : 56, **d.** in me, and I in him.
14 : 17, he **d.** with you, and shall be in you.
Acts 7 : 48; 17 : 24, God **d.** not in temples.
Rom. 7 : 17, sin that **d.** in me.
8 : 11, by his Spirit that **d.** in you.
Col. 2 : 9, in him **d.** all the fulness of the
Godhead.
3 : 16, word of Christ **d.** in you richly.
1 Tim. 6 : 16, **d.** in the light.
2 Tim. 1 : 14, Holy Ghost who **d.** in us.
2 Pet. 3 : 13, wherein **d.** righteousness.
1 John 3 : 17, how **d.** the love of God in him.
4 : 12, God **d.** in us.
Dyed, Ex. 25 : 5; Isa. 63 : 1; Ezek. 23 : 15.
Dying, 2 Cor. 4 : 10, the **d.** of the Lord Jesus.
2 Cor. 6 : 9, as **d.**, and, behold, we live.
Heb. 11 : 21, by faith Jacob, when **d.**

E

Each, Gen. 40 : 5; 41 : 11, 12, **e.** man according
to.
Ezek. 40 : 16, upon **e.** post were palms.
Luke 13 : 15, doth not **e.** one of you ?
Acts 2 : 3, cloven tongues upon **e.** of them.
Phil. 2 : 3, **e.** esteem other better.
2 Thess. 1 : 3, charity toward **e.** other.
Eagle [Heb. nesher]. This bird was not our
eagle, but the Griffon vulture, and the word
is so rendered in the R.V. (Mic. 1 : 16,
margin). The characteristics of this fine
bird are frequently referred to in the Bible
—its bared neck (Mic. 1 : 15), its swiftness
(Job 39 : 28, 29), its building in high cliffs
(Jer. 49 : 16), its powerful sight (Job 39;
Deut. 28 : 49), its great powers of flight
(Prov. 30 : 19), and its teaching its young
to fly (Deut. 32 : 11). Like all the birds
that fed on animal food, it was unclean. It
devours living as well as dead prey.
unclean, Lev. 11 : 13.
described, Job 9 : 26; 39 : 27; Ezek. 17 : 3;
Obad. 4.
one of the four living creatures in the vision
of heaven, Ezek. 1 : 10; Rev. 4 : 7.

Ex. 19 : 4, I bare you on e. wings.
Deut. 32 : 11, as an e. stirreth her nest.
2 Sam. 1 : 23, swifter than e.
Ps. 103 : 5, youth renewed like e.
Isa. 40 : 31, mount up with wings as e.
Matt. 24 : 28; Luke 17 : 37, e. be gathered.
Ear, the, 2 Sam. 7 : 22; Ps. 45 : 10; 78 : 1;
    94 : 9; Prov. 15 : 31; 20 : 12; 22 : 17; Isa.
    50 : 4; 55 : 3; Matt. 10 : 27.
he that hath, to hear, Matt. 11 : 15; 13 : 16;
    Mark 4 : 9, 23; 7 : 16.
have, but hear not, Ps. 115 : 6; Isa. 42 : 20;
    Ezek. 12 : 2; Matt. 13 : 14; Mark 8 : 18;
    Rom. 11 : 8.
the Lord's, open to prayer, 2 Sam. 22 : 7; Ps.
    18 : 6; 34 : 15; Jas. 5 : 4; 1 Pet. 3 : 12.
opened by God, Job 33 : 16; 36 : 15; Ps.
    40 : 6; Mark 7 : 35.
Ex. 21 : 6; Deut. 15 : 17, master shall bore e.
2 Ki. 19 : 16; Ps. 31 : 2, bow down thine e.
Neh. 1 : 6, 11, let thy e. be attentive.
Job 42 : 5, heard by hearing of e.
Ps. 10 : 17, cause thine e. to hear.
    94 : 9, he that planted the e.
Prov. 18 : 15, e. of wise seek knowledge.
Isa. 59 : 1, e. heavy that it cannot hear.
Matt. 10 : 27, what ye hear in the e.
1 Cor. 2 : 9, eye hath not seen nor e. heard.
1 Sam. 8 : 12; Isa. 30 : 24, e. the ground.
Early, Ps. 46 : 5, God shall help her and that
    right e.
    63 : 1, my God, e. will I seek thee.
    90 : 14, satisfy us e. with thy mercy.
Prov. 8 : 17, seek me e. shall find me.
Hos. 5 : 15, in affliction will seek me e.
    6 : 4; 13 : 3, as the e. dew.
Jas. 5 : 7, the e. and latter rain.
Early Rising, Gen. 19 : 27; 26 : 31; 28 : 18;
    Josh. 3 : 1; Judg. 6 : 38; 1 Sam. 9 : 26;
    15 : 12; 17 : 20; Mark 1 : 35; 16 : 2; John
    8 : 2; 20 : 1; Acts 5 : 21.
Earnest, Job 7 : 2, as servant e. desireth.
Luke 22 : 44, in agony he prayed more e.
Rom. 8 : 19, the e. expectation of the creature.
1 Cor. 12 : 31, covet e. the best gifts.
2 Cor. 1 : 22; 5 : 5, the e. of the Spirit.
Eph. 1 : 14, the e. of our inheritance.
Jude 3, e. contend for the faith.
Earth created, Gen. 1 : 1; made fruitful, Gen.
    1 : 11; cursed, Gen. 3 : 17; covered by the
    flood, Gen. 7 : 10; to be consumed by fire,
    Mic. 1 : 4; Zeph. 3 : 8; 2 Pet. 3 : 7; Rev.
    20 : 9.
a new (and heaven), 2 Pet. 3 : 13; Rev. 21 : 1.
Gen. 1 : 10, God called the dry land e.
    6 : 11, e. was corrupt before God.
Ex. 9 : 29; Deut. 10 : 14; Ps. 24 : 1; 1 Cor.
    10 : 26, e. is the Lord's.
Num. 14 : 21, all the e. filled with glory of
    the Lord.
    16 : 30, if the e. open her mouth.
Deut. 32 : 1, O e., hear the words of my
    mouth.
Josh. 23 : 14, going way of all the e.
1 Sam. 2 : 8, pillars of the e. are Lord's.
1 Ki. 8 : 27; 2 Chr. 6 : 18, will God dwell on
    the e. ?
Job 19 : 25, stand at latter day upon the e.
    38 : 4, when I laid foundations of the e.

Ps. 2 : 8, uttermost parts of the e.
    33 : 5, e. is full of the goodness of the Lord
    46 : 2, not fear, though e. be removed.
    58 : 11, a God that judgeth in the e.
    65 : 9, thou visitest the e., and waterest it.
    72 : 19, let the whole e. be filled with his
    glory.
    73 : 25, none on e. I desire beside thee.
    99 : 1, Lord reigneth, let e. be moved.
    102 : 25; 104 : 5; Prov. 8 : 29; Isa. 48 : 13,
    laid the foundation of the e.
Ps. 148 : 13, his glory is above the e.
Prov. 3 : 19, Lord founded the e.
    8 : 23, from everlasting, or ever e. was.
Eccl. 1 : 4, the e. abideth for ever.
    12 : 7, dust return to e.
Isa. 11 : 9, e. full of knowledge of the Lord.
    40 : 28, Creator of ends of e. fainteth not.
    45 : 22, be saved, all ends of the e.
Jer. 22 : 29; Mic. 1 : 2, O e., e., e., hear word
    of the Lord.
Ezek. 34 : 27, the e. shall yield her increase.
Hos. 2 : 22, the e. shall hear the corn.
Zech. 4 : 10, eyes of Lord run through e.
Matt. 5 : 5, meek shall inherit the e.
Mark 4 : 28, e. bringeth forth fruit of herself.
Luke 2 : 14, on e. peace.
    23 : 44, darkness over all the e.
John 3 : 31, he that is of e. is e., and speaketh
    of the e.
    12 : 32, Son of man lifted up from the e.
Acts 8 : 33, his life is taken from the e.
1 Cor. 15 : 47, first man is of the e., c.
Col. 3 : 2, set your affection not on things on
    the e.
Heb. 6 : 7, e. drinketh in the rain.
    12 : 25, refused him that spake on e.
2 Pet. 3 : 10, the e. shall be burned up.
Rev. 5 : 10, we shall reign on the e.
    21 : 1, a new e.
Earthen, 2 Cor. 4 : 7, treasure in e. vessels.
Earthly, 1 Cor. 15 : 49, have borne the image of
    the e.
    2 Cor. 5 : 1, our e. house of this tabernacle.
    Phil. 3 : 19, who mind e. things.
Jas. 3 : 15, this wisdom is e.
Earthquakes, 1 Ki. 19 : 11; Isa. 29 : 6; Amos
    1 : 1; Matt. 27 : 54; Acts 16 : 26; Rev.
    6 : 12; 8 : 5; 11 : 13; 16 : 18.
1 Ki. 19 : 11, Lord was not in the e.
Zech. 14 : 5, ye fled before the e.
Matt. 24 : 7; Mark 13 : 8; Luke 21 : 11,
    famines and e.
Matt. 27 : 54, centurion saw the e.
    28 : 2; Acts 16 : 26; Rev. 6 : 12, there was
    a great e.
Ease, Deut. 28 : 65, shalt thou find no e.
Job 12 : 5, thought of him that is at e.
    21 : 23, dieth, being wholly at e.
Ps. 25 : 13, his soul shall dwell at e.
Isa. 32 : 9, rise up, ye women at e.
Amos 6 : 1, woe to them that are at e.
Matt. 9 : 5; Mark 2 : 9; Luke 5 : 23, whether
    is e. to say.
Matt. 11 : 30, my yoke is e. and burden light.
    19 : 24; Mark 10 : 25; Luke 18 : 25, e. for
    camel.
Luke 12 : 19, take thine e. and be merry.
1 Cor. 13 : 5, charity is not e. provoked.

Heb. 12 : 1, sin which doth so e. beset us.
East, men of the, Job 1 : 3.
glory of God proceeding from, etc., Ezek.
　43 : 2; 47 : 8.
wise men from, worship Christ, Matt. 2 : 1.
Gen. 3 : 24, e. of the garden of Eden.
29 : 1, land of the people of the e.
41 : 6, 23, 27, thin ears blasted with e. wind.
Ex. 10 : 13; 14 : 21, Lord brought an e. wind.
Job 1 : 3, greatest of all the men of the e.
38 : 24, scattereth e. wind on the earth.
Ps. 48 : 7, breakest ships with e. wind.
75 : 6, promotion cometh not from e.
103 : 12, as far as e. from west.
Isa. 27 : 8, stayeth rough wind in day of e.
　wind.
43 : 5;　Zech. 8 : 7, bring thy seed from
　the e.
Ezek. 8 : 16, faces toward the e.
Hos. 12 : 1, Ephraim followeth e. wind.
13 : 15, an e. wind shall come.
Jonah 4 : 5, sat on e. side of city.
Matt. 2 : 1, wise men from the e.
8 : 11; Luke 13 : 29, many come from e.
24 : 27, as lightning out of the e.
Easter. The Christian name for this season,
derived from that of a pagan goddess,
corresponds to the Greek " pascha," the
time of the celebration of the feast of the
Passover.
Peter imprisoned till after, Acts 12 : 4.
Eat, Gen. 2 : 16, of every tree thou mayest e.
3 : 17, in sorrow shalt thou e.
1 Ki. 19 : 5; Acts 10 : 13; 11 : 7, angel said,
arise and e.
2 Ki. 6 : 28, give thy son, that we may e.
him.
Neh. 5 : 2, corn, that we may e., and live.
8 : 10, e. the fat, drink the sweet.
Ps. 22 : 26, the meek shall e. and be satisfied.
69 : 9; John 2 : 17, zeal of thine house hath
e. me up.
Ps. 78 : 25; man did e. angels' food.
109 : 9, have e. ashes like bread.
Prov. 1 : 31; Isa. 3 : 10, e. fruit of own way.
Cant. 5 : 1, e. O friends; drink, yea, drink
abundantly.
Isa. 1 : 19, if obedient, ye shall e. the good of
the land.
7 : 15, 22, butter and honey shall he e.
11 : 7; 65 : 25, lion e. straw like ox.
55 : 1, come ye, buy and e.
65 : 13, my servants shall e., but ye shall be
hungry.
Jer. 31 : 29; Ezek. 18 : 2, the fathers have e.
sour grapes.
Hos. 4 : 10; Mic. 6 : 14; Hag. 1 : 6, e., and
not have enough.
Matt. 6 : 25; Luke 12 : 22, what ye shall e.
Matt. 12 : 4, e. shewbread, which was not
lawful to e.
14 : 16; Mark 6 : 37; Luke 9 : 13, give ye
them to e.
Matt. 15 : 20, to e. with unwashen hands.
15 : 27; Mark 7 : 28, dogs e. of crumbs.
Matt. 26 : 26; Mark 14 : 22; 1 Cor. 11 : 24,
take e., this is my body.
Mark 6 : 31, no leisure so much as to e.
11 : 14, no man e. fruit of thee.

Luke 10 : 8, e. such things as are set before
you.
12 : 19, take thine ease, e., drink.
15 : 23, let us e. and be merry.
24 : 43, he took it, and did e. before them.
John 4 : 32, meat to e. ye know not of.
6 : 53, except ye e. the flesh.
Acts 2 : 46, did e. their meat with gladness.
9 : 9, Saul did neither e. nor drink.
Rom. 14 : 2, one believeth he may e. all things.
1 Cor. 10 : 31, whether ye e. or drink.
11 : 29, he that e. unworthily.
2 Thess. 3 : 10, any work not, neither e.
2 Tim. 2 : 17, e. as doth a canker.
Jas. 5 : 3, e. your flesh as fire.
Rev. 2 : 7, e. of the tree of life.
2 : 17, give to e. of hidden manna.
19 : 18, e. flesh of kings.
Ebed-melech (ē-́bĕd-mĕl-́ĕch) [king's servant],
Ethiopian eunuch, intercedes for and delivers Jeremiah, etc., Jer. 38 : 7; 39 : 16.
Eben-ezer (ĕb-́ĕn-ē-́zĕr) [stone of help], Israelites
smitten by Philistines at, 1 Sam. 4 : 1.
" hitherto hath the Lord helped us " (stone
raised by Samuel in memory of defeat of
the Philistines), 1 Sam. 7 : 12.
Eber (ē-́bĕr) [region beyond], a name of the
Hebrew people, Gen. 10 : 24; Num.
24 : 24.
Ebony [Heb. hobnim or hobenim]. The hard
wood known by this name is the inner
heart wood of a tree growing in Southern
India. Ebony is mentioned in Ezek. 27 : 15,
in connection with ivory, as brought to
Tyre by merchants trading from the East.
Ecclesiastes, Book of.
Title.—The book of Ecclesiastes, like Proverbs, is one of the class of didactic com-
positions or mashals. It does not, however,
like that work, consist of a number of
maxims loosely connected with one another,
but forms a continuous soliloquy on the
vanity of human wishes, put by the author
into the mouth of Solomon, the wise king
of Israel. The title assigned to the king
in the book is Koheleth.
In the LXX. the book bears the title
Ecclesiastes, i.e., Preacher, and this name
has been adopted in a Latinised form by
the Vulgate, and has passed over into the
English version.
Author and Date.—The common opinion in
ancient times was that the author of the
book was King Solomon. It would appear,
however, from indications in the Targum,
Talmud, and other writers, that that
opinion was not entirely accepted by Jewish
scholars. Others consider that it was
written somewhat later, about 200 B.C.
The language of Ecclesiastes is unique. In
many of its features it bears a strong resemblance to the later books of the Old
Testament; in others it approximates to the
language of post-Biblical literature.
Contents.—In chapters 1 and 2 the writer
demonstrates the " vanity of all things " by
illustrations drawn from the fields of
human activity; man's labour, the pursuit
of wisdom, or pleasure, or riches, are all of

no avail, for the end of the wise and foolish is the same, and riches, amassed with toil and care, bring no satisfaction. The only result he arrives at is that there is "nothing better for a man than that he should eat and drink," and enjoy such pleasures as God provides for him during his short sojourn on earth. In ch. 3 : 1-15, he shows that everything has its own proper time and season, but who can be certain that he has discovered this season ? Man's efforts to grasp success are thus of no avail, and all he can do is to enjoy the present. In ch. 3 : 16-22, he contrasts the lot of man with that of the beasts that perish—the fate of both is alike—and he again draws the same conclusion, to enjoy the present. In ch. 4 : 1-3, he depicts the evils of oppression, for which there is no redress (4-6) of rivalry (7-12) of isolation, and (13-16) the vanity of political life. In ch. 5 : 1-9 he points out how certain of the vexations of life may be avoided by care and prudence, and in ver. 10-17 moralises on the vanity of riches, which are often fraught with care and trouble, and (ver. 18-20) can only be regarded as blessings when God grants the opportunity and power to enjoy them. This, however (ch. 6 : 1-6), God often denies, and (ver. 7-9), though man toils and labours, he cannot obtain his desire, for (ver. 10-12) he is powerless to contend with " him that is mightier than he." In ch. 7 : 1-24 the writer points out how a man may alleviate the troubles of life by avoiding frivolity and practising patience and resignation, and instead of brooding over the ills of life, by seeking after wisdom, which, though diffi-cult to find, is the best guide for man. In ver. 25-29 he emphatically insists on the fact that one of the greatest hindrances to human happiness is the wicked woman, " whose heart is snares and nets, and her hands as bands." In ch. 8 : 1-9, the writer urges prudence in all matters affecting the king and those in authority. The memory of the righteous (ver. 10-15) speedily passes away, while the wicked are honoured and rewarded, so that man's best course is to derive all the enjoyment he can from life, while God permits him. Ch. 8 : 16 to 9 : 6, man's efforts to grasp God's purposes are of no avail, life is naught but evil, and death quickly comes, with no certain hope of im-mortality (a judgment to come is affirmed in ch. 12 : 14), therefore (ver. 7-10) man must get all the pleasure he can out of life. In ch. 4 : 11-16 he points out that merit is not always sufficiently rewarded, wisdom is often of more avail than strength, yet wisdom, that has accomplished much, is often forgotten. Chaps. 9 : 17 to 10 : 15 forms a collection of proverbs on wisdom, and the consequences of folly, and (ver. 16-20) the wretched condition of a country under the rule of a feeble king. In ch. 11 : 1-8, the writer urges the importance of benevolence, and that life, in spite of its troubles, ought to be enjoyed. Especially

(ch. 11 : 9 to 12 : 8) ought the young man to rejoice in the season of his youth before old age overtakes him; yet in his joy he should not be unmindful of God who created him. The book concludes with the epilogue, ch. 12 : 8-14, which some main-tain to be the work of a different author.

Eden (ē-děn) [pleasure or delight], described, Gen. 2 : 8; Adam driven from, Gen. 3 : 24. figuratively mentioned, Isa. 51 : 3; Ezek. 28 : 13; 31 : 9; 36 : 35; Joel 2 : 3.

Edification, Rom. 14 : 19; 15 : 2; 1 Cor. 8 : 1; 10 : 33; 14 : 5; 2 Cor. 12 : 19; 13 : 10; Eph. 4 : 12, 29; 1 Thess. 5 : 11.

Edify, Rom. 14 : 19, one may e. another. 15 : 2, please his neighbour to e. 1 Cor. 8 : 1, charity e. 10 : 23, all things lawful, but e. not. 14 : 26, let all things be done to e. Eph. 4 : 12, the e. of the body of Christ. 1 Tim. 1 : 4, minister questions rather than e.

Edom (ē-dŏm) [red], see **Idumea,** Gen. 25 : 30. prophecies concerning, Jer. 25 : 21; 49 : 7; Ezek. 25 : 13; 35; Amos 1 : 11; Obad. 1.

Edomites (ē-dŏm-ites), the descendants of Esau, Gen. 36. deny the Israelites passage through Edom, Num. 20 : 18. their possessions, Deut. 2 : 5; Josh. 24 : 4. not to be abhorred, Deut. 23 : 7. subdued by David, 2 Sam. 8 : 14. revolt, 2 Ki. 8 : 20; 2 Chr. 21 : 8. subdued by Amaziah, 2 Ki. 14 : 7; 2 Chr. 25 : 11.

Effect, Ps. 33 : 10, devices of people of none e. Isa. 32 : 17, the e. of righteousness, quiet-ness. Matt. 15 . 6, Mark 7 : 13, command of God of none e. Rom. 4 : 14; Gal. 3 : 17, promise of none e. 1 Cor. 1 : 7, lest cross of Christ be of none e. Gal. 5 : 4, Christ has become of no e.

Effectual, 1 Cor. 16 : 9, a great door and e. Eph. 3 : 7; 4 : 16, the e. working. Jas. 5 : 16, the e. prayer of a righteous man. See 1 Thess. 2 : 13.

Egg, Job 6 : 6, any taste in white of e. ? Job 39 : 14, ostrich leaveth e. in earth. Isa. 59 : 5, hatch cockatrice' e. Jer. 17 : 11, partridge sitteth on e. Luke 11 : 12, if he ask an e.

Eglah (ĕg-läh) [heifer, calf], 2 Sam. 3 : 5.

Eglon (ĕg-lŏn) [calf-like], king of Moab, op-presses Israel, Judg. 3 : 14. slain by Ehud, Judg. 3 : 21.

Egypt (ē-gўpt) [Heb. Mizraim], a dual name properly equal to the two Egypts, i.e., Upper and Lower, Gen. 10 : 6. Abram goes down into, Gen. 12 : 10. Joseph sold into, Gen. 37 : 36; his advance-ment, imprisonment, and restoration there, Gen. 39; 40 : 41. Jacob's sons go to buy corn in, Gen. 41. Jacob and all his family go there, Gen. 46 : 6. Israelites' bondage there, Ex. 1 : 12; 5, etc. their departure from, Ex. 13 : 17; Ps. 78 : 12. army of, pursue and perish in the Red Sea, Ex. 14. kings of, harass Judah, 1 Ki. 14 : 25; 2 Ki.

23 : 29; 2 Chr. 12 : 2; 35 : 20; 36 : 3; Jer. 37 : 5.

the " remnant of Judah " taken there, Jer. 43 : 7.

Jesus taken to, Matt. 2 : 13.

prophecies concerning, Gen. 15 : 13; Isa. 11 : 11; 19; 20; 27 : 12; 30 : 1; Jer. 9 : 26; 25 : 19; 43 : 8; 44 : 28; 46; Ezek. 29 : 32; Dan. 11 : 8; Hos. 9 : 3; 11; Joel 3 : 19; Zech. 10 : 10; 14 : 18.

Egyptian Mummy.

Egyptian (ĕ-gўp-'tĭ-ăn), slain by Moses, Ex. 2 : 12.

to know the Lord, Ex. 14 : 18.

slain by Benaiah, 2 Sam. 23 : 21.

Ehud (ē-'hŭd) [derivation unknown], a judge, delivers Israel, Judg. 3 : 15.

Ekron (ĕk-'rŏn) [rooting up], men of, smitten with emerods, 1 Sam. 5 : 12; 6 : 17.

prophecies concerning Amos, 1 : 8; Zeph. 2 : 4; Zech. 9 : 5.

Elah (ē-'lăh) [oak, terebinth], Gen. 36 : 41.

king of Israel, 1 Ki. 16 : 8, 10.

valley of, battle in, 1 Sam. 17 : 2.

David slays Goliath there, 1 Sam. 17 : 49.

Elam (ē-'lăm) [probably highland], son of Shem, Gen. 10 : 22.

Chedorlaomer, king of, Gen. 14.

Elath (ē-'lăth) [grove, probably of palms], 2 Ki. 14 : 22, a town at the head of the Arabian

Gulf, on the route of the Israelites, Deut. 2 : 8.

El Belka, a division of modern Palestine.

El-beth-el (ĕl-bĕth-'ĕl) [God of Bethel], Gen. 35 : 7.

Eldad (ĕl-'dăd) or **Elidad** [God loves], and Medad prophesy, Num. 11 : 26.

Elath.

Elder, Gen. 25 : 23; Rom. 9 : 12, e. serve younger.

Job 15 : 10, aged men, much e. than thy father.

Ps. 107 : 32, praise in assembly of e.

Matt. 15 : 2; Mark 7 : 3, tradition of the e.

Titus 1 : 5, ordain e. in every city.

Heb. 11 : 2, by faith the e. obtained a good report.

Jas. 5 : 14, call for e. of church.

1 Pet. 5 : 1, the e. I exhort, who am an e.

Elders. " The Elders of Israel " (Ex. 3 : 16), were a Senate of the people in Moses' time, which continued through all the vicissitudes of the Hebrew history (Ezra 5 : 5; Jer. 29 : 1). " The elders " are often mentioned in the New Testament as acting co-ordinately with (1) the chief priests (Matt. 21 : 23); (2) the chief priests and scribes (Matt. 16 : 21); (3) all the Council (Matt. 26 : 59). In the New Testament Church " the elders " are the presbyters or ministers (Acts 20 : 17).

seventy, Ex. 24 : 1; Num. 11 : 16.

officers so called, Gen. 50 : 7; Lev. 4 : 15; Deut. 21 : 19; 1 Sam. 16 : 4; Ezra 5 : 5; Ps. 107 : 32; Ezek. 8 : 1.

of the Church, Acts 14 : 23; 15 : 4, 23; 16 : 4; 20 : 17; Titus 1 : 5; Jas. 5 : 14; 1 Pet. 5 : 1.

Paul's charge to, Acts 20 : 17.

Peter's charge to, 1 Pet. 5.

twenty-four, in heaven, Rev. 4 : 4; 7 : 11; 14 : 3.

Eleazar (ĕl-ē-ā-'zär) or **Eliezer** (ĕ-lĭ-ē-'zĕr) [God helpeth], son of Aaron, and chief priest, Ex. 6 : 23; 28; 29; Lev. 8; Num. 3 : 2; 4 : 16; 16 : 36; 20 : 26; 27 : 22; 31 : 13; 34 : 17; Josh. 17 : 4; 24 : 33.

son of Abinadab, keeps the ark, 1 Sam. 7 : 1.

one of David's captains, 2 Sam. 23 : 9; 1 Chr. 11 : 12.

Elect, Christ so called, 1 Pet. 2 : 6; Isa. 42 : 1.
God's chosen, Isa. 45 : 1; 65 : 9.
under the Gospel, Matt. 24 : 22; Mark
13 : 20; Luke 18 : 7; Rom. 8 : 33; 11 : 5;
Col. 3 : 12; 2 Tim. 2 : 10; Titus 1 : 1;
1 Pet. 1 : 2; 2 John 1 : 13.
Isa. 42 : 1, mine e., in whom my soul delighteth.
65 : 9, mine e. shall inherit it.
Matt. 24 : 22; Mark 13 : 20, for e. sake those
days shortened.
Matt. 24 : 31; Mark 13 : 27, gather together
his e.
Luke 18 : 7, God avenge his own e.
Rom. 8 : 33, lay anything to charge of God's e.
Col. 3 : 12, put on as the e. of God.
1 Tim. 5 : 21, charge thee before e. angels.
1 Pet. 1 : 2, e. according to the foreknowledge.
2 : 6, corner stone, e., precious.
Election, of God, 1 Thess. 1 : 4.
its privileges and duties, Mark 13 : 20; Luke
18 : 7; Rom. 8 : 29; 1 Cor. 1 : 27; 2 Pet.
1 : 10.
Rom. 9 : 11, purpose of God according to e.
1 Thess. 1 : 4, knowing your e. of God.
2 Pet. 1 : 10, your calling and e. sure.
Elect Lady, Epistle to, 2 John.
El-elohe-Israel (ĕl-ĕl-ōhē-ĭs̱-rā-ĕl) [God, the God
of Israel], Gen. 33 : 20.
Elements, Gal. 4 : 9, the weak and beggarly e.
2 Pet. 3 : 10, the e. melt with heat.
Elhanan (ĕl-hā-̣năn) [God is gracious], one of
David's warriors, 2 Sam. 21 : 19; 23 : 24;
1 Chr. 11 : 26; 20 : 5.
Eli (ē-̣lī) [lifting up, or (God) nurtured; or
possibly a contraction for Eliah, lofty is
Jah (?)], high priest and judge, blesses
Hannah, 1 Sam. 1 : 17.
Samuel brought to, 1 Sam. 1 : 25.
wickedness of his sons, 1 Sam. 2 : 22.
rebuked by man of God, 1 Sam. 2 : 27.
destruction of his house foretold, 1 Sam. 3 : 11.
his sons slain, 1 Sam. 4 : 10, 11.
his death, 1 Sam. 4 : 18.
Eli, Eli, lama sabachthani ? Matt. 27 : 46;
Mark 15 : 34.
Eliab (ē-lī-̣ăb) [God is my father, or God of the
Father], Deut. 11 : 6; Num. 1 : 9; 1 Sam.
16 : 6; 1 Chr. 12 : 9.
Eliada (ē-lī-̣ă-dă) [God knows], 2 Sam. 5 : 16;
1 Ki. 11 : 23; 1 Chr. 3 : 8.
Eliakim (ē-lī-̣ă-kĭm) [God raises], chief minister
of Hezekiah, conference with Rab-shakeh,
2 Ki. 18 : 18; Isa. 36 : 11.
sent to Isaiah, 2 Ki. 19 : 2; Isa. 37 : 2.
prefigures kingdom of Christ, Isa. 22 : 20-25.
son of Josiah, made king by Pharaoh, and
named Jehoiakim, 2 Ki. 23 : 34; 2 Chr.
36 : 4.
Elias (ē-lī-̣ăs), New Testament form of Elijah,
Matt. 27 : 47, 49 ; Mark 15 : 35, 36.
Eliashib (ē-lī-̣ăsh-ĭb) [God will restore], high
priest, builds the wall, Neh. 3 : 1.
allied unto Tobiah, Neh. 13 : 4.
Eliel (ē-lī-̣ĕl) [God is God], a chief of Manasseh,
1 Chr. 5 : 24.
a Gadite, 1 Chr. 12 : 11.
an overseer in reign of Hezekiah, 2 Chr.
31 : 13.

Eliezer (ĕl-ĭ-ē-̣zĕr) [my God is help], Abraham's
steward, Gen. 15 : 2.
son of Moses, Ex. 18 : 4; 1 Chr. 23 : 15.
prophet, reproves Jehoshaphat, 2 Chr. 20 : 37.
Elihu (ē-lī-̣hū) [God is he!], reproves Job's
friends, Job 32; and Job's impatience, Job
33 : 8; and self-righteousness, Job 34 : 5.
declares God's justice, Job 33 : 12; 34 : 10;
35 : 13; 36; and power, Job 33; 37; and
mercy, Job 33 : 23, 24; 34 : 28.
Elijah (ē-lī-̣jăh) [my God is Jah], the Tishbite,
predicts a great drought, 1 Ki. 17 : 1; Luke
4 : 25; Jas. 5 : 17.
miraculously fed, 1 Ki. 17 : 5; 19 : 5.
raises the widow's son, 1 Ki. 17 : 21.
slays the priests of Baal, 1 Ki. 18 : 40.
flees into the wilderness of Beersheba, 1 Ki.
19; Rom. 11 : 2.
anoints Elisha, 1 Ki. 19 : 19.
denounces Ahab in Naboth's vineyard, 1 Ki.
21 : 17.
his prediction fulfilled, 2 Ki. 9 : 36; 10 : 10.
rebukes Ahaziah, 2 Ki. 1 : 3, 16.
calls down fire from heaven, 2 Ki. 1 : 10; Luke
9 : 54.
divides Jordan, 2 Ki. 2 : 8.
carried up into heaven in a chariot of fire,
2 Ki. 2 : 11.
his mantle taken by Elisha, 2 Ki. 2 : 13.
appears at Christ's transfiguration, Matt.
17 : 3; Mark 9 : 4; Luke 9 : 30.
precursor of John the Baptist, Mal. 4 : 5;
Matt. 11 : 14; 16 : 14; Luke 1 : 17; 9 : 8,
19; John 1 : 21.
Elimelech (ē-lĭm-ē-lĕch) [my God is king], Ruth
1 : 2; 4 : 3.
Eliphaz (ē-lī-̣phăz) [my God is strength], reproves Job, Job 4 : 5; 15 : 22.
God's anger against him appeased, Job 42 : 7, 8.
Elisabeth (ē-lĭs̱-ă-bĕth) [Græcised form of
Elisheba, God is the oath, i.e., I swear by
God], mother of John the Baptist, Luke
1 : 5.
her salutation to Mary, Luke 1 : 42.
Eliseus (ĕl-ĭ-sē-̣ŭs), incorrect Greek form of
Elisha, found in A.V., Luke 4 : 27. The
correct Greek form is Elis-sai-̣os.
Elisha (ē-lī-̣shă) [my God is salvation], appointed to succeed Elijah, 1 Ki. 19 : 16.
receives his mantle, 2 Ki. 2 : 13.
heals the waters with salt, 2 Ki. 2 : 22.
bears destroy the children who mock him,
2 Ki. 2 : 24.
his miracles : water, 2 Ki. 3 : 16; oil, 2 Ki.
4 : 4; Shunammite's son, 2 Ki. 4 : 32;
death in the pot, 2 Ki. 4 : 40; feeds a
hundred men with twenty loaves, 2 Ki.
4 : 44; Naaman's leprosy, 2 Ki. 5 : 14;
Luke 4 : 27; the iron swims, 2 Ki. 6 : 5;
Syrians struck blind, 2 Ki. 6 : 18.
prophesies plenty in Samaria when besieged,
2 Ki. 7 : 1.
sends to anoint Jehu, 2 Ki. 9 : 1.
his death, 2 Ki. 13 : 20.
miracle wrought by his bones, 2 Ki. 13 : 21.
Elishah (ē-lī-̣shăh), Gen. 10 : 4; Ezek. 27 : 7.
Elisheba (ē-lĭsh-ē-bă), Ex. 6 : 23. See Elisabeth.
Elkanah (ĕl-kā-năh) [God created], father of
Samuel, 1 Sam. 1 : 1.

Elm. This word only occurs in Hos. 4 : 13. The R.V. translates the Hebrew word 'elah as terebinth or teil.

Elnathan (ĕl-nā-́thăn) [God hath given, or the gift of God; compare Theodore], 2 Ki. 24 : 8.

Elohim (ĕl-ō-hîm) [the Hebrew for God]. The word is a plural form of a lost singular, possibly the plural of majesty. It is also applied to the shades or spirits of the dead, cf. 1 Sam. 28 : 13, " I saw gods ascending out of the earth." This may be a relic of a more primitive ancestor worship.

Eloi (ē-lō-́ī) [my God], Mark 15 : 34.

Elon (ē-́lŏn) [oak tree], judges Israel, Judg. 12 : 11.
See Gen. 26 : 34; 46 : 14.

Eloquent, Ex. 4 : 10, I am not e.
Isa. 3 : 3, Lord doth take away e. orator.
Acts 18 : 24, an e. man.

Elul (ē-́lŭl) [Assyrian U-lu-lu], the month of September, Neh. 6 : 15.

Elymas (ĕl-ý-măs), wise man, magician [Bar-Jesus], Acts 13 : 8.

Embalming of Jacob, Gen. 50 : 2; of Joseph, Gen. 50 : 26; of Christ, John 19 : 39.

Emerald = Carbuncle of A.V. [Heb. Barequeth and Bareqath; Σμαραγδος; Smaragdus], Ex. 28 : 17; Rev. 4 : 3. The word translated carbuncle in A.V. should have been emerald. Smaragdus, as understood by the ancients, was a generic term for a number of green stones which probably included the emerald. A possible source of the true emerald existed in certain mines at Zabara, on the borders of Egypt. Whether emeralds were ever found in the far east is doubtful. Ex. 28 : 18; 39 : 11; Rev. 4 : 3; 21 : 19.

Emerods [hæmorrhoids, tumours, piles], threatened, Deut. 28 : 27.
Philistines smitten with, 1 Sam. 5 : 6.

Emmanuel (ĕm-măn-́ū-ĕl) [Immanuel, God with us], Isa. 7 : 14; 8 : 8; Matt. 1 : 23.

Emmaus (ĕm-mā-́ŭs) [hot springs (Cheyne)], a village near Jerusalem, Christ's journey to, and discourse, Luke 24 : 15.

Empire, Esther 1 : 20.

Employ, Deut. 20 : 19; 1 Chr. 9 : 33; Ezek. 39 : 14.

Empty, Gen. 31 : 42; Mark 12 : 3; Luke 1 : 53; 20 : 10, sent e. away.
Ex. 23 : 15; 34 : 20; Deut. 16 : 16, none shall appear before me e.
Eccl. 11 : 3, clouds e. themselves on the earth.
Isa. 24 : 1, the Lord maketh earth e.
29 : 8, hungry awaketh, his soul is e.
Hos. 10 : 1, Israel is an e. vine.
Matt. 12 : 44, when come, he findeth it e.

Emulations [jealousies], Rom. 11 : 14, may provoke to e.
Gal. 5 : 20, works of the flesh are e.

Enabled, 1 Tim. 1 : 12, Lord, who hath e. me.

Encamp, Ps. 27 : 3, though an host e. against me.
34 : 7, angel of Lord e. round.
53 : 5, bones of him that e. against thee.

Enchantments forbidden, Lev. 19 : 26; Deut. 18 : 9; Isa. 47 : 9.

Encourage, Deut. 1 : 38; 3 : 28; 2 Sam. 11 : 25, e. him.

Ps. 64 : 5, they e. themselves in an evil matter.
Isa. 41 : 7, carpenter e. goldsmith.

End, Gen. 6 : 13, the e. of all flesh is come.
Num. 23 : 10, let my last e. be like his.
Deut. 32 : 29, consider their latter e.
Job 6 : 11, what is mine e., that I should prolong ?
16 : 3, shall vain words have an e. ?
Ps. 9 : 6, destructions come to perpetual e.
37 : 37, the e. of that man is peace.
39 : 4, make me to know my e.
102 : 27, thy years have no e.
107 : 27, are at their wit's e.
Prov. 14 : 12, the e. thereof are ways of death.
19 : 20, be wise in thy latter e.
Eccl. 4 : 8, no e. of all his labour.
7 : 8, better is the e. of a thing than.
12 : 12, of making books there is no e.
Isa. 9 : 7, of his government shall be no e.
Jer. 8 : 20, harvest past, summer e.
31 : 17, there is hope in thine e.
Lam. 4 : 18; Ezek. 7 : 2; Amos 8 : 2, e. is near, e. is come.
Ezek. 21 : 25; 35 : 5, iniquity shall have an e.
Dan. 8 : 19, at the time appointed e. shall be.
Dan. 12 : 8, what shall be the e. of these ?
Hab. 2 : 3, at the e. it shall speak, and not tarry.
Matt. 10 : 22; 24 : 13; Mark 13 : 13, endureth to e.
Matt. 13 : 39, harvest is the e. of the world.
24 : 3, what sign of the e. of the world ?
24 : 6; Mark 13 : 7; Luke 21 : 9, the e. is not yet.
Matt. 24 : 31, gather from one e. of heaven.
28 : 20, I am with you, even unto the e.
Mark 3 : 26, cannot stand, but hath an e.
Luke 1 : 33, of his kingdom there shall be no e.
22 : 37, things concerning me have an e.
John 18 : 37, to this e. was I born.
Rom. 6 : 21, the e. of those things is death.
6 : 22, the e. everlasting life.
10 : 4, Christ is e. of law for righteousness.
1 Tim. 1 : 5, the e. of commandment is charity.
Heb. 6 : 8, whose e. is to be burned.
7 : 3, neither beginning nor e. of life.
9 : 26, once in the e. hath he appeared.
13 : 7, considering e. of their conversation.
Jas. 5 : 11, ye have seen e. of the Lord.
1 Pet. 1 : 9, receiving the e. of your faith.
4 : 11, what shall the e. be of them that obey not Gospel ?
Rev. 21 : 6; 22 : 13, the beginning and the e.

Endanger, Eccl. 10 : 9; Dan. 1 : 10.

Endeavour, Ps. 28 : 4, wickedness of the e.
Eph. 4 : 3, e. to keep the unity.
1 Thess. 2 : 17, e. the more abundantly.
2 Pet. 1 : 15, e. that ye may be able.

Endless, 1 Tim. 1 : 4, heed to e. genealogies.
Heb. 7 : 16, after power of an e. life.

Endor (ĕn-́dôr) [fountain of Dor], a city south of Mount Tabor, memorable for the interview there between Saul and the witch, Josh. 17 : 11; 1 Sam. 28 : 7.

Endue, Gen. 30 : 20, e. me with good dowry.
2 Chr. 2 : 13, cunning man e. with understanding.
Luke 24 : 49, till ye be e. with power.

Jas. 3 : 13, **e.** with knowledge.
Endure, Gen. 33 : 14, as children be able to **e.**
Esther 8 : 6, can I **e.** to see the evil ?
Ps. 9 : 7; 102 : 12; 104 : 31, Lord shall **e.** for ever.
30 : 5, weeping may **e.** for a night.
72 : 5, fear thee as long as the sun and moon **e.**
72 : 17, his name shall **e.** for ever.
106 : 1; 107 : 1; 118 : 1; 136 : 1; 138 : 8; Jer. 33 : 11, his mercy **e.** for ever.
Ps. 111 : 3; 112 : 3, 9, his righteousness **e.** for ever.
Prov. 27 : 24, doth crown **e.** to every generation ?
Ezek. 22 : 14, can thy heart **e.** ?
Matt. 24 : 13; Mark 13 : 13, he that shall **e.** to the end.
Mark 4 : 17, **e.** but for a time.
1 Cor. 13 : 7, charity **e.** all things.
2 Tim. 2 : 3, **e.** hardness as a good soldier.
Heb. 10 : 34, in heaven a better and **e.** substance.
12 : 7, if ye **e.** chastening.
Jas. 1 : 12, blessed is man that **e.** temptation.
5 : 11, we count them happy who **e.**
1 Pet. 1 : 25, the word of the Lord **e.** for ever.
2 : 19, for conscience **e.** grief.
Enemies, treatment of, Ex. 23 : 4; 1 Sam. 24 : 10; 26 : 9; Job 31 : 29; Prov. 24 : 17; 25 : 21; Matt. 5 : 44; Luke 6 : 35.
God delivers from, 1 Sam. 12 : 11; Ezra 8 : 31; Ps. 18 : 48; 59; 61 : 3.
of God, their punishment, Ex. 15 : 6; Deut. 32 : 41; Judg. 5 : 31; Esther 7; 8; Ps. 68 : 1; 92 : 9; Isa. 1 : 24; 37 : 36; 2 Thess. 1 : 8; Rev. 21 : 8.
Ex. 23 : 22, I will be **e.** to thine **e.**
Deut. 32 : 31, our **e.** themselves being judges.
Judg. 5 : 31, so let all thine **e.** perish.
1 Ki. 21 : 20, hast thou found me, O mine **e.** ?
Ps. 8 : 2, mightiest still the **e.** and avenger.
72 : 9, his **e.** shall lick the dust.
127 : 5, speak with **e.** in the gate.
Prov. 25 : 21; Rom. 12 : 20, if **e.** hunger give bread.
Isa. 59 : 19, when **e.** shall come in like a flood.
63 : 10, he was turned to be their **e.**
Mic. 7 : 6, man's **e.**, men of his own house.
Matt. 5 : 43, said, thou shalt hate thine **e.**
Luke 19 : 43, thine **e.** shall cast a trench.
Rom. 5 : 10, if when **e.** we were reconciled.
Gal. 4 : 16, am I become your **e.** ?
Jas. 4 : 4, friend of the world is the **e.** of God.
En-gedi (ĕn-gē′-dĭ) [fountain of the kid], David dwells there, 1 Sam. 23 : 29; 24 : 1.
See Cant. 1 : 14; Ezek. 47 : 10.
Engines of war, 2 Chr. 26 : 15; Ezek. 26 : 9.
Engrave, Zech. 3 : 9, I will **e.** the graving thereof.
2 Cor. 3 : 7, ministration of death **e.**
Engraving on stones, Ex. 28 : 11; Zech. 3 : 9.
Enjoin, Job 36 : 23, who hath **e.** him his way ?
Philem. 8, to **e.** what is convenient.
Heb. 9 : 20, blood which God hath **e.**
Enjoy, Lev. 26 : 34; 2 Chr. 36 : 21, land **e.** her Sabbaths.
Eccl. 2 : 1, **e.** pleasure, this also is vanity.
2 : 24; 3 : 13; 5 : 18, his soul **e.** good.
1 Tim. 6 : 17, giveth all things to **e.**

Heb. 11 : 25, than **e.** pleasures of sin.
Enlarge [to set at large, to make free].
Ps. 4 : 1, thou hast **e.** me when I was in distress.
Gen. 9 : 27, God shall **e.** Japheth.
Deut. 12 : 20, when the Lord shall **e.** thy border.
Ps. 25 : 17, troubles of my heart are **e.**
119 : 32, when thou shalt **e.** my heart.
Isa. 5 : 14, hell hath **e.** herself.
60 : 5, heart shall fear and be **e.**
Matt. 23 : 5, **e.** borders of garments.
2 Cor. 6 : 11, our heart is **e.**
Enlighten, Ps. 18 : 28, Lord will **e.** my darkness.
19 : 8, command of Lord is pure, **e.** the eyes.
97 : 4, his lightnings **e.** world.
Eph. 1 : 18, eyes of understanding **e.**
Heb. 6 : 4, impossible for those once **e.**
Enmity between God and man, Rom. 8 : 7; Jas. 4 : 4.
how abolished, Eph. 2 : 15; Col. 1 : 20.
Gen. 3 : 15, I will put **e.** between them.
Rom. 8 : 7, carnal mind is **e.** against God.
Eph. 2 : 15, abolished in his flesh the **e.**
Jas. 4 : 4, friendship of world is **e.** with God.
Enoch (ē′-nŏch), dedicated, Gen. 4 : 17.
his godliness and translation, Gen. 5 : 24.
his faith, Heb. 11 : 5; his prophecy, Jude 14.
Enos (ē′-nŏs) [man], Gen. 4 : 26.
Enough, Gen. 33 : 9, I have **e.**
45 : 28, it is **e.**, Joseph is yet alive.
Ex. 36 : 5, people bring more than **e.**
2 Sam. 24 : 16; 1 Ki. 19 : 4; 1 Chr. 21 : 15; Mark 14 : 41; Luke 22 : 38, it is **e.**
Prov. 30 : 15, four things say not, it is **e.**
Hos. 4 : 10; Hag. 1 : 6, eat, and have not **e.**
Mal. 3 : 10, not room **e.** to receive it.
Matt. 10 : 25, it is **e.** for disciple.
25 : 9, lest there be not **e.**
Luke 15 : 17, bread **e.** and to spare.
Enquire, Ex. 18 : 15, people come to **e.** of God.
2 Sam. 16 : 23, as if a man **e.** at oracle of God.
Ps. 27 : 4, to **e.** in his temple.
78 : 34, returned and **e.** early after God.
Eccl. 7 : 10, thou dost not **e.** wisely.
Isa. 21 : 12, if ye will **e.**, **e.** ye.
Ezek. 14 : 3, should I be **e.** of at all by them ?
36 : 37, I will yet for this be **e.** of.
Matt. 10 : 11, **e.** who in it is worthy.
Luke 22 : 23, to **e.** among themselves.
1 Pet. 1 : 10, of which salvation the prophets **e.**
Enrich, 1 Sam. 17 : 25, king will **e.** them.
Ps. 65 : 9, greatly **e.** it with river of God.
Ezek. 27 : 33, didst **e.** kings of earth.
2 Cor. 9 : 11, being **e.** in everything.
En-rogel (ĕn-rō′-gĕl) [fuller's fountain], Josh. 15 : 7; 18 : 6; 1 Ki. 1 : 9.
Ensample, 1 Cor. 10 : 11, happened to them for **e.**
Phil. 3 : 17, as ye have us for an **e.**
2 Thess. 3 : 9, to make ourselves an **e.**
1 Pet. 5 : 3, being **e.** to the flock.
Ensign, Ps. 74 : 4, set up their **e.** for signs.
Isa. 5 : 26, he will lift up an **e.**
11 : 12, set up an **e.** for the nations.
30 : 17, till ye be left as **e.** on hill.
Ensue [follow after until one attains], 1 Pet. 3 : 11, seek peace and **e.** it.
Entangle, Matt. 22 : 15, how they might **e.** him.

Gal. 5 : 1, be not e. with yoke of bondage.
2 Tim. 2 : 4, e. himself with affairs of life.
Enter, Job 22 : 4, will he e. into judgment ?
Ps. 100 : 4, e. his gates with thanksgiving.
  118 : 20, gate into which righteous e.
Isa. 2 : 10, e. into the rock.
  26 : 2, righteous nation may e. in.
  26 : 20, e. thou into thy chambers.
Matt. 5 : 20, in no case e. into kingdom of heaven.
  6 : 6, when thou prayest, e. into thy closet.
  7 : 13; Luke 13 : 24, e. in at strait gate.
Matt. 18 : 8; Mark 9 : 43, better to e. into life halt.
Matt. 19 : 17, if thou wilt e. into life, keep commandments.
  25 : 21, e. into joy of Lord.
Mark 14 : 38; Luke 22 : 46, watch and pray, lest ye e. into temptation.
Luke 13 : 24, many will seek to e., but not able.
John 3 : 5, he cannot e. into kingdom of God.
  10 : 9, by me if any man e. in.
Acts 14 : 22, through much tribulation e. kingdom of God.
Rom. 5 : 12, sin e. into the world.
1 Cor. 2 : 9, neither have e. into heart of man.
Heb. 4 : 6, e. not in because of unbelief.
  6 : 20, forerunner is for us e.
  10 : 19, e. into holiest by blood of Jesus.
Rev. 21 : 27, e. into it, anything that defileth.
Entice, Judg. 14 : 15, e. thy husband, that he may declare.
Prov. 1 : 10, if sinners e. thee.
1 Cor. 2 : 4; Col. 2 : 4, with e. words.
Enticers to idolatry to be stoned, Deut. 13 : 10.
Entrance, 2 Chr. 12 : 10, kept the e. of the king's house.
Ps. 119 : 130, e. of thy word giveth light.
2 Pet. 1 : 11, e. shall be ministered unto you.
Entreat, Matt. 22 : 6, e. them spitefully.
Acts 7 : 6, and e. them evil.
1 Thess. 2 : 2, were shamefully e.
Envious, Ps. 73 : 3, I was e. at the foolish.
Envy described, Prov. 14 : 30; 27 : 4; Eccl. 4 : 4; Matt. 27 : 18; Acts 7 : 9; Rom. 1 : 29; 1 Cor. 3 : 3; 2 Cor. 12 : 20; Gal. 5 : 21; 1 Tim. 6 : 4; Titus 3 : 3; Jas. 4 : 5.
  forbidden, Ps. 37 : 1; Prov. 3 : 31; 24 : 1, 19; Rom. 13 : 13; 1 Pet. 2 : 1.
  its evil consequences, Job 5 : 2; Ps. 106 : 16; Prov. 14 : 30; Isa. 26 : 11; Jas. 3 : 16.
Joseph sold for, Acts 7 : 9; Gen. 37 : 28.
Job 5 : 2, e. slayeth the silly one.
Prov. 14 : 30, e. is the rottenness of the bones.
  27 : 4, who is able to stand before e. ?
Eccl. 9 : 6, their e. is perished.
Isa. 26 : 11, ashamed for their e.
Matt. 27 : 18; Mark 15 : 10, for e. they delivered him.
Acts 7 : 9, patriarchs moved with e.
  13 : 45, Jews filled with e.
Rom. 1 : 29, full of e.
1 Cor. 3 : 3, among you e. and strife.
  13 : 4, charity e. not.
2 Cor. 12 : 20, I fear lest there be e.
Gal. 5 : 21, works of flesh are e., murders.
Phil. 1 : 15, preach Christ even of e.
Titus 3 : 3, living in malice and e.

Jas. 4 : 5, spirit in us lusteth to e.
Epaphras (ĕp-ă-phrăs), a Greek name, commended, Col. 1 : 7; 4 : 12.
Epaphroditus (ĕp-ăph-rō-dī-tŭs), Paul's joy at his recovery, Phil. 2 : 25; his kindness, Phil. 4 : 18.
Ephah (ē-phäh) [darkness], Gen. 25 : 4.
a measure of capacity, Ex. 16 : 36; Lev. 19 : 36; Ezek. 45 : 10; Zech. 5 : 6.
Ephesians, Epistle to the.
Date.—This Epistle belongs to the group which is called " the Epistles of the Imprisonment " or " of the Captivity," i.e., his Roman imprisonment, during which St. Paul wrote Philippians, Philemon, Colossians, and Ephesians. The letter was probably written and sent near to the close of the imprisonment, about the year A.D. 63.
Occasion.—The fact that Tychicus was going from Rome to Colossæ (Col. 4 : 7) was an opportunity of sending a letter not only to that city, but to other Christians in Asia (Eph. 6 : 21). There is little doubt that this magnificent Epistle was originally a circular one, and that Ephesus was only one of the cities in the Roman province of Asia to which it was addressed.
Character.—As we might expect from the fact of their being written almost at the same time, there is great resemblance between the letters to the Colossians and to the Ephesians. Out of the hundred and fifty-five verses in Ephesians, seventy-eight contain expressions identical with those in Colossians. But the two Epistles, although similar, are not the same. In Colossians the glory of Christ as Head of the Universe and of the Church is magnified. In Ephesians it is the catholicity of the Church itself that is set forth as the outcome of the doctrine of adoption in Christ. In Colossians it is the glory of Christ that is emphasised : in Ephesians the work of the Spirit, for it is through the Spirit that the presence and energy of Christ is continued in the Church (1 : 13; 2 : 22; 4 : 3, 30; 5 : 18; 6 : 17, 18).
Contents.—The Epistle expounds the conception of the ideal Church and draws practical conclusions from it. The Church is the Body of Christ, and the fulness of Him, that filleth all in all (1 : 23; 4 : 12-16); the holy Temple of God (2 : 20-22); and the spotless Spouse of Christ (5 : 25-28). As the fulness of the Godhead resides in Christ, so the fulness of Christ resides in His Church. This ideal Church is in process of being realised. The actual Church has many defects and blemishes. But " the measure of the stature of the fulness of Christ " will be reached at last (4 : 13); and it is the duty of each individual member to work towards this end, especially through the Christian family, which is a symbol and likeness of the Church.
The usual Salutation (1 : 1, 2) and Thanksgiving (1 : 3-14) are followed by a corresponding Intercession (1 : 15–2 : 10)

and a Contrast between unconverted and converted Gentiles (2:11-22). The Apostle's special interest in the Conversion of the Gentiles (3 : 1-21) leads up to exhortations respecting the Unity of the Catholic Church and the Duties of its members (4 : 1–6 : 20); after which comes a Personal Explanation, and the concluding Benediction (6 : 21-24).

Ruins of the Theatre at Ephesus.

Ephesus (ĕph-ĕ-sŭs), a celebrated city of Asia Minor, scene of Paul's labours for three years, visited by Paul, Acts 18 : 19; 19 : 1; miracles there, Acts 19 : 11; tumult there, Acts 19 : 24.

Paul's address to the elders of, Acts 20 : 17.

Paul's fight with beasts there, 1 Cor. 15 : 32; Paul tarries there, 1 Cor. 16 : 8.

Message to Church of, Rev. 1 : 11; 2 : 1.

Ephod of the priest, Ex. 28 : 4; 39 : 2.

of Gideon, Judg. 8 : 27.

of Micah, Judg. 17 : 5.

Ephphatha (ĕph-phă-thă) [be opened], Mark 7 : 34.

Ephraim (ĕ-phră-ĭm) [double fruitfulness], younger son of Joseph, Gen. 41 : 52.

Jacob blesses Ephraim and Manasseh, Gen. 48 : 14.

his descendants numbered, Num. 1 : 10, 32; 2 : 18; 26 : 35; 1 Chr. 7 : 20.

their possessions, Josh. 16 : 5; 17 : 14; Judg. 1 : 29.

chastise the Midianites, Judg. 7 : 24.

their quarrel with Gideon, Judg. 8 : 1; and Jephthah, Judg. 12.

revolt from the house of David, 1 Ki. 12 : 25.

chastise Ahaz and Judah, 2 Chr. 28 : 6, 7.

release their prisoners, 2 Chr. 28 : 12.

carried into captivity, 2 Ki. 17 : 5; Ps. 78 : 9, 67; Jer. 7 : 15.

repenting, called God's son, Jer. 31 : 20.

prophecies concerning, Isa. 7; 9 : 9; 11 : 13; 28 : 1; Hos. 51–4; Zech. 9 : 10; 10 : 7.

allotment of, Josh. 16 : 5.

a mountain, Josh. 17 : 5; Judg. 2 : 9; 7 : 24.

a city eight miles from Jerusalem, John 11 : 54.

Ephron (ĕ-phrŏn) [connected with, or belonging to, a calf], the Hittite, sells Machpelah to Abraham, Gen. 23 : 10.

Epicurean (ĕp-ĭ-c-ūrē-ăn) [belonging to the school of Greek philosophy founded by Epicurus],

philosophers, encounter Paul at Athens, Acts 17 : 18.

Epistle, 2 Cor. 3 : 2, ye are our e.

2 Thess. 2 : 15, taught by word or e.

2 Pet. 3 : 16, as in all his e. speaking.

Equal, Ps. 17 : 2, eyes behold things that are e.

55 : 13, a man mine e.

Prov. 26 : 7, legs of lame not e.

Isa. 40 : 25; 46 : 5, to whom shall I be e. ?

Ezek. 18 : 25, way of the Lord is not e.

33 : 17, their way is not e.

Matt. 20 : 12, hast made them e. to us.

Luke 20 : 36, e. to the angels.

John 5 : 18; Phil. 2 : 6, e. with God.

Col. 4 : 1, give servants what is e.

Equity, Ps. 98 : 9, judge the people with e.

Prov. 1 : 3, receive instruction of e.

2 : 9, understand judgment and e.

Eccl. 2 : 21, a man whose labour is in e.

Isa. 11 : 4, reprove with e.

59 : 14, truth is fallen, and e. cannot enter.

Mal. 2 : 6, he walked with me in e.

Erastus (ē-răs-tŭs) [amiable], ministers to Paul, Acts 19 : 22; Rom. 16 : 23; 2 Tim. 4 : 20.

Coins of Ephesus.

Err, Ps. 95 : 10, people that do e. in their heart.

119 : 21, do e. from thy commandments.

Prov. 19 : 27, instruction that causeth to e.

Isa. 3 : 12; 9 : 16, that lead thee cause to e.

35 : 8, wayfaring men shall not e.

Matt. 22 : 29; Mark 12 : 24, do e., not knowing Scriptures.

1 Tim. 6 : 21, have e. concerning the faith.

Jas. 1 : 16, do not e., my brethren.

5 : 19, if any do e. from truth.

Error, Ps. 19 : 12, who can understand his e. ?

Eccl. 5 : 6, neither say it was an e.

10 : 5, an evil I have seen as an e.

Isa. 32 : 6, to utter e. against the Lord.

Matt. 27 : 64, last e. worse than first.

Heb. 9 : 7, offered for e. of people.

Jas. 5 : 20, converteth sinner from e.

2 Pet. 3 : 17, led away with e. of the wicked.

1 John 4 : 6, the spirit of e.

Jude 11, ran after e. of Balaam.

Esarhaddon (ē-sär-hăd-dọn) [Assyrian, Asurkha-iddin; Asshur has given a brother], king of Assyria, 2 Ki. 19 : 37; Ezra 4 : 2; Isa. 37 : 38.

Esau (ē-saü) [hairy], son of Isaac, Gen. 25 : 25; (Mal. 1 : 2; Rom. 9 : 10).

sells his birthright, Gen. 25 : 29; (Heb. 12 : 16).

deprived of the blessing, Gen. 27 : 26.

his anger against Jacob, Gen. 27 : 41; and reconciliation, Gen. 33.
his descendants, Gen. 36; 1 Chr. 1 : 35.
Escape, Gen. 19 : 17, e. for thy life, e. to mountain.
1 Ki. 18 : 40; 2 Ki. 9 : 15, let none of them e.
Job 11 : 20, the wicked shall not e.
19 : 20, e. with the skin of my teeth.
Ps. 55 : 8, hasten my e. from storm.
Ps. 71 : 2, deliver me, and cause me to e.
Prov. 19 : 5, he that speaketh lies shall not e.
Eccl. 7 : 26, whoso pleaseth God shall e.
Isa. 20 : 6, how shall we e. ?
Matt. 23 : 33, how e. damnation of hell ?
Luke 21 : 36, accounted worthy to e.
Acts 27 : 44, they e. all safe to land.
1 Cor. 10 : 13, with temptation make a way to e.
Heb. 12 : 25, if they e. not who refused.
2 Pet. 1 : 4, e. corruption in the world.
Eschew [flee from, shun], Job 1 : 1, feared God and e. evil.
1 Pet. 3 : 11, let him e. evil, do good.
Esdraelon (ĕs-drǽ-lŏn), Plain of, an extensive valley in which many battles were fought.
Esek (ē-sĕk) [contention], Gen. 26 : 20.
Eshcol (ĕsh-cŏl) [cluster of grapes], Gen. 14 : 13; Num. 13 : 23, 24.
Especially, Ps. 31 : 11, e. among my neighbours.
Gal. 6 : 10, e. the household of faith.
1 Tim. 5 : 17, e. they who labour in word.
2 Tim. 4 : 13, e. the parchments.
Espy, Gen. 42 : 27, e. the money.
Josh. 14 : 7, sent me to e. out.
Jer. 48 : 19, stand by the way, and e.
Ezek. 20 : 6, land I had e. for them.
Establish, Gen. 17 : 19, I will e. my covenant.
Ps. 40 : 2, e. my goings.
89 : 2, faithfulness shalt e. in heavens.
90 : 17, e. work of our hands.
Prov. 3 : 19, Lord hath e. the heavens.
16 : 12, throne is e. by righteousness.
20 : 18, every purpose is e. by counsel.
Isa. 16 : 5, in mercy shall throne be e.
Jer. 10 : 12; 51 : 15, he e. world by wisdom.
Matt. 18 : 16, two witnesses, every word e.
Rom. 3 : 31, yea, we e. the law.
10 : 3, going about to e. their own righteousness.
Heb. 8 : 6, e. upon better promises.
13 : 9, the heart be e. with grace.
1 Pet. 5 : 10, God of all grace e. you.
Estate, Ps. 136 : 23, remembered us in low e.
Eccl. 1 : 16, I am come to great e.
Luke 1 : 48, low e. of his handmaiden.
Rom. 12 : 16, condescend to men of low e.
Jude 6, angels who kept not first e.
Estates [persons of high rank]. " Lords, high captains, and chief estates of Galilee," Mark 6 : 21. Compare the " three estates of the realm."
Esteem, Deut. 32 : 15, lightly e. rock of salvation.
1 Sam. 2 : 30, despise me shall be lightly e.
Job 36 : 19, will he e. thy riches ?
Ps. 119 : 128, I e. all thy precepts.
Isa. 53 : 4, did e. him smitten.
Luke 16 : 15, highly e. among men, is.

Rom. 14 : 5, one man e. one day above another.
14 : 14, that e. anything unclean.
Phil. 2 : 3, let each e. other better.
1 Thess. 5 : 13, e. highly for work's sake.
Heb. 11 : 26, e. reproach of Christ greater riches.
Esther (ĕs-thĕr) [star], a Persian name (Hadassah), made queen in place of Vashti, Esther 2 : 17.
intercedes for her people, Esther 7 : 3, 4, etc.
Esther, Book of.
Title and Date.—The book takes its name from Esther, the principal character in it, one of the heroines of the Jewish race. The date is hard to fix, but from the tone of the book with its intense nationalism, and the occurrence of late linguistic forms it can probably be assigned as late in the history of the " Chosen People." Most scholars now place it as one of the products of the Maccabean struggle—135 B.C. or later—with the character of Haman modelled on that of Antiochus Epiphanes.
Object.—The object of the book is to explain the origin of the Feast of Purim or Lots, the real beginning of which is shrouded in mystery. Here it is traced to the triumph of the Jews over their enemies.
Contents.—The narrative relates how Esther, a Jewish maiden, dwelling in Susa, the Persian capital, became queen of Ahasuerus or Xerxes (485-465 B.C.), and was instrumental in rescuing her compatriots from the destruction prepared for them by Haman, the king's favourite.
The name of God occurs nowhere in the book. The omission is perhaps intentional, in order to avoid irreverence, for the book was designed to be read in the Jewish houses during the festive banquets customary at the celebration of Purim (9 : 27).
In later times the book attained a great popularity among the Jews, who considered it superior to the writings of the prophets, and the other parts of the Hagiographa.
Estranged, Job 19 : 13, acquaintance are e.
Ps. 58 : 3, wicked e. from the womb.
78 : 30, not e. from their lust.
Ezek. 14 : 5, they are all e. from me.
Eternal, Deut. 33 : 27, the e. God is thy refuge.
Isa. 60 : 15, make thee an e. excellency.
Matt. 19 : 16; Mark 10 : 17; Luke 10 : 25; 18 : 18, do that I may have e. life.
Matt. 25 : 46, righteous unto life e.
Mark 3 : 29, in danger of e. damnation.
10 : 30, receive in world to come e. life.
John 3 : 15, believeth in him have e. life.
4 : 36, gathereth fruit unto life e.
5 : 39, Scriptures, in them e. life.
6 : 54, drinketh my blood hath e. life.
6 : 68, thou hast words of e. life.
10 : 28, I give unto my sheep e. life.
12 : 25, hateth life, shall keep it to life e.
17 : 2, give e. life to as many.
Acts 13 : 48, as many as were ordained to e. life.
Rom. 2 : 7, who seek for glory, e. life.
5 : 21, grace reign to e. life.

6 : 23, gift of God is e. life.
2 Cor. 4 : 17, an e. weight of glory.
4 : 18, things not seen are e.
5 : 1, an house e. in the heavens.
Eph. 3 : 11, according to e. purpose.
1 Tim. 1 : 17, to king e. be honour.
6 : 12, 19, lay hold on e. life.
Titus 1 : 2; 3 : 7, in hope of e. life.
Heb. 5 : 9, author of e. salvation.
6 : 2, doctrine of e. judgment.
9 : 12, obtained e. redemption for us.
1 Pet. 5 : 10, called to e. glory by Christ.
1 John 1 : 2, e. life which was with the Father.
2 : 25, this is the promise, even e. life.
5 : 11, record that God hath given e. life.
5 : 20, this is true God, and e. life.
Jude 7, vengeance of e. fire.
Eternity, Isa. 57 : 15, lofty one that inhabiteth e.
Ethiopia (ē-thĭ-ō-pĭ-ă) [in Hebrew " Cush "], 2 Ki. 19 : 9.
Ethiopians, invading Judah, subdued by Asa, 2 Chr. 14 : 9.
See Num. 12 : 1; 2 Ki. 19 : 9; Esther 1 : 1; Job 28 : 19.
prophecies concerning, Ps. 68 : 31; 87 : 4; Isa. 18; 20; 43 : 3; 45 : 14; Jer. 46 : 9; Ezek. 30 : 4; 38 : 5; Nah. 3 : 9; Zeph. 3 : 10.
eunuch baptized, Acts 8 : 27.
Eunice (ēū-nī-çē), Greek female name, commended; (Acts 16 : 1); 2 Tim. 1 : 5.
Eunuchs, promise to those who please God, Isa. 56 : 3.
Christ's declaration concerning, Matt. 19 : 12.
Ashpenaz, master of the king's eunuchs, Dan. 1 : 3.
Ethiopian, baptized by Philip, Acts 8 : 27.
Euroclydon (ēū-rŏc-lȳ-dǫn), north-east wind, Acts 27 : 14.
Eutychus (ēū-tȳ-chŭs), a Greek name [fortunate], his fall and recovery, Acts 20 : 7.
Evangelist, Philip the, receives Paul's company, Acts 21 : 8.
work of, Eph. 4 : 11; 2 Tim. 4 : 5.
Eve [life, or living], created, Gen. 1 : 27; 2 : 18.
her fall and fate, Gen. 3. See Adam.
Even, Gen. 6 : 17, I, e. I, do bring a flood.
19 : 1, angels to Sodom at e.
27 : 34, 38, bless me, e. me.
Lev. 23 : 32, from e. unto e.
Judg. 9 : 40, e. unto the entering of the gate.
Ps. 40 : 3, e. praise unto our God.
48 : 14, guide e. unto death.
Prov. 14 : 13, e. in laughter the heart.
Jer. 23 : 33, will e. forsake you.
Matt. 11 : 26, e. so, Father.
Luke 10 : 11, e. the very dust of your city.
John 17 : 16, not of the world, e. as I.
Rom. 15 : 3, e. Christ pleased not himself.
Rev. 22 : 20, e. so, come, Lord Jesus.
Evening, Judg. 19 : 9, day draweth towards e.
1 Sam. 14 : 24, cursed that eateth till e.
1 Ki. 17 : 6, brought bread morning and e.
Ps. 90 : 6, in the e. it is cut down.
104 : 23, goeth to his labour until the e.
141 : 2, prayer be as the e. sacrifice.
Eccl. 11 : 6, in e. withhold not thine hand.
Jer. 6 : 4, shadows of e. stretched out.
Zech. 14 : 7, at e. time shall be light.

Matt. 14 : 23, when e. was come, he was there alone.
Luke 24 : 29, abide, for it is toward e.
Event, Eccl. 2 : 14; 9 : 3, one e. to them all.
9 : 2, one e. to righteous and wicked.
Ever, Gen. 3 : 22, lest he eat, and live for e.
Deut. 5 : 29; 12 : 28, be well with them for e.
32 : 40, lift up hand and say, I live for e.
Job 4 : 7, who e. perished innocent.
Ps. 9 : 7, Lord shall endure for e.
22 : 26, your heart shall live for e.
23 : 6, dwell in the house of the Lord for e.
33 : 11, counsel of the Lord standeth for e.
45 : 6; Heb. 1 : 8, thy throne, O God, is for e. and e.
51 : 3, my sin is e. before me.
61 : 4, I will abide in tabernacle for e.
73 : 26, God is my strength and portion for e.
93 : 5, holiness becometh thine house for e.
102 : 12, thou shalt endure for e.
103 : 9, not keep his anger for e.
132 : 14, this is my rest for e.
146 : 6, Lord keepeth truth for e.
Prov. 27 : 24, riches are not for e.
Eccl. 1 : 4, the earth abideth for e.
Isa. 26 : 4, trust in Lord for e.
32 : 17, quietness and assurance for e.
40 : 8, word of God shall stand for e.
Lam. 3 : 31, Lord will not cast off for e.
Matt. 21 : 19; Mark 11 : 14, no fruit grow on thee for e.
John 6 : 51, he that eateth shall live for e.
12 : 34, heart that Christ abideth for e.
14 : 16, comforter abide for e.
1 Thess. 4 : 17, so shall we e. be with the Lord.
Heb. 7 : 25, he e. liveth to make intercession.
13 : 8, Christ the same yesterday, today, and for e.
Everlasting, Gen. 21 : 33; Isa. 40 : 28; Rom. 16 : 26, the e. God.
Ex. 40 : 15; Num. 25 : 13, an e. priesthood.
Deut. 33 : 27, underneath are e. arms.
Ps. 24 : 7, be ye lift up, ye e. doors.
90 : 2, from e. to e. thou art God.
103 : 17, mercy of Lord from e. to e.
119 : 142, thy righteousness is e.
139 : 24, lead me in the way e.
Prov. 8 : 23, I was set up from e.
10 : 25, righteousness is an e. foundation.
Isa. 9 : 6, called the e. Father.
26 : 4, in Jehovah is e. strength.
35 : 10; 51 : 11; 61 : 7, e. joy.
45 : 17, with e. salvation.
54 : 8, with e. kindness.
55 : 5; 63 : 12, an e. name.
56 : 5; 63 : 12, an e. name.
60 : 19, 20, Lord shall be an e. light.
Jer. 31 : 3, loved thee with an e. love.
Dan. 4 : 34; 7 : 14, an e. dominion.
Mic. 5 : 2, goings forth of old from e.
Hab. 3 : 6, the e. mountains.
Matt. 18 : 8; 25 : 41, into e. fire.
19 : 29, shall inherit e. life.
25 : 46, go into e. punishment.
Luke 16 : 9, into e. habitations.
John 3 : 16, 36, believeth shall have e. life.
4 : 14, water springing up into e. life.
12 : 50, his commandment is life e.

Rom. 6 : 22, ye have the end e. life.
Gal. 6 : 8, of the spirit reap life e.
2 Thess. 1 : 9, punished with e. destruction.
  2 : 16, given us e. consolation.
Jude 6, angels reserved in e. chains.
Rev. 14 : 6, having the e. Gospel.
Evermore, Ps. 16 : 11, pleasures for e.
  37 : 27, do good, and dwell for e.
  86 : 12, will glorify thy name for e.
  113 : 2, blessed be name of Lord for e.
  121 : 8, Lord preserve thy going out e.
  133 : 3, the blessing, life for e.
John 6 : 34, Lord, e. give us this bread.
1 Thess. 5 : 16, rejoice e.
Heb. 7 : 28, Son, who is consecrated for e.
Rev. 1 : 18, I am alive for e.
Every, Gen. 6 : 5, e. imagination of heart evil.
Deut. 4 : 4, alive e. one of you this day.
Ps. 32 : 6, for this shall e. one that is godly.
  119 : 101, refrained from e. evil way.
Prov. 2 : 9, e. good path.
  14 : 15, simple beneath e. word.
  30 : 5, e. word of God is pure.
Eccl. 3 : 1, a time to e. purpose.
Isa. 45 : 23; Rom. 14 : 11, e. knee shall bow.
Matt. 4 : 4, by e. word that proceedeth.
Luke 19 : 26, to e. one which hath.
2 Cor. 10 : 5, bringing into captivity e. thought.
Eph. 1 : 21; Phil. 2 : 9, far above e. name.
1 Tim. 4 : 4, e. creature of God is good.
2 Tim. 2 : 1, prepared to e. good work.
Heb. 12 : 1, lay aside e. weight.
Jas. 1 : 17, e. good and perfect gift.
1 John 4 : 1, believe not e. spirit.
Evidence, Jer. 32 : 10, I subscribed the e.
Heb. 11 : 1, faith e. of things not seen.
Evident, Job 6 : 28, it is e. to you if I lie.
Gal. 3 : 1, Christ hath been e. set forth.
  3 : 11, no man justified by the law is e.
Phil. 1 : 28, an e. token of perdition.
Heb. 7 : 14, it is e. our Lord sprang out of Judah.
Evil, Gen. 6 : 5; 8 : 21, thoughts of heart only e.
  37 : 20, 33, an e. beast hath devoured him.
  47 : 9, few and e. days of life been.
Deut. 29 : 21, Lord shall separate him to e.
  30 : 15, set before thee death and e.
  31 : 29, e. befall you in latter days.
Job 2 : 10, receive good and not e.
  30 : 26, looked for good, then e. came.
Ps. 23 : 4, I will fear no e.
  34 : 21, e. shall slay the wicked.
  91 : 10, no e. shall befall thee.
  97 : 10, ye that love the Lord, hate e.
Prov. 12 : 21, no e. shall happen to the just.
  15 : 3, beholding the e. and good.
Isa. 5 : 20, call e. good and good e.
  7 : 15, refuse the e. and choose the good.
  57 : 1, righteous taken from the e. to come.
Jer. 17 : 17, art my hope in the day of e.
  44 : 11, set my face against you for e.
Ezek. 7 : 5, an e., an only e. is come.
Jonah 3 : 10; 4 : 2, God repented of the e.
Hab. 1 : 13, purer eyes than to behold e.
Matt. 5 : 11, all manner of e. against you.
  6 : 34, sufficient unto day is e. thereof.
  7 : 11; Luke 11 : 13, if ye, being e.

Matt. 27 : 23; Mark 15 : 14; Luke 23 : 22, what e. hath he done ?
Mark 9 : 39, lightly speak e. of me.
Luke 6 : 35, kind to the unthankful and e.
John 3 : 20, doeth e. hateth light.
  18 : 23, if I have spoken e.
Acts 23 : 5, not speak e. of ruler.
Rom. 7 : 19, the e. I would not, that I do.
  12 : 17, recompense to no man e. for e.
  12 : 21, overcome e. with good.
1 Cor. 13 : 5, charity thinketh no e.
Eph. 5 : 16, because the days are e.
1 Thess. 5 : 15; 1 Pet. 3 : 9, let no man render e. for e.
1 Thess. 5 : 22, abstain from all appearance of e.
1 Tim. 6 : 10, love of money root of all e.
Titus 3 : 2, speak e. of no man.
Jas. 3 : 8, tongue an unruly e.
3 John 11, follow not e. but good.
Evildoers, Ps. 37 : 1, fret not thyself because of e.
Ps. 37 : 9, e. shall be cut off.
  119 : 115, depart ye e.
Isa. 1 : 4, a seed of e.
  9 : 17, hypocrite and an e.
1 Pet. 3 : 16, speak evil of you, as of e.
  4 : 15, e. or as a busybody.
Evil-mero-dach (ĕ-vĭl-mĕr-̄ō-dăch) [man of Merodach. Babyl. Awel-Mardak], king of Babylon, restores Jehoiachin, 2 Ki. 25 : 27; Jer. 52 : 31.
Exact, Deut. 15 : 2, shall not e. it of neighbour.
Neh. 5 : 10, might e. of them.
Ps. 89 : 22, enemy not e. upon him.
Isa. 58 : 3, in fast you e. all labours.
  60 : 17, will make e. righteousness.
Luke 3 : 13, e. no more than is appointed.
Exaction (usury, etc.) forbidden, Lev. 25 : 35; Deut. 15 : 2; Prov. 28 : 8; Ezek. 22 : 12; 45 : 9; Luke 3 : 13; 1 Cor. 5 : 10.
disclaimed, Neh. 5 : 1; 10 : 31.
Exactors, Isa. 60 : 17, I will make thine e. righteousness.
Exalt, Ex. 15 : 2, my father's God, I will e. him.
1 Sam. 2 : 10, shall e. horn of anointed.
1 Chr. 29 : 11, thou art e. as head above all.
Ps. 34 : 3, let us e. his name together.
  89 : 16, in righteousness shall they be e.
  92 : 10, my horn shalt thou e.
  97 : 9, art e. far above all gods.
  108 : 5, be thou e. above the heavens.
Prov. 4 : 8, e. her, and she shall promote thee.
  11 : 11, by blessing of upright the city is e.
  14 : 34, righteousness e. a nation.
Isa. 2 : 2; Micah 4 : 1, mountain of Lord's house be e. above the hills.
Isa. 40 : 4, every valley shall be e.
  52 : 13, my servant shall be e.
Ezek. 21 : 26, e. him that is low.
Matt. 11 : 23; Luke 10 : 15, e. to heaven.
Matt. 23 : 12; Luke 14 : 11; 18 : 14, e. himself shall be abased.
Acts 5 : 31, him hath God e.
2 Cor. 12 : 7, be e. above measure.
Phil. 2 : 9, God hath highly e. him.
2 Thess. 2 : 4, e. himself above all called God.
1 Pet. 5 : 6, may e. you in due time.
Examine, Ezra 10 : 16, sat down to e. matter.
Ps. 26 : 2, e. me, O Lord, prove me.

Acts 4 : 9, if we this day be e.
22 : 24, be e. by scourging.
1 Cor. 11 : 28, let a man e. himself.
2 Cor. 13 : 5, e. yourselves, prove.
Example of Christ, Matt. 11 : 29; John 13 : 15;
   Rom. 15 : 5; Phil. 2 : 5; 1 Pet. 2 : 21.
of the prophets, Heb. 6 : 12; Jas. 5 : 10.
of the apostles, 1 Cor. 4 : 16; 11 : 1; Phil.
   3 : 17; 4 : 9; 1 Thess. 1 : 6.
for warning, 1 Cor. 10 : 6; Heb. 4 : 11; 1 Pet.
   5 : 3; Jude 7.
John 13 : 15, I have given you an e.
1 Cor. 10 : 6, these things were our e.
Phil. 3 : 17, ye have us for an e.
1 Tim. 4 : 12, an e. of believers.
Heb. 4 : 11, fall after same, e. of unbelief.
1 Pet. 2 : 21, Christ suffered, leaving an e.
Jude 7, set forth for an e. suffering.
Exceed, Deut. 25 : 3, forty stripes, and not e.
Matt. 5 : 20, except righteousness e.
2 Cor. 3 : 9, ministration e. in glory.
Exceeding, Gen. 15 : 1, thy e. great reward.
27 : 34, an e. bitter cry.
Num. 14 : 7, land is e. good.
Ps. 21 : 6, e. glad with thy countenance.
43 : 4, God, my e. joy.
119 : 96, thy commandment is e. broad.
Prov. 30 : 24, four things are e. wise.
Eccl. 7 : 24, which is e. deep.
Jonah 1 : 16, men feared the Lord e.
3 : 3, an e. great city.
4 : 6, e. glad of the gourd.
Matt. 2 : 10, rejoiced with e. great joy.
4 : 8, an e. high mountain.
5 : 12, rejoice and be e. glad.
19 : 25, they were e. amazed.
26 : 38; Mark 14 : 34, my soul is e. sorrowful.
Mark 6 : 26, king was e. sorry.
9 : 3, his raiment e. white.
Luke 23 : 8, Herod was e. glad.
Acts 7 : 20, Moses was e. fair.
26 : 11, being e. mad against them.
Rom. 7 : 13, sin might become e. sinful.
2 Cor. 4 : 17, e. weight of glory.
7 : 4, e. joyful in tribulation.
Gal. 1 : 14, e. zealous of traditions.
Eph. 1 : 19, e. greatness of his power.
2 : 7, the e. riches of his grace.
3 : 20, able to do e. abundantly.
1 Thess. 3 : 10, praying e. that.
2 Thess. 1 : 3, your faith groweth e.
1 Pet. 4 : 13, be glad with e. joy.
2 Pet. 1 : 4, e. great and precious promises.
Jude 24, present you faultless with e. joy.
Excel, Gen. 49 : 4, unstable as water, shalt not
   e.
Ps. 103 : 20, angels that e. in strength.
Prov. 31 : 29, thou e. them all.
Eccl. 2 : 13, wisdom e. folly.
2 Cor. 3 : 10, the glory that e.
Excellency, Gen. 49 : 3, e. of dignity.
Ex. 15 : 7, the greatness of thine e.
Job 4 : 21, doth not their e. go away ?
37 : 4, thundereth with voice of his e.
40 : 10, deck with majesty and e.
Ps. 62 : 4, cast him down from his e.
Isa. 60 : 15, I will make thee an eternal e.
1 Cor. 2 : 1, I came not with e. of speech.

2 Cor. 4 : 7, that the e. of the power may be
   of God.
Phil. 3 : 8, count all things but loss for the e.
Excellent, Job 37 : 23, Almighty is e. in power.
Ps. 8 : 1, 9, how e. is thy name in earth!
16 : 3, e. in whom is all my delight.
36 : 7, how e. is thy lovingkindness!
Prov. 8 : 6, I will speak of e. things.
12 : 26, righteous more e. than neighbour.
17 : 27, of an e. spirit.
Isa. 12 : 5, Lord hath done e. things.
28 : 29, e. in working.
Dan. 5 : 12; 6 : 3, e. spirit in Daniel.
Rom. 2 : 18; Phil. 1 : 10, things that are e.
1 Cor. 12 : 31, a more e. way.
Heb. 1 : 4, obtained a more e. name.
2 Pet. 1 : 17, a voice from the e. glory.
Except, Gen. 32 : 26, not let go, e. thou bless me.
Deut. 32 : 30, e. their Rock had sold them.
Ps. 127 : 1, e. the Lord build the house.
Isa. 1 : 9; Rom. 9 : 29; e. Lord had left
   remnant.
Amos 3 : 3, can two walk, e. agreed ?
Matt. 5 : 20, e. your righteousness exceed that
   of the scribes.
18 : 3, e. ye be converted.
24 : 22; Mark 13 : 20, e. days be shortened.
Mark 7 : 3, Pharisees e. they wash oft.
Luke 13 : 3, e. ye repent, ye shall perish.
John 3 : 2, do miracles e. God be with him ?
3 : 3, e. a man be born again.
4 : 48, e. ye see signs and wonders.
6 : 53, e. ye eat flesh of the Son of man.
19 : 11, no power, e. it were given from above.
20 : 25, e. I see print of the nails.
Acts 15 : 1, e. ye be circumcised, ye cannot.
26 : 29, as I am, e. these bonds.
Rom. 10 : 15, how preach, e. they be sent ?
1 Cor. 15 : 36, not quickened, e. it die.
2 Thess. 2 : 3, e. there come a falling away.
2 Tim. 2 : 5, not crowned, e. he strive lawfully.
Excess forbidden, Eph. 5 : 18; 1 Pet. 4 : 3.
Matt. 23 : 25, within are full of e.
Eph. 5 : 18, wine wherein is e.
1 Pet. 4 : 4, that ye run not to the same e.
Exchange, Gen. 47 : 17, bread in e. for.
Matt. 16 : 26; Mark 8 : 37, give in e. for his
   soul.
Exchanger [banker], Matt. 25 : 27.
Exclude, Rom. 3 : 27, where is boasting ? it is e.
Gal. 4 : 17, they would e. you, that.
Excuse, Luke 14 : 18, they began to make e.
Rom. 1 : 20, they are without e.
2 : 15, thoughts accusing or e.
2 Cor. 12 : 19, think we e. ourselves.
Execute, Num. 8 : 11, that they may e. service
   of the Lord.
Deut. 33 : 21, he e. justice of the Lord.
1 Chr. 6 : 10; 24 : 2; Luke 1 : 8, e. priest's
   office.
Ps. 9 : 16, Lord is known by the judgment
   he e.
103 : 6, Lord e. righteousness and judgment.
149 : 7, to e. vengeance upon heathen.
John 5 : 27, authority to e. judgment.
Rom. 13 : 4, minister of God to e. wrath.
Jude 15, to e. judgment on all.
Exercise, Ps. 131 : 1, e. myself in things too
   high.

Jer. 9 : 24, e. lovingkindness.
Matt. 20 : 25; Mark 10 : 42; Luke 22 : 25, e. dominion.
Acts 24 : 16, I e. myself to have a conscience.
1 Tim. 4 : 7, e. thyself to godliness.
Heb. 5 : 14, senses e. to discern good and evil.
12 : 11, fruit of righteousness unto them which are e.
2 Pet. 2 : 14, heart e. with covetous practises.
Exhort, Acts 2 : 40, with many words did he e.
27 : 22, I e. you to be of good cheer.
Rom. 12 : 8, he that e., on e.
1 Tim. 6 : 2, these things teach and e.
2 Tim. 4 : 2, e. with all longsuffering.
Titus 1 : 9, able to e. and convince.
2 : 15, e. and rebuke with authority.
Heb. 3 : 13, e. one another daily.
13 : 22, suffer the word of e.
Exhortation, 1 Thess. 4 : 18; 5 : 11; Heb. 3 : 13; 10 : 25.
Exodus, Book of.
Title.—The name (" departure," in reference to the great event in the book; cf. Heb. 11 : 22) is derived from the Greek title in the LXX., through the Latin Version. The Hebrew title is Shemoth (names) or Eleh Shemoth (these are the names), from the beginning of ver. 1.
Contents.—The book continues the history of Israel, from the death of Joseph down to the giving of the law at Sinai, and the erection of the Tabernacle. It may be divided into two parts—(1) Ch. 1-18 describes the oppression of the Israelites in Egypt, the history of Moses and his dealings with Pharaoh, the plagues, the exodus, and overthrow of the Egyptians, and the arrival at Sinai. (2) Ch. 19-40 contains an account of the sojourn at Sinai, the giving of the law, the directions respecting the Tabernacle and its services, the story of the sin of the golden calf, and its subsequent punishment, the giving of the new tables, and the erection and dedication of the Tabernacle.
Exorcists [persons who professed to cast out demons], Acts 19 : 13, vagabond Jews, e.
Expectation, Ps. 9 : 18, e. of poor shall not perish.
62 : 5, wait on God, my e. from him.
Prov. 10 : 28; 11 : 7, e. of wicked perish.
Isa. 20 : 5, ashamed of their e.
Rom. 8 : 19, e. of creature.
Phil. 1 : 20, my earnest e. and hope.
Expedient, John 11 : 50, e. for us that one man die.
16 : 7, e. for you that I go away.
1 Cor. 6 : 12; 10 : 23, all things not e.
2 Cor. 8 : 10, this is e. for you.
12 : 1, it is not e. for me to glory.
Experience, Gen. 30 : 27, by e. the Lord blessed me.
Eccl. 1 : 16, my heart had e. of wisdom.
Rom. 5 : 4, patience worketh e., and e. hope.
Expound, Judg. 14 : 14, they could not e. riddle.
Mark 4 : 34, when alone, he e. all things.
Luke 24 : 27, he e. to them the scriptures.
Acts 28 : 23, e. the kingdom of God.
Express [exactly resembling an original, per-

fectly like], Heb. 1 : 3, the e. image of His person.
1 Tim. 4 : 1, Spirit speaketh e. some.
Extend, Ps. 16 : 2, my goodness e. not to thee.
109 : 12, none to e. mercy.
Isa. 66 : 12, I will e. peace like river.
Extinct, Job 17 : 1, my days are e.
Isa. 43 : 17, they are e., they are quenched.
Extol, Ps. 30 : 1; 145 : 1, I will e. thee.
68 : 4, e. him that rideth on heavens.
Isa. 52 : 13, my servant shall be e.
Dan. 4 : 37, I e. the king of heaven.
Extortion, Ezek. 22 : 12, thou hast gained by e.
Matt. 23 : 25, within they are full of e.
Extortioner, Ps. 109 : 11, let e. catch all he hath.
Isa. 16 : 4, the e. is at an end.
Luke 18 : 11, I am not as other men, e.
1 Cor. 5 : 11, if any be an e.
6 : 10, nor e. inherit kingdom of God.
Eye, Gen. 3 : 7, e. of both were opened.
27 : 1, his e. were dim.
Ex. 21 : 24; Lev. 24 : 20; Deut. 19 : 21; Matt. 5 : 38, e. for e.
Num. 10 : 31, be to us instead of e.
Deut. 4 : 19, lest thou lift up e. to heaven.
16 : 19, gift doth blind e. of wise.
32 : 10, kept him as apple of his e.
34 : 7, his e. was not dim.
1 Ki. 1 : 20, e. of all Israel upon thee.
8 : 29, 52; 2 Chr. 6 : 20, 40, e. open towards this house.
2 Ki. 6 : 17, Lord opened e. of young man.
2 Chr. 16 : 9; Zech. 4 : 10, e. of Lord run to and fro.
Job 10 : 18, and no e. had seen me.
19 : 27, mine e. shall behold, and not another.
29 : 11, when the e. saw me.
29 : 15, I was e. to the blind.
Ps. 11 : 4, his e. try children of men.
19 : 8, commandment enlightening the e.
33 : 18, e. of Lord on them that fear him.
34 : 15; 1 Pet. 3 : 12, e. of Lord on the righteous.
36 : 1, no fear of God before his e.
94 : 9, formed e. shall he not see ?
119 : 18, open mine e.
121 : 1, lift up mine e. to hills.
132 : 4, not give sleep to mine e.
141 : 8, mine e. are unto thee, O God.
145 : 15, e. of all wait upon thee.
Prov. 10 : 26, as smoke to the e.
20 : 12, the seeing e. Lord hath made.
22 : 9, bountiful e. shall be blessed.
23 : 29, who hath redness of e. ?
27 : 20, e. of man are never satisfied.
Eccl. 1 : 8, e. not satisfied with seeing.
2 : 14, wise man's e. are in his head.
11 : 7, pleasant for the e. to behold the sun.
Isa. 1 : 15, I will hide mine e. from you.
32 : 3, e. of them that see not be dim.
33 : 17, thine e. shall see the king in his beauty.
42 : 7, to open the blind e. to bring.
52 : 8, they shall see e. to e.
64 : 4; 1 Cor. 2 : 9, neither hath e. seen.
Jer. 5 : 21; Ezek. 12 : 2, have e. and see not.
Jer. 9 : 1, mine e. a fountain of tears.
13 : 17, mine e. shall weep sore.

GALILEE FROM SITE OF SERMON ON THE MOUNT

MARKET IN NAZARETH

14 : 17, mine e. run down with tears.
16 : 17, mine e. are on their ways.
24 : 6, I will set mine e. upon them for good.
Ezek. 24 : 16, 25, the desire of thine e.
Hab. 1 : 13, of purer e. than to behold evil.
Matt. 6 : 22; Luke 11 : 34, light of the body is the e.
Matt. 13 : 16, blessed are your e.
18 : 9, if e. offend thee, pluck it out.
Mark 8 : 18, having e., see ye not ?
Luke 4 : 20, e. were fastened on him.
24 : 16, their e. were holden.
John 9 : 6, anointed e. of blind man.
11 : 37, could not this man, which opened e. ?
Gal. 3 : 1, before whose e. Christ has been set.
Eph. 1 : 18, e. of your understanding enlightened.
Heb. 4 : 13, all things are opened unto e. of him.
1 John 2 : 16, the lust of the e.
Eyeservice forbidden, Eph. 6 : 6; Col. 3 : 22.
Eyes of the Lord, Deut. 11 : 12; 2 Chr. 16 : 9; Prov. 15 : 3; upon the righteous, Ezra 5 : 5; Ps. 32 : 8; 33 : 18; 34 : 15; 1 Pet. 3 : 12.
See John 10 : 21.
Ezekiel (ē-zēk-iēl) [Latin form of Hebrew Ye-hez-kal, the strength of God], sent to house of Israel, Ezek. 2; 3; 33 : 7.
intercedes for his people, Ezek. 9 : 8; 11 : 13.
his dumbness, Ezek. 3 : 26; 24 : 26; 33 : 22.
his parables, Ezek. 15; 16; 17; 19; 23; 24.
exhorts Israel against idols, Ezek. 14 : 1; 20 : 1; 33 : 30.
rehearses Israel's rebellions, Ezek. 20; and the sins of the rulers and people of Jerusalem, Ezek. 22; 23; 24.
Ezekiel, Book of.
Author and Date.—Ezekiel was one of those who were carried captive to Babylonia with King Jehoiachin, 597 B.C., and lived there at Tel-abib, on the banks of the canal or river of Chebar, a name which is distinct from Habor, a river mentioned in 2 Ki. 17 : 6; 18 : 11. He was a priest, the son of Buzi (1 : 3), and as such belonged to the aristocracy of Jerusalem. He received the prophetic call in the fifth year of the captivity (1 : 2), and prophesied for at least twenty-two years among his fellow-exiles (cf. 29 : 17; his last dated prophecy was in the twenty-seventh year of the captivity). His prophetic ministry was possibly of longer duration. As to his subsequent fate nothing is known. An uncertain tradition states that he died a martyr's death at the hands of his fellow-exiles, who resented the tone of his prophecies. He was a younger contemporary of Jeremiah, and like him prophesied both before and after the destruction of Jerusalem by the Chaldeans. His prophecies, however, were all composed in Babylonia.
Contents.—The book may be divided into three parts, each dealing with a different subject. (1) Ch. 1–24, the impending downfall of Jerusalem. (a) The opening chapters

(1-3 : 21) contain an account of the prophet's call, and the wonderful vision of the four living creatures (cherubim), with the four faces, and four wings encircling the four-wheeled chariot. (b) Ch. 3 : 22–7 is a symbolic description of the fate of Jerusalem. (c) Ch. 8–11, a vision of the destruction of Jerusalem. (d) Ch. 12–19, the certainty of the impending ruin is further demonstrated by the prophet. Its ground is the nation's sinfulness. (e) Ch. 20–24, the further development of the same theme. The song in ch. 21, the allegory in ch. 23, and the parable in ch. 24 : 1-14, are all characteristic of the prophet. (2) Ch. 25–32, the prophecies against the foreign nations who rejoice at the fall of Jerusalem, and regard it as a sign that Jehovah cannot defend His city. Jehovah will bring a similar misfortune upon them. (a) Ch. 25 : 1-7, against Ammon; (b) 8-11, against Moab; (c) 12-14, concerning Edom; (d) 15-17, on the Philistines; (e) ch. 26–28 : 19, against Tyre; (f) 28 : 20-26, against Sidon; (g) ch. 29–32, prophecies against Egypt. (3) Ch. 33–47, Israel's Restoration. (a) Ch. 33 (which was probably delivered shortly before the news of the capture of Jerusalem) describes the duties of the prophet towards the people. (b) Ch. 34, the bad shepherd and the good shepherd; the advent of the Messiah (God's servant David). (c) Ch. 35–36 : 15, Edom, on account of its hostility to Israel, will become an utter desolation, but the land of Israel shall again be peopled with those of the house of David, and its ruins rebuilt. (d) Ch. 36 : 16-38, the reason why Israel is to be restored. (e) Ch. 37 : 1-14, the vision of the dry bones in the valley; the resurrection of all Israel to a new life, and (ver. 15-28) the reunion of Ephraim and Judah, who will be united together under the rule of the Messianic king. (f) Ch. 38, 39, Jehovah's final triumph over the world is set forth in the allegory of Gog and Magog. (g) Ch. 40–43, describes the buildings and dedication of a new Temple. (h) Ch. 44–46 gives the order of Divine service, the position of strangers, Levites, and priests in the Sanctuary; ordinances with reference to the sacrifices. (i) Ch. 47 : 1-12, the stream of living water that flows from the Sanctuary. (j) Ch. 47 : 13–48, the boundaries and divisions of the land in the restored earth. They are found to agree in many details with the description of the New Jerusalem given in Rev. 21. Compare Ezek. 40 : 2 with Rev. 21 : 10; Ezek. 37 : 27 with Rev. 21 : 3; Ezek. 48 : 30, 31 with Rev. 21 : 12, 13.
Ezel (ē-zĕl) [walk, side], 1 Sam. 20 : 19.
Ezra (ĕz-rä) [help], 1 Chr. 4 : 17; scribe, goes up from Babylon to Jerusalem, Ezra 7 : 1; 8 : 1.
the commission from Artaxerxes, Ezra 7 : 11.
fast ordered by, Ezra 8 : 21.
his prayer, Ezra 9 : 5.
reproves the people, Ezra 10 : 9.

reforms various corruptions, Ezra 10; Neh. 13.

Ezra and Nehemiah, Books of.
These books were regarded in ancient times as one, but in later editions of the Hebrew Bible they are divided into two books.

The books record the expeditions to Jerusalem for the purpose of rebuilding the Temple and the Wall of Jerusalem. These expeditions were authorized by the decree of Cyrus made in the first year of his reign (536 B.C.). His part in the matter is specifically prophesied in Isa. 44 : 28 and 45 : 1-6. Ezra records the first expedition, made under Zerubbabel, in chapters 1–6 and the second under himself in chapters 7–10.

Nehemiah records a later expedition (445 B.C.) during the reign of Artaxerxes Longimanus for the purpose of rebuilding the wall of the city.

Contents.—The books may be divided into four parts. (1) Ezra 1–6 describes the first return of the Jews under Sheshbazzar or Zerubbabel and Joshua, the high priest, in the first year of Cyrus (536 B.C.), and the beginning of the rebuilding of the temple. Under this period are included the prophetic ministries of Haggai and Zechariah. (2) Ezra 7–10 narrates the migration from Babylon, under Ezra, in the seventh year of Artaxerxes II. (398-397 B.C.), and includes Ezra's prayer and confession (Chap. 9) and the expulsion of the foreign wives. (3) Neh. 1–7 relates how Nehemiah came to Jerusalem in the twentieth year of Artaxerxes I., Longimanus (445-444 B.C.), and rebuilt the walls of the city despite the hostility of Sanballat, Tobiah, and Geshem, the Arabian, who desired to lord it over the people of Israel. (4) Neh. 8–13 describes the efforts of Ezra to effect the restoration of religion, including the solemn reading of the Law, the celebration of the Feast of Tabernacles, the confession of the Levites, the sealing of the Covenant by the people, a list of the inhabitants of Jerusalem and of other cities, the dedication of the walls, and the removal of certain abuses.

Ezrahite (ĕz'-rā-hīte), descendant of Ezrah (not of Ezra), or of Zerah, 1 Ki. 4 : 31.

F

Fables, unedifying, 1 Tim. 1 : 4; 4 : 7; 2 Tim. 4 : 4; Titus 1 : 14.
1 Tim. 1 : 4, nor give heed to f.
2 Tim. 4 : 4, shall be turned unto f.
Titus 1 : 14, not giving heed to f.
2 Pet. 1 : 16, have not followed cunningly devised f.

Face [often explainable by the word " before " from the literal " to the face of " of the Hebrew idiom], of God set against them that do evil, Ps. 34 : 16; Isa. 59 : 2; Ezek. 39 : 23.
to be sought, 2 Chr. 7 : 14; Ps. 31 : 16; 80 : 2; Dan. 9 : 17.

seen by Jacob, Gen. 32 : 30.
Gen. 3 : 19, in sweat of f. eat bread.
16 : 8, I flee from f. of my mistress.
32 : 30, I have seen God f. to f.
Ex. 3 : 6, Moses hid his f.
33 : 11, Lord spake to Moses f. to f.
34 : 29, skin of his f. shone.
34 : 33; 2 Cor. 3 : 13, put a veil on his f.
Lev. 19 : 32, honour the f. of old man.
Num. 6 : 25, Lord make his f. shine on thee.
Deut. 1 : 17, not be afraid of f. of man.
1 Sam. 5 : 3, Dagon was fallen on his f.
1 Ki. 19 : 13, wrapped his f. in his mantle.
2 Ki. 4 : 29, lay staff on f. of child.
2 Chr. 6 : 42; Ps. 132 : 10, turn not away the f. of thine anointed.
Ezra 9 : 7; Dan. 9 : 8, confusion of f.
Job 1 : 11; 2 : 5, curse thee to thy f.
13 : 24; Ps. 44 : 24; 88 : 14, wherefore hidest thou thy f. ?
Ps. 17 : 15, I will behold thy f. in righteousness.
27 : 9; 69 : 17; 102 : 2; 143 : 7, hide not thy f.
31 : 16; 119 : 135, make thy f. to shine.
34 : 5, their f. were not ashamed.
84 : 9, look upon f. of thine anointed.
89 : 14, mercy and truth go before f.
Prov. 27 : 19, in water f. answereth to f.
Eccl. 8 : 1, wisdom maketh f. to shine.
Isa. 25 : 8, wipe tears from off all f.
53 : 3, hid as it were our f. from him.
Jer. 2 : 27, turned their back, and not f.
16 : 17, ways not hid from my f.
50 : 5, to Zion, with f. thitherward.
Dan. 10 : 6, his f. as appearance of lightning.
Hos. 5 : 5, testifieth to his f.
Matt. 6 : 17, anoint head, and wash f.
11 : 10; Mark 1 : 2; Luke 7 : 27, messenger before f.
Matt. 16 : 3; Luke 12 : 56, discern f. of sky.
Matt. 17 : 2, his f. did shine as sun.
18 : 10, angels behold f. of my father.
Luke 2 : 31, prepared before f. of all people.
22 : 64, struck him on f.
Acts 2 : 25, I foresaw Lord before my f.
1 Cor. 13 : 12, then see f. to f.
2 Cor. 3 : 18, we all with open f. beholding.
Gal 2 : 11, I withstood him to the f.
Jas. 1 : 23, beholding natural f. in a glass.
Fade, Isa. 1 : 30, whose leaf f.
40 : 7, grass withereth, flower f.
64 : 6, we all f. as a leaf.
Jer. 8 : 13, the leaf shall f.
Ezek. 47 : 12, whose leaf shall not f.
Jas. 1 : 11, rich man shall f. away.
1 Pet. 1 : 4; 5 : 4, inheritance that f. not away.
Fail, Gen. 47 : 16, for your cattle, if money f.
Deut. 28 : 32, eyes shall f. with longing.
Josh. 21 : 45; 23 : 14; 1 Ki. 8 : 56, there f. not any good thing.
1 Sam. 17 : 32, let no man's heart f.
1 Ki. 2 : 4; 8 : 25, shall not f. a man on throne.
17 : 14, neither shall cruse of oil f.
Job 14 : 11, as waters f. from the sea.
Ps. 12 : 1, the faithful f. among men.
31 : 10; 38 : 10, my strength f. me.
77 : 8, doth his promise f. for ever ?

119 : 123, mine eyes f. for thy salvation.
Eccl. 10 : 3, wisdom f. him.
  12 : 5, desire shall f.
Isa. 15 : 6, the grass f.
  19 : 5, waters shall f.
  32 : 10, the vintage shall f.
  38 : 14, mine eyes f. with looking.
  42 : 4, not f. nor be discouraged.
Jer. 15 : 18, as waters that f.
Lam. 3 : 22, his compassions f. not.
Hab. 3 : 17, labour of olive shall f.
Luke 12 : 33, treasure in heaven that f.
  16 : 17, one tittle of law to f.
  21 : 26, hearts f. them for fear.
  22 : 32, that thy faith f. not.
1 Cor. 13 : 8, charity never f.
Heb. 1 : 12, thy years shall not f.
  11 : 32, time would f. me to tell.
  12 : 15, lest any man f. of grace of God.
Fain, Job 22 : 22, f. flee out of his hand.
Luke 15 : 16, f. fill belly with husks.
Faint, Gen. 25 : 29, came from field and was f.
Deut. 25 : 18, smote when thou wast f.
Judg. 8 : 4, f., yet pursuing.
Ps. 27 : 13, I had f., unless I had believed.
  107 : 5, their soul f. in them.
Isa. 1 : 5, whole heart f.
  40 : 28, creator of earth f. not.
  40 : 29, giveth power to the f.
  40 : 30; Amos 8 : 13, even youths shall f.
Isa. 40 : 31, walk, and not f.
Matt. 15 : 32; Mark 8 : 3, lest they f. by the way.
Luke 18 : 1, always to pray, and not f.
2 Cor. 4 : 1, 16, as we have received mercy, we f. not.
Gal. 6 : 9, in due season shall reap, if we f. not.
Heb. 12 : 3, wearied and f. in your minds.
  12 : 5, nor f. when thou art rebuked.
Fainthearted, Deut. 20 : 8, fearful and f.
Isa. 7 : 4, fear not, neither be f.
Jer. 49 : 23, they are f.
Faintness, Lev. 26 : 36, send a f. into their hearts.
Fair, Gen. 6 : 2, daughters of men were f.
Job 37 : 22, f. weather out of the north.
Ps. 45 : 2, f. than children of men.
Prov. 11 : 22, a f. woman without discretion.
Cant. 1 : 8; 5 : 9; 6 : 1, thou f. among women.
  6 : 10, f. as the moon.
Isa. 5 : 9, many houses great and f.
  54 : 11, lay stones with f. colours.
Jer. 12 : 6, though they speak f. words.
Dan. 1 : 15, their countenances appeared f.
Matt. 16 : 2, it will be f. weather.
Acts 7 : 20, Moses was exceeding f.
Rom. 16 : 18, by f. speeches deceive.
Gal. 6 : 12, to make f. shew in flesh.
Faith described, Heb. 11.
justification by, Rom. 3 : 28; 5 : 1, 16; Gal. 2 : 16.
purification by, Acts 15 : 9.
sanctification by, Acts 26 : 18.
object of, Father, Son, and Holy Ghost, Mark 11 : 22; John 6 : 29; 14 : 1; 20 : 31; Acts 20 : 21; 2 Cor. 13 : 14.
the gift of God, Rom. 12 : 3; 1 Cor. 2 : 5; 12 : 9; Eph. 2 : 8.

in Christ, Acts 8 : 12; 2 Tim. 3 : 15.
unity of, Eph. 4 : 5, 13; Jude 3.
leads to salvation, etc., Mark 16 : 16; John 1: 12; 3 : 16, 36; 6 : 40, 47; Acts 16 : 31; Gal. 3 : 11; Eph. 2 : 8; Heb. 11 : 6; 1 Pet. 1 : 9; 1 John 5 : 10.
works by love, 1 Cor. 13; Gal. 5 : 6; Col. 1 : 4; 1 Thess. 1 : 3; 1 Tim. 1 : 5; Philem. 5; Heb. 10 : 23; 1 Pet. 1 : 22; 1 John 3 : 14, 23.
without works is dead, Jas. 2 : 17, 20.
produces peace, joy, hope, etc., Rom. 5 : 1; 15 : 13; 2 Cor. 4 :13; 1 Pet. 1 : 8.
excludes boasting, etc., Rom. 3 : 27; 4 : 2; 1 Cor. 1 : 29; Eph. 2 : 9.
blessings received through, Mark 16 : 16; John 6 : 40; 12 : 36; 20 : 31; Acts 10 : 43; 16 : 31; 26 : 18; Rom. 1 : 17; (Hab. 2 : 4); Rom. 3 : 21; 4 : 16; 5 : 1; 2 Cor. 5 : 7; Gal. 2 : 16; 3 : 14, 26; Eph. 1 : 13; 3 : 12, 17; 1 Tim. 1 : 4; Heb. 4 : 3; 6 : 12; 10 : 38; 1 Pet. 1 : 5; Jude 20.
miracles performed through, Matt. 9 : 22; Luke 8 : 50; Acts 3 : 16.
power of, Matt. 17 : 20; Mark 9 : 23; 11 : 23; Luke 17 : 6.
trial of, 2 Thess. 1 : 4; Heb. 11 : 17; Jas. 1 : 3, 13; 1 Pet. 1 : 7.
overcometh the world, 1 John 5 : 4.
shield of the Christian, Eph. 6 : 16; 1 Thess. 5 : 8.
exhortations to continue in, 1 Cor. 16 : 13; 2 Cor. 13 : 5; Eph. 6 : 16; Phil. 1 : 27; Col. 1 : 32; 2 : 7; 1 Thess. 5 : 8; 1 Tim. 1 : 19; 4 : 12; 6 : 11; 2 Tim. 2 : 22; Titus 1 : 13; Heb. 10 : 22; Jude 3.
Examples of :—
  Caleb, Num. 13 : 30.
  Shadrach, Meshach, and Abednego, Dan. 3 : 17.
  Daniel, Dan. 6 : 10.
  Ninevites, Jonah 3 : 5.
  Peter, Matt. 16 : 16.
  Nathanael, John 1 : 49.
  Martha, John 11 : 27.
  Stephen, Acts 6 : 5.
  Ethiopian eunuch, Acts 8 : 37.
  Barnabas, Acts 11 : 24.
Deut. 32 : 20, children in whom is no f.
Hab. 2 : 4; Rom. 1 : 17; Gal. 3 : 11; Heb. 10 : 38, just shall live by f.
Matt. 6 : 30; 8 : 26; 14 : 31; 16 : 8; Luke 12 : 28, O ye of little f.
Matt. 8 : 10; Luke 7 : 9, so great f.
Matt. 9 : 2; Mark 2 : 5; Luke 5 : 20, Jesus seeing their f.
Matt. 9 : 22; Mark 5 : 34; 10 : 52; Luke 8 : 48; 17 : 19, thy f. hath made thee whole.
Matt. 15 : 28, great is thy f.
  17 : 20, f. as a grain of mustard seed.
  21 : 21, if we have f., and doubt not.
  23 : 23, judgment, mercy, and f.
Mark 4 : 40, how is it ye have no f. ?
  11 : 22, have f. in God.
Luke 7 : 50, thy f. hath saved thee.
  8 : 25, where is your f. ?
  17 : 5, Lord, increase our f.
  18 : 8, shall Son of man find f. on earth ?
  22 : 32, that thy f. fail not.

Acts 3 : 16, the **f.** which is by him.
6 : 5; 11 : 24, a man full of **f.**
14 : 9, perceiving he had **f.** to be healed.
14 : 22, exhorting to continue in the **f.**
14 : 27, opened the door of **f.**
15 : 9, purifying their hearts by **f.**
16 : 5, established in the **f.**
20 : 21, **f.** toward our Lord Jesus Christ.
26 : 18, sanctified by **f.**
Rom. 1 : 5, grace for obedience to **f.**
1 : 17, righteousness of God revealed from **f.** to **f.**
3 : 3, make **f.** of God without effect.
3 : 28; 5 : 1; Gal. 2 : 16; 3 : 24, justified by **f.**
4 : 5, **f.** counted for righteousness.
5 : 2, we have access by **f.**
10 : 8, the word of **f.**, which we preach.
10 : 17, **f.** cometh by hearing.
12 : 3, the measure of **f.**
12 : 6, prophesy according to proportion of **f.**
14 : 1, weak in **f.** receive ye.
14 : 23, what is not of **f.** is sin.
1 Cor. 2 : 5, your **f.** not stand in wisdom.
13 : 2, though I have all **f.**
13 : 13, now abideth **f.**
15 : 14, your **f.** is also vain.
16 : 13, stand fast in the **f.**
2 Cor. 4 : 13, having the same spirit of **f.**
5 : 7, we walk by **f.** not by sight.
13 : 5, examine whether ye be in the **f.**
Gal. 1 : 23, preach the **f.** which once destroyed.
2 : 20, I live by the **f.** of Son of God.
3 : 2, by the hearing of **f.**
3 : 12, the law is not of **f.**
3 : 23, before **f.** came, we were under.
5 : 6, **f.** which worketh by love.
5 : 22, fruit of the spirit is **f.**
6 : 10, the household of **f.**
Eph. 3 : 12, access by **f.**
4 : 5, one Lord, one **f.**
4 : 13, in the unity of the **f.**
6 : 16, taking shield of **f.**
Phil. 1 : 27, striving for the **f.** of the Gospel.
Col. 2 : 5, the stedfastness of your **f.**
1 Thess. 1 : 3; 2 Thess. 1 : 11, your work of **f.**
1 Thess. 5 : 8, the breastplate of **f.**
2 Thess. 1 : 11, fulfil work of **f.** with power.
3 : 2, all men have not **f.**
1 Tim. 1 : 5; 2 Tim. 1 : 5, **f.** unfeigned.
1 Tim. 1 : 19, holding **f.** and a good conscience.
2 : 15, if they continue in **f.**
3 : 13, great boldness in the **f.**
4 : 1, some shall depart from the **f.**
5 : 8, he hath denied the **f.**
6 : 10, 21, erred from the **f.**
6 : 12, fight the good fight of **f.**
2 Tim. 2 : 18, overthrow **f.** of some.
3 : 8, reprobate concerning the **f.**
4 : 7, I have kept the **f.**
Titus 1 : 1, the **f.** of God's elect.
Heb. 4 : 2, word, not being mixed with **f.**
6 : 1, not laying again the foundation of **f.**
10 : 22, draw near in full assurance of **f.**
10 : 23, hold fast the profession of our **f.**
11 : 1, **f.** is substance of things hoped for.
11 : 6, without **f.** it is impossible to please God.

11 : 39, a good report through **f.**
12 : 2, author and finisher of our **f.**
13 : 7, whose **f.** follow.
Jas. 1 : 3; 1 Pet. 1 : 7, the trying of your **f.**
Jas. 1 : 6, let him ask in **f.**
2 : 1, have not **f.** with respect of persons.
2 : 14, man say he hath **f.**, can **f.** save him ?
2 : 17, **f.** without works is dead.
2 : 22, **f.** wrought with his works.
5 : 15, the prayer of **f.** shall save.
1 Pet. 1 : 9, the end of your **f.**
5 : 9, resist stedfast in the **f.**
2 Pet. 1 : 1, like precious **f.** with us.
1 : 5, add to your **f.** virtue.
1 John 5 : 4, overcometh the world, even our **f.**
Jude 3, earnestly contend for the **f.**
20, your most holy **f.**
Rev. 2 : 13, hast not denied my **f.**
2 : 19, I know thy works, and **f.**
13 : 10, patience and **f.** of the saints.
14 : 12, that keep the **f.** of Jesus.
Faithful, Num. 12 : 7; Heb. 3 : 2, 5, Moses **f.** in house.
2 Sam. 20 : 19, one of them that are **f.** in Israel.
Neh. 7 : 2, a **f.** man, and feared God.
9 : 8, found his heart **f.** before thee.
Ps. 12 : 1, the **f.** fail among men.
89 : 37, a **f.** witness in heaven.
101 : 6, the **f.** of the land.
119 : 86, thy commandments are **f.**
119 : 138, thy testimonies are very **f.**
Prov. 11 : 13, a **f.** spirit concealeth.
13 : 17, a **f.** ambassador is health.
14 : 5; Jer. 42 : 5, a **f.** witness.
Prov. 20 : 6, a **f.** man, who can find ?
27 : 6, **f.** are the wounds of a friend.
28 : 20, **f.** man shall abound with blessings.
Isa. 1 : 21, 26, **f.** city.
Matt. 24 : 45; Luke 12 : 42, who is a **f.** and wise servant ?
Matt. 25 : 21, well done, good and **f.** servant.
25 : 23; Luke 19 : 17, **f.** in a few things.
Luke 16 : 10, **f.** in least is **f.** also in much.
Acts 16 : 15, if ye have judged me **f.**
1 Cor. 1 : 9; 10 : 13, God is **f.**
4 : 2, required in stewards that a man be **f.**
Eph. 6 : 21; Col. 1 : 7; 4 : 7, a **f.** minister.
1 Thess. 5 : 24, **f.** is he that calleth you.
2 Thess. 3 : 3, Lord is **f.**, who shall stablish you.
1 Tim. 1 : 15; 4 : 9; 2 Tim. 2 : 11; Titus 3 : 8, a **f.** saying.
2 Tim. 2 : 13, he abideth **f.**
Heb. 2 : 17, a **f.** high priest.
3 : 2, **f.** to him that appointed him.
10 : 23; 11 : 11, he is **f.** that promised.
1 Pet. 4 : 19, as unto a **f.** creator.
1 John 1 : 9, he is **f.** and just to forgive.
Rev. 2 : 10, be thou **f.** unto death.
17 : 14, called, and chosen, and **f.**
21 : 5; 22 : 6, these words are true and **f.**
Faithfully, 2 Ki. 12 : 15; 22 : 7, they dealt **f.**
2 Chr. 34 : 12, men did the work **f.**
Jer. 23 : 28, let him speak my word **f.**
3 John 5, thou doest **f.** whatsoever thou doest.
Faithfulness commended in the service of God, 2 Ki. 12 : 15; 2 Chr. 31 : 12; Matt. 24 : 45; 2 Cor. 2 : 17; 4 : 2; 3 John 5.

towards men, Deut. 1 : 16; Ps. 141 : 5; Prov.
11 : 13; 13 : 17; 14 : 5; 20 : 6; 25 : 13;
27 : 6; 28 : 20; Luke 16 : 10; 1 Cor. 4 : 2;
1 Tim. 3 : 11; 6 : 2; Titus 2 : 10.
of Abraham, Gen. 22; Gal. 3 : 9.
of Joseph, Gen. 39 : 4, 22.
of Moses, Num. 12 : 7; Heb. 3 : 5.
of David, 1 Sam. 22 : 14.
of Daniel, Dan. 6 : 4.
of Paul, Acts 20 : 20.
of Timothy, 1 Cor. 4 : 17.
of God, Ps. 36 : 5; 40 : 10; 88 : 11; 89 : 1;
92 : 2; 119 : 75; Isa. 25 : 1; Lam. 3 : 23.
1 Sam. 26 : 23, Lord render to man his f.
Ps. 5 : 9, no f. in their mouth.
36 : 5, thy f. reacheth unto the clouds.
40 : 10, I have declared thy f.
89 : 8, or to thy f. round about thee ?
92 : 2, good to shew forth thy f. every night.
119 : 90, thy f. is unto all generations.
143 : 1, in thy f. answer me.
Isa. 11 : 5, f. shall be the girdle of his reins.
25 : 1, thy counsels of old are f.
Lam. 3 : 23, great is thy f.
Faithless, Matt. 17 : 17; Mark 9 : 19; Luke
9 : 41, O f. generation.
John 20 : 27, be not f. but believing.
Fall of man, Gen. 3.
its consequences, sin and death, Gen. 3 : 19;
Rom. 5 : 12; 1 Cor. 15 : 21.
Gen. 45 : 24, see ye f. not out by the way.
1 Sam. 3 : 19, let none of his words f. to
ground.
14 : 45; 2 Sam. 14 : 11; 1 Ki. 1 : 52; Acts
27 : 34, not hair of head f. to ground.
2 Sam. 1 : 19, 25, how are the mighty f.
3 : 38, a great man f. this day.
24 : 14; 1 Chr. 21 : 13, let us f. into the hand
of God.
2 Ki. 10 : 10, shall f. nothing of word of the
Lord.
Job 4 : 13; 33 : 15, deep sleep f. on men.
Ps. 5 : 10, let them f. by their own counsels.
16 : 6, lines f. in pleasant places.
37 : 24, though he f., not utterly cast down.
56 : 13; 116 : 8, deliver my feet from f.
72 : 11, kings shall f. down before him.
91 : 7, a thousand shall f. at thy side.
145 : 14, Lord upholdeth all that f.
Prov. 11 : 5, wicked shall f. by his own
wickedness.
11 : 14, where no counsel is, the people f.
16 : 18, haughty spirit before a f.
24 : 16, wicked shall f. into mischief.
24 : 17, rejoice not when thine enemy f.
26 : 27; Eccl. 10 : 8, diggeth a pit shall f.
therein.
Eccl. 4 : 10, if they f. one will lift up.
11 : 3, where the tree f., there it shall be.
Isa. 14 : 12, how art thou f. from heaven!
40 : 30, the young men shall utterly f.
Jer. 8 : 4, shall they f. and not arise!
46 : 6, they shall stumble and f.
49 : 21, earth moved at noise of f.
49 : 26; 50 : 30, young men f. in her streets.
Ezek. 6 : 7, slain shall f. in the midst.
Dan. 3 : 5, f. down and worship image.
Hos. 10 : 8; Luke 23 : 30; Rev. 6 : 16, say to
hills, f. on us.

Mic. 7 : 8, O mine enemy, when I f. I shall
arise.
Matt. 7 : 27, great was the f. of it.
10 : 29, not one sparrow f. to ground.
12 : 11, if it f. into a pit on Sabbath.
Matt. 15 : 14; Luke 6 : 39, both f. into the
ditch.
Matt. 15 : 27, crumbs which f. from master's
table.
21 : 44; Luke 20 : 18, whoso shall f. on this
stone.
Matt. 24 : 29; Mark 13 : 25, stars shall f.
from heaven.
Luke 2 : 34, child set for the f. and rising of
many.
8 : 13, in time of temptation f. away.
10 : 18, Satan as lightning f. from heaven.
John 12 : 24, except a corn of wheat f. into
ground.
Rom. 11 : 12, if f. of them be riches of world.
Rom. 14 : 13, occasion to f. in brother's
way.
1 Cor. 10 : 12, standeth, take heed lest he f.
15 : 6, 18, some are f. asleep.
Gal. 5 : 4, ye are f. from grace.
1 Tim. 3 : 6, f. into condemnation of the devil.
6 : 9, rich f. into temptation.
Heb. 4 : 11, lest any f. after same example.
10 : 31, fearful thing to f. into hands of
living God.
Jas. 1 : 2, joy when ye f. into temptations.
5 : 12, lest ye f. into condemnation.
2 Pet. 1 : 10, do these things, ye shall never f.
3 : 17, lest ye f. from your stedfastness.
Rev. 14 : 8; 18 : 2, Babylon is f., is f.
Falling, Ps. 56 : 13; 116 : 8, deliver my feet
from f.
Luke 22 : 44, great drops of blood f. down
Acts 1 : 18, Judas f. headlong.
1 Cor. 14 : 25, so f. down, he will worship
God.
2 Thess. 2 : 3, except there come a f. away.
Jude 24, that is able to keep from f.
Fallow, Jer. 4 : 3; Hos. 10 : 12.
Fallow Deer [Heb. yachmur] There is a great
deal of uncertainty as to what animal is
meant by this name. It was permitted to be
eaten as food (Deut. 14 : 5), and was
included among the beasts daily slain for
Solomon's table, it would therefore seem
to have been common in the land.
False, Ex. 20 : 16; Deut. 5 : 20; Matt. 19 : 18,
thou shalt not bear f. witness.
Ex. 23 : 1, thou shalt not raise a f. report.
2 Ki. 9 : 12, it is f., tell us now.
Job 36 : 4, my words shall not be f.
Ps. 27 : 12, f. witnesses are risen up.
119 : 104, 128, I hate every f. way.
120 : 3, thou f. tongue.
Prov. 6 : 19; 12 : 17; 14 : 5; 19 : 5; 21 : 28;
25 : 18, a f. witness.
11 : 1; 20 : 23, a f. balance.
Zech. 8 : 17, love no f. oath.
Matt. 24 : 24; Mark 13 : 22, f. Christs and f.
prophets.
Matt. 26 : 59; Mark 14 : 56, f. witness against
Christ.
Luke 19 : 8, any thing by f. accusation.
Acts 6 : 13, set up f. witnesses, who said.

1 Cor. 15 : 15, we are found f. witnesses of God.

2 Cor. 11 : 26, in perils among f. brethren.

2 Pet. 2 : 1, there shall be f. teachers.

witnesses condemned. See Deceit, Witness.

Falsehood, 2 Sam. 18 : 13, should have wrought f.

Job 21 : 34, in answers remaineth f.

Ps. 7 : 14, he hath brought forth f.

144 : 8, 11, right hand of f.

Isa. 28 : 15, under f. have we hid ourselves.

57 : 4, a seed of f.

59 : 13, words of f.

Hos. 7 : 1, they commit f.

Mic. 2 : 11, walking in the spirit and f.

Falsely, Lev. 6 : 3; 19 : 12; Jer. 5 : 2; 7 : 9; Zech. 5 : 4, swear f.

Ps. 44 : 17, nor have we dealt f.

Jer. 5 : 31; 29 : 9, prophets prophesy f.

Matt. 5 : 11, say evil against you f.

Luke 3 : 14, nor accuse any f.

1 Tim. 6 : 20, opposition of science f. so called.

1 Pet. 3 : 16, f. accuse good conversation.

Fame, Num. 14 : 15, have heard f. of thee.

Josh. 9 : 9, we heard the f. of God.

1 Ki. 10 : 1; 2 Chr. 9 : 1, f. of Solomon.

Job 28 : 22, we have heard f. with ears.

Isa. 66 : 19, isles that have not heard f.

Zeph. 3 : 19, get them f. in every land.

Matt. 4 : 24; Mark 1 : 28; Luke 4 : 14, 37; 5 : 15, f. of Jesus.

Matt. 9 : 26, the f. thereof went abroad.

14 : 1, Herod heard of the f. of Jesus.

Familiar spirits not to be sought after, Lev. 19 : 31; Isa. 8 : 19.

possessors of, to die, Lev. 20 : 27.

inquired of by Saul, 1 Sam. 28 : 7; 1 Chr. 10 : 13.

inquired of by Manasseh, 2 Ki. 21 : 6.

Job 19 : 14, my f. friends have forgotten me.

Ps. 41 : 9, my f. friend lifted heel.

Isa. 8 : 19; 19 : 3, f. spirits.

Familiars [those of the same family, intimate friends], Jer. 20 : 10, all my f.

Family, Gen. 12 : 3; 28 : 14, in thee all f. be blessed.

Deut. 29 : 18, lest a f. turn away from God.

Ps. 68 : 6, setteth the solitary in f.

Jer. 31 : 1, God of all the f. of Israel.

Zech. 12 : 12, every f. apart.

Eph. 3 : 15, whole f. in heaven and earth.

Famine occurs in Canaan, Gen. 12 : 10; Egypt, Gen. 41; Israel, Ruth 1 : 1; 2 Sam. 21 : 1; 1 Ki. 18 : 2; 2 Ki. 6 : 25; 7; Luke 4 : 25.

threatened, Jer. 14 : 15; 15 : 2; Ezek. 5 : 12; 6 : 11; Matt. 24 : 7; Acts 11 : 28.

described, Jer. 14; Lam. 4; Joel 1.

(of God's word), Amos 8 : 11.

Gen. 12 : 10, f. was grievous in land.

41 : 27, seven years f.

2 Sam. 21 : 1, a f. in days of David.

1 Ki. 8 : 37; 2 Chr. 20 : 9, if there be f.

1 Ki. 18 : 2; 2 Ki. 6 : 25, sore f. in Samaria.

2 Ki. 8 : 1, the Lord hath called for a f.

Job 5 : 20, in f. he shall redeem thee.

Ps. 33 : 19, to keep them alive in f.

37 : 19, in days of f. they shall be satisfied.

Isa. 51 : 19, destruction, f., and sword.

Jer. 24 : 10; 29 : 17, I will send f. among them.

Lam. 5 : 10, skin black, because of f.

Ezek. 5 : 16, evil arrows of f.

36 : 29, I will lay no f. upon you.

Amos 8 : 11, a f., not of bread.

Matt. 24 : 7; Mark 13 : 8; Luke 21 : 11, f. in divers places.

Luke 15 : 14, a mighty f. in that land.

Famish, Gen. 41 : 55, all land of Egypt was f.

Prov. 10 : 3, Lord will not suffer righteous to f.

Isa. 5 : 13, their honourable men are f.

Zeph. 2 : 11, he will f. gods of earth.

Fan, winnowing, for separating the grain from the chaff by the action of the wind, the heavy grain falling again to the ground while the light chaff is blown away.

Isa. 30 : 24, provender winnowed with the f.

Jer. 15 : 7, I will f. them with a f.

51 : 2, send fanners that shall f. her.

Matt. 3 : 12; Luke 3 : 17, whose f. is in his hand.

Far, Gen. 18 : 25, that be f. from thee.

Deut. 12 : 21; 14 : 24, too f. from thee.

Judg. 19 : 11; Mark 6 : 35; Luke 24 : 29, day f. spent.

1 Sam. 2 : 30; 22 : 15; 2 Sam. 20 : 20; 23 : 17, be it f. from me.

Job 5 : 4, his children f. from safety.

11 : 14; 22 : 23, put iniquity f. away.

19 : 13, he hath put my brethren f. from me.

34 : 10, f. be it from God to do wickedness.

Ps. 22 : 1, why so f. from helping me ?

22 : 11; 35 : 22; 38 : 21; 71 : 12, be not f. from me.

97 : 9, Lord exalted f. above all gods.

103 : 12, as f. as east from west, so f.

Prov. 31 : 10, her price is f. above rubies.

Eccl. 2 : 13, as f. as light excelleth darkness.

Isa. 43 : 6; 60 : 9, bring sons from f.

57 : 19, peace to him that is f. off.

Matt. 16 : 22, be it f. from thee, Lord.

Mark 12 : 34, not f. from the kingdom.

13 : 34, as a man taking a f. journey.

Acts 17 : 27, not f. from every one of us.

2 Cor. 4 : 17, f. more exceeding weight of glory.

Eph. 1 : 21, f. above all principality.

2 : 13, who were f. off, are made nigh.

4 : 10, ascended up f. above all heavens.

Phil. 1 : 23, with Christ, which is f. better.

Heb. 7 : 15, it is yet f. more evident.

Fare, 1 Sam. 17 : 18, look how thy brethren f.

Jonah 1 : 3, he paid the f.

Luke 16 : 19, f. sumptuously.

Acts 15 : 29, f. ye well.

Farthing, or Quadrans. See Money.

Matt. 5 : 26, till hast paid the uttermost f.

10 : 29, are not two sparrows sold for a f. ?

Mark 12 : 42, two mites, which make a f.

Fashion, Job 10 : 8; Ps. 119 : 73, thine hands have f. me.

Ps. 33 : 15, he f. hearts alike.

139 : 16, in continuance were f.

Isa. 45 : 9, shall the clay say to him that f. it ?

Mark 2 : 12, never saw it on this f.

Luke 9 : 29, the f. of his countenance.

1 Cor. 7 : 31, the **f.** of this world passeth away.
Phil. 2 : 8, found in **f.** as a man.
3 : 21, be **f.** like to his glorious body.
Jas. 1 : 11, the grace of **f.** perisheth.
Fast proclaimed, Lev. 23 : 27, 29; 2 Chr. 20 : 3; Ezra 8 : 21; Neh. 9; Esther 4 : 16; Joel 2 : 15; Jonah 3 : 5.
the true and the false, Isa. 58; Zech. 7; Matt. 6 : 16.
2 Sam. 12 : 23, child is dead, wherefore should I **f.** ?
Ps. 33 : 9, he commanded, and it stood **f.**
65 : 6, strength setteth **f.** the mountains.
Isa. 58 : 4, ye **f.** for strife.
58 : 6, is not this the **f.** that I have chosen ?
Zech. 7 : 5, did ye at all **f.** unto me ?
Matt. 6 : 16, when ye **f.** be not as hypocrites.
Mark 2 : 19, can children of bridechamber **f.**?
Luke 18 : 12, I **f.** twice in the week.
Fasten, Eccl. 12 : 11, as nails **f.** by masters of assemblies.
Isa. 22 : 25, nail **f.** in the sure place.
Luke 4 : 20, eyes of all were **f.** on him.
Acts 11 : 6, when I had **f.** mine eyes.
Fasting turned into gladness, Zech. 8 : 19.
Christ defends his disciples for not, Matt. 9 : 14; Mark 2 : 18; Luke 5 : 33.
of Moses (twice) for forty days, Ex. 24 : 18; 34 : 28; Deut. 9 : 9, 18.
of David, 2 Sam. 12 : 16.
of Elijah, 1 Ki. 19 : 8.
of Christ, Matt. 4 : 2, etc.
of Barnabas and Paul, Acts 14 : 23.
recommended, 1 Cor. 7 : 5.
Neh. 9 : 1, were assembled with **f.**
Ps. 35 : 13, I humbled my soul with **f.**
69 : 10, chastened my soul with **f**
109 : 24, my knees weak through **f.**
Matt. 17 : 21; Mark 9 : 29, this kind goeth not out but by **f.**
Mark 8 : 3, send them away **f.**
1 Cor. 7 : 5, give yourselves to **f.** and prayer.
2 Cor. 11 : 27, in **f.** often.
Fat not to be eaten, Lev. 3 : 17; 7 : 22.
of sacrifices to be burnt, Ex. 29 : 13; Lev. 3 : 3.
Gen. 45 : 18, shall eat the **f.** of the land.
Lev. 3 : 16, all the **f.** is the Lord's.
Deut. 32 : 15, Jeshurun waxed **f.,** and kicked.
Neh. 8 : 10, eat the **f.,** and drink the sweet.
Ps. 17 : 10, inclosed in their own **f.**
92 : 14, shall be **f.** and flourishing.
Prov. 11 : 25, liberal soul be made **f.**
13 : 4, soul of diligent be made **f.**
15 : 30, good report maketh the bones **f.**
Isa. 25 : 6, feast of **f.** things.
Fat, a cistern or large tub. Same as Vat (Joel 3 : 24).
Father, the, God, 1 Chr. 29 : 10; Isa. 9 : 6; 63 : 16; 64 : 8; Matt. 6 : 9; Luke 11 : 2; John 20 : 17.
duty of, Deut. 21 : 18; Prov. 3 : 12; 13 : 24; 19 : 18; 22 : 6, 15; 23 : 13; 29 : 15, 17; Luke 11 : 11; Eph. 6 : 4; Col. 3 : 21; Heb. 12 : 9.
children to obey, Ex. 20 : 12; Prov. 6 : 20; Eph. 6 : 1; Col. 3 : 20.

Gen. 17 : 4; Rom. 4 : 17, a **f.** of many nations.
Ex. 20 : 5; Num. 14 : 18, iniquity of **f.** upon children.
Judg. 17 : 10; 18 : 19, be to me a **f.** and a priest.
2 Sam. 7 : 14, I will be his **f.,** he my son.
1 Ki. 19 : 4, not better than my **f.**
2 Ki. 2 : 12; 13 : 14, cried, my **f.,** my **f.**
6 : 21, my **f.,** shall I smite them ?
Ezra 7 : 27, blessed be the Lord God of our **f.**
Job 29 : 16, I was a **f.** to the poor.
31 : 18, brought up with me as with a **f.**
38 : 28, hath the rain a **f.** ?
Ps. 27 : 10, when my **f.** and mother forsake me.
68 : 5, a **f.** of fatherless is God.
103 : 13, as a **f.** pitieth his children.
Prov. 3 : 12, correcteth, as **f.** the son.
4 : 1, hear the instruction of a **f.**
10 : 1; 15 : 20, wise son maketh a glad **f.**
Isa. 9 : 6, name called everlasting **F.**
63 : 16; 64 : 8, doubtless thou art our **f.**
Jer. 31 : 9, I am a **f.** to Israel.
31 : 29; Ezek. 18 : 2, **f.** have eaten sour grapes.
Mal. 1 : 6, if I be a **f.,** where is mine honour ?
2 : 10, have we not all one **f.** ?
Matt. 5 : 16, 45, your **F.** in heaven.
6 : 9; Luke 11 : 2, our **F.** which art in heaven.
Matt. 10 : 37, he that loveth **f.** or mother more than me.
23 : 9, call no man **f.** on earth.
Matt. 25 : 34, ye blessed of my **F.**
Mark 13 : 32, hour knoweth to man but the **F.**
14 : 36; Rom. 8 : 15; Gal. 4 : 6, Abba, **F.**
Luke 10 : 22, who the **F.** is, but Son.
Luke 11 : 11, if a son ask bread of a **f.**
15 : 21, **F.,** I have sinned.
16 : 27, I pray thee **f.** send him.
22 : 42, **F.,** if thou be willing, remove cup.
23 : 34, **F.,** forgive them.
John 1 : 14, as of the only begotten of the **F.**
3 : 35; 5 : 20, **F.** loveth the Son.
4 : 23, shall worship the **F.** in spirit.
5 : 22, the **F.** judgeth no man.
5 : 37; 8 : 16; 12 : 49; 14 : 24, the **F.** which hath sent me.
6 : 46; 14 : 9, hath seen the **F.**
10 : 15, as the **F.** knoweth me.
12 : 27, **F.,** save me from this hour.
13 : 1, I should depart unto the **F.**
14 : 6, no man cometh to the **F.,** but by me.
15 : 1, my **F.** is the husbandman.
16 : 32, not alone, for the **F.** is with me.
17 : 1, **F.,** the hour is come.
20 : 17, I ascend to my **F.** and your **F.**
Rom. 4 : 11, the **f.** of all that believe.
1 Cor. 8 : 6, is but one God, the **F.**
2 Cor. 1 : 3, **F.** of mercies, God of all comfort.
6 : 18, I will be a **f.** unto you.
Gal. 1 : 14, zealous of the traditions of my **f.**
4 : 2, the time appointed of the **f.**
Eph. 4 : 6, one God and **F.** of all.
Phil. 2 : 11, to the glory of the **F.**
Col. 1 : 19, it pleased the **F.** that in him.

Heb. 1 : 5, I will be to him a f.
7 : 3, without f., without mother.
12 : 9, the F. of spirits.
Jas. 1 : 17, the F. of lights.
1 John 1 : 2, life which was with the F.
2 : 1, an advocate with the F.
3 : 1, what manner of love the F. hath bestowed.
5 : 7, three bear record, the F., the Word, and Holy Ghost.

Fatherless protected by God, Deut. 10 : 18; Ps. 10 : 14; 68 : 5; 146 : 9; Jer. 49 : 11; Hos. 14 : 3.
duty towards, Ex. 22 : 22; Deut. 14 : 29; 24 : 17; Prov. 23 : 10; Isa. 1 : 17; Jer. 7 : 6; Jas. 1 : 27.
the wicked oppress, Job 6 : 27; 22 : 9; Ps. 94 : 6; Isa. 1 : 23; 10 : 2; Jer. 5 : 28; Ezek. 22 : 7.
Ex. 22 : 22, not afflict f.
Deut. 10 : 8; Ps. 82 : 3; Isa. 1 : 17, execute judgment of f.
Ps. 10 : 14, the helper of the f.
109 : 9, let his children be f.
Prov. 23 : 10, the fields of the f.
Isa. 1 : 23; Jer. 5 : 28, judge not f.
Jer. 49 : 11, leave thy f. children.
Hos. 14 : 3, in thee the f. findeth mercy.
Mal. 3 : 5, witness against those that oppress f.
Jas. 1 : 27, pure religion to visit f.

Fathom [Gk. ὀργυιά], a measure of length of a little over six feet, Acts 27 : 28.

Fatness, Gen. 27 : 39, thy dwelling be f. of the earth.
Ps. 36 : 8, satisfied with f. of thine house.
63 : 5, satisfied as with marrow and f.
65 : 11, thy paths drop f.
73 : 7, their eyes stand out with f.
Isa 55 : 2, let soul delight itself in f.
Rom. 11 : 17, partakest of f. of olive tree.

Fault, how to deal with, Matt. 18 : 15; Gal. 6 : 1.
exhortation to confess, Jas. 5 : 16.
Gen. 41 : 9, I remember my f. this day.
1 Sam. 29 : 3, I found no f. in him.
Ps. 19 : 12, cleanse me from secret f.
Dan. 6 : 4, find no occasion or f. in him.
Matt. 18 : 15, tell him his f.
Luke 23 : 4; John 18 : 38; 19 : 4, I find no f. in this man.
Rom. 9 : 19, why doth he yet find f. ?
1 Cor. 6 : 7, utterly a f. among you.
Gal. 6 : 1, if a man be overtaken in a f.
Heb. 8 : 8, finding f. with them.
Jas. 5 : 16, confess your f. one to another.
1 Pet. 2 : 20, if, when buffeted for your f.
Rev. 14 : 5, without f. before throne.

Faultless, Heb. 8 : 7, if first covenant had been f.
Jude 24, able to present you f.

Favour, of God bestowed on Christ, Matt. 3 : 16; Luke 2 : 52; John 11 : 41; 12 : 28; on the righteous, Job 33 : 26; Ps. 5 : 12; Prov. 3 : 4; on Abraham, Gen. 18 : 17; on David, Acts 7 : 46; on Job, Job 42 : 10; on the Israelites, Ps. 44 : 3; 85 : 1; on the Virgin Mary, Luke 1 : 30.
Gen. 39 : 21, Joseph f. in the sight of the keeper.

Ex. 3 : 21; 11 : 3; 12 : 36, f. in sight of Egyptians.
Ps. 5 : 12, with f. wilt thou compass him.
30 : 5, in his f. is life.
45 : 12, rich shall entreat thy f.
89 : 17, in thy f. our horn exalted.
102 : 13, set time to f. her is come.
112 : 5, a good man showeth f.
Prov. 13 : 15, good understanding giveth f.
14 : 35; 19 : 12, the king's f.
31 : 30, f. is deceitful.
Isa. 60 : 10, in my f. I had mercy.
Dan. 1 : 9, brought Daniel into f.
Luke 2 : 52, Jesus increased in f.
Acts 2 : 47, having f. with all the people.

Favourable, Judg. 21 : 22, be f. for our sakes.
Job 33 : 26, God will be f. unto him.
Ps. 77 : 7, will Lord be f. no more ?
85 : 1, hast been f. to thy land.

Fear, what causes fear, the source of fear. There is the feeling of fear, and the cause of fear. Both occur in : " Then were they in great fear, where no fear was," Ps. 53 : 5.
of God, described, Job 28 : 28; Ps. 19 : 9; Prov. 1 : 7; 8 : 13; 9 : 10; 14 : 27; 15 : 33.
enjoined, Deut. 10 : 12; Josh. 4 : 24; Job 13 : 11; Ps. 2 : 11; 76 : 7; 130 : 4; Jer. 10 : 7; Matt. 10 : 28; Luke 12 : 5; Heb. 12 : 28; Rev. 14 : 7; 15 : 4.
blessings resulting from, Ps. 15 : 4; 25 : 14; 31 : 19; 33 : 18; 60 : 4; 61 : 5; 85 : 9; 103 : 11; 111 : 5; 112 : 1; 145 : 19; 147 : 11; Prov. 10 : 27; 14 : 26; 15 : 33; 19 : 23; 22 : 4; Eccl. 8 : 12; Mal. 3 : 16; 4 : 2; Luke 1 : 50; 2 Cor. 7 : 1; Rev. 11 : 18.
exhortations to, Lev. 19 : 14; Deut. 4 : 10; 6 : 2; 28 : 58; Josh. 24 : 14; 1 Sam. 12 : 14; 2 Ki. 17 : 38; 1 Chr. 16 : 30; Ps. 2 : 11; 33 : 8; Prov. 3 : 7; 23 : 17; 24 : 21; Eccl. 5 : 7; 8 : 12; 12 : 13; Isa. 8 : 13; Rom. 11 : 20; Eph. 6 : 5; Phil. 2 : 12; Col. 3 : 22; Heb. 4 : 1; 1 Pet. 2 : 17.
(of punishment), causing torment, Gen. 3 : 8; 4 : 14; Prov. 28 : 1; Isa. 2 : 19; 33 : 14; Luke 19 : 21; Acts 24 : 25; Rom. 8 : 15; Heb. 10 : 27; 1 John 4 : 18; Rev. 6 : 16; 21 : 8.
Gen. 9 : 2, the f. of you on every beast.
20 : 11, the f. of God not in this place.
Ex. 15 : 16, f. shall fall upon them.
Deut. 2 : 25; 1 Chr. 14 : 17, f. of thee on nations.
Ps. 2 : 11, serve the Lord with f.
5 : 7, in thy f. will I worship.
19 : 9, f. of the Lord is clean.
34 : 11, I will teach you the f. of the Lord.
36 : 1; Rom. 3 : 18, no f. of God before his eyes.
53 : 5, in f., where no f. was.
90 : 11, to thy f. so is thy wrath.
111 : 10; Prov. 9 : 10, f. of Lord beginning of wisdom.
Prov. 1 : 7, f. of Lord beginning of knowledge.
1 : 26, mock when f. cometh.
3 : 25, not afraid of sudden f.
14 : 26, in f. of Lord is strong confidence.
19 : 23, f. of the Lord tendeth to life.
29 : 25, f. of man bringeth a snare.

Isa. 8 : 12, neither f. ye their f.
14 : 3, Lord shall give thee rest from f.
24 : 17, f. and the pit are upon thee.
29 : 13, their f. toward me is taught by men.
Jer. 30 : 5, a voice of f., not of peace.
32 : 40, I will put my f. in their hearts.
Mal. 1 : 6, if master, where is my f. ?
Matt. 14 : 26, disciples cried out for f.
28 : 4, for f. of him keepers did shake.
Luke 21 : 26, hearts failing them for f.
Rom. 13 : 7, f. to whom f. is due.
1 Cor. 2 : 3, with you in weakness and f.
2 Cor. 7 : 11, what f., what desire!
Eph. 6 : 5; Phil. 2 : 12, with f. and trembling.
Heb. 2 : 15, through f. of death.
12 : 28, with reverence and godly f.
1 Pet. 1 : 17, pass time of sojourning in f.
1 John 4 : 18, no f. in love, cast out f.
Jude 23, others save with f.
(verb) Gen. 42:18, this do, and live, for I f. God.
Ex. 14 : 13, f. not, stand still, and see.
Deut. 4 : 10, that they may learn to f. me.
25 : 58, f. this glorious name.
2 Ki. 17 : 39, the Lord your God ye shall f.
1 Chr. 16 : 30; Ps. 96 : 9, f. before him, all the earth.
Job 1 : 9, doth Job f. God for nought ?
Ps. 23 : 4, I will f. no evil, for thou.
27 : 1, whom shall I f. ?
31 : 19, goodness for them that f. thee.
34 : 9, f. the Lord, ye his saints.
52 : 6, righteous also shall see and f.
72 : 5, f. thee as long as sun endureth.
86 : 11, unite my heart to f. thy name.
103 : 11, great is his mercy to them that f. him.
115 : 11, ye that f. the Lord, trust in the Lord.
118 : 4, f. Lord say, his mercy endureth.
130 : 4, forgiveness that thou mayest be f.
145 : 19, fulfil desire of them that f. him.
Prov. 3 : 7, f. the Lord, depart from evil.
28 : 14, happy is the man that f. always.
Eccl. 3 : 14, that men should f. before him.
5 : 7, but f. thou God.
12 : 13, f. God. and keep his commandments.
Isa. 35 : 5, say to them of fearful heart, f. not.
41 : 10; 43 : 5, f. not, I am with thee.
Jer. 5 : 24, nor say they, let us f. the Lord.
10 : 7, who would not f. thee ?
23 : 4, and they shall f. no more.
Dan. 6 : 26, that men f. before God of Daniel.
Mal. 4 : 2, to you that f. my name shall sun of righteousness arise.
Matt. 10 : 28; Luke 12 : 5, f. him who is able.
Matt. 21 : 26; Mark 11 : 32; Luke 20 : 19, we f. the people.
Mark 4 : 41, they f. exceedingly.
5 : 33, woman f. and trembling came.
6 : 20, Herod f. John.
Luke 1 : 50, his mercy on them that f. him.
9 : 34, f. as they entered cloud.
12 : 32, f. not, little flock.
18 : 2, a judge who f. not God.
19 : 21, I f. thee, because thou art an austere man.
23 : 40, dost not thou f. God ?
John 9 : 22, because they f. the Jews.
12 : 15, f. not, daughter of Zion.

Acts 10 : 22, one that f. God.
13 : 16, that f. God, give audience.
13 : 26, whosoever among you f. God.
Rom. 8 : 15, spirit of bondage again to f.
11 : 20, be not highminded, but f.
2 Cor. 12 : 20, I f. lest I shall not find you such as.
1 Tim. 5 : 20, rebuke, that others may f.
Heb. 4 : 1, let us f., lest a promise being made.
5 : 7, was heard, in that he f.
13 : 6, not f. what man can do.
1 John 4 : 18, that f. is not perfect in love.
Rev. 2 : 10, f. none of those things.
Fearful, Ex. 15 : 11, like thee, f. in praises.
Ps. 139 : 14, f. and wonderfully made.
Isa. 35 : 4, say to them of f. heart.
Matt. 8 : 26; Mark 4 : 40, why are ye f. ?
Luke 21 : 11, f. sights in divers places.
Heb. 10 : 27, f. looking for of judgment.
10 : 31, f. thing to fall into hands of God.
Fearfulness, Ps. 55 : 5, f. and trembling are come.
Isa. 21 : 4, f. affrighted me.
33 : 14, f. surprised the hypocrites.
Feast, the three annual, Ex. 23 : 14; 34 : 23; Lev. 23; Num. 29; Deut. 16.
of Ahasuerus, Esther 1.
of Job's children, Job 1 : 4.
of Belshazzar, Dan. 5.
of Herod, Mark 6 : 21, etc.
given by Levi, Matt. 9 : 10; Luke 5 : 29.
of charity, 1 Cor. 11 : 22; 2 Pet. 2 : 13; Jude 12.
Num. 29 : 12, ve shall keep a f. to Lord.
Job 1 : 4, his sons f. in their houses.
Ps. 35 : 16, hypocritical mockers in f.
Prov. 15 : 15, merry heart continual f.
Eccl. 7 : 2; Jer. 16 : 8, the house of f.
Eccl. 10 : 19, a f. is made for laughter.
Isa. 1 : 14, your appointed f. my soul hateth.
25 : 6, Lord make to all people a f.
Amos 8 : 10, turn your f. into mourning.
Matt. 23 : 6; Mark 12 : 39; Luke 20 : 46, uppermost rooms at f.
Matt. 26 : 5; Mark 14 : 2, not on the f. day.
Luke 2 : 42, after the custom of the f.
14 : 13, when thou makest a f.
23 : 17, release one at the f.
John 6 : 4, the passover, a f. of the Jews.
7 : 8, go ye up to this f.
7 : 37, that great day of the f.
13 : 29, buy what we need against the f.
Acts 18 : 21, I must keep this f.
1 Cor. 5 : 8, let us keep the f. not with old leaven.
10 : 27, that believe not bid to f.
Jude 12, spots in your f. of charity.
Feathers, Job 39 : 13, f. unto the ostrich.
Ps. 68 : 13, her f. with yellow gold.
91 : 4, cover thee with his f.
Ezek. 39 : 17, unto every f. fowl.
Dan. 4 : 33, grown like eagles' f.
Fed, Gen. 48 : 15, God who f. me all my life.
Deut. 8 : 3, he f. thee with manna.
Ps. 37 : 3, verily thou shalt be f.
81 : 16, f. them with finest of wheat.
Isa. 1 : 11, I am full of fat of f. beasts.
Jer. 5 : 7, when I f. them to the full.
Ezek. 34 : 8, shepherds f. themselves. not flock.

Matt. 25 : 37, hungered, and f. thee.
Luke 16 : 21, desiring to be f. with crumbs.
1 Cor. 3 : 2, I have f. you with milk.
Feeble, Neh. 4 : 2, what do these f. Jews ?
Job 4 : 4; Isa. 35 : 3; Heb. 12 : 12, the f. knees.
Ps. 105 : 37, not one f. person.
Prov. 30 : 26, the conies a f. folk.
Jer. 6 : 24, our hands wax f.
Ezek. 7 : 17; 21 : 7, all hands shall be f.
1 Thess. 5 : 14, comfort the f. minded.
Feed, Gen. 37 : 12, to f. their father's flock.
46 : 32, their trade to f. cattle.
1 Ki. 17 : 4, commanded ravens to f. thee.
22 : 27; 2 Chr. 18 : 26, f. him with bread and water of affliction.
Ps. 28 : 9, f. them, and lift them up.
49 : 14, death shall f. on them.
Prov. 10 : 21, lips of righteous f. many.
30 : 8, f. me with food convenient.
Isa. 5 : 17, lambs shall f. after their manner.
11 : 7, cow and bear shall f.
40 : 11, he shall f. his flock like a shepherd.
61 : 5, strangers shall f. your flocks.
65 : 25, the wolf and lamb shall f. together.
Jer. 3 : 15, pastors, f. you with knowledge.
6 : 3, f. every one in his place.
Lam. 4 : 5, f. delicately are desolate.
Hos. 12 : 1, Ephraim f. on wind.
Zech. 11 : 4, f. flock of the slaughter.
Matt. 6 : 26, your heavenly Father f. them.
Luke 12 : 24, sow not, yet God f. them.
John 21 : 15, f. my lambs.
Rom. 12 : 20, if enemy hunger, f. him.
1 Pet. 5 : 2, f. the flock of God.
Rev. 7 : 17, lamb shall f. and lead them.
Feel, Gen. 27 : 21, that I may f. thee.
Acts 17 : 27, if haply they might f. after.
Feeling, Eph. 4 : 19, who being past f.
Heb. 4 : 15, touched with f. of our infirmities.
Feet of Gamaliel. Paul was " brought up at the feet of Gamaliel " (Acts 22 : 3), for the Rabbis sat on elevated seats and their pupils sat at their feet. Jewish boys preparing to become Rabbis entered Rabbinical schools at the age of thirteen. Gamaliel was grandson of the great Hillel, and so much renowned for learning that he was called " the glory of the law." He was the first of the seven Rabbis to whom the higher title of Rabban was given.
Feet, Gen. 49 : 10, lawgiver from between his f.
Ex. 3 : 5; Acts 7 : 33, shoes off thy f.
Deut. 2 : 28, I will pass through on my f.
Josh. 3 : 15, f. of priests dipped in Jordan.
1 Sam. 2 : 9, keep f. of his saints.
2 Sam. 22 : 34; Ps. 18 : 33; Hab. 3 : 19, he maketh my f. like hinds' f.
2 Sam. 22 : 37; Ps. 18 : 36, my f. did not slip.
2 Ki. 13 : 21, dead man stood on his f.
Neh. 9 : 21, their f. swelled not.
Job 29 : 15, f. was I to the lame.
Ps. 8 : 6; 1 Cor. 15 : 27; Eph. 1 : 22, all things under his f.
Ps. 22 : 16, pierced my hands and f.
25 : 15, pluck my f. out of the net.
40 : 2, set my f. on a rock.
56 : 13; 116 : 8, deliver my f. from falling.
73 : 2, my f. were almost gone.

115 : 7, f. have they, but walk not.
119 : 105, thy word is a lamp to my f.
122 : 2, our f. shall stand within thy gates.
Prov. 1 : 16; 6 : 18; Isa. 59 : 7, f. run to evil.
Prov. 4 : 26, ponder the path of thy f.
19 : 2, he that hasteth with his f.
Cant. 7 : 1; Isa. 52 : 7, how beautiful are f.
Isa. 52 : 7; Nah. 1 : 15, the f. of him that bringeth good tidings.
60 : 13, place of my f. glorious.
Ezek. 24 : 17, put shoes upon thy f.
Dan. 10 : 6; Rev. 1 : 15; 2 : 18, f. like brass.
Nah. 1 : 3, clouds are the dust of his f.
Matt. 7 : 6, trample them under f.
10 : 14; Mark 6 : 11; Luke 9 : 5; Acts 13 : 51, dust of f.
Matt. 18 : 8, rather than having two f.
Luke 1 : 79, guide our f. into way of peace.
7 : 38, she kissed his f., and anointed them.
10 : 39, Mary sat at Jesus' f.
24 : 39, behold my hands and my f.
John 11 : 2; 12 : 3, wiped f. with her hair.
John 13 : 5, wash disciples' f.
Acts 3 : 7, his f. received strength.
5 : 9, f. of them that buried thy husband.
14 : 8, a man impotent in his f.
22 : 3, at f. of Gamaliel.
Rom. 3 : 15, f. swift to shed blood.
10 : 15, the f. of them that preach Gospel.
16 : 20, bruise Satan under your f.
1 Cor. 12 : 21, nor head to the f., I have no need.
Eph. 6 : 15, your f. shod with preparation.
Heb. 12 : 13, straight paths for your f.
Rev. 1 : 17, I fell at his f. as dead.
22 : 8, I fell at his f. to worship.
Feign, 1 Sam. 21 : 13, David f. himself mad.
1 Ki. 14 : 5, f. herself another woman.
Ps. 17 : 1, prayer not out of f. lips.
Luke 20 : 20, f. themselves just men.
2 Pet. 2 : 3, with f. words make merchandise.
Feignedly, Jer. 3 : 10, turned to me f., saith the Lord.
Felix (fē-lĭx) [happy or prosperous], governor of Judea, Paul sent to, Acts 23 : 24.
Paul's defence before him, Acts 24 : 10.
trembles at Paul's preaching, but leaves him bound, Acts 24 : 25.
Fell, Gen. 4 : 5, his countenance f.
44 : 14, Joseph's brethren f. before him.
Josh. 6 : 20; Heb. 11 : 30, the wall f. down.
1 Ki. 18 : 38, fire of Lord f. and consumed sacrifice.
Ps. 78 : 64, their priests f. by sword.
Dan. 4 : 31, there f. a voice from heaven.
Jonah 1 : 7, lot f. on Jonah.
Matt. 2 : 11, wise men f. down and worshipped.
7 : 25; Luke 6 : 48, house f. not.
Matt. 18 : 29, servant f. down, saying.
Luke 5 : 8, Peter f. down at Jesus' knees.
10 : 30, 36, f. among thieves.
13 : 4, on whom tower f.
15 : 20, his father f. on his neck.
John 18 : 6, went backwards and f.
Acts 1 : 25, Judas by transgression f.
1 : 26, lot f. on Matthias.
7 : 60, said this, he f. asleep.
9 : 4, Saul f. and heard a voice.

2 Pet. 3 : 4, since fathers f. asleep.
Fellow, Gen. 19 : 9, this f. came in to sojourn.
Ex. 2 : 13, why smitest thou thy f. ?
1 Sam. 21 : 15, this f. to play the madman.
2 Sam. 6 : 20, as one of the vain f.
1 Ki. 22 : 27; 2 Chr. 18 : 26, put this f. in prison.
Ps. 45 : 7; Heb. 1 : 9, oil of gladness above thy f.
Zech. 13 : 7, the man that is my f.
Matt. 11 : 16, like children calling to their f.
24 : 49, begin to smite his f. servants.
26 : 61, this f. said, I am able to destroy.
26 : 71; Luke 22 : 59, this f. was also with Jesus.
Luke 23 : 2, found this f. perverting nation.
John 9 : 29, as for this f.
Acts 17 : 5, lewd f. of the baser sort.
22 : 22, away with such a f.
24 : 5, found this man a pestilent f.
Eph. 2 : 19, f. citizens with the saints.
Phil. 4 : 3, f. labourers.
3 John 8, f. helpers to the truth.
Rev. 19 : 10; 22 : 9, thy f. servant.
Fellowship of the saints, Acts 2 : 42; 2 Cor. 8 : 4; Gal. 2 : 9; Phil. 1 : 5; 1 John 1 : 3.
See Eph. 2 : 19.
of Christ, 1 Cor. 1 : 9; 12 : 27; 2 Cor. 4 : 11; Phil. 3 : 10.
See 1 Cor. 10 : 16.
of the Spirit, Phil. 2 : 1.
with evil, forbidden, 1 Cor. 10 : 20; 2 Cor. 6 : 14; Eph. 5 : 11.
Acts 2 : 42, in doctrine and f.
1 Cor. 1 : 9, called to the f. of his son.
10 : 20, not have f. with devils.
2 Cor. 6 : 14, what f. hath righteousness!
6 : 4, f. of ministering to saints.
Gal. 2 : 9, gave the right hand of f.
Eph. 3 : 9, what is f. of the mystery.
5 : 11, have no f. with works of darkness.
Phil. 1 : 5, your f. in the Gospel.
2 : 1, if there be any f. of the spirit.
3 : 10, the f. of his sufferings.
1 John 1 . 3, our f. is with the Father.
1 : 7, we have f. one with another.
Female, Matt. 19 : 4; Mark 10 : 6, made them male and f.
Gal. 3 : 28, in Christ neither male nor f.
Ferret [Heb. ánakah] occurs among the unclean animals mentioned in Lev. 11 : 30.
Fervent, Acts 18 : 25; Rom. 12 : 11, f. in spirit.
2 Cor. 7 : 7, your f. mind toward me.
Jas. 5 : 16, f. prayer of righteous availeth.
1 Pet. 1 : 22, with a pure heart f.
4 : 8, have f. charity among yourselves.
2 Pet. 3 : 10, melt with f. heat.
Festivals, Annual. Of these there were three chief ones in the course of the Hebrew year, Ex. 23 : 14. These were (1) the Feast of Unleavened Bread, Ex. 23 : 15, in the month of Abib or Nisan (March-April), with which the Passover became associated, Ex. 34 : 25. (2) Seven weeks later followed the Feast of Harvest or Weeks, concluding with Pentecost in the month of Sivan (May-June). (3) Succoth or Booths, the Feast of the Autumnal Ingathering, Ex. 23 : 16,

came in the month Tishri (September-October).
Subsidiary to these were the lesser festivals, also three in number : (1) Feast of Trumpets at the beginning of the civil year in the month Tishri. (2) Day of Atonement, a great and solemn fast, ten days later. (3) Tabernacles, five days thereafter.
After the return from the Exile further feasts were added, such as Purim to celebrate the deliverance of the Jews from Haman, Dedication, instituted by Judas Maccabæus in commemoration of the rededication of the purified temple, and other minor festivals.
Festus (fĕs-tŭs) [joyful], governor of Judea, Acts 24 : 27.
Paul brought before him, Acts 25.
Paul's defence before, Acts 25 : 8; 26.
acquits Paul, Acts 25 : 14; 26 : 31.

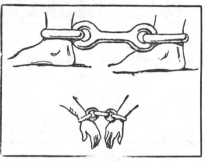

Fetters and Manacles from Nineveh.

Fetters, Judg. 16 : 21; Ps. 149 : 8; Mark 5 : 4.
Fever threatened for disobedience, Deut. 28 : 22.
healed, Matt. 8 : 14; John 4 : 52.
Few, Gen. 29 : 20, they seemed but a f. days.
47 : 9, f. and evil have the days of my life been.
1 Sam. 14 : 6, to save by many or f.
Neh. 7 : 4, city large, but people f.
Job 14 : 1, man is of f. days.
16 : 22, when a f. years are come.
Eccl. 5 : 2, let thy words be f.
12 : 3, grinders cease because f.
Matt. 7 : 14, f. there be that find it.
9 : 37; Luke 10 : 2, the labourers are f.
Matt. 20 : 16; 22 : 14, many called, f. chosen.
25 : 21, faithful in a f. things.
Luke 13 : 23, are there f. that be saved ?
Heb. 12 : 10, for a f. days chastened us.
Rev. 2 : 14, 20, a f. things against thee.
Fewest, Deut. 7 : 7, were the f. of all people.
Fewness, Lev. 25 : 16, according to the f. of years.
Fidelity (shewing good), Titus 2 : 10.
Field, Gen. 23 : 20, f. and cave made sure.
Deut. 5 : 21, neither shalt covet his f.
21 : 1, if one be found slain in f.
Ps. 96 : 12, let the f. be joyful.
Prov. 24 : 30, the f. of the slothful.
Isa. 5 : 8, woe to them that lay f. to f.
Jer. 26 : 18; Mic. 3 : 12, plowed like a f.

Matt. 6 : 28, consider lilies of the **f.**
13 : 38, the **f.** is the world.
13 : 44, treasure hid in a **f.**
27 : 8; Acts 1 : 19, the **f.** of blood.
John 4 : 35, lift up eyes, and look on **f.**
Jas. 5 : 4, labourers which reaped your **f.**
Fierce, Gen. 49 : 7, their anger, for it was **f.**
Deut. 28 : 50, nation of a **f.** countenance.
Dan. 8 : 23, a king of **f.** countenance.
Matt. 8 : 28, devils, exceeding **f.**
Luke 23 : 5, they were more **f.**
2 Tim. 3 : 3, men shall be incontinent, **f.**
Jas. 3 : 4, ships driven of **f.** winds.
Fiery, Num. 21 : 6, Lord sent **f.** serpents.
Deut. 33 : 2, a **f.** law for them.
Ps. 21 : 9, make them as a **f.** oven.
Isa. 14 : 29, a **f.** flying serpent.
Dan. 3 : 6, a **f.** furnace.
Eph. 6 : 16, able to quench **f.** darts.
Heb. 10 : 27, judgment and **f.** indignation.
1 Pet. 4 : 12, concerning the **f.** trial.
Fiery serpents, plague of, Num. 21 : 6; Deut. 8 : 15.
means of deliverance from, Num. 21 : 8.
See John 3 : 14.

The Fig Tree.

Fig [Heb. teênah]. This useful tree abounds everywhere in Palestine. It is the first tree mentioned in the Bible (Gen. 3 : 7). From a remote antiquity it has been cultivated for its fruit, which in most warm, but not tropical countries, forms an essential portion of the food of the inhabitants, either in a fresh or dried state. The Promised Land was described as a land of vines and fig trees. It lives to a great age, and reaches a very considerable size. Its thick rigid leaves form a dense shade, and bear a great heat without flagging. It puts forth its fruiting stems before its leaf buds expand, and these green figs (paggah) remain through the winter, the first small ripe figs (bikkurah) sometimes appearing in the early summer. " The fig tree ripeneth her green figs, and the vines are in blossom " (Song of Sol. 2 : 13). Joel refers to the destruction of fig trees by barking the stems (Joel 1 : 7). Fig trees were then, as now, planted in the corners of the vineyards (Luke 13 : 6). Cakes of dried and pressed figs were, and are still, used as an article of food. The Egyptian found famished by the brook Besor, was given by David, among other food, a piece of a cake of figs (debelah) (1 Sam. 30 : 12). Its power of retaining heat and moisture made the fruit highly prized as a poultice (Isa. 38 : 21).
Gen. 3 : 7, sewed **f.** leaves for aprons.
1 Ki. 4 : 25; Mic. 4 : 4, dwelt under **f.** tree.
2 Ki. 18 : 31; Isa. 36 : 16, eat every one of his **f.** tree.
2 Ki. 20 : 7; Isa. 38 : 21, take lump of **f.**
Hab. 3 : 17, although **f.** tree shall not blossom.
Matt. 7 : 16; Luke 6 : 44, do men gather **f.** of thistles ?
Matt. 21 : 19; Mark 11 : 13, saw **f.** tree in way.
Luke 21 : 29, behold the **f.** tree.
Jas. 3 : 12, can the **f.** tree bear olive berries ?
Rev. 6 : 13, **f.** tree casteth untimely **f.**
Fight, Ex. 14 : 14; Deut. 1 : 30; 3 : 22; 20 : 4, Lord **f.** for you.
Deut. 1 : 41, we will go up and **f.**
Josh. 23 : 10, Lord God that **f.** for you.
1 Sam. 4 : 9, quit like men, and **f.**
17 : 10, give me a man that we may **f.**
25 : 28, **f.** the battles of the Lord.
Ps. 35 : 1, **f.** against them that **f.** against me.
144 : 1, teacheth my fingers to **f.**
John 18 : 36, then would my servants **f.**
Acts 5 : 39; 23; 9, **f.** against God.
1 Cor. 9 : 26, so **f.** I, not as one that.
2 Cor. 7 : 5, without were **f.**
Jas. 4 : 1, wars and **f.** among you.
of faith, 1 Tim. 6 : 12; 2 Tim. 4 : 7; Heb. 10 : 32; 11 : 34.
Figs, Hezekiah cured by, 2 Ki. 20 : 7; Isa. 38 : 21.
Jeremiah's vision of, Jer. 24 : 1.
Fig Tree, the barren, Matt. 21 : 19; Mark 11 : 13.
parables of, Matt. 24 : 32; Luke 13 : 6; 21 : 29.
Figure (or type), Rom. 5 : 14; 1 Cor. 4 : 6; Heb. 9 : 9, 24; 1 Pet. 3 : 21.
Deut. 4 : 16, the similitude of any **f.**
Rom. 5 : 14, **f.** of him that was to come.
Heb. 9 : 9, which was a **f.** for time.
11 : 19, whence he received him in a **f.**
1 Pet. 3 : 21, the like **f.** even baptism.
Fill, Gen. 1 : 22, **f.** waters in the seas.
Num. 14 : 21; Ps. 72 : 19; Hab. 2 : 14, earth **f.** with glory of Lord.
Ps. 81 : 10, open mouth, I will **f.** it.
104 : 28, openest hand, are **f.** with good.
Prov. 1 : 31, be **f.** with own devices.
3 : 10, barns be **f.** with plenty.
14 : 14, **f.** with his own ways.

20 : 17, mouth be f. with gravel.
Matt. 5 : 6, hunger, shall be f.
Mark 7 : 27, let the children first be f.
Luke 1 : 15; Acts 4 : 8; 9 : 17; 13 : 9, f. with Holy Ghost.
Luke 1 : 53, hath f. hungry with good.
John 16 : 6, sorrow hath f. your heart.
Acts 14 : 17, f. our hearts with food and gladness.
Rom. 15 : 14, f. with all knowledge.
Eph. 1 : 23, fulness of him that f. all in all.
3 : 19, be f. with fulness of God.
5 : 18, be f. with the Spirit.
Phil. 1 : 11, f. with fruits of righteousness.
Col. 1 : 24, f. up what is behind.
Rev. 15 : 1, in them is f. up wrath of God.
Filth, Isa. 4 : 4, washed away the f. of Zion.
1 Cor. 4 : 13, as the f. of the world.
Filthiness, figurative of sin, Job 15 : 16; Ps. 14 : 3; Isa. 1 : 6; 64 : 6; Ezek. 24 : 13.
purification from, Isa. 4 : 4; Ezek. 22 : 15; 36 : 25; Zech. 3 : 3; 13 : 1; 1 Cor. 6 : 11; 2 Cor. 7 : 1.
2 Cor. 7 : 1, cleanse ourselves from all f.
Eph. 5 : 4, nor let f. be once named.
Jas. 1 : 21, lay apart all f.
Rev. 17 : 4, cup full of abominations and f.
Filthy, Job 15 : 16, how much more f. is man ?
Ps. 14 : 3; 53 : 3, altogether become f.
Isa. 64 : 6, all our righteousness as f. rags.
Zech. 3 : 3, Joshua clothed with f. garments.
Col. 3 : 8, put off f. communication.
1 Tim. 3 : 3; Titus 1 : 7; 1 Pet. 5 : 2, f. lucre.
2 Pet. 2 : 7, Lot vexed with f. communication.
Jude 8, f. dreamers defile the flesh.
Rev. 22 : 11, he that is f., let him be f.
Finally, 2 Cor. 13 : 11; Eph. 6 : 10; Phil. 3 : 1; 4 : 8; 2 Thess. 3 : 1; 1 Pet. 3 : 8, f. brethren.
Find, Num. 32 : 23, be sure your sin will f. you out.
2 Chr. 2 : 14, to f. out every device.
Job 9 : 10, things past f. out.
23 : 3, where I might f. him.
Prov. 2 : 5, shalt f. knowledge of God.
4 : 22, my words life to those that f. them
8 : 17; Jer. 29 : 13, seek me early shall f. me.
Prov. 8 : 35, whoso f. me, f. life.
18 : 22, whoso f. a wife, f. a good thing.
Eccl. 9 : 10, what thy hand f. to do, do it.
11 : 1, shalt f. it after many days.
Isa. 58 : 13, not f. thine own pleasure.
Jer. 6 : 16; Matt. 11 : 29, f. rest to your souls.
Matt. 7 : 7; Luke 11 : 9, seek, and ye shall f.
Matt. 10 : 39, loseth life, shall f. it.
Mark 13 : 36, lest he f. you sleeping.
Luke 6 : 7, they might f. accusation.
13 : 7, seeking fruit, and f. none.
15 : 8, seek diligently till she f. it.
Rom. 7 : 21, I f. a law that when I would do good.
11 : 33, his ways past f. out.
2 Tim. 1 : 18, may f. mercy in that day.
Heb. 4 : 16, f. grace to help.
Rev. 9 : 6, seek death, and shall not f. it.
Fine, Job 28 : 1, place for gold where they f. it.
Ps. 19 : 10, more to be desired than f. gold.
81 : 16; 147 : 14, the f. of the wheat.
Prov. 8 : 19, wisdom better than f. gold.
25 : 12, as an ornament of f. gold.

Isa. 13 : 12, man more precious than f. gold.
Mark 15 : 46, Joseph bought f. linen.
Rev. 19 : 8, granted to be arrayed in f. linen.
Finger of God, Ex. 8 : 19; 31 : 18; Luke 11 : 20; John 8 : 6.
Ex. 8 : 19, this is the f. of God.
31 : 18; Deut. 9 : 10, tables written with f. of God.
1 Ki. 12 : 10; 2 Chr. 10 : 10, little f. thicker.
Ps. 8 : 3, thy heavens, work of thy f.
144 : 1, who teacheth my f. to fight.
Prov. 7 : 3, bind them on thy f.
Isa. 58 : 9, putting forth of the f.
Dan. 5 : 5, the f. of a man's hand.
Matt. 23 : 4; Luke 11 : 46, not move with f.
Luke 11 : 20, with f. of God cast out.
16 : 24, the tip of his f.
John 8 : 6, with his f. wrote on ground.
20 : 25, put my f. into print of nails.
20 : 27, reach hither thy f.
Finish, Gen. 2 : 1, heavens and earth were f.
1 Chr. 28 : 20, not fail till thou hast f.
Dan. 9 : 24, f. transgression.
Luke 14 : 28, sufficient to f.
John 4 : 34, to do his will, and f. his work.
5 : 36, works given me to f.
17 : 4, I have f. the work.
19 : 30, he said, It is f.
Acts 20 : 24, I might f. my course.
Rom. 9 : 28, he will f. the work.
2 Cor. 8 : 6, f. in you the same grace.
Heb. 4 : 3, works f. from foundation of world.
12 : 2, Jesus, author and f. of faith.
Jas. 1 : 15, sin, when it is f.
Fir [Heb. berosh]. Referred to very frequently in the Old Testament, as a wood used for floors, rafters, ceilings, and decks of ships. The word may also be used in a general sense for any cone-bearing tree, and thus the musical instruments may have been made of the wood of some cypress (2 Sam. 6 : 5). The pine mentioned in Isa. 41 : 13 is by some thought to be a conifer, by others, an elm. Isa. 41 : 19; 55 : 13; 60 : 13; Hos. 14 · 8
Fire, pillar of, Ex. 13 : 21; Neh. 9 : 12.
God appears by, Ex. 3 : 2; 13 : 21; 19 : 18; Deut. 4 : 12; 2 Sam. 22 : 13; Isa. 6 : 4; Ezek. 1 : 4; Dan. 7 : 10; Mal. 3 : 2; Matt. 3 : 11; Rev. 1 : 14; 4 : 5.
sacrifices consumed by, Gen. 15 : 17; Lev. 9 : 24; Judg. 13 : 20; 1 Ki. 18 : 38; 2 Chr. 7 : 1.
not to be kindled on the Sabbath, Ex. 35 : 3.
emblem of God's word, Jer. 23 : 29.
See Acts 2 : 3.
instrument of judgment, Gen. 19 : 24; Ex. 9 : 23; Lev. 10; Num. 11 : 1; 16 : 35; 2 Ki. 1 : 10; Amos 7 : 4; 2 Thess. 1 : 8; Rev. 8 : 8.
everlasting, Deut. 32 : 22; Isa. 33 : 14; 66 : 24; Mark 9 : 44; Jude 7; Rev. 20 : 10.
God is a consuming, Heb. 12 : 29.
Gen. 22 : 7, behold the f. and the wood.
Ex. 3 : 2, the bush burned with f.
Lev. 10 : 2, f. from the Lord, and devoured.
18 : 21; Deut. 18 : 10; 2 Ki. 17 : 17; 23 : 10, pass through f.
Num. 16 : 46, take censer, and put f. therein.

Deut. 4 : 11, mountain burned with f.
5 : 5, ye were afraid by reason of the f.
Judg. 6 : 21, rose up f. out of rock.
1 Ki. 18 : 24, God that answereth by f.
19 : 12, the Lord was not in the f.
1 Chr. 21 : 26, Lord answered by f.
Ps. 39 : 3, I was musing, the f. burned.
46 : 9, he burneth chariot in the f.
74 : 7, they have cast f. into thy sanctuary.
Prov. 6 : 27, can man take f. in bosom ?
26 : 20, where no wood is, the f. goeth out.
Isa. 9 : 19, as the fuel of the f.
43 : 2, walkest through f. not be burned.
64 : 2, when melting f. burneth.
66 : 15, the Lord will come with f.
66 : 24; Mark 9 : 44, neither their f. be quenched.
Jer. 20 : 9, word as a f. in my bones.
Ezek. 36 : 5; 38 : 19, in the f. of my jealousy.
Dan. 3 : 27, upon bodies, f. had no power.
Hos. 7 : 6, it burneth as a flaming f.
Nah. 1 : 6, fury poured out like f.
Zech. 2 : 5, a wall of f. round about.
3 : 2, a brand plucked out of the f.
Mal. 3 : 2, like a refiner's f.
Matt. 3 : 10; 7 : 19; Luke 3 : 9; John 15 : 6, every tree that bringeth not good fruit, cast into f.
Matt. 3 : 11; Luke 3 : 16, baptize with f.
Matt. 13 : 42, cast them into furnace of f.
17 : 15; Mark 9 : 22, oft he falleth into f.
Matt. 18 : 8; 25 : 41; Mark 9 : 43, everlasting f.
Luke 9 : 54, wilt thou that we command f. ?
12 : 49, come to send f. on earth.
17 : 29, same day it rained f. and brimstone.
Acts 2 : 3, cloven tongues like as of f.
1 Cor. 3 : 13, revealed by f., and the f. shall try.
3 : 15, saved, yet so as by f.
2 Thess. 1 : 8, in flaming f. taking vengeance.
Heb. 1 : 7, his ministers a flame of f.
11 : 34, through faith, quenched violence of f.
Jas. 3 : 5, matter, little f. kindleth.
1 Pet. 1 : 7, gold tried with f.
2 Pet. 3 : 7, reserved unto f.
3 : 12, heavens being on f.
Jude 7, vengeance of eternal f.
23, pulling them out of the f.
Rev. 3 : 18, buy gold tried in the f.
15 : 2, a sea of glass mingled with f.
20 : 9, f. came down from God.
20 : 14, death and hell cast into lake of f.
Firebrand, Judg. 15 : 4, turned tail to tail, and put a f.
Prov. 26 : 18, mad man casteth f.
Isa. 7 : 4, these smoking f.
Amos 4 : 11, as a f. plucked out of.
Firm, Josh. 3 : 17, covenant of the Lord stood f.
Ps. 73 : 4, their strength is f.
Dan. 6 : 7, make a f. decree.
Heb. 3 : 6, f. unto the end.
Firmament, Gen. 1 : 6; Ps. 19 : 1; Ezek. 1 : 22; Dan. 12 : 3.
First, Deut. 9 : 18, 25, I fell before the Lord, as at the f.
Ezra 3 : 12; Hag. 2 : 3, the glory of the f. house.
Job 15 : 7, art thou the f. man born ?

Prov. 3 : 9, honour the Lord with f. fruits.
18 : 17, f. in his own cause.
Isa. 43 : 27, thy f. father hath sinned.
Matt. 5 : 24, f. be reconciled to thy brother.
6 : 33, seek ye f. the kingdom of God.
7 : 5; Luke 6 : 42, f. cast beam out of own eye.
Matt. 8 : 21; Luke 9 : 59, f. to go and bury my father.
Matt. 12 : 45, last state of that man worse than f.
17 : 10; Mark 9 : 12, Elias must f. come.
Matt. 22 : 38; Mark 12 : 28, the f. commandment.
Mark 4 : 28, f. the blade, then the ear.
9 : 35, if any desire to be f., same shall be last.
13 : 10, Gospel must f. be published.
Luke 11 : 38, that he had not f. washed.
14 : 28, sitteth not down f.
17 : 25, but f. must he suffer many things.
John 1 : 41, he f. findeth his own brother.
5 : 4, whosoever f. stepped in.
Acts 11 : 26, called Christians f. at Antioch.
26 : 23, Christ f. that should rise from the dead.
Rom. 2 : 9, of the Jew f.
8 : 23, the f. fruits of the Spirit.
8: 29, f. born among many brethren.
11 : 16, if the f. fruit be holy.
1 Cor. 12 : 28, f. apostles, secondarily prophets.
15 : 20, 23, Christ the f. fruits of them that slept.
15 : 45, the f. man was made a living soul.
15 : 47, the f. man is of the earth.
2 Cor. 8 : 5, f. gave own selves to the Lord.
8 : 12, if there be f. a willing mind.
Eph. 1 : 12, who f. trusted in Christ.
6 : 2, f. commandment with promise.
Col. 1 : 15, f.-born of every creature.
1 Thess. 4 : 16, dead in Christ shall rise f.
2 Thess. 2 : 3, a falling away f.
1 Tim. 1 : 16, in me f. Christ might shew.
5 : 4, learn f. to shew piety at home.
2 Tim. 2 : 6, husbandman must be f. partaker.
Titus 3 : 10, after f. and second admonition.
Heb. 5 : 12, which be the f. principles.
7 : 27, offer f. for his own sins.
10 : 9, he taketh away the f.
Jas. 3 : 17, wisdom from above is f. pure.
1 Pet. 4 : 17, if judgment f. begin at us.
1 John 4 : 19, because he f. loved us.
Jude 6, angels who kept not f. estate.
Rev. 2 : 4, thou hast left thy f. love.
20 : 5, this is the f. resurrection.
21 : 1, f. heaven and f. earth passed away.
Firstborn, privileges of the, Gen. 43 : 33; Deut. 21 : 15; 2 Chr. 21 : 3; Col. 1 : 15; (Heb. 12 : 23).
dedicated to God, Ex. 13 : 2, 12; 22 : 29; 34 : 19; Deut. 15 : 19.
redemption of, Ex. 34 : 20; Num. 3 : 41; 8 : 18.
in Egypt slain, Ex. 11 : 4; 12 : 29.
Firstfruits, offering of, Ex. 22 : 29; 23 : 16; 34 : 26; Lev. 23 : 9; Num. 28 : 26.
confession at, Deut. 26 : 5.

given to the priests, Num. 18 : 12; Deut. 18 : 4.

Fish. Fresh-water fishes were known to the Jews while in Egypt. In the Mosaic Law fishes without scales were forbidden as food. Fish abounded in the Lake of Galilee, in the Jordan, and in the rivers flowing into the Mediterranean Sea.

the waters bring forth, Gen. 1 : 20.

of Egypt destroyed, Ex. 7 : 21.

prepared for Jonah, Jonah 1 : 17.

caught for tribute, Matt. 17 : 27.

miraculous draught of, Luke 5 : 6; John 21 : 6.

Gen. 1 : 26; Ps. 8 : 8, dominion over f. of sea.

Deut. 4 : 18, likeness of any f. in waters.

Eccl. 9 : 12, f. taken in an evil net.

Hab. 1 : 14, makest men as f. of the sea.

Matt. 7 : 10, if he ask a f. ?

14 : 17; Mark 6 : 38; Luke 9 : 13; John 6 : 9, five loaves and two f.

Matt. 17 : 27, take up the f. that first cometh.

Luke 24 : 42, gave him piece broiled f.

John 21 : 9, they saw f. laid.

1 Cor. 15 : 39, one flesh of beasts, another of f.

Fishermen, occupation of several of the apostles, Matt. 4 : 18; Mark 1 : 16; Luke 5; John 21 : 7.

Fishers, Jer. 16 : 16, f., and they shall fish them.

Matt. 4 : 19; Mark 1 : 17, make you f. of men.

John 21 : 7, girt f. coat to him.

Fit, Lev. 16 : 21, away by hand of a f. man.

Job 34 : 18, is it f. to say to a king ?

Luke 9 : 62, is f. for kingdom of God.

14 : 35, not f. for land or dunghill.

Acts 22 : 22, it is not f. that he should live.

Rom. 9 : 22, vessels of wrath f. to destruction.

Col. 3 : 18, submit, as it is f. in the Lord.

Fitches. Two different Hebrew words are thus translated. The first ketzach, is, in the Revised Version (Isa. 28 : 25, 27), rendered in the margin, " black cummin," the fruit of a small annual often grown in our own gardens. The seeds are black, and used as a condiment; the dried fruit requires a smart blow to beat out its seeds. The second word, cussemeth, is thus wrongly translated in the Authorised Version (Ezek. 4 : 9). The R.V. translates **Spelt.**

Fitly, Prov. 25 : 11, a word f. spoken, apples of gold.

Eph. 2 : 21, all the building f. framed.

4 : 16, whole body f. joined.

Flag, Ex. 2 : 3; Job 8 : 11; Isa. 19 : 6. See **Bulrush.**

Flagon [a bottle or flask]. " Flagon of wine " should be pressed grapes, or a cake of raisins. " To every one . . . a good piece of flesh and a flagon of wine " (cake of raisins), 2 Sam. 6 : 19; also, Isa. 22 : 24; Hos. 3 : 1.

Flame, Gen. 3 : 24, at Garden of Eden a f. sword.

Ex. 3 : 2; Acts 7 : 30, angel in f. of fire.

Judg. 13 : 20, angel ascended in f.

Job 41 : 21, a f. goeth out of his mouth.

Ps. 29 : 7, voice of Lord divideth f. of fire.

Isa. 5 : 24, as the f. consumeth chaff.

29 : 6, the f. of devouring fire.

43 : 2, neither shall f. kindle.

66 : 15, rebuke with f. of fire.

Ezek. 20 : 47, the f. shall not be quenched.

Joel 2 : 3, behind them a f. burneth.

Luke 16 : 24, tormented in this f.

Heb. 1 : 7, who maketh ministers a f. of fire.

Rev. 1 : 14; 2 : 18; 19 : 12, eyes as f. of fire.

Flatter, Job 17 : 5, that speaketh f. to friends.

32 : 21, 22, give f. titles.

Ps. 5 : 9, they f. with their tongue.

12 : 2, with f. lips and double heart.

36 : 2, he f. himself in his own eyes.

Prov. 20 : 19, meddle not with him that f.

26 : 28, a f. mouth worketh ruin.

29 : 5, man that f. spreadeth a net.

1 Thess. 2 : 5, neither used we f. words.

Flattery, condemned, Job 17 : 5; 32 : 21; Ps. 5 : 9; 12 : 2; 78 : 36; Prov. 2 : 16; 20 : 19; 24 : 24; 28 : 23; 29 : 5; 1 Thess. 2 : 5.

Flax [Linum usitatissimum]. The oldest known textile fibre. It was woven into garments by the ancient Egyptians, and was swathed around their bodies after they were embalmed. It was an important crop in Egypt (Ex. 9 : 31), and was known and used in Canaan before the entrance of the Israelites. The custom of blanching the flax fibre by exposure to the sun and air, practised to this day in many parts of Europe, is referred to in Josh. 2 : 6. While woollen garments were probably worn by many of the people (Prov. 31 : 13), the robes of the priests were made of linen (Ex. 39 : 27). A mingled stuff—wool and flax together, was strictly prohibited (Lev. 19 : 19; Deut. 20 : 11). " The smoking flax shall he not quench " (Isa. 42 : 3) is, in Revised Version, margin, translated " the dimly burning wick shall he not quench," lamp wicks being of flax. Some of the linen mentioned in the New Testament may have been made of cotton fibre.

Flea [Heb. par ósh] is twice referred to by David in addressing Saul—" after whom dost thou pursue ? after a dead dog, after a flea "— evidently as something of extreme insignificance (1 Sam. 24 : 14; 26 : 20).

Flee, Gen. 19 : 20, this city is near to f. unto.

Lev. 26 : 17, 36, shall f. when none pursueth.

Num. 10 : 35; Ps. 68 : 1, that hate thee, f. before thee.

Neh. 6 : 11, should such a man as I f. ?

Job 14 : 2, he f. as a shadow.

27 : 22, would fain f. out of his hand.

Ps. 11 : 1, how say ye to my soul, f. as.

139 : 7, whither shall I f. from presence ?

Prov. 28 : 1, the wicked f. when no man pursueth.

Cant. 2 : 17; 4 : 6, till shadows f. away.

Isa. 35 : 10; 51 : 11, sighing shall f. away.

Amos 5 : 19, as if a man did f. from a lion.

Matt. 3 : 7; Luke 3 : 7, to f. from wrath to come.

Matt. 10 : 23, when persecuted in one city, f. to another.

24 : 16; Mark 13 : 14; Luke 21 : 21, f. to mountains.

John 10 : 5, stranger not follow, but **f.** from
   him.
10 : 13, the hireling **f.**
1 Tim. 6 : 11, **f.** these things.
2 Tim. 2 : 22, **f.** youthful lusts.
Jas. 4 : 7, resist the devil, he will **f.**
Rev. 9 : 6, death shall **f.** from them.
Fleece, Gideon's, Judg. 6 : 37.
Flesh allowed for food, Gen. 9 : 3.
   figuratively contrasted with Spirit, Rom.
   7 : 5; 8 : 1; Gal. 3 : 3; 5 : 17; 6 : 8.
   lusts of the, to be mortified, 2 Cor. 7 : 1;
   Gal. 5 : 16; 6 : 8; Col. 2 : 11; 1 Pet. 4 : 2;
   1 John 2 : 16.
   God manifest in the, John 1 : 14; 1 Tim.
   3 : 16; 1 Pet. 3 : 18; 4 : 1; to be acknowledged, 1 John 4 : 2; 2 John 7.
Flesh, Gen. 2 : 24; Matt. 19 : 5; Mark 10 : 8;
   1 Cor. 6 : 16; Eph. 5 : 31, one **f.**
   Gen. 6 : 12, all **f.** had corrupted his way.
   6 : 13, end of all **f.** is come.
   7 : 21, all **f.** died that moved.
   Lev. 17 : 14, life of all **f.** is the blood.
   19 : 28, not make cuttings in your **f.**
   Num. 16 : 22; 27 : 16, God of spirits of all **f.**
   1 Ki. 17 : 6, ravens brought bread and **f.**
   2 Chr. 32 : 8, with him is an arm of **f.**
   Neh. 5 : 5, our **f.** is as **f.** of our brethren.
   Job 10 : 11, clothed me with skin and **f.**
   19 : 26, in my **f.** shall I see God.
   Ps. 16 : 9; Acts 2 : 26, my **f.** shall rest in hope.
   Ps. 65 : 2, to thee shall all **f.** come.
   Prov. 4 : 22, my sayings health to **f.**
   11 : 17, the cruel troubleth his own **f.**
   Eccl. 12 : 12, much study is weariness of **f.**
   Isa. 40 : 6; 1 Pet. 1 : 24, all **f.** is grass.
   Ezek. 11 : 19; 36 : 26, a heart of **f.**
   Joel 2 : 28; Acts 2 : 17, pour Spirit on all **f.**
   Matt. 16 : 17, **f.** and blood hath not revealed
   it.
   24 : 22; Mark 13 : 20, there should no **f.** be
   saved.
   Matt. 26 : 41; Mark 14 : 38, Spirit willing,
   f. weak.
   Luke 24 : 39, Spirit hath not **f.** and bones.
   John 1 : 14, the Word was made **f.**
   6 : 52, can this man give us his **f.** ?
   6: 63, the **f.** profiteth nothing.
   17 : 2, power over all **f.**
   Acts 2 : 30; Rom. 1 : 3, seed of David
   according to **f.**
   Rom. 3 : 20, shall no **f.** be justified.
   8 : 3, God sending Son in likeness of sinful **f.**
   8 : 9, not in the **f.**, but in the Spirit.
   Rom. 9 : 5, of whom as concerning the **f.**
   Christ came.
   13 : 14, make not provision for the **f.**
   1 Cor. 1 : 29, that no **f.** should glory.
   15 : 50, **f.** and blood cannot inherit kingdom.
   2 Cor. 4 : 11, life of Jesus be manifest in **f.**
   12 : 7, a thorn in the **f.**
   Gal. 1 : 16, I conferred not with **f.** and blood.
   2 : 16, works of law no **f.** be justified.
   2 : 20, life I now live in the **f.**
   5 : 17, the **f.** lusteth against the Spirit.
   Eph. 2 : 3, lusts of **f.**, desires of **f.**
   Phil. 3 : 3, no confidence in the **f.**
   Heb. 2 : 14, children are partakers of **f.** and
   blood.

9 : 13, to the purifying of the **f.**
1 Pet. 4 : 1, Christ hath suffered in the **f.**
1 John 4 : 3; 2 John 7, confess not that Christ
   is come in **f.**
Fleshly, 2 Cor. 1 : 12, not with **f.** wisdom.
   3 : 3, in **f.** tables of the heart.
   Col. 2 : 18, puffed up by his **f.** mind.
   1 Pet. 2 : 11, abstain from **f.** lusts.
Flies. The word probably refers to a number
   of two-winged insects.
   Egyptians plagued by, Ex. 8 : 21, 31; Ps.
   78 : 45; 105 : 31.
Flint [Heb. Challāmīsh; Εκλήρας], Deut.
   8 : 15; 32 : 13; Job 28 : 9; Ps. 114 : 8;
   Isa. 50 : 7; Ezek. 3 : 9.
   water brought from, Num. 20 : 11; Deut.
   8 : 15; Ps. 114 : 8; 1 Cor. 10 : 4.
Flock, Isa. 40 : 11, he shall feed **f.** like a shep-
   herd.
   Jer. 13 : 20, where is the **f.**, thy beautiful **f.** ?
   Ezek. 24 : 5, take the choice of the **f.**
   34 : 12, as a shepherd seeketh out his **f.**
   34 : 31, the **f.** of my pasture, are men.
   Hab. 3 : 17, though the **f.** shall be cut off.
   Zech. 11 : 7, the poor of the **f.**
   Matt. 26 : 31, sheep of **f.** shall be scattered.
   Luke 12 : 32, fear not, little **f.**
   Acts 20 : 28, take heed to all the **f.**
   1 Pet. 5 : 2, feed the **f.** of God.
   5 : 3, being ensamples to the **f.**
Flood threatened, Gen. 6 : 17; sent, Gen. 7 : 11;
   Matt. 24 : 38; 2 Pet. 2 : 5.
   assuaged, Gen. 8.
   Gen. 6 : 17, even I, bring a **f.** of waters.
   Job 22 : 16, foundation overflown with **f.**
   28 : 11, he bindeth **f.** from overflowing.
   Ps. 29 : 10, Lord sitteth upon the **f.**
   32 : 6, in **f.** of great waters.
   66 : 6, they went through **f.** on foot.
   90 : 5, carriest them away as with a **f.**
   Cant. 8 : 7, neither can **f.** drown love.
   Isa. 44 : 3, I will pour **f.** on dry ground.
   59 : 19, enemy come in like a **f.**
   Matt. 7 : 25, the **f.** came, and the winds blew.
   24 : 38, in days before the **f.**
   24 : 39; Luke 17 : 27, knew not till **f.**
   came.
   2 Pet. 2 : 5, bringing in **f.** on world of ungodly.
   the river Euphrates. " The other side of the
   flood," Josh. 24 : 3.
Floor, 2 Sam. 24 : 21, to buy the threshing-**f.** of
   thee.
   1 Ki. 6 : 30, overlaid **f.** of house with gold.
   Hos. 9 : 1, loved a reward on every corn-**f.**
   Mic. 4 : 12, gather as sheaves into the **f.**
   Matt. 3 : 12; Luke 3 : 17, purge his **f.**
Flour, employed in sacrifices, Ex. 29 : 2; Lev.
   2 : 2.
Flourish, Ps. 72 : 7, in his days shall the righteous
   Ps. 90 : 6, in the morning it **f.**
   92 : 12, righteous shall **f.** like the palm tree.
   92 : 13, they shall **f.** in courts of our God.
   103 : 15, as flower, so he **f.**
   132 : 18, upon himself shall crown **f.**
   Prov. 11 : 28, righteous shall **f.** as branch.
   14 : 11, tabernacle of upright shall **f.**
   Eccl. 12 : 5, when the almond tree shall **f.**

Isa. 17 : 11, in morning thou shalt make seed f.
Ezek. 17 : 24, have made dry tree to f.
Phil. 4 : 10, your care of me hath f. again.
Flow, Ps. 147 : 18, wind to blow, and waters f.
Cant. 4 : 16, that the spices may f. out.
Isa. 2 : 2, all nations shall f. unto it.
   48 : 21, caused waters to f. out of rock.
Isa. 60 : 5, shalt see, and f. together.
Jer. 31 : 12, shall f. to the goodness of the Lord.
Mic. 4 : 1, people shall f. to mountain of Lord.
John 7 : 38, shall f. living water.
Flower, 1 Sam. 2 : 33, shall die in f. of age.
Job 14 : 2, cometh forth as a f.
Cant. 2 : 12, the f. appear on the earth.
Isa. 28 : 1, 4, glorious beauty is a fading f.
   40 : 6, as the f. of the field.
   40 : 7; Nah. 1 : 4; Jas. 1 : 10; 1 Pet. 1 : 24, f. fadeth.
Flute, a musical instrument operated by blowing, Dan. 3 : 5.
Fly, Job 5 : 7, as sparks f. upward.
Ps. 55 : 6, then would I f. away.
   90 : 10, soon cut off, and we f. away.
Prov. 23 : 5, riches f. away.
Isa. 60 : 8, f. as a cloud.
Hab. 1 : 8, they shall f. as the eagle.
Rev. 14 : 6, angel f. in midst of heaven.
   19 : 17, fowls that f. in midst of heaven.
Fold, Isa. 13 : 20, shepherds make their f.
Hab. 3 : 17, flock cut off from the f.
John 10 : 16, one f., and one shepherd.
Follow, Ex. 23 : 2, shalt not f. multitude to do evil.
Num. 14 : 24, hath f. me fully.
   32 : 12; Deut. 1 : 36, wholly f. Lord.
Ps. 23 : 6, goodness and mercy shall f. me.
   63 : 8, my soul f. hard after thee.
Isa. 5 : 11, that they may f. strong drink.
Hos. 6 : 3, if we f. on to know the Lord.
Matt. 4 : 19; 8 : 22; 9 : 9; 16 : 24; 19 : 21; Mark 2 : 14; 8 : 34; 10 : 21; Luke 5 : 27; 9 : 23; John 1 : 43; 21 : 22, Jesus said, f. me.
Matt. 8 : 19; Luke 9 : 57, 61, Master, I will f. thee.
Mark 10 : 28; Luke 18 : 28; we left all, and f. thee.
Mark 16 : 17, signs f. them that believe.
Luke 22 : 54, Peter f. afar off.
John 10 : 27, my sheep hear my voice, and f. me.
   13 : 37, Lord, why cannot I f. thee ?
Rom. 14 : 19, f. things that make for peace.
1 Cor. 10 : 4, drank of rock that f. them.
   14 : 1, f. after charity.
Phil. 3 : 12, I f. after, if that I may.
1 Thess. 5 : 15, f. that which is good.
1 Tim. 5 : 24, some men they f. after.
   6 : 11; 2 Tim. 2 : 22, f. righteousness.
Heb. 12 : 14, f. peace with all men.
   13 : 7, whose faith f. considering end.
1 Pet. 1 : 11, testified glory that should f.
   2 : 21, example, that ye should f. his steps.
2 Pet. 1 : 16, not f. cunningly devised fables.
   2 : 2, shall f. pernicious ways.
3 John 11, f. not that which is evil.

Rev. 14 : 4, they that f. the Lamb.
   14 : 13, and their works do f. them.
Follower, Eph. 5 : 1, be ye f. of God, as dear children.
1 Thess. 1 : 6, f. of us and of the Lord.
Heb. 6 : 12, f. of them who through faith.
1 Pet. 3 : 13, if ye be f. of that which is good.
Folly [base sin], Josh. 7 : 15, Achan wrought f. in Israel.
1 Sam. 25 : 25, and f. is with him.
Job 4 : 18, his angels he charged with f.
   24 : 12, God layeth not f. to them.
Job 42 : 8, lest I deal with you after f.
Ps. 49 : 13, this their way is their f.
   85 : 8, let them not turn again to f.
Prov. 5 : 23, in his f. he shall go astray.
   13 : 16, a fool layeth open his f.
   14 : 8, the f. of fools is deceit.
   16 : 22, instruction of fools is f.
   26 : 4, answer not a fool according to his f.
Eccl. 1 : 17, to know wisdom and f.
   2 : 13, wisdom excelleth f.
Eccl. 7 : 25, the wickedness of f.
   10 : 6, f. is set in great dignity.
Isa. 9 : 17, every mouth speaketh f.
2 Cor. 11 : 1, bear with me a little in my f.
2 Tim. 3 : 9, their f. shall be manifest.
Food for all creatures, Gen. 1 : 29; 9 : 3; Ps. 104 : 14; 145 : 16; 147 : 8.
Gen. 3 : 6, tree good for f.
Deut. 10 : 18, in giving stranger f.
Job 23 : 12, esteemed his words more than f.
   38 : 41, who provideth for raven f. ?
Ps. 78 : 25, man did eat angels' f.
   104 : 14, bring forth f. out of the earth.
   136 : 25, giveth f. to all flesh.
Prov. 30 : 8, feed me with f. convenient.
Ezek. 48 : 18, increase thereof be for f.
Acts 14 : 17, filling our hearts with f.
2 Cor. 9 : 10, minister bread for your f.
1 Tim. 6 : 8, having f. and raiment.
Jas. 2 : 15, destitute of daily f.
Fool [one wickedly blind], their character and conduct, Ps. 14 : 1; 49 : 13; 53 : 1; 92 : 6; Prov. 10 . 8, 23, 12 : 15, 16; 13 : 16; 14 : 16; 15 : 5; 17 : 7, 10, 12, 16, 21, 28; 18 : 2, 6, 7; 19 : 1; 20 : 3; 26 : 4; 27 : 3, 22; Eccl. 4 : 5; 5 : 1, 3; 7 : 4, 9; 10 : 2, 14; Isa. 44 : 25; Matt. 7 : 26; 23 : 17; 25 : 2; Luke 12 : 20; Rom. 1 : 22.
1 Sam. 26 : 21, I have played the f.
2 Sam. 3 : 33, died Abner as a f. dieth ?
Ps. 14 : 1; 53 : 1, f. said in his heart.
   92 : 6, neither doth f. understand this.
Prov. 1 : 7, f. despise wisdom.
   10 : 8, 10, a prating f. shall fall.
   10 : 21, f. die for want of wisdom.
   11 : 29, the f. shall be servant to the wise.
   12 : 15, way of f. right in own eyes.
   13 : 20, companion of f. shall be destroyed.
   14 : 9, f. make a mock at sin.
   15 : 5, a f. despiseth his father's instruction.
   16 : 22, the instruction of f. is folly.
   17 : 28, a f., when he holdeth his peace, is counted wise.
   18 : 2, a f. hath no delight in understanding.
   20 : 3, every f. will be meddling.
   29 : 11, a f. uttereth all his mind.

Eccl. 2 : 14, f. walketh in darkness.
2 : 16, no remembrance of wise more than f.
5 : 3, a f. voice known by multitude of words.
7 : 4, heart of f. in house of mirth.
Isa. 35 : 8, wayfaring men, though f.
Jer. 17 : 11, at his end he shall be a f.
Matt. 5 : 22, whoso shall say, thou f.
23 : 17; Luke 11 : 40, ye f. and blind.
Luke 12 : 20, thou f., this night.
24 : 25, O f., and slow of heart.
1 Cor. 3 : 18, let him become a f.
15 : 36, thou f. that thou sowest.
2 Cor. 11 : 16, let no man think me a f.
12 : 11, I am become a f. in glorying.
Eph. 5 : 15, walk not as f., but as wise.
Foolish, Deut. 32 : 6, O f. people.
2 Sam. 24 : 10; 1 Chr. 21 : 8, I have done
very f.
Job 1 : 22, nor charged God f.
2 : 10, as one of the f. women.
5 : 3, I have seen the f. taking root.
Ps. 5 : 5, f. not stand in thy sight.
73 : 3, I was envious at the f.
Prov. 9 : 6, forsake the f., and live.
17 : 25; 19 : 13, a f. son is grief.
Eccl. 7 : 17, neither be thou f.
Jer. 4 : 22, my people are f.
Matt. 7 : 26, be likened unto a f. man.
25 : 2, five were wise, and five f.
Rom. 1 : 21, their f. heart was darkened.
2 : 20, an instructor of the f.
1 Cor. 1 : 20, made f. wisdom of this world.
Gal. 3 : 1, O f. Galatians.
Eph. 5 : 4, nor f. talking.
2 Tim. 2 : 23; Titus 3 : 9, f. questions avoid.
Titus 3 : 3, we were sometimes f.
Foolishness, the Gospel so designated, 1 Cor.
1 : 18; 2 : 14.
worldly wisdom is, with God, 1 Cor. 1 : 20;
2 : 7; 3 : 19.
2 Sam. 15 : 31, counsel into f.
Ps. 69 : 5, O God, thou knowest my f.
Prov. 22 : 15, f. is bound in heart of child.
24 : 9, thought of f. is sin.
Eccl. 10 : 13, the beginning of words is f.
1 Cor. 1 : 18, to them that perish f.
1 : 21, the f. of preaching.
1 : 23, Christ crucified, to Greeks f.
1 : 25, the f. of God is wiser than men.
2 : 14, things of Spirit are f. to him.
3 : 19, wisdom of world f. with God.
Foot, Gen. 41 : 44, without thee no man lift f.
Deut. 8 : 4, nor did thy f. swell.
29 : 5, shoe is not waxen old on f.
Ps. 26 : 12, my f. standeth in an even place.
38 : 16, when my f. slippeth.
66 : 6, went through the flood on f.
91 : 12; Matt. 4 : 6; Luke 4 : 11, dash f.
against a stone.
Ps. 121 : 3, not suffer f. to be moved.
Prov. 3 : 23, thy f. shall not stumble.
4 : 27, remove thy f. from evil.
25 : 17, withdraw f. from neighbour's house.
Eccl. 5 : 1, keep thy f. when thou goest.
Isa. 1 : 6, from sole of f. to head no soundness.
Matt. 5 : 13, salt trodden under f.
14 : 13, people followed on f.
18 : 8; Mark 9 : 45, if thy f. offend thee.
John 11 : 44, dead, bound hand and f.

1 Cor. 12 : 15, if the f. say, because I am not.
Heb. 10 : 29, trodden under f. the Son of God.
Footsteps, Ps. 17 : 5, that my f. slip not.
Ps. 77 : 19, thy f. are not known.
89 : 51, f. of thine anointed.
Footstool of God : the temple so called, 1 Chr.
28 : 2; Ps. 99 : 5; 132 : 7.
the earth called, Isa. 66 : 1; Matt. 5 : 35;
Acts 7 : 49.
God's enemies made, Ps. 110 : 1; Matt.
22 : 44; Heb. 10 : 13.
Forbear, 2 Chr. 35 : 21, f. from meddling with
God.
Neh. 9 : 30, many years didst thou f. them.
Job 16 : 6, though I f., what am I eased ?
Ezek. 2 : 5; 3 : 11, whether hear or f.
1 Cor. 9 : 6, power to f. working ?
Eph. 4 : 2; Col. 3 : 13, f. one another in love.
1 Thess. 3 : 1, we could no longer f.
Forbearance, exhortations to, Matt. 18 : 33;
Eph. 4 : 2; 6 : 9; Col. 3 : 13; 2 Tim.
2 : 24.
of God, Ps. 50 : 21; Isa. 30 : 18; Rom.
2 : 4; 3 : 25; 1 Pet. 3 : 20; 2 Pet. 3 : 9.
Forbid, Num. 11 : 28, Joshua said f. them.
Mark 9 : 39; Luke 9 : 50, f. him not.
Mark 10 : 14; Luke 18 : 16, suffer little chil-
dren and f. them not.
Luke 6 : 29, f. not to take coat.
23 : 2, f. to give tribute.
Acts 10 : 47, can any f. water ?
1 Cor. 14 : 39, f. not to speak with tongues.
1 Thess. 2 : 16, f. us to speak to Gentiles.
Force, Deut. 34 : 7, nor natural f. abated.
Ezra 4 : 23, made them cease by f.
Matt. 11 : 12, the violent take it by f.
John 6 : 15, perceived they would take him
by f.
Heb. 9 : 17, a testament is of f. after.
Forefathers, Jer. 11 : 10, turned to iniquities of f.
2 Tim. 1 : 3, whom I serve from my f.
Forehead, Ex. 28 : 38, it shall always be on his f.
1 Sam. 17 : 49, stone sunk in his f.
Ezek. 3 : 9, as adamant I made thy f.
16 : 12, put jewel on thy f.
Rev. 7 : 3; 9 : 4, sealed in their f.
22 : 4, his name shall be in their f.
Foreigner, Ex. 12 : 45, a f. not eat thereof.
Deut. 15 : 3, of a f. exact it again.
Eph. 2 : 19, ye are no more f.
Foreknow, Rom. 8 : 29, whom he did f., he also.
11 : 2, not cast away people he f.
Foreknowledge of God, Acts 2 : 23; Rom.
8 : 29; 11 : 2; Gal. 3 : 8; 1 Pet. 1 : 2.
Foreordained, 1 Pet. 1 : 20, who verily was f.
Forerunner, Heb. 6 : 20, whither f. is for us
entered.
Foresee, Prov. 22 : 3; 27 : 12, prudent man f.
the evil.
Gal. 3 : 8, the scripture f. that God.
Forest, Ps. 50 : 10, every beast of f. is mine.
104 : 20, beasts of f. do creep forth.
Isa. 29 : 17; 32 : 15, field esteemed as f.
44 : 23, break forth into singing, O f.
Jer. 5 : 6, lion out of f. shall slay them.
21 : 14, will kindle a fire in the f.
26 : 18; Mic. 3 : 12, high places of the f.
Jer. 46 : 23, they shall cut down her f.
Amos 3 : 4, will a lion roar in the f. ?

Forewarn, Luke 12 : 5, will f. whom ye shall fear.
1 Thess. 4 : 6, as we also have f. you.
Forgat, Judg. 3 : 7, children of Israel f. Lord.
Ps. 78 : 11, they f. his works.
106 : 21, f. God their Saviour.
Lam. 3 : 17, I f. prosperity.
Forgave, Ps. 32 : 5, f. iniquity of my sin.
78 : 38, he f. their iniquity.
Matt. 18 : 27, f. him the debt.
Luke 7 : 42, he frankly f. them both.
2 Cor. 2 : 10, if I f. anything, for your sakes, f. I it.
Col. 3 : 13, as Christ f. you, so do ye.
Forget, Deut. 4 : 9, lest thou f. things eyes have seen.
6 : 12; 8 : 11, beware lest thou f. the Lord.
2 Ki. 17 : 38, covenant ye shall not f.
Job 8 : 13, so are the paths of all that f. God.
Ps. 9 : 17, all nations that f. God.
10 : 12, O Lord, f. not the humble.
13 : 1, how long wilt thou f. me ?
50 : 22, consider, ye that f. God.
74 : 19, f. not congregation of thy poor.
78 : 7, that they might not f. works of God.
102 : 4, I f. to eat my bread.
103 : 2, f. not all his benefits.
137 : 5, if I f. thee, O Jerusalem.
Prov. 2 : 17, f. the covenant of her God.
3 : 1, f. not my law.
31 : 5, lest they drink, and f. law.
Isa. 49 : 15, can a woman f. child ?
51 : 13, f. Lord thy Maker.
Jer. 2 : 32, can a maid f. her ornaments ?
23 : 27, cause my people to f. my name.
Lam. 5 : 20, why dost f. us for ever ?
Phil. 3 : 13, f. those things which are behind.
Heb. 6 : 10, God not unrighteous to f.
13 : 16, to communicate f. not.
Jas. 1 : 24, f. what manner of man.
Forgetfulness of God, condemned, Deut. 4 : 9;
6 : 12; Ps. 78 : 7; 103 : 2; Prov. 3 : 1;
4 : 5; 31 : 5; Heb. 13 : 16.
punishment of, Job 8 : 13; Ps. 9 : 17; 50 : 22;
Isa. 17 : 10; Jer. 2 : 32; Hos. 8 : 14.
Forgive, Ex. 32 : 32, if thou wilt f. their sin.
34 : 7; Num. 14 : 18, f. iniquity and transgression.
1 Ki. 8 : 30; 2 Chr. 6 : 21, hearest, f.
2 Chr. 7 : 14, then will I hear, and f.
Ps. 25 : 18, f. all my sins.
32 : 1; Rom. 4 : 7, whose transgression is f.
Ps. 86 : 5, good and ready to f.
103 : 3, who f. all thine iniquities.
Jer. 31 : 34, I will f. their iniquity.
Dan. 9 : 19, O Lord, hear, O Lord, f.
Matt. 6 : 12; Luke 11 : 4, f. us, as we f.
Matt. 9 : 6; Mark 2 : 10; Luke 5 : 24, power to f. sins.
Matt. 18 : 35, if he from your hearts f. not.
Mark 2 : 7; Luke 5 : 21, who can f. sins ?
Mark 11 : 25, f. that your Father may f.
Luke 6 : 37, f., and ye shall be f.
7 : 49, who is this f. sins also ?
17 : 3, if brother repent, f. him.
23 : 34, Father f. them, they know not.
2 Cor. 2 : 7, ye ought rather to f.
2 : 10, to whom ye f. I f. also.
Eph. 4 : 32, as God hath f. you.

Col. 2 : 13, quickened, having f. all trespasses.
1 John 1 : 9, faithful and just to f.
Forgiveness, mutual, commanded, Gen. 50 : 17;
Matt. 5 : 23; 6 : 14; 18 : 21, 35; Mark
11 : 25; Luke 11 : 4; 17 : 4; 2 Cor. 2 : 7;
Eph. 4 : 32; Col. 3 : 13; Jas. 2 : 13.
of enemies, Matt. 5 : 44; Luke 6 : 27; Rom.
12 : 14, 19.
of sin, prayed for, Ex. 32 : 32; 1 Ki. 8 : 30;
2 Chr. 6 : 21; Ps. 25 : 18; 32; 51; 79 : 9;
130; Dan. 9 : 19; Amos 7 : 2; Matt.
6 : 12.
promised, Lev. 4 : 20; 2 Chr. 7 : 14; Isa.
33 : 24; 55 : 7; Jer. 3 : 12; 31 : 20, 34;
33 : 8; Ezek. 36 : 25; Hos. 14 : 4; Mic.
7 : 18; Luke 24 : 47; Acts 5 : 31; 26 : 18;
Eph. 1 : 7; Col. 1 : 14; Jas. 5 : 15; 1 John
1 : 9.
Ps. 130 : 4, f. with thee, that thou mayest be feared.
Dan. 9 : 9, to the Lord our God belong f.
Mark 3 : 29, hath never f.
Acts 5 : 31, exalted to give f.
13 : 38, through this man is preached f. of sins.
Eph. 1 : 7; Col. 1 : 14, in whom we have f.
Forgotten, Deut. 32 : 18, f. God that formed thee.
Job 19 : 14, my familiar friends have f. me.
Ps. 9 : 18, needy not always be f.
10 : 11, said in heart, God hath f.
31 : 12, I am f. as a dead man.
42 : 9, why hast thou f. me ?
44 : 20, if we have f. name of our God.
77 : 9, hath God f. to be gracious ?
119 : 61, I have not f. thy law.
Eccl. 2 : 16, in days to come all f.
9 : 5, memory of them is f.
Isa. 17 : 10, f. the God of thy salvation.
49 : 14, Zion said, Lord hath f. me.
65 : 16, the former troubles are f.
Jer. 2 : 32; 13 : 25; 18 : 15, my people have f.
3 : 21, have f. the Lord their God.
30 : 14, all thy lovers have f. thee.
50 : 6, have f. their restingplace.
Ezek. 22 : 12; 23 : 35, thou hast f. me.
Hos. 8 : 14, Israel hath f. his Maker.
Matt. 16 : 5; Mark 8 : 14, f. to take bread.
Luke 12 : 6, not one f. before God.
Heb. 12 : 5, ye have f. the exhortation.
2 Pet. 1 : 9, f. that he was purged.
Form, Gen. 1 : 2, the earth was without f.
1 Sam. 28 : 14, what f. is he of ?
Job 4 : 16, I could not discern the f.
Isa. 52 : 14, his f. more than sons of men.
53 : 2, he hath no f. nor comeliness.
Ezek. 10 : 8, the f. of a man's hand.
43 : 11, shew them f. of the house.
Dan. 3 : 19, f. of visage changed.
3 : 25, f. of fourth like Son of God.
Mark 16 : 12, he appeared in another f.
Rom. 2 : 20, hast f. of knowledge.
6 : 17, obeyed that f. of doctrine.
Phil. 2 : 6, being in f. of God.
2 Tim. 1 : 13, f. of sound words.
3 : 5, having a f. of godliness.
Formed, Gen. 2 : 7, God f. man of the dust.
Deut. 32 : 18, forgotten God that f. thee.
2 Ki. 19 : 25; Isa. 37 : 26, that I have f. it.

Job 26 : 13, his hand f. crooked serpent.
33 : 6, I also am f. of clay.
Ps. 90 : 2, or ever thou hadst f. the earth.
94 : 9, he that f. the eye.
95 : 5, his hands f. the dry land.
Prov. 26 : 10, great God that f. all things.
Isa. 43 : 1, he that f. thee, O Israel.
43 : 7; 44 : 21, I have f. him.
43 : 10, before me was no god f.
43 : 21, this people have I f. for myself.
44 : 2, f. thee from the womb.
45 : 18, God that f. the earth.
54 : 17, no weapon f. against thee.
Rom. 9 : 20, shall thing f. say to him that f. it.
Gal. 4 : 19, till Christ be f. in you.
Former, 1 Sam. 17 : 30, answered after f. manner.
Job 8 : 8, inquire of the f. age.
Ps. 79 : 8, remember not f. iniquities.
89 : 49, where are thy f. lovingkindnesses ?
Eccl. 1 : 11, no remembrance of f. things.
7 : 10, f. days better than these.
Isa. 42 : 9, f. things are come to pass.
43 : 18, remember not the f. things.
46 : 9, remember the f. things of old.
Isa. 48 : 3, declared f. things from beginning.
65 : 16, f. troubles are forgotten.
Jer. 5 : 24; Hos. 6 : 3; Joel 2 : 23, f. and latter rain.
Jer. 10 : 16; 51 : 19, the f. of all things.
Hag. 2 : 9, greater than glory of f. house.
Mal. 3 : 4, pleasant as in f. years.
Eph. 4 : 22, concerning the f. conversation.
Rev. 21 : 4, the f. things are passed away.
Fornication denounced, Ex. 22 : 16; Lev. 19 : 20; Num. 25; Deut. 22 : 21; 23 : 17; Prov. 2 : 16; 5 : 3; 6 : 25; 7; 9 : 13; 22 : 14; 23 : 27; 29 : 3; 31 : 3; Eccl. 7 : 26; Hos. 4 : 11; Matt. 15 : 19; Mark 7 : 21; Acts 15 : 20; Rom. 1 : 29; 1 Cor. 5 : 9; 6 : 9; 2 Cor. 12 : 21; Gal. 5 : 19; Eph. 5 : 5; Col. 3 : 5; 1 Thess. 4 : 3; 1 Tim. 1 : 10; Heb. 13 : 4; 1 Pet. 4 : 3; Jude 7; Rev. 2 : 14; 21 : 8; 22 : 15.
spiritual, idolatry, etc., Ezek. 16 : 29; Hos. 1; 2; 3; Rev. 14 : 8; 17 : 2; 18 : 3; 19 : 2.
Forsake, Deut. 4 : 31; 31 : 6; 1 Chr. 28 : 20, he will not f. thee.
Deut. 31 : 16, this people will f. me.
32 : 15, he f. God that made him.
Josh. 1 : 5; Heb. 13 : 5, I will not fail nor f. thee.
1 Chr. 28 : 9, if thou f. him, he will cast thee off.
2 Chr. 15 : 2, if ye f. him, he will f. you.
Neh. 10 : 39, we will not f. house of our God.
13 : 11, why is house of God f. ?
Job 6 : 14, he f. fear of the Almighty.
Ps. 22 : 1; Matt. 27 : 46; Mark 15 : 34, why hast thou f. me ?
Ps. 37 : 8, cease from anger, f. wrath.
37 : 25, not seen the righteous f.
94 : 14, nor will he f. his inheritance.
119 : 8, f. me not utterly.
138 : 8, f. not works of thine own hands.
Prov. 2 : 17, f. the guide of her youth.
4 : 6, f. her not, she shall preserve thee.
Isa. 17 : 9, as a f. bough.
32 : 14; Jer. 4 : 29; Ezek. 36 : 4, f. city.

Isa. 55 : 7, let the wicked f. his way.
62 : 4, no more be termed f.
Jer. 2 : 13; 17 : 13, f. fountain of living waters.
Matt. 19 : 27; Luke 5 : 11, we have f. all.
Matt. 26 : 56; Mark 14 : 50, disciples f. him, and fled.
Luke 14 : 33, whoso f. not all he hath.
2 Cor. 4 : 9, persecuted, but not f.
Heb. 10 : 25, not f. assembling of ourselves.
11 : 27, by faith Moses f. Egypt.
2 Pet. 2 : 15, have f. right way.
Forsaking God, danger of, Deut. 28 : 20; Judg. 10 : 13; 2 Chr. 15 : 2; 24 : 20; Ezra 8 : 22; 9 : 10; Isa. 1 : 28; Jer. 1 : 16; 5 : 19; 17 : 13; Ezek. 9 : 9.
Forswear, Matt. 5 : 33, not f. thyself.
Forth, Gen. 1 : 11, 12, earth bring f. grass.
Gen. 8 : 10, sent f. his dove.
Ex. 8 : 5, stretch f. thine hand.
2 Sam. 19 : 7, arise, go f.
Job 14 : 2, cometh f. like a flower.
Ps. 19 : 6, his going f. is from the end.
113 : 2; 115 : 18, this time f. and for evermore.
Prov. 27 : 1, knowest not what a day may bring f.
Isa. 11 : 1, there shall come f. a rod.
49 : 13; 54 : 1, break f. into singing.
Matt. 13 : 3, sower went f. to sow.
Luke 6 : 8, arose and stood f.
Rom. 7 : 4, 5, bring f. fruit.
Fortress, the Lord compared to a, 2 Sam. 22 : 2; Ps. 18 : 2; Jer. 16 : 19.
Fortunatus (fôr-tū-nā-tŭs) [fortunate], ministers to Paul, 1 Cor. 16 : 17.
Forty days, period of the flood, Gen. 7 : 17.
giving of the law, Ex. 24 : 18.
spying land of Canaan, Num. 13 : 25.
Goliath's defiance, 1 Sam. 17 : 16.
Elijah's journey to Horeb, 1 Ki. 19 : 8.
Jonah's warning to Nineveh, Jonah 3 : 4.
fasting of Christ, Matt. 4 : 2; Mark 1 : 13; Luke 4 : 2.
Christ's appearance during, Acts 1 : 3.
Forty stripes, Deut. 25 : 3; save one, 2 Cor. 11 : 24.
Forty years, manna sent, etc., Ex. 16 : 35; Num. 14 : 33; Ps. 95 : 10.
of peace, Judg. 3 : 11; 5 : 31; 8 : 28.
Forward, Job 23 : 8, I go f., but he is not there.
Jer. 7 : 24, backward, and not f.
Ezek. 1 : 9; 10 : 22, every one straight f.
Mark 14 : 35, went f. a little.
Gal. 2 : 10, I also was f. to do.
Forwardness, 2 Cor. 9 : 2, know the f. of your mind.
Fought, Josh. 10 : 14, the Lord f. for Israel.
Josh. 23 : 3, he that f. for you.
1 Cor. 15 : 32, have f. with beasts.
2 Tim. 4 : 7, I have f. a good fight.
Foul, Job 16 : 16, my face is f. with weeping.
Matt. 16 : 3, it will be f. weather.
Mark 9 : 25, he rebuked the f. spirit.
Rev. 18 : 2, Babylon, hold of every f. spirit.
Found, Gen. 6 : 8, Noah f. grace in eyes of the Lord.
8 : 9, the dove f. no rest.
27 : 20, how hast thou f. it so quickly ?
44 : 16, God hath f. out the iniquity.

Num. 15 : 32, **f.** a man gathering sticks.
1 Ki. 21 : 20, hast thou **f.** me, mine enemy?
2 Ki. 22 : 8, I **f.** book of the law.
2 Chr. 19 : 3, good things **f.** in thee.
Job 33 : 24, I have **f.** a ransom.
Ps. 32 : 6, when thou mayest be **f.**
69 : 20, comforters, but **f.** none.
84 : 3, sparrow hath **f.** an house.
107 : 4, **f.** no city to dwell in.
Eccl. 7 : 28, one man among a thousand have I **f.**
Song of Sol. 3 : 4, I **f.** him whom my soul loveth.
Isa. 65 : 1; Rom. 10 : 20, **f.** of them that sought me not.
Ezek. 22 : 30, I sought for a man, but **f.** none.
Dan. 5 : 27, weighed, and **f.** wanting.
Matt. 8 : 10; Luke 7 : 9, not **f.** so great faith.
Matt. 13 : 46, **f.** one pearl of great price.
20 : 6, **f.** others standing idle.
21 : 19; Mark 11 : 13; Luke 13 : 6, **f.** nothing thereon.
Matt. 26 : 43; Mark 14 : 40; Luke 22 : 45, he **f.** them asleep.
Mark 7 : 2, they **f.** fault.
Luke 2 : 46, they **f.** him in the temple.
7 : 10, they **f.** the servant whole.
15 : 6, I have **f.** the sheep.
15 : 9, I have **f.** the piece of money.
15 : 32, was lost, and is **f.**
23 : 14, I have **f.** no fault.
24 : 2, **f.** the stone rolled away.
John 1 : 41, 45, we have **f.** the Messias.
Acts 7 : 11, our fathers **f.** no sustenance.
9 : 2, if he **f.** any of this way.
17 : 23, I **f.** an altar with inscription.
24 : 5, **f.** this man a pestilent fellow.
Rom. 7 : 10, to life, I **f.** to be unto death.
1 Cor. 15 . 15, we are **f.** false witnesses.
Phil. 2 : 8, **f.** in fashion as a man.
Heb. 11 : 5, Enoch was not **f.**
12 : 17, he **f.** no place of repentance.
Rev. 3 : 2, not **f.** thy works perfect.
Foundation, Christ the one, Isa. 28 : 16, I lay in Zion for a **f.** a stone; Ps. 118 : 22; Matt. 21 : 42; Acts 4 : 11; Rom. 9 : 33; 1 Cor. 3 : 11; Eph. 2 : 20; 1 Pet. 2 : 6.
of the world, Matt. 13 : 35, kept secret from **f.** of the world.
John 17 : 24, lovedst me before **f.** of the world.
Heb. 4 : 3, works finished from **f.** of world.
Rev. 13 : 8, Lamb slain from **f.** of world. (Matt. 25 : 34; Luke 11 : 50; Eph. 1 : 4; 9 : 26; 1 Pet. 1 : 20; Rev. 17 : 8).
stones of New Jerusalem, jasper, sapphire, chalcedony, emerald, sardonyx, sardius, chrysolite, beryl, topaz, chrysoprasus, jacinth, amethyst (Rev. 21 : 19, **f.**). See **Precious Stones.**
Josh. 6 : 26; 1 Ki. 16 : 34, lay the **f.** in firstborn.
2 Sam. 22 : 16; Ps. 18 : 7, 15, **f.** were discovered.
Job 4 : 19, whose **f.** is in the dust.
38 : 4, when I laid **f.** of earth ?
Ps. 11 : 3, if **f.** be destroyed.
82 : 5, all the **f.** out of course.
102 : 25, of old laid **f.** of earth.

137 : 7, rase it even to the **f.**
Prov. 10 : 25, righteous an everlasting **f.**
48 : 13, my hand laid **f.** of the earth.
58 : 12, the **f.** of many generations.
Luke 6 : 48, laid the **f.** on a rock (cf. 49).
14 : 29, lest haply, after he hath laid the **f.**
Rom. 15 : 20, build on another man's **f.**
1 Cor. 3 : 10, wise masterbuilder, laid **f.**
3 : 11, other **f.** can no man lay (cf. 12).
Eph. 2 : 20, on the **f.** of the apostles and prophets.
1 Tim. 6 : 19, laying up a good **f.**
2 Tim. 2 : 19, the **f.** of God standeth sure.
Heb. 1 : 10, hast laid the **f.** of the earth.
6 : 1, not laying **f.** of repentance.
Rev. 21 : 14, walls of the city had twelve **f.**
Founder, Judg. 17 : 4; Jer. 6 : 29; 10 : 9, 14 **f.**; 51 : 17.
Fountain, of life, Ps. 36 : 9, with thee is the **f.** of life.
Prov. 13 : 14, the law of the wise a **f.** of life.
14 : 27, fear of the Lord a **f.** of life.
of living waters, Jer. 2 : 13; 17 : 13, forsaken the **f.** of living waters (cf. Ps. 36 : 9; Joel 3 : 18; Zech. 14 : 8; Rev. 7 : 17).
Gen. 7 : 11; 8 : 2, **f.** of deep.
16 : 7, found Hagar by a **f.**
Deut. 8 : 7, a land of **f.**
Ps. 114 : 8, flint into a **f.** of waters.
Prov. 5 : 18, let thy **f.** be blessed.
8 : 24, no **f.** abounding with water.
25 : 26, as a troubled **f.**
Eccl. 12 : 6, pitcher broken at the **f.**
Song of Sol. 4 : 12, a **f.** sealed.
4 : 15, a **f.** of gardens.
Jer. 9 : 1, mine eyes a **f.** of tears.
Zech. 13 : 1, in that day shall be a **f.** opened.
Mark 5 : 29, **f.** of her blood dried up.
Jas. 3 : 11, doth a **f.** send forth ?
Rev. 7 : 17, lead them to living **f.**
21 : 6, of the **f.** of the water of life freely (cf. Isa. 12 : 3; 44 : 3; 51 : 1; John 4 : 10; Rev. 7 : 17).
Four, living creatures, vision of, Ezek. 1 : 5-14; 10 : 10-14; Rev. 4 : 6-8; 5 : 14; 6 : 1-7.
kingdoms, Daniel's vision of, Dan. 7 : 3-28; 8 : 22. See **Daniel, Book of.**
Nebuchadnezzar's vision of, Dan. 2 : 36-45.
winds, Dan. 7 : 2, **f.** winds strove on the sea. (Ezek. 37 : 9; Dan. 11 : 4; Matt. 24 : 31; Mark 13 : 27).
Fourfold compensation, Ex. 22 : 1; 2 Sam. 12 : 6; Luke 19 : 8.
Fourfooted beasts, Acts 10 : 12; 11 : 6; Rom. 1 : 23.
Four thousand, Matt. 15 : 38; Mark 8 : 9; 8 : 20; 16 : 10; Acts 21 : 38.
Fourscore, Ex. 7 : 7; 2 Sam. 19 : 32; Ps. 90 : 10; Jer. 41 : 5; Luke 16 : 7.
Foursquare, Ex. 28 : 16; Ezek. 48 : 20; Rev. 21 : 16.
Fowl, winged, Gen. 1 : 21; Deut. 4 : 17.
Gen. 1 : 20; 7 : 8; Ps. 104 : 12; 148 : 10; Matt. 6 : 26; 13 : 4; Luke 12 : 24; Acts 10 : 12. See **Cock and Hen.**
Fowler, Ps. 91 : 3; 124 : 7; Prov. 6 : 5; Hos. 9 : 8.
Fox. Under this term it is probable both foxes (Canis vulpes) and jackals (C. aureus) are

comprehended; the former are more or less solitary in their habits; the latter hunt in packs. While both are omnivorous, the fox prefers to capture his prey; the jackal will eat carrion; foxes will destroy grapes. The three hundred animals caught by Samson were no doubt jackals (Judg. 15 : 4). Jackals hide among rocks, foxes in holes of the earth (Matt. 8 : 20). Both animals are very common in Palestine.
Samson's stratagem with, Judg. 15 : 4.
Neh. 4 : 3; Ps. 63 : 10; Song of Sol. 2 : 15; Lam. 5 : 18; Ezek. 13 : 4; Matt. 8 : 20; Luke 9 : 58; 13 : 32.

Fragments, Matt. 14 : 20; Mark 6 : 43; Luke 9 : 17; John 6 : 13, took up the f.
Mark 8 : 19, how many baskets of f. ?
John 6 : 12, gather up f. that remain.

Frail, Ps. 39 : 4, may know how f. I am.

Frame, Judg. 12 : 6, could not f. to pronounce it.
Ps. 50 : 19, thy tongue f. deceit.
94 : 20, f. mischief by a law.
103 : 14, he knoweth our f.
Isa. 29 : 16, shall thing f. say of him that f. it.
Ezek. 40 : 2, was as the f. of a city.
Eph. 2 : 21, in whom the building fitly f.
Heb. 11 : 3, worlds f. by word of God. (Jer. 18 : 11; Hos. 5 : 4.)

Frankincense, a resinous gum, bitter to taste, obtained as a milky exudation from various trees of the genus " Boswellia," an ally of the terebinth. It burns with a steady flame for a long time; and it derives its name from the " freeness " with which it gives off its delightful odour. Found, according to Herodotus, in Arabia only (cf. Isa. 60 : 6; Jer. 6 : 20, R.V.), it is now known to be in tropical Africa. It was used, sometimes as a constituent of incense (Ex. 30 : 34), for sacrificial fumigation. Often in association with myrrh (Song of Sol. 3 : 6; 4 : 6), it was presented as one of the gifts of the wise men to Jesus (Matt. 2 : 11). It was offered with the shewbread (Lev. 24 : 7), and became a usual accompaniment of the meat offering (cf. Jer. 6 : 20, R.V.). An ancient commentator records that it was the symbol of deity (Jer. 6 : 20) as gold was of kingship and myrrh of mortification.
It should be read for " incense " in six passages, viz. : Isa. 43 : 23; 60 : 6; 66 : 3; Jer. 6 : 20; 17 : 26; 41 : 5.
See also Lev. 2 : 1; Rev. 18 : 13.

Frankly, Luke 7 : 42, he f. forgave them both.

Fraud condemned, Lev. 19 : 13; Mal. 3 : 5; Mark 10 : 19; 1 Cor. 6 : 8; 1 Thess. 4 : 6. See **Deceit.**
Ps. 10 : 7, mouth is full of f.
Jas. 5 : 4, hire kept back by f.

Fray, now obsolete, is a shortened form of " afray " (ptcp. " afraid," in use), Deut. 28 : 26; Jer. 7 : 33; Zech. 1 : 21.

Freckled, Lev. 13 : 39, it is a f. spot.

Free, Ex. 21 : 2; Deut. 15 : 12, in seventh year go out f.
Deut. 24 : 5, shall be f. at home one year.
2 Chr. 29 : 31, as were of f. heart offered.
Ps. 51 : 12, uphold me with thy f. Spirit.
88 : 5, f. among the dead.

Isa. 58 : 6, to let the oppressed go f.
Matt. 17 : 26, then are the children f.
Mark 7 : 11, say it is Corban, he shall be f.
John 8 : 32, truth shall make you f.
8 : 36, if Son make you f., ye shall be f.
Acts 22 : 28, I was f. born.
Rom. 5 : 15, not as offence, so is f. gift.
6 : 18, being made f. from sin.
8 : 2, f. from the law of sin and death.
1 Cor. 9 : 1, am I not f. ?
12 : 13; Eph. 6 : 8, whether bond or f.
Gal. 3 : 28; Col. 3 : 11, there is neither bond nor f.
Gal. 5 : 1, liberty wherewith Christ made us f.
2 Thess. 3 : 1, word have f. course.
1 Pet. 2 : 16, as f., and not using liberty.
Rev. 19 : 18, both bond and f.

Freely, Gen. 2 : 16, of every tree f. eat.
Hos. 14 : 4, I will love them f.
Matt. 10 : 8, f. ye have received, f. give.
Rom. 3 : 24, justified f. by his grace.
8 : 32, with him f. give us all things.
2 Cor. 11 : 7, preached the gospel of God f.
Rev. 21 : 6, of the fountain of the water of life f.
22 : 17, water of life f.

Freeman, 1 Cor. 7 : 22, the Lord's f.
Rev. 6 : 15, bond and f. hid themselves.

Freewill offerings, Lev. 22 : 18; Num. 15 : 3; Deut. 16 : 10; Ezra 3 : 5; 7 : 16; 8 : 28.

Freewoman and bondwoman, allegory of, Gal. 4 : 22-31.

Frequent, 2 Cor. 11 : 23, in prisons more f.

Fresh, Num. 11 : 8; Job 29 : 20; 33 : 25; Ps. 92 : 10; Jas. 3 : 12.

Fret, Ps. 37 : 1, 7, 8; Prov. 24 : 19, f. not thyself.
Prov. 19 : 3, his heart f. against the Lord.
Isa. 8 : 21, when hungry they shall f.

Friend of God, title of Abraham, 2 Chr. 20 : 7; Isa. 41 : 8; Jas. 2 : 23.

Friends, advantages of, Prov. 18 : 24; 27 : 6, 9, 17; John 15 : 13.
danger arising from evil, Deut. 13 : 6; Prov. 22 : 24; 25 : 19; Mic. 7 : 5; Zech. 13 : 6.
the disciples so called, Luke 12 : 4; John 15 : 14; 3 John 14.
Ex. 33 : 11, as a man to his f.
Deut. 13 : 6, if thy f. entice thee.
2 Sam. 19 : 6, lovest thine enemies, and hatest f.
Job 6 : 14, pity be shewed from his f.
19 : 14, my f. have forgotten me.
42 : 10, when he prayed for his f.
Ps. 35 : 14, as though he had been my f.
41 : 9, my familiar f. hath lifted heel.
88 : 18, lover and f. hast put far from me.
Prov. 6 : 1, if thou be surety for thy f.
14 : 20, the rich hath many f.
17 : 17, a f. loveth at all times.
18 : 24, a f. that sticketh closer than a brother.
19 : 4, wealth maketh many f.
27 : 6, faithful are wounds of a f.
27 : 17, man sharpeneth countenance of his f.
Song of Sol. 5 : 16, beloved, this is my f.
Isa. 41 : 8, seed of Abraham my f.
Lam. 1 : 2, her f. have dealt treacherously.
Mic. 7 : 5, trust not in a f.

Matt. 11 : 19; Luke 7 : 34, a **f.** of publicans.
Matt. 20 : 13, **f.**, I do thee no wrong.
22 : 12, **f.**, how camest thou hither ?
26 : 50, **f.**, wherefore art thou come ?
Mark 3 : 21, when his **f.** heard of it.
5 : 19, Jesus saith, go home to thy **f.**
Luke 11 : 5, which of you shall have a **f.**
14 : 10, **f.**, go up higher.
14 : 12, a dinner, call not thy **f.**
16 : 9, **f.** of the mammon.
John 3 : 29, **f.** of bridegroom rejoiceth.
11 : 11, our **f.** Lazarus sleepeth.
15 : 13, lay down his life for his **f.**
19 : 12, thou art not Cæsar's **f.**
Jas. 2 : 23, Abraham was called the **f.** of God.
4 : 4, a **f.** of the world is the enemy of God.
Friends of Jesus, Matt. 10 : 2-4; 17 : 1 f.;
21 : 17; 26 : 14-17, 37-46, 50; 27 : 55-61;
Mark 5 : 37; 13 : 3 f.; Luke 8 : 1-3; 10 :
38-42; 12 : 4; John 1 : 35-51; 11; 12 : 1-7;
13 : 1-5, 23; 15 : 13-15; 19 : 27.
Friendship of Jonathan and David, 1 Sam.
18 : 1; 19; 20; 2 Sam. 1 : 26.
with the world, forbidden, Rom. 12 : 2;
2 Cor. 6 : 17; Jas. 4 : 4; 1 John 2 : 15.
Fringes, how worn, Num. 15 : 37 ff.; Deut.
22 : 12; Matt. 23 : 5. (cf. Matt. 9 : 20;
14 : 36; Mark 6 : 56; Luke 8 : 44.)
See **Hem.**
Fro, to and, Gen. 8 : 7; 2 Chr. 16 : 9; Job
1 : 7; Ps. 107 : 27; Isa. 24 : 20; Zech.
6 : 7; Eph. 4 : 14.

Egyptian Frogs.

Frogs are mentioned only in Ex. 8 : 2, 7; Ps.
78 : 45; 105 : 30, where the reference is to
the second plague of Egypt. They abounded
in the irrigation canals of Egypt, and in the
Holy Land there were many edible frogs
and green tree-frogs. In Rev. 16 : 13, they
are compared to unclean spirits.
Front, 2 Sam. 10 : 9, **f.** of battle against him.

Frontiers, Ezek. 25 : 9.
Frontlets, or **Phylacteries,** Ex. 13 : 16; Deut.
6 : 8; 11 : 18; Matt. 23 : 5. They were
ribands of parchment on which, in ink only
used for that purpose, were written four
passages of the law (Ex. 13 : 2-10, 11-17;
Deut. 6 : 4-9; 11 : 13-22). The strips were
then rolled up in cylinders of black calf-skin
and enclosed in a case of similar material.
This was attached to a small piece of leather
about one and a half inches square. The
case was closed by folding back the lower
half of the stiff piece of leather from which
it projected. At the fold room was left for
the passage of a long strap, blackened on
the upper side, which bound the phylactery
in position on the forehead. This strap
was knotted at the back of the head to
form the Hebrew letter " daleth." For the
arm there was also a phylactery, but unlike
the other its case consisted of a single com-
partment containing only one parchment
with the four passages thereon. It was
fastened by means of a strap to the bend of
the left arm, the loop forming the letter
" yod." These two letters together with the
" shin " which was written on two sides of
the case were supposed to form the sacred
name " Shaddai," " Almighty " (sh, dd, y).
At the age of three a Jewish boy put on
the fringed clothing (Num. 15 : 38); at
five he was taught the law, the creed (Deut.
6 : 4), the Hallel (Ps. 114–118, 136); on his
thirteenth birthday he became a member of
the Jewish Church, was brought to the
Synagogue on " the Sabbath of Phylacteries," and presented with the Phylacteries,
whioh ho honooforth woro at hio daily
prayer.
When Jesus said, " They make broad
their phylacteries " (Matt. 23 : 5), the reference was not to the phylactery itself, which
was of a prescribed breadth, but to the case
containing the parchment. To impress
people with their devotion (cf. Mark 7 : 3, 4,
Luke 5 : 33, etc.), the Pharisees made the
cases as large as possible and wore them
always. The common people reserved them
for times of prayer.
Frost, Gen. 31 : 40; Ex. 16 : 14; Job 37 : 10;
Ps. 78 : 47; Jer. 36 : 30.
Froward, Deut. 32 : 20, a very **f.** generation.
2 Sam. 22 : 27; Ps. 18 : 26, with **f.** wilt shew
thyself **f.**
Ps. 101 : 4, a **f.** heart shall depart.
Prov. 2 : 12, man that speaketh **f.** things.
3 : 32, the **f.** is abomination to the Lord.
4 : 24, put away **f.** mouth.
11 : 20; 17 : 20, a **f.** heart.
16 : 28, a **f.** man soweth strife.
21 : 8, the way of man is **f.**
22 : 5, thorns are in way of the **f.**
1 Pet. 2 : 18, servants, be subject to the **f.**
Frowardly, Isa. 57 : 17, went on **f.** in the way.
Frowardness, Prov. 2 : 14; 6 : 14; 10 : 32.
results of, Deut. 32 : 20; 2 Sam. 22 : 27; Job
5 : 13; Prov. 2 : 12; 3 : 32; 4 : 24; 10 : 31;
11 : 20; 16 : 28; 17 : 20; 21 : 8; 22 : 5.
Frozen, Job 38 : 30, face of the deep is **f.**

Fruit, first three years not to be touched, Lev. 19 : 23.

blessed to the obedient, Deut. 7 : 13; 28 : 4.

of faith meet for repentance, etc., Matt. 3 : 8; 7 : 16; John 4 : 36; 15 : 16; Rom. 7 : 4; 2 Cor. 9 : 10; Gal. 5 : 22; Col. 1 : 6; Heb. 12 : 11; Jas. 3 : 17.

Gen. 1 : 29, every tree in the which is f.

Num. 13 : 26, shewed them the f. of the land.

Deut. 26 : 2, take the first of all f.

Ps. 72 : 16, f. thereof shake like Lebanon.

132 : 11, of f. of thy body will I set upon thy throne.

Prov. 8 : 19, my f. is better than gold.

11 : 30, f. of the righteous a tree of life.

12 : 14; 18 : 20, satisfied by the f. of mouth.

Song of Sol. 2 : 3, his f. was sweet to my taste.

Isa. 3 : 10; Mic. 7 : 13, f. of their doings.

27 : 6, fill face of the world with f.

28 : 4, the hasty f. before summer.

57 : 19, I create the f. of the lips.

Jer. 17 : 10; 21 : 14; 32 : 19, according to f. of doings.

Hos. 10 : 13, ye have eaten the f. of lies.

Amos 8 : 1, a basket of summer f.

Mic. 6 : 7, f. of body for sin of soul.

Hab. 3 : 17, neither shall f. be in the vines.

Hag. 1 : 10, earth is stayed from her f.

Matt. 3 : 8; Luke 3 : 8, f. meet for repentance.

12 : 33, make tree good, and his f. good.

21 : 19, let no f. grow on thee.

26 : 29; Mark 14 : 25, drink of f. of the vine.

Mark 4 : 28, earth bringeth forth f. of herself.

Luke 13 : 7, I come seeking f. on this fig tree.

John 4 : 36, f. to life eternal.

15 : 4, branch cannot bear f. of itself.

Rom. 6 : 21, what f. had ye in those things ?

7 : 4, bring forth f. unto God.

Gal. 5 : 22; Eph. 5 : 9, the f. of the Spirit.

Phil. 4 : 17, I desire f. that may abound.

2 Tim. 2 : 6, first partaker of the f.

Heb. 12 : 11, peaceable f. of righteousness.

13 : 15, offer f. of our lips.

Jas. 5 : 7, waiteth for the precious f.

Jude 12, trees whose f. withereth, without f.

Fruit trees, to be preserved in time of war, Deut. 20 : 19.

Fruitful, Gen. 1 : 22; 35 : 11; Isa. 5 : 1; Ezek. 19 : 10; Hos. 13 : 15; Acts 14 : 17; Col. 1 : 10.

Frustrate, Ezra 4 : 5, hired to f. their purpose.

Isa. 44 : 25, f. the tokens of the liars.

Gal. 2 : 21, I do not f. the grace of God.

Fryingpan, Lev. 2 : 7; 7 : 9.

Fuel, Isa. 9 : 5, 19; Ezek. 15 : 4; 21 : 32.

Fugitive, servant, law of, Deut. 23 : 15.

cf. Gen. 4 : 12, 14; 1 Sam. 30 : 15; Ezek. 17 : 21.

Fulfil, Ps. 20 : 4, the Lord f. all thy counsel.

145 : 19, f. desire of them that fear him.

Matt. 3 : 15, to f. all righteousness.

5 : 17, not come to destroy, but to f.

5 : 18; 24 : 34, till all be f.

Mark 13 : 4, what sign when all shall be f. ?

Luke 21 : 22, all written may be f.

22 : 16, till it be f. in kingdom of God.

John 3 : 29; 17 : 13, my joy is f.

Acts 13 : 22, who shall f. all my will.

13 : 33, God hath f. the same unto us.

Rom. 8 : 4, righteousness of law be f. in us.

13 : 10, love is the f. of the law.

Gal. 5 : 14, all the law is f. in one word.

6 : 2, so f. the law of Christ.

Phil. 2 : 2, f. ye my joy.

Col. 1 : 25, to f. the Word of God.

2 Thess. 1 : 11, f. good pleasure of his goodness.

Jas. 2 : 8, if ye f. the royal law.

Rev. 20 : 3, till the thousand years be f.

Fulfilling, Ps. 148 : 8, stormy wind f. his word.

Rom. 13 : 10, love is the f. of the law.

Eph. 2 : 3, f. desires of flesh and mind.

Full, Num. 22 : 18; 24 : 13, give house f. of silver.

Deut. 6 : 11, houses f. of good things.

34 : 9, Joshua was f. of spirit of wisdom.

Ruth 1 : 21, I went out f.

2 Ki. 6 : 17, the mountain was f. of horses.

Job 5 : 26, come to grave in f. age.

14 : 1, of few days, and f. of trouble.

Ps. 10 : 7; Rom. 3 : 14, his mouth is f. of cursing.

Ps. 73 : 10, waters of a f. cup.

74 : 20, f. of habitations of cruelty.

119 : 64, the earth is f. of thy mercy.

Prov. 27 : 20, hell and destruction are never f.

30 : 9, lest I be f., and deny thee.

Eccl. 1 : 7, yet the sea is not f.

Isa. 1 : 11, I am f. of burnt offerings.

11 : 9, earth shall be f. of knowledge of the Lord.

Jer. 6 : 11, I am f. of the fury of the Lord.

Hab. 3 : 3, earth f. of his praise.

Zech. 8 : 5, streets f. of boys and girls.

Matt. 6 : 22; Luke 11 : 36, body f. of light.

Luke 6 : 25, woe unto you that are f.

John 1 : 14, f. of grace and truth.

15 : 11; 16 : 24, that your joy might be f.

Acts 6 : 3; 7 : 55, f. of Holy Ghost.

1 Cor. 4 : 8, now ye are f.

Phil. 4 : 12, I am instructed to be f.

2 Tim. 4 : 5, make f. proof of thy ministry.

Heb. 5 : 14, meat to them of f. age.

1 Pet. 1 : 8, joy unspeakable and f. of glory.

Fuller, 2 Ki. 18 : 17; Isa. 7 : 3; Mal. 3 : 2; Mark 9 : 3.

Fully, Num. 14 : 24, Caleb hath followed me f.

Eccl. 8 : 11, heart is f. set to do evil.

Acts 2 : 1, day of Pentecost was f. come.

Rom. 14 : 5, let every man be f. persuaded.

Rev. 14 : 18, her grapes are f. ripe.

Fulness, 1 Chr. 16 : 32; Ps. 96 : 11; 98 : 7, let sea roar, and f. thereof.

Ps. 16 : 11, in thy presence is f. of joy.

24 : 1; 1 Cor. 10 : 26, 28, earth is Lord's, and f. thereof.

John 1 : 16, of his f. have we received.

Rom. 11 : 25, the f. of the Gentiles.

Gal. 4 : 4, when f. of time was come.

Eph. 1 : 23, the f. of him that filleth all in all.

3 : 19, filled with the f. of God.

4 : 13, the stature of the f. of Christ.

Col. 1 : 19, in him should all f. dwell.

2 : 9, the f. of the Godhead bodily.

Furbish, Jer. 46 : 4; Ezek. 21 : 9, 10, 11, 28.

Furious, Prov. 22 : 24, with a f. man thou shalt not go.

29 : 22, a f. man aboundeth in transgression.

Nah. 1 : 2, the Lord is f.
See 2 Ki. 9 : 20; Ezek. 5 : 15; 23 : 25; 25 : 17.
Furlongs, Luke 24 : 13; John 6 : 19; Rev. 14 : 20; 21 : 16. A Greek furlong = 202 yards. See Measures.
Furnace, burning fiery, Dan. 3 : 6, 11, 15, 17, etc.
figurative, Deut. 4 : 20; Isa. 48 : 10; Ezek. 22 : 18.
Gen. 19 : 28, smoke went as smoke of a f.
Deut. 4 : 20, Lord hath taken you out of f.
Ps. 12 : 6, as silver tried in a f.
Prov. 17 : 3; 27 : 21, f. for gold.
Isa. 48 : 10, in f. of affliction.
Dan. 3 : 6, 11, into midst of fiery f.
Matt. 13 : 42, into a f. of fire.
Furnish, Ps. 78 : 19, can God f. table in wilderness ?
Matt. 22 : 10, wedding f. with guests.
Mark 14 : 15; Luke 22 : 12, shew a room f.
2 Tim. 3 : 17, f. unto all good works.
Furniture, Gen. 31 : 34; Ex. 31 : 7, 8, 9; 39 : 33; Nah. 2 : 9.
of tabernacle. See Tabernacle.
Furrows, Job 31 : 38; 39 : 10; Ps. 65 : 10; 129 : 3; Ezek. 17 : 7, 10; Hos. 12 : 11.
Further, Job 38 : 11, hitherto shalt thou come, but no f.
Matt. 26 : 65; Mark 14 : 63; Luke 22 : 71, what f. need of witnesses ?
Luke 24 : 28, as though he would have gone f.
Acts 4 : 17, that it spread no f.
2 Tim. 3 : 9, they shall proceed no f.
Furtherance, Phil. 1 : 12, 25.
Furthermore, Ex. 4 : 6; Deut. 4 : 21; Ezek. 8 : 6.
Fury, Gen. 27 : 44, till thy brother's f. turn.
Isa. 27 : 4, f. is not in me.
51 : 20, they are full of f. of the Lord.
Jer. 21 : 5, I will fight against you in f.
25 : 15, the wine cup of this f.
Zech. 8 : 2, I was jealous with great f.

G

Gaal (gā-ăl) [loathing], Judg. 9 : 26-41.
Gaash (gā-ăsh) [shaking], Josh. 24 : 30; Judg. 2 : 9; 2 Sam. 23 : 30; 1 Chr. 11 : 32.
Gabbatha (găb-bă-thă) [elevated], Hebrew for pavement, John 19 : 13. It was a raised stone pavement or platform fronting the Temple courts, from which Pilate delivered up Jesus to be crucified. Its stones are said to be in the cellars of the convent of the Sisters of Zion.
Gabriel (gā-brī-ĕl) [hero of God], archangel, appears to Daniel, Dan. 8 : 16; 9 : 21.
to Zacharias, Luke 1 : 19.
to Mary, Luke 1 : 26.
Gad (găd) [a troop, fortune], son of Jacob, Gen. 30 : 11.
his descendants, Gen. 46 : 16.
blessed by Jacob, Gen. 49 : 19.
tribe of, blessed by Moses, Deut. 33 : 20.
numbered, Num. 1 : 24; 26 : 15.
their possessions, Num. 32; 34 : 14.
commended by Joshua, Josh. 22 : 1.
accused of idolatry, Josh. 22 : 11.

their defence, Josh. 22 : 21.
seer, his message to David, 2 Sam. 24 : 11; 1 Chr. 21 : 9; 2 Chr. 29 : 25.
Gadarenes (găd-ă-rēnes) [people of Gadara], or Gergesenes, miracle wrought in the country of, Matt. 8 : 28; Mark 5 : 1; Luke 8 : 26 ff.
Gaddest, Jer. 2 : 36, why g. thou to change ?
Gaddi (găd-dī) [fortunate], Num. 13 : 11.
Gaddiel (găd-dī-ĕl) [God is my fortune], Num. 13 : 10.
Gadi (gā-dī), father of Menahem, king of Israel, 2 Ki. 15 : 14, 17.
Gadites (găd-ītes), Deut. 3 : 12, 16. See Gad, tribe of.
Gaham (gā-hăm), son of Nahor, Gen. 22 : 24.
Gahar (gā-här) [hiding-place], Ezra 2 : 47; Neh. 7 : 49.
Gain, Job 22 : 3, is it g. to make ways perfect ?
Prov. 1 : 19; 15 : 27, greedy of g.
3 : 14, the g. thereof better than gold.
28 : 8, by usury and unjust g.
Ezek. 22 : 13, 27, dishonest g.
Dan. 11 : 39, he shall divide the land for g.
Mic. 4 : 13, consecrate their g. to the Lord.
Matt. 16 : 26; Mark 8 : 36; Luke 9 : 25, if he g. the world.
Matt. 25 : 22, have g. other two talents.
Luke 19 : 15, had g. by trading.
Acts 16 : 16, brought masters much g.
19 : 24, no small g. to craftsmen.
1 Cor. 9 : 19, that I might g. the more.
2 Cor. 12 : 17, did I make a g. of you ?
Phil. 1 : 21, to die is g.
3 : 7, what things were g. to me.
1 Tim. 6 : 5, supposing that g. is godliness.
Jas. 4 : 13, buy and sell, and get g.
Gainsay, Luke 21 : 15, adversaries not able to g.
Acts 10 : 29, came without g.
Rom. 10 : 21, stretched hands to a g. people.
Jude 11, perished in the g. of Core.
Gainsayers, Titus 1 : 9, able to convince g.
Gaius (gā-ŭs), Greek form of Caius, Paul's host and companion, Acts 20 : 4; Rom. 16 : 23; 1 Cor. 1 : 14.
of Macedonia, Acts 19 : 29.
commended by John, 3 John 1-11.
Galatians (gă-lā-ťäns), Paul visits, Acts 16 : 6.
reproved, Gal. 1 : 6; 3; and exhorted, Gal. 5 : 6.
their love to Paul, Gal. 4 : 13.
Galatians, Epistle to the.
Time of writing is still debatable. Perhaps the best date to assign to it is A.D. 57 (cf. Gal. 2 : 1 and Acts 15; Gal. 2 : 3; 5 : 11, and Acts 16 : 3; 1 Cor. 16 : 8; Rom. 15 : 25). Later than 1 Cor., it is probably earlier than Romans. This date leaves open the question as to the position of the Galatian churches.
The Galatian Churches.—We are uncertain whether it is the Churches in the Roman province of Galatia, which included part of Phrygia, Pisidia, and Lycaonia, or only those in Galatia proper (in the north), which are addressed by the Apostle. The latter, even allowing for the fact that Paul's custom was to think in terms of Roman provinces, is the more probable alternative. In the Acts St. Luke seems to mean Galatia

proper, and not the Roman province, when he mentions the country. Its inhabitants were a mixed people, with a strong Celtic element from its Gallic conquerors; and in the want of stability, for which St. Paul rebukes them, some have seen an example of Celtic fickleness.

The Occasion of the Epistle.—We gather from 4 : 13 that St. Paul was detained among the Galatians by illness; and this led to their conversion. They received his preaching with enthusiasm, and became personally devoted to him (4 : 15, 19). But after he left them some Judaising teachers arrived, who had the prestige of coming from the mother Church of Jerusalem, and the advantage of being able to say that Paul was a mere convert and not one of the Twelve, in whose name they claimed to speak. They affirmed that, in order to be loyal Christians, the Galatians must become loyal Jews and keep the Mosaic law : and to this persistent dogmatism the Galatians succumbed. It was probably after he had written Corinthians that St. Paul received news of the apostasy of the Galatians. He visited them a second time (1 : 9; 5 : 3), found that some one in a high position had been perverting their faith (5 : 10), and this burning appeal is the result.

Contents.—(a) 1 : 1-10, Introduction. (b) 1 : 11-2 : 21, Personal—The challenge to his apostleship; his gospel independent of man and given by God; his early relations with Peter and the rest of the apostles. (c) 3-5 : 11, Dogmatic—The challenge to his doctrine; the Law and the Spirit; the Law merely provisional (Abraham and his faith); the Law superseded (Hagar); freedom and finality in Christianity. (d) 5 : 126 : 10.   Ethical and Hortatory—The application of his principles to conduct; the freedom of Christians; Paul's is a gospel of liberty but not licence; fruit and ethics of Spirit. (e) 6 : 11—18, Epilogue, stressing ver. 12-14 in " large letters " (ver. 11) as the crux of the matter.

Galbanum (găl-bă-nŭm), a heavy smelling resin which was used as one of the ingredients of the perfume which Moses was ordered to make (Ex. 30 : 34).

Galeed (gă-lĕed) [" cairn of witness "], Gen. 31 : 47 f.

Galileans. " Galilee of the Gentiles," north of Samaria, was thickly inhabited by a mixed population, as it had been for a long time, in consequence of its position, Phœnicians, Arabians, Greeks, and Syrians having penetrated among the Jews who had settled there, and whose descendants, in spite of being despised by their Judæan co-religionists, remained, in the time of our Lord, faithful to the God and the law of Israel. They were a brave people, but too ready for sedition and too liberal in their religious views to please the orthodox Jews. They were despised by the Judæans (John 1 : 46; 7 : 52), though Deborah, Barak, Jonah, Elisha, and perhaps Hosea were among

their children. Their provincialisms, such as the confusion of gutterals in speaking, jarred upon the ears of their more sensitive Judæan brethren (Matt. 26 : 73). Add, too, that they were inferior in education to the Jews and that they held frequent intercourse with the heathen, and you have the reason for their being despised as " unclean." killed by Pilate, Luke 13 : 1. disciples so called, Acts 1 : 11; 2 : 7.

Galilee (gă-lĭ-lēe) [ring, circuit, district], prophecy concerning, Isa. 9 : 1; Matt. 4 : 15. scene of most of Christ's life, Matt. 2 : 22; 4 : 23;   15 : 29;   26 : 32;   27 : 55;   28 : 7; Mark 1 : 9; Luke 4 : 14;   23 : 5;   24 : 6; Acts 10 : 37; 13 : 31. mountain in, Matt. 28 : 16. Sea of, called also the Sea of Chinnereth, Num. 34 : 11, the Sea of Tiberias, John 6 : 1, and the Sea of Gennesaret, Luke 5 : 1. See Palestine, Lakes.

Gall. The Hebrew word " rosh," thus translated, is, in Hos. 10 : 4, translated " hemlock." It is also, in other passages variously translated. It was evidently some bitter vegetable extract from a plant which grew up quickly in the furrows of fields, and may have been the poppy; but nothing more than conjecture is possible. " Their grapes are grapes of gall " (Deut. 32 : 32) would seem to indicate " their grapes are bitter grapes." The vinegar mingled with gall (Matt. 27 : 34) may have been an acid wine mingled with myrrh (Mark 15 : 23). Ps. 69 : 21, gave me g. for meat. Lam. 3 : 19, wormwood and g. Amos 6 : 12, turned judgment into g. Acts 8 : 23, in g. of bitterness.

Gallant, Isa. 33 : 21, nor shall g. ship pass.

Galleries, Ezek. 41 : 15 f; 42 : 3, 5. curls of hair, Song of Sol. 7 : 5.

Galley, Isa. 33 : 21, shall go no g.

Gallio (găl-lĭ-ō), a Roman proconsul, deputy of Achaia, and elder brother of Seneca, dismisses Paul, Acts 18 : 12, 14, 17.

Gallows, Esther 5 : 14; 7 : 10; 9 : 13.

Gamaliel (gă-mā-lĭ-ĕl) [recompense of God], Num. 1 : 10. advises the council, Acts 5 : 34. See Feet of Gamaliel.

Games, public, 1 Cor. 9 : 24;   Phil. 3 : 12; 1 Tim. 6 : 12; 2 Tim. 2 : 5; 4 : 7; Heb. 12 : 1.

Gap, Ezek. 13 : 5; 22 : 30.

Gaped, Job 16 : 10; Ps. 22 : 13.

Garden of Eden, Gen. 2 : 8. of Gethsemane, John 18 : 1. Gen. 3 : 23, sent him forth from g. 13 : 10, as the g. of the Lord. Deut. 11 : 10; 1 Ki. 21 : 2, as a g. of herbs. Song of Sol. 4 : 12, a g. enclosed. 5 : 1, I am come into my g. 6 : 2, gone down into his g. Isa. 1 : 8, as a lodge in a g. 1 : 30, as a g. that hath no water. 58 : 11; Jer. 31 : 12, like a watered g. Isa. 61 : 11, as the g. causeth things sown to spring forth. Jer. 29 : 5, plant g., and eat the fruit.

Ezek. 28 : 13, in Eden the g. of God.
36 : 35, desolate land like g. of Eden.
Joel 2 : 3, land as g. of Eden before them.
John 18 : 1, over brook Cedron, where was a g.
18 : 26, did not I see thee in the g. ?
19 : 41, a g. and in g. a new sepulchre.
Gareb (gâr-ĕb) [scabby], one of David's " Thirty," 2 Sam. 23 : 38; 1 Chr. 11 : 40.
a hill near Jerusalem, Jer. 31 : 39.
Garlands, Acts 14 : 13.
Garlick, mentioned among the good things of Egypt, in Num. 11 : 5.
Garments of the priests, Ex. 28; 39.
manner of purifying, Lev. 13 : 47 (Eccl. 9 : 8; Zech. 3 : 3; Jude 23).
not to be made of diverse materials, Lev. 19 : 19; Deut. 22 : 11.
of the sexes not to be exchanged, Deut. 22 : 5
of Christ, lots cast for (Ps. 22 : 18); Matt. 27 : 35; John 19 : 23.
Gen. 39 : 16, laid up his g.
Josh. 7 : 21, a goodly Babylonish g.
2 Ki. 5 : 26, is it a time to receive g. ?
7 : 15, all the way was full of g.
Ps. 22 : 18, they part my g. among them.
102 : 26; Isa. 50 : 9; 51 : 6; Heb. 1 : 11, wax old as a g.
Ps. 104 : 2, cover with light, as with a g.
109 : 18, clothed with cursing as with his g.
Prov. 20 : 16; 27 : 13, his g. that is surety.
30 : 4, who hath bound the waters in a g. ?
Isa. 52 : 1, put on thy beautiful g.
61 : 3, g. of praise for spirit of heaviness.
Joel 2 : 13, rend your heart and not your g.
Matt. 9 : 16; Mark 2 : 21; Luke 5 : 36, new cloth to old g.
Matt. 9 : 20; Mark 5 : 27; Luke 8 : 44, hem of a g.
Matt. 21 : 8; Mark 11 : 8, spread g. in way.
Matt. 23 : 5, enlarge borders of g.
27 : 35; Mark 15 : 24, parted g., casting lots.
Mark 11 : 7; Luke 19 : 35, cast g. on colt.
Mark 13 : 16, not turn back again to take g.
Luke 24 : 4, in shining g
Acts 9 : 39, showing the coats and g.
Jas. 5 : 2, your g. are moth eaten.
Jude 23, the g. spotted by the flesh.
Rev. 3 : 4, not defiled their g.
Garner, Ps. 144 : 13, our g. may be full.
Joel 1 : 17, g. are laid desolate.
Matt. 3 : 12; Luke 3 : 17, gather his wheat into the g.
Garnish, 2 Chr. 3 : 6, he g. the house.
Job 26 : 13, by Spirit he g. the heavens.
Matt. 12 : 44; Luke 11 : 25, swept and g.
Rev. 21 : 19, foundations of the walls were g.
Garrison, 1 Sam. 13 : 3, Jonathan smote g. of Philistines.
2 Sam. 8 : 6; 1 Chr. 18 : 6, David put g. in Syria.
Ezek. 26 : 11, thy strong g. shall go down.
2 Cor. 11 : 32, kept the city with a g.
Gashmu (găsh-mû), probably N. Arabian pronunciation of Geshem, Neh. 6 : 6.
Gatam (gā-tăm) [small and thick], Gen. 36 : 11, 16; 1 Chr. 1 : 36.
Gates. The ancients held their meetings for council, business, and amusement at the

gates of their cities. They were to them what law-courts, town-halls, and newsrooms are in the present day.
of heaven, Gen. 28 : 17; Ps. 24 : 7; Isa. 26 : 2.
of death and hell, Ps. 9 : 13; Matt. 16 : 18.
of the grave, Isa. 38 : 10.
the strait and wide, Matt. 7 : 13; Luke 13 : 24.
Gen. 34 : 20, 24, unto the g. of the city.
Ps. 118 : 19, open the g. of righteousness.
118 : 20, this g. of the Lord.
Isa. 60 : 11, thy g. shall be open continually.
60 : 18, thy walls salvation, and g. praise.
Ezek. 38 : 11, neither bars nor g.
Nah. 2 : 6, g. of the rivers shall be opened.
Acts 3 : 10, at the beautiful g.
12 : 14, Peter stood before the g.
Heb. 13 : 12, Jesus suffered without the g.
Rev. 21 : 25, g. not shut at all by day.
22 : 14, enter in through the g.

City Gate.

Gath (găth) [a wine press], one of the famous five Philistine cities, Josh. 11 : 2; 2 Sam. 1 : 20, tell it not in G.
Goliath of, 1 Sam. 17 : 4.
men of, smitten with emerods, 1 Sam. 5 : 8.
David flees to, 1 Sam. 27 : 4.
taken by David, 1 Chr. 18 : 1.
taken by Hazael, 2 Ki. 12 : 17.
Uzziah breaks down the wall of, 2 Chr. 26 : 6.
Gather, Gen. 41 : 35, let them g. all the food.
Ex. 16 : 17, g. some more, some less.
Deut. 30 : 3; Ezek. 36 : 24, will g. thee from all nations.
Ps. 26 : 9, g. not my soul with sinners.
104 : 28, that thou givest them, they g.
Prov. 10 : 5, that g. in summer is wise son.
Isa. 27 : 12, ye shall be g. one by one.
40 : 11, he shall g. the lambs.
54 : 7, with great mercies will I g. thee.
Matt. 3 : 12; Luke 3 : 17, g. wheat into garner.
Matt. 6 : 26, nor g. into barns.
7 : 16; Luke 6 : 44, do men g. grapes of thorns ?
Matt. 12 : 30; Luke 11 : 23, he that g., not scattereth.
Matt. 13 : 28, wilt thou that we g. them up ?
23 : 37, as a hen g. her chickens.
25 : 24, g. where thou hast not strawed.
25 : 32, before him shall be g. all nations.

John 6 : 12, g. up fragments.
15 : 6, men g. them, and cast them.
Acts 12 : 12, were g. together praying.
1 Cor. 16 : 2, no g. when 1 come.
2 Cor. 8 : 15, that had g. much had nothing over.
Rev. 20 : 8, to g. Gog and Magog.
Gath-hepher (găth-hē-phĕr) [wine press of the pit or well], the home of the prophet Jonah, 2 Ki. 14 : 25.
Gave, Josh. 21 : 44; 2 Chr. 15 : 15; 20 : 30, Lord g. them rest.
Job 1 : 21, the Lord g.
Ps. 21 : 4, he asked life, and thou g. it.
Eccl. 12 : 7, spirit return to God, who g. it.
Matt. 21 : 23; Mark 11 : 28; Luke 20 : 2, who g. thee this authority ?
Matt. 25 : 35, hungered and ye g. me meat.
Luke 15 : 16, no man g. unto him.
John 1 : 12, he g. power to become sons of God.
3 : 16, God g. his only begotten Son.
10 : 29, my Father, who g. them.
17 : 4, work thou g. me to do.
Acts 2 : 4, as the Spirit g. them utterance.
26 : 10, I g. my voice against them.
1 Cor. 3 : 6, God g. the increase.
Gal. 2 : 20, loved me, and g. himself for me.
Eph. 4 : 8, g. gifts unto men.
1 Tim. 2 : 6, who g. himself a ransom.
Rev. 13 : 2, dragon g. him his power.
Gay, Jas. 2 : 3, him that weareth g. cloth.
Gaza (gā-ză) [strong], a border city of the Philistines. Modern city is Ghuzzeh, with about 16,000 of a population, Gen. 10 : 19; Josh. 10 : 41; 11 : 22; 15 : 47.
Samson carries away the gates of, Judg. 16.
destruction of, foretold, Jer. 47; Amos 1 : 6; Zeph. 2 : 4; Zech. 9 : 5.

Gaza.

Gaze, Ex. 19 : 21; Acts 1 : 11.
Gazer (gā-zĕr), 2 Sam. 5 : 25; 1 Chr. 14 : 16.
Gazez (gā-zĕz), 1 Chr. 2 : 46.
Gazingstock, Nah. 3 : 6; Heb. 10 : 33.
Gazzam (găz-zăm), Ezra 2 : 48; Neh. 7 : 51.
Geba (gē-bă) [a hill], a town of Benjamin assigned to the priests, Josh. 18 : 24; 21 : 17. Also a town near Samaria.
Gebal (gē-băl) [hill country], a city of the Giblites on the coast of Phœnicia, famous for its masonry and shipbuilding, 1 Ki.

5 : 18 (R.V.); Ezek. 27 : 9. It is now a small town, Jebeil. Also a place, south of Dead Sea, now known as Jebal, Ps. 83 : 7.
Gebalites, or Giblites, people of Gebal or of Byblus, Josh. 13 : 5.
Geber (gē-bĕr), 1 Ki. 4 : 13, 19.
Gebim (gē-bĭm) [cisterns], Isa. 10 : 31.
Gecko. This word occurs in Lev. 11 : 30, where in the Authorised Version it is translated "ferret," but more correctly in the Revised Version, "gecko." The latter is a small lizard-like reptile with flattened pads to each toe; several forms are common in Palestine.
Gedaliah (gĕd-ă-lī-ăh) [great is Jah, i.e., Jehovah], governor of the remnant of Judah, 2 Ki. 25 : 22; (Jer. 40 : 5).
treacherously slain by Ishmael, 2 Ki. 25 : 25; (Jer. 41).
Gedeon (gĕd-ē-ǫn), Heb. 11 : 32.
Geder (gē-dĕr), or Gederah (gĕ-dē-răh) [wall], Josh. 12 : 13; 15 : 36.
Gederathite (gĕ-dē-ră-thīte), 1 Chr. 12 : 4.
Gederite (gĕ-dē-rīte), belonging to Geder, 1 Chr. 27 : 28.
Gederoth (gĕ-dē-rōth) [sheep-folds], Josh. 15 : 41; 2 Chr. 28 : 18.
Gehazi (gē-hā-zī) [valley of vision], servant of Elisha, 2 Ki. 4 : 12.
his covetousness and its punishment, 2 Ki. 5 : 20.
Gehenna. See Hell.
Gemariah (gĕm-ă-rī-ăh) [Jah, i.e., Jehovah has accomplished], Jer. 29 : 3; 36 : 10 ff.
Gender, Lev. 19 : 19; Job 38 : 29; Gal. 4 : 24; 2 Tim. 2 : 23.
Genealogies : Generations of Adam, Gen. 5; 1 Chr. 1; Luke 3; of Noah, Gen. 10; 1 Chr. 1 : 4; of Shem, Gen. 11 : 10; of Terah, Gen. 11 : 27; of Abraham, Gen. 25; 1 Chr. 1 : 28; of Jacob, Gen. 29 : 31; 30; 46 : 8; Ex. 1 : 2; Num. 26 ; 1 Chr. 2; of Essau, Gen. 36; 1 Chr. 1 : 35; of the tribes, 1 Chr. 2; 4; 5; 6; 7; of David, 1 Chr. 3; of Saul, 1 Chr. 8; 9 : 35; of Christ, Matt. 1; Luke 3 : 23; endless, 1 Tim. 1 : 4.
Genealogies are useful, not only for the history of individuals, but also as evidence for the movements of peoples and clans (cf. Gen. 10).
General Epistles, The.
St. James, with the six writings which follow it, constitutes the group known as "the Catholic Epistles." This name is of Eastern origin. They are called "catholic" or "general," not so much because they are the work of the apostles generally as distinct from Paul, nor yet because they contain "catholic," as against "orthodox" teaching; they were so called neither because they gave "general" as opposed to "particular" instruction nor because they were "generally" accepted, but because they are not addressed to any particular Church but to a wide circle of readers. True 2 John and 3 John are addressed to a particular church and individual respectively, but for convenience they would be associated with

1 John, and thus make up the sacred number seven. St. Paul had written to seven churches;—Thessalonica, Corinth, Galatia, Rome, Philippi, Colossæ, Ephesus. And here we have seven Epistles without address to any particular Church; therefore they may be called " general " or " catholic." This group was anciently placed immediately after the Acts, a place which suits their character very well; and in the group itself the Epistle of St. James has almost always stood first.

Generation, Gen. 7 : 1, righteous in g.
Deut. 32 : 5, a perverse and crooked g.
Ps. 14 : 5, God is in the g. of the righteous.
22 : 30, it shall be accounted for a g.
78 : 4, to g. to come praises of Lord.
95 : 10; Heb. 3 : 10, grieved with this g.
Ps. 145 : 4, one g. shall praise thy works.
Prov. 27 : 24, doth crown endure to every g. ?
30 : 12, there is a g. pure in own eyes.
Eccl. 1 : 4, one g. passeth away.
Isa. 34 : 10, from g. to g. it shall lie waste.
53 : 8; Acts 8 : 33, who shall declare his g. ?
Dan. 4 : 3, 34, his dominion from g. to g.
Matt. 3 : 7; 12 : 34; 23 : 33; Luke 3 : 7, g. of vipers.
Matt. 11 : 16; Luke 7 : 31, whereunto shall I liken this g. ?
Matt. 17 : 17; Mark 9 : 19; Luke 9 : 41, faithless, perverse g.
Matt. 24 : 34; Mark 13 : 30; Luke 21 : 32, this g. shall not pass.
Mark 8 : 38, ashamed of me in this sinful g.
Luke 16 : 8, children of world in g. wiser.
1 Pet. 2 : 9, ye are a chosen g.

Genesis.
Title.—The word " Genesis," signifying generation or origin, is the title the book bears in the LXX. version, evidently with an allusion to its contents. Its Hebrew name is Bereshith, " in the beginning."
Authorship, Date and Contents.—Genesis is the first of the Five Books of Moses, called the Pentateuch. It was undoubtedly written during the wilderness journey of the Israelites from Egypt to Canaan, approximately fifteen centuries before Christ. As has been shown by friends and enemies of the Mosaic authorship, Genesis has a distinct plan which is followed logically from beginning to end. First of all, the beginning of the universe is accounted for, then follow the beginning of life, vegetable, animal, and human, the entrance of sin, the divine provision for forgiveness, the spread of iniquity, the judgment of the Flood, the covenant with Noah and the repeopling of the earth, the division of the nations according to families and their separation by the confusion of tongues. All this material is compressed into the first eleven chapters of Genesis. From the twelfth chapter onward, the record has to do with Abraham, the chosen of God, and his descendants down to the death of Joseph. The history may well be grouped around the names of five men : Adam, Noah, Abraham, Isaac, Jacob.

Scope of the Book.—While primarily written to define man's relationship to God, Genesis touches all sciences, philosophies and industries. Here are recorded five hundred beginnings of things. The first verse of Genesis, seven Hebrew words, sets aside Polytheism, Materialism, Pantheism and Fatalism (after Murphy). Through the Protevangelium, Gen. 3 : 15, and through the covenant with Abraham, frequently repeated to him and his descendants, the entire program of Redemption is forecast.

Gennesaret (gĕn-nĕś-ă-rĕt) [garden of the prince], a lake of Palestine, miracles wrought there, Matt. 17 : 27; Luke 5 : 1; John 21 : 6. See **Palestine, Lakes.**

Gentiles, origin of, Gen. 10 : 5.
their state by nature, Rom. 1 : 21; 1 Cor. 12 : 2; Eph. 2; 4 :17; 1 Thess. 4 : 5.
their conversion predicted, Isa. 11 : 10; 42 : 1; 49 : 6; (Matt. 12 : 18; Luke 2 : 32; Acts 13 : 47); 62 : 2; Jer. 16 : 19; Hos. 2 : 23; Mal. 1 : 11; Matt. 8 : 11.
prediction fulfilled, John 10 : 16; Acts 8 : 37; 10; 14; 15; Eph. 2 : 1; 1 Thess. 1 : 1.
calling of, Rom. 9 : 24.
See Isa. 66 : 19.
Christ made known to, Col. 1 : 27.
Isa. 11 : 10, root of Jesse, to it shall **G.** seek.
60 : 3, the **G.** shall come to thy light.
Matt. 6 : 32, after all these things **G.** seek.
10 : 5, go not into way of **G.**
John 7 : 35, to the dispersed among **G.**
Acts 9 : 15, to bear my name before **G.**
18 : 6, from henceforth I will go to the **G.**
Rom. 3 : 9, proved Jews and **G.** under sin.
11 : 12, diminishing of them riches of the **G.**
15 : 11, praise the Lord, all ye **G.**
Eph. 3 : 8, preach among **G.**, unsearchable riches.
2 Tim. 1 : 11, I am appointed a teacher of **G.**
1 Pet. 2 : 12, conversation honest among **G.**
Rev. 11 : 2, the court is given to the **G.**

Gentle, 1 Thess. 2 : 7, we were g. among you.
2 Tim. 2 : 24, servant of Lord must be g.
Titus 3 : 2, g., shewing all meekness.
Jas. 3 : 17, wisdom from above pure and g.
1 Pet. 2 : 18, subject not only to the g.
cf. 2 Sam. 18 : 5; Isa. 40 : 11.

Gentleness of Christ, 2 Cor. 10 : 1; Matt. 11 : 29; (Isa. 40 : 11).
the fruit of the Spirit, Gal. 5 : 22.
exhortations to (1 Thess. 2 : 7), 2 Tim. 2 : 24; Titus 3 : 2; Jas. 3 : 17.
See 2 Sam. 22 : 36; Ps. 18 : 35.

Gera (gē-rä) [bean], one of Benjamin's sons, Gen. 46 : 21 (cf. 1 Chr. 8 : 3, 5, 7); a well-known Benjamite clan, Judg. 3 : 15; 2 Sam. 16 : 5; 19 : 16, 18; 1 Ki. 2 : 8.

Gerah (gē-räh), the smallest weight. The twentieth part of a shekel, it would amount to about 12.65 grams Troy weight, Ex. 30 : 13; Lev. 27 : 25. See **Weights.**

Gergesenes (gĕr-gĕ-sēnĕś) [inhabitants of Gergesa or Gadara], Matt. 8 : 28; Mark 5 : 1.

Gershom (gĕr-shŏm) [driving away] (Gershon), son of Levi, Gen. 46 : 11; Num. 3 : 17.
son of Moses, Ex. 2 : 22; 18 : 3.

Gershonites (gĕr-shŏn-ītes), their duties in the

service of the tabernacle, Num. 4 : 27; 10 : 17.

Geshem (gē-́shĕm) [firmness], Neh. 2 : 19; 6 : 1, 2. In Neh. 6 : 6, the form Gashmu occurs.

Geshur (gē-́shûr) [bridge], 2 Sam. 3 : 3.
Absalom dwells there, 2 Sam. 13 : 37; 14 : 23; (Josh. 13 : 13).

Get, Gen. 12 : 1; Acts 7 : 3, g. thee out of thy country.
Ps. 119 : 104, through thy precepts, I g. understanding.
Prov. 4 : 5, g. wisdom, g. understanding.
4 : 7, with all thy g., g. understanding.
21 : 6, g. of treasures by a lying tongue.
Jer. 17 : 11, he that g. riches, and not by right.
Matt. 16 : 23; Mark 8 : 33; Luke 4 : 8, g. thee behind me, Satan.

Garden of Gethsemane.

Gethsemane (gĕth-sĕm-́ă-nē) [oil-press].
garden of, our Lord's agony there, Matt. 26 : 36; Mark 14 : 32; Luke 22 : 39; John 18 : 1.

Geuel (gēu-́ĕl), Num. 13 : 15.

Gezer (gē-́zĕr) [a precipice], a city of Ephraim, Josh. 10 : 33; 1 Ki. 9 : 16; 1 Chr. 20 : 4.

Gezrites (gĕz-́rītes), 1 Sam. 27 : 8.

Ghost, Gen. 25 : 8; 35 : 29; 49 : 33; Job 14 : 10; Matt. 27 : 50, Jesus yielded up g. Holy. See God.

Giants, before the flood, Gen. 6 : 4.
in Canaan terrify the spies, Num. 13 : 33; Deut. 1 : 28; (2 : 10, 11, 19, 20; 9 : 2).
several slain by David and his servants, 1 Sam. 17; 2 Sam. 21 : 16; 1 Chr. 20 : 4.

Gibbethon (gĭb-́bĕ-thŏn) [high place], Josh. 19 : 44; 21 : 23; 1 Ki. 15 : 27; 16 : 15 ff.

Gibeah (gĭb-́ĕ-ăh) [a hill], a city of Benjamin. Judg. 19 : 14.
its wickedness, Judg. 19 : 22.
punishment of its inhabitants, Judg. 20.
the city of Saul, 1 Sam. 10 : 26; 11 : 4; 14 : 2; 15 : 34; 2 Sam. 21 : 6; Isa. 10 : 29.

Gibeon (gĭb-́ĕ-ŏn) [hill], a city N. of Jerusalem; modern, El Jib; craft of its inhabitants, Josh. 9.
delivered by Joshua, Josh. 10.
Saul persecutes them, 2 Sam. 21 : 1; and David makes atonement, 2 Sam. 21 : 3-9.
Solomon's dream at, 1 Ki. 3 : 5.
tabernacle of the Lord kept at, 1 Chr. 16 : 39; 21 : 29; (Isa. 28 : 21).

Gibeonites (gĭb-́ĕ-ŏ-nītes), 2 Sam. 21 : 1-4, 9.

Giblites (gĭb-́lītes), inhabitants of Gebal, Josh. 13 : 5.

Giddalti (gĭd-dăl-́tī) [I praise God], 1 Chr. 25 : 4, 29.

Giddel (gĭd-́dĕl) [very great], Ezra 2 : 47 = Neh. 7 : 49; Ezra 2 : 56 = Neh. 7 : 58.

Gideon (gĭd-́ĕ-ŏn) [tree feller], angel of the Lord appears to, Judg. 6 : 11.
destroys the altar and grove of Baal, Judg. 6 :25, 27.
God gives him two signs, Judg. 6 : 36-40.
his army reduced, etc., Judg. 7 : 2-7.
his stratagem, Judg. 7 : 16.
subdues the Midianites, Judg. 7 : 19; 8.
makes an ephod of the spoil, Judg. 8 : 24-27.
his death, Judg. 8 : 32.
See Heb. 11 : 32.

Gideoni (gĭd-ĕ-ō-́nī) [=Gideon], Num. 1 : 11; 2 : 22; 7 : 60, 65; 10 : 24.

Gier eagle. The Egyptian vulture or Pharaoh's hen (Neophron percnopterus), included among the unclean birds in Lev. 11 : 13 and Deut. 14 : 17; is common in the Holy Land during spring and summer. In Egypt and the East generally, it is protected, on account of its great use as a scavenger, eating up, as it does, every kind of filth.

Gift of God, John 4 : 10; unspeakable, 2 Cor. 9 : 15.
the Holy Ghost, Acts 2 : 38; 8 : 20; 10 : 45.
gifts, spiritual, Ps. 29 : 11; 68 : 18, 35 ; 84 : 11; Prov. 2 : 6; Ezek. 11 : 19; Acts 11 : 17; Rom. 12 : 6; 1 Cor. 1 : 7; 12; 13 : 2; 14; Eph. 2 : 8; Jas. 1 : 5, 17; 4 : 6; 1 Pet. 4 : 10.
temporal, Gen. 1 : 26; 9 : 3; 27 : 28; Lev. 26 : 4; Ps. 34 : 10; 65 : 9; 104; 136 : 25; 145 : 15; 147; Isa. 30 : 23; Acts 14 : 17.
(Corban), Matt. 15 : 5; Mark 7 : 11.
Ex. 23 : 8; Deut. 16 : 19, take no g., for g. blindeth.
2 Chr. 19 : 7, with Lord is no taking of g.
Ps. 45 : 12, daughter of Tyre with a g.
68 : 18; Eph. 4 : 8, g. for men.
Ps. 72 : 10, kings of Sheba shall offer g.
Prov. 17 : 8, a g. is as a precious stone.
Eccl. 3 : 13; 5 : 19, it is the g. of God.
7 : 7, a g. destroyeth the heart.
Isa. 1 : 23, every one loveth g.
Matt. 5 : 23, bring thy g. to the altar.
7 : 11; Luke 11 : 13, know how to give good g.
Matt. 15 : 5; Mark 7 : 11, a g., by whatsoever thou mightest be profited.
Luke 21 : 1, casting g. into treasury.
John 4 : 10, if thou knewest the g. of God.
Acts 8 : 20, the g. of God may be purchased.
Rom. 1 : 11, some spiritual g.
5 : 15, not as offence, so is free g.
6 : 23, the g. of God is eternal life.
11 : 29, g. of God without repentance.
12 : 6, g. differing according to grace.
1 Cor. 12 : 4, diversities of g.
12 : 9, 30, the g. of healing.
14 : 1, 12, desire spiritual g.
2 Cor. 9 : 15, thanks to God for unspeakable g.
Eph. 2 : 8, faith is the g. of God.
Phil. 4 : 17, not because I desire a g.

1 Tim. 4 : 14, neglect not g. in thee.
2 Tim. 1 : 6, stir up g. in thee.
Heb. 2 : 4, g. of the Holy Ghost.
  6 : 4, tasted of heavenly g.
Jas. 1 : 17, every good and perfect g.

Valley of Gihon.

Gihon (gī'hŏn) [bursting forth], or **Araxes**, a river in Armenia, Gen. 2 : 13.
pools and valleys of, near Jerusalem, 1 Ki. 1 : 45; 2 Chr. 32 : 30; 33 : 14.
Gilead (gĭl'ĕ-ăd) [hard, rough country], land of, granted to the Reubenites, etc., Num. 32.
invaded by the Ammonites, Judg. 10 : 17.
Jephthah made captain of, Judg. 11.
Gileadites (gĭl'ĕ-ă-dītes), Num. 26 : 29; Judg. 12 : 4, 5.
Gilgal (gĭl'găl) [wheel, whirlwind], site of first Israelite encampment (Joshua) after crossing the Jordan. Joshua encamps there, Josh. 4 : 19; 9 : 6.
Saul made king there, 1 Sam. 10 : 8; 11 : 14.
sacrifices at, 1 Sam. 13 : 8; 15 : 12.
Giloh (gī'lōh), **Gilohnite** (gī-lōh-nīte) [exile ?], Josh. 15 : 51; 2 Sam. 15 : 12; 23 : 34; birthplace of Ahithopel.
Gin [ar.], a snare or trap; contraction of "engine," Job 18 : 9; Ps. 140 : 5; Isa. 8 : 14; Amos 3 : 5.
Gird, 2 Sam. 22 : 40; Ps. 18 : 39, hast g. me with strength.
Ps. 45 : 3, g. sword on thy thigh.
Joel 1 : 13, g. yourselves, and lament.
John 21 : 18, when old, another shall g. thee.
Eph. 6 : 14, having your loins g.
Girdle of the High Priest, Ex. 28 : 4.
typical, Jer. 13 : 1.
Isa. 11 : 5, righteousness be g. of loins.
Matt. 3 : 4; Mark 1 : 6, John had a leathern g.
Rev. 1 : 13, girt about with golden g.
Girgashites (gĭr'gă-shītes) [dwellers in clay], a tribe of the Canaanites, W. of Jordan. Descendants of Canaan Gen. 10 : 15; 15 : 21.
intercourse with, forbidden, Deut. 7 : 1.
driven out, Josh. 3 : 10; 24 : 11.
Girl, Joel 3 : 3, they have sold g. for wine.
Zech. 8 : 5, streets full of g.
Gispa (gĭs'pă), Neh. 11 : 21.
Gittah-hepher (gĭt'täh-hē'phĕr), Josh. 19 : 13.
Gittaim (gĭt-tā'ĭm) [two wine presses], 2 Sam. 4 : 3; Neh. 11 : 21. Site unknown.

Gittite (gĭt'tīte) [belonging to Gath], Josh. 13 : 3; 2 Sam. 6 : 10; 21 : 19. See **Gath**.
Gittith (gĭt'tĭth) [set to], found in the titles to Ps. 8, 81, and 84, means properly, "belonging to Gath," and is by some scholars supposed to be the name of a musical instrument; by others to denote a style or method of singing common in Gath. Inasmuch, also, as the word gath in Hebrew means a wine press, it has also been suggested that "upon Gittith" refers to some tune commonly used at the vintage season; but these Psalms, especially 84, have no suitability to this.
Give, Gen. 28 : 22, I will g. the tenth.
Deut. 16 : 17; Ezek. 46 : 5, 11, every man g. as he is able.
Ps. 2 : 8, I shall g. thee the heathen.
  29 : 11, Lord will g. strength.
  37 : 4, g. thee the desires of thine heart.
  84 : 11, Lord will g. grace and glory.
Prov. 23 : 26, my son, g. me thine heart.
Isa. 55 : 10, that it may g. seed to the sower.
Jer. 17 : 10; 32 : 19, g. every man according to ways.
Hos. 11 : 8, how shall I g. thee up ?
Matt. 5 : 42, g. to him that asketh.
  6 : 11; Luke 11 : 3, g. us daily bread.
Matt. 7 : 7, ask, and i shall be g. you.
  10 : 8, freely ye have received, freely g.
  16 : 26; Mark 8 : 37, what shall a man g. in exchange for soul ?,
Matt. 19 : 21; Mark 10 : 21, go sell, and g. to the poor.
Matt. 25 : 29, unto every one that hath shall be g.
Luke 6 : 38, g., and it shall be g.
John 4 : 14, the water I shall g. him.
  6 : 37, all that the Father g. me.
  10 : 28, I g. to them eternal life.
  14 : 16, he shall g. you the Comforter.
  14 : 27, not as the world g., g. I.
Acts 3 : 6, such as I have, g. I thee.
  6 : 4, we will g. ourselves to prayer,
  20 : 35, more blessed to g. than to receive.
Rom. 8 : 32, with him also freely g. us all things.
1 Cor. 2 : 12, things freely g. of God.
  15 : 57, God, which g. us the victory.
2 Cor. 9 : 7, g. not grudgingly.
Eph. 5 : 2, and hath g. himself.
1 Tim. 4 : 13, g. attendance to reading.
  6 : 17, who g. us richly.
2 Tim. 3 : 16, all scripture is g. by inspiration.
Jas. 1 : 5, that g. to all men liberally.
  4 : 6, g. more grace, g. grace to humble.
1 Pet. 4 : 11, of the ability that God g.
Rev. 11 : 17, we g. thee thanks, Lord God Almighty.
Glad, Ex. 4 : 14, he will be g. in heart.
Job 3 : 22, g. when they can find the grave.
Ps. 16 : 9, my heart is g.
  21 : 6, made him g. with thy countenance.
  34 : 2; 69 : 32, humble shall hear, and be g.
  46 : 4, streams make g. the city of God.
  90 : 15, make us g.
  122 : 1, I was g. when they said.
  126 : 3, great things, whereof we are g.

Prov. 10 : 1; 15 : 20, a wise son maketh a g. father.

Isa. 35 : 1, wilderness be g. for them.

Luke 8 : 1, g. tidings of the kingdom.

15 : 32, make merry, and be g.

John 8 : 56, saw my day, and was g.

11 : 15, I am g. for your sakes.

Acts 11 : 23, when he had seen grace of God, was g.

1 Pet. 4 : 13, ye may be g. also.

Gladness, Num. 10 : 10, in day of g. ye shall blow.

2 Sam. 6 : 12, David brought ark with g.

Neh. 8 : 17, there was very great g.

Ps. 4 : 7, thou hast put g. in my heart.

45 : 7; Heb. 1 : 9, the oil of g.

Ps. 51 : 8, make me to hear joy and g.

97 : 11, g. is sown for the upright.

100 : 2, serve the Lord with g.

Isa. 35 : 10; 51 : 11, they shall obtain joy, and g.

Acts 2 : 46, did eat with g. of heart.

12 : 14, opened not gate for g.

14 : 17, filling our hearts with food and g.

Glass, 1 Cor. 13 : 12, we see through a g.

2 Cor. 3 : 18, beholding as in a g.

Jas. 1 : 23, man beholding face in a g.

Rev. 4 : 6, sea of g. like unto crystal.

21 : 18, 21, city pure gold, like clear g.

Glean, Lev. 19 : 10; Deut. 24 : 21, not g. vineyard.

Ruth 2 : 19, where hast thou g. to day.

Jer. 6 : 9, they shall g. the remnant.

Mic. 7 : 1, as grape g. of the vintage.

Gleaning, to be left for the poor and stranger, Lev. 19 : 9; 23 : 22; Deut. 24 : 21.

liberality of Boaz concerning, Ruth 2 : 15.

Glede. Only mentioned in Deut. 14 : 13 among the unclean birds, as were all the birds of prey. Tristram thinks it may have been the buzzard.

Glistering, 1 Chr. 29 : 2; Luke 9 : 29.

Glittering, Deut. 32 : 41; Job 20 : 25; 39 : 23; Hab. 3 : 11.

Gloominess, Joel 2 : 2; Zeph. 1 : 15.

Glorify, God, exhortations to, 1 Chr. 16 : 28; Ps. 22 : 23; 50 : 15; Rom. 15 : 6; 1 Cor. 6 : 20; 10 : 31; 1 Pet. 2 : 12; Rev. 15 : 4.

Ps. 22 : 23, all seed of Jacob g. him.

50 : 23, offereth praise g. me.

86 : 9, all nations shall g. thy name.

Isa. 60 : 7, I will g. house of my glory.

Dan. 5 : 23, God hast thou not g.

Matt. 5 : 16, g. your Father in heaven.

15 : 31, they g. the God of Israel.

Luke 2 : 20, g. and praising God.

4 : 15, being g. of all.

John 7 : 39, because Jesus was not yet g.

11 : 4, that the Son of God might be g.

12 : 16, when Jesus was g.

12 : 28, Father, g. thy name.

13 : 32, God shall also g. him.

14 : 13, that Father may be g. in Son.

15 : 8, herein is my Father g.

17 : 1, g. thy Son, that thy Son may g.

21 : 19, by what death he should g. God.

Acts 4 : 21, men g. God for what was done.

Rom. 1 : 21, they g. him not as God.

8 : 17, suffer with him, that we may be g.

1 Cor. 6 : 20, g. God in body and spirit.

2 Thess. 1 : 10, to be g. in his saints.

3 : 1, that word of Lord may be g.

Heb. 5 : 5, Christ g. not himself.

1 Pet. 4 : 14, on your part he is g.

Rev. 15 : 4, fear thee, and g. thy name.

Glorious, Ex. 15 : 11, g. in holiness.

15 : 21, he hath triumphed g.

Deut. 28 : 58; 1 Chr. 29 : 13, this g. name.

Neh. 9 : 5, blessed be thy g. name.

Ps. 45 : 13, king's daughter g. within.

66 : 2, make his praise g.

72 : 19, blessed be his g. name for ever.

87 : 3, g. things are spoken of thee.

145 : 5, speak of g. honour of majesty.

Isa. 28 : 1, whose g. beauty is a fading flower.

60 : 13, place of my feet g.

63 : 1, g. in his apparel.

Jer. 17 : 12, a g. high throne.

Luke 13 : 17, rejoiced for g. things done.

Rom. 8 : 21, g. liberty of children of God.

2 Cor. 3 : 8, ministration of spirit rather g.

4 : 4, light of g. gospel.

Eph. 5 : 27, present it a g. church.

1 Tim. 1 : 11, the g. gospel of the blessed.

Titus 2 : 13, the g. appearing of the great.

Glory, Ex. 33 : 18, show me thy g.

Num. 14 : 21; Ps. 72 : 19; Isa. 6 : 3, earth filled with g. of Lord.

1 Sam. 4 : 21, the g. is departed from Israel.

Ps. 8 : 1, thy g. above the heavens.

24 : 7, 10, the king of g.

73 : 24, afterward receive me to g.

84 : 11, Lord will give grace and g.

85 : 9, that g. may dwell in our land.

89 : 17, thou art g. of their strength.

145 : 11, speak of the g. of thy kingdom.

Prov. 3 : 35, the wise shall inherit g.

17 : 6, the g. of children are their fathers.

20 : 29, the g. of young men is their strength.

Isa. 24 : 16, songs, even g. to the righteous.

42 : 8, my g. will I not give to another.

60 : 7, will glorify house of my g.

Jer. 2 : 11, my people have changed their g.

Ezek. 31 : 18, to whom art thou thus like in g. ?

Dan. 2 : 37; 7 : 14, God hath given power and g.

Hos. 4 : 7, change their g. into shame.

Hag. 2 : 7, I will fill this house with g.

Matt. 6 : 2, that they may have g. of men.

6 : 29; Luke 12 : 27, Solomon in all his g.

Matt. 16 : 27; Mark 8 : 38, come in g. of Father.

Matt. 24 : 30; Mark 13 : 26; Luke 21 : 27, son coming with power and g.

Luke 2 : 14; 19 : 38, g. to God.

4 : 6, power will I give thee and g.

9 : 31, appeared in g., and spake.

24 : 26, to enter into his g.

John 1 : 14, we beheld his g.

8 : 50, I seek not mine own g.

17 : 5, the g. I had with thee.

17 : 24, that they may behold my g.

Acts 7 : 2, God of g. appeared.

12 : 23, he gave not God the g.

Rom. 3 : 23, come short of g. of God.

8 : 18, not worthy to be compared with the g.

9 : 23, he had afore prepared unto g.

11 : 36;   Gal. 1 : 5;   2 Tim. 4 : 18;   Heb. 13 : 21;   1 Pet. 5 : 11, to whom be g.

1 Cor. 2 : 8, not crucified the Lord of g.

5 : 6, your g. is not good.

9 : 15, make my g. void.

10 : 31, do all to the g. of God.

15 : 40, g. of celestial, g. of terrestrial.

15 : 43, sown in dishonour, raised in g.

2 Cor. 3 : 18, are changed from g. to g.

4 : 17, an eternal weight of g.

Eph. 1 : 6, praise of g. of his grace.

3 : 21, to him be g. in the church.

Phil. 4 : 19, according to his riches in g.

Col. 1 : 27, Christ in you, the hope of g.

3 : 4, appear with him in g.

1 Tim. 3 : 16, received up into g.

Heb. 1 : 3, the brightness of his g.

2 : 10, in bringing many sons to g.

3 : 3, this man was counted worthy of more g.

Jas. 2 : 1, faith of Jesus, Lord of g.

1 Pet. 1 : 8, joy unspeakable and full of g.

1 : 24, the g. of man as flower of grass.

2 : 20, what g. is it, if when buffeted?

4 : 14, the spirit of g. and of God.

5 : 10, called us to eternal g.

2 Pet. 1 : 17, voice from the excellent g.

Rev. 4 : 11;   5 : 12, worthy to receive g.

7 : 12, blessing and g. to our God.

21 : 23, the g. of God did lighten it.

See God.

Gluttony condemned, Deut. 21 : 20;   Prov. 23 : 1, 20;   25 : 16;   1 Pet. 4 : 3.

See Matt. 11 : 19; Luke 13 : 28.

Gnash, Job 16 : 9; Ps. 37 : 12, he g. on me.

Ps. 35 : 16, they g. on me with teeth.

Mark 9 : 18, he foameth, and g. with teeth.

Acts 7 : 54, they g. on him with teeth.

Gnashing of teeth, Matt. 8 : 12; 13 . 42, 22 . 13, 24 : 51; 25 : 30; Luke 13 : 28.

Gnat. Only mentioned in Matt. 23 : 24, "which strain at a gnat," or rather, as in the Revised Version, "strain out the gnat." It is a small two-winged insect, smaller than the mosquito, but belonging to the same genus (Culex).

Gnaw, Zeph. 3 : 3; Rev. 16 : 10.

Go, Gen. 32 : 26, let me g.

Ex. 23 : 23;   32 : 34, angel shall g. before.

33 : 14, my presence shall g. with thee.

Deut. 31 : 6, thy God, he it is that doth g.

Ruth 1 : 16, whither thou g., I will go.

2 Sam. 12 : 23, I shall g. to him, he shall not return.

1 Ki. 2 : 2, I g. the way of all the earth.

Ps. 32 : 8, teach thee in way thou shalt g.

139 : 7, whither shall I g. from thy spirit ?

Prov. 22 : 6, train child in way he should g.

30 : 29, three things which g. well.

Matt. 5 : 41, to g. a mile, g. twain.

8 : 9, I say g., and he g.

10 : 6, g. rather to lost sheep of Israel.

28 : 19, g. ye, and teach all nations.

Luke 10 : 37, g. and do likewise.

John 6 : 68, Lord, to whom shall we g. ?

14 : 2, I g. to prepare a place for you.

19 : 12, if thou let this man g.

Go about [ar.], frame plans, adopt measures, take steps, John 7 : 19 f.

Go beyond [ar.], injure by craft, overreach artfully, I Thess. 4 : 6.

Go to [ar.], come on, be quick, take heed, Jas. 5 : 1.

Goad, Judg. 3 : 31;   1 Sam. 13 : 21.   Eccl. 12 : 11, words of the wise are as g.

Goat. This well-known animal (Capra hircus) ranked with the cattle, camels, and sheep, as the chief wealth of the Israelites in their pastoral days. Its flesh, with the exception of the fat, was eaten. A kid of the goat's was, in a warm country, a quickly prepared article of food (Gen. 27 : 9). Goats' milk was largely consumed in the household (Prov. 27 : 27); its hair was manufactured into a durable texture, used for raiment and curtains. Goatskins were used as coverings, and, when sewed up, as "bottles" for water and wine. The goats are said to be " the price of the field " (Prov. 27 : 26). It was killed for sacrifice, and on the day of atonement, one of a pair was sent alive into the wilderness (Lev. 16 : 10).

Goat, Wild. This goat is possibly an ibex (probably the fine Capra beden), a goat with large horns, those of the male being sometimes three feet long. It loves the desolate and rocky parts, where the " high hills are a refuge for the wild goats " (Ps. 104 : 18).

Matt. 25 : 32, divideth sheep from g.

Heb. 9 : 12, by the blood of g.

11 : 37, in sheepskins and g.-skins.

The Beden or Mountain Goat.

Goblet, Song of Sol. 7 : 2.

God.—The existence of God is never questioned in the Bible. When seemingly it is (Ps. 14 : 1;   53 : 1) the words probably imply that God does not concern Himself with man (cf. Ps. 10 : 4).

The Lord God Almighty, Gen. 17 : 1;   Ex. 6 : 3; Num. 24 : 4; Ruth 1 : 20; Job 5 : 17; Ps. 68 : 14; 91 : 1; Isa. 13 : 6; Ezek. 1 : 24; Joel 1 : 15; 2 Cor. 6 : 18; Rev. 1 : 8.

The Creator, Gen. 1 : 2; Deut. 4 : 19; Neh. 9 : 6; Job 33 : 4; 38; Ps. 8; 19 : 1; 33 : 6; 89 : 11; 94 : 9; 104; 136; 146 : 6; 148; Prov. 3 : 19; 8 : 22; Eccl. 12 : 1; Isa. 37 : 16; 40 : 28; 43 : 7; 44 : 8; Jer. 10 : 12;

32 : 17; Zech. 12 : 1; John 1 : 3; Acts 17 : 24; Rom. 1 : 25; 11 : 36; Col. 1 : 16; Heb. 1 : 10; 3 : 4; 11 : 3; 1 Pet. 4 : 19; Rev. 4 : 11.

His Dealings with
our first parents, Gen. 3.
Noah and the sinful world, Gen. 6–9.
Abraham and Lot, Gen. 12–24.
Isaac, Jacob, and Esau, Gen. 22; 25; 26; 28.
Joseph, Gen. 39.
Moses and Aaron, Ex. 3; 7.
Pharaoh and Egypt, Ex. 7; 8.
causes the plagues of blood, Ex. 7 : 19; frogs, lice, and flies, Ex. 8; murrain, boils, and hail, Ex. 9; locusts and darkness, Ex. 10; death of the firstborn in Egypt, Ex. 12 : 29.
institutes the passover, Ex. 11; 12; 13.
the children of Israel during their forty years wandering in the wilderness :
preserves the Israelites in their passage through the Red Sea, Ex. 14.
sends manna, Ex. 16 : 15.
gives the ten commandments, Ex. 20.
reveals his glory to Moses, Aaron, and the elders, Ex. 24.
makes a covenant with Israel, Ex. 34.
commands the tabernacle to be made, Ex. 35; to be reared and anointed, Ex. 40.
delivers the law concerning sacrificial offerings, Lev. 1; Num. 28.
sanctifies Aaron, Lev. 8; 9.
institutes blessings and curses, Lev. 26; Deut. 27.
punishes the revolt of Korah, Dathan, and Abiram, Num. 16.
causes Aaron's rod to blossom, Num. 17.
excludes Moses and Aaron from the promised land for unbelief, Num. 20 : 12.
sends fiery serpents, and heals with brazen serpent, Num. 21.
Balaam and Balak, Num. 22–24.
Joshua at Jericho and Ai, Josh. 1; 3; 4; 6; 7; 8.
kings of Canaan, Josh. 10–12.
Gideon, Judg. 6.
Jephthah, Judg. 11.
Samson, Judg. 13.
Naomi and Ruth, Ruth 1–4.
Hannah, Eli, and Samuel, 1 Sam. 1–3.
Saul, 1 Sam. 9-31; 1 Chr. 10.
David, 1 Sam. 16–31; 2 Sam. 1–24; 1 Ki. 1–2 : 11; 1 Chr. 11–23; 28; 29.
Solomon, 1 Ki. 1-11; 2 Chr. 1-9.
Rehoboam, Jeroboam, 1 Ki. 12-15; 2 Chr. 10–12.
Ahab, 1 Ki. 16–22; 2 Chr. 18.
Elijah, 1 Ki. 17–22; 2 Ki. 2.
Elisha, 2 Ki. 2–9.
Hezekiah, 2 Ki. 18–20; 2 Chr. 29–32; Isa. 36–39.
Josiah, 2 Ki. 22; 23; 2 Chr. 34 ; 35.
the captive Jews in Persia, Esther 1–10.
the liberated Jews, Ezra 1-10; Neh. 1–13.
Job and his friends, Job 1; 2; 38–42.
Isaiah, 2 Ki. 19; 20; 2 Chr. 26; 32.
Jeremiah, 2 Chr. 35; 36; Jer. 26 : 34–43.
Daniel at Babylon, Dan. 1–10.
Nebuchadnezzar, Dan. 4.
Shadrach, Meshach, and Abed-nego, Dan. 3.

Jonah, Jonah 1–4.
His Revelations to
Isaiah, warning Judah and Israel, Isa. 1–12.
warning surrounding nations, Isa. 13–23.
of impending judgment, Isa. 24–66.
comforting his people, Isa. 40–44, etc.
Jeremiah, respecting Judah's overthrow on account of sin, Jer. 1–25; 27–33; 44.
Ezekiel, concerning
Judah's captivity, Ezek. 3–7.
the defiled temple, Ezek. 8–11.
warnings to Judah, Ezek. 12–19.
impending judgments, Ezek. 20–23.
Jerusalem's overthrow, Ezek. 24.
judgments on other nations, Ezek. 25–32.
exhortations and promises, Ezek. 32–39.
the New Jerusalem, Ezek. 40–48.
His Goodness :
Ex. 34 : 6; Ps. 25 : 8; 33 : 5; 52 : 1; 65 : 4; 104 : 24; 145 : 9; Jer. 31 : 12, 14; Nah. 1 : 7; Zech. 9 : 17; Matt. 5 : 45; 19 : 17; Rom. 2 : 4.
how manifested, Ps. 31 : 19; 68 : 10; 86 : 5; 119 : 68; Lam. 3 : 25; Acts 14 : 17.
His Gifts :
Num. 14 : 8; Rom. 8 : 32; Jas. 1 : 17; 2 Pet. 1 : 3.
dispensed according to his will, Eccl. 2 : 26; Dan. 2 : 21; Rom. 12 : 6; 1 Cor. 7 : 7.
His Spiritual Gifts :
Ps. 21 : 2; 29 : 11; 68 : 35; Ezek. 11 : 19; Rom. 11 : 29.
are through Christ, Ps. 68 : 18, with Eph. 4 : 7, 8.
Christ the chief of, Isa. 42 : 6; 55 : 4; John 3 : 16; 4 : 10; 6 : 32, 33.
to be prayed for, Matt. 7 : 7, 11; John 16 : 23, 24.
the Holy Ghost, Luke 11 : 13; Acts 8 : 20.
rest, Matt. 11 : 28; 2 Thess. 1 : 7.
grace, Ps. 84 : 11; Jas. 4 : 6.
wisdom, Prov. 2 : 6; Jas. 1 : 5.
glory, Ps. 84 : 11; John 17 : 22.
repentance, Acts 11 : 18.
righteousness, Rom. 5 : 16, 17.
eternal life, John 6 : 27; Rom. 6 : 23.
faith, Eph. 2 : 8; Phil. 1 : 29.
to be used for mutual profit, 1 Pet. 4 : 10.
His Temporal Gifts :
rain and fruitful seasons, Gen. 27 : 28; Lev. 26 : 4, 5; Isa. 30 : 23; Acts 14 : 17.
should make us remember God, Deut. 8 : 18.
all good things, Ps. 34 : 10; 1 Tim. 6 : 17.
all creatures partake of, Ps. 136 : 25; 145 : 15, 16.
to be used and enjoyed, Eccl. 3 : 13; 5 : 19, 20; 1 Tim. 4 : 4, 5.
food and raiment, etc., Matt. 6 : 25-33.
to be prayed for, Zech. 10 : 1; Matt. 6 : 11.
His Joy over His People :
1 Chr. 29 : 17; Ps. 147 : 11; 149 : 4; Prov. 11 : 20; 15 : 8; Zeph. 3 : 17; Luke 15 : 7, 10; Heb. 11 : 5, 6.
leads him to do them good, etc., Num. 14 : 8; Deut. 28 : 63; 30 : 9; 2 Sam. 22 : 20; Isa. 65 : 19; Jer. 32 : 41; 1 Pet. 1 : 4.
His Glory :
exhibited in his power, Ex. 15 : 1, 6; Rom. 6 : 4; holiness, Ex. 15 : 11; name, Deut.

28 : 58; Neh. 9 : 5; majesty, Job 37 : 22; Ps. 93 : 1; 104 : 1; 145 : 5, 12; Isa. 2 : 10; works, Ps. 19 : 1; 111 : 3.
described as exalted, Ps. 8 : 1; 113 : 4; eternal, Ps. 104 : 31; great, Ps. 138 : 5; rich, Eph. 3 : 16.
exhibited to Moses, Ex. 34 : 5-7, with Ex. 33 : 18-23; his Church, Deut. 5 : 24; Ps. 102 : 16; Isa. 60 : 1, 2; Rev. 21 : 11, 23; Stephen, Acts 7 : 55.
exhibited in Christ, John 1 : 14; 2 Cor. 4 : 6; Heb. 1 : 3.
See Num. 14 : 21; 1 Chr. 16 : 24; Ps. 57 : 5; 63 : 2; 79 : 9; 90 : 16; 145 : 5, 11; Isa. 6 : 3; 42 : 8; 59 : 19; Hab. 2 : 14.

His Law :
Given to Adam, Gen. 2 : 16, 17, with Rom. 5 : 12-14.
to Noah, Gen. 9 : 6.
to the Israelites, Ex. 20 : 2 ff.; Ps. 78 : 5.
through Moses, Ex. 31 : 18; John 7 : 19.
through the ministration of angels, Acts 7 : 53; Gal. 3 : 19; Heb. 2 : 2.
described as perfect, Ps. 19 : 7; Rom. 12 : 2; pure, Ps. 19 : 8; exceeding broad, Ps. 119 : 96; truth, Ps. 119 : 142; holy, just, and good, Rom. 7 : 12; spiritual, Rom. 7 : 14; not grievous, 1 John, 5 : 3.
requires perfect obedience, Deut. 27 : 26; Gal. 3 : 10; Jas. 2 : 10.
requires obedience of the heart, Ps. 51 : 6, Matt. 22 : 37.
man cannot render perfect obedience to, 1 Ki. 8 : 46; Eccl. 7 : 20; Rom. 3 : 10.
man cannot be justified by, Acts 13 : 39; Rom. 3 : 20, 28; Gal. 2 : 16; 3 : 11.
all men have transgressed, Rom. 3 : 9, 19.
gives the knowledge of sin, Rom. 3 : 20; 7 : 7.
love is the fulfilling of, Rom. 13 . 8, 10, Gal. 5 : 14; Jas. 2 : 8.
designed to lead to Christ, Gal. 3 : 24.
blessedness of keeping, Ps. 119 : 1; Matt. 5 : 19; 1 John 3 : 22, 24; Rev. 22 : 14.
Christ came to fulfil, Matt. 5 : 17; (Isa. 42 : 21).
explained by Christ, Matt. 7 : 12; 22 : 37-40.
the wicked forsake, etc., 2 Chr. 12 : 1; Ps. 78 : 10; Isa. 5 : 24; 30 : 9; Jer. 9 : 13; Hos. 4 : 6.
saints should observe, etc., Ex. 13 : 9; Ps. 119 : 55, 77, 97, 113; Jer. 31 : 33; Mal. 4 : 4; Heb. 8 : 10.
punishment for disobeying, Neh. 9 : 26, 27; Isa. 65 : 11-13; Jer. 9 : 13-16.

His Attributes :
Eternal, Gen. 21 : 33; Ex. 3 : 14; Deut. 32 : 40; 33 : 27; Job 10 : 5; 36 : 26; Ps. 9 : 7; 90 : 2; 92 : 8; 93 : 2; 102 : 12; 104 : 31; 135 : 13; 145 : 13; Eccl. 3 : 14; Isa. 9 : 6; 40 : 28; 41 : 4; 43 : 13; 48 : 12; 57 : 15; 63 : 16; Jer. 10 : 10; Lam. 5 : 19; Dan. 4 : 3, 34; 6 : 26; Mic. 5 : 2; Hab. 1 : 12; Rom. 1 : 20; 16 : 26; Eph. 3 : 9; 1 Tim. 1 : 17; 6 : 16; 2 Pet. 3 : 8; Rev. 1 : 8; 4 : 9; 22 : 13.
Immutable, Num. 23 : 19; 1 Sam. 15 : 29; Ps. 33 : 11; 119 : 89; Mal. 3 : 6; Acts 4 : 28; Eph. 1 : 4; Heb. 1 : 12; 6 : 17; 13 : 8; Jas. 1 : 17.

Invisible, Ex. 33 : 20; Job 23 : 8; John 1 : 18; 4 : 24; 5 : 37; Rom. 1 : 20; Col. 1 : 15; 1 Tim. 1 : 17; 6 : 16; Heb. 11 : 27; 1 John 4 : 12.
Incomprehensible, Job 5 : 9 9 : 10; 11 : 7; 26 : 14; 36 : 26; 37 : 5; Ps. 36 : 6; 40 : 5; 106 : 2; 139 : 6; Eccl. 3 : 11; 8 : 17; 11 : 5; Isa. 40 : 12; 45 : 15; Mic. 4 : 12; 1 Tim. 6 : 16.
Unsearchable, Job 11 : 7; 26 : 14; 37 : 15; Ps. 145 : 13; Eccl. 8 : 17; Rom. 11 : 33.
Omniscient, Job 26 : 6; 34 : 21; Ps. 139; Prov. 15 : 3; Isa. 44 : 7; Ezek. 11 : 5; Matt. 12 : 25; John 2 : 24; Rom. 1 : 20.
Omnipresent, Job 23 : 9; 26; 28; Acts 17 : 27.
Holiness, Gen. 35 : 2; Ex. 3 : 5; 28 : 36; 34 : 5 ff.; 39 : 30; Lev. 11 : 44; 21 : 8; Josh. 5 : 15; 1 Sam. 2 : 2; 1 Chr. 16 : 10; Ps. 22 : 3; 30 : 4; 60 : 6. See Psalms. Isa. 6 : 3; 43 : 15; 49 : 7; 57 : 15; Jer. 23 : 9; Luke 1 : 49; Acts 3 : 14; Rom. 7 : 12; 1 John 2 : 20; Rev. 4 : 8; 19 : 1.
Justice, Gen. 2 : 16; 3 : 8 ff.; 4 : 9; 6 : 7; 9 : 4 ff.; 18 : 17; Ex. 32 : 33; Lev. 4; 7 : 20; 18 : 4; 26 : 21; Num. 11; 14; 16; 17; 20; 25; 26 : 64; 27 : 12; 35; Deut. 1 : 31 ff.; 4 : 24; 5; 6; 9 : 4; 10 : 17; 25 : 15 f.; 28 : 15; 31 : 16; 32 : 35, 41; Josh. 7 : 1; Judg. 1 : 7; 2 : 14; 9 : 56; 1 Sam. 2 : 30; 3 : 11; 6 : 19; 15 : 17; 2 Sam. 6 : 7; 12 : 1; 22; 24 : 11; 1 Ki. 8 : 20; 2 Chr. 6 : 17; 19 : 7; Neh. 9 : 33; Ezra 8 : 22; Job 4 : 17; 8; 10 : 3; 11 : 11; 12 : 6; 13 : 15; 14 : 15; 34 : 10; 35 : 13; 37 : 23; 40 : 8. See Psalms. Prov. 11 : 21; 15 : 8; 28 : 9; 30 : 5; Eccl. 5 : 8; 8 : 12; 9 : 2; Isa. 45 : 21; Jer. 5 : 3; 9 : 24; 23 . 20, 32 . 19, 50 . 7, 51 . 9, Lam. 1 : 18; Ezek. 7 : 27; 16 : 35; 18 : 10; 33 : 17; Dan. 4 : 37; 9 : 14; Hos. 4; 5; Nah. 1 : 3; Hab. 1 : 13; Zeph. 3 : 5; Mal. 2 : 17; 4 : 1; Matt. 10 : 15; 20 : 13; 23 : 14; Luke 12 : 47; 13 : 27; John 7 : 18; Acts 10 : 34; 17 : 31; Rom. 2 : 2; Gal. 6 : 7; Eph. 6 : 8; Col. 3 : 25; Jas. 1 : 13; 1 John 1 : 9; Rev. 15 : 3; 16 : 7.
Knowledge, Wisdom, and Power, Gen. 1 : 3; 6-9; 41 : 16; Ex. 4 : 1, 11; 7-10; 12 : 29; 14; 15; 33 : 18 f.; 34 : 5; 35 : 30 ff.; 36; Num. 11 : 23; 12; 22 : 9; 23 : 4 f.; 24 : 16; Deut. 3; 4 : 32; 5 : 24; 6 : 22; 7; 10; 26; 28 : 58; 29 : 29; 32 : 4; Josh. 3 ; 6; 7 : 10; 23 : 9; 24; Judg. 2; 1 Sam. 2; 4; 5; 12 : 18; 14 : 6; 16 : 7; 17 : 37, 46; 18 : 10; 23; 2 Sam. 7 : 22; 1 Ki. 8 : 27; 22 : 22; 1 Chr. 16 : 24; 17 : 4; 22 : 18; 28 : 9; 29 : 11; 2 Chr. 6 : 18; 14 : 11; 20 : 6; Neh. 9 : 5; Job 4 : 9; 5 : 9; 9; 10 : 4; 11; 12; 19 : 6; 21 : 17; 22 : 23; 26 : 6; 33; 34 : 22; 35-41. See Psalms. Prov. 3 : 19; 5 : 21; 8 : 22; 15 : 3; 16 : 9; 10 : 21; 21 : 30; Eccl. 3 : 11; 7 : 13; Isa. 2 : 10; 6 : 3; 12 : 5; 14 : 24; 28 : 29; 29 : 16; 30 : 18; 33 : 13; 40 : 29; 41 : 20; 42 : 8; 43 : 13; 44 : 6, 23; 45 : 20; 46 : 5; 47 : 4; 48 : 3; 52 : 10; 55 : 11; 59 : 1; 60 : 1; 66 : 1; Jer. 3 : 14; 5 : 22; 10 : 6; 14 : 22; 29 : 23; 32 : 17; Lam. 3 : 37; Ezek. 8 : 12;

11 : 5; 22 : 14; Dan. 2 : 20; 3 : 17, 29;
4 : 34; 6 : 26; Joel 2 : 11; Amos 5 : 12;
8 : 7; Hab. 2 : 14; Mal. 3 : 16; Matt.
5 : 48; 6 : 13; 9 : 38; 10 : 29; 12 : 25;
19 : 26; 22 : 29; Mark 5 : 30; 12 : 15;
Luke 1 : 49; 12 : 5; 18 : 27; John 1 : 14;
2 : 24; 5 : 26; 6 : 64; 11 : 25; 16 : 19;
18 : 4; 19 : 28; 20 : 17; Acts 1 : 24; 2 : 17;
7 : 55; 15 : 18; Rom. 1 : 20; 4 : 17; 8 : 29;
11 : 34; 15 : 19; 16 : 27; 1 Cor. 2 : 9; 2
Cor. 4 : 6; 12 : 9; 13 : 4; Gal. 2 : 8; Eph.
1 : 19; 3 : 7; 6 : 10; Phil. 1 : 6; 3 : 21;
Col. 3 : 4; 1 Tim. 1 : 12, 17 ; Heb. 1 : 3;
2 : 10; 4 : 12; Jas. 4 : 6; 1 Pet. 1 : 2, 20;
1 John 1 : 5; 3 : 20; Jude 24; Rev. 1 : 8;
4 : 11; 5 : 13; 11 : 17; 19 : 6; 21 : 3.
Faithfulness and Truth, Num. 23 : 19; Deut.
7 : 8; Josh. 21 : 45; 2 Sam. 7 : 28; 1 Ki.
8 : 56; Ps. 19 : 9; 89 : 34; 105 : 8; 111 : 7;
117; 119 : 89, 160; 146 : 6; Isa. 25 : 1;
31 : 2; 46 : 11; 65 : 16; Jer. 4 : 28; Lam.
2 : 17; Ezek. 12 : 25; Matt. 24 : 35; John
7 : 28; Rom. 3 : 4; 1 Cor. 1 : 9; 15 : 58;
2 Cor. 1 : 18; 1 Thess. 5 : 24; 2 Thess. 3 : 3;
2 Tim. 2 : 13; Titus 1 : 2; Heb. 6 : 18;
10 : 23; 11 : 11; 13 : 5; 2 Pet. 3 : 9; Rev.
1 : 5; 3 : 7; 15 : 3; 16 : 7.
Goodness, Mercy, and Love, Gen. 1 : 28;
4 : 4; 8; 9; 15 : 4; 16 : 7; 17; 18 : 16;
19 : 12; 21 : 12; 22 : 15; 24 : 12; 26 : 24;
28 : 10 f.; 29 : 31; 32 : 49, 2; 39 : 2; 46;
Ex. 1 : 20; 2 : 23; 3 : 7; 6; 16; 17; 20 : 6;
22 : 27; 23 : 20; 29 : 45; 32 : 14; 33 : 12;
34 : 6; Lev. 4 : 35; 26 : 3, 40; Num.
14 : 18; 21 : 7; Deut. 4 : 29; 7 : 7; 8;
10 : 15; 18 : 15; 20 : 4; 23 : 5; 28 : 1; 30;
32 : 7, 43; 33; Josh. 20; Judg. 2 : 16;
6 : 36; 10 : 15; 13; 15 : 18; 1 Sam. 2 : 9;
7; 25 : 32; 2 Sam. 12 : 13; 1 Ki. 8 : 56;
2 Chr. 15 : 9; 30 : 9; Ezra 8 : 18; Neh.
2 : 18; 9 : 17; Job 5 : 17; 7 : 17; 11 : 6;
33 : 14; 36 : 11; 37 : 23; Ps. 34 : 8; 36 : 5;
69 : 16; Prov. 8 : 30; 11 : 20; 18 : 10;
28 : 13; Eccl. 2 : 26; 8 : 12; Isa. 25 : 4;
27 : 3; 30 : 18; 38 : 17; 40 : 29; 43 : 1;
48 : 9, 17; 49 : 15; 54 : 7; 55 : 3; 63 : 7;
Jer. 3 : 12; 9 : 24; 16 : 14; 17 : 7; 31 : 3,
12; 32 : 39; 33 : 11; 46 : 28; Lam. 3 : 22,
31; Ezek. 20 : 17; 33 : 11; Dan. 9 : 9;
Hos. 2 : 19; 11 : 4; 13 : 14; 14 : 3; Joel
2 : 13; Mic. 7 : 18; Nah. 1 : 7; Hab.
3 : 18; Zeph. 3 : 17; Mal. 3 : 6, 16; 4;
Matt. 5 : 45; 19 : 17; 23 : 37; Luke 1 : 50,
78; 5 : 21; 6 : 35; 12 : 6; John 1 : 4, 9;
3 : 16; 4 : 10; 14; 15 : 9; 16 : 7; 17; Acts
14 : 17; Rom. 2 : 4; 3 : 25; 5 : 5; 8 : 32;
9 : 22; 11; 2 Cor. 1 : 3; 12 : 9; 13 : 11;
Gal. 1 : 4; Eph. 2 : 4, 19; 4 : 6; 1 Tim.
2 : 4; 6 : 17; 2 Tim. 1 : 8; Titus 3 : 4;
Heb. 12 : 6; Jas. 1 : 5, 17; 5 : 11; 1 Pet.
1 : 3; 3 : 20; 2 Pet. 3 : 9, 15; 1 John 1;
Jude 21; Rev. 2 : 7. See Psalms.
Jealousy, Ex. 20 : 5; 34 : 14; Deut. 4 : 24;
5 : 9; 6 : 15; 29 : 20; 32 : 16; Josh.
24 : 19; Ps. 78 : 58; 79 : 5; Ezek. 16; 23;
Hos. 1; 2; Joel 2 : 18; Zeph. 1 : 18; Zech.
1 : 14; 1 Cor. 10 : 22; Rev. 2 : 4.
His Characters :
The Supreme Governor, Gen. 6–9; 11 : 8;

12; 14 : 20; 18 : 14; 22; 25 : 23; 26;
Ex. 9 : 16; Deut. 7 : 7; 1 Sam. 2 : 6;
9 : 15; 13 : 14; 15 : 17; 16 ; 2 Sam. 7 : 8;
22 : 1; Ps. 10 : 16; 22 : 28; 24; 33;
74 : 12; 75; Isa. 6 : 5; 40 : 13; 43–45;
64 : 8; Jer. 8 : 19; 10 : 10; 18; 19; Dan.
4; 5; Zech. 14 : 9; Luke 10 : 21; Rom. 9;
Eph. 1; 1 Tim. 1 : 17; 6 : 15; Jas. 4 : 12.
Judge of All, Gen. 18 : 25; Deut. 32 : 36;
Judg. 11 : 27; Ps. 7 : 11; 9 : 7; 50;
58 : 11; 68 : 5; 75 : 7; 94 : 2; Eccl.
3 : 17; 11 : 9; 12 : 14; Isa. 2 : 4; 3 : 13;
Jer. 11 : 20; Acts 10 : 42; Rom. 2 : 16;
2 Tim. 4 : 8; Heb. 12 : 23; Jude 6; Rev.
11 : 18; 18 : 8; 19 : 11.
Searcher of Hearts, 1 Chr. 28 : 9; Ps. 7 : 9;
44 : 21; 139 : 23; Prov. 17 : 3; 24 : 12;
Jer. 17 : 10; Acts 1 : 24; Rom. 8 : 27;
Rev. 2 : 23.
Refuge and Sanctuary, Deut. 33 : 27; 2 Sam.
22 : 3; Ps. 9 : 9; 46 : 1; 57 : 1; 59 : 16;
62; 71 : 7; 91; 94 : 22; 142 : 5; Isa.
8 : 14; Ezek. 11 : 16; Heb. 6 : 18.
The Saviour, Ps. 106 : 21; Isa. 43 : 3. 11;
45 : 15; 49 : 26; 60 : 16; 63 : 8; Jer.
14 : 8; Hos. 13 : 4; Luke 1 : 47.
His Names :
Jehovah, Ex. 6 : 3; Ps. 83 : 18; Isa. 12 : 2;
26 : 4; usually rendered Lord.
I Am, Ex. 3 : 14.
Living God, Deut. 5 : 26; Josh. 3 : 10.
God of Heaven, Ezra 5 : 11; Neh. 1 : 4;
2 : 4.
God of Hosts, Ps. 80 : 7, 14, 19.
Holy One, Job 6 : 10; Ps. 16 : 10; Isa.
10 : 17; Hos. 11 : 9; Hab. 1 : 12.
Holy One of Israel, 2 Ki. 19 : 22; Ps. 71 : 22;
Isa. 1 : 4; Jer. 51 : 5; Ezek. 39 : 7.
Lord of Hosts, 1 Sam. 1 : 11; Isa. 1 : 24.
Lord of Lords, Deut. 10 : 17; 1 Tim. 6 : 15;
Rev. 17 : 14.
Mighty God, Ps. 50 : 1; Isa. 9 : 6; 10 : 21;
Jer. 32 : 18.
Most High, Num. 24 : 16; Deut. 32 : 8;
2 Sam. 22 : 14; Ps. 7 : 17.
Most High God, Gen. 14 : 18; Ps. 57 : 2;
Dan. 3 : 26.
Father of Lights, Jas. 1 : 17.
Lord of Sabaoth, Rom. 9 : 29; Jas. 5 : 4.
King of Kings, 1 Tim. 6 : 15; Rev. 17 : 14.
The Father, Matt. 11 : 25; 28 : 19; Mark
14 : 36; Luke 10 : 21; 22 : 42; John 1 : 14;
Acts 1 : 4; 2 : 33; Rom. 6 : 4; 8 : 15;
1 Cor. 8 : 6; 15 : 24; 2 Cor. 1 : 3; 6 : 18;
Gal. 1 : 1; 3, 4; Eph. 1 : 17; Col. 1 : 19;
2 : 2; 1 Thess. 1 : 1; Jas. 1 : 27; 3 : 9;
2 Pet. 1 : 17; 1 John 1 : 2; Jude 1.
The Son, Matt 11 : 27; Luke 1 : 32; John
1 : 18; Acts 8 : 37; 9 : 20; Rom. 1 : 4;
2 Cor. 1 : 19; Gal. 2 : 21; Eph. 4 : 13;
Heb. 4 : 14; 1 John 2 : 22; Rev. 2 : 18.
See Christ.
Holy Ghost :
As a Spirit :
" The Holy Ghost," John 4 : 24; 2 Cor. 3 : 17.
Eternal, Heb. 9 : 14.
Omnipresent, Ps. 139 : 7.
Omniscient, 1 Cor. 2 : 10.
Omnipotent, Luke 1 : 35; Rom. 15 : 19.

Author of the new birth, John 3 : 5, 6; 5 : 4.

the source of wisdom, Isa. 11 : 2; John 14 : 26; 16 : 13; 1 Cor. 12 : 8.

the source of miraculous power, Matt. 12 : 28; Luke 11 : 20; Acts 19 : 11; Rom. 15 : 19.

inspiring Scripture, 2 Tim. 3 : 16; 2 Pet. 1 : 21.

appointing ministers, Acts 13 : 2, 4; 20 : 28.

directing where to preach the Gospel, Acts 16 : 6, 7.

dwelling in saints, John 14 : 17; 1 Cor. 6 : 19.

sanctifying the Church, Rom. 15 : 16; (Ezek. 37 : 28).

the witness, Heb. 10 : 15; 1 John 5 : 8.

convincing of sin, of righteousness, and of judgment, John 16 : 8-11.

Personality of :

he strives with sinners, Gen. 6 : 3.

he creates and gives life, Job 33 : 4.

he commissions his servants, etc., Isa. 48 : 16; Acts 8 : 29; 10 : 19, 20; 1 Cor. 2 : 13.

he teaches, etc., John 14 : 26; 15 : 26; 16 : 8; 16 : 13, 14; 1 Cor. 12 : 13.

helps our infirmities, Rom. 8 : 26.

searches all things, Rom. 11 : 33, 34; 1 Cor. 2 : 10, 11.

works according to his own will, 1 Cor. 12 : 11.

he spoke in, and by, the prophets, Acts 1 : 16; 1 Pet. 1 : 11, 12; 2 Pet. 1 : 21.

See Acts 7 : 51; 9 : 31; Rom. 15 : 16.

The Comforter :

given by Christ, Luke 4 : 18; John 14 : 26; 15 : 26; 16 : 7.

edifies the Church, Acts 9 : 31.

imparts the love of God, Rom. 5 : 5.

communicates joy, Rom. 14 : 17; Gal. 5 : 22; 1 Thess. 1 : 6.

imparts hope, Rom. 15 : 13; Gal. 5 : 5.

The Teacher :

as the Spirit of wisdom, Isa. 11 : 2; 40 : 13, 14.

given to saints, Neh. 9 : 20; 1 Cor. 2 : 12, 13; Eph. 1 : 16, 17.

See Ezek. 36 : 27; Mark 13 : 11; Luke 2 : 26; 12 : 12; John 16 : 13, 14; Acts 15 : 28; 1 Cor. 12 : 8.

Emblems of :

Water, John 3 : 5; 7 : 38; Eph. 5 : 26; Heb. 10 : 22; Rev. 22 : 17; (Isa. 55 : 1).

Fire, Ex. 13 : 21; Ps. 78 : 14; Isa. 4 : 4; Mal. 3 : 2, 3; Matt. 3 : 11; Heb. 12 : 29.

Wind, 1 Ki. 19 : 11; John 3 : 8; Acts 2 : 2.

Oil, Isa. 61 : 1, 3; Heb. 1 : 9; 1 John 2 : 20, 27.

Rain and Dew, Ps. 68 : 9; 72 : 6; Hos. 6 : 3; 10 : 12; 14 : 5.

A Dove, Matt. 3 : 16.

A Voice, Isa. 6 : 8; 30 : 21; John 16 : 13; Heb. 3 : 7.

Seal, 2 Cor. 1 : 22; Eph. 1 : 13, 14; 4 : 30; Rev. 7 : 2.

Cloven Tongues, Acts 2 : 3, 6-11.

The Gift of the Holy Ghost, Ps. 68 : 18; Isa. 32 : 15; 59 : 21; Ezek. 39 : 29; Hag. 2 : 5; Luke 11 : 13; John 3 : 34; 20 : 22; Acts 2 : 38; 5 : 32; 10 : 44, 45; 15 : 8; 2 Cor. 5 : 5; Gal. 3 : 14; 1 John 3 : 24; 4 : 13.

Gen. 5 : 22; 6 : 9, walked with G.

16 : 13, thou G. seest me.

32 : 28, power with G.

48 : 21, G. shall be with you.

Num. 23 : 19, G. is not a man, that he should lie.

Deut. 33 : 27, the eternal G. is thy refuge.

1 Sam. 17 : 46, may know there is a G. in Israel.

2 Sam. 16 : 16, G. save the king.

22 : 32; Ps. 18 : 31, who is G. save the Lord ?

1 Ki. 18 : 21, if the Lord be G., follow him.

18 : 39, the Lord, he is the G.

2 Ki. 19 : 15, thou art G., even thou.

Job 22 : 13; Ps. 73 : 11, how doth G. know ?

Ps. 14 : 1; 53 : 1, fool said, there is no G.

22 : 1; Matt. 27 : 46, my G., my G., why hast thou forsaken me ?

Ps. 86 : 10; Isa. 37 : 16, thou art G. alone.

Eccl. 5 : 2, G. is in heaven.

Isa. 44 : 8, is there a G. beside me ?

45 : 22, I am G., there is none else.

Jer. 31 : 33; 32 : 38, I will be their G.

Hos. 11 : 9, I am G., and not man.

Jonah 1 : 6, arise, call upon thy G.

Mic. 6 : 8, walk humbly with thy G.

Matt. 1 : 23, G. with us.

6 : 24; Luke 16 : 13, ye cannot serve G. and mammon.

Matt. 19 : 17; Mark 10 : 18; Luke 18 : 19, there is none good but one, that is G.

Matt. 22 : 32, G. is not G. of the dead.

Mark 12 : 32, there is one G., and none other.

John 1 : 1, the Word was G.

3 : 2, do miracles, except G. be with him.

4 : 24, G. is a Spirit.

17 : 3, life eternal, to know thee, the only true G.

Acts 10 : 34, G. is no respecter of persons.

Rom. 8 : 31, if G. be for us, who against us ?

1 Cor. 8 : 6, but one G., the Father.

15 : 28, that G. may be all in all.

2 Cor. 13 : 11, G. of love and peace shall be with you.

2 Thess. 2 : 4, above all that is called G.

1 Tim. 3 : 16, G. was manifest in the flesh.

Heb. 3 : 4, he that built all things is G.

8 : 10, I will be to them a G.

11 : 16, not ashamed to be called their G.

1 John 1 : 5, G. is light.

4 : 8, 16, G. is love.

Rev. 21 : 4, G. shall wipe away all tears.

God (an idol), Ex. 32 : 1, make us g.

Judg. 6 : 31, if he be a g., let him plead.

17 : 5, Micah had a house of g.

Ps. 16 : 4, hasten after another g.

Isa. 44 : 15, maketh a g., and worshippeth.

45 : 20, pray to a g. that cannot save.

Amos 5 : 26; Acts 7 : 43, star of your g.

Jonah 1 : 5, cried every man to his g.

Acts 12 : 22, the voice of a g., not of a man.

14 : 11, the g. are come down to us.

1 Cor. 8 : 5, there be g. many.

Goddess, 1 Ki. 11 : 5, 33; Acts 19 : 27, 35, 37.

Godhead, Acts 17 : 29, not to think g. is like unto gold.

Rom. 1 : 20, his eternal power and g.

Col. 2 : 9, all the fulness of the g. bodily.

Godliness, 1 Tim. 3 : 16, the mystery of g.
4 : 8, g. is profitable unto all things.
6 : 5, supposing that gain is g.
2 Tim. 3 : 5, a form of g.
Titus 1 : 1, the truth which is after g.
2 Pet. 1 : 3, pertain to life and g.
3 : 11, in all holy conversation and g.
Godly, Ps. 12 : 1, the g. man ceaseth.
2 Cor. 1 : 12, in g. sincerity.
7 : 10, g. sorrow worketh repentance.
2 Tim. 3 : 12, all that will live g. in Christ.
Titus 2 : 12, live g. in this world.
Heb. 12 : 28, reverence and g. fear.
2 Pet. 2 : 9, Lord knoweth how to deliver g.
3 John 6, bring forward after a g. sort.
Gods, judges described as, Ex. 22 : 28; Ps.
82 : 1; 138 : 1; John 10 : 34; 1 Cor. 8 : 5.
false, worship of, forbidden, Ex. 20 : 3;
34 : 17; Deut. 5 : 7; 8 : 19; 18 : 20.
Godward, Ex. 18 : 19; 2 Cor. 3 : 4; 1 Thess.
1 : 8.
Gog and Magog (gŏg, mā⸗gŏg), Ezek. 38; 39;
Rev. 20 : 8.
Going, 2 Sam. 5 : 24; 1 Chr. 14 : 15, sound of
g. in trees.
Ps. 17 : 5, hold up my g.
19 : 6, his g. forth is from the end of the
heaven.
40 : 2, establish my g.
Prov. 5 : 21, pondereth all his g.
14 : 15, man looketh well to his g.
20 : 24, man's g. are of the Lord.
Mic. 5 : 2, whose g. forth have been from of
old.
1 Tim. 5 : 24, sins g. before to judgment.
1 Pet. 2 : 25, as sheep g. astray.
Jude 7, g. after strange flesh.
Gold [Heb. Zāhab; χρυσίον; aurum], 1 Ki.
9 : 28. There are six different names for
gold, besides various qualifying terms, prefixed to zāhab, used in the Bible. These
names refer to the characteristics or various
attributes of gold, and testify to the high
position of esteem which it occupied. As
a medium of exchange, by weight, it was
used in the time of Abraham, but does not
appear to have been actually coined till the
time of Ezra. There is no indication of its
having been obtained in Palestine, but some
may have come from Egypt or even Midian.
The Jews were mainly dependent, however,
on supplies from Arabia (Sheba), Africa,
and Ophir on the west coast of India.
Possibly some may have come too through
Tarshish (Tartessus) in Spain.
Gen. 2 : 11; Job 22 : 24; Ps. 19 : 10; 21 : 3;
Zech. 4 : 2.
mentioned figuratively, Rev. 3 : 18; 21 : 18.
Ex. 20 : 23, neither shall ye make unto you
gods of g.
Deut. 8 : 13, when thy g. is multiplied.
1 Ki. 20 : 3, silver and g. is mine.
Job 28 : 1, a vein for silver, a place for g.
31 : 24, if I made g. my hope.
Ps. 19 : 10, more to be desired than g.
Prov. 16 : 16, better to get wisdom than g.
25 : 11, like apples of g.
Isa. 60 : 17, for brass I will bring g.
Lam. 4 : 1, how is g. become dim ?

Hag. 2 : 8, the silver is mine, and the g. is
mine.
Zech. 13 : 9, I will try them as g. is tried.
Matt. 23 : 16, swear by g. of the temple.
Acts 3 : 6, silver and g. have I none.
1 Cor. 3 : 12, build on this foundation, g.
2 Tim. 2 : 20, vessels of g. and silver.
Heb. 9 : 4, ark overlaid with g.
Jas. 2 : 2, man with a g. ring.
5 : 3, your g. is cankered.
1 Pet. 1 : 7, trial of your faith more precious
than of g.
Rev. 3 : 18, to buy of me g. tried.
21 : 18, city was pure g.
Golden, candlestick, Ex. 25 : 31; Rev. 1 : 12,
20; 2 : 1.
Goldsmith, Neh. 3 : 8, 31, 32; Isa. 40 : 19;
41 : 7; 46 : 6. See **Handicraft.**
Golgotha (gŏl⸗gŏ-thǎ) [place of a skull], Matt.
27 : 33; Mark 15 : 22; Luke 23 : 33; John
19 : 17. See **Calvary.**
Goliath (gō-li⸗ǎth) [shining], 1 Sam. 17 : 4;
21 : 9; 22 : 10.
Gomer (gō⸗mĕr) [complete ?], wife of Hosea,
Hos. 1 : 3.
Gomorrah (gō-mŏr⸗răh) [overflowed] (and
Sodom), Gen. 19 : 24, 28; Isa. 1 : 9; Matt.
10 : 15.
Gone, Num. 16 : 46, wrath g. out from the Lord.
Deut. 23 : 23, that which is g. out of thy lips.
Ps. 42 : 4, I had g. with the multitude.
73 : 2, my feet were almost g.
77 : 8, is his mercy clean g. for ever ?
103 : 16, wind passeth over, it is g.
109 : 23, I am g. like the shadow.
Song of Sol. 2 : 11, the rain is over and g.
Isa. 53 : 6, all we like sheep have g. astray.
Mark 5 : 30; Luke 8 : 46, virtue had g. out of
him.
John 12 : 19, the world is g. after him.
Acts 16 : 19, hope of their gains was g.
Rom. 3 : 12, they are all g. out of the way.
Jude 11, g. in the way of Cain.
Good (noun), Gen. 27 : 46, what g. shall my life
do me ?
32 : 12, I will surely do thee g.
50 : 20, God meant it unto g.
Neh. 5 : 19; 13 : 31, think upon me for g.
Job 2 : 10, shall we receive g. ?
22 : 21, thereby g. shall come to thee.
Ps. 4 : 6, who will show us any g. ?
14 : 1; 53 : 1; Rom. 3 : 12, none doeth g.
Ps. 34 : 12, loveth days that he may see g.
86 : 17, show me a token for g.
Prov. 3 : 27, withhold not g. from them.
11 : 17, doeth g. to his own soul.
Eccl. 7 : 20, that doeth g., and sinneth not.
9 : 18, one sinner destroyeth much g.
Acts 10 : 38, who went about doing g.
14 : 17, he did g. and gave us rain.
Rom. 8 : 28, all things work together for g.
13 : 4, minister of God for g.
1 John 3 : 17, this world's g.
(adj.), Gen. 1 : 4, 12, 31, God saw it was g.
2 : 18, not g. that man should be alone.
26 : 29, we have done nothing but g.
Deut. 2 : 4; Josh. 23 : 11, take g. heed.
1 Sam. 2 : 24, it is no g. report I hear.
12 : 23, I will teach you the g. way.

25 : 15, men were very g. to us.
1 Ki. 8 : 56, no word of g. promise failed.
2 Ki. 20 : 19; Isa. 39 : 8, g. is word of the Lord.
Ezra 8 : 18, g. hand of our God upon us.
Neh. 9 : 20, thy g. spirit to instruct.
Ps. 25 : 8, g. and upright is the Lord.
34 : 8, taste and see that the Lord is g.
37 : 23, steps of g. man ordered by Lord.
45 : 1, my heart is inditing a g. matter.
112 : 5, a g. man showeth favour.
145 : 9, the Lord is g. to all.
Prov. 12 : 25, a g. word maketh the heart glad.
15 : 23, word in season, how g. is it ?
22 : 1, a g. name rather to be chosen than riches.
Eccl. 9 : 2, one event to the g. and clean.
Isa. 55 : 2, eat ye that which is g.
Jer. 6 : 16, the g. way, and walk therein.
29 : 10, I will perform my g. work.
Lam. 3 : 27, it is g. that a man bear yoke.
Zech. 1 : 13, Lord answereth with g. words.
Matt. 7 : 11; Luke 11 : 13, how to give g. gifts.
Matt. 9 : 22; Luke 8 : 48, be of g. comfort.
Matt. 19 : 17; Luke 18 : 19, none g., save one.
Matt. 25 : 21, well done, thou g. servant.
26 : 24, been g. for that man.
Mark 9 : 50; Luke 14 : 34, salt is g., but.
Luke 2 : 14, peace on earth, g.-will to men.
6 : 38, g. measure pressed down.
10 : 42, Mary hath chosen that g. part.
12 : 32, your Father's g. pleasure to give.
23 : 50, Joseph was a g. man, and a just.
John 1 : 46, can any g. thing come out of Nazareth ?
2 : 10, kept g. wine until now.
10 : 11, I am the g. shepherd.
10 : 33, for a g. work we stone thee not.
Rom. 7 : 12, the commandment holy, just, and g.
12 : 2, that g. and perfect will of God.
1 Cor. 15 : 33, evil communications corrupt g. manners.
2 Cor. 9 : 8, abound to every g. work.
Gal. 6 : 6, communicate in all g. things.
Col. 1 : 10, fruitful in every g. work.
1 Thess. 5 : 21; hold fast that which is g.
1 Tim. 1 : 8, the law is g.
4 : 4, every creature of God is g.
Titus 2 : 14, zealous of g. works.
Heb. 6 : 5, tasted the g. word of God.
Jas. 1 : 17, every g. gift.
Goodliness, Isa. 40 : 6, g. thereof is as the flower.
Goodly, Gen. 39 : 6, Joseph was a g. person.
49 : 21, he giveth g. words.
Ex. 2 : 2, he was a g. child.
Num. 24 : 5, how g. are thy tents, O Jacob!
Deut. 3 : 25, let me see that g. mountain.
6 : 10, g. cities which thou buildest not.
8 : 12, when thou hast built g. houses.
Josh. 7 : 21, a g. Babylonish garment.
1 Sam. 9 : 2, a choice young man, and a g.
16 : 12, David was g. to look to.
Ps. 16 : 6; Jer. 3 : 19, a g. heritage.
Ps. 80 : 10, boughs were like g. cedars.
Zech. 11 : 13, a g. price I was prized at.
Matt. 13 : 45, seeking g. pearls.

Jas. 2 : 2, a man in g. apparel.
Goodman [ar.], man of the house, husband.
Used as polite designation of those below rank of gentry, Prov. 7 : 19; Matt. 20 : 11; Mark 14 : 14; Luke 22 : 11.
Goodness, Ex. 33 : 19, I will make all my g. pass before thee.
34 : 6, the Lord God abundant in g.
2 Chr. 6 : 41, let thy saints rejoice in g.
Ps. 16 : 2, my g. extendeth not to thee.
23 : 6, g. and mercy shall follow me.
27 : 13, believed to see the g. of the Lord.
31 : 19, how great is thy g.
33 : 5, earth is full of g. of the Lord.
65 : 11, thou crownest the year with thy g.
107 : 9, he filleth the hungry soul with g.
145 : 7, the memory of thy g.
Prov. 20 : 6, proclaim every one his g.
Jer. 31 : 12, flow together to g. of the Lord.
Hos. 6 : 4, your g. is as a morning cloud.
Rom. 2 : 4, the riches of his g.
11 : 22, the g. and severity of God.
2 Thess. 1 : 11, fulfil good pleasure of his g.
Goods, Matt. 12 : 29; Mark 3 : 27, spoil his g.
Luke 12 : 19, much g. laid up.
15 : 12, the portion of g.
16 : 1, accused that he had wasted his g.
19 : 8, half of my g. I give to the poor.
Rev. 3 : 17, rich, and increased with g.
Gopher wood, mentioned in Gen. 6 : 14 only. The Hebrew word is left untranslated, but tradition asserts it to be " cypress." Perhaps " cedar " is more correct. The ark was made of this wood.
Gore, Ex. 21 : 28, 31.
Gorgeous, Ezek. 23 : 12; Luke 7 : 25; 23 : 11.
Goshen (gō̄-shĕn), land of (Egypt), Israelites placed there, Gen. 45 : 10; 46 : 34; 47 : 4.
no plagues there, Ex. 8 : 22; 9 : 26.
(Canaan), Josh. 10 : 41; 11 : 16.
Gospel of Christ, characterised, Matt. 4 : 23; 24 : 14; Mark 1 : 14; Luke 2 : 10; 20 : 21; Acts 13 : 26; 14 : 3; 20 : 21; Rom. 1 : 2, 9, 16; 2 : 16; 10 : 8; 16 : 25; 1 Cor. 1 : 18; 2 : 13; 15 : 1; 2 Cor. 4 : 4; 5 : 19; 6 : 1; Eph. 1 : 13; 3 : 2; 6 : 15; Phil. 2 : 16; Col. 1 : 5; 3 : 16; 1 Thess. 1 : 5; 2 : 8; 3 : 2; 1 Tim. 1 : 11; 6 : 3; Heb. 4 : 2; 1 Pet. 1 : 12, 25; 4 : 17.
preached to Abraham, Gal. 3 : 8.
preached to the poor and others, Matt. 11 : 5; Mark 1 : 14 f.; 13 : 10; 16 : 15; Luke 4 : 18; 24 : 47; Acts 13 : 46; 14; 1 Cor. 1 : 17; 9 : 16; Gal. 2 : 2; Rev. 14 : 6.
its effects, Mark 1 : 14 f.; 8 : 35; Luke 2 : 10, 14; 19 : 8; Acts 4 : 32; Rom. 1 : 16; 12; 13; 15 : 29; 16 : 26; 2 Cor. 8; 9; Gal. 1 : 16; 2 : 14; Eph. 4–6; Phil. 1 : 5, 17, 27; Col. 1 : 23; 3; 4; 1 Thess. 1; 2; Titus 2 : 3; Jas. 1; 1 and 2 Pet.; 1 John 3; Jude 3.
from whom hid, 1 Cor. 1 : 23; 2 : 8; 2 Cor. 4 : 3.
rejected by the Jews, Acts 13 : 46; 28 : 25; Rom. 9; 10; 11; 1 Thess. 2 : 16.
Mark 1 : 15, repent, and believe the g.
8 : 35, lose life for my sake and g.
13 : 10, the g. must be published.

Acts 20 : 24, the g. of the grace of God.
Rom. 1 : 16, I am not ashamed of g. of Christ.
 15 : 29, the blessing of the g. of Christ.
2 Cor. 4 : 3, if our g. be hid.
Gal. 1 : 7, pervert g. of Christ.
 2 : 7, the g. of uncircumcision, g. of circumcision.
Eph. 6 : 15, preparation of the g. of peace.
Col. 1 : 23, be not moved from the hope of
 the g.
1 Tim. 1 : 11, g. of the blessed God.
2 Tim. 1 : 10, immortality to light through g.
Rev. 14 : 6, having everlasting g. to preach.

Gospels, The Four.
 The name Gospel (lit. " God's story ") was
 given to the accounts of the " good tidings "
 of the salvation of the world through the
 coming of Jesus Christ as Saviour (Isa.
 52 : 7; Matt. 1 : 21–23; 4 : 23). From the
 Greek word given to our Lord's mission,
 " euangelion," those who reported or
 preached the " good message " were called
 " euangelistai " or " evangelists " (Eph.
 4 : 11; 2 Tim. 4 : 5; Acts 21 : 8).
 While there are various accounts given of
 the life and mission of Jesus, the Western
 Church has accepted four as historical,
 viz. : those attributed to Matthew, Mark,
 Luke, and John.
 Matthew writes for Jews, his theme being
 " the kingdom of heaven " (in Mark and
 Luke, " the kingdom of God ") as opposed
 to the earthly kingdom, which the Jews
 were then expecting. Mark's Gospel has
 a Roman aspect; his theme is Christ's
 practical service as the servant of God for
 man. His very name is Roman. The
 Gospel of Luke, whose name is Greek, has
 a Greek aspect; his theme is Christ " the
 Son of Man " in his sympathising humanity
 and as Saviour of sinners (7 : 36; 15 : 18).
 John writes for the Spiritual of every race;
 his theme is the Son of God manifested as
 our Light and Life. His Gospel is the
 complement of the three Synoptists (i.e., the
 first three Gospels). Christ appears as—
 (1) the Son of David in Matthew; (2) the
 servant of God in Mark; (3) the Son
 of Man in Luke; (4) the Son of God in
 John.
 Date.—The first three Gospels were composed during the latter part of the first
 century, and probably between the years
 A.D. 63 and 85. John is rather later, perhaps between A.D. 90 and 110. (See
 articles on separate Gospels.) By the end
 of the second century they were accepted as
 authentic.
 Origin.—Great erudition has been brought to
 the task of tracing the Gospels to a common literary source. The complete absence
 of any external evidence of the existence of
 such a source embarrasses each hypothesis
 that is offered. The true source of the
 materials recorded is the life, work, teaching, death, resurrection and ascension of
 the Lord Jesus. These facts made up the
 body of truth that was the common possession of the church of the first century.

Many attempts were made to record these
 facts systematically. Out of the many
 writings, four only had the complete confidence of the church from the first. The
 writings of the Fathers abundantly sustain
 this position. Irenæus (martyred 202 A.D.)
 says that the four Gospels were so well
 authenticated among the churches that even
 the heretics could not confute them. Ter-
 tullian ascribes the authorship of two of the
 Gospels to apostles and two to the disciples
 of apostles. The authenticity of all four
 rests upon their apostolic origin.

Gourd. There has been a great deal of discussion as to what plant is referred to in Jonah
 4 : 6-10, but the balance of opinion is in
 favour of its being, as translated in our
 Bible, the gourd (Cucurbita pepo). All
 practical experience seems opposed to its
 being the castor oil plant (Ricinus); it certainly was not the ivy, as St. Jerome
 thought. In the East, or in warm countries,
 gourds are grown to cover booths or
 arbours, and the plant, growing up rapidly,
 a grub destroying the root would cause the
 whole stem and foliage quickly to wither.

Gourd, Wild (2 Ki. 4 : 38-40). Probably the
 Citrullus colocynthus or colocynth, which
 is common in Palestine, and of bitter taste.

Government, Isa. 9 : 7, of increase of his g. shall
 be no end.
 22 : 21, I commit thy g. to his hand.
1 Cor. 12 : 28, g. diversities of tongues.
2 Pet. 2 : 10, them that despise g.

Governor, Gen. 42 : 6; 45 : 26, Joseph g. over
 the land.
 Neh. 5 : 18, I required not the bread of g.
 Ps. 22 : 28, g. among the nations.
 Matt. 2 : 6, shall come a g. that shall rule.
 28 : 14, if this come to the g. ears.
 Acts 23 : 34, g. had read the letter.
 24 : 1, informed g. against Paul.
 [ar.], helmsman, pilot, Jas. 3 : 4, whitherso-
 ever the g. listeth.

Grace (=French " grâce," derived from Latin
 " gratia," meaning " favour " either received from, or extended towards, another),
 of God and Jesus Christ, Ps. 84 : 11; Zech.
 4 : 7; Luke 2 : 40; John 1 : 16; Acts
 20 : 24; 1 Cor. 15 : 10; 2 Cor. 8 : 9; 2 Tim.
 1 : 9.
 salvation through, Acts 15 : 11; Rom. 3 : 24;
 4 : 4; Eph. 2 : 5; 2 Thess. 2 : 16; Titus
 3 : 7; 1 Pet. 1 : 10.
 effects of, 2 Cor. 1 : 12; Titus 2 : 11; 1 Pet.
 4 : 10.
 See **Gospel.**
 prayer for, Rom. 16 : 20; 1 Tim. 1 : 2; Heb.
 4 : 16.
 danger of abusing, Rom. 6; Jude 4; and
 departing from, Gal. 5 : 4.
 exhortations concerning, 2 Tim. 1 : 9; Heb.
 12 : 15, 28; 2 Pet. 3 : 18.
 Ps. 45 : 2, g. is poured into thy lips.
 84 : 11, Lord will give g.
 Prov. 1 : 9, an ornament of g.
 3 : 34; Jas. 4 : 6, giveth g. to the lowly.
 Zech. 4 : 7, crying g., g. unto it.
 12 : 10, spirit of g. and supplications.

John 1 : 14, full of g. and truth.
1 : 17, g. and truth came by Jesus Christ.
Acts 4 : 33, great g. was upon them all.
14 : 3, the word of his g.
Rom. 1 : 7; 1 Cor. 1 : 3; 2 Cor. 1 : 2; Gal.
1 : 3; Eph. 1 : 2; Phil. 1 : 2; Col. 1 : 2;
1 Thess. 1 : 1; 2 Thess. 1 : 2, g. and peace.
Rom. 3 : 24, justified freely by his g.
5 : 2, access into this g.
5 : 20, where sin abounded, g. did much
more abound.
6 : 14, under g.
11 : 5, the election of g.
2 Cor. 4 : 15, g. redound to the glory of God.
8 : 9, know the g. of our Lord.
12 : 9, my g. is sufficient for thee.
Gal. 5 : 4, ye are fallen from g.
Eph. 1 : 7, forgiveness, according to riches
of g.
2 : 5, 8, by g. ye are saved through faith.
4 : 29, minister g. to hearers.
6 : 24, g. be with all that love our Lord.
Col. 4 : 6, let your speech be always with g.
2 Thess. 2 : 16, good hope through g.
1 Tim. 1 : 2; 2 Tim. 1 : 2; Titus 1 : 4; 2 John
3, g., mercy, and peace.
2 Tim. 2 : 1, be strong in the g. in Christ.
Heb. 4 : 16, come boldly to the throne of g.
10 : 29, done despite to the spirit of g.
12 : 28, let us have g. to serve God.
13 : 9, heart established with g.
Jas. 1 : 11, the g. of the fashion perisheth.
4 : 6, he giveth more g.
1 Pet. 1 : 2; 2 Pet. 1 : 2, g. and peace be
multiplied.
1 Pet. 3 : 7, heirs of g.
5 : 5, giveth g. to the humble.
2 Pet. 3 : 18, grow in g.
Jude 4, turning g. of God into lasciviousness.
Rev. 1 : 4, g. from him, who is, and was.
Gracious, Gen. 43 : 29, God be g. to thee.
Ex. 22 : 27, I will hear, for I am g.
33 : 19, I will be g. to whom I will be g.
Num. 6 : 25, Lord be g. unto thee.
2 Sam. 12 : 22, tell whether God will be g. ?
Neh. 9 : 17, 31, a God g., merciful.
Ps. 77 : 9, hath God forgotten to be g. ?
Isa. 30 : 18, Lord will wait that he may be g.
Amos 5 : 15, may be the Lord will be g.
Jonah 4 : 2, I knew that thou art a g. God.
Mal. 1 : 9, beseech God, he will be g. to us.
Luke 4 : 22, wondered at the g. words.
1 Pet. 2 : 3, tasted that the Lord is g.
Graciously, Gen. 33 : 5, children which God hath
g. given.
33 : 11, God hath dealt g. with me.
Ps. 119 : 29, and grant me thy law g.
Hos. 14 : 2, receive us g.
Graffed, Rom. 11 : 17, 19, 23, 24.
Grain, of mustard seed, Matt. 13 : 31; 17 : 20;
Mark 4 : 31; Luke 13 : 19; 17 : 6.
Amos 9 : 9; 1 Cor. 15 : 37.
Grandmother, 2 Tim. 1 : 5.
Grant, 1 Sam. 1 : 17, God g. thee thy petition.
1 Chr. 4 : 10, God g. what he requested.
Job 6 : 8, God g. the thing I long for.
Prov. 10 : 24, desire of righteous shall be g.
Matt. 20 : 21; Mark 10 : 37, g. that my two
sons may sit.

2 Tim. 1 : 18, Lord g. he may find mercy.
Rev. 3 : 21, will I g. to sit with me in my
throne.
Grapes, laws concerning, Lev. 19 : 10; Num.
6 : 3; Deut. 23 : 24; 24 : 21.
See Jer. 31 : 29; Ezek. 18 : 2.
Gen. 49 : 11, washed clothes in blood of g.
Lev. 19 : 10, nor gather g. of vineyard.
Deut. 32 : 14, drink the blood of the g.
Song of Sol. 2 : 13, vines with tender g. give
good smell.
Isa. 5 : 2, looked it should bring forth g.
17 : 6; 24 : 13, gleaning g.
Jer. 6 : 9, thine hand as a g.-gatherer.
8 : 13, there shall be no g. on the vine.
31 : 29; Ezek. 18 : 2, fathers have eaten sour
g.
Mic. 7 : 1, g. gleanings of the vintage.
Matt. 7 : 16, do men gather g. of thorns ?
Luke 6 : 44, nor of brambles gather they g.
Rev. 14 : 18, her g. are fully ripe.
See Vine.
Grass, Gen. 1 : 11, let the earth bring forth g.
Deut. 32 : 2, as showers upon the g.
2 Ki. 19 : 26; Ps. 129 : 6; Isa. 37 : 27, as g.
on housetops.
Ps. 72 : 6, like rain upon the mown g.
90 : 5, like g. which groweth up.
102 : 4, my heart is withered like the g.
103 : 15, as for man, his days are as g.
Prov. 27 : 25, the tender g. sheweth itself.
Isa. 40 : 6; 1 Pet. 1 : 24, all flesh is g.
Mic. 5 : 7, as showers upon the g.
Matt. 6 : 30; Luke 12 : 28; if God so clothe
the g.
Jas. 1 : 10, as g. he shall pass away.
cf. Ps. 37 : 2; Jer. 50 : 11.
Grasshopper [Heb. chagab]. This insect, mentioned in Lev. 11 : 22, belongs, with the
other insects enumerated in the same place,
to the straight-winged or orthopterous
insects. This order includes the locusts,
crickets, and cockroaches.
Num. 13 : 33, were in our sight as g.
Judg. 6 : 5, came as g. for multitude.
Eccl. 12 : 5, g. shall be a burden.
Grate, Ex. 27 : 4; 38 : 4, 5.
Grave, law of, Num. 19 : 16.
triumphed over, Hos. 13 : 14; John 5 : 28;
1 Cor. 15 : 55; Rev. 20 : 13.
(noun), Gen. 37 : 35, will go down to g. to
my son.
42 : 38; 44 : 31, with sorrow to the g.
Ex. 14 : 11, no g. in Egypt.
Job 5 : 26, come to g. in full age.
7 : 9, goeth down to the g. shall come up no
more.
14 : 13, hide me in the g.
17 : 1, the g. are ready for me.
33 : 22, his soul draweth near to the g.
Ps. 6 : 5, in g. who shall give thanks ?
30 : 3, brought my soul from the g.
49 : 15; Hos. 13 : 14, the power of the g.
Eccl. 9 : 10, no wisdom in the g.
Isa. 38 : 18, the g. cannot praise thee.
53 : 9, he made his g. with the wicked.
Matt. 27 : 52, the g. were opened.
Luke 11 : 44, as g. which appear not.
John 5 : 28, all in the g. shall hear his voice.

1 Cor. 15 : 55, O g., where is thy victory ?
(verb =cut), 2 Chr. 2 : 7, send a man that can
  skill to g.
Job 19 : 24, were g. with an iron pen.
Isa. 49 : 16, I have g. thee upon palms of
  hands.
Jer. 17 : 1, is g. upon table of heart.
Hab. 2 : 18, that the maker hath g. it.
Grave-clothes, John 11 : 44.
Gravel, Prov. 20 : 17; Isa. 48 : 19; Lam. 3 : 16.
Graven image, Ex. 20 : 4; Lev. 26 : 1; Deut.
  5 : 8; Ps. 78 : 58; Isa. 42 : 17; Mic. 5 : 13.
Gravings, 1 Ki. 7 : 31; 2 Chr. 2 : 14; Zech. 3 : 9.
Gravity, 1 Tim. 3 : 4, in subject with all g.
  Titus 2 : 7, in doctrine showing g.
Gray, Gen. 42 : 38; 44 : 29, g. hairs with
  sorrow.
  Hos. 7 : 9, g. hairs are here and there.
Gray-headed, 1 Sam. 12 : 2; Ps. 71 : 18, I am
  old and g.
  Job 15 : 10, with us are the g.
Grease, Ps. 119 : 70, heart is as fat as g.
Great, Gen. 12 : 2; 18 : 18; 46 : 3, make a g.
  nation.
  48 : 19, he also shall be g.
  Deut. 10 : 17; 2 Chr. 2 : 5, the Lord your
  God is a g. God.
  Deut. 29 : 24, the heat of this g. anger.
  2 Sam. 22 : 36; Ps. 18 : 35, thy gentleness
  hath made me g.
  2 Ki. 5 : 13, bid thee do some g. thing.
  2 Chr. 2 : 5, the house is g., for g. is our God.
  Job 32 : 9, g. men are not always wise.
  36 : 18, a g. ransom.
  Ps. 14 : 5; 53 : 5, there were they in g. fear.
  31 : 19, how g. is thy goodness!
  92 : 5, how g. are thy works!
  139 : 17, how g. is the sum of them!
  Isa. 53 : 12, divide him a portion with the g.
  Jer. 32 : 19, g. in counsel.
  Matt. 5 : 12; Luke 6 : 23, g. is your reward.
  Matt. 20 : 26, whosoever will be g. among you.
  22 : 38, the first and g. commandment.
  Luke 10 : 2, the harvest is g.
  16 : 26, a g. gulf is fixed.
  Acts 8 : 9, giving out that he was some g. one.
  19 : 28, 34, g. is Diana of Ephesians.
  1 Tim. 3 : 16, g. is mystery of godliness.
  Heb. 2 : 3, so g. salvation.
  12 : 1, so g. a cloud of witnesses.
  Jas. 3 : 5, how g. a matter a little fire kindleth !
Greater, Gen. 4 : 13, punishment g. than I can
  bear.
  Ex. 18 : 11, Lord is g. than all gods.
  Deut. 1 : 28, people g. and taller than we.
  Job 33 : 12, that God is g. than man.
  Hag. 2 : 9, glory of latter house g. than
  former.
  Matt. 11 : 11; Luke 7 : 28, not risen a g. than
  John.
  Matt. 12 : 6, one g. than the temple.
  12 : 42; Luke 11 : 31, a g. than Solomon is
  here.
  John 1 : 50, thou shalt see g. things.
  4 :12; 8 : 53, art thou g. than our father ?
  5 : 20; 14 : 12, g. works than these.
  10 : 29; 14 : 28, my Father is g. than I.
  13 : 16; 15 : 20, servant not g. than lord.
  15 : 13, g. love hath no man than this.

19 : 11, he that delivered me hath g. sin.
Heb. 6 : 13, he could swear by no g.
  9 : 11, g. and more perfect tabernacle.
  11 : 26, the reproach of Christ g. riches.
1 John 3 : 20, God is g. than our heart.
  4 : 4, g. is he in you than he in the world.
  5 : 9, witness of God is g.
3 John 4, no g. joy than to hear that.
Greatest, Jer. 31 : 34; Heb. 8 : 11, all know me
  from least to the g.
  Matt. 13 : 32, it is the g. among herbs.
  18 : 1, who is g. in kingdom of heaven ?
  Mark 9 : 34; Luke 9 : 46, who should be g.
  1 Cor. 13 : 13, the g. of these is charity.
Greatly, Gen. 3 : 16, I will g. multiply thy
  sorrow.
  Ex. 19 : 18, whole mount quaked g.
  1 Sam. 12 : 18, the people g. feared the Lord.
  2 Sam. 24 : 10; 1 Chr. 21 : 8, I have sinned, g.
  1 Chr. 16 : 25; Ps. 48 : 1; 96 : 4; 145 : 3, the
  Lord is g. to be praised.
  Ps. 21 : 1, in thy salvation g. rejoice.
  28 : 7, my heart g. rejoiceth.
  47 : 9, God is g. exalted.
  89 : 7, God is g. to be feared in the assembly
  of saints.
  Dan. 9 : 23; 10 : 11, thou art g. beloved.
  Mark 5 : 38, wept and wailed g.
  12 : 27, ye do g. err.
Greatness, Ex. 15 : 7, g. of thine excellency.
  Deut. 32 : 3, ascribe ye g. unto our God.
  1 Chr. 29 : 11, thine is the g., power, and
  glory.
  Ps. 79 : 11, according to g. of thy power.
  145 : 3, his g. is unsearchable.
  Prov. 5 : 23, in g. of folly go astray.
  Isa. 40 : 26, by g. of his might.
  63 : 1, travelling in g. of strength.
  Dan. 4 : 22, thy g. reacheth unto heaven.
  Eph. 1 : 19, the exceeding g. of his power.
Greaves, armour for the legs below the knees.
  1 Sam. 17 : 6, Goliath had g. of brass.
Grecians. The " Grecians " were Greek-speaking Jews as distinguished from Jews who
  spoke Hebrew. " Greeks," on the other
  hand, were either Greeks by race (Acts
  16 : 1-3), or Gentiles of any nation (Rom.
  2 : 9, 10). The " Greeks " were Hellenes,
  the " Grecians " were Hellenists. The
  " murmuring of the Grecians against the
  Hebrews " (Acts 6 : 1) was that of foreign
  Jews who spoke Greek, against Palestinian
  Jews who spoke Hebrew.
Greece, prophecies of, Dan. 8 : 21; 10 : 20;
  11 : 2; Zech. 9 : 13.
  Paul preaches in, Acts 16; 20.
Greedy, Ps. 17 : 12, a lion that is g. of prey.
  Prov. 1 : 19; 15 : 27, g. of gain.
  Isa. 56 : 11, they are g. dogs.
  1 Tim. 3 : 3, not g. of filthy lucre.
  See Prov. 21 : 26; Eph. 4 : 19; Jude 11.
Greek (grēek), Luke 23 : 38; Acts 21 : 37; Rev.
  9 : 11.
Greeks, would see Jesus, John 12 : 20.
  believe in him, Acts 11 : 21; 17 : 4.
Green, Gen. 1 : 30; Lev. 2 : 14; Job 8 : 16;
  Jer. 11 : 16; Hos. 14 : 8; Mark 6 : 39; Rev.
  8 : 7.
Greenish, Lev. 13 : 49; 14 : 37.

Greenness, Job 8 : 12.
Greet, 1 Sam. 25 : 5; Rom. 16 : 3, 5, 6, 8, 11;
  1 Thess. 5 : 26; 3 John 14.
Greetings, in the markets, Matt. 23 : 7; Luke
  11 : 43; 20 : 46.
  send g., Acts 15 : 23; 23 : 26.
  2 Tim. 4 : 21; Jas. 1 : 1.
Grew, Gen. 21 : 8; 1 Sam. 2 : 21; Luke 1 : 80;
  Acts 7 : 17; 12 : 24; 19 : 20.
Greyhound [Heb. zarzir-mothnayim; girt-in-the-
  loins] occurs in Prov. 30 : 31, but the
  translation, war horse, given in the margin,
  is preferable.
Grief, 1 Sam. 1 : 16, out of abundance of g.
  2 Chr. 6 : 29, every one shall know his own g.
  Job 6 : 2, oh that my g. were weighed!
  Ps. 31 : 10, my life is spent with g.
  Eccl. 1 : 18, in much wisdom is much g.
  Isa. 53 : 3, a man of sorrows, and acquainted
  with g.
  Heb. 13 : 17, do it with joy and not g.
Grievance, Hab. 1 : 3, cause me to behold g.
  cf. Ezek. 28 : 24.
Grieve, Gen. 6 : 6, it g. Lord that he had made
  man.
  45 : 5, be not g. that ye sold me.
  1 Sam. 2 : 33, the man to g. thy heart.
  Ps. 78 : 40, how oft did they g. him ?
  95 : 10, forty years was I g.
  139 : 21, am not I g. with those that rise
  against thee.
  Lam. 3 : 33, doth not willingly g. men.
  Mark 3 : 5, being g. for hardness of their
  hearts.
  10 : 22, he went away g.
  John 21 : 17, Peter was g. because.
  Acts 4 : 2, being g. that they taught the
  people.
  Rom. 14 : 15, if brother be g. with meat.
  Eph. 4 : 30, g. not the Holy Spirit of God.
Grievous, Gen. 12 : 10, famine was g. in the land.
  50 : 11, a g. mourning to the Egyptians.
  Ps. 10 : 5, his ways are always g.
  Prov. 15 : 1, g. words stir up anger.
  Eccl. 2 : 17, work that is wrought under the
  sun is g.
  Isa. 21 : 2, a g. vision is declared.
  Jer. 30 : 12; Nah. 3 : 19, thy wound is g.
  Matt. 23 : 4; Luke 11 : 46, burdens g. to be
  borne.
  Acts 20 : 29, g. wolves enter in among you.
  Phil. 3 : 1, to me indeed is not g.
  Heb. 12 : 11, no chastening joyous, but g.
  1 John 5 : 3, his commandments are not g.
  cf. Luke 9 : 1; Ezek. 14 : 13; Matt. 15 : 22.
Grievousness, Isa. 10 : 1; 21 : 15.
Grind, Isa. 3 : 15, g. the faces of the poor.
  Lam. 5 : 13, took young men to g.
  Matt. 21 : 44; Luke 20 : 18, it will g. him
  to powder.
  Matt. 24 : 41; Luke 17 : 35, two women shall
  be g.
  See Eccl. 12 : 3, 4.
Grisled, Gen. 31 : 10, 12; Zech. 6 : 3, 6.
Groan, Job 24 : 12, men g. from out of the city.
  Joel 1 : 18, how do the beasts g. ?
  Rom. 8 : 23, we ourselves g. within.
  2 Cor. 5 : 2, we g. desiring to be clothed.
Groaning, Ex. 2 : 24, God heard their g.

John 11 : 38, Jesus g. within himself.
  Rom. 8 : 26, with g. which cannot be uttered.
Grope, Deut. 28 : 29; Job 5 : 14; 12 : 25; Isa.
  59 : 10.
Gross, Isa. 60 : 2, g. darkness shall cover the
  people.
  Matt. 13 : 15; Acts 28 : 27, waxed g.
Ground, Gen. 2 : 5, not a man to till g.
  Ex. 3 : 5; Acts 7 : 33, holy g.
  Job 5 : 6, nor trouble spring out of g.
  Ps. 107 : 33, turneth springs into dry g.
  Isa. 35 : 7, parched g. shall become a pool.
  Jer. 4 : 3; Hos. 10 : 12, break your fallow g.
  Zech. 8 : 12, g. shall give her increase.
  Matt. 13 : 8; Luke 8 : 8, fell into good g.
  Mark 4 : 26, cast seed into g.
  Luke 13 : 7, why cumbereth it the g. ?
  14 : 18, I have bought a piece of g.
  19 : 44, lay thee, even with the g.
  John 8 : 6, he wrote on the g.
  12 : 24, a corn of wheat fall into g.
Grounded, Isa. 30 : 32, where g. staff shall pass.
  Eph. 3 : 17, being rooted and g. in love.
  Col. 1 : 23, in the faith, g. and settled.
Grove. The Hebrew word " eshel " thus translated (A.V.) in Gen. 21 : 33; 1 Sam. 22 : 6
  and 31 : 13, is translated in the R.V.,
  " tamarisk." This tree belongs to the
  genus Tamarix, of which one shrubby
  species (T. gallica) is common in our
  gardens. Some species grow to the size of
  large trees. In many places the word
  " Asherah " is translated in the A.V.
  " grove," but in the R.V. it is untranslated. It is the Assyrian " Asirat "—the
  productive goddess (Deut. 16 : 21; Judg.
  6 : 25, 30); called also " Astarte," and worshipped as the moon-goddess.
  for worship, Gen. 21 : 33.
  idolatrous, forbidden, Deut. 16 : 21; Judg.
  6 : 25; 1 Ki. 14 : 15; 15 : 13; 16 : 33;
  2 Ki. 17 : 16; 21 : 3; 23 : 4.
Grow, Gen. 48 : 16, let them g. into a multitude.
  2 Sam. 23 : 5, though he make it not to g.
  Ps. 92 : 12, g. like cedar on Lebanon.
  104 : 14; 147 : 8, grass to g. for cattle.
  Isa. 53 : 2, he shall g. up before him.
  Hos. 14 : 5, he shall g. as the lily.
  Mal. 4 : 2, ye shall g. up as calves.
  Matt. 6 : 28; Luke 12 : 27, consider the lilies
  how they g.
  Matt. 13 : 30, let both g. together.
  21 : 19, no fruit g. on thee henceforward.
  Mark 4 : 27, seed g. up, he knoweth not how.
  Acts 5 : 24, doubted whereunto this would g.
  Eph. 2 : 21, g. unto a holy temple.
  2 Thess. 1 : 3, your faith g. exceedingly.
  1 Pet. 2 : 2, milk of word that ye may g.
  2 Pet. 3 : 18, g. in grace.
Growth, Amos 7 : 1, shooting up of latter g.
Grudge, Lev. 19 : 18, not bear g. against people.
  Jas. 5 : 9, g. not one against another.
  1 Pet. 4 : 9, use hospitality without g.
Grudgingly, 2 Cor. 9 : 7, let him give, not g.
Guard, Gen. 37 : 36; 40 : 4; 1 Ki. 14 : 27;
  2 Ki. 11 : 11; Dan. 2 : 14; Acts 28 : 16.
Guest, Prov. 9 : 18; Matt. 22 : 10, 11; Luke
  19 : 7.

Guestchamber, Mark 14 : 14; Luke 22 : 11.
Guide (noun), Ps. 48 : 14, be our g. even unto
   death.
   55 : 13, it was thou, a man, my g.
   Prov. 2 : 17, forsaketh g. of her youth.
   6 : 7, having no g., overseer, or ruler.
   Jer. 3 : 4, thou art the g. of my youth.
   Mic. 7 : 5, put not confidence in g.
   Matt. 23 : 16, 24, ye blind g.
   Rom. 2 : 19, a g. of the blind.
   (verb), Job 38 : 32, canst thou g. Arcturus ?
   Ps. 25 : 9, meek will he g. in judgment.
   32 : 8, I will g. thee with mine eye.
   73 : 24, g. me with thy counsel.
   112 : 5, g. his affairs with discretion.
   Isa. 58 : 11, Lord shall g. thee continually.
   Luke 1 : 79, g. our feet into the way of peace.
   John 16 : 13, he will g. you into all truth.
Guile, Ex. 21 : 14, if a man slay with g.
   Ps. 32 : 2, in whose spirit is no g.
   34 : 13; 1 Pet. 3 : 10, keep lips from speaking
   g.
   John 1 : 47, an Israelite, in whom is no g.
   2 Cor. 12 : 16, I caught you with g.
   1 Pet. 2 : 1, laying aside malice and g.
   2 : 22, nor was g. found in his mouth.
   Rev. 14 : 5, in mouth was found no g.
Guilt, Deut. 19 : 13; 21 : 9.
Guiltiness, Gen. 26 : 10; Ps. 51 : 14.
Guiltless, Ex. 20 : 7; Deut. 5 : 11, Lord will not
   hold him g.
   Josh. 2 : 19, we will be g.
   2 Sam. 3 : 28, g. of blood.
   Matt. 12 : 7, ye would not have condemned
   the g.
Guilty, Gen. 42 : 21, verily g. concerning our
   brother.
   Ex. 34 : 7; Num. 14 : 18, by no means clear
   the g.
   Rom. 3 : 19, all the world become g. before
   God.
   1 Cor. 11 : 27, g. of the body and blood.
   Jas. 2 : 10, offend in one point, he is g. of all.
Gulf, Luke 16 : 26.
Gum tragacanth, Gen. 37 : 25, Revised Version
   in the margin, for " spicery." It is the
   gum from a species of Astragalus, possible
   A. gummifer.
Guni (gū-nī), Gen. 46 : 24; 1 Chr. 5 : 15; 7 : 13.
   cf. Num. 26 : 48.
Gur (gūr) [place of sojourn], 2 Ki. 9 : 27.
Gur-baal (gùr-bā-ăl) [" dwelling of Baal "],
   2 Chr. 26 : 7.
Gush, Ps. 105 : 41; Isa. 48 : 21; Jer. 9 : 18;
   Acts 1 : 18.
Gutter, Gen. 30 : 38, 41; 2 Sam. 5 : 8.

H

Ha, Job 39 : 25, saith among the trumpets,
   h., h.
Haahashtari (hā-ă-hăsh-tă-rī), 1 Chr. 4 : 6.
Habaiah (hă-bā-ăh) [Jehovah hath hidden],
   Neh. 7 : 63; Ezra 2 : 61.
Habakkuk (hă-băk-kŭk) [embrace], Hab. 1 : 1;
   3 : 1, eighth of the minor prophets.
Habakkuk, Book of.
   Author.—Nothing is known about the

prophet outside the book itself. He belonged to the kingdom of Judah and may
have been either a priest, or a member of
the Levitical Choir (cf. the use of musical
terms in 3 : 1, 3, 13-19).
Date.—While Duhm's view that the book
refers to the invasion of Alexander the
Great (fourth century) can be substantiated,
it is best to assert with most critics that our
author was a contemporary of Jeremiah (c.
600 B.C.). The book was written some
time during the reigns of Josiah (639–608)
and Jehoiakim (608–597).
Contents.—Ch. 1 : 1, Title. Ch. 1 : 2-4,
Prevalent injustice. Ch. 1 : 5-11, Agent of
retribution (Chaldeans), sent by God. Ch.
1 : 12-17, Knowledge of such agent's work
causes him to doubt God's part in it.
Ch. 2 : 1-4, Religious solution, faithfulness,
gained on the watch-tower. Ch. 2 : 5-20,
A series of woes amplifying 2 : 4a. Ch. 3,
A psalm on Jehovah's coming, amplifying
2 : 4b.
Habergeon, " coat of mail " for neck and
   shoulders, Ex. 28 : 32; Neh. 4 : 16. cf.
   Eph. 6 : 4, " breastplate."
Habitable, Prov. 8 : 31.
Habitation, Ex. 15 : 2, I will prepare him an h.
   15 : 13, guided them to thy holy h.
   2 Chr. 6 : 2, have built an house of h.
   Ps. 26 : 8, I have loved h. of thy house.
   33 : 14, from the place of his h.
   69 : 25, let their h. be desolate.
   71 : 3, be thou my strong h.
   74 : 20, full of h. of cruelty.
   89 : 14, justice and judgment the h. of thy
   throne.
   91 : 9, made the Most High thy h.
   107 : 7, 36, might go to a city of h.
   132 : 13, Lord hath desired it for his h.
   Prov. 3 : 33, he blesseth the h. of the just.
   Isa. 32 : 18, dwell in a peaceable h.
   Luke 16 : 9, receive you into everlasting h.
   Acts 17 : 26, hath determined bounds of h.
   Eph. 2 : 22, an h. of God through the Spirit.
   Jude 6, angels which left their own h.
Habor (hā-bôr), *i.e.,* river **Chebar.**
Hachaliah (hăch-ă-lī-ăh) [Jehovah saddens],
   Neh. 1 : 1; 10 : 1.
Hachilah (hă-chī-lăh), 1 Sam. 23 : 19; 26 : 1, 3.
Hachmoni (hăch-mō-nī) [wise], 1 Chr. 27 : 32.
Hachmonite (hăch-mō-nīte), 1 Chr. 11 : 11, for
   Hachmoni.
Hadad (hā-dăd) [clashing], name of a Syrian
   god. An Edomite, Gen. 36 : 35; 1 Ki.
   11 : 14.
   [sharpness], 1 Chr. 1 : 30.
Hazadezer (hăd-ă-dē-zĕr) [Hadad is help]
   (Hadarezer), king of Zobah, David's wars
   with, 2 Sam. 8; 10 : 15; 1 Chr. 18.
Hadadrimmon (hā-dăd-rīm-mǫn) [Hadad the
   thunderer], a city in the valley of Megiddo,
   Zech. 12 : 11.
Hadar (hā-där), Gen. 25 : 15; 36 : 39. See
   Hadad.
Hadarezer (hăd-ă-rē-zĕr) [Hadar is help], 2 Sam.
   10 : 16; 1 Chr. 18 : 3, 9. See **Hadadezer.**
Hades. See **Hell.**
Hadid (hā-dīd), Ezra 2 : 33; Neh. 7 : 37; 11 : 34.

Hadoram (hă-dôr-ăm), contraction of "Adoniram, lord of the height," 2 Chr. 10 : 18; cf. 2 Sam. 20 : 24.

Haft, Judg. 3 : 22.

Hagar (hā-gär) [emigrant, fugitive], mother of Ishmael, Gen. 16.

fleeing from Sarah, is comforted by an angel, Gen. 16 : 10, 11.

dismissed with her son, Gen. 21 : 14; allegory of, Gal. 4 : 24.

Haggai (hăg-gāi) [feast of Jehovah? (festal)], the prophet, Ezra 5 : 1; 6 : 14. See Hag. 1 : 2.

Haggai, Book of.

Author.—The prophet Haggai was a contemporary of Zerubbabel, "the governor of Judah," with whom he returned to Jerusalem. Together with Zechariah the prophet (cf. Ezra 4 : 24; 5 : 1-2), he came forward in the second year of Darius (520 B.C.) to urge the people to undertake again the building of the Temple, already commenced in the second year of Cyrus (535 B.C.), but abandoned owing to the opposition met with (cf. Ezra 4 and 5). The exhortations of the two prophets were not without effect, and that work was completed at the expiration of four years (cf. Ezra 6 : 14, 15).

Contents.—The book consists of four addresses, delivered between September and December, 520 B.C., and their results.—(1) Ch. 1 : 1-11, Drought a penalty for neglect to build Temple; ch. 1 : 12-15, effect was to cause people to begin building on twenty-fourth day of sixth month of second year of Darius (Sept. 24th). (2) Ch. 2 : 1-9, Jehovah will make new Temple grander than the old, despite scanty resources at their disposal. (3) Ch. 2 : 10-19, Loyal devotion will ensure success and blessing. (4) Ch. 2 : 20-23, Zerubbabel is promised a unique place in the Messianic kingdom. The Messianic prophecy is referred to in Heb. 12 : 26-28. In 2 : 7, "desire of all nations" is not a title of the Messiah, however, but implies that "the desirable things" of all the world shall beautify the second Temple.

Haggeri (hăg-gē-rī), 1 Chr. 11 : 38.

Haggi (hăg-gī) [" born on a festival "—masculine], Gen. 46 : 16; Num. 26 : 15.

Haggiah (hăg-gī-äh) [feast of Jehovah], 1 Chr. 6 : 30.

Haggites (hăg-gītes), Num. 26 : 15.

Haggith (hăg-gīth) [" born on a festival "—feminine], 2 Sam. 3 : 4; 1 Ki. 1 : 5; 2 : 13.

Hagiographa (hăg-ĭ-ŏ-grăph-ă) (or Kethubim), third division of the Jewish Bible. See **Old Testament.**

Hai (hā-ī), Gen. 12 : 8.

Hail, plague of, Ex. 9 : 23; Josh. 10 : 11; Ps. 18 : 12; 78 : 47; Isa. 28 : 2; Ezek. 13 : 11; Hag. 2 : 17; Rev. 8 : 7; 11 : 19; 16 : 21.

to salute, Matt. 26 : 49; 27 : 29; Mark 15 : 18; Luke 1 : 28; John 19 : 3.

Job 38 : 22, hast thou seen the treasures of the h.?

Ps. 105 : 32, he gave them h. for rain.

148 : 8, fire and h., snow and vapours.

Isa. 28 : 17, the **h.** shall sweep away the refuge of lies.

Ezek. 38 : 22, great **h.**, fire and brimstone.

Hair, Gen. 42 : 38; 44 : 29, bring down gray **h.** with sorrow.

Judg. 20 : 16, sling stones at **h.** breadth.

1 Ki. 1 : 52, not an **h.** fall to earth.

Job 4 : 15, the **h.** of my flesh stood up.

Ps. 40 : 12; 69 : 4, more than the **h.** of my head.

Matt. 3 : 4; Mark 1 : 6, raiment of camel's **h.**

Matt. 5 : 36, not make one **h.** white or black.

10 : 30; Luke 12 : 7, the **h.** of your head are numbered.

John 11 : 2; 12 : 3, wiped his feet with her **h.**

1 Cor. 11 : 14, if a man have long **h.**

1 Tim. 2 : 9, not with broided **h.**

1 Pet. 3 : 1, plaiting the **h.**

Hairy, Gen. 25 : 25; 27 : 11, 23; 2 Ki. 1 : 8; Ps. 68 : 21.

Hakkatan (hăk-kă-tăn) [the smallest], Ezra 8 : 12.

Hakkoz (hăk-kŏz), 1 Chr. 24 : 10; Ezra 2 : 61; Neh. 3 : 4.

Hakupha (hă-kū-phă), Ezra 2 : 51; Neh. 7 : 53.

Halah (hā-läh), 2 Ki. 17 : 6; 18 : 11; 1 Chr. 5 : 26.

Halak (hā-lăk) [bare, smooth mountain], Josh. 11 : 17; 12 : 7.

Hale [ar.], to haul, drag by force, Luke 12 : 58; Acts 8 : 3.

Halhul (hăl-hŭl) [hollow?], a mountain city of Judah, Josh. 15 : 58.

Hali (hā-lī), a border city of Asher, Josh. 19 : 25.

Hall, Matt. 27 : 27; Mark 15 : 16; Luke 22 : 55.

of judgment, John 18 : 28, 33; 19 : 9; Acts 23 : 35.

Hallelujah (hăl-lē-lū-jäh) (Alleluia) [praise ye Jehovah], Ps. 104–106; 111–113; 115–117; 135; 146–150; Rev. 19 : 1, 3 f., 6.

Hallow, Ex. 20 : 11, blessed the Sabbath day and h. it.

Lev. 22 : 32, I am the Lord, who h. you.

25 : 10, shall h. the fiftieth year.

1 Ki. 9 : 3, I have h. this house.

Jer. 17 : 22, h. ye the Sabbath day.

Ezek. 20 : 20; 44 : 24, and h. my Sabbaths.

Matt. 6 : 9; Luke 11 : 2, h. be thy name.

Num. 5 : 10, everyman's h. things.

1 Sam. 21 : 6, priest gave him h. bread.

Halt, 1 Ki. 18 : 21, how long h. ye between two opinions?

Ps. 38 : 17, I am ready to h.

Jer. 20 : 10, my familiars watched for my h.

(lame), Matt. 18 : 8; Mark 9 : 45, better to enter into life h.

Luke 14 : 21, bring hither h. and blind.

John 5 : 3, blind, h., waiting for moving of the water.

Ham [black], son of Noah, cursed, Gen. 9 : 22.

his descendants, Gen. 10 : 6; 1 Chr. 1 : 8; Ps. 105 : 23; smitten by the Simeonites, 1 Chr. 4 : 40.

Haman (hā-măn) [magnificent], probably connected with the Sanskrit "Heman," name of the planet Mercury; advancement, Esther 3.

hatred to Mordecai, Esther 3 : 8.

fall, Esther 7.

Hamath (hā-̱măth) [fortification], a city and province of Syria, in the valley of Orontes, Num. 13 : 21; Judg. 3 : 3; Ezek. 48 : 1.

conquered, 2 Ki. 18 : 34; Isa. 37 : 13; Jer. 49 : 23.

See Num. 34 : 8; Josh. 13 : 5; 2 Ki. 14 : 28; 17 : 24.

Hamath-zobah (hā-̱măth-zō-̱băh) [fortress of Zobah], 2 Chr. 8 : 3.

Hammath (hăm-̱măth) [hot springs] (5 Dc; 14 Ab; 16 Dc), a fenced city of Naphtali, now called Hammam, Josh. 19 : 35.

Hammedatha (hăm-mĕ-dā-̱thă) [given of the moon], Esther 3 : 1, 10; 8 : 5; 9 : 10, 24.

Hammelech (hăm-̱mĕ-lĕch) [the king], Jer. 36 : 26; 38 : 6.

Hammer, Judg. 4 : 21; 1 Ki. 6 : 7; Ps. 74 : 6; Isa. 44 : 12; Jer. 10 : 4; 23 : 29; 50 : 23.

Hammoleketh (hăm-mō-̱lĕ-kĕth) [the queen ?], 1 Chr. 7 : 18.

Hammon (hăm-̱mŏn) [hot spring], 1 Chr. 6 : 76.

Hammoth-dor (hăm-̱mōth-dôr) [hot springs], Josh. 21 : 32.

Hammurabi. See Chronology Old Testament.

Hamonah (hă-mō-̱näh) [multitude], Ezek. 39 : 16.

Hamon-gog (hā-̱mŏn-gŏg) [Gog's multitude], Ezek. 39 : 11, 15.

Hamor (hā-̱môr) [he-ass], Gen. 34 : 2.

Hamuel (hăm-̱ū-ĕl) [God is warmth], 1 Chr. 4 : 26.

Hamul (hăm-̱ŭl) [spared], Num. 26 : 21.

Hamulites (hăm-ū-̱lītes), Num. 26 : 21.

Hamutal (hă-mū-̱tăl) [warmth of dew ?], 2 Ki. 23 : 31; 24 : 18; Jer. 52 : 1.

Hanameel (hăn-̱ă-mēēl), corrupt form of Hananeel, Jer. 32 : 7-9, 12.

Hanan (hā-̱năn) [gracious], Ezra 2 : 46; Neh. 7 : 49.

Hananeel (hăn-̱ă-nēel) [God is gracious], Neh. 3 : 1; 12 : 39; Jer. 31 : 38; Zech. 14 : 10. See Hanameel.

Hanani (hă-nā-̱nī) [inclined to grace], a prophet, 2 Chr. 16 : 7.

brother of Nehemiah, Neh. 1 : 2; 7 : 2; 12 : 36.

father of Jehu, 1 Ki. 16 : 1.

Hananiah (hăn-ă-nī-̱ăh) [Jehovah is gracious], false prophet, Jer. 28.

his death, Jer. 28 : 17.

Hand, of God, for blessing, 2 Chr. 30 : 12; Ezra 7 : 9; 8 : 18; Neh. 2 : 18.

for chastisement, Deut. 2 : 15; Ruth 1 : 13; Job 2 : 10; 19 : 21; 1 Pet. 5 : 6.

laying on of, Num. 8 : 10; 27 : 18; Acts 6 : 6; 13 : 3; 1 Tim. 4 : 14; 2 Tim. 1 : 6.

washing, as mark of innocence, Deut. 21 : 6; Ps. 26 : 6; Matt. 27 : 24.

lifting up, in prayer, Ex. 17 : 11; Ps. 28 : 2; 63 : 4; 141 : 2; 143 : 6; 1 Tim. 2 : 8.

Gen. 3 : 22, put forth his h. and take of the tree.

16 : 12, his h. against every man.

24 : 2; 47 : 29, put thy h. under my thigh.

Ex. 14 : 8; Num. 33 : 3, Israel went out with an high h.

Ex. 21 : 24; Deut. 19 : 21, h. for h.

Ex. 33 : 22, cover with my h. while I pass.

Num. 11 : 23, is Lord's h. waxed short ?

22 : 29, would there were a sword in mine h.

Deut. 8 : 17, my h. hath gotten this wealth.

33 : 3, all his saints are in thy h.

Judg. 7 : 2, saying, my own h. hath saved me.

1 Sam. 5 : 6, h. of Lord heavy on them.

12 : 3, of whose h. have I received any bribe ?

26 : 18, what evil is in mine h. ?

28 : 21, I have put my life in my h.

2 Sam. 24 : 14; 1 Chr. 21 : 13, let us fall into h. of Lord.

1 Ki. 18 : 44, cloud like a man's h.

Ezra 7 : 9; 8 : 18; Neh. 2 : 8, good h. of God.

Neh. 2 : 18, strengthened their h. for work.

Job 12 : 10, in whose h. is soul of every living thing.

17 : 9, hath clean h. shall be stronger.

40 : 14, that thine own h. can save.

Ps. 16 : 11, at right h. pleasures for evermore.

24 : 4, clean h. and pure heart.

31 : 5, into thy h. I commit my spirit.

32 : 4, day and night thy h. heavy.

80 : 17, thy h. on man of thy right h.

90 : 17, establish thou the work of our h.

119 : 73, thy h. made and fashioned me.

137 : 5, let my right h. forget her cunning.

139 : 10, there shall thy h. lead me.

Prov. 3 : 16, in left h. riches and honour.

10 : 4, h. of diligent maketh rich.

11 : 21; 16 : 5, though h. join in h.

12 : 24, h. of diligent shall bear rule.

19 : 24; 26 : 15, slothful man hideth his h.

22 : 26, be not of them that strike h.

Eccl. 2 : 24, this was from h. of God.

9 : 10, whatsoever thy h. findeth to do.

11 : 6, in evening withhold not thine h.

Isa. 1 : 12, who hath required this at your h.?

5 : 25; 9 : 12; 10 : 4; 14 : 27, his h. is stretched out still.

40 :12, measured waters in hollow of h.

53 : 10, pleasure of Lord shall prosper in his h.

56 : 2, keepeth his h. from doing evil.

Jer. 18 : 6, as clay in the potter's h.

Ezek. 7 : 17; 21 : 7, all h. shall be feeble.

Dan. 4 : 35, none can stay his h.

Joel 2 : 1, day of Lord is nigh at h.

Mic. 7 : 3, do evil with both h. earnestly.

Matt. 3 : 2; 4 : 17; 10 : 7, kingdom of heaven at h.

3 : 12; Luke 3 : 17, whose fan is in his h.

Matt. 18 : 8; Mark 9 : 43, if thy h. offend.

Matt. 26 : 18, my time is at h.

Mark 14 : 41, Son of man is betrayed into h. of sinners.

16 : 19, sat on right h. of God.

Luke 9 : 44, delivered into h. of men.

22 : 21, h. that betrayeth is with me.

John 10 : 29, to pluck out of my Father's h.

20 : 27, reach hither thy h.

1 Cor. 12 : 15, because I am not the h.

2 Cor. 5 : 1, house not made with h.

Phil. 4 : 5, the Lord is at h.

Col. 2 : 11, circumcision without h.

1 Thess. 4 : 11, work with your own h.

2 Thess. 2 : 2, the day of Christ is at h.

1 Tim. 2 : 8, lifting up holy h.

Heb. 9 : 24, not entered places made with **h.**
10 : 31, fall into **h.** of living God.
Jas. 4 : 8, cleanse your **h.**
1 Pet. 4 : 7, end of all things is at **h.**
1 John 1 : 1, our **h.** have handled of Word of life.
Handbreadth, Ex. 25 : 25; 37 : 12; 2 Chr. 4 : 5; Ps. 39 : 5.
Handful, Gen. 41 : 47, earth brought forth by **h.**
Ex. 9 : 8, **h.** of ashes.
Ruth 2 : 16, let fall also some of the **h.**
1 Ki. 17 : 12, **h.** of meal in a barrel.
Ps. 72 : 16, be an **h.** of corn.
Eccl. 4 : 6, better is an **h.** with quietness.
Jer. 9 : 22, as the **h.** after the harvestman.
Handicraft, Acts 18 : 3; 19 : 25, 27; Rev. 18 : 22. See **Craft.**
    In later Judaism fathers were considered in duty bound to teach their sons a trade. " Craftsman " (2 Ki. 24 : 14) and " artificer " (1 Chr. 29 : 5) translate the general term which is derived from a word meaning " to cut." Since this is frequently qualified by the name of the material, we suggest the following division :
1. Clay-workers.—(*a*) Brickmaking, Ex. 1 : 14; 5 : 7. (*b*) Plaistering, Lev. 14 : 42; Dan. 5 : 5. These were too simple to be called " crafts." (*c*) Pottery, Jer. 18 : 2-6, was the oldest craft.
2. Leather-workers.—(*a*) Tanning, Acts 9 : 43. Owing to its unpleasant circumstances tanning was forbidden within the city (cf. Acts 10 : 32).
3. Metal-workers or Smiths.—(*a*) Coppersmith, 2 Tim. 4 : 14; Gen. 4 : 22; 1 Ki. 7 : 14. " Brass " in O.T. (except in Deut. 8 : 9, where the pure metal is meant) probably always stands for " bronze," or copper alloyed with tin. The coppersmith was the chief metal-worker of the earlier period. (*b*) Ironsmith, 1 Sam. 13 : 19; 2 Chr. 24 : 12, later supplanted the coppersmith. (*c*) Goldsmith, Neh. 3 : 18, 21, 32; Isa. 40 : 19; 41 : 7; 46 : 6, produced beaten work (Ex. 25 : 18), plating (Ex. 30 : 3), and wire or thread for embroidery (Ex. 39 : 3). (*d*) Silversmith, Acts 19 : 24.
4. Stone-workers.—1 Chr. 22 : 15. (*a*) Mason, 2 Sam. 5 : 11; 1 Chr. 14 : 1, was general term for stone-squarer (1 Ki. 5 : 18) or dresser of stones. The Phœnicians were clever masons. (*b*) Builder, Ps. 118 : 22, worked from a prepared plan (1 Chr. 28 : 11).
5. Woodworkers.—1 Chr. 22 : 15. (*a*) Carpenter, Gen. 6 : 14; Ex. 37; Isa. 44 : 13; Matt. 13 : 55; Mark 6 : 3, was also cabinet-maker, ploughwright, woodcarver, etc.
6. Miscellaneous Crafts.—(*a*) Apothecaries or Perfumers formed a guild, Neh. 3 : 8. (cf. Ex. 30 : 25, 35; 2 Chr. 16 : 14; Eccl. 7 : 1; 10 : 1.) (*b*) Bakers had a street named from their trade, Jer. 37 : 21. (cf. Hos. 7 : 4.) (*c*) Barber, Num. 6 : 5, 19; Ezek. 5 : 1. (*d*) Butcher, 1 Cor. 10 : 25. (*e*) Dyer, Ex. 26 : 14. (*f*) Embroiderer, Ex. 28 : 39. (*g*) Fuller, Isa. 7 : 3; Mal. 3 : 2; Mark 9 3:. (*h*) Shipbuilder, 1 Ki. 9 : 26 f.;

Hebrews making bricks, from Tomb at Thebes.

22 : 48; 2 Chr. 20 : 36 f. (*i*) Tentmaker, Acts 18 : 3. (*j*) Weavers were women in olden times, Ex. 35 : 25 f.; Lev. 19 : 19; Deut. 22 : 11; 1 Sam. 17 : 7; 2 Ki. 23 : 7; Ezek. 16 : 16; Prov. 31 : 13, 24.
    The well-known valley of Tyropœon probably derived its name from the cheese-making that obtained there.
    See various references to above crafts passim.

Handkerchiefs, Acts 19 : 12.
Handle, Gen. 4 : 21, father of such as h. harp.
Judg. 5 : 14, that h. pen of writer.
Ps. 115 : 7, hands, but they h. not.
Prov. 16 : 20, that h. a matter wisely.
Song of Sol. 5 : 5, drop myrrh on h. of lock.
Jer. 2 : 8, they that h. the law.
Ezek. 27 : 29, all that h. the oar.
Mark 12 : 4, sent him away shamefully h.
Luke 24 : 39, h. me, and see.
2 Cor. 4 : 2, not h. word of God deceitfully.
Col. 2 : 21, taste not, h. not.
1 John 1 : 1, have h. of Word of life.
Handmaid, Ps. 86 : 16, save the son of thy h.
116 : 16, thy servant, and son of thy h.
Luke 1 : 38, behold the h. of the Lord.
Handstaves, Ezek. 39 : 9.
Handwriting, Col. 2 : 14.
Handywork, Ps. 19 : 1.

Egyptian operations in metals.

Hang, Job 26 : 7, he h. the earth on nothing.
Ps. 137 : 2, we h. our harps upon the willows.
Matt. 18 : 6; Mark 9 : 42; Luke 17 : 2, mill-stone h. about neck.
Matt. 22 : 40, on these h. all the law and the prophets.
27 : 5, Judas went and h. himself.
Heb. 12 : 12, lift up the hands which h. down.
Hanging, a punishment, Gen. 40 : 22; Num. 25 : 4; Esther 7 : 10.
the hanged accursed, Deut. 21 : 22; Gal. 3 : 13.
Hannah (hăn-năh) [grace], her vow and prayer, 1 Sam. 1 : 11; answered, 1 Sam. 1 : 19.
song, 1 Sam. 2.
Hanun (hā-nŭn) [favoured], king of the Ammonites, dishonours David's messengers, 2 Sam. 10 : 4; chastised, 2 Sam. 12 : 30.
Hap, Ruth 2 : 3, her h. was to light on a part.
Haply, Mark 11 : 13, if h. he might find fruit.
Luke 14 : 29, lest h. after he hath laid foundation.
Acts 5 : 39, h. ye be found to fight against God.
17 : 27, if h. they might feel after him.
Happen, Prov. 12 : 21, no evil h. to the just.
Eccl. 2 : 14, one event h. to them all.
Isa. 41 : 22, let them show us what shall h.
Jer. 44 : 23, therefore this evil is h.
Luke 24 : 14, talked of things that had h.
Rom. 11 : 25, blindness is h. to Israel.
1 Cor. 10 : 11, things h. for ensamples.
Phil. 1 : 12, things which h. to me.

1 Pet. 4 : 12, as though some strange thing h.
2 Pet. 2 : 22, it is h. according to proverb.
Happier, 1 Cor. 7 : 40.
Happy, Deut. 33 : 29, h. art thou, O Israel.
Job 5 : 17, h. is the man whom God correcteth.
Ps. 144 : 15, h. is that people whose God is the Lord.
Prov. 3 : 13, h. that findeth wisdom.
14 : 21, he that hath mercy on the poor, h. is he.
16 : 20, whoso trusteth in the Lord, h. is he.
28 : 14, h. is the man that feareth alway.
Jer. 12 : 1, why are they h. that deal treacherously ?
Mal. 3 : 15, now we call the proud h.
John 13 : 17, if ye know these things, h. if ye do them.
Rom. 14 : 22, h. is he that condemneth not.
Jas. 5 : 11, we count them h. that endure.
1 Pet. 3 : 14; 4 : 14, h. are ye.
Haran (hâr-ăn) [mountainous], a town of Padanaram, Gen. 11 : 32.
Abram comes to, Gen. 11 : 31; departs from, Gen. 12 : 4.
Jacob flees to Laban at, Gen. 27 : 43; 28 : 10; 29.
son of Terah, Gen. 11 : 26.
Hard, Gen. 18 : 14, is any thing too h. for the Lord ?
Deut. 1 : 17, cause that is too h.
26 : 6, Egyptians laid on h. bondage.
2 Sam. 3 : 39, sons of Zeruiah too h.
1 Ki. 10 : 1; 2 Chr. 9 : 1, to prove with h. questions.
2 Ki. 2 : 10, thou hast asked a h. thing.
Job 41 : 24, as h. as a piece of nether millstone.
Prov. 13 : 15, way of transgressors is h.
18 : 19, brother offended is h. to be won.
Jer. 32 : 17, 27, there is nothing too h. for thee.
Ezek. 3 : 5, 6, to a people of h. language.
3 : 7, Israel, impudent and h.-hearted.
Matt. 25 : 24, I knew thou art an h. man.
Mark 10 : 24, how h. for them that trust in riches.
John 6 : 60, this is an h. saying.
Acts 9 : 5; 26 : 14, h. to kick against the pricks.
Heb. 5 : 11, many things h. to be uttered.
2 Pet. 3 : 16, things h. to be understood.
Jude 15, convince all of h. speeches.
Hardly, Luke 18 : 24, h. shall they that have riches. (cf. Matt. 19 : 23; Mark 10 : 23).
Harden, Ex. 4 : 21; 7 : 3; 14 : 4, I will h. Pharaoh's heart.
14 : 17, h. hearts of Egyptians.
Deut. 15 : 7, shalt not h. thy heart.
2 Ki. 17 : 14; Neh. 9 : 16, h. their necks.
Job 6 : 10, I would h. myself in sorrow.
9 : 4, who hath h. himself against him ?
Ps. 95 : 8; Heb. 3 : 8, 15; 4 : 7, h. not your hearts.
Prov. 21 : 29, a wicked man h. his face.
28 : 14, he that h. his heart.
29 : 1, he that, being often reproved, h. his neck.
Isa. 63 : 17, why hast thou h. our heart ?
Dan. 5 : 20, his mind was h. in pride.
Mark 6 : 52; 8 : 17, their heart h.

John 12 : 40, he hath h. their heart.
Rom. 9 : 18, whom he will he h.
Heb. 3 : 13, lest any of you be h.
Hardened heart, deprecated, Deut. 15 : 7; 1 Sam. 6 : 6; Ps. 95 : 8; Heb. 3 : 8.
results of, Ex. 7 : 13; 8 : 15; Prov. 28 : 14; Dan. 5 : 20; John 12 : 40.
Hardness, Mark 3 : 5, grieved for h. of their hearts.
16 : 14, upbraided them for h. of heart.
Rom. 2 : 5, h. and impenitent heart.
2 Tim. 2 : 3, endure h., as a good soldier.
Hare. One of the unclean animals mentioned in Lev. 11 : 6.
Hareph (hâr-ĕph), 1 Chr. 2 : 51.
Hareth (hâr-ĕth), 1 Sam. 22 : 5.
Harhaiah (här-hâi-ăh) [zeal of Jehovah], Neh. 3 : 8.
Harhas (här-hăs), 2 Ki. 22 : 14.
Harhur (här-hŭr) [fever], Ezra 2 : 51.
Harim (hâr-ïm) [flat-nose], 1 Chr. 24 : 8; Ezra 2 : 32.

Hariph (hâr-ïph), Neh. 7 : 24; 10 : 19.
Harlots, Gen. 34 : 31; Lev. 19 : 29; 21 : 7; Deut. 23 : 17; Isa. 57 : 3; Jer. 3 : 3; Matt. 21 : 32; 1 Cor. 6 : 15.
Rahab of Jericho, Josh. 2 : 1.
priests forbidden to marry, Lev. 21 : 14.
Solomon's judgment between two, 1 Ki. 3 : 16.
figurative of idolatry, Isa. 1 : 21; Jer. 2 : 20; Ezek. 16 : 28; Hos. 2; Rev. 17; 18.
Harm, Lev. 5 : 16, make amends for h. done.
2 Ki. 4 : 41, no h. in the pot.
1 Chr. 16 : 22; Ps. 105 : 15, do prophets no h.
Prov. 3 : 30, if he have done thee no h.
Acts 16 : 28, do thyself no h.
28 : 5, he felt no h.
1 Pet. 3 : 13, who will h. you, if followers of good ?
Harmless, Matt. 10 : 16, wise as serpents, h. as doves.
Phil. 2 : 15, may be h., the sons of God.
Heb. 7 : 26, holy, h., undefiled.

Harmony of the Gospels.

DATE.	CONTENTS.	MATT.	MARK.	LUKE.	JOHN.
B.C.	**Incidents of the birth and boyhood of Jesus Christ till he was twelve years of age.**				
	1. Introduction	..	..	1 : 1-4	1 : 1-14
	2. The Genealogies—Matthew the legal, Luke the natural descent	1 : 1-17	..	3 : 23-38	..
6, Nov.	3. Birth of John announced to Zacharias	..	..	1 : 5-25	..
5, May	4. Birth of Jesus announced to Mary at Nazareth six months later	..	..	1 : 26-38	..
	5. Mary's visit to Elizabeth, and her hymn	..	..	1 : 39-56	..
Aug.	6. John the Baptist's birth, and Zacharias' hymn	..	..	1 : 57-80	..
	7. The Angel appears to Joseph	1 : 18-25	..	..	..
4, Feb.	8. Birth of Jesus at Bethlehem	..	..	2 : 1-7	..
	9. Angelic announcement to the shepherds. (In spring, flocks were watched by night)	..	..	2 : 8-20	..
Apr.	10. Circumcision of Jews, and presentation in the Temple, where He is welcomed by Simeon and Anna, 41 days after nativity (Lev. 12 : 3, 4)	..	..	2 : 21-38	..
	11. Visit of the Magi, in the house—no longer in manger ; Epiphany to Gentiles	2 : 1-12	..	..	..
3, Apr.	12. Flight into Egypt	2 : 13-15	..	..	..
	13. Herod's murder of the Innocents	2 : 16-18	..	..	..
A.D. 9	14. Return to Nazareth, fearing Archelaus' cruelty	2 : 19-23	..	2 : 39-40	..
	15. Jesus, at age of twelve, goes up to the Passover, and is found with the doctors in the Temple ; then follow his 18 years' retirement	..	..	2 : 41-52	..
26	**Inauguration of Christ's Public Ministry.**				
27, Jan.	16. Preparatory preaching of John the Baptist	3 : 1-12	1 : 1-8	3 : 1-18	..
	17. Christ's baptism in river Jordan at Perean Bethany	3 : 13-17	1 : 9-11	3 :21-23	..
	18. The Spirit leads Him to desert of Judæa, where Satan tempts Him	4 : 1-11	1 : 12, 13	4 : 1-13	..
	19. The Baptist's witness to Jesus	..	..	..	1 : 15-34
	20. Two of John's disciples follow Jesus ; Andrew brings his brother Simon	..	..	..	1 : 35-42
27	21. Christ returns to Galilee ; finds Philip, who in turn finds Nathanael	..	..	..	1 : 43-51
	22. First miracle at Cana, and visit to Capernaum	..	..	..	2 : 1-12
	Public Ministry of Christ from the First Passover to the Second.				
Apr.	23. Christ goes up to Jerusalem for the Passover, and, with a scourge, expels the sellers and money-changers from the Temple ; works miracles, convincing many	..	..	..	2 : 13-25
	24. Nicodemus convinced, has a night interview with Jesus	..	..	..	3 : 1-21
	25. Christ leaves Jerusalem, stays eight months in N.E. Judæa, and baptises by His disciples	..	..	..	3 : 22
	26. John, baptising in Ænon, again witnesses to the Christ.	..	..	..	3 : 23-36
	27. Imprisonment of John	..	..	3 : 19, 20	..
	28. John being cast into prison, Jesus leaves Judæa for Galilee ; John beheaded—not till A.D. 28 (Matt. 14 : 12-21)	..	..	..	..
Dec.	29. Passing through Samaria, He converts a woman of Sychar, and through her many of the Samaritans, four months before harvest	4 : 12	1 : 14	4 : 14, 15	4 : 1-3
	30. Commencement of His public ministry in Galilee	4 : 17	1 : 14, 15	4 : 14, 15	4 : 41-42 4 : 43-45

DATE.	CONTENTS.	MATT.	MARK.	LUKE.	JOHN.
	31. Visiting Cana again. He heals a nobleman's son sick at Capernaum	..	..	..	4 : 46-54
	From His Second to His Third Passover				
28 Apr.	32. Returns to Jerusalem at the Passover, " *the* feast." His second Passover. From this to the third, His main Galilean ministry. Jesus cures an infirm man at Bethesda pool on the Sabbath. The Jews seek to kill Him for declaring himself one with the Father in working	..	..	..	5 : 1-47
	33. Returns to Galilee. Rejected at Nazareth . .	..	..	4 : 14-30	..
	34. He settles at Capernaum, and teaches in public . .	4 : 13-17	1 : 21, 22	4 : 31, 32	..
	35. Miraculous draught of fishes ; call of Simon, Andrew, James, and John	4 : 18-22	1 : 16-20	5 : 1-11	..
A.D. 28	36. Jesus casts out a demon		1 : 23-28	4 : 33-37	..
	37. Cure of Simon's wife's mother, and other sick people .	8 : 14-17	1 : 29-34	4 : 38-41	..
	38. Circuit with the disciples through Galilee . .	4 : 23-25	1 : 35-39	4 : 42-44	..
	39. He heals a leper, and. shunning popularity, retires to the desert	8 : 1-4	1 : 40-45	5 : 12-16	..
	40. Returning to Capernaum, he heals a palsied man let down through the roof	9 : 2-8	2 : 1-12	5 : 17-26	..
	41. Call of Matthew, the feast, and discourse at his house—the new garment and new wine . . .	9 : 9-13	2 : 13-17	5 : 27-32	..
	42. He answers objections as to the reason of His not fasting	9 : 14-17	2 : 18-22	5 : 22-39	..
	43. Returning towards Galilee, the disciples pluck corn-ears on the Sabbath	12 : 1-8	2 : 23-28	6 : 1-5	..
	44. Healing a man's withered hand on the Sabbath, the Pharisees plot His death with the Herodians .	12 : 9-14	3 : 1-6	6 : 6-11	..
	45. He withdraws to the Lake, and heals many. . .	12 : 15-21	3 : 7-12	..	..
	46. Ascending a hill west of the Lake, after prayer all night, He chooses the twelve ; His charge . .	10 : 1-42	3 : 13-19	6 : 12-19	..
	47. Sermon on the mount, on the level below the hill-top .	5 : 1-8 : 1	..	6 : 20-49	..
	48. Healing of the centurion's servant	8 : 5-13	..	7 : 1-10	..
	49. Raising of the widow's son at Nain . . .	..	..	7 : 11-17	..
	50. John Baptist's mission of inquiry from his dungeon at Machærus	11 : 2-19	..	7 : 18-35	..
	51. Jesus upbraids Chorazin, Bethsaida, and Capernaum, and invites the heavy-laden	11 : 20-30	..	..	..
	52. Anointing of His feet in the Pharisee Simon's house by the sinful, but forgiven woman	..	..	7 : 36-50	..
	53. Short circuit of two days' preaching through Galilee; women ministering	..	..	8 : 1-3	..
	54. Returning to Capernaum, He heals a blind and demoniac, the Pharisees attributing the miracle to Beelzebub .	12 : 22-37	3 : 22-30	11 : 14, 15, [17-23	..
	55. Seeking a sign, and the answer	12 : 38-45	..	11:16,24-36	..
	56. His kinsfolk try to lay hold on Him as mad .	12 : 46-50	3 : 19-21	8 : 19-21	..
	57. From a fishing vessel He speaks a series of seven parables, beginning with the parable of the sower . .	13 : 1-53	.31-35 4 : 1-34	8 : 4-18	..
	58. Jesus crosses the Lake with His disciples, and calms a storm	8 : 18-27	4 : 35-41	8 : 22-25	..
	59. He cures two demoniacs of Gadara, one being prominent	8 : 28-34	5 : 1-20	8 : 26-40	..
	60. Returning to the West shore, He raises Jairus' daughter, and heals a woman with an issue of blood . .	9 : 1, 18-26 9 : 27-34	5 : 21-43	8 : 40-56	..
	61. He heals two blind men and casts out a demon .	9 : 27-34	..	..	..
	62. Jesus visits Nazareth again, when His countrymen disbelieve in Him	13 : 54-58	6 : 1-6	..	..
	63. Christ teaches throughout Galilee	9 : 35-38	6 : 6	..	..
	64. Sends forth the Twelve	10 : 1-11:1	6 : 7-13	9 : 1-6	..
	65. Herod, who has murdered John the Baptist, fears that Jesus is John risen from the dead . . .	14 : 1-12	6 : 14-29	9 : 7-9	..
	66. The Twelve return to Jesus, telling all they have done and taught. He withdraws with them to a desert on the other side of the Sea of Galilee, and feeds five thousand people	14 : 13-21	6 : 30-44	9 : 10-17	6 : 1-14
	67. He sends the disciples across the Lake westward to Bethsaida (close to Capernaum, distinct from Bethsaida Julias, N.E. of the Lake, Luke 9 : 10), and at night comes walking to them upon the water .	14 : 22-33	6 : 45-56	..	6 : 15-21
	68. The miraculously-fed multitude seek and find Jesus at Capernaum. His discourse in the synagogue and Peter's confession	..	..	..	6 : 22-71
29, Apr.	**From the Third Passover to the beginning of the last Passover Week.**				
	69. Healings in the Gennesaret plain for a few days .	14 : 34-36	6 : 55, 56	..	..
	70. Pharisees from Jerusalem object to His neglect of washing hands	15 : 1-20	7 : 1-23	..	..
	71. Jesus goes northward towards Tyre and Sidon. The Syro-Phenician woman's faith gains a cure for her daughter	15 : 21-28	7 : 24-30	..	..
	72. He returns through Decapolis, and, ascending a mount near the Sea of Galilee, heals many and feeds four thousand	15 : 29-38	7 : 31-8 : 9	..	..
	73. He crosses the Lake to Dalmanutha . . .	15 : 39	8 :10	..	..
	74. Pharisees and Sadducees require a sign . . .	16 : 1-4	8 : 11, 12	..	..

178

Date.	Contents.	Matt.	Mark.	Luke.	John.
	75. Embarking in the ship, He comes to Bethsaida (Julias). He warns against leaven of doctrine	16 : 4-12	8 : 13-21	..	..
	76. Healing of a blind man	..	8 : 22-26	..	..
	77. Journey to the region of Cesarea Philippi. Peter's confession	16 : 13-20	8 : 27-30	9 : 18-2	..
	78. He foretells His death and resurrection. Reproof of Peter	16 : 21-28	8 : 31-38, [9 : 1	9 : 22-27	..
29	79. The transfiguration on Mount Hermon six days later	17 : 1-13	9 : 2-13	9 : 28-36	..
	80. Descending, the following day He casts out a demon which the disciples could not cast out	17 : 14-21	9 : 14-29	9 : 37-43	..
	81. Jesus again foretells His death and resurrection	17 : 22, 23	9 : 30-32	9 : 44, 45	..
	82. Temple-tribute money miraculously provided from a fish at Capernaum	17 : 24-27	..	..	..
A.D. Oct.	83. The disciples strive which should be greatest. Jesus teaches a childlike, forgiving spirit. John tells of the disciples forbidding one who cast out demons in Jesus' name	18 : 1-35	9 : 33-50	9 : 46-50	..
	Journey to the Feast of Tabernacles, six months after the third Passover ; his period ends with His arrival at Bethany before the last Passover	..	..	..	7 : 1-10
	84. He goes up from Galilee about the midst of the feast and teaches in the Temple	..	..	..	7 : 14
	85. The people are divided in opinion ; the rulers try to seize him ; Nicodemus remonstrates	..	..	..	7 : 11-53
	86. His charity, yet faithfulness, towards the adulteress	..	..	..	8 : 1-11
	87. Jesus, in the Temple, declares Himself the Light of the World, pre-existent before Abraham. The Jews seek to stone Him	..	..	..	8 : 12-59
	88. Healing of the beggar, blind from his birth	..	..	..	9
	89. Christ's Discourse on Himself as the Good Shepherd and the Door	..	..	..	10 : 1-21
	90. Final departure for Jerusalem from Galilee through Samaria	..	..	9 : 51-56	..
	91. Warnings to certain who would follow	..	..	9 : 57-62	..
	92. Sending forth of the seventy	..	..	10 : 1-16	..
	93. The seventy return, announcing their successful mission	..	..	10 : 17-24	..
	94. Christ speaks the parable of the good Samaritan	..	..	10 : 25-37	..
	95. Jesus in Bethany visits Mary and Martha	..	..	10 : 38-42	..
	96. He again teaches the disciples how to pray	..	..	11 :1-3	..
	97. Cure of the dumb demoniac ; the Pharisees again attribute His miracles to Beelzebub ; dines with one ; woes to hypocritical lawyers ; doom of the nation	..	..	11 : 14-54	..
	98. Exhortation to disciples	..	..	12 : 1-12	..
	99. Appeal to Jesus to arbitrate about inheritance ; parable of the rich fool	..	..	12 : 13-21	..
	100. Discourses	..	..	12 : 22-59	..
	101. God's judgments, motive to repentance	..	..	13 : 1-5	..
	102. Parable of the barren fig-tree	..	..	13 : 6-9	..
	103. Cure of a woman with a spirit of infirmity	..	..	13 : 10-17	..
	104. Jesus, at the Feast of Dedication in Jerusalem, proclaims His divine Oneness with God. The Jews a third time seek to kill Him, when consequently He withdraws to Peræa	..	..	..	10 . 22-42
	105. Discourses—Parables of the mustard seed and of the leaven ; the strait gate	..	..	13 : 18-30	..
	106. Pharisees urge Him to depart quickly from Peræa, on the plea that Herod would kill Him, and His answer	..	..	13 : 31-35	..
	107. Cure of a man with the dropsy	..	..	14 : 61-	..
30, Jan.	108. Parable of the great supper	..	..	14 : 7-24	..
	109. He warns the multitude to count the cost of discipleship	..	..	14 : 25-35	..
	110. Many publicans crowd to Him, and on the Pharisees murmuring, He uttered the parables of the lost sheep, the lost coin, and the prodigal son	..	..	15	..
	111. To the disciples He spake the parables of the unjust steward, and the rich man and Lazarus	..	..	16	..
	112. Sayings as to offences ; mutual forgiveness and profitableness never exceeding duty	..	..	17 : 1-10	..
	113. Journey to Bethany, where He raises Lazarus from the dead	..	..	..	11 : 1-46
	114. Caiaphas and the Sanhedrin determine to put Jesus to death : unconscious prophecy	..	..	..	11 : 47-53
	115. Jesus withdraws to Ephraim on borders of Samaria	..	..	..	11 : 54
Mar.	*The Last Journey to Jerusalem through the midst of Samaria and Galilee.*				
	116. He heals ten lepers on the Samaritan frontier	..	..	17 : 11-19	..
	117. The Pharisees ask when the kingdom of God should come ; He foretells its concomitants	..	..	17 : 20-37	..
	118. Parables of importunate widow, and the Pharisee and Publican	..	..	18 : 1-14	..
	119. Journey from Galilee through Peræa	19 : 1, 2	10 : 1	..	..
	120. Pharisees question Him about divorce	19 : 3-12	10 : 2-12	..	..
	121. Parents bring their children to Jesus to bless them	19 : 13-15	10 : 13-16	18 : 15-17	..
	122. The rich young ruler declines the discipleship ; Peter contrasts the disciples' self-sacrifice	19 : 16-30	10 : 17-31	18 : 18-30	..

DATE.	CONTENTS.	MATT.	MARK.	LUKE.	JOHN.
	123. Parable of the labourers in the vineyard to warn against mercenary service	20 : 1-16	..	..	..
30	124. Jesus goes before on his way to Jerusalem, and a third time foretells His death and resurrection	20 : 17-19	10 : 32-34	18 : 31-34	..
	125. James and John desire highest places next to Christ in the temporal kingdom	20 : 20-28	10 : 35-45	..	..
	126. He heals two blind men near Jericho	20 : 29-34	10 : 46-52	18:35-19:1	..
	127. Zacchæus climbs a sycamore tree, and is called down by Jesus. Salvation comes to his house	..	..	19 : 2-10	..
	128. Nigh Jerusalem, when men thought the kingdom of God should immediately appear, Jesus checks this thought by the parable of the pounds	..	..	19 : 11-27	..
	The Last Sabbath, Saturday, beginning at Friday sunset.				
A.D. 30	129. The hostile Jews seek Him at Jerusalem ; Pharisees command to take Him. Jesus reaches Bethany six days before the Passover. In the house of Simon the leper, Mary anoints His head and feet	26 : 6-13	14 : 3-9	..	11 : 55-57: [12 : 1-8
	130. Jews come to Bethany to see Jesus	..	..	..	12 : 9-11
Mar.	**The Last Passover Week, ending with the Crucifixion.**				
	First Day of the Week—Sunday, April 1.				
	131. Jesus triumphantly enters Jerusalem. He weeps over the city as doomed. At eventide He returns to Bethany, having first entered the Temple, and sternly looked round about upon all things (Zeph. 1 : 12)	21:1-11, 17	11 : 1-11	19 : 28-44	12 : 12-19
Apr.	*Second Day—Monday, April 2.*				
	132. On His way from Bethany, Jesus curses the barren fig tree. He purges the Temple at the close of His ministry as at the beginning, but without the scourge, and again returns to Bethany	21 : 12-16, [18, 19	11 : 12-19	19 : 45-48	..
	Third Day—Tuesday, April 3.				
	133. On His way to Jerusalem, the fig tree being withered up, Jesus teaches the lesson " that believing prayer can move mountains of hindrance "	21 : 20-22	11 : 20-26	..	..
	134. Teaches in the Temple. Deputation from the Sanhedrin challenge His authority. Parables of the two sons and vineyard	21 : 23-46	[12 : 1-12 11 : 27-33	20 : 1-19	..
	135. Parable of the marriage feast	22 : 1-14	..	..	..
	136. The Pharisees, with the Herodians, try to entangle Him in His words. His reply from Cæsar's image on the coin	22 : 15-22	12 : 13-17	20: 20-26	..
	137. He baffles the Sadducees' cavil about the resurrection	22 : 23-33	12 : 18-27	20 : 27-40	..
	138. He replies to a lawyer on which one is the great commandment	22 : 34-40	12 : 28-34	..	..
	139. Our Lord leaves them without answer to His question : " If Christ be Son of David, how does David call him Lord ? "	22 : 41-46	12 : 35-37	20 : 41-44	..
	140. Warns against Scribes and Pharisees. Woe to Jerusalem	23	12 : 38-40	20 : 45-47	..
	141. He commends the widow's offering to God's treasury	..	12 : 41-44,	21 : 1-4	..
	142. Some Greeks desire to see Jesus. He accepts this as a pledge of His coming glory, and the gathering-in of the Gentiles	..	..	..	12 : 20-36
	143. Leaving the Temple, Jesus, sitting on Olivet, with Peter, James, John, and Andrew, foretells the destruction of the Temple and Jewish theocracy. The last days	24 : 1-42	13 : 1-37	21 : 5-38	..
	144. Parables :—The goodman of the house, the wise and evil servant, the ten virgins, the talents, sheep and goats	[25 24 :43-51;	..	..	..
	Fourth Day—Wednesday, April 4.				
	145. *Beginning at sunset*; Jesus, two days before the Passover, announced His betrayal and crucifixion ; the Sanhedrin consult to kill Jesus by subtlety. Judas, availing himself of his Master's retirement from them, covenants to betray Him. Most disbelieved ; some rulers believed, but loving men's praise confessed Him not. Jesus' judgment	[14-16 26 : 1-5,	[10, 11 14 : 1, 2,	22 : 1-6	14 : 36-50
	Fifth Day—Thursday, April 5.				
	146. Jesus sends two disciples into the city to prepare for the Passover ; follows with the rest in the afternoon	26 : 17-19	14 : 12-16	22 : 7-13	..
	Sixth Day—Friday, April 6.				
	147. *At sunset*; Jesus celebrates the Passover by anticipation	26 : 20	14 : 17	22 : 14	..
	148. Reproves the ambition of disciples, yet promises the kingdom	..	..	22 : 24-30	

Date.	Contents.	Matt.	Mark.	Luke.	John.
	149. He teaches love and humility by washing disciples' feet	..	..	..	13 : 1-20
	150. He indicates His betrayer, who, however, did not leave till after the Lord's Supper (Luke 22 : 21).	26 : 21-25	14 : 18-21	22 : 21-23	13 : 21-35
	151. He foretells Peter's sifting by Satan, and restoration by His intercession ; and scattering of the twelve	26 : 31-35	14 : 27-31	22 : 31-38	13 : 36-38
	152. Ordains the Lord's Supper (1 Cor. 11 : 23-25)	26 : 26-29	14 : 22-25	22 : 15-20	..
	153. Farewell address and intercessory prayer in the Paschal chamber, all standing (John 14 : 31)				14 : 17-26
	154. His agony in Gethsemane	26 : 30, [36-46	14 : 26, [32-42	22 : 39-46	18 : 1, 4
	155. His betrayal with a kiss, and apprehension. Peter cuts off, and Jesus heals, Malchus' ear	26 : 47-56	14 : 43-52	22 : 47-53	18 : 2-12
	156. He is brought before Annas first at night. Peter's three denials	26 : 57, 58,	14 : 53, 54, [66-72	22 : 54-62	18 : 13, 18, [25-27
	157. Before Caiaphas, at first dawn, Jesus avows his Messiahship and Godhead. He is condemned for blasphemy, and mocked	26 : 59-68	14 : 55-65	22 : 63-71	18 : 19-24
A.D. 30	158. Brought before Pilate for sentence of crucifixion	27 : 1, 2, [11-14	15 : 1-5	23 : 1-5	18 : 28-38
	159. Pilate sends Him to Herod ; Herod sends Him back to Pilate	..	..	23 : 6-12	..
	160. Pilate sought to release Him, but the Jews demanded Barabbas. To appease them, Pilate scourges Him ; the Jews clamour for His crucifixion as making Himself a King. Pilate, notwithstanding his wife's warning, sentences Him	27 : 15-26	15 : 6- 15	23 : 13-25	[19 : 1-11 18 : 39,
	161. Jesus mocked by Roman soldiers with scarlet robe, crown of thorns, and reed	27 : 27-30	15 : 16-19	..	..
	162. Judas' remorse, presumptuously enters Temple, flings down the silver, and hangs himself (Acts 1 : 18, 19)	27 : 3-10	..	..	..
	163. Jesus bears His own cross to the city gate, where He is relieved by Simon of Cyrene ; refuses stupefying myrrhed wine	27 : 31-34	15 : 20-23	23 : 26-32	19 : 16, 17
	164. Crucified at Golgotha, probably outside the Damascus gate ; Seven sayings on cross, *three* relating to *others*, *four* to *Himself*;—(1) For His murderers—" Father, forgive them," etc.	27 : 35-44	15 : 24-32	23 : 33-38	19 : 18-27
	165. (2) The penitent thief promised Paradise, "To-day," etc.	..	..	23 : 39-43	..
	166. His garments divided and vesture cast lots for ; (3) commends His mother to the care of John, " Behold thy son," etc.	..	..	..	19 : 23-27
	167. Darkness over the land from sixth to ninth hour. Jesus' loud cry : (4) " Eli, Eli," etc. Saith (5) " I thirst," and receives the vinegar to fulfil Scripture ; (6) " It is finished ; " (7) " Father, into Thy hands I commend My Spirit ; " gives up the ghost ; the veil of the Temple rent. Centurion's testimony.	27 : 45-56	15 : 33-41	23 : 44-49	19 : 28-30
	168. The side pierced by the soldier's spear, and the blood and water attest His death and the truth of Scripture, Gen. 2 : 21-23 ; Eph. 5 : 30, 32 ; 1 John 5 : 6; Zech. 12 : 10. The body taken down, is wrapped up with Nicodemus' aloes and myrrh, and buried in new tomb of Joseph of Arimathea	27 : 57-61	15 : 42-47	23 : 50-56	19 : 31-42
	Seventh Day—Saturday, April 7.				
	169. Pilate grants a guard, and they set a seal upon sepulchre	27 : 62-66	..	..	..
	Christ's Resurrection, His Appearances during forty days, and Ascension.				
	First Day—Easter Sunday, April 8.				
	170. Resurrection at first dawn	28 : 2-4	..	..	..
	171. The women coming with spices find the sepulchre open and empty. Mary Magdalene returns to tell Peter and John	28 : 1	16 : 1-4	24 : 1-3	20 : 1, 2
	172. The other women remaining see two angels, who declare the Lord's resurrection	28 : 5-7	16 : 5-7	24 : 4-8	..
	173. Mary Magdalene returns to the sepulchre. Jesus reveals Himself to her. She reports to the disciples— *First* appearance	..	16 : 9-11	..	20 : 11-18
	174. Jesus meets the women (Mary mother of James, Salome, and Joanna) on their return to the city— *Second* appearance	28 : 8-10	16 : 8	24 : 9-11	20 : 3-10
	175. Peter and John find the sepulchre empty			24 : 12	
	176. Report of the watch to the chief priests, who bribe them	28 : 11-15	..		
	177. Jesus seen by Peter (Cephas, 1 Cor. 15 : 5)—*Third* appearance	..	..	24 : 34	..
	178. Seen by the two disciples on way to Emmaus—*Fourth* appearance	..	16 : 12, 13	24 : 13-35	..
	179. Jesus appears to the ten, Thomas being absent— *Fifth* appearance	..	16 : 14	24 : 36-49	20 : 19-23

DATE.	CONTENTS.	MATT.	MARK.	LUKE.	JOHN.
	Subsequent Appearances.				
Apr. 15	180. Evening of Sunday after Easter Day. Jesus appears to them again, Thomas being present—*Sixth* appearance	..	..	..	20 : 24-29
	181. The eleven go into Galilee, to a mountain appointed. Jesus appears, and commands them to teach all nations—*Seventh* appearance . .	28 : 16-20	16 : 15-18	..	..
	182. Jesus shows Himself at the Sea of Tiberias—*Eighth* appearance. Charges Simon to feed his lambs, sheep, and young sheep	..	..	..	21 : 1-24
	183. Seen of above five hundred brethren at once (1 Cor. 15 : 6), probably along with the eleven—*Ninth* appearance	28 : 16	..	..	..
	184. He is seen by James, then by all the Apostles (Acts 1 : 3-8 ; 1 Cor. 15 : 7)—*Tenth* appearance. In all 538 (549 if the Eleven, Matt. 28 : 16, be distinct from the 500) persons are *specified* as having seen the risen Saviour ; also, after His ascension, St. Paul (1 Cor. 15 : 8)				
May 17	185. The Ascension, forty days after Easter (Acts 1 : 9-12) .	..	16 : 19, 20	24 : 50-53	..
	186. Purpose and conclusion	..	..	..	20 : 30, 31, [21, 25

Harness [ar.], body armour, 1 Ki. 20 : 11; 22 : 34; 2 Chr. 18 : 33.
(verb), Ex. 13 : 18; Jer. 46 : 4.
Harod (hăr-ŏd) [fear, terror], Judg. 7 : 1.
Harodite (hăr-ŏd-īte), 2 Sam. 23 : 25.
Haroeh (hă-rō-ĕh) [the seer], 1 Chr. 2 : 52.
Harorite (hăr-ō-rīte), 1 Chr. 11 : 27.
Harosheth (hă-rō-shĕth) [working in stone or wood], Judg. 4 : 2.

Egyptian Harps.

Harp. St. Paul alludes to the harp (Greek κιθάρα) in 1 Cor. 14 : 7; and harps and harpers are frequently mentioned in the book of the Revelation—5 : 8; 14 : 2; 15 : 2; 18 : 22. First mentioned in Gen. 4 : 21, it had eight, ten, or twelve strings and was played by the fingers or by a plectrum when size permitted.
played on by David, 1 Sam. 16 : 23; 2 Sam. 6 : 5.
used in public worship, 1 Chr. 25 : 3; Ps. 33 : 2; 81 : 2; 150 : 3.
in heaven, Rev. 14 : 2.
See Gen. 4 : 21; Ps. 71 : 22; 98 : 5.
1 Sam. 16 : 16, cunning player on an h.
Job 30 : 31, my h. is turned to mourning.
Ps. 49 : 4, dark saying upon the h.
137 : 2, hanged h. on the willows.

Isa. 5 : 12, h. and viol are in their feasts.
1 Cor. 14 : 7, whether pipe or h.
Harper, Rev. 14 : 2; 18 : 22.
Harrow, 2 Sam. 12 : 31; 1 Chr. 20 : 3; **Job** 39 : 10.
Hart, Hind. It is difficult to form a conjecture as to which species of the deer tribe these words refer. The animal must have been common, for not only has it given its name to a city (Josh. 21 : 24; Judg. 12 : 12), but to Mount Ajilon. It was used as food, and appears among the game daily provided for Solomon's table, while the references to its habits, timidity, swiftness, gracefulness, etc., are most numerous.
a clean animal, Deut. 12 : 15; 1 Ki. 4 : 23; Isa. 35 : 6; Ps. 42 : 1.
Harvest, promise concerning, Gen. 8 : 22.
feast of, Ex. 23 : 16; 34 : 21; Lev. 19 : 9; Isa. 9 : 3; 16 : 9.
of the world, Jer. 8 : 20; Matt. 13 : 30, 39; Rev. 14 : 15.
1 Sam. 6 : 13, men reaping their h.
12 : 17, is it not wheat h. to-day ?
Job 5 : 5, whose h. the hungry eateth up.
Prov. 6 : 8, the ant gathereth food in h.
10 : 5, he that sleepeth in h.
25 : 13, cold of snow in time of h.
26 : 1, as rain in h.
Isa. 17 : 11, h. shall be a heap in day of grief.
18 : 4, dew in heat of h.
Jer. 5 : 17, they shall eat up thine h.
8 : 20, the h. is past, the summer ended.
Joel 3 : 13; Rev. 14 : 15, put in sickle, for the h. is ripe.
Matt. 9 : 37, the h. is plenteous.
9 : 38; Luke 10 : 2, the Lord of the h.
Matt. 13 : 30, both grow together until h.
Mark 4 : 29, he putteth in sickle, because h. is come.
John 4 : 35, the fields are white to h.
Harvestman, Isa. 17 : 5, as when h. gathereth corn.
Jer. 9 : 22, fall as the handful after h.
Harvest-time, Jer. 50 : 16.
Hasadiah (hăs-ă-dī-ăh) [Jehovah is kind], 1 Chr. 3 : 20.
Hasenuah (hăs-ĕ-nū-ăh), 1 Chr. 9 : 7.

Hashabiah (hăsh-ă-bī-ăh) [Jehovah provides], Neh. 10 : 11.
Hashabnah (hă-shăb-näh), Neh. 10 : 25. See Hashabiah.
Hashabniah (hăsh-ăb-nī-ăh), Neh. 3 : 10; 9 : 5.
Hashub (hăsh-ŭb), Neh. 3 : 11, 23; 10 : 23; 11 : 15.
Hashum (hăsh-ŭm), Ezra 2 : 19; 10 : 33; Neh. 7 : 22; 10 : 18.
Hast, Matt. 19 : 21; Mark 10 : 21; Luke 18 : 22, sell all thou h.
Matt. 25 : 25, there thou h. that is thine.
Rev. 2 : 6, but this thou h., that.
3 : 11, hold that fast which thou h.
Haste, Ex. 12 : 11, shall eat it in h.
1 Sam. 21 : 8, king's business required h.
Ps. 31 : 22; 116 : 11, I said in my h.
Prov. 19 : 2, he that h. with feet sinneth.
28 : 22, he that h. to be rich.
Isa. 52 : 12, ye shall not go out with h.
60 : 22, the Lord will h. it.
Zeph. 1 : 14, day of the Lord h. greatly.
Mark 6 : 25, came in h. to the king.
Hastily, Prov. 20 : 21; John 11 : 31.
Hasty, Prov. 14 : 29, he that is h. of spirit exalteth folly.
29 : 20, seest thou a man h. in words ?
Eccl. 5 : 2, let not thy heart be h.
7 : 9, be not h. in thy spirit.
Isa. 28 : 4, as h. fruit before summer.
Dan. 2 : 15, why is the decree so h. ?
Hatach (hă-tăch) [truth ?], Esther 4 : 5 f., 9 f.
Hatch, Isa. 34 : 15; 59 : 5; Jer. 17 : 11.
Hate, Gen. 24 : 60, possess gate of those that h. them.
Lev. 19 : 17, shalt not h. thy brother.
26 : 17, that h. you shall reign over you.
Num. 10 : 35, let them that h. thee flee.
2 Chr. 19 : 2, shouldest thou love them that h. the Lord ?
Ps. 34 : 21, that h. righteous shall be desolate.
83 : 2, that h. thee have lifted up the head.
97 : 10, ye that love the Lord, h. evil.
139 : 21, do not I h. them that h. thee ?
Prov. 1 : 22, how long will ye h. knowledge ?
8 : 13, fear of the Lord is to h. evil.
13 : 24, he that spareth his rod h. his son.
15 : 10, he that h. reproof shall die.
Eccl. 3 : 8, a time to h.
Isa. 1 : 14, your feasts my soul h.
61 : 8, I h. robbery for burnt offering.
Amos 5 : 15, h. the evil and love the good.
Mic. 3 : 2, who h. good and love evil.
Zech. 8 : 17, these are things that I h.
Mal. 1 : 3; Rom. 9 : 13, loved Jacob and h. Esau.
Matt. 5 : 44; Luke 6 : 27, do good to them that h. you.
Matt. 6 : 24, either he will h. the one.
10 : 22; Mark 13 : 13; Luke 21 : 17, ye shall be h.
Matt. 24 : 10, betray and h. one another.
Luke 6 : 22, blessed are ye when men h. you.
14 : 26, h. not his father and mother.
John 3 : 20, h. the light.
7 : 7, the world cannot h. you.
12 : 25, he that h. his life.
15 : 18; 1 John 3 : 13, marvel not if the world h. you.

John 15 : 23, he that h. me h. my Father also.
Rom. 7 : 15, what I h., that do I.
Eph. 5 : 29, no man ever yet h. his own flesh.
1 John 2 : 9; 3 : 15; 4 : 20, h. his brother.
Rev. 2 : 6, deeds of the Nicolaitanes I h.
Hateful, Ps. 36 : 2, iniquity be found to be h.
Titus 3 : 3, were h. and hating one another.
Rev. 18 : 2, cage unclean and h. bird.
Haters, Ps. 81 : 15, h. of the Lord.
Rom. 1 : 30, h. of God.
Hatred forbidden, Ex. 23 : 5; Lev. 19 : 17; Deut. 19 : 11; Prov. 10 : 12, 18; 15 : 17; Matt. 5 : 43; Gal. 5 : 20; Titus 3 : 3; 1 John 2 : 9; 3 : 15; 4 : 20.
Hats, Dan. 3 : 21.
Haughtiness censured, 2 Sam. 22 : 28; Prov. 6 : 17; 21 : 4, 24; Isa. 2 : 11; 13 : 11; 16 : 6; Jer. 48 : 29.
Haughty, 2 Sam. 22 : 28, thine eyes are upon h.
Ps. 131 : 1, my heart is not h.
Prov. 16 : 18, a h. spirit before a fall.
Isa. 3 : 16, daughters of Zion are h.
10 : 33, the h. shall be humbled.
Zeph. 3 : 11, no more be h.
Haunt, 1 Sam. 30 : 31; Ezek. 26 : 17.
Haven, Gen. 49 : 13; Ps. 107 : 30; Acts 27 : 8, 12.
Havoc, Acts 8 : 3, Saul made h. of the church.
Havoth-jair (hā-vŏth-jā-ĭr) [villages of Jair], Num. 32 : 41; Deut. 3 : 14; Josh. 13 : 20.

Hawk.

Hawk. The name is used in a very general sense for one of the smaller birds of prey.
unclean, Lev. 11 : 16.
described, Job 39 : 26.
Hay. See Grass.

Hazael (hă-zā-'ĕl) [God sees], king of Syria, 1 Ki. 19 : 15.
Elisha's prediction concerning, 2 Ki. 8 : 8 ff.
slays Ben-hadad, 2 Ki. 8 : 15.
oppresses Israel, 2 Ki. 9 : 14; 10 : 32; 12 : 17; 13 : 22. See **Chronology, Old Testament**.

Hazaiah (hă-zâi-'ah) [Jehovah sees], Neh. 11 : 5.

Hazar-addar (hā-'zär-ăd-'där) [village of Addar], Num. 34 : 4.

Hazar-enan (hā-'zär-ē-'năn) [village of fountains], Num. 34 : 9, 10.

Hazar-gaddah (hā-'zär-găd-'däh) [village of fortune], Josh. 15 : 27.

Hazar-hatticon (hā-'zär-hăt-'tĭ-cŏn) [village of the midway], Ezek. 47 : 16.

Hazar-maveth (hā-'zär-vĕth) [village of death], land occupied by descendants of Hazar-maveth (Joktan), Gen. 10 : 26; 1 Chr. 1 : 20.

Hazar-shual (hā-'zär-shû-'ăl) [village of jackals], Josh. 15 : 28; 1 Chr. 4 : 28.

Hazar-susah (hā-'zär-sū-'săh) [village of the horse], Josh. 19.

Hazar-susim (hā-'zär-sū-'sim), 1 Chr. 4 : 31.

Hazazon-tamar. See **Hazezon-tamar.**

Hazel, occurs only once in the A.V., Gen. 30 : 37. In the R.V. it is translated " almond," which is the tree intended.

Hazelelponi (hăz-ĕl-ĕl-pō-'nī) [give shade], O thou that turnest thyself towards me, 1 Chr. 4 : 3.

Hazerim (hă-zē-'rĭm), Deut. 2 : 23.

Hazeroth (hă-zē-'rōth) [villages], encampment of the Israelites in the wilderness, Num. 11 : 35; 12 : 16.

Hazezon-tamar (hăz-'ĕ-zŏn-tā-'mär), ancient name of Engedi, on west of Salt Sea, Gen. 14 : 7; 2 Chr. 20 : 2.

Haziel (hā-'zĭ-ĕl) [seen of God], 1 Chr. 23 : 9.

Hazo (hā-'zō), Gen. 22 : 22.

Hazor (hā-'zôr) [court, castle], 12 Ab, principal royal Canaanite city, near Lake Merom, Josh. 11 : 10; 15 : 25; 19 : 36.

He, fifth letter of Hebrew alphabet. Used to designate the fifth part of Ps. 119, each verse of which part begins with this letter.
Deut. 32 : 39, I, even I, am h.
Luke 24 : 6, they said, h. is not here.
John 7 : 25, is not this h. ?

Head, of the Church, Christ, Eph. 1 : 22; 4 : 15; 5 : 23; Col. 1 : 18; 2 : 10.
not holding the, Col. 2 : 19.
Gen. 3 : 15, it shall bruise thy h.
Josh. 2 : 19, blood be upon his h.
Judg. 13 : 5, no razor come on his h.
2 Ki. 2 : 3, take thy master from h. to-day.
4 : 19, said, My h., my h.
Esther 9 : 25, device return on own h.
Ps. 7 : 16, mischief return on own h.
27 : 6, now shall my h. be lifted up.
38 : 4, iniquities gone over mine h.
110 : 7, therefore shall he lift up the h.
141 : 5, oil, which shall not break my h.
Prov. 10 : 6, blessings on h. of the just.
25 : 22; Rom. 12 : 20, coals of fire on his h.
Eccl. 2 : 14, the wise man's eyes are in his h.
Isa. 1 : 5, the whole h. is sick.
51 : 11, everlasting joy upon their h.

58 : 5, bow down h. as bulrush.
59 : 17, helmet of salvation on h.
Jer. 9 : 1, oh that my h. were waters.
Dan. 2 : 38, thou art this h. of gold.
Amos 8 : 10, bring baldness on every h.
Zech. 1 : 21, no man did lift up his h.
6 : 11, set crowns on h. of Joshua.
Matt. 5 : 36, neither swear by thy h.
27 : 30; Mark 15 : 19, smote him on h.
Luke 7 : 46, my h. thou didst not anoint.
21 : 18, not an hair of h. perish.
John 13 : 9, also my hands and my h.
1 Cor. 11 : 3, the h. of every man is Christ.
Eph. 5 : 23, husband is h. of the wife.
Rev. 19 : 12, on his h. many crowns.

Headbands, Isa. 3 : 20.

Headdress was at first unused among the Hebrews, except in the case of war or other special occasions (1 Ki. 20 : 31 f.). For cases of long exposure to the sun they would probably wear something after the fashion of the ordinary headdress of the Bedouin. This consists of the " keffieh," a square handkerchief, generally of red and yellow cotton or cotton and silk, folded so that three of the corners hang down over the back and shoulders, leaving the face exposed, and bound round the head by a cord. The " tsânîph " (something like a turban), the best attested covering, was worn by nobles, Job 29 : 14; ladies, Isa. 3 : 23; and kings, Isa. 62 : 3; while the " peer " was an article of holiday dress, Isa. 61 : 3, A.V. " beauty," Ezek. 24 : 17, 23, and was worn at weddings, Isa. 61 : 10. A kindred word is used of the high priest's turban, Ex. 28 : 4. The " hats " of Dan. 3 : 21 were a variety of the conical Babylonian headdress, not " mantles," as in R.V.

Headlong, Job 5 : 13; Luke 4 : 29; Acts 1 : 18.

Headstone, Zech. 4 : 7.

Heady, 2 Tim. 3 : 4.

Heal, Ex. 15 : 26, I am the Lord that h. thee.
Deut. 32 : 39, I wound and I h.
2 Ki. 2 : 22, waters were h.
Ps. 6 : 2, O Lord, h. me.
41 : 4, h. my soul, for I have sinned.
103 : 3, who h. all thy diseases.
107 : 20, sent his word, and h. them.
Isa. 6 : 10, lest they convert, and be h.
53 : 5, with his stripes we are h.
Jer. 6 : 14; 8 : 11, they have h. the hurt slightly.
17 : 14, h. me, and I shall be h.
Lam. 2 : 13, who can h. thee ?
Hos. 6 : 1, he hath torn, and he will h. us.
14 : 4, I will h. their backsliding.
Matt. 8 : 7, I will come and h. him.
10 : 8; Luke 9 : 2; 10 : 9, h. the sick.
12 : 10; Luke 14 : 3, is it lawful to h. on Sabbath ?
Matt. 13 : 15; John 12 : 40; Acts 28 : 27, be converted, and I should h. them.
Mark 3 : 2; Luke 6 : 7, whether he would h. on Sabbath day.
Luke 4 : 18, to h. the broken hearted.
5 : 17, power of the Lord present to h.
John 4 : 47, come and h. his son.
5 : 13, he that was h. wist not who it was.

Acts 4 : 30, stretching forth thine hand to h.
14 : 9, that he had faith to be h.
Heb. 12 : 13, let it rather be h.
Jas. 5 : 16, pray that ye may be h.
1 Pet. 2 : 24, by whose stripes ye were h.
Healer, Isa. 3 : 7.
Healing, Jer. 14 : 19, there is no h. for us.
Nah. 3 : 19, no h. of thy bruise.
Mal. 4 : 2, arise with h. in his wings.
Matt. 4 : 23, h. all manner of sickness.
Luke 9 : 11, healed them that had need of h.
1 Cor. 12 : 9, 28, the gifts of h.
Rev. 22 : 2, for the h. of the nations.
Health, of body, Gen. 43 : 28; 3 John 2.
spiritual, Ps. 42 : 11; Prov. 3 : 8; 12 : 18;
  Isa. 58 : 8; Jer. 8 : 15; 30 : 17; 33 : 6.
2 Sam. 20 : 9, art thou in h., my brother ?
Ps. 42 : 11; 43 : 5, the h. of my countenance.
67 : 2, thy saving h. may be known.
Prov. 4 : 22, they are h. to all their flesh.
13 : 17, a faithful ambassador is h.
16 : 24, h. to the bones.
Isa. 58 : 8, thy h. shall spring forth.
Jer. 8 : 15, looked for a time of h.
8 : 22, why is not h. of my people recovered ?
Heap, Deut. 13 : 16, shall be an h. for ever.
32 : 23, h. mischiefs upon them.
Josh. 7 : 26, over him a h. of stones.
Job 16 : 4, I could h. up words.
27 : 16, though he h. up silver.
Ps. 39 : 6, he h. up riches.
Prov. 25 : 22; Rom. 12 : 20, h. coals of fire.
Eccl. 2 : 26, to gather and to h. up.
Isa. 17 : 11, harvest shall be a h.
25 : 2, thou hast made of a city an h.
Jer. 30 : 18, city shall be builded on own h.
Ezek. 24 : 10, h. on wood.
Mic. 1 : 6, Samaria as an h. of the field.
3 : 12, Jerusalem shall become h.
Hab. 1 : 10, they shall h. dust.
2 Tim. 4 : 3, h. to themselves teachers.
Jas. 5 : 3, ye have h. treasures for last days.
Hear, Deut. 4 : 10, I will make them h. my
  words.
31 : 12, h. and fear the Lord.
1 Sam. 2 : 23, I h. your evil dealings.
15 : 14, lowing of oxen which I h.
1 Ki. 8 : 42, they shall h. of thy great name.
18 : 26, saying, O Baal, h.
2 Ki. 7 : 6, h. a noise of chariots.
18 : 28; Isa. 36 : 13, h. words of the great
  king.
1 Chr. 14 : 15, when thou h. a sound of going.
Neh. 8 : 2, all that could h. with understanding.
Job 5 : 27, h. it, and know thou it.
34 : 2, h. my words, ye wise men.
42 : 4, h. I beseech thee.
Ps. 4 : 1; 39 : 12; 54 : 2; 84 : 8; 102 : 1;
  143 : 1, h. my prayer.
20 : 1, Lord, h. thee in day of trouble.
27 : 7, h., O Lord, when I cry.
51 : 8, make me h. joy and gladness.
59 : 7, who, say they, doth h. ?
66 : 16, come and h., all ye that fear God.
85 : 8, I will h. what God the Lord will speak.
102 : 20, h. groaning of the prisoner.
143 : 8, to h. thy loving-kindness.
Prov. 8 : 33, h. instruction and be wise.
22 : 17, h. the words of the wise.

Eccl. 5 : 1, more ready to h. than give.
7 : 5, better to h. rebuke of wise.
12 : 13, h. conclusion of the whole matter.
Isa. 1 : 2, h. O heavens, and give ear.
6 : 9; Mark 4 : 12, h., but understand not.
Isa. 33 : 13, h., ye that are afar off.
34 : 1, let the earth h.
42 : 18, h. ye deaf.
55 : 3; John 5 : 25, h., and your soul shall
  live.
Ezek. 3 : 27, he that h., let him h.
Dan. 9 : 17, h. prayer of thy servant.
Matt. 11 : 5; Mark 7 : 37; Luke 7 : 22, the
  deaf h.
Matt. 13 : 17; Luke 10 : 24, h. those things
  which ye h.
Matt. 17 : 5; Mark 9 : 7, my beloved Son,
  h. him.
Mark 4 : 24; Luke 8 : 18, take heed what
  ye h.
Luke 5 : 1, pressed on him to h. word.
6 : 17, came to h. him and be healed.
9 : 9, who is this of whom I h.?
10 : 16, he that h. you h. me.
16 : 2, how is it I h. this of thee ?
19 : 48, people very attentive to h.
John 5 : 25, dead shall h. voice of Son of God.
5 : 30, as I h., I judge.
6 : 60, an hard saying, who can h. it ?
8 : 47, he that is of God, h. God's words.
9 : 31, God h. not sinners.
12 : 47, if any man h. my words.
14 : 24, the word ye h. is not mine.
Acts 2 : 8, how h. we every man in our own
  tongue.
13 : 44, whole city together to h. word.
17 : 21, to tell or h. some new thing.
Rom. 10 : 14, how shall they h, without a
  preacher ?
1 Cor. 11 : 18, I h. there be divisions.
2 Thess. 3 : 11, we h. that some walk disorderly.
1 Tim. 4 : 16, save thyself, and them that h.
  thee.
Jas. 1 : 19, swift to h.
1 John 5 : 15, we know that he h. us.
3 John 4, than to h. that children walk in
  truth.
Rev. 3 : 20, if any man h. my voice.
9 : 20, neither see, nor h., nor walk.
Heard, Gen. 3 : 8, they h. voice of the Lord.
16 : 11, Lord h. thy affliction.
21 : 26, neither yet h. I of it.
Ex. 2 : 24, God h. their groaning.
3 : 7, I have h. their cry.
Num. 11 : 1; 12 : 2, the Lord h. it.
Deut. 4 : 12, only ye h. a voice.
1 Ki. 6 : 7, nor any tool of iron h.
2 Ki. 19 : 25; Isa. 37 : 26, hast thou not h.
  long ago ?
Ezra 3 : 13; Neh. 12 : 43, noise was h. afar off.
Job 15 : 8, hast thou h. the secret of God ?
19 : 7, cry out of wrong, but I am not h.
29 : 11, when the ear h. me, it blessed me.
Ps. 6 : 9, Lord hath h. my supplication.
10 : 17, hast h. the desire of the humble.
34 : 4, I sought the Lord, and he h.
38 : 13, I as a deaf man h. not.
61 : 5, thou hast h. my vows.

97 : 8, Zion h. and was glad.
116 : 1, I love the Lord, because he hath h.
Song of Sol. 2 : 12, voice of turtle is h.
Isa. 40 : 21, have ye not h. ?
52 : 15, that had not h., shall they consider.
60 : 18, violence no more be h. in land.
64 : 4, not h. what he hath prepared.
65 : 19, weeping no more be h.
66 : 8, who hath h. such a thing ?
Jer. 7 : 13, rising early, but ye h. not.
51 : 46, rumour shall be h. in land.
Ezek. 26 : 13, harps shall no more be h.
Dan. 12 : 8, I h., but understood not.
Jonah 2 : 2, I cried unto Lord, and he h.
Mal. 3 : 16, the Lord hearkened, and h. it.
Matt. 6 : 7, be h. for much speaking.
26 : 65; Mark 14 : 64, ye have h. the blasphemy.
Luke 12 : 3, shall be h. in the light.
John 4 : 42, we have h. him ourselves.
8 : 6, as though he h. not.
11 : 41, I thank thee thou hast h. me.
18 : 21, ask them which h. me.
Acts 2 : 37, when they h. this, they were pricked.
4 : 4, many which h. believed.
4 : 20, cannot but speak things we have h.
22 : 15, witness of what thou hast seen and h.
Rom. 10 : 14, of whom they have not h.
1 Cor. 2 : 9, eye hath not seen, nor ear h.
2 Cor. 12 : 4, h. unspeakable words.
Eph. 4 : 21, if so be ye have h. him.
Heb. 2 : 3, confirmed by them that h.
4 : 2, not mixed with faith in them that h.
5 : 7, was h. in that he feared.
Jas. 5 : 11, ye have h. of patience of Job.
1 John 1 : 1, that which we have h. and seen.
Rev. 3 : 3, remember how thou hast h.
10 : 4; 14 : 2; 18 : 4, h. a voice from heaven.
Hearer, Rom. 2 : 13, not the h. of law are just.
Eph. 4 : 29, minister grace unto the h.
2 Tim. 2 : 14, to subverting of the h.
Jas. 1 : 22, be ye doers of the Word, not h.
Hearing, Deut. 31 : 11, read this law in their h.
2 Ki. 4 : 31, was neither voice nor h.
Job 42 : 5, by the h. of the ear.
Prov. 20 : 12, the h. ear, the Lord hath made.
Eccl. 1 : 8, nor ear filled with h.
Isa. 33 : 15, stoppeth ears from h. blood.
Amos 8 : 11, a famine of h. the words of the Lord.
Matt. 13 : 13, h., they hear not.
Mark 6 : 2, many h. were astonished.
Luke 2 : 46, h. them and asking questions.
Acts 9 : 7, h. a voice, but seeing no man.
Rom. 10 : 17, faith cometh by h.
1 Cor. 12 : 17, where were the h. ?
Gal. 3 : 2, or by the h. of faith ?
Heb. 5 : 11, seeing ye are dull of h.
Hearken, Deut. 18 : 15, a prophet, to him ye shall h.
28 : 13; 1 Ki. 11 : 38, if thou h. to commandments.
Josh. 1 : 17, so will we h. unto thee.
1 Sam. 15 : 22, to h. better than the fat of rams.
Ps. 103 : 20, angels h. to voice of his word.
Isa. 55 : 2, h. diligently unto me.
Dan. 9 : 19, O Lord, h. and do.

Mic. 1 : 2, h., O earth, and all therein.
Mark 7 : 14, h. to me, every one of you.
Acts 7 : 2, men, brethren, and fathers, h.
Heart of man, Gen. 6 : 5; 8 : 21; Eccl. 8 : 11; 9 : 3; Jer. 17 : 9; Matt. 12 : 34; 15 : 19; Luke 6 : 45; Rom. 2 : 5.
searched and tried by God, 1 Chr. 28 : 9; 29 : 17; Ps. 44 : 21; 139 : 23; Prov. 21 : 2; 24 : 12; Jer. 12 : 3; 17 : 10; 20 : 12; Rev. 2 : 23.
enlightened, etc., by him, Ps. 27 : 14; Prov. 16 : 1; 2 Cor. 4 : 6; 1 Thess. 3 : 13; 2 Pet. 1 : 19.
a new, promised, Jer. 24 : 7; 31 : 33; 32 : 39; Ezek. 11 : 19; 36 : 26.
Gen. 45 : 26, Jacob's h. fainted.
Ex. 23 : 9, ye know the h. of a stranger.
35 : 35, hath he filled with wisdom of h.
Deut. 11 : 13; Josh. 22 : 5; 1 Sam. 12 : 20, serve him with all your h.
Deut. 13 : 3; 30 : 6; Matt. 22 : 37; Mark 12 : 30; Luke 10 : 27, love the Lord with all your h.
Judg. 5 : 16, great searchings of h.
1 Sam. 10 : 9, God gave him another h.
16 : 7, the Lord looketh on the h.
1 Ki. 3 : 9, give an understanding h.
8 : 17; 2 Chr. 6 : 7, it was in the h. of David.
1 Ki. 11 : 4, not perfect as was the h. of David.
14 : 8, followed me with all his h.
1 Chr. 12 : 33, not of double h.
16 : 10; Ps. 105 : 3, let the h. of them rejoice that seek the Lord.
1 Chr. 29 : 17; Jer. 11 : 20, thou triest the h.
2 Chr. 15 : 12, seek God of fathers with all h.
31 : 21, he did it with all his h.
32 : 25, his h. was lifted up.
Neh. 2 : 2, nothing else but sorrow of h.
Job 9 : 4, wise in h. and mighty.
29 : 13, I caused the widow's h. to sing.
38 : 36, given understanding to the h.
Ps. 19 : 8, statutes rejoicing the h.
27 : 3, my h. shall not fear.
34 : 18, Lord is nigh them of broken h.
44 : 21, he knoweth secrets of the h.
64 : 6, the h. is deep.
73 : 7, more than h. could wish.
78 : 37, their h. was not right.
97 : 11, gladness sown for upright in h.
139 : 23, search me, and know my h.
Prov. 4 : 23, keep thy h. with all diligence.
14 : 10, the h. knoweth his own bitterness.
23 : 7, as he thinketh in his h.
31 : 11, h. of her husband doth trust.
Eccl. 8 : 5, a wise man's h. discerneth.
Isa. 30 : 29, ye shall have gladness of h.
35 : 4, say to them of fearful h.
57 : 1; Jer. 12 : 11, no man layeth it to h.
Isa. 57 : 15, revive h. of contrite.
65 : 14, sing for joy of h.
Jer. 11 : 20, triest reins and h.
17 : 9, h. is deceitful above all things.
24 : 7, give them a h. to know me.
Lam. 3 : 65, give sorrow of h.
Ezek. 11 : 19, stony h. out of flesh.
18 : 31, make you a new h.
36 : 26, give you a h. of flesh.
44 : 7; Acts 7 : 51, uncircumcised in h.
Joel 2 : 13, end your h.

Mal. 4 : 6, turn h. of fathers to children.
Matt. 5 : 8, blessed are the pure in h.
6 : 21; Luke 12 : 34, there will your h. be also.
11 : 29, meek and lowly in h.
12 : 34; Luke 6 : 45, out of abundance of the h.
Matt. 15 : 19; Mark 7 : 21, out of h. proceed evil thoughts.
Mark 2 : 8, why reason ye in your h.
10 : 5; 16 : 14, hardness of h.
21 : 14, settle it in your h.
24 : 25, slow of h. to believe.
John 14 : 1, 27, let not your h. be troubled.
Acts 2 : 46, with singleness of h.
7 : 54, were cut to the h.
11 : 23, with purpose of h.
Rom. 10 : 10, with the h. man believeth.
1 Cor. 2 : 9, neither entered into h. of man.
2 Cor. 3 : 3, in fleshy tables of the h.
5 : 12, glory in appearance, not in h.
Eph. 3 : 17, that Christ may dwell in your h. by faith.
Col. 3 : 22, in singleness of h.
Heb. 4 : 12, discerner of intents of the h.
10 : 22, draw near with true h.
Jas. 4 : 8, purify your h.
1 Pet. 3 : 4, the hidden man of the h.
3 : 15, sanctify the Lord in your h.
Hearth, Gen. 18 : 6; Jer. 36 : 22, 23; Zech. 12 : 6.
Heartily, Col. 3 : 23, whatsoever ye do, do it h.
Heat, Gen. 8 : 22, cold and h., summer and winter.
18 : 1, in h. of the day.
Deut. 29 : 24, the h. of this great anger.
Ps. 19 : 6, nothing hid from h. thereof.
Isa. 4 : 6; 25 : 4, shadow from h.
18 : 4, cloud of dew in h. of harvest.
49 : 10, neither shall h. smite them.
Matt. 20 : 12, borne burden and h. of the day.
Acts 28 : 3, came viper out of the h.
Jas. 1 : 11, sun risen with burning h.
2 Pet. 3 : 10, elements melt with fervent h.
Dan. 3 : 19, seven times more than wont to be h.
Hos. 7 : 4, as an oven h. by the baker.
Heath. The Hebrew " ar ar " and " aro er," thus translated in Jer. 17 : 6 and 48 : 6, are in the R.V. translated in the margin " tamarisk." Others, as Tristram, think the low-growing " Juniperus Sabina," which is a dwarf juniper, is meant, for which a similar word is used by the Arabs.
Heathen, described, Eph. 2 : 12; 4 : 18.
gospel preached to, Matt. 24 : 14; 28 : 19; Rom. 10 : 14; 16 : 26; Gal. 1 : 16.
conversion of, Acts 10 : 35; Rom. 15 : 16.
Ps. 2 : 1; Acts 4 : 25, why do the h. rage ?
Ps. 2 : 8, give thee h. for inheritance.
9 : 5, thou hast rebuked the h.
33 : 10, bringeth counsel of h. to nought.
102 : 15, the h. shall fear the name of the Lord.
Matt. 6 : 7, vain repetitions, as the h. do.
18 : 17, let him be as an h. man.
Gal. 3 : 8, that God would justify the h.
Heave offering, Ex. 29 : 27; Num. 15 : 19, 20; 18 : 8, 30, 32.

Heaven. The word heaven is used in the Scriptures in essentially the same senses in which it is commonly used to-day. (1) The airy spaces in which the birds fly. (2) The visible, starry sky. (3) God's house. When it states in Isa. 65 : 18 and 2 Peter 3 : 13 that there will be new heavens and a new earth, the heaven referred to is the visible sky above us.
The firmament, created, Gen. 1 : 1, 8; Ps. 8; 19; Isa. 40 : 22; Rev. 10 : 6.
God's dwelling-place, 1 Ki. 8 : 30; Ps. 2 : 4; 115 : 3; 123 : 1; Isa. 6 : 1; 66 : 1; Ezek. 1; 10; Matt. 6 : 9; Acts 7 : 49; Heb. 8 : 1; Rev. 4.
its happiness, Ps. 16 : 11; Isa. 49 : 10; Dan. 12 : 3; Matt. 5 : 12; 13 : 43; John 12 : 26; 14 : 1, 2; 17 : 24; 1 Cor. 2 : 9; 13 : 12; 1 Pet. 1 : 4; Rev. 7 : 16; 14 : 13; 21 : 4; 22 : 3.
who enter, Matt. 5 : 3; 25 : 34; Rom. 8 : 17; Heb. 12 : 23; 1 Pet. 1 : 4; Rev. 7 : 9, 14.
who excluded from, Matt. 7 : 21; 25 : 41; Luke 13 : 27; 1 Cor. 6 : 9; Gal. 5 : 21; Rev. 21 : 8; 22 : 15.
the new, Rev. 21 : 1.
Gen. 28 : 17, the gate of h.
Ex. 20 : 22, talked with you from h.
Deut. 10 : 14; 1 Ki. 8 : 27; Ps. 115 : 16, the h. and h. of h.
Deut. 33 : 13, the precious things of h.
2 Ki. 7 : 2, if the Lord would make windows in h. ?
Job 15 : 15, the h. are not clean in his sight.
22 : 14, he walketh in the circuit of h.
Ps. 8 : 3, when I consider thy h.
73 : 25, whom have I in h. ?
89 : 6, who in h. can be compared unto the Lord ?
103 : 11, as the h. is high above the earth.
Prov. 8 : 27, when he prepared the h., I was there.
25 : 3, the h. for height.
Eccl. 5 : 2, for God is in h.
Isa. 40 : 12, who hath meted out h. ?
65 : 17; Rev. 21 : 1, new h., and new earth.
Isa. 66 : 1; Acts 7 : 49, h. is my throne.
Jer. 7 : 18, make cakes to queen of h.
23 : 24, do not I fill h. and earth ?
31 : 37, if h. can be measured.
51 : 15, hath stretched out the h.
Ezek. 32 : 7, I will cover the h.
Dan. 4 : 35, doeth according to his will in army of h.
7 : 13, with clouds of h.
Hag. 1 : 10, the h. over you is stayed from dew.
Mal. 3 : 10, if I will not open windows of h.
Matt. 5 : 18, till h. and earth pass.
5 : 34; Jas. 5 : 12, nor swear by h.
Matt. 24 : 30; 26 : 64; Mark 14 : 62, Son of man coming in clouds of h.
Mark 13 : 27, elect to uttermost part of h.
Luke 3 : 21, the h. was opened.
15 : 18, I have sinned against h.
John 1 : 51, ye shall see h. open.
6 : 31, bread from h.
Acts 3 : 21, whom the h. must receive.
4 : 12, none other name under h.

Rom. 1 : 18, wrath of God revealed from h.
1 Cor. 8 : 5, whether in h. or in earth.
2 Cor. 5 : 1, house eternal in the h.
Gal. 1 : 8, though an angel from h. preach.
Eph. 1 : 10, gather in one all things in h.
3 : 15, whole family in h. is named.
6 : 9; Col. 4 : 1, your master is in h.
Phil. 3 : 20, our conversation is in h.
Col. 1 : 16, by him all things created in h.
Heb. 10 : 34, have in h. a better substance.
12 : 23, written in h.
1 John 5 : 7, three that bear record in h.
Rev. 4 : 1, a door opened in h.
8 : 1, silence in h.
11 : 19, temple of God in h.
12 : 1, a great wonder in h.
Heavenly, Matt. 6 : 26, your h. Father feedeth them.
Luke 2 : 13, multitude of the h. host.
John 3 : 12, if I tell you of h. things.
Acts 26 : 19, not disobedient to h. vision.
1 Cor. 15 : 48, as is the h., such are they.
Eph. 1 : 3; 2 : 6; 3 : 10, in h. places.
Heb. 3 : 1, partakers of the h. calling.
6 : 4, have tasted of the h. gift.
8 : 5, shadow of h. things.
11 : 16, an h. country.
Heavenly Father, Matt. 6 : 14 f.; 18 : 26; Luke 11 : 13.
Heaviness, Ps. 69 : 20, full of h.
119 : 28, my soul melteth for h.
Prov. 12 : 25, h. in the heart maketh it stoop.
14 : 13, the end of that mirth is h.
Isa. 61 : 3, garment of praise for spirit of h.
Rom. 9 : 2, have great h. and sorrow.
Jas. 4 : 9, let your joy be turned to h.
1 Pet. 1 : 6, if need be, ye are in h.
Heavy, Ex. 17 : 12, Moses' hands were h.
18 : 18, this thing is too h. for thee.
1 Ki. 14 : 6, sent with h. tidings.
Neh. 5 : 18, the bondage was h.
Ps. 32 : 4, thy hand was h. upon me.
Prov. 25 : 20, songs to a h. heart.
31 : 6, wine to those of h. hearts.
Isa. 6 : 10, and make their ears h.
58 : 6, to undo the h. burdens.
Matt. 11 : 28, all ye that are h. laden.
23 : 4, they bind h. burdens.
26 : 37, he began to be very h.
26 : 43; Mark 14 : 40, their eyes were h.
Heber (hē-́běr) [association, society], the Kenite, Judg. 4 : 11, 17. A name Heber, differently spelled, meaning a "passer over" (the Euphrates), is used in Gen. 10 : 21; 11 : 15; Num. 24 : 24. It is spelled in A.V. "Eber," but is connected with the word "Hebrew."
Hebrewess, Jer. 34 : 9.
Hebrews [descendants of Heber, or dwellers on the other side (of the Euphrates), or passers over], Phil. 3 : 5.
Abraham and his descendants so called, Gen. 14 : 13; 40 : 15; 43 : 32; Ex. 2 : 6; 2 Cor. 11 : 22; Phil. 3 : 5.
Hebrews, Epistle to the.
Authenticity.—For a century after it was written, no voice was raised among orthodox Christians against the canonicity of the epistle. It is freely quoted by Clement writing from Rome, acknowledged by

Justin Martyr and by the compilers of the Peshito N.T. Later on when church writers adopted Latin in place of Greek as their vehicle, for some unknown reason the church of Rome and of Northern Africa questioned the authority of Hebrews. The book still maintained its place in the Eastern and Greek-speaking churches. At the end of the fourth century, all the evidence for and against the book was weighed by Jerome who decided emphatically in its favour, Augustine concurred. In 397 A.D., the third Council of Carthage confirmed this decision.
Authorship.—While there is no external authority for the superscription, "The Epistle of Paul, the Apostle, to the Hebrews," the opinion was current at first, apparently everywhere but in Northern Africa, that Paul was the author. Olshausen is authority for the statement that among the Greek fathers no one is mentioned in Egypt, Syria, Palestine, Asia or Greece who doubted Paul's authorship. In Alexandria questions arose on the basis of differences of vocabulary and style on this point. A large literature has grown up around the subject. Apollos, Barnabas, Luke, Silvanus and Clement have been named among possible authors.
Occasion of the Epistle.—At first Hebrew Christians continued attendance at Temple and Synagogue. Later they were excluded from such fellowship. The Epistle was written to show that their possessions in Christ were far better than those surrendered. The theme of the Epistle centres about the person of Christ and his Highpriesthood. In the first chapter, he is the anointed one; in the second, a faithful Highpriest able to succour the tempted; in the fourth, in all points tempted yet without sin; in the fifth, the author of eternal salvation; sixth, a priest forever after the order of Melchizedek; seventh, ever living to make intercession; eighth, the mediator of a better covenant; ninth, the Priest manifested to put away sin by the sacrifice of himself, and to appear again on earth apart from a sin offering for the complete deliverance of his people. In the tenth, the Highpriest is seen seated at the right hand of God awaiting the subjugation of his enemies. Believers are exhorted to have great boldness since he is faithful that promised. The eleventh chapter immortalizes the heroes of faith; the twelfth exhorts to like fidelity, and the thirteenth is a covering letter with salutations and benediction.
Hebron (hē-́brŏn) [association], ancient city in Canaan; present population 10,000, Jewish and Moslem. An ancient enclosure surrounds the probable site of the cave of Machpelah (Gen. 23 : 9).
Abraham dwells there, Gen. 13 : 18; 23 : 2.
the spies come to, Num. 13 : 22.
taken, Josh. 10 : 36, 37.
given to Caleb, Josh. 14 : 13; 15 : 13.
David reigns there, 2 Sam. 2 : 1-4; 5 : 1-5; 1 Chr. 11 : 1-3; 12 : 38; 29 : 27.
Hebronites, Num. 3 : 27.

Hebron, with the cave of Machpelah.

Hedge, Job 1 : 10, hast not thou made an h. about him ?
Prov. 15 : 19, way of slothful as an h. of thorns.
Eccl. 10 : 8, whoso breaketh an h.
Hos. 2 : 6, I will h. up thy way.
Matt. 21 : 33, vineyard, h. it round.
Mark 12 : 1, set an h. about it.
Luke 14 : 23, the highways and h.
Heed, 2 Sam. 20 : 10, took no h. to the sword.
2 Ki. 10 : 31, Jehu took no h.
Ps. 119 : 9, by taking h. to thy word.
Eccl. 12 : 9, preacher gave good h.
Jer. 18 : 18, let us not give h. to any words.
Acts 3 : 5, he gave h. unto them.
1 Tim. 1 : 4; Titus 1 : 14, neither give h. to fables.
1 Tim. 4 : 1, giving h. to seducing spirits.
Heb. 2 : 1, we ought to give the more earnest h.
Heel, Gen. 3 : 15, thou shalt bruise his h.
Gen. 25 : 26; Hos. 12 : 3, hold on brother's h.
Ps. 41 : 9; John 13 : 18, hath lifted up h. against me.
Ps. 49 : 5, iniquity of my h.
Jer. 13 : 22, thy h. made bare.
Heifer, for sacrifice, Gen. 15 : 9; Num. 19 : 2; Deut. 21 : 3; Heb. 9 : 13.
Height, 1 Sam. 16 : 7, look not on h. of stature.
17 : 4, Goliath's h.
Job 22 : 12, is not God in h. of heaven ?
Ps. 102 : 19, Lord looked from h. of sanctuary.
Prov. 25 : 3, the heaven for h.
Isa. 7 : 11, ask it in the h. above.
Rom. 8 : 39, nor h., nor depth.
Eph. 3 : 18, 19, the h. of the love of Christ.
Heinous, Job 31 : 11.
Heirs, of God, Rom. 8 : 17; Gal. 3 : 29; 4 : 7; Eph. 3 : 6; Heb. 6 : 17; Jas. 2 : 5.
2 Sam. 14 : 7, we will destroy the h.
Prov. 30 : 23, handmaid that is h. to her mistress.
Matt. 21 : 38; Mark 12 : 7; Luke 20 : 14, this is the h.
Titus 3 : 7, h. according to hope of eternal life.
Heb. 1 : 14, who shall be h. of salvation.
11 : 7, became h. of righteousness.
1 Pet. 3 : 7, as h. together of the grace.

Helah (hē-lăh) [rust], 1 Chr. 4 : 5, 7.
Helam (hē-lăm) [strength of the people ?], 2 Sam. 10 : 16.
Helbah (hĕl-băh), Judg. 1 : 31.
Helbon (hĕl-bŏn) [fat, fruitful], a city of Syria, famed for its excellent wine, Ezek. 27 : 18.
Heldai (hĕl-dâi) [worldly], 1 Chr. 27 : 15; Zech. 6 : 10.
Heleb (hē-lĕb) [fatness], 2 Sam. 23 : 29.
Heled (hē-lĕd) [worldly], 1 Chr. 11 : 30.
Helek (hē-lĕk) [a portion], Num. 26 : 30; Josh. 17 : 2.
Helekites, Num. 26 : 30.
Helem (hē-lĕm) [a stroke], 1 Chr. 7 : 35.
Heleph (hē-lĕf) [exchange], Josh. 19 : 33.
Helez (hē-lĕz) [strong], 1 Chr. 2 : 39; the Pelonite, 1 Chr. 11 : 27; 27 : 10.
Heli (hē-lī) i.q., Eli, Luke 3 : 23.
Heliopolis. See Baalbek.
Helkai (hĕl-kā-ī) [Jehovah his portion], Neh. 12 : 15.
Helkath (hĕl-kăth) [portion], Josh. 21 : 31.
Helkath-hazzurim (hĕl-kăth-hăz-zū-rĭm) [the field of the sword-edges], 2 Sam. 2 : 16.
Hell. This word in the Old Testament translates " Sheol," which comes from an Assyrian root meaning " chamber." It was regarded as an underworld of the dead, often called the " grave," in which the shades live, whether active or not is hard to determine (cf. Ps. 88 : 13; 94 : 17; 30 : 10; Job 14 : 13; and Ezek. 32 : 27).
Two words are translated in the New Testament by " hell," namely, " Hades " and " Gehenna." " Hades " is the Latin translation of " Sheol," and means literally " the unseen world," or " the grave " (Acts 2 : 31; 1 Cor. 15 : 55; Rev. 20 : 13). So the creeds say of Jesus, " He descended into hell," without implying misery. The notion of torment is certainly seen elsewhere (Matt. 11 : 23; Luke 16 : 23; 2 Pet. 2 : 4, etc.); and the double use of the word has led people to look on hell as a place or state intermediate between death and resurrection and divided into the abode of the blessed and that of the lost. " Gehenna " is, however, the word oftenest used for future punishment. Originally the valley of Hinnom (Ge-Hinnom), where possibly Molech and Tammuz were worshipped (2 Ki. 23 : 18; 2 Chr. 28 : 3; 33 : 6; Jer. 7 : 31; 32 : 35), its sinister character caused its defilement by Josiah (2 Ki. 23 : 6, 10). It became the place for burning the refuse of the city, dead animals, and the bodies of criminals; and it was regarded as a fit symbol of the destruction of wicked souls.
(Hades), the grave, Acts 2 : 31; 1 Cor. 15 : 55; Rev. 20 : 13.
place of torment, Matt. 11 : 23; 13 : 42; 25 : 41, 46; Rev. 14 : 10.
for whom reserved, Ps. 9 : 17; Prov. 5 : 5; 7 : 27; 9 : 18; Matt. 23 : 15; 25 : 41.
Deut. 32 : 22, fire shall burn to lowest h.
2 Sam. 22 : 6; Ps. 18 : 5, sorrows of h. compassed me.
Job 11 : 8, deeper than h.
26 : 6, h. is naked before him.

Ps. 16 : 10; Acts 2 : 27, not leave soul in h.
Ps. 55 : 15, let them go down quick into h.
116 : 3, pains of h. gat hold on me.
139 : 8, if I make my bed in h.
Prov. 15 : 11, h. and destruction are before the Lord.
15 : 24, that he may depart from h. beneath.
23 : 14, deliver his soul from h.
27 : 20, h. and destruction are never full.
Isa. 5 : 14, h. hath enlarged herself.
14 : 9, h. from beneath is moved.
28 : 15, with h. are we at agreement.
Ezek. 31 : 16, when I cast him down to h.
32 : 21, shall speak out of the midst of h.
Amos 9 : 2, though they dig into h.
Jonah 2 : 2, out of the belly of h.
Hab. 2 : 5, enlargeth his desire as h.
Matt. 5 : 22, in danger of h. fire.
10 : 28; Luke 12 : 5, destroy soul and body in h.
Matt. 16 : 18, gates of h. shall not prevail.
18 : 9; Mark 9 : 47, having two eyes to be cast into h.
Luke 10 : 15, thrust down to h.
16 : 23, h. he lifted up his eyes.
Jas. 3 : 6, tongue set on fire of h.
2 Pet. 2 : 4, cast angels down to h.
Rev. 1 : 18, keys of h. and death.
20 : 13, death and h. delivered up dead.
See Isa. 33 : 14; Matt. 3 : 12.
Hellenes, or Greeks. This word denotes persons of Greek descent in the narrowest sense (Acts 16 : 1; 18 : 4; Rom. 1 : 14), or implies all those who are not of Jewish extraction (John 12 : 20; Rom. 1 : 16; 10 : 12; Gal. 3 : 28). See **Greeks.**
Hellenists or Grecians were Greek-speaking foreign Jews who were to the Hebrews who spoke Aramaic (" Hebrew ") and kept strictly by the law. The contact between Greece and Judæa produced a sort of dualistic Judaism. See **Grecians.**
Helm, Jas. 3 : 4.
Helmet, 1 Sam. 17 : 5, 38, h. of brass.
Isa. 59 : 17; Eph. 6 : 17, the h. of salvation.
Jer. 46 : 4, stand forth with your h.
Help, Gen. 2 : 18, an h. meet for him.
Deut. 33 : 29, the shield of thy h.
Job 6 : 13, is not my h. in me ?
Ps. 20 : 2, Lord send h. from sanctuary.
33 : 20, he is our h. and our shield.
42 : 5, the h. of his countenance.
46 : 1, God a very present h. in trouble.
60 : 11; 108 : 12, vain is the h. of man.
63 : 7, thou hast been my h.
89 : 19, laid h. upon one that is mighty.
94 : 17, unless the Lord had been my h.
121 : 1, the hills, from whence cometh my h.
124 : 8, our h. is in the name of the Lord.
146 : 3, trust not in man, in whom is no h.
Isa. 10 : 3, to whom will ye flee for h. ?
30 : 5, nor be an h. nor profit.
Hos. 13 : 9, in me is thine h.
Acts 26 : 22, having obtained h. of God.
27 : 17, used h., undergirding the ship.
Ps. 22 : 19; 38 : 22, haste to h. me.
Mark 9 : 24, h. thou mine unbelief.
Acts 21 : 28, men of Israel, h.
Rom. 8 : 26, Spirit also h. our infirmities.

2 Cor. 1 : 11, h. together by prayer.
Heb. 4 : 16, grace to h. in time of need.
Helper, Ps. 10 : 14, thou art h. of the fatherless.
72 : 12, deliver him that hath no h.
Heb. 13 : 6, Lord is my h., I will not fear.
Helve, Deut. 19 : 5.
Hem, of garment, Matt. 9 : 20; 14 : 36.
See Num. 15 : 38, 39; Matt. 23 : 5.
Hemlock, Hos. 10 : 4, is one translation of the Hebrew " rosh." Others are " wormwood " (Deut. 29 : 18) and " gall " (Amos 6 : 12). See **Gall.**
Hen (hĕn) [grace, favour], son of Zephaniah, Zech. 6 : 14.
fowl, Matt. 23 : 37; Luke 13 : 34.
Hence, Judg. 6 : 18, depart not h.
Matt. 4 : 10, get thee h., Satan.
John 14 : 31, arise, let us go h.
18 : 36, my kingdom not from h.
Acts 22 : 21, far h. unto the Gentiles.
Henceforth, Ps. 125 : 2; 2 Tim. 4 : 8; Rev. 14 : 13.
Henceforward, Num. 15 : 23; Matt. 21 : 19.
Hephzi-bah (hĕph-zĭ-băh) [my delight is in her], Isa. 62 : 4.
queen of Hezekiah, 2 Ki. 21 : 1.
Herald, Dan. 3 : 4.
Herb. This word is used with varying shades of meaning, according to the Hebrew word it translates. (1) " Green thing," Ex. 10 : 15; Isa. 15 : 6; cf. Deut. 11 : 10; 1 Ki. 21 : 2. (2) " Herbage " in general, Gen. 1 : 11. See **Grass.** (3) " Herb," Deut. 32 : 2; 2 Ki. 19 : 26; Job 38 : 27; Ps. 37 : 2; Isa. 37 : 27; 66 : 14. (4) " Herbs," 2 Ki. 4 : 39, either the colewort or any eatable plant which escaped the drought.
The word " oroth," which is used in this sense is connected with the idea of " light," light and bloom being cognate ideas. Hence the difference of translation in Isa. 18 : 4, " like clear heat upon herbs," A.V., but in R.V., " like clear heat in sunshine "; and Isa. 26 : 19, " dew of herbs " or " dew of lights."
See Gen. 1 : 30; Prov. 15 : 17; Ps. 104 : 14.
Herd, 2 Sam. 12 : 4; Mark 5 : 11, 13; Luke 8 : 32.
Herdman, Gen. 13 : 7; Amos 7 : 14.
Here, Ex. 3 : 4; 1 Sam. 3 : 5, 6, said, h. am I.
Matt. 28 : 6, he is not h.; for he is risen.
Luke 9 : 33, good for us to be h.
19 : 20, h. is thy pound.
John 11 : 21, 32, Lord, if thou had been h.
Heb. 13 : 14, h. have we no continuing city.
Hereafter, Matt. 26 : 64; John 1 : 51; 14 : 30; Rev. 9 : 12.
Hereby, Gen. 42 : 33; 1 John 3 : 16; 4 : 13.
Herein, John 15 : 8; 1 John 4 : 17.
Hereof, Matt. 9 : 26; Heb. 5 : 3.
Heresies, deprecated, 1 Cor. 11 : 19; Gal. 5 : 20; 2 Pet. 2 : 1.
See Rom. 16 : 17; 1 Cor. 1 : 10; 3 : 3; 14 : 33; Phil. 2 : 3; 4 : 2; Jude 19.
Heretic, Titus 3 : 10.
Heretofore, 1 Sam. 4 : 7; 2 Cor. 13 : 2.
Hereunto, 1 Pet. 2 : 21.
Herewith, Mal. 3 : 10.
Heritage, Job 20 : 29, h. appointed by God.

Ps. 16 : 6; Jer. 3 : 19, a goodly **h.**
Ps. 61 : 5, **h.** of those that fear thy name.
111 : 6, give them **h.** of the heathen.
127 : 3, children are an **h.** of the Lord.
Isa. 54 : 17, **h.** of servants of the Lord.
Mic. 7 : 14, feed flock of thine **h.**
1 Pet. 5 : 3, lords over God's **h.**

Hermon (hĕr-ʹmọn) [rugged], a mountain on the north-eastern boundary of Palestine, dome-shaped and rugged, a main feature in Palestine scenery as far south as Shechem, Deut. 4 : 48; Josh. 12 : 5; 13 : 5; Ps. 89 : 12; 133 : 3.

Hermonites (hĕr-ʹmō-nītes), Ps. 42 : 6.

Herod (hĕr-ʹŏd) [hero-like], the Great, king of Judæa, Matt. 2 : 1, 3.
slays the children of Bethlehem, Matt. 2 : 16.
Agrippa, persecutes the church, Acts 12 : 1.
his pride and miserable death, Acts 12 : 23.
Agrippa II., Acts 25 : 13.
Antipas, reproved by John the Baptist, imprisons him, Luke 3 : 19, 20.
beheads him, Matt. 14; Mark 6 : 14-29.
desires to see Christ, Luke 9 : 9.
scourges him, and is reconciled to Pilate. Luke 23 : 8 ff.; Acts 4 : 27.

Herodians (hĕ-rō-ʹdĭ-ăns), a political party among the Jews, and supporters of the Herod dynasty, especially of Antipas. The natural issue of Sadduceeism, they preserved an outward friendliness for the Roman rule while in reality aiming at "home rule." Their chief characteristics were a readiness for compromise and a remarkable ability for evading the rigidity of the Mosaic requirements. Few in number, they made no marked impression on the community. cf. Matt. 22 : 16; Mark 3 . 6, 12 . 13.

Herodias (hĕ-rō-ʹdĭ-ăs), married to Herod Antipas, Mark 6 : 17.

her revenge on John the Baptist, Matt. 14; Mark 6 : 24.

Heron. The Hebrew word (anāphāh) really designates an unclean bird; but occurring (Lev. 11 : 19; Deut. 14 : 18), immediately after " stork " and followed by the phrase " after her kind," it should be taken in a general sense.

Heth [dread], father of Hittites, Gen. 10 : 15; 23 : 3; 25 : 10.
his sons' kindness to Abraham, Gen. 23 : 3 ff.; 25 : 10.

Hew, Ex. 34 : 4, **h.** two tables of stone.
Jer. 2 : 13, **h.** them out cisterns.
Matt. 3 : 10; Luke 3 : 9, **h.** down and cast into the fire.
Mark 15 : 46, sepulchre which was **h.** out.

Hewer, Josh. 9 : 21; 1 Ki. 5 : 15; Jer. 46 : 22.

Hezekiah (hĕz-ē-kīʹäh) [Jehovah is strength], king of Judah, 2 Ki. 16 : 20; (2 Chr. 28 : 27).
abolishes idolatry, 2 Ki. 18.
his message to Isaiah, when attacked by the Assyrians, 2 Ki. 19 : 4, 5.
his life lengthened, etc., 2 Ki. 20; (Isa. 38).
celebrates the passover, 2 Chr. 30.
rebuked for displaying his treasures, 2 Ki. 20 : 16, 17; (Isa. 39).
his piety and good reign, 2 Chr. 29.
his death, 2 Ki. 20 : 21.
men of, edit sacred writings. See **Proverbs.**

Hezron (hĕz-ʹrŏn) [fortified], Gen. 46 : 9; Ex. 6 : 14; Num. 26 : 6; 1 Chr. 5 : 3.

Hid, Gen. 3 : 8, Adam and his wife **h.**
Ex. 2 : 2, she **h.** Moses three months.
3 : 6, Moses **h.** his face.
2 Ki. 4 : 27, the Lord hath **h.** it from me.
Job 17 : 4, **h.** heart from understanding.
Ps. 22 : 24, neither **h.** his face from him.
35 : 7, they **h.** for me their net.
119 : 11, thy word have I **h.** in my heart.

Herodian Family Table in connection with the New Testament.

Antipater, an Idumean, made procurator of Judæa by Julius Cæsar, 47 B.C., m. Cypros, an Arabian.

Phasael.   Herod the Great, " the king " (Matt. 2 : 1 ; Luke 1 : 5).
Made by Antony joint tetrarchs of Judæa, 41 B.C. Herod, made by the Senate king of Judæa, 40 B.C. After battle of Actium, Octavian confirmed him in the kingdom, 31 B.C. Died, 4 B.C.
m. 1. Doris.   m. 2. Mariamne, grand-daughter of Hyrcanus.

Aristobulus m. Berenice.   m. 3. Mariamne. daughter of Simon, high priest.

Herodias, wife of (1) Philip I., and (2) Herod Antipas (Matt. 14 : 3-11 ; Mark 6 : 17-28 ; Luke 3 : 19).   Herod Agrippa I. (Acts 12 : 1.)   m. Cypros, a cousin.   Herod Philip I. m. Herodias.   m. 4 Malthace, a Samaritan.

Agrippa II. (Acts 25 : 13).

Bernice m. her uncle, Herod, king of Chalcis, at whose death she re-returned to her brother (Acts 25 : 13, 23), Agrippa II., with whom she was suspected of intimacy. He and she heard Paul's defence before Festus.

Drusilla, a Jewess (Acts 24 : 24), m. 1, Aziz, king of Emesa. m. 2, Felix.

Salome m. Herod Philip II., son of Herod the Great and Cleopatra, Tetrarch of Ituræa and Trachonitis (Luke 3 : 1).

Herod Antipas (" the tetrarch," Matt. 14 : 1 ; Luke 3 : 1, 19 ; 9 : 7), called " King Herod," Mark 6 : 14. Deposed, A.D. 40.   m. Herodias.

Archelaus (Matt. 2 : 22). Deposed and banished A.D. 6.

Isa. 53 : 3, and we h. our faces from him.
Matt. 10 : 26; Mark 4 : 22, there is nothing h.
Matt. 11 : 25; Luke 10 : 21, h. from wise.
Matt. 25 : 18, went and h. his lord's money.
Luke 19 : 42, now they are h. from thine eyes.
Acts 26 : 26, none of these things are h.
2 Cor. 4 : 3, if our Gospel be h.
Col. 1 : 26, mystery h. from ages.
    3 : 3, your life is h. with Christ.
1 Pet. 3 : 4, the h. man of the heart.
Hid treasure, parable of, Matt. 13 : 44. See
    Parables.
Hide, Gen. 18 : 17, shall I h. from Abraham ?
Job 14 : 13, h. me in the grave.
    40 : 13, h. in dust together.
Ps. 17 : 8, h. me under the shadow of thy
    wings.
    27 : 5, h. me in pavilion.
    31 : 20, h. them in secret of thy presence.
    89 : 46, how long wilt thou h. thyself ?
    139 : 12, darkness h. not from thee.
    143 : 9, I flee unto thee to h. me.
Isa. 1 : 15, I will h. mine eyes from you.
    2 : 10, and h. thee in the dust.
    26 : 20, h. thyself for a little moment.
    45 : 15, thou art a God that h. thyself.
Ezek. 28 : 3, no secret they can h. from thee.
Jas. 5 : 20, and h. a multitude of sins.
Rev. 6 : 16, h. us from the face of him.
Lev. 8 : 17; 9 : 11, h. flesh be burnt.
Hiding, Ps. 119 : 114, my h. place and my shield.
Isa. 32 : 2, a man shall be as an h. place.
Hiel (hī-ĕl) [God lives], 1 Ki. 16 : 34. See
    Jericho.
Higgaion (hĭg-gāi-ŏn), occurs with " Selah " in
    Ps. 9 : 16, where it seems to be a musical
    note. In Ps. 92 : 3 (R.V.) it is translated
    " a solemn sound," and in Ps. 19 : 14
    (R.V.) as " meditation."
High, Gen. 29 : 7, lo, it is yet h. day.
Job 11 : 8, it is as h. as heaven.
    22 : 12, behold stars, how h. they are.
    41 : 34, he beholdeth all h. things.
Ps. 18 : 27, bring down h. looks.
    62 : 9, men of h. degree are a lie.
    68 : 18, thou hast ascended on h.
    103 : 11, as the heaven is h. above the earth.
    131 : 1, in things too h. for me.
    138 : 6, though the Lord be h.
    139 : 6, it is h., I cannot attain unto it.
Eccl. 12 : 5, afraid of that which is h.
Isa. 6 : 1, Lord, h. and lifted up.
    32 : 15, Spirit poured on us from on h.
    57 : 15, thus saith the h. and lofty One.
Luke 1 : 78, dayspring from on h.
John 19 : 31, sabbath was an h. day.
Rom. 12 : 16, mind not h. things.
    13 : 11, it is h. time to awake.
2 Cor. 10 : 5, casting down every h. thing.
Phil. 3 : 14, prize of the h. calling of God.
Rev. 21 : 12, Jerusalem had a wall h.
High places, forbidden, Deut. 12 : 2; 1 Ki.
    3 : 2; 12 : 31; 13 : 2; 14 : 23; Jer. 3 : 6.
High priest.—(1) His consecration is by an
    elaborate ritual of washing, vesting with
    robes, anointing with oil, and sacrificial
    rites. The sacrificial ceremonies lasted
    seven days (Ex. 29; Lev. 8). The office
    passed to the eldest son of each occupant,

and Aaron was the first to be consecrated
(Ex. 28). Inasmuch as he alone was
anointed (Lev. 8 : 12), one of the distinctive
epithets of the high priest was " the
anointed priest " (Lev. 4 : 3, 5, 7, 16;
21 : 10. cr. Num. 35 : 25).

Costume of High Priest.

(2) Distinctive vestments marked him out
from the ordinary priest, who wore "linen"
breeches, coats of checkerwork, head-tires
and girdles (cf. Ex. 28 : 42; 29 : 8 f.; Lev.
8 : 13). In addition the high priest wore (a)
the seamless robe of blue, knee-length, with
a hole for the head; (b) the turban with the
crown engraved " Holy to Jahweh " (Ex.
28 : 36); (c) the ephod of curiously wrought
embroidered work, made in two parts (one
of which covered the back, the other the
breast and upper part of the body) which
were joined on the shoulder by two large
onyx stones each bearing six names of the
tribes of Israel and by a girdle round the
waist; (d) the breastplate (" breastplate of
judgment," Ex. 28 : 15, 29 f.), worn square
in shape and bearing on it twelve precious
stones each named after one of the children
of Israel and arranged in three columns of
four. This was attached to the ephod. cf.
Lev. 8 : 7.

(3) Special duties were (a) the offering of a
daily meal offering (Lev. 6 : 19 f.); (b) the
performing of ceremonial sprinklings in
regard to the sin offerings of the whole
people (Lev. 4 : 13-21); (c) the special
ceremony on the Day of Atonement (Lev.
16), when he alone, attired only in the

GOLDEN GATE – JERUSALEM

SOLOMON'S POOL — NEAR HEBRON

priestly linen garb, entered the "Holy of Holies" to sprinkle the blood of the sin offering on the mercy seat and to burn incense.

(4) Qualifications. 2 Chr. 31 : 17 gives twenty as the usual age for entering the priesthood, but no one was actually prohibited the office if he had reached puberty. To have a blemish, however, was to suffer an unsurmountable block (Lev. 21 : 17-21).

Higher, Ps. 61 : 2, lead me to the Rock that is h.
Isa. 55 : 9, heaven h. than the earth.
Luke 14 : 10, friend, go up h.
Rom. 13 : 1, be subject to h. powers.
Heb. 7 : 26, high priest made h. than the heavens.

Highest, Ps. 18 : 13, the H. gave his voice.
Luke 1 : 32, shall be called the Son of the H.
2 : 14, glory to God in the h.

Highly, Luke 1 : 28, thou art h. favoured.
Rom. 12 : 3, think of himself more h. than he ought.
Phil. 2 : 9, God also hath h. exalted him.
1 Thess. 5 : 13, esteem them very h. in love.

High-minded, Rom. 11 : 20; 1 Tim. 6 : 17.

Highness, Job 31 : 23; Isa. 13 : 3.

Highway, Isa. 35 : 8, an h. shall be there.
Matt. 22 : 9; Luke 14 : 23, go into the h.

Hilkiah (hĭl-kĭ-ăh) [Jehovah is my portion], 2 Ki. 22 : 8; 23 : 4 ff.

Hill, Gen. 49 : 26, the everlasting h.
Deut. 11 : 11, a land of h. and valleys.
Ps. 2 : 6, set my king on holy h.
24 : 3, who shall ascend the h. of the Lord ?
43 : 3, bring me to thy holy h.
50 : 10, cattle on a thousand h. are mine.
95 : 4, strength of the h. is his.
98 : 8, let the h. be joyful together.
121 : 1, I will lift up mine eyes to the h.
Prov. 8 : 25, before the h. was I brought forth.
Isa. 2 : 2, shall be exalted above h.
40 : 12, weighed the h. in balance.
Hos. 10 : 8; Luke 23 : 30, to the h., Fall on us.
Matt. 5 : 14, city set on an h.
Luke 3 : 5, every h. be brought low.
Acts 17 . 22, Paul stood in Mars' h.

Hill country, Josh. 13 : 6; Luke 1 : 39, 65.

Him, Rom. 11 : 36, of h., through h. and to h. are all things.

Hin, a measure, Lev. 19 : 36. See **Measures.**

Hind, Gen. 49 : 21; Ps. 18 : 33; Prov. 5 : 19.

Hinder, Gen. 24 : 56, h. me not.
Neh. 4 : 8, h. the building.
Job 9 : 12; 11 : 10, who can h. him ?
Luke 11 : 52, them entering in ye h.
Acts 8 : 36, what doth h. me to be baptized ?
1 Cor. 9 : 12, lest we should h. the gospel of Christ.
Gal. 5 : 7, ye did run well; who did h. you ?
1 Thess. 2 : 18, Satan h. us.
1 Pet. 3 : 7, that your prayers be not h.

Hinder end, 2 Sam. 2 : 23.

Hinder sea, Zech. 14 : 8.

Hinges, 1 Ki. 7 : 50; Prov. 26 : 14.

Hinnom (hĭn-nom) [lamentation], valley of, (Josh. 15 : 8); 2 Ki. 23 : 10; 2 Chr. 28 : 3; 33 : 6; Jer. 7 : 31; 19 : 6; 32 : 35. See **Tophet** and **Moloch,** and cf. **Gehenna.**

Hip, Judg. 15 : 8.

Hippopotamus. See **Behemoth** (Job 40 : 15).

Hiram (hĭ-răm) or **Huram** [noble], king of Tyre, sends aid to David and Solomon, 2 Sam. 5 : 11; 1 Ki. 5; 9 : 11; 10 : 11; 1 Chr. 14 : 1; 2 Chr. 2 : 11.
brass worker of Solomon's, 1 Ki. 7 : 13.

Hire, for labour, not to be withheld, Lev. 19 : 13; Deut. 24 : 15; Jas. 5 : 4.
1 Ki. 5 : 6, unto thee will I give h.
Mic. 3 : 11, priests teach for h.
Matt. 20 : 8, give them their h.
Luke 10 : 7, labourer worthy of his h.

Hired servants, Ex. 12 : 45; Lev. 25 : 6; Mark 1 : 20; Luke 15 : 17.

Hireling, Job 7 : 1, 2; Mal. 3 : 5; John 10 : 12, 13.

His [ar.], its, 1 Cor. 15 : 38.

Hiss, Job 27 : 23; Jer. 25 : 18; Lam. 2 : 15, 16.

Hit, 1 Sam. 31 : 3; 1 Chr. 10 : 3.

Hither, Ex. 3 : 5; Josh. 3 : 9; Matt. 8 : 29; John 20 : 27; Rev. 11 : 12.

Hitherto, Josh. 17 : 14, the Lord hath blessed me h.
1 Sam. 7 : 12, h. hath the Lord helped us.
Job 38 : 11, h. shalt thou come, but no further.
John 5 : 17, my Father worketh h.
16 : 24, h. have ye asked nothing in my name.
1 Cor. 3 : 2, h. ye were not able to hear it.

Hittites. The Hittites were descended from Heth, the second son of Canaan, and seem to have been a considerable power at a comparatively early date. During the patriarchal period a portion of them had settled in the neighbourhood of Hebron, and Abraham's contract with the sons of Heth for the cave of Machpelah is well known. Their chief cities seem to have been Kadesh, on the Lake of Homs (Emesa or Kadas), and Carchemish, now Jerablus, south of Biredjik, on the Euphrates—a great trading centre. This city seems to have been the centre of a powerful kingdom until captured by Sargon the Later, in 717 B.C., though it had given tribute to Assyria long before that time. We may say that they played an important part on the stage of history from 1500–700 B.C., that they formed small city-kingdoms and were not politically united, and that their religion had many Semitic features about it.

Hivites (hī-vītes) [villagers ?], a Canaanite tribe whose racial affinities are unknown but who may have lived near Jerusalem. (cf. 2 Sam. 24 : 7.) The Israelites dispossessed them (Gen. 10 : 17; Ex. 3 : 17; Josh. 9 : 7). See **Palestine, Early Inhabitants.**

Ho, Isa. 55 : 1, h., every one that thirsteth.
Zech. 2 : 6, h., h., come forth and flee.

Hoar, Ex. 16 : 14, h. frost on the ground.
1 Ki. 2 : 9, his h. head bring thou down to the grave.
Ps. 147 : 16, scattereth the h. frost like ashes.
Prov. 16 : 31, h. head is a crown of glory.

Hoary, Job 41 : 32.

Hobab (ho-bab) [beloved] entreated to dwell with Israel, Num. 10 : 29.
his descendants, Judg. 4 : 11.

Hobah (hō-bah) [hidden] (3 Fb), a town near Damascus, Gen. 14 : 15.

Hod (hŏd) [majesty], 1 Chr. 7 : 37.
Hodaiah (hō-dāi-ăh) [thanks to Jah], 1 Chr. 3 : 24.
Hodaviah (hō-dă-vī-ăh) [give thanks to Jehovah], 1 Chr. 5 : 24.
Hodesh (hō-děsh) [born at the new moon], 1 Chr. 8 : 9.
Hodevah (hō-dě-väh), Neh. 7 : 43.
Hodiah (hō-dī-ăh) [Jehovah is praise], 1 Chr. 4 : 19.
Hodijah (hō-dī-jăh) [Jah is praise], Neh. 8 : 7; 9 : 5; 10 : 13.
Hoglah (hŏg-lăh) [patridge], Num. 26 : 33; 36 : 11.
Hoham (hō-hăm), Josh. 10 : 3.
Hoised, Acts 27 : 40.
Hold, Gen. 21 : 18, h. him in thine hand.
  Ex. 20 : 7; Deut. 5 : 11, Lord will not h. him guiltless.
  Esther 4 : 11, king h. out golden sceptre.
  Job 9 : 28, thou wilt not h. me innocent.
  Ps. 18 : 35, thy right hand hath h. me up.
  119 : 117, h. me up, and I shall be safe.
  Prov. 11 : 12, man of understanding h. his peace.
  17 : 28, a fool when he h. his peace.
  Isa. 41 : 13, Lord will h. thy hand.
  62 : 6, never h. their peace day nor night.
  Jer. 4 : 19, I cannot h. my peace.
  Matt. 6 : 24; Luke 16 : 13, he will h. to the one.
  Mark 1 : 25; Luke 4 : 35, h. thy peace, come out.
  Rom. 1 : 18, h. the truth in unrighteousness.
  Phil. 2 : 16, h. forth the word.
  2 : 29, h. such in reputation.
  Col. 2 : 19, not h. the Head.
  1 Thess. 5 : 21, h. fast that which is good.
  1 Tim. 1 : 19, h. faith and a good conscience.
  2 Tim. 1 : 13, h. fast form of sound words.
  Heb. 3 : 14, h. beginning of confidence.
  4 : 14; 10 : 23, h. fast our profession.
  Rev. 2 : 25, h. fast till I come.
  3 : 11, h. that fast which thou hast.
  See Judg. 9 : 46; 1 Sam. 22 : 4; Jer. 51 : 30; Ezek. 19 : 9; Acts 4 : 3; Rev. 18 : 2.
Hole, Ex. 28 : 32, be an h. in the top of it.
  Isa. 11 : 8, child shall play on h. of asp.
  51 : 1, h. of pit whence ye are digged.
  Ezek. 8 : 7, a h. in the wall.
  Hag. 1 : 6, to put it into a bag with h.
  Matt. 8 : 20; Luke 9 : 58, foxes have h.
Holier, Isa. 65 : 5.
Holiest, Heb. 9 : 3, 8; 10 : 19.
Holily, 1 Thess. 2 : 10.
Holiness, enjoined, Ex. 19 : 22; Lev. 11 : 44; 20 : 7; Num. 15 : 40; Deut. 7 : 6; 26 : 19; 28 : 9; Luke 1 : 75; Rom. 12 : 1; 2 Cor. 7 : 1; Eph. 1 : 4; 4 : 24; Col. 3 : 12; 1 Thess. 2 : 12; 1 Tim. 2 : 15; Heb. 12 : 14; 1 Pet. 1 : 15; 2 Pet. 3 : 11; Rev. 22 : 11.
  Ex. 15 : 11, glorious in h.
  28 : 36; Zech. 4 : 20, h. to the Lord.
  1 Chr. 16 : 29; 2 Chr. 20 : 21; Ps. 29 : 2; 96 : 9, beauty of h.
  Ps. 30 : 4; 97 : 12, at remembrance of his h.
  47 : 8, God sitteth on throne of his h.
  60 : 6; 108 : 7, God hath spoken in his h.
  93 : 5, h. becometh thine house.

  110 : 3, people willing, in beauties of h.
  Isa. 35 : 8, the way of h.
  63 : 15, habitation of thy h.
  Jer. 31 : 23, O mountain of h.
  Obad. 17, upon mount Zion there shall be h.
  Luke 1 : 75, might serve him in h.
  Acts 3 : 12, as though by our h.
  Rom. 1 : 4, according to the Spirit of h.
  6 : 22, fruit unto h.
  2 Cor. 7 : 1, perfecting h. in fear of God.
  Eph. 4 : 24, created in righteousness and h.
  1 Thess. 3 : 13, stablish your hearts in h.
  1 Tim. 2 : 15, continue in faith and h.
  Titus 2 : 3, in behaviour as becometh h.
  Heb. 12 : 10, partakers of his h.
  12 : 14, h. without which no man shall see the Lord.
Hollow, Gen. 32 : 25; Isa. 40 : 12.
Holpen, helped, Ps. 86 : 17; Dan. 11 : 34; Luke 1 : 54.
Holy, Ex. 3 : 5; Josh. 5 : 15, place whereon thou standest is h.
  Ex. 16 : 23, the h. sabbath.
  19 : 6; 1 Pet. 2 : 9, an h. nation.
  Ex. 20 : 8; 31 : 14, sabbath day to keep it h.
  Lev. 10 : 10, difference between h. and unholy.
  20 : 7, be ye h.
  Num. 16 : 5, Lord will show who is h.
  1 Sam. 2 : 2, there is none h. as the Lord.
  2 Ki. 4 : 9, an h. man of God.
  Ps. 20 : 6, hear from h. heaven.
  22 : 3, thou art h. that inhabitest the praises of Israel.
  28 : 2, lift hands toward thy h. oracle.
  86 : 2, preserve my soul, for I am h.
  98 : 1, his h. arm hath gotten victory.
  145 : 17, the Lord is h. in all his works.
  Isa. 6 : 3; Rev. 4 : 8, h., h., h. is the Lord.
  Isa. 27 : 13, worship in h. mount.
  52 : 10, Lord made bare his h. arm.
  58 : 13, call sabbath a delight, h. of the Lord.
  64 : 11, our h. and beautiful house.
  Ezek. 22 : 26, put no difference between h. and profane.
  Matt. 7 : 6, give not that which is h. unto the dogs.
  Mark 8 : 38; Luke 9 : 26, in glory with h. angels.
  John 17 : 11, h. Father, keep those.
  Acts 4 : 27, against thy h. child Jesus.
  Rom. 1 : 2, promised in the h. scriptures.
  7 : 12, the commandment is h., just, and good.
  11 : 16, if first-fruit be h., if root be h.
  12 : 1, a living sacrifice, h., acceptable unto God.
  1 Cor. 3 : 17, the temple of God is h.
  Eph. 1 : 4; 5 : 27, be h. and without blame.
  2 : 21, groweth unto an h. temple in the Lord.
  Col. 1 : 22, present you h. and unblameable.
  1 Thess. 5 : 27, the h. brethren.
  1 Tim. 2 : 8, lifting up h. hands.
  2 Tim. 1 : 9, called us with an h. calling.
  Titus 1 : 8, bishop must be h.
  Heb. 3 : 1, h. brethren, partakers of heavenly calling.
  7 : 26, high priest became us, who is h.

1 Pet. 1 : 15; 2 Pet. 3 : 11, **h.** in all conversation.
1 Pet. 2 : 5, an **h.** priesthood.
2 Pet. 1 : 18, with him in the **h.** mount.
Rev. 3 : 7, saith he that is **h.**
6 : 10, O Lord, **h.** and true.
15 : 4, for thou only art **h.**
21 : 10, the **h.** Jerusalem.
22 : 11, that is **h.,** let him be **h.**
Holy Ghost, Matt. 3 : 11; Mark 1 : 8; Luke 3 : 16, John 1 : 33; Acts 1 : 5, baptize with **H.** Ghost.
Matt. 12 : 31; Mark 3 : 29, blasphemy against **H.** Ghost.
Mark 13 : 11, not ye that speak, but **H.** Ghost.
Luke 1 : 15, filled with the **H.** Ghost.
3 : 22, **H.** Ghost descended in bodily shape.
4 : 1, Jesus being full of the **H.** Ghost.
12 : 12, **H.** Ghost shall teach you.
John 7 : 39, **H.** Ghost was not yet given.
14 : 26, Comforter, who is the **H.** Ghost.
20 : 22; Acts 2 : 38, receive ye the **H.** Ghost.
Acts 2 : 4; 4 : 31, all filled with **H.** Ghost.
5 : 3, to lie to the **H.** Ghost.
6 : 3, men full of the **H.** Ghost.
7 : 51, ye do always resist the **H.** Ghost.
8 : 15, prayed that they might receive the **H.** Ghost.
9 : 31, in comfort of the **H.** Ghost.
10 : 38, God anointed Jesus with **H.** Ghost.
15 : 28, it seemed good to the **H.** Ghost.
16 : 6, forbidden of **H.** Ghost to preach.
19 : 2, have ye received the **H.** Ghost ?
20 : 28, **H.** Ghost hath made you overseers.
Rom. 14 : 17, kingdom of God is joy in the **H.** Ghost.
1 Cor. 2 : 13, words which the **H.** Ghost teacheth.
2 Cor. 13 : 14, communion of the **H.** Ghost.
1 Pet. 1 : 12, the **H.** Ghost sent down from heaven.
See **God** (The Holy Ghost).
Holy gifts, Heb. 28 : 38.
Holy of holies. See **Tabernacle.**
Holy place, laws concerning, Ex. 28 : 29; Lev. 6 : 16; 16 : 2; 2 Chr. 29 : 5; Heb. 9 : 12.
Holy Spirit. Without examining too closely the Christian doctrine of the Holy Spirit we may summarise its teaching as follows. The Holy Spirit is God; the Third Person within the Godhead, knowledge of whom depends on the Revelation of the Father and the Son; from both of these He proceeds. Before the " Word became flesh " He spoke by the prophets, and His was the agency by which the " Word became flesh." The atonement was consummated through Him. He is the life-giving presence within the Church; He communicates His power to the individual Christian, is the mediator to him of new birth and of forgiveness, strengthens and purifies his whole personality, and knits him closely into the fabric of the body of saints, crowning all by bringing him to eternal life through the resurrection of the body. See **God** (The Holy Ghost).
Holy things, laws respecting, Ex. 28 : 38; Lev.

5 : 15; 22 : 2; Num. 4 : 19, 20; 1 Chr. 23 : 28; Neh. 10 : 33; Ezek. 20 : 40; 22 : 8.
Home, Gen. 43 : 16, bring these men **h.**
Ex. 9 : 19, shall not be brought **h.**
Deut. 24 : 5, free at **h.** one year.
Ruth 1 : 21, Lord hath brought me **h.** empty.
2 Sam. 14 : 13, not fetch **h.** his banished.
1 Chr. 13 : 12, bring ark of God **h.**
Job 39 : 12, bring **h.** thy seed.
Ps. 68 : 12, she that tarried at **h.**
Eccl. 12 : 5, man goeth to his long **h.**
Lam. 1 : 20, at **h.** there is as death.
Hag. 1 : 9, when ye brought it **h.**
Matt. 8 : 6, my servant lieth at **h.** sick.
Mark 5 : 19, go **h.** to thy friends.
Luke 9 : 61, bid them farewell at **h.**
John 19 : 27, disciple took her to his own **h.**
20 : 10, went away to their own **h.**
1 Cor. 11 : 34, let him eat at **h.**
14 : 35, ask their husbands at **h.**
2 Cor. 5 : 6, whilst we are at **h.** in the body.
1 Tim. 5 : 4, learn to show piety at **h.**
Titus 2 : 5, discreet, chaste, keepers at **h.**
Homeborn, Ex. 12 : 49; Jer. 2 : 14.
Homer, Ezek. 45 : 11; Hos. 3 : 2. See **Measure.**
Honest, Luke 8 : 15, an **h.** and good heart.
Acts 6 : 3, men of **h.** report.
Rom. 12 : 17, 2 Cor. 8 : 21, things **h.**
Phil. 4 : 8, whatsoever things are **h.**
1 Pet. 2 : 12, conversation **h.** among Gentiles.
Honestly, Rom. 13 : 13, let us walk **h.** as in the day.
Heb. 13 : 18, in all things willing to live **h.**
Honesty, 1 Tim. 2 : 2, in all godliness and **h.**
Honey, Gen. 43 : 11; 1 Sam. 14 : 25; Ps. 19 : 10; Prov. 24 : 13; 25 : 16; Isa. 7 : 15; Song of Sol. 4 : 11; Rev. 10 : 9.
not to be used in burnt sacrifices, Lev. 2 : 11. See **Bee.**
Honeycomb, 1 Sam. 14 : 27; Ps. 19 : 10; Prov. 5 : 3; 16 : 24; 24 : 13; 27 : 7; Luke 24 : 42.
Honour, due to God, Ps. 29 : 2; 71 : 8; 145 : 5; 1 Tim. 1 : 17; Rev. 5 : 13.
given by God, 1 Ki. 3 : 13; Esther 8 : 16; Prov. 4 : 8; 22 : 4; 29 : 23; Dan. 5 : 18; John 12 : 26.
(noun), Num. 22 : 17, promote thee to **h.**
24 : 11, Lord hath kept thee from **h.**
2 Sam. 6 : 22, of them shall I be had in **h.**
1 Chr. 29 : 12, riches and **h.** come of thee.
2 Chr. 1 : 11, not asked riches or **h.**
Esther 1 : 20, wives shall give their husbands **h.**
Job 14 : 21, his sons come to **h.**
Ps. 7 : 5, lay mine **h.** in the dust.
8 : 5; Heb. 2 : 7, thou hast crowned him with **h.**
Ps. 26 : 8, place where thine **h.** dwelleth.
49 : 12, being in **h.** abideth not.
66 : 2, sing forth the **h.** of his name.
96 : 6, **h.** and majesty are before him.
104 : 1, thou art clothed with **h.**
Prov. 3 : 16, in left hand riches and **h.**
8 : 18, riches and **h.** are with me.
15 : 33; 18 : 12, before is **h.** is humility.
20 : 3, an **h.** to cease from strife.
25 : 2, **h.** of kings to search a matter.

26 : 1, **h.** is not seemly for a fool.
Eccl. 6 : 2, to whom God hath given **h.**
Mal. 1 : 6, where is mine **h.** ?
Matt. 13 : 57; Mark 6 : 4; John 4 : 44, prophet not without **h.**
John 5 : 41, I receive not **h.** from men.
Rom. 2 : 7, in well-doing seek for **h.**
12 : 10, in **h.** preferring one another.
13 : 7, **h.** to whom **h.** is due.
2 Cor. 6 : 8, by **h.** and dishonour.
Col. 2 : 23, not in any **h.** to the satisfying of the flesh.
1 Tim. 5 : 17, elders worthy of double **h.**
6 : 1, count masters worthy of **h.**
6 : 16, to whom be **h.** and power everlasting.
2 Tim. 2 : 20, some to **h.**, some to dishonour.
Heb. 3 : 3, more **h.** than the house.
5 : 4, no man taketh this **h.** unto himself.
1 Pet. 1 : 7, found to praise, **h.**, and glory.
3 : 7, giving **h.** to the wife.
Rev. 4 : 11; 5 : 12, worthy to receive glory and **h.**
(verb), Ex. 20 : 12; Deut. 5 : 16; Matt. 15 : 4; 19 : 19; Mark 7 : 10; 10 : 19; Luke 18 : 20; Eph. 6 : 2, **h.** thy father and mother.
Lev. 19 : 32, thou shalt **h.** the face of the old man.
1 Sam. 2 : 30, them that **h.** me I will **h.**
Esther 6 : 6, the king delighteth to **h.**
Ps. 15 : 4, he **h.** them that fear the Lord.
91 : 15, I will deliver him and **h.** him.
Prov. 3 : 9, **h.** the Lord with thy substance.
12 : 9, better than he that **h.** himself.
Isa. 29 : 13, people with lips do **h.** me.
Dan. 4 : 37, I extol and **h.** King of heaven.
Mal. 1 : 6, a son **h.** his father.
Matt. 15 : 8; Mark 7 : 6, **h.** me with their lips.
John 5 : 23, **h.** the Son as they **h.** the Father.
8 : 54; if I **h.** myself, my **h.** is nothing.
Acts 28 : 10, **h.** us with many **h.**
1 Tim. 5 : 3, **h.** widows that are widows indeed.
1 Pet. 2 : 17, **h.** all men, **h.** the king.
Honourable, Num. 22 : 15, sent princes more **h.**
1 Chr. 4 : 9, more **h.** than brethren.
Ps. 45 : 9, daughters among **h.** women.
111 : 3, his work is **h.** and glorious.
Isa. 3 : 3, Lord doth take away **h.** man.
42 : 21, magnify the law, and make it **h.**
Luke 14 : 8, lest a more **h.** man be bidden.
1 Cor. 4 : 10, ye are strong, ye are **h.**
Hoods, Isa. 3 : 23.
Hoof, Ex. 10 : 26; Jer. 47 : 3; Ezek. 26 : 11; Mic. 4 : 13.
Hook, Ex. 26 : 32; Isa. 18 : 5; Matt. 17 : 27.
Hope, Ps. 16 : 9; 22 : 9; Acts 24 : 15; Rom. 15 : 13.
of the wicked will perish, Job 8 : 13; 11 : 20; 27 : 8.
comfort of, Job 11 : 18; Prov. 10 : 28; 14 : 32; Lam. 3 : 21; Acts 24 : 15; Rom. 12 : 12; 15 : 4; Eph. 1 : 18; 4 : 4; Col. 1 : 5; Heb. 3 : 6.
exhortations to, Ps. 130 : 7; Lam. 3 : 26; Col. 1 : 23; Titus 2 : 13; Heb. 3 : 6; 6 : 11; 1 Pet. 1 : 13.

prisoners of, Zech. 9 : 12.
effect of, Rom. 8 : 24; 15 : 4; 1 Cor. 13 : 7; 1 John 3 : 3.
gift of God, Gal. 5 : 5; 2 Thess. 2 : 16; Titus 1 : 2; 1 Pet. 1 : 3.
a reason to be given for, 1 Pet. 3 : 15.
Job 7 : 6, my days are spent without **h.**
19 : 10, my **h.** hath he removed.
Ps. 22 : 9, thou didst make me **h.**
31 : 24, all ye that **h.** in the Lord.
39 : 7, my **h.** is in thee.
42 : 5; 43 : 5, **h.** thou in God.
71 : 14, I will **h.** continually.
78 : 7, set their **h.** in God.
119 : 116, let me not be ashamed of my **h.**
131 : 3, let Israel **h.** in the Lord.
146 : 5, happy he whose **h.** is in the Lord.
Prov. 13 : 12, **h.** deferred maketh the heart sick.
26 : 12; 29 : 20, more **h.** of a fool.
Eccl. 9 : 4, to all the living is **h.**
Jer. 17 : 7, blessed whose **h.** the Lord is.
31 : 17, there is **h.** in thine end.
Hos. 2 : 15, for a door of **h.**
Luke 6 : 35, lend, **h.** for nothing again.
Acts 2 : 26, my flesh shall rest in **h.**
23 : 6, **h.** and resurrection of the dead.
28 : 20, for the **h.** of Israel I am bound.
Rom. 5 : 5, **h.** maketh not ashamed.
8 : 25, if we **h.** for that we see not.
15 : 13, that ye may abound in **h.**
1 Cor. 13 : 7, believeth all things, **h.** all things.
13 : 13, faith, **h.**, charity.
15 : 19, if in this life only we have **h.**
Eph. 2 : 12, having no **h.** and without God.
Col. 1 : 27, Christ in you the **h.** of glory.
1 Thess. 4 : 13, even as others who have no **h.**
5 : 8, for an helmet the **h.** of salvation.
Titus 3 : 7, the **h.** of eternal life.
Heb. 6 : 18, lay hold on **h.** set before us.
1 Pet. 1 : 13, be sober, and **h.** to the end.
Hophni (hŏph´-nī) [pugilist] and Phinehas, sons of Eli, 1 Sam. 1 : 3.
their sin and death, 1 Sam. 2 : 12, 22; 4 : 11.
Horeb (hōr´-ĕb) [desert], a mountain in Arabia, near Mount Sinai, Ex. 3 : 1; 17 : 6; 33 : 6; Deut. 1 : 6; 4 : 10.
law given on, Ex. 19 : 20; Deut. 4 : 10; 5 : 2; 18 : 16; 1 Ki. 8 : 9; Mal. 4 : 4.
Moses twice there forty days, Ex. 24 : 18; 34 : 28; Deut. 9 : 9.
Elijah there forty days, 1 Ki. 19 : 8. See **Sinai.**
Horites (hōr´-ītes) [cave-men], Gen. 36 : 20, 21. See **Palestine, Early Inhabitants.**
Horns. Horns might be wrought into vessels for storing (1 Ki. 1 : 39) or carrying oil (1 Sam. 16 : 1), and for holding eye-paint (Job 42 : 14), or into a kind of trumpet (Josh. 6 : 4). In poetry " horns " symbolised strength and honour, from their being the weapons and ornaments of the animals using them (cf. the unicorn, Deut. 33 : 17). Common were the expressions " to exalt one's horn " or " cause one's horn to bud " (= " to strengthen and prosper," 1 Sam. 2 : 1; Ezek. 29 : 21), " to lift one's own horn " (= " to be arrogant,"

Ps. 75 : 4 f.), and " to break, or cut off, one's horn " (= " to crush," Jer. 48 : 25; Lam. 2 : 3). In prophecy " horns " symbolised kings and military powers (Dan. 7 : 8; 8 : 21, etc.). The altar " horns " (Ex. 27 : 2), projecting from the four corners thereof and peculiarly sacred (Ex. 30 : 10, etc.), offered asylum to fugitives who clung to them (1 Ki. 1 : 50, etc.).

seen in vision, Dan. 7 : 7; 8 : 3; Hab. 3 : 4; Rev. 5 : 6; 12 : 3; 13 : 1; 17 : 3.

of the altar, 1 Ki. 1 : 50; 2 : 28.

2 Sam. 22 : 3; Ps. 18 : 2, the h. of my salvation.

Ps. 89 : 17, in thy favour our h. shall be exalted.

132 : 17, make h. of David to bud.

Luke 1 : 69, raised up h. of salvation.

Hornet, Ex. 23 : 28; Deut. 7 : 20; Josh. 24 : 12, a name applying to several species of large wasp-like insects armed with stings. Whether taken literally, or metaphorically as used of armies, they are in all the references mentioned as the Lord's instrument for driving out the Canaanites.

Horrible, Ps. 11 : 6, upon the wicked he shall rain an h. tempest.

Ps. 40 : 2, brought me up out of h. pit.

Jer. 5 : 30, h. thing committed in land.

Horribly, Jer. 2 : 12; Ezek. 32 : 10.

Horror, Gen. 15 : 12, a h. of great darkness.

Ps. 55 : 5, h. hath overwhelmed me.

119 : 53, h. hath taken hold upon me.

Horse. The horse does not appear to have been known to the Israelites in the days of the patriarchs. Possibly Jacob became acquainted with the horse in Egypt; he refers to it in his prophecy about Dan. In Egypt the horse was known from a very remote antiquity; during the great famine Joseph brought up the horses of the people for food, and thus enormously increased the war material of Pharaoh. In Solomon's day large numbers were purchased for that king in Egypt. In their progress into Palestine the Jews found the Canaanites with horses and chariots very many (Josh. 11 : 4), but when David defeated the King of North Eastern Syria, he kept from the slaughter horses enough for an hundred chariots (2 Sam. 8 : 4), and a little later, King Solomon had 12,000 cavalry horses. All through the Bible we read of horses in connection with war; the ass and the ox were kept for more peaceful labours. In O.T. times horses were apparently unshod (Isa. 5 : 28).

Ex. 15 : 21, h. and rider thrown into sea.

Deut. 17 : 16, shall not multiply h. to himself.

Ps. 32 : 9, be not as the h. or mule.

33 : 17, a h. is a vain thing for safety.

147 : 10, he delighteth not in strength of h.

Prov. 21 : 31, h. is prepared against day of battle.

Isa. 63 : 13, led through deep, as a h.

Jer. 8 : 6, a h. rusheth into battle.

Hos. 14 : 3, we will not ride upon h.

Zech. 14 : 20, upon bells of the h.

Jas. 3 : 3, we put bits in h. mouths.

Horseback, 2 Ki. 9 : 18, went one on h. to meet him.

Esther 8 : 10, sent letters by posts on h.

Horse gate, 2 Chr. 23 : 15; Neh. 3 : 28; Jer. 31 : 40.

Horseleech, Prov. 30 : 15. Common in Palestine, it is larger than the medicinal leech, and causes trouble, even sickness and death, to man and beast. It is voracious for blood.

Horseman, Ex. 14 : 9; Joel 2 : 4; Nah. 3 : 3; Acts 23 : 32.

Hosanna [Save, I beseech thee], children sing to Christ, Matt. 21 : 9, 15; Mark 11 : 9; John 12 : 13; (Ps. 118 : 26).

Hosea, Book of.

Hosea is the first in the list of the Minor Prophets and first in order of time, unless he was preceded by Jonah, as many assert. He prophesied, as did Isaiah, during the reigns of Uzziah, Jotham, Ahaz and Hezekiah, Kings of Judah, and Jeroboam II., King of Israel. It is believed that his ministry covered at least forty years, at most seventy years (according to Ussher, 785–725). He was the son of Beeri, and his prophesying was done in the northern kingdom. He lived during a time of great abandonment to sin in that kingdom, and, like his contemporaries, Amos and Micah, arraigned the leaders of the people in most scathing terms. The sins of the people are likened to the faithlessness of an adulterous woman. Tragedy is brought into the life of the prophet himself by his marriage with such a woman, and the figure is carried out in the relationship between God and Israel. The style of Hosea is most lofty and sententious. A great number of the most striking texts of the Bible are found in these fourteen chapters.

The sins of Israel for which punishment was announced through Hosea were idolatry, fornication, drunkenness, bribery and bloodshed. " Because thou hast rejected knowledge, I also will reject thee." The national judgment fell in the captivity of Samaria to Assyria in 722 B.C. " For they have sown the wind and they shall reap the whirlwind," 8 : 7. Hosea utters many specific promises of blessing to be fulfilled in the messianic kingdom.

Hosen [ar.], stockings and trousers combined, Dan. 3 : 21.

Hoshea (hō-shē-ă), last king of Israel; his wicked reign, defeat, and captivity, 2 Ki. 15 : 30; 17 : 1-4.

Hospitality, exhortations to, Rom. 12 : 13; Titus 1 : 8; Heb. 13 : 2; 1 Pet. 4 : 9.

of Abraham, Gen. 18; Lot, Gen. 19; Laban, Gen. 24 : 31; Jethro, Ex. 2 : 20; Manoah, Judg. 13 : 15; Samuel, 1 Sam. 9 : 22; David, 2 Sam. 6 : 19; Barzillai, etc., 2 Sam. 17 : 27-29; 19 : 32; the Shunammite, 2 Ki. 4 : 8; Nehemiah, Neh. 5 : 18; Matthew, Luke 5 : 29; Zaccheus, Luke 19 : 6; Lydia, Acts 16 : 15; Publius, etc., Acts 28 : 2; Gaius, 3 John 5.

Host, the heavenly, Luke 2 : 13.

of the Lord, Gen. 32 : 2; Josh. 5 : 14; 1 Chr. 9 : 19.

See, 1 Chr. 12 : 22; Ps. 103 : 21; 148 : 2.

Host of heaven = (1) the object of idolatrous worship, Deut. 4 : 19; 2 Ki. 21 : 5; 23 : 4 f. (2) Angels, 1 Ki. 22 : 19. cf. Host, the heavenly. From the popular idea of the stars as being animate these two meanings were held simultaneously by later thought. cf. Rev. 9 : 1, 11.

Hot, Deut. 9 : 19, anger and **h.** displeasure.

2 Sam. 11 : 15, forefront of the **h.** battle.

Ps. 6 : 1; 38 : 1, neither chasten in thy **h.** displeasure.

Prov. 6 : 28, can one go upon **h.** coals ?

1 Tim. 4 : 2, conscience seared with **h.** iron.

Rev. 3 : 15, art neither cold nor **h.**

Hotly, Gen. 31 : 36, **h.** pursued after me.

Hough, Josh. 11 : 6; 2 Sam. 8 : 4.

Hour, of day, the third, Matt. 20 : 3; Mark 15 : 25; Acts 2 : 15; 23 : 23.

the sixth, Matt. 27 : 45; Mark 15 : 33; Luke 23 : 44; John 4 : 6; 19 : 14; Acts 10 : 9.

the ninth, Acts 3 : 1; 10 : 3, 30.

at hand, Matt. 26 : 45; John 4 : 21; 5 : 25; 12 : 23; 13 : 1; 16 : 21; 17 : 1.

of temptations, Rev. 3 : 10.

of judgment, Rev. 14 : 7; 18 : 10.

knoweth no man, Matt. 24 : 36, 42; 25 : 13; Mark 13 : 32; Rev. 3 : 3.

figurative, Rev. 8 : 1; 9 : 15.

Dan. 4 : 19, astonied for one **h.**

Matt. 10 : 19; Luke 12 : 12, shall be given you in that same **h.**

Matt. 20 : 12, these have wrought but one **h.**

24 : 36; Mark 13 : 32, of that **h.** knoweth no man.

Matt. 25 : 13, ye know neither day nor **h.**

26 : 40; Mark 14 : 37, could ye not watch one **h.** ?

Mark 14 : 35, if possible, the **h.** might pass.

Luke 10 : 21, in that **h.** Jesus rejoiced.

12 : 39, what **h.** the thief would come.

22 : 59, about the space of one **h.**

John 2 : 4, mine **h.** is not yet come.

5 : 25; 16 : 32, the **h.** is coming, and now is.

12 : 27, Father, save me from this **h.**

Acts 3 : 1, at the **h.** of prayer.

1 Cor. 4 : 11, to this present **h.**

Gal. 2 : 5, gave place, no, not for an **h.**

Rev. 3 : 10, **h.** of temptation.

See Matt. 8 : 13; 9 : 22; 15 : 28; Luke 12 : 12; John 4 : 53; Acts 22 : 13; 1 Cor. 4 : 11; 8 : 7.

House. The caves used by the Hebrews as places of refuge in times of danger (Judg. 6 : 2; 1 Sam. 13 : 6) and persecution (Heb. 11 : 38) were the houses inhabited about 2500 B.C. The patriarchs and their descendants, of course, dwelt in tents; afterwards came booths made of leafy boughs, and later still mud huts. In all periods of Jewish history known to us, houses were made of clay in the form of crude bricks (Job 4 : 19 f.; Ezek. 12 : 5; Matt. 6 : 19 f.) and of stone (Lev. 14 : 40 ff.; Isa. 9 : 10).

From the recent excavations at Gezer we can judge the general plan of Hebrew houses, for they have hardly altered in four

thousand years. The Canaanite houses provided the model (Deut. 6 : 10). The rooms were built on one or more sides of an open court (2 Sam. 17 : 18; Jer. 32 : 2) and were of small size (some twelve or fifteen feet square). The house of a peasant consisted of a walled enclosure within which was a small court. At the farther end of this a single room closed it in, and this further was divided into two parts, the one on a level with the door to house the domestic animals at night (1 Sam. 28 : 24), and the other, raised eighteen inches above this, for the family.

A better class house consisted in two or three rooms, the largest being the living-room and bed-room, a second for the cattle, and a third for use as a general store-room (namely, the " closet," Matt. 6 : 6). If occasion arose (such as the marriage of a son) the house was enlarged by building another room or so on another side of the court.

A wealthy man's house would consist of two or more courts, the rooms round the " inner court " being set apart for the women-folk (Esther 4 : 11). In the court of many houses would be the cistern for catching the precious rain that fell in the rainy season (2 Sam. 17 : 18). Moreover, the houses of the wealthier classes would be of two or three storeys, the highest consisting of only one room, extending over the whole house; this was the upper room. It was in such an " upper room " the Lord observed the passover (Luke 22 : 12; cf. Acts 1 : 13; 9 : 37; 20 : 8). Over the upper room, or if the house had only one room, there was a flat roof with a parapet or palisade around it for protection (Deut. 22 : 8). This was the usual place of recreation in the evening, and is called the " house-top." Here all news would be mentioned, hence the words of Jesus, " that which ye have spoken in the ear in closets [inner chambers or rooms] shall be proclaimed upon the housetops " (Luke 12 : 3). Access to the housetops was by a staircase or ladder on the outside. By such an approach the bearers of the paralytic ascended, when they broke open the floor and let down the sufferer into the room where Jesus was (Mark 2 : 3).

of God, Judg. 20 : 18; 2 Chr. 5 : 14; Ezra 5 : 8, 15; Neh. 6 : 10; Ps. 84 : 10; Isa. 6 : 4; 60 : 7; 64 : 11; Zech. 7 : 2; Matt. 12 : 4; Acts 7 : 49; 1 Tim. 3 : 15; Heb. 10 : 21; 1 Pet. 4 : 17. See **Temple.**

Gen. 28 : 17, none other but the **h.** of God.

Ex. 20 : 17; Deut. 5 : 21, shalt not covet neighbour's **h.**

2 Sam. 6 : 12, Lord blessed **h.** of Obededom.

Neh. 13 : 11, why is the **h.** of God forsaken ?

Job 30 : 23, the **h.** appointed for all living.

Ps. 65 : 4, satisfied with the goodness of thy **h.**

69 : 9; John 2 : 17, the zeal of thine **h.**

Ps. 84 : 3, the sparrow hath found an **h.**

Prov. 2 : 18, her **h.** inclineth to death.

9 : 1, wisdom hath builded her **h.**

12 : 7, the **h.** of the righteous shall stand.
14 : 11, the **h.** of wicked be overthrown.
Eccl. 7 : 2, **h.** of mourning, **h.** of feasting.
  12 : 3, the keepers of the **h.** shall tremble.
Isa. 5 : 8, woe unto them that join **h.** to **h.**
Mic. 4 : 2, let us go up to the **h.** of God.
Hag. 1 : 4, and this **h.** lie waste.
Matt. 7 : 25; Luke 6 : 48, beat upon that **h.**
Matt. 10 : 12, ye come into an **h.**
  12 : 25;   Mark   3 : 25,   **h.** divided cannot stand.
Matt. 23 : 38, your **h.** is left to you desolate.
Luke 10 : 7, go not from **h.** to **h.**
  14 : 23, that my **h.** may be filled.
  15 : 8, light candle, and sweep **h.**
  18 : 14, went down to his **h.** justified.
John 12 : 3, the **h.** was filled with odour of ointment.
  14 : 2, in my Father's **h.** are many mansions.
Acts 2 : 2, sound from heaven filled **h.**
  2 : 46, breaking bread from **h.** to **h.**
2 Cor. 5 : 1, **h.** not made with hands.
2 Tim. 2 : 20, in a great **h.** vessels of gold.
Heb. 3 : 4, every **h.** is built by some man.
Household, Gen. 18 : 19, command his **h.** after him.
2 Sam. 6 : 20, returned to bless his **h.**
Prov. 31 : 27, looketh well to her **h.**
Matt. 10 : 36, a man's foes shall be they of his own **h.**
Gal. 6 : 10, the **h.** of faith.
Eph. 2 : 19, of the **h.** of God.
Householder, Matt. 13 : 27, 52; 21 : 33.
Household servants, Acts 10 : 7.
Household stuff, Gen. 31 : 37; Neh. 13 : 8.
Housetops, Ps. 129 : 6;   Matt. 10 : 27; Luke 5 : 19; Acts 10 : 9.
How, Gen. 28 : 17, Jacob said, **h.** dreadful is this place ?
  39 : 9, **h.** then can I do this great wickedness.
  44 : 16, **h.** shall we clear ourselves ?
Num. 25 : 5, **h.** goodly are thy tents.
Deut. 32 : 30, **h.** should one chase a thousand?
1 Sam. 10 : 27, **h.** shall this man save us ?
  14 : 28, see **h.** mine eyes have been en lightened ?
2 Sam. 1 : 4, **h.** went the matter ?
  1 : 19, **h.** are the mighty fallen!
1 Ki. 3 : 7, I know not **h.** to go out or come in.
Job 9 : 2, but **h.** should a man be just with God ?
Ps. 11 : 1, **h.** say ye to my soul, flee as a bird.
  104 : 24, **h.** manifold are thy works.
Eccl. 11 : 5, **h.** the bones grow in the womb.
Isa. 52 : 7, **h.** beautiful are the feet.
Matt. 6 : 23, **h.** great is the darkness.
  10 : 19, take no thought **h.** ye shall speak.
  12 : 14, **h.** they might destroy him.
Rev. 6 : 10, **h.** long, Lord, holy and true.
Howbeit, 2 Chr. 21 : 7;   Mark 5 : 19; John 16 : 13; 1 Tim. 1 : 16.
Howl, Deut. 32 : 10;   Isa. 65 : 14; Jer. 47 : 2; Jas. 5 : 1.
Howlings, Isa. 15 : 8; Amos 8 : 3; Zeph. 1 : 10.
Howsoever, Judg. 19 : 20; 2 Sam. 18 : 22, 23.
Huge, 2 Chr. 16 : 8.
Huldah (hŭl-dăh) [weasel], 2 Ki. 22 : 14; 2 Chr. 34 : 22.

Humble, Deut. 8 : 2, to **h.** thee and prove thee.
Job 22 : 29, he shall save **h.** person.
Ps. 9 : 12, forgetteth not cry of the **h.**
  34 : 2, the **h.** shall hear thereof.
  69 : 32, **h.** shall see this and be glad.
  113 : 6, **h.** himself to behold things in heaven.
Prov. 16 : 19, better be of a **h.** spirit.
Isa. 57 : 15, of contrite and **h.** spirit.
Matt. 18 : 4;   23 : 12;   Luke 14 : 11;   18 : 14, **h.** himself.
2 Cor. 12 : 21, God will **h.** me.
Phil. 2 : 8, he **h.** himself, and became obedient to death.
Jas. 4 : 6;   1 Pet. 5 : 5, giveth grace to the **h.**
Humbleness, Col. 3 : 12.
Humbly, 2 Sam. 16 : 4, **h.** beseech thee that I may find.
Mic. 6 : 8, and to walk **h.**
Humiliation, Acts 8 : 33.
Humility, Prov. 15 : 33; 22 : 4.
enjoined, Mic. 6 : 8;   Matt. 18;   20 : 25 ff.; Mark 9 : 34, 35;   10 : 43, 44;   Luke 9 : 46;   14 : 7;   22 : 24;   Eph. 4 : 2;   Phil. 2 : 3; Col. 3 : 12;   Jas. 4 : 10;   1 Pet. 5 : 5.
benefits of, Ps. 34 : 2;   69 : 32;   Prov. 3 : 34; Isa. 57 : 15;   Matt. 18 : 4;   Luke 14 : 11; Jas. 4 : 6.
Hundred, Lev. 26 : 8;   1 Sam. 18 : 25;   25 : 18; Ezra 2 : 69; Isa. 65 : 20; Amos 5 : 3; Matt. 18 : 12; Luke 15 : 4.
Hundredfold, Matt. 13 : 8, 23;   Mark 10 : 30; Luke 8 : 8.
Hunger, Ex. 16 : 3;   Jer. 38 : 9; Lam. 4 : 9; Luke 15 : 17; 2 Cor. 11 : 27; Rev. 6 : 8.
(and thirst), figurative, Ps. 107 : 5;   Matt. 5 : 6; John 6 : 35.
Deut. 8 : 3, he suffered thee to **h.**
Ps. 34 : 10, young lions do lack, and suffer **h.**
Prov. 19 : 15, an idle soul shall suffer **h.**
Isa. 49 : 10, shall not **h.** nor thirst.
Matt. 25 : 35, I was an **h.**, and ye gave me meat.
Luke 6 : 21, blessed are ye that **h.**
  6 : 25, woe unto full, ye shall **h.**
Rom. 12 : 20, if thine enemy **h.**, feed him.
1 Cor. 4 : 11, we both **h.** and thirst.
  11 : 34, if any man **h.**, let him eat at home.
Rev. 7 : 16, they shall **h.** no more.
See Ps. 146 : 7;   Prov. 25 : 21;   Isa. 58 : 7; Luke 1 : 53; Acts 10 : 10; 1 Cor. 11 : 21.
Hungerbitten, Job 18 : 12.
Hungry, Job 22 : 7, withholden bread from **h.**
Ps. 50 : 12, if I were **h.**, I would not tell thee.
  107 : 9, he filleth **h.** soul with goodness.
Prov. 27 : 7, to the **h.** every bitter thing is sweet.
Isa. 29 : 8, as when a **h.** man dreameth.
  32 : 6, to make empty the soul of the **h.**
  65 : 13, my servants eat, but ye shall be **h.**
Mark 11 : 12, come from Bethany, he was **h.**
Luke 1 : 53, filled **h.** with good things.
Phil. 4 : 12, instructed both to be full and to be **h.**
Hunt, Gen. 27 : 5, Esau went to **h.** venison.
1 Sam. 26 : 20, as when one doth **h.** a partridge.
Job 10 : 16, thou **h.** me as a fierce lion.
Jer. 16 : 16, **h.** them from every mountain.
Mic. 7 : 2, they **h.** every man his brother.

Hunter, Gen. 10 : 9; 25 : 27; Prov. 6 : 5; Jer. 16 : 16.

Hur (hûr) [noble], son of Caleb, Ex. 17 : 10; 24 : 14; 1 Chr. 2 : 19.

a prince of Midian, Num. 31 : 8.

Huram (hū-́răm), 1 Chr. 8 : 5; 2 Chr. 4 : 11. See Hiram.

Hurl, Num. 35 : 20; 1 Chr. 12 : 2; Job 27 : 21.

Hurt, Gen. 4 : 23, slain young man to my h.

Gen. 26 : 29, that thou wilt do us no h.

31 : 29, in power of my hand to do h.

Ps. 15 : 4, that sweareth to his own h.

Eccl. 8 : 9, ruleth over another to his own h.

Isa. 11 : 9, they shall not h. nor destroy.

Jer. 6 : 14; 8 : 11, have healed h. slightly.

8 : 21, for the h. of my people.

25 : 7, ye provoke me to your own h.

Dan. 6 : 23, no manner of h. found upon him.

Mark 16 : 18, deadly thing, it shall not h.

Luke 10 : 19, nothing shall by any means h. you.

Acts 18 : 10, no man set on thee to h. thee.

27 : 10, this voyage be with h.

Rev. 7 : 3, h. not earth, neither sea.

Hurtful, Ps. 144 : 10; 1 Tim. 6 : 9.

Husband, Gen. 2 : 24; Matt. 19 : 4; 1 Cor. 7 : 2; Eph. 5 : 25; 1 Pet. 3 : 7.

God the husband of his church, Isa. 54 : 5; Hos. 2 : 7.

Ex. 4 : 25, a bloody h. art thou.

Prov. 12 : 4, a virtuous woman is a crown to her h.

31 : 11, heart of her h. doth trust in her.

John 4 : 16, go, call thy h.

Rom. 7 : 2, h. dead, she is loosed.

1 Cor. 7 : 16, whether thou shalt save thy h.

14 : 35, ask their h. at home.

Eph. 5 : 22, wives, submit yourselves to your h.

Col. 3 : 19, h. love your wives.

1 Tim. 3 : 12, the h. of one wife.

Titus 2 : 4, teach young women to love their h.

1 Pet. 3 : 1, subjection to own h.

Rev. 21 : 2, as bride adorned for her h.

Husbandman, parable of the, Matt. 21 : 33; Mark 12 : 1; Luke 20 : 9.

Gen. 9 : 20, Noah began to be an h.

John 15 : 1, I am true vine, my Father is h.

2 Tim. 2 : 6, h. that laboureth.

Jas. 5 : 7, the h. waiteth for fruit of earth.

Husbandry, 2 Chr. 26 : 10; 1 Cor. 3 : 9.

Husks, Luke 15 : 16, is used to designate the pods of the locust tree (Ceratonia siliqua). Varying in length from six to ten inches, and being about a finger's breadth, they are used in the East for feeding cattle and are often eaten by the poor.

Hymenæus (hȳ-mĕ-nāē-́ŭs) [nuptial song], 1 Tim. 1 : 20; 2 Tim. 2 : 17.

Hymn, Matt. 26 : 30; Mark 14 : 26, sung an h.

Eph. 5 : 19; Col. 3 : 16, speaking in psalms and h.

Hypocrisy, Isa. 32 : 6, iniquity, to practise h.

Matt. 23 : 28, within ye are full of h.

Mark 12 : 15, he, knowing their h.

Luke 12 : 1, leaven of Pharisees, which is h.

1 Tim. 4 : 2, speaking lies in h.

Jas. 3 : 17, wisdom is pure, and without h.

1 Pet. 2 : 1, lay aside all guile and h.

Hypocrite, Job 8 : 13, the h. hope shall perish.

Job 15 : 34, congregation of h. shall be desolate.

20 : 5, the joy of the h. but for a moment.

36 : 13, h. in heart heap up wrath.

Isa. 9 : 17, every one is an h.

33 : 14, fearfulness surprised h.

Matt. 6 : 2, 5, 16, as the h. do.

7 : 5, Luke 6 : 42, thou h., first cast out beam.

Matt. 15 : 7; 16 : 3; Mark 7 : 6; Luke 12 : 56, ye h.

Matt. 22 : 18, why tempt ye me, ye h. ?

23 : 13; Luke 11 : 44, woe unto you, h.

Matt. 24 : 51, appoint him portion with h.

Hypocritical, Ps. 35 : 16; Isa. 10 : 6.

Hyssop was used for sprinkling blood (Ex. 12 : 22), and in the ritual of leper-cleansing (Lev. 14 : 4; Num. 19 : 6). An insignificant plant growing out of the wall (1 Ki. 4 : 33), it could supply a branch to support a wet sponge (John 19 : 29). All the references may not be to a single species. Marjoram, or, better, the caper-plant, is the best suggestion of its identity.

Ps. 51 : 7, purge me with h.

Heb. 9 : 19, took blood, with h., and sprinkled.

I

I am, the divine name, Ex. 3 : 14.

See John 8 : 58; Rev. 1 : 18.

Ibhar (ĭb-̍här) [he (God) chooses], 2 Sam. 5 : 15.

Ibleam (ĭb-̍lē-ăm), Josh. 17 : 11.

Ibneiah (ĭb-neῒ-ăh) [Jah builds], 1 Chr. 9 : 8.

Ibnijah (ĭb-nῒ-jăh) [Jah builds], 1 Chr. 9 : 8.

Ibri (ĭb-̍rῒ), 1 Chr. 24 : 27.

Ibzan (ĭb-̍zăn) [illustrious], Judg. 12 : 8, 10.

Ice, Job 6 : 16; Ps. 147 : 17.

Ichabod (ῒ-̍chă-bŏd) [inglorious], 1 Sam. 4 : 21; 14 : 3.

Iconium (ῒ-cō-́nῒ-ŭm), the capital of Lycaonia (now Konia) in Asia Minor.

gospel preached at, Acts 13 : 51; 14 : 1; 16 : 2.

Paul persecuted at, 2 Tim. 3 : 11.

Idle, Ex. 5 : 8, they be i.

Prov. 19 : 15, an i. soul shall suffer hunger.

Matt. 12 : 36, every i. word men speak.

20 : 3, standing i. in market-place.

Luke 24 : 11, words seemed as i. tales.

1 Tim. 5 : 13, they learn to be i.

Idleness, reproved, Prov. 6 : 6; 18 : 9; 24 : 30; 31 : 27; Rom. 12 : 11; 1 Thess. 4 : 11; 2 Thess. 3 : 10; Heb. 6 : 12.

evil of, Prov. 10 : 4; 12 : 24; 13 : 4; 19 : 15; 20 : 4, 13; 21 : 25; Eccl. 10 : 18; 1 Tim. 5 : 13.

Idolaters, 1 Cor. 5 : 10; 10 : 7; Rev. 21 : 8.

Idolatrous, 2 Ki. 23 : 5.

Idolatry. The desire to propitiate gods who were dispossessed when their worshippers were conquered by the Israelites, intermarriage with other peoples, and political relationships, caused the rise of idolatry among the Hebrews. In essence it was the worship of Baal (the male principle in nature), nature-

worship, astrolatry, or a mixture of
Jehovah-worship with that of other gods.
forbidden, Ex. 20 : 3-5; 22 : 20; 23 : 13;
Lev. 26 : 1; Deut. 4 : 15-19; 5 : 7; 11 : 16;
17 : 2, 3; 18 : 9; 27 : 15; Ps. 97 : 7; Jer.
2 : 11; 1 John 5 : 21.
folly of, 1 Ki. 18 : 26; Ps. 115 : 4-8; 135 :
15-18; Isa. 40 : 19; 41 : 29; 44 : 9; 46 : 1;
Jer. 2 : 26-28; 10.
monuments of, to be destroyed, Ex. 23 : 24;
34 : 13; Deut. 7 : 5.
Israelites guilty of, Ex. 32; Num. 25; Judg.
2 : 11; 3 : 7; 8 : 33; 18 : 30; 2 Ki. 17 : 12;
Micah, Judg. 17; Solomon, 1 Ki. 11 : 5;
Jeroboam, 1 Ki. 12 : 28; Ahab, etc., 1 Ki.
16 : 31; 18 : 18; Manasseh, 2 Ki. 21 : 4;
Ahaz, 2 Chr. 28 : 2; Nebuchadnezzar, etc.,
Dan. 3 : 5, inhabitants of Lystra, Acts
14 : 11; Athenians, Acts 17 : 16;¦Ephesians,
Acts 19 : 28.
zeal of Asa against, 1 Ki. 15 : 12; of Jehoshaphat, 2 Chr. 17 : 6; of Hezekiah, 2 Chr.
30 : 14; of Josiah, 2 Chr. 34.
punishment of, Deut. 7 : 16; 17 : 2-7; Jer.
8 : 1-3; 16 : 11-13; 44 : 22; Hos. 8 : 5;
1 Cor. 6 : 9; Eph. 5 : 5; Rev. 14 : 9-11;
21 : 8; 22 : 15.
Idols, meats offered to, Rom. 14 : 14; 1 Cor. 8.
1 Ki. 15 : 13; 2 Chr. 15 : 16, made an i. in a
grove.
Ps. 96 : 5, all gods of the nations are i.
115 : 4; 135 : 15, their i. are silver and gold.
Isa. 66 : 3, as if he blessed an i.
Jer. 50 : 38, mad upon their i.
Hos. 4 : 17, Ephraim is joined to i.
Acts 7 : 41, offered sacrifice to the i.
15 : 20, abstain from pollutions of i.
1 Cor. 8 : 4, we know an i. is nothing.
2 Cor. 6 : 16, what agreement hath temple of
God with i. ?
1 Thess. 1 : 9, ye turned to God from i.
1 John 5 : 21, keep yourselves from i.
Idumea (ĭ-dū-mē̆-ă̆) [Heb. " Edom "], Isa.
34 : 5; Ezek. 35 : 15; 36 : 5; (Mark 3 : 8).
Ignominy, Prov. 18 : 3.
Ignorance, sin offerings for, Lev. 4; Num.
15 : 22-29.
effects of, Rom. 10 : 3; 2 Pet. 3 : 5.
Paul's deprecation of, 1 Cor. 10 : 1; 12;
2 Cor. 1 : 8; 1 Thess. 4 : 13; 2 Pet. 3 : 8.
Acts 3 : 17, through i. ye did it.
17 : 30, times of this i. God winked at.
Eph. 4 : 18, alienated through i.
1 Pet. 2 : 15, put to silence i. of foolish men.
Ignorant, Ps. 73 : 22, so foolish was I, and i.
Isa. 56 : 10, watchmen all i., they are all
dumb.
63 : 16, though Abraham be i. of us.
Acts 4 : 13, perceived they were i. men.
Rom. 10 : 3, being i. of God's righteousness.
11 : 25, should be i. of this mystery.
1 Cor. 14 : 38, if any man be i., let him be i.
2 Cor. 2 : 11, not i. of Satan's devices.
Heb. 5 : 2, can have compassion on the i.
2 Pet. 3 : 8, be not i. of this one thing.
Ignorantly, Num. 15 : 28; Acts 17 : 23; 1 Tim.
1 : 13.
Ill, Gen. 41 : 3, 4; Ps. 106 : 32; Isa. 3 : 11;
Mic. 3 : 4; Rom. 13 : 10.

Illuminated, Heb. 10 : 32.
Image, Gen. 1 : 26, let us make man in our i.
Ps. 73 : 20, shalt despise their i.
Matt. 22 : 20; Mark 12 : 16; Luke 20 : 24,
whose is this i. ?
Acts 19 : 35, i. which fell from Jupiter.
Rom. 1 : 23, changed glory of God into an i.
8 : 29, be conformed to i. of his Son.
1 Cor. 15 : 49, we have borne i. of earthy.
2 Cor. 3 : 18, changed into the same i.
Col. 3 : 10, after i. of him that created.
Heb. 1 : 3, the express i. of his person.
10 : 1, not the very i. of things.
Rev. 14 : 11, have no rest, who worship i.
Imagery [ar.], paintings of images or idols, Ezek.
8 : 12.
Images, prohibited, Ex. 20 : 4; Lev. 26 : 1;
Deut. 16 : 22.
Imagination, of man, evil, Gen. 6 : 5; 8 : 21;
Deut. 31 : 21; Jer. 23 : 17.
Gen. 8 : 21, i. of heart evil.
Deut. 29 : 19, walk in i. of heart.
1 Chr. 28 : 9, Lord understandeth all i. of the
thoughts.
Luke 1 : 51, scattered the proud in i. of their
hearts.
Rom. 1 : 21, became vain in their i.
2 Cor. 10 : 5, casting down i.
Imagine, Ps. 2 : 1; Acts 4 : 25, why do people
i. vain things ?
Ps. 62 : 3, how long will ye i. mischief ?
Nah. 1 : 9, what do ye i. against the Lord ?
Zech. 7 : 10; 8 : 17, let none i. evil.
Immanuel (ĭm-măn-ʹu-el) [God with us], Isa.
7 : 14; (Matt. 1 : 23).
Immediately, Matt. 4 : 22; Mark 1 : 12; John
6 : 21; Rev. 4 : 2.
Immer (ĭm-ʹmer) [talkative], 1 Chr. 9 : 12;
24 : 14; Jer. 20 : 1; Ezra 2 : 59; Neh.
7 : 61.
Immortality, of God, 1 Tim. 1 : 17; 6 : 16.
of man, Rom. 2 : 7; 1 Cor. 15 : 54.
Immutability, Heb. 6 : 17, 18.
Impart, Job 39 : 17, nor i. to her understanding.
Luke 3 : 11, let him i. to him that hath none.
Rom. 1 : 11, may i. some spiritual gift.
1 Thess. 2 : 8, willing to have i. souls.
Impediment, Mark 7 : 32.
Impenitent, Rom. 2 : 5.
Imperious, Ezek. 16 : 30.
Implacable, Rom. 1 : 31.
Implead, Acts 19 : 38.
Importunity, Luke 11 : 8.
Impose, Ezra 7 : 24, not be lawful to i. toll.
Heb. 9 : 10, carnal ordinances, i. on them.
Impossible, Matt. 17 : 20, nothing shall be i.
unto you.
19 : 26; Mark 10 : 27; Luke 18 : 27, with
men it is i.
Luke 1 : 37; 18 : 27, with God nothing i.
17 : 1, it is i. but that offences will come.
Heb. 6 : 4, i. for those enlightened.
11 : 6, without faith it is i. to please God.
Impotent, John 5 : 3, 7; Acts 4 : 9; 14 : 8.
Impoverish, Judg. 6 : 6; Isa. 40 : 20; Jer.
5 : 17; Mal. 1 : 4.
Imprisoned, Acts 22 : 19.
Imprisonment, Ezra 7 : 26; 2 Cor. 6 : 5; Heb.
11 : 36.

Impudent, Prov. 7 : 13; Ezek. 2 : 4.

Impute, Lev. 17 : 4, blood shall be i. to that man.
Ps. 32 : 2; Rom. 4 : 8, to whom the Lord i. not iniquity.
Rom. 5 : 13, sin is not i. when there is no law.
2 Cor. 5 : 19, not i. trespasses to them.
Jas. 2 : 23, it was i. unto him.

Inasmuch, Matt. 25 : 40, 45; Rom. 11 : 13; 1 Pet. 4 : 13.

Incense was burned [Latin, " to burn "] with the meat-offering (Lev. 2 : 1 f., 15 f.; 6 : 15), and offered with the shewbread (Lev. 24 : 7-9). See **Frankincense.** The holy incense (Ex. 30 : 34) was compounded of stacte, onycha, galbanum, and frankincense, no other ingredients being permitted (Ex. 30 : 9).
figurative, Rev. 8 : 3.
offered, Lev. 10 : 1; 16 : 13; Num. 16 : 46.
cf. Ex. 30 : 27; 37 : 29; Luke 1 : 9.

Incensed, Isa. 41 : 11; 45 : 24.

Incest, forbidden, Lev. 18; 20 : 17; Deut. 22 : 30; 27 : 20; Ezek. 22 : 11; Amos 2 : 7.
cases of, Gen. 19 : 33; 35 : 22; 38 : 18; 2 Sam. 13; 16 : 21; Mark 6 : 17; 1 Cor. 5 : 1.

Incline, Josh. 24 : 23, i. your heart to the Lord.
1 Ki. 8 : 58, that he may i. our hearts to keep the law.
Ps. 78 : 1, i. your ears to the words of my mouth.
116 : 2, i. his ear unto me.
119 : 36, i. my heart to thy testimonies.
Prov. 2 : 18, her house i. unto death.
Jer. 7 : 24; 11 : 8; 17 : 23; 34 : 14, nor i. ear.

Inclosed, Ex. 28 : 20; 39 : 6; Ps. 22 : 16; Luke 5 : 6.

Inclosings, Ex. 28 : 20.

Incontinency, 1 Cor. 7 : 5.

Incontinent, 2 Tim. 3 : 3.

Incorruptible, 1 Cor. 9 : 25, to obtain an i. crown.
15 : 52, the dead shall be raised i.
1 Pet. 1 : 4, an inheritance i.

Incorruption, 1 Cor. 15 : 42, 50, 53 f.

Increase, Lev. 26 : 4, the land shall yield her i.
Deut. 14 : 22, tithe all i. of thy seed.
Job 8 : 7, thy latter end greatly i.
11 : 24, that scattereth, and yet i.
Ps. 62 : 10, if riches i., set not heart on them.
Ps. 67 : 6; Ezek. 34 : 27, earth shall yield her i.
115 : 14, Lord shall i. you more and more.
Prov. 18 : 20, with the i. of his lips.
Prov. 1 : 5; 9 : 9, a wise man will i. learning.
Eccl. 1 : 18, he that i. knowledge, i. sorrow.
Eccl. 5 : 10, not be satisfied with i.
Isa. 9 : 7, of i. of his government shall be no end.
Isa. 40 : 29, he i. strength.
Dan. 12 : 4, knowledge shall be i.
Hos. 12 : 1, he daily i. lies.
Luke 2 : 52, Jesus i. in wisdom.
17 : 5, Lord, i. our faith.
John 3 : 30, he must i., I decrease.
Acts 6 : 7, word of God i.
16 : 5, churches i. daily.
1 Cor. 3 : 6, God gave the i.

Col. 1 : 10, i. in the knowledge of God.
2 : 19, body i. with i. of God.
1 Thess. 4 : 10, that ye i. more and more.
Rev. 3 : 17, I am rich, and i. with goods.
[ar.], interest, Lev. 25 : 36.
offspring, 1 Sam. 2 : 33.

Incredible, Acts 26 : 8.

Incurable, Job 34 : 6; Jer. 30 : 15; Mic. 1 : 9.

Indebted, Luke 11 : 4.

Indeed, Gen. 37 : 8, shalt thou i. reign over us ?
1 Ki. 8 : 27, will God i. dwell on the earth?
1 Chr. 4 : 10, thou wouldest bless me i.
Isa. 6 : 9, hear ye i., see ye i.
Mark 11 : 32, a prophet i.
Luke 24 : 34, the Lord is risen i.
John 1 : 47, an Israelite i.
4 : 42, that this is i. the Christ.
6 : 55, my flesh is meat i., and my blood is drink i.
8 : 36, ye shall be free i.

Indignation, Ps. 69 : 24, pour out thine i. upon them.
Ps. 78 : 49, wrath, i., and trouble.
Isa. 26 : 20, till the i. be overpast.
Nah. 1 : 6, who can stand before his i. ?
Matt. 20 : 24, moved with i.
26 : 8, they had i.
Acts 5 : 17, they were filled with i.
2 Cor. 7 : 11, yea, what i.
Heb. 10 : 27, fearful looking for of fiery i.
Rev. 14 : 10, the cup of his i.

Inditing, Ps. 45 : 1.

Industrious, 1 Ki. 11 : 28.

Industry, command, Gen. 2 : 15; 3 : 23; Prov. 6 : 6; 10 : 4; 12 : 24; 13 : 4; 21 : 5; 22 : 29; 27 : 23; Eph. 4 : 28; 1 Thess. 4 : 11; 2 Thess. 3 : 12; Titus 3 : 14.
rewarded, Prov. 13 : 11; 31 : 13.

Inexcusable, Rom. 2 : 1.

Infallible, Acts 1 : 3.

Infamous, Ezek. 22 : 5.

Infamy, Prov. 25 : 10; Ezek. 36 : 3.

Infant, Job 3 : 16; Isa. 65 : 20; Luke 18 : 15.

Inferior, Job 12 : 3; 2 Cor. 12 : 13.

Infidel (=unbeliever), 2 Cor. 6 : 15, he that believeth with an i. ?
1 Tim. 5 : 8, is worse than an i.

Infinite, Job 22 : 5; Ps. 147 : 5; Nah. 3 : 9.

Infirmity, Ps. 77 : 10, this is mine i.
Prov. 18 : 14, spirit of man will sustain his i.
Matt. 8 : 17, himself took our i.
Rom. 6 : 19, the i. of your flesh.
8 : 26, the Spirit also helpeth our i.
15 : 1, strong bear the i. of the weak.
2 Cor. 12 : 10, take pleasure in i.
Heb. 4 : 15, touched with the feeling of our i.

Inflame, Isa. 5 : 11.

Inflammation, Lev. 13 : 28; Deut. 28 : 22.

Inflicted, 2 Cor. 2 : 6.

Influences, Job 38 : 31.

Infolding, Ezek. 1 : 4.

Inform, Deut. 17 : 10; Dan. 9 : 22; Acts 21 : 24.

Ingathering, feast of, Ex. 23 : 16; 34 : 22.

Ingrafted, Jas. 1 : 21.

Ingratitude, to God, Rom. 1 : 21.
exemplified : Israel, Deut. 32 : 18; Saul, 1 Sam. 15; 24 : 17; David, 2 Sam. 12 : 7, 9; Nebuchadnezzar, Dan. 5; the lepers, Luke 17.

punishment of, Prov. 17 : 13; Jer. 18 : 20.
Inhabit, Ps. 22 : 3, O thou that i. the praises of Israel.
Isa. 57 : 15, lofty One that i. eternity.
65 : 21, build houses and i. them.
Amos 9 : 14, build waste cities and i. them.
Zeph. 1 : 13, build houses, not i. them.
Inhabitant, Gen. 19 : 25, overthrew i. of cities.
Num. 13 : 32, land eateth up i.
Judg. 5 : 23, curse bitterly the i.
Isa. 5 : 9, houses great without i.
6 : 11, cities be wasted without i.
24 : 17, snare on the, O i. of the earth.
33 : 24, the i. shall not say, I am sick.
Jer. 44 : 22, land without an i.
Amos 1 : 8, I will cut off i.
Inherit, Gen. 15 : 8, shall I know that I shall i. it?
Ex. 32 : 13, they shall i. it for ever.
Ps. 25 : 13, his seed shall i. the earth.
37 : 11; Matt. 5 : 5, the meek shall i. the earth.
Prov. 3 : 35, the wise shall i. glory.
14 : 18, the simple i. folly.
Isa. 65 : 9, mine elect shall i. it.
Matt. 19 : 29, shall i. everlasting life.
25 : 34, i. the kingdom prepared.
Mark 10 : 17; Luke 10 : 25; 18 : 18, i. eternal life.
1 Cor. 6 : 9; 15 : 50; Gal. 5 : 21, not i. the kingdom.
Heb. 6 : 12, through faith i. the promises.
12 : 17, when he would have i. the blessing.
Rev. 21 : 7, he that overcometh shall i. all things.
Inheritance, law of, Num. 27 : 6-11; Deut. 21 : 15.
in Christ, Eph. 1 : 11; Col. 1 : 12; 3 : 24; 1 Pet. 1 : 4.
Gen. 31 . 14, is there any i. for us ?
Ex. 15 : 17, plant them in thine i.
Ps. 16 : 5, Lord is portion of mine i.
47 : 4, choose our i. for us.
79 : 1, heathen are come into thine i.
Prov. 13 : 22, a good man leaveth i.
20 : 21, an i. may be gotten hastily.
Eccl. 7 : 11, wisdom is good with an i.
Matt. 21 : 38, let us seize on his i.
Mark 12 : 7; Luke 20 : 14, the i. shall be ours.
Luke 12 : 13, divide the i. with me.
Acts 20 : 32; 26 : 18, an i. among the sanctified.
Eph. 1 : 14, the earnest of our i.
Heb. 1 : 4, he hath by i. obtained more excellent name.
9 : 15, receive promise of eternal i.
11 : 8, place he should receive for i.
Iniquity, Gen. 15 : 16, the i. of the Amorites.
Ex. 20 : 5; 34 : 7; Num. 14 : 18; Deut. 5 : 9, visiting the i. of the fathers.
Ex. 34 : 7; Num. 14 : 18, forgiving i. and transgression.
Deut. 32 : 4, a God of truth without i.
Job 4 : 8, they that plow i. reap the same.
5 : 16, i. stoppeth her mouth.
34 : 32, if I have done i., I will do no more.
Ps. 25 : 11, pardon mine i., for it is great.
32 : 2, blessed to whom Lord imputeth not i.
51 : 5, I was shapen in i.
66 : 18, if I regard i. in my heart.

69 : 27, add i. to their i.
90 : 8, thou hast set our i. before thee.
103 : 3, who forgiveth all thine i.
130 : 3, if thou shouldest mark i.
Prov. 22 : 8, he that soweth i. shall reap vanity.
Isa. 1 : 4, a people laden with i.
5 : 18, woe to them that draw i.
6 : 7, thine i. is taken away.
40 : 2, her i. is pardoned.
53 : 5, he was bruised for our i.
Dan. 9 : 24, make reconciliation for i.
Hos. 14 : 2, take away i., receive us graciously.
Hab. 1 : 13, canst not look on i.
Matt. 24 : 12, i. shall abound.
Acts 1 : 18, purchased field with reward of i.
8 : 23, in bond of i.
Rom. 6 : 19, servants to i. unto i.
2 Thess. 2 : 7, the mystery of i. doth work.
2 Tim. 2 : 19, depart from i.
Titus 2 : 14, redeem us from i.
Jas. 3 : 6, tongue is a world of i.
Rev. 18 : 5, God hath remembered i.
Injured, Gal. 4 : 12.
Injurious, 1 Tim. 1 : 13.
Injustice, forbidden, Ex. 22 : 21; 23 : 6; Lev. 19 : 15; Deut. 16 : 19; 24 : 17; Job 31 : 16, 21, 28; Ps. 82 : 2; Prov. 22 : 16; 29 : 7; Jer. 22 : 3; Luke 16 : 10.
results of, Prov. 11 : 7; 28 : 8; Amos 5 : 11; 8 : 5; Mic. 6 : 10; 1 Thess. 4 : 6; 2 Pet. 2 : 9.
Ink, Jer. 36 : 18, wrote them with i. in a book.
2 Cor. 3 : 3, not with i., but the Spirit.
2 John 12; 3 John 13, I would not write with i.
Inkhorn, Ezek. 9 : 2, 3, 11.
Inn. In the O.T., " inns " in the later sense can hardly be said to have existed. Hospitality provided for the ordinary traveller. The " mālōn " (Gen. 42 : 27, cf. Ex. 4 : 24) was merely a place where travelling caravans passed the night. The " lodge of wayfaring men " (Jer. 9 : 2) may refer to a building of some kind.
In N.T. times, under Greek and Roman influence, great changes occurred and inns were numerous. Those on the highways would be not unlike the " khans " of to-day, providing rest and entertainment. Such was the inn of the Good Samaritan's choosing (Luke 10 : 34). Their reputation was not high; hence Christians are enjoined to avoid them and practise hospitality among themselves (1 Pet. 4 : 9).
Ex. 4 : 24, in the i. the Lord met him.
Luke 2 : 7, no room for them in the i.
Inner, Acts 16 : 24.
Inner man, Eph. 3 : 16.
Innermost, Prov. 18 : 8; 26 : 22.
Innocency, Ps. 26 : 6; Dan. 6 : 22; Hos. 8 : 5.
Innocent, Deut. 27 : 25, taketh reward to slay i.
Job 4 : 7, who ever perished, being i. ?
9 : 23, laugh at the trial of the i.
27 : 17, the i. shall divide the silver.
Ps. 15 : 5, taketh reward against the i.
19 : 13, i. from the great transgression.
Prov. 28 : 20, haste to be rich shall not be i.
Jer. 19 : 4, filled this place with blood of i.

Matt. 27 : 24, I am i. of the blood.
Innumerable, Ps. 40 : 12, i. evils compassed about.
Ps. 104 : 25, things creeping i.
Heb. 11 : 12, sand by the seashore i.
12 : 22, come to i. company of angels.
Inordinate, Ezek. 23 : 11; Col. 3 : 5.
Inquisition, Deut. 19 : 18, judges shall make diligent i.
Esther 2 : 23, i. was made of the matter.
Ps. 9 : 12, when he maketh i. for blood.
Inscription, Acts 17 : 23.
Inside, 1 Ki. 6 : 15.
Insomuch, Mal. 2 : 13; Matt. 15 : 31; Mark 1 : 45; 2 Cor. 1 : 8.
Inspiration of the Bible. " The Scriptures may be compendiously described as the record by inspired writers of a revelation, or rather a series of revelations, from God to man."
—Angus. " They (the Fathers) teach us that Inspiration is an operation of the Holy Spirit acting through men according to the laws of their constitution, which is not neutralized by His influence, but adopted as a vehicle for the full expression of the Divine message."—Bishop Westcott. " We verily believe that the Holy Ghost was so breathed into the mind of the writer, so illumined his spirit and pervaded his thoughts, that while nothing that individualized him as a man was taken away, everything that was necessary to enable him to declare Divine Truth in all its fullness was bestowed and superadded."
—Bishop Ellicott.
Instant, Isa. 29 : 5, it shall be at an i. suddenly.
Luke 7 : 4, they besought him i.
Acts 26 : 7, twelve tribes i. serving God.
[ar.], urgent, importunate.
Rom. 12 : 12, continuing i. in prayer.
2 Tim. 4 : 2, be i. in season, out of season.
Instead, Num. 10 : 31; Ps. 45 : 16; Isa. 55 : 13.
Instruct, Neh. 9 : 20, thy good Spirit to i. them.
Ps. 16 : 7, my reins i. me in the night seasons.
32 : 8, I will i. thee, and teach thee.
Isa. 28 : 26, God doth i. him to discretion.
40 : 14, who i. him, and taught him ?
Matt. 13 : 52, every scribe i. unto the kingdom.
Rom. 2 : 18, being i. out of the law.
Phil. 4 : 12, in all things I am i.
Instruction, Job 33 : 16, he openeth the ears, sealeth their i.
Ps. 50 : 17, seeing thou hatest i.
Prov. 1 : 3, to receive the i. of wisdom.
10 : 17, in way of life that keepeth i.
15 : 32, refuseth i. despiseth his soul.
16 : 22, the i. of fools is folly.
23 : 12, apply thine heart to i.
2 Tim. 3 : 16, scripture is profitable for i.
Instructor, Gen. 4 : 22; Rom. 2 : 20; 1 Cor. 4 : 15.
Instrument, Gen. 49 : 5, i. of cruelty in habitations.
Ps. 7 : 13, prepared the i. of death.
33 : 2; 92 : 3, sing with i. of ten strings.
Isa. 38 : 20, my songs to the stringed i.
41 : 15, sharp threshing i.
Ezek. 33 : 32, one that can play on an i.
Rom. 6 : 13, members i. of unrighteousness.

See Ps. 150 : 4; Amos 6 : 5; Hab. 3 : 19.
Insurrection, Ezra 4 · 19; Ps. 64 : 2; Mark 15 : 7; Acts 18 : 12.
Integrity, Gen. 20 : 5, in i. of my heart have I done this.
Job 2 : 3, he holdeth fast his i.
31 : 6, that God may know my i.
Ps. 7 : 8, according to my i.
25 : 21, let i. preserve me.
26 : 1, I have walked in i.
41 : 12, thou upholdest me in my i.
Prov. 11 : 3, the i. of the upright.
19 : 1, poor that walketh in i.
20 : 7, just man walketh in his i.
Intelligence, Dan. 11 : 30, i. with them that forsake.
Intend, 2 Chr. 28 : 13, i. to add more to our sins.
Acts 5 : 35, ye i. to do as touching these.
See Acts 5 : 28; 12 : 4.
Intent, Acts 10 : 29, for what i. ye have sent for me ?
Eph. 3 : 10, to the i. that now unto the principalities.
Heb. 4 : 12, discerner of i. of heart.
Intercession, of Christ, Luke 23 : 34; Rom. 8 : 34; 1 John 2 : 1.
of the Holy Spirit, Rom. 8 : 26.
to be made for all men, Eph. 6 : 18; 1 Tim. 2 : 1; for kings, 1 Tim. 2 : 2.
asked for by Paul, Rom. 15 : 30; 2 Cor. 1 : 11; Col. 4 : 3; 1 Thess. 5 : 25; 2 Thess. 3 : 1; Heb. 13 : 18.
Intercessor, Isa. 59 : 16.
Intermeddle, Prov. 14 : 10; 18 : 1.
Intermission, Lam. 3 : 49.
Interpret, Gen. 41 : 8; 1 Cor. 12 : 30.
Interpretation (of dreams) is of God, Gen. 40 : 8; Prov. 1 : 6; Dan. 2 : 27.
Interpreter, Job 33 : 23; 1 Cor. 14 : 28.
Intreat, Ruth 1 : 16, i. me not to leave thee.
1 Sam. 2 : 25, if a man sin, who shall i. ?
Ps. 45 : 12, rich shall i. favour.
Isa. 19 : 22, he shall be i. of them.
1 Cor. 4 : 13, being defamed, we i.
1 Tim. 5 : 1, i. him as a father.
Jas. 3 : 17, wisdom is easy to be i.
Intreaties, Prov. 18 : 23; 2 Cor. 8 : 4.
Intruding, Col. 2 : 18, i. into things.
Invade, 1 Sam. 23 : 27; Hab. 3 : 16.
Invasion, 1 Sam. 30 : 14.
Invent, 2 Chr. 26 : 15, engines, i. by cunning men.
Amos 6 : 5, i. to themselves instruments.
Inventions, Ps. 106 : 29, provoked him to anger with i.
Prov. 8 : 12, knowledge of witty i.
Eccl. 7 : 29, have sought out many i.
Inventors, Rom. 1 : 30, i. of evil things.
Invisible, Rom. 1 : 20, i. things are clearly seen.
Col. 1 : 15, the image of the i. God.
1 Tim. 1 : 17, King immortal, i.
Heb. 11 : 27, as seeing him who is i.
Invited, 1 Sam. 9 : 24; 2 Sam. 13 : 23; Esther 5 : 12.
Inward, Job 38 : 36, wisdom in the i. parts.
Ps. 51 : 6, truth in the i. parts.
64 : 6, i. thought of every one is deep.
Jer. 31 : 33, I will put my law in their i. parts.

Luke 11 : 39, i. part is full of ravening.
Rom. 7 : 22, law of God after the i. man.
2 Cor. 4 : 16, the i. man is renewed.
Inwardly, Ps. 62 : 4; Matt. 7 : 15; Rom. 2 : 29.
Iphedeiah (iph-ĕ-dêi'-ăh) [Jah redeems], 1 Chr. 8 : 25.
Ir (ir), a Benjamite, 1 Chr. 7 : 12.
Ira (ir'-ă) [a watcher], 2 Sam. 20 : 26; 1 Chr. 11 : 28.
Irad (i'-răd) [wild ass], Gen. 4 : 18.
Iram (i'-răm) [citizen], Gen. 36 : 43; 1 Chr. 1 : 54.
Iri (i'-ri), 1 Chr. 7 : 7. See Ir.
Irijah (i-ri'-jäh) [Jah sees], Jer. 37 : 14.
Irnahash (ir-nā'-hăsh), a city, 1 Chr. 4 : 12.
Iron and steel, Gen. 4 : 22; Deut. 8 : 9; Jer. 9 : 12. Simple and rude as the process is by which semi-savage tribes in Africa and the East are able to produce iron of excellent quality, still by some it has been doubted whether the art is one of very great antiquity. On the other hand, there is evidence that the manufacture of iron in Assyria, Egypt, India, and China was practised at very remote periods.
pen of, Job 19 : 24.
rod of, figurative, Ps. 2 : 9; Rev. 2 : 27.
See Deut. 3 : 11; 2 Sam. 23 : 7; Job 28 : 2; Prov. 27 : 17; Isa. 45 : 2; Ezek. 27 : 12; Dan. 2 : 33, 40.
Isaac (i'-săăc) [laughter], his birth promised, Gen. 15 : 4; 17 : 16; 18 : 10; born, Gen. 21 : 2.
offered by Abraham, Gen. 22 : 7 ff.
marries Rebecca, Gen. 24 : 51.
blesses his sons, Gen. 27 : 27-40; 28 : 1.
his death, Gen. 35 : 29.
Isaiah (i-sai'-ah) [the salvation of Jah], (Esaias), prophet, Isa. 1 : 1; 2 : 1.
sent to Ahaz, Isa. 7; and to Hezekiah, Isa. 37 : 6; 38 : 4; 39 : 3.
prophecies concerning various nations, Isa. 7; 8; 10; 13–23; 45–47.
referred to, Matt. 3 : 3; 5 : 17; 8 : 17; 12 : 17; 13 : 14; 15 : 7; Mark 1 : 2; Luke 3 : 4; 4 : 17; John 1 : 23; 12 : 38; Acts 8 : 32; 28 : 25; Rom. 9 : 29; 10 : 16; 15 : 12.
Isaiah, Book of the Prophet.
Authorship and Date.—The information given by the first verse of the book is that Isaiah was the son of Amoz, about whom nothing more is known; that his vision concerned Judah and Jerusalem, and that it was given during the reigns of Uzziah, Jotham, Ahaz and Hezekiah, Kings of Judah. We learn that his wife was called the prophetess (8 : 3) and that Isaiah had two sons. According to tradition, he was placed in a hollow log and sawn asunder by Manasseh, and it is therefore to him that Hebrews 11 : 37 is supposed to refer. He was closely related to affairs of state and the messages from God through him steadied Kings in the midst of great crises. A case in point is Rabshakeh's challenge and Isaiah's reassurance to Hezekiah recorded in 2 Kings 19 : 6, 7.

Duration of his ministry.—Beginning near the close of Uzziah's reign and continuing through the reign of Hezekiah, his testimony must have covered forty and more years (760-698 B.C.). If the vision of the sixth chapter marked the beginning of Isaiah's prophesying, this beginning was four years later than is commonly assumed. There is no reason, however, why this vision may not have been given after he had already received other revelations from God. That the prophet was able to keep himself so far in the background during so long and so statesmanlike a ministry is an added testimony to the divine origin of his messages.

Unity of the Book.—Two major divisions are commonly recognized, chapters 1 to 39 and 40 to 66. These divisions are made upon the basis of the general character of the contents. The earlier portion has to do with moral and political conditions in the nation of Israel and in the surrounding nations that had dealings with her. The later portion has largely to do with eschatology and with the completion of Redemption. However, these distinctions do not apply with any measure of exclusiveness, for chapters 24 to 27 are called the Little Apocalypse of Isaiah, and chapters 11 and 35 are clearly millennial pictures.

The critical question as to the authorship of these two parts has been discussed with great ability and spirit by liberal and conservative critics. A Deutero Isaiah and even a Trito Isaiah have been posited. The question hinges primarily on the possibility of predictive prophecy. According to the words of Delitsch, " If we only allow that the prophet was a prophet, it is of no essential consequence to what age he belonged." Assertions made with confidence to sustain the Two-Isaiah theory, when put under scientific examination by those competent for the task, have been found to be unconvincing. Those who believe that the messages of Isaiah have primarily a divine origin will continue to regard the book as a unity. Those who believe in the human origin of the book will insist that the parts that have had fulfilment were penned after the events recorded.

Contents of the Book.—The first chapter opens with a most solemn call to attention, Hear, O heavens, and give ear, O earth, for the Lord hath spoken. God's people, more foolish than the ox and the ass, have forsaken the Lord and have provoked to anger the Holy One of Israel. This last appellation, Holy One of Israel, is one which occurs twenty-six times in this book and only eight times in the rest of the O. T. This holy God is weary of the sin and hypocrisy of His people and now calls upon them to reason with Him and be restored to favour and prosperity.

Chapter 2 is regarded as a summary of the entire book. It is apocalyptic in content and its fulfilment is to be in the last days. The loftiness of man will then be humbled and the Lord alone exalted.

Chapter 3 depicts the degradation of Jerusalem and the wantonness of her people.

Chapter 4 indicates something of the method by which glory is to be restored to Zion. It is parallel with Zech. 14 : 6, 7 and Isa. 24 : 23.

Chapter 5 is the Vineyard song and pictures the Lord's people as bringing forth poisonous grapes. Therefore this vineyard is to be desolated.

Chapter 6 gives us Isaiah's great vision of God (1-4), of self and others (5), his cleansing and commissioning to a difficult work (6-13).

Chapters 7 and 8 record Isaiah's reassurance to Ahaz in the face of invasion by Rezin of Syria and Pekah of Israel. Judah will be safe for, Immanuel : God is with us!

Chapter 9 announces the Messiah, Wonderful, Counsellor, Mighty God, Everlasting Father, Prince of Peace.

Chapter 10 forecasts God's punishment of Israel's corruption by the hand of the Assyrian and then the breaking of the rod of correction.

Chapter 11 presents the rod from the stock of Jesse upon whom is to rest the spirit of wisdom, understanding, counsel, might, knowledge and fear of the Lord. He is to bring about the blessings of the kingdom in a renewed earth with Ephraim and Judah united and the earth filled with the knowledge of the Lord.

Chapter 12 is the song that will be sung by the restored people in the day of their great gladness.

Chapters 13 to 23 contain the doom songs of Babylon, Moab, Damascus, Egypt, Dumah, Arabia, Tyre and Zidon.

Chapters 24 to 27 are called the Little Apocalypse of Isaiah and contain much of the most specific description of the coming glory when the kingdom of Heaven has been established on earth. " He hath swallowed up death forever." " Lo, this is our God; we have waited for him, and he will save us : this is Jehovah." Ch. 25 : 8, 9.

Chapters 28, 29, 30, 31 contain five woes to the sinners of Israel and Judah who have turned from God to idols or to surrounding nations for help.

Chapter 32 represents a King reigning in righteousness, now that judgment on Jerusalem has been finished.

Chapter 33 presents God's judgment on Sennacherib and the future glory of Zion.

Chapter 34 details the judgment upon Edom.

Chapter 35 is a song of the Kingdom.

Chapters 36–39 relate Sennacherib's invasion, Hezekiah's prayer and its answer, Hezekiah's illness and recovery and the ill-considered display of his treasures to the delegation from Babylon. This closes the first portion of the book.

Chapters 40–66 comprise the second portion of the book. Summarized in a phrase, they appear as follows : 40, Comfort ye my people; 41, Fear not for I will——; 42, The isles shall wait for his law; 43, Fear not, I have redeemed thee; 44, Jehovah contrasted with idols; 45, Prophecy concerning Cyrus; 46, Idolaters carry their idols; Jehovah carries Israel; 47, Judgment on Babylon; 48, No peace to the wicked; 49, A light to the Gentiles; 50, Is my hand shortened; 51, Hearken, awake, stand up; 52, Awake, arise, sing, be clean; 53, The man of sorrows; 54, Sing, O barren; 55, Ho, every one that thirsteth; 56, Yet will I gather others to him; 57, Wicked are like the troubled sea; 58, The fast that God approves; 59, The Lord's hand is not shortened; 60, Zion's coming glory; 61, Beauty for ashes; 62, Pray for Jerusalem; 63, I have trodden the winepress alone; 64, Oh that thou wouldest rend the heavens; 65, The new heavens and the new earth; 66, Ye shall be comforted in Jerusalem.

Iscah (ĭs'-cäh) [looking out], Gen. 11 : 29.

Iscariot (ĭs-cär'-ĭ-ŏt) [a man of Kerioth], Matt. 10 : 4.

Ishbah (ĭsh'-băh), 1 Chr. 4 : 17.

Ishbi-benob (ĭsh'-bĭ-bē'-nŏb) [whose dwelling is in Nob], 2 Sam. 21 : 16.

Ish-bosheth (ĭsh-bŏsh'-ĕth) [a man of shame] (i.e., of Baal), Saul's son, called also **Eshbaal**, 2 Sam. 2 : 8; 3 : 7; 4 : 5.

Ishiah (ĭsh-ī'-äh), 1 Chr. 7 : 3.

Ishijah (ĭsh-ī'-jäh), Ezra 10 : 31.

Ishmael (ĭsh'-mā-ĕl) [God hears], son of Abraham, Gen. 16 : 15; 17 : 20; 21 : 17; 25 : 17.

his descendants, Gen. 25 : 12; 1 Chr. 1 : 29.

country of the descendants of Ishmael.

son of Nethaniah, slays Gedaliah, Jer. 40 : 14; 41.

high priest. See **Chronology, New Testament.**

Ishmaelites (ĭsh'-mā-ĕl-ītes), descendants of Ishmael, cf. 1 Chr. 1 : 29-31.

Ishmaiah (ĭsh-mā'-äh) [heard by Jehovah], 1 Chr. 27 : 19.

Ishmerai (ĭsh'-mĕ-rāi), a Benjamite, 1 Chr. 8 : 18.

Ishod (ī'-shŏd), 1 Chr. 7 : 18.

Ishpan (ĭsh'-păn), 1 Chr. 8 : 22.

Ish-tob (ĭsh'-tŏb) [man of Tob], 2 Sam. 10 : 6, 8.

Ishuah (ĭsh'-ū-äh) [likeness], Gen. 46 : 17.

Ishuai (ĭsh'-ū-âi), 1 Chr. 7 : 30.

Ishui (ĭsh'-ū-ī), 1 Sam. 14 : 49.

Island, Acts 27 : 26; 28 : 7; Rev. 6 : 14; 16 : 20.

Isles of the Gentiles, Asia Minor and Europe so named, Gen. 10 : 5; Isa. 49 : 1; 66 : 19.

Ismachiah (ĭs-mă-kī'-äh), 2 Chr. 31 : 13.

Ismaiah (ĭs-mă-ī'-äh) [heard by Jah], 1 Chr. 12 : 4.

Ispah (ĭs'-păh), 1 Chr. 8 : 16.

Israel (ĭs'-rä-ĕl) [God fights], Jacob so called, Gen. 32 : 28; 35 : 10.

kingdom of the ten tribes, 1 Ki. 11 : 38.

Israelites, their bondage in Egypt, Ex. 1–12.

the first passover instituted, Ex. 12.

their departure from Egypt, Ex. 12 : 31.

pass through the Red Sea, Ex. 14.

miraculously fed, Ex. 15 : 23; 16; 17 : 1; Num. 11 : 20.

God's covenant with, Ex. 19; 20; Deut. 29; 30.

their idolatry, Ex. 32.

their rebellious conduct, Deut. 1; 2; 9.

enter and divide Canaan under Joshua, Josh. 12–19.

governed by Judges, Judg. 2; and by kings, 1 Sam. 10; 2 Sam.; 1 and 2 Ki.; 1 and 2 Chr.

their captivity in Assyria, 2 Ki. 17; in Babylon, 2 Ki. 25; 2 Chr. 36; Jer. 39; 52.

their return, Ezra; Neh.; Hag.; Zech. See 2 Ki. 17; Ezra 9; Neh. 9; Ps. 78; 105; 106; Ezek. 20; 22; 23; Acts 7 : 39; 1 Cor. 10 : 1-6. See Chronology, Old Testament.

Issachar (ĭs-ʹsă-chär) [he brings pay, or recompense], son of Jacob, Gen. 30 : 18; 35 : 23.

descendants of, Gen. 46 : 13; Judg. 5 : 15; 1 Chr. 7 : 1; Num. 26 : 23-25.

allotment of, Josh. 19 : 17. See Gen. 49 : 14; Num. 1 : 8; 26 : 23; Deut. 33 : 18; Ezek. 48 : 33; Rev. 7 : 7.

Issue, Gen. 48 : 6; Matt. 9 : 20.

Issued, Josh. 8 : 22; Ezek. 47 : 1, 12; Dan. 7 : 10; Rev. 9 : 17, 18.

Issues, Ps. 68 : 20, to God belong the i. from death.

Prov. 4 : 23, out of heart are i. of life.

Italian (ĭ-tăl-ʹĭ-ăn), Acts 10 : 1.

Itch, Deut. 28 : 27.

Itching, 2 Tim. 4 : 3.

Ithamar (ĭth-ʹă-mär) [island of the palm tree], son of Aaron, Ex. 6 : 23; Lev. 10 : 6.

his charge, Num. 4 : 28.

Ithiel (ĭ'thĭ ĕl), R.V., Prov. 30 : 1.

Ithmah (ĭth-ʹmăh), 1 Chr. 11 : 46.

Ithnan (ĭth-ʹnăn) [strong], Josh. 15 : 23.

Ithra (ĭth-ʹră), 2 Sam. 17 : 25.

Ithran (ĭth-ʹrăn), Gen. 36 : 26.

Ithream (ĭth-ʹrē-ăm) [overflowing of the people], 2 Sam. 3 : 5.

Ithrite (ĭth-ʹrīte), 1 Chr. 11 : 40.

Its, Lev. 25 : 5.

Itself, Prov. 23 : 31, moveth i. aright. Matt. 12 : 25, house divided against i. 1 Cor. 13 : 4, vaunteth not i. 13 : 5, not behave i. unseemly. 3 John 12, of the truth i.

Ivory, the tusk or canine tooth of the elephant, and greatly valued from the earliest times.

beds, Amos 6 : 4.

horns, Ezek. 27 : 15.

imported from Ophir, 1 Ki. 10 : 22.

palaces, 1 Ki. 22 : 39; Ps. 45 : 8; Amos 3 : 15.

Solomon's throne of, 1 Ki. 10 : 18-20.

tower of, Song of Sol. 7 : 4.

See Rev. 18 : 12.

Iyyar, or Zif, April-May. See Months.

Izehar (ĭ-zĕ-här) [oil], Num. 3 : 19.

Izharites (ĭz-här-ʹītes), 1 Chr. 24 : 22.

Izrahiah (ĭz-ră-hī-ʹăh), 1 Chr. 7 : 3.

Izrahite (ĭz-ʹră-hīte), 1 Chr. 27 : 8.

Izri (ĭz-ʹrī), a descendant of Jezer, 1 Chr. 25 : 11.

J

Jaakan (jā-ʹă-kăn), Deut. 10 : 6.

Jaakobah (jā-ă-kō-ʹbăh) [heel-catcher], 1 Chr. 4 : 36.

Jaala (jā-ʹă-lă), Neh. 7 : 58.

Jaalah (jā-ʹă-lăh), Ezra 2 : 56.

Jaalam (jā-ʹă-lăm) [hidden], Gen. 36 : 5; 1 Chr. 1 : 25.

Jaanai (jā-ʹă-nâi) [mourner], 1 Chr. 5 : 12.

Jaare-oregim (jā-ʹă-rĕ-ôr-ʹĕ-gĭm), 2 Sam. 21 : 19.

Jaasau (jā-ʹă-saû) [fabricator], Ezra 10 : 37.

Jaasiel (jā-ăs-ʹĭ-ĕl) [made by God], 1 Chr. 27 : 21.

Jaazaniah (jā-ăz-ă-nī-ʹăh) [Jah will hear], 2 Ki. 25; 23; Jer. 35 : 3; Ezek. 8 : 11.

Jaazer (jā-ă-ʹzĕr) [he helps], Num. 21 : 32.

Jaaziah (jā-ă-zī-ʹăh) [Jehovah comforts], 1 Chr. 24 : 26, 27.

Jaaziel (jā-ă-ʹzĭ-ĕl) [comforted by God], 1 Chr. 15 : 18.

Jabal (jā-ʹbăl) [stream], Gen. 4 : 20.

River Jabbok.

Jabbok (jăb-ʹbọk) [pouring out], river on east side of Jordan, Gen. 32 : 22; Deut. 2 : 37. Jabesh (jā-ʹbĕsh) [dry], 1 Sam. 11 : 1; 2 Ki. 15 . 10.

Jabesh-gilead (jā-ʹbĕsh-gĭl-ʹĕ-ăd) [Jabesh of Gilead], inhabitants of, slain, Judg. 21; threatened by Ammonites, 1 Sam. 11 : 1; delivered by Saul, 1 Sam. 31 : 11.

Jabin (jā-ʹbĭn) [he understands], king of Hazor, conquered by Joshua, Josh. 11; another, subdued by Barak, Judg. 4 : 10-17.

Jabneel (jăb-ʹnéel) [God causes to build], Josh. 15 : 11; Josh. 19 : 33.

Jabneh (jăb-ʹnēh) [building], city of Dan, 2 Chr. 26 : 6.

Jachan (jā-ʹchăn) [mourner], 1 Chr. 5 : 13.

Jachin (jā-ʹchĭn) [he strengthens], one of the pillars of the temple, 1 Ki. 7 : 21; 2 Chr. 3 : 17.

Jacinth. The breastplates of the visionary horsemen of Rev. 9 : 17 are compared to jacinth, cf. Rev. 21 : 20. (R.V. hyacinth.) This designates the modern sapphire, but whether the true sapphire was known in O.T. times we cannot say. The modern hyacinth was known as the ligure. See Precious Stones.

Jackal [Heb. shua'al]. See **Fox**. In Isa. 13 : 22 and 34 : 13, this word is in the Revised Version translated jackal. See **Dragon** and **Leviathan**.

Jacob (jā-cǫb) [he supplants], his birth, Gen. 25 : 26.
birthright, Gen. 25 : 33.
obtains the blessing, Gen. 27 : 27.
sent to Padan-aram, Gen. 27 : 43; 28 : 2.
his vision and vow, Gen. 28 : 20.
marriages, Gen. 29.
his sons, Gen. 29 : 31; 30.
dealings with Laban, Gen. 31.
his vision of God's host, Gen. 32 : 1.
his prayer, Gen. 32 : 9.
wrestles with an angel, Gen. 32 : 24; Hos. 12 : 4.
reconciled with Esau, Gen. 33.
builds an altar, Gen. 35 : 1.
his grief for Joseph and Benjamin, Gen. 37; 42 : 38; 43.
goes down to Egypt, Gen. 46.
brought before Pharaoh, Gen. 47 : 7.
blesses his sons, Gen. 48; 49.
his death and burial, Gen. 49 : 33; 50.
See Ps. 105 : 23; Mal. 1 : 2; Rom. 9 : 10; Heb. 11 : 21.

Jacob's well, a fountain near Shechem, John 4 : 6. Once of great depth (John 4 : 11), it has been filled up with rubbish, and to-day it is perhaps some seventy-five feet deep.

Jada (jā-dǎ) [he knoweth], 1 Chr. 2 : 28.

Jaddua (jăd-dū-ǎ) [much-knowing], Neh. 10 : 21.

Jadon (jā-dŏn) [he that judgeth], Neh. 3 : 7.

Jael (jā-ĕl) [goat, climber], Judg. 4 : 17.

Jagur (jā-gúr) [place of sojourn], Josh. 15 : 21.

Jah, contracted form of " Jehovah." The form appears in poetry (Ex. 15 : 2; Ps. 68 : 4), in proper names, and in Hallelujah.

Jahath (jā-hǎth) [union], 1 Chr. 23 : 10; 24 : 22.

Jahaz (jā-hǎz) [trodden down], **Jahaza, Jahazah** (jā-hā-zǎh), Num. 21 : 23; Josh. 13 : 18; 21 : 36; Jer. 48 : 21.

Jahaziah (jā-hā-zī-ǎh) [Jehovah seeth], Ezra 10 : 15.

Jahaziel (jā-hā-zī-ĕl) [God seeth], comforts Jehoshaphat, 2 Chr. 20 : 14; Ezra 8 : 5.

Jahdai (jäh-dā-ī) [grasper], 1 Chr. 2 : 47.

Jahdiel (jäh-dī-ĕl), 1 Chr. 5 : 24.

Jahdo (jäh-dō), 1 Chr. 5 : 14.

Jahleel (jäh-lēĕl), **Jahleelites**, Num. 26 : 26.

Jahmai (jäh-mā-ī), 1 Chr. 7 : 2.

Jahzah (jäh-zäh), 1 Chr. 6 : 78.

Jahzeel (jäh-zēĕl) [allotted by God], **Jahze-elites**, Gen. 46 : 24; Num. 26 : 48.

Jahzerah (jäh-zĕ-räh) [returner], 1 Chr. 9 : 12.

Jahziel (jäh-zī-ĕl), 1 Chr. 7 : 13.

Jailor, Acts 16 : 23.

Jair (jā-ĭr) [he enlightens], Gileadite judge, Judg. 10 : 3; others, Num. 32 : 41; 1 Chr. 2 : 22; 20 : 5; Esther 2 : 5.

Jairus (jā-ĭ-rŭs) **daughter of**, raised, Matt. 9 : 18; Mark 5 : 22; Luke 8 : 41.

Jambres (jăm-brēŝ), corruption of " Mambres," or " Mamre," an Egyptian magician, 2 Tim. 3 : 8. The name meant " to oppose," and, along with Jannes (which see) is quoted by Numeninus (second century

A.D.) and Eusebius, and by the fourth century " Gospel of Nicodemus." Jews were fond of the names. Some described them as sons of Balaam, others assert that they were drowned in the Red Sea; others say they were killed for inciting Aaron to build the Golden Calf.

James (jām(e)ŝ), apostle, son of Zebedee, called Matt. 4 : 21; Mark 1 : 19; Luke 5 : 10.
ordained one of the Twelve, Matt. 10 : 2; Mark 3 : 14; Luke 6 : 13.
present at Christ's transfiguration, Matt. 17 : 1; Mark 9 : 2; Luke 9 : 28.
present at the passion, Matt. 26 : 36; Mark 14 : 33.
slain by Herod, Acts 12 : 2.
(apostle), son of Alpheus, Matt. 10 : 3; Mark 3 : 18; 6 : 3; Luke 6 : 15; Acts 1 : 13; 12 : 17.
his decision concerning circumcision, etc., Acts 15 : 13-29.
See Acts 21 : 18; 1 Cor. 15 : 7; Gal. 1 : 19; 2 : 9.

James, Epistle of.
Authorship and Date.—Many have argued against the tradition that our Lord's brother wrote this Epistle, for two reasons : (1) Why does so conspicuous a Christian, writing for believers, mention Jesus' name only twice, and pass Him by in favour of Job as the supreme example of endurance (Jas. 5 : 11). (2) Why did this, if really James's, remain outside the Canon until almost the very last stages of its growth ? For these reasons a late date is assigned.
With regard to the first objection, James was writing for unconverted Jews (cf. 4 : 1-4; 5 : 1-6) who looked to him as the only Christian leader they could regard. Hence he does not mention Jesus' name, since that would keep them from reading. Instead, he records many of Christ's sayings, in the hope that these would by their beauty prepare a place for their Author's being loved. When, however, James was martyred as a Christian, veneration turned into fanatical hatred, and his Jewish following melted away. Neither would the Christians regard too favourably a work intended for narrow Judaistic circles. Therefore it was some time before the rights of the Epistle to enter the Canon were recognised.
We may urge, then, that the letter was written before A.D. 62 or 63, when James was martyred.
Contents.—Chap. 1 : 1, Address. Chap. 1 : 2-12, Reason and reward of man's trial. Chap. 1 : 12-18, Trial in relation to God. Chaps. 1 : 19-2 : 26, Deeds are the results and proof of religion. Chap. 3 : 1-18, The bridling of the tongue, etc. Chaps. 4 : 1-5 : 12, Counsel against worldliness, faultfinding, presumption, injustice, impatience, and swearing. Chap. 5 : 13-20, Conclusion, advice on worship, sickness, prayer, and winning back the lapsed.

James, Protevangelium of, apocryphal gospel. See **Apocrypha, New Testament.**

Jamin (jā-mĭn), Num. 26 : 12; 1 Chr. 4 : 24.

Jaminites (jā-mĭn-ītes), Num. 26 : 12.

Jamlech (jăm-lĕch) [may cause to reign], 1 Chr. 4 : 34.

Jamnia (jăm-nĭ-ă), modern town Yebna.

Jangling, 1 Tim. 1 : 6.

Janna (jăn-nă), corruption of " Jannai " or " John," Luke 3 : 24.

Jannes (jăn-nēs), magician of Egypt, 2 Tim. 3 : 8; (Ex. 7 : 11). The name is probably a corruption of Johannes or John. It was traditional as a magician's name before the Christian era, being used by Pliny the Elder (A.D. 23–79). See Jambres.

Japheth (jā-phĕth) [he enlarges], son of Noah, blessed, Gen. 9 : 27.

descendants, Gen. 10 : 1; 1 Chr. 1 : 5.

Japhia (jă-phī-ă) [shining], a city of Zebulon, Josh. 19 : 12.

son of David, 2 Sam. 5 : 15.

king of Lachish, Josh. 10 : 3.

Japhlet (jăph-lĕt), 1 Chr. 7 : 32.

Japhleti (jăph-lē-tī), Josh. 16 : 3.

Japho (jā-phō) [beauty], a seaport town, now Joppa, Josh. 19 : 46.

Jarah (jăr-ăh), 1 Chr. 9 : 42.

Jareb (jăr-ĕb) [contentious], Hos. 5 : 13; 10 : 6.

Jared (jăr-ĕd) [descent], Gen. 5 : 15; Luke 3 : 37.

Jaresiah (jăr-ĕ-sī-ăh), 1 Chr. 8 : 27.

Jarha (jär-hă), 1 Chr. 2 : 34.

Jarib (jăr-ĭb) [adversary], 1 Chr. 4 : 24.

Jarmuth (jär-mûth) [height], city of Judah now called Yarmuk, Josh. 10 : 5; 21 : 29.

Jaroah (jă-rō-ăh), 1 Chr. 5 : 14.

Jashen (jăsh-ĕn) [sleeping], 2 Sam. 23 : 32.

Jasher (jăsh-ĕr), properly Jashar (jā-shăr) [upright], ancient book of national songs, Josh. 10 : 13; 2 Sam. 1 : 18.

Jashobeam (jă-shŏb-ĕ-ăm) [to whom the people turn], one of David's warriors, 1 Chr. 11 : 11; 27 : 2.

Jashub (jăsh-ŭb) [returner], 1 Chr. 7 : 1.

Jashubites (jăsh-ū-bītes), Num. 26 : 24.

Jashubi–lehem (jă-shu-bī-lĕ-hĕm), 1 Chr. 4 : 22.

Jasiel (jăs-ĭ-ĕl), 1 Chr. 11 : 47.

Jason (jāson), Acts 17 : 5, etc.

Jasper, jade (?). The modern jasper is a completely opaque form of various shades of chalcedony which was usually regarded as a semi-transparent silica. This, at least, we would infer from Rev. 21 : 11, where reference is made to jasper " clear as crystal." We may take it to mean a fine variety of jade or nephrite.

Ex. 28 : 20; Ezek. 28 : 13; Rev. 4 : 3; 21 : 18 f.

Javan (jā-văn), son of Japheth, Gen. 10 : 2. Greece, Isa. 66 : 19; Ezek. 27 : 13, 19.

Javelin, Num. 25 : 7; 1 Sam. 18 : 10; 19 : 10.

Jaw, Judg. 15 : 19; Hos. 11 : 4.

Jawbone, of an ass, Samson uses, Judg. 15 : 15, 16, 17.

Jawteeth, Prov. 30 : 14.

Jealous, Ex. 34 : 14; Deut. 4 : 24; 5 : 9; 6 : 15; Josh. 24 : 19, a j. God.

1 Ki. 19 : 10, 14, I have been j. for the Lord. Ezek. 39 : 25, be j. for my holy name.

Joel, 2 : 18, then will the Lord be j.

Nah. 1 : 2, God is j.

2 Cor. 11 : 2, I am j. over you.

Jealousy, offering of, Num. 5 : 11-31. A wife, suspected of unfaithfulness, had to demonstrate her innocence by drinking the " Water of Bitterness " (Num. 5 : 11-31).

Idolatry is adultery; Jehovah is Israel's husband; hence the idea of the jealous God who desires a sure relation between Himself and His people.

Deut. 32 : 16; 1 Ki. 14 : 22, they provoked him to j.

Ps. 79 : 5, shall thy j. burn like fire ?

Prov. 6 : 34, j. is the rage of a man.

Song of Sol. 8 : 6, j. is cruel as the grave.

Isa. 42 : 13, stir up j. like man of war.

Ezek. 36 : 5, in fire of j. have I spoken.

1 Cor. 10 : 22, do we provoke the Lord to j. ?

Jearim (jē-ă-rīm) [forests], Josh. 15 : 10.

Jeaterai (jē-ăt-ĕ-raī), 1 Chr. 6 : 21.

Jeba (jē-bă), a village of Nablus.

Jebel–jermuk (jĕb-ĕl-jĕr-mŭk), name of a mountain.

Jeberechiah (jĕ-bĕr-ĕ-chī-ăh) [Jehovah will bless], Isa. 8 : 2.

Jebus (jē-bŭs) [trodden under], the ancient name of Jerusalem, Judg. 19 : 10.

Jebusi (jĕb-ū-sī), Josh. 18 : 16, 28. See Jebus.

Jebusites (jĕb-ū-sītes), Gen. 15 : 21; Num. 13 : 29; Josh. 15 : 63; Judg. 1 : 21; 19 : 11; 2 Sam. 5 : 8. See Palestine, Ancient Inhabitants.

Jeconiah (jĕc-ŏ-nī-ăh), contracted form, Coniah, Jer. 27 : 20. See Jehoiachin, 2 Chr. 36 : 8.

Jedaiah (jĕ-dā-ăh) [invoker of Jehovah], Neh. 3 : 10.

priest, 1 Chr. 9 : 10; 24 : 7.

a Simeonite, 1 Chr. 4 : 37.

Jediael (jĕd-ĭ-ā-ĕl), 1 Chr. 7 : 11.

Jedidah (je-dī-dăh) [beloved], 2 Ki. 22 : 1.

Jedidiah (jĕd-ĭ-dī-ăh) [beloved of Jehovah], 2 Sam. 12 : 25.

Jeduthun (jĕ-dū-thŭn) [appointed for praise], 1 Chr. 16 : 42.

Jeezer (jē-ē-zĕr), Num. 26 : 30.

Jeezerites (jē-ē-zĕr-ites), Num. 26 : 30.

Jegar–sahadutha (jē-găr-să-hă-dū-thă) [heap of witness], Gen. 31 : 47.

Jehaleleel (jĕ-hăl-ĕ-lēĕl), 1 Chr. 4 : 16.

Jehdeiah (jĕh-dĕl-ăh), 1 Chr. 24 : 20.

Jehezekel (jĕ-hĕz-ĕk-ĕl), 1 Chr. 24 : 16.

Jehiah (jĕ-hī-ăh) [Jehovah liveth], 1 Chr. 15 : 24.

Jehiel (jĕ-hī-ĕl), 1 Chr. 15 : 18; 27 : 32.

Jehieli (jĕ-hē-ĕ-lī), 1 Chr. 26 : 21.

Jehizkiah (jĕ-hĭz-kī-ăh) [Jehovah strengthens], 2 Chr. 28 : 12.

Jehoadah (jĕ-hō-ă-dăh), 1 Chr. 8 : 36.

Jehoaddan (jĕ-hō-ăd-dăn) [Jehovah his ornament], 2 Ki. 14 : 2; 2 Chr. 25 : 1.

Jehoahaz (jĕ-hō-ă-hăz) [Jehovah holdeth], after Jehu, was for seventeen years king of Israel, 2 Ki. 10 : 35; 13 : 4.

(Shallum, A.V., margin), king of Judah, 2 Ki. 23 : 31; 2 Chr. 36 : 1.

Jehoiachin (jĕ-hŏī-ă-chĭn) [Jehovah strengthens], 2 Ki. 24 : 6.

Jehoiada (jĕ-hŏī-ă-dăh) [Jehovah knoweth], high priest, slays Athaliah, and restores Jehoash, 2 Ki. 11 : 4; 2 Chr. 23.

repairs the temple, 2 Ki. 12 : 7; 2 Chr. 24 : 6.

abolishes idolatry, 2 Chr. 23 : 16.

Jehoiakim (jĕ-hŏĭ-ă-kĭm [Jehovah will raise], 2 Ki. 23 : 36; 24 : 1; 2 Chr. 36 : 4; Dan. 1 : 2.

See Jer. 22 : 18. Placed on the throne by Pharaoh Necho, his reign of eleven years was unpopular and evil. The abuses Josiah had tried to abolish came back with greater strength. Extravagant and impious, he persecuted Jeremiah's party (Jer. 22 : 13-19; 36 : 1-26; 26 : 20-24). He died while a Babylonian army was on the march to depose him for his loyalty to Egypt.

Jehoiarib (jĕ-hŏĭ-ă-rĭb) [Jehovah will plead], 1 Chr. 9 : 10.

Jehonadab (jĕ-hŏn-ă-dăb) [Jehovah impels], 2 Sam. 13 : 3; Jer. 35 : 6. See **Jonadab.**

Jehonathan (jĕ-hŏn-ă-thăn) [whom Jehovah gave], 1 Chr. 27 : 25; 2 Chr. 17 : 8.

Jehoram (jĕ-hôr-ăm) [Jehovah is exalted], king of Judah, 1 Ki. 22 : 50; 2 Ki. 8 : 16.

his cruelty and death, 2 Chr. 21 : 4, 18.

(Joram), king of Israel, son of Ahab, 2 Ki. 1 : 17; 3 : 1.

his evil reign, 2 Ki. 3 : 2.

slain by Jehu, 2 Ki. 9 : 24.

Jehoshabeath (jĕ-hŏ-shăb-ĕ-ăth), 2 Chr. 22 : 11.

Jehoshaphat (jĕ-hŏsh-ă-phăt) [Jehovah judges], king of Judah, 1 Ki. 15 : 24; 2 Chr. 17.

his death, 1 Ki. 22 : 50; 2 Chr. 21 : 1.

valley of, Joel 3 : 2.

Jehosheba (jĕ-hŏsh-ĕ-bă), 2 Ki. 11 : 2.

Jehoshua (jĕ-hŏsh-ū-ă), 1 Chr. 7 : 27.

Jehovah (properly Jahweh = Yahweh), the name of God. It was already in existence in pre-Mosaic times (Gen. 4 : 26) and was already embedded in names (e.g., "Joche-bed," the name of Moses' mother, Ex. 6 : 20). Originally it may have meant " to blow " or " to breathe " or " to fall " or " to be " or even " to cause to be," i.e., Creator. From Moses' time onwards there is no doubt as to its meaning (cf. Ex. 3 : 10 ff.), for it was derived from the imperfect tense of the verb " to be." Hence it means " I am " or " I will be." That is, it denotes active and self-manifesting existence. Jehovah denotes the friendly personal God who communes with man as compared with His nature as creator and governor of the universe when He is known as Elohim. cf. Num. 16 : 22; John 4 : 24.

The form Jehovah dates only from A.D. 1518. The name Jahweh was so sacred that, in later Jewish times, it was not pronounced at all, owing to an overmeticulous anxiety to keep the Third Commandment. In reading it, the name " Adonai " was substituted, and its vowels came to be attached to the consonants " J h w h," to form the hybrid " Jehovah."

Jehovah-jireh (jĕ-hŏ-văh-jĭ-rĕh) [Jehovah sees or provides], Gen. 22 : 14.

Jehovah-nissi (jĕ-hŏ-văh-nĭs-sĭ) [Jehovah my banner], Ex. 17 : 15.

Jehovah-shalom (jĕ-hŏ-văh-shă-lŏm) [Jehovah is peace], Judg. 6 : 24.

Jehovah-shammah (jĕ-hŏ-văh-shăm-măh) [Jehovah is there], Ezek. 48 : 35, margin.

Jehovah-tsidkenu (jĕ-hŏ-văh-tsĭd-kĕ-nū) [Jehovah our righteousness], Jer. 23 : 6, margin.

Jehozabad (jĕ-hŏ-ză-băd) [Jehovah bestowed], 1 Chr. 26 : 4.

Jehozadak (jĕ-hŏ-ză-dăk) [Jehovah is righteous], 1 Chr. 6 : 15.

Jehu (jĕ-hū) [Jehovah is he], prophesies against Baasha, 1 Ki. 16 : 1.

rebukes Jehoshaphat, 2 Chr. 19 : 2; 20 : 34.

son of Nimshi, to be anointed king of Israel, 1 Ki. 19 : 16; 2 Ki. 9 : 2.

his reign, 2 Ki. 10. It was certain that Ahab's house must fall. The skill of Jehu lay in making the most important men in the kingdom the partners of his crime. See Chronology, Old Testament.

Jehubbah (jĕ-hŭb-băh), 1 Chr. 7 : 34.

Jehucal (jĕ-hū-căl) [able], Jer. 37 : 3.

Jehud (jĕ-hŭd), Josh. 19 : 45.

Jehudi (jĕ-hū-dĭ) [a Jew], Jer. 36 : 14, 21.

Jehudijah (jĕ-hū-dĭ-jăh) [Jewess], 1 Chr. 4 : 18.

Jehush (jĕ-hŭsh), 1 Chr. 8 : 39.

Jeil (jĕ-ĭ-ĕl), 1 Chr. 16 : 5; 2 Chr. 20 : 14.

Jekabzeel (jĕ-kăb-zĕĕl) [God assembleth], Neh. 11 : 25.

Jekameam (jĕ-kăm-ĕ-ăm) [may raise a people], 1 Chr. 23 : 19; 24 : 22.

Jekamiah (jĕk-ă-mĭ-ăh) [may Jehovah raise up], 1 Chr. 2 : 41.

Jekuthiel (jĕ-kū-thĭ-ĕl), 1 Chr. 4 : 18.

Jemima (jĕ-mĭ-mă) [dove], Job 42 : 14.

Jemuel (jĕ-mū-ĕl), Gen. 46 : 10.

Jenin, same as **Engannim.**

Jeoparded, Judg. 5 : 18.

Jeopardy, 1 Chr. 11 : 19, have put their lives in j.

Luke 8 : 23, and were in j.

1 Cor. 15 : 30, stand in j. every hour.

Jephthah (jĕph-thăh) or **Jephthæ** [God opens], a judge. The story of Jephthah's vow is a mixture of two ancient beliefs and shows that Israel's religion was not wholly different from that of her neighbours. The first belief was that a human being must be sacrificed in times of special stress. The second was the " Weeping for Tammuz " (i.e., Adonis, cf. Ezek. 8 : 14). Tammuz was a beautiful youth who was killed by a boar, symbolising the conquest over Summer of Winter. The rite of celebrating the death and resurrection of vegetation was celebrated annually, the women folk's wailing for Tammuz (Judg. 11 : 40) giving place on the second day to joy at the re-appearance of life.

his covenant with the Gileadites, Judg. 11 : 4-11.

his message to the Ammonites, Judg. 11 : 14.

his rash vow, Judg. 11 : 30, 34.

chastises the Ephraimites, Judg. 12.

his faith, Heb. 11 : 32.

Jephunneh (jĕ-phŭn-nĕh) [prepared for the way], Num. 13 : 6.

Jerach, a city on the coast of Hazarmaveth.

Jerah (jĕ-răh) [the moon], 1 Chr. 1 : 20.

Jerahmeel (jĕ-răh-mĕĕl) [God have mercy], 1 Chr. 2 : 9.

Jered (jĕ-rĕd), 1 Chr. 1 : 2.

Jeremai (jĕr-ĕ-māⁱ), Ezra 10 : 33.
Jeremiah (jĕr-ĕ-mīⁱăh) [Jehovah foundeth],
prophet, his call and visions, Jer. 1.
his mission, Jer. 1 : 17; 7.
his complaint, Jer. 20 : 14.
his message to Zedekiah, Jer. 21 : 3; 34 : 1.
foretells the seventy years' captivity, Jer. 25.
apprehended, but delivered by Ahikam,
Jer. 26.
denounces Hananiah, Jer. 28 : 5.
his letter to the captives in Babylon, Jer. 29.
praying, is comforted, Jer. 32 : 16; 33.
writes a roll of a book, Jer. 36 : 4; Baruch
reads it, Jer. 36 : 8.
imprisoned by Zedekiah, Jer. 32; 37; 38.
released by Ebed-melech, Jer. 38 : 7.
carried into Egypt, Jer. 43 : 6, 7.
various predictions, Jer. 46–51; 51 : 59.
See Matt. 2 : 17; 16 : 14; 27 : 9.
Jeremiah, Book of.
Authorship.—In 626 B.C. Jeremiah, the
young and inexperienced son of Hilkiah
(1 : 6; cf. 1 : 2; 25 : 3) received the call to
become a prophet of God. Although he
never entirely forsook his birthplace,
Anathoth, where his father had been a priest
(cf. 11 : 21; 37 : 12), yet his main work
was in the nearby city of Jerusalem. On
the destruction of Jerusalem by Nebuchadrezzar he settled in Mizpah (40 : 6) but
was later carried off to Egypt, where tradition has it that the Jews killed him because
of his prophecies (43 : 6 ff.). The book as
we have it is the result of Jeremiah's dictat-
ing from memory part of his life story to
Baruch the scribe (cf. 36); to Baruch's
filling in of the account as nearly as possible
in the prophet's spirit and words (cf.
36 : 24); to additions over many years in
the interests of homiletics.
Situation.—The Scythians were in Western
Asia; Judah had still twenty years of
vassalage to Nineveh to endure until her
overlord should fall (606 B.C.). The
Reformation of 621 was still in the future,
and that, when it came, was unable to undo
the mischief of the idolatry of King
Manasseh, grandfather of Josiah (cf. 7 : 9).
Josiah's death at Megiddo in 609 B.C. was
a blow to the reforming minority, and
sceptics urged that this was a result of
God's displeasure. After Assyria ceased to
trouble her, Judah became subject to
Egypt, then to Babylon. A succession of
weak kings, faithless priests and superficial
prophets (23 : 9–40; 28; 26; 7 : 21 f.), and
Jeremiah, faced with this situation, in spite
of persecution and false accusation (9),
preached that there was no salvation in
ritual, but only in the circumcised heart
(17 : 9; 4 : 4; 29 : 13). He spiritualised the
conception of religion, and pointed to the
renewal of the Covenant by God. (For
references to the Messianic idea see 23 : 5–8;
30 : 4–11; 33 : 14–26.)
Contents.—(a) Prophecies concerning Judah
and the kingdom of God (chaps. 1–45, but
see (b)). (b) Personal allusions to Jeremiah
(11 : 21; 20 : 1–3; 26; 28; 36–43 : 8).

(c) Nine oracles against foreign nations
(chaps. 46–51). (d) Late addition (after
562 B.C. cf. 52 : 31 ff. with 51 : 64),
namely, Chapter 52 (cf. 2 Ki. 24 : 18–
25 : 30).
Only at intervals can we discern logical
or chronological order in the prophesies as
we have them.
Jeremias (jĕr-ĕ-mīⁱăs), Greek form of "Jeremiah," Matt. 16 : 14.
Jeremy (jĕrⁱĕ-mў), shortened English form of
"Jeremiah," Matt. 2 : 17; 27 : 9.

Jericho.

Jericho (jĕrⁱĭ-chō) [moon city], a royal city of
great antiquity about five miles from the
north end of the Dead Sea.
spies sent there, Josh. 2 : 1.
capture of, Josh. 6 : 20; (Heb. 11 : 30).
rebuilt by Hiel, 1 Ki. 16 : 34.
See Josh. 6 : 26.
Jeriel (jĕrⁱĭ-ĕl), 1 Chr. 7 : 2.
Jerijah (jĕ-rīⁱ-jăh), 1 Chr. 26 : 31.
Jerimoth (jĕrⁱĭ-mŏth) [high places], 1 Chr. 7 : 8;
24 : 30; 2 Chr. 11 : 18.
Jerioth (jĕrⁱĭ-ŏth), 1 Chr. 2 : 18.
Jeroboam (jĕr-ŏ-bōⁱăm) [struggler for the
people], the first king of the northern tribes
after the division of Israel and Judah into
two kingdoms, 937 B.C.; he reigned for
twenty-two years; promoted by Solomon,
1 Ki. 11 : 28.
Ahijah's prophecy to, 1 Ki. 11 · 29.
made king, 1 Ki. 12 : 20; 2 Chr. 10.
his idolatry, 1 Ki. 12 : 28.
his hand withers, 1 Ki. 13 : 4.
judgment denounced upon his house, 1 Ki.
14 : 7.
his death, 1 Ki. 14 : 20.
evil example, 1 Ki. 15 : 34.
Jeroboam II., the grandson of Jehu, 2 Ki.
13 : 13; 14 : 23–29.

Jeroham (jĕ-rō-́hăm) [cherished], 1 Sam. 1 : 1; 1 Chr. 27 : 22; 12 : 7; 2 Chr. 23 : 1.

Jerusalem [foundation, abode of peace].

(*a*) Site.—The chief town of Palestine, Jerusalem is situated 31° 46′ 45″ N. latitude, and 35° 13′ 25″ E. longitude. It stands 2500 feet above sea level on the Judæan mountain-summit. Deep valleys divide and define the elevated plateau on which the city stands.

(*b*) Defining Valleys.—There are two of these: (1) Wady en-Nār or the Biblical Kidron, or the Valley of Jehoshaphat. It begins north of Jerusalem, runs south-east, turns south and deepens quickly, now cutting off the city from the ridge of olives on the east. Traversing the Judæan desert, it opens out west of the Dead Sea. (2) Wady er-Rabābi, identified as the " Valley of the son of Hinnom," begins west of Jerusalem and joins the first about half a mile south of the city. The city thus stands in the junction of the valleys, as though in the fork of a Y.

(*c*) Dividing Valleys.—(1) The Tyropœon (Josephus) begins in the north of the city (between the arms of the Y), and, growing ever deeper, cuts through the city and enters the Wady en-Nār just above the mouth of the Wady er-Rabābi. (2) A smaller valley cutting the above at right angles and running across the city from west to east.

(*d*) Hills.—Thus the city is in four divisions, each built on a hill. North-west is the hill Acra, north-east is Bezetha, and south-west is Zion. In the south-east is Ophel, which is subdivided into Ophel and Moriah (the higher north end). These names are still debatable. The latter was the site of the Temple. (cf. 2 Chr. 3 : 1; Gen. 22 : 2.)

(*e*) Water-supply—was naturally available only from the sporadic activity of a spring in Kidron. Hence, from the earliest times, we find cisterns built to catch and store rain-water, while conduits were used to bring external supplies into the city. The oldest enters the city from the north, and consists of a channel hewn in the rock. From reservoirs beyond Bethlehem a second, " the low-level aqueduct " (attributed to Solomon), brings supplies. In Roman times was built " the high-level aqueduct " (cf. 2 Ki. 20 : 20; 2 Chr. 32 : 30; Isa. 7 : 3; Eccl. 1 : 3). The famous " Well of Job " (Enrogel) lies at the fork where the two defining valleys meet, south of Jerusalem.

king of, slain by Joshua, Josh. 10.

borders of, Josh. 15 : 8.

ark brought there, 2 Sam. 6.

David reigns there, 2 Sam. 5 : 6.

preserved from the pestilence, 2 Sam. 24 : 16.

temple built at, 1 Ki. 5–8; 2 Chr. 2–7.

sufferings from war, 1 Ki. 14 : 25; 2 Ki. 14 : 14; 25; 2 Chr. 12; 25 : 24; 36; Jer. 39; 52.

capture and destruction by Nebuchadrezzar, Jer. 52 : 12-15.

captives return, and Cyrus begins to rebuild the temple, Ezra 1 : 2; 3; continued by Artaxerxes, Neh. 2.

wall rebuilt and dedicated, Neh. 12 : 38.

presentation of Christ at, Luke, 2 : 22.

his public entry into, Matt. 21 : 1; Mark 11 : 7; Luke 19 : 35; John 12 : 14; laments over it, Matt. 23 : 37; Luke 13 : 34; 19 : 41; foretells its destruction, Matt. 24; Mark 13; Luke 13 : 35; 19 : 41; 21.

disciples filled with the Holy Ghost at, Acts 2 : 4.

which is above, Gal. 4 : 26.

the new, Rev. 21 : 2.

Jerusha (jĕ-rū-́shă) [possession], 2 Ki. 15 : 33.

Jesaiah (jĕ-sāi-́äh), i.q. **Isaiah**, 1 Chr. 3 : 21.

Jeshaiah (jĕ-shāi-́äh) [deliverance of Jah], 1 Chr. 26 : 25; Ezra 8 : 7.

Jeshanah (jĕ-shā-́näh), 2 Chr. 13 : 19.

Jesharelah (jĕsh-ă-rē-́läh) [upright toward God], 1 Chr. 25 : 14.

Jeshebeab (jĕ-shĕb-́ĕ-ăb), 1 Chr. 24 : 13.

Jesher (jē-́shĕr) [uprightness], 1 Chr. 2 : 18.

Jeshimon (jĕ-shī-́mọn) [desolation], 1 Sam. 23 : 24.

Jeshishai (jĕ-shĭsh-́āī), 1 Chr. 5 : 14.

Jeshohaiah (jĕsh-ō-hāi-́äh), 1 Chr. 4 : 36.

Jeshua (jĕsh-́ū-ă), Ezra 2 : 36; 2 Chr. 31 : 15; Neh. 7 : 7.

form of " Joshua," Neh. 8 : 17.

Jeshurun (jĕ-shū-́rŭn) [the upright one], a "pet" name for Israel, from the patriotic notion that Israel was the " Jashar-El " or " upright of God " and her people the " upright little people," Deut. 32 : 15; 33 : 5, 26.

Jesse (jĕs-́sē) [Jehovah is], David's father, Ruth 4 : 22.

and his sons sanctified by Samuel, 1 Sam. 16 : 5.

his son David anointed to be king, 1 Sam. 16 : 13.

his posterity, 1 Chr. 2 : 13.

See Isa. 11 : 1.

Jesting, Eph. 5 : 4.

Jesus (jē-́sŭs) (see **Joshua**, **Jeshua**), twice used in the A.V. for " Joshua," Acts 7 : 45; Heb. 4 : 8. The name, of course, was one of those given to our Lord from His supreme office as " Saviour." As such we may almost say that this is " God's Christian name." See further under **Christ, Messiah,** etc.

Jethro (jĕth-́rō) [excellence], Ex. 3 : 1; 18 : 12.

Jewels, Prov. 20 : 15, knowledge a precious j.

Isa. 61 : 10, adorneth herself with j.

Hos. 2 : 13, decked with earrings and j.

Mal. 3 : 17, when I make up my j.

Jewess, Acts 16 : 1; 24 : 24.

Jewish (jēw-́ĭsh), Titus 1 : 14.

Jewry, Dan. 5 : 13; Luke 23 : 5; John 7 : 1.

Jews, derived from " Judah," Israelites first so called, 2 Ki. 16 : 6.

Christ's mission to, Matt. 15 : 34; 21 : 37; Acts 3 : 26.

Christ rejected by, Matt. 11 : 20; 13 : 15; John 5 : 16, 38; Acts 3 : 13; 1 Thess. 2 : 15.

gospel first preached to, Matt. 10 : 6; Luke 24 : 27; Acts 1 : 8.

St. Paul's teaching rejected by, Acts 13 : 46; 28 : 24, 26.

Jezebel (jĕz'-ĕ-bĕl) [chaste] **Isabella,** wife of Ahab, 1 Ki. 16 : 31. Of strong character and very ambitious, she was unshrinking in her attitude against Jahwism. During the twenty-two years of her husband's reign and the thirteen years of her two sons, she exercised her evil influence in Israel.

kills the prophets, 1 Ki. 18 : 4; 19 : 2.

causes Naboth to be put to death, 1 Ki. 21.

her violent death, 2 Ki. 9 : 30. See Rev. 2 : 20.

Jezer (jē'-zĕr), **Jezerites** (jē'-zĕr-ītes), Num. 26 : 49.

Jeziah (jĕ-zī'-ăh), Ezra 10 : 25.

Jeziel (jē'-zĭ-ĕl), 1 Chr. 12 : 3.

Jezliah (jĕz-lī'-ăh), 1 Chr. 8 : 18.

Jezoar (jĕ-zō'-är), 1 Chr. 4 : 7.

Jezrahiah (jĕz-rä-hī'-ăh) [Jehovah appeareth], Neh. 12 : 42.

Jezreel (jĕz'-rēĕl) [God sows], a village of 500 inhabitants, on a spur of Gilboa, with springs near by, and ruined winepresses to the east, where Naboth's vineyards might have been (2 Ki. 21 : 1), Josh. 19 : 18; 1 Ki. 21 : 1; 2 Ki. 9 : 30-37; Hos. 1 : 4.

Jezreelite (jĕz'-rēĕl-īte), 1 Ki. 21 : 1.

Jezreelitess (jĕz-rēĕl-ī'-tĕss), 1 Sam. 27 : 3.

Jibsam (jĭb'-săm) [agreeable], 1 Chr. 7 : 2.

Jidlaph (jĭd'-lăph) [he shed tears], Gen. 22 : 22.

Jiljulieh (16 Cd), probably the site of ancient Gilgal.

Jimna (jĭm'-nă), **Jimnah** (jĭm'-năh), **Jimnites** (jĭm'-nītes), Gen. 46 : 17; Num. 26 : 44.

Jiphtah (jĭph-tăh), Josh. 15 : 43.

Jiphthah-el (jĭph'-thăh-ĕl), Josh. 19 : 14.

Joab (jō'-ăb) [Jah is father], captain of the host, 2 Sam. 8 : 16.

kills Abner, 2 Sam. 3 : 23.

intercedes for Absalom, 2 Sam. 14.

slays him in an oak, 2 Sam. 18 : 14.

reproves David's grief, 2 Sam. 19 : 5.

treacherously kills Amasa, 2 Sam. 20 : 9, 10.

unwillingly numbers the people, 2 Sam. 24 : 3; (1 Chr. 21 : 3).

supports Adonijah, 1 Ki. 1 : 7.

slain by Solomon's command, 1 Ki. 2 : 5, 28.

Joanna (jō-ăn'-nă) [Jah graciously gives], Luke 3 : 27; 8 : 3; 24 : 10.

Joash (jō'-ăsh) or **Jehoash** [Jah bestows], king of Israel, 2 Ki. 13 : 10.

visits Elisha sick, 2 Ki. 13 : 14.

defeats the Syrians, 2 Ki. 13 : 25.

chastises Amaziah, 2 Ki. 14 : 8; 2 Chr. 25 : 27.

king of Judah, 2 Ki. 11 : 2; 2 Chr. 23.

repairs the temple, 2 Ki. 12; 2 Chr. 24.

kills Zechariah, 2 Chr. 24 : 20-22.

slain by his servants, 2 Ki. 12 : 20; 2 Chr. 24 : 25.

Job (jōb) [he cries], Gen. 46 : 13.

different in Hebrew from the preceding; in O.T., found only in the book of Job and in Ezek. 14 : 14, 20; probably " hostile," or " towards whom God turns."

his character, Job 1 : 1, 8; 2 : 3; (Ezek. 14 : 14, 20).

his afflictions, Job 1 : 13; 2 : 7.

his patience, Job 1 : 20; 2 : 10; (Jas. 5 : 11).

complains of his life, Job 3.

reproves his friends, Job 6 : 7; 12; 13; 16; 17; 19; 21; 23; 24; 26-30.

declares his integrity, Job 31.

humbles himself, Job 40 : 3; 42 : 1.

his redoubled prosperity, Job 42 : 10.

Job, Book of.

Author and Date.—The only external evidence of the identity of the author comes to us through Aben Ezra (about 1150 A.D.) who says that " the sages of blessed memory " ascribe the book to Moses. That the book is one of great antiquity is apparent from the patriarchal conditions of life which it portrays. None of the great events of Hebrew history are mentioned in it, and the age it reflects probably antedated Abraham. Strong arguments are advanced for indentifying Job with Jobab, youngest son of Joktan. Young gives Jobab's date as 2200 B.C.

Theme of Job.—The question, " Why do the righteous suffer ? " may be said to be the theme of the book. Psalms 37 and 73 had not been written. The prevailing idea of the time was that of Eliphaz, Bildad and Zophar; that suffering was an evidence of sin. Elihu, however, brings to the discussion the thought that God uses suffering as a refining agent and that it is not necessarily an evidence of His displeasure. Throughout the dialogue, Job maintains that he is innocent of the charges lodged against him. In the 38th chapter, God himself speaks to Job out of the whirlwind, saying, " Who is this that darkeneth counsel by words without knowledge ? " He spreads before Job the wonders of creation and the majesty of the Godhead. Overwhelmed, Job replies, " Behold, I am vile; what shall I answer thee ? I will lay mine hand upon my mouth." (40 : 4). At the end of the divine revelation, Job cries out in complete humility, " I had heard of thee by the hearing of the ear; but now mine eye seeth thee. Wherefore I abhor myself, and repent in dust and ashes." (42 : 5.) It is after this, and after Job has prayed for his friends that God gives him redoubled wealth, a new family and a hundred and forty years of satisfied prosperity.

Jochebed (jŏch'-ĕ-bĕd) [Jah is glory], mother of Moses, Ex. 6 : 20; Num. 26 : 59.

Joel (jō'-ĕl) [Jah is God], delivers God's judgments, Joel 1-3.

proclaims a fast and declares the mercy of God, Joel 1 : 14; 2 : 15; 3 (cf. Acts 2 : 16).

fourteen of name.

Joel, Book of.

Authorship and Date.—Nothing is known of Joel nor of his father except what is found in the brief reference of verse 1. For want of definite evidence to the contrary, most commentators have conceded to him the date which the Jewish scribes have assigned him between Hosea and Amos.

Contents of the Book.—The first chapter describes a visitation of drought and locusts then in progress or immediately

213

impending as a judgment of God. Priests and people are called upon to humble themselves and seek forgiveness. In the second and third chapters the scene shifts to a similar calamity that will overtake the land in the last days. The details are almost identical with those given in Revelation 9. In Joel 2 : 18, begins the statement of the purposed deliverance of Jehovah. Encouragement rings out in verse 21, " Fear not, O land, be glad and rejoice for the Lord will do great things." This refrain is wholly in harmony with the joyous pæan of Isa. 62 : 1-5. The point of view is in the glad days of Israel's Messiah. The passage in 2 : 28-32 is familiar from its place in Peter's Pentecost sermon, Acts 2 : 17-21.

Joelah (jō-ē-ʹlăh), 1 Chr. 12 : 7.

Joezer (jō-ē-ʹzĕr) [Jah is help], 1 Chr. 12 : 6.

Jogbehah (jŏgʹbē-häh) city in Gilead, Num. 32 : 35.

Jogli (jŏgʹlī) [carried into exile], Num. 34 : 22.

Joha (jōʹhă), probably a corruption of " Joah," 1 Chr. 8 : 16; 11 : 45.

John, N.T. form of " Johanan," the apostle, called, Matt. 4 : 21; Mark 1 : 19; Luke 5 : 10.

ordained, Matt. 10 : 2; Mark 3 : 17.

reproved, Matt. 20 : 20; Mark 10 : 35; Luke 9 : 50.

declares the divinity and humanity of Jesus Christ, John 1; 1 John 1; 4; 5.

Christ's love for, John 13 : 23; 19 : 26; 21 : 7, 20, 24.

his care for Mary, the Lord's mother, John 19 : 27.

accompanies Peter before the council, Acts 4 : 13.

exhorts to obedience, and warns against false teachers, 1 John 1-5.

sees Christ's glory in heaven, Rev. 1 : 12 ff.

writes the Revelation, Rev. 1 : 19.

forbidden to worship the angel, Rev. 19 : 10; 22 : 8.

the Baptist, his coming foretold, Isa. 40 : 3; Mal. 4 : 5; Luke 1 : 17.

his birth and circumcision, Luke 1 : 57.

office, preaching, and baptism, Matt. 3; Mark 1; Luke 3; John 1 : 6; 3 : 26; Acts 1 : 5; 13 : 24.

John, Gospel according to.

Author and Date.—The writer carefully avoids the use of his own name, but that he was the Apostle John was the universal belief of the early Church and is abundantly established by both internal and external evidence. " We beheld his glory," the testimony of 1 : 14, evidently places him among the three who were with Jesus on the Mount. " This is the disciple (the one whom Jesus loved) who wrote these things "; the testimony of 21 : 24 amounts almost to a signature. Parallelisms in thought and word are so marked between the Gospel and the First Epistle of John as to leave no doubt of their common authorship. External evidence is no less positive than internal evidence. Irenæus, the pupil

of Polycarp, who was a disciple of St. John, states that John wrote this Gospel in Ephesus after the other Gospels had been written. Quotations from writings at the very beginning of the second century testify that the fourth Gospel was known and recognized as authoritative in 100 A.D.

Characteristics of John's Gospel.—It is elemental, vital. Statements of profound truth crowd one upon another with axiomatic clearness and simplicity. Knowledge of the major facts of the birth and ministry of Christ is assumed. John steps to the heart of the significance of this Life that was manifested. The purpose of his writing is stated in 20 : 31. It is that readers may believe and may have life in Jesus' name. " Faith rests on evidence, not on explanation."—White. And John proceeds to bring the evidence of the Baptist, the Father, Jesus' own mighty works, the testimony of friends, of enemies. And finally the last doubter among the disciples cries out, " My Lord and my God! "

Summary.—Chap. 1 : 1-18, Prologue—The Logos, etc. Chap. 1 : 19-51, Preparation and witness of John and early disciples. Chaps. 2 : 1-4 : 42, Early ministry in Galilee, Jerusalem, Samaria. Chaps. 4 : 43-6 : 71, ministry of Galilee, Jerusalem, Galilee. Chaps. 7 : 1-10 : 42, Controversy with priests and Pharisees in Jerusalem. Chaps. 11-12, Controversy with priests and Pharisees in Judæa. Chaps. 13-17, Jesus confides in disciples—family worship. Chaps. 18-19, The passion. Chap. 20, The Resurrection and three appearances. Chap. 21, Appendix (Scene : the lake of Galilee).

John, First Epistle of.

Author, Date, and Characteristics.—From the general tone of the letter we may say that it is from the same hand as the fourth Gospel, and was written probably from Ephesus about A.D. 90. (John's authorship need not be denied in either of these two writings. See above.) Frequent references to the Gospel seem to confirm its views. It was perhaps a letter designed for all the churches which came under John's influence.

Purpose.—The readers were in danger at the hands of certain heretical doctrines. Docetism reduced the Incarnation merely to an appearance of union of the Divine and human, on the theory that matter was intrinsically evil (1 John 1 : 1-3; 2 : 22; 4 : 1-3). Another form of Docetism was that of Cerenthus and Basilides, who taught that the Divine Christ united with the Human Christ at the Baptism and departed again prior to the Crucifixion (cf. 1 John 5 : 6). These Gnostic theories our author discounts, and points to the ethical working out in the lives of men of Christianity which is the only gnosis.

Summary.—Chap. 1 : 1-4, Introduction. Chaps. 1 : 5-2 : 17, Darkness and light (sins and love); Chap. 2 : 18-29, Truth and falsehood (the Antichrist); Chap. 3 : 1-12, Character of fellowship. Chaps. 3 : 13–5 : 12, Brotherly love and its results. Chap. 5 : 13-21, Epilogue and Recapitulation.

John, Second Epistle of.
The author of this and the Third Epistle we take to be the same as in the two previous writings. Whether this Epistle is addressed to the " Church of Pergamum " (concealed under a metaphor) or to a real lady (cf. 2 John 1) makes no difference to the sense. The danger is, as in the First Epistle, from Docetic gnosticism. This and the following Epistle became attached through time to 1 John, and were thus saved from oblivion and inserted in the Canon (though both are absent ₍from the Syriac Version of the N.T.).
Summary.—Ver. 1-3, Greeting. Ver. 4-11, Warning against heretics made in love. Ver. 12-13, Salutations.

John, Third Epistle of.
An interesting light is shed on the early Church by the writer, for whose identity we need look no further than in the case of 1 and 2 John. Addressed to Gaius, a prosperous layman, it deplores the rise of that independence which led to Diotrephes asserting his influence against the apostle's, and forbidding hospitality to travelling evangelists (cf. Rom. 12 : 13; 1 Tim. 3 : 2; 5 : 10; Titus 1 : 8; Heb. 13 : 2; 1 Pet. 4 : 9. That bitter feeling existed is seen in such phrases as " prating against us with malicious words " (ver. 10).
Summary.—Ver. 1, Greeting. Ver. 2-4, Gaius is praised. Ver. 5-8. His hospitality commended. Ver. 9-12, Diotrephes is rebuked and Demetrius commended. Ver. 13-14, Salutations.

John Mark, Acts 12 : 12, 25. See **Mark.**
John the Baptist. It was not without reason that Herod feared the popular temper in regard to the Baptist, whose influence must have been widespread and lasting if the priests were afraid to slight him for fear of being stoned (cf. Matt. 21 : 26; Mark 11 : 32; Luke 20 : 6).
his coming foretold, Isa. 40 : 3; Mal. 4 : 5; Luke 1 : 17.
his birth and circumcision, Luke 1 : 57.
his office, preaching, and baptism, Matt. 3; Mark 1; Luke 3; John 1 : 6; 3 : 26; Acts 1 : 5; 13 : 24.
baptizes Christ, Matt. 3; Mark 1; Luke 3; John 1 : 6; 3 : 26.
imprisoned by Herod, Matt. 4 : 12; Mark 1 : 14; Luke 3 : 20.
sends his disciples to Christ, Matt. 11 : 2; Luke 7 : 18.
beheaded, Matt. 14; Mark 6 : 14.
Christ's testimony to, Matt. 11 : 10, 11; 17 : 12; Mark 9 : 11; Luke 7 : 27.
his disciples receive the Holy Ghost, Acts 18 : 24; 19 : 1.
Join, Prov. 11 : 21; 16 : 5, hand j. in hand.
Isa. 5 : 8, that j. house to house.

Jer. 50 : 5, let us j. ourselves to the Lord.
Hos. 4 : 17, Ephraim is j. to idols.
Matt. 19 : 6; Mark 10 : 9, what God hath j.
Acts 5 : 13, durst no man j. himself.
8 : 29, go near, and j. thyself to this chariot.
1 Cor. 1 : 10, perfectly j. in same mind.
6 : 17, j. to the Lord.
Eph. 4 : 16, the whole body fitly j.
Joining, 1 Chr. 22 : 3.
Joint, Gen. 32 : 25, thigh out of j.
Ps. 22 : 14, all my bones are out of j.
Prov. 25 : 19, like foot out of j.
Eph. 4 : 16, which every j. supplieth.
Col. 2 : 19, body by j. and bands knit together.
Heb. 4 : 12, dividing of j. and marrow.
Joint heirs, Rom. 8 : 17.
Jokdeam (jŏk-́dĕ-ăm), Josh. 15 : 56.
Jokim (jō-́kĭm), 1 Chr. 4 : 22.
Jokmeam (jŏk-́mĕ-ăm) [may Jehovah raise up a people], 1 Chr. 6 : 68.
Jokneam (jŏk-́nĕ-ăm) [may Jehovah found a people], a city of Zebulon now called Tell Keimun, Josh. 12 : 22.
Jokshan (jŏk-́shăn) [bird catcher], Gen. 25 : 2.
Joktan (jŏk-́tăn) [small], land occupied by the descendants of Joktan, Gen. 10 : 25; 1 Chr. 1 : 19.
Joktheel (jŏk-́théel) [subdued by God], Josh. 15 : 38; 2 Ki. 14 : 7.
Jona (jō-́nă), John 1 : 42.
Jonadab (jŏn-́ă-dăb), contracted form of " Jehonadab," son of Rechab, 2 Ki. 10 : 15.
Jonah (jō-́năh) [a dove], prophet, 2 Ki. 14 : 25.
his disobedience and punishment, Jonah 1.
his prayer and deliverance, Jonah 2.
preaches to the Ninevites, Jonah 3.
reproved for murmuring at God's mercy, Jonah 4.
a type of Christ, Matt. 12 : 39; Luke 11 : 29.
Jonah, Book of.
Contents.—Jonah, a Hebrew prophet, to avoid being sent to the heathen and hostile Nineveh, flees in a ship bound for the west, but a storm overtakes him. After being thrown into the sea (the sailors having discovered by lot that he it is upon whom the wrath of his god is falling), he is swallowed by a great fish and remains in its belly three days and three nights (1). The prophet prays, and is thrown upon the dry land (2). He now obeys God's command, and Nineveh repents and is spared (3). Jonah, angry that the enemy should have escaped, by a miracle is taught the folly of his little narrow nationalism and the infinite love of God (4).
Author and Date.—The Prophet Jonah was the son of Amittai, and we learn from 2 Kings 14 : 25 that he had prophesied the restoration of the boundary of Israel from Hamath to the Dead Sea. Syria had bitterly oppressed Israel and it was under Jeroboam II., son of Joash, King of Israel, that the deliverance was wrought. He reigned 41 years from about 790 B.C. The date of Jonah must be before or during this long reign. Jonah's home was Gath-Hepher, of

Zebulun, midway between Mt. Carmel and the Sea of Galilee.

The task assigned to Jonah.—That Jonah should be sent to a hostile city with a message so sombre, was enough to try the mettle of the bravest man. He quailed and disobeyed. When again commissioned, he obeyed, and met with the success that God intended, for the city repented and was spared for the later destruction prophesied by Nahum from which there was to be no escape.

Jonas (jō-năs), Greek form of "Jonah," Matt. 12 : 39, 40; John 21 : 15-17.

Jonathan (jŏn-ă-thăn) [Jah gave], son of Saul, smites the Philistines, 1 Sam. 13 : 3; 14.

his love for David, 1 Sam. 18 : 1; 19; 20; 23 : 16.

slain by the Philistines, 1 Sam. 31 : 2.

David's lamentation for, 2 Sam. 1 : 17.

son of Abiathar, 2 Sam. 15 : 27; 1 Ki. 1 : 42.

one of David's nephews, 2 Sam. 21 : 21; 1 Chr. 20 : 7.

Jonath-elem-rechokim (jō-năth-ē-lĕm-rĕ-chō-kĭm), Ps. 56, title. Tradition, following the vocalised Hebrew text, translates this "the dove of the silence of them that are distant," but more probably, following the consonants, we should take it to be "the dove of the distant terebinths." The word "upon" should read "set to," the idea being that Psalm 56 was "set to" the tune of the well-known song beginning "the dove of the distant terebinths."

Accra, now Jaffa.

Joppa (jŏp-pă) [beauty], the modern Jaffa, a seaport town on the Mediterranean, 2 Chr. 2 : 16; Jonah 1 : 3.

Tabitha raised at, Acts 9 : 36.

Peter dwells at, Acts 10 : 5; 11 : 5.

Joram (jō-răm) or Jorim (jō-rĭm) [Jehovah is exalted], 2 Ki. 8 : 16; Luke 3 : 29.

Jordan (jŏr-dăn) [the descender], is the longest river in Palestine. It rises among the foot-hills of Mount Hermon, and, flowing tortuously south through lakes Huleh and Galilee, follows the bed of a rapidly "descending" geological fissure to empty itself in the Dead Sea, 1292 feet below Mediterranean level. Only one hundred

miles long, it descends about three thousand feet, and runs below the level of the ocean throughout the greater part of its course. Hence the name.

Its sources are principally (1) the Hasbani River, rising on the western slopes of Hermon at an altitude of 1700 feet; (2) the Leddan, most copious supply of all, rising 500 feet up; and (3) the Banias, issuing from a cavern near Cæsarea Philippi (Banias), some 1200 feet up (cf. Matt. 16 : 13; Mark 8 : 27). Its chief tributaries are the Yarmuk and the Jabbok. The combined waters of the sources flow after seven miles into Lake Huleh, identified as "the waters of Merom" (Josh. 11 : 5, 7), which is about four miles long.

Its fords are numerous (1 Sam. 13 : 7; 2 Sam. 10 : 17). It was perhaps by "ferry" that David and his household were conveyed across. It formed a natural boundary to Palestine (cf. Num. 34 : 12; Josh. 22 : 25). Hence the frequent references "on this side" and "on the other side Jordan" (Josh. 1 : 14). The Jordan valley [Heb. "Arabah"] is a long plain, three miles broad at the northern, twelve at the southern end, and sloping nine feet to the mile. The climate is hot, the Lower Jordan especially so, since it is shut in by two walls of mountains. "Esh-Sheriah," "the watering-place," is the modern name.

waters divided for the Israelites, Josh. 3 : 14 ff.; Ps. 114 : 3; by Elijah and Elisha, 2 Ki. 2 : 8, 13.

Naaman's leprosy cured at, 2 Ki. 5 : 10.

John baptizes there, Matt. 3; Mark 1 : 5; Luke 3 : 3.

See Job 40 : 23; Ps. 42 : 6; Jer. 12 : 5; 49 : 19; Zech. 11 : 3.

Jose (jō-sē) or Joses [whom Jehovah helps], abbreviation of Joseph, Luke 3 : 29; Matt. 13 : 55.

Joseph (jō-sĕph) [may add], son of Jacob, Gen. 30 : 24. Has earned for himself a high place among the founders of Israel. The great feature of his life is that he could bear failure and success with equal equanimity, allowing neither to eclipse for him the sense of his Divine election.

his dreams and the jealousy of his brethren, Gen. 37 : 5.

sold to the Ishmaelites, Gen. 37 : 28.

servant to Potiphar, Gen. 39.

resists temptation, Gen. 39 : 7.

interprets the dreams of Pharaoh's servants, Gen. 40; and of Pharaoh, Gen. 41 : 25.

made governor of Egypt, Gen. 41 : 39-43.

prepares for the famine, Gen. 41 : 48.

receives his brethren and father, Gen. 42–46.

his charge concerning his bones, Gen. 50 : 25.

death, Gen. 50 : 26.

See Ps. 105 : 17; Acts 7 : 9; Heb. 11 : 22.

husband of the Virgin, Matt. 1 : 19; 2 : 13, 19; Luke 1 : 27; 2 : 4.

of Arimathea, Matt. 27 : 57; Mark 15 : 43; Luke 23 : 50, 51; John 19 : 38.

(Barsabas), Justus, Acts 1 : 23.

Joshah (jō-shäh) [establisher], 1 Chr. 4 : 34.

Joshaphat (jŏsh-ă-phăt), 1 Chr. 11 : 43.
Joshaviah (jŏsh-ă-vī-ăh) [Jehovah sufficient], 1 Chr. 11 : 46.
Joshbekashah (jŏsh-bĕ-kăsh-ăh) [hardness], 1 Chr. 25 : 4.
Joshua (jŏsh-ū-ă) [Jah is salvation] (Hoshea, Oshea, Jehoshua, Jeshua, and Jesus), son of Nun or Non, 1 Chr. 7 : 27; Heb. 4 : 8.
discomfits Amalek, Ex. 17 : 9.
ministers to Moses, Ex. 24 : 13; 32 : 17; 33 : 11.
spies out Canaan, Num. 13 : 16.
appointed Moses' successor, Num. 27 : 18; 34 : 17; Deut. 1 : 38; 3 : 28; 34 : 9.
encouraged by God, Josh. 1.
commands his officers, Josh. 1 : 10-15.
crosses Jordan, Josh. 3.
erects memorial pillars, Josh. 4.
renews circumcision, Josh. 5.
takes Jericho, Josh. 6.
punishes Achan, Josh. 7.
subdues Ai, Josh. 8.
his victories, Josh. 10–12.
divides the land, Josh. 14–21.
his charge to the Reubenites, etc., Josh. 22.
exhorts the people, Josh. 23.
rehearses God's mercies, Josh. 24.
renews the covenant, Josh. 24 : 14-27.
his death, Josh. 24 : 29; Judg. 2 : 8.
his curse, Josh. 6 : 26; fulfilled, 1 Ki. 16 :34.
Joshua, Book of.
The account of the Conquest of Canaan resumes where the account of the Exodus has terminated. God's commands to occupy the land and His promises to supply the power to do so, are among the most majestic of the O.T. Scriptures. Evidently the author is Joshua, for the words of Jehovah are given in great detail, and the plans of conquest are outlined as they could scarcely be except by the general in command. That the inhabitants of the land were to be destroyed has been the subject of much criticism. It should be remembered that judgment upon their sins was long deferred. To have preserved the people in the midst of Israel would have involved a physical and moral menace that could not be justified.
Summary.—(a) Chaps. 1–12, The Conquest of Canaan (mainly by J.E.); (b) Chaps. 13–22, Settlement of the land (mainly by P.); (c) Chaps. 23–24, Last words and death of Joshua.
Josiah (jō-sī-ăh) [Jah heals]. A just king, he was very popular, as we see after his death at Megiddo in 608 B.C., when the people went into a long mourning for him.
prophecy concerning, 1 Ki. 13 : 2; fulfilled, 2 Ki. 23 : 16.
his good reign, 2 Ki. 22.
repairs the temple, 2 Ki. 22 : 3.
hears the word of the book of the law, 2 Ki. 22 : 10.
Huldah's message from God to him, 2 Ki. 22 : 16.
ordains the reading of the book, 2 Ki. 23.
his solemn passover, 2 Chr. 35.
slain by Pharaoh-nechoh, 2 Ki. 23 : 29.

Jot and tittle, Matt. 5 : 18; Luke 16 : 17. The Greek "iota" and "keraia" were so translated by Tindale ("iott" and "tytle"), and these forms were retained in all other translations. "Iota" is the smallest letter in the Greek alphabet, as "yod" was of the later Hebrew. The "keraia" or "little horn" is any small mark like the crosspiece of a "t," but great confusion arises when this is ignored. The phrase is applied to the smallest minutiæ of anything.
Jotham (jō-thăm) [Jejovah is perfect], son of Gideon, his parable, Judg. 9 : 7-15.
king of Judah, 2 Ki. 15 : 32; 2 Chr. 27.
Journey, Gen. 24 : 21, Lord made j. prosperous.
Josh. 9 : 11, take the victuals for your j.
1 Ki. 18 : 27, or he is in a j.
Neh. 2 : 6, how long shall thy j. be ?
Matt. 10 : 10; Mark 6 : 8; Luke 9 : 3, nor scrip for your j.
Luke 11 : 6, a friend in his j.
15 : 13, took his j. into a far country.
John 4 : 6, Jesus, wearied with his j.
2 Cor. 11 : 26, in j. often.
Journeyed, Gen. 12 : 9; Acts 9 : 3.
Joy—In no other religion and in no other literature is joy so conspicuous as in Christianity and in the Bible. Physically and psychologically speaking, it is the criterion of health whereby all the powers and affections are enriched and harmonised. So in religion it denotes the satisfaction of the soul at attaining its desire; and Christianity stands firm so long as men who have it are invested with joy.
1 Chr. 12 : 40; Ezra 6 : 16; Ps. 89 : 15; 149 : 2; Isa. 35 : 2; 60 : 15; 61 : 10; Hab. 3 : 18, Luke 10 . 17, John 15 : 11; Phil. 3 : 3; 1 Thess. 1 : 6.
of the wicked, folly, Prov. 15 : 21; Eccl. 2 : 10; 7 : 6; 11 : 9; Isa. 16 : 10; Jas. 4 : 9.
follows grief, Prov. 14 : 10; Isa. 61 : 3; 66 : 10; John 16 : 20; 2 Cor. 6 : 10.
in heaven over repentant sinners, Luke 15 . 7, 10.
of Paul over the churches, 2 Cor. 1 : 24; 2 : 3; 7 : 13; Phil. 1 : 4; 2 : 2; 4 : 1; 1 Thess. 2 : 19; 3 : 9; 2 Tim. 1 : 4; Philem. 7.
of John over his spiritual children, 3 John 4.
expressed by psalmody, Eph. 5 : 19; Col. 3 : 16; Jas. 5 : 13.
1 Chr. 15 : 25, went to bring ark with j.
Neh. 8 : 10, the j. of the Lord is your strength.
Job 20 : 5, the j. of the hypocrite but for a moment.
29 : 13, widow's heart to sing for j.
33 : 26, he shall see his face with j.
41 : 22, sorrow is turned into j.
Ps. 16 : 11, in thy presence fulness of j.
30 : 5, j. cometh in the morning.
43 : 4, to God my exceeding j.
48 : 2; Lam. 2 : 15, the j. of the whole earth.
Ps. 51 : 12, restore j. of thy salvation.
126 : 5, that sow in tears shall reap in j.
Prov. 21 : 15, j. to the just to do judgment.
Eccl. 9 : 7, eat thy bread with j.
Isa. 9 : 3, not increased the j.

12 : 3, with **j**. shall ye draw water.
24 : 8, the **j**. of the harp ceaseth.
29 : 19, meek shall increase their **j**.
35 : 10; 51 : 11, with everlasting **j**.
65 : 14, my servants shall sing for **j**. of heart.
Jer. 15 : 16, thy word was the **j**. of my heart.
31 : 13, turn their mourning into **j**.
Matt. 13 : 20; Luke 8 : 13, with **j**. receiveth it.
Matt. 13 : 44, for **j**. goeth and selleth.
25 : 21, 23, the **j**. of thy Lord.
Luke 15 : 10, there is **j**. in presence of the angels.
24 : 41, they believed not for **j**.
John 3 : 29, this my **j**. is fulfilled.
16 : 24, that your **j**. might be full.
Acts 20 : 24, finish my course with **j**.
Rom. 14 : 17, kingdom of God is **j**.
Heb. 12 : 2, for the **j**. that was set before him.
Jas. 1 : 2, count it all **j**.
1 Pet. 4 : 13; Jude 24, with exceeding **j**.
Joyful, Ezra 6 : 22, Lord had made them **j**.
Ps. 35 : 9, my soul shall be **j**. in the Lord.
63 : 5, praise thee with **j**. lips.
66 : 1; 95 : 1; 98 : 6, make a **j**. noise.
Eccl. 7 : 14, in day of prosperity be **j**.
Isa. 56 : 7, **j**. in house of prayer.
61 : 10, soul shall be **j**. in God.
2 Cor. 7 : 4, **j**. in all our tribulation.
Joyfully, Luke 19 : 6; Heb. 10 : 34.
Joyous, Isa. 32 : 13; Heb. 12 : 11.
Jubal (jû-̍băl) [sound], inventor of harp and organ, Gen. 4 : 21.
Jubilee, year of. At the end of seven times seven years (49 years) the fiftieth was observed as the year of *Jubilee*, a word of uncertain meaning. The directions for its observance are given in Lev. 25 : 9, 10; 25 : 31; 27 : 17.
Juda (**Judah**), Matt. 2 : 6; Heb. 7 : 14; Rev. 5 : 5.
Judah [praise], fourth son of Jacob and Leah (Gen. 29 : 35). He married a daughter of Shuah, a Canaanite, by whom he had three sons, Er, Onan and Shelah. The first two displeased God and were slain. (38 : 1-10). By Tamar, widow of Er, Judah becomes the father of Perez and Zerah, twins. The royal line of David came through Perez. Because of the sin of Reuben (Gen. 35 : 22), and because of the cruelty of Simeon and Levi (49 : 5-7), these eldest sons were passed over when Jacob bestowed his prophetic blessing, and the sceptre was given to Judah (49 : 8-10). The tribe of Judah makes David King (2 Sam. 2 : 4), and in the division of the kingdom adheres to his house (1 Ki. 12).
Judas, Græcised form of " Judah " (Jude, Lebbeus, Thaddeus), apostle, brother of James, Matt. 10 : 3; Mark 3 : 18; Luke 6 : 16; Acts 1 : 13.
his question to our Lord, John 14 : 22.
exhorts to perseverance in the faith, Jude 3, 20.
the Lord's brother, Matt. 13 : 55; Mark 6 : 3.
Barsabas, Acts 15 : 22.
Iscariot, Matt. 10 : 4; Mark 3 : 19; Luke 6 : 16; John 6 : 70.
betrays Jesus, Matt. 26 : 14, 47; Mark

14 : 10, 43; Luke 22 : 3, 47; John 13 : 26; 18 : 2.
hangs himself, Matt. 27 : 5; (Acts 1 : 18).
Jude, Epistle of.
Author and Date.—There is no need to place the Epistle in the second century. The writer may be regarded as Judas, the brother of James, our Lord's brother (Mark 6 : 3; Matt. 13 : 55). Mention is made of his grandsons being arrested in the reign of Domitian (Eusebius Eccl. Hist. 3 : 19 f.). He probably joined the apostles before Pentecost (Acts 1 : 14) and soon rose to a high place in the Church (cf. 1 Cor. 9 : 5). The Epistle was written before A.D. 80 (Jude was dead in the reign of Domitian, see Eusebius), and after A.D. 63 (v. 24 f. depends on Romans and v. 18 on the Pastorals). The object was to warn the brethren against the monstrous vices and libertinism which were beginning even so early to appear (cf. 1 Cor. and Gnosticism of the second century for the beginnings and the results). He writes " as a Hebrew Christian to Gentile Christians " (Chase), (v. 3, " Our common salvation ").
Summary.—Ver. 1-2, Salutation; ver. 3-4, Occasions ver. 5-11, Errorists denounced and warned; ver. 12-19, Their exposure and characteristics; ver. 20-23, Treatment by Christians; ver. 24-25, Benediction.
Judge, Gen. 18 : 25, the **J**. of all the earth.
16 : 5, Lord **j**. between me and thee.
Ex. 2 : 14; Acts 7 : 27, who made thee a **j**. over us ?
Deut. 32 : 36; Ps. 7 : 8; 50 : 4; Heb. 10 : 30, Lord shall **j**. people.
Ps. 50 : 6, God is **j**. himself.
58 : 11, he is a God that **j**. in the earth.
68 : 5, a **j**. of the widows.
94 : 2, thou **J**. of the earth.
96 : 13; 98 : 9; Acts 17 : 31, he shall **j**. the world with righteousness.
Ps. 110 : 6, he shall **j**. among the heathen.
Isa. 1 : 17, **j**. the fatherless.
3 : 2, take away the **j**.
5 : 3, **j**. betwixt me and my vineyard.
Mic. 7 : 3, the **j**. asketh a reward.
Matt. 5 : 25; Luke 12 : 58, adversary deliver thee to the **j**.
Matt. 7 : 1, **j**. not, that ye be not **j**.
Luke 7 : 43, thou hast rightly **j**.
12 : 14, who made me **j**. over you ?
18 : 6, the unjust **j**.
John 7 : 24, **j**. righteous judgment.
16 : 11, prince of this world is **j**.
Acts 10 : 42, the **J**. of quick and dead.
Rom. 14 : 13, let us not **j**. one another.
2 Tim. 4 : 8, the Lord, the righteous **J**.
Heb. 12 : 23, to God, the **J**. of all.
Jas. 4 : 11, not a doer of the law, but a **j**.
5 : 9, the **J**. standeth before the door.
Rev. 20 : 13, **j**. every man according to works.
Judges. The judges were temporary and special deliverers sent by God to deliver the Israelites from their oppressors; not supreme magistrates, succeeding to the authority of Moses and Joshua. Their power only extended over portions of the

country, and some of them were ruling at the same time. Their first work was that of deliverers and leaders in war, they then administered justice to the people, and their authority supplied the want of a regular government. The Book of Judges gives a history of the rise and rule of thirteen judges, a list of whom follows with a brief reference to their work.

1st Judge—Othniel (Judg. 3 : 7-11), against " Mesopotamia."

2nd Judge—Ehud (3 : 12-30), against Eglon of Moab.

3rd Judge—Shamgar (3 : 31), against the Philistines. (Probably a later addition.)

4th Judge—Deborah and Barak (Chaps. 4–5), against Jabin and Sisera.

5th Judge—Gideon (6–8), against Midian.

6th Judge—Abimelech (9) against Shechem.

7th Judge—Tola (10 : 1-2).

8th Judge—Jair (10 : 3-5).

9th Judge—Jephthah (11 : 1–12 : 7), against Ammon.

10th Judge—Ibzan (12 : 8-10).

11th Judge—Elon (12 : 11-12).

12th Judge—Abdon (12 : 13-15).

13th Judge—Samson (13–16), against the Philistines.

Then come Eli and Samuel.

Of these, Samson was a popular folklore hero, and legends hide the truth which lies behind the stories. The most valuable portions of the book are those dealing with Deborah and Barak, Gideon, Ehud, and Jephthah. (cf. Ex. 18 : 21; Lev. 19 : 15; Deut. 1 : 16; 16 : 18; 17 : 8; 1 Sam. 8 : 3; 2 Chr. 19 . 6, Ezra 7 . 25, Ps. 82; Prov. 17 : 15; 18 : 5; 24 : 23 f.; Isa. 1 : 23; 10 : 1; Luke 18 : 2.)

Judges, Book of.

Contents.—The book derives its title from its contents. A brief summary would be : (a) Chaps. 1 : 1–2 : 5, Introduction. (b) Chaps. 2 : 6–3 : 6, The moral stated, viz., Infidelity to Jehovah brings disaster; fidelity and penitence obtain forgiveness. (c) Chaps. 3 : 7–16 : 31, The moral elaborated by historical illustration. (d) Chaps. 17 : 1–21 : 25, Two appendices : (1) 17–18, Origin of sanctuary at Dan. (2) 19–21, Israel's vengeance on Benjamin for an outrage at Gibeah.

Composition and Date.—The historical period covered by Judges is the time of adjustment between the theocracy which had been established under Moses and continued under Joshua and the later founding of the kingdom. The conquest and occupation of the land was incomplete, and trouble constantly arose from the neighbours of Israel. The Judges were often military leaders providentially raised up to deliver Israel. The book is thought to have been written in the time of Samuel and probably by himself. If this is true, there are perhaps some editorial additions of a later date, such as ch. 18 : 30, in which

the captivity of the land is referred to. Some critics ascribe all the historical books from Judges to 2 Kings to one source. The chronology of the book presents many problems. Various hypotheses have been advanced for harmonizing the difficulties. It can hardly be said that any of these is certain enough to remain unchallenged. Eli and Samuel belong in the same category as the Judges though they are not included among those mentioned in the Book of Judges. If we omit Abimelech, who ruled more as a King than as a Judge, and add the names of Eli and Samuel, the number of the Judges was 14. The Book of Ruth belongs to this stormy era and was originally a part of the Book of Judges, but was later given a separate place.

Hence the book in its final form belongs to about B.C. 450.

Judgment, cautions concerning, Matt. 7 : 1; Luke 6 : 37; 12 : 57; John 7 : 24; Rom. 2 : 1; Jas. 4 : 11.

the last, foretold, 1 Chr. 16 : 33; Ps. 96 : 13; 98 : 9; Eccl. 3 : 17; 11 : 9; 12 : 14; Acts 17 : 31; Rom. 2 : 16; 2 Cor. 5 : 10; 2 Pet. 3 : 7.

described, Ps. 50; Dan. 7 : 9; Matt. 25 : 31; 2 Thess. 1 : 8; Rev. 6 : 12; 20 : 11.

hope of Christians respecting, Rom. 8 : 33; 1 Cor. 4 : 5; 2 Tim. 4 : 8; 1 John 2 : 28; 4 : 17.

Ex. 12 : 12, against the gods execute j.

Deut. 1 : 17, the j. is God's.

16 : 18, judge people with just j.

32 : 4, all his ways are j.

2 Sam. 8 : 15; 1 Chr. 18 : 14, executed j. and justice.

Ps. 1 : 5, ungodly shall not stand in j.

9 : 7, prepared his throne for j.

25 : 9, the meek will he guide in j.

37 : 6, bring forth thy j. as the noon-day.

89 : 14; 97 : 2, justice and j. are habitation of throne.

101 : 1, I will sing of mercy and j.

Prov. 2 : 9, then shalt thou understand j.

29 : 26, j. cometh from the Lord.

Eccl. 8 : 6, to every purpose there is time and j.

11 : 9; 12 : 14, God will bring into j.

Isa. 26 : 9, when thy j. are in the earth.

28 : 17, I will lay j. to the line.

53 : 8, taken from prison and from j.

Jer. 5 : 1, if there be any that executeth j.

Hos. 12 : 6, keep mercy and j.

Matt. 5 : 21, in danger of the j.

Luke 11 : 42, pass over j. and the love of God.

John 5 : 22, committed all j. to the Son.

9 : 39, for j. I am come.

12 : 31, now is the j. of this world.

16 : 8, reprove the world of j.

Acts 8 : 33, his j. was taken away.

24 : 25, reasoned of j. to come.

Rom. 5 : 18, j. came on all to condemnation.

14 : 10, we shall all stand before j. seat.

Heb. 9 : 27, after this the j.

10 : 27, certain fearful looking for of j.

1 Pet. 4 : 17, j. begin at house of God.

Rev. 16 : 7; 19 : 2, righteous are thy j.

Judgment hall or prætorium. In four places the A.V. translates " prætorium " by " judgment hall," and many see in John 18 : 28, 33; 19 : 9, and Acts 23 : 35, two distinct places implied, the first being the Tower of Antonia which Pilate made his headquarters, the second referring to the hall of the palace of Herod the Great described in Josephus. All four, however, may equally refer to the latter only, on the supposition, largely supported, that Pilate made Herod's palace his headquarters when he visited Jerusalem.

The reference in Phil. 1 : 13, which also translates " prætorium," is probably to the barracks of the prætorians, or emperor's bodyguard, on Mount Palatine in Rome.

Judith (jū-dīth) [Jewess], Gen. 26 : 34.

Juice, Song of Sol. 8 : 2.

Julius (jū-lĭ-ŭs), Latin masculine name, Acts 27 : 1; 28 : 16.

Jumping, Nah. 3 : 2.

Juniper (1 Ki. 19 : 4, 5). In the Revised Version the Hebrew word " rothem " is translated in the margin " broom." It is supposed to be " Retama rœtam," a broom-like shrub, " frequently met with near Sinai, round the Dead Sea, and in the ravines leading down to the Jordan Valley." The roots seem to have been converted into charcoal (Ps. 120 : 4). Men gaunt with famine are said to have had the roots of broom for their meat (Job 30 : 4, Revised Version).

Jupiter (jū-pĭ-tĕr), Latin name of " Zeus," Acts 14 : 12, 13; 19 : 35.

Jurisdiction, Luke 23 : 7.

Just, Gen. 6 : 9, Noah was a j. man.
Deut. 32 : 4, a God of truth, j. and right is he.
Job 9 : 2, how should man be j. with God ?
Prov. 3 : 33, God blesseth the habitation of the j.
4 : 18, path of j. as shining light.
10 : 7, the memory of the j. is blessed.
12 : 21, no evil happen to the j.
Eccl. 7 : 20, not a j. man on earth that sinneth not.
Isa. 26 : 7, way of j. is uprightness.
45 : 21, a j. God, and a Saviour.
Hab. 2 : 4; Rom. 1 : 17; Gal. 3 : 11; Heb. 10 : 38, the j. shall live by faith.
Matt. 5 : 45, sendeth rain on j. and unjust.
Luke 14 : 14, recompensed at resurrection of the j.
15 : 7, ninety and nine j. persons.
23 : 50, good man and a j.
Acts 24 : 15, resurrection of j. and unjust.
Rom. 2 : 13, not hearers of law are j.
3 : 26, that he might be j.
Phil. 4 : 8, whatsoever things are j.
Heb. 2 : 2, a j. recompense of reward.
12 : 23, spirits of j. men made perfect.
1 Pet. 3 : 18, the j. for the unjust.
1 John 1 : 9, he is j. to forgive sins.

Justice. The administration of justice was at first in the hands of the head of the family (Gen. 38 : 24), thence passing into the office of the " elders " of a tribe or clan (Num. 11 : 16). In the monarchical period this latter form continued (1 Ki. 21 : 8-13) with the addition of two other interested parties, namely, the king (1 Sam. 8 : 20; 2 Sam. 15 : 2-6; 2 Ki. 15 : 5, etc.) and the priests (Deut. 19 : 15-21). In the time of Ezra the law was administered by the " elders " of the city in the law courts (Ezra 7 : 25; 10 : 14), while in N.T. days the system was the famous Roman legal procedure (cf. Acts 24 ff.).

The word " justice " here means "righteousness" and what we mean by "justice" is seen in the O.T. under the name " judgment " (which see).
of God, Job 4 : 17; 8 : 3; 34 : 12; Zeph. 3 : 5; Rev. 15 : 3.
to do, enjoined, Lev. 19 : 36; Deut. 16 : 18; Prov. 11 : 1; Jer. 22 : 3; Ezek. 18 : 5; 45 : 9; Mic. 6 : 8; Matt. 7 : 12; Rom. 13 : 7; 2 Cor. 8 : 21; Col. 4 : 1.
Gen. 18 : 19, keep way of Lord to do j.
2 Sam. 15 : 4, I would do j.
Ps. 82 : 3, do j. to afflicted and needy.
Prov. 8 : 15, by me princes decree j.
Isa. 9 : 7, to establish his throne with j.
59 : 4, none calleth for j.
Jer. 23 : 5, execute judgment and j. in the earth.
31 : 23; 50 : 7, habitation of j.

Justification, by faith. To Paul, " justification " was synonymous with " reconciliation " (Rom. 3 : 23 f.; 5 : 11, 15–21; 2 Cor. 5 : 19). The ground is the grace of God (Rom. 3 : 23 f.; 14 : 4; 5 : 6, 8, 21; 6 : 23; cf. Heb. 2 : 9), the means is Jesus' vicarious death (Rom. 3 : 24 f.; 5 : 9; 2 Cor. 5 : 14; cf. Heb. 9 : 12, etc.), the only condition is faith sealed by baptism, both implying repentance (Rom. 6 : 3 f., 21; 1 Cor. 6 : 11; Gal. 3 : 26 f., etc.). Note that Christ did not make Himself a substitute for man from the outside of humanity, but from within, rendered obedience, thereby affording us an ethical justification (Rom. 5 : 15, 20).
Hab. 2 : 4; Acts 13 : 39; Rom. 1 : 17; 3; 4; 5; Gal. 3 : 11.
by works, Jas. 2 : 14-26.
Rom. 4 : 25, Christ raised again for our j.
5 : 18, free gift came on all men to j.

Justifier, Rom. 3 : 26.

Justify, Job 9 : 20, if I j. myself, my mouth shall condemn me.
Job 25 : 4, how can man be j. with God ?
Ps. 51 : 4, be j. when thou speakest.
143 : 2, in thy sight shall no man living be j.
Isa. 5 : 23, j. the wicked for reward.
53 : 11, my righteous servant j. many.
Matt. 11 : 19; Luke 7 : 35, wisdom is j. of her children.
Matt. 12 : 37, by thy words thou shalt be j.
Luke 10 : 29, he, willing to j. himself.
16 : 15, ye j. yourselves before men.
18 : 14, j. rather than the other.
Rom. 3 : 24; Titus 3 : 7, j. freely by his grace.
Rom. 5 : 1, being j. by faith.
8 : 30, whom he j. he also glorified.
Gal. 2 : 16, man is not j. by the law.
1 Tim. 3 : 16, j. in the Spirit.

Justle, Nah. 2 : 4.
Justly, Mic. 6 : 8, what doth the Lord require, but to do j. ?
Luke 23 : 41, indeed j.; for we receive the due reward.
1 Thess. 2 : 10, how holily and j. we behaved.
Justus (jŭs-tŭs) [upright], Acts 1 : 23; 18 : 7; Col. 4 : 11.

K

Kab, 2 Ki. 6 : 25.
Kabzeel (kăb-zéel) [God assembles], Josh. 15 : 21; 2 Sam. 23 : 20.
Kades. See Kadesh.
Kadesh (kā-dĕsh) [holy], a city on the borders of the promised land, twelve miles east-southeast of Beer-sheba, Num. 13 : 26; Ezek. 47 : 19.
Israelites murmur there, Num. 13 : 31; 14.
Kadesh-barnea (kā-dĕsh-bär-nĕ-ă) [holy desert], Deut. 1 : 19. See Kadesh.
Kadmiel (kăd-mĭ-ĕl) [before God], Ezra 2 : 40; Neh. 9 : 4.
Kadmonites (kăd-mō-nītes) [men of the east], a people supposed to have resided by Mount Hermon, Gen. 15 : 19; 25 : 15.
Kallai (kăl-lā-ī), Neh. 12 : 20.
Kanah (kă-năh) [reeds] (13 Cd), city of Asher, Josh. 19 : 28.
Kanah brook (5 Bd, 16 Cd 17 Cd), Josh. 16 : 8; 17 : 9.
Kara (kā-ră), a mountain chain in Media.
Kareah (kă-rē-ăh) [bald], Jer. 40 : 8; 41 : 11.
Karkaa (kär-kă-ă) [a floor], Josh. 15 : 3.
Karkar, a city near Kadesh.
Karkor (kär-kôr) [foundation], Judg. 8 : 10.
Kartah (kär-tăh) [city], Josh. 21 : 34.
Kartan (kär-tăn) [double city], Josh. 21 : 32.
Kattath (kăt-tăth), Josh. 19 : 15.
Kedar (kē-där) [blackness], son of Ishmael, Gen. 25 : 13; 1 Chr. 1 : 29; Ps. 120 : 5; Song of Sol. 1 : 5; Jer. 2 : 10; Ezek. 27 : 21.
tribe of, prophecies concerning, Isa. 21 : 16; 42 : 11; 60 : 7; Jer. 49 : 28. They were Bedouin, lived in black tents, rich as far as nomadic tribes may be so termed, and skilful in war.
Kedron (kē-drŏn), Kidron, Cedron, brook near Jerusalem, crossed by David in affliction, 2 Sam. 15 : 23; and by Christ, John 18 : 1.
idols destroyed there, 1 Ki. 15 : 13; 2 Ki. 23 : 6; 2 Chr. 29 : 16; Jer. 31 : 40.
Keep, Gen. 18 : 19, they shall k. the way of the Lord.
28 : 15, 20, I am with thee, and will k. thee.
Num. 6 : 24, the Lord bless thee and k. thee.
1 Sam. 2 : 9, he will k. the feet of his saints.
Job 14 : 13, O that thou wouldest k. me.
Ps. 17 : 8, k. me as the apple of the eye.
19 : 13, k. me from presumptuous sins.
34 : 13, k. thy tongue from evil.
91 : 11, his angels charge to k. thee.
103 : 9, neither will he k. his anger for ever.
121 : 3, he that k. thee will not slumber.
127 : 1, except the Lord k. the city.
141 : 3, k. the door of my lips.

Prov. 4 : 6, love wisdom, she shall k. thee.
4 : 23, k. thy heart with all diligence.
Eccl. 3 : 6, a time to k., and a time to cast away.
5 : 1, k. thy foot when thou goest.
12 : 13, fear God, and k. his commandments.
Isa. 26 : 3, thou wilt k. him in perfect peace.
27 : 3, I the Lord do k. it.
Jer. 3 : 5, 12, will he k. his anger ?
Mic. 7 : 5, k. the doors of thy mouth.
Hab. 2 : 20, let the earth k. silence.
Matt. 19 : 17, k. the commandments.
Luke 11 : 28, blessed are they that hear the word and k. it.
19 : 43, enemies shall k. thee in on every side.
John 8 : 51, k. my saying.
12 : 25, he that hateth his life shall k. it.
14 : 23, if a man love me, he will k. my words.
17 : 15, k. them from the evil.
Acts 5 : 3, to k. back part of the price.
16 : 4, delivered the decrees to k.
1 Cor. 5 : 8, let us k. the feast.
9 : 27, I k. under my body.
15 : 2, k. in memory what I preached.
Eph. 4 : 3, k. the unity of the Spirit.
Phil. 4 : 7, the peace of God shall k. your hearts.
1 Tim. 5 : 22, k. thyself pure.
6 : 20, k. that committed to thy trust.
Jas. 1 : 27, to k. himself unspotted.
1 John 5 : 21, k. yourselves from idols.
Jude 24, to him that is able to k. you.
Rev. 3 : 10, I will k. thee from hour of temptation.
Keeper, Gen. 4 : 9, am I my brother's k. ?
Ps. 121 : 5, the Lord is thy k.
Eccl. 12 : 3, when k. of the house shall tremble.
Song of Sol. 1 : 6, made me k. of the vineyards.
Acts 16 : 27, k. of the prison.
Titus 2 : 5, chaste, k. at home.
Kehelathah (kĕ-hă-lā-thăh) [assembly], Num. 33 : 22, 23.
Keilah (kē-ī-lăh) [mountain-back], Josh. 15 : 44; 1 Sam. 23 : 1-12.
Kelaiah (kĕ-lāī-ăh), Ezra 10 : 23.
Kelita (kĕ-lī-tă), Ezra 10 : 23; Neh. 8 : 7.
Kemuel (kĕ-mū-ĕl) [raised by God], Gen. 22 : 21.
Kenakir, a city in El Hauran.
Kenan (kē-năn), 1 Chr. 1 : 2.
Kenath (kē-năth) [possession], a town of Manasseh, Num. 32 : 42.
Kenaz (kē-năz) [hunt], Josh. 15 : 17.
Kenezite (kē-nĕz-īte), Num. 32 : 12. See Palestine, Ancient Inhabitants.
Kenizzites (kĕ-nĭz-zītes), Gen. 15 : 19. See Palestine, Ancient Inhabitants.
Kenites (kē-nītes), connected with Cain, Gen. 15 : 19; Num. 24 : 21, 22. See Palestine, Ancient Inhabitants.
Kept, Luke 2 : 19, Mary k. all these things.
2 Tim. 4 : 7, I have k. the faith.
1 Pet. 1 : 5, k. by the power of God.
Jude 6, k. not their first estate.
Rev. 3 : 8, and hast k. my word.

Kerchief [ar.], a covering for the head, idolatrously used, Ezek. 13 : 18, 21. They seem to have varied with the height of the wearer, and were probably similar to long veils worn by the female prisoners from Lachish.

Keren, or cornet. See Musical Instruments.

Kernels, Num. 6 : 4.

Kethubim, or Hagiographa. See Old Testament.

Kettle, 1 Sam. 2 : 14.

Keturah (kĕ-tū-'răh) [incense], Abraham's descendants by, Gen. 25; 1 Chr. 1 : 32.

Key, of David, Rev. 3 : 7; Judg. 3 : 25; Isa. 22 : 22.

Keys, of heaven, Matt. 16 : 19.
of hell, Rev. 1 : 18.
See Isa. 22 : 22; Luke 11 : 52.
Rev. 9 : 1, k. of the bottomless pit.

Kibroth-hattaavah (kĭb-'rŏth-hăt-tā-'ă-väh) [the graves of lust], Num. 11 : 34.

Kick, Deut. 32 : 15, Jeshurun waxed fat and k.
1 Sam. 2 : 29, k. ye at my sacrifice ?
Acts 9 : 5; 26 : 14, to k. against the pricks.

Kid, law concerning, Ex. 23 : 19; Deut. 14 : 21; Lev. 4 : 23; 16 : 5; 23 : 19.

Kidneys, burnt for sacrifices, Ex. 29 : 13; Lev. 3 : 4, 5.
of wheat, fat of, Deut. 32 : 14.

Kill, Ex. 20 : 13; Deut. 5 : 17; Matt. 5 : 21; Rom. 13 : 9, thou shalt not k.
Num. 16 : 13, to k. us in the wilderness.
Deut. 32 : 39, I k., and I make alive.
2 Ki. 5 : 7, am I God, to k. ?
7 : 4, if they k. us, we shall but die.
Ps. 44 : 22, for thy sake are we k.
Eccl. 3 : 3, a time to k.
Matt. 10 : 28; Luke 12 : 4, fear not them that k. the body.
Mark 3 : 4, is it lawful to save life, or to k. ?
John 7 : 19; 7 : 1, the Jews sought to k. him.
7 : 19, why go ye about to k. me ?
8 : 22, will he k. himself ?
10 : 10, thief cometh to steal and k.
Rom. 8 : 36, for thy sake we are k. all the day.
2 Cor. 3 : 6, the letter k., spirit giveth life.
6 : 9, as chastened and not k.
Jas. 4 : 2, ye k. and desire to have.
5 : 6, ye condemned and k. the just.
Rev. 13 : 10, he that k. with sword must be k.

Kin, Lev. 18 : 6; Ruth 2 : 20; Mark 6 : 4. The next of kin stood in a civic and legal relationship to his nearest kinsman (cf. Jer. 32 : 8 ff.; Lev. 25 : 25; Ruth 2 : 1; 4 : 5). Above all he was the avenger should a feud remove his kinsman (cf. Ex. 21 : 13; Deut. 19 : 1-13; 24 : 16; Num. 35 : 9-34).

Kind, 2 Chr. 10 : 7, if thou be k. to this people.
Matt. 13 : 47, garnered of every k.
17 : 21; Mark 9 : 29, this k. goeth not out.
Luke 6 : 35, God is k. to unthankful and evil.
1 Cor. 13 : 4, charity suffereth long and is k.
Jas. 1 : 18, a k. of first-fruits.

Kindle, Num. 11 : 33; Deut. 11 : 17; 2 Ki. 22 : 13; Ps. 106 : 40, wrath of the Lord was k.
Ps. 2 : 12, his wrath is k. but a little.
Prov. 26 : 21, a contentious man to k. strife.
Hos. 11 : 8, my repentings are k. together.

Luke 12 : 49, what will I, if it be already k.

Jas. 3 : 5, how great a matter a little fire k.

Kindly, Gen. 24 : 49; 47 : 29; Josh. 2 : 14, deal k. and truly.

Kindness, exhortations to, Prov. 19 : 22; 31 : 26; Rom. 12 : 10; 1 Cor. 13 : 4; Eph. 4 : 32; Col. 3 : 12.
Josh. 2 : 12, show k. to my father's house.
Ruth 3 : 10, showed more k. in latter end.
2 Sam. 2 : 6, I will requite you this k.
Neh. 9 : 17, God gracious, of great k.
Ps. 117 : 2, his merciful k. is great.
141 : 5, let the righteous smite me, it shall be a k.
Isa. 54 : 8, with everlasting k.
Jer. 2 : 2, I remember the k. of thy youth.
Joel 2 : 13; Jonah 4 : 2, Lord is of great k.
2 Cor. 6 : 6, by long-suffering, by k.
2 Pet. 1 : 7, brotherly k., to k. charity.

Kindred, Gen. 24 : 4; Ruth 3 : 2; Acts 3 : 25; Rev. 11 : 9.

Kine, Pharaoh's dream of, Gen. 41 : 2; two take back the ark, 1 Sam. 6 : 7.

King, of kings. Jesus has been called our Prophet, Priest, and King, but apart from the first two offices the last has no content. His kingship implies that He has done the work of Prophet and Priest perfectly, in that He has brought God to man and man to God. In order, therefore to comprehend our idea of Christ as Mediator, we would be better to use the phrase, " Kingly Prophet and Kingly Priest."
Ps. 2 : 6; 10 : 16; 24 : 7; 110; Zech. 9 : 9; Luke 23 : 2; 1 Tim. 1 : 17; 6 : 15; Rev. 15 : 3; 17 : 14.
parable of the king and his servants, Matt. 18 : 23-35; of the king and his guest, Matt. 22 : 2-14.
kings, chosen by God, Deut. 17 : 14; 1 Sam. 9 : 17; 16 : 1; 1 Ki. 11 : 35; 19 : 15; 1 Chr. 28 : 4; Dan. 2 : 21.
honour due to, Prov. 24 : 21; 25 : 6; Eccl. 8 : 2; 10 : 20; Matt. 22 : 21; Rom. 13; 1 Pet. 2 : 13, 17.
to be prayed for, 1 Tim. 2 : 1, 2.
See Ps. 2 : 10; Prov. 25 : 2; 31 : 4; Isa. 49 : 23.
Gen. 14 : 18; Heb. 7 : 1, Melchizedek, k. of Salem.
Num. 23 : 21, the shout of a k. is among them.
Judg. 8 : 18, resembled children of a k.
9 : 8, trees went forth to anoint a k.
1 Sam. 8 : 5, now make us a k.
10 : 24; 2 Sam. 16 : 16; 2 Ki. 11 : 12, God save the k.
Job 18 : 14, the k. of terrors.
Ps. 2 : 6, I set my K. upon a holy hill.
5 : 2; 84 : 3, my K. and my God.
10 : 16; 29 : 10, the Lord is K. for ever.
20 : 9, let the K. hear us when we call.
24 : 10, Lord of hosts is K. of glory.
45 : 1, things I have made touching the K.
72 : 1, give the k. thy judgments.
74 : 12, God is my K. of old.
149 : 2, children of Zion joyful in their K.
Prov. 8 : 15, by me k. reign.
22 : 29, the diligent shall stand before k.

24 : 21, fear the Lord and the k.

Eccl. 2 : 12, what can the man do that cometh after the k. ?

10 : 16, woe to thee when thy k. is a child.

10 : 20, curse not the k.

Isa. 6 : 5, mine eyes have seen the K.

32 : 1, a k. shall reign in righteousness.

33 : 17, thine eyes shall see the K. in his beauty.

49 : 23, k. shall be thy nursing fathers.

Jer. 10 : 10, the Lord is an everlasting K.

23 : 5, a K. shall reign and prosper.

Matt. 22 : 11, when the k. came in to see the guests.

Luke 14 : 31, what k. going to war ?

19 : 38, blessed be the K. that cometh.

23 : 2, saying that he is Christ a k.

John 6 : 15, by force, to make him a k.

19 : 14, behold your k.

Acts 17 : 7, there is another k., one Jesus.

1 Tim. 1 : 17, now to the K. eternal.

Rev. 1 : 6; 5 : 10, k. and priests unto God.

15 : 3, thou K. of saints.

Kingdom, of God. A close study of all the passages relating to the Kingdom of God will show that it is regarded both as a present possession and as a future inheritance.

Ps. 22 : 28; 45 : 6; 145 : 11; Isa. 24 : 23; Dan. 2 : 44.

of Christ, Isa. 2; 4; 9; 11; 32; 35; 52; 61; 66; Matt. 16 : 28; 26 : 29; John 18 : 36; 2 Pet. 1 : 11.

of heaven, Matt. 3 : 2; 8 : 11; 11 : 11; 13 : 11.

who shall enter, Matt. 5 : 3; 7 : 21; Luke 9 : 62; John 3 : 3; Acts 14 : 22; Rom. 14 : 17; 1 Cor. 6 : 9; 15 : 50; 2 Thess. 1 : 5.

parables concerning, Matt. 13.

Ex. 19 : 6, a k. of priests.

1 Sam. 18 : 8, what can he have more but the k. ?

1 Chr. 29 : 11; Matt. 6 : 13, thine is the k., O Lord.

Ps. 103 : 19, k. ruleth over all.

145 : 12, the glorious majesty of his k.

Dan. 4 : 3, his k., is an everlasting k.

Matt. 4 : 23; 9 : 35; 24 : 14, gospel of the k.

8 : 12, children of k. cast out.

12 : 25; Mark 3 : 24; Luke 11 : 17, K. divided against itself.

Matt. 13 : 38, good seed are children of the k.

25 : 34, inherit the k. prepared for you.

26 : 29, drink it new in Father's k.

Luke 12 : 32, Father's good pleasure to give you the k.

22 : 29, I appoint unto you a k.

John 18 : 36, my k. is not of this world.

Acts 1 : 6, restore k. again to Israel.

1 Cor. 15 : 24, when he shall have delivered up the k.

Col. 1 : 13, translated us into k. of his Son.

Heb. 12 : 28, a k. that cannot be moved.

Jas. 2 : 5, heirs of the k. which he hath promised.

2 Pet. 1 : 11, entrance into everlasting k.

Rev. 12 : 10, now is come k. of our God.

Kingly, Dan. 5 : 20.

Kings, First and Second Books of. Composition and Date.—The books rest on early sources, e.g., the " Acts of Solomon " (1 Ki. 11 : 41), the " Chronicles of the kings of Israel " and the " Chronicles of the kings of Judah." These contained narratives of conquests, plots, wars, buildings, etc. (cf. 1 Ki. 14 : 19; 15 : 23; 16 : 20). There were two redactions or editings of the writings under the influence of the Deuteronomic Reformation (see Joshua, etc.), namely, between 621 and 597 B.C., and also c. 560 B.C. (called D, and D¹ respective'y), (cf. 2 Ki. 24 : 5; 25 : 27, etc.). Our books were known then by 560 B.C., though in Hebrew MSS. they are regarded as one. The LXX. and Vulgate refer to them as Third and Fourth Kings (Samuel being known as First and Second Kings).

The sources of these books were no doubt the historical documents of Judah and Israel. The two books of Kir.gs were called in the Septuagint the third and fourth, the books of Samuel were called the first and second, and the Chronicles the fifth and sixth.

The time covered by the books of the Kings is the entire period after Saul and David down to the close of the Israelite monarchies. Under Solomon, the boundaries extended from the Euphrates to the Mediterranean and the border of Egypt (1 K. 4 : 21). Corruption entered and the dominion dwindled to a pitiful dependency. The decline was marked by the division of the kingdom after Solomon (975 B.C.) and the suicidal wars between the north, Samaria, and the south, Jerusalem, often with allies hired from heathen neighbours. Idolatry and moral corruption kept pace with wrong political alliances, until punishment fell in the form of the captivities. (Samaria, 722 B.C.; Judah, 606-586.)

Kinnor. See **Musical Instruments.**

Kinsfolk, Job 19 : 14; Luke 21 : 16.

Kinsman, Ruth 3 : 12, 13; 4 : 1-8.

Kinswoman, Lev. 18 : 17; Prov. 7 : 4.

Kir (kĭr) [a wall, fortress], 2 Ki. 16 : 9; Isa. 15 : 1; 22 : 6; Amos 1 : 5; 9 : 7.

Kir-hareseth (kĭr-hăr-́ĕ-sĕth) [a city of the hill], Isa. 16 : 7.

Kiriathaim (kĭr-ĭ-ă-thā-́ĭm) [twofold city], Jer. 48 : 1, 23.

Kirioth (kĭr-ĭ-ŏth), Amos 2 : 2.

Kirjath (kĭr-jăth) [city], Josh. 18 : 28.

Kirjathaim (kĭr-jă-thā-́ĭm) (3 Ef), Num. 32 : 37.

Kirjath-arba (kĭr-jăth-är-́bă) [city of Arba], the ancient name of Hebron, Gen. 23 : 2; Josh. 14 : 15.

Kirjath-baal (kĭr-́jă.h-bā-́ăl) [city of Baal], Josh. 16 : 60.

Kirjath-huzoth (kĭr-́jăth-hū-́zŏth) [city of streets], Num. 22 : 39.

Kirjath-jearim (kĭr-́jăth-jē-́ă-rĭm) or **Kirjatharim** [city of the woods], Josh. 9 : 17; 18 : 14; 1 Chr. 13 : 5.

the ark brought to, 1 Sam. 7 : 1.

the ark fetched from, 1 Chr. 13 : 6; 2 Chr. 1 : 4.

Kirjath-Jearim.

Kirjath-sannah (kĭr-́jăth-săn-́năh) [city of palm-spikes], Josh. 15 : 49.
Kirjath-sepher (kĭr-́jăth-sē-́phĕr) [city of books], Josh. 15 : 15.
Kir Moab, one of the two chief strongholds of Moab.
Kish (kĭsh) [a bowl], 1 Sam. 9 : 1, 3; Acts 13 : 21.
Kishi (kĭsh-́ī), 1 Chr. 6 : 44.
Kishion (kĭsh-́iŏn) [hardness], Josh. 19 : 20.
Kishon (kĭ-́shŏn) [wending], a rivulet which rises in Mount Tabor, and falls into the Mediterranean, Judg. 4 : 7; 5 : 21; Ps. 83 : 9.
Kislev, month of (Nov.-Dec.). See **Months**.
Kison. See **Kishon**.
Kiss, holy, salute with, Rom. 16 : 16; 2 Cor. 13 : 12; 1 Thess. 5 : 26; 1 Pet. 5 : 14.
given as a mark of affection, Gen. 27 : 27; 29 : 11; 45 : 15; 48 : 10; 1 Sam. 10 : 1; 20 : 41; Luke 7 : 38; 15 : 20; Acts 20 : 37.
given treacherously, 2 Sam. 20 : 9; Matt. 26 : 48; Luke 22 : 48.
idolatrous, 1 Ki. 19 : 18; Job 31 : 27; Hos. 13 : 2.
Ps. 2 : 12, k. the Son, lest he be angry.
85 : 10, righteousness and peace k. each other.
Luke 7 : 45, thou gavest me no k.
1 Cor. 16 : 20, salute with an holy k.
Kite. The red, black, and Egyptian kites are all found in Palestine, and are regarded as among the unclean birds (Lev. 11 : 14; Deut. 14 : 13; Job 28 : 7, R.V.; Isa. 34 : 15, R.V.). "Vulture," "falcon," "glede," all translate the Hebrew words.
Knead, Ex. 8 : 3; 1 Sam. 28 : 24; Jer. 7 : 18.
Knee, Gen. 41 : 43; Matt. 27 : 29.
Kneeling, in prayer, 2 Chr. 6 : 13; Ezra 9 : 5; Ps. 95 : 6; Dan. 6 : 10; Acts 7 : 60; 9 : 40; 21 : 5; Eph. 3 : 14.
Knew, Gen. 28 : 16, the Lord is in this place, and I k. it not.
Job 23 : 3, k. where I might find him.
Jer. 1 : 5, before I formed thee I k. thee.
Matt. 7 : 23, I never k. you, depart.
25 : 24, I k. thee, thou art an hard man.
John 2 : 25, Jesus k. what was in man.
4 : 10, if thou k. the gift of God.
1 Cor. 1 : 21, world by wisdom k. not God.
2 : 8, none of princes of world k.
2 Cor. 5 : 21, who k. no sin.
Rev. 19 : 12, name written no man k.

Knife, Gen. 22 : 6, 10; Judg. 19 : 29; Prov. 30 : 14.
Knit, 1 Sam. 18 : 1; Acts 10 : 11; Col. 2 : 2, 19.
Knock, Matt. 7 : 7; Luke 11 : 9, k. and it shall be opened unto you.
Luke 12 : 36, he cometh and k.
Acts 12 : 16, Peter continued k.
Rev. 3 : 20, I stand at the door and k.
Knop, a bud-shaped carving, Ex. 25 : 33; 1 Ki. 6 : 18.
Know. In many cases, where the Bible speaks of God as "knowing" a person it implies more than mere comprehension. It suggests affection, and we may often paraphrase "knoweth" by "careth for," e.g., Isa. 1 : 3.
Gen. 3 : 22, to k. good and evil.
1 Sam. 3 : 7, Samuel did not yet k. the Lord.
Job 5 : 27, k. thou it is for thy good.
8 : 9, we are but of yesterday, and k. nothing.
19 : 25, I k. that my Redeemer liveth.
22 : 13, Ps. 73 : 11, how doth God k. ?
Ps. 39 : 4, make me to k. mine end.
46 : 10, be still, and k. that I am God.
103 : 16, the place shall k. it no more.
139 : 23, k. my heart.
143 : 8, to k. way wherein I should walk.
Eccl. 1 : 17, gave my heart to k. wisdom.
9 : 5, the living k. they shall die.
11 : 9, k. that God will bring to judgment.
Isa. 1 : 3, the ox k. his owner.
52 : 6, my people shall k. my name.
Jer. 17 : 9, the heart is deceitful, who can k. it ?
31 : 34; Heb. 8 : 11, k. the Lord : for all shall k. me.
Hos. 2 : 20, thou shalt k. the Lord.
Matt. 6 : 3, let not thy left hand k. what.
7 : 11, if ye k. how to give good gifts.
13 : 11; Mark 4 : 11; Luke 8 : 10, it is given to you to k.
Luke 19 : 42, if thou hadst k.
22 : 57, I k. him not.
John 4 : 42, we k. that this is the Christ.
7 : 17, he shall k. of the doctrine.
10 : 14, I k. my sheep, and am k. of mine.
13 : 7, thou shalt k. hereafter.
Acts 1 : 7, not for you to k. the times.
Rom. 8 : 28, we k. that all things work for good.
1 Cor. 2 : 14, neither can he k.
13 : 9, we k. in part.
Eph. 3 : 19, k. the love of Christ.
2 Tim. 1 : 12, I k. whom I have believed.
3 : 15, thou hast k. the scriptures.
1 John 3 : 2, we k. that when he shall appear.
Rev. 2 : 2; 3 : 1, 8, I k. thy works.
3 : 9, make them k. I have loved thee.
Knowledge, given by God, Ex. 8 : 10; 18 : 16; 31 : 3; 2 Chr. 1 : 12; Ps. 119 : 66; Prov. 1 : 4; 2 : 6; Eccl. 2 : 26; Isa. 28 : 9; Jer. 24 : 7; 31 : 33; Dan. 2 : 21; Matt. 11 : 25; 13 : 11; 1 Cor. 1 : 5; 2 : 12; 12 : 8.
advantages of, Ps. 89 : 15; Prov. 1 : 4; 3 : 13; 4; 9 : 10; 10 : 14; Eccl. 7 : 12; Mal. 2 : 7; Eph. 3 : 17, 18; 4 : 13; Jas. 3 : 13; 2 Pet. 2 : 20.
want of, Prov. 1 : 22; 10 : 13; Jer. 4 : 22; Hos. 4 : 6; Rom. 1 : 28; 1 Cor. 15 : 34.
to be prayed for, Col. 1 : 9.

JOPPA

IN THE WILDERNESS (SELA)

to be sought for, 1 Cor. 14 : 1; Heb. 6 : 1; 2 Pet. 1 : 5.
abuse of, 1 Cor. 8 : 1.
responsibility of, Num. 15 : 30; Deut. 17 : 12; Luke 12 : 47; John 15 : 22; Rom. 1 : 21; 2 : 21; Jas. 4 : 17.
vanity of human, Eccl. 1 : 18; Isa. 44 : 25; 1 Cor. 1 : 19; 3 : 19; 2 Cor. 1 : 12.
of good and evil, tree of, Gen. 2 : 9.
Num. 24 : 16, k. of the Most High.
2 Chr. 1 : 11, thou hast asked k.
Job 21 : 14, we desire not k. of thy ways.
Ps. 19 : 2, night to night showeth k.
73 : 11, is there k. in Most High ?
94 : 10, he that teacheth man k.
139 : 6, such k. is too wonderful.
144 : 3, what is man that thou takest k. ?
Prov. 1 : 7, fear of Lord is beginning of k.
14 : 18, prudent are crowned with k.
17 : 27, he that hath k. spareth his words.
30 : 3, nor have the k. of the holy.
Eccl. 9 : 10, nor k. in the grave.
Isa. 11 : 2, the spirit of k.
40 : 14, who taught him k. ?
53 : 11, by his k. justify many.
Dan. 12 : 4, k. shall be increased.
Hab. 2 : 14, earth filled with k. of Lord.
Luke 11 : 52, taken away key of k.
Acts 4 : 13, took away k. of them.
24 : 22, more perfect k. of that way.
Rom. 3 : 20, by law is k. of sin.
10 : 2, zeal of God, but not according to k.
1 Cor. 13 : 8, k. shall vanish away.
2 Cor. 4 : 6, like of k. of the glory of God.
Eph. 3 : 19, love of Christ, which passeth k.
Phil. 3 : 8, all things loss for the k. of Christ.
Col. 2 : 3, treasures of wisdom and k.
1 Tim. 2 : 4; 2 Tim. 3 : 7, the k. of the truth.
2 Pet. 3 : 10, grow in grace and k. of Lord.

Kohath (kō-hăth) [congregation], son of Levi, Gen. 46 : 11.
his descendants, Ex. 6 : 18; 1 Chr. 6 : 2.
their duties, Num. 4 : 15; 10 : 21; 2 Chr. 29 : 12; 34 : 12.
Korah (kôr-ăh), Greek **Core** [baldness], and Dathan, their sedition and punishment, Num. 16; 26 : 9; 27 : 3; Jude 11.
sons of, psalms ascribed to. See **Psalms.**
Korahites (kôr-ă-hītes), 1 Chr. 9 : 19.
Korathites (kôr-ă-thītes), Num. 26 : 58.
Kore (kôr-ē) [partridge], **Korhites** (kôr-hītes), Ex. 6 : 24; 1 Chr. 26 : 1; 2 Chr. 31 : 14.
Koz (kŏz) [thorn], Ezra 2 : 61.
Kushaiah (kū-shā-ĭăh), 1 Chr. 15 : 17.
Kutha, a city near Babylon.

L

Laadah (lā-ă-dăh), 1 Chr. 4 : 21.
Laadan (lā-ă-dăn) [order], 1 Chr. 7 : 26.
Laban (lā-băn) [white]. By no means pleasing in character, reflecting as he does the more odious characteristics of his nephew Jacob, Laban nevertheless occasionally shows a generous spirit (e.g., at his final parting from Jacob).
hospitality of, Gen. 24 : 29.
gives Jacob his two daughters, Gen. 29.

envies and oppresses him, Gen. 30 : 27; 31 : 1.
his covenant with him, Gen. 31 : 43.
Labour, appointed for man, Gen. 3 : 19; Ps. 104 : 23; 1 Cor. 4 : 12.
when blessed by God, Prov. 13 : 11; Eccl. 2 : 24; 4 : 9; 5 : 12, 19.
Ex. 20 : 9; Deut. 5 : 13, six days shalt thou l.
Job 9 : 29, why then l. in vain ?
Ps. 90 : 10, is their strength l. and sorrow.
127 : 1, except Lord build, they l. in vain.
128 : 2, shalt eat the l. of thy hands.
144 : 14, our oxen may be strong to l.
Prov. 10 : 16, l. tendeth to life.
14 : 23, in all l. there is profit.
23 : 4, l. not to be rich.
Eccl. 1 : 8, all things are full of l.
2 : 22, what hath man of all his l. ?
4 : 8, for whom do I l. ?
5 : 12, sleep of a l. man is sweet.
9 : 9, portion in thy l. under the sun.
Hab. 3 : 17, the l. of the olive shall fail.
Matt. 11 : 28, come unto me, all ye that l.
John 4 : 38, reap where ye bestow no l.
6 : 27, l. not for meat that perisheth.
1 Cor. 15 : 58, your l. is not in vain.
2 Cor. 5 : 9, we l. to be accepted of God.
Eph. 4 : 28, rather l., working with his hands.
1 Thess. 1 : 3; Heb. 6 : 10, your l. of love.
1 Thess. 3 : 5, our l. be in vain ?
1 Tim. 4 : 10, l. and suffer reproach.
5 : 17, that l. in word and doctrine.
Heb. 4 : 11, l. to enter into that rest.
Rev. 2 : 2, I know thy l. and patience.
14 : 13, rest from their l.
Labourer, worthy of hire, Luke 10 : 7; 1 Tim. 5 : 18.
parable of the, Matt. 20.
with God, 1 Cor. 3 : 9.
Lace, Ex. 28 : 28; 39 : 21, 31.
Lachish (lā-chĭsh) [Assyr. " Lakisu "; impregnable], a city of Judah.
conquered, Josh. 10 : 13; 12 : 11.
Amaziah slain at, 2 Ki. 14 : 19.
Lack, Hos. 4 : 6, people destroyed for l. of knowledge.
Ps. 34 : 10, young lions do l. ?
Matt. 19 : 20, what l. I yet ?
Mark 10 : 21, one thing thou l.
Phil. 4 : 10, but ye l. opportunity.
Jas. 1 : 5, if any l. wisdom, ask of God.
Lad, Gen. 22 : 12; 44 : 22, 30; John 6 : 9.
Ladder, Gen. 28 : 12.
Lade, 1 Ki. 12 : 11; Luke 11 : 46.
Laden, Isa. 1 : 4, a people l. with iniquity.
Matt. 11 : 28, all that are heavy l.
2 Tim. 3 : 6, women l. with sins.
Lading, Neh. 13 : 15; Acts 27 : 10.
Lady, Esther 1 : 18; Isa. 47 : 5, 7; 2 John 1 : 5.
Lael (lā-ĕl), Num. 3 : 24.
Lahad (lā-hăd), 1 Chr. 4 : 2.
Lahai-roi (lā-hāi-rŏi), Gen. 24 : 62. See **Beer-lahai-roi.**
Lahmam (lăh-măm) [head], Josh. 15 : 40.
Lahmi (lăh-mī) [my bread], 1 Chr. 20 : 5.
Laish (lā-ĭsh) [lion], original name of the city of Dan, Judg. 18 : 7; Isa. 10 : 30.
Lake, Luke 5 : 1, stood by the l.
8 : 33, down a steep place into the l.

Rev. 19 : 20; 20 : 10, 14, 15, into the l. of fire.

Lama (lä-mä) [why], Matt. 27 : 46; Mark 15 : 34.

Lamb. The idea of the sacrifice of the Paschal Lamb was present in John's mind when he treated of the Crucifixion as occurring at the time of the Passover. When numerous lambs were being prepared for an offering, the Lamb of God was offering Himself a ransom for many.

for sacrifices, Gen. 22 : 7; Ex. 12 : 3; Lev. 3 : 7; Isa. 1 : 11.

Gen. 22 : 8, God will provide a l.

Isa. 11 : 6, the wolf shall dwell with the l.

53 : 7; Jer. 11 : 19, as a l. to the slaughter.

John 1 : 29, 36, behold the L. of God.

Acts 8 : 32, like a l. dumb before shearer.

1 Pet. 1 : 19, as of a l. without blemish.

Rev. 13 : 8, L. slain from foundation of world.

15 : 3, sons of Moses and of the L.

Lame, the, excluded from the priest's office, Lev. 21 : 18.

animals, not to be offered for sacrifices, Deut. 15 : 21; Mal. 1 : 8, 13.

healed by Christ, Matt. 11 : 5; 21 : 14; Luke 7 : 22; and the apostles, Acts 3; 8 : 7.

Job 29 : 15, feet to the l.

Prov. 26 : 7, legs of l. are not equal.

Isa. 35 : 6, l. man leap as an hart.

Heb. 12 : 13, lest that l. be turned out of the way.

Lamech (lä-měch) [strong youth], descendant of Cain, Gen. 4 : 18.

father of Noah, Gen. 5 : 25, 28.

Lament, Isa. 3 : 26; Mic. 2 : 4; John 16 : 20; Rev. 18 : 9.

Lamentable, Dan. 6 : 20.

Lamentation, for Jacob, Gen. 50 : 10.

David's, for Saul and Jonathan, 2 Sam. 1 : 17; for Abner, 2 Sam. 3 : 31.

for Josiah, 2 Chr. 35 : 25.

for Tyrus, Ezek. 26 : 17; 27 : 30; 28 : 12.

for Pharaoh, Ezek. 32.

for Christ, Luke 23 : 27.

for Stephen, Acts 8 : 2.

for Babylon, Rev. 18 : 10.

Lamentations of Jeremiah, The.

Occasion and Purpose.—The prophecy of Jeremiah is a statesmanlike and impassioned appeal to Judah and Jerusalem to forsake the sins that were bringing judgment upon the nation. This warning went unheeded, and the judgment fell in the very terms predicted. Jeremiah voices in Lamentations the sorrow of the people and his own overwhelming grief. The five poems are so composed as to form a memorial to be repeated at stated times lest God's people should forget their sin. It was long the custom after the captivity to read Lamentations with fasting and weeping on the 9th of Ab (July) in order that the people might remember the depths of misery from which they had been delivered. The acrostic form in which four of the five poems are constructed, though confessedly the most difficult to compose, is admirably adapted to memorizing, and the very dignity of this elegiac verse has made Lamentations the appropriate expression of sorrow in widely differing conditions of disaster.

Summary.—The subject is the destruction and subsequent sorrows of Jerusalem at the hands of Nebuchadrezzar (586 B.C.).

(a) Four Elegies, three of which (1, 2, and 4) have twenty-two verses, each of which begins with a different and successive letter of the Hebrew alphabet, each poem thus using all the letters once in rotation. The third, consisting of sixty-six verses, uses each letter three times. (cf. Ps. 119, which is also alphabetical.)

(1) Chaps. 1 : 1-11, Jerusalem has lost her glory and her sanctuary; 12-22, she bewails her doom. (2) Chap. 2 : 1-10, Her sorrow is due to God's judgment; 11-17, her shame and distress; 18-22, appeals to God. (3) Chap. 3 : 1-21, The city laments bitterly; 22-36, God's love gives her hope and encourages submission; 37-54, prayer of penitence; 55-66, prayer for vengeance upon the enemy. (4) Chap. 4 : 1-6, The fate of the people of Jerusalem; 7-11, and of the princes; 12-16, of the priests and prophets; 17-20, the king's fate; 21-22, doom to the Edomites. (cf. Ps. 137 : 7.)

(b) A Prayer.—(5) Chap. 5 : 1-18, The city laments her sorrows; 19-22, prayer for deliverance.

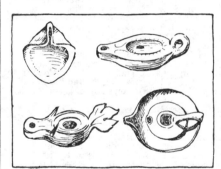

Lamps.

Lamp. Illuminants are early mentioned in the Bible. (1) Earliest of all were those pieces of resinous wood known as " torches " (Judg. 7 : 16, 20. A.V. = " lamps "). (2) From excavations, the development of the " lamp " has been built up, and two main forms, the open lamp and the closed, have been discovered. Some lamps, as against the majority which favoured the single wick, allowed for three, four, and even seven lights through spouts punched in their rims. Made usually of clay (the Temple lamps being of gold), they generally burned olive oil and even naphtha, while their wicks were made of twisted flax (Isa. 42 : 3, R.V.m.). The lamps were placed in poorer houses in a niche in the wall; the wealthy placed them on " lampstands."

(A.V. = candlestick, but cf. Matt. 5 : 15, R.V.)

In the East in ancient times (as even yet they are) the household lamps were kept alight continually. This custom lies behind such passages as 1 Ki. 11 : 36; 2 Ki. 8 : 19; Job 18 : 6; Prov. 13 : 9.

The A.V. frequently uses the word " candles " when " lamps " would be more appropriate. Our candles were not known then.

Of the Temple lamps we merely refer by pointing to such passages as Ex. 25 : 37; 30 : 7 f.; 1 Ki. 7 : 49; 2 Chr. 4 : 20; 13 : 11; Zech. 4 : 2.

in the tabernacle, Ex. 27 : 20; Lev. 24 : 2; Num. 8.

seen in visions, Gen. 15 : 17; Rev. 4 : 5.

parable concerning, Matt. 25 : 1.

1 Sam. 3 : 3, ere l. went out.

Ps. 119 : 105, thy word a l. to my feet.

132 : 17, ordained a l. for mine anointed.

Prov. 13 : 9, l. of wicked shall be put out.

Matt. 25 : 1, ten virgins took l.

See **Candle, Candlestick.**

Lance, Jer. 50 : 42.

Lancets, 1 Ki. 18 : 28.

Land, Gen. 1 : 9, let the dry l. appear.

Gen. 12 : 1, unto a l. that I will show thee.

Ex. 14 : 21, made the sea dry l.

Num. 21 : 22, let me pass through thy l.

Deut. 32 : 49, behold the l. of Canaan.

Josh. 4 : 22, over this Jordan on dry l.

Ps. 66 : 1; 100 : 1, make a joyful noise all ye l.

Ezek. 34 : 13, will bring them to their own l.

Mic. 7 : 13, l. shall be desolate.

Mark 15 : 33, darkness over the whole l.

Heb. 11 : 9, sojourned in the l. of promise.

See Acts 18 : 22; 28 : 12.

Landmark. Single stones set on end, or piles of stones some distance apart, constituted the boundary between the land of one owner and that of another. These stones could be easily moved by a dishonest man; hence the curse (Deut. 27 : 17).

Deut. 19 : 14; Job 24 : 2; Prov. 22 : 28; 23 : 10.

Lanes, Luke 14 : 21.

Languages, confounded, Gen. 11.

gift of, by Holy Ghost, Acts 2 : 7, 8; 10 : 46; 19 : 6; 1 Cor. 12 : 10.

Gen. 11 : 1, whole earth of one l.

Ps. 19 : 3, no l. where voice is not heard.

Acts 2 : 6, heard them speak in his own l.

Languages of the Bible. The languages in which the originals of the sacred Scriptures have come down to us are three in number, namely :—

1. Hebrew.—The Hebrew language is a branch of the great Semitic family of languages spoken in Palestine, Phœnicia, Syria, Mesopotamia, Babylonia, Assyria, and Arabia. The territory in which the Semitic language was indigenous embraced the countries bounded by the Mediterranean Sea on the west, and extended east beyond the great rivers, the Euphrates and the Tigris. It stretched from the mountains of Armenia in the north to the south coast of Arabia. The Semitic spread in very early times from Arabia into Africa, and ultimately became the common language of Abyssinia where it still preserves its hold. It was also extended by means of the Phœnician colonies over very considerable districts of North Africa, and even became common in several of the islands of the Mediterranean, notably in Cyprus and Malta. The Canaanites who dwelt in Palestine prior to the settlement of the Israelites in the country spoke a Semitic language, as is clear from the names they gave to their cities. The Israelites probably borrowed their language, in spite of attempts to show that Abram brought it with him (e.g., " eber " = " beyond," i.e., Abram's crossing the Euphrates named the language he brought). There is no doubt there were considerable dialectic differences between the Hebrew language as spoken in the north, and that which prevailed in the south of Palestine; some few remains of those peculiarities have been traced by scholars. But the written language of the Law and the Prophets was essentially one and the same, and all the books of the Old Testament were written in Hebrew, with the exception of the portions noted in the next paragraph. It is at once grave and simple, depending for its effect not on involved sentences but in co-ordinated sentences stark and realistic. Hence, though unsuitable for dialectic, it is pre-eminently successful as the medium of God's revelation. It died out of common use after 587 B.C. (destruction of Jerusalem) but is still used in the synagogues and in some educated circles.

2. Biblical Aramaic.—Several portions of the books of the Old Testament are written in a peculiar Aramaic dialect often miscalled Chaldee, a mistake which arose from a misconception of Dan. 1 : 4 with Dan. 2 : 4. Jerome the translator of the Latin Vulgate, perpetuated and popularised this mistake. Although Aramaic seems to have been extensively used as the language of trade and commerce, and occasionally employed in official proclamations, it was not the language of the court of Babylonia. The Biblical Aramaic has certain marked peculiarities, but is closely akin to the Aramaic of the Targums and to Syriac. The following portions of the Old Testament are in this language :—(1) Ezra 4 : 8 to ch. 6 : 18, and ch. 7 : 12-26. (2) Jeremiah 10 : 11. (3) Daniel 2 : 4, after the words in the English version " in Syriac," up to ch. 7 : 28. Jesus and His disciples spoke Aramaic (" Hebrew "). cf. Matt. 5 : 22; 6 : 24; 16 : 17; 27 : 46; Mark 5 : 41; 7 : 34; 14 : 36; Luke 16 : 9, 13; John 1 : 42; 19 : 13; Acts 1 : 19; 1 Cor. 16 : 22.

3. Greek.—All the books of the New Testament have come down to us in Greek only. It is a question whether St. Matthew's Gospel was not originally composed in

Hebrew. If that be so, the original is lost for the Greek only is extant. The Greek o the New Testament is not, however, the Greek of the classical writers, but Greek as spoken by Jews, and modified accordingly. It is generally termed Hellenistic Greek, that is, the Greek spoken by the Hellenists, or Greek-speaking Jews. The Jews who settled in Alexandria in Egypt, when Alexander the Great founded that city, and whose numbers were swelled by constant deportations, as well as by immigration, became distinguished in after times for their literary ability, and wrote in this Greek dialect, which, though peculiar, was easily understood by persons acquainted with the classical language. The Septuagint Version (LXX.), including the Apocryphal Books of the Old Testament is written in Hellenistic Greek.

Languish, Ps. 41 : 3, upon the bed of l.
    Isa. 19 : 8, upon the waters shall l.
    24 : 4, the world l. and fadeth.
    Jer. 14 : 2, the gates thereof l.
    Nah. 1 : 4, the flower of Lebanon l.

Lanterns.

Lantern. A common kind (John 18 : 3) was made by stretching oiled canvas round a frame of wood or round a coil of wire. Such a " torch " (rather than " lantern ") was carried by a servant in front of his master to show a safe path through the unpaved streets.

Laodicea (lā-ŏd-ĭ-cē-ă), a city of Phrygia, near Colossæ, Col. 2 : 1; 4 : 13; Rev. 1 : 11.
    a city of Syria, near Antioch.

Laodiceans (lā-ŏd-ĭ-cē-ăns), Rev. 3 : 14.
    Paul's epistle to, Col. 4 : 16.

Lap, Judg. 7 : 5, that l. water as a dog.
    Prov. 16 : 33, lot is cast into the l.

Lapwing, Lev. 11 : 19; Deut. 14 : 18.

Large, Neh. 4 : 19; Ps. 18 : 19; Luke 22 : 12; Rev. 21 : 16.

Largeness, 1 Ki. 4 : 29.

Lasciviousness, source of, Mark 7 : 21; Gal. 5 : 19.

censured, 2 Cor. 12 : 21; Eph. 4 : 19; 1 Pet 4 : 3; Jude 4.

Last, Num. 23 : 10, let my l. end be like his.
    Prov. 23 : 32, at the l. it biteth like a serpent.
    Lam. 1 : 9, she remembereth not her l. end.
    Matt. 12 : 45; Luke 11 : 26, l. state of that man worse.
    Matt. 19 : 30; 20 : 16; Mark 10 : 31; Luke 13 : 30, first shall be l.
    Matt. 27 : 64, l. error worse than first.
    John 6 : 39; 11 : 24, the l. day.
    Heb. 1 : 2, spoken in l. days by his Son.

Latchet, Isa. 5 : 27; Mark 1 : 7.

Late, Ps. 127 : 2; Mic. 2 : 8; John 11 : 8.

Lately, Acts 18 : 2.

Latin. Luke 23 : 38; John 19 : 20. Latin was the official and legal language of the province of Judæa, Greek was the language of commerce, and Aramaic (" Hebrew ") the medium of common conversation among the Jews. Hence all three were used in the inscription on the Cross.

Latter, Deut. 11 : 14, first and l. rain.
    Job 19 : 25, Redeemer stand at l. day.
    Prov. 19 : 20, be wise in l. end.
    1 Tim. 4 : 1, in l. times some depart from faith.

Lattice, Judg. 5 : 28; 2 Ki. 1 : 2; Song of Sol. 2 : 9.

Laud, Rom. 15 : 11.

Laugh, Job 5 : 22, at famine thou shalt l.
    Ps. 2 : 4, that sitteth in heaven shall l.
    Prov. 1 : 26, I will l. at your calamity.
    Eccl. 3 : 4, a time to weep, a time to l.
    Luke 6 : 25, woe unto you that l.

Laughter, Gen. 18 : 13; Eccl. 2 : 2; 3 : 4; 7 : 3; Ps. 126 : 2; Prov. 14 : 13.

Launch, Luke 5 : 4; Acts 27 : 2, 4; Luke 8 : 22.

Supposed form of the Laver.

Laver (1) Ex. 30 : 17-21. The bronze laver near the altar contained water for the ablutions of the priests, (cf. 38 : 8 (R.V.) for an anachronism). (2) 1 Ki. 7 : 27-39. Ten brazen lavers, facsimiles of the brazen sea, were placed five on the north side and five on the south of the priests' court in Solomon's Temple, cf. 2 Chr. 4 : 6.

Lavish, Isa. 46 : 6.

Law. In John 1 : 17, a primary fact is stated and a New Testament truth set forth : " For the law was given through Moses; grace and truth came through Jesus Christ." The law as recorded in the Pentateuch is that to which the word refers in the vast majority of instances in the Bible. This law was given at Sinai and proceeded from God, who in His own capacity as moral governor of the universe and as the Redeemer of His people, has authority to legislate for the well-being of all His creatures and for the establishment of righteousness in the earth.

of God, given to Adam, Gen. 2 : 16; to Noah, Gen. 9 : 3.
promulgated through Moses, Ex. 19 : 20; Deut. 1 : 5; 5; 6.
requires perfect obedience, Deut. 27 : 26; Gal. 3 : 10; Jas. 2 : 10.
described, Ps. 19 : 7; 119 : 1; Rom. 7 : 12.
all guilty under, Rom. 3 : 20.
of Moses, ordained, Ex. 21; Lev. 1; Num. 3; Deut. 12.
preserved on stone, Deut. 27 : 1; Josh. 8 : 32.
read every seventh year, Deut. 31 : 9.
preserved in the ark, Deut. 31 : 24.
read by Joshua, Josh. 8 : 34; by Ezra, Neh. 8.
book of, discovered by Hilkiah, 2 Ki. 22 : 8; and read by Josiah, 2 Ki. 23 : 2.
fulfilled by Christ, Rom. 5 : 18.
abolished in Christ, Acts 15 : 24; 28 : 23; Gal. 2-6; Eph. 2 : 15; Col. 2 : 14; Heb. 7.
Christians redeemed from curse of, John 1 : 17; Acts 13 : 39; Gal. 3 : 13.
Deut. 33 : 2, from right hand went fiery l.
Ps. 1 : 2, in his l. he meditates.
37 : 31, the l. of his God is in his heart
119 : 70, I delight in thy l.
119 : 97, how I love thy l.
Prov. 13 : 14, the l. of the wise is a fountain o life.
29 : 18, that keepeth the l., happy is he.
Isa. 42 : 4, the isles shall wait for his l.
Mal. 2 : 6, the l. of truth was in his mouth
Matt. 5 : 17, not come to destroy the l.
22 : 40, on two commandments hang l.
23 : 23, the weightier matters of the l.
Luke 16 : 17, for one tittle of the l. to fail.
John 1 : 17, the l. was given by Moses.
7 : 51, doth our l. judge any man ?
19 : 7, by our l. he ought to die.
Rom. 2 : 13, not hearers of the l. are just.
3 : 20, by deeds of l. no flesh be justified.
7 : 12, the l. is holy.
7 : 16; 1 Tim. 1 : 8, the l. is good.
Rom. 8 : 3, what the l. could not do.
10 : 4, Christ is the end of the l.
Gal. 3 : 24, the l. was our schoolmaster.
5 : 14, all the l. is fulfilled in one word.
6 : 2, so fulfil the l. of Christ.
1 Tim. 1 : 9, the l. is not made for a righteous man.
Heb. 10 : 1, the l. having a shadow of good things.
Jas. 1 : 25, perfect l. of liberty.
2 : 8, the royal l.
1 John 3 : 4, transgresseth also the l.

Lawful, Matt. 12 : 10; Mark 3 : 4; Luke 6 : 9, is it l. to heal on the sabbath ?
John 18 : 31, not l. to put to death.
1 Cor. 6 : 12; 10 : 23, all things l. to me.
2 Cor. 12 : 4, words not l. to utter.
Lawfully, 1 Tim. 1 : 8, if a man use it l.
2 Tim. 2 : 5, except he strive l.
Lawgiver, God, Isa. 33 : 22; Num. 21 : 18; Jas. 4 : 12.
Lawless, 1 Tim. 1 : 9.
Lawsuits, censured, 1 Cor. 6 : 7.
Lawyers, Christ reproves, Luke 10 : 25; 11 : 46; 14 : 3.
Lay, Ps. 7 : 5, l. mine honour in the dust.
Eccl. 7 : 2, the living will l. it to heart.
Isa. 26 : 5, lofty city he l. low.
Matt. 8 : 20; Luke 9 : 58, not where to l. his head.
Matt. 28 : 6, place where the Lord l.
Acts 7 : 60, l. not sin to their charge.
Col. 1 : 5, hope which is l. up for you.
1 Tim. 6 : 12, l. hold on eternal life.
Heb. 6 : 18, l. hold on hope set before us.
12 : 1, l. aside every weight.
1 Pet. 2 : 6, l. in Zion a chief corner stone.
Laying on of hands. This symbolises the idea that through actual physical contact one person identifies himself with another before God. In the Old Testament it implies the transfer of (a) a Divine blessing (e.g., Gen. 48 : 14); (b) a burden of guilt (e.g., Lev. 1 : 4; 4 : 3 f.). In the New Testament the general idea is always that of blessing (cf. Matt. 19 : 13 ff.; Mark 6 : 5; 8 : 23; Luke 4 : 40; 13 : 13). It has come to be the symbol in ordination to deaconship, eldership, ministry, etc.
Lazarus (lăz-ă-rŭs) [whom God helps], **Eleazar.** and the rich man, Luke 16 : 19-25, brother of Mary and Martha, raised from the dead, John 11 : 1-46; 12 : 1.
Lead, Ex. 13 : 21, pillar of cloud to l. them.
Deut. 32 : 12, Lord alone did l. him.
Ps. 23 : 2, he l. me beside still waters.
43 : 3, send light and truth, let them l. me.
61 : 2, l. me to Rock higher than I.
139 : 24, l. me in the way everlasting.
143 : 10, l. me to land of uprightness.
Isa. 11 : 6, a little child shall l. them.
40 : 11, gently l. those with young.
42 : 16, l. them in paths not known.
Matt. 6 : 13; Luke 11 : 4, l. us not into temptation.
Matt. 7 : 14, way, which l. unto life.
15 : 14; Luke 6 : 39, if the blind l. the blind.
1 Tim. 2 : 2, we may l. a quiet life.
Rev. 7 : 17, Lamb feed and l. them.
Lead (metal), was used in the smelting of silver (Jer. 6 : 29; Ezek. 22 : 18-22), was used to suggest weight (Ex. 15 : 10), and to fill in inscriptions chiselled on rock to make them more durable (Job 19 : 24). In Zech. 5 : 7 f. the " ephah " has a lead covering, cf. Num. 31 : 22. Mined in the Sinaitic rocks, it was an article of commerce at Tyre.
Leaf, Gen. 8 : 11, in dove's mouth was olive l.
Ps. 1 : 3, his l. also shall not wither.
Isa. 64 : 6, fade as a l.
Jer. 8 : 13, on the fig tree and the l. shall fade.

League, Josh. 9 : 6; 2 Sam. 5 : 3; Job 5 : 23; Dan. 11 : 23; 2 Chr. 16 : 3.
Leah (lē-äh) [wearied], Gen. 29 : 31; 30 : 17; 31 : 4; 33 : 2; 49 : 31.
See Ruth 4 : 11.
Lean, Judg. 16 : 26, may l. on the pillars.
Prov. 3 : 5, l. not to own understanding.
Amos 5 : 19, l. his hand on the wall.
John 21 : 20, l. on his breast at supper.
Heb. 11 : 21, l. on top of staff.
Lean (fleshed), Gen. 41 : 3, 4, 19 f.
Leanness, Ps. 106 : 15.
Leap, Isa. 35 : 6, lame man l. as an hart.
Luke 6 : 23, and l. for joy.
Acts 3 : 8, he l. up, stood, and walked.
19 : 16, man in whom the evil spirit was l. on them.
Learn, Gen. 30 : 27, I have l. by experience.
Deut. 31 : 13, l. to fear the Lord.
Isa. 1 : 17, l. to do well.
2 : 4; Mic. 4 : 3, neither shall they l. war any more.
Isa. 26 : 9, inhabitants l. righteousness.
Matt. 9 : 13, go and l. what that meaneth.
11 : 29, l. of me.
Acts 7 : 22, Moses was l. in wisdom of Egyptians.
Eph. 4 : 20, ye have not so l. Christ.
Phil. 4 : 9, which ye have both l. and received.
4 : 11, have l. to be content.
Titus 3 : 14, l. to maintain good works.
Heb. 5 : 8, yet l. he obedience.
Learning, advantage of, Prov. 1 : 5; 9 : 9; 16 : 21, 23.
Dan. 1 : 17, God gave them skill in l.
Acts 26 : 24, much l. doth make thee mad.
Rom. 15 : 4, things written for our l.
2 Tim. 3 : 7, ever l. and never able.
Leasing [ar.], speaking lies, Ps. 4 : 2; 5 : 6.
Least, Gen. 32 : 10, not worthy l. of mercies.
Matt. 5 : 19, one of these l. commandments.
11 : 11; Luke 7 : 28, he that is l. in kingdom of heaven.
Matt. 25 : 40, 45, done it to the l. of these.
Luke 16 : 10, faithful in that which is l.
Eph. 3 : 8, less than the l. of all saints.
Leather, 2 Ki. 1 : 8.
Leathern, Matt. 3 : 4.
Leave, Gen. 2 : 24; Matt. 19 : 5; Mark 10 : 7; Eph. 5 : 31, l. father and mother.
Ruth 1 : 16, entreat me not to l. thee.
Ps. 16 : 10; Acts 2 : 27, not l. my soul in hell.
Ps. 27 : 9; 119 : 121, l. me not.
Matt. 18 : 12; Luke 15 : 4, l. the ninety and nine.
Matt. 23 : 23, and not to l. the other undone.
John 14 : 27, peace I l. with you.
Heb. 13 : 5, I will never l. thee.
1 Pet. 2 : 21, l. us an example.
Leaven, not to be used at the passover, Ex. 12 : 15; 13 : 7; or in meat offerings, Lev. 2 : 11; 6 : 17; 10 : 12. Possibly this is an illustration of how conservative ritualism tends to be, preserving as it did the fact that the ancestors of the Hebrews, a nomadic race, were accustomed to feast on un-leavened bread. Its exclusion also implied the fact that fermentation in a measure pointed to corruption of the dough and

therefore could not be offered to an in-corruptible God.
figuratively mentioned, Matt. 13 : 33; 16 : 6; Luke 13 : 21; 1 Cor. 5 : 6.
Leaves, Gen. 3 : 7, sewed fig. l. together.
Jer. 36 : 23, read three or four l.
Mark 11 : 13, he found nothing but l.
Rev. 22 : 2, l. of the trees were for the healing.
Lebanon (lĕb-ă-nǫn) [white mountain], its cedars, 2 Ki. 14 : 9; 2 Chr. 2 : 8; Ps. 92 : 12; Song of Sol. 3 : 9; Isa. 40 : 16; Hos. 14 : 5.
Lebbæus (lĕb-bǣ-ŭs) [courageous], Matt. 10 : 3.
Led, Gen. 24 : 48, l. me in the right way.
Deut. 29 : 5, l. you forty years.
Prov. 4 : 11, have l. thee in right paths.
Ps. 68 : 18; Eph. 4 : 8, l. captivity captive.
Ps. 77 : 20, l. thy people like a flock.
Luke 4 : 1; Rom. 8 : 14; Gal. 5 : 18, l. of the Spirit.
Acts 8 : 32, l. as a sheep to the slaughter.
2 Pet. 3 : 17, being l. away with the error.
Ledges, 1 Ki. 7 : 28, 35, 36.
Leek (Allium porrum) is a favourite in Palestine, where it is largely grown. The Hebrew " châtsir " (= " grass " or " herbs ") is, in Num. 11 : 5, rendered " leeks," as being the herb of herbs.
Lees [ar.], sediment (settling at bottom of wine-jars and composed of stalks, husks, etc.). Refined wines, the lees of which had all settled down, were known as " Wines on the lees."
Isa. 25 : 6, feast of wines on the l.
Jer. 48 : 11, Moab hath settled on his l.
Zeph. 1 : 12, punish men settled on l.
Left, Prov. 3 : 16, in her l. hand riches and honour.
4 : 27, to the right hand nor to the l.
Matt. 25 : 33, the goats on the l.
24 : 40, 41, one taken, the other l.
10 : 28, l. all, and have followed thee.
13 : 2, not be l. one stone.
Left-handed slingers, Judg. 20 : 16.
Leg, Ps. 147 : 10; Prov. 26 : 7; Isa. 47 : 2.
Legion (of devils), Mark 5 : 9; Luke 8 : 30.
legions of angels, Matt. 26 : 53.
Leisure, Mark 6 : 31.
Lemuel (lĕm-ū-ĕl) [consecrated to God], Prov. 31 : 1, 4.
Lend, Deut. 15 : 6, thou shalt l. to many nations.
Ps. 37 : 26; 112 : 5, merciful, and l.
Prov. 19 : 17, he that hath pity on poor l. to the Lord.
Luke 6 : 34, if ye l. to them.
Lender, Prov. 22 : 7; Isa. 24 : 2.
Lending, laws concerning, Ex. 22 : 25; Lev. 25 : 37; Deut. 15 : 2; 23 : 19; 24 : 10.
Length, Prov. 3 : 2, l. of days and long life.
Rom. 1 : 10, at l. I might have a prosperous journey.
Rev. 21 : 16, l., and the breadth.
Lengthened, Deut. 25 : 15, thy days may be l. in the land.
Lentils, a small reddish bean from a small leguminous plant six to eight inches high, which ripens in June-July. From it the " revalenta," or food for invalids, is made. In Palestine, a kind of pottage is made, which is popular and is the original of the

"red pottage" (Gen. 25 : 30). cf. Gen. 25 : 34; 2 Sam. 17 : 28; 23 : 11; Ezek. 4 : 9.

Leopard, still found in the wilder parts of Palestine, though rarely, it was at one time common.
vision of, Dan. 7 : 6; Rev. 13 : 2.
cf. Num. 32 : 3, 36; Song of Sol. 4 : 8; Isa. 11 : 6; 15 : 6; Jer. 5 : 6; 48 : 34; Hos. 13 : 7; Hab. 1 : 8.

Lepers, expelled from the camp, Lev. 13 : 46; Num. 5 : 2; 12 : 14.
four of Samaria, 2 Ki. 7 : 3.

Leprosy, a contagious skin disease of the most loathsome kind.
in a house, Lev. 14 : 33.
of Miriam, Num. 12 : 10.
of Naaman and Gehazi, 2 Ki. 5.
of Uzziah, 2 Chr. 26 : 19.
symptoms of, Lev. 13.
rites observed in healing, Lev. 14; 22 : 4: Deut. 24 : 8.
cured by Christ, Matt. 8 : 3; Mark 1 : 41; Luke 5 : 12; 17 : 12.

Leprous, Ex. 4 : 6; Lev. 13 : 44.

Lepton, mite, smallest coin. See **Money.**

Less, Isa. 40 : 17, l. than nothing, and vanity.
2 Cor. 12 : 15, though the more I love, the l. I be loved.
Heb. 7 : 7, the l. is blessed of the better.

Lesser, Gen. 1 : 16; Isa. 7 : 25.

Let, Isa. 43 : 13, who shall l. it ?
John 19 : 12, thou l. this man go.
2 Thess. 2 : 7, who now l. will l.
Heb. 2 : 1, lest we should l. them slip.

Lethech, measure, forty gallons. See **Measures.**

Letter, and the spirit, Rom. 2 : 27; 7 : 6; 2 Cor. 3 : 6. Every generation of Christians is puzzled as to the exact application of Christianity to life. Christ wisely left not precepts but a spirit. The Jews had too many applications in the Law. These applications demanded new sanctions and hid from view the greatest sanction, the spirit. Men are still lost to Christ because of the tendency on the part of the Church to create too many applications. A man must grow (wisely guided perhaps) into his own method of applying the Spirit.

Letters, of David to Joab, 2 Sam. 11 : 14; of Jezebel, 1 Ki. 21 : 9; of king of Syria, 2 Ki. 5 : 5; of Jehu, 2 Ki. 10 : 1; of Elijah to Jehoram, 2 Chr. 21 : 12; of Hezekiah, 2 Chr. 30 : 1; to Artaxerxes, Ezra 4 : 7; of Tatnai, Ezra 5 : 6; of Sennacherib, Isa. 37 : 10, 14; of Jeremiah, Jer. 29 : 1; of the apostles, Acts 15 : 23; of Claudius Lysias to Felix, Acts 23 : 25.
Luke 23 : 38, over him in l. of Greek.
Rom. 2 : 27, by l. and circumcision.
7 : 6, not in the oldness of the l.
2 Cor. 3 : 6, not of l., but of the spirit.
10 : 11, in word by l. when absent.
Gal. 6 : 11, how large a l. I have written.
See John 7 : 15.

Levi (lē-vī) [adhesion], son of Jacob, Gen. 29 : 34.
avenges Dinah, Gen. 34 : 25; 49 : 5.
See **Matthew.**

Leviathan (lē-vī-ă-thăn) [that which twists round]. Most Biblical references to this point to the crocodile (cf. Job 41 : 1-34; Ps. 74 : 14). Isa. 27 : 1 distinguishes the flying serpent and the coiled serpent—these two leviathans representing two heathen kingdoms. It is a fresh-water reptile, and is now almost extinct in Palestine. Lam. 4 : 3, "sea monsters" is rendered "jackals" in the R.V.

Levites, descendants of Levi, Ex. 32 : 26.
their service, Ex. 38 : 21.
appointed over the tabernacle, Num. 1 : 50.
their divisions, Gershonites, Kohathites, Merarites, Num. 3.
their charge, Num. 3 : 23; 4; 8 : 23-26; 18.
their inheritance, Num. 35; Deut. 18; Josh. 21.
duty towards, Deut. 12 : 19.
their genealogies, 1 Chr. 6-9.
charged with the temple service, 1 Chr. 23; 24.
their sin censured, Ezek. 22 : 23-26; Mal. 1; 2.

Levitical, Heb. 7 : 11.

Leviticus, Book of.
Holiness is the theme of this third book of the Bible. It tells how a sinful man may approach a holy God under the old covenant. The instruction is specifically for the priests and the Levites and concerns their service in the Tabernacle. Central in the book is the Day of Atonement (ch. 16) and explanatory of all the sacrifices is ch. 17 : 11, which says that the life or soul is in the blood, and that animal blood may be shed upon the altar to make atonement for human life or soul which has been forfeited because of sin (Gen. 2 : 17).
Summary.—Chs. 1-7, Law of the offerings : Burnt, Meal, Peace, Sin of ignorance, Sin of concealing knowledge, Trespass or Guilt. Chs. 8, 9, Consecration of the Priests. Ch. 10, Judgment on Nadab and Abihu. Ch. 11, Distinction between clean and unclean beasts. Chs. 12-15, Laws of diagnosis and sanitation. Ch. 16, Day of Atonement. Ch. 17, Sacredness of blood because it contains life. Ch. 18, Laws of chastity. Ch. 19, Repetition of various laws. Ch. 20, Warnings against idolatry, spiritism, incest and all heathen corruption. Chs. 21, 22, The sanctity of the priests and rules for their conduct. Chs. 23, 24, 25, The Feasts of Jehovah : Sabbath, Passover or Unleavened Bread, Harvest, Pentecost, Trumpets, Tabernacles, Sabbatical year, Year of Jubilee. Chs. 26, 27, Warnings against disobedience. Promise of rewards for fidelity.

Levy, Num. 31 : 28; 1 Ki. 9 : 15.

Lewd, Ezek. 16 : 27; 23 : 48; Acts 17 : 5; 18 : 14.

Liars, instances : the devil, Gen. 3 : 4; Cain, Gen. 4 : 9; Sarah, Gen. 18 : 15; Jacob, Gen. 27 : 19; Joseph's brethren, Gen. 37 : 31, 32; Saul, 1 Sam. 15 : 13; Michal, 1 Sam. 19 : 14; David, 1 Sam. 21 : 2; prophet of Bethel, 1 Ki. 13 : 18; Gehazi, 2 Ki. 5 : 22; Ninevites, Nah. 3 : 1; Peter,

Matt. 26 : 72; Ananias, Acts 5 : 3; Cretians, Titus 1 : 12.
their doom, Rev. 21 : 8, 27; 22 : 15.
Deut. 33 : 29, enemies found l. unto thee.
Ps. 116 : 11, said in my haste, All men are l.
Rev. 21 : 8, all l. have their part in lake.
Liberal, Prov. 11 : 25, l. shall be made fat.
Isa. 32 : 5, the vile shall not be called l.
32 : 8, the l. deviseth l. things.
Jas. 1 : 5, God, who giveth to all men l.
Liberality, commended, Deut. 15 : 14; Prov. 11 : 25; Isa. 32 : 8; 2 Cor. 9 : 13.
of the Israelites, Ex. 35 : 21; Num. 7.
of the early Christians, Acts 2 : 45; 4 : 34.
of the Macedonians, 2 Cor. 8 : 2; Phil. 4 : 15.
Libertines (lĭb-ẽr-tīn(e)s̱) [freedmen], the descendants of Jews taken to Rome as slaves and emancipated in later times. They formed a large and distinct class.
synagogue of, Acts 6 : 9.
Liberty, of the gospel, Luke 4 : 18; Rom. 8 : 21; Gal. 5 : 1; Jas. 1 : 25; 2 : 12.
not to be misused, 1 Cor. 8 : 9; Gal. 5 : 13; 1 Pet. 2 : 16.
Ps. 119 : 45, I will walk at l.
Isa. 61 : 1; Jer. 34 : 8; Luke 4 : 18, to proclaim l.
Acts 26 : 32, man might have been set at l.
Rom. 8 : 21, the glorious l. of children of God.
2 Cor. 3 : 17, where the Spirit is, there is l.
Gal. 5 : 1, stand fast in the l.
2 Pet. 2 : 19, promise them l.
Libnah (lĭb-năh) [whiteness], subdued, Josh. 10 : 29; 21 : 13.
revolts, 2 Ki. 8 : 22.
besieged by Assyrians, 2 Ki. 19 : 8; Isa. 37 : 8.
Libya (lĭb- y̆-ă) [Heb., " Phut "], Ezek. 30 : 5; Acts 2 : 10.
Lice, Ex. 8 : 16-18; Ps. 105 : 31, a parasite common among the dirty.
Licence, Acts 21 : 40; 25 : 16.
Lick, Num. 22 : 4, as the ox l. up the grass.
1 Ki. 18 : 38, l. up the water that was in the trench.
Ps. 72 : 9, enemies shall l.
Mic. 7 : 17, l. dust like a serpent.
Luke 16 : 21, came and l. his sores.
Lid, 2 Ki. 12 : 9.
Lie, Ps. 23 : 2, l. down in green pastures.
Prov. 19 : 9, speaketh l. shall perish.
Acts 5 : 3, filled thine heart to l.
23 : 21, l. in wait for him.
Rom. 1 : 25, truth of God into a l.
Heb. 6 : 18, impossible for God to l.
Rev. 22 : 15, loveth and maketh a l.
Liers in wait, Judg. 9 : 25; 16 : 12; 20 : 33, 37.
Lieutenants, Ezra 8 : 36; Esther 3 : 12; 8 : 9.
Life. The Old Testament is much concerned with the brevity and vanity of life, yet it never reaches the assurance of life to come. Suggestions we do get, it is true, in Job 14 : 14 and Ps. 16; but it was left to Jesus to turn this into actual trust in a future life. Jesus never bewailed the brevity of this life (cf. Matt. 11 : 19; Luke 12 : 6, etc.), and condemned over-anxiety about it and its goods (Matt. 6 : 19, 31; Luke 12 : 15). He has, moreover, caused the phrase, "Eternal Life " to be written large across the pages of the New Testament. It is life lived primarily under God's rule and is therefore a matter of moral and spiritual concerns (John 17 : 3). From this follows the notion of everlastingness, for God will not allow what He considers precious to be destroyed (Matt. 25 : 46; Mark 10 : 30). It is, however, also a present possession (John 3 : 36; 5 : 24, etc.), and Jesus guarantees us this life (John 1 : 4, etc.).
the gift of God, Gen. 2 : 7; Job 12 : 10; Ps. 36 : 9; 66 : 9; Dan. 5 : 23; Acts 17 : 28.
long, to whom promised, Ex. 20 : 12; Deut. 5 : 33; 6 : 2; Prov. 3 : 2; 9 : 11; 10 : 27; Eph. 6 : 3.
its shortness and vanity, Job 7 : 1; 9 : 25; 14 : 1; Ps. 39 : 5; 73 : 19; 89 : 47; 90 : 5, 9; Eccl. 6 : 12; Isa. 38 : 12; Jas. 4 : 14; 1 Pet. 1 : 24.
of Hezekiah, prolonged, 2 Ki. 20; 2 Chr. 32 : 24; Isa. 38.
how to be passed, Luke 1 : 75; Rom. 12 : 18; 14 : 8; Phil. 1 : 21; 1 Pet. 1 : 17.
spiritual, Rom. 6 : 4, 8; Gal. 2 : 19; Eph. 2 : 1.
eternal, the gift of God through Jesus Christ, John 6 : 27, 54; 10 : 28; 17 : 3; Rom. 2 : 7; 6 : 23; 1 John 1 : 2; 2 : 25; Jude 21; Rev. 2 : 7; 21 : 6.
to whom promised, John 3 : 16; 5 : 24; 1 Tim. 1 : 16.
Gen. 2 : 9; 3 : 24; Rev. 2 : 7, the tree of l.
Lev. 17 : 11, the l. is in the blood.
Deut. 30 : 15; Jer. 21 : 8, I have set before thee l.
Josh. 2 : 14, our l. for yours.
1 Sam. 25 : 29, bound in the bundle of l.
2 Sam. 15 : 21, whether in death or l.
Ps. 16 : 11, show me the path of l.
21 : 4, asked l. of thee, thou gavest it.
30 : 5, in his favour is l.
34 : 12, what man is he that desireth l.
36 : 9, with thee is the fountain of l.
91 : 16, with long l. will I satisfy him.
133 : 3, even l. for evermore.
Prov. 3 : 22, so shall they be l. to thy soul.
8 : 35, whoso findeth me, findeth l.
14 : 27, fear of Lord is a fountain of l.
15 : 24, way of l. is above to the wise.
Jer. 8 : 3, death shall be chosen rather than l.
Matt. 6 : 25; Luke 12 : 22, take no thought for your l.
Matt. 18 : 8; Mark 9 : 43, to enter into l.
Luke 12 : 23, l. is more than meat.
John 1 : 4, in him was l.
5 : 26, as the Father hath l. in himself.
5 : 40; 10 : 10, will not come that ye might have l.
6 : 35, the bread of l.
8 : 12, shall have the light of l.
11 : 25, resurrection and the l.
14 : 6, the way, the truth, and the l.
20 : 31, believing, ye might have l.
Acts 17 : 25, seeing he giveth to all l.
Rom. 5 : 17, reign in l. by one.
8 : 6, to be spiritually minded is l.
11 : 15, l. from the dead.
1 Cor. 3 : 22, l. or death, all are yours.

2 Cor. 2 : 16, the savour of l. unto l.
5 : 4, mortality swallowed up of l.
Eph. 4 : 18, alienated from the l. of God.
Col. 3 : 3, your l. is hid with Christ.
1 Tim. 4 : 8; 2 Tim. 1 : 1, promise of l.
2 Tim. 1 : 10, brought l. to light through the Gospel.
Heb. 7 : 16, made after power of an endless l.
Jas. 1 : 12, a crown of l.
1 John 2 : 16, the pride of l.
5 : 12, he that hath the Son, hath l.
Rev. 22 : 1, 17, river of water of l.
Lifetime, 2 Sam. 18 : 18; Luke 16 : 25; Heb. 2 : 15.
Lift, Ps. 24 : 7, l. up your heads, O ye gates.
147 : 6, Lord l. up the meek.
Luke 17 : 13, l. up their voices.
John 3 : 14, Son of man be l. up.
1 Tim. 2 : 8, l. up holy hands.
Jas. 4 : 10, he shall l. you up.
Lifter, Ps. 3 : 3.
Light. The ancients held light to be holy. Hence the Bible associates it with God He not only lives in light (Ex. 24 : 10;' 1 Tim. 6 : 16) and is clothed with it (Ps. 104 : 2), but He is light (1 John 1 : 5). Hence when God becomes Incarnate, He is called " the Light of the world " (cf. John 1 : 1-18; 8 : 12). To walk in the light brings salvation (John 8 : 12; 12 : 36; 1 John 1 : 7; 2 Cor. 4 : 6 etc.), while a life lived without God is darkness (John 3 : 19; 12 : 46, etc.).
type of God's favour, Ex. 10 : 23; Ps. 4 : 6; Isa. 9 : 2; 60 : 19.
God's word is, Ps. 19 : 8; 119 : 130; Prov. 6 : 23.
instances of miraculous, Matt. 17 : 2; Acts 9 : 3.
Christ the light of the world, Luke 2 : 32; John 3 : 19; 8 : 12; 12 : 35.
disciples called children of, Eph. 5 : 8; 1 Thess. 5 : 5.
God is, 1 Tim. 6 : 16.
Gen. 1 : 3, God said, Let there be l.
Neh. 9 : 19, pillar of fire to show l.
Job 18 : 5, the l. of the wicked shall be put out.
Ps. 27 : 1, the Lord is my l.
36 : 9, in thy l. shall we see l.
37 : 6, bring forth righteousness as l.
97 : 11, l. is sown for the righteous.
104 : 2, who coverest thyself with l.
119 : 105, a l. to my path.
139 : 12, darkness and l. alike to thee.
Prov. 4 : 18, path of just as shining l.
Eccl. 11 : 7, the l. is sweet.
Isa. 5 : 20, darkness for l., and l. for darkness.
30 : 26, l. of moon as l. of sun.
60 : 1, shine, for thy l. is come.
Jer. 31 : 35, sun for l. by day.
Hab. 3 : 4, his brightness was as l.
Zech. 14 : 6, the l. shall not be clear.
Matt. 5 : 14; John 8 : 12, the l. of the world.
Matt. 5 : 16, let your l. so shine before men.
6 : 22; Luke 11 : 34, the l. of the body is the eye.
Luke 8 : 16; 11 : 33, enter in may see the l.
16 : 8, wiser than children of l.

John 1 : 4, life was the l. of men.
5 : 35, a burning and shining l.
Acts 22 : 6, there shone a great l. round.
26 : 23, l. to people and to the Gentiles.
1 Cor. 4 : 5, to l. hidden things.
2 Cor. 4 : 4, l. of the gospel.
4 : 6, commanded l. to shine out of darkness.
Eph. 5 : 14, Christ shall give thee l.
1 Thess. 5 : 5, children of the l.
2 Pet. 1 : 19, a l. shining in a dark place.
1 John 1 : 5, God is l.
Rev. 21 : 23, the Lamb is the l. thereof.
22 : 5, no candle, neither l. of the sun.
Lighter, 1 Ki. 12 : 4; Ps. 62 : 9.
Lightly, Isa. 9 : 1; Jer. 4 : 24; Mark 9 : 39.
Lightness, Jer. 23 : 32; 2 Cor. 1 : 17.
Lightning, surrounding God's throne, Ezek. 1 : 13; Rev. 4 : 5.
2 Sam. 22 : 15, sent l. and discomfited.
Job 28 : 26, way for l. of thunder.
38 : 25, who divided a way for the l.
Ps. 18 : 14, shot out l. and discomfited them.
77 : 18; 97 : 4, l. lightened the world.
144 : 6, cast forth l. and scatter.
Matt. 24 : 27; Luke 17 : 24, as l. cometh out of the east.
Luke 10 : 18, Satan as l. fall from heaven.
Lign aloes, Num. 24 : 6.
Ligure, a precious stone, the hyacinth or jacinth, Ex. 28 : 19.
Like, Ex. 15 : 11; Deut. 33 : 29; 1 Ki. 8 : 23; Ps. 35 : 10; Jer. 11 : 19; Hos. 4 : 9; Matt. 13 : 31; Acts 14 : 15, etc.
Like-minded, Rom. 15 : 5; Phil. 2 : 2, 20.
Liken, Isa. 40 : 18; Lam. 2 : 13; Matt. 7 : 24; 11 : 16.
Likeness, Gen. 1 : 26, make man after our l.
Ex. 20 : 4, not make l. of anything.
Ps. 17 : 15, when I awake, with thy l.
Isa. 40 : 18, what l. will ye compare ?
Acts 14 : 11, gods are come down in l. of men.
Rom. 6 : 5, l. of his death, l. of his resurrection.
8 : 3, in the l. of sinful flesh.
Phil. 2 : 7, was made in the l. of men.
Likewise, Matt. 18 : 35; Luke 3 : 11; 15 : 10; 22 : 20; Rom. 8 : 26.
Liking [ar.], state of body as to health, condition, Job 39 : 4; Dan. 1 : 10.
Lily, a comprehensive term including lilies, irises, gladioli, etc. The " lily-work " of 1 Ki. 7 : 19, etc., was perhaps modelled after the lotus.
2 Chr. 4 : 5; Song of Sol. 2 : 1 f., 16; 4 : 5; 5 : 13; 6 : 3; Hos. 14 : 5; Matt. 6 : 28; Luke 12 : 27.
Lime, Isa. 33 : 12; Amos 2 : 1.
Limit, Ps. 78 : 41, l. the Holy One of Israel.
Heb. 4 : 7, he l. a certain day.
Line, Ps. 19 : 4, their l. is gone through the earth.
Isa. 28 : 10, l. upon l.; here a little.
28 : 17, judgment will I lay to the l.
2 Cor. 10 : 16, boast in another man's l.
Lineage, Luke 2 : 4.
Linen, cloth made from the prepared fibre of flax. There were three classes : (1) Common, Lev. 6 : 10; Ezek. 9 : 2; Dan. 10 : 5;

Rev. 15 : 6. (2) Superior, Ex. 26 : 1; 39 : 27.
(3) Costliest, Esther 8 : 15; 1 Chr. 15 : 27;
Rev. 19 : 8.
Lines, 2 Sam. 8 : 2; Ps. 16 : 6.
Lingered, Gen. 19 : 16; 43 : 10; 2 Pet. 2 : 3.
Lintel, Ex. 12 : 22, 23; Amos 9 : 1.
Lion. There are five classes of words in Scripture : (1) the full-grown lion, Gen. 49 : 9;
Judg. 14 : 8 f., etc. (2) The young strong
lion, Judg. 14 : 5; Job 4 : 10; Ezek. 19 : 2,
etc. (3) The lioness, Gen. 49 : 9; Num.
23 : 24; Job 4 : 11, etc. (4) Poetic terms,
Job 4 : 10 f.; 10 : 16; Prov. 30 : 30; Isa.
30 : 6; Hos. 5 : 14, etc. (5) The ' lion's
whelps " of Job 28 : 8 should be " sons of
pride " (R.V.m.). Extinct in Palestine since
the time of the Crusades, they were a source
of terror to shepherds and sheep. They lay
in cover (Jer. 4 : 7; 25 : 38) and filled their
holes with prey (Nah. 2 : 12). They were
captured by hunting or by means of pits
(2 Sam. 23 : 20).
Samson kills one, Judg. 14 : 5, 6.
David kills one, 1 Sam. 17 : 34, 35.
Daniel in the den of, Dan. 6 : 16-23.
prophets slain by, 1 Ki. 13 : 24; 20 : 36.
parable of young, Ezek. 19 : 1-9.
mentioned figuratively, Num. 24 : 9; 2 Sam.
17 : 10.
Satan likened to a, 1 Pet. 5 : 8; (Ps. 10 : 9).
visions of, Ezek. 1 : 10; 10 : 14; Dan. 7 : 4;
Rev. 4 : 7.
Ps. 17 : 12, like a l. greedy of his prey.
91 : 13, thou shalt tread on the l.
Prov. 28 : 1, the righteous are bold as a l.
Eccl. 9 : 4, living dog better than dead l.
Isa. 35 : 9, no l. shall be there.
2 Tim. 4 : 17, delivered out of mouth of l.
Heb. 11 : 33, by faith stopped mouths of l.
1 Pet. 5 : 8, devil as a roaring l.
" Lion of the tribe of Judah," Rev. 5 : 5.
Lips, Ps. 12 : 4, our l. are our own.
Ps. 17 : 1, goeth not out of feigned l.
63 : 5, mouth praise thee with joyful l.
140 : 3, poison is under their l.
Prov. 15 : 7, the l. of wise disperse knowledge.
Song of Sol. 7 : 9, causing l. of those asleep
to speak.
Isa. 6 : 5, a man of unclean l.
29 : 13; Matt. 15 : 8, people with l. do
honour me.
Heb. 13 : 15, fruit of our l. giving thanks.
Liquor, Ex. 22 : 29; Num. 6 : 3; Song of Sol.
7 : 2.
Listed, Matt. 17 : 12; Mark 9 : 13.
Listen, Isa. 49 : 1.
Listeth [ar.], desireth, chooseth, John 3 : 8;
Jas. 3 : 4.
Litters, Isa. 66 : 20.
Little, Gen. 30 : 30, it was l. thou hadst.
Ps. 8 : 5; Heb. 2 : 7, a l. lower than the
angels.
Ps. 37 : 16, a l. that a righteous man hath.
Prov. 15 : 16, better is l. with the fear of the
Lord.
30 : 24, four things l. on earth.
Isa. 26 : 20, hide thyself for a l. moment.
28 : 10, here a l., and there a l.
40 : 15, taketh up isles as a l. thing.

Luke 7 : 47, to whom l. is forgiven.
19 : 17, been faithful in a very l.
1 Tim. 4 : 8, bodily exercise profiteth l.
Jas. 4 : 14, life a vapour that appeareth for a
l. time.
Live, Gen. 3 : 22, take of tree of life, and l. for
ever.
42 : 18, this do, and l.
Ex. 33 : 20, shall no man see me and l.
Lev. 18 : 5; Neh. 9 : 29; Ezek. 20 : 11, he
shall l. in them.
Deut. 8 : 3; Matt. 4 : 4; Luke 4 : 4, not l. by
bread alone.
Job 14 : 14, if a man die, shall he l. again ?
Ps. 69 : 32, heart shall l. that seek God.
Isa. 26 : 19, dead men shall l.
55 : 3, hear, and your soul shall l.
Ezek. 3 : 21; 18 : 9; 33 : 13, he shall surely l.
Hos. 6 : 2, we shall l. in his sight.
Hab. 2 : 4; Rom. 1 : 17, the just shall l. by
faith.
Luke 10 : 28, this do, and thou shalt l.
John 5 : 25, hear voice of God, and l.
11 : 25, though he were dead, yet shall he l.
Acts 17 : 28, in him we l. and move.
Rom. 6 : 8, we believe we shall l. with him.
8 : 12, not to l. after the flesh.
14 : 8, whether we l., we l. unto the Lord.
1 Cor. 9 : 14, should l. of the Gospel.
2 Cor. 6 : 9, as dying, and behold we l.
13 : 4, l. with him by power of God.
Gal. 2 : 20, I l. by faith of Son of God.
5 : 25, if we l. in the Spirit.
Phil. 1 : 21, to me to l. is Christ.
Jas. 4 : 15, if the Lord will, we shall l.
Rev. 1 : 18, I am he that l., and was dead.
3 : 1, a name that thou l.
20 : 4, l. with Christ.
Lively, Ps. 38 : 19, my enemies are l.
(=living), Acts 7 : 38, received l. oracles.
1 Pet. 1 : 3, begotten us again to l. hope.
2 : 5, ye as l. stones are built.
Liver, Ex. 29 : 13; Prov. 7 : 23; Ezek. 21 : 21.
Living, water given by Christ, John 4 : 10;
7 : 38; Rev. 7 : 17.
Gen. 2 : 7, man became a l. soul.
Job 28 : 13; Ps. 27 : 13; 116 : 9, the land of
the l.
Job 30 : 23, the house appointed for all l.
Ps. 69 : 28, blotted out of book of the l.
143 : 2, in thy sight shall no man l. be
justified.
145 : 16, satisfiest every l. thing.
Eccl. 7 : 2, the l. will lay it to heart.
9 : 5, the l. know that they shall die.
Song of Sol. 4 : 15; John 4 : 14, a well of l.
water.
Isa. 38 : 19; the l. shall praise thee.
53 : 8, cut off out of the land of the l.
Lam. 3 : 39, wherefore doth a l. man com-
plain ?
Matt. 22 : 32; Mark 12 : 27; Luke 20 : 38,
God is the God of the l.
John 6 : 51, I am the l. bread.
Rom. 12 : 1, your bodies a l. sacrifice.
Heb. 10 : 20, a new and l. way.
1 Pet. 2 : 4, coming as to a l. stone.
Mark 12 : 44, cast in all her l.
Luke 8 : 43, spent all her l.

Lizard, Lev. 11 : 30 (cf. Lev. 11 : 29, R.V.).
Lizards occur in great varieties in Palestine.
Lo, Ps. 73 : 26; Isa. 25 : 9; Matt. 24 : 23.
Loaden, Isa. 46 : 1, carriages were heavy l.
Loadeth, Ps. 68 : 19, daily l. us with benefits.
Lo-ammi (lō-ăm-'mĭ) [not my people], Hos. 1 : 9.
Loan, 1 Sam. 2 : 20.
Loathe, Job 7 : 16; Prov. 13 : 5.
Loaves, miraculous multiplication of, Matt.
14 : 17; 15 : 32 ff.; Mark 6 : 35 ff.; Luke
9 : 12 ff.; John 6 : 5 ff.
Lock, Song of Sol. 5 : 5.

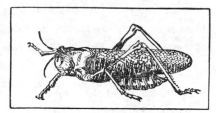

The Locust.

Locust. These voracious insects are migratory,
and often appear in huge darkening swarms,
settling on and devouring every green
thing and leaving barrenness behind. They
are still prized as food (cf. Lev. 11 : 22;
Matt. 3 : 4).
Ex. 10 : 4; Deut. 28 : 38; Ps. 105 : 34; Prov.
30 : 27; Nah. 3 : 17; Rev. 9 : 3, 7.
Locust tree. See Husks.
Lodge, Ruth 1 : 16; Jer. 9 : 2; Matt. 13 : 32;
Acts 21 : 16.
Lodging, Josh. 4 : 3; Acts 28 : 23.
Loft, 1 Ki. 17 : 19.
Loftiness, Isa. 2 : 17, l. of man shall be bowed
down.
Lofty, Ps. 131 : 1, heart not haughty, nor eyes l.
Isa. 2 : 11; 5 : 15, l. looks be humbled.
26 : 5, the l. city he layeth low.
57 : 15, the high and l. One.
Loftily, Ps. 73 : 8, they speak l.
Log, a liquid measure, Lev. 14 : 10. See
Measures.
Loins, Prov. 31 : 17, girdeth her l. with strength.
Matt. 3 : 4, girdle about his l.
Eph. 6 : 14, your l. girt about with truth.
1 Pet. 1 : 13, gird up the l. of your mind.
Lois (lō-'is), commended, 2 Tim. 1 : 5.
Long, Job 6 : 8, that God would grant the thing
I l. for.
Ps. 63 : 1, my flesh l. for thee in a dry land.
84 : 2, my soul l. for courts of the Lord.
Longer, Jer. 44 : 22; Luke 16 : 2; Rev. 10 : 6.
Longsuffering, Num. 14 : 18; Gal. 5 : 22; Eph.
4 : 2; 1 Tim. 1 : 16.
Look, Gen. 19 : 17, l. not behind thee.
Job 3 : 9, l. for light, but have none.
33 : 27, he l. on men.
Ps. 34 : 5, they l. to him and were lightened.
40 : 12, that I am not able to l. up.
84 : 9, l. upon the face of thine anointed.
123 : 2, as eyes of servants l. to masters.
Isa. 17 : 7, **at that day shall a man l.** to his
Maker.

45 : 22, l. unto me, and be ye saved.
66 : 2, to this man will I l.
Jer. 8 : 15; 14 : 19, we l. for peace.
40 : 4, I will l. well to thee.
Mic. 7 : 7, I l. to the Lord.
Matt. 11 : 3; Luke 7 : 19, do we l. for
another ?
Matt. 24 : 50, in a day he l. not for.
Luke 9 : 62, no man l. back is fit for the
kingdom.
21 : 28, then l. up.
John 13 : 22, disciples l. one on another.
Acts 3 : 4, 12, said, L. on us.
6 : 3, l. ye out seven men.
2 Cor. 4 : 18, we l. not at things seen.
Phil. 2 : 4, l. not every man on his own things.
3 : 20, we l. for the Saviour.
Titus 2 : 13, l. for that blessed hope.
Heb. 9 : 28, to them that l. shall he appear.
11 : 10, he l. for a city.
12 : 2, l. unto Jesus.
1 Pet. 1 : 12, angels desire to l. into.
2 Pet. 3 : 13, we l. for new heavens.
Look in the face [ar.], meet in order to fight,
2 Ki. 14 : 8.
Looking-glasses, Ex. 38 : 8; Job 37 : 18.
Loops, Ex. 26 : 4, 5; 36 : 11.
Loose, Josh. 5 : 15, l. thy shoe from off thy foot.
Job 38 : 31, canst thou l. the bands of Orion ?
Ps. 102 : 20, l. those appointed to death.
116 : 16, thou hast l. my bonds.
Eccl. 12 : 6, or ever the silver cord be l.
Isa. 58 : 6, to l. the bands of wickedness.
Matt. 16 : 19; 18 : 18, l. on earth, be l. in
heaven.
John 11 : 44, l. him, and let him go.
Acts 2 : 24, having l. the pains of death.
Lop, Isa. 10 : 33.
Lord (lôrd) Applied to Christ the title is the
highest confession of His person (1 Cor.
12 : 3; Rom. 10 : 9; Rev. 19 : 16, etc.).
Gen. 18 : 14, is any thing too hard for the
L. ?
28 : 21, then shall the L. be my God.
Ex. 34 : 6, the L., the L. God, merciful and
gracious.
Deut. 4 : 35; 1 Ki. 18 : 39, the L. is God.
Deut. 6 : 4, the L. our God is one L.
Ruth 1 : 17; 1 Sam. 20 : 13, L. do so to me,
and more.
1 Sam. 3 : 18; John 21 : 7, it is the L.
Neh. 9 : 6; Isa. 37 : 20, that art L. alone.
Ps. 33 : 12, blessed is the nation whose God is
the L.
100 : 3; 118 : 27, the L. is God.
Zech. 14 : 9, one L., and his name one.
Matt. 7 : 21, not every one that saith, L., L.
25 : 21, the joy of thy L.
Mark 2 : 28; Luke 6 : 5, Son of man is L. of
the Sabbath.
Luke 6 : 46, why call ye me L., L. ?
John 6 : 68, L., to whom shall we go ?
13 : 13, ye call me Master and L.
Acts 2 : 36, crucified, both L. and Christ.
9 : 5; 26 : 15, who art thou, L. ?
Rom. 10 : 12, same L. over all.
14 : 9, L. of the dead and of the living.
1 Cor. 2 : 8, L. of glory.
15 : 47, L. from heaven.

Eph. 4 : 5, one **L.**, one faith.

Phil. 2 : 11, confess Jesus Christ is L.

1 Tim. 6 : 15, King of kings, L. of l. See God and Christ.

Lordly, Judg. 5 : 25.

Lord of Hosts, a title applied 282 times in the Old Testament to God, and mainly of prophetic usage. It includes the idea of God as leader of the Israelite forces (1 Sam. 17 : 45), of the spiritual forces standing at His disposal (Josh. 5 : 13 f.), or of all the forces in the universe (Isa. 6 : 3). (See Rom. 9 : 29; Jas. 5 : 4.)

Lordship, Mark 10 : 42; Luke 22 : 25.

Lord's Day, Rev. 1 : 10.

Lord's Prayer, Matt. 6 : 9; Luke 11 : 1.

Lord's Supper. See **Communion**.

Lo-ruhamah (lō-rû-hä-măh) [not pitied], Hos. 1 : 6, 8.

Lose, Eccl. 3 : 6, a time to get, and a time to l.

Matt. 10 : 39; 16 : 25; Mark 8 : 35; Luke 9 : 24, he that findeth his life shall l. it.

Matt. 16 : 26; Mark 8 : 36; Luke 9 : 25, l. his own soul.

Luke 15 : 4, if he l. one sheep.

John 12 : 25, that loveth his life shall l. it.

Loss, Acts 27 : 21, gained this harm and l.

1 Cor. 3 : 15, he shall suffer l.

Phil. 3 : 8, I count all things but l. for Christ.

Lost, Ps. 119 : 176, gone astray like l. sheep.

Matt. 10 : 6; 15 : 24, l. sheep of the house of Israel.

18 : 11; Luke 19 : 10, to save that which was l.

Luke 15 : 24, son was l.

John 6 : 12, gather fragments, that nothing be l.

17 : 12, none is l. but son of perdition.

2 Cor. 4 : 3, Gospel hid to them that are l.

Lot (lŏt), Abraham's nephew, his choice, Gen. 13 : 10.

rescued from captivity by Abram, Gen. 14.

entertains angels, Gen. 19 : 1.

saved by destruction of Sodom, Gen. 19 : 16; 2 Pet. 2 : 7.

his wife turned into a pillar of salt, Gen. 19 : 26; Luke 17 : 28, 32.

Lot, the, decided by God, Lev. 16 : 8; Prov. 16 : 33.

Canaan divided by, Num. 26 : 55; Josh. 15.

Saul chosen king by, 1 Sam. 10 : 17.

Christ's garments divided by, Matt. 27 : 35; Mark 15 : 24; (Ps. 22 : 18).

Matthias chosen by, Acts 1 : 26.

1 Chr. 16 : 18; Ps. 105 : 11, the l. of your inheritance.

Ps. 16 : 5, thou maintainest my l.

125 : 3, not rest on l. of the righteous.

Prov. 1 : 14, cast in thy l. among us.

16 : 33, the l. is cast into the lap.

18 : 18, the l. causeth contentions to cease.

Isa. 34 : 17, he hath cast the l. for them.

Dan. 12 : 13, shall stand in thy l. at end.

Matt. 27 : 35; Mark 15 : 24, parted garments, casting l.

Acts 8 : 21, thou hast no l. in this matter.

Loud, Neh. 12 : 42; Esther 4 : 1; Ps. 98 : 4; Acts 16 : 28.

Love. As in the case of joy, so in love, the

Christian religion is outstanding. It implies the mutual and reciprocated affection of God and His people. Other religions make the gods so far above men that no such relation is possible. Christianity does not detract from God's superiority to man. By stressing the idea, however, that man's love of God is not spontaneous, but rather won from him by seeing the Divine love in Christ, the proper balance is preserved (1 John 4 : 19; Eph. 3 : 19; Rom. 5 : 17, etc.).

to God, commanded, Deut. 6 : 5; 11 : 1; Josh. 22 : 5; Ps. 31 : 23; Dan. 9 : 4; Matt. 22 : 37; 1 John 4 : 7.

blessings of, Neh. 1 : 5; Ps. 145 : 20; 1 Cor. 2 : 9; 8 : 3.

of husbands, etc., Gen. 29 : 20; 2 Sam. 1 : 26; Eph. 5 : 25; Titus 2 : 4.

to Christ, Matt. 10 : 37; Rev. 2 : 4.

of the world, censured, 1 John 2 : 15.

Lev. 19 : 18; Matt. 19 : 19; 22 : 39; Mark 12 : 31, thou shalt l. thy neighbour.

Deut. 10 : 12; 19 : 9; 30 : 6; Matt. 22 : 37; Mark 12 : 30; Luke 10 : 27, l. the Lord thy God.

2 Sam. 1 : 26, passing the l. of women.

13 : 15, hatred greater than l.

Ps. 5 : 11, let them that l. thy name be joyful.

18 : 1, I will l. thee, O Lord, my strength.

34 : 12, what man is he that l. many days ?

69 : 36, they that l. his name.

97 : 10, ye that l. the Lord hate evil.

122 : 6, they shall prosper that l. thee.

Prov. 8 : 17, I l. them that l. me.

10 : 12, l. covereth all sins.

15 : 17, better a dinner of herbs where l. is.

17 : 17, a friend l. at all times.

Eccl. 3 : 8, a time to l.

9 : 6, their l. and hatred is perished.

Song of Sol. 2 : 4, his banner over me was l.

8 : 7, many waters cannot quench l.

Jer. 31 : 3, loved thee with everlasting l.

Hos. 11 : 4, the bands of l.

14 : 4, I will l. them freely.

Amos 5 : 15, hate the evil, and l. the good.

Mic. 6 : 8, to l. mercy, and walk humbly.

Matt. 5 : 44; Luke 6 : 27, I say, L. your enemies.

24 : 12, l. of many shall wax cold.

Luke 7 : 42, which will l. him most ?

John 5 : 42, ye have not the l. of God in you.

11 : 3, he whom thou l. is sick.

15 : 12, 17, that ye l. one another.

15 : 13, greater l. hath no man than this.

17 : 26, l. wherewith thou hast loved me.

21 : 15, l. thou me ?

Rom. 8 : 28, for good to them that l. God.

8 : 35, separate from l. of Christ ?

13 : 8, owe no man any thing, but to l. one another.

13 : 10, l. worketh no ill.

2 Cor. 5 : 14, the l. of Christ constraineth us.

Gal. 5 : 6, faith which worketh by l.

Eph. 3 : 19, to know the l. of Christ.

6 : 24, grace be with them that l. our Lord.

1 Thess. 5 : 8, breastplate of faith and l.

1 Tim. 6 : 10, l. of money is the root of all evil.

Heb. 6 : 10, your work and labour of l.
13 : 1, let brotherly l. continue.
1 Pet. 1 : 8, whom having not seen ye l.
2 : 17, l. the brotherhood.
1 John 4 : 7, l. is of God.
4 : 10, herein is l., not that we loved God.
4 : 18, there is no fear in l.
4 : 19, we l. him, because he first l. us.
Rev. 2 : 4, thou hast left thy first l.
3 : 19, as many as I l., I rebuke.
Lovely, 2 Sam. 1 : 23, l. in their lives.
Song of Sol. 5 : 16, he is altogether l.
Phil. 4 : 8, whatsoever things are l.
Lover, Ps. 88 : 18, l. and friend hast thou put far from me.
2 Tim. 3 : 4, l. of pleasure more than l. of God.
Titus 1 : 8, l. of hospitality, l. of good men.
Lovingkindness, Ps. 17 : 7; 92 : 2, show thy l.
Ps. 51 : 1, have mercy according to thy l.
63 : 3, thy l. is better than life.
143 : 8, cause me to hear thy l.
Jer. 31 : 3, with l. have I drawn thee.
See Ps. 36 : 7; 69 : 16; 103 : 4; Isa. 63 : 7.
Low, 1 Sam. 2 : 7, the Lord bringeth l.
Job 5 : 11, set on high those that be l.
Ps. 49 : 2, high and l., rich and poor.
62 : 9, men of l. degree are vanity.
136 : 23, remembered us in l. estate.
Isa. 26 : 5, the lofty city he layeth l.
Luke 1 : 52 exalted them of l. degree.
Rom. 12 : 16, men of l. estate.
Jas. 1 : 10, rich in that he is made l.
Lower, Ps. 8 : 5; Heb. 2 : 7, l. than the angels.
Ps. 63 : 9, go into l. parts of the earth.
Eph. 4 : 9, descended into l. parts.
Lowest, Deut. 32 : 22; Ps. 86 : 13; Luke 14 : 9 f.
Lowliness, Eph. 4 : 2, walk with l. and meekness.
Phil. 2 : 3, in l. of mind.
Lowly, Ps. 138 : 6, yet hath he respect to the l.
Prov. 3 : 34, he giveth grace to the l.
11 : 2, with the l. is wisdom.
Zech. 9 : 9, l., and riding upon an ass.
Matt. 11 : 29, I am meek and l.
Lowring, Matt. 16 : 3.
Lucifer (lū-cĭ-fẽr) [bringer of light], Isa. 14 : 12. " Helel " is taken to mean " the morning-star," hence the phrase " L. son of the morning "; but more probably it refers to the moon waning at daybreak, i.e., the waning luminary. From a supposed reference in Luke 10 : 18; Rev. 9 : 1-11, " Lucifer " was identified with Satan.
Lucius (lū-cĭ-ŭs), of Cyrene, a teacher, Acts 13 : 1; Rom. 16 : 21.
Lucre, greed of, forbidden, 1 Tim. 3 : 3; Titus 1 : 7; 1 Pet. 5 : 2.
Lud, son of Shem, Gen. 10 : 22.
Luke. The name Luke or Lucas is an abbreviation, possibly of Lucilius, but almost certainly of Lucanus. Some of the oldest Latin MSS. have Secundum Lucanum as the title of the Third Gospel. Lucas, like Apollos, Artemas, Demas, Hermas, and Nymphas (which are similar abbreviations), is a form not found in classical literature, whereas Lucanus is common in inscriptions. These contracted proper names are frequent as the names of slaves; and slaves

were sometimes physicians. It is quite possible that St. Luke was a manumitted slave. Antistius, the surgeon of Julius Cæsar, and Antonius Musa, the physician of Augustus, were freed-men. Luke nowhere gives his name in either of the two writings which from the first have been assigned to him; but he is three times named by St. Paul (Col. 4 : 10, 14; Philem. 24; 2 Tim. 4 : 11). These notices of him tell us that he was a Gentile and a physician, very dear to the Apostle, as being his fellow-worker in spreading the faith and his attendant in both his Roman imprisonments. It is worth noting that in all three places his brother Evangelist Mark is mentioned also. In four other passages in the New Testament Luke, by using the first person, tells us a good deal about himself (Luke 1 : 1-4; Acts 16 : 10-17; 20 : 5-21 : 18; 27 : 1-28 : 16): and these seven passages contain all that is really known about the life of St. Luke. The attempts to identify him with other persons mentioned in Scripture all break down either through lack of evidence or through being at variance with evidence which we possess. That Lucius of Cyrene (Acts 13 : 1) is Luke is highly improbable : we do not even know that Lucius was ever shortened into Lucas. If Luke was a Gentile, and not an eye-witness, he cannot be the same as Lucius, Paul's kinsman (Rom. 16 : 21), nor one of the Seventy (Luke 10 : 1-7), nor one of two at Emmaus (24 : 13), nor one of the Greeks who came to see Jesus (John 12 : 20), nor Silvanus or Silas (Acts 15 : 22). All these were either Jews or eye-witnesses, or both. Luke was probably a Syrian of Antioch, and may have been converted by St. Paul. He gives us much information about Antioch (Acts 11 : 19-30, where ver. 26 is specially remarkable; 13 : 1-3; 14 : 26-15 : 3; 15 : 22-41); and in enumerating the seven deacons appointed at Jerusalem he tells us the nationality of only one, Nicolas of Antioch. The tradition that he was a painter, although legendary, is more ancient than is commonly supposed. It can be traced to the eighth or even the sixth century, and bears witness to the influence which the scenes recorded by St. Luke have had upon Christian art. His opportunities of collecting the very best information were very great, owing to his residence at Antioch, at Jerusalem, at Cæsarea, and at Rome, where we lose sight of him. At all these places he would meet, or from them could easily reach, Apostles and many others who had seen Jesus Christ in the flesh. He is rightly called the " father of Christian Church History." A trustworthy tradition says that he died in Bithynia, aged 74.
Luke, Gospel according to.
Authorship and Date.—As early as A.D. 140 there was a reference to Luke's name being attached to the third Gospel; and though some would give this another meaning, no

other construction can be put upon statements in Irenæus and in the Muratorian
Fragment (c. A.D. 180). A comparison
with Acts shows that this is from the same
hand, and that, with the exception perhaps
of Hebrews, the hand of the greatest stylist
in the New Testament (cf. the "we"
passages, etc.). There is no need to doubt
that the author of both was the same as the
"beloved physician" (Col. 4 : 14). If A.D.
85 be taken as the date of Acts, then the
Gospel must be assigned to the years around
A.D. 80. This would explain certain
linguistic differences between the two books,
while it accounts for the intimate knowledge
of the destruction of Jerusalem (Luke
21 : 20-24), and for the author's knowledge
of Mark's chronology.

Summary.—(1) Preface (1 : 1-4). (2) John
Baptist and Jesus, their birth and infancy
(1 : 5–2 : 52). (3) John's mission—Jesus
baptized and tempted (3 : 1–4 : 13). (4)
The ministry in Galilee—the earlier (4 : 14
–7 : 50); the later (8 : 1–9 : 50). (5) The
journey to Jerusalem (9 : 51–19 : 28).
(6) Last days, death and resurrection (19 : 29
–24 : 53).

Distinguishing Features.—Rénan's dictum
that the Gospel is "the most beautiful
book ever written" would find many who
agree. It is interesting to note :—
    (1) Luke's self-revelation in the type of
story he chooses. In the summary above,
section (1), (2), and most of (5) are peculiarly
his. His sympathy with the "down and
outs," the sick, the poor, etc., justify his
title "beloved physician" (cf. especially
that supreme "chapter of lost things,"
Luke 15).
    (2) His emphasising of Christ's liberality
of outlook (cf. 4 : 25-27; 2 : 32; 3 : 6;
9 : 52 ff.; 10 : 30 ff.; 17 : 15-19). He is
interested not so much in a Jewish Messiah
as in a Saviour in the world. In this he
was no doubt inspired by his friend and
master, Paul.
    (3) The prominence given to women
(e.g., Elizabeth, Virgin, Anna, Widow of
Nain, the repentant sinner, Mary Magdalene, Martha and Mary, the women at the
tomb, etc.).

Sources and Style.—Luke based his narrative
on oral tradition (cf. 1 : 1-4) and on Mark,
Q., and a narrative told by Joanna (cf.
Luke 8 : 3; 24 : 10, and see Gospels, the
Four). Using Mark's framework he
wedged in much of his own material holus
bolus (see Summary), and worked up the
whole with consummate skill. An accurate
historian, Luke has also a poetic flair (cf.
1 : 28, 46-55, 68-79; 2 : 14, 28-32).

Lukewarm, Rev. 3 : 16.
Lump, Rom. 9 : 21; 1 Cor. 5 : 6.
Lunatic, Matt. 4 : 24; 17 : 15.
Lurk, Ps. 10 : 8; Prov. 1 : 18.
Lust. Now restricted to sexual desire, this word
formerly expressed any kind of intense
desire. Hence Gal. 5 : 17 can speak of the
Spirit lusting against the flesh.

Ps. 81 : 12, gave them up to their own l.
Rom. 7 : 7, I had not known l., except by
law.
Gal. 5 : 24, crucified flesh with l.
1 Tim. 6 : 9, foolish and hurtful l.
2 Tim. 2 : 22, flee youthful l.
Titus 2 : 12, denying worldly l.
Jas. 1 : 14, when he is drawn of his own l.
1 Pet. 2 : 11, abstain from fleshy l.
1 John 2 : 16, the l. of the flesh.
    2 : 17, the world passeth away, and the l.
    thereof.
Jude 16, 18, walking after their l.
    See Deut. 12 : 15; 14 : 26; Matt. 5 : 28.
Lusty [ar.], robust, Judg. 3 : 29.
Luz (lŭz) [almond tree], Gen. 28 : 19; 35 : 6;
48 : 3; Josh. 16 : 2; 18 : 13; Judg. 1 : 23-
26. A close examination and comparison of
these places brings out the fact that Luz
and Bethel need not be regarded as occupying the same site and as being therefore
identical. Perhaps the name Luz applied
to the old city of Canaan while Bethel was
the pillar and altar of Jacob outside that
city.
LXX., an abbreviation for "Septuagint," which
see.
Lycaonia (lȳ-cā-ō-'nĭ-ă), province of Asia Minor,
Acts 14 : 6.
Lycia (lȳc-'ĭ-ă) [a wolf], a province of Asia
Minor, Acts 27 : 5.
Lydda (lȳd-'dă). (or Ludd).
    miracle at, Acts 9 : 32.
Lydia (lȳd-'ĭ-ă), of Thyatira, Acts 16 : 14, 40.
Lying, hateful to God, Prov. 6 : 16-19; 12 :
22.
    forbidden, Lev. 19 : 11; Col. 3 : 9.
    devil, father of, John 8 : 44; Acts 5 : 3.
Ps. 31 : 18, let the l. lips be put to silence.
Prov. 6 : 17, Lord hateth a l. tongue.
    12 : 19, a l. tongue is but for a moment.
Jer. 7 : 4, trust not in l. words.
Jonah 2 : 8, observe l. vanities, forsake mercy.
Ps. 119 : 29, remove from me the way of l.
    119 : 163, I hate and abhor l.
Isa. 59 : 13, l. against the Lord.
Eph. 4 : 25, putting away l.
Lysias (lȳs-'ĭ-ăs), Acts 23 : 26; 24 : 7.
Lystra (lȳs-'tră), miracle at, Acts 14 : 8.
    Paul and Barnabas taken for gods at, Acts
14 : 11.
    Paul stoned at, Acts 14 : 19.

M

Maacah (mā-'ă-căh) [oppressed], queen, her
idolatry, 2 Sam. 3 : 3.
Maachah (mā-'ă-chäh), 1 Ki. 15 : 13; 2 Chr.
15 : 16. See Maacah.
Maachathi (mā-ăch-'ă-thĭ), 2 Sam. 23 : 34.
Maachathite (mā-ăch-'ă-thĭte), Deut. 3 : 14.
Maadai (mā-ă-dā-'ĭ), Ezra 10 : 34; shortened
form of Maadiah (mā-ă-dī-'ăh) [ornament of
Jah], Neh. 12 : 5.
Maai (mā-ā-'ĭ), Neh. 12 : 36.
Maaleh-acrabbim (mā-ă-lēh-ăc-răb-'bĭm) [ascent
of scorpions], Josh. 15 : 3.
Maarath (mā-'ă-răth) [desolation], Josh. 15 : 59.

Maaseiah (mā-ă-sēı̆-äh) [work of Jehovah], Neh. 11 : 5.

Maasiai (mā-ăs-ĭ-ā-ı̄), 1 Chr. 9 : 12. See Maaseiah.

Maath (mā-äth) [small], Luke 3 : 26.

Maaz (mā-ăz), 1 Chr. 2 : 27.

Maaziah (mā-ă-zı̆-äh) [strength of Jehovah], 1 Chr. 24 : 18; Neh. 10 : 8.

Maccabæus, Judas. See Chronology, Period between Old and New Testaments.

Macedonia (măc-ē-dō-nı̆-ă), a large Greek province lying between the Adriatic and Ægean seas.

Paul's mission there, Acts 16 : 9; 20.

liberality of, 2 Cor. 8; 9; 11 : 9; Phil. 4 : 15.

its churches, 1 and 2 Thess.

Coin of Macedonia Prima.

Machbanai (măch-bā-nāı̆) [cloak], 1 Chr. 12 : 13.

Machbenah (măch-bē-näh), 1 Chr. 2 : 49.

Machi (mā-chı̆), Num. 13 : 15.

Machir (mā-chı̆r) [sold], Gen. 50 : 23; Num. 26 : 29; Josh. 17 : 1.

Machnadebai (măch-năd-ĕ-bāı̆), Ezra 10 : 40.

Machpelah (măch-pē-läh) [doubling], field of, Gen. 23 : 19.

patriarchs buried there, Gen. 23 : 19; 25 : 9; 35 : 29; 49 : 30; 50 : 12.

Mad. The ancients respected persons who were mad, and believed them to be possessed by supernatural spirits, good or evil.

1 Sam. 21 : 13, feigned himself m.

Ps. 102 : 8, are m. against me.

Eccl. 2 : 2, I said of laughter, It is m.

John 10 : 20, he hath a devil, and is m.

Acts 26 : 24, much learning doth make thee m.

1 Cor. 14 : 23, will they not say that ye are m. ?

Made, Ex. 2 : 14, who m. thee a prince over us ?

Ps. 104 : 24, thy works in wisdom hast thou m.

118 : 24, this is the day the Lord hath m.

139 : 14, I am wonderfully m.

Prov. 16 : 4, Lord m. all things for himself.

Eccl. 3 : 11, he hath m. every thing beautiful.

7 : 29, God hath m. man upright.

John 1 : 3, all things were m. by him.

Acts 7 : 50, hath not my hand m. all these things ?

Rom. 1 : 20, understood by the things that are m.

1 Cor. 9 : 22, m. all things to all men.

2 Cor. 5 : 21, he hath m. him to be sin for us.

Gal. 4 : 4, m. of a woman, m. under the law.

Eph. 3 : 7; Col. 1 : 23, I was m. a minister.

Phil. 2 : 7, m. in the likeness of men.

Heb. 2 : 9, m. a little lower than the angels.

2 : 17, to be m. like unto his brethren.

1 John 2 : 19, that they might be m. manifest.

Madian (mā-dı̆-ăn), Acts 7 : 29.

Madmannah (măd-măn-näh) [dunghill], Josh. 15 : 31.

Madmen (măd-mĕn), **Madmenah** (măd-mē-näh) [dungheap], Isa. 10 : 31; Jer. 48 : 2.

Madness, feigned by David, 1 Sam. 21 : 23.

threatened, Deut. 28 : 28.

Madon (ma-dŏn) [strife], Josh. 11 : 1; 12 : 19.

Magbish (măg-bı̆sh), Ezra 2 : 30.

Magdala (măg-dă-lă) [tower], a town on the shore of the Sea of Galilee, Matt. 15 : 39.

Magdalene (măg-dă-lĕne), or **Magdalen** (măg-dă-lĕn), inhabitant of Magdala, Luke 8 : 2.

Magic is due to a belief in supernatural powers and is a method used by man to obtain from these, if possible, knowledge of the future or help for the present. Hard to distinguish from religion in its first stages, magic is encouraged only in the lower stages. For examples in the Old Testament see Ex. 22 : 18; 1 Sam. 28 : 3; Isa. 2 : 6; Jer. 10 : 2; 2 Ki. 21 : 6; 23 : 24; Dan. 2 : 2; Isa. 47 : 12 f.; Ezek. 21 : 21, etc.

Magicians, of Egypt, Ex. 7 : 11; 8 : 19.

of Chaldea, preserved, Dan. 2.

Magistrates, to be obeyed, Ex. 22 : 9; Rom. 13; Titus 3 : 1; 1 Pet. 2 : 14.

See Ezra 7 : 25; Luke 12 : 11.

Magnifical [magnificent], 1 Chr. 22 : 5.

Magnificat, the hymn contained in Luke 1 : 46-55.

Magnificence, Acts 19 : 27.

Magnify, Josh. 3 : 7, this day will I begin to m. thee.

Job 7 : 17, what is man, that thou shouldest m. him ?

Ps. 34 : 3, m. the Lord with me.

40 : 16; 70 : 4, say, Lord be m.

138 : 2, thou hast m. thy word above all.

Isa. 42 : 21, he will m. the law.

Luke 1 : 46, my soul doth m. the Lord.

Acts 10 : 46, speak with tongues, and m. God.

Rom. 11 : 13, I m. mine office.

Magog (mā-gŏg) [land of Gugu], Gen. 10 : 2.

Magor-missabib (mā-gŏr-mı̆s-să-bı̆b) [fear round about], Jer. 20 : 3.

Magus (mā-gŭs) [magician], not a proper name, a sorcerer, Acts 13 : 6 ff.

239

Mahalah (mă-hā-läh) [disease], 1 Chr. 7 : 18.

Mahalaleel (mă-hăl-ă-lēe) [praise of God], Gen. 5 : 12 f., 15 ff.; 1 Chr. 1 : 2.

Mahalath (mā-hă-lăth) [sickness ? song], occurs in the title of Ps. 53; and in the title of Ps. 88, it is followed by " Leannoth." Since the expression is preceded by " al " [" to (the tune of) " rather than " upon "] it implies a song concerning the spiritual " sickness " of Judah or Israel (Jer. 8 : 21 f.), and is to be sung to a mournful tune. cf. **Jonath-elem-rehokim.**

Mahali (mā-hă-lī), Ex. 6 : 19.

Mahanaim (mā-hă-nā-īm) [two camps of two hosts], a city east of the Jordan, Jacob's vision at, Gen. 32. See 2 Sam. 2 : 8; 17 : 24.

Mahaneh-dan (mā-hă-nĕh-dăn), Judg. 18 : 12.

Maharai (mā-hă-râ̄), 1 Chr. 27 : 13.

Mahath (mā-hăth) [grasping], 1 Chr. 6 : 35; 2 Chr. 29 : 12.

Mahazioth (mă-hā-zĭ-ŏth), 1 Chr. 25 : 4.

Maher-shalal-hash-baz (mā-hĕr-shăl-ăl-hăsh-băz) [haste spoil, speed prey], Isa. 8 · 1, 3.

Mahlon (măh-lŏn) [sick], and Chilion, die in Moab, Ruth 1 : 2, 5; 4 : 10.

Maid, 2 Ki. 5 : 2, of the land of Israel a little m. Matt. 9 : 24, the m. is dead. 26 : 71, another m. saw him.

Maid child, Lev. 12 : 5.

Maidens, Ex. 2 : 5, m. walked along by the river's side. Ps. 148 : 12, both young men and m.

Maidservant, Ex. 20 : 10; 21 : 7; Deut. 15 : 17.

Mail, 1 Sam. 17 : 5, 38.

Maimed, healed by Christ, Matt. 15 : 30. animal unfit for sacrifice, Lev. 22 : 22.

Mainsail, Acts 27 : 40.

Maintain, 1 Ki. 8 : 45; 2 Chr. 6 : 35, 39, m. their cause. Ps. 16 : 5, thou m. my lot. Titus 3 : 8, 14, careful to m. good works.

Maintenance, Ezra 4 : 14; Prov. 27 : 27.

Majesty, of God, 1 Chr. 29 : 11; Ps. 93; 96; Isa. 24 : 14; Nah. 1; Hab. 3. See **God.** of Christ, 2 Pet. 1 : 16. See **Christ.** Job 37 : 22, with God is terrible m. Ps. 29 : 4, voice of the Lord is full of m. 96 : 6, honour and m. are before him. 104 : 1, thou art clothed with m. 145 : 12, glorious m. of his kingdom. Heb. 1 : 3; 8 : 1, on right hand of m. Jude 25, to God be glory and m.

Make, Gen. 1 : 26; Mal. 2 : 15; Rev. 21 : 5.

Maker. The idea of God as Maker or Creator of Man is the beginning and end of religion. For no one wishes harm to the thing he has made. Creation implies pursuing love. And God loves the work of His hand and desires to save man for Himself. Job 4 : 17, shall a man be more pure than his M. ? 32 : 22, my M. would soon take me away. 35 : 10, none saith, Where is God my M. ? 36 : 3, ascribe righteousness to my M. Ps. 95 : 6, kneel before the Lord our M. Prov. 14 : 31; 17 : 5, reproacheth his M. 22 : 2, the Lord is M. of them all.

Isa. 17 : 7, shall a man look to his M. 45 : 9, woe to him that striveth with his M. 51 : 13, forgetteth the Lord thy M. 54 : 5, thy M. is thine husband. Hos. 8 : 14, Israel hath forgotten his M. Hab. 2 : 18, imagine the m. hath graven. Heb. 11 : 10, whose builder and m. is God.

Makheloth (măk-hē-lŏth) [stations], Num. 33 : 25, 26.

Makkedah (măk-kē-dăh) [place of shepherds], Josh. 10 : 10, 16, 17.

Maktesh (măk-tĕsh) [mortar-shaped], Zeph. 1 : 11.

Maktua, a stream flowing into Chaldean Lake.

Malachi (măl-ă-chī) [my messenger], complains of Israel's ingratitude, Mal. 1 : 4. foretells the coming of Messiah and his messenger, Mal. 3 : 4.

Malachi, Book of. The name Malachi signifies " My messenger " and has been thought by some to refer to the office of the writer rather than to his name. The opinion is more general that Malachi was the name of the prophet and that he lived in the time of Nehemiah, since the sins he rebukes are identical with those condemned in Nehemiah. The probable date of the book is c. 420 B.C. Great unity marks the book and it contains some of the most striking of the messianic and eschatological passages (e.g., 3 : 1-3, 16-18; 4 : 1-3). The sin of the people finds expression in seven insolent questions hurled in the face of Jehovah : Wherein hast thou loved us ? (1 : 2); Wherein have we despised thy name ? (1 : 6); Wherein have we polluted thee ? (1 : 7); Wherein have we wearied him ? (2 : 17); Wherein shall we return ? (3 : 7); Wherein have we robbed thee ? (3 : 8); Wherein have we spoken against thee ? (3 : 13 R.V.). Such has been the sinfulness of God's people that but for his changelessness they would be consumed. In the New Testament Malachi is quoted frequently. Compare Mal. 1 : 2 with Rom. 9 : 13; ch. 3 : 1 and 4 : 5, 6 with Matt. 11 : 10, 14; 17 : 11; Mark 1 : 2; 9 : 11, 12; Luke 1 : 17, 76, 78; 7 : 27.

Malcham (măl-chăm) [their king], Zeph. 1 : 5.

Malchiah (măl-chī-ăh), Jer 38 : 6.

Malchijah (măl-chī-jăh) [Jehovah is king], 1 Chr. 24 : 9; Jer. 38 : 6.

Malchiel (măl-chī-ĕl) [God is king], Gen. 46 : 17; Num. 26 : 45; 1 Chr. 7 : 31.

Malchielites (măl-chī-ĕ-lītes), Num. 26 : 45.

Malchiram (măl-chī-răm) [high king], 1 Chr. 3 : 18.

Malchi-shua (măl-chī-shû-ă), 1 Chr. 8 : 33.

Melchi-shua (mĕl-chī-shû-ă) [my king is salvation], 1 Sam. 14 : 49.

Malchus (măl-chŭs), Greek form of " Malluch ", wounded by Peter, John 18 : 10; Matt. 26 : 51; Mark 14 : 47. healed by Jesus, Luke 22 : 51.

Male children saved from Pharaoh, Ex. 1 : 15. males to appear before the Lord three times a year, Ex. 23 : 17; Deut. 16 : 16.

Malefactors, execution of, Deut. 21 : 22.

crucified with Christ, Luke 23 : 32.

Malice. The word meant " evil " generally. Only since the seventeenth century has it been confined to " spite."
condemned, Prov. 17 : 5; 24 : 17; 1 Cor. 5 : 8; Col. 3 : 8; Titus 3 : 3; Jas. 5 : 9.
1 Cor. 14 : 20, in m. be ye children.
Eph. 4 : 31, put away from you all m.
1 Pet. 2 : 1, laying aside all m.

Malicious, 3 John 10.

Maliciousness, Rom. 1 : 29; 1 Pet. 2 : 16.

Malignity, Rom. 1 : 29.

Mallow, Job 30 : 4 (R.V. " salt-wort "). The sea orache is meant (Atriplex halinus). This is a perennial shrub which grows on salt marshes and has leaves like the olive.

Mammon (măm-mŏn) [riches], worship of, Matt. 6 : 24; Luke 16 : 9, 11, 13. The word is not a proper noun, though it comes near to personification in the phrase " God and mammon." Probably all that is meant is the literal meaning " God and gain " (cf. Phil. 3 : 19).

Man, created, Gen. 1 : 26.
his original dignity, Gen. 1 : 27; 2 : 25; Eccl. 7 : 29.
his fall, Gen. 3.
his iniquity, Gen. 6 : 5, 12; 1 Ki. 8 : 46; Job 14 : 16; 15 : 14; Ps. 14; 51; Eccl. 9 : 3; Isa. 43 : 27; 53 : 6; Jer. 3 : 25; 17 : 9; John 3 : 19; Rom. 3 : 9; 5 : 12; 7 : 18; Gal. 3 : 10; 5 : 17; Jas. 1 : 13; 1 John 1 : 8.
his weakness, etc., 2 Chr. 20 : 12; Matt. 6 : 27; Rom. 9 : 16; 1 Cor. 3 : 7; 2 Cor. 3 : 5.
liable to suffering, Job 14 : 1; Ps. 39 : 4; Eccl. 3 : 2; Acts 14 : 22; Rom. 8 : 22; Rev. 7 : 14.
his ignorance, Job 8 : 9; 28 : 12; Prov. 16 : 25; 27 : 1; Eccl. 8 : 17; Isa. 59 : 10; 1 Cor. 1 : 20; 8 : 2; (Isa. 47 : 10); Jas. 4 : 14.
mortality of, Ps. 39; 49; 78 : 39; 89 : 48; 103 : 14; 144 : 4; 146 : 4; Eccl. 1 : 4; 12 : 7; Rom. 5 : 12; Heb. 9 : 27.
vanity of his life, Ps. 49; Eccl. 1 : 2.
his whole duty, Eccl. 12 : 13; Mic. 6 : 8; 1 John 3 : 23.
his redemption, Rom. 5; 1 Cor. 15 : 49; Gal. 3; 4; Eph. 3; 5 : 25; Phil. 3 : 21; Col. 1; Heb. 1; 2; Rev. 5.
Gen. 2 : 7, Lord God formed m. of the dust.
3 : 22, the m. is become as one of us.
Num. 23 : 19, God is not a m.
2 Sam. 12 : 7, thou art the m.
Job 4 : 17, shall m. be more just than God ?
5 : 7, m. is born to trouble.
11 : 12, vain m. would be wise.
14 : 1, m. that is born of a woman.
33 : 12, God is greater than m.
Ps. 49 : 12, m. being in honour abideth not.
80 : 17, let thy hand be on the m.
90 : 3, thou turnest m. to destruction.
104 : 23, m. goeth forth to his work.
118 : 6, I will not fear : what can m. do ?
Prov. 12 : 2, a good m. obtaineth favour.
20 : 24, m. goings are of the Lord.

Eccl. 6 : 12, who knoweth what is good for m. ?
Isa. 2 : 22, cease ye from m.
32 : 2, a m. shall be as an hiding-place.
53 : 3, a m. of sorrows.
Jer. 10 : 23, it is not in m. to direct his steps.
Lam. 3 : 27, it is good for a m. that he bear the yoke.
Hos. 11 : 9, I am God, and not m.
Matt. 6 : 24, no m. can serve two masters.
8 : 9; Luke 7 : 8, I am a m. under authority.
Mark 2 : 27, sabbath was made for m.
John 1 : 18; 1 John 4 : 12, no m. hath seen God.
John 2 : 25, he knew what was in m.
19 : 5, behold the m.
1 Cor. 2 : 11, what m. knoweth things of m. ?
2 Cor. 4 : 16, though our outward m. perish.
Eph. 3 : 16, by his Spirit in the inner m.
4 : 24, that ye put on the new m.
Phil. 2 : 8, found in fashion as a m.
1 Tim. 2 : 5, the m. Christ Jesus.
1 Pet. 3 : 4, hidden m. of the heart.
Note : " man " can also stand for the indefinite " one " (Zech. 13 : 5; Mark 8 : 4).

Manaen (măn-ā-ĕn) [consoler], Greek form of " Menahem," Acts 13 : 1.

Manahath (măn-ă-hăth), a city near Jerusalem, Gen. 36 : 23; 1 Chr. 8 : 6.

Manahethites (măn-ă-hē-thītes), 1 Chr. 2 : 52, 54.

Manasseh (mă-năs-sĕh) [one who makes to forget], firstborn son of Joseph, Gen. 41 : 51.
his blessing, Gen. 48.
his descendants, numbered, etc., Num. 1 : 34; 26 : 29; Josh. 22 : 1; 1 Chr. 5 : 23; 7 : 14
incline to David's cause, 1 Chr. 9 : 3; 12 : 19; 2 Chr. 15 : 9; 30 : 11.
their inheritance, Num. 32 : 33; 34 : 14; Josh. 13 : 29; 17 : 1.
king of Judah, his evil reign, 2 Ki. 21; 2 Chr. 33.

Manasses (mă-năs-sĕs), Matt. 1 : 10; Rev. 7 : 6.

Mandrakes, Gen. 30 : 14-16; Song of Sol. 7 : 13, a low-growing plant with dark leaves something like lettuce, it is of the potato family and is allied to the deadly nightshade. Its fruit ripens in May and grows to the size of a small apple. It is reddish or yellowish in colour, and emits such a pleasing odour that the Arabs call it " Devil's Apple " from its enticing the appetites.

Maneh (mā-nĕh), a weight, Ezek. 45 : 12. See **Weights.**
money. See **Money.**

Manger, Luke 2 : 7, 12, 16. Jesus' birth, according to an ancient tradition, was in a cave near Bethlehem. Such caves, built beneath the houses, are often used as stables; and cut in the side is the " manger," an excellent " crib " for a baby.

Manifest, Mark 4 : 22, nothing hid that shall not be m.
John 2 : 11, m. forth his glory.
14 : 22, how is it thou wilt m. thyself ?

1 Cor. 4 : 5, make m. the counsels of the heart.
15 : 27, it is m. he is excepted.
2 Cor. 2 : 14, maketh m. savour of knowledge.
Gal. 5 : 19, the works of the flesh are m.
2 Thess. 1 : 5, a m. token of righteous judgment.
1 Tim. 3 : 16, God was m. in the flesh.
Heb. 4 : 13, no creature that is not m.
1 John 1 : 2, the life was m.
3 : 5, he was m. to take away our sins.
4 : 9, in this was m. the love of God.
Manifestation, of Christ, Matt. 17; John 1 : 14; 1 John 3 : 5.
of God's righteousness, Rom. 3 : 21; and love, 1 John 4 : 9.
of the sons of God, Rom. 8 : 19.
of the Spirit, 1 Cor. 12 : 7.
Manifestly, 2 Cor. 3 : 3.
Manifold, Ps. 104 : 24, how m. are thy works.
Luke 18 : 30, receive m. more.
Eph. 3 : 10, m. wisdom of God.
1 Pet. 1 : 6, through m. temptations.
4 : 10, stewards of the m. grace of God.
Mankind, Job 12 : 10; Jas. 3 : 7.
Manna (" the-what-is-it "), a small, white, flaky substance like the seed or fruit of the coriander (Ex. 16 : 31; Num. 11 : 7). It tasted like wafers made with honey. Seen when the dew began to disappear, it melted under the heat of the sun. The miraculous character of the manna was emphasized by the fact that it ceased instantly when no longer needed, Josh. 5 : 12.
promised, Ex. 16 : 4.
sent, Ex. 16 : 14; Deut. 8 : 3; Neh. 9 : 20; Ps. 78 : 24; John 6 : 31.
an omer of, laid up in the ark of the covenant, Ex. 16 : 32; Heb. 9 : 4.
Israelites murmur at, Num. 11 : 6.
ceases on entering Canaan, Josh. 5 : 12.
the hidden, Rev. 2 : 17.
Manner, Lev. 23 : 31, ye shall do no m. of work.
2 Sam. 7 : 19, is this the m. of man ?
Ps. 107 : 18, all m. of meat.
Song of Sol. 7 : 13, all m. of pleasant fruits.
Isa. 5 : 17, lambs shall feed after their m.
Matt. 5 : 11, say all m. of evil against you.
8 : 27; Mark 4 : 41; Luke 8 : 25, what m. of man is this ?
John 19 : 40, m. of Jews to bury.
1 Cor. 15 : 33, evil communications corrupt good m.
2 Tim. 3 : 10, my m. of life.
Heb. 10 : 25, as the m. of some.
Jas. 1 : 24, forgetteth what m. of man.
1 Pet. 1 : 15, holy in all m. of conversation.
2 Pet. 3 : 11, what m. of persons ought ye to be ?
1 John 3 : 1, what m. of love.
Manoah (mă-nō-ʻăh) [rest], father of Samson, Judg. 13 : 2; 16 : 31.
Man of sin, 2 Thess. 2 : 3 ff.
Manservant, Deut. 5 : 14; Jer. 34 : 9.
Mansion [ar.], an abiding place, John 14 : 2.
Manslaughter, Gen. 9 : 6; Ex. 21 : 12; Num. 35 : 6, 22; Deut. 19 : 4; Josh. 20 : 1; 1 Tim. 1 : 9.
Manstealing, Ex. 21 : 16; Deut. 24 : 7.

Mantle, 1 Ki. 19 : 19; 2 Ki. 2 : 8, 13, 14.
Manuscripts of the Bible. There are three sources of material open to the textual critic, namely, Greek MSS., Versions (Latin, Syriac, Egyptian, etc. See **Versions**), and Quotations in Patristic Writings (*e.g.*, Justin, Irenæus, Clement, etc.).
The MSS. fall into two classes :
(1) Uncials, *i.e.*, " inch-high " or " capital " letters are used. Dating, broadly speaking, from the fourth to the ninth centuries, the more important are :—
Aleph, or Codex Sinaiticus, discovered by Tischendorf in a monastery on Mount Sinai in 1859, is now in the British Museum, having been bought by the Nation for £100,000 from the U.S.S.R. Containing parts of the LXX., the Epistle of Barnabas, and the whole of the New Testament, it is made up of 346 leaves (13⅜″ x 14⅞″) each of four columns with forty-eight lines. It dates from the middle of the fourth century, A.D., as does also
B, or Codex Vaticanus, at Rome. The pages are of three columns of forty-two lines. Except for parts of Genesis, some Psalms and Pastoral Epistles, Philemon, Revelation, and part of Hebrews, it contains the whole Bible. With Aleph it is the best and fullest of our MSS.
A, or Codex Alexandrinus, was given by the Patriarch of Constantinople, Cyril Lukar, to the British Ambassador there in 1621. Dating from the fifth century, it is now one of the treasures of the British Museum, and includes one of the apocryphal epistles, part of the LXX., the greater part of the New Testament.
C, or Codex Ephræmi Syri, in the National Library in Paris. This is a palimpsest, *i.e.*, a text (of the New Testament) which has become faint and over which another work (of Ephræm the Syrian) has been written. It gives about two-thirds of the New Testament, and dates from the fifth century.
D, or Codex Bezae, now at Cambridge University, it formerly belonged to the reformer Cardinal Beza. It dates from the sixth century, and contains the Gospels and Acts (in Greek on the left-hand pages and Latin on the right), and some verses of 3 John in Latin. It is very daring in some of its readings, many of which are authenticated by other means.
(2) Minuscules or " Cursives," *i.e.*, those written in a running hand. They date generally from the tenth to the fifteenth centuries. They are usually numbered by Arabic figures. The two chief groups are:—
(a) Codex 1 or fam.[1] (Nos. 1, 118, etc., four in number).
(b) Fam.[13], or the Ferrar group (Nos. 13, 69, etc., eight in number).
Notes.—Before the thirteenth century the Greek MSS. are usually of vellum; after the fourteenth century they are of paper. Account must be taken of Greek service-books or lectionaries, which contain por-

tions of the New Testament for public reading.

While many New Testament MSS. are dated prior to the tenth century, only a few Old Testament MSS. are prior to the twelfth century.

The oldest MS. of the whole Old Testament is dated A.D. 1010; the earliest known Hebrew MS. is dated circa B.C. 100 (the book of Isaiah which was found in 1947 amongst the Dead Sea Scrolls).

In conclusion, the original autographed MSS. of the Bible are gone. Hence arises the need for Textual Criticism, the aim of which is to present us with a copy as near to the original as possible.

Many, Ps. 3 : 2; Luke 13 : 24; 21 : 8; John 1 : 12; Rom. 12 : 5; 1 Cor. 1 : 26; Gal. 6 : 16.

Mar, Lev. 19 : 27, not m. the corners of thy beard.

Isa. 52 : 14, his visage m. more than any man.

Mark 2 : 22, wine is spilled, and the bottles will be m.

Mara (mâr-ā) [bitter], Ruth 1 : 20.

Maran-atha (măr-ăn-ā-thă) [our Lord cometh] (R.V., Maran atha), 1 Cor. 16 : 22. See **Anathema.**

Marble [Heb. " shayish "; Marmor Parium] 1 Chr. 29 : 2; Esther 1 : 6; Song of Sol. 5 : 15. " Shayish " appears to have been a variety of marble used for building.

March, Ps. 68 : 7; Jer. 46 : 22; Hab. 1 : 6.

Marchesvan, or **Bul.** See **Months.**

Marcus (mär-cŭs). See **Mark.**

Mariners, Ezek. 27 : 8, 9, 29; Jonah 1 : 5.

Marish [ar.], a marsh or swampy place, Ezek. 47 : 11.

Mark The Evangelist's full name was John Mark (Acts 12 : 12, 25; 15 : 37), a combination of Hebrew (John or Johanan = Jehovah is gracious) with Roman (Marcus = Hammer or Mallet), which symbolises his mission. As in the case of Peter and Paul, the original Hebrew name (Acts 13 : 5, 13) seems to have gone out of use (Acts 15 : 39); Col. 4 : 10; Philem. 24; 2 Tim. 4 : 11). His mother, Mary, was a friend of Peter (Acts 12 : 12), and Peter probably converted Mark, and hence calls him his son (1 Pet. 5 : 13). The young man mentioned in Mark 14 : 51, 52, is possibly the Evangelist. It is difficult to see why so trivial an occurrence is mentioned, unless it was of personal interest to the narrator. Mark was cousin to Barnabas (Col. 4 : 10), and perhaps in this way came in contact with St. Paul (Acts 12 : 25; 13 : 5), who dismissed him for slackness (Acts 15 : 38, 39), on which his cousin was less severe. But nine or ten years later we find him a welcome companion of St. Paul during his first Roman captivity (Col. 4 : 11; Philem. 24), and a much desired fellow-worker during his second (2 Tim. 4 : 11). Mark was with Peter in " Babylon," i.e., Rome, when he wrote his First Epistle (5 : 13). The date and manner of his death are unknown.

Mark, Gospel according to.

Date.—Mark's is now acknowledged to be the earliest of the Gospels. Its scope is more limited than Matthew's or Luke's (cf. Acts 1 : 22); and where these diverge from Mark it is in a secondary sense.

Of the primitive material, oral or written, which is employed by all three Synoptists, St. Mark gives us the most. His Gospel contains little else, and there are only about twenty-four verses in it which are not contained in Matthew or in Luke, or in both (e.g., 4 : 26-29; 7 : 4, 31-37; 12 : 32, 33). Even this small portion may be part of the primitive material known to all three, although neither Matthew nor Luke make any use of it. This, however, does not extend to the history of the Passion. There it would seem that St. Mark has made use of St. Matthew's account, or vice versa. There is good reason for believing that the source of most of this common material is the preaching of St. Peter. That which is found in all three Gospels, or in Mark and Matthew, or in Mark and Luke, is just that part of Christ's life of which Peter would have personal knowledge. The earliest witnesses, from Papias (A.D. 130) downwards, state that Mark recorded the things which were related by Peter. He was called Peter's " interpreter," because he communicated to others what he had heard from Peter's own lips. It is remarkable with what exactness the summary of the Gospel narrative given by St. Peter (Acts 10 : 36-40) fits the contents of the Second Gospel. The graphic details, which are so abundant in Mark, indicate that the writer was an eye-witness or obtained his information from an eye-witness (e.g., 3 : 5, 34; 5 : 32; 8 : 33; 9 : 35; 10 : 23, 32, etc.). St. Mark sometimes specially mentions the presence of Peter where Matthew and Luke are silent on the point (1 : 36; 11 : 21; 13 : 3; 16 : 7). He begins the ministry of Christ with the call of Peter and his brother Andrew (1 : 16), and ends his Gospel with a message to Peter (16 : 7). He tells us that at the Transfiguration Peter " wist not what to answer." He alone tells us that Peter was warming himself " in the light of the fire " (14 : 54), so as to attract attention, when he denied his Master; and that the cock crew twice (14 : 72). And possibly it is Peter's humility which suppresses notice of Peter where others tell what is to his honour (contrast Mark 6 : 50, 51 with Matt. 14 : 28-31; Mark 9 : 33 with Matt. 17 : 24-27; Mark 8 : 29, 30 with Matt. 16 : 17-19).

If, then, Mark's Gospel is a record of Peter's preaching, it cannot have been written before A.D. 63. The prophecies in Chapter 13 show no knowledge of the destruction of Jerusalem, and implies a date prior to A.D. 70. Between these two dates is the probable date of the Gospel.

Intention.—The early tradition that St. Mark

wrote his Gospel in Rome for Gentiles, and primarily for Romans. is probably correct. It is confirmed by the internal evidence of the Gospel itself. In his own person he quotes only two passages from the Old Testament (1 : 2, 3). He makes no references to the Mosaic Law, and gives no genealogy of the Messiah. He explains Jewish words, localities, and customs (3 : 17; 5 : 41; 7 : 3, 11; 10 : 46; 12 : 18, 42; 13 : 3; 14 : 1, 12, 36; 15 : 6, 16, 34, 42). The Latin words which he uses may be the result of life in Rome (6 : 27; 7 : 4; 12 : 42; 15 : 39, 44, 45); but that he originally wrote his Gospel in Latin is a late and baseless statement. He represents Christ as the Son of God, exhibiting the Divine power in mighty wonders, especially in vanquishing the powers of evil by healing demoniacs. The people are thus led to recognise in Him a spiritual conqueror, an aspect of the crucified which would be acceptable to heathen and especially to the Romans.

Summary.—Chap. 1 : 1-8, Introduction. 1 : 9 —13 : 37, Ministry (Galilee, Peræa, Jerusalem). 14 : 1—16 : 8, Passion and Resurrection.

Mark, Gen. 4 : 15, the Lord set a m. on Cain.
Job 18 : 2, m. and we will speak.
22 : 15, hast thou m. the old way ?
Ps. 37 : 37, m. the perfect man.
48 : 13, m. well her bulwarks.
130 : 3, if thou shouldest m. iniquities.
Luke 14 : 7, m. how they chose out the chief rooms.
Gal. 6 : 17, the m. of the Lord Jesus.
Phil. 3 : 14, I press towards the m. for the prize.

Marks. Six classes are here enumerated : (1) Marks of circumcision (Gen. 17 : 14, the mark of a Jahweh-worshipper); (2) Mark of Cain (Gen. 4 : 15); (3) Mark of the prophet (1 Ki. 20 : 35-43); (4) Incisions for the dead (Lev. 19 : 28; Deut. 14 : 1); (5) Marks as signs of Jahweh-worship (Ex. 13 : 9, 16); (6) Stigmata (2 Cor. 11 : 23 f.; Gal. 6 : 17).

Market, Ezek. 27 : 17; Matt. 23 : 7; Luke 20 : 46; Acts 17 : 17.

Marriage, instituted, Gen. 2 : 18.
honourable, Ps. 128 : 3; Prov. 31 : 10; Heb. 13 : 4.
Christ's discourses about, Matt. 19; Mark 10.
its obligations, Matt. 19 : 4; Rom. 7 : 2; 1 Cor. 6 : 16; 7 : 10; Eph. 5 : 31.
parables concerning, Matt. 22 : 25.
confined to this world, Matt. 22 : 30; Mark 12 : 25.
Paul's opinion on, 1 Cor. 7; 1 Tim. 5 : 14.
of the Lamb, typical, Rev. 19 : 7.
unlawful marriages, Lev. 18; Deut. 7 : 3; Josh. 23 : 12; Ezra 9; 10; Neh. 13 : 23.

Marrow, Ps. 63 : 5, soul satisfied as with m.
Prov. 3 : 8, health and m. to the bones.
Isa. 25 : 6, feast of fat things full of m.
Heb. 4 : 12, to the dividing asunder of joints and m.

Mars' Hill, Acts 17 : 22. See Areopagus.

Mart, Isa. 23 : 3. See Market.

Martha, instructed by Christ, John 11 : 5, 21 ff.
reproved by him, Luke 10 : 38.

Martyr, Stephen the first, Acts 7; 22 : 20.
See Rev. 2 : 13; 17 : 6.

Marvel, Eccl. 5 : 8, m. not at the matter.
Matt. 8 : 10; Mark 6 : 6; Luke 7 : 9, Jesus m.
Mark 5 : 20, all men did m.
John 5 : 28, m. not at this.
Acts 3 : 12, why m. ye at this ?
1 John 3 : 13, m. not if world hate you.

Marvellous, Job 5 : 9, m. things without number.
Ps. 17 : 7, show m. lovingkindness.
98 : 1, he hath done m. things.
118 : 23; Matt. 21 : 42; Mark 12 : 11, m. in our eyes.
John 9 : 30, herein is a m. thing.
1 Pet. 2 : 9, called you into his m. light.

Marvellously, Job 37 : 5; Hab. 1 : 5.

Mary (Miriam), the Virgin, mother of Jesus, Gabriel sent to, Luke 1 : 26.
believes and magnifies the Lord, Luke 1 : 38, 46; John 2 : 5.
Christ born of, Matt. 1 : 18; Luke 2.
present at the marriage at Cana, John 2 : 1.
desires to speak with Christ, Matt. 12 : 46; Mark 3 : 31; Luke 8 : 19.
commended to John by Christ at his crucifixion, John 19 : 25.
Magdalene, out of whom were cast seven devils, Luke 8 : 2.
at the cross, Matt. 27 : 56; Mark 15 : 40; John 19 : 25.
Christ appears first to, Matt. 28 : 1; Mark 16 : 1; Luke 24 : 10; John 20 : 1.
sister of Lazarus, commended, Luke 10 : 42.
Christ's affection for, John 11 : 5, 33.
anoints Christ, Matt. 26 : 7; Mark 14 : 3; John 12 : 3.

Maschil (măs-́chîl) [instructing], is found in the titles of Ps. 32; 42; 44 f.; 52-55; 74; 78; 88 f.; 142. The term implies a didactic poem, but further than that we cannot go.

Masons, 2 Ki. 22 : 6; 2 Chr. 24 : 12; Ezra 3 : 7. See Handicraft.

Massah (măs-́săh) [trial, temptation], Israel's rebellion at, Ex. 17 : 7; Deut. 9 : 22; 33 : 8. Except in Deut. 6 : 11; 9 : 22, Massah never stands alone. It is coupled in Ex. 17 : 1-7 with Meribah. See Meribah.

Master, duty of, Ex. 20 : 10; Lev. 19 : 13; 25 : 40; Deut. 24 : 14; Job 31 : 13; Jer. 22 : 13; Col. 4 : 1; Jas. 5 : 4.
Mal. 1 : 6, if I be a m. where is my fear ?
2 : 12, the Lord will cut off the m. and the scholar.
Matt. 6 : 24; Luke 16 : 13, no man can serve two m.
Matt. 10 : 24; Luke 6 : 40, disciple is not above his m.
Matt. 23 : 8, 10, one is your M., even Christ.
Mark 5 : 35; Luke 8 : 49, why troublest thou the M. ?
Mark 9 : 5; Luke 9 : 33, M., it is good for us to be here.
Mark 10 : 17; Luke 10 : 25; 18 : 18, good M., what shall I do ?
Luke 13 : 25, when the m. of the house is risen.

John 3 : 10, art thou a **m.** of Israel ?
11 : 28, the **M.** is come, and calleth for thee.
13 : 13, ye call me **M.** and ye say well.
Rom. 14 : 4, to his own **m.** he standeth or falleth.
Eph. 6 : 9, **M.** is in heaven.
1 Tim. 6 : 1, count **m.** worthy of honour.
Jas. 3 : 1, be not many **m.**
Masterbuilder, 1 Cor. 3 : 10.
Mastery, Ex. 32 : 18; 1 Cor. 9 : 25; 2 Tim. 2 : 5.
Masts, Ezek. 27 : 5; Prov. 23 : 34; Isa. 33 : 23.
Mate, Isa. 34 : 15, 16.
Matrix, Ex. 13 : 13; Num. 18 : 15.
Mattan (măt-tăn) [gift], priest of Baal, slain, 2 Ki. 11 : 18; 2 Chr. 23 : 17.
Mattanah (măt-tā-năh) [a gift], Num. 21 : 18, 19.
Mattaniah (măt-tă-nī-ăh) [gift of Jehovah], 2 Ki. 24 : 17; Neh. 11 : 17; 13 : 13.
Mattatha (măt-tă-thă), Luke 3 : 31.
Mattathias (măt-tă-thī-ăs), Luke 3 : 25 f.
Mattathah (măt-tă-thăh), Ezra 10 : 33.
Mattenai (măt-tē-nâî), Ezra 10 : 33; Neh. 12 : 19.
Matter, Deut. 17 : 8, if there arise a **m.** too hard.
Job 19 : 28, the root of the **m.** is found in me.
32 : 18, I am full of **m.**
Ps. 45 : 1, my heart is inditing a good **m.**
Prov. 16 : 20, that handleth a **m.** wisely.
18 : 13, answereth a **m.** before he heareth it.
Eccl. 10 : 20, that which hath wings shall tell the **m.**
12 : 13, hear conclusion of the whole **m.**
Matt. 23 : 23, omitted the weightier **m.**
Acts 18 : 14, if it were a **m.** of wrong.
24 : 22, I will know uttermost of the **m.**
1 Cor. 6 : 1, dare any having a **m.** go to law ?
2 Cor. 9 . 5, ready as a **m.** of bounty.
Jas. 3 : 5, how great a **m.** a little fire kindleth.
Matthew (măt-thēw), Greek form of " Mattai," probably shortened from " Mattithiah," (Levi) apostle, called, Matt. 9 : 9; Mark 2 : 14; Luke 5 : 27.
sent out, Matt. 10 : 3; Mark 3 : 18; Luke 6 : 15; Acts 1 : 13.
Matthew, Gospel according to.
Summary.—Chaps. 1–2, The birth and infancy of Jesus. 3 : 1-12, Mission of John Baptist. 3 : 13–4 : 17, Baptism and temptation. 4 : 18–15 : 20, Work in Galilee (teaching, healing, call of disciples; effects on the populace, officials, and Himself). 15 : 21–18 : 35, Work outside Galilee (Cæsarea-Philippi). 19–20, Journey to Jerusalem. 21–28, Passion and resurrection.
Authorship and Date.—The authorship of the gospel has been from the end of the first century ascribed to Matthew, the Publican, a disciple of Christ. It was probably written in 80 or 90 A.D. Certain of the Fathers, Papias, Irenæus, Pantænus, Origen, Eusebius, Epiphanius, Jerome and others assert that it was first written in Hebrew, that is, in the vernacular of Palestine, Aramaic. There are, however, strong arguments that the original was written in Greek. Among those who hold this view are, Erasmus, Calvin, Le Clerc, Fabricius,

Lightfoot, Wetstein, Paulus, Lardner, Hey, Hales, Hug, Schott, De Wette, Stewart, Fritsche, Credner, Thiersch, and others. No one ever claims to have seen a Hebrew original, and the arguments for it are not altogether convincing. However, this truth is clear,—that the gospel was written from the Jewish standpoint and with a Jewish audience in view. It is the gospel of the Kingdom and each fact is presented with this subject logically in mind. Christ is announced as the Son of David, the Son of Abraham (1 : 1). His genealogy through Joseph is given, for it is through his mother's husband that the crown rights will descend. It is as Son of Man that he inherits the covenants. The spiritual laws of the Kingdom are declared with all authority on the Mount (5–7). In chapters 8, 9, authority is seen in action. In 10 the Twelve are commissioned and given the credentials of the King as his messengers. Chapter 11 records the varied reception given to the Kingdom message. Those with hearts of babes accept. Collisions with the Pharisees over the question of authority begin to multiply. The kingdom indeed is wanted, but not so spiritual a King. He foretells this rejection and prepares His followers for a long period when the King will be absent. In chapters 24 and 25, He depicts the events connected with His return and the establishment of the Kingdom of Heaven upon the earth.
Matthias (măth-ī-ăs) [gift of Jah], chosen apostle, Acts 1 : 26.
Mattock, 1 Sam. 13 : 20, 21; Isa. 7 : 25.
Maul, Prov. 25 : 18.
Maw, Deut. 18 : 3.
Meadow, Gen. 41 : 2, 18; Judg. 20 : 33.
Meal, 1 Ki. 17 : 12, an handful of **m.** in a barrel.
1 Ki. 17 : 16, the **m.** wasted not.
Matt. 13 : 33; Luke 13 : 21, hid in three measures of **m.**
Mealtime, Ruth 2 : 14.
Mean, Ex. 12 : 26, what **m.** ye by this service ?
Deut. 6 : 20, what **m.** the testimonies ?
Josh. 4 : 6, 21, what **m.** these stones ?
Prov. 22 : 29, not stand before **m.** men.
Isa. 2 : 9; 5 : 15, the **m.** man.
Mark 9 : 10, what the rising from the dead should **m.**
Acts 21 : 39, a citizen of no **m.** city.
Means, Ex. 34 : 7; Num. 14 : 18, by no **m.** clear the guilty.
Ps. 49 : 7 none can by **m.** redeem his brother.
Matt. 5 : 26, shalt by no **m.** come out.
Luke 5 : 18, sought **m.** to bring him.
10 : 19, nothing shall by any **m.** hurt you.
John 9 : 21, by what **m.** he now seeth.
Acts 4 : 9, by what **m.** he is made whole.
1 Cor. 9 : 22, that I might by all **m.** save some.
2 Cor. 11 : 3, lest by any **m.**, as the serpent.
Gal. 2 : 2, lest by any **m.** I should run in vain.
Phil. 3 : 11, by any **m.** attain.
2 Thess. 2 : 3, no man deceive you by any **m.**
Meantime, Luke 12 : 1.
Meanwhile, John 4 : 31; Rom. 2 : 15.

Measure, Num. 35 : 5, ye shall **m.** from without the city.
Deut. 25 : 15, a just **m.** shalt thou have.
Job 11 : 9, the **m.** is longer than the earth.
28 : 25, he weigheth the waters by **m.**
Ps. 39 : 4, to know the **m.** of my days.
80 : 5, tears to drink in great **m.**
Isa. 40 : 12, who hath **m.** the waters ?
40 : 12, comprehended dust of earth in a **m.**
65 : 7, I will **m.** former work into bosom.
Jer. 30 : 11; 46 : 28, correct thee in **m.**
31 : 37, if heaven can be **m.**
33 : 22; Hos. 1 : 10, sand of the sea cannot be **m.**
Ezek. 4 : 11, thou shalt drink water by **m.**
Matt. 7 : 2; Mark 4 : 24; Luke 6 : 38, with what **m.** ye mete.
Matt. 13 : 33; Luke 13 : 21, three **M.** of meal.
Matt. 23 : 32, fill up **m.** of your fathers.
Mark 6 : 51, were amazed beyond **m.**
Luke 6 : 38, good **m.**, pressed down.
John 3 : 34, God giveth not the Spirit by **m.**
Rom. 12 : 3, to every man the **m.** of faith.
12 : 7, exalted above **m.**
2 Cor. 10 : 12, **m.** themselves by themselves.
10 : 13, not boast of things without our **m.**
Gal. 1 : 13, beyond **m.** I persecuted.
Eph. 4 : 7, the **m.** of the gift of Christ.
4 : 13, to the **m.** of the stature.
Rev. 6 : 6, a **m.** of wheat for a penny.
11 : 1, rise, and **m.** the temple of God.
21 : 15, a golden reed to **m.** the city.
21 : 17, according to the **m.** of a man.

Measures of Capacity.
Assuming an ephah to contain 8 gallons, we obtain the following fairly accurate measures :—
1 Log = $\frac{7}{8}$ pint (Lev. 14 : 10 f., 21).
1 Cab = 4 Logs = $3\frac{1}{2}$ pints (2 Ki. 6 : 25).
1 Hin = 3 Cabs = $1\frac{1}{3}$ gallons (Ex. 29 : 40).
1 Omer = $1\frac{4}{5}$ Cabs = 6 pints (Ex. 16 : 36; Lev. 5 : 11; 14 : 10).
1 Seah = $3\frac{1}{2}$ Omers = 2 Hins = $2\frac{2}{3}$ gallons.
1 Ephah or Bath = 3 Seahs = 8 gallons (Isa. 5 : 10; Ezek. 45 : 11).
1 Lethech = 5 Ephahs = 40 gallons.
1 Homer = 10 Ephahs = 80 gallons (Isa. 5 : 10; Ezek. 45 : 14).

Measures of Length.
The Royal System measures $1\frac{4}{25}$ for every 1 unit in the Common System. We give approximate measures of the Common System.
1 Digit or fingerbreadth = $\frac{3}{4}$ inch.
1 Palm = 4 Digits = 3 inches (Ex. 25 : 25; Ps. 39 : 5).
1 Span = 3 Palms = 9 inches (Ex. 28 : 16; 1 Sam. 17 : 4).
1 Cubit = 2 Spans = $1\frac{1}{2}$ feet (Gen. 6 : 15 f.; Deut. 3 : 11).
1 Reed = 6 Cubits = 9 feet.
The following were the Measures prevalent in the Greek and Roman periods :—
1 Roman Foot = 11.65 inches.
1 Roman passus = 4 feet $10\frac{1}{4}$ inches.
1 Roman Mile = 0.92 English mile (*i.e.*, 1615 yards).
1 Greek Foot = 12.135 inches.
1 Greek Fathom = 6 feet 1 inch (Acts 27 : 28).
1 Greek Furlong = 202 yards (Luke 24 : 13; John 11 : 18).
1 Persian Parasang = $3\frac{1}{2}$ miles (nearly).

Measuring of the holy city and new Jerusalem, Ezek. 40; Zech. 2 : 1; Rev. 11 : 1; 21 : 15.

Meat. The word is used in A.V., as it still is in Scotland, to represent " food " in general.
clean and unclean, Lev. 11; Deut. 14; Acts 15 : 29; Rom. 14; 1 Cor. 8 : 4; Col. 2 : 16; 1 Tim. 4 : 3.
Gen. 1 : 29, it shall be for **m.**
27 : 4, savoury **m.**
1 Ki. 19 : 8, he went in strength of that **m.**
Job 33 20, his soul abhorreth dainty **m.**
38 : 41, wander for lack of **m.**
Ps. 42 : 3, tears have been my **m.**
59 : 15, wander up and down for **m.**
69 : 21, they gave me gall for my **m.**
104 27, thou mayest give them their **m.**
145 : 15; Matt. 24 : 45, **m.** in due season.
Prov. 6 : 8, the ant provideth her **m.**
31 : 15, giveth **m.** to her household.
Isa. 65 : 25, dust shall be the serpent's **m.**
Ezek. 4 : 10, thy **m.** shall be by weight.
Dan. 1 : 8, not defile himself with king's **m.**
Hab. 3 : 17, fields yield no **m.**
Matt. 6 : 25; Luke 12 : 23, is not the life more than **m.** ?
Matt. 10 : 10, workman worthy of his **m.**
15 : 37; Mark 8 : 8, of the broken **m.**
Matt. 25 : 35, hungered, and ye gave me **m.**
Luke 8 : 55, he commanded to give her **m.**
24 : 41; John 21 : 5, have ye any **m.** ?
John 4 : 34, my **m.** is to do the will of him that sent me.
6 : 27, labour not for the **m.** that perisheth.
Acts 2 : 46, eat their **m.** with gladness.
Rom. 14 : 15, if thy brother be grieved with thy **m.**
14 : 17, kingdom of God is not **m.** and drink.
1 Cor. 3 : 2, fed with milk, not with **m.**
6 : 13, **m.** for the belly.
8 : 8, **m.** commendeth us not to God.
10 : 3, eat the same spiritual **m.**
Col. 2 : 16, let no man judge you in **m.**
Heb. 5 : 14, strong **m.** belongeth to them of full age.
12 : 16, for one morsel of **m.** sold birthright.

Meat offering, Lev. 2; 6 : 14; Num. 15 : 9; Neh. 10 : 33.

Medad (mē-dăd), Num. 11 : 26. See **Eldad.**

Meddle, 2 Ki. 14 : 10; 2 Chr. 25 : 19, why **m.** to thy hurt ?
Prov. 20 : 19, **m.** not with him that flattereth.
24 : 21, **m.** not with them given to change.
26 : 17, that **m.** with strife.

Medes (mēdeṡ) and **Persians,** capture Babylon, Isa. 21; Dan. 5 : 28.

Media (mē-dĭ-ă), the country of the Medes, Esther 1.
ten tribes carried there, 2 Ki. 17 : 6; 18 : 11.
prophecy concerning, Dan. 8 : 20.

Mediator, Gal. 3 : 19, by angels in hand of a **m.**
1 Tim. 2 : 5, there is one **m.**, Jesus Christ.
Heb. 8 : 6, the **M.** of a better covenant.
9 : 15, the **M.** of the new testament.

12 : 24, Jesus the M. of the new covenant.
Medicine, Prov. 17 : 22, doeth good like a m.
Jer. 30 : 13, thou hast no healing m.
Ezek. 47 : 12, the leaf shall be for m.
Meditate, Gen. 24 : 63, Isaac went out to m.
Josh. 1 : 8, thou shalt m. therein.
Ps. 1 : 2, in his law doth he m.
63 : 6, m. in night watches.
77 : 12; 143 : 5, m. of all thy work.
Isa. 33 : 18, thine heart shall m. terror.
Luke 21 : 14, settle not to m. what ye shall answer.
1 Tim. 4 : 15, m. on these things.
Meditation, encouraged, Ps. 19 : 14; 104 : 34; 119 : 97.
exhortations to, Josh. 1 : 8; Ps. 4 : 4; Prov. 4 : 26.
Meek, Num. 12 : 3, Moses was very m.
Ps. 22 : 26, the m. shall eat and be satisfied.
25 : 9, the m. will he guide in judgment.
37 : 11; Matt. 5 : 5, the m. shall inherit the earth.
Ps. 147 : 6, the Lord lifteth up the m.
149 : 4, beautify the m. with salvation.
Isa. 29 : 19, the m. shall increase their joy.
61 : 1, good tidings to the m.
Matt. 11 : 29, I am m. and lowly.
21 : 5, thy king cometh to thee, m.
1 Pet. 3 : 4, ornament of a m. and quiet spirit.
Meekness. Originally simply a fine virtue (Num. 12 : 3), meekness came to be applied to those who were thrust into the background by the rich and the oppressors (Ps. 10 : 8-10; cf. Isa. 53 : 9). In Jesus' day the term was one of those applied to the humble godly people, living in quiet fashion (Luke 2 : 25, 38). By sharing their humility Jesus magnified them to His glory.
Christ an example of, Matt. 11 : 29; (Isa. 53 : 2; John 18 : 19).
exhortations to, Zeph. 2 : 3; Gal. 5 : 23; 6 : 1; Eph. 4 : 2; Phil. 2 : 3; 1 Tim. 6 : 11; Jas. 3 : 13.
blessed of God, Ps. 22 : 26; 25 : 9; 37 : 11; (Matt. 5 : 5); 69 : 32; 76 : 9; 147 : 6; 149 : 4; Isa. 11 : 4; 29 : 19; 61 : 1
of Moses, Num. 12 : 3; David, 2 Sam. 16 : 10; Jeremiah, Jer. 26 : 14.
Ps. 45 : 4, because of truth and m.
1 Cor. 4 : 21, shall I come in spirit of m. ?
2 Cor. 10 : 1, by the m. of Christ.
Gal. 5 : 23, fruit of the Spirit is m.
6 : 1, restore in the spirit of m.
Col. 3 : 12, put on m.
2 Tim. 2 : 25, in m. instructing.
Titus 3 : 2, showing all m. to all.
Jas. 1 : 21, receive with m. the ingrafted word.
1 Pet. 3 : 15, give reason of hope in you with m.
Meet, Gen. 2 : 18, an help m. for him.
Prov. 22 : 2, the rich and poor m. together.
Isa. 14 : 9, hell is moved to m. thee.
Amos 4 : 12, prepare to m. thy God.
Matt. 3 : 8, fruits m. for repentance.
8 : 34, city came to m. Jesus.
15 : 26; Mark 7 : 27, not m. to take children's bread.
Matt. 25 : 1, went forth to m. the bridegroom.
Acts 26 : 20, works m. for repentance.

1 Cor. 15 : 9, not m. to be called an apostle.
Col. 1 : 12, made us m. to be partakers.
1 Thess. 4 : 17, in the clouds, to m. the Lord.
Heb. 6 : 7, herbs m. for them by whom it is dressed.
Megiddo (mĕ-gĭd´dō), a city of the tribe of Manasseh, Josh. 17 : 11; Judg. 1 : 27; 5 : 19.
Ahaziah and Josiah slain there, 2 Ki. 9 : 27; 23 : 29.
Megilloth, or Rolls. The Jews gave this name to certain books of the Old Testament, Song of Solomon, Ruth, Lamentations, Ecclesiastes, and Esther. On special occasions during the year they were appointed to be read publicly in the synagogues.
Mehetabel (mĕ-hĕt´ă-bĕl) [God does good], Gen. 36 : 30; Neh. 6 : 10.
Mehida (mĕ-hī´dă), Ezra 2 : 52; Neh. 7 : 54.
Meholathite (mĕ-hō´lă-thīte), 1 Sam. 18 : 19.
Mehujael (mĕ-hū´jā-ĕl) [struck by God], Gen. 4 : 18.
Mehunim (mĕ-hū´nĭm) [habitation], Ezra 2 : 50; 2 Chr. 26 : 7.
Mejarkon (mĕ-jär´kŏn), Josh. 19 : 46.
Mekonah (mĕ-kō´năh) [foundation], Neh. 11 : 28.
Melchi (mĕl´chī), probably " Malchiah " [Jah is king], Luke 3 : 24, 28.
Melchizedek (mĕl-chĭz´ĕd-ĕk), or Melchisedec [king of righteousness], king of Salem, blesses Abram, Gen. 14 : 18.
his priesthood above Aaron's, Ps. 110 : 4; Heb. 5 : 6, 10; 6 : 20; 7 : 1.
Melita (mĕl´ĭ-tă), now called Malta.
Paul shipwrecked near, Acts 28 : 1.
shakes off the viper at, Acts 28 : 5.
Melody, Isa. 23 : 16, make sweet m.
Amos 5 : 23, not hear m. of thy viols.
Eph. 5 : 19, making m. to the Lord.
Melon, the common melon and its varieties, and the watermelon, Num. 11 : 5.
Melt, Josh. 2 : 11; Ps. 107 : 26; Isa. 64 : 2; Nah. 2 : 10; Ps. 58 : 8; 68 : 2.
Members of the body, types of the church, Rom. 12 : 4; 1 Cor. 12 : 12.
Ps. 139 : 16, in thy book all my m. written.
Matt. 5 : 29, one of thy m. should perish.
Rom. 7 : 23, another law in m. warring.
1 Cor. 6 : 15, your bodies are m. of Christ.
12 : 14, the body is not one m.
Eph. 4 : 25, we are m. one of another.
5 : 30, m. of his body.
Jas. 3 : 5, the tongue is a little m.
4 : 1, lusts that war in your m.
Memorials, ordained, Ex. 17 : 14; 28 : 12; 30 : 16; Num. 16 : 40.
offerings of, Lev. 2 : 2; Num. 5 : 15.
Memory, of the just, blessed, Prov. 10 : 7.
of the wicked, cut off, Ps. 109 : 15; Isa. 26 : 14.
Ps. 145 : 7, utter the m. of thy goodness.
Eccl. 9 : 5, the m. of them is forgotten.
Isa. 26 : 14, made their m. to perish.
1 Cor. 15 : 2, keep in m. what I preached.
Memphis (mĕm´phĭs) [Heb. " Moph "]. The Egyptian name is variously explained; most probably " place of worshipping Ptah." Hos. 9 : 6. Ancient city of Egypt.

Memucan (mĕ-mū-́căn) [dignified], Persian name, Esther 1 : 14, 16, 21.

Men, 1 Sam. 2 : 26, in favour with Lord and **m.**
2 Chr. 6 : 18, will God dwell with **m.** ?
Ps. 9 : 20, know themselves to be but **m.**
82 : 7, ye shall die like **m.**
Eccl. 12 : 3, the strong **m.** shall bow themselves.
Isa. 31 : 3, the Egyptians are **m.**, and not God.
46 : 8, show yourselves **m.**
Matt. 7 : 12; Luke 6 : 31, that **m.** should do to you, do ye even so to them.
1 Cor. 16 : 13, quit you like **m.**
1 Thess. 2 : 4, not as pleasing **m.**, but God.
1 Pet. 2 : 17, honour all **m.**

Menahem (mĕn-́ă-hĕm), New Testament form " Manaen " [comforter], king of Israel, his evil reign, 2 Ki. 15 : 14, 18.

Mend, 2 Chr. 24 : 12; Matt. 4 : 21; Mark 1 : 19.

Mene, Mene, Tekel, Upharsin, Dan. 5 : 25-28. These are the words of the " Writing on the Wall " and are best interpreted as weights, thus : " A mina, a mina, a shekel and half-minas," or " He has counted, counted, weighed, and they assess." The mystery is heightened by the double meaning implicit in each word and by the fact that in Aramaic cursive the words would be very difficult to distinguish. See Daniel's interpretation.

Menpleasers, Eph. 6 : 6; Col. 3 : 22.

Mention, Ex. 23 : 13; Josh. 23 : 7, make no **m.** of other gods.
Ps. 71 : 16, I will make **m.** of thy righteousness.
Isa. 12 : 4, make **m.** that his name is exalted.
26 : 13, we will make **m.** of thy name.
63 : 7, I will **m.** the lovingkindness of the Lord.
Amos 6 : 10, may not **m.** name of Lord.
Rom. 1 : 9; Eph. 1 : 16; 1 Thess. 1 : 2, **m.** of you in my prayers.
Heb. 11 : 22, made **m.** of departing of Israel.

Mephibosheth (mĕ-phĭb-́ŏ-shĕth), variously explained as meaning " he that blows upon " (*i.e.*, treats contemptuously), " shame " or " the idol "; or, as a corruption for Merribosheth, " contender against shame " (the idol), son of Jonathan, 2 Sam. 9 : 6.
his lameness, 2 Sam. 4 : 4.
David's kindness to, 2 Sam. 9 : 1 ff.
slandered by Ziba, 2 Sam. 16 : 1; 19 : 24.
spared by David, 2 Sam. 21 : 7.

Merab (mĕ-́răb) [increasing], Saul's daughter, 1 Sam. 14 : 49; 18 : 17.
her five sons hanged by the Gibeonites, 2 Sam. 21 : 8.

Merarites (mĕ-rā-́rītes), Num. 26 : 57; descendants of Levi, Ex. 6 : 19; 1 Chr. 6 : 1; 23 : 21; 24 : 26.
their duties and dwellings, Num. 4 : 29; 7 : 8; 10 : 17; Josh. 21 : 7; 1 Chr. 6 : 63.

Merchandise, Prov. 3 : 14, **m.** of it better than **m.** of silver.
Isa. 23 : 18, her **m.** shall be holiness to the Lord.
Matt. 22 : 5, one to his farm, another to his **m.**

John 2 : 16, my Father's house an house of **m.**
2 Pet. 2 : 3, make **m.** of you.
Rev. 18 : 11, no man buyeth their **m.** any more.

Merchants, Gen. 37 : 25; 1 Ki. 10 : 15; Neh. 13 : 20; Ezek. 27 : 3.
parable of one seeking pearls, Matt. 13 : 45.
Gen. 23 : 16, current money with the **m.**
Isa. 23 : 8, whose **m.** are princes.
47 : 15, thy **m.** shall wander.
Rev. 18 : 3, the **m.** of the earth are waxed rich.
18 : 23, thy **m.** were great men of the earth.

Merchantman, Gen. 37 : 28; 1 Ki. 10 : 15; Matt. 13 : 45.

Merciful, Ex. 34 : 6, Lord God, **m.** and gracious.
2 Sam. 22 : 26; Ps. 18 : 25, with the **m.** thou wilt show thyself **m.**
Ps. 37 : 26, the righteous is ever **m.**
67 : 1, God be **m.** to us.
Prov. 11 : 17, the **m.** man doeth good to his own soul.
Isa. 57 : 1, **m.** men are taken away.
Jer. 3 : 12, I am **m.**, saith the Lord.
Jonah 4 : 2, I knew that thou art a gracious God, and **m.**
Matt. 5 : 7, blessed are the **m.**
Luke 6 : 36, be ye **m.** as your Father is **m.**
18 : 13, God be **m.** to me a sinner.
Heb. 2 : 17, a **m.** High Priest.
8 : 12, I will be **m.** to their unrighteousness.

Mercurius (mĕr-cū-́rĭ-ŭs), name of a Roman god, Acts 14 : 12. The corresponding Greek God was Hermes, the spokesman of Olympus, and worshipped therefore as the god of eloquence.

Mercy. Originally from the Latin " merces," a reward, it was probably the cry of the recipient, " Merci " [=reward to you (in heaven)], which gave it its meaning. From being merely acknowledgment of bounty given, the term came to be used of the spirit prompting the gift. Note the shades of meaning in the instances given.
supplication for, Deut. 21 : 8; 1 Ki. 8 : 30; Neh. 9 : 32; Ps. 51; Dan. 9 : 16; Hab. 3 : 2; Matt. 6 : 12.
of God, Ps. 78 : 38; 103 : 11; Isa. 30 : 18; 54 : 7; Lam. 3 : 32.
exhortations to show, Prov. 3 : 3; Zech. 7 : 9; Luke 6 : 36; Rom. 12 : 19; (Prov. 25 : 21); Phil. 2 : 1; Col. 3 : 12.
Gen. 19 : 19, thou hast magnified thy **m.**
32 : 10, not worthy of the least of all the **m.**
Ex. 33 : 19, I will show **m.**
34 : 7; Dan. 9 : 4, keeping **m.** for thousands.
Num. 14 : 18; Ps. 103 : 11; 145 : 8, the Lord is of great **m.**
1 Chr. 16 : 34, 41; 2 Chr. 5 : 13; 7 : 3, 6; Ezra 3 : 11; Ps. 106 : 1; 118 : 1; 136 : 1; Jer. 33 : 11, his **m.** endureth for ever.
Ps. 23 : 6, goodness and **m.** shall follow me.
25 : 10, all the paths of the Lord are **m.**
33 : 18, that hope in his **m.**
52 : 8, I trust in the **m.** of God.
59 : 10, the God of my **m.**
62 : 12, unto thee belongeth **m.**
66 : 20, not turned his **m.** from me.

77 : 8, is his **m.** clean gone for ever ?
85 : 10, **m.** and truth met together.
89 : 2, **m.** shall be built up for ever.
90 : 14, satisfy us carly with thy **m.**
101 : 1, I will sing of **m.**
103 : 17, **m.** of the Lord is from everlasting.
130 : 7, with the Lord there is **m.**
Prov. 14 : 21, he that hath **m.** on the poor.
21 : 21, followeth after **m.** findeth life.
Isa. 54 : 10, the Lord that hath **m.** on thee.
60 : 10, in my favour had **m.** on thee.
Jer. 6 : 23, they are cruel, and have no **m.**
Lam. 3 : 22, it is the Lord's **m.**
Hos. 6 : 6; Matt. 9 : 13, I desired **m.** and not sacrifice.
Hos. 14 : 3, in thee the fatherless find **m.**
Mic. 6 · 8, to do justly, and love **m.**
7 : 18, he delighteth in **m.**
Matt. 5 : 7, the merciful, for they shall obtain **m.**
9 : 27; 15 : 22; 20 : 30; Mark 10 : 47; Luke 18 : 38, thou son of David, have **m.** on me.
Matt. 23 : 23, omitted judgment and **m.**
Rom. 9 : 15, 18, I will have **m.** on whom I will have **m.**
11 : 30, obtained **m.** through unbelief.
2 Cor. 1 : 3, the Father of **m.**
4 : 1, as we have received **m.**
Eph. 2 : 4, God who is rich in **m.**
Titus 3 : 5, according to his **m.** he saved us.
Heb. 4 : 16, that we may obtain **m.**
10 : 28, despised the law, died without **m.**
Jas. 2 : 13, judgment without **m.**
5 : 11, Lord is pitiful and of tender **m.**
1 Pet. 1 : 3, according to his abundant **m.**
2 : 10, had not obtained **m.**, but now have obtained **m.**
Jude 21, looking for the **m.** of our Lord Jesus Christ.
Mercyseal, described, Ex. 25 : 17; 26 : 34;
37 : 6; Lev. 16 : 13; 1 Chr. 28 : 11; Heb. 9 : 5. See **Tabernacle.**
Meribah (měr-ĭ-bäh) [contention], Israel's rebellion there, Ex. 17 : 7; Num. 20 : 13; 27 : 14; Deut. 32 : 51; 33 : 8; Ps. 81 : 7.
Meribbaal (měr-ĭh-hā-ăl), 1 Chr. 8 · 34 See **Mephibosheth.**
Merodach (měr-ō-dăch) [Assyr.-Bab., " Mar(u)duk "; Akkad., " Amur-uduk "; brightness(?) of day], chief god of Babylonian pantheon, Jer. 50 : 2.
Merodach-baladan (měr-ō-dăch-băl-ă-dăn) [**Berodach-b.** Marduk gave a son], " Mar(u)duk-able-iddina," king of Babylon, his embassy to Hezekiah, 2 Ki. 20 : 12; Isa. 39 : 1.
Merrily, Esther 5 : 14.
Merry, Gen. 43 : 34, they drank and were **m.**
Judg. 16 : 25, their hearts were **m.**
19 : 6; 1 Ki. 21 : 7, let thine heart be **m.**
Prov. 15 : 13, **m.** heart maketh cheerful countenance.
17 : 22, **m.** heart doeth good like a medicine.
Eccl. 8 : 15, nothing better than to eat and be **m.**
10 : 19, wine maketh **m.**
Luke 12 : 19, take thine ease, eat, drink, and be **m.**
15 : 32, it was meet we should be **m.**

Jas. 5 : 13, is any **m.** ?
Rev. 11 : 10, rejoice and make **m.**
Merryhearted, Isa. 24 : 7.
Meshach (mē-shăch) [who is as Aku (?)], moongood, Dan. 1 : 7.
Meshech (mē-shěch) [perhaps " Moshech "; Assyrian " Muski "], a people inhabiting mountain ranges between Iberia, Armenia, and Colchis. The word has no connection with Moscow. Ezek. 32 : 26; 38 : 2; 39 : 1.
traders of, Ezek. 27 : 13.
son of Japheth, Gen. 10 : 2.
Meshelemiah (me-shěl-ě-mī-äh) [Jah recompenses], 1 Chr. 9 : 21.
Meshezabeel (mě-shěz-ă-bēel) [freed by God] Neh. 3 : 4; 10 : 21; 11 : 24.
Meshillemith (mě-shĭl-lě-mĭth), 1 Chr. 9 : 12.
Meshillemoth (mě-shĭl-lě-mōth), Neh. 11 : 13.
Meshobab (mě-shō-băb), 1 Chr. 4 : 34.
Meshullam (mě-shŭl-lăm) [one devoted], Ezra 8 : 16; 10 : 15; Neh. 3 : 6; 10 : 7, 20.
Meshullemeth (mě-shŭl-lě-měth) [a devoted female], 2 Ki. 21 : 19.
Mesobaite (mě-sōb-ă-īte), 1 Chr. 11 : 47.
Mesopotamia (měs-ō-pō-tā-mĭ-ă) [between the rivers], Greek name of the country between Euphrates and Tigris (cf. Gen. 24 : 10).
king of, slain by Othniel, Judg. 3 : 8.
See Acts 2 : 9; 7 : 2.
Mess, Gen. 43 : 34; 2 Sam. 11 : 8.
Message, Judg. 3 : 30, a **m.** from God to thee.
Luke 19 : 14, citizens sent a **m.** after him.
1 John 1 : 5; 3 : 11, the **m.** we have heard.
Messenger, Job 33 : 23, if there be a **m.** with him.
Prov. 25 : 13, faithful **m.**
Isa. 42 : 19, my **m.** that I sent.
Mal. 3 : 1, **m.** of the covenant
2 Cor. 12 : 7, the **m.** of Satan to buffet.
Messias (měs-sī-ăs) [anointed; Greek, Χριστος, cf. Christ], better known to us as Messiah. The term was first used of any who were anointed with holy oil. The kings of Israel were consecrated by anointing (1 Sam. 2 · 10, 35; 12 : 3, 5). Then it was extended to the Anointed one, par excellence, whose coming to rescue and redeem Israel was foretold by the prophets. Jesus was conscious that He was the Messiah, though He enlarged the idea and made it more universal. For the idea in Jesus' mind, cf. Matt. 3 : 13-17; 4 : 1-11; 11 : 1-6; 16 : 13-20; 17 : 1-9; 21 : 1-11; 26 : 57-68. The name occurs in John 1 : 41; 4 : 25.
Met, Gen. 32 : 1; Num. 23 : 4; Mark 11 : 4; Heb. 7 : 1.
Metal workers. See **Handicraft.**
Mete, Ex. 16 : 18; Ps. 60 : 6; Matt. 7 : 2.
Meteyard [ar.], yardstick, Lev. 19 : 35.
Methusael (mě-thū-să-ēl) [man of God], Gen. 4 : 18.
Methuselah (mě-thū-sě-läh) [man of the javelin], Gen. 5 : 21, 27; 1 Chr. 1 : 3.
Metsiltaim, musical instrument. See **Musical Instruments.**
Micah (mī-căh), shortened form of **Micaiah** [who is like Jah ?], makes and worships idols, Judg. 17; 18.

prophet prophesies against Jerusalem, Jer. 26 : 18.

denounces Israel's sin, Mic. 1–3; 6; 7.

predicts Messiah's coming, Mic. 4; 5; 7.

Micah, Book of.
The prophecy is the work of Micah of Moresheth-Gath. He is thus to be distinguished from Micaiah the son of Imlah (1 Kings 22 : 8) who prophesied in the time of Ahab of Israel and Jehoshaphat of Judah. Both names mean, " Who is like Jehovah ? " The time of Micah's testimony was in the reigns of Jotham, Ahaz and Hezekiah. He was a contemporary of Isaiah, Hosea and Amos. His messages are concerning Samaria and Jerusalem, and are clarion calls to repentance and righteousness. National disasters threaten. Shalmanezer comes against Samaria (2 Ki. 17 : 4, 6) and Sennacherib comes against Judah (2 Ki. 18 : 13). Since the political situation confronted by Isaiah, Hosea, Amos and Micah is the same, since the moral issues are identical, and since each of these prophets is the messenger of Jehovah, it is not strange that there are similarities in the messages given by all of them. In the brief compass of seven chapters, Micah covers many of the majestic Kingdom announcements of the great prophet Isaiah.

Summary of the Book.—Ch. 1, The first verse states the author's name, the time of his testimony and the subject matter. The earth and all peoples are called upon to hear the indictment pronounced against his people by Jehovah. For the sins of Samaria and Jerusalem, they are to be desolated. Ch. 2, Woes are pronounced upon the corrupt and violent. Ch. 3, A cry to the rulers of Jacob who hate the good and love the evil to cease from their cruelty to their subjects. Night shall overtake the false prophets that cry, " Peace," and that divine for hire " for there is no answer of God." Ch. 4, The opening verses are practically identical with Isa. 2 : 2-4. They depict the last days when the house of the Lord shall be established in the top of the mountains and all nations shall seek it. War shall cease and the Lord shall reign in Jerusalem for ever. Though captivity immediately confronts the city, ultimately a glorious deliverance will come. Ch. 5, Verse 2 proclaims Bethlehem as the birthplace of the coming Ruler of Israel. Ch. 6, God pleads with his people to do justly, love mercy, and walk humbly with Him. Ch. 7, Though all human relationships fail and prove false, God will vindicate Jacob as he has sworn to the fathers.

Micaiah (mĭcâ-̱äh), forewarns Ahab, 1 Ki. 22 : 8, etc.; 2 Chr. 18 : 8, etc.

Mice, 1 Sam. 6 : 4, 5, 11, 18.

Michael (mĭchaĕl) [who is like God ?], Dan. 10 : 13, 21; 12 : 1.

archangel, Jude 9; Rev. 12 : 7.

Michal (mĭ-̱chăl), probably shortened form of " Michael," used as a feminine, Saul's daughter, 1 Sam. 14 : 49.

becomes David's wife, 1 Sam. 18 : 27.

given to another, 1 Sam. 25 : 44.

restored to David, 2 Sam. 3 : 13.

rebuked for mocking his religious dancing, 2 Sam. 6 : 16, 20; 1 Chr. 15 : 29.

Michmash (mĭch-̱măsh) [hidden], a city of Benjamin, 1 Sam. 13 : 5; Neh. 11 : 31.

Michmas (mĭch-̱măs), Ezra 2 : 27.

Michmethah (mĭch-mē-̱thăh) [hiding-place], Josh. 16 : 6.

Michtam (mĭch-̱tăm), occurs in the titles of Pss. 16 and 56–60. Luther rendered it a " golden psalm "; others, a " psalm of deep meaning "; the LXX. renders " an inscription song," possibly meaning wholly inscribed on David's palace. All we can say is that the character of the poem is in some way described.

Midday, 1 Ki. 18 : 29; Neh. 8 : 3; Acts 26 : 13.

Middle, Josh. 12 : 2; Judg. 7 : 19; Ezek. 1 : 16; Eph. 2 : 14.

Middlemost, Ezek. 42 : 5.

Midian (mĭd-̱ĭ-ăn) [strife], sons of, Gen. 25 : 4.

See 1 Ki. 11 : 18; Isa. 60 : 6; Hab. 3 : 7.

Midianites (mĭd-ĭ-ă-nītes), their cities destroyed by Moses, Num. 31 : 2, etc.

subdued by Gideon, Judg. 6—8.

See Ps. 83 : 9; Isa. 9 : 4; 10 : 26.

Midnight, Egyptians smitten at, Ex. 12 : 29.

prayer made at, Ps. 119 : 62; Acts 16 : 25; 20 : 7.

See Matt. 25 : 6; Mark 13 : 35.

Midst, Gen. 2 : 9, tree of life in the **m.**

Ps. 46 : 5, God is in the **m.**

102 : 24, in the **m.** of my days.

Prov. 23 : 34, lieth down in **m.** of the sea.

Isa. 6 : 5, I dwell in the **m.** of a people of unclean lips.

12 : 6; Hos. 11 : 9, the Holy One in the **m.** of thee.

Dan. 3 : 25, walking in **m.** of the fire.

9 : 27, in the **m.** of the week.

Matt. 10 : 16, as sheep in the **m.** of wolves.

18 : 2; Mark 9 : 36, a little child in the **m.**

Matt. 18 : 20, there am I in the **m.**

Luke 24 : 36; John 20 : 19, Jesus himself in the **m.**

Rev. 2 : 7, in the **m.** of the paradise of God.

4 : 6; 5 : 6; 7 : 17, in the **m.** of the throne.

8 : 13, flying through **m.** of heaven.

Midwives, Ex. 1 : 15, 20.

Migdal-gad (mĭg-dăl-găd) [tower of fortune], Josh. 15 : 37, a town in the territory of Judah. The derivation implies that it was a seat of idolatry. Perhaps the Canaanites worshipped " Gad " (the god of " Good Luck " or " Fortune ") in that place.

Migdol (mĭg-̱dŏl) [tower], Ex. 14 : 2; Num. 33 : 7.

Might, Deut. 6 : 5, love thy God with all thy **m.**

8 : 17, the **m.** of mine hand hath gotten wealth.

Judg. 6 : 14, go in thy **m.**

2 Sam. 6 : 14, David danced with all his **m.**

1 Chr. 29 : 12; 2 Chr. 20 : 6, in thine hand is power and **m.**

Ps. 145 : 6, speak of the **m.** of thy terrible acts.

Eccl. 9 : 10, do it with thy **m.**

Isa. 40 : 29, to them that have no **m.**
Jer. 9 : 23, let not mighty man glory in his **m.**
Zech. 4 : 6, not by **m.** nor by power.
Eph. 3 : 16; Col. 1 : 11, strengthened with **m.**
Rev. 7 : 12, glory and **m.** be unto God.
Mighty, Gen. 10 : 9, he was a **m.** hunter.
Gen. 18 : 18, become a **m.** nation.
Judg. 5 : 23, to the help of the Lord against the **m.**
2 Sam. 1 : 19, how are the **m.** fallen.
Job 9 : 4, God is wise in heart and **m.** in strength.
　34 : 20, the **m.** shall be taken away.
Ps. 24 : 8, Lord strong and **m.**, the Lord **m.** in battle.
　45 : 3, gird thy sword, O Most **M.**
　68 : 33, his voice, a **m.** voice.
　89 : 13, thou hast a **m.** arm.
　89 : 19, laid help upon one that is **m.**
　93 : 4, Lord mightier than **m.** waves.
　112 : 2, his seed shall be **m.** on earth.
Prov. 16 : 32, that is slow to anger better than **m.**
　23 : 11, their Redeemer is **m.**
Isa. 1 : 24; 30 : 29; 49 : 26; 60 : 16, the **m.** One of Israel.
　63 : 1, **m.** to save.
Jer. 32 : 19, **m.** in work.
Amos 2 : 14, neither shall **m.** deliver himself.
Matt. 11 : 20; 13 : 54; 14 : 2; Mark 6 : 2, **m.** works.
Luke 1 : 52, he hath put down the **m.**
　9 : 43, the **m.** power of God.
　24 : 19, a prophet **m.** in deed and word.
Acts 18 : 24, **m.** in the Scriptures.
1 Cor. 1 : 26, not many **m.**
2 Cor. 10 : 4, weapons of warfare **m.** through God.
Eph. 1 : 19, the working of his **m.** power.
Mightily, Jonah 3 : 8; Acts 19 : 20; Col. 1 : 29; Rev. 18 : 2.
Migron (mĭg-rŏn) [overthrown], 1 Sam. 14 : 2.
Mikloth (mĭk-lŏth), 1 Chr. 8 : 32.
Mijamin (mĭ-jă-mĭn) [at the right hand], 1 Chr. 24 : 9.
Milalai (mĭl-ă-lā) [eloquent], Neh. 12 : 36.
Milcah (mĭl-cäh) [queen], Gen. 11 : 29; 22 : 20.
Milch, Gen. 32 : 15; 1 Sam. 6 : 7.
Milcom (mĭl-cŏm) [their king], the god Molech, 1 Ki. 11 : 5, 33; 2 Ki. 23 : 13.
Mile. See **Measures.**
Miletus (mĭ-lē-tŭs) (Miletum), a seaport city south of Ephesus, Paul takes leave of elders at, Acts 20 : 15.
Trophimus left at, 2 Tim. 4 : 20.
Milk, Gen. 18 : 8, butter and **m.**
Gen. 49 : 12, his teeth be white with **m.**
Josh. 5 : 6, land that floweth with **m.** and honey.
Judg. 5 : 25, he asked water, she gave **m.**
Prov. 30 : 33, churning of **m.**
Isa. 55 : 1, buy wine and **m.**
Lam. 4 : 7, Nazarites whiter than **m.**
Ezek. 25 : 4, eat fruit and drink **m.**
1 Cor. 3 : 2, I have fed you with **m.**
Heb. 5 : 12, such as have need of **m.**
1 Pet. 2 : 2, the sincere **m.** of the word.
Mill. There were two kinds : (1) worked by hand; (2) worked by an ass. The upper

stone of the hand-mill was moved by a wooden spoke or handle, which two women, at opposite sides, worked as men work a crosscut saw—" Two women shall be grinding at the mill " (Matt. 24 : 41). The stones of the ass-mill were much larger. The lower, called " the nether millstone," was solidly fixed, the upper was made to go round by the traction of the animal. It is to the ass millstone Jesus refers in Matt. 18 : 6, " a millstone hanged about his neck . . . and drowned in the depths of the sea."

See also **Mortar.**

Hand-mill.

Millet. Only once referred to, in Ezek. 4 : 9, where it is named as one of the ingredients of bread. There are many species of grain-producing grasses in the East and Africa which are to this day largely cultivated.
Millions, Gen. 24 : 60.
Millo (mĭl-lō) [rampart], Judg. 9 : 6; 2 Sam. 5 : 9.
Millstones, Isa. 47 : 2; Jer. 25 : 10; Matt. 18 : 6; Rev. 18 : 21, 22.
Mina, equal to 30 shekels. See **Money.**
Mincing, Isa. 3 : 16.
Mind, devoted to God, Mark 12 : 30; Rom. 7 : 25.
willingness of, 1 Chr. 28 : 9; Neh. 4 : 6.
united, 1 Cor. 1 : 10; 2 Cor. 13 : 11; Phil. 2 : 2; 1 Pet. 3 : 8.
Job 23 : 13, he is in one **m.**, and who can turn him ?
Ps. 31 : 12, as a dead man out of **m.**
Prov. 29 : 11, a fool uttereth all his **m.**
Isa. 26 : 3, whose **m.** is stayed on thee.
Matt. 22 : 37; Luke 10 : 27, love the Lord with all thy **m.**

Mark 5 : 15; Luke 8 : 35, clothed, and in his right **m.**
Luke 12 : 29, neither be of doubtful **m.**
Acts 17 : 11, with all readiness of **m.**
20 : 19, humility of **m.**
Rom. 8 : 5, **m.** the things of the flesh.
  8 : 7, the carnal **m.** is enmity against God.
  11 : 34, who hath known the **m.** of the Lord?
  12 : 16, be of the same **m.**
  14 : 5, fully persuaded in his own **m.**
1 Cor. 2 : 16, we have the **m.** of Christ.
2 Cor. 8 : 12, if there be first a willing **m.**
Eph. 2 : 3, desires of the flesh and **m.**
Phil. 1 : 27, be of one **m.**
  2 : 3, in lowliness of **m.**
  2 : 5, let this **m.** be in you.
  4 : 2, be of the same **m.** in the Lord.
Col. 3 : 12, humbleness of **m.**
2 Tim. 1 : 7, spirit of sound **m.**
Titus 3 : 1, put them in **m.** to be subject.
Heb. 8 : 10, put my laws into their **m.**
1 Pet. 1 : 13, the loins of your **m.**
Rev. 17 : 13, these have one **m.**
See Rom. 12 : 16; Phil. 3 : 16.
Mindful, Ps. 8 : 4; Heb. 2 : 6, what is man, that thou art **m.** of him ?
Ps. 115 : 12, Lord hath been **m.** of us.
Isa. 17 : 10, not been **m.** of the rock.
Heb. 11 : 15, been **m.** of that country.
2 Pet. 3 : 2, be **m.** of words spoken.
Mine, Ex. 19 : 5; Ps. 50 : 12, all the earth is **m.**
Hag. 2 : 8, silver is **m.,** and gold is **m.**
Mal. 3 : 17, they shall be **m.,** saith the Lord.
Matt. 20 : 23; Mark 10 : 40, is not **m.** to give.
John 17 : 10, all **m.** are thine, and thine are **m.**
Mingle, Isa. 5 : 22; Ps. 102 : 9; Dan. 2 : 43; Mark 15 : 23; Rev. 15 : 2.
Minish [ar.], to diminish, Ex. 5 : 19; Ps. 107 : 39; (Isa. 19 : 6, R.V.).
Ministers, God's, Ps. 103 : 21; 104 : 4; Heb. 1 : 7.
  (priest), Ex. 28; Heb. 10 : 11.
  to be honoured, etc., 1 Thess. 5: 12, 13; 1 Tim. 5 : 17; Heb. 13 : 17.
  Christ's, 1 Cor. 3 : 5; 4 : 1; Eph. 3 : 7; 6 : 21.
  qualifications of, 1 Tim. 3; Titus 1; 1 Pet. 5.
Deut. 21 : 5, God hath chosen them to **m.**
1 Sam. 2 : 11, the child did **m.** to the Lord.
1 Ki. 10 : 5; 2 Chr. 9 : 4, the attendance of his **m.**
1 Chr. 15 : 2, chosen to **m.** for ever.
Ps. 9 : 8, **m.** judgment to people.
Isa. 60 : 10, their kings shall **m.** to thee.
Matt. 20 : 26; Mark 10 : 43, let him be your **m.**
Matt. 20 : 28; Mark 10 : 45, not to be **m.** unto, but to **m.**
Luke 4 : 20, gave the book to the **m.**
Rom. 13 : 4, he is the **m.** of God to thee.
2 Cor. 3 : 6, able **m.** of new testament.
  9 : 10, **m.** bread for your food.
  11 : 23, are they **m.** of Christ ?
Gal. 2 : 17, is Christ the **m.** of sin ?
Eph. 3 : 7; Col. 1 : 23, whereof I was made a **m.**
Eph. 4 : 29, **m.** grace to the hearers.
  6 : 21; Col. 1 : 7, a faithful **m.**
1 Tim. 4 : 6, a good **m.** of Christ.

Heb. 1 : 7, his **m.** a flame of fire.
  8 : 2, a **m.** of the sanctuary.
Ministering spirits, Heb. 1 : 14.
See Rom. 15 : 25, 27.
Ministration, Luke 1 : 23, days of **m.** were accomplished.
Acts 6 : 1, widows neglected in daily **m.**
2 Cor. 3 : 7, if **m.** of death was glorious.
  9 : 13, by the experiment of this **m.**
Ministry, of the gospel, Acts 6 : 4; 20 : 24; 1 Cor. 16 : 15; 2 Cor. 5 : 18; 1 Tim. 1 : 12.
Acts 1 : 25, that he may take part of **m.**
Rom. 12 : 7, or **m.,** let us wait on our ministering.
2 Cor. 4 : 1, seeing we have this **m.**
  5 : 18, the **m.** of reconciliation.
Eph. 4 : 12, for the work of the **m.**
Col. 4 : 17, take heed to the **m.**
2 Tim. 4 : 5, make full proof of thy **m.**
Heb. 8 : 6, obtained a more excellent **m.**
Minstrel, 2 Ki. 3 : 15, bring me a **m.**
Matt. 9 : 23, when Jesus saw the **m.**
Mint. Several species of the genus " Mentha," to which our common mint (Mentha sativa) belongs, grow in Palestine, and to this reference is made in Matt. 23 : 23; Luke 11 : 42.
Miracles of the Bible. The miracles are called signs or works, not portents or exhibitions of power nor even deeds exciting wonder or contrary to expectation. They are in harmony with the divine purpose and are to be expected if there is an omnipotent Creator who has intervened in Earth's affairs in such a way as to become a Redeemer. They are cognate to the divine procedure and in their results often prophetic of ultimate ideal conditions in Messiah's Kingdom. The evidence *for* miracles must ever be positively authenticated fact : the evidence *of* miracles may be any truth of sufficient importance to merit divine attestation. The miraculous element of prophecy lies rather in the prediction than in the fulfilment. It involves events immediately pending as well as remote consummations.
I.—Old Testament.
Destruction of Sodom and Gomorrah, Gen. 19 : 24.
Lot's wife turned to a pillar of salt, Gen. 19 : 26.
Birth of Isaac, Gen. 21 : 1-3.
The burning bush not consumed, Ex. 3 : 2.
Aaron's rod changed into a serpent, Ex. 7 : 10-12.
The plagues of Egypt—
  (1) The waters made blood, Ex. 7 : 20-25; (2) The frogs, Ex. 8 : 5-14; (3) The lice, Ex. 8 : 16-18; (4) The flies, Ex. 8 : 20-24; (5) The murrain, Ex. 9 : 3-6; (6) The boils, Ex. 9 : 8-11; (7) The thunder, hail, etc., Ex. 9 : 22-26; (8) The locusts, Ex. 10 : 12-19; (9) The darkness, Ex. 10 : 21-23; (10) The death of the firstborn, Ex. 12 : 29, 30.
The Red Sea divided by east wind; Israel passes through, Ex. 14 : 21-31.
The waters of Marah sweetened, Ex. 15 : 23-25.

The manna sent daily—Sabbath excepted, Ex. 16 : 14-35.

The water from the smitten rock at Rephidim, Ex. 17 : 5-7.

Nadab and Abihu consumed for offering " strange fire," Lev. 10 : 1, 2.

Part of Israel burned for ungrateful and faithless discontent, Num. 11 : 1-3.

The earth swallows Korah, etc., fire and plague follow, Num. 16 : 32 ff.

Aaron's rod budding, Num. 17 : 1 ff.

Water from the rock smitten twice at Meribah, Num. 20 : 7-11.

The brazen serpent, Num. 21 : 8, 9.

Balaam's ass speaking, Num. 22 : 21-30.

The river Jordan stopped; Israel crosses dryshod, Josh. 3 : 14-17.

The walls of Jericho fall down, Josh. 6 : 6-20.

Sun and moon stayed (?); hail-storm in aid of Israel, Josh. 10 : 11-14.

Strength of Samson, Judg. 14–16.

The water flows from the hollow place, " in Lehi " (Heb.), Judg. 15 : 19.

Dagon falls twice before the ark; emerods on Philistines, 1 Sam. 5 : 1-12.

The men of Beth-shemesh smitten for looking into the ark, 1 Sam. 6 : 19.

A thunderstorm causes a panic in the Philistines' army, 1 Sam. 7 : 10-12.

The thunder and rain in harvest, 1 Sam. 12 : 17, 18.

The sound in the mulberry trees, i.e., God goeth before, 2 Sam. 5 : 23-35.

Uzzah struck dead for touching the ark, 2 Sam. 6 : 7.

Jeroboam's hand withered and his new altar destroyed, 1 Ki. 13 : 4-6.

The widow of Zarephath's meal and oil increased by Elijah, 1 Ki. 17 : 14-16.

The widow's Son raised from death, 1 Ki. 17 : 17-24.

Drought, fire from heaven, and rain at the prayer of Elijah; Elijah wondrously fed, 1 Ki. 17–19.

Wall of Aphek falls upon thousands of Syrians, 1 Ki. 20 : 30.

Ahaziah's captains and men consumed by fire, 2 Ki. 1 : 10-12.

The river Jordan divided by Elijah and Elisha successively, 2 Ki. 2 : 7, 7, 14.

Elijah translated to heaven, 2 Ki. 2 : 11.

The waters of Jericho healed with salt, 2 Ki. 2 : 21, 22.

Bears destroy forty-two mocking " young men " (Heb.), 2 Ki. 2 : 24.

Water for Jehoshaphat and the allied army, 2 Ki. 3 : 16-20.

The widow's oil multiplied, 2 Ki. 4 : 2-7.

The gift of a son to the Shunammite, and the raising afterwards of that son from the dead, 2 Ki. 4 : 14-37.

The deadly pottage cured with meal, 2 Ki. 4 : 38-41.

The hundred men fed with twenty loaves, 2 Ki. 4 : 42-44.

Naaman cured of leprosy, and the disease transferred to Gehazi, 2 Ki. 5 : 10-27.

The iron axe head made to swim, 2 Ki. 6 : 5-7.

The Syrian army smitten with blindness, and cured, 2 Ki. 6 : 18-20.

Elisha's bones revive the dead, 2 Ki. 13 : 21.

Sennacherib's army destroyed by a blast, 2 Ki. 19 : 35.

The shadow of the sun goes back ten degrees on the sundial of Ahaz, 2 Ki. 20 : 9-11.

Uzziah struck with leprosy, 2 Chr. 26 : 16-21.

Shadrach, Meshach, and Abednego delivered from the furnace, Dan. 3 : 19-27.

Daniel saved in the den of lions, Dan. 6 : 16-23.

Deliverance of Jonah, Jonah 2 : 1-10.

Ex. 7 : 9, saying Shew a m.

Deut. 29 : 3, thine eyes have seen m.

Judg. 6 : 13, where be all his m. ?

II.—Miracles of our Lord—
   1. Peculiar to St. Matthew.

Two blind men cured, Matt. 9 : 27-31.

Dumb spirit cast out, Matt. 9 : 32, 33.

Tribute money provided, Matt. 17 : 24-27.
   2. Peculiar to St. Mark.

Deaf and dumb man cured, Mark 7 : 31-37.

Blind man cured, Mark 8 : 22-26.
   3. Peculiar to St. Luke.

Jesus passes through crowd at Nazareth, Luke 4 : 28-30.

Draught of fishes, Luke 5 : 1-11.

Widow's son raised to life at Nain, Luke 7 : 11-17.

Woman's infirmity cured, Luke 13 : 11-17.

Dropsy cured, Luke 14 : 1-6.

Ten lepers cleansed, Luke 17 : 11-19.

The ear of Malchus healed, Luke 22 : 50, 51.
   4. Peculiar to St. John.

Water made wine at Cana, John 2 : 1-11.

Nobleman's son cured of fever, John 4 : 46-54.

Impotent man cured at Jerusalem, John 5 : 1-9.

Jesus passes through crowd in the temple, John 8 : 59.

Man born blind cured at Jerusalem, John 9 : 1-7.

Lazarus raised from the dead at Bethany, John 11 : 38-44.

Falling backwards of the soldiers, John 18 : 5, 6.

Draught of 153 fishes, John 21 : 1-14.
   5. Common to Matthew and Mark.

Syrophenician's daughter cured, Matt. 15 : 28; Mark 7 : 24.

The four thousand fed, Matt. 15 : 32; Mark 8 : 1.

The fig-tree blasted, Matt. 21 : 19; Mark 11 : 13.
   6. Common to Matthew and Luke.

Centurion's palsied servant cured, Matt. 8 : 5; Luke 7 : 1.

Blind and dumb demoniac cured, Matt. 12 : 22; Luke 11 : 14.
   7. Common to Mark and Luke.

Demoniac in synagogue cured, Mark 1 : 23; Luke 4 : 33.
   8. Common to Matthew, Mark, and Luke.

Peter's mother-in-law cured, Matt. 8 : 14; Mark 1 : 30; Luke 4 : 38.

The tempest stilled, Matt. 8 : 23; Mark 4 : 37; Luke 8 : 22.

The demoniacs cured, Matt. 8 : 28; Mark 5 : 1; Luke 8 : 26.
The leper cured, Matt. 8 : 2; Mark 1 : 40; Luke 5 : 12.
The daughter of Jairus raised to life, Matt. 9 : 23; Mark 5 : 23; Luke 8 : 41.
Woman's issue of blood cured, Matt. 9 : 20; Mark 5 : 25; Luke 8 : 43.
A Paralytic cured, Matt. 9 : 2; Mark 2 : 3; Luke 5 : 18.
Man's withered hand cured, Matt. 12 : 10; Mark 3 : 1; Luke 6 : 6.
Devil cast out of boy, Matt. 17 : 14; Mark 9 : 14; Luke 9 : 37.
Blind men cured, Matt. 20 : 30; Mark 10 : 46; Luke 18 : 35.
  9. Common to Matthew, Mark, and John.
Christ walks on the sea, Matt. 14 : 25; Mark 6 : 48; John 6 : 19.
  10. Common to all the Evangelists.
The five thousand fed, Matt. 14 : 15; Mark 6 : 30; Luke 9 : 10; John 6 : 1-14.
III.—Miracles recorded in the Acts of the Apostles—
The outpouring of the Holy Spirit, with the accompanying signs, Acts 2.
The gift of tongues, Acts 2 : 4-11; 10 : 44-46.
Lame man at Beautiful Gate of the Temple, Acts 3.
Death of Ananias and Sapphira, Acts 5.
Healing of sick in streets by Peter, etc., Acts 5 : 15, 16.
Prison opened for apostles by angels, Acts 5 : 19; 12 : 7-11.
Stephen's dying vision of Christ, Acts 7 : 55, 56.
Unclean spirits cast out by Philip, Acts 8 : 6, 7.
Christ's appearance to Saul on his way to Damascus, Acts 9 : 3 ff.; 22 : 6 ff.; 26 : 13-19.
Saul's recovery of his sight, Acts 9 : 17, 18; 22 : 12, 13.
Eneas healed of palsy by Peter, Acts 9 : 33, 34.
Raising of Dorcas to life by Peter, Acts 9 : 40.
Vision of Cornelius, Acts 10 : 3, 4, 30-32.
Vision of Peter, Acts 10 and 11.
Peter miraculously released from prison, Acts 12 : 7-11.
Elymas stricken with blindness by Paul, Acts 13 : 11.
Healing of cripple at Lystra, Acts 14 : 8-18.
Vision of " man of Macedonia " seen by Paul, Acts 16 : 9.
Spirit of divination cast out of a damsel by Paul, Acts 16 : 16-18.
Earthquake at Philippi, Acts 16 : 25, 26.
Special miracles wrought by Paul at Ephesus, Acts 19 : 11, 12.
Evil spirit puts to flight Sceva's sons, Acts 19 : 13-16.
Raising of Eutychus to life by Paul, Acts 20 : 9-12.
Prophecies of Agabus, Acts 11 : 28; 21 : 11.
Appearance of Christ to Paul, Acts 9 : 3 ff.; 22 : 17-21; 23 : 11; 27 : 23, 24.

Paul unharmed by bite of viper, Acts 28 : 3-5.
Paul heals Publius' father and other sick at Melita, Acts 28 : 8, 9.
IV.—Miracles referred to in the Epistles and Revelation—
Miracles wrought by Paul and others, Rom. 15 : 18, 19; 1 Cor. 12 : 9, 10, 28-31; 14 : 18; Gal. 3 : 5; 1 Tim. 1 : 20.
Miracle of tongues, 1 Cor. 14 : 27-33.
Appearance of Christ after his resurrection, 1 Cor. 15 : 4-8.
Visions and revelations of Paul, 2 Cor. 12 : 1-5, with 12.
" Powers of the world to come " (i.e., of gospel times), Heb. 2 : 4; 6 : 5.
The visions of John in Patmos, Rev. 1 : 10; 4 to end of book.
Mark 9 : 39, no man which shall do a m. in my name.
Luke 23 : 8, hoped to have seen some m.
John 2 : 11, this beginning of m.
  4 : 54, this is the second m.
  10 : 41, said, John did no m.
  11 : 47, this man doeth many m.
Acts 2 : 22, approved of God by m. and signs.
  4 : 16, a notable m. has been done.
1 Cor. 12 : 29, are all workers of m. ?
Heb. 2 : 4, God bearing witness with m.
Mire, Job 8 : 11; Ps. 69 : 2; 2 Pet. 2 : 22.
Miriam (mĭr-ĭ-ăm) [bitterness, sorrow] (Greek, " Mariam," " Maria "; English, " Mary "), sister of Moses and Aaron, Ex. 15 : 20; Num. 26 : 59.
her song, Ex. 15 : 20.
her sedition against Moses, Num. 12 : 1, 2.
is smitten with leprosy, Num. 12 : 10, 15.
her death, Num. 20 : 1.
Mirth, vanity of, Eccl. 2; 7 : 4.
Neh. 8 : 12, the people went to make m.
Ps. 137 : 3, they that wasted us required of us m.
Eccl. 2 : 1, prove thee with m.
Isa. 24 : 11, the m. of the land is gone.
See Jer. 7 : 34; 16 : 9; Hos. 2 : 11.
Miry, Ps. 40 : 2, brought me out of m. city.
Dan. 2 : 41, iron mixed with m. clay.
Miscarrying, Hos. 9 : 14.
Mischief, Punishment of, Ps. 7 : 14; 9 : 15; 140 : 2; Prov. 26 : 27; Isa. 33 : 1.
Gen. 42 : 4, lest m. befall him.
Job 15 : 35, they conceive m. and vanity.
Ps. 36 : 4, the wicked deviseth m.
  52 : 1, why boastest thou thyself in m. ?
  62 : 3, how long will ye imagine m. ?
Prov. 10 : 23, as sport to a fool to do m.
  24 : 16; 28 : 14, wicked shall fall into m.
Ezek. 7 : 26, m. shall come upon m.
Acts 13 : 10, O full of all subtility and m.
Mischievous, Ps. 21 : 11; Mic. 7 : 3.
Miserable, Job 16 : 2; 1 Cor. 15 : 19; Rev. 3 : 17.
See Matt. 21 : 41.
Misery, Job 11 : 16, thou shalt forget thy m.
Prov. 31 : 7, remember his m. no more.
Eccl. 8 : 6, the m. of man is great.
Jas. 5 : 1, howl for your m.
See Job 16 : 2; Matt. 21 : 41; 1 Cor. 15 : 19; Rev. 3 : 17.
Misgab (mĭs-găb) [height], Jer. 48 : 1.

Mishael (mǐ-shā-ĕl) [who is what God is ?], Ex. 6 : 22; Dan. 1 : 11, 19.
Mishal (mǐ-shăl), a town of Asher, given to the Gershonite Levites (Josh. 21 : 30).
Misham (mǐ-shăm), 1 Chr. 8 : 12.
Misheal (mǐ-shē-ăl) [request], Josh. 19 : 26.
Mishma (mǐsh-mă) [hearing], Gen. 25 : 14.
Mishmannah (mǐsh-măn-năh) [fatness], 1 Chr. 12 : 10.
Mishraites (mǐsh-rā-ītes), 1 Chr. 2 : 53.
Mispereth (mǐs-pĕ-rĕth), Neh. 7 : 7.
Misrephoth-maim (mǐs-rĕ-phŏth-mā-ĭm) [burnings of the waters], smelting works by the water, Josh. 11 : 8.
Miss, Judg. 20 : 16; 1 Sam. 20 : 18; 25 : 7.
Mist, Gen. 2 : 6, went up a m. from the earth.
Acts 13 : 11, there fell on him a m.
2 Pet. 2 : 17, the m. of darkness.
Mistress, Gen. 16 : 8; 1 Ki. 17 : 17; Isa. 24 : 2; Nah. 3 : 4.
Misused, 2 Chr. 36 : 16.
Mite, Mark 12 : 42; Luke 12 : 59; 21 : 2. See Money.
Mitre, a wrapping for the head of the high priest. It consisted of eight yards of fine linen folded round the head like a turban. The words " Holiness to the Lord " were inscribed on a gold plate and fixed to the front. cf. Ex. 28 : 4, 37, 39; 28 : 30; Lev. 8 : 9.
Mixed, Prov. 23 : 30, that go to seek m. wine.
Isa. 1 : 22, thy wine m. with water.
Heb. 4 : 2, not being m. with faith.
Mixture, Ps. 75 : 8; John 19 : 39; Rev. 14 : 10.
Mizpah (mǐz-păh) (Mizpeh) [watch-tower], Jacob and Laban meet at, Gen. 31 : 49.
Israelites assemble there, Judg. 10 : 17; 11 : 11; 20 : 1; 1 Sam. 7 : 5; 10 : 17.
(Moab), 1 Sam. 22 : 3.

2 Sam. 8 : 2; by Jehoshaphat and Jehoram, 2 Ki. 3.
their destruction, 2 Chr. 20 : 23.
prophecies concerning, Ex. 15 : 15; Num. 21 : 29; 24 : 17; Ps. 60 : 8; 83 : 6; Isa. 11 : 14; 15; 16; 25 : 10; Jer. 9 : 26; 25 : 21; 48. Ezek. 25 : 8; Amos 2 : 1; Zeph. 2 : 8.
Moabitess, Ruth 1 : 22; 2 Chr. 24 : 26.
Mock, Gen. 19 : 14, he seemed as one that m.
1 Ki. 18 : 27, Elijah m. them.
2 Chr. 36 : 16, they m. the messengers of God.
Prov. 1 : 26, I will m. when your fear cometh.
17 : 5, whoso m. the poor reproacheth his Maker.
30 : 17, the eye that m. at his father.
Luke 14 : 29, begin to m. him.
Acts 2 : 13, others m. said.
Gal. 6 : 7, God is not m.
Mocker, Prov. 20 : 1, wine is a m.
Isa. 28 : 22, be ye not m.
Jude 18, there should be m. in the last time.
Mocking, censured, Prov. 17 : 5; 30 : 17; Jer. 15 : 17; Jude 18.
punished, Gen. 21 : 9; 2 Ki. 2 : 23.
of Christ, Matt. 27 : 29; Luke 23 : 11.
See 2 Chr. 30 : 10.
Moderation, Phil. 4 : 5.
Moderately, Joel 2 : 23.
Modest apparel, 1 Tim. 2 : 9; 1 Pet. 3 : 3.
Moist, Num. 6 : 3.
Moisture, Ps. 32 : 4; Luke 8 : 6.
Mole, Lev. 11 : 30, in which A.V. has " mole "; R.V., " chameleon."
Mollified, Isa. 1 : 6.
Moloch (Molech) [king], god of the Phœnicians and Ammonites, Lev. 18 : 21; 20 : 2.
worship of, 1 Ki. 11 : 7; 2 Ki. 23 : 10; Jer. 32 : 35; Amos 5 : 26; Acts 7 : 43.

View in the land of Moab.

Egyptian Ring Money.

Moab (mō-ăb) [progeny of a father], son of Lot, Gen. 19 : 37.
an ancient kingdom east of the Dead Sea, Gen. 19 : 37; Num. 21 : 13, 15; 34 : 5.
Moabite Stone, The, discovered in 1868 by Rev. F. A. Klein, at Dhiban (=biblical Dibon), in Moab. It records in Phœnician characters the wars of Mesha, king of Moab, with Israel (2 Ki. 3 : 4). The names recorded on the stone witness to the accuracy of names in Scripture.
Moabites, excluded from the congregation, Deut. 23 : 3.
subdued by Ehud, Judg. 3 : 15-30; by David,

Molten, Ex. 32 : 4; Deut. 27 : 15; Mic. 1 : 4; Hab. 2 : 18.
Moment, Ex. 33 : 5, into midst of thee in a m.
Num. 16 : 21, consume them in a m.
Job 7 : 18, try him every m.
34 : 20, in a m. shall they die.

Ps. 30 : 5, his anger endureth but a m.
Isa. 26 : 20, hide thyself as it were for a m.
27 : 3, I will water it every m.
54 : 8, I hid my face from thee for a m.
Luke 4 : 5, kingdoms of world in a m.
1 Cor. 15 : 52, all be changed in a m.
2 Cor. 4 : 17, affliction, which is but for a m.
Money. Before money was coined the precious metals were weighed and kept in some such form as rings (cf. Gen. 17 : 13; 20 : 16, 20; 37 : 28, for examples). The following table is given for rough computation.

	Troy Weight	Money Value	
	lb. oz. dwt. gr.	£ s. d.	dols. cts.
I. Old Testament Period.			
(a) Silver.			
1 Shekel (Holy Shekel)	0 0 9 8.8	0 2 8	0 64
1 Maneh (mina) (=50 shekels)	1 11 8 8	6 13 4	32 0
1 Talent (=60 manehs)	117 (about)	400 0 0	1920 0
(b) Gold.			
1 Shekel	0 0 10 13	2 0 0	9 60
1 Maneh or mina (=50 shekels)	2 2 6 22	100 0 0	480 0
1 Talent (=60 manehs)	131 8 14 14	6000 0 0	28,800 0
II. New Testament Period.			
(a) Copper.			
Lepton (mite)	about	0 0 0	0 ⅛
Quadrans (farthing) =2 lepta	"	0 0 0⅛	0 ¼
Assarion or As (penny) =4 quadrantes	"	0 0 0½	0 1
(b) Silver.			
Denarius (penny)= drachma= 16 asses	"	0 0 8	0 16
Didrachm= 2 drachmas or denarii		0 1 4	0 32
Stater or tetradrachm= shekel		0 2 8	0 64
Mina or pound (Attic)=30 shekels		4 0 0	19 10
Talent = 60 minæ (Attic)		240 0 0	1146 0
(c) Gold.			
Imperial Aureus		1 1 0	5 4
Stater		1 2 0	5 28

cf. Ezra 2 : 69; 8 : 27; Neh. 7 : 70, 71, 72, for Persian money. cf. Matt. 17 : 24-27, 22 : 15-21; Luke 20 : 19-25.
love of, censured, 1 Tim. 6 : 10.
Gen. 23 : 9, as much m. as field is worth.
2 Ki. 5 : 26, is it a time to receive m. ?
Ps. 15 : 5, putteth not out m. to usury.
Eccl. 7 : 12, m. is a defence.
10 : 19, m. answereth all things.
Isa. 52 : 3, redeemed without m.
55 : 1, he that hath no m.
Matt. 25 : 18, hid his lord's m.
28 : 12, gave large m. to soldiers.
Acts 8 : 20, thy m. perish with thee.
See Gen. 17 : 27; 42 : 25; Jer. 32 : 9; Mark 12 : 41; 14 : 11.
Monsters, Lam. 4 : 3.
Months of the Hebrew year. The Jews reckoned the " civil " day from sunset to sunset (cf. Lev. 23 : 32. Gen. 1 : 5 is not clear, and cannot be quoted here). The lunar month contained from twenty-nine to thirty days, and, like the Babylonian, began with the evening of the first observation of the new moon. The year, consisting of twelve lunar months, was three hundred and fifty-four days in duration, but, as in the Babylonian system, an inter-calary month or second Adar (" Ve-adar ") was added to balance the lunar with the solar year.
Monthly, Isa. 47 : 13.
Monuments, Isa. 65 : 4.
Moon, the lesser light, Gen. 1 : 16.
referred to, Deut. 33 : 14; Josh. 10 : 12; Ps. 8 : 3; 89 : 37; 104 : 19; 121 : 6.
idolatrously worshipped, Deut. 17 : 3; Job 31 : 26; Jer. 44 : 17.
feasts of the new, 1 Sam. 20 : 5; 1 Chr. 23 : 31; Ps. 81 : 3; Isa. 1 : 13; Hos. 2 : 11.
Mordecai (môr-dĕ-cā-ī) [consecrated to Merodach], discovers conspiracy against Ahasuerus, Esther 2 : 21. See **Purim.**
excites Haman's enmity, Esther 3 : 5.
his appeal to Esther, Esther 4.
honoured by the king, Esther 6.
his advancement, Esther 8; 9; 10.
See Ezra 2 : 2; Neh. 7 : 7.
More, Ex. 16 : 17; 1 Sam. 3 : 17; John 21 : 15, etc.
Moreh (mō-rĕh) [teacher], probably the name of a Canaanite, Gen. 12 : 6; Judg. 7 : 1.
Moreover, Ps. 19 : 11; Heb. 11 : 36.
Moriah (mō-rī-ăh) [provided by Jah], Gen. 22 : 2; 2 Chr. 3 : 1.
David's sacrifice there, 2 Sam. 24 : 18; 1 Chr. 21 : 18; 22 : 1.
site of the temple, 2 Chr. 3 : 1.
Morning, Gen. 1 : 5, 8, 13, evening and the m.
Job 38 : 7, m. stars sang together.
Ps. 30 : 5, joy cometh in the m.
90 : 6, in the m. it flourisheth.
130 : 6, they that watch for the m.
Eccl. 11 : 6, in the m. sow thy seed.
Hos. 6 : 4, goodness is as a m. cloud.
Mark 16 : 2, very early in the m.
Rev. 22 : 16, the bright and m. star.
Morrow, Prov. 27 : 1, boast not thyself of to-m.
Isa. 22 : 13; 1 Cor. 15 : 32, to-m. we die.
Isa. 56 : 12, to-m. shall be as this day.
Matt. 6 : 34, take no thought for the m.
Jas. 4 : 14, ye know not what shall be on the m.
Morsel, 1 Ki. 17 : 11; Prov. 17 : 1; Heb. 12 : 16.
Mortal, Job 4 : 17, shall m. man be more just than God ?
Rom. 6 : 12, your m. body.
1 Cor. 15 : 53, this m. must put on immortality.
Mortality of man, Job 19 : 26; Rom. 8 : 11; 2 Cor. 4 : 11; 5 : 4.
Mortar. Corn for bread was prepared by bruising or crushing it in a hollow stone by another stone. Ex. 1 : 14; Ezek. 13 : 10 f., 14; Nah. 3 : 14.
Mortgaged, Neh. 5 : 3.
Mortify, Rom. 8 : 13; Col. 3 : 5.
Moses (mō-sĕs) [saved from water], an Egyptian name. Moses is portrayed in the threefold capacity of (1) Leader; (2) Promoter of Jahweh-religion; and (3) Lawgiver and

Sacred Year.	Civil Year.	Jewish Calendar, with Lists of Fasts and Festivals.	Agricultural Seasons.
1	7	Abib or Nisan (March-April). 1st—New Moon. *Beginning of the* SACRED YEAR. 14th—Preparation for *Passover*—paschal lamb eaten in the evening. 15th—Sabbath and Holy Convocation. Week of unleavened bread begins. 16th—The offering of *Omer* or *First Sheaf* (Lev. 23 : 10-12). 21st—Holy Convocation.	Latter or spring rains (Deut. 11 : 14). Barley harvest begins.
2	8	Iyyar or Zif (April-May). 1st—New Moon. 10th—*Fast* to commemorate the death of Elijah. 14th—*Second* or *Little Passover.* 28th—*Fast* for the death of Samuel.	Barley harvest (Ruth 1 : 22).
3	9	Sivan (May-June). 1st—New Moon. 6th and 7th—*Pentecost* or *Feast of Weeks,* marking the close of harvest.	Wheat harvest.
4	10	Tammuz (June-July). 1st—New Moon. 17th—*Fast* to commemorate the breach in the wall of Jerusalem (Jer. 52 : 5-7).	
5	11	Ab (July-August). 1st—New Moon. 9th—*Fast* for the destruction of the temple by Nebuzaradan.	Grapes, figs, and olives begin to ripen as the month progresses.
6	12	Elul (August-September). 1st—New Moon. 7th—*Feast* for the dedication of the walls by Nehemiah.	Vintage begins, also harvest of maize. Pomegranates ripen.
7	1	Tishri or Ethanim (September-October). 1st—New Moon. *New Year's Day. Beginning of the* CIVIL YEAR. *Feast of Trumpets.* 3rd—*Fast* for Gedaliah's assassination (Jer. 41 : 2-6 ; 2 Ki. 25 : 25). 10th—*Kippurim* or *Day of Atonement.* 15th-22nd—*Feast of Tabernacles* or *Booths.* 21st—*Feast of Branches* or *Palms.*	Former or early rains (Joel 2 : 23). Plowing and sowing begin.
8	2	Marchesvan or Bul (October-November). 1st—New Moon.	Wheat and barley sown.
9	3	Kislev (November-December). 1st New Moon. 25th—*Chanuccah*—*Feast of Dedication.*	
10	4	Tebet (December-January). 1st—New Moon. 10th—*Fast* commemorating the beginning of Nebuchadnezzar's siege of Jerusalem (2 Ki. 25 : 1).	
11	5	Shebat (January-February). 1st—New Moon.	
12	6	Adar (February-March). 1st—New Moon. 13th—*Fast of Esther.* 14th and 15th—*Feast of Purim.*	Almond tree blossoms.
13		Veadar (intercalary month).	

Moral Teacher or Prophet. As the representative figure in the Old Dispensation our Lord often paralleled his case to the New.
his birth and preservation, Ex. 2; (Acts 7 : 20; Heb. 11 : 23).
escapes to Midian, Ex. 2 : 15.
called by the Lord, Ex. 3.
signs shown to, Ex. 4.
returns to Egypt, Ex. 4 . 20.
intercedes with Pharaoh for Israel, Ex. 5–12.
leads Israel forth from Egypt, Ex. 14.
meets God in Mount Sinai, Ex. 19 : 3; (24 : 18).
delivers the law to the people, Ex. 19 : 25; 20–23; 34 : 10; 35 : 1; Lev. 1; Num. 5; 6; 15; 27–30; 36; Deut. 13–26.
instructed to build the tabernacle, Ex. 25–31; 35; 40; Num. 4; 8; 9; 10; 18; 19.
his anger at Israel's idolatry, Ex. 32 : 19.
his intercession, Ex. 32 : 11; (33 : 12).
again meets God in the mount, Ex. 34 : 2.
skin of his face shines, Ex. 34 : 29; (2 Cor. 3 : 7, 13).
consecrates Aaron, Lev. 8 : 9.
numbers the people, Num. 1; 26.
sends out the spies to Canaan, Num. 13.
intercedes for the people, Num. 14 : 13.
Korah's sedition against, Num. 16.
for his unbelief not permitted to enter Canaan, Num. 20 : 12; 27 : 12; Deut. 1 : 35; 3 : 23.
leads Israel in the wilderness, Num. 20; 21.
makes the brazen serpent, Num. 21 : 9; (John 3 : 14).

recounts Israel's history, etc., Deut. 1; 3–12, 27–31.
his charge to Joshua, Deut. 3 : 28; 31 : 7, 23.
his death, Deut. 34 : 5.
his body, Jude 9.
seen at Christ's transfiguration, Matt. 17 : 3; Mark 9 : 4; Luke 9 : 30.
his meekness, Num. 12 : 3; dignity, Deut. 34 : 10; faithfulness, Num. 12 : 7; Heb 3 : 2.
addresses of, to the people, Deut.
Mote, Matt. 7 : 3; Luke 6 : 41, m. in brother's eye.
Moth, the fragile and easily destroyed insect, the clothes-moth. Possible allusions to its house and to the larva appear in Job 27 : 18 and Isa. 51 : 8.
Ps. 39 : 11; Isa. 50 : 9; Hos. 5 : 12; Matt. 6 : 19.
Motheaten, Job 13 : 28; Jas. 5 : 2.
Mother, of all living, Eve, Gen. 3 : 20.
love of, Isa. 49 : 15.
examples of, Gen. 21 : 10; Ex. 2; 1 Sam. 1 : 22; 1 Ki. 3 : 26; 2 Tim. 1 : 5; 2 John.
duty towards, Ex. 20 : 12; Prov. 1 : 8; 19 : 26; 23 : 22; Eph. 6 : 2.
Judg. 5 : 7; 2 Sam. 20 : 19, a m. in Israel.
Job 17 : 14, said to worm, Thou art my m.
Ps. 113 : 9, a joyful m. of children.
Isa. 66 : 13, as one whom his m. comforteth.
Mic. 7 : 6; Matt. 10 : 35; Luke 12 : 53, daughter riseth against her m.
Matt. 12 : 48; Mark 3 : 33, who is my m. ?

John 2 : 1; Acts 1 : 14, the m. of Jesus.
Gal. 4 : 26, Jerusalem the m. of us all.
Motions, Rom. 7 : 5.
Mouldy, Josh. 9 : 5, 12.
Mount, Ex. 18 : 5; 1 Ki. 19 : 8, the m. of God.
Job 20 : 6; Ps. 107 : 26, m. to heaven.
Isa. 40 : 31, m. up with wings as eagles.
Mountain, Gen. 19 : 17; Isa. 14 : 23; Matt. 14 : 23; Mark 11 : 23; Ps. 11 : 1; Isa. 2 : 3.
Mourn, Gen. 37 : 34, Jacob m. for his son.
Ps. 55 : 2, I m. in my complaint.
Prov. 5 : 11, thou m. at the last.
Eccl. 3 : 4, a time to m.
Isa. 61 : 2, to comfort all that m.
Matt. 5 : 4, blessed are they that m.
Luke 6 : 25, for ye shall m.
Jas. 4 : 9, m. and weep.
Mourners, comfort for, Job 29 : 25; Rom. 12 : 15; 2 Cor. 1 : 4; 1 Thess. 4 : 18.
See 2 Sam. 14 : 2; Eccl. 12 : 5.
Mournfully, Mal. 3 : 14.
Mourning, when blessed, Eccl. 7 : 2; Matt. 5 : 4; Luke 6 : 21.
for the dead, Gen. 50 : 3; Num. 20 : 29; Deut. 14 : 1; 2 Sam. 1 : 17; 3 : 31; 12 : 16; 18 : 33; 19 : 1; Eccl. 12 : 5; Jer. 6 : 26; 9 : 17; 22 : 18.
of the priests, Lev. 21 : 1; Ezek. 44 : 25.
Mouse, Lev. 11 : 29; Isa. 66 : 17, refer to the rodent of that name or to the rat. 1 Sam. 6 : 4 may apply to the field mice. All these animals are common in the Holy Land.
Mouth, of God, Deut. 8 : 3; Matt. 4 : 4.
of babes, Ps. 8 : 2.
of fools, Prov. 14 : 3; 15 : 2; 18 : 7; 26 : 7.
of the righteous, etc., Ps. 37 : 30; Prov. 10 : 31; Eccl. 10 : 12.
of the wicked, Ps. 32 : 9; 107 : 42; 109 : 2; 144 : 8; Prov. 4 : 24; 5 : 3; 6 : 12; 19 : 28; Rom. 3 : 14; Rev. 13 : 5.
Ps. 63 : 11, m. that speaketh lies.
103 : 5, satisfieth thy m. with good things.
Prov. 18 : 7, a fool's m. is his destruction.
Eccl. 6 : 7, labour of man is for his m.
Isa. 29 : 13; Matt. 15 : 8, people draw near me with m.
Mal. 2 : 6, the law of truth was in his m.
Matt. 12 : 34; Luke 6 : 45, of abundance of heart the m. speaketh.
Matt. 21 : 16, out of the m. of babes.
Luke 21 : 15, I will give you a m. and wisdom.
Rom. 10 : 10, with the m. confession is made unto salvation.
1 Cor. 9 : 9, not muzzle m. of ox.
Jas. 3 : 10, out of same m. proceedeth.
Move, Deut. 32 : 21, m. them to jealousy.
Ps. 10 : 6; 16 : 8; 30 : 6; 62 : 2, I shall not be m.
Matt. 21 : 10; Acts 21 : 30, the city was m.
Matt. 23 : 4, they will not m. them.
Acts 17 : 28, in him we live and m.
20 : 24, none of these things m. me.
See John 5 : 3; Heb. 12 : 28.
Moveable, Prov. 5 : 6.
Mover, Acts 24 : 5.
Mower, Ps. 129 : 7.
Mowings, Amos 7 : 1.
Mown, Ps. 72 : 6.
Much, Luke 12 : 48.

Mufflers, Isa. 3 : 19.
Mulberry, 2 Sam. 5 : 23 f.; 1 Chr. 14 : 14 f. (R.V. margin, " balsam trees "); Ps. 84 : 6 (A.V. margin. R.V., " balsam trees "). Probably the aspen tree was intended. For Luke 17 : 4, 6cf. Sycamine tree.
Mules, 1 Ki. 18 : 5; Esther 8 : 10; Gen. 36 : 24 (R.V., " hot springs ").
Multiply, Gen. 1 : 22; 8 : 17; 35 : 11, be fruitful and m.
Ps. 16 : 4, their sorrows shall be m.
Isa. 9 : 3, thou hast m. the nation.
Dan. 4 : 1; 6 : 25; 1 Pet. 1 : 2; 2 Pet. 1 : 2; Jude 2, peace be m.
Acts 12 : 24, word of God grew and m.
2 Cor. 9 : 10, m. your seed sown.
Multitude, Gen. 28 : 3, God Almighty make thee a m.
Ex. 23 : 2, not follow a m. to do evil.
Deut. 1 : 10; 10 : 22; 28 : 62; Heb. 11 : 12, as the stars for m.
Josh. 11 : 4; Judg. 7 : 12; 1 Sam. 13 : 5; 2 Sam. 17 : 11; 1 Ki. 4 : 20, as sand on seashore for m.
Job 32 : 7, m. of years should teach wisdom.
Ps. 5 : 7; 51 : 1; 69 : 13, m. of thy mercy.
33 : 16, no king saved by the m. of an host.
94 : 19, in the m. of my thoughts.
Prov. 10 : 19, in the m. of words there wanteth not sin.
11 : 14; 15 : 22; 24 : 6, in the m. of counsellors.
Eccl. 5 : 3, through the m. of business.
Jas. 5 : 20, hide a m. of sins.
1 Pet. 4 : 8, charity shall cover the m. of sins.
Munition [ar.], stronghold, Isa. 29 : 7; 33 : 16; Nah. 2 : 1.
Murder, forbidden, Gen. 9 : 6; Ex. 20 : 13; Lev. 24 : 17; Deut. 5 : 17; 21 : 9; Matt. 5 : 21; 1 John 3 : 15.
examples, Gen. 4; Judg. 9; 2 Sam. 3 : 27; 4; 12 : 9; 20 : 10; 1 Ki. 16 : 10; 21; 2 Ki. 15 : 10; 21 : 23; 2 Chr. 24 : 21.
its penalty, Gen. 4 : 12; 9 : 6; Num. 35 : 30; Jer. 19 : 4 ff.; Ezek. 16 : 38; Gal. 5 : 21; Rev. 22 : 15.
source of, Matt. 15 : 19.
Murmur, Ex. 16 : 7, that ye m. against us.
John 6 : 43, m. not among yourselves.
1 Cor. 10 : 10, neither m. as some of them m.
Murmuring, rebuked, Lam. 3 : 39; Phil. 2 : 14.
of Israel, Ex. 15 : 24; 16; 17; Num. 11; 16; 20; 21.
Murrain, plague of, Ex. 9 : 3; Ps. 78 : 50.
Muse, Ps. 39 : 3, while I was m., the fire burned.
143 : 5, I m. on work of thy hands.
Luke 3 : 15, all men m. in their hearts.
Music, soothes Saul, 1 Sam. 16 : 23. Used in worship, 2 Sam. 6 : 5; 1 Chr. 15 : 28; 16 : 42; 2 Chr. 29 : 25; Ps. 33; 81; 92; 108; 150; Dan. 3 : 5.
at festivities, Isa. 5 : 12; 14 : 11; Amos 6 : 5; 1 Cor. 14 : 7.
in heaven, Rev. 5 : 8; 14 : 2.
1 Sam. 18 : 6, meet Saul with m.
2 Chr. 7 : 6, instruments of m.
Luke 15 : 25, his elder son heard m.
See Gen. 4 : 21.

Hebrew music was probably of a loud and piercing nature, and whether it ever advanced beyond unison is open to question. Antiphonal settings were in use (cf. Pss. 13, 20, 38, 68, 89). Music was connected indissolubly with religion.

Stringed Instruments.

Musical Instruments.

I.—Stringed Instruments.
(a) Harp (kinnor).
(b) Psaltery (nĕbel).
Both favourites with the Hebrews, and used rather for joyous than mournful occasions (Ps. 137 : 2).
The "kinnor" has been variously rendered as "lyre," "cithern," "harp." Josephus tells us it was a ten-stringed instrument struck by a plectrum. (Note however, 1 Sam. 16 : 23.)
While "nĕbel" has been taken to be the "lute," the "viol," and the "dul cimer," it is best to take it as above, and to think of it as a larger "kinnor," though played with the hand. (cf. Amos 6 : 5; Isa. 5 : 12; 14 : 11;—1 Sam. 10 : 5; 2 Sam. 6 : 5.)
(c) "Sackbut" (sabbĕkha), a large harp of many strings and rich tone; at other periods, very small and of high pitch.
(d) "Gittith" (Pss. 8, 81, 84 titles), a probable reference to a harp which David brought from Gath. So Targum.
II.—Wind Instruments.
(a) "Pipe," "Flute," or "Reed Pipe" (chălīl) was the most common of this type. For usage, cf. 1 Sam. 10 : 5; 1 Ki. 1 : 40; —Isa. 30 : 29;—Jer. 48 : 36; Matt. 9 : 23; —Isa. 5 : 12;—Dan. 3 : 5.
(b) "Organ" (ūgāb), the Pandean pipes [Gr. Syrinx], Gen. 4 : 21.
(c) "Flute" (mȧshrōkītha), similar to (a).
(d) "Bagpipes" (sumpōnya).
(e) "Cornet," "Castanet," "Horn" or "Trumpet" (shōphār). (cf. 1 Chr. 15 : 28; 2 Chr. 15 : 14; Ps. 98 : 6; Hos. 5 : 8;—Judg. 3 : 27;—1 Ki. 1 : 34, 39.)
(f) "Trumpet" (hatsōtsĕrāh), long and straight (2 Ki. 12 : 13; 1 Chr. 13 : 8).
III.—Percussion Instruments.
(a) "Tabret," "Timbrel" (tōph), a kind of drum, of various shapes and sizes, without

allowing of the skin being tightened or loosed.
(b) "Cymbals" (mĕtsiltaim, tseltsĕlīm).
(c) "Castanets," "Sistra" (mena-anim), (R.V and R.V.m., 2 Sam. 6 : 5).
(d) Shālīshīm (1 Sam. 18 : 6, R.V.m., "triangles," etc.), probably a particular kind of (c). cf. Ps. 150 : 3-5.
Musician, chief, used in titles of fifty-five psalms. See Psalms.
Musicians, Rev. 18 : 22.
Must, Mark 9 : 31; John 3 : 7; Acts 4 : 12, etc.
Mustard, of the ordinary black variety is common in Palestine, and is a tree among herbs, growing sometimes to a height of 8 to 10 feet.
Mustard seed, parable of, Matt. 13 : 31 f.; Mark 4 : 30-32; Luke 13 : 18, f.
Mustered, 2 Ki. 25 : 19; Jer. 52 : 25.
Muthlabben (mŭth-lăb-bĕn) [die for the son], Ps. 9, title. The reference is possibly to the opening words of some song and the Psalm is "set to" (A.V. "upon ") the tune of that song. See Maschil.
Mutter, Isa. 8 : 19; 59 : 3.
Mutual, Rom. 1 : 12.
Muzzling the ox, law concerning, Deut. 25 : 4; 1 Cor. 9 : 9; 1 Tim. 5 : 18.
Myrrh, an aromatic resin of several species. The oil for anointing had it as an ingredient (Ex. 30 : 23), and it was also used for embalming (John 19 : 39).
Esther 2 : 12; Ps. 45 : 8; Song of Sol. 1 : 13; Matt. 2 : 11; Mark 15 : 23.
Myrtle, a shrub of great beauty, whose branches were used to decorate the booths made during the Feast of Tabernacles (Neh. 8 : 15).
Isa. 55 : 13, instead of the brier shall come up the m.
Zech. 1 : 8, he stood among the m. trees.
Mystery, of the kingdom of God, made known by Christ, Eph. 1 : 9; 3 : 3; 1 Tim. 3 : 16; by the disciples to the world, 1 Cor. 4 : 1; 13 : 2; Eph. 6 : 19.
of iniquity, 2 Thess. 2 . 7, Rev. 17 . 5.
Mark 4 : 11, to know the m. of the kingdom.
Rom. 11 : 25, not be ignorant of m.
16 : 25, according to revelations of the m.
1 Cor. 15 : 51, I show you a m.
Eph. 5 : 32, this is a great m.
Col. 2 : 2, acknowledgment of the m. of God.
1 Tim. 3 : 16, great is the m. of godliness.

N

Naaman (nā-ă-măn) [pleasantness], the Syrian, his leprosy healed, 2 Ki. 5 : 1 ff., etc.
See Luke 4 : 27.
Naamathite (nā-ăm-ă-thīte), inhabitant of Naamah, Job 2 : 11.
Naamites (nā-ă-mītes), Num. 26 : 40.
Naarah (nā-ă-răh), 1 Chr. 4 : 5 f.
Naarai (nā-ă-rāi) [youthful], 1 Chr. 11 : 37.
Naaran (nā-ă-răn), 1 Chr. 7 : 28.
Naarath (nā-ă-răth), Josh. 16 : 7.
Naashon (nā-ăsh-ŏn) [enchanter], Ex. 6 : 23.

Naasson (nā-ăs-sŏn), Luke 3 : 32. See Naashon, Nahshon.

Nabal (nā-băl) [fool], his conduct towards David, 1 Sam. 25 : 10.

Abigail's intercession for, 1 Sam. 25 : 18.

his death, 1 Sam. 25 : 38.

Naboth (nā-bŏth) [fruits?], slain by Jezebel, 1 Ki. 21.

his murder avenged, 2 Ki. 9 : 21.

Nadab (nā-dăb) [noble], son of Aaron, his trespass and death, Lev. 10.

king of Israel, slain by Baasha, 1 Ki. 14 : 20; 15 : 25.

Nagge (năg-gē) (Naggai) [bright], Luke 3 : 25.

Nahaliel (nă-hăl-ĭ-ĕl) [valley of God], Num. 21 : 19.

Nahallal (nă-hăl-lăl) [pasture], a town of Zebulon, Josh. 19 : 15.

Naham, 1 Chr. 4 : 19.

Nahamani (nā-hă-mā-nĭ) [comforter], Neh. 7 : 7.

Naharai (nā-hă-râi) [snorer], 2 Sam. 23 : 37.

Nahash (nā-hăsh) [serpent], the Ammonite, subdued by Saul, 1 Sam. 11 : 1, etc.

Nahath (nā-hăth) [rest], Gen. 36 : 13, 17.

Nahbi (năh-bĭ) [hidden], Num. 13 : 14.

Nahor (nā-hôr) [snoring], Abram's brother, Gen. 11 : 26; 22 : 20; 24 : 10.

Nahshon (năh-shŏn) [diviner], Num. 1 : 7.

Nahum (nā-hŭm) [comforting], a prophet of Judah, his vision, Nah. 1–3.

Nahum, Book of.

Nahum was an inhabitant of Elkosh in Galilee. Nothing is known of him except what is found in his book. This was thought to have been written from 660 to 640 B.C. It is a sequel to Jonah. When the earlier prophet announced the destruction of Nineveh, the people repented and the city was spared. They returned to their sins and their cruelties to Israel, and the message of Nahum leaves to them no hope. The city, thought to be impregnable, was completely destroyed (625-606 B.C.). The passage in Nah. 1 : 15 much resembles Isa. 52 : 6, 7. " Behold upon the mountains the feet of him that bringeth good tidings, that publisheth peace."

Nails, figuratively mentioned, Ezra 9 : 8; Eccl. 12 : 11; Isa. 22 : 23.

Judg. 5 : 26, she put her hand to the n.

Isa. 22 : 23, fasten him as a n. in a sure place.

Dan. 4 : 33, his n. like bird's claws.

John 20 : 25, put finger into print of n.

Col. 2 : 14, n. it to his cross.

Naked, Job 1 : 21, n. came I, and n. shall I return.

Matt. 25 : 36, was n., and ye clothed me.

1 Cor. 4 : 11, to this hour we are n.

2 Cor. 5 : 3, we shall not be found n.

Heb. 4 : 13, all things are n. to eyes of him.

Jas. 2 : 15, if a brother be n.

Rev. 3 : 17, poor, and blind, and n.

Nakedness, Rom. 8 : 35; 2 Cor. 11 : 27.

Name. In ancient times the name of a god called up the character of that deity, not only in the mind of the suppliant, but also objectively. The same crude idea has often been read into the phrase " praying in the name of Jesus," as though by itself the sound of the name had magic power to

charm an answer. In reality, the phrase is far richer, implying that our prayers should be in the spirit of our Lord.

of God, Ex. 34 : 5, 14.

to be reverenced, Ex. 20 : 7; Deut. 5 : 11; 28 : 58; Ps. 34 : 3; 72 : 17; 111 : 9; Mic. 4 : 5; 1 Tim. 6 : 1.

of Christ, prayer in, John 14 : 13; 16 : 23; Rom. 1 : 8; Eph. 5 : 20; Heb. 13 : 15.

miracles performed in, Acts 3 : 6; 4 : 10; 19 : 13.

to be honoured, 2 Tim. 2 : 19.

given to children at circumcision, Luke 1 : 59; 2 : 21.

value of a good, Prov. 22 : 1; Eccl. 7 : 1.

changed by God, Gen. 17 : 5, 15; 32 : 28; 2 Sam. 12 : 25; by man, Dan. 1 : 7; by Christ, Mark 3 : 16, 17.

(noun), Gen. 32 : 29, why ask after my n. ?

48 : 16, let my n. be named on them.

Ex. 3 : 15, this is my n. for ever.

20 : 24, where I record my n.

Deut. 9 : 14, blot out n. from under heaven.

Neh. 9 : 10, so didst thou get thee a n.

Job 18 : 17, he shall have no n.

Ps. 20 : 1, n. of God of Jacob.

20 : 5, in n. of God set up our banners.

44 : 20, if we forget n. of our God.

Prov. 10 : 7, the n. of the wicked shall rot.

18 : 10, the n. of the Lord is a strong tower.

Song of Sol. 1 : 3, thy n. is an ointment poured forth.

Isa. 55 : 13, it shall be to the Lord for a n.

56 : 5; 63 : 12, an everlasting n.

57 : 15, whose n. is Holy.

62 : 2, called by a new n.

Jer. 10 : 6, thou art great, and thy n. is great.

44 : 26, sworn by my great n.

Zech. 14 : 9, one Lord, and his n. one.

Mal. 1 : 6, wherein have we despised thy n. ?

4 : 2, to you that fear my n.

Matt. 6 : 9; Luke 11 : 2, hallowed by thy n.

Matt. 10 : 41, receiveth prophet in n. of a prophet.

18 : 20, gathered together in my n.

24 : 5; Mark 13 : 6; Luke 21 : 8, many shall come in my n.

Mark 6 : 14, his n. was spread abroad.

9 : 39, do a miracle in my n.

Luke 6 : 22, cast out your n. as evil.

10 : 20, n. written in heaven.

24 : 47, remission of sins in his n.

John 5 : 43, if another shall come in his own n.

15 : 16, whatsoever ye ask in my n.

20 : 31, ye might have life through his n.

Acts 3 : 16, his n. through faith in his n.

4 : 12, none other n. under heaven.

Eph. 1 : 21, far above every n. that is named.

Phil. 2 : 10, at n. of Jesus every knee should bow.

4 : 3, whose n. are in the book of life.

Col. 3 : 17, do all in the n. of the Lord Jesus.

Heb. 1 : 4, obtained a more excellent n.

Jas. 2 : 7, that worthy n.

1 Pet. 4 : 14, reproached for n. of Christ.

Rev. 2 : 17, a n. written, which no man knoweth.

3 : 1, hast a n. that thou livest.

14 : 1; 22 : 4, Father's n. in their foreheads.

15 : 4, who shall not fear, and glorify thy **n.** ?

(verb), Eccl. 6 : 30, that which hath been is **n.** already.

Isa. 61 : 6, shall be **n.** priests of the Lord.

Rom. 15 : 20 not where Christ was **n.**

Eph. 3 : 15, whole family in heaven and earth is **n.**

Namely, Mark 12 : 31.

Naomi (nā-ō-mĭ) [pleasant], Ruth 1–2, etc.

Naphtali (năph-tă-lĭ) [struggle for], son of Jacob, Gen. 30 : 8; 35 : 25; 46 : 24; 49 : 21; Deut. 33 : 23.

tribe of, numbered, etc., Num. 1 : 42; 10 : 27; 13 : 14; 26 : 48; Judg. 1 : 33; Isa. 9 : 1; Matt. 4 : 13.

subdue the Canaanites, Judg. 6 : 35; 7 : 23.

carried captive, 2 Ki. 15 : 29.

Napkin, Luke 19 : 20, laid up in a **n.**

John 11 : 44, bound about with a **n.**

Narcissus (när-cĭs-sŭs) [daffodil], a Roman, Rom. 16 : 11.

Nard. See **Spikenard.**

Narrow, Num. 22 : 26, angel of Lord stood in **n.** place.

Isa. 28 : 20, **n.** than that he can wrap himself.

49 : 19, land of destruction too **n.**

Matt. 7 : 14, **n.** is way that leadeth to life.

Narrowly, Isa. 14 : 16, shall **n.** look upon thee.

Nathan (nā-thăn) [he gave], the prophet, 2 Sam. 7.

his parable condemning David, 2 Sam. 12 : 1.

anoints Solomon king, etc., 1 Ki. 1 : 34.

son of David, 2 Sam. 5 : 14; Zech. 12 : 12; Luke 3 : 31.

Nathanael (nă-thăn-ă-ĕl)[God gave],commended, John 1 : 45; 21 : 2.

Nation, Gen. 20 : 4, wilt thou slay a righteous **n.** ?

Num. 14 : 12; Deut. 9 : 14, I will make thee a greater **n.**

Deut. 28 : 50, a **n.** of fierce countenance.

2 Sam. 7 : 23; 1 Chr. 17 : 21, what **n.** like thy people ?

Ps. 33 : 12, blessed is the **n.** whose God is the Lord.

105 : 13, went from one **n.** to another.

147 : 20, he hath not dealt so with any **n.**

Prov. 14 : 34, righteousness exalteth a **n.**

Isa. 1 : 4, sinful **n.**

2 : 4; Mic. 4 : 3, **n.** shall not lift sword against **n.**

Isa. 3 : 1, thou hast multiplied the **n.**

26 : 2, that the righteous **n.** may enter in.

40 : 17, all **n.** before him are as nothing.

55 : 5, shalt call a **n.** thou knowest not.

60 : 22, small one become a strong **n.**

66 : 8, shall a **n.** be born at once ?

Jer. 10 : 7, O king of **n.**

27 : 7; Dan. 7 : 14, all **n.** serve him.

Zech. 2 : 11, many **n.** be joined to the Lord.

Matt. 24 : 7; Mark 13 : 8; Luke 21 : 10, **n.** rise against **n.**

Luke 7 : 5, he loveth our **n.**

John 11 : 50, that the whole **n.** perish not.

Acts 2 : 5, devout men out of every **n.**

10 : 35, in every **n.** he that feareth God.

17 : 26, made of one blood all **n.**

Rom. 10 : 19, by a foolish **n.** I will anger you.

Phil. 2 : 15, in midst of a crooked **n.**

1 Pet. 2 : 9, a holy **n.**

Rev. 5 : 9, redeemed out of every **n.**

21 : 24, the **n.** who are saved.

Native, Jer. 22 : 10.

Nativity, Ezek. 16 : 3, 4; 21 : 30; 23 : 15.

Natural, Deut. 34 : 7; Rom. 1 : 31; 1 Cor. 2 : 14; 15 : 44; 2 Tim. 3 : 3; Jas. 1 : 23.

Nature, Rom. 2 : 14, do by **n.** the things in the law.

11 : 24, olive tree which is wild by **n.**

1 Cor. 11 : 14, doth not **n.** teach you ?

Gal. 4 : 8, which by **n.** are no gods.

Eph. 2 : 3, by **n.** the children of wrath.

Heb. 2 : 16, took not the **n.** of angels.

Jas. 3 : 6, the course of **n.**

2 Pet. 1 : 4, partakers of the divine **n.**

Naught, 2 Ki. 2 : 19, water **n.**, and the ground barren.

Prov. 20 : 14, is it **n.**, saith the buyer.

See **Nought.**

Naughtiness, 1 Sam. 17 : 28, the **n.** of thy heart.

Prov. 11 : 6, taken in their own **n.**

Jas. 1 : 21, all superfluity of **n.**

Naughty, Prov. 6 : 12; 17 : 4.

[ar.], worthless, Jer. 24 : 2.

Navel, Prov. 3 : 8; Song of Sol. 7 : 2.

Naves, 1 Ki. 7 : 33.

Navy, of Solomon, 1 Ki. 9 : 26; 2 Chr. 8 : 17, f.; of Jehoshaphat, 1 Ki. 22 : 48.

Nay, Matt. 5 : 37; Jas. 5 : 12, let your communication be, N., **n.**

Rom. 3 : 27, **n.**; but by the law of faith.

9 : 20, **n.** but, O man, who art thou ?

2 Cor. 1 : 18, our word was not yea and **n.**

Nazarene (năz-ă-rēne) [man of Nazareth], Matt. 2 : 23; Acts 24 : 5.

Nazareth (năz-ă-rĕth) [twig, brushwood], a town of Galilee where Christ spent His early years, and where He afterwards preached. The town Nazareth is not mentioned in the Old Testament. In Isa. 11 : 1; 14 : 19, however, it is connected with the word rendered " branch." Arising from the obscurity of Old Testament times, it sank again on the death of Christ, into obscurity. Later it was a centre of pilgrimage, and under the Crusaders became a bishopric. The population has been estimated as 6000.

See Matt. 2 : 23; 21 : 11; Luke 1 : 26; 2 : 39, 51; 4 : 16; John 1 : 45; 18 : 5; Acts 2 : 22; 3 : 6.

Nazarites, law of the, Num. 6. More correctly, **Nazirites.**

Near, Gen. 19 : 20, this city is **n.** to flee to.

Judg. 20 : 34, knew not evil was **n.**

Ps. 22 : 11, trouble is **n.**

Prov. 27 : 10, better a neighbour that is **n.**

Isa. 55 : 6, call upon the Lord while he is **n.**

Obad. 15; Zep. 1 : 14, the day of the Lord is **n.**

Matt. 24 : 33, it is **n.**, even at the doors.

13 : 28, ye know that summer is **n.**

Rom. 13 : 11, our salvation is **n.**

Heb. 10 : 22, draw **n.** with a true heart.

Nebai (nē-bā-ī), Neh. 10 : 19.

Nebaioth (nē-bāī-ōth) [heights], Isa. 60 : 7.

Nebajoth (nē-bā-jōth), Gen. 25 : 13. See **Nebaioth.**

Nazareth.

Neballat (nĕ-băl-lăt) [secret wickedness], Neh. 11 : 34.

Nebat (nĕ-băt) [a look], 1 Ki. 11 : 26.

Nebatiyeh, a village in Beirut.

Nebel, musical instrument. See **Musical Instruments.**

Nebo (nĕ-bō) [speaker], the planet Mercury, worshipped by Babylonians, Isa. 46 : 1.
mountain in the land of Moab and scene of Moses' death, Deut. 32 : 49.

Nebuchadnezzar (nĕb-ū-chăd-nĕz-zär) [Baby.-Assyr., " Nabû-kudurri-usur "; Nebo protect my landmark], also **Nebuchadrezzar** (Jer. 25 · 9), variously spelled in Hebrew; king of Babylon, Jer. 20; 21; 25; 27; 28; 32; 34; Ezek. 26 : 7; 29 : 19. He was king of Babylon from 604 to 561 B.C., and under him that land reached the zenith of her power. He conquered Palestine (596) and carried captive King Jehoiachin and the nobles, and later (586) destroyed Jerusalem and the Temple and scattered the people.
captures Jerusalem, 2 Ki. 24; 25; 2 Chr. 36; Jer. 37–39; 52; Dan. 1 : 1.
his dreams, Dan. 2 : 4.
sets up the golden image, Dan. 3.
his degradation, Dan. 4 : 33.
his restoration and confession, Dan. 4 : 34.

Nebuzar-adan (nĕb-ū-zär-ăd-ăn) [Bab., "Nabû-zĕra-iddina "; Nebo has given seed], 2 Ki. 25 : 8. Captain of the Chaldeans, he showed kindness towards Jeremiah (Jer. 39 : 11; 40 : 1).

Necessary, Job 23 : 12, his words more than n. food.
Acts 15 : 28; 28 : 10, n. things.
Titus 3 : 14, good works for n. uses.

Heb. 9 : 23, it was n. patterns should be purified.

Necessity, Luke 23 : 17, of n. he must release one.
Acts 20 : 34, ministered unto my n.
Rom. 12 : 13, distributing to n. of saints.
1 Cor. 9 : 16, n. is laid upon me.
2 Cor. 6 : 4, in afflictions, in n.
9 : 7; Philem. 14, give not as of n.
2 Cor. 12 : 10, reproaches, in n.
Heb. 9 : 16, there must of n. be death of testator.

Nechiloth may be a general name for wind instruments, as " neginoth " is for stringed instruments.

Necho (nĕ-chō) [Egyptian " Neka-û "], 2 Chr. 35 : 20, 22.

Neck, Prov. 3 : 3; 6 : 21, bind them about thy n.
Matt. 18 : 6; Mark 9 : 42; Luke 17 : 2, a millstone about his n.
Luke 15 : 20; Acts 20 : 37, fell on his n.
Acts 15 : 10, yoke on n. of the disciples.

Necromancer, Deut. 18 : 11.

Need, Deut. 15 : 8, lend sufficient for his n.
Prov. 31 : 11, he shall have no n. of spoil.
Matt. 6 : 8; Luke 12 : 30, what things ye have n. of.
Matt. 26 : 65; Mark 14 : 63; Luke 22 : 71, what further n. of witnesses ?
John 13 : 29, buy things we have n. of.
Acts 2 : 45; 4 : 35, as every man had n.
1 Cor. 12 : 21, cannot say, I have no n. of thee.
Phil. 4 : 12, to abound and to suffer n.
4 : 19, God shall supply all your n.
Heb. 4 : 16, grace to help in time of n.
5 : 12, ye have n. that one teach you.
7 : 11, what n. that another priest rise ?
1 John 3 : 17, seeth his brother have n.
Rev. 3 : 17, rich, and have n. of nothing.
21 : 23, city had no n. of the sun.
Matt. 9 : 12; Mark 2 : 17; Luke 5 : 31, whole n. not a physician.
Matt. 14 : 16, they n. not depart.
Luke 15 : 7, just persons, which n. no repentance.
2 Cor. 3 : 1, n. we epistles of commendation ?
2 Tim. 2 : 15, workman that n. not to be ashamed.
Rev. 22 : 5, they n. no candle.

Needful, Luke 10 : 42, one thing is n.
Jas. 2 : 16, things n. to the body.

Needle, Matt. 19 : 24; Mark 10 : 25.

Needlework, Ex. 26 : 36; Judg. 5 : 30; Ps. 45 : 14.

Needy, Deut. 15 : 11, open thy hand to the n.
Job 24 : 4, they turn the n. out of the way.
Ps. 9 : 18, the n. shall not always be forgotten.
40 : 17; 70 : 5; 86 : 1; 109 : 22, I am poor and n.
72 : 13, he shall spare the poor and n.
113 : 7, he lifteth the n.
Prov. 31 : 9, plead the cause of the poor and n.
Isa. 25 : 4, been a strength to the n.
Jer. 22 : 16, he judgeth cause of the n.

Neesings [ar.], sneezing, Job 41 : 18.

Neginah (nĕ-gĭ-näh), Ps. 61, title. Singular of **Neginoth.**

Neginoth (nĕ-gĭ⸗nōth) occurs in the titles of Ps. 4; 6; 54; 55; 67; 76. It is a general name for stringed instruments (cf. Hab. 3 : 19; Isa. 38 : 20; Ps. 77 : 7; Job 30 : 9).

Neglect, Matt. 18 : 17, if he shall n. to hear.
1 Tim. 4 : 14, n. not the gift in thee.
Heb. 2 : 3, how escape, if we n. so great salvation ?

Negligent, 2 Chr. 29 : 11; 2 Pet. 1 : 12.

Nehemiah (nē-hĕ-mĭ⸗ăh) [Jah comforts], his grief and prayer for Jerusalem, Neh. 1; his visit, Neh. 2 : 9; his conduct there, Neh. 4–6; 8–10; 13.

Nehemiah, Book of. See Ezra and Nehemiah, Books of.

Nehiloth (nĕ-hĭl⸗ōth), Ps. 5, title. Denotes perforated wind instruments.

Nehushtan (nĕ-hŭsh⸗tăn) [brazen], the brazen serpent, destroyed by Hezekiah, 2 Ki. 18 : 4.

Neighbour. Christ summed up the whole Law in Matt. 22 : 38 f. The man who has a right love for God and a proper self-love must equally show love for his neighbour. The last is conditioned, however, by the two first. To love one's neighbour as oneself, note, implies, a true self-love also.
duty towards one's, Ex. 22 : 26; Lev. 19 : 18; Deut. 15 : 2; 27 : 17; Prov. 3 : 28; 24 : 28; 25 : 8, 17; Mark 12 : 31; Rom. 13 : 9; Gal. 5 : 14; Jas. 2 : 8.
Ex. 20 : 16, not bear false witness against thy n.
Ps. 15 : 3, doeth evil to his n.
Prov. 14 : 20, the poor is hated even of his n.
27 : 10, better is a n. near, than a brother far off.
Eccl. 4 : 4, a man is envied of his n.
Jer. 22 : 13, useth his n. service without wages.
31 : 34; Heb. 8 : 11, teach no more every one his n.
Hab. 2 : 15, that giveth his n. drink.
Zech. 8 : 16; Eph. 4 : 25, speak every man truth to his n.
Matt. 19 : 19; 22 : 39, thou shalt love thy n. as thyself.
Mark 12 : 33, to love his n. as himself.
Luke 10 : 29, who is my n. ?
Rom. 13 : 10, love worketh no ill to his n.
15 : 2, every one please his n.

Neighed, Jer. 5 : 8.

Neighing, Jer. 8 : 16; 13 : 27.

Nekeb (nē⸗kĕb) [cavern], a place south-west of the water of Galilee, Josh. 19 : 33.

Nekoda (nĕ-kō⸗dă), Ezra 2 : 48, 60; Neh. 7 : 50.

Nemuel (nĕm⸗ū-ĕl) [day of God], Num. 26 : 9; 1 Chr. 4 : 24.

Nepheg (nēph⸗ĕg), Ex. 6 : 21; 2 Sam. 5 : 15.

Nephew [ar.], grandchild, Job 18 : 19; Judg. 12 : 14; 1 Tim. 5 : 4.

Nephishesim (nĕ-phĭsh⸗ĕ-sĭm), Neh. 7 : 52.

Nephthalim (nĕph⸗thă-lĭm), Matt. 4 : 13, 15; Rev. 7 : 6.

Nephtoah (nĕph-tō⸗ăh) [opened], Josh. 15 : 9; 18 : 15.

Nephusim (nĕ-phū⸗sĭm), Ezra 2 : 50.

Ner (nĕr) [lamp], 1 Sam. 14 : 50; 1 Chr. 8 : 33.

Nereus (nē⸗rēŭs), a Greek name, Rom. 16 : 15.

Nergal (nĕr⸗găl), 2 Ki. 17 : 30.

Nergal-sharezer (nĕr⸗găl-shă-rē⸗zĕr), Jer. 39 : 3, 13.

Neri (nē⸗rī), Luke 3 : 27. See Neriah.

Neriah (nē-rī⸗ăh) [my light is Jah], Jer. 32 : 12.

Nero, Roman emperor. A comparatively young man when he died (in A.D. 68, in his thirty-first year), he instituted a persecution against Christians.

Nest, Num. 24 : 21, thou puttest thy n. in a rock.
Deut. 32 : 11, as an eagle stirreth up her n.
Job 29 : 18, I shall die in my n.
Ps. 84 : 3, the swallow hath found a n.
Prov. 27 : 8, as a bird that wandereth from her n.
Matt. 8 : 20; Luke 9 : 58, birds of the air have n.

Net, Ps. 25 : 15; 31 : 4, shall pluck my feet out of n.
66 : 11, thou broughtest us into n.
Prov. 1 : 17, in vain the n. is spread.
Eccl. 9 : 12, as fishes taken into an evil n.
Mic. 7 : 2, hunt his brother with a n.
Matt. 4 : 18; Mark 1 : 16, casting n. into sea.
Matt. 13 : 47, kingdom of heaven like a n.
Mark 1 : 18, they forsook their n.
Luke 5 : 5, I will let down the n.
John 21 : 11, drew the n. to land.

Nether, Ex. 19 : 17; Deut. 24 : 6; Ezek. 31 : 14, 16, 18.

Nethermost, 1 Ki. 6 : 6.

Nettles (1) Isa. 34 : 13; Hos. 9 : 6; Prov. 24 : 31, the stinging nettle or " thorns."
(2) Prov. 24 : 31, R.V. margin, " wild vetches." Prov. 24 : 31 has both words.

Network, Ex. 27 : 4; Isa. 19 : 9.

Never, Matt. 7 : 23; Mark 14 : 21; John 7 : 46; 1 Cor. 13 : 8; Heb. 13 : 5.

Nevertheless, Matt. 26 : 39; 2 Tim. 1 : 12; Rev. 2 : 4.

New, Num. 16 : 30, if Lord make a n. thing.
Job 32 : 19, like n. bottles.
Ps. 33 : 3; 96 : 1; 98 : 1; 149 : 1; Isa. 42 : 10, sing to the Lord a n. song.
Eccl. 1 : 9, no n. thing under the sun.
Isa. 42 : 9; 48 : 6, n. things I declare.
62 : 2, called by a n. name.
65 : 17; 66 : 22, create n. heavens, n. earth.
Lam. 3 : 23, Lord's mercies are n. every morning.
Matt. 9 : 16; Mark 2 : 21; Luke 5 : 36, n. cloth to old garment.
Matt. 13 : 52, things n. and old.
Mark 1 : 27; Acts 17 : 19, what n. doctrine is this ?
John 13 : 34, n. commandment I give unto you.
Acts 17 : 21, to tell or hear some n. thing.
2 Cor. 3 : 6, able ministers of n. testament.
5 : 17; Gal. 6 : 15, a n. creature.
Eph. 4 : 24; Col. 3 : 10, put on the n. man.
Heb. 10 : 20, a n. and living way.
1 Pet. 2 : 2, as n.-born babes, desire milk of the word.
Rev. 2 : 17; 3 : 12, a n. name.
21 : 5, I make all things n.

New birth, John 3 : 3, 6; 1 Pet. 1 : 23.

New Moon, Festival of. In the Reformation of the seventh century, B.C., and in Post-

Exilic days, this was probably heralded on the first day of the month by the blowing of trumpets and the celebration of burnt-offerings and peace-offerings (Num. 10 : 10). How it was first instituted among the early local sanctuaries we do not know.

New Testament.
miracles. See **Miracles.**
parables. See **Parables.**
versions. See **Versions.**

Newly, Deut. 32 : 17; Judg. 7 : 19.

Newness, Rom. 6 : 4; 7 : 6.

News, Prov. 25 : 25, good n. from a far country.

Next, Ex. 12 : 4; Esther 10 : 3; Mark 1 : 38; John 1 : 29; Acts 4 : 3.

Nicanor (nĭ-cā-nôr) [conqueror], one of the seven deacons, Acts 6 : 5.

Nicodemus (nĭc-ŏ-dē-́mŭs) [victory of the people], visits Jesus by night, John 3 : 1.
defends him before the Pharisees, John 7 : 50.
assists at Christ's burial, John 19 : 39.

Nicolaitanes (nĭc-ō-lā-ĭ-tān(e)ŝ) [followers of Nicolas], their doctrines condemned, Rev. 2 : 6, 15.

Nicolas (nĭc-́ŏ-lăs) [conquering the people], Acts 6 : 5.

Niger (nī-́gĕr) [black], Latin name, Acts 13 : 1.

Nigh, Deut. 30 : 14; Rom. 10 : 8, the word is n. thee.
Ps. 34 : 18, Lord is n. to them of broken heart.
85 : 9, his salvation n. them that fear him.
145 : 8, Lord is n. unto all them that call upon him.
Joel 2 : 1, day of the Lord is n. at hand.
Eph. 2 : 13, made n. by the blood of Christ.
Heb. 6 : 8, is n. unto cursing.

Night, Gen. 1 : 5, the darkness God called N.
Ex. 12 : 42, a n. to be much observed.
Job 7 : 4, when shall the n. be gone ?
Ps. 19 : 2, n. unto n. sheweth knowledge.
30 : 5, weeping may endure for a n.
136 : 9, moon to rule by n.
139 : 11, the n. shall be light about me.
Isa. 21 : 11, watchman, what of the n. ?
Jonah 4 : 10, came up in a n., perished in a n.
Luke 6 : 12, he continued all n. in prayer.
12 : 20, this n. thy soul shall be required.
John 9 : 4, the n. cometh, when no man can work.
11 : 10, if a man walk in the n., he stumbleth.
Rom. 13 : 12, the n. is far spent.
1 Cor. 11 : 23, the same n. he was betrayed.
1 Thess. 5 : 2; 2 Pet. 3 : 10, cometh as a thief in the n.
Rev. 21 : 25; 22 : 5, shall be no n. there.

Night hawk, Lev. 11 : 16; Deut. 14 : 15, was perhaps the night jar, several species of which are found in Palestine.

Night watches, Ps. 63 : 6; 119 : 148.

Nile [blue], a celebrated river of Egypt, referred to as " Sihor " in Isa. 23 : 3; Jer. 2 : 18; and in Gen. 41 : 1, " the river."

Nimrod (nĭm-́rŏd) [upstart ?], mighty hunter, Gen. 10 : 9; 1 Chr. 1 : 10.

Nine, Luke 17 : 17, where are the n. ?

Ninety, Matt. 18 : 12, 13; Luke 15 : 4, 7, n. and nine.

Nineveh (nĭn-́ĕ-vēh) [Assyrian, "Ninaa, Ninua"], one of the oldest and largest cities of the

Drawing water from the Nile.

world, situated on the left bank of the Tigris; Jonah's mission to, Jonah 1 : 1; 3 : 2.
repenting, is spared by God, Jonah 3 : 5-10; (Matt. 12 : 41; Luke 11 : 32).
the burden of, Nah. 1 : 1; 2 : 8 (cf. Gen. 10 : 11).

Ninth hour, Matt. 20 : 5; 27 : 45 f.; Mark 15 : 33 f.; Acts 10 : 3.

Nisan (nī-́săn) [Assyr.-Bab., " Nisannu "; flower month], April, Neh. 2 : 1; Esther 3 : 7. See **Months.**

Nisroch (nĭs-́rŏch), idol of Ninevites, 2 Ki. 19 : 37; Isa. 37 : 38.

Nitre. In tropical countries, where there are underlying strata of volcanic origin, carbonate of soda or nitre is produced from lakes and rivers, Prov. 25 : 20; Jer. 2 : 22.

No [city] (**No-Amod**), the Egyptian Thebes, prophecy concerning, Jer. 46 : 25; Ezek. 30 : 14; Nah. 3 : 8.

Noah (nō-́ăh) [rest], son of Lamech, Gen. 5 : 29.
finds grace with God, Gen. 6 : 8.
builds the ark, Gen. 6 : 14; enters it, Gen. 7; goes forth from it, Gen. 8 : 18.
God makes a covenant with, Gen. 9 : 1, 8.
is drunken, Gen. 9 : 21.
his death, Gen. 9 : 29.

Winged Lion from Nineveh.

[movement], daughter of Zelophehad, Num. 26 : 33; 27 : 1.

Nob (nŏb) [height], city of, David comes to, 1 Sam. 21 : 1.

smitten by Saul, 1 Sam. 22 : 19.

Noble, Neh. 3 : 5, the **n.** put not their necks to work.

Job 29 : 10, the **n.** held their peace.

Isa. 43 : 14, brought down all the **n.**

Jer. 2 : 21, a **n.** vine.

Acts 17 : 11, Bereans were more **n.**

1 Cor. 1 : 26, not many **n.** are called.

Nobleman, Luke 19 : 12; John 4 : 46, 49.

Nobles, Neh. 5 : 7; Esther 1 : 3; Jer. 14 : 3; Nah. 3 : 18.

Nod (nŏd) [flight, exile], Gen. 4 : 16.

Noe (nō-ē), Matt. 24 : 37, 38; Luke 3 : 36. See **Noah.**

Noise, Ps. 66 : 1; 81 : 1; 95 : 1; 98 : 4; 100 : 1, make a joyful **n.**

93 : 4, Lord mightier than **n.** of waters.

2 Pet. 3 : 10, heavens pass away with great **n.** See Mark 2 : 1; Acts 2 : 6.

Noisome [strongly offensive to the senses], Ps. 91 : 3, deliver thee from **n.** pestilence.

Rev. 16 : 2, a **n.** and grievous sore.

None to save, 2 Sam. 22 : 42; Ps. 18 : 41.

Noonday, Deut. 28 : 29; Job 11 : 17; Ps. 91 : 6.

Noontide, Jer. 20 : 16.

Noph (nŏph) (**Moph**) [Egyptian for " Memphis "], city warned, Isa. 19 : 13; Jer. 2 : 16; 46 : 14; Ezek. 30 : 13.

North and south, conflicts of, Dan. 11.

Northern, Jer. 15 : 12; Joel 2 : 20.

Northward, Gen. 13 : 14; Deut. 2 : 3.

Nose. A man with a " flat " or " slit " nose could not make an offering (Lev. 21 : 18). It is the organ of breath which gives life (Gen. 2 : 7). Since it is easy to stop the breath and to expirate it, the figure is called up of the brevity of life (Isa. 2 : 22). Anger led to excited breathing and a distention of the nostrils, and explains the figurative use of "nose" as wrath (Gen. 27 : 45). The Romans considered it the mark of culture to possess a fine nose, and of an intelligent man they would say " nasum habet " (he has a nose).

Assyrian God Nisroch.

2 Ki. 19 : 28; Isa. 37 : 29, put my hook in thy **n.**

Ps. 115 : 6, **n.** have they, but smell not.

Prov. 30 : 33, the wringing of the **n.**

Isa. 3 : 21, the **n.** jewels.

Nostrils, Gen. 2 : 7, into his **n.** the breath of life.

Isa. 2 : 22, whose breath is in his **n.**

Notable, Matt. 27 : 16, a **n.** prisoner.

Acts 2 : 20, before **n.** day of Lord come.

4 : 16, a **n.** miracle hath been done.

Note, Isa. 30 : 8; Dan. 10 : 21; 2 Thess. 3 : 14; Rom. 16 : 7.

Nothing, Ex. 16 : 18; 2 Cor. 8 : 15, gathered much had **n.** over.

2 Sam. 24 : 24, neither offer of that which costs **n.**

2 Chr. 14 : 11, it is **n.** with thee to help.

Neh. 8 : 10, portions to them for whom **n.** is prepared.

Job 8 : 9, we are of yesterday, and know **n.**

34 : 9, it profiteth a man **n.**

Ps. 39 : 5, mine age is as **n.** before thee.

49 : 17, dieth, he shall carry **n.** away.

119 : 165, **n.** shall offend them.

Prov. 13 : 4, the sluggard desireth, and hath **n.**

13 : 7, that maketh himself rich, yet hath **n.**

Eccl. 5 : 15, he shall take **n.** of his labour.

Isa. 40 : 17, all nations before him are as **n.**

Lam. 1 : 12, is it **n.** to you ?

Dan. 4 : 35, inhabitants of earth as **n.**

Matt. 17 : 20; Luke 1 : 37, **n.** shall be impossible.

Matt. 21 : 19; Mark 11 : 13, **n.** but leaves.

Luke 7 : 42, they had **n.** to pay.

23 : 41, this man hath done **n.** amiss.

John 14 : 30, prince of this world hath **n.** in me.

15 : 5, without me ye can do **n.**

1 Cor. 1 : 19, bring to **n.** the understanding of prudent.

4 : 5, judge **n.** before the time.

2 Cor. 6 : 10, having **n.**, yet possessing all things.

13 : 8, can do **n.** against the truth.

Gal. 5 : 2, Christ shall profit you **n.**

1 Tim. 4 : 4, **n.** to be refused.

6 : 7, we brought **n.** into this world.

Heb. 7 : 19, the law made **n.** perfect.

Jas. 1 : 4, perfect and entire, wanting **n.**

Notice, 2 Sam. 3 : 36; 2 Cor. 9 : 5.

Notwithstanding, Luke 10 : 11, 20; 1 Tim. 2 : 15.

Nought, Prov. 1 : 25, set at **n.** my counsel.

Isa. 49 : 4, spent strength for **n.**

52 : 3, ye have sold yourselves for **n.**

Acts 4 : 11, stone which was set at **n.**

5 : 38, it will come to **n.**

Rom. 14 : 10, why set at **n.** thy brother ?

1 Cor. 1 : 28, to bring to **n.** things that are.

Rev. 18 : 17, riches is come to **n.**

Nourish, Isa. 1 : 2, **n.** and brought up children.

Acts 12 : 20, was **n.** by the king's country.

1 Tim. 4 : 6, in words of faith.

Jas. 5 : 5, have **n.** your hearts.

Nourisher, Ruth 4 : 15.

Nourishment, Col. 2 : 19.

Novice, one newly received into the church, 1 Tim. 3 : 6.

Now, Luke 14 : 17; John 13 : 7; 16 : 12; 1 Cor. 13 : 12.

Number (noun), Job 5 : 9; 9 : 10, things without **n.**

Ps. 139 : 18, more in **n.** than the sand.

147 : 4, he telleth the **n.** of the stars.

Isa. 40 : 26, bringeth out their hosts by **n.**

Hos. 1 : 10; Rom. 9 : 27, **n.** of Israel shall be as the sand.

John 6 : 10, men sat down, in **n.** about five thousand.

Acts 6 : 1, **n.** of disciples was multiplied.

16 : 5, the churches increased in **n.**

2 Cor. 10 : 12, not make ourselves of the **n.**

Rev. 13 : 17, the **n.** of his name.

(verb), Gen. 13 : 16, if a man can **n.** the dust.

15 : 5, tell stars, if able to **n.** them.

2 Sam. 24 : 2; 1 Chr. 21 : 2, **n.** the people.

Job 38 : 37, who can **n.** the clouds ?

Ps. 40 : 5, more than can be **n.**

90 : 12, so teach us to **n.** our days.

Eccl. 1 : 15, that which is wanting cannot be **n.**

Isa. 53 : 12; Mark 15 : 28, he was **n.** with the transgressors.

Matt. 10 : 30; Luke 12 : 7, hairs of head are all **n.**

Acts 1 : 17, he was **n.** with us.

Rev. 7 : 9, a multitude which no man could **n.**

Numbering, of the people, by Moses, Num. 1 : 26; by David, 2 Sam. 24; 1 Chr. 21.

of the Levites, Num. 3 : 14; 4 : 34.

Numbers, Book of.

This, the fourth book of the Pentateuch, is among the most dramatic and forceful of the O.T. writings. Moses is confronted with a murmuring host crying for flesh to eat. The quails are sent in overwhelming abundance. Miriam and Aaron murmur, and Miriam becomes leprous. Korah, Dathan and Abiram murmur, and the earth swallows them up. Jealousy against the priestly position of the tribe of Levi is finally set at rest by the test of the twelve rods in which Aaron's rod for Levi puts forth buds. Again the people speak against Moses and against God, and are punished by the serpents. The brazen serpent here becomes the distinguished type that is the basis of John 3 : 14. Balaam, hired by Balak to curse Israel, gives utterance to many of the most significant and glowing prophecies of Israel's worldwide dominion. Two numberings of the people are given in chapters 1, 3, 4 and 26. In connection with the first, there was the organization of the camp, ch. 2, and the division of labour among the Levites, chs. 4, 7. The sons of Levi were Gershon, Kohath, Merari. One of the sons of Kohath was Amram the father of Moses and Aaron. To Aaron and his sons was committed the priesthood. The other descendants of Kohath had charge of the furniture of the Tabernacle and carried it upon their shoulders when on the march. The sons of Gershon carried the draperies and cords of the sanctuary with the aid of two wagons and four oxen. The sons of Merari carried the boards, bars, sockets and pins, aided by four wagons and eight oxen.

Nun (nŭn) [fish], Ex. 33 : 11; Num. 27 : 18.

Nurse, Ex. 2 : 7, a **n.,** that she may **n.** the child.

Isa. 60 : 4, daughters shall be **n.** at thy side.

1 Thess. 2 : 7, as a **n.** cherisheth her children.

See Gen. 35 : 8; 2 Sam. 4 : 4; 1 Thess. 2 : 7.

Nursing, Num. 11 : 12; Isa. 49 : 23.

Nurture, Eph. 6 : 4, in the **n.** of the Lord.

Nuts, of the pistachio variety, were among the presents of Joseph, Gen. 43 : 11. In Song of Sol. 6 : 11, the walnut is intended.

O

Oak, 1 Chr. 10 : 12; Isa. 2 : 13; Zech. 11 : 2. Various species, such as the evergreen oak, are implied, and oak forests in the early settlement in Israel were probably extensive. There are six Hebrew words thus translated, one of which refers to the teil tree or terebinth. See **Elm, Teil.**

Oar, Isa. 33 : 21; Ezek. 27 : 6, 29.

Oaths, God ratifies his purpose by, Ps. 132 : 11; Acts 2 : 30; Heb. 6 : 17.

laws about, Lev. 5 : 4; 6 : 3; 19 : 12; Num. 30 : 2; Ps. 15 : 4; Matt. 5 : 33.

demanded, Ex. 22 : 11; Num. 5 : 21; 1 Ki. 8 : 31; Ezra 10 : 5.

examples of, Gen. 14 : 22; 21 : 31; 24 : 2; Josh. 14 : 9; 1 Sam. 20 : 42; 28 : 10; Ps. 132 : 2.

rash, of Esau, Gen. 25 : 33; of Israel to the Gibeonites, Josh. 9 : 19; of Jephthah, Judg. 11 : 30; of Saul at Bethaven, 1 Sam. 14 : 24; of Herod to Herodias' daughter, Matt. 14 : 7; of the forty Jews, Acts 23 : 12, 21.

1 Sam. 14 : 26, people feared the **o.**

Eccl. 9 : 2, as he that feareth an **o.**

Luke 1 : 73, the **o.** which he sware.

Heb. 6 : 16, an **o.** for confirmation.

Jas. 5 : 12, swear not by earth, nor other **o.**

Obadiah (ō-bă-dī-äh) [servant of Jah], sent by Ahab to find water, 1 Ki. 18 : 3; meets Elijah, 1 Ki. 18 : 7.

hides a hundred prophets, 1 Ki. 18 : 4, 13.

prophet, his prediction, Obad. 17.

thirteen of name.

Obadiah, Book of.

The shortest of the Minor Prophets is placed between Amos and Jonah, thus showing that the Hebrew scribes gave to it an early date. From the evidence of verses 11 and 12, it would seem that the captivity of Judah by Chaldea had occurred, and that therefore the date, 587 B.C., assigned by Ussher, is not far from correct. Obadiah is concerned with the sins of Edom and the doom that is to follow them. Esau or Edom was brother of Jacob. The Edomites gave aid to the enemies of Israel, refused asylum to Jewish fugitives and gloated over their calamities. The prophet says, " Thy dealing shall return upon thine own head " (15, R.V.). The last five verses contain a glimpse of the deliverance that shall come to Zion and have its complete fulfilment in the last days : " And saviours shall come up on mount Zion to judge the mount of Esau; and the kingdom shall be the Lord's."

Obed (ō-bĕd) [worshipper, servant], son of Boaz, Ruth 4 : 17; Matt. 1 : 5; Luke 3 : 32.

Obed-edom (ō-bĕd-ē-dǫm) [servant of Edom], blessed while keeping the ark, 2 Sam. 6 : 10; 1 Chr. 13 : 14; 15 : 18, 24; 16 : 5.
his sons, 1 Chr. 26 : 4, 5.

Obedience, to God, enjoined, Ex. 19 : 5; 23 : 21; Lev. 26 : 3; Deut. 4–8; 11 : 29; Isa. 1 : 19; Jer. 26 : 13; 38 : 20; Jas. 1 : 25.
its blessings, Ex. 23 : 22; Deut. 28 : 10; Isa. 1 : 19; Heb. 11 : 8; Rev. 22 : 14.
preferred before sacrifice, 1 Sam. 15 : 22; Ps. 50 : 8; Mic. 6 : 6.
of Christ, Phil. 2 : 8; Heb. 5 : 8.
of the faith, Rom. 1 : 5; 2 Chr. 7 : 15.
due to parents, Col. 3 : 20.
to masters, Col. 3 : 22; Titus 2 : 9.
of wives to husbands, Titus 2 : 5.
to rulers, Titus 3 : 1.
Rom. 5 : 19; by the o. of one.
16 : 26, for the o. of faith.
2 Cor. 10 : 5, every thought to o. of Christ.
1 Pet. 1 : 2, sanctification of the Spirit to o.

Obedient, Ex. 24 : 7, all will we do, and be o.
Deut. 4 : 30, be o. to voice of Lord.
Prov. 25 : 12, wise reprover upon an o. ear.
Isa. 1 : 19, if o. ye shall eat good of land.
Acts 6 : 7, priests were o. to the faith.
2 Cor. 2 : 9, o. in all things.
Eph. 6 : 5, servants, be o. to your masters.
1 Pet. 1 : 14, as o. children.

Obeisance, Gen. 37 : 7, 9; 2 Chr. 24 : 17.

Obey, Ex. 5 : 2, who is the Lord, that I should o. his voice ?
Deut. 11 : 27, a blessing, if ye o. commandments.
Josh. 24 : 24, Lord's voice will we o.
1 Sam. 15 : 22, to o. is better than sacrifice.
Jer. 7 : 23, o. my voice, and I will be your God.
Zech. 6 : 15, amend ways, and o. voice of the Lord.
Acts 5 : 29, we ought to o. God rather than men.
Rom. 6 : 16, his servants ye are to whom ye o.
Eph. 6 : 1, children, o. your parents in the Lord.
2 Thess. 1 : 8; 1 Pet. 4 : 17, that o. not the gospel.
Heb. 5 : 9, salvation to all that o. him.
13 : 17, o. them that have rule over you.
1 Pet. 1 : 22, purified souls in o. the truth.
3 : 1, if any o. not the word.

Object, Acts 24 : 19.

Oblations, Lev. 2 : 3.
of the spoil, Num. 31 : 28.

Obscure, Prov. 20 : 20.

Obscurity, Isa. 29 : 18, eyes of blind see out of o.
Isa. 58 : 10, then shall thy light rise in o.

Observation, Luke 17 : 20.

Observe, Gen. 37 : 11, his father o. the saying.
Ps. 107 : 43, whoso is wise, and will o. these things.

119 · 34, o. with whole heart.
Prov. 23 : 26, let thine eyes o. my ways.
Jonah 2 : 8, that o. lying vanities.
Matt. 28 : 20, teaching them to o. all things.
Mark 10 : 20, all these have I o.
Acts 16 : 21, customs not lawful to o.
Gal. 4 : 10, ye o. days.

Observer, Deut. 18 : 10.

Observation, Luke 17 : 20.

Obstinate, Deut. 2 : 30; Isa. 48 : 4.

Obtain, Prov. 8 : 35, shall o. favour of the Lord.
Isa. 35 : 10; 51 : 11, they shall o. joy and gladness.
Luke 20 : 35, worthy to o. that world.
1 Cor. 9 : 24, so run, that ye may o.
1 Thess. 5 : 9; 2 Tim. 2 : 10, to o. salvation.
Heb. 4 : 16, o. mercy, and find grace to help.
11 : 35, might o. a better resurrection.
Jas. 4 : 2, ye desire to have, and cannot o.

Occasion, Gen. 43 : 18, that he may seek o. against us.
2 Sam. 12 : 14, great o. to enemies to blaspheme.
Dan. 6 : 4, sought to find o.
Rom. 7 : 8, sin taking o. by commandment.
14 : 13, an o. to fall in his brother's way.
2 Cor. 5 : 12, give you o. to glory.
11 : 12, cut off o. from which desire o.
1 Tim. 5 : 14, give none o. to the adversary.
1 John 2 : 10, none o. of stumbling.

Occupation, Gen. 46 : 33; Jonah 1 : 8, what is your o.
Acts 18 : 3, by o. they were tentmakers.
19 : 25, with the workmen of like o.

Occupiers, Ezek. 27 : 27.

Occupy, Ezek. 27 : 9; Luke 19 : 13; 1 Cor. 14 : 16.

Occurrent, 1 Ki. 5 : 4.

Odd, Num. 3 : 48.

Odious, Chr. 19 : 6; Prov. 30 : 23.

Odour, John 12 : 3, the o. of the ointment.
Phil. 4 : 18, an o. of a sweet smell.
Rev. 5 : 8, golden vials full of o.

Of, Hag. 2 : 3 (=with); Matt. 4 : 1 (=by); Luke 18 : 3 (=on); Luke 23 : 8 (=for or during); Acts 13 : 29 (=concerning); 1 Cor. 11 : 23 (=from).

Offence, Mount of, the southern peak of the Mount of Olives, in Jerusalem. The idol temple of Solomon gave it its name, 1 Ki. 11 : 1-8.

Offences, to be avoided, Matt. 18 : 7; 1 Cor. 10 : 32.
how to remedy, Matt. 5 : 29; Mark 9 : 43; Rom. 16 : 17.
Christ delivered for our, Rom. 4 : 25.
1 Sam. 25 : 31, this shall be no o.
Eccl. 10 : 4, yielding pacifieth great o.
Isa. 8 : 14; Rom. 9 : 33; 1 Pet. 2 : 8, a rock of o.
Matt. 16 : 23, thou art an o. to me.
Luke 17 : 1, woe to the world because of o.
Acts 24 : 16, a conscience void of o.
Rom. 5 : 15, not as the o., so also is the free gift.
2 Cor. 6 : 3, give none o.
Gal. 5 : 11, then is o. of the cross ceased.
Phil. 1 : 10, without o. till the day of Christ.

Offend, Job 34 : 31, I will not o. any more.

Ps. 119 : 165, nothing shall o. them.
Prov. 18 : 19, a brother o. is harder to be won.
Hab. 1 : 11, he shall pass over and o.
Matt. 13 : 41, gather all things that o.
18 : 16; Mark 9 : 42; Luke 17 : 2, whoso o. one of these.
Matt. 18 : 9; Mark 9 : 47, if thine eye o. thee.
Matt. 26 : 31, be o. because of me.
Rom. 14 : 21, whereby thy brother is o.
Jas. 2 : 10, yet o. in one point.
Offender, 1 Ki. 1 : 21; Isa. 29 : 21; Acts 25 : 11.
Offer, Ex. 22 : 29, to o. the first of thy ripe fruits.
Judg. 5 : 2, people willingly o. themselves.
Ps. 50 : 23, whoso o. praise.
116 : 17, o. sacrifice of thanksgiving.
Matt. 5 : 24, then come and o. thy gift.
8 : 4, o. the gift that Moses commanded.
Luke 6 : 29, one cheek, o. also the other.
Phil. 2 : 17, o. in the service of your faith.
2 Tim. 4 : 6, now ready to be o.
Heb. 9 : 28, Christ was once o. to bear the sins of many.
See Mal. 1 : 10; Eph. 5 : 2; Heb. 10 : 18.
Offerings, laws for, Lev. 1; 22 : 21; Deut. 15 : 21; Mal. 1 : 13.
types of Christ, Heb. 9 : 1; 10 : 10.
Office, Gen. 41 : 13, me he restored to o.
1 Sam. 2 : 36, put me into priest's o.
Neh. 13 : 13, their o. was to distribute.
Ps. 109 : 8, let another take his o.
Rom. 11 : 13, I magnify mine o.
1 Tim. 3 : 1, the o. of a bishop.
Heb. 7 : 5, the o. of the priesthood.
Officer, Gen. 37 : 36; 1 Ki. 22 : 9; Matt. 5 : 25.
Offscouring, Lam. 3 : 45, made us as the o.
1 Cor. 4 : 13, the o. of all things unto this day.
Offspring, Acts 17 : 29, we are the o. of God.
Rev. 22 : 16, I am the o. of David.
Oft, 1 Cor. 11 : 25, as o. as ye drink.
Often, Prov. 29 · 1, he that being o. reproved.
Mal. 3 : 16, spake o. one to another.
Matt. 23 : 37; Luke 13 : 34, how o. would I have gathered.
1 Cor. 11 : 26, as o. as ye eat this bread.
2 Cor. 11 : 26, in journeyings o.
1 Tim. 5 : 23, thine o. infirmities.
Heb. 9 : 25, nor offer himself o.
Oftentimes, Luke 8 : 29; John 18 : 2; Rom. 1 : 13; 2 Cor. 8 : 22; Heb. 10 : 11.
Og (ŏg), king of Bashan, Num. 21 : 33; Deut. 3 : 1; Ps. 135 : 11; 136 : 20.
Oil, for the lamps, Ex. 27 : 20; Lev. 24 : 2.
for anointing, Ex. 30 : 31; 37 : 29.
used in meat offerings, Lev. 2 : 1.
miraculously increased, 1 Ki. 17 : 12; 2 Ki. 4 : 1-6.
figurative, Ps. 23 : 5; Isa. 61 : 3; Zech. 4 : 12; Matt. 25 : 1.
Ex. 25 : 6, take o. for the light.
Ps. 45 : 7; Heb. 1 : 9, with o. of gladness.
Ps. 104 : 15, o. to make his face to shine.
141 : 5, an excellent o., which shall not break my head.
Mic. 6 : 7, will the Lord be pleased with rivers of o. ?
Matt. 25 : 3, took no o. with them.
Luke 7 : 46, my head with o. thou didst not anoint.

10 : 34, pouring in o. and wine.
Oil tree, oleaster, wild olive. 1 Ki. 6 : 23, A.V., " olive trees "; A.V., margin, " oily tree "; R.V., " olive wood." Neh. 8 : 15, A.V., " pine branches "; R.V., " wild olive." Isa. 41 : 19, A.V. and R.V., " oil tree "; R.V., margin, " oleaster." The oleaster, common in Palestine, yields an oil and must not be confused with the olive tree.
Ointment, Christ anointed with, Matt. 26 : 7; Luke 7 : 37; John 11 : 2.
Ex. 30 : 25, make oil of holy o.
Ps. 133 : 2, like the precious o.
Prov. 27 : 9, o. and perfume rejoice the heart.
Eccl. 7 : 1, a good name better than o.
Song of Sol. 1 : 3, thy name is as o. poured forth.
Isa. 1 : 6, nor mollified with o.
Mark 14 : 3; John 12 : 3, box of precious o.
Luke 23 : 56, prepared spices and o.
Old, Deut. 8 : 4; 29 : 5; Neh. 9 : 21, thy raiment waxed not o.
Ps. 37 : 25, I have been young and now am o.
71 : 18, when I am o., O God, forsake me not.
Prov. 22 : 6, when o. he will not depart from it.
23 : 10, remove not o. landmark.
Isa. 50 : 9, they shall wax o. as a garment.
58 : 12, build the o. waste places.
65 : 20, child shall die a hundred years o.
Jer. 6 : 16, ask for the o. paths.
Matt. 9 : 17; Mark 2 : 22; Luke 5 : 37, new wine into o. bottles.
John 21 : 18, when thou shalt be o.
1 Cor. 5 : 7, purge out the o. leaven.
2 Cor. 5 : 17, o. things are passed away.
Heb. 8 : 13, hath made the first o.
2 Pet. 2 : 5, if God spared not the o. world.
1 John 2 : 7, the o. commandment is the word.
Old age, Job 30 : 2; Ps. 90 : 10; Eccl. 12; Titus 2 : 2.
reverence due to, Lev. 19 : 32; Prov. 23 : 22; 1 Tim. 5 : 1.
Old man, to put off, Rom. 6 : 6; Eph. 4 : 22; Col. 3 : 9.
Oldness, Rom. 7 : 6.
Old Testament, apocrypha. See **Apocrypha, Old Testament.**
ancient versions. See **Versions.**
English versions. See **Versions, English.**
chronology. See **Chronology, Old Testament.**
languages. See **Languages of the Bible.**
miracles. See **Miracles.**
parables. See **Parables.**
Jewish arrangement of.—This differed from the order observed in our Bibles. There were three parts :—
(1) The Law or Torah, *i.e.*, the Pentateuch or five " books of Moses."
(2) The Prophets—(a) The former prophets (Joshua, Judges, Samuel, Kings).
(b) The latter prophets (Isaiah, Jeremiah, Ezekiel, and the twelve minor prophets).
(3) The Holy Writings or Hagiographa.
—(a) Psalms, Proverbs, Job. (b) Song of Solomon, Ruth, Lamentations, Ecclesiastes, Esther. (c) Daniel, Ezra, Nehemiah,

Chronicles. Another name given to this class was Kethubim or "Writings."

Olive. Originating in South-western Asia, olives and vines were among the discoveries of the Israelites when they entered Canaan. The oil is produced from the fruits, does not easily dry, and can be made to the very end of the extreme age of the tree. At first green, the leaves become silvery white in colour.

trees, vision of, Zech. 4 : 3; Rev. 11 : 4.
yards, Ex. 23 : 11; 1 Sam. 8 : 14; Neh. 9 : 25.

Olive Tree.

Olives, Mount of, or **Olivet** (ŏ-lǐ-vĕt), not a single peak but a range of limestone mountains, east of Jerusalem, which reaches to a height of 2600 feet above sea level, and commands a fine view of the Jordan valley. Its connection with our Lord is famous.

2 Sam. 15 : 30; Matt. 21 : 1; 24 : 3; Mark 11 : 1; 13 : 3; Luke 21 : 37; John 8 : 1; Acts 1 : 12.

Omega (ō-mē-găg), final letter of Greek alphabet, Rev. 1 : 8, 11; 21 . 6; 22 . 13.

Omer (ō-měr), a measure, Ex. 16 . 16, 33, 36. See **Measures.**

Omitted, Matt. 23 : 23.

Omnipotent, Rev. 19 : 6.

Omri (ŏm-rǐ) [my portion is Jah], king of Israel, 1 Ki. 16 : 16, 23; Mic. 6 : 16.

Once, Gen. 18 : 32; Judg. 6 : 39, I will speak but this **o.**

2 Ki. 6 : 10, he saved himself not **o.**
Job 33 : 14; Ps. 62 : 11, God speaks **o.**
Isa. 66 : 8, shall a nation be born at **o.** ?
Rom. 6 : 10, he died unto sin **o.**
7 : 9, I was alive without the law **o.**
Heb. 9 : 26, now **o.** in end of the world.

Jude 3, contend for faith **o.** delivered unto the saints.

One, Gen. 27 : 38, hast thou but **o.** blessing ?
Job 9 : 3; 33 : 23, **o.** of a thousand.
Ps. 89 : 19, help on **o.** that is mighty.
Eccl. 4 : 9, two are better than **o.**
Isa. 27 : 12, ye shall be gathered **o.** by **o.**
Matt. 5 : 18, **o.** jot or **o.** tittle shall in no wise pass from law.
19 : 17; Mark 10 : 18; Luke 18 : 19, none good but **o.**
Mark 10 : 21; Luke 18 : 22, **o.** thing thou lackest.
Luke 10 : 42, **o.** thing is needful.
John 9 : 25, **o.** thing I know.
Eph. 4 : 5, **o.** Lord, **o.** faith, **o.** baptism.
Phil. 3 : 13, this **o.** thing I do.

Onesimus (ō-něs-ǐ-mŭs) [serviceable], Col. 4 : 9; Philem. 10.

Onesiphorus (ō-něs-ǐph-ǒ-rŭs) [bringing gain], 2 Tim. 1 : 16; 4 : 19.

Onion, Num. 11 : 5.

Only, Gen. 22 : 2; Rom. 16 : 27.

Onward, Ex. 40 : 36.

Onycha (ŏn-ȳ-chă), Ex. 30 : 34. This was mixed with various spices and used in the preparation of holy incense. Found with a kind of shell-fish, it is roasted and ground to powder.

Onyx [finger-nail], a precious stone, reddish or brown, overlaid with a translucent bluish-white layer, Ex. 28 : 20; 39 : 13. See **Precious Stones.**

Open, Num. 16 : 30, if the earth **o.** her mouth.
Ps. 49 : 4, I will **o.** my dark saying.
78 : 2, I will **o.** my mouth in a parable.
81 : 10, **o.** thy mouth wide.
104 : 28, thou **o.** thine hand.
118 : 19, **o.** to me the gates of righteousness.
119 : 18, **o.** thou mine eyes.
Prov. 31 : 8, **o.** thy mouth for the dumb.
Isa. 22 : 22, he shall **o.,** and none shall shut.
26 : 2, **o.** gates, that righteous may enter.
42 : 7, to **o.** the blind eyes.
60 : 11, thy gates shall be **o.** continually.
Mal. 3 : 10, **o.** the windows of heaven.
Matt. 25 : 11; Luke 13 : 25, Lord **o.** to us.
Luke 24 : 32, while he **o.** to us the scriptures.
Acts 26 : 18, to **o.** their eyes.
Col. 4 : 3, that God would **o.** to us a door of utterance.
Heb. 4 : 13, all things are **o.** to him.
Rev. 3 : 7, and no man **o.**
5 : 2, who is worthy to **o.** the book ?

Opening, Job 12 : 14; Isa. 61 : 1.

Openly, Matt. 6 : 4, 6, 18, shall reward thee **o.**
John 7 : 4, seeketh to be known **o.**
Acts 16 : 37, have beaten us **o.**

Operation, Ps. 28 : 5, they regard not **o.** of his hands.
Isa. 5 : 12, nor consider **o.** of his hands.
1 Cor. 12 : 6, there are diversities of **o.**
Col. 2 : 12, through faith of the **o.** of God.

Ophir (ō-phír), a country celebrated for its gold and precious stones, Gen. 10 : 29. It is regarded by some as being on the Arabian coast, by others as on the coast of Somaliland, and by others again as part of India, namely, Abhira, at the mouth of the Indus, the Hebrew "tukkiyyim," "peacocks," which came from Ophir, being compared with the Tamil "tōgei." Gen. 10 : 29 would lead us to place it in South Arabia, between Sheba and Havilah, thus supporting the first suggestion.

gold of, 1 Ki. 9 : 28; 10 : 11; 22 : 48; 1 Chr. 29 : 4; 2 Chr. 8 : 18; Job 22 : 24; Ps. 45 : 9; Isa. 13 : 12.

Opinion, 1 Ki. 18 : 21, how long halt ye between two o. ?

Job 32 : 6, durst not show you mine o.

Opportunity, Matt. 26 : 16; Luke 22 : 6, sought o. to betray him.

Gal. 6 : 10, as we have o., let us do good.

Phil. 4 : 10, ye lacked o.

Heb. 11 : 15, had o. to have returned.

Oppose, Job 30 : 21, with strong hand o. thyself.

2 Thess. 2 : 4, o. and exalteth himself.

2 Tim. 2 : 25, instructing those that o. themselves.

Oppositions, 1 Tim. 6 : 20.

Oppress, Ex. 23 : 9, shalt not o. a stranger.

Lev. 25 : 17, ye shall not o. one another.

Deut. 23 : 16, shalt not o. servant.

1 Sam. 12 : 3, whom have I o. ?

Ps. 10 : 18, man of earth no more o.

Prov. 22 : 16, he that o. the poor.

22 : 22, nor o. the afflicted.

Jer. 7 : 6, if ye o. not the stranger.

Hos. 12 : 7, he loveth to o.

Zech. 7 : 10, o. not widow nor fatherless.

Acts 10 : 38, Jesus healed all that were o.

Jas. 2 : 6, do not rich men o. you ?

Oppression, forbidden and threatened, Ex. 22 : 21; Lev. 25 : 14; Deut. 24 : 14; Ps. 12 : 5; Prov. 14 : 31; Eccl. 5 : 8; Isa. 1 : 17; 10; 58 : 6; Jer. 22 : 17; Ezek. 22 : 7; Amos 4 : 1; 8 : 4; Mic. 2 : 2; Mal. 3 : 5; Jas. 4.

Deut. 26 : 7, the Lord looked on our o.

Job 36 : 15, openeth their ears in o.

Ps. 42 : 9; 43 : 2, o. of the enemy.

62 : 10, trust not in o.

119 : 134, deliver me from o. of man.

Eccl. 4 : 1, I considered the o. done.

7 : 7, o. maketh a wise man mad.

Isa. 54 : 14, thou shalt be far from o.

Oppressor, Ps. 72 : 4; Jer. 21 : 12; 22 : 3.

Or ever [ar.], before, Ps. 90 : 2.

Oracle, the holy of holies containing the ark, 1 Ki. 6 : 16; 8 : 6; 2 Chr. 4 : 20.

See 2 Sam. 16 : 23; Ps. 28 : 2.

Oracles, supposed answers or revelations of the gods, and sought in various ways. Jehovah responded through the mysterious media of Urim and Thummim.

"lively oracles," Acts 7 : 38; the communications to Moses at Sinai.

"oracles of God," i.e., the Holy Scriptures, Rom. 3 : 2; Heb. 5 : 12; 1 Pet. 4 : 11.

Oration, Acts 12 : 21.

Orator, Isa. 3 : 3; Acts 24 : 1.

Orchard, Song of Sol. 4 : 13; Eccl. 2 : 5.

Ordain, 1 Chr. 17 : 9, I will o. a place for my people.

Ps. 8 : 2, out of mouth of babes hast thou o. strength.

132 : 17, I have o. a lamp for mine anointed.

Isa. 26 : 12, thou wilt o. peace for us.

30 : 33, Tophet is o. of old.

Jer. 1 : 5, I o. thee a prophet.

Mark 3 : 14, and he o. twelve to be with him.

John 15 : 16, have o. you, that ye should bring forth fruit.

Acts 10 : 42, o. of God to be the judge.

13 : 48, o. to eternal life.

17 : 31, by that man whom he hath o.

Rom. 7 : 10, commandment o. to life.

13 : 1, powers that be are o. of God.

1 Cor. 2 : 7, hidden wisdom God o.

Gal. 3 : 19, the law was o. by angels.

Eph. 2 : 10, good works, which God hath before o.

Heb. 5 : 1; 8 : 3, every high priest is o.

Jude 4, of old o. to this condemnation.

Order, necessary in the churches, 1 Cor. 14 : 40; Titus 1 : 5.

2 Ki. 20 : 1; Isa. 38 : 1, set thine house in o.

Job 10 : 22, a land without o.

23 : 4, would o. my cause.

Ps. 37 : 23, steps of a good man are o. by the Lord.

50 : 21, I will set them in o.

110 : 4; Heb. 5 : 6; 6 : 20; 7 : 11, the o. of Melchizedek.

1 Cor. 15 : 23, every man shall rise in his o.

Orderings, 1 Chr. 24 : 19.

Orderly, Acts 21 : 24.

Ordinance, Ex. 15 : 25, made a statute and an o.

Isa. 58 : 2; Rom. 13 : 2, the o. of God.

Mal. 3 : 7, gone away from mine o.

Eph. 2 : 15, commandments contained in o.

Col. 2 : 14, handwriting of o.

Heb. 9 : 10, in carnal o.

1 Pet. 2 : 13, submit to every o. of man.

Ordinary, Ezek. 16 : 27.

Ordination, mode and use of, Acts 6 : 6; 14 : 23; 1 Tim. 2 : 7; 3; 4 : 14; 5 : 22; 2 Tim. 2 : 2; Titus 1 : 5.

Oreb (ōr′ĕb) [raven], Judg. 7 : 25; Isa. 10 : 26. See Zeeb.

Organ, Gen. 4 : 21; Job 21 : 12; Ps. 150 : 4.

Orion (ō-rī′ŏn) [giant ?], name given to a constellation, Job 9 : 9.

Ornaments, of apparel, etc., Gen. 24 : 22; Prov. 4 : 9; 25 : 12; Isa. 3 : 18; 1 Pet. 3 : 4.

of covering of king of Tyre, Ezek. 28 : 13.

Prov. 1 : 9, an o. of grace to thy head.

Isa. 61 : 10, decketh himself with o.

Jer. 2 : 32, can a maid forget her o. ?

1 Pet. 3 : 4, the o. of a meek and quiet spirit.

Orpah (ôr′păh) [wild goat], Ruth 1 : 4, 14.

Orphans, Lam. 5 : 3.

Osee (ō-sē′ē), New Testament form of "Hosea," Rom. 9 : 25.

Ospray, one of the unclean birds, perhaps the fish-eating eagle which is found in Palestine. Lev. 11 : 13; Deut. 14 : 12.

Ossifrage [bone-breaker], one of the largest of vultures and "unclean," Lev. 11 : 13. It carried small animals, tortoises, bones, up in the air and dropped them, so that, when broken in pieces the portions for food might be reached. Hence the name.

Ostentation condemned, Prov. 25 : 14; 27 : 2; Matt. 6 : 1.

Ostrich was well known to the Jews. A.V. has

"owl," where R.V. reads "ostrich" in Lev. 11 : 16; Deut. 14 : 15; Job 30 : 29; Isa. 13 : 21; 34 : 13; 43 : 20; Jer. 50 : 39; Mic. 1 : 8. Its habits may be gathered from these passages, and from Job 39 : 13-18. Its feathers, speed, and " wailing " cry not unlike that of the jackals are all mentioned. Job 39 : 14 f. gives the popular view that this bird neglects its eggs, but this is true only in so far as meaning that when the nests are full of eggs to be hatched a few further eggs are scattered to be used later as food for the chicks.

Other, Gen. 28 : 17; 1 Sam. 20 : 25; Luke 18 : 11; Acts 4 : 12.

Otherwise, Ps. 38 : 16; Rom. 11 : 6; Gal. 5 : 10; 1 Tim. 6 : 3.

Othniel (ŏth-nĭ-ĕl) [my strength is God], Josh. 15 : 17; Judg. 1 : 13; 3 : 9.

Ouches [ar.], sockets, Ex. 28 : 11; 39 : 6.

Ought, Matt. 5 : 23, if thy brother hath o. against thee.
   23 : 23; Luke 11 : 42, these o. ye to have done.
   Acts 4 : 32, neither said o. was his own.
   5 : 29, we o. to obey God.
   Rom. 8 : 26, what we should pray for as we o.
   Jas. 4 : 15, ye o. to say, If the Lord will.
   2 Pet. 3 : 11, what manner of persons o. ye to be ?

Ours, Mark 12 : 7; Luke 20 : 14, and the inheritance shall be o.
   1 Cor. 1 : 2, Jesus, both theirs and o.
   2 Cor. 1 : 14, ye are o. in day of the Lord.

Ourselves, Heb. 10 : 25; 1 John 1 : 8.

Out, Num. 32 : 23, sin will find you o.
   Matt. 12 : 34, o. of abundance of heart.
   2 Tim. 4 : 2, in season, o. of season.

Outcasts, of Israel, promised restoration, Isa. 11 : 12; 16 : 3; 27 : 13; Rom. 11.
   Ps. 147 : 2, the o. of Israel.
   Jer. 30 : 17, they called thee o.

Outer, Ezek. 10 : 5; Matt. 8 : 12.

Outer Court of Tabernacle. See **Tabernacle.**

Outgoings, Josh. 17 : 18, the o. of it shall be thine.
   Ps. 65 : 8, thou makest o. of morning to rejoice.

Outlandish [ar.], out-of-the-land, foreign, Neh. 13 : 26.

Outlived, Judg. 2 : 7.

Outmost, Num. 34 : 3; Deut. 30 : 4; Isa. 17 : 6.

Outrageous, Prov. 27 : 4.

Outrun, John 20 : 4.

Outside, Judg. 7 : 19; Ezek. 40 : 5; Matt. 23 : 25.

Outstretched, Deut. 26 : 8; Jer. 21 : 5.

Outward, 1 Sam. 16 : 7, man looketh on o. appearance.
   Matt. 23 : 27, appear beautiful o.
   2 Cor. 4 : 16, though our o. man perish.

Outwardly, Matt. 23 : 28; Rom. 2 : 28.

Outwent, Mark 6 : 33.

Oven. (a) The Bowl Oven—consisting of a large clay bowl inverted, has a movable lid. Heated bricks are covered by it, and hold the cakes which are to be baked, while dung is heaped on the outside of the bowl further to heat it.

(b) The Jar Oven—a large jar of earthenware, is heated by placing in the bottom stubble (Mal. 4 : 1), grass (Matt. 6 : 30), dry twigs (1 Ki. 17 : 12), etc. The cakes are applied to the inside walls when the jar is thoroughly heated.

(c) The Pit Oven—is a development of the jar oven, and was built partly in the ground and partly by clay raised above the ground, the whole shaped not unlike a jar and narrowing from the bottom upwards. Most families had a movable oven such as the Bowl or Jar Ovens.
   cf. Ex. 8 : 3; Lev. 26 : 26; Ps. 21 : 9; Hos. 7 : 4.

Over, Num. 27 : 16; Song of Sol. 2 : 11.

Overcharge [ar.], press too heavily upon, Luke 21 : 34; 2 Cor. 2 : 5.

Overcome, Gen. 49 : 19, a troop shall o. him.
   Jer. 23 : 9. a man whom wine hath o.
   Luke 11 : 22, a stronger shall o.
   John 16 : 33, I have o. the world.
   Rom. 12 : 21, be not o. of evil, but o. evil with good.
   1 John 5 : 4, victory that o. the world.
   Rev. 2 : 7, to him that o. will I give to eat of tree of life.

Overcoming, glory and reward of, 1 John 2 : 13; Rev. 2 : 11; 17 : 14; 3 : 5, 12, 21; 21 : 7.

Overdrive, Gen. 33 : 13.

Overflow, Deut. 11 : 4; Josh. 3 : 15; Ps. 69 : 2; Isa. 43 : 2.

Overlaid, Ex. 36 : 34; Heb. 9 : 4.

Overlived, Josh. 24 : 31.

Overmuch, 2 Cor. 2 : 7.

Overpast, Ps. 57 : 1, refuge, until calamities be o.
   Isa. 26 : 20, hide, until indignation be o.

Overplus, Lev. 25 : 27.

Overran, 2 Sam. 18 : 23.

Overrunning, Nah. 1 : 8.

Overseers. in building the temple, 1 Chr. 9 : 29; 2 Chr. 2 : 18.
   2 Chr. 34 : 17, delivered money into hand of o.
   Prov. 6 : 7, the ant having no o.
   Acts 20 : 28, Holy Ghost made you o.

Overshadow, Matt. 17 : 5; Luke 1 : 35; Acts 5 : 15.

Oversight, Gen. 43 : 12, peradventure it was an o.
   Neh. 13 : 4, the o. of the house of God.
   1 Pet. 5 : 2, taking the o., not by constraint.

Overspread, Gen. 9 : 19; Dan. 9 : 27.

Overtake, Deut. 28 : 2, blessings shall come and o. thee.
   Gal. 6 : 1, man be o. in a fault.
   1 Thess. 5 : 4, day should o. you as a thief.

Overthrow, Gen. 19 : 21, I will not o. this city.
   Ex. 23 : 24, thou shalt o. their gods.
   Ps. 140 : 4, purposed to o. my goings.
   Jonah 3 : 4, yet forty days, and Nineveh shall be o.
   Acts 5 : 39, if it be of God, ye cannot o. it.
   2 Tim. 2 : 18, o. the faith of some.

Overturn, Job 12 : 15, sendeth waters, they o. the earth.
   Ezek. 21 : 27, I will o., o., o. it.

Overwhelm, Job 6 : 27, ye o. the fatherless.

Ps. 55 : 5, horror hath o. me.
    61 : 2, when my heart is o.
    77 : 3; 142 : 3; 143 : 4, my spirit was o.
    124 : 4, then the water had o. us.
Overwise, Eccl. 7 : 16.
Owe, Matt. 18 : 28, pay me that thou o.
    Luke 16 : 5, 7, how much o. thou ?
    Rom. 13 : 8, o. no man any thing.
    See Philem. 18, f.
Owl. The most common species of this " un-
    clean " genus was the little bōmeh, with its
    melancholy cry which is set up at twilight.
    It is tame. Next in order comes the Egyp-
    tian eagle-owl, which is almost two feet
    long, and frequents ruins.
    See Lev. 11 : 18; Deut. 14 : 6, and cf. **Ostrich**.
Own, 1 Chr. 29 : 14, of thine o. have we given
    thee.
    Ps. 12 : 4, our lips are our o.
    Matt. 20 : 15, do what I will with mine o.
    John 1 : 11, he came to his o., and his o.
    received him not.
    13 : 1, having loved his o.
    15 : 19, world would love his o.
    1 Cor. 6 : 19, ye are not your o.
    10 : 24, let no man seek his o.
    13 : 5, charity seeketh not her o.
    Phil. 2 : 21, all seek their o. things.
Owner, Eccl. 5 : 13, riches kept for o. to their
    hurt.
    Isa. 1 : 3, the ox knoweth his o.
    Luke 19 : 33, o. said, Why loose ye the colt ?
    Acts 27 : 11, the o. of the ship.
Ox, treatment of, Ex. 21 : 28; 22 : 1; 23 : 4;
    Lev. 17 : 3; Deut. 5 : 14; 22 : 1.
    not to be muzzled when treading out the
    corn, Deut. 25 : 4; 1 Cor. 9 : 9; 1 Tim.
    5 : 18.
    Ex. 20 : 17; Deut. 5 : 21, not covet neigh-
    bour's o.
    1 Sam. 12 : 3, whose o. have I taken ?
    Isa. 11 : 7, lion shall eat straw like o.
    Luke 13 : 15, doth not each loose his o. on
    sabbath.
    14 : 19, bought five yoke of o.
    John 2 : 14, those in temple sold o.
    Acts 14 : 13, priest of Jupiter brought o.
Ozem (ō-zĕm) [angry], 1 Chr. 2 : 15; 2 : 25.
Ozias (ō-zī-ăs), New Testament form of
    " Uzziah," Matt. 1 : 8, 9.
Ozni (ŏz-nĭ), Num. 26 : 16.
Oznites (ŏz-nītes), Num. 26 : 16.

P

Paces, 2 Sam. 6 : 13.
Pacify, Prov. 16 : 14, a wise man p. wrath.
    21 : 14, a gift in secret p. anger.
    Eccl. 10 : 4, yielding p. great offences.
Padan-aram (pā-dăn-âr-ăm) [field of Aram],
    country in Mesopotamia, whither Jacob
    was sent, Gen. 25 : 20; 28 : 2.
Paddle, Deut. 23 : 13.
Padon (pā-dŏn), Ezra 2 : 44; Neh. 7 : 47.
Pagiel (pā-ġĭ-ĕl) [fortune of God], Num. 1 : 13.
Pahath-moab (pā-hăth-mō-ăb) [governor of
    Moab], Ezra 2 : 6; 8 : 4; Neh. 10 : 14.
Pai (pā-ĭ), 1 Chr. 1 : 50.

Pain, Ps. 25 : 18, look on mine affliction and p.
    116 : 3, the p. of hell gat hold upon me.
    Acts 2 : 24, having loosed the p. of death.
    Rom. 8 : 22, the whole creation travaileth
    in p.
    Rev. 21 : 4, neither shall there be any more p.
Painful, Ps. 73 : 16.
Painfulness [ar.], much painstaking, 2 Cor.
    11 : 27.
Painted, 2 Ki. 9 : 30, Jezebel p. her face.
    Jer. 22 : 14, p. with vermilion.
    Ezek. 23 : 40, p. thine eyes.
Painting, Jer. 4 : 30, rentest face with p.
Pair, Amos 2 : 6; Luke 2 : 24; Rev. 6 : 5.
Palace, the temple so called, 1 Chr. 29 : 1; Ps.
    48 : 3; 78 : 69.
    Ezra 4 : 14, maintenance from the p.
    Ps. 45 : 15, shall enter into king's p.
    122 : 7, prosperity within thy p.
    144 : 12, after similitude of a p.
    Isa. 25 : 2, hast made p. of strangers to be no
    city.
    Luke 11 : 21, a strong man keepeth his p.
    Phil. 1 : 13, bonds are manifest in thy p.
Pale, Isa. 29 : 22; Jer. 30 : 6; Rev. 6 : 8.
Palestina (păl-ĕs-tī-nä) or **Palestine** (păl-ĕs-tīne)
    [Heb., " Pelesheth "; wandering], meant
    in Old Testament times Philistia; later it
    included all of Canaan. See Ex. 15 : 14;
    Isa. 14 : 29.
    The name was never applied to Israel in
    the Bible. Such names as " Canaan " (Ps.
    105 : 11), " Israel " (1 Sam. 13 : 19),
    " Judea " (Matt. 19 : 1; Mark 10 : 1) were
    preferred in the pre-monarchic, the mon-
    archic, and the exilic and post-exilic
    periods respectively. It was only at the
    beginning of the Christian Era that the
    name Palestina attached itself to the whole
    land. Down through the Middle Ages and
    even in our own day the commonest name
    has been the " Terra sancta " or " Holy
    Land."
Palestine.
    (1) Limits.—The range of mountains which
    runs parallel to the Mediterranean, south-
    wards from the Taurus to the tongue of
    the Sinaitic peninsula, is bounded by the
    valleys of the Orontes and the Jordan, and
    extends 600 miles, with a mean breadth of
    40 miles, having on the west a narrow
    plain, which gradually broadens into the
    plateau of the desert of Beersheba. This
    region includes three districts : (a) the
    Lebanon, extending 200 miles south to
    Hermon; (b) **Western Palestine**, from Dan
    under Hermon (143 miles) to Beersheba at
    the foot of the Hebron Hills, with an area
    of 6000 square miles; (c) the **Sinaitic
    desert**, descending in steps from the Beer-
    sheba plateau to the granitic group of the
    Sinai mountains.
    (2) Mountains.—The Lebanon (Jebel Libnan,
    Josh. 13 : 6; 1 Ki. 5 : 6; Ps. 29 : 5; Isa.
    14 : 8; Ezra 3 : 7) is a very narrow, rugged
    range of hard limestone, well watered, and
    with good soil near its feet. " Lebanon
    towards the sun-rising " (Jebel esh Sherki,
    Josh. 13 : 5; Judith 1 : 7), is the **Anti-**

Libanus—an arid and desert chain, ending in white peaks of chalk on the north, near Palmyra. **Mount Hermon,** also called Sirion (Deut. 3 : 9), Shenir (the later Sanir), and Sion (Jebel esh Sheikh, Deut. 4 : 48), is a dome-shaped, rugged mountain, which is a main feature in Palestine scenery as far south as Shechem and Jericho. It commands a very fine view on all sides, and is still covered with vineyards. **Carmel** is a long ridge rising on the south-east (1 Ki. 18 : 19; 2 Ki. 2 : 25; 4 : 25; Isa. 33 : 9; 35 : 2; Jer. 46 : 18; Mic. 7 : 14). The site of Elijah's sacrifice appears to have been at the south end, overlooking the plain of Esdraelon. **Tabor** is an outlier of the chain of upper Galilee (Josh. 19 : 22; Judg. 4 : 6; 8 : 18, 19). **Gilboa** is a very barren chain between the Jordan Valley and the plain of Esdraelon (1 Sam. 31 : 1). **Ebal** and **Gerizim** are lofty summits on the watershed divided by the Vale of Shechem; Gerizim, on the south, is the sacred mountain of the Samaritans. The reading of the Law occurred in the valley between them (Deut. 11 : 26-30; John 4 : 20). **Baal Hazor** is a remarkable summit south of Shiloh, rising 3300 feet above the sea (2 Sam. 13 : 23). **Olivet,** a long range of white chalky limestone, dotted with olives; it commands a fine view over the Jordan Valley (1 Ki. 11 : 7; 2 Sam. 15 : 30; Ezek. 11 : 23; Zech. 14 : 4; Mark 13 : 3). Other hills are **Moriah** (2 Chr. 3 : 1; = Gen. 22 : 1 ?), **Sion** (Ps. 133 : 3), **Horeb** or **Sinai, Bashan** (Ps. 68 : 15), **Abarim** (Num. 27 : 12; Deut. 32 : 49; 34 : 1), **Gilead,** and **Mount Seir** (see various references).

(3) Rivers.—The **Orontes** is not mentioned in the Bible. It rises from deep springs in the plain of Cœle Syria, east of the Lebanon, and flows north. The **Eleutherus** (1 Macc. 12 : 30) is a stream rising west of Emesa, and flowing to the sea north of Tripoli. **Abana** and **Pharpar,** the "rivers of Damascus," flow eastwards from the Anti-Lebanon and from Hermon respectively (2 Ki. 5 : 12). The river **Adonis,** not mentioned in the Bible, was celebrated in Phœnician mythology. The **Leontes** forms the natural division of Syria and Palestine; it rises not far from the source of the Orontes, and runs south-west of Hermon. The **Kishon** drains the whole plain of Esdraelon, and reaches the sea north of Carmel (Judg. 4 : 7-13; 5 : 21; 1 Ki. 18 : 40). The **Jabbok** is the only affluent of Jordan, from the east, mentioned in the Bible (Deut. 3 : 6; Gen. 32 : 22; cf. 33 : 14). The **Arnon** (Num. 21 : 13; Josh. 13 : 16), was in early times the north border of Moab, while in later books of the Old Testament Moab extends to Heshbon. The **Brook Zered,** the north border of Edom (Deut. 2 : 14, 15), flows into the south end of the Dead Sea. **The River of Egypt** (Nakhal, Num. 34 : 5; 1 Ki. 8 : 65; Isa. 27 : 12) is to be distinguished from the Nile (Gen. 15 : 18; Josh. 13 : 3; Jer.

11 : 18), and is the great torrent which bounds the Holy Land on the south, rising near Beersheba.

There are several minor streams watering Palestine, both those which flow west into the sea (the Crocodile River, the 'Aujeh, and others in the plain of Sharon, the Belus, near Accho) and those which join the Jordan, of which the most important is the **Hieromax.** The perennial streams of Syria are more numerous than those of Palestine, and in Judæa there are no streams that run all the year, as there are in Galilee. See **Jordan.**

(4) Lakes.—The principal lakes in Palestine are the **Sea of Galilee** (of Gennesaret or of Tiberias) and the **Dead Sea.** The former is a pear-shaped basin, twelve miles north and south by eight miles east and west at its broadest, and which has a depth of 160 feet. The waters of the lake are sweet, but somewhat turbid near the Jordan. The basin is subject to sudden storms, such as are mentioned in the New Testament (Matt. 8 : 24; 14 : 24; Mark 4 : 37; Luke 8 : 23).

The **Dead Sea** extends forty miles in length by ten in breadth, and its level is kept down entirely by evaporation, which makes a difference of fifteen feet in the winter and summer water marks. The saltness is greater than that of any known body of water, twenty-five per cent. of various chlorides having been found in the analysis of specimens. No fish can live in the waters, which are extremely buoyant. The greatest depth near the east shore is about 1300 feet.

(5) Springs.—We mention these briefly, merely to present a complete conspectus. Those calling for attention are **En Rogel** or **Gihon** (1 Ki. 1 : 9, etc.), **Bethesda** (John 5 : 2), **Jacob's Well** (John 4 : 6), **Serah** (2 Sam. 3 : 26), and **Hammath** (Josh. 19 : 35).

(6) Sea Coast.—The Palestine coast has only one natural harbour—the open roadstead under Carmel, at the south end of the Bay of Accho. The small ports of Gaza, Jabneel, Joppa, and Cæsarea, are formed by dangerous reefs. **Tyre** possessed two ports, still extant, but both small, and formed by reefs. **Sidon** had a larger port of the same character. The other Phœnician cities had also unimportant harbours, except Tripoli, which is said to be the best on the coast. This disadvantage may account for the small maritime power of the Hebrews, as compared with the Phœnicians, Egyptians, and Greeks.

(7) Plains.—Lower Galilee includes the large **plain of Jezreel** or **Esdraelon** (fourteen miles by ten miles), of triangular shape. The seaside plains of **Sharon** and **Philistia** are remarkable for the fertility of the soil; on the north of the former there was an open woodland of oaks, which still exist, though much injured. The smaller Plain of Sepphoris ("Josephus' Life," sec. 45, etc.), north of the Nazareth Hills, opens into the

plateau east of Tabor, which has, like it, a rich basaltic soil. The Plains of **Bashan** are also remarkable for the same rich volcanic soil, suitable for cornland. The plain or valley of **Jericho** and **Shittim** is less naturally fertile, owing to the saltness of the soil, and is only tilled towards the north, while on the south it is scattered with acacias, and near the Dead Sea grows only the alkali plant. Corn is still grown in the upper part of the Jordan valley, where a few stunted palms represent the remains of former palm gardens (" Josephus' Ant." XVIII. 11 : 2). The plateau of Beersheba is entirely pastoral, and still sustains large flocks watered at deep wells. The corn plains cease on the south near Gaza.

(8) Deserts.—These are " **the desert of Judæa** " (Matt. 3 : 1), " **the rocks of the wild goats** " (1 Sam. 24 : 2), the deserts of **Beersheba** and **Arabah** (1 Ki. 19 : 4 f.), and the true **Sinaitic desert** in the south. Although the first name is one of the most desolate regions in the world, the total proportion of desert to cultivated land is probably not greater than in England.

(9) Climate.—The climate of Syria is not unlike that of Italy, and its seasons are the same. In summer, when the west wind blows, beginning about 10 a.m., the heat is rarely above 90° Fahr.; but in May, with the east wind from the Syrian Desert, it ranges to 104° Fahr. In the Jordan Valley, in summer, it is as high as 120° Fahr., or even higher, in the shade. The summits of Lebanon and Hermon are, however, annually covered with snow, which sometimes is not altogether melted even in autumn. Snow also falls, at times, on the hills of Samaria and Judæa.

(10) Early Inhabitants of the Land.—Syria and Palestine were early occupied by Canaanite tribes (Gen. 10 : 15), which were of the same stock with the early inhabitants of Mesopotamia (verse 6) and not of the Semitic race to which Assyrians, Hebrews, Phœnicians, and Arabs belonged. The invasion of Syria, about 2500 B.C., by the Akkadian prince, Gudea, as found recorded at Tell Loh, agrees with the Biblical account : He cut cedars in the northern Lebanon, and even brought diorite for statues from Sinai. The Canaanite tribes were probably related to the Akkadians, and included in the north the Hittites, a powerful race, ruling from Carchemish on the Euphrates to Hermon (Josh. 1 : 4), to which stock belonged probably the six divisions of Arkites (at Arca, near Tripoli), Sinites (at Sinna, of Strabo), Arvadites (on the island of Arvad, thirty miles north of Tripoli), Zemarites (inland of Arvad) Hivites, and Hamathites (in Hamath, on the Orontes). The early inhabitants of Sidon, and of the Phœnician coast, appear to have been related to the Canaanites. In Palestine itself the Canaanites proper, or people of the " lowlands " (as the word is used geographically on Phœnician coins),

were found in the plains of Gaza, and in the Jordan Valley (Gen. 10 : 19; Josh. 11 : 3). The **Amorites** were a tribe who are represented on Egyptian monuments as civilised inhabitants of the Hebron Mountains, where also a **Hittite** tribe dwelt (Gen. 23 : 5), the **Perizzites** (compare Caphrath Perazi, 1 Sam. 6 : 18), who were " rustics " in the centre of Palestine (Gen. 34 : 30), and in Lower Galilee (Josh. 17 : 15). Hivites also lived in the hills north of Jerusalem, and as far as Shechem (Gen. 34 : 2; Josh. 9 : 17), as well as in Lebanon (Judg. 3 : 3); the Jebusites inhabited Jerusalem, and the Girgashites some region unknown. Of the early aborigines, Rephaim, Zuzim Zamzummim, and Emim (Deut. 2 : 11), and the Anakim in the southern mountains (2 Sam. 21 : 16), nothing is known save the names. They were attacked by Chaldean conquerors at an early period (Gen. 14 : 1), probably by the Akkadians above mentioned. The **Horim**, or " cave men," were early aborigines of Edom (Deut. 2 : 12), and the **Avim** dwelt in " enclosures " (Deut. 2 : 26), and were conquered by the Philistines, who as we are expressly told (Gen. 10 : 14), were a tribe of Mizraimite or Egyptian origin. The **Amalekites** inhabited the Sinaitic deserts (Gen. 14 : 7); these tribes appear to have been all of distinct race and " language " (Gen. 10 : 20) from the Semitic peoples.

That the appearance of Semitic tribes in Syria occurred before 1600 B.C., is proved by the names of about 119 cities conquered by Thothmes III. in 1600 B.C.; many of these are the same mentioned in the book of Joshua. The **Phœnicians** were a Semitic race, whose traditions (" Strabo " XVI., 3 : 4) derived them from the Persian Gulf, and whose civilisation was similar to that of the Babylonians, and their language very close to the Hebrew. Their great cities, Tyre, Sidon, etc., are mentioned in monumental texts as early as the seventeenth century, B.C., bearing Semitic names. They probably migrated to the Syrian coast about the same time with the Hebrews, whose ancestors finally settled in the plains of Beersheba (Gen. 21 : 14, etc.); about the same time also the kindred **Moabites** and **Ammonites** (Gen. 19 : 37) began to spread over Moab and Gilead, and the Ishmaelites (Gen. 23 : 16) over the Sinaitic desert, and the region east of the Gulf of Akabah. A half-Hebrew, half-Hittite race then conquered the aborigines of **Edom** (Gen. 36 : 1-43), and to the same stock perhaps belonged the **Kenites** (Gen. 15 : 19), who may have been named from Cain, " the nest of the Kenite " (Num. 24 : 21; Josh. 15 : 57), and who remained in the same region south of Hebron in David's time (1 Sam. 30 : 29), but from whom the family of Hobab (cf. Judg. 1 : 16) separated to dwell on the plains of Tabor (Judg. 4 : 11). The **Kenizzites** (see Gen. 15 : 19) were also probably Semitic, with the **Kadmonites** or

" southerners," who also dwelt in the south (Gen. 15 : 19; cf. 1 Sam. 30 : 29). The language of the whole of Palestine appears from the recently discovered letters from Tell 'Amarna (1500-1450 B.C.), to have been similar to that of Assyria, during the period immediately preceding and following the Exodus.

For the first division of the country into districts, see Josh. 12 : 1—19 : 51.

Palm. See **Measures.**

Palm [Heb. " tamar "; " Phœnix dactylifera "], was at one time a characteristic tree of Palestine. Differing in its erect make of growth without forming branches, with a tapering stem and great summit clusters of leaves, it stood out from all other trees of the country. Its Hebrew name, " tamar," was given to towns and to people. In some districts it was found in dense groves; in others, isolated trees served as landmarks. Its stem and leaves were favourite subjects for architectural embellishments, from the period of Solomon's Temple. With a suitable climate it will flourish in almost any soil if it gets moisture. Its fruit, the date, is not mentioned in the Bible, unless in the margin to 2 Chr. 31 : 5, and yet it must have been largely used as an article of food. The immense branch-like leaves are mentioned as symbols of triumph and were used on occasions of rejoicing.

tree and branches, Ex. 15 : 27; Lev. 23 : 40; Deut. 34 : 3; Judg. 1 : 16; 3 : 13; 2 Chr. 28 : 15; John 12 : 13.

Ps. 92 : 12, righteous flourish like p. tree.

Rev. 7 : 9, white robes, p. in their hands.

(of the hand), Isa. 49 : 16, graven thee on p. of hands.

Matt. 26 : 67; Mark 14 : 65, smote Jesus with p. of hands.

Palmer worm, Joel 1 : 4; 2 : 25; Amos 4 : 9. See **Locust.**

Palsy, cured by Christ, Matt. 4 : 24; 8 : 6; 9 : 2; Mark 2 : 3; Luke 5 : 18; by his disciples, Acts 8 : 7; 9 : 33.

Pan, 2 Sam. 13 : 9; 1 Chr. 9 : 31; Ezek. 4 : 3.

Pangs, Isa. 13 : 8; 21 : 3.

Pannag (păn̈-năg). This word which occurs in Ezek. 27 : 17, has been left untranslated. The R.V. gives in the margin, " a kind of confection." Some think, with the Syriac Version, that millet, a product of Palestine of which bread is made, is intended.

Pant, Ps. 42 : 1, as hart p., so p. my soul.

Amos 2 : 7, that p. after the dust.

Paper, Isa. 19 : 7, the p. reeds shall wither.

2 John 12, I would not write with p.

Paphos (pā̇-phŏs), a city of Cyprus. Elymas the sorcerer at, Acts 13 : 6-8.

Paps, Ezek. 23 : 21; Luke 11 : 27.

Papyrus, paper reed. See **Bulrush.**

Parables of the Bible. A fable, by making animals speak, etc., violates probability. An allegory is, on the other hand, very artificial, representing something " other " than itself (Greek = " speaking other "), e.g., the language of a journey being used for the spiritual life. A parable in the technical sense is not only a natural and self-sufficient story, but it also points to a deeper spiritual meaning, and whereas, in the allegory, every detail may be pressed, in the parable, which merely seeks to bring out a general truth, such a proceeding would be disastrous. The five " perfect " parables in the Old Testament are 2 Sam. 12 : 1-4; 14 : 6; 1 Ki. 20 : 39; Isa. 5 : 1-6; 28 : 24-28.

I.—Old Testament :

The trees making a king, addressed by Jotham to the men of Shechem, Judg. 9 : 7-15.

Riddle put forth by Samson to his marriage guests, Judg. 14 : 14.

The poor man's ewe lamb, told by Nathan to David, 2 Sam. 12 : 1-6.

Parable of the woman of Tekoah and her two sons, 2 Sam. 14 : 6-11.

The escaped prisoner, addressed to Ahab by the unknown prophet, 1 Ki. 20 : 35-40.

The vision of Micaiah, told by him to Ahab, 1 Ki. 22 : 19-23.

The thistle and cedar, addressed by Jehoash to Amaziah, 2 Ki. 14 : 9.

The drunkard, addressed to the people of Israel, Prov. 23 : 29-35.

The sluggard and his vineyard, to the people of Israel, Prov. 24 : 30-34.

The unfruitful vineyard, to the people of Israel, Isa. 5 : 1-6.

The plowman, or good out of evil, to the people of Israel, Isa. 28 : 23-29.

The great eagles and the vine, Ezek. 17 : 3-10.

The lion's whelps, Ezek. 19 : 2-9.

The two harlots, addressed to the people of Israel, Ezek. 23.

The boiling pot and its scum, addressed to the people of Israel, Ezek. 24 : 3-5.

The cedar in Lebanon, Ezek. 31.

The sea monster, Ezek. 32 : 1-16.

The shepherds and the flock, Ezek. 34.

The dry bones in the valley, Ezek. 37.

The living waters, Ezek. 47.

Many others, as in Amos 7-9; Zech. 1 : 7— 6 : 15, and the true and the false shepherd in Zech. 11.

II.—New Testament, Parables of our Lord :
   1. Peculiar to St. Matthew.

The tares, Matt. 13 : 24-30.

The hidden treasure, Matt. 13 : 44.

The pearl of great price, Matt. 13 : 45, 46.

The drag net, Matt. 13 : 47.

The unmerciful servant, Matt. 18 : 23-35.

Labourers in the vineyard, Matt. 20 : 1-17.

The father and two sons, Matt. 21 : 28-32.

The marriage of the king's son, Matt. 22 : 1-14.

The ten virgins, Matt. 25 : 1-13.

The talents, Matt. 25 : 14-30.

The sheep and goats, Matt. 25 : 31-46.
   2. Peculiar to St. Mark.

Growth of seed, Mark 4 : 26-29.

The household watching, Mark 13 : 34-37.
   3. Peculiar to St. Luke.

The two debtors, Luke 7 : 36-50.

The good Samaritan, Luke 10 : 25-37.

The friend at midnight, Luke 11 : 5-8.

The rich fool, Luke 12 : 16-21.
The servants watching, Luke 12 : 35-40.
The steward on trial, Luke 12 : 42-48.
The barren fig-tree, Luke 13 : 6-9.
The great supper, Luke 14 : 16-24.
The tower and the warring king, Luke 14 : 28-33.
The lost piece of money, Luke 15 : 8-10.
The prodigal son and his elder brother, Luke 15 : 11-32.
The unjust steward, or dishonest land agent, Luke 16 : 1-13.
The rich man and Lazarus, Luke 16 : 19-31.
The master and servant, Luke 17 : 7-10.
The importunate widow, Luke 18 : 1-8.
The Pharisee and the publican, Luke 18 : 9-14.
The pounds, Luke 19 : 12-27.
    4. Peculiar to St. John.
The bread of life, John 6.
The shepherd and the sheep, John 10.
The vine and the branches, John 15.
    5. Common to Matthew and Luke.
House built on rock and on sand, Matt. 7 : 24; Luke 6 : 48.
The leaven, Matt. 13 : 33; Luke 13 : 20.
The lost sheep, Matt. 18 : 12; Luke 15.
    6. Common to Matthew, Mark, Luke.
The candle under a bushel, Matt. 5 : 15 f.: Mark 4 : 21 f.; Luke 8 : 16 f.
The new cloth on old garment, Matt. 9 : 16; Mark 2 : 21; Luke 5 : 36.
New wine and old bottles, Matt. 9 : 17; Mark 2 : 22; Luke 5 : 37 ff.
The sower, Matt. 13; Mark 4; Luke 8.
The mustard seed, Matt. 13 : 31, 32; Mark 4 : 31, 32; Luke 13 : 18, 19.
The vineyard and husbandmen, Matt. 21 : 33 ff.; Mark 12 : 1 ff.; Luke 20 : 9 ff.
The fig tree and its young leaves, Matt. 24 : 32 ff.; Mark 23 : 28 ff.; Luke 21 : 29 ff.
Num. 23 : 7, Balaam took up **p.**
Ps. 49 : 4, I will incline mine ear to a **p.**
Mic. 2 : 4, take up a **p.** against you.
See also Num. 24 : 5, 16; 2 Chr. 25 : 18; Job 27; Ps. 78 : 2; Prov. 26 : 9; Isa. 5 : 1; Jer. 13 : 1; 18; 24; 27; Ezek. 16 : 33.
Paradise. This word is of Persian origin, and was applied to the garden or park connected with the royal residence. Owing to the Persians regarding their kings as gods (which explains why the laws of the Medes and Persians were unchangeable) the residence of the king and its surrounding grounds were looked upon as a divine abode. Accordingly paradise came to mean the precincts of the divine dwelling-place.
Luke 23 : 43, to-day shalt thou be with me in **p.**
2 Cor. 12 : 4, caught up into **p.**
Rev. 2 : 7, midst of **p.** of God.
Paramours, Ezek. 23 : 20.
Parasang, a Persian measure of distance of about 3½ miles. See **Measures.**
Parcel, Gen. 33 : 19; 1 Chr. 11 : 13.
Parched, Ruth 2 : 14; Isa. 35 : 7; Jer. 17 : 6.
Parchments, 2 Tim. 4 : 13.
Pardon, of sin, Job 7 : 21; Ps. 25 : 11; Jer. 33 : 8; 50 : 20.

Ex. 23 : 21, not **p.** your transgressions.
34 : 9, **p.** our iniquity.
2 Ki. 5 : 18, the Lord **p.** thy servant.
2 Chr. 30 : 18, the good Lord **p.** every one.
Neh. 9 : 17, a God ready to **p.**
Isa. 55 : 7, he will abundantly **p.**
Mic. 7 : 18, who is a God like unto thee that **p.** iniquity ?
Pare, Deut. 21 : 12.
Parents, duty of, Prov. 13 : 24; 19 : 18; 22 · 6, 15; 23 : 13; 29 : 15; Luke 11 : 13; Eph. 6 : 4; Col. 3 : 21; 1 Tim. 5 : 8; Titus 2 : 4.
duty to. See **Obedience.**
Matt. 10 : 21; Mark 13 : 12, children shall rise up against **p.**
Luke 18 : 29, no man that hath left **p.**
21 : 16, ye shall be betrayed by **p.**
John 9 : 2, who did sin, this man or his **p.** ?
Rom. 1 : 30; 2 Tim. 3 : 2, disobedient to **p.**
2 Cor. 12 : 14, children ought not to lay up for **p.**
Eph. 6 : 1; Col. 3 : 20, children, obey your **p.**
1 Tim. 5 : 4, learn to requite their **p.**
Parlour, Judg. 3 : 20, 23, 24, 25; 1 Sam. 9 : 22; 1 Chr. 28 : 11.
Parmashta (pär-măsh-tă) [strong-fisted], Esther 9 : 9.
Parmenas (pär-mĕ-năs) [constant], Acts 6 : 5.
Parnach (pär-năch), Num. 34 : 25.
Parosh (pär-ŏsh) [a flea], Ezra 2 : 3.
Parshandatha (pär-shăn-dā-thä) Old Persian [granted to prayer ?], Esther 9 : 7.
Part, Josh. 22 : 25, ye have no **p.** in the Lord.
Ruth 1 : 17, if ought but death **p.** thee and me.
2 Sam. 20 : 1, we have no **p.** in David.
Ps. 5 : 9, their inward **p.** is very wickedness.
22 : 18, they **p.** my garments.
51 : 6, in hidden **p.** make me know wisdom.
118 : 7, the Lord taketh my **p.**
Mark 9 : 40, he that is not against us is on our **p.**
Luke 10 : 42, Mary hath chosen that good **p.**
24 : 51, while he blessed them, he was **p.** from them.
John 13 : 8, thou hast no **p.** with me.
19 : 23, four **p.**, to every soldier a **p.**
Acts 2 : 45, **p.** them to all men.
Acts 8 : 21, thou hast neither **p.** nor lot in this matter.
1 Cor. 13 : 9, we know in **p.**, and we prophesy in **p.**
2 Cor. 6 : 15, what **p.** hath he that believeth with an infidel ?
Heb. 2 : 14, himself took **p.** of the same.
Partaker, Ps. 50 : 18, **p.** with adulterers.
Matt. 23 : 30, not been **p.** in blood of prophets.
Rom. 15 : 27, **p.** of their spiritual things.
1 Cor. 9 : 13, **p.** with the altar ?
10 : 17, **p.** of that one bread.
10 : 21, **p.** of the Lord's table.
Heb. 3 : 1, **p.** of the heavenly calling.
1 Pet. 4 : 13, **p.** of Christ's sufferings.
5 : 1, a **p.** of the glory.
2 Pet. 1 : 4, be **p.** of the divine nature.
See Rom. 11 : 17.
Parthians (pär-thĭ-ăns), Acts 2 : 9.
Partial, Mal. 2 : 9, have been **p.** in the law.
Jas. 2 : 4, are ye not **p.** in yourselves ?
Partiality, condemned, Lev. 19 : 15; Deut.

1 : 17; 16 : 19; Prov. 18 : 5; 24 : 23;
1 Tim. 5 : 21; Jas. 3 : 17; Jude 16.
Particular, 1 Cor. 12 : 27; Eph. 5 : 33; Heb.
9 : 5.
Parties, Ex. 22 : 9.
Parting, Ezek. 21 : 21.
Partition, 1 Ki. 6 : 21, he made a p. by chains of
gold.
Eph. 2 : 14, the middle wall of p.
Partly, Dan. 2 : 42; 1 Cor. 11 : 18; Heb.
10 : 33.
Partner, Luke 5 : 10; 2 Cor. 8 : 23; Philem. 17.
Partridge is common in the Holy Land, but is
only twice referred to in the Bible, 1 Sam.
26 : 20; Jer. 17 : 11.
Pass, Gen. 41 : 32, God will bring it to p.
Ex. 12 : 13, when I see the blood, I will p. over.
33 : 22, cover thee while I p. by.
Isa. 43 : 2, when thou p. through waters.
Matt. 5 : 18, till heaven and earth p.
26 : 39; Mark 14 : 36, let this cup p.
Luke 16 : 26, neither can they p. to us.
John 5 : 24; 1 John 3 : 14, is p. from death to
life.
1 Cor. 7 : 31, fashion of this world p. away.
2 Cor. 5 : 17, old things are p.
Eph. 3 : 19, love of Christ, which p. knowledge.
Phil. 4 : 7, peace of God, which p. all understanding.
2 Pet. 3 : 10, the heavens shall p. away.
Passage, Num. 20 : 21; Isa. 10 : 29.
Passengers, Prov. 9 : 15; Ezek. 39 : 11 ff.
Passion, Acts 1 : 3, showed himself alive after
his p.
14 : 15, we are men of like p.
Passover, Feast of the. This covenant of Israel
was associated with the Feast of Unleavened
Bread (Ex. 34 : 25; Deut. 16 : 1 f.), which
lasted a week (Lev. 23 : 6-8). The Passover-
lamb (a male, and without blemish) was
slain at sunset closing the fourteenth day
of the month Abib (or, as it was afterwards
called, Nisan), and it was then roasted and
eaten, no remnant of the flesh being allowed
to remain till the following morning (Deut.
16 : 4) since decay or putrefaction, which
rapidly sets in under a semi-tropical
climate, was regarded as ritual defilement.
It was strictly ordained that all leaven should
be removed from the dwellings of the
Hebrews on the 14th Nisan. The removal
of the leaven was, by a much later enact-
ment, prescribed for the period from the
evening of the 13th till that of the 14th
Nisan. This was the preparation for the
Passover referred to in John's Gospel
(19 : 14), on which every head of a family
made diligent search for leaven by the
light of a lamp (" Mishna Pesachim,"
1 : 1). Leaven might indeed be eaten until
midday of the 14th. After that every fragment of leavened bread that was discovered
was burned. The presence of women as
well as men was permitted at this as well
as other festivals (Luke 2 : 41; comp.
1 Sam. 1 : 24), for the festival, though
national, was domestic. The examples just
cited show that the same privilege was

extended to boys and little children.
Legislation was generous in its rules respecting the victims. It might be either a
lamb or a kid (Ex. 12 : 5), and it was to be
selected four days beforehand, *i.e.,* 10th
Nisan, by the head of the family. If a
household was too small, it might unite
with another small household in providing
a single lamb for both. Doubtless this
regulation arose in part as a consequence
of the rule which enforced the consumption
of the entire victim before the following
morning. For the lamb was slain at sunset
of the 14th Nisan, and whatever remained
uneaten was consumed by fire. The blood
of the animal was sprinkled with a bunch
of hyssop on the two side posts and lintel
of the house-door. The paschal feast was
eaten by the family with unleavened cakes
and bitter herbs, with loins girded, sandals
on the feet, and staff in hand. The animal
was eaten entire, head, legs, and entrails,
without breaking a bone (Ex. 12 : 7-11), so
far as this was possible.
The rule was stringently laid down that
all males should unite with their brethren
in celebrating this great national feast.
Non-performance involved excommunica-
tion (Num. 9 : 13). Defilement, however,
as by contact with a dead body, constituted
a disqualification. For the temporary unclean, therefore, a second and later passover
was instituted at the corresponding time in
the following month (Num. 9 : 10, 11).
While the Jews still observe the Passover,
they now omit the eating of the roasted
lamb.
instituted, Ex. 12 : 12.
law relating to, Lev. 23 : 5; Num. 9; 28 : 16;
Deut. 16.
observed under Moses, Ex. 12 : 28; Num.
9 : 5; under Joshua, Josh. 5 : 10; by
Hezekiah, 2 Chr. 30; by Josiah, 2 Ki.
23 : 21; 2 Chr. 35; by Ezra, Ezra 6 : 16.
kept by Christ, Matt. 26 : 19; Mark 14 : 12;
Luke 22 : 7; John 13.
a type of Christ's death, 1 Cor. 5 : 7.
Past, 1 Sam. 15 : 32, bitterness of death is p.
Eccl. 3 : 15, God requireth that which is p.
Jer. 8 : 20, the harvest is p.
Rom. 11 : 33, ways p. finding out.
Eph. 4 : 19, being p. feeling.
Pastor, Jer. 2 : 8, p. transgressed against me.
Jer. 23 : 1, woe to p. that destroy sheep.
Eph. 4 : 11, gave some p. and teachers.
Pastoral Epistles. 1 and 2 Timothy and Titus
(especially the second) are by no means
entirely "pastoral." Hence the title,
which is applied to them, is somewhat
misleading. They are treated, however,
from the point of view of the minister, not
that of the congregation. For dates and
fuller particulars the reader is referred to
the separate articles on these three Epistles.
Pasture, spiritual, Ps. 23 : 2; 79 : 13; 95 : 7;
100 : 3; Ezek. 34 : 14.
Ps. 74 : 1, sheep of p.
Ezek. 34 : 31, flock of my p. are men.
John 10 : 9, go in and out, and find p.

Pate, Ps. 7 : 16.
Path, Num. 22 : 24, angel of Lord stood in p.
Job 28 : 7, a p. which no fowl knoweth.
Ps. 16 : 11, show me the p. of life.
27 : 11, lead me in a plain p.
77 : 19, thy p. is in the great waters.
119 : 105, thy word is a light unto my p.
139 : 3, thou compassest my p.
Prov. 4 : 18, the p. of the just.
Isa. 2 : 3; Mic. 4 : 2, we will walk in his p.
Isa. 42 : 16, in p. they have not known.
Jer. 6 : 16, ask for the old p.
Matt. 3 : 3; Mark 1 : 3; Luke 3 : 4, make his
    p. straight.
Heb. 12 : 13, make straight p. for feet.
Pathway, Prov. 12 : 38.
Patience, commended, Eccl. 7 : 8; Isa. 30 : 15;
    40 : 31; 1 Thess. 5 : 14; 2 Thess. 3 : 5;
    1 Tim. 3 : 3; 6 : 11.
blessings resulting from, Rom. 15 : 4; 2 : 2.
Matt. 18 : 26, 29, have p. with me.
Luke 8 : 15, bring forth fruit with p.
21 : 19, in p. possess your souls.
Rom. 5 : 3, tribulation worketh p.
8 : 25, with p. wait for it.
15 : 5, the God of p.
2 Cor. 6 : 4, as ministers of God in much p.
Col. 1 : 11, strengthened with all might to
    all p.
2 Thess. 1 : 4, glory in you for your p.
Titus 2 : 2, faith, charity, p.
Heb. 6 : 12, through p. inherit the promises.
10 : 36, ye have need of p.
12 : 1, let us run with p.
Jas. 1 : 3, trying of your faith worketh p.
5 : 7, the husbandman hath long p.
5 : 11, ye have heard of the p. of Job.
2 Pet. 1 : 6, add to temperance p.
Rev. 3 : 10, thou hast kept word of p.
13 : 10; 14 : 12, here is the p. of the saints.
Patient, Eccl. 7 : 8; Rom. 2 : 7; 12 : 12.
Patiently, Ps. 37 : 7, rest in the Lord, wait p.
Ps. 40 : 1, I waited p. for the Lord.
Heb. 6 : 15, after he had p. endured.
1 Pet. 2 : 20, if, when ye be buffeted, ye take
    it p.
Patriarchs, history of, Gen. 5. cf. Acts 7 : 8.
Patrimony, Deut. 18 : 8.
Pattern, of the tabernacle, etc., Ex. 25 : 9, 40;
    (Ezek. 43 : 10); Heb. 8 : 5.
Num. 8 : 4, p. which the Lord had showed.
1 Tim. 1 : 16, in me Christ might show p.
Titus 2 : 7, showing thyself a p. of good
    works.
Heb. 9 : 23, was necessary that p. of things.
Paul or Paulus [small, little], as a persecutor,
    Acts 7 : 58; 8 : 1; 9 : 1; 22 : 4; 26 : 9;
    1 Cor. 15 : 9; Gal. 1 : 13; Phil. 3 : 6;
    1 Tim. 1 : 13.
his miraculous conversion, Acts 9 : 3; 22 : 6;
    26 : 12.
as a preacher, Acts 9 : 19, 29; 13 : 1, 4, 14;
    17 : 18; (2 Cor. 11 : 32; Gal. 1 : 17).
stoned at Lystra, Acts 14 : 8, 19.
contends with Barnabas, Acts 15 : 36.
persecuted at Philippi, Acts 16.
the Holy Ghost given by his hands, Acts
    19 : 6.
restores Eutychus, Acts 20 : 10.

his charge to the elders of Ephesus, Acts
    20 : 17.
returns to Jerusalem, and persecution there,
    Acts 21.
his defence before the people, Acts 22; before
    the council, Acts 23; before Felix, Acts 24;
    Festus, Acts 25; and Agrippa, Acts 26.
appeals to Cæsar at Rome, Acts 25.
his voyage and shipwreck, Acts 27.
miracles wrought by, at Melita, Acts 28 : 3, 8.
arrives at Rome, Acts 28 : 14.
reasons with the Jews, Acts 28 : 17.
his love to the churches, Rom. 1 : 8; 15;
    1 Cor. 1 : 4; 4 : 14; 2 Cor. 1; 2; 6; 7;
    Phil. 1; Col. 1; 1 and 2 Thess.
his sufferings, 1 Cor. 4 : 9; 2 Cor. 11 : 23;
    12 : 7; Phil. 1 : 12; 2 Tim. 2 : 11.
divine revelations to, 2 Cor. 12 : 1.
defends his apostleship, 1 Cor. 9; 2 Cor.
    11 : 12; 2 Tim. 3 : 10.
commends Timothy, etc., 1 Cor. 16 : 10;
    Phil. 2 : 19; 1 Thess. 3 : 2.
commends Titus, 2 Cor. 7 : 13; 8 : 23.
pleads for Onesimus, Philem.
his epistles mentioned by Peter, 2 Pet. 3 : 15.
The following order of events has been
    suggested :
Ascension, Pentecost, A.D. 30 or 31.
Stoning of Stephen, A.D. 33 or 32.
Conversion of Saul near Damascus, A.D.
    34 or 33.
Saul's first visit to Jerusalem (9 : 26), after
    visiting Arabia and Damascus again,
    A.D. 38 or 37.
Barnabas and Saul go to Antioch; disciples
    called " Christians " there, A.D. 40.
Agabus' prophecy about the same time
    (11 : 28 implies) was before Claudius,
    whose reign began Jan. 24th (Suet. Cal.
    58), A.D. 41.
Saul's second visit to Jerusalem (11 : 30),
    A.D. 41 or 42.
Martyrdom of James the Elder; death of
    Herod Agrippa (12 : 2, 23) (" Joseph
    Antiq.," 19 : 8, 2), A.D. 44.
First missionary journey of Barnabas and
    Saul (henceforward Paul) (13 : 1; 14 :
    28), A.D. 44.
Fourteen years after his first visit (Gal. 2 : 1
    and Acts 15), Paul's third visit to Jeru-
    salem on the question of circumcising
    Gentiles. Second missionary journey
    with Silas (15 : 40) and Timothy (16 : 3),
    A.D. 52 or 51.
At Corinth he writes First and Second
    Epistles to Thessalonians, A.D. 53.
Fourth visit to Jerusalem, A.D. 54.
Third missionary journey; stay (19 : 10;
    20 : 31) between two and three years at
    Ephesus; where First Epistle to Corin-
    thians was written (1 Cor. 16 : 8); Second
    Epistle to Corinthians from Macedonia
    (2 Cor. 9 : 2), A.D. 55-57.
Epistle to Romans (and perhaps Epistle to
    Galatians) from Corinth (Rom. 16 : 1,
    23), A.D. 58.
Fifth visit to Jerusalem (21 : 16, 17), before
    Pentecost, issuing in his imprisonment
    for two years in Cæsarea under Felix;

Porcius Festus (" Joseph. Antiq.," 20 : 8, 9) succeeds A.D. 60, A.D. 58.

Arrives at Rome, spring of A.D. 61, where for two years he is in a hired house (28 : 11-31), A.D. 61.

During these two years at Rome he writes Epistles to Ephesians, Colossians, Philemon, and probably at the close, Philippians; the Book of Acts finished, A.D. 63.

Paul's martyrdom at Rome (Eusebius), A.D. 67.

Paved, Ex. 24 : 10; Song of Sol. 3 : 16.

Pavement, 2 Ki. 16 : 17; Ezek. 40 : 17, 18; John 19 : 13.

Pavilion, 2 Sam. 22 : 12; Ps. 18 : 11, he made darkness his p.

Ps. 27 : 5, he shall hide me in his p.

31 : 20, keep them secretly in a p.

Paw, 1 Sam. 17 : 37.

Paweth, Job 39 : 21.

Pay, Deut. 23 : 21, shalt not slack to p. vow.

Ps. 22 : 25; 66 : 13; 116 : 14, will p. my vows.

76 : 11, vow, and p. to the Lord.

Eccl. 5 : 4, defer not to p. it.

Matt. 18 : 26, I will p. thee all.

18 : 28, p. that thou owest.

23 : 23, ye p. tithe of mint, arise.

Rom. 13 : 6, for this cause p. tribute.

Payment, Matt. 18 : 25.

Peace. In the Old Testament the word implied " welfare," and is external. The New Testament sense is that of " heartpeace " and is more internal.

to be prayed for, Jer. 29 : 7; 1 Tim. 2 : 2.

bestowed by God, Lev. 26 : 6; 1 Ki. 2 : 33; 4 : 24; 2 Ki. 20 : 19; Prov. 16 : 7; Jer. 14 : 13.

exhortations to maintain, Matt. 5 : 9; Rom. 12 : 18; 14 : 19; 2 Tim. 2 : 22; 1 Pet. 3 : 11.

spiritual, gift of God, Acts 10 : 36; Rom. 8 : 6; 1 Thess. 5 : 23; 2 Thess. 3 : 16; Rev. 1 : 4.

preached to the Gentiles, Zech. 9 : 10; Eph. 3.

the fruit of the Spirit, Gal. 5 : 22.

on earth, Luke 2 : 14.

in heaven, Luke 19 : 38.

denied to the wicked, 2 Ki. 9 : 31; Isa. 48 : 22; (Rom. 3 : 17); Jer. 12 : 12.

to whom promised, Ps. 29 : 11; 125 : 5; 128 : 6; 147 : 14; Gal. 6 : 16; Eph. 6 : 23.

king of, Melchisedec, Heb. 7 : 2.

Prince of, Christ, Isa. 9 : 6.

Gen. 28 : 21, I come to my father's house in p.

41 : 16, an answer of p.

Num. 6 : 26, Lord give thee p.

25 : 12, my covenant of p.

Deut. 29 : 19, I shall have p., though I walk.

1 Sam. 25 : 6; Luke 10 : 5, p. be to thine house.

2 Ki. 9 : 19; what hast thou to do with p. ?

Job 22 : 21, acquaint thyself with him, and be at p.

Ps. 4 : 8, I will lay me down in p.

7 : 4, evil to him that was at p.

34 : 14, seek p., and pursue it.

37 : 37, end of upright man is p.

72 : 3, the mountains shall bring p.

85 : 8, he will speak p. to his people.

122 : 6, pray for the p. of Jerusalem.

Eccl. 3 : 8, a time of war, a time of p.

Isa. 26 : 3, thou wilt keep him in perfect p.

32 : 17, work of righteousness shall be p.

45 : 7, I make p., and create evil.

48 : 18, thy p. been as a river.

52 : 7; Nah. 1 : 15, the feet of him that publisheth p.

53 : 5, chastisement of our p. was upon him.

57 : 21, no p. to the wicked.

59 : 8, the way of p. they know not.

Jer. 6 : 14; 8 : 11, saying, P., p.; when there is no p.

8 : 15; 14 : 19, we looked for p.

Ezek. 7 : 25, seek p., there shall be none.

Dan. 4 : 1; 6 : 25; 1 Pet. 1 : 2; 2 Pet. 1 : 2; Jude 2, p. be multiplied.

Matt. 10 : 13, let your p. come upon it.

10 : 34; Luke 12 : 51, to send p. on earth.

Mark 9 : 50, have p. one with another.

Luke 1 : 79, to guide our feet in way of p.

19 : 42, things which belong unto thy p.

24 : 36; John 20 : 19, Jesus said, P. be unto you.

John 14 : 27, p. I leave with you, my p. I give unto you.

16 : 33, in me ye might have p.

Rom. 1 : 7; 1 Cor. 1 : 3; 2 Cor. 1 : 2; Gal. 1 : 3; Eph. 1 : 2; Phil. 1 : 2, p. from God our Father.

Rom. 5 : 1, we have p. with God.

10 : 15; Eph. 6 : 15, the gospel of p.

Rom. 14 : 17, the kingdom of God is p.

15 : 33; 16 : 20; 2 Cor. 13 : 11; Phil. 4 : 9; Heb. 13 : 20, the God of p.

1 Cor. 7 : 15, God hath called us to p.

2 Cor. 13 : 11, live in p.

Eph. 2 : 14, he is our p.

2 : 17, came and preached p.

4 : 3, unity of Spirit in bond of p.

Phil. 4 : 7, p. of God, which passeth all understanding.

Col. 1 : 2; 1 Thess. 1 : 1; 2 Thess. 1 : 2; 1 Tim. 1 : 2; 2 Tim. 1 : 2; Titus 1 : 4; Philem. 3; 2 John 3, grace and p. from God.

Col. 3 : 15, let the p. of God rule in your hearts.

1 Thess. 5 : 13, be at p. among yourselves.

Heb. 12 : 14, follow p. with all men.

Jas. 2 : 16, depart in p.

3 : 18, fruit of righteousness is sown in p.

2 Pet. 3 : 14, be found of him in p.

Peaceable, Isa. 32 : 18, people dwell in a p. habitation.

1 Tim. 2 : 2, lead a quiet and p. life.

Heb. 12 : 11, yieldeth the p. fruit of righteousness.

Jas. 3 : 17, wisdom from above is first pure, then p.

Peaceably, Gen. 37 : 4; Rom. 12 : 18.

Peacemakers, Matt. 5 : 9.

Peace offerings, laws concerning, Ex. 20 : 24; 24 : 5; Lev. 3 : 6; 7 : 11; 19 : 5.

Peacock. This Asiatic bird was imported by Solomon in the ships of Tarshish from Ceylon, 2 Chr. 9 : 21; Job 39 : 13.

Pearls, a well-known concretion formed within

the mantle and shell of an oyster which is dredged in the Red Sea, Persian Gulf, etc.
parable of, Matt. 7 : 6; 13 : 45.
Matt. 13 : 46, one **p.** of great price.
1 Tim. 2 : 9, not with **p.**, or costly array.
Rev. 18 : 11, 12, no man buyeth the merchandise of **p.**
21 : 21, every gate was of one **p.**
See Rev. 17 : 4.
Peculiar [ar.], what is one's own, people of God, Deut. 14 : 2; Ps. 135 : 4.
See Titus 2 : 14; 1 Pet. 2 : 9.
Pedigrees, Num. 1 : 18; Heb. 7 : 3, 6.
Peeled [stripped, plundered], Isa. 18 : 2, 7; Ezek. 29 : 18.
Peep [cry as a young bird], Isa. 8 : 19; 10 : 14.
Pekah (pē-́käh) [open-eyed], king of Israel, 2 Ki. 15 : 25.
his victory over Judah, 2 Chr. 28 : 6.
prophecy against, Isa. 7 : 1.
Pekahiah (pĕk-ä-hī-́äh) [Jah opens eyes], king of Israel, 2 Ki. 15 : 22.
Pekod (pē-́kŏd) [visitation], allegorical name of Babylon, possibly in reference to the people Pukudu, Jer. 50 : 21; Ezek. 23 : 23.
Pelethites (pĕl-́ĕ-thītes), 2 Sam. 8 : 18; 20 : 23.
See **Cherethites.**
Pelican. Several species of the genus "Pelicanus" are found in Palestine. It is fond of damp places, and after feeding it often seeks places of solitude. Lev. 11 : 18; Deut. 14 : 17; Ps. 102 : 6. See **Cormorant.**
Pen, Judg. 5 : 14, they that handle the **p.**
Job 19 : 24. graven with an iron **p.**
Ps. 45 : 1, my tongue is the **p.** of a ready writer.
3 John 13, I will not with ink and **p.** write.
Pence, Matt. 18 : 28; Luke 10 : 35; John 12 : 5.
Peniel (pĕ-́nī-ĕl) or **Penuel** (pĕ-́nū-ĕl) [face of God], a place on the east of Jordan, scene of Jacob's wrestling with an angel, Gen. 32 : 24, 30.
Gideon's vengeance upon, Judg. 8 : 17.
Penknife, Jer. 36 : 23.
Penny, a Roman coin equal to about sixteen cents, Matt. 20 : 2; Mark 12 : 15; Rev. 6 : 6. See **Money.**
Pennyworth, Mark 6 : 37; John 6 : 7.
Pentateuch, The. "Pentateuch" is a Greek name, meaning "the five-volumed" book. Its equivalent in Hebrew is "the Law," or "the book of the law of Moses," or, according to the later Jews, "the five-fifth parts of the law."

That Moses was the author of the Pentateuch was universally assumed by those who had it in their power to verify the facts. So complete unity in a matter of this kind constitutes evidence of the utmost cogency. Added to this is the testimony of the other Scriptures and the testimony of the Saviour himself (John 5 : 45-47). He not only says that Moses wrote of him but that it is to be expected that if the Jews reject Moses' record in written letters (grammata) they will reject Jesus' spoken words. The internal evidence is no less convincing than the external that Moses

wrote the Pentateuch. First, the language of the five books uses archaic forms not evident in other books. The references to Egypt are those of an eye-witness and of a resident now escaped. Many passages could not have been written in later times, for the conditions involved had passed away. That Moses was the author of the books does not preclude the probability that he made use of written records and oral tradition that had been transmitted to him. But that he had information direct from God is a part of his own declaration. The subject matter of the creation story is such that it could not have been penned without supernatural information. It is upon this precise point that the weight of the assault upon the Mosaic authorship has focused. If the records are accurate accounts of the contacts of men with God; if God has indeed spoken to man then the rest of the argument for the supernatural may be conceded. The Documentary Hypothesis created libraries of speculation, and an amazing monument in the Polychrome Bible. The Fragmentary and Supplementary Hypothesis have left us still without an acceptable basis for the reconstruction of the books upon a rationalistic foundation.

Pentecost, Feast of. Pentecost is a Greek word, η πεντηκοστη (ἡμέρα), the fiftieth day. This followed the last day of the seven weeks reckoned from " the morrow of the Sabbath " (Lev. 23 : 11, 15, 16). Without stirring the dust of dead controversies that once prevailed among the Jewish schools as to what the Sabbath here referred to was, it is enough to say that the " morrow after the Sabbath," on which the " wave offering " (Tenûfah) of the omer or sheaf was presented in the temple, was the 16th Nisan. The Feast of Weeks thus fell on the 6th Sivan. This day of Pentecost was marked by the offering of two loaves made with leaven to be presented by way of Tenûfah as a first-fruit. They were accompanied by burnt-offerings of seven lambs without blemish, of a year old, together with meal-offerings and drink-offerings. In addition to these there was a sin-offering of a he-goat and a peace-offering consisting of two male lambs of the first year. These likewise were to be presented as a wave-offering by the priest. The sacrificial details are not referred to in Deut. 16, but are to be found in Lev. 23 : 16-20 (Num. 28 : 26-30). This again was a day of festal assembly, or, as the phrase in the book of Leviticus expresses it, a day of " holy convocation " on which no servile work was done (Lev. 23 : 21).

This festival is not connected in the Old Testament with any national event in Israel's history. It coincided, however, with the exact time of the year when the law was given from Sinai, according to the record in the book of Exodus, and this coincidence was probably realised by the

Jews in the days of Christ, as it certainly was in later times.

manner observed, Lev. 23 : 9; Deut. 16 : 9.

Holy Spirit given at that time, Acts 2.

Penuel. See Peniel.

Penury, Prov. 14 : 23, talk of lips tendeth to p.

Luke 21 : 4, she of her p. cast in all.

People, of God, their blessings and privileges, Deut. 7 : 6; 32 : 9; 33; 1 Sam. 12 : 22; 2 Sam. 7 : 23; Ps. 3 : 8; 29 : 11; 33 : 12; 50 : 23; 65 : 4; 77 : 15; 85; 89 : 15; 94 : 14; 95 : 7; 100; 110; 111 : 6; 121; 125; 148 : 14; 149 : 4; Isa. 11 : 11; 14 : 32; 30 : 19; 33 : 24; 49 : 13; 51 : 22; 65 : 18; Dan. 7 : 27; Joel 2 : 18; 3 : 16; Zeph. 3 : 9, 20; Matt. 1 : 21; Acts 15 : 14; Rom. 11; 2 Cor. 6 : 16; Heb. 8 : 10; 1 Pet. 2 : 9; Rev. 21 : 3.

Ex. 6 : 7; Deut. 4 : 20; 2 Sam. 7 : 24; Jer. 13 : 11, I will take you for a p.

Deut. 4 : 33, did ever p. hear voice of God and live ?

33 : 29, who is like unto thee, O p.

2 Sam. 22 : 44; Ps. 18 : 43, p. I knew not shall serve me.

Ps. 62 : 8, ye p., pour out your heart.

144 : 15, happy is that p.

Prov. 14 : 34, sin is a reproach to any p.

30 : 25, the ants are a p. not strong.

Isa. 1 : 4, a p. laden with iniquity.

30 : 9; 65 : 2, this is a rebellious p.

Jer. 6 : 22; 50 : 41, a p. cometh from the north.

Jonah 1 : 8, of what p. art thou ?

Mic. 4 : 1, p. shall flow unto it.

Luke 1 : 17, a p. prepared for the Lord.

Rom. 10 : 19, by them that are no p.

Titus 2 : 14, purify to himself a peculiar p.

Heb. 4 : 9, remaineth a rest to p. of God.

Rev. 5 : 9, redeemed us out of every p.

Peor (pē-ôr) [hole, split], (Baal), Num. 23 : 28; 25 : 3, 18; Josh. 22 : 17.

Peradventure, Gen. 18 : 24, 32; Num. 22 : 6, 11; Rom. 5 : 7; 2 Tim. 2 : 25.

Perceive, Deut. 29 : 4, a heart to p.

Josh. 22 : 31, we p. that the Lord is among us.

Job 23 : 8, I cannot p. him.

Eccl. 3 : 22, p. that there is nothing better.

Isa. 6 : 9, see ye indeed, but p. not.

33 : 19, deeper speech than thou canst p.

64 : 4, nor p. what God hath prepared.

Matt. 13 : 14; Mark 4 : 12; Acts 28 : 26, ye shall see, and not p.

Mark 8 : 17, p. ye not, neither understand ?

Luke 6 : 41, p. not the beam.

8 : 46, I p. that virtue is gone out of me.

John 4 : 19, I p. that thou art a prophet.

12 : 19, p. ye how ye prevail nothing ?

Acts 10 : 34, p. that God is no respecter of persons.

14 : 9, p. that he had faith.

1 John 3 : 16, hereby p. we the love of God.

Perdition, what leads to, Phil. 1 : 28; 1 Tim. 6 : 9; Heb. 10 : 39; 2 Pet. 3 : 7; Rev. 17 : 8.

the son of, John 17 : 12; 2 Thess. 2 : 3.

Perez-uzza (pē-rĕz-ŭz-ză) [the breach of Uzzah], 2 Sam. 6 : 8; 1 Chr. 13 : 11.

Perfect, Gen. 6 : 9, Noah was a just man and p.

17 : 1, walk before me, and be thou p.

Deut. 18 : 13, thou shalt be p. with the Lord.

Job 1 : 1, 8; 2 : 3, that man was p.

Ps. 18 : 30, his way is p.

19 : 7, law of Lord is p.

37 : 37, mark the p. man.

101 : 2, behave myself in a p. way.

Prov. 4 : 18, path of just shineth to p. day.

Ezek. 28 : 15, thou wast p. in thy ways.

Matt. 5 : 48, be ye p., as your Father is p.

19 : 21, if thou wilt be p.

John 17 : 23, may be made p. in one.

Acts 24 : 22, having more p. knowledge.

Rom. 12 : 2, that p. will of God.

1 Cor. 2 : 6, wisdom among them that are p.

2 Cor. 12 : 9, strength made p. in weakness.

Eph. 4 : 13, till we come unto a p. man.

Phil. 3 : 15, as many as be p.

Col. 1 : 28, present every man p. in Christ.

4 : 12, may stand p. and complete.

Heb. 2 : 10, made p. through sufferings.

7 : 19, the law made nothing p.

11 : 40, without us should not be made p.

12 : 23, spirits of just men made p.

13 : 21, make you p., in every good work.

Jas. 1 : 4, let patience have her p. work.

1 : 17, every good and p. gift.

2 : 22, by works was faith made p.

3 : 2, the same is a p. man.

1 John 4 : 18, p. love casteth out fear.

1 Thess. 3 : 10, p. that which is lacking.

Perfection. The word might mean (a) wholeness; (b) reaching an ideal or end; (c) full adjustment; or (d) fully fitted for a given task. A close study of the various passages will show these shades in all their depth.

of God, Deut. 32 : 4; 2 Sam. 22 : 31; Job 36 : 4; Matt. 5 : 48.

of Christ, Heb. 5 : 9; 7 : 28.

of God's law, Ps. 19 : 7; 119; Jas. 1 : 25.

of saints, Eph. 4 : 12; Col. 3 : 14; 2 Tim. 3 : 17.

Job 11 : 7, canst thou find out the Almighty unto p. ?

Ps. 50 : 2, out of Zion p. of beauty.

Luke 8 : 14, bring no fruit to p.

Heb. 6 : 1, let us go on unto p.

Perfectly, Acts 18 : 26; 1 Cor. 1 : 10.

Perfectness, Col. 3 : 14.

Perform, Gen. 26 : 3; Deut. 9 : 5; Luke 1 : 72, p. oath I sware to Abraham.

Ex. 18 : 18, not able to p. it thyself.

Job 5 : 12, hands cannot p. their enterprise.

Ps. 65 : 1, unto thee shall the vow be p.

119 : 106, I have sworn, and I will p. it.

Isa. 9 : 7, zeal of the Lord will p. this.

Jer. 29 : 10; 33 : 14, I will p. my good word.

Matt. 5 : 33, unto the Lord thine oaths.

Rom. 4 : 21, was able also to p.

7 : 18, how to p. that which is good I find not.

Phil. 1 : 6, p. it until day of Christ.

Performance, Luke 1 : 45; 2 Cor. 8 : 11.

Perfume, Ex. 30 : 35; Prov. 7 : 17; 27 : 9.

Pergamos (pĕr-gă-mŏs), a city of Mysia, epistle to the church of, Rev. 1 : 11; 2 : 12.

Perhaps, Philem. 15.

Peril, Rom. 8 : 35, shall **p.** separate us from Christ ?

2 Cor. 11 : 26, in **p.** of waters.

Perilous, 2 Tim. 3 : 1.

Perish, Num. 17 : 12, we **p.,** we all **p.**

Deut. 26 : 5, a Syrian ready to **p.**

Esther 4 : 16, if I **p.,** I **p.**

Job 4 : 7, who ever **p.,** being innocent ?

29 : 13, blessing of him that was ready to **p.**

Ps. 2 : 12, lest ye **p.** from the way.

49 : 12, like the beasts that **p.**

102 : 26, they shall **p.,** but thou shalt endure.

Prov. 11 : 10; 28 : 28, when the wicked **p.**

29 : 18, no vision, the people **p.**

31 : 6, strong drink to him that is ready to **p.**

Isa. 27 : 13, they shall come that were ready to **p.**

Jonah 1 : 6; 3 : 9, God will think on us, that we **p.** not.

Matt. 8 : 25; Luke 8 : 24, save us; we **p.**

Matt. 26 : 52, shall **p.** with the sword.

Mark 4 : 38, carest thou not that we **p.** ?

Luke 15 : 17, I **p.** with hunger.

21 : 18, there shall not an hair of your head **p.**

John 3 : 15 f., believeth on Son of God should not **p.**

6 : 27, labour not for the meat which **p.**

Acts 8 : 20, thy money **p.** with thee.

2 Cor. 4 : 16, though outward man **p.**

2 Pet. 3 : 9, not willing that any should **p.**

Perizzites (pĕ-rĭz-zītes) [villagers], a tribe of the ancient Canaanites, Gen. 13 : 7; 15 : 20; Judg. 1 : 4.

See **Palestine, Early Inhabitants.**

Perjury, forbidden, Ex. 20 : 16; Lev. 6 : 3; 19 : 12; Deut. 5 : 20; Ezek. 17 : 16; Zech. 5 : 4; 8 : 17; 1 Tim. 1 : 10.

Permission, 1 Cor. 7 : 6.

Permit, Acts 26 : 1, thou art **p.** to speak for thyself.

1 Cor. 16 : 7, tarry awhile, if the Lord **p.**

Heb. 6 : 3, this will we do, if God **p.**

Pernicious, 2 Pet. 2 : 2.

Perpetual, Ex. 29 : 9, priest's office be for **p.** statute.

31 : 16, keep sabbath for **p.** covenant.

Ps. 9 : 6, destructions are come to a **p.** end.

74 : 3; Jer. 25 : 9; Ezek. 35 : 9; Zeph. 2 : 9, **p.** desolation.

Jer. 8 : 5, a **p.** backsliding.

15 : 18, why is my pain **p.** ?

50 : 5, join the Lord in a **p.** covenant.

Hab. 3 : 6, the **p.** hills.

Perpetually, 1 Ki. 9 : 3; Amos 1 : 11.

Perplexed, Luke 9 : 7; 24 : 4; 2 Cor. 4 : 8.

Perplexity, Mic. 7 : 4, now shall be their **p.**

Luke 21 : 25, distress of nations, with **p.**

Persecute, Job 19 : 22, why do ye **p.** me as God ?

Ps. 7 : 1, save me from them that **p.** me.

71 : 11, **p.** and take him, none to deliver.

Matt. 5 : 11, blessed are ye when men shall **p.** you.

5 : 44, pray for them that **p.** you.

John 15 : 20, they will also **p.** you.

Acts 9 : 4; 22 : 7; 26 : 14, why **p.** thou me ?

22 : 4, **p.** this way unto the death.

Rom. 12 : 14, bless them which **p.** you.

1 Cor. 4 : 12, being **p.,** we suffer it.

15 : 9; Gal. 1 : 13, I **p.** the church of God.

2 Cor. 4 : 9, are **p.** but not forsaken.

Phil. 3 : 6, **p.** the church.

Persecution, foretold, Matt. 13 : 21; 23 : 24; Luke 11 : 49; John 15 : 20, etc.

conduct under, Matt. 10 : 22; Acts 5 : 41; Phil. 1 : 28; Heb. 10 : 33 f.; 1 Pet. 4 : 13-19.

results of, Matt. 5 : 10; Luke 6 : 22; 9 : 24; Jas. 1 : 2; 1 Pet. 4 : 14; Rev. 6 : 9; 7 : 13-17.

Mark 4 : 17, when **p.** ariseth.

10 : 30, shall have lands with **p.**

Rom. 8 : 35, shall **p.** separate us from Christ ?

2 Cor. 12 : 10, I take pleasure in **p.**

Gal. 6 : 12, lest they should suffer **p.**

2 Tim. 3 : 12, godly shall suffer **p.**

Persecutor, Ps. 119 : 157; 142 : 6; Lam. 4 : 19; 1 Tim. 1 : 13.

Perseverance, enjoined, Matt. 24 : 13; Mark 13 : 13; Luke 9 : 62; Acts 13 : 43; 1 Cor. 15 : 58; 16 : 13; Eph. 6 : 18; Col. 1 : 23; 2 Thess. 3 : 13; 1 Tim. 6 : 14; Heb. 3 : 6, 13; 10 : 23, 38; 2 Pet. 3 : 17; Rev. 2 : 10, 25.

Persia (pĕr-ŝĭ-ă), kingdom of, 2 Chr. 36 : 20; Esther 1 : 3; Ezek. 27 : 10; 38 : 5.

prophecies concerning, Dan. 5 : 28; 8 : 10; 10 : 13; 11 : 2.

Head of Persian from Persepolis.

Persian, Neh. 12 : 22; Esther 1 : 19; Dan. 6 : 28.

Person of Christ. In systematic Theology this problem centres round the self-consciousness of Jesus and the experience of the Church concerning His various titles, e.g., Jesus of Nazareth (i.e., His humanity), the Messiah, the Son of Man, and the Son of God.

Persons, God no respecter of, Deut. 10 : 17; 2 Chr. 19 : 7; Job 34 : 19; Acts 10 : 34; Rom. 2 : 11; Gal. 2 : 6; Eph. 6 : 9; Col. 3 : 25; 1 Pet. 1 : 17.

Lev. 19 : 15, nor honour **p.** of mighty.

2 Sam. 14 : 14, neither doth God respect any **p.**
Job 22 : 29, shall save the humble **p.**
Ps. 15 : 4; Isa. 32 : 5; vile **p.**
Ps. 26 : 4; Prov. 12 : 11; 28 : 19, vain **p.**
Ps. 101 : 4, I will not know wicked **p.**
Matt. 22 : 16; Mark 12 : 14, regardest not **p.** of men.
Matt. 27 : 24, innocent of blood of this just **p.**
2 Cor. 2 : 10, forgave it in the **p.** of Christ.
Heb. 1 : 3, the express image of his **p.**
2 Pet. 3 : 11, what manner of **p.** ought ye to be ?
Jude 16, having men's **p.** in admiration.
Persuade, Matt. 28 : 14, we will **p.** him, and secure you.
Luke 16 : 31, will not be **p.** though one rose from dead.
Acts 26 : 28, almost thou **p.** me to be a Christian.
    28 : 23, **p.** them concerning Jesus.
Rom. 14 : 5, let every man be fully **p.**
2 Cor. 5 : 11, we **p.** men.
Gal. 1 : 10, do I now **p.** men or God ?
2 Tim. 1 : 12, am **p.** that he is able to keep.
Heb. 6 : 9, are **p.** better things of you.
Persuasion, Gal. 5 : 8.
Pertain, Rom. 15 : 17, things which **p.** to God.
1 Cor. 6 : 3, things that **p.** to this life.
Heb. 5 : 1, things **p.** to God.
2 Pet. 1 : 3, all things that **p.** to life.
Perverse, Deut. 32 : 5, a **p.** generation.
Job 6 : 30, cannot my taste discern **p.** things ?
Prov. 4 : 24, **p.** lips put far from thee.
    17 : 20, **p.** tongue falleth into mischief.
    23 : 33, thine heart shall utter **p.** things.
Matt. 17 : 17; Luke 9 : 41, O **p.** generation.
Phil. 2 : 15, in the midst of a **p.** nation.
1 Tim. 6 : 5, **p.** disputings.
Perversely, 1 Ki. 8 : 47, sinned and have done **p.**
Ps. 119 : 78, dealt **p.** with me.
Perverseness, Prov. 11 : 3; Isa. 59 : 3; Ezek. 9 : 9.
Pervert, Deut. 16 : 19, a gift doth **p.** words of righteous.
Deut. 24 : 17, thou shalt not **p.** judgment of stranger.
Job 8 : 3, doth God **p.** judgment ?
Prov. 10 : 9, he that **p.** his ways shall be known.
Jer. 23 : 36, ye have **p.** the words of God.
Mic. 3 : 9, ye that **p.** equity.
Acts 13 : 10, wilt thou not cease to **p.** right ways ?
Gal. 1 : 7, would **p.** the gospel of Christ.
Pestilence, threatened for disobedience, Lev. 26 : 25; Num. 14 : 12; Deut. 28 : 21; Jer. 14 : 12; 27 : 13; Ezek. 5 : 12; 6 : 11; 7 : 15; Luke 21 : 11.
inflicted, Num. 14 : 37; 16 : 46; 25 : 9; 2 Sam. 24 : 15; Ps. 78 : 50.
removed, Num. 16 : 47; 2 Sam. 24 : 16.
Ex. 9 : 15, smite thee with **p.**
Ps. 91 : 3, deliver thee from noisome **p.**
Hab. 3 : 5, before him went **p.**
Matt. 24 : 7, there shall be **p.**
Pestilent, Acts 24 : 5.
Pestle, Prov. 27 : 22.
Peter (pē-tẽr) [rock, stone], apostle, called, Matt.

4 : 18, 19; Mark 1 : 16, 17; Luke 5; John 1 : 35.
sent forth, Matt. 10 : 2; Mark 3 : 16; Luke 6 : 14.
confesses Jesus to be the Christ, Matt. 16 : 16; Mark 8 : 29; Luke 9 : 20.
present at the transfiguration, Matt. 17; Mark 9; Luke 9 : 28; 2 Pet. 1 : 16.
his self-confidence reproved, Luke 22 : 31; John 13 : 36.
thrice denies Christ, Matt. 26 : 69; Mark 14 : 66; Luke 22 : 57; John 18 : 17.
his repentance, Matt. 26 : 75; Mark 14 : 72; Luke 22 : 62.
his address to the disciples, Acts 1 : 15.
preaches to the Jews, Acts 2 : 14; 3 : 12.
brought before the council, Acts 4.
rebukes Ananias and Sapphira, Acts 5.
denounces Simon the sorcerer, Acts 8 : 20.
restores Eneas and Tabitha, Acts 9 : 32-40.
sent for by Cornelius, Acts 10.
imprisoned, and liberated by an angel, Acts 12.
his decision about circumcision, Acts 15 : 7.
rebuked by Paul, Gal. 2 : 14.
bears witness to Paul's teaching, 2 Pet. 3 : 15.
his death foretold, John 21 : 18; 2 Pet. 1 : 14.
comforts the church, and exhorts to holy living, etc., 1 and 2 Pet.
Peter, First Epistle of.
That the apostle Peter was the author of this epistle has not been seriously questioned, and the evidence, both internal and external, is overwhelmingly favourable to this view. It was probably written in 64 or 65 A.D. The mention of the provinces of Asia Minor, beginning in the east and moving west, is in harmony with the view that he wrote from Babylon (5 : 13). The people addressed were those evangelized by Paul, and that many of them were Gentiles is clear from such passages as 1 : 14; 2 : 9, 10; 4 : 3. This epistle is referred to in 2 Pet. 3 : 1. The goal of Redemption is the revelation of Jesus Christ (1 : 8, 13). Holiness is the norm of the Christian life (1 : 15, 16). The style of the writing is vigorous and full of metaphor. There are at least 15 figures in the 2nd chapter. That Peter was thinking in Hebrew while writing 2 : 4-8 is evident from his play upon the words representing house, stone, son, daughter. (Clarke *in loco*). In relation to human governments, Peter's direction in 2 : 13, 14 are parallel with Paul's in Rom. 13 : 1-7. Concerning wives and husbands, ch. 3 : 1-7, recalls Eph. 5 : 22-33 and Col. 3 : 18-25. Concerning humility and the mind of Christ, ch. 4 : 1, 2 recalls Phil. 2 : 5-11. The church was suffering from persecution. The spirit of Nero reached beyond Rome. The fiery trial was upon believers (4 : 12-19). This trial must be met in the spirit of Rom. 8 : 18-25. One can endure much if his eyes are upon a worthy goal. " Wherefore girding up the loins of your mind, be sober, and set your hope perfectly on the grace

that is to be brought unto you at the revelation of Jesus Christ " (ch. 1 : 13).

Peter, Second Epistle of.
The author was Simon Peter, a bondservant and apostle of Jesus Christ. He was among those present on the mount and saw the kingly glory that descended upon the Saviour. He also heard the attestation of the Father to the Son (1 : 16-18). In spite of these strong points of identification, the Petrine authorship of the epistle has been challenged chiefly on account of the difference in vocabulary and style from the first epistle. Jerome suggests that the difference may be accounted for by a difference in interpreters. The loftiness of the language was called out largely by the loftiness of his theme. No prophecy ever came through the prophet's own disclosure, but men spake from God borne along by the Holy Ghost (1 : 21) Gnosticism was denying primary truths of revelation, therefore Peter states with all authority (ch. 3) truth concerning the re-making of the first earth by judgment waters and the expected re-making of the present earth by judgment fires.

Pethuel (pĕ-thŭ-ĕl) [godly simplicity], Joel 1 : 1.

Petition, 1 Sam. 1 : 17, God grant thee thy **p.**
1 Ki. 2 : 20, I desire one small **p.**
Esther 5 : 6; 7 : 2; 9 : 12, what is thy **p.**?
Ps. 20 : 5, the Lord fulfil all thy **p.**
Dan. 6 : 13, maketh his **p.** three times a day.
1 John 5 : 15, we have the **p.** that we desired.

Phalti (phăl-tī) (*i.e.,* **Phaltiel**) [God is deliverance], 1 Sam. 25 : 44; 2 Sam. 3 : 15.

Pharaoh (Gr. form. The Heb. is " par-ōh "; Egypt., " phe-rā-o) [great house], title of the kings of Egypt, Gen. 12 : 15.
reproves Abraham, Gen. 12 : 18.
his dreams interpreted by Joseph, Gen. 41.
his kindness to Jacob and his family, Gen. 47.
oppresses the Israelites, Ex. 1 : 8.
miracles performed before, and plagues sent, Ex. 7; 8; 9; 10.
grants Moses' request, Ex. 12 : 31.
repenting, pursues Israel and perishes in the Red Sea, Ex. 14; (Neh. 9 : 10; Ps. 135 : 9; 136 : 15; Rom. 9 : 17).
Solomon's affinity with, 1 Ki. 3 : 1.
receives Hadad, Solomon's adversary, 1 Ki. 11 : 19.

Pharaoh-hophra (phâr-āoh-hŏph-ră), his fate predicted, Jer. 44 : 30.
See Ezek. 29 : 3; 30; 31 : 32.

Pharaoh-nechoh (phâr-āoh-nē-chōh), slays Josiah, 2 Ki. 23 : 29.
dethrones Jehoahaz, 2 Ki. 23 : 33; 2 Chr. 36 : 3.
See Necho.

Pharaoh's daughter, saves Moses, Ex. 2 : 5, 10; Acts 7 : 21.

Pharisee.
(1) Origin and Name.—Post-Exilic Israel was faced with the difficulty of building up a new type of community to replace the bankrupt monarchy. Their solution was a sort of half-Church, half-State hybrid; their leaders were drawn not so much from

the prophets now as from teachers, who stressed the Jewish idea of monotheism. Superiority to the idolatrous heathen as regards the idea of God brought with it a tendency to withdraw from contact with alien races (cf. Ezra 10 : 11). Thus, when, in the third century, B.C., Hellenism began to threaten Judaism with extermination, the stricter Jews or Puritans (" Hasidim " or " Holy Men ") drew apart from innovating tendencies. Their " separating " themselves earned them the name Pharisees.
(2) Leading Characteristics.—In religion they did lean to the new views concerning the apocalyptic or divine intervention, with its doctrine of angels and of the resurrection (cf. the Sadducees, who in this were more conservative). Politics they regarded as useless for the true Jew in light of the sudden coming of the Messiah, when the earth was to be straightened by a cataclysmic effort on God's part. Their strict adherence to the " jot and tittle " of the Law led them to be charged with sanctimonious hypocrisy. They held that the will was free, and the soul was immortal and all life was predestined. While never very numerous, their influence was enormous, and they were respected by the people as conservers of all that was best in the faith (cf. Gal. 2 : 12 ff.; Matt. 23 : 2). Their weaknesses arose from their over-anxiety to conserve the Law and thus to externalise.
See Sadducees.
censured by Christ, Matt. 5 : 20; 16 : 6; 21 : 43; 23 : 2, 13; Luke 11 : 39, 42.
Christ's controversies with, Matt. 9 : 34; 19 : 3; Mark 2 : 18; Luke 5 : 30; 11 : 39; 16 : 14.
celebrated ones : Nicodemus, John 3 : 1; Simon, Matt. 26 : 6; Gamaliel, Acts 5 : 34; Saul of Tarsus, Acts 23 : 6; 26 : 5; Phil. 3 : 5.
Christ entertained by, Luke 11 : 37; 14 : 1.
people cautioned against, Mark 8 : 15; Luke 12 : 1.
seek a sign from Christ, Matt. 12 : 38; 16 : 1.
take counsel against Christ, Matt. 12 : 14; Mark 3 : 6.
send officers to take him, John 7 : 32.
Nicodemus remonstrates with, John 7 : 50.
contend about circumcision, Acts 15 : 5.
their belief in the resurrection, Acts 23 : 8.

Pharosh (phâr-ōsh), Ezra 8 : 3.

Pharpar (phär-pär) [rapid], a river of Damascus, 2 Ki. 5 : 12.

Pharzites (phär-zītes), Num. 26 : 20.

Phaseah (phă-sē-äh), Neh. 7 : 51.

Phaseal, son of Antipater.

Phebe or **Phœbe** (phē-bē), Rom. 16 : 1.

Phenice, Phenicia (phē-ni-çē, phē-nĭç-jä), Paul and Barnabas pass through, Acts 11 : 19; 15 : 3; 21 : 2.

Phenice (**Phœnix**) [palm], a port of Crete, Acts 27 : 12.

Phichol (phī-chŏl) [mouth of all], Gen. 21 : 32.

Philadelphia, a city of Lydia, church of, commended, Rev. 1 : 11; 3 : 7.

Philemon (phī-lē-mon), Philem. 1.

Philemon, Epistle to.

Characteristics and Date.—This exquisite relic stands alone among the writings of St. Paul and almost alone in the Bible. It is a private letter from an Apostle, to a private individual. The Pastoral Epistles are addressed to individuals; but they are not private. They are partly official, being written to persons who hold office in the Church, and are to be read by others besides Titus and Timothy. The letter to Philemon is entirely domestic. St. Paul may have written many such letters in the course of his long ministry, but this is the only one of which we have any knowledge; and, short as it is, it reveals the Apostle to us in a new, but not unexpected character, as the perfect Christian gentleman, with all a gentleman's courtesy and delicacy of feeling. It was written at the same time as the Epistle to the Colossians (viz., A.D. 63), and Onesimus, the bearer of it, was accompanied by Tychicus, who had charge of the two longer Epistles.

Immediate Occasion.—Philemon of Colossæ had been converted by St. Paul. Apphia was probably his wife, and Archippus possibly his son (ver. 2). Onesimus, his slave, had robbed him and fled to Rome, the common hiding-place of countless criminals. His name means "profitable," and hence the play on words (ver. 11, 20). While he was in Rome he came in contact with St. Paul, who converted him and became deeply attached to him. But at great personal sacrifice he restored him to his master, whom he begs to welcome the former slave and thief as now a brother and the Apostle's child.

Paul and Slavery.—Neither here nor in other Epistles, in which he treats of slaves and their masters, does St. Paul order, or even recommend, emancipation. But he enjoins a treatment of slaves which would render emancipation either inevitable or unnecessary. If a slave is treated as a beloved brother, slavery has become an empty form. Of the effect of this letter we have no certain knowledge; but we need not doubt that Onesimus was forgiven and kindly received.

Philip (phĭ-lĭp) [lover of horses], apostle, called, John 1 : 43.

ordained, Matt. 10 : 3; Mark 3 : 18; Luke 6 : 14; John 12 : 22; Acts 1 : 13.

reproved by Christ, John 14 : 8.

deacon, elected, Acts 6 : 5.

preaches in Samaria, Acts 8 : 5.

baptizes the eunuch, Acts 8 : 38.

his daughter's prophecy, Acts 21 : 8.

brother of Herod, Matt. 14 : 3; Mark 6 : 17; Luke 3 : 1, 19.

Philippi (phĭ-lĭp-pī), Paul persecuted at, Acts 16 : 12.

church at, commended and exhorted, Phil. 1; 2; 3; 4.

Philippians, Epistle to the.

Characteristics, Occasion, and Date.—Like Romans and Ephesians, this Epistle is not called forth by any reported error in doctrine or in conduct; but, unlike them, it expounds no doctrinal system. It is a spontaneous expression of love and gratitude in return for the affectionate generosity of the Philippians, and is a beautiful reflection of the Apostle's mind and character in its noblest and tenderest moods.

The Epistle to the Philippians is the only one of St. Paul's letters to the Churches in which there is no word of rebuke or disappointment. It overflows with Christian cheerfulness. " Rejoice in the Lord alway; again I will say, rejoice " (4 : 4). Like the First Epistle to the Thessalonians, it approaches the character of a private letter as an exhibition of personal feeling; hence there is very little arrangement of topics. He looks forward to visiting them again (2 : 24); and it would seem that this hope was fulfilled in the interval between the two Roman imprisonments (1 Tim. 1 : 3); but in the New Testament we are told no more about Philippi. The letter was sent by Epaphroditus, who had brought help from the Philippians to their imprisoned master in Rome, at the cost of a severe illness, which almost proved fatal, and which left him rather homesick. St. Paul generously seconded his desire to return home, and with him sent this affectionate letter (2 : 25-30). Although Epaphras is a shortened form of Epaphroditus, yet Epaphroditus of Philippi is not to be identified with Epaphras of Colossæ (Col. 1 : 7; 4 : 12; Philem. 23). The date is 63 A.D.

Summary.—Salutation and Thanksgiving (1 : 1-11), Personal Narrative (1 : 12-26); Exhortation to follow Christ (1 : 27—2 : 18); the Missions of Timothy and Epaphroditus (2 : 19-30); Final Charge, interrupted by a Caution against those who debase the Gospel (3 : 1—4 : 1); and resumed (4 : 2-9); Gratitude for their Bounty (4 : 10-20); Greetings and Blessing (4 : 21-23).

Paul and the Church at Philippi.—Philippi, founded by Philip, the father of Alexander the Great, and immortalised by the battle which ended the Roman republic and ushered in the empire (42 B.C.), had been thereupon raised to the rank of a Roman military colony, and made a miniature likeness of Rome. Greeks, Roman officials and colonists, and a small colony of Jews, who had a place of prayer by the river, formed the population. St. Paul's first visit to Philippi, in company with Silas, Timothy, and Luke, is narrated by Luke with exceptional detail in one of the " we " sections (16 : 11-40). This was on the second missionary journey, in or near A.D. 52. The three converts whom St. Luke mentions, and the order of their conversion, are typical; first the proselyte purple-seller from Thyatira; next the Greek slave-girl with the spirit of divination; and lastly, the Roman gaoler. The Gospel is for both Jew and Gentile, for both bond and free, for both male and female; and it passed through the Jew and the proselyte to the Greek, and from the Greek to the Roman. Nowhere, in spite of very great persecution, was the Apostle's success so great, and nowhere had he more loyal converts. They were the only congregation from which he accepted pecuniary help (4 : 15), and that more than once. He was deeply attached to them as his " joy and crown "; and visited them a second time towards the end of 57, when he wrote 2 Corinthians and perhaps Galatians, on his way to Corinth; and yet a third time on his return to Asia for the last journey to Jerusalem, in the spring of 58, when he stayed and kept Easter with them. They contributed, not only to his support, but to the relief of the poor Christians in Judæa—a charitable work which St. Paul had very much at heart.

Philistia, Gen. 21 : 34; Ex. 13 : 17; Josh. 13 : 2; 2 Ki. 8 : 2; Ps. 60 : 8; 87 : 4; 108 : 9.

Philistines [wanderers], people of Philistia, Gen. 26 : 1; 1 Chr. 1 : 12. See **Palestine, Early Inhabitants.**

Ancient Philistines from Ancient Scriptures.

fill up Isaac's wells, Gen. 26 : 15.
contend with Joshua, Josh. 13; Shamgar, Judg. 3 : 31; Samson, Judg. 14; 15; 16; Samuel, 1 Sam. 4 : 7; Jonathan, 1 Sam. 14; Saul, 1 Sam. 17; David, 1 Sam. 17 : 38.
their wars with Israel, 1 Sam. 4 : 1; 28; 29; 31; 2 Chr. 21 : 16.
mentioned, Ps. 83 : 7; Isa. 2 : 6; 9 : 12; 11 : 14; Jer. 25 : 20.

their destruction foretold, Jer. 47; Ezek. 25 : 15; Amos 1 : 8; Obad. 19; Zeph. 2 : 5; Zech. 9 : 6.

Philosophers mentioned, Acts 17 : 18.

Philosophy, vanity of, Col. 2 : 8.

Phinehas (phĭn-ĕ-hăs) [mouth of brass, or negro ?], son of Eleazar, Ex. 6 : 25.
slays Zimri and Cozbi, Num. 25 : 7, 8, 14, 15; Ps. 106 : 30.
sent against the Midianites, etc., Num. 31 : 6; Josh. 22 : 13; Judg. 20 : 28.
son of Eli, his sin and death, 1 Sam. 1 : 3; 2 : 22; 4 : 11.

Phygellus (phȳ-ġĕl-lŭs) and Hermogenes, censured, 2 Tim. 1 : 15.

Phylacteries. See **Frontlets.**

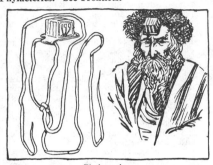

Phylacteries.

Physician, Job 13 : 4, ye are all p. of no value.
Jer. 8 : 22, is there no p. there ?
Matt. 9 : 12; Mark 2 : 17; Luke 5 : 31, they that be whole need not a p.
Mark 5 : 26, suffered many things of many p.
Luke 4 : 23, p., heal thyself.
8 : 43, spent all her living upon p.
Col. 4 : 14, the beloved p.

Pick, Prov. 30 : 17.

Pictures, Num. 33 : 52, shall destroy all their p.
Prov. 25 : 11, like apples of gold in p. of silver.
Isa. 2 : 16, day of Lord on pleasant p.

Piece, 1 Sam. 2 : 36; Prov. 6 : 26; 28 : 21, a p. of bread.
Ps. 50 : 22, lest I tear you in p.
Jer. 23 : 29, hammer that breaketh rock in p.
Zech. 11 : 13; Matt. 27 : 6, 9, thirty p. of silver.
Luke 14 : 18, bought a p. of ground.

Pierce, Num. 24 : 8, p. them with arrows.
2 Ki. 18 : 21; Isa. 36 : 6, it will go into his hand and p. it.
Ps. 22 : 16, p. my hands and my feet.
Zech. 12 : 10; John 19 : 37, they shall look on me whom they have p.
1 Tim. 6 : 10, p. themselves with many sorrows.
Heb. 4 : 12, p. to the dividing asunder.
Rev. 1 : 7, they also which p. him.

Piercings, Prov. 12 : 18.

Piety [ar.], filial affection, 1 Tim. 5 : 4.

Pigeon, as an offering, Lev. 1 : 14; 12 : 6; Num. 6 : 10; Luke 2 : 24. See **Dove.**

Pilate (pī-lāte) [armed with a dart], Pontius, governor of Judæa, Luke 3 : 1.

destroys the Galileans, Luke 13 : 1.

declares Christ's innocence, but delivers him to be crucified, Matt. 27; Mark 15; Luke 23; John 18; 19.

grants the request of Joseph of Arimathea, Matt. 27 : 57; Mark 15 : 42; Luke 23 : 50; John 19 : 38.

See Acts 3 : 13; 4 : 27; 13 : 28; 1 Tim. 6 : 13.

Pile, Isa. 30 : 33; Ezek. 24 : 9.

Pilgrimage, Gen. 47 : 9; Ex. 6 : 4; Ps. 119 : 54.

Pilgrims, Heb. 11 : 13; 1 Pet. 2 : 11.

Pillars. Pillars seem to have been an essential part of every "high place." Erected originally perhaps as suitable resting-places if the spirits of the departed came back to the scene of their burial, they became the abode of any numina, and later still were regarded merely as symbolic of deities whose abodes were elsewhere.

erected by Jacob, Gen. 28 : 18; 35 : 20; and Absalom, 2 Sam. 18 : 18.

in porch of the temple, 1 Ki. 7 : 21; 2 Chr. 3 : 17.

pillar of cloud and fire, Ex. 13 : 21; 33 : 9; Ps. 99 : 7.

Gen. 19 : 26, a p. of salt.

Neh. 9 : 12, leddest them by cloudy p.

Job 9 : 6; 26 : 11, the p. thereof tremble.

1 Tim. 3 : 15, the p. and ground of the truth.

Rev. 3 : 12, him that overcometh will I make a p.

Pilled, Gen. 30 : 37 f.

Pillow, Gen. 28 : 11, Jacob put stones for p.

1 Sam. 19 : 13, 16, a p. of goat's hair.

Ezek. 13 : 18, woe to women that sew p.

Mark 4 : 38, Jesus was asleep on a p.

Pilots, Ezek. 27 : 8, 27, 28, 29.

Pin, Judg. 16 : 14; Ezek. 15 : 3.

Pine tree, Isa. 41 : 19; 60 : 13. See **Fir.**

Pinnacle, Matt. 4 : 5; Luke 4 : 9.

Pipe. Minstrels are mentioned in Matt. 9 : 23, and the words used there denotes persons playing on the pipe.

1 Ki. 1 : 40, the people p. with p.

Isa. 5 : 12, the harp and p. are in their feasts.

Matt. 11 : 17; Luke 7 : 32, we have p. unto you.

1 Cor. 14 : 7, how shall it be known what is p. ?

Pipers, Rev. 18 : 22.

Pisgah (pĭs-găh), **Mount** [piece, peak], ridge in Moab, Num. 23 : 14; Deut. 3 : 27; 34 : 1. See **Nebo.**

Pit, the grave, death, Job 17 : 16; 33 : 18; Ps. 28 : 1; 30 : 9; 88 : 4; Isa. 14 : 15; 38 : 17; Ezek. 26 : 20; 32 : 18.

as a prison, Isa. 24 : 22; Zech. 9 : 11.

Gen. 37 : 20, cast him into some p.

Ex. 21 : 33, if a man dig a p.

Num. 16 : 30, 33, go down into the p.

Job 33 : 24, deliver him from going down to the p.

Ps. 40 : 2, brought me out of horrible p.

88 : 4; 143 : 7; Prov. 1 : 12, them that go down into p.

Prov. 28 : 10, fall into his own p.

Isa. 24 : 17, p. and the snare are on thee.

38 : 17, the p. of corruption.

Matt. 12 : 11; Luke 14 : 5, fall into a p. on sabbath.

Pitch, used for the ark, etc., Gen. 6 : 14; Ex. 2 : 3; Isa. 34 : 9.

Pitched, Gen. 12 : 8; 13 : 12; 26 : 17; 2 Ki. 25 : 1.

Pitcher, Gen. 24 : 15, 20; Luke 22 : 10.

Gideon's use of, Judg. 7 : 16 ff.

Eccl. 12 : 6, or the p. be broken at the fountain.

Lam. 4 : 2, esteemed as earthen p.

Mark 14 : 13, man bearing a p.

Pitiful, Lam. 4 : 10; Jas. 5 : 11; 1 Pet. 3 : 8.

Pity, Deut. 7 : 16; 19 : 13, thine eye shall have no p.

Ps. 69 : 20, I looked for some to take p.

Prov. 19 : 17, he that hath p. on the poor lendeth to Lord.

Isa. 13 : 18, they shall have no p.

63 : 9, in his p. he redeemed them.

Jer. 15 : 5, who shall have p. on thee ?

21 : 7, he shall not spare them, neither have p.

Ezek. 36 : 21, I had p. for my holy name.

Matt. 18 : 33, as I had p. on thee.

Zech. 11 : 5, their shepherds p. them not.

cf. Deut. 13 : 8; 25 : 12; 2 Sam. 12 : 6; Job 19 : 21; Ps. 103 : 13; Joel 2 : 18.

Place, idolatrous, 1 Ki. 11 : 7; 12 : 31; 13 : 22; Ps. 78 : 58; Ezek. 16 : 24.

destruction of, Lev. 26 : 30; 2 Ki. 18 : 4; 23 : 5; 2 Chr. 14 : 3; 17 : 6; 34 : 3; Ezek. 6 : 3.

Ex. 3 : 5; Josh. 5 : 15, the p. whereon thou standest is holy.

1 Ki. 8 : 29, thine eyes may be open toward this p.

2 Ki. 6 : 1; Isa. 49 : 20, the p. is too strait.

Ps. 26 : 8, the p. where thine honour dwelleth.

32 : 7; 119 : 114, thou art my hiding-p.

33 : 14, from the p. of his habitation.

103 : 16, the p. thereof shall know it no more.

Prov. 15 : 3, the eyes of the Lord are in every p.

Eccl. 3 : 20, all go to one p.

Isa. 60 : 13, the p. of my feet glorious.

66 : 1, where is the p. of my rest ?

Mic. 1 : 3, the Lord cometh out of his p.

Mal. 1 : 11, incense be offered in every p.

Matt. 28 : 6; Mark 16 : 6, see the p. where the Lord lay.

Mark 6 : 10, in what p. soever.

Luke 10 : 1, two and two into every p.

14 : 9, give this man p.

John 8 : 37, my word hath no p. in you.

Acts 2 : 1, with one accord in one p.

4 : 31, the p. was shaken.

8 : 32, the p. of the scripture.

Rom. 12 : 19, rather give p. unto wrath.

Eph. 4 : 27, neither give p. to the devil.

Heb. 12 : 17, no p. of repentance.

Plagues, of Egypt. See **Egypt.**

of Israel. See **Pestilence.**

Ex. 12 : 13, the p. shall not be on you.

Deut. 28 : 61, every p. not written.

2 Sam. 24 : 21; 1 Chr. 21 : 22, the p. may be stayed.

1 Ki. 8 : 38, know every man the **p.** of his heart.

Ps. 91 : 10, neither any **p.** come nigh thy dwelling.

Hos. 13 : 14, O death, I will be thy **p.**

Mark 5 : 34, go in peace, and be whole of **p.**

Rev. 22 : 18, God shall add to him the **p.** written.

Plain, Cities of the. These were five in number, viz., Sodom, Gomorrah, Admah, Zeboiim, and Bela (or Zoar). They were situated in the " plain " (or " circle ") of Jordan, Gen. 18, 19.

Plain, Gen. 25 : 27, Jacob was a **p.** man.

Ps. 27 : 11, lead me in a **p.** path.

Prov. 8 : 9, they are **p.** to him that understandeth.

15 : 19, the way of righteous is made **p.**

Isa. 40 : 4, rough places made **p.**

Mark 7 : 35, he spake **p.**

Plainly, Ex. 21 : 5, if the servant **p.** say.

Deut. 27 · 8, write this law very **p.**

Isa. 32 : 4, stammerers shall speak **p.**

John 10 : 24, if thou be Christ, tell us **p.**

16 : 29, now speakest thou **p.**

Heb. 11 : 14, declare **p.**

Plainness, 2 Cor. 3 : 12.

Plaister, Isa. 38 : 21.

Plaiting, 1 Pet. 3 : 3.

Planes, Isa. 44 : 13.

Planets, 2 Ki. 23 : 5.

Planks, 1 Ki. 6 : 15; Ezek. 41 : 25, 26.

Plant, figuratively mentioned, Ps. 128 : 3; Song of Sol. 4 : 13; Jer. 2 : 21.

Job 14 : 9, bring forth boughs like a **p.**

Ps. 144 : 12, sons as **p.** grown up.

Isa. 5 : 7, his pleasant **p.**

53 : 2, as a tender **p.**

Ezek. 34 : 29, a **p.** of renown.

Matt. 15 : 13, every **p.** my Father hath not planted.

2 Sam. 7 : 10; 1 Chr. 17 : 9, I will **p.** them.

Ps. 1 : 3; Jer. 17 : 8, like a tree **p.**

Ps. 92 : 13, **p.** in the house of the Lord.

94 : 9, he that **p.** the ear.

Isa. 40 : 24, they shall not be **p.**

Luke 17 : 6, be thou **p.** in the sea.

Rom. 6 : 5, if we have been **p.** together.

1 Cor. 3 : 6, I have **p.**

Plantation, Ezek. 17 : 7.

Planters, Jer. 31 : 5.

Planting, Isa. 61 : 3.

Plaster, Deut. 27 : 2; Dan. 5 : 5.

Plat, 2 Ki. 9 : 26.

Plate, Ex. 28 : 36; 39 : 30.

Platted, Matt. 27 : 29; John 19 : 2.

Platter, Matt. 23 : 25, 26; Luke 11 : 39.

Play, Ex. 32 : 6; 1 Cor. 10 : 7, people rose up to **p.**

1 Sam. 16 : 17, a man that can **p.** well.

2 Sam. 6 : 21, I will **p.** before the Lord.

10 : 12, let us **p.** the men.

Job 40 : 20 where beasts of field **p.**

41 : 5, wilt thou **p.** with him.

Ps. 33 : 3, **p.** skilfully with a loud noise.

Isa. 11 : 8, sucking child shall **p.**

Ezek. 33 : 32, can **p.** well on an instrument.

Zech. 8 : 5, boys and girls **p.** in the streets.

Player, 1 Sam. 16 : 16; Ps. 68 : 25.

Plea, Deut. 17 : 8.

Plead, Judg. 6 : 31, will ye **p.** for Baal ?

Job 9 : 19, who shall set me a time to **p.** ?

13 : 19, who will **p.** with me ?

16 : 21, might **p.** for a man with God.

Isa. 1 : 17, **p.** for the widow.

3 : 13, the Lord standeth up to **p.**

43 : 26, let us **p.** together.

Jer. 2 : 9, I will yet **p.** with you.

Lam. 3 : 58, O Lord, thou hast **p.**

Hos. 2 : 2, **p.** with your mother, **p.**

Pleading, of God with Israel, Isa. 1; 3 : 13; Jer. 2-6; 13; Ezek. 17 : 20; 20 : 36; 22; Hos. 2 ff.; Joel 3 : 2; Mic. 2.

of Job with God, Job 16 : 21.

Pleasant, Gen. 3 : 6, **p.** to the eyes.

2 Sam. 1 : 23, were **p.** in their lives.

Ps. 16 : 6, lines have fallen in **p.** places.

106 : 24, they despised the **p.** land.

133 : 1, how **p.** for brethren to dwell together.

Prov. 2 : 10, knowledge is **p.** to thy soul.

9 : 17, bread eaten in secret is **p.**

15 : 26, the words of the pure are **p.** words.

16 : 24, **p.** words are as honeycomb.

Eccl. 11 : 7, it is **p.** to behold the sun.

Isa. 32 : 12, lament for **p.** fields.

64 : 11, our **p.** things are laid waste.

Jer. 31 : 20, is Ephraim a **p.** child ?

Ezek. 33 : 32, song of one that hath a **p.** voice.

Dan. 10 : 3, I ate no **p.** bread.

Pleasantness, Prov. 3 : 17.

Please, 2 Sam. 7 : 29; 1 Chr. 17 : 27, let it **p.** thee.

Ps. 51 : 19, then shalt thou be **p.** with sacrifices.

69 : 31, this also shall **p.** the Lord.

115 : 3, God hath done whatsoever he **p.**

Prov. 16 : 7, when a man's ways **p.** the Lord.

Isa. 53 : 10, it **p.** the Lord to bruise him.

55 : 11, accomplish that which I **p.**

Mic. 6 : 7, will the Lord be **p.** with rams ?

Mal. 1 : 8, will he be **p.** with thee ?

John 8 : 29, I do always those things that **p.** him.

Rom. 8 : 8, they that are in the flesh cannot **p.** God.

15 : 3, Christ **p.** not himself.

1 Cor. 1 : 21, it **p.** God by the foolishness of preaching.

Gal. 1 : 10, do I seek to **p.** men ?

Heb. 11 : 6, without faith it is impossible to **p.** God.

Pleasers, Eph. 6 : 6.

Pleasures, vanity of worldly, Eccl. 2; effects of, Luke 8 : 14; Jas. 5; 2 Pet. 2 : 13; exhortations against, 2 Tim. 3 : 4; Titus 3 : 3; Heb. 11 : 25; 1 Pet. 4.

1 Chr. 29 : 17, thou hast **p.** in uprightness.

Esther 1 : 8, according to every man's **p.**

Job 21 : 21, what **p.** hath he in his house ?

22 : 3, is it any **p.** to the Almighty ?

Ps. 5 : 4, not a God that hath **p.** in wickedness.

16 : 11, at thy right hand **p.** for evermore.

51 : 18, do good in thy good **p.**

102 : 14, thy servants take **p.** in her stones.

103 : 21, ministers that do his **p.**

111 : 2, sought out of all that have **p.** therein.

149 : 4, the Lord taketh **p.** in his people.

Prov. 21 : 17, he that loveth **p.** shall be poor.

Eccl. 12 : 1, I have no **p.** in them.

BETHANY

VALE OF JEZREEL

Isa. 53 : 10, the **p.** of the Lord shall prosper.

58 : 13, from doing thy **p.** on my holy day.

Jer. 48 : 38; Hos. 8 : 8, a vessel wherein is no **p.**

Ezek. 18 : 23; 33 : 11, have I any **p.** that wicked should die ?

Mal. 1 : 10, I have no **p.** in you, saith the Lord.

Luke 12 : 32, Father's good **p.**

Eph. 1 : 5, good **p.** of his will.

Phil. 2 : 13, both to will and to do of his good **p.**

1 Tim. 5 : 6, she that liveth in **p.**

Heb. 10 : 38, my soul shall have no **p.** in him.

12 : 10, chastened us after their own **p.**

Jas. 5 : 5, ye have lived in **p.** on earth.

Rev. 4 : 11, for thy **p.** they were created.

Pledges, limitations of, Ex. 22 : 26; Deut. 24 : 6.

See Job 22 : 6; 24 : 3; Ezek. 18 : 7; Amos 2 : 8.

Pleiades (plê-ă-dēś), Job 9 : 9; 38 : 31; Amos 5 : 8.

Plenteous, Deut. 28 : 11; 30 : 9, Lord shall make thee **p.**

Ps. 86 : 5; 103 : 8, **p.** in mercy.

130 : 7, with the Lord is **p.** redemption.

Matt. 9 : 37, the harvest truly is **p.**

Plenteousness, Gen. 41 : 53; Prov. 21 : 5.

Plentiful, Ps. 68 : 9, thou didst send a **p.** rain

Jer. 48 : 33, gladness is taken from **p.** field.

Plentifully, Luke 12 : 16.

Plenty, the gift of God, Deut. 16 : 10; 28 : 11; Ps. 65; 68 : 9; 104 : 10; 144 : 13; Joel 2 : 26; Acts 14 : 17.

Gen. 27 : 28, **p.** of corn and wine.

Job 22 : 25, **p.** of silver.

37 : 23, **p.** of justice.

Prov. 3 : 10, barns filled with **p.**

Jer. 44 : 17, **p.** of victuals.

Plotteth, Ps. 37 : 12.

Ploughing with one-handed plough.

Plow. From the modern Syrian counterpart we learn what a plow was like in Biblical times. The " body " consisted of a piece of tough wood bent at the foot and pointed. This was to receive the sheath or share of iron (1 Sam. 13 : 20). A short cross-piece at the upper end formed the handle. There were two parts to the pole; through the lower end of the first, which is curved and strong, the " body " is passed slightly above the share, through the upper end of the second, which is also the lighter part of the pole, a pin is passed, to act as a means for attaching the " yoke."

Job 4 : 8, that **p.** iniquity reap the same.

Prov. 20 : 4, sluggard will not **p.**

Isa. 28 : 24, doth the plowman **p.** all day to sow ?

1 Cor. 9 : 10, he that **p.** should **p.** in hope.

See Amos 6 : 12; Isa. 30 : 24; Deut. 22 : 10.

Plowman, Isa. 61 : 5; Jer. 14 : 4; Amos 9 : 13.

Plowshares, beaten into swords, Joel 3 : 10.

swords to be beaten into plowshares, Isa. 2 : 4; Mic. 4 : 3.

Pluck, Deut. 23 : 25, thou mayest **p.** the ears.

2 Chr. 7 : 20, then will I **p.** them up.

Job 24 : 9, they **p.** the fatherless from the breast.

Ps. 25 : 15, he shall **p.** my feet out of the net.

52 : 5, **p.** thee out of thy place.

80 : 12, they which pass **p.** her.

Eccl. 3 : 2, a time to **p.** up.

Amos 4 : 11; Zech. 3 : 2, a firebrand **p.** out of the burning.

Matt. 5 : 29; 18 : 9; Mark 9 : 47, if eye offend thee, **p.** it out.

Matt. 12 : 1; Mark 2 : 23, began to **p.** ears of corn.

John 10 : 28, nor shall any **p.** them out of my hand.

Jude 12, twice dead, **p.** up by the roots.

Plumbline, Amos 7 : 8.

Plummet, 2 Ki. 21 : 13; Isa. 28 : 17; Zech. 4 : 10.

Plunge, Job 9 : 31.

Poets, heathen, quoted, Acts 17 : 28; Titus 1 : 12.

Point, Gen. 25 : 32, at the **p.** to die.

Jer. 17 : 1, written with the **p.** of a diamond.

Mark 5 : 23, John 4 : 47, at the **p.** of death.

Heb. 4 : 15, in all **p.** tempted.

Jas. 2 : 10, yet offend in one **p.**

Poison, Deut. 32 : 24, the **p.** of serpents.

Ps. 140 : 3, adders' **p.** is under their lips.

Jas. 3 : 8, tongue is full of deadly **p.**

See Ps. 58 : 4; Rom. 3 : 13.

Pole, Num. 21 : 8, 9.

Policy, Dan. 8 : 25.

Polished, Ps. 144 : 12; Isa. 49 : 2; Dan. 10 : 6.

Politarch. This is the word rendered " rulers of the city " in Acts 17 : 6. " Politarch " does not occur in Greek literature, and for a long time was not known to have been used elsewhere, but it has been found carved on an arch (now in the possession of the British Museum) at Thessalonica, of the date of A.D. 69-79.

Poll, Num. 3 : 47; Mic. 1 : 16.

Pollute, Num. 18 : 32, neither **p.** holy things.

Ps. 106 : 38, land was **p.** with blood.

Ezek. 20 : 31; 23 : 30; 36 : 18, ye **p.** yourselves with idols.

Mal. 1 : 12, say, The Table of the Lord is **p.**

Acts 21 : 28, **p.** this holy place.

Pollutions, under the law, Lev. 5 : 11; 13; 15; 21; 22; Num. 5; 9 : 6; Ezek. 22.

of the heathen, Lev. 18 : 24; 19 : 31; 20 : 3; Acts 15 : 20.

of the sabbath, Neh. 13 : 15; Isa. 56 : 2; Ezek. 20 : 13.

of God's altar, etc., Ex. 20 : 25; 2 Chr. 33 : 7; 36 : 14; Ezek. 8 : 6; 44 : 7; Dan. 8 : 11; Zeph. 3 : 4; Mal. 1 : 7.

Pomegranate, a lovely tree—evergreen in warm countries—bearing large orange-scarlet flowers, and large apple-like fruits. The bright pink seeds are beautifully arranged within the rind of the fruit. This fruit was cultivated from early days in Egypt. The spies brought from Eschol grapes, figs, and pomegranates. See Ex. 38 : 33.

Pommel, 2 Chr. 4 : 12.

Pomp, Isa. 5 : 14; Ezek. 7 : 24; Acts 25 : 23.

Ponder, Prov. 4 : 26, p. the path of thy feet.
5 : 21, the Lord p. all his goings.
Luke 2 : 19, Mary p. them in her heart.

Ponds, Ex. 7 : 19; 8 : 5; Isa. 19 : 10.

Pontius (pŏn-tĭŭs). See **Pilate.**

Pool, Isa. 35 : 7, ground shall become a p.
41 : 18, wilderness a p. of water.
John 5 : 2, by the sheep market, a p.
5 : 7, put me into the p.
9 : 7, wash in the p. of Siloam.

Poor. An interesting study is to note all the instances in which the word " poor " occurs in the Old Testament. The prophets especially seem to imply that the " poor " are righteous, the " rich " wicked. The Hebrews were very alert to the problem of the poor and their attitude, on the whole, was very humane.
always to be found, 1 Sam. 2 : 7; Matt. 26 : 11; John 12 : 8.
their condition described, Job 24 : 4; Prov. 13 : 8; 14 : 20; 18 : 23; 19 : 4; Eccl. 9 : 15.
causes of poverty, Prov. 6 : 11; 13 : 4; 19 : 15; 20 : 13; 23 : 21; 28 : 19.
not to be despised, Deut. 1 : 17; 16 : 19; Prov. 24 : 23; 28 : 21; Jas. 2.
oppression of, censured, Ex. 22 : 25; 23 : 3; Deut. 24 : 12; Job 24 : 9; Ps. 12 : 5; 14 : 6; 82 : 3; Prov. 14 : 31; 28 : 3; Eccl. 5 : 8; Isa. 3 : 14; Jer. 22 : 3; Amos 4; 5 : 11; 8 : 4; Zech. 7 : 10; Jas. 2 : 3.
kindly treatment of, Ex. 23 : 11; Lev. 19 : 10; 23 : 22; 25 : 25; Deut. 15 : 7; Isa. 58 : 7; Gal. 2 : 10.
God's consideration of, Job 5 : 15; Ps. 69 : 33; 72 : 2; 102 : 17; 113 : 7; Zech. 11 : 7.
provision for, in the church, Acts 6 : 1; 1 Cor. 16 : 2; 2 Cor. 8 : 9.
in spirit, blessed by Christ, Matt. 5 : 6; Luke 6 : 20.
Ex. 30 : 15, the p. shall not give less.
Lev. 19 : 15, shalt not respect person of p.
Deut. 15 : 11, the p. shall never cease.
1 Sam. 2 : 8; Ps. 113 : 7, Lord raiseth up the p.
Job 5 : 16, the p. hath hope.
29 : 16, I was a father to the p.
36 : 15; Ps. 72 : 12, deliver p. in affliction.
Ps. 9 : 18, expectation of the p.
10 : 14, the p. committeth himself to thee.
34 : 6, this p. man cried.
41 : 1, blessed is he that considereth the p.
68 : 10, prepared of thy goodness for the p.
82 : 4, deliver the p. and needy.
132 : 15, I will satisfy her p. with bread.
140 : 12, Lord will maintain the right of the p.

Prov. 10 : 4, he becometh p. that dealeth with a slack hand.
13 : 7, there is that maketh himself p.
14 : 21, that hath mercy on the p., happy is he.
17 : 5, whoso mocketh the p. reproacheth his Maker.
22 : 2, the rich and p. meet together.
30 : 9, lest I be p., and steal.
Isa. 14 : 32, the p. of his people shall trust.
41 : 17, when p. and needy seek water.
66 : 2, to him that is p. and of a contrite spirit.
Amos 2 : 6, they sold the p. for a pair of shoes.
Zech. 11 : 11, the p. of the flock waited on me.
Matt. 5 : 3, blessed are the p. in spirit.
11 : 5, the p. have the Gospel preached.
Mark 14 : 7, ye have the p. always with you.
2 Cor. 6 : 10, as p., yet making many rich.
8 : 9, for your sakes he became p.
Jas. 2 : 5, hath not God chosen the p. ?
Rev. 3 : 17, thou knowest not that thou art p.
See Prov. 15 : 16; 16 : 8; 19 : 4; 28 : 6, 11; 1 John 3 : 17.

Poplar. The Hebrew word " libneh " occurs only twice. In both places (Gen. 30 : 37 and Hos. 4 : 13) it is translated " poplar," but the R.V. gives in the margin " storax tree." The storax tree grows commonly in the East, and has pale whitish leaves, but the white poplar is also found in Palestine.

Populous, Deut. 26 : 5; Nah. 3 : 8.

Porch, 1 Ki. 7 : 7; 2 Chr. 29 : 17; John 10 : 23.

Porpoise. This word occurs in the margin of Ex. 25 : 5, R.V., where in the text it is given as " sealskins "; but A.V. translates " badgers' skins." See **Badger.**

Port [ar.], gate, Neh. 2 : 13.

Porter, 1 Chr. 9 : 21; Mark 13 : 34; John 10 : 3.

Portion, Gen. 31 : 4, is there yet any p. for us ?
Deut. 32 : 9, the Lord's p. is his people.
2 Ki. 2 : 9, a double p. of thy spirit.
Job 20 : 29, this is the p. of a wicked man.
31 : 2, what p. of God is there from above ?
Ps. 16 : 5, the Lord is the p. of mine inheritance.
63 : 10, they shall be a p. for foxes.
73 : 26, God is my p. for ever.
119 : 57; 142 : 5, thou art my p., O Lord.
Prov. 31 : 15, giveth a p. to her maidens.
Eccl. 2 : 10, this was my p. of all my labour.
3 : 22; 5 : 18; 9 : 9, for that is his p.
9 : 6, neither have they any more p. for ever.
11 : 2, give a p. to seven.
Isa. 53 : 12, divide him a p. with the great.
61 : 7, they shall rejoice in their p.
Jer. 12 : 10, made my pleasant p. a desolate wilderness.
Lam. 3 : 24, the Lord is my p.
Dan. 1 : 8, with p. of king's meat.
Mic. 2 : 4, changed the p. of my people.
Matt. 24 : 51, appoint him his p. with the hypocrites.
Luke 12 : 42, their p. in due season.
15 : 12, the p. of goods that falleth to me.

Possess, Gen. 22 : 17; 24 : 60, thy seed shall p. the gate.

Job 7 : 3, made to p. months of vanity.
13 : 26, to p. iniquities of youth.
Ps. 139 : 13, thou hast p. my reins.
Prov. 8 : 22, the Lord p. me in the beginning.
Luke 18 : 12, I give tithes of all I p.
21 : 19, in patience p. ye your souls.
1 Cor. 7 : 30, as though they p. not.
2 Cor. 6 : 10, yet p. all things.
Possession, Gen. 17 : 8; 48 : 4, for an everlasting p.
Ps. 2 : 8, uttermost parts of the earth for thy p.
Prov. 28 : 10, good things in p.
Matt. 19 : 22; Mark 10 : 22, had great p.
Acts 2 : 45, sold their p.
Eph. 1 : 14, redemption of purchased p.
Possessor, Gen. 14 : 19; Acts 4 : 34.
Possible, Matt. 19 : 26; Mark 10 : 27, with God all things are p.
Matt. 24 : 24; Mark 13 : 22, if p. deceive the very elect.
Matt. 26 : 39; Mark 14 : 35, if p., let this cup pass from me.
Mark 9 : 23, all things are p. to him that believeth.
14 : 36; Luke 18 : 27, all things are p. to thee.
Acts 2 : 24, not p. he should be holden.
Rom. 12 : 18, if p., live peaceably.
Heb. 10 : 4, not p. that the blood of bulls.
Post, Ex. 12 : 7, 22, 23; Deut. 11 : 20; Esther 3 : 13, 15.
Posterity, Gen. 45 : 7, preserve your p. in the earth.
Ps. 49 : 13, yet their p. approve their sayings.
Dan. 11 : 4, not be divided to his p.
Post-exilic. The Jews were in exile in Babylon until 537 B.C. Anything after this date may be referred to as post-exilic. For instance, that school of writers who were interested in Judah and ritual, and edited much of the Old Testament rigorously, as in the case of the Pentateuch, was post-exilic. Known as P., they are believed to have flourished about 150 B.C., and thus we can date many books in which we trace their hand.
Pot, Ex. 16 : 33, take a p., and put manna therein.
2 Ki. 4 : 2, not any thing save a p. of oil.
4 : 40, there is death in the p.
Job 41 : 31, maketh the deep boil like a p.
Prov. 17 : 3; 27 : 21, fining p. for silver.
Zech. 14 : 21, every p. shall be holiness.
Mark 7 : 4, the washing of cups and p.
Heb. 9 : 4, the golden p. with manna.
Potentate, 1 Tim. 6 : 15.
Potiphar (pŏt-ĭ-phär), contraction of **Potipherah** [belonging to Ra, the sun-god], Joseph's master, Gen. 37 : 36; 39 : 1-20.
Potsherd, Job 2 : 8; Prov. 26 : 23.
Pottage, Esau's birthright sold for, Gen. 25 : 29.
unwholesome, healed by Elisha, 2 Ki. 4 : 38.
Potter, as a type of God's power, Ps. 2 : 9; Isa. 64 : 8; Jer. 18 : 2; Rom. 9 : 21.
ancient, 1 Chr. 4 : 23. See **Handicraft.**
Pounds, parable of, Luke 19 : 12-27.
Pour, Ex. 4 : 9, p. water on the dry land.

Job 30 : 16, my soul is p. out.
36 : 27, p. rain according to vapour.
Ps. 42 : 4, I p. out my soul.
45 : 2, grace is p. into thy lips.
62 : 8, p. out your heart before him.
Prov. 1 : 23; Isa. 44 : 3; Joel 2 : 28; Acts 2 : 17, I will p. out my Spirit.
Song of Sol. 1 : 3, name is as ointment p. forth.
Isa. 44 : 3, I will p. water on him that is thirsty.
53 : 12, p. out his soul to death.
Lam. 2 : 19, p. out thine heart like water.
Nah. 1 : 6, fury is p. out like fire.
Zech. 12 : 10, I will p. on house of David.
Mal. 3 : 10, if I will not p. out a blessing.
Matt. 26 : 7; Mark 14 : 3, p. ointment on his head.
John 2 : 15, he p. out the changers' money.
Rev. 14 : 10, wine of wrath of God which is p. out.
Pouring out, of God's wrath, Ps. 69 : 24; 79 : 6; Jer. 10 : 25; Ezek. 7 : 8; Hos. 5 : 10; of the Holy Spirit, Isa. 32 : 15; Ezek. 39 : 29; Acts 2; 10 : 45; of the vials, Rev. 16.
Pourtray, Ezek. 4 : 1; 8 : 10; 23 : 14.
Poverty, Prov. 6 : 11; 24 : 34, p. come as one that travelleth.
10 : 15, destruction of poor is their p.
13 : 18, p. to him that refuseth instruction.
20 : 13; 23 : 21, come to p.
28 : 19, shall have p. enough.
30 : 8, give me neither p. nor riches.
31 : 7, forget his p.
2 Cor. 8 : 9, that ye through his p. might be rich.
Rev. 2 : 9, I know thy works and p.
Powder, Ex. 32 : 20, Moses ground the calf to p.
Deut. 28 : 24, Lord shall make the rain of thy land p.
2 Ki. 23 : 15, stamped the altar to p.
2 Chr. 34 : 7, beaten the images to p.
Matt. 21 : 44; Luke 20 : 18, it will grind him to p.
Power, bestowed by God, Isa. 40 : 29; Acts 6 : 8; Rom. 15 : 13; 1 Cor. 5 : 4; 2 Cor. 12 : 9.
powers, heavenly, Matt. 24 : 29; Eph. 3 : 10.
earthly, to be obeyed, Rom. 13; Titus 3; 1 Pet. 2 : 13.
Gen. 32 : 28, as a prince thou hast p. with God.
Ex. 15 : 6, right hand glorious in p.
Lev. 26 : 19, I will break your p.
Deut. 8 : 18, giveth thee p. to get wealth.
2 Sam. 22 : 33, God is my strength and p.
1 Chr. 29 : 11; Matt. 6 : 13, thine is the p.
2 Chr. 25 : 8, God hath p. to help.
Job 21 : 7, why are the wicked mighty in p. ?
26 : 2, helped him that is without p. ?
37 : 23, excellent in p. and judgment.
Ps. 49 : 15, redeem my soul from p. of the grave.
62 : 11, p. belongeth unto God.
65 : 6, being girded with p.

66 : 7, he ruleth by his **p.**
90 : 11, who knoweth **p.** of thine anger ?
110 : 3, people be willing in the day of thy **p.**
145 : 11, they shall talk of thy **p.**
Prov. 3 : 27, it is in **p.** of thy hand.
18 : 21, in **p.** of the tongue.
Eccl. 5 : 19; 6 : 2, **p.** to eat thereof.
8 : 4, where word of king is, there is **p.**
Jer. 10 : 12; 51 : 15, made earth by his **p.**
Ezek. 30 : 6, pride of her **p.** shall come down.
Dan. 2 : 37, God hath given thee **p.**
Mic. 3 : 8, full of **p.** by the Spirit.
Hab. 2 : 9, delivered from the **p.** of evil.
Zech. 4 : 6, not by might, nor by **p.**
Matt. 9 : 6; Mark 2 : 10; Luke 5 : 24, Son of man hath **p.** to forgive.
Matt. 24 : 30; Luke 21 : 27, coming in clouds with **p.**
Matt. 28 : 18, all **p.** is given me.
Mark 9 : 1, kingdom of God come with **p.**
Luke 1 : 35, **p.** of the Highest.
4 : 6, all this **p.** will I give thee.
4 : 32, his word was with **p.**
5 : 17, the **p.** of the Lord was present.
9 : 43, amazed at the mighty **p.** of God.
12 : 5, that hath **p.** to cast into hell.
22 : 53, the **p.** of darkness.
24 : 49, endued with **p.** from on high.
John 1 : 12, **p.** to become sons of God.
10 : 18, I have **p.** to lay it down.
17 : 2, given him **p.** over all flesh.
19 : 10, **p.** to crucify, **p.** to release.
Acts 1 : 8, receive **p.**, after Holy Ghost is come.
3 : 12, as though by our own **p.**
5 : 4, was it not in thine own **p.** ?
8 : 10, this man is the great **p.** of God.
26 : 18, from the **p.** of Satan unto God.
Rom. 1 : 20, his eternal **p.** and Godhead.
9 : 21, hath not potter **p.** over clay ?
13 : 2, whosoever resisteth the **p.**
1 Cor. 4 : 20, not in word, but in **p.**
15 : 43, sown in weakness, raised in **p.**
2 Cor. 4 : 7, excellency of **p.** be of God.
Eph. 1 : 19, exceeding greatness of his **p.**
2 : 2, prince of the **p.** of the air.
3 : 7, by the effectual working of his **p.**
Phil. 3 : 10, the **p.** of his resurrection.
Col. 1 : 13, delivered us from the **p.** of darkness.
2 Tim. 1 : 7, God hath given spirit of **p.**
3 : 5, a form of godliness, but denying the **p.**
Heb. 1 : 3, all things by the word of his **p.**
2 : 14, might destroy him that had **p.** of death.
7 : 16, the **p.** of an endless life.
Rev. 4 : 11; 5 : 12, thou art worthy to receive **p.**
Powerful, Ps. 29 : 4; 2 Cor. 10 : 10; Heb. 4 : 12.
Practice, Ps. 141 : 4; Mic. 2 : 1.
Practices, 2 Pet. 2 : 14.
Praise. This is an important element in religion and in the psychological life of the worshipper. Over-concentration on our own unworthiness and sin would lead

to morbidity ; the recognition of God's glory and the praise of His good works towards men is necessary for our psychological as well as our spiritual salvation.
God worthy of, Deut. 10 : 21; Judg. 5 : 2; Isa. 12; 25; 42 : 10; Jer. 31 : 7; Dan. 2 : 23; Joel 2 : 26; Luke 1 : 46, 68; Eph. 1 : 6; Rev. 19 : 5.
of man, vanity of, Prov. 27 : 2; Matt. 6 : 1.
Ex. 15 : 11, fearful in **p.**
Judg. 5 : 3; Ps. 7 : 17; 9 : 2; 57 : 7; 61 : 8; 104 : 33, I will sing **p.**
1 Chr. 29 : 13, **p.** thy glorious name.
2 Chr. 23 : 13, taught to sing **p.**
Neh. 9 : 5, exalted above **p.**
Ps. 22 : 3, thou that inhabitest the **p.** of Israel.
22 : 23, ye that fear the Lord, **p.** him.
22 : 25, my **p.** shall be of thee.
30 : 9, shall the dust **p.** thee ?
33 : 1; 147 : 1, **p.** is comely.
34 : 1, his **p.** shall continually be in my mouth.
35 : 28, tongue shall speak of thy **p.**
42 : 5, 11; 43 : 5, I shall yet **p.** him.
45 : 17, therefore shall the people **p.** thee.
49 : 18, men will **p.** thee when thou doest well.
50 : 23, whoso offereth **p.** glorifieth me.
63 : 3, my lips shall **p.** thee.
65 : 1, **p.** waiteth for thee, O God.
66 : 2, make his **p.** glorious.
67 : 3, let the people **p.** thee, O God.
69 : 34, let heaven and earth **p.** him.
71 : 8, let my mouth be filled with thy **p.**
71 : 14, I will yet **p.** thee more and more.
72 : 15, daily shall he be **p.**
76 : 10, wrath of man shall **p.** thee.
88 : 10, shall the dead arise and **p.** thee ?
99 : 3, let them **p.** thy great name.
100 : 4, enter his courts with **p.**
106 : 2, who can show all his **p.** ?
107 : 32, **p.** him in the assembly.
115 : 17, the dead **p.** not the Lord.
119 : 164, seven times a day I **p.** thee.
138 : 4, kings of the earth shall **p.** thee.
145 : 4, one generation shall **p.** thy works.
145 : 10, all thy works shall **p.** thee.
148 : 3, **p.** him, sun and moon.
Prov. 27 : 2, let another **p.** thee.
27 : 21, so is a man to his **p.**
31 : 31, let her own works **p.** her.
Isa. 38 : 19, the living shall **p.** thee.
42 : 12, declare his **p.** in the islands.
60 : 18, call thy gates **P.**
61 : 3, garment of **p.**
62 : 7, a **p.** in the earth.
Jer. 13 : 11, that they might be to me for a **p.**
Dan. 2 : 23, I thank and **p.** thee, O God.
Joel 2 : 26, **p.** the name of the Lord.
Hab. 3 : 3, the earth was full of his **p.**
Zeph. 3 : 19, get them **p.** and fame.
Matt. 21 : 16, thou hast perfected **p.**
John 9 : 24, give God the **p.**
12 : 43, loved of men.
Rom. 2 : 29, whose **p.** is not of men.
13 : 3, thou shalt have **p.** of the same.

15 : 11, **p.** the Lord, all ye Gentiles.
1 Cor. 4 : 5, then shall every man have **p.** of God.
11 : 22, I **p.** you not.
2 Cor. 8 : 18, whose **p.** is in the Gospel.
Eph. 1 : 12, **p.** of his glory.
Phil. 4 : 8, if there be any **p.**
Heb. 2 : 12, in church will I sing **p.**
13 : 15, offer sacrifice of **p.**
1 Pet. 1 : 7, trial of faith might be found to **p.**
2 : 14, for **p.** of them that do well.
Rev. 19 : 5, saying, **P.** our God.
Prancing, Judg. 5 : 22; Nah. 3 : 2.
Prating, Prov. 10 : 8, a **p.** fool shall fall.
3 John 10, **p.** against us with malicious words.
Pray, Gen. 20 : 7, he shall **p.** for thee.
1 Sam. 7 : 5, I will **p.** for you to the Lord.
12 : 23, I should sin in ceasing to **p.**
2 Sam. 7 : 27, found in his heart to **p.**
2 Chr. 6 : 24, **p.** and make supplication.
Ezra 6 : 10, **p.** for the life of the king.
Job 21 : 15, what profit if we **p.** to him ?
Ps. 5 : 2, my God, to thee will I **p.**
55 : 17, evening, and morning, and at noon will I **p.**
122 : 6, **p.** for the peace of Jerusalem.
Isa. 16 : 12, come to sanctuary to **p.**
45 : 20, **p.** to a god that cannot save.
Jer. 37 : 3; 42 : 2, 20, **p.** for us to the Lord.
Zech. 7 : 2, they sent men to **p.** before the Lord.
Matt. 5 : 44, **p.** for them which despitefully use you.
6 : 5, love to **p.** standing in the synagogue.
14 : 23; Mark 6 : 46; Luke 9 : 28, apart to **p.**
Mark 11 . 24, what ye desire, believe when ye **p.**
14 : 38; Luke 22 : 40, watch and **p.** lest ye enter into temptation.
Luke 11 : 1, Lord, teach us to **p.**
18 : 1, men ought always to **p.**
John 14 : 16; 16 : 26, I will **p.** the Father.
17 . 9, I **p.** for them : I **p.** not for the world.
Acts 9 : 11, behold, he **p.**
10 : 9, on housetop to **p.**
Rom. 8 : 26, know not what we should **p.** for.
1 Cor. 14 : 15, I will **p.** with the spirit.
1 Thess. 5 : 17, **p.** without ceasing.
1 Tim. 2 : 8, that men **p.** everywhere.
Jas. 5 : 14, let them **p.** over him.
5 : 16, **p.** one for another.
1 John 5 : 16, I do not say that he shall **p.** for it.
Prayer. One of the gravest obstacles in the way of believing that God answers prayer is that to do so would be to alter His own natural and moral laws, and hence to " change His mind." The answer must be along such lines as to ask, " What is God's mind ? " According to Jesus, it is fellowship with man and that for ever. All else subserves that great plan, and prayer, the medium whereby man enters into communion with his God,

is surely provided for in the scheme of creation. Christians do, in fact, experience answer to prayer, whether it be direct or indirect, immediate or deferred; and the final answer to prayer is summed up for us in Jesus' words : " How much more shall your heavenly Father give the Holy Spirit." Whatever we want, all that we really need is God; and prayer brings us God.
occasions and objects of, 1 Chr. 16 : 35; Job 33 : 26; Matt. 9 : 38; Luke 18 : 13; 38; Rom. 15 : 30; 1 Cor. 7 : 5; Jas. 5 : 13; 1 Pet. 3 : 7.
commanded, Isa. 55 : 6; Matt. 7 : 7; 26 : 41; Luke 21 : 36; Col. 4 : 2.
encouragements to, Ps. 6 : 9; 32 : 6; 66 : 19; Isa. 65 : 24 ; Zech. 13 : 9; Matt. 18 : 19; Luke 11 : 9; Rom. 10 : 13; Jas. 1 : 5.
how to be offered, Ps. 145 : 18; Prov. 15 : 29; Eccl. 5 : 2; Matt. 6 : 7; Luke 11 : 1; John 9 : 31; 15 : 7; Rom. 12 : 12; 1 Tim. 5 : 5; Heb. 11 : 6; Jas. 1 : 6; 4 : 8.
through Christ, Eph. 2 : 18; Heb. 10 : 19.
God's hearing of, Ps. 10 : 17; 99 : 6; Isa. 58 : 9; 65 : 24; Amos 5 : 4; Zech. 13 : 9; Matt. 6 : 6; John 11 : 42; 14 : 13.
examples of public : Joshua, Josh. 7 : 6-9; David, 1 Chr. 29 : 10, 12; 2 Sam. 6 : 18; Solomon, 2 Chr. 6 : 12; Jews, Luke 1 : 10; early church, Acts 2 : 46; 4 : 24; 12 : 5; Peter and John, Acts 3 : 1; Paul and Silas, Acts 16 : 25; Paul with the elders, Acts 20 : 36; 21 : 5.
examples of private, Gen. 18 : 23-32; 19 : 19; 24 : 12; 32 : 9; Judg. 6 : 13, 22; 1 Sam. 1; 2 Sam. 7 . 18, 1 Ki. 18 : 36; 2 Ki. 20 : 2, 11; 1 Chr. 4 : 10; 2 Chr. 33 : 19; Ezra 9 : 5; Neh. 2 : 4; Jer. 32 : 16; Dan. 9 : 3; Jonah 2 : 1; Luke 2 : 37; Acts 10 : 2, 30 ; 1 Thess. 5 : 23.
of the hypocrite, condemned, Ps. 109 : 7; Prov. 1 . 28, 28 . 9.
the Lord's, Matt. 6 : 9; Luke 11 : 2.
of the dying malefactor, Luke 23 : 42.
prayers of Christ, Matt. 26 : 36; 27 : 46; Mark 14 : 32; 15 : 34; Luke 6 : 12; 23 : 34, 46.
1 Ki. 8 : 28, respect **p.** of thy servant.
2 Chr. 7 : 15, ears be attent unto the **p.**
Neh. 1 : 6, thou mayest hear the **p.**
Job. 15 : 4, thou restrainest **p.**
22 : 27, shalt make thy **p.** to him.
Ps. 65 : 2, O thou that hearest **p.**
72 : 15, **p.** shall be made continually.
102 : 17, he will regard **p.** of the destitute.
109 : 4, I give myself to **p.**
Prov. 15 : 8, **p.** of upright his delight.
Isa. 1 : 15, when ye make many **p.**
56 : 7; Matt. 21 : 13; Mark 11 : 17; Luke 19 : 46, house of **p.**
Dan. 9 : 17, hear **p.** of thy servant.
Matt. 17 : 21; Mark 9 : 29, but by **p.** and fasting.
Matt. 21 : 22, whatsoever ye ask in **p.**
23 : 14; Mark 12 : 40; Luke 20 : 47, long **p.**

Luke 1 : 13, thy **p.** is heard.
6 : 12, continued all night in **p.**
Acts 3 : 1, the hour of **p.**
6 : 4, we will give ourselves to **p.**
10 : 31, thy **p.** is heard.
12 : 5, **p.** was made without ceasing.
16 : 13, where **p.** was wont to be made.
Eph. 6 : 18, praying with all **p.**
Phil. 4 : 6, by **p.** let your requests be made known.
1 Tim. 4 : 5, it is sanctified by **p.**
Jas. 5 : 15, the **p.** of faith shall save the sick.
5 : 16, the effectual fervent **p.**
1 Pet. 4 : 7, watch unto **p.**
Rev. 5 : 8; 8 : 3, the **p.** of saints.
See Num. 16 : 22; Ps. 28 : 2; 88 : 1; 95 : 6; Dan. 6 : 10; Mark 11 : 25; Luke 22 : 41.
Preach, Neh. 6 : 7, appointed prophets to **p.**
Isa. 61 : 1, anointed me to **p.** good tidings.
Jonah 3 : 2, **p.** the preaching I bid thee.
Matt. 4 : 17, Jesus began to **p.**
11 : 1, he departed thence to **p.**
Mark 1 : 4, John did **p.** the baptism of repentance.
2 : 2, he **p.** the word to them.
3 : 14; Luke 9 : 2, send them forth to **p.**
Mark 6 : 12, they **p.** that men should repent.
16 : 20, went forth, and **p.** everywhere.
Luke 9 : 60, go and **p.** the kingdom of God.
Acts 5 : 42, ceased not to **p.** Christ.
10 : 42, he commanded us to **p.**
13 : 38, through this man is **p.** forgiveness.
15 : 21, in every city them that **p.** him.
17 : 3, this Jesus, whom I **p.** unto you, is Christ.
Rom. 2 : 21, thou that **p.** a man should not steal.
10 : 15, how shall they **p.**, except they be sent ?
1 Cor. 1 : 23, **p.** Christ crucified.
9 : 16, woe is unto me, if I **p.** not the Gospel.
9 : 27, lest when I have **p.** to others.
15 : 11, so we **p.**, and so ye believed.
2 Cor. 4 : 5, we **p.** not ourselves.
Gal. 2 : 2, gospel which I **p.**
Phil. 1 : 15, some **p.** Christ of envy and strife.
Col. 1 : 28, whom ye **p.**, warning every man.
2 Tim. 4 : 2, **p.** the word; be instant.
Heb. 4 : 2, the word **p.** did not profit.
1 Pet. 3 : 19, **p.** to spirits in prison.
Preacher, Eccl. 12 : 10, the **p.** sought to find words.
Rom. 10 : 14, how shall they hear without a **p.** ?
1 Tim. 2 : 7; 2 Tim. 1 : 11, am ordained a **p.**
Preaching, of Jonah, Jonah 3; Matt. 12 : 41; Luke 11 : 32.
of John the Baptist, Matt. 3; Mark 1; Luke 3.
of Noah, 2 Pet. 2 : 5, etc.
of the gospel, Matt. 4 : 23; 5; 28 : 18; Mark 1 : 14; 16 : 15; Luke 4 : 18; 24 : 47; Acts 2 : 14; 3 : 12; 4 : 8; 13 : 16.
See Rom. 10 : 8; 1 Cor. 1 : 17; 2; 15 : 1; Gal. 1; Eph. 1–3; Titus 1 : 3.
Precept, Neh. 9 : 14, commandest them **p.**

Ps. 119 : 40, I have longed after thy **p.**
Isa. 28 : 10, 13, **p.** must be upon **p.**
29 : 13, taught by **p.** of men.
Dan. 9 : 5, departing from thy **p.**
Mark 10 : 5, he wrote you this **p.**
Precious, Gen. 24 : 53; Deut. 33 : 13, **p.** things.
1 Sam. 3 : 1, the word of the Lord was **p.**
26 : 21, my soul was **p.** in thine eyes.
2 Ki. 1 : 13, let my life be **p.**
Job 28 : 16, it cannot be valued with **p.** onyx.
Ps. 49 : 8, the redemption of their souls is **p.**
72 : 14, **p.** shall their blood be in his sight.
116 : 15, **p.** in sight of Lord is death of saints.
126 : 6, bearing **p.** seed.
133 : 2, like **p.** ointment upon the head.
139 : 17, how **p.** are thy thoughts, O God.
Prov. 3 : 15, wisdom is more **p.** than rubies.
20 : 15, lips of knowledge are a **p.** jewel.
Eccl. 7 : 1, good name better than **p.** ointment.
Isa. 13 : 12, a man more **p.** than gold.
28 : 16; 1 Pet. 2 : 6, a **p.** corner stone.
Isa. 43 : 4, thou wast **p.** in my sight.
Jer. 15 : 19, take the **p.** from the vile.
Lam. 4 : 2, the **p.** sons of Zion.
Jas. 5 : 7, husbandman waiteth for **p.** fruit of earth.
1 Pet. 1 : 7, trial of your faith more **p.** than of gold.
1 : 19, the **p.** blood of Christ.
2 : 7, to you which believe he is **p.**
2 Pet. 1 : 1, obtained like **p.** faith.
1 : 4, exceeding great and **p.** promises.
Precious Stones in the Bible.
(1) Stones in the Breastplate of the High Priest (Ex. 28 : 17-20).

A.V.	Hebrew.	Modern Names.
Sardius	'Odem	Sard
Topaz	Pitdah	Chrysolite
Carbuncle	Barekheth	Emerald
Emerald	Nophek	Garnet, or Carbuncle
Sapphire	Sappir	Lapis Lazuli
Diamond	Yahalom	Corundum (?)
Ligure	Leshem	Hyacinth
Agate	Shebo	Agate
Amethyst	'Ahlamah	Amethyst
Beryl	Tarshish	Beryl
Onyx	Shoham	Onyx
Jasper	Yashepeh	Jade (?)

(2) The Ornaments in the Covering of the King of Tyre (Ezek. 28 : 13).

Sard	'Odem	Sard
Topaz	Pitdah	Chrysolite
Diamond	Yahalom	Corundum (?)
Beryl	Tarshish	Beryl
Onyx	Shoham	Onyx
Jasper	Yashepeh	Jade (?)
Sapphire	Sappir	Lapis Lazuli
Emerald	Nophek	Carbuncle
Carbuncle	Barekheth	Emerald

(3) The Foundations of the Heavenly City (Rev. 21 : 10-20).

A.V.		Modern Names.
Jasper	– –	Jade (?)
Sapphire	– –	Lapis Lazuli
Chalcedony	–	Chalcedony

Emerald   –   – Emerald
Sardonyx –   – Sardonyx
Sardius   –   – Sard
Chrysolite   – Topaz
Beryl   –   – Beryl
Topaz   –   – Chrysolite
Chrysoprasus   – Chrysoprase
Jacinth   –   – Sapphire
Amethyst –   – Amethyst
Predestination, Rom. 8 : 29; 9; 10; 11; Eph. 1 : 5.
Pre-eminence, Eccl. 3 : 19, a man hath no p. above a beast.
Col. 1 : 18, that he might have the p.
3 John 9, Diotrephes, who loveth to have the p.
Pre-exilic, before the Exile, *i.e.*, before 587 B.C. See Post-exilic.
Prefer, Ps. 137 : 6, if I p. not Jerusalem.
John 1 : 15, he that cometh after me is p. before me.
Rom. 12 : 10, in honour p. one another.
Premeditate, Mark 13 : 11.
Preparation. The word was used of the day preceding the Sabbath, or any of the Jewish festivals, and especially that day preceding the Passover.
Prov. 16 : 1, p. of the heart of man.
Matt. 27 : 62; Mark 15 : 42; Luke 23 : 54; John 19 : 14, the day of p.
Eph. 6 : 15, feet shod with p. of the gospel of peace.
Prepare, Ex. 15 : 2, I will p. him an habitation.
1 Sam. 7 : 3, p. your hearts unto the Lord.
Ps. 61 : 7, O p. mercy and truth.
68 : 10, thou hast p. of thy goodness for the poor.
107 : 36, they may p. a city.
Prov. 8 : 27, when he p. the heavens.
30 : 25, they p. their meat in summer.
Isa. 21 : 5, p. the table, watch in the watch tower.
40 : 3; Mal. 3 : 1; Matt. 3 : 3; Mark 1 : 3; Luke 1 : 76, p. the way of the Lord.
Isa. 62 : 10, p. the way of the people.
Amos 4 : 12, p. to meet thy God.
Matt. 11 : 10, shall p. way before thee.
20 : 23; Mark 10 : 40, given to them for whom it is p.
Matt. 26 : 17; Mark 14 : 12; Luke 22 : 9, where wilt thou that we p. ?
John 14 : 2, I go to p. a place for you.
Rom. 9 : 23, vessels of mercy afore p.
1 Cor. 2 : 9, things God hath p.
14 : 8, who shall p. to battle ?
Heb. 10 : 5, a body hast thou p. me.
11 : 16, hath p. for them a city.
Presbytery, 1 Tim. 4 : 14.
Prescribe, Ezra 7 : 22; Isa. 10 : 1.
Presence, of God, 1 Chr. 16 : 27; Ps. 18 : 7; 68 : 8; Isa. 64 : 1; Jer. 5 : 22; Ezek. 1; Dan. 7 : 9; Nah. 1; Hab. 3; Rev. 1.
angels and elders stand in, Luke 1 : 19; Rev. 5 : 8, 11.
Christ has entered, Heb. 9 : 24.
Gen. 3 : 8, hid from p. of the Lord.
47 : 15, why should we die in thy p. ?

Ex. 33 : 14, my p. shall go with thee.
1 Chr. 16 : 33, trees sing at p. of the Lord.
Job 23 : 15, I am troubled at his p.
Ps. 16 : 11, in thy p. is fulness of joy.
31 : 20, in the secret of thy p.
51 : 11, cast me not away from thy p.
97 : 5, hills melted at the p. of the Lord.
100 : 2, come before his p. with singing.
139 : 7, whither shall I flee from thy p. ?
Prov. 14 : 7, go from p. of a foolish man.
Isa. 63 : 9, the angel of his p. saved them.
64 : 2, nations may tremble at thy p.
Jer. 23 : 39; 52 : 3, I will cast you out of my p.
Jonah 1 : 3, to flee from p. of the Lord.
Nah. 1 : 5, earth is burned at his p.
Zeph. 1 : 7, hold thy peace at p. of the Lord.
Luke 13 : 26, we have eaten and drunk in thy p.
Acts 3 : 19, times of refreshing from p. of the Lord.
1 Cor. 1 : 29, no flesh should glory in his p.
2 Cor. 10 : 10, his bodily p. is weak.
2 Thess. 1 : 9, destruction from the p. of the Lord.
Jude 24, present you faultless before his p.
Present, 1 Ki. 10 : 25; 2 Chr. 9 : 24, brought every man his p.
Ps. 46 : 1, God is a very p. help in trouble.
Luke 5 : 17, power of the Lord was p.
John 14 : 25, being yet p. with you.
Acts 10 : 33, all here p. before God.
Rom. 7 : 21, do good, evil is p. with me.
8 : 18, the sufferings of this p. time.
2 Cor. 5 : 8, to be p. with the Lord.
Gal. 1 : 4, deliver us from this p. evil world.
2 Tim. 4 : 10, having loved this p. world.
Titus 2 : 12, live godly in this p. world.
Heb. 12 : 11, no chastening for the p. seemeth joyous.
2 Pet. 1 : 12, established in the p. truth.
Rom. 12 : 1, p. your bodies a living sacrifice.
Col. 1 : 22, to p. you holy, unblameable.
Presently, Prov. 12 : 16; Matt. 21 : 19; Phil. 2 : 23.
Presents made, Gen. 32 : 13; 33 : 10; 43 : 11; Judg. 3 : 15; 1 Sam. 9 : 7; 2 Ki. 8 : 8; 20 : 12; Matt. 2 : 11.
Preserve, Gen. 32 : 30, I have seen God, and life is p.
45 : 7, God sent me to p. you a posterity.
Deut. 6 : 24, that he might p. us alive.
Job 29 : 2, in the days when God p. me.
Ps. 25 : 21, let uprightness p. me.
36 : 6, thou p. man and beast.
79 : 11, p. thou those that are to die.
121 : 8, Lord shall p. thy going out, and thy coming in.
Prov. 2 : 11, discretion shall p. thee.
20 : 28, mercy and truth p. the king.
22 : 12, eyes of the Lord p. knowledge.
Isa. 49 : 8, I will p. thee.
Luke 17 : 33, whosoever shall lose his life shall p. it.
Preserver, of the faithful, Ps. 31 : 23; 37 : 28; 97 : 10; 145 : 20; Prov. 2 : 8.

of men, Josh. 24 : 17; 2 Sam. 8 : 6; Job 7 : 20; Ps. 116 : 6; 146 : 9.

Presidents, Dan. 6 : 2, 4, 6, 7.

Press, Mark 2 : 4; Luke 8 : 19, could not come nigh for the **p.**

Mark 5 : 30, Jesus turned about in the **p.**

Ps. 38 : 2, thy hand **p.** me sore.

Amos. 2 : 13, I am **p.** under you, as a cart is **p.**

Mark 3 : 10, they **p.** on him to touch him.

Luke 6 : 38, good measure, **p.** down.

16 : 16, every man **p.** into it.

2 Cor. 1 : 8, were **p.** out of measure.

Phil. 3 : 14, I **p.** toward the mark.

Pressfat, Hag. 2 : 16.

Presumption, of Israelites, Num. 14 : 44; Deut. 1 : 43; prophets, Deut. 18 : 20; builders of Babel, Gen. 11; Korah, etc., Num. 16; Beth-shemites, 1 Sam. 6 : 19; Uzzah, 2 Sam. 6 : 6; Uzziah, 2 Chr. 26 : 16; Jewish exorcists, Acts 19 : 13.

Presumptuous, sins, Ex. 21 : 14; Num. 15 : 30; Deut. 17 : 12; Ps. 19 : 13; 2 Pet. 2 : 10.

Pretence, Matt. 23 : 14; Mark 12 : 40, for a **p.** make long prayers.

Phil. 1 : 18, whether in **p.** or truth.

Prevail, Gen. 32 : 28, power with God, and hast **p.**

Ex. 17 : 11, when Moses held up his hand, Israel **p.**

1 Sam. 2 : 9, by strength shall no man **p.**

2 Chr. 14 : 11; Ps. 9 : 19, let not man **p.**

Ps. 65 : 3, iniquities **p.** against me.

Eccl. 4 : 12, if one **p.** against him.

Matt. 16 : 18, gates of hell shall not **p.**

John 12 : 19, perceive ye how ye **p.** nothing ?

Acts 19 : 20, so mightly grew the word of God and **p.**

Prevent [anticipate, come before, precede], 2 Sam. 22 : 6; Ps. 18 : 5, snares of death **p.** me.

Ps. 59 : 10, God of mercy shall **p.** me.

88 : 13, in morning shall my prayer **p.** thee.

119 : 147, I **p.** the dawning of the morning.

Matt. 17 : 25, Jesus **p.** him.

1 Thess. 4 : 15, shall not **p.** them which are asleep.

Prey, Gen. 49 : 27, in morning he shall devour the **p.**

Ps. 17 : 12, like a lion greedy of **p.**

124 : 6, who hath not given us as a **p.**

Isa. 49 : 24, shall the **p.** be taken from the mighty ?

Ezek. 34 : 22, my flock shall no more be a **p.**

Price, of redemption, the blood of Christ, 1 Cor. 6 : 20; 7 : 23; 1 Pet. 1 : 19.

pearl of great, Matt. 13 : 46.

ornament of, 1 Pet. 3 : 4.

2 Sam. 24 : 24; 1 Chr. 21 : 22, I will buy it at a **p.**

Job 28 : 18, **p.** of wisdom above rubies.

Isa. 55 : 1, buy wine and milk without **p.**

Matt. 13 : 46, one pearl of great **p.**

27 : 6, it is the **p.** of blood.

Acts 5 : 2, kept back part of the **p.**

See Job 28 : 13; Prov. 31 : 10; Zech. 11 : 12; Matt. 26 : 15.

Pricked, Ps. 73 : 21; Acts 2 : 37.

Pricks, Num. 33 : 35, those that remain shall be **p.** in your eyes.

Acts 9 : 5; 26 : 14, it is hard for thee to kick against the **p.**

Pride, 1 Sam. 2 : 3; Prov. 6 : 16; 16 : 5; 21 : 4; Dan. 5 : 20; Mark 7 : 20; Rom. 12 : 3, 16.

instances of, 2 Ki. 20 : 13; Zeph. 3 : 11; Luke 18 : 11; 1 Cor. 8 : 1.

evil results of, Ps. 10 : 2; Prov. 21 : 24; 28 : 25; Jer. 43 : 2; Obad. 3.

followed by shame, etc., Prov. 11 : 2; 18 : 12; 29 : 23; Isa. 28 : 3.

exhortations against, Jer. 13 : 15.

Job 33 : 17, that he may hide **p.** from man.

Ps. 59 : 12, let them be taken in their **p.**

Prov. 8 : 13, **p.** do I hate.

13 : 10, by **p.** cometh contention.

14 : 3, in mouth of foolish is rod of **p.**

16 : 18, **p.** goeth before destruction.

Isa. 28 : 1, woe to the crown of **p.**

Jer. 49 : 16, the **p.** of thine heart hath deceived thee.

1 Tim. 3 : 6, being lifted up with **p.**

1 John 2 : 16, **p.** of life is not of the Father.

Priesthood, of Christ, Aaron, and Melchisedec, Rom. 8 : 34; Heb. 2 : 17; 3; 5; 7; 1 John 2 : 1.

Ex. 40 : 15; Num. 25 : 13, an everlasting **p.**

Heb. 7 : 24, hath an unchangeable **p.**

1 Pet. 2 : 5, an holy **p.**

2 : 9, ye are a royal **p.**

Priests, high, see **High Priest.** Ex. 28; 39; Lev. 8; 16; Levitical, Ex. 28 : 1; Lev. 8.

their duties, etc., Lev. 1; 9; 21; 22; Num. 3; Deut. 31 : 9; Josh. 3; 4; 1 Ki. 8 : 3.

slain by command of Saul, 1 Sam. 22 : 17.

divided by lot by David, 1 Chr. 24.

denounced for unfaithfulness, Jer. 1 : 18; Hos. 5 : 6; Zeph. 3 : 4; Mal. 2.

of Baal, slain, 1 Ki. 18 : 40; 2 Ki. 10 : 19; 11 : 18.

Christians called, 1 Pet. 2 : 5; Rev. 1 : 6; 20 : 6.

For the method whereby the priests were supported financially, see (a) Num. 18 : 26; (b) Num. 18 : 12-18; Lev. 7 : 30-34; (c) Num. 18 : 9; Lev. 5 : 13; 6 : 16; Num. 18 : 11; Lev. 7 : 8; Lev. 24 : 9.

Gen. 14 : 18; Heb. 7 : 1, **p.** of the most high God.

1 Sam. 2 : 35, I will raise up a faithful **p.**

2 Chr. 6 : 41; Ps. 132 : 16, let thy **p.** be clothed with salvation.

2 Chr. 15 : 3, Israel without a teaching **p.**

Ps. 110 : 4; Heb. 5 : 6, **p.** for ever after order of Melchisedec.

Isa. 24 : 2, as with people, so with **p.**

28 : 7, **p.** and prophet have erred.

61 : 6, be named the **P.** of the Lord.

Jer. 5 : 31, **p.** bear rule.

23 : 11, prophet and **p.** are profane.

Mic. 3 : 11, the **p.** teach for hire.

Mal. 2 : 7, the **p.** lips should keep knowledge.

Luke 10 : 31, there came down a certain **p.**

17 : 14, show yourselves unto the **p.**

Acts 6 : 7, **p.** were obedient to the faith.

14 : 13, the **p.** of Jupiter.

Heb. 7 : 3, abideth a p. continually.
Rev. 5 : 10, made us unto our God kings and p.
Prince, of Peace, Isa. 9 : 6; of life, Acts 3 : 15.
  of this world, John 14 : 30; 16 : 11; of the power of the air, Eph. 2 : 2.
  of devils, Christ's miracles ascribed to, Matt. 12 : 24; Mark 3 : 22; Luke 11 : 15.
  princes of the tribes, Num. 1 : 5 ff.; their offerings, Num. 7.
Gen. 32 : 28, as a p. hast thou power with God.
Ex. 2 : 14, who made thee a p. over us ?
2 Sam. 3 : 38, a p. is fallen in Israel.
Job 12 : 21; Ps. 107 : 40, he poureth contempt on p.
Job 21 : 28, where is the house of the p. ?
  34 : 19, that accepteth not the person of p.
Ps. 45 : 16, p. in all the earth.
  118 : 9, than to put confidence in p.
  146 : 3, put not your trust in p.
Prov. 8 : 15, by me p. decree justice.
  28 : 16, a p. that wanteth understanding.
  31 : 4, it is not for p. to drink strong drink.
Eccl. 10 : 7, p. walking as servants.
Isa. 10 : 8, are not my p. altogether kings ?
  23 : 8, whose merchants are p.
  32 : 1, p. shall rule in judgment.
  34 : 12, all her p. shall be nothing.
Hos. 3 : 4, Israel shall abide many days without a p.
Mic. 7 : 3, the p. and judge asketh for reward.
Matt. 9 : 34, casteth out devils by p. of devils.
John 12 : 31, p. of this world.
Acts 5 : 31, him hath God exalted to be a P.
1 Cor. 2 : 6, nor the wisdom of the p. of this world.
Princess, 1 Ki. 11 : 3; Lam. 1 : 1.
Principal, Prov. 4 : 7; Acts 25 : 23.
Principalities, and powers, Eph. 3 : 10; Col. 2 : 15.
  Christ the head of all, Col. 1 : 16; 2 : 10.
Rom. 8 : 38, nor p., nor powers, shall be able to separate.
Eph. 1 : 21, far above all p.
  6 : 12, we wrestle against p., against powers.
Titus 3 : 1, to be subject to p.
Principles, Heb. 5 : 12; 6 : 1.
Print, Job 13 : 27, thou settest a p. upon heels of my feet.
  19 : 23, O that my words were p. in a book.
John 20 : 25, except I see p. of nails.
Prisca [ancient], diminutive of Priscilla, 2 Tim. 4 : 19.
Priscilla, wife of Aquila, Acts 18 : 2; Rom. 16 : 3; 1 Cor. 16 : 19.
Prison, Gen. 40 : 3, put butler and baker in p.
Ps. 142 : 7, bring my soul out of p.
Eccl. 4 : 14, out of p. he cometh to reign.
Isa. 53 : 8, he was taken from p. and from judgment.
  61 : 1, opening of the p.
Matt. 5 : 25, thou be cast into p.
  25 : 36, in p., and ye came unto me.

Luke 22 : 33, to go with thee to p. and to death.
Acts 5 : 18, put apostles in common p.
1 Pet. 3 : 19, the spirits in p.
Prisoner, Ps. 79 : 11, let sighing of the p. come.
  102 : 20, to hear groaning of the p.
Zech. 9 : 12, turn to stronghold, p. of hope.
Matt. 27 : 15, release to the people a p.
Eph. 3 : 1; 4 : 1; Philem. 1, 9, the p. of Jesus.
Private, 2 Pet. 1 : 20.
Privately, Matt. 24 : 3, came unto him p.
Acts 23 : 19, with him aside p.
Gal. 2 : 2, p. to them of reputation.
Privily, Ps. 11 : 2, may p. shoot at the upright.
Prov. 1 : 11, lurk p. for the innocent.
Acts 16 : 37, do they thrust us out p.
2 Pet. 2 : 1, p. bring in heresies.
Privy, 1 Ki. 2 : 44; Acts 5 : 2.
Prize, 1 Cor. 9 : 24, one receiveth the p.
Phil. 3 : 14, I press for the p.
Proceed, Gen. 24 : 50, the thing p. from the Lord.
Deut. 8 : 3; Matt. 4 : 4, every word that p. out of mouth of God.
Job 40 : 5, I will p. no further.
Isa. 29 : 14, I will p. to do a marvellous work.
  51 : 4, a law shall p. from me.
Jer. 9 : 3, they p. from evil to evil.
Matt. 15 : 18, things which p. out of the mouth.
John 8 : 42, I p. forth from God.
Eph. 4 : 29, let no corrupt communication p.
Jas. 3 : 10, out of same mouth p. blessing and cursing.
Process, Gen. 4 : 3; Ex. 2 : 23.
Prochorus (prŏch-ŏ-rŭs), Acts 6 : 5.
Proclaim, Ex. 33 : 19, I will p. the name of the Lord.
Isa. 61 : 1, p. liberty to captives.
  62 : 11, the Lord hath p., Behold, thy salvation cometh.
Luke 12 : 3, shall be p. upon the housetops.
Rev. 5 : 2, p. with a loud voice.
Proclamation, Ex. 32 : 6; 1 Ki. 22 : 36; Dan. 5 : 29.
Procure, Prov. 11 : 27; Jer. 4 : 18; 26 : 19.
Prodigal son, parable of, Luke 15 : 11.
Produce, Isa. 41 : 21.
Profane, outside the temple, Ezek. 42 : 20. This is its root meaning. Hence came the general meaning " to make ceremoniously unclean," " to render unholy "; and thereafter it was expanded to include varying shades, e.g., not distinctly sacred or religious, as sacred and profane history, Heb. 12 : 16.
  given to swearing, 1 Tim. 1 : 9.
Lev. 20 : 3; 21 : 6; 22 : 2, neither shalt thou p. name of God.
Matt. 12 : 5, priests in temple p. sabbath.
Acts 24 : 6, gone about to p. temple.
Jer. 23 : 11, prophet and priest are p.
1 Tim. 6 : 20; 2 Tim. 2 : 16, avoid p. babblings.
Heb. 12 : 16, lest there be any p. person.

Profaneness, Jer. 23 : 15.
Profanity, forbidden, Lev. 18 : 21; 19 : 12; Neh. 13 : 18.
Profess, Matt. 7 : 23, will I p., I never knew you.
Rom. 1 : 22, p. themselves to be wise.
1 Tim. 6 : 12, hast p. a good profession.
Titus 1 : 16, they p. that they know God.
Profession, of Christ, to hold fast, Heb. 3 : 1; 4 : 14; 10 : 23.
Profit, Gen. 25 : 32, what p. shall birthright do to me ?
37 : 26, what p. is it if we slay our brother ?
Job 21 : 15, what p., if we pray unto him ?
Ps. 30 : 9, what p. is in my blood ?
Prov. 14 : 23, in all labour there is p.
Eccl. 1 : 3; 3 : 9; 5 : 16, what p. hath a man of his labour ?
2 : 11, there was no p. under the sun.
5 : 9, the p. of the earth is for all.
7 : 11, by wisdom there is p.
Jer. 16 : 19, things wherein is no p.
Mal. 3 : 14, what p. that we have kept his ordinance ?
Rom. 3 : 1, what p. of circumcision ?
1 Cor. 10 : 33, not seeking mine own p.
2 Tim. 2 : 14, about words to no p.
Heb. 12 : 10, he chasteneth us for our p.
1 Sam. 12 : 21, vain things which cannot p.
Job 34 : 9, it p. nothing to delight in God.
Prov. 10 : 2, treasures of wickedness p. nothing.
11 : 4, riches p. not in the day of wrath.
Isa. 30 : 5, a people that could not p.
Jer. 2 : 11, changed for that which doth not p.
7 : 8, lying words that cannot p.
Matt. 16 : 26; Mark 8 : 36, what is a man p. if he gain the world ?
1 Cor. 12 : 7, given to every man to p. withal.
13 : 3, charity, it p. me nothing.
Gal. 5 : 2, Christ shall p. you nothing.
1 Tim. 4 : 8, bodily exercise p. little.
Heb. 4 : 2, the word preached did not p.
Jas. 2 : 14, what doth it p. ?
Profitable, Job 22 : 2, can a man be p. to God ?
Eccl. 10 : 10, wisdom is p. to direct.
Matt. 5 : 29, p. that one of thy members perish.
1 Tim. 4 : 8, godliness is p. to all things.
2 Tim. 3 : 16, scripture is p. for doctrine.
Profiting, 1 Tim. 4 : 15, that thy p. may appear.
Profound, Hos. 5 : 2.
Progenitors, Gen. 49 : 26.
Prolong, Deut. 4 : 26; 30 : 18, ye shall not p. your days.
Job 6 : 11, what is mine end, that I should p. my life ?
Prov. 10 : 27, the fear of the Lord p. days.
Isa. 53 : 10, he shall p. his days.
Promise, Num. 14 : 34, know my breach of p.
1 Ki. 8 : 56, not failed one word of his good p.
Neh. 5 : 13, performeth not p.
Ps. 77 : 8, doth his p. fail ?

Luke 24 : 49; Acts 1 : 4, p. of the Father.
Acts 2 : 39, the p. is to you and your children.
7 : 17, the time of the p.
26 : 6, hope of the p. made of God.
Rom. 4 : 14, the p. is made of none effect.
9 : 4, to whom pertain the p.
2 Cor. 1 : 20, p. of God in him are yea and amen.
Gal. 3 : 17, should make the p. of none effect.
Eph. 2 : 12, strangers from covenants of p.
1 Tim. 4 : 8, having p. of the life that now is.
Heb. 6 : 12, through faith inherit the p.
9 : 15; 10 : 36, the p. of eternal inheritance.
2 Pet. 3 : 4, where is the p. of his coming ?
3 : 9, Lord is not slack concerning his p.
1 John 2 : 25, this is the p. he hath p. us.
Ex. 12 : 25, give according as he p.
Num. 14 : 40, will go to place the Lord p.
Deut. 1 : 11; 15 : 6, Lord bless you, as he hath p.
19 : 8; 27 : 3, give thee the land which he p.
26 : 18, to be his people, as he p.
1 Ki. 8 : 56, Lord hath given rest, as he p.
2 Ki. 8 : 19; 2 Chr. 21 : 7, he p. to give him a light.
Matt. 14 : 7, Herod p. with an oath.
Mark 14 : 11, they p. to give him money.
Luke 1 : 72, mercy p. to our fathers.
Rom. 4 : 21, what he had p. he was able to perform.
Titus 1 : 2, p. before the world began.
Heb. 10 : 23; 11 : 11, faithful that p.
Promises, of God, Ps. 89 : 3; Rom. 1 : 2; Eph. 3 : 6; 2 Tim. 1 : 1; Heb. 6 : 17; 8 : 6.
inviolable and precious, Num. 23 : 19; Deut. 7 : 9; Josh. 23 : 14; Ps. 105 : 42; Gal. 3 : 21; Heb. 6 : 17; 2 Pet. 1 : 4.
of pardon and reconciliation, Ex. 34 : 7; Ps. 65 : 3; 130 : 4; Isa. 1 : 18; 27 : 5; 43 : 25; 44 : 22; 46 : 13; 53; 55; Jer. 31 : 34; 33 : 8; Ezek. 33 : 16; 36 : 25; Rom. 4; 5; 2 Cor. 6 : 18; 7 : 1; Eph. 2 : 13.
of strength and help, etc., Ps. 23; 37 : 17; 42 : 8; 73 : 26; 84 : 11; 94 : 14; 103 : 13; Isa. 25 : 8; 30 : 18; 40 : 29; 41 : 10; 43 : 4; 46 : 3; 49 : 13; 63 : 9; Jer. 31 : 3; Hos. 13 : 10; 14 : 4; Zeph. 3 : 17; Zech. 2 : 9; 10; Rom. 16 : 20; 1 Cor. 10 : 13; 15 : 57; 2 Cor. 6 : 18; 12 : 9; Eph. 1 : 3; 1 Pet. 1 : 3; 5 : 7.
to Adam, Gen. 3 : 15; to Noah, Gen. 8 : 21; 9 : 9; to Abraham, Gen. 12 : 7; 13 : 14; 15; 17; 18 : 10; 22 : 15; to Hagar, Gen. 16 : 10; 21 : 17; to Isaac, Gen. 26 : 2; to Jacob, Gen. 28 : 13; 31 : 3; 32 : 12; 35 : 10; 46 : 3; to David, 2 Sam. 7 : 11; 1 Chr. 17 : 10; to Solomon, 1 Ki. 9; 2 Chr. 1 : 7; 7 : 12.
of Christ to his disciples, Matt. 6 : 4, 33; 7 : 7; 10; 11 : 28; 12 : 50; 16 : 18, 25; 17 : 20; 19 : 28; 28 : 20; Luke

9–11; 12 : 32; 22 : 29; John 14–16; 20 : 21.

to the poor, fatherless, etc., Deut. 10 : 18; Ps. 9 : 8; 10 : 14; 12 : 5; 68 : 5; 69 : 33; 72 : 12; 102 : 17; 107 : 41; 109 : 31; 113 : 7; 146 : 9; Prov. 15 : 25; 23 : 10; Jer. 49 : 11; Hos. 14 : 3.

of temporal blessings, Ex. 23 : 25; Lev. 26 : 6; Ps. 34 : 9; 37 : 3; 91; 102 : 28; 112; 121 : 3; 128; Prov. 3 : 10; Isa. 32 : 18; 33 : 16; Matt. 6 : 25; Phil. 4 : 19; 1 Tim. 4 : 8.

exhortation concerning, Heb. 4 : 1.

fulfilled in Christ, 2 Sam. 7 : 12; (Acts 13 : 23); Luke 1 : 69-73.

Promote, Num. 22 : 17; 24 : 11, **p.** thee to honour.

Prov. 4 : 8, wisdom shall **p.** thee.

Promotion, Ps. 75 : 6, **p.** cometh not from east.

Prov. 3 : 35, shame be **p.** of fools.

Pronounce, Judg. 12 : 6; Jer. 36 : 7, 18.

Proof, Acts 1 : 3, showed himself alive by many **p.**

2 Cor. 2 : 9, might know the **p.** of you.

13 : 3, ye seek a **p.** of Christ.

2 Tim. 4 : 5, make full **p.** of thy ministry.

Proper, 1 Chr. 29 : 3, mine own **p.** good.

one's own, Acts 1 : 19, in their **p.** tongue, Aceldama.

1 Cor. 7 : 7, every man hath his **p.** gift of God.

goodly, Heb. 11 : 23, Moses was a **p.** child.

Prophecies, we must remember, are not so much mere prediction of happenings in the near future as the ideas of prophets or seers, men of vision, who can picture the certainty of the overruling of the universe on the part of God. Their actual categories or modes of thought may not satisfy all our ideas, but their faith and their seeing is eternally true. " God's in His heaven " and His kingdom must prevail. Since God is a person, we can think of no higher category than that of personality, and the purpose of God is linked with the fortunes of a Person, Christ. This Person is vaguely foreshadowed in the Old Testament, and it is interesting to see how certain prophecies point to the Messiah, and how the New Testament realises these pictures.

Gen. 3 : 15—Gal. 4 : 4.

22 : 18—Gal. 3 : 16.

Ex. 12 : 46; Ps. 34 : 20—John 19 : 33, 36.

Ps. 2 : 7—Luke 1 : 32, 35.

16 : 10—Acts 2 : 31.

22 : 1—Matt. 27 : 46.

22 : 7, 8—Matt. 27 : 39-44.

22 : 14, 15—Luke 22 : 42, 44.

22 : 16—John 19 : 18; 20 : 25.

22 : 18—Matt. 27 : 35.

45 : 7; Isa. 11 : 2; 61 : 1—Matt. 3 : 16; John 3 : 34; Acts 10 : 38.

68 : 18—Luke 24 : 51; Acts 1 : 9.

69 : 9—John 2 : 17.

69 : 21—Matt. 27 : 34.

72 : 8 ; Dan. 7 : 14—Phil. 2 : 9, 11.

78 : 2—Matt. 13 : 34, 35.

110 : 1—Heb. 1 : 3.

118 : 22—Matt. 21 : 42; John 7 : 48.

132 : 11; Jer. 23 : 5—Acts 13 : 23; Rom. 1 : 3.

Isa. 7 : 14—Matt. 1 : 18; Luke 2 : 7.

9 : 7; Dan. 7 : 14—Luke 1 : 32, 33.

11 : 10; 42 : 1—Matt. 1 : 17, 21; John 10 : 16; Acts 10 : 45.

28 : 16—1 Pet. 2 : 6, 7.

40 : 3; Mal. 3 : 1—Matt. 3 : 1; Luke 1 : 17.

40 : 11; 42 : 3—Matt. 12 : 15, 20; Heb. 4 : 15.

50 : 6—John 19 : 1.

52 : 14; 53 : 3—John 19 : 5.

53 : 2—Mark 6 : 3; Luke 9 : 58.

53 : 4-6; Dan. 9 : 26—Matt. 20 : 28.

53 : 7—Matt. 26 : 63; 27 : 12-14.

53 : 12—Matt. 27 : 50; Mark 15 : 28.

Hos. 11 : 1—Matt. 2 : 15.

Mic. 5 : 1—Matt. 27 : 30.

5 : 2—Matt. 2 : 1.

Zech. 6 : 13—Rom. 8 : 34.

9 : 9—Matt. 21 : 1-5.

11 : 12—Matt. 26 : 15.

11 : 13—Matt. 27 : 7.

13 : 7—Matt. 26 : 31.

Prophecy, God author of, Isa. 44 : 7; 45 : 21; Luke 1 : 70; Rev. 1 : 1.

gift of Christ, Eph. 4 : 11; Rev. 11 : 3; of Holy Ghost, 1 Cor. 12 : 10.

Christ the great subject of, Luke 24 : 44; Acts 3 : 22-24; 10 : 43; 1 Pet. 1 : 10, 11.

how to be received, 2 Chr. 20 : 20; Luke 24 : 25; 1 Thess. 5 : 20.

false, how tested, Deut. 13 : 1, 18 : 20; Jer. 14 : 15; 23 : 16; Ezek. 13 : 3.

Matt. 13 : 14, is fulfilled the **p.** of Esaias.

1 Cor. 13 : 8, whether there be **p.,** they shall fail.

1 Tim. 4 : 14, gift given thee by **p.**

2 Pet. 1 : 19, a more sure word of **p.**

1 : 21, **p.** came not by the will of man.

Rev. 1 : 3, blessed that hear this **p.**

19 : 10, the testimony of Jesus is the spirit of **p.**

22 : 19, if any man take from this **p.**

Prophesy, Num. 11 : 25, they **p.,** and did not cease.

1 Ki. 22 : 8, he doth not **p.** good.

Isa. 30 : 10, **p.** not to us right things.

Jer. 5 : 31, the prophets **p.** falsely.

14 : 14; 23 : 25, the prophets **p.** lies.

Joel 2 : 28; Acts 2 : 17, your sons shall **p.**

Amos 2 : 12; Mic. 2 : 6, saying, **P.** not.

Amos 3 : 8, Lord hath spoken, who can but **p.** ?

Mic. 2 : 11, I will **p.** of wine.

Matt. 26 : 68; Mark 14 : 65; Luke 22 : 64, **p.** unto us, thou Christ.

Rom. 12 : 6, whether prophecy, let us **p.**

1 Cor. 13 : 9, we **p.** in part.

14 : 3, he that **p.** speaketh unto men.

14 : 39, covet to **p.**

Prophetess, Anna, Luke 2 : 36; Deborah,

Judg. 4 : 4; Huldah, 2 Ki. 22 : 14; Miriam, Ex. 15 : 20; Noadiah, Neh. 6 : 14.

Prophets, sent by God, Isa. 58 : 1; Jer. 1 : 4; 23 : 28; 25 : 4; Ezek. 2 : 3.

Christ so called, Matt. 21 : 11; Luke 7 : 16; 22 : 64: (Deut. 18 : 15).

others so called : Aaron, Ex. 7 : 1; Abraham, Gen. 20 : 7; Ahijah, 1 Ki. 11 : 29; Amos, Amos 7 : 14; Balaam, Num. 24 : 2; Daniel, Dan. 10 : 11; Matt. 24 : 15; David, Matt. 13 : 35; Acts 2 : 30; Eldad, Num. 11 : 26; Elijah, 1 Ki. 18 :36; Elisha, 2 Ki. 6 : 12; Ezekiel, Ezek. 1 : 3; Gad, 1 Sam. 22 : 5; Habakkuk, Hab. 1 : 1; Haggai, Ezra 5 : 1; 6 : 14; Hag. 1 : 1; Hananiah, Jer. 28 : 17; Hosea, Hos. 1 : 1; Rom. 9 : 25; Iddo, 2 Chr. 13 : 22; Isaiah, 2 Ki. 20 : 11; Isa. 1 : 1; Matt. 3 : 3; Jehu, 1 Ki. 16 : 7; Jeremiah, 2 Chr. 36 : 12; Jer. 1 : 5; Joel, Joel 1 : 1; Acts 2 : 16; John the Baptist, Luke 7 : 28; Jonah, 2 Ki. 14 : 25; Jonah 1 : 1; Matt. 12 : 39; Joshua, 1 Ki. 16 : 34; Malachi, Mal. 1 : 1; Medad, Num. 11 : 26; Micah, Jer. 26 : 18; Mic. 1 : 1; Moses, Deut. 34 : 10; Nahum Nah. 1 : 1; Nathan, 1 Ki. 1 : 32; Obadiah, Obad. 1; Oded, 2 Chr. 15 : 8; Paul, Acts 13 : 9; 27 : 10; Samuel, 1 Sam. 3 : 20; Zacharias, Luke 1 : 67; Zechariah, Zech. 1 : 1; Zephaniah, Zeph. 1 : 1.

false, Zedekiah, 1 Ki. 22 : 11; Jer. 29 : 21; Bar-jesus, Acts 13 : 6.

denounced, Deut. 13; 18 : 20; Isa. 9 : 15; Jer. 6 : 13; 14 : 15; 23 : 34; 28 : 15; 29 : 31; Ezek. 13 : 3; 14 : 9.

Num. 11 : 29, would that all the Lord's people were p.

Deut. 13 : 1, if there arise a p.

18 : 15; Acts 3 : 22; 7 : 37, the Lord will raise up a P.

1 Sam. 10 : 12; 19 : 24, is Saul also among the p. ?

1 Ki. 13 : 18, I am a p. as thou art.

18 : 22, I only remain a p. of the Lord.

22 : 7; 2 Ki. 3 : 11; 2 Chr. 18 : 6, is there not here a p. of the Lord.

2 Ki. 5 : 13, if the p. had bid thee do some great thing.

1 Chr. 16 : 22; Ps. 105 : 15, do my p. no harm.

Ps. 74 : 9, there is no more any p.

Isa. 3 : 2, the Lord taketh away the p.

Jer. 37 : 19, where are now your p.

Ezek. 2 : 5; 33 : 33, there hath been a p. among them.

Hos. 9 : 7, the p. is a fool.

Amos 7 : 14, I was no p., neither was I a p. son.

Mic. 3 : 11, the p. divine for money.

Zech. 1 : 5, the p., do they live forever ?

Matt. 2 : 5, thus it is written by the p.

10 : 41, he that receiveth a p. in the name of a p.

13 : 57; Mark 6 : 4; Luke 4 : 24; John 4 : 44, a p. not without honour.

Luke 4 : 24, no p. is accepted in his own

country.

7 : 28, there hath not arisen a greater p. than John.

13 : 13, it cannot be that a p. perish out of Jerusalem.

24 : 19, Jesus who was a p. mighty in deed.

John 4 : 19, thou art a p.

7 : 40, of a truth this is the P.

Acts 8 : 34, of whom speaketh the p. this ?

13 : 15, reading of the Law and the P.

26 : 27, believest thou the P ?

1 Cor. 12 : 29, are all p. ?

14 : 32, spirits of p. are subject to the p.

Eph. 2 : 20, built on foundation of p.

4 : 11, he gave some p.

Heb. 1 : 1, spake to fathers by the p.

Jas. 5 : 10, take the p., who have spoken.

1 Pet. 1 : 10, of which salvation the p. enquired.

Rev. 22 : 9, I am of thy brethren the p.

Propitiation for sin, Rom. 3 : 25; 1 John 2 : 2; 4 : 10.

Proportion, 1 Ki. 7 : 36, to the p. of every one.

Job 41 : 12, not conceal his comely p.

Rom. 12 : 6, according to p. of faith.

Proselytes, Jewish, Acts 2 : 10; 6 : 5; 13 : 43. These were Gentiles won from the heathen world and converted to Judaism. The " proselytes of righteousness " were circumcised and fully initiated into the Jewish legal requirements. " The devout " worshipped " in the court of the Gentiles," and though they kept the commandments they could hardly be termed " proselytes " in the strict sense of the term. This was the class which supplied many of the early Gentile Christians.

Prospect, Ezek. 40 : 44, etc.; 42 : 15; 43 : 4.

Prosper, Gen. 24 : 42, if now thou do p. my way.

39 : 3, the Lord made all Joseph did to p.

Num. 14 : 41, transgress, but it shall not p.

Deut. 28 : 29, thou shalt not p. in thy ways.

1 Chr. 22 : 13, shalt p., if thou takest heed.

2 Chr. 20 : 20, believe his prophets, so shall ye p.

Neh. 2 : 20, God of heaven will p. us.

Ps. 1 : 3, whatsoever he doeth shall p.

73 : 12, ungodly who p. in the world.

122 : 6, they shall p. that love thee.

Prov. 28 : 13, he that covereth sins shall not p.

Eccl. 11 : 6, knowest not whether shall p.

Isa. 53 : 10, pleasure of Lord shall p.

54 : 17, no weapon that is found against thee shall p.

55 : 11, it shall p. in the thing whereto I sent it.

Jer. 12 : 1, wherefore doth way of wicked p. ?

23 : 5, a king shall reign and p.

Dan. 11 : 27, speak lies, but it shall not p.

1 Cor. 16 : 2, as God hath p. him.

Prophetical Books, Table Concerning the

Name.	Approximate Date.	Contemporary King.	Notes.
	B.C.		
Isaiah	760-701	Uzziah, Jotham, Ahaz, Hezekiah	The Prophet of Holiness.
Jeremiah	629-585	Josiah to Zedekiah	The Prophet unto the Nations.
Ezekiel	592-570	Nebuchadrezzar of Babylon	The Prophet of Israel's Deliverance by Jehovah.
Daniel	605-534	Nebuchadrezzar, Darius Cyrus	The Prophet of the Lions' Den.
Hosea	750-722	Uzziah, Jotham, Ahaz, Hezekiah	The Prophet of God's Yearning Love.
Joel	750-710	Jotham, Ahaz, Hezekiah	The Prophet of Armageddon.
Amos	775-750	Uzziah, Jeroboam II.	The Prophet of Righteousness.
Obadiah	587	Zedekiah	The Prophet of Edom's Doom.
Jonah	862	Jehoshaphat	The Prophet of Nineveh's Repentance.
Micah	740-700	Jotham, Ahaz, Hezekiah	The Prophet of Messiah's Birthplace.
Nahum	660-640	Manasseh	The Prophet of Nineveh's Doom.
Habakkuk	626	Josiah, Jehoiakim	The Prophet of Joy in God.
Zephaniah	630	Josiah	The Prophet of Zion's Glory.
Haggai	520	Darius I. of Persia	The Prophet of Encouragment for Zerubbabel.
Zachariah	520	Darius I. of Persia	The Prophet of the Day of the Lord.
Malachi	420	Darius Nothus	The Prophet of the Son of Righteousness.

3 John 2, I wish that thou mayest **p.**

Prosperity, of the righteous, Ps. 36 : 8; 37 : 11, 18; 75 : 10; 84 : 11; 92 : 12; Prov. 3 : 2; Eccl. 8 : 12.

of the wicked, Job 12 : 6; 20 : 5; 21 : 7; Ps. 37; 92 : 7; Eccl. 8 : 14; 9 : 2; Jer. 12.

dangers of, Deut. 6 : 10; Prov. 30 : 8; Luke 6 : 24; 12 : 16; 16 : 19; Jas. 5 : 1.

Deut. 23 : 6, thou shalt not seek their **p.**

1 Sam. 25 : 6, say to him that liveth in **p.**

1 Ki. 10 : 7, thy wisdom and **p.**

Job 36 : 11, spend their days in **p.**

Ps. 30 : 6, in my **p.** I shall never be moved.

73 : 3, when I saw the **p.** of the wicked.

118 : 25, O Lord, send now **p.**

122 : 7, **p.** within thy palaces.

Prov. 1 : 32, the **p.** of fools shall destroy them.

Eccl. 7 · 14, in the day of **p.** be joyful.

Jer. 22 : 21, I spake to thee in thy **p.**

Lam. 3 : 17, I forgat **p.**

Prosperous, Gen. 24 : 21, Lord made his journey **p.**

39 : 2, he was a **p.** man.

Josh. 1 : 8, thou shalt make thy way **p.**

Rom. 1 : 10, might have a **p.** journey.

Prosperously, Ps. 45 : 4.

Prostitute (verb), Lev. 19 : 29.

Protection, Deut. 32 : 38.

Protest, Gen. 43 : 3, the man did solemnly **p.**

Zech. 3 : 6, the angel of the Lord **p.**

1 Cor. 15 : 31, I **p.** by rejoicing in Christ.

Proud, Job 26 : 12, he smiteth through the **p.**

40 : 11, behold every one that is **p.**

Ps. 31 : 23, rewardeth the **p.** doer.

40 : 4, blessed is the man that respecteth not the **p.**

94 : 2, render a reward to the **p.**

101 : 5, him that hath a **p.** heart.

119 : 21, thou hast rebuked the **p.**

123 : 4, soul filled with contempt of the **p.**

138 : 6, the **p.** he knoweth afar off.

Prov. 6 : 17, Lord hateth a **p.** look.

15 : 25, the Lord will destroy the house of the **p.**

21 : 4, high look and a **p.** heart is sin.

Eccl. 7 : 8, patient in spirit better than the **p.**

Hab. 2 : 5, he is a **p.** man.

Mal. 3 : 15, we call the **p.** happy.

Luke 1 : 51, he hath scattered the **p.**

1 Tim. 6 : 4, he is **p.**, knowing nothing.

Jas. 4 : 6; 1 Pet. 5 : 5, God resisteth the **p.**

Proudly, 1 Sam. 2 : 3; Ps. 17 : 10; Isa. 3 : 5; Obad. 12.

Prove, Ex. 16 : 4, I may **p.** them.

20 · 20, God is come to **p.** you.

Deut. 8 : 2, 16, humble thee, and **p.** thee.

Judg. 6 : 39, let me **p.** thee but this once.

1 Sam. 17 : 39, I have not **p.** them.

1 Ki. 10 : 1; 2 Chr. 9 : 1, she came to **p.** Solomon.

Ps. 17 : 3, thou hast **p.** my heart.

26 : 2, examine me, O Lord, and **p.** me.

95 : 9; Heb. 3 : 9, when your fathers **p.** me.

Eccl. 2 : 1, I will **p.** thee with mirth.

Mal. 3 : 10, **p.** me now herewith.

Luke 14 : 19, I go to **p.** them.

John 6 : 6, this he said to **p.** him.

Acts 9 : 22, **p.** that this is very Christ.

Rom. 12 : 2, **p.** what is that good will of God.

2 Cor. 13 : 5, **p.** your own selves.

1 Thess. 5 : 21, **p.** all things.

Provender, Gen. 24 : 25, 32; Isa. 30 : 24.

Proverbs, of Solomon, Prov. 1-25; collected under Hezekiah, Prov. 25-29.

various, 1 Sam. 10 : 12; Luke 4 : 23.

Deut. 28 : 37, become a **p.** and a by-word.

1 Sam. 24 : 13, as saith of ancients.

Ps. 69 : 11, I became a **p.** to them.

Eccl. 12 : 9, preacher set in order many **p.**

Hab. 2 : 6, take up a **p.** against him.

John 16 : 29, speakest plainly and speakest no **p.**

2 Pet. 2 : 22, it is happened according to the **p.**

Proverbs, Book of.

Title.—The Hebrew title of the book is Mishle, the singular of which is Mashal, usually translated "proverb." The word really signifies "likeness," and then a similitude or "parable." It is frequently employed for short maxims or sententious sayings, which often consist in comparisons, or for longer or shorter didactic poems.

Literary Analysis.—Just as the Psalms are attributed to David as the fount of Hebrew psalmody, so the Proverbs were ascribed to Solomon as the source of Hebrew wisdom. That he is not responsible for the whole collection is seen in the marked divisions into which the book falls: (a) Praise of wisdom, 1-9 (6: 1-19, and 9: 7-12 are misplaced). (b) Proverbs of Solomon, 10 : 1—22 : 16. (c) Two collections to the professional sages or "wise," 22 : 17—24 : 22, and 24 : 23-34. (d) The Hezekiah collection, 25-29 (i.e., "collected by the men of Hezekiah"). (e) Four appendices, 30-31: (1) words of Agur (30 : 1-9); (2) Proverbs numerical, etc. (30 : 10-33); (3) words of King Lemuel (31 : 1-9); (4) the virtuous woman —an acrostic poem (31 : 10-31).

Date.—The date must be connected with each particular division. The general finding is as follows: (b) is ascribed to Solomon as the father of Hebrew wisdom (1 Ki. 4 : 29-34). That many actual sayings are here preserved is doubtful. In political, social and religious outlook the section betrays Persian and Greek influences. There are no strong national characteristics. These considerations and others suggest that while an older stratum can be observed, this collection has its origin somewhere between 400 and 300 B.C. (d) and (c) are regarded as slightly later than (b), the main consideration being the date of the class of literary sages, who most naturally fall into the post-exilic period. (a) is a unity and not a string of aphorisms. There are definite Greek traces herein, and we can assign it to the years 300-250 B.C., and probably to the editor of (b), (c), and (d). (e) is a collection added to the above edition later; (1) and (4) especially bear the stamp of a late date.

Characteristics.—The poetry makes great use of parallelism, which is antithetic in form (i.e., the thought of one line couplet balanced by a contrasted of a thought in the other) or synonymous i.e., the thought in the second line repeats in a different form the thought of the first).

Provide, Gen. 22 : 8, God will p. himself a lamb.

30 : 30, when shall I p. for mine own house ?

Job 38 : 41, p. for the raven his food.

Ps. 78 : 20, can he p. flesh for his people ?

Matt. 10 : 9, p. neither gold nor silver.

Luke 12 : 33, p. bags that wax not old.

Rom. 12 : 17, p. things honest.

1 Tim. 5 : 8, if any p. not for his own house.

Heb. 11 : 40, God having p. some better thing for us.

Providence, of God, Gen. 8 : 22; 1 Sam. 6 : 5; Ps. 36 : 6; 104; 136; 145; 147; Prov. 16; 19; 20; Matt. 6 : 26; 10 : 29; Luke 21 : 18; Acts 17 : 26.

Province, Esther 1 : 22; 3 : 12; Acts 23 : 34.

Provision, Gen. 42 : 25; 45 : 21, p. for the way.

Ps. 132 : 15, I will bless her p.

Dan. 1 : 5, king appointed a daily p.

Rom. 13 : 14, make not p. for the flesh.

Provocation, 1 Ki. 21 : 22; Neh. 9 : 18, 26; Ps. 95 : 8; Heb. 3 : 8, 15.

Provoke, Ex. 23 : 21, obey his voice, p. him not.

Num. 14 : 11, how long will this people p. me ?

Deut. 31 : 20, p. me, and break my covenant.

Job 12 : 6, they that p. God are secure.

Ps. 78 : 40, how oft did they p. him.

106 : 29, they p. him with their inventions.

Luke 11 : 53, began to urge, and p. him to speak.

Rom. 10 : 19; 11 : 11, p. to jealousy.

1 Cor. 13 : 5, charity is not easily p.

Eph. 6 : 4, p. not your children to wrath.

Heb. 3 : 16, when they heard, did p.

10 : 24, p. to love and good works.

Prudence, 2 Chr. 2 : 12; Prov. 8 : 12; Eph. 1 : 8.

Prudent, Prov. 12 : 16, a p. man covereth shame.

12 : 23, a p. man concealeth knowledge.

14 : 8, wisdom of p. is to understand.

15 : 5, that regardeth reproof is p.

16 : 21, the wise shall be called p.

19 : 14, a p. wife is from the Lord.

22 : 3; 27 : 12, a p. man foreseeth evil.

Isa. 5 : 21, woe to them that are p. in their own sight.

Jer. 49 : 7, is counsel perished from p. ?

Hos. 14 : 9, who is p. ?

Amos 5 : 13, the p. shall keep silence.

Matt. 11 : 25; Luke 10 : 21, hid these things from the wise and p.

1 Cor. 1 : 19, bring to nothing the understanding of the p.

Prudently, Isa. 52 : 13.

Prune, Lev. 25 : 3, 4; Isa. 5 : 6.

Pruning-hooks, Isa. 2 : 4; Joel 3 : 10; Mic. 4 : 3.

Psalmist, 2 Sam. 23 : 1.

Psalmody, service of song, Jewish, Ex. 15 : 1; 1 Chr. 6 : 31; 13 : 8; 2 Chr. 5 : 13; 20 : 22; 29 :30; Neh. 12 : 27.

Christian, Matt. 26 : 30; Mark 14 : 26; Jas. 5 : 13.

spiritual songs, Eph. 5 : 19; Col. 3 : 16.

Psalms, Book of.

Compilation and Date.—(a) Collection in book form of the Psalms " of David " (this included Ps. 3-32, 34-41); (b) a second hymn-book entitled " of David "

(Ps. 51–72, with certain exceptions), (c) compilation entitled " of Asaph " (cf. Ezra 2 : 41, where we see " Asaph " is a guild of singers); (d) book " of the sons of Korah " (cf. (c) and see 2 Chr. 20 : 19); (e) the " Elohistic Psalter " (compiled from (b), (c), and (d), and substituting " Elohim " for " Jahweh "); (f) (e) enlarged by adding Ps. 84–89; (g) compilation of " Songs of the Ascents."

All we can say regarding the date is that the Psalter was compiled between the sixth and second centuries B.C., and that, as Solomon was regarded as the father of Hebrew wisdom, so David was considered the pioneer of Hebrew psalmody, and his name was affixed not only to the completed edition, but also to various collections and to individual psalms.

Divisions.—In the Hebrew and in the Revised Version the Psalter is divided into five books. This division was probably due to the similar division of the Pentateuch, and dates back to a period before the LXX. translation.

(1) Book I. contains Psalms 1–41. Thirty-seven of the Psalms in this book are ascribed in the titles to David. Psalms 1 and 2 are without titles. Psalms 9 and 10 were originally one, as appears from the alphabetical arrangement of the verses, and the absence of a title to Ps. 10. They form but one in the LXX. and Vulgate. Ps. 33 has no superscription in the Hebrew, but in the LXX. is ascribed to David. Psalms 2, 16, and 22 are Messianic, and probably Ps. 8 (see Heb. 2), so also Ps. 40. In Book I. the usual title of God is Jehovah; Elohim is rarely used.

(2) Book II. comprises Psalms 42–72. In ,this book Psalms 42–49 are ascribed to the sons of Korah, Ps. 50 to Asaph, and Psalms 51–65, 68–70, to David. Psalms 66, 67, and 71 are without titles, and Ps. 72 is headed " a Psalm of Solomon." Ps. 67 is ascribed in the LXX. to David. Ps. 43 probably forms part of Ps. 42; the former is without a title, and in some Hebrew MSS. is united with Ps. 42. In the majority of the Psalms in this book the Divine title Elohim is used, Jehovah being employed only thirty times. Two psalms which are in Book I. Jehovistic (Psalms 14 and 40 : 13-17) are here Elohistic, viz., Psalms 53 and 70. The Messianic Psalm in this first book is Ps. 72, but the New Testament recognises Messianic elements in Psalms 45, 68, and 69.

(3) Book III. consists of Psalms 73–89. Psalms 73–83 inclusive, are ascribed to Asaph; Psalms 84, 85, 87 to the sons of Korah. Ps. 86 is entitled " a prayer of David." Ps. 88 is assigned both to the sons of Korah and to Heman the Ezrahite; and Ps. 89 to Ethan the Ezrahite.

Ps. 89 is applied to the Messiah in the New Testament.

(4) Book IV. contains Psalms 90–106. Ps. 90 is ascribed in the title to " Moses the man of God," and Psalms 101, 103 to David. All the others are anonymous, though the LXX. assigns 91, 93–99, and 104 to David. Ps. 91 is applied to the Messiah in the New Testament.

(5) Book V. comprises Ps. 107 to end. Fifteen of these are, according to the Hebrew titles, Davidic. One (Ps. 127) is Solomonic. Psalms 116 and 147 are each divided into two psalms in the LXX. version. The titles prefixed to the psalms in this book in the LXX., Syriac, and Vulgate versions, differ considerably from those in the Hebrew. Ps. 110 is an important Messianic psalm, and Messianic elements are recognised in the New Testament in Ps. 118. The fifteen psalms (120–134) are entitled " Songs of Degrees." These psalms were probably intended to be sung by the pilgrims on their way to Jerusalem.

At the end of each of the first four books of the Psalter a doxology is inserted, which in each case serves to conclude the book. These doxologies are found in all the ancient versions, as an evidence of the antiquity of the fivefold division.

Titles.—Only thirty-four psalms are without titles. The superscriptions of the others indicate the supposed author, or the liturgical character of the psalm, e.g., " For the precentor," or " chief musician," or the musical or religious features of the psalm, " a Maschil," " a Shiggaion," " a Michtam," " a prayer," " a song of praise." Others specify the instrument to be used in playing the accompaniment to the psalm, or the measure or melody to which it was to be sung. In other cases the title indicates the event which prompted the composition of the psalm, or the occasion on which it was to be used (e.g., the Songs of Degrees, see above). In some cases the psalm is provided with two titles (e.g., Ps. 88). The Psalms without titles have been named " Orphan " Psalms; seven psalms (viz., 6, 32, 38, 51, 102, 130, 143) are also called Penitential Psalms. The various classifications of the Psalter are more or less unsatisfactory.

General Remarks.—Its subject-matter is varied. It contains prayers, songs of praise, lamentations, reflections on God's providence and His moral government of the world, expressions of faith, resignation, joy in God's presence, psalms referring to the personal circumstances of the Psalmist; national, historical, and royal psalms (many of Messianic import); others of a didactic character, referring to matters of religion or morality (cf. Driver, " Introd.," p. 346 ff.). The theology of the Psalter does not differ from that of the prophetical books. The psalms were used both in the public services of the Israelites and also in their private devotions, and afford a striking picture of the religious life and thought of the pious portion of Israel.

The Psalms may be divided into five parts as follows : (1) Davidic (1–41); (2) Davidic (42–72); (3) Asaphic (73–89); (4) of the captivity (90–106); (5) of restoration (107–150); or may be classified according to their subjects, thus :—

(a) Psalms of Supplication—
1. On account of sin, Ps. 6; 25; 32; 38; 51; 102; 130.
2. Affliction, Ps. 7; 10; 13; 17; 22; 31; 35; 41–43; 54–57; 59; 64; 69–71; 77; 86; 88; 94; 109; 120; 140–143.
persecution, Ps. 44; 60; 74; 79; 80; 83; 89; 94; 102; 133; 137.
4. Relative to public worship, Ps. 26; 27; 42; 43; 63; 65; 84; 92; 95–100; 118; 122; 132; 144; 145–150.
5. Expressing trust in God, Ps. 3–5; 11; 12; 16; 20; 23; 27; 28; 31; 42; 43; 52; 54; 56; 57; 59; 61–64; 71; 77; 86; 108; 115; 118; 121; 125; 131; 138; 141.
6. The Psalmist's integrity, Ps. 7; 17; 26; 35; 101; 119.

(b) Gratitude—
1. For mercies shown to the Psalmist, Ps. 9; 18; 30; 32; 34; 40; 61–63; 75; 103; 108; 116; 118; 138; 144.
2. To the Church, Ps. 33; 36; 47; 65; 66; 68; 75; 76; 81; 85; 87; 95; 98; 105; 106; 107; 124; 126; 129; 134; 135; 136; 149.

(c) Adoration—
1. Of God's goodness and mercy, Ps. 3; 4; 9; 16; 18; 30–34; 36; 40; 46; 65–68; 84; 85; 91; 99; 100; 103; 107; 111; 113; 116; 117; 121; 126; 145; 146.
2. Of God's power, majesty, and glory, Ps. 2; 3; 8; 18; 19; 24; 29; 33; 45–48; 50; 65–68; 76; 77; 89; 91–100; 104–108; 110; 111; 113–118; 135; 136; 139; 145–150.

(d) Didactic.
1. Shewing the blessings of God's people and the misery of His enemies, Ps. 1; 3; 4; 5; 7; 9–15; 17; 24; 25; 32; 34; 36; 37; 41; 50; 52; 53; 58; 62; 73; 75; 82; 84; 91; 92; 94; 101; 112; 119; 121; 125; 127–129; 133; 149.
2. The excellence of God's law, Ps. 19; 119.
3. The vanity of human life, etc., Ps. 14; 39; 49; 53; 73; 90.

(e) Prophetical, Typical and Historical—
Ps. 2; 16; 22; 24; 31; 35; 40; 41; 45; 50; 55; 68; 69; 72; 78; 87; 88; 102; 105; 106; 109; 110; 118; 132; 135; 136.

Luke 20 : 42, David saith in book of P.
24 : 44, written in the P.
Eph. 5 : 19, speaking to yourselves in p.
Col. 3 : 16, admonishing one another in p.
Jas. 5 : 13, is any merry ? let him sing p.
Psaltery, 2 Sam. 6 : 5; 2 Chr. 9 : 11. Dan. 3 : 5, 10, 15. See Musical Instruments.
Publick, Matt. 1 : 19.
Publickly, Acts 18 : 28; 20 : 20.
Publicans. These were not dealers in spirituous liquors, but native Jews who acted as tax and tribute raisers. Roman officers contracted with their government to levy certain revenues. Local agents, who knew the people and their ways, were employed to raise the required amounts. These had authority to assess taxes on land, produce, and live stock, and to exact their own remuneration in addition. The practice reeked with extortion, oppression, and cruelty; consequently, " publicans " were the most odious members of the community, and were regarded as traitors to their race.
some believe in Jesus, Matt. 21 : 32; Luke 5 : 27; 7 : 29; 15 : 1; 19 : 2.
parable of Pharisee and publican, Luke 18 : 10.
See Matt. 5 : 46; 9 : 11; 11 : 19; 18 : 17; Luke 3 : 12.
Publish, Deut. 32 : 3, I will p. the name of the Lord.
2 Sam. 1 : 20, p. it not in Askelon.
Ps. 26 : 7, may p. it with the voice of thanksgiving.
68 : 11, great was the company that p. it.
Isa. 52 : 7; Nah. 1 : 15, that p. peace.
Jonah 3 : 7, he caused it to be p.
Mark 1 : 45; 5 : 20, he began to p. it much.
Luke 8 : 39, p. throughout whole city.
Acts 13 : 49, word of the Lord was p.
Publius (pŭb-li-ŭs), of Melita, entertains Paul, Acts 28 : 7.
Puffed, 1 Cor. 4 : 6, 18; 13 : 4; 2 Cor. 8 : 1.
Pul (pŭl) [Assyr., " Pulu," wild beast], king of Assyria, 2 Ki. 15 : 19; 1 Chr. 5 : 26.
Pull, Ps. 31 : 4, p. me out of net they laid.
Jer. 12 : 3, p. them out like sheep for the slaughter.
Amos 9 : 15, shall no more be p. up.
Matt. 7 : 4; Luke 6 : 42, p. mote out of thine eye.
Luke 12 : 18, I will p. down my barns.
14 : 5, will not p. him out on sabbath ?
2 Cor. 10 : 4, mighty to p. down of strong holds.
Jude 23, p. them out of the fire.
Pulpit, Neh. 8 : 4, stood upon a p. of wood.
Pulse, in Dan. 1 : 12 ff., seems to refer to any kind of farinaceous food. The Hebrew word simply means seeds (2 Sam. 19 : 28).
Punish, Prov. 17 : 26, to p. the just is not good.
Isa. 13 : 11, I will p. the world for their evil.
26 : 21, Lord cometh to p. inhabitants of the earth.
Jer. 21 : 14, p. according to your doings.

Acts 4 : 21, how they might p. them.

26 : 11, I p. them in every synagogue.

2 Thess. 1 : 9, p. with everlasting destruction.

2 Pet. 2 : 9, unto the day of judgment to be p.

Punishment, by burning, Gen. 38 : 24; Lev. 20 : 14; 21 : 9.

hanging, Gen. 40 : 22; Deut. 21 : 22; Ezra 6 : 11; Esther 2 : 23; 7 : 10.

scourging, Lev. 19 : 20; Deut. 25 : 1; Matt. 27 : 26; Acts 22 : 25.

stoning, Lev. 20 : 2; 24 : 14; 1 Ki. 21 : 10; John 8 : 59; Acts 7 : 58; 14 : 19.

beheading, 2 Ki. 6 : 31; 10 : 7; Matt. 14 : 10.

crucifying, Matt. 20 : 19; 27 : 31 ff.

Gen. 4 : 13, my p. is greater than I can bear.

1 Sam. 28 : 10, no p. shall happen to thee.

Job 31 : 3, a strange p. to workers of iniquity.

Prov. 19 : 19, a man of wrath shall suffer p.

Lam. 3 : 39, a man for p. of his sins ?

4 : 6, p. is greater than p. of Sodom.

Ezek. 14 : 10, bear p. of their iniquity.

Matt. 25 : 46, go away into everlasting p.

Heb. 10 : 29, of how much sorer p. ?

1 Pet. 2 : 14, the p. of evil doers.

See Heb. 11 : 36.

Pur (pŭr) [lot], **Purim** (lots), Esther 3 : 7; 9 : 26. See **Purim.**

Purchase, Gen. 25 : 10, Abraham p. of sons of Heth.

Ruth 4 : 10, I p. to be my wife.

Ps. 74 : 2, congregation thou hast p.

Acts 1 : 18, this man p. a field.

8 : 20, thought that the gift of God may be p. with money.

20 : 28, he hath p. with his own blood.

Eph. 1 : 14, redemption of p. possession.

1 Tim. 3 : 13, p. to themselves a good degree.

Pure, 2 Sam. 22 : 27; Ps. 18 : 26, with the p. thou wilt show thyself p.

Job 4 : 17, shall a man be more p. than his Maker?

8 : 6, if thou wert p. and upright.

11 : 4, my doctrine is p.

16 : 17, my prayer is p.

25 : 5, stars are not p. in his sight.

Ps. 12 : 6, words of the Lord are p.

19 : 8, commandment of Lord is p.

Prov. 15 : 26, words of the p. are pleasant.

20 : 29, who can say, I am p. from sin?

Mic. 6 : 11, shall I count them p. ?

Zeph. 3 : 9, a p. language.

Acts 20 : 26, I am p. from blood of all men.

Rom. 14 : 20, all things indeed are p.

Phil. 4 : 8, whatsoever things are p.

1 Tim. 3 : 9; 2 Tim. 1 : 3, a p. conscience.

1 Tim. 5 : 22, keep thyself p.

Titus 1 : 15, to the p. all things are p.

Heb. 10 : 22, bodies washed with p. water.

Jas. 1 : 27, p. religion.

3 : 17, wisdom from above is first p.

2 Pet. 3 : 1, I stir up your p. minds.

1 John 3 : 3, purifieth himself even as he is p.

Rev. 22 : 1, p. river of water of life.

Purely, Isa. 1 : 25, and I will p. purge away.

Pureness, Job 22 : 30, delivered by p. of hands.

Prov. 22 : 11, he that loveth p. of heart.

2 Cor. 6 : 6, approving ourselves by p.

Purer, Lam. 4 : 7, Nazarites p. than snow.

Hab. 1 : 13, thou art of p. eyes.

Purge, Ps. 51 : 7, p. me with hyssop.

Ps. 65 : 3, transgressions, thou shalt p.

Isa. 1 : 25, purely p. away thy dross.

6 : 7, thy sin is p.

Ezek. 24 : 13, I have p. thee, and thou wast not p.

Mal. 3 : 3, p. them as gold.

Matt. 3 : 12; Luke 3 : 17, he will throughly p. his floor.

John 15 : 2, branch that beareth fruit, he p.

1 Cor. 5 : 7, p. out the old leaven.

2 Tim. 2 : 21, if a man p. himself from these.

Heb. 9 : 14, p. your conscience.

10 : 2, worshippers once p.

2 Pet. 1 : 9, hath forgotten he was p.

Purification, laws concerning, Lev. 13–16; Num. 19; 31 : 19; (Acts 21 : 24; Heb. 9 : 13).

of women, Lev. 12; Esther 2 : 12; Luke 2 : 22.

of the heart by faith, Acts 15 : 9; 1 Pet. 1 : 22.

Purifier, Mal. 3 : 3, as a p. of silver he shall purify.

Purify, Titus 2 : 14, p. to himself a peculiar people.

Jas. 4 : 8, p. your hearts, ye double minded.

See Dan. 12 : 10.

Purim (pū-rĭm), Esther 9 : 26. On the 14th and 15th March, 473 B.C., the Jews were delivered from Haman, who had plotted their extermination throughout the Persian Empire. In commemoration of this, the Feast of Lots or Purim was celebrated annually. (In 2 Macc. 15 : 36 it is called " Mordecai's Day.") At first merely local and marked by no religious sentiment, a time when presents were given and received, it became more universal, and by the time of Christ was attended with much ceremonial. The book of Esther is read, and after the service merrymaking occurs. See Esther passim.

Purity, moral, enjoined, Gal. 5 : 16; Eph. 5 : 3; Phil. 2 : 15; 4 : 8; Col. 3 : 5; 1 Tim. 5 : 22; 1 Pet. 2 : 11.

of God's word and law, Ps. 12 : 6; 19 : 8; 119 : 140; Prov. 30 : 5.

Purloining, Titus 2 : 10.

Purple. The famous Tyrian purple dye was obtained from the bodies of several species of shellfish. Ex. 25 : 4; Mark 15 : 17.

Purpose, Prov. 20 : 18, every p. is established by counsel.

Eccl. 3 : 1, 17; 8 : 6, a time to every p.

Isa. 1 : 11, to what p. are your sacrifices ?

14 : 27, Lord hath p., who shall disannul it ?

Acts 11 : 23, with p. of heart.

Rom. 8 : 28, called according to his **p.**
  9 : 11, that **p.** of God might stand.
2 Cor. 1 : 17, do I **p.** according to the flesh ?
  9 : 7, every man as he **p.** in heart.
Eph. 1 : 11, according to the **p.** of him who worketh.
  3 : 11, eternal **p.** in Christ.
1 John 3 : 8, for this **p.** the Son of God.
Purse, Prov. 1 : 14, let us have one **p.**
Matt. 10 : 9, neither silver nor brass in your **p.**
Mark 6 : 8, take no money in their **p.**
Luke 10 : 4, carry neither **p.** nor scrip.
Pursue, Deut. 19 : 6; Josh. 20 : 5, lest avenger **p.**
Job 30 : 15, terrors **p.** my soul.
Ps. 34 : 14, seek peace, and **p.** it.
Prov. 11 : 19, he that **p.** evil **p.** death.
  28 : 1, wicked flee when no man **p.**
Pursuer, Josh. 2 : 16; 8 : 20; Lam. 1 : 6.
Purtenance, Ex. 12 : 9.
Push, Deut. 33 : 17; Ps. 44 : 5; Dan. 11 : 40.
Put, Gen. 3 : 15, I will **p.** enmity.
Ex. 23 : 1, **p.** not thine hand with the wicked.
Lev. 26 : 8; Deut. 32 : 30, **p.** ten thousand to flight.
Num. 23 : 5, Lord **p.** word in Balaam's mouth.
Judg. 12 : 3; 1 Sam. 28 : 21, I **p.** my life in my hands.
1 Sam. 2 : 36, **p.** me into one of the priest's offices.
1 Ki. 9 : 3; 11 : 36; 14 : 21, to **p.** my name there.
1 Chr. 11 : 19, **p.** their lives in jeopardy.
Neh. 2 : 12, what God **p.** in my heart.
Job 19 : 13, hath **p.** my brethren far from me.
Ps. 4 : 7, thou hast **p.** gladness in my heart.
  8 : 6; Eph. 1 : 22; Heb. 2 : 8, thou hast **p.** all things under his feet.
Ps. 88 : 18, lover and friend hast thou **p.** far from me.
Isa. 5 : 20, that **p.** darkness for light.
  42 : 1; Matt. 12 : 18, I have **p.** my Spirit upon him.
Matt. 19 : 6; Mark 10 : 9, let not man **p.** asunder.
Mark 10 : 16, he **p.** his hands on them.
John 5 : 7, no man to **p.** me into the pool.
1 Cor. 15 : 25, **p.** all his enemies under his feet.
Eph. 4 : 22; Col. 3 : 9, **p.** off old man.
Philem. 18, **p.** that on my account.
Heb. 6 : 6, **p.** him to an open shame.
  9 : 26, to **p.** away sin by the sacrifice of himself.
2 Pet. 1 : 14, I must **p.** off this my tabernacle.
Jude 5, will **p.** you in remembrance.
Rev. 2 : 24, **p.** on you none other burden.
Putrifying, Isa. 1 : 6.
Pygarg, mentioned in Deut. 14 : 5, among the clean animals allowed for food. Some form of antelope is intended, probably " Antilope addax." This is a large animal, and was possibly once numerous enough in Canaan's borders to be used as food.

Even to-day it approaches the eastern and southern frontiers.

Q

Quadrans, a farthing. See **Money.**
Quail. This well-known bird is found all over Europe, Asia, and Africa ; it is more or less a migratory bird. Some quails, according to Tristram, are found in Palestine all through the winter. In March they make their appearance in myriads, in the course of a single night.
Israel fed with, Ex. 16 : 12.
sent in wrath, Num. 11 : 31; Ps. 78 : 27; 105 : 40.

The Quail.

Quake, Ex. 19 : 18, mount **q.** greatly.
Dan. 10 : 7, great **q.** fell upon them.
Joel 2 : 10, earth shall **q.** before them.
Matt. 27 : 51, earth did **q.**
Heb. 12 : 21, Moses said, I exceedingly fear and **q.**
Quantity, Isa. 22 : 24.
Quarrel, 2 Ki. 5 : 7, see how he seeketh a **q.**
Mark 6 : 19, Herodias had a **q.** against John.
Col. 3 : 13, if any man have a **q.**
Quarrelling. See **Strife.**
Quarries, Judg. 3 : 19, 26.
Quarter, Gen. 19 : 4; Mark 1 : 45; Rev. 20 : 8.
Quaternion, a set of four persons, or things. The " four quaternions of soldiers " (Acts 12 : 4) were four bodies of four men. Each set of four soldiers did duty for six hours in the twenty-four. Peter was chained to two of the quaternion, the other two standing guard.
Queen, of heaven, idolatrous worship of, Jer. 44 : 17, 25.
1 Ki. 10 : 1; 2 Chr. 9 : 1, the **q.** of Sheba.
Ps. 45 : 9, the **q.** in gold of Ophir.
Isa. 49 : 23, their **q.** thy nursing mothers.
Dan. 5 : 10, **q.** came into banquet house.
Matt. 12 : 42; Luke 11 : 31, the **q.** of the south shall rise up in judgment.
Rev. 18 : 7, I sit a **q.** and am no widow.
Quench, Num. 11 : 2, the fire was **q.**

2 Sam. 14 : 7, they shall q. my coal.
21 : 17, q. not the light of Israel.
Song of Sol. 8 : 7, many waters cannot q. love.
Isa. 34 : 10, shall not be q. night nor day.
42 : 3; Matt. 12 : 20, smoking flax shall he not q.
Isa. 66 : 24, neither shall their fire be q.
Mark 9 : 44, 46, 48, where fire is not q.
Eph. 6 : 16, able to q. fiery darts of wicked.
1 Thess. 5 : 19, q. not the Spirit.
Heb. 11 : 34, q. the violence of fire.
Question, 1 Ki. 10 : 1; 2 Chr. 9 : 1, to prove him with a q.
Matt. 22 : 46, neither durst ask any more q.
Mark 9 : 16, what q. ye with them ?
11 : 29, I will ask of you one q.
Acts 18 : 15, if it be a q. of words.
19 : 40, in danger to be called in q.
1 Cor. 10 : 25, asking no q. for conscience' sake.
1 Tim. 6 : 4, doting about q.
2 Tim. 2 : 23; Titus 3 : 9, unlearned q. avoid.
Quick, Num. 16 : 30; Ps. 55 : 15, they go down q.
Ps. 124 : 3, they had swallowed us up q.
Isa. 11 : 3, make him of q. understanding.
Heb. 4 : 12, the word of God is q. and powerful.
living, Acts 10 : 42; 2 Tim. 4 : 1; 1 Pet. 4 : 5, judge the q. and the dead.
Quicken, Ps. 71 : 20, thou shalt q. me again.
Ps. 80 : 18, q. us, and we will call on thy name.
119 : 25, q. me according to thy word.
143 : 11, q. me, O Lord, for thy name's sake.
Rom. 8 . 11, shall q. your mortal bodies.
1 Cor. 15 : 36, that which thou sowest is not q.
Eph. 2 : 1, you hath he q., who were dead.
2 : 5; Col. 2 : 13, q. us together with Christ.
1 Pet. 3 : 18, q. by the Spirit.
Quickening, spiritual, John 5 : 21; 6 : 63; Rom. 4 : 17; 1 Cor. 15 : 45; 2 Cor. 3 : 6; 1 Tim. 6 : 13.
Quickly, Gen. 27 : 20, how hast thou found it so q. ?
Ex. 32 : 8; Deut. 9 : 12, have turned q. out of the way.
Num. 16 : 46, go q. to congregation.
Josh. 2 : 5, pursue q., overtake them.
Eccl. 4 : 12, threefold cord not q. broken.
Matt. 5 : 25, agree with thine adversary q.
John 13 : 27, that thou doest, do q.
Rev. 2 : 5, 16, repent, else I come q.
3 : 11; 22 : 7, 12, 20, behold I come q.
Quicksands, Acts 27 : 17.
Quiet, the faithful shall dwell in, Prov. 1 : 33; Isa. 30 : 15; 32 : 17, 18.
to be enjoined, 1 Thess. 4 : 11; 1 Tim. 2 : 2.
Job 21 : 23, one dieth, being at ease and q.
Ps. 107 : 30, glad, because they be q.
Eccl. 9 : 17, words of wise men are heard in q.
Isa. 7 : 4, take heed, and be q.

14 : 7, the earth is at rest, and is q.
32 : 18, in q. resting places.
Jer. 49 : 23, sorrow on the sea; it cannot be q.
Ezek. 16 : 42, I will be q.
Acts 19 : 36, ye ought to be q.
1 Pet. 3 : 4, ornament of a meek and q. spirit.
Quietly, 2 Sam. 3 : 27; Lam. 3 : 26.
Quietness, Judg. 8 : 28, the country was in q.
Prov. 17 : 1, better a dry morsel and q.
Eccl. 4 : 6, better a handful with q.
Isa. 32 : 17, effect of righteousness, q.
Acts 24 : 2, by thee we enjoy great q.
2 Thess. 3 : 12, exhort that with q. they work.
Quit, 1 Sam. 4 : 9; 1 Chr. 16 : 13, q. you like men.
[ar.], set free, Ex. 21 : 19, that smote him be q.
Josh 2 : 20, we will be q. of the oath.
Quite, Gen. 31 : 15; Num. 17 : 10; 2 Sam. 3 : 24.
Quiver, Ps. 127 : 5, happy is the man that hath his q. full.
Isa. 49 : 2, in his q. hath he hid me.
Jer. 5 : 16, their q. is as an open sepulchre.
Hab. 3 : 16, my lips q. at the voice.

R

Raamah (rā-ă-mäh) [trembling], land occupied by the descendants of Ham, Gen. 1 : 7; 1 Chr. 1 : 9.
Raamiah (rā-ă-mī-ăh) [trembling before Jah], Neh. 7 : 7.
Raamses (rā-ăm-sēs), Ex. 1 : 11.
Rabbah (răb-băh) [the great], the chief city of the Ammonites, besieged and taken by Joab, 2 Sam. 11 : 1; 12 : 26.
prophecies concerning, Jer. 49 : 2; Ezek. 25; Amos 1 : 14.
Rabbath (rab-bath), Ezek. 21 : 20. See Rabbah.
Rabbath-ammon, the metropolis and very strong fortress of the Ammonites, Deut. 3 : 11.
Rabbath-Moab, capital of Moab, also called Ar.
Rabbi [master], Matt. 23 : 7, 8; John 1 : 38; 3 : 2, 26; 6 : 25. The Jewish teachers simply quoted Rabbi after Rabbi (much as we might quote Professors) to prove all the minutiæ of the Law. No one ventured to express his own beliefs or to come down to the level of the people until Jesus charmed them by His simplicity and daring. He was His own authority. He made religion a natural thing, rather than the study of a few.
Rabboni (răb-bō-nī) [my master], Christ so named by Mary, John 20 : 16.
Rabsaris (răb-să-rĭs) [chief of the princes], 2 Ki. 18 : 17.
Rabshakeh (răb-shă-kĕh) [Assyr., " Rabsaki,"

commander-in-chief], 2 Ki. 18 : 17, 19;
Isa. 36 : 2, 4.
Raca (rā-cä) [worthless], Matt. 5 : 22.
Race, Ps. 19 : 5, strong man to run a r.
Eccl. 9 : 11, the r. is not to the swift.
1 Cor. 9 : 24, they which run in a r.
Heb. 12 : 1, run with patience the r.
Rachel (rā-chĕl) or Rahel [ewe], and Jacob,
Gen. 29 : 10, 28; 31 : 4, 19, 34; 35 :
16.
tomb of, near Bethlehem, Gen. 48 : 7.
See Jer. 31 : 15.

Rachel's Grave.

Rafters, Song of Sol. 1 : 17.
Rage, censured, 2 Ki. 19 : 28; Ps. 2 : 1.
2 Ki. 5 : 12, Naaman turned away in a r.
Isa. 37 : 28, I know thy r.
Prov. 6 : 34, jealousy is the r. of a man.
14 : 16, the fool r., and is confident.
29 : 9, whether he r. or laugh.
Acts 4 : 25, why did the heathen r. ?
Ragged, Isa. 2 : 21.
Raging, Ps. 89 : 9, thou rulest the r. of the
sea.
Prov. 20 : 1, strong drink is r.
Jonah 1 : 15, the sea ceased from her r.
Luke 8 : 24, he rebuked the r. of the
water.
Jude 13, r. waves of the sea.
Rags, Prov. 23 : 21, shall clothe a man with r.
Isa. 64 : 6, our righteousness as filthy r.
Jer. 38 : 11, took rotten r.
Rahab (rā-hăb) [arrogance, raging], used of
the crocodile, Job 26 : 12, R.V.; of Egypt,
Isa. 30 : 7; 51 : 9, R.V.
the harlot, in the original spelled differently
from the former word [wide, large], Josh.
2 : 1; 6 : 23.
See Matt. 1 : 5; Heb. 11 : 31; Jas. 2 : 25.
Railer, 1 Cor. 5 : 11.
Railing, 1 Sam. 25 : 14; 2 Sam. 16 : 7;
Mark 15 : 29; 1 Tim. 6 : 4; 1 Pet. 3 : 9;
2 Pet. 2 : 11; Jude 9.

Raiment, Gen. 27 : 15, goodly r.
28 : 20, if the Lord will give me r.
Deut. 8 : 4, thy r. waxed not old.
24 : 17, nor take a widow's r. to pledge.
2 Ki. 5 : 5, ten changes of r.
Job 27 : 16, though he prepare r. as clay.
Ps. 45 : 14, be brought to the king in r. of
needlework.
Isa. 63 : 3, I will stain all my r.
Zech. 3 : 4, I will clothe thee with r.
Matt. 3 : 4, his r. of camel's hair.
6 : 25; Luke 12 : 23, the body more
than r.
Matt. 11 : 8; Luke 7 : 25, a man clothed
in soft r. ?
Matt. 17 : 2; Mark 9 : 3; Luke 9 : 29, his
r. white as light.
Luke 23 : 34; John 19 : 24, they parted
his r.
1 Tim. 6 : 8, having food and r., let us be
content.
Jas. 2 : 2, a poor man in vile r.
Rev. 3 : 18, buy white r.
Rain, the deluge, Gen. 7; Ex. 9 : 34; 1 Sam.
12 : 17; Ps. 105 : 32.
withheld, Jer. 14; Zech. 14 : 17.
emblematic, Lev. 26 : 4; Ps. 68 : 9; Hos.
10 : 12.
the gift of God, Matt. 5 : 45; Acts 14 : 17.
There are two seasons of rain in Palestine
with an interval of dry weather. The
first rains after summer begin to fall
generally in November. These soften
the hard-baked soil and allow the sower
to sow his seeds. The " latter " rains water
the seed.
Gen. 2 : 5, Lord had not caused it to r.
8 : 2, r. from heaven was restrained.
Ex. 16 : 4, I will r. bread from heaven.
Deut. 11 : 11, drinketh of the r. of heaven.
11 : 14; 28 : 12, r. in due season.
32 : 2, my doctrine shall drop as r.
1 Ki. 17 : 1, there shall be no dew nor r.
18 : 41, a sound of abundance of r.
Ezra 10 : 13, a time of much r.
Job 5 : 10, who giveth r. upon earth.
28 : 26, he made a decree for the r.
37 : 6, to small r., and to great r.
38 : 28, hath the r. a father ?
Ps. 11 : 6, upon the wicked he shall r.
snares.
72 : 6, like r. on the mown grass.
78 : 24, 27, and r. down manna.
Prov. 25 : 14, like clouds without r.
25 : 23, north wind driveth away r.
26 : 1, as r. in harvest.
Eccl. 11 : 3, if the clouds be full of r.
12 : 2, nor clouds return after the r.
Song of Sol. 2 : 11, the r. is over and gone.
Isa. 4 : 6, a covert from storm and from r.
30 : 23, then shall he give the r.
55 : 10, as the r. cometh down from heaven.
Ezek. 38 : 22, I will r. an overflowing r.
Hos. 6 : 3, he shall come unto us as the r.
Matt. 7 : 25, the r. descended, and the floods
came.
Heb. 6 : 7, earth drinketh in the r.
Jas. 5 : 17, Elias prayed that it might
not r.

See Prov. 27 : 15.

Rainbow, sign of God's covenant with Noah, Gen. 9 : 12; Ezek. 1 : 28.
in heaven, Rev. 4 : 3; 10 : 1.

Rainy, Prov. 27 : 15.

Raise, Deut. 18 : 15; Acts 3 : 22, Lord will r. up a prophet.
1 Sam. 2 : 8; Ps. 113 : 7, he r. poor out of the dust.
Ps. 145 : 14; 146 : 8, he r. those that be bowed down.
Isa. 44 : 26, I will r. up decayed places.
Hos. 6 : 2, in the third day he will r. us up.
Matt. 11 : 5; Luke 7 : 22, dead are r. up.
John 2 : 19, in three days I will r. it up.
6 : 40, I will r. him up at the last day.
Acts 26 : 8, why incredible that God should r. the dead ?
Rom. 4 : 25, was r. again for our justification.
6 : 4, as Christ was r. from the dead.
1 Cor. 6 : 14, God will r. up us by his power.
2 Cor. 1 : 9, trust in God which r. the dead.
4 : 14, he shall r. up us by Jesus.
Eph. 2 : 6, r. us up together.
Heb. 11 : 19, accounting that God was able to r. him.
Jas. 5 : 15, the Lord shall r. him up.
1 Pet. 1 : 21, believe in God that r. him.

Raiser, Dan. 11 : 20.

Raisins, dried grapes, 1 Sam. 25 : 18; 1 Chr. 12 : 40.

Ram (răm) [high, elevated], Ruth 4 : 19.
used in sacrifices, Gen. 15 : 9; 22 : 13; Ex. 29 : 15; Lev. 9; Num. 5 : 8.
typical, Dan. 8 : 10.
horns of, used as trumpets, Josh. 6 : 4.
See Sheep.

Ramah.

Ramah (rā-mǎh), a city of Benjamin, now called el-Ram, Josh. 18 : 25; Judg. 4 : 5; 1 Sam. 1 : 19; 7 : 17; 8 : 4; 19 : 18; 25 : 1; Jer. 31 : 15; 40 : 1.

Ramathaim-zophim (rā-mǎ-thā-ĭm-zō-phĭm) [the two heights of the Zophites], 1 Sam. 1 : 1; 1 Chr. 6 : 26.

Ramathite (rā-mǎth-īte), 1 Chr. 27 : 27.

Ramath-lehi (rā-mǎth-lē-hī) [height of Lehi], Judg. 15 : 17.

Ramath-mizpeh (rā-mǎth-mĭz-pĕh), Josh. 13 : 26.

Rameses (răm-ĕ-sēś), Gen. 47 : 11.

Rameses II. (rā-mē-sēś), king of Egypt. See Chronology, Old Testament.

Ramia, a city of Beirut.

Ramiah (rā-mī-ǎh) [Jah has overthrown], Ezra 10 : 25.

Ramleh, a village famous for its tower.

Ramoth (rā-mŏth) [high places], a city of Issachar, 1 Chr. 6 : 73.

Ramoth-gilead (rā-mŏth-gil-ĕ-ǎd) [heights of Gilead], city of refuge in Gad, Deut. 4 : 43; 1 Ki. 22 : 3; 2 Ki. 8 : 28; 9 : 1; 2 Chr. 18 : 2, 3 ; 22 : 5.

Rampart, Lam. 2 : 8; Nah. 3 : 8.

Ran, Gen. 33 : 4; 1 Sam. 20 : 36; Luke 8 : 33; Acts 27 : 41.

Rang, 1 Sam. 4 : 5; 1 Ki. 1 : 45.

Range, Lev. 11 : 35; Job 39 : 8; Prov. 28 : 15.

Rank, Gen. 41 : 5, 7; 1 Chr. 12 : 38; Mark 6 : 40.

Ransom, Christ a, Matt. 20 : 28; 1 Tim. 2 : 6.
Ex. 21 : 30, he shall give for the r. of his life.
30 : 12, give every man a r. for his soul.
Job 33 : 24, I have found a r.
36 : 18, a great r. cannot deliver thee.
Ps. 49 : 7, nor give to God a r. for him.
Prov. 6 : 35, he will not regard any r.
13 : 8, r. of a man's life are his riches.
Isa. 35 : 10, r. of the Lord shall return.
43 : 3, I gave Egypt for thy r.
Mark 10 : 45, to give his life a r. for many.
Hos. 13 : 14, I will r. them from grave.

Rare, Dan. 2 : 11.

Rase, Ps. 137 : 7.

Rash, Eccl. 5 : 2, be not r. with thy mouth.
Isa. 32 : 4, the r. shall understand knowledge.

Rashly, Acts 19 : 36, be quiet, do nothing r.

Rate, Ex. 16 : 4; 2 Ki. 25 : 30.

Rather, Matt. 10 : 6, go r. to the lost sheep of Israel.
Matt. 25 : 9, go r. to them that sell.
Mark 5 : 26, but r. grew worse.
Rom. 8 : 34, yea r., that is risen again.

Rattling, Job 39 : 23; Nah. 3 : 2.

Raven is common in Palestine; its fine glossy back plumage is noted in Song of Sol. 5 : 11; its feeding on dead animals is hinted at in Gen. 8 : 7; and its habit of picking out the eyes of its victims, in Prov. 30 : 17.
1 Ki. 17 : 4, r. to feed thee there.
Job 38 : 41, provideth for the r.
Ps. 147 : 9, to the young r. which cry.
Luke 12 : 24, consider the r.

Ravening, Matt. 7 : 15; Luke 11 : 39.

Ravenous, Isa. 35 : 9; 46 : 11.

Ravin [ar.], to take prey violently, Gen. 49 : 27; Nah. 2 : 12.

Ravished, Song of Sol. 4 : 9; Isa. 13 : 16.

Raw, Ex. 12 : 9; Lev. 13 : 10.

Razor, Num. 6 : 5; Ps. 52 : 2; Ezek. 5 : 1.

Reach, Gen. 11 : 4, tower may **r.** to heaven.

John 20 : 27, **r.** hither thy finger.

2 Cor. 10 : 13, a measure to **r.** unto you.

Phil. 3 : 13, **r.** forth unto those things which are before.

Read, Ex. 24 : 7, **r.** in audience of the people.

Deut. 17 : 19, the king shall **r.** therein.

Isa. 34 : 16, seek out book of the Lord, and **r.**

Matt. 12 : 3; Mark 2 : 25; Luke 6 : 3, have ye not **r.** ?

2 Cor. 1 : 13, none other things than what ye **r.**

3 : 2, our epistle known and **r.**

Rev. 1 : 3, blessed is he that **r.**

1 Tim. 4 : 13, give attendance to **r.**

Readiness, Acts 17 : 11; 2 Cor. 8 : 11; 10 : 6.

Reading, of the law, Josh. 8 : 34; 2 Ki. 23 : 2; Neh. 8 : 9.

of the prophets, Luke 4 : 16.

of the epistles, Col. 4 : 16; 1 Thess. 5 : 27.

See Acts 13 : 15.

Ready, Deut. 26 : 5, a Syrian **r.** to perish.

Neh. 9 : 17, a God **r.** to pardon.

Job 29 : 13, blessing of him **r.** to perish.

Ps. 38 : 17, I am **r.** to halt.

45 : 1, pen of a **r.** writer.

86 : 5, Lord good, and **r.** to forgive.

Prov. 31 : 6, strong drink unto him **r.** to perish.

Eccl. 5 : 1, be more **r.** to hear.

Isa. 27 : 13, shall come which were **r.** to perish.

32 : 4, tongue of stammerers **r.** to speak plainly.

Matt. 22 : 4; Luke 14 : 17, all things are **r.**

Matt. 24 : 44; Luke 12 : 40, be ye also **r.**

Matt. 25 : 10, they that were **r.** went in.

Mark 14 : 38, the spirit is **r.**, but the flesh is weak.

Luke 22 : 33, **r.** to go with thee.

John 7 : 6, your time is always **r.**

Acts 21 : 13, I am **r.** not to be bound only.

Rom. 1 : 15, I am **r.** to preach the gospel at Rome.

2 Cor. 8 : 19, declaration of your **r.** mind.

1 Tim. 6 : 18, **r.** to distribute.

2 Tim. 4 : 6, I am now **r.** to be offered.

Titus 3 : 1, **r.** to every good work.

Heb. 8 :13, old is **r.** to vanish.

1 Pet. 1 : 5, **r.** to be revealed in last time.

3 : 15, be **r.** always to give an answer.

5 : 2, but of a **r.** mind.

Rev. 3 : 2, the things that are **r.** to die.

Reap, Lev. 19 : 9, when ye **r.** harvest.

Lev. 25 : 11, in jubilee ye shall not sow nor **r.**

Job. 24 : 6, they **r.** every one his corn.

Ps. 126 : 5, they that sow in tears shall **r.** in joy.

Eccl. 11 : 4, he that regardeth clouds shall not **r.**

Hos. 8 : 7, shall **r.** the whirlwind.

10 : 12, sow in righteousness, **r.** in mercy.

Mic. 6 : 15, thou shalt sow, but not **r.**

Matt. 6 : 26; Luke 12 : 24, they sow not, neither **r.**

Matt. 25 : 26; Luke 19 : 22, I **r.** where I sowed not.

John 4 : 38, to **r.** that whereon ye bestowed no labour.

2 Cor. 9 : 6, that soweth sparingly, shall **r.** sparingly.

Gal. 6 : 7, that shall he also **r.**

Jas. 5 : 4, cries of them which have **r.**

Rev. 14 : 15, thrust in sickle, and **r.**

Reaper, Ruth 2 : 3, 7; 2 Ki. 4 : 18; Amos 9 : 13.

Reaping, Lev. 23 : 10, 22; 25 : 5.

figurative, Job 4 : 8; Prov. 22 : 8; Matt. 13 : 30; John 4 : 36; 1 Cor. 9 : 11.

Rear, Ex. 26 : 30; 1 Ki. 16 : 32; John 2 : 20.

Reason, Prov. 26 : 16, seven men that can render a **r.**

Eccl. 7 : 25, to search out the **r.** of things.

Rom. 8 : 20, by **r.** of him who hath subjected.

1 Pet. 3 : 15, a **r.** of the hope that is in you.

1 Sam. 12 : 7, that I may **r.** with you.

Job 9 : 14, choose words to **r.** with him.

13 : 3, I desire to **r.** with God.

Isa. 1 : 18, let us **r.** together.

Matt. 16 : 18; Mark 2 : 8, why **r.** ye among yourselves ?

Luke 5 : 22, what **r.** ye in your hearts ?

24 : 15, while they **r.**, Jesus drew near.

Acts 24 : 25, as he **r.** of righteousness.

Reasonable, Rom. 12 : 1.

Rebecca (rĕ-bĕc⸗că), Rom. 9 : 10. See **Rebekah.**

Rebekah (rĕ-bĕ⸗käh) [noose], history of, Gen. 22; 24 : 15, 67; 27 : 6, 42; 49 : 31.

Rebel, Num. 14 : 9, only **r.** not against the Lord.

1 Sam. 12 : 15, if ye will not obey the Lord, but **r.**

Neh. 2 : 19, will ye **r.** against the king ?

Ps. 107 : 11, they **r.** against words of God.

Isa. 1 : 2, have nourished children, and they **r.**

63 : 10, they **r.**, and vexed his Holy Spirit.

Hos. 13 : 16, Samaria **r.** against God.

Rebels, Num. 17 : 10; 20 : 10; Ezek. 20 : 38.

Rebellion, Josh. 22 : 22, if it be in **r.**

1 Sam. 15 : 23, **r.** is as the sin.

Job 34 : 37, addeth **r.** unto his sins.

Jer. 28 : 16, taught **r.** against the Lord.

Rebellious, Deut. 9 : 7; 31 : 27, **r.** against the Lord.

Ps. 66 : 7, let not the **r.** exalt themselves.

78 : 8, a **r.** generation.

Isa. 65 : 2, have spread out my hands unto a **r.** people.

Jer. 5 : 23, this people hath a **r.** heart.

Ezek. 24 : 3, utter parable to the **r.** house.

Rebuke, Deut. 28 : 20, Lord shall send on thee **r.**

2 Ki. 19 : 3; Isa. 37 : 3, this is a day of **r.**

Ps. 6 : 1; 38 : 1, **r.** me not in anger.

18 : 15, at thy **r.**, at blast of breath of thy nostrils.

80 : 16, perish at **r.** of thy countenance.

104 : 7, at thy **r.** they fled.

Prov. 9 : 8, **r.** a wise man, and he will love thee.

13 : 1, a scorner heareth not r.
27 : 5, open r. is better than secret love.
28 : 23, he that r. shall find favour.
Eccl. 7 : 5, better to hear r. of wise.
Isa. 2 : 4; Mic. 4 : 3, he shall r. many nations.
30 : 17, thousand flee at r. of one.
Zech. 3 : 2; Jude 9, the Lord r. thee.
Matt. 8 : 26; Mark 4 : 39; Luke 8 : 24, he r. the wind.
Matt. 16 : 22; Mark 8 : 23, Peter began to r. him.
Luke 17 : 3, if brother trespass, r. him.
19 : 39, r. thy disciples.
Phil. 2 : 15, without r.
1 Tim. 5 : 1, r. not an elder.
2 Tim. 4 : 2, r. with all longsuffering.
Titus 1 : 13; 2 : 15, r. sharply.
Heb. 12 : 5, nor faint when thou art r.
Rev. 3 : 19, as many as I love, I r.
Rebuker, Hos. 5 : 2.
Recall, Lam. 3 : 21.
Receipt [ar.], place of receiving, Matt. 9 : 9; Mark 2 : 14; Luke 5 : 27.
Receive, Job 2 : 10, shall we r. good, and not r. evil ?
22 : 22, r. the law from his mouth.
Ps. 6 : 9, the Lord will r. my prayer.
24 : 5, he shall r. blessing from the Lord.
49 : 15, God shall r. me.
68 : 18, hast r. gifts for men.
73 : 24, afterward r. me to glory.
Prov. 2 : 1, if thou wilt r. my words.
Isa. 40 : 2, she hath r. of the Lord's hand double.
Hos. 14 : 2, r. us graciously.
Matt. 11 : 14, if ye will r. it, this is Elias.
19 : 12, he that is able to r. it, let him r. it.
21 : 22, whatsoever ye ask, believing ye shall r.
Mark 4 : 16; Luke 8 : 13, r. the word with joy.
Mark 11 : 24, when ye pray, believe that ye r.
16 : 19; Acts 1 : 9, he was r. up into heaven.
Luke 16 : 9, may r. you into everlasting habitations.
23 : 41, r. reward of our deeds.
John 1 : 12, as many as r. him.
3 : 27, a man can r. nothing, except it be given him.
5 : 43, come in his own name, him ye will r.
16 : 24, ask, and ye shall r.
Acts 2 : 38, ye shall r. the gift of the Holy Ghost.
10 : 43, shall r. remission of sins.
20 : 35, more blessed to give than to r.
Rom. 5 : 11, by whom we have r. atonement.
14 : 1, him that is weak in faith r. ye.
1 Cor. 3 : 8, every man shall r. his own reward.
11 : 23, I r. of the Lord that which I delivered.
2 Cor. 5 : 10, every one may r. things done in his body.
Col. 3 : 25, he shall r. for the wrong done.

Jas. 4 : 3, ye ask and r. not.
1 John 3 : 22, whatsoever we ask, we r.
Rev. 3 : 3, remember how thou hast r.
Receiver, Isa. 33 : 18.
Rechab (rē-chăb) [rider], 2 Sam. 4 : 2, 5, 6.
Rechabites (rĕchăb-ites), Jer. 35 : 2, 3.
Reckon, Lev. 25 : 50, he shall r. with him that bought him.
Ps. 40 : 5, thy thoughts cannot be r. up.
Matt. 18 : 24, when he had begun to r.
25 : 19, lord of those servants cometh, and r. with them.
Rom. 4 : 4, the reward is not r. of grace.
6 : 11, r. yourselves dead to sin.
8 : 18, I r. that the sufferings of this present time.
Recompense, Num. 5 : 7, he shall r. his trespass.
Deut. 32 : 35, to me belongeth r.
Ruth 2 : 12, the Lord r. thy work.
2 Sam. 19 : 36, why should the king r. me ?
Job 15 : 31, vanity shall be his r.
34 : 33, he will r. it whether.
Prov. 12 : 14, r. shall be rendered.
20 : 22, say not, I will r. evil.
Isa. 35 : 4, God will come with a r.
65 : 6, I will r., even r. into their bosom.
Jer. 16 : 18, I will r. their iniquity.
25 : 14; Hos. 12 : 2, I will r. them according to their deeds.
Hos. 9 : 7, the days of r. are come.
Joel 3 : 4, will ye render me a r. ?
Luke 14 : 12, and a r. be made thee.
14 : 14, for they cannot r. thee.
Rom. 11 : 9, let their table be made a r.
12 : 17, r. to no man evil for evil.
2 Cor. 6 : 13, now for a r., be ye also enlarged.
Heb. 10 : 30, that hath said, I will r.
10 : 35, great r. of reward.
Reconcile, 1 Sam. 29 : 4, should he r. himself ?
Matt. 5 : 24, first be r. to thy brother.
Rom. 5 : 10, if when enemies we were r. to God.
2 Cor. 5 : 20, be ye r. to God.
Eph. 2 : 16, that he might r. both to God.
Col. 1 : 20, to r. all things to himself.
See 2 Cor. 5 : 18; Heb. 2 : 17.
Reconciliation with God, Isa. 53 : 5; Dan. 9 : 24; Rom. 5; 2 Cor. 5 : 19; Eph. 2 : 16; Col. 1 : 20; Heb. 2 : 17.
Record, Ex. 20 : 24, in places where I r. my name.
Deut. 30 : 19, I call heaven and earth to r.
Job 16 : 19, my r. is on high.
John 1 : 32, 34, bare r.
8 : 13, thou bearest r. of thyself.
19 : 35, he that saw bare r., and his r. is true.
Rom. 10 : 2, I bear them r. they have a zeal of God.
2 Cor. 1 : 23, I call God for a r.
Phil. 1 : 8, God is my r. how greatly I long.
1 John 5 : 7, three that bear r.
5 : 11, this is the r. that God hath given.
3 John 12, we bear r. and our r. is true.
Recount, Nah. 2 : 5.

Recover, 2 Ki. 1 : 2, enquire whether I shall r.
5 : 3, the prophet would r, him.
Ps. 39 : 13, that I may r. strength.
Isa. 38 : 16, r. me, and make me live.
Jer. 8 : 22, why is not my people r. ?
Mark 16 : 18, lay hands on sick, and they shall r.
Luke 4 : 18, r. of sight to the blind.
2 Tim. 2 : 26, they may r. themselves.

Red, Gen. 25 : 30, r. pottage.
49 : 12, his eyes shall be r. with wine.
2 Ki. 3; 22, water r. as blood.
Ps. 75 : 8, the wine is r.
Prov. 23 : 31, look not on wine when r.
Isa. 1: 18, though your sins be r. like crimson.
27 : 2, a vineyard of r. wine.
63 : 2, wherefore art thou r. in thine apparel ?
Matt. 16 : 2, fair weather, for sky is r.

Red Dragon, Rev. 12 : 3.

Red Horse, vision of, Zech. 1 : 8; 6 : 2; Rev. 6 : 4.

Redeem, Ex. 6 : 6, I will r. you.
15 : 13, people whom thou hast r.
2 Sam. 7 : 23, what nation like Israel whom God went to r. ?
Neh. 5 : 5, nor is it in our power to r. them.
Job 5 : 20, in famine he shall r. thee.
6 : 23, r. me from hand of mighty.
Ps. 25 : 22, r. Israel out of all his troubles.
26 : 11, r. me and be merciful to me.
34 : 22, the Lord r. the soul of his servants.
49 : 15, God will r. my soul from the grave.
72 : 14, he shall r. their soul from deceit.
130 : 8, he shall r. Israel.
Isa. 35 : 9 the r. shall walk there.
44 : 22, return to me, I have r. thee.
50 : 2, is my hand shortened, that it cannot r. ?
51 : 11, the r. of Lord shall return.
52 : 3, ye shall be r. without money.
Hos. 13 : 14, I will r. them from death.
Luke 1 : 68, Lord hath visited and r. his people.
24 : 21, he who should have r. Israel.
Gal. 3 : 13, r. us from curse of the law.
4 : 5, to r. them that were under law.
Titus 2 : 14, that he might r. us from all iniquity.
1 Pet. 1 : 18, not r. with corruptible things.
Rev. 5 : 9, thou hast r. us to God.

Redeemer, Job 19 : 25, I know that my R. liveth.
Ps. 19 : 14, O Lord, my strength, and my R.
78 : 35, the high God was their R.
Prov. 23 : 11, their R. is mighty.
Isa. 49 : 26; 60 : 16, I the Lord am thy R.
59 : 20, the R. shall come to Zion.
63 : 16, thou art our Father, our R.
Jer. 50 : 34, their R. is strong.

Redemption, Lev. 25 : 51, give price of his r.
Ps. 49 : 8, the r. of their soul is precious.
111 : 9, he sent r. to his people.
130 : 7, with Lord is plenteous r.
Luke 2 : 38, them that looked for r.

21 : 28, your r. draweth nigh.
Rom. 8 : 23, the r. of our body.
Eph. 1 : 7; Col. 1 : 14, have r. through his blood.
Eph. 4 : 30, ye are sealed unto the day of r.
Heb. 9 : 12, obtained eternal r. for us.

Redness, Prov. 23 : 29, r. of eyes.

Reed, bruised, 2 Ki. 18 : 21; Isa. 42 : 3; Matt. 12 : 20. See **Bulrush.**
a measure, Ezek. 40 : 3; Rev. 11 : 1; 21 : 15. See **Measures.**

References to the Old Testament histories in the New Testament.
(1) The Pentateuch.
   (a) Genesis.—The Creation generally, Gen. 1.—Acts 14 : 15; 2 Pet. 3 : 4, 5. Creation out of nothing, Heb. 11 : 3; of light, 2 Cor. 4 : 6; of man and woman in God's image and from dust, 1 Cor. 11 : 7-12; 15 : 45-47. God's rest, Gen. 2—see Heb. 4 : 4; cf. Mark 2 : 27, 28. Garden of Eden, Rev. 2 : 7; 22 : 1, 2. Tree of Life, Rev. 2 : 7; 22 : 2, 14. Man first formed, then woman, 1 Tim. 2 : 13; 1 Cor. 11 : 9. Woman out of man, 1 Cor. 11 : 8. Creation subject to man, Heb. 1 : 8. Institution of marriage, Matt. 19 : 4-6; 1 Cor. 6 : 16. Temptation of the serpent, Gen. 3—see John 8 : 44; 1 Cor. 11 : 3; 2 Cor. 2 : 11; 1 John 3 : 8; Rev. 12 : 9; cf. 20 : 2. Adam tempted by Eve, 1 Tim. 2 : 14. Sin and consequences, Rom. 5 : 12-19; 1 Cor. 15 : 22; Heb. 9 : 27. Creation cursed for man's sake, Rom. 8 : 22. Struggle between good and evil, 1 John 3 : 8, 10; and victory of good, Rom. 16 : 20; 2 Tim. 1 : 10; Heb. 2 : 14, 15. Abel's faith, Gen. 4—see Heb. 11 : 4. Murdered by Cain, 1 John 3 : 12; cf. John 8 : 44; Jude 11. Blood of Abel, Matt. 23 : 35; Luke 11 : 51; Heb. 12 : 24. Like begets like, Gen. 5 : 1—see John 3 : 6. Enoch's life and translation, Gen. 5 : 21-24—see Jude, 14, 15; Heb. 11 : 5. Story of Noah, Gen. 6 ff.—see 2 Pet. 2 : 5. Preparation of the ark, Heb. 11 : 7; 1 Pet. 3 : 20. The flood, Gen. 79;—see Matt. 24 : 37-39; Luke 17 : 26, 27; 1 Pet. 3 : 20; 2 Pet. 2 : 5; 3 : 6. History of Abraham, Gen. 12 ff.—see Acts 7 : 2 ff.; Rom. 4 : 3 ff. Promise to Abraham, Luke 1 : 73; Acts 3 : 25, 26; Gal. 3 : 8. His sojourn in Canaan, Acts 7 : 4; Heb. 11 : 8-10. Promise of the land, Acts 7 : 5. Melchisedec and Abraham, Gen. 14—see Heb. 7. Abraham's seed as the stars, Gen. 15 : 5—see Heb. 11 : 12; Rom. 4 : 3 ff. Abraham's faith (ver. 6)—see Rom. 4 : 3, 9, 18-22; Gal. 3 : 6; Jas. 2 : 23. Bondage of his seed (ver. 13), Luke 1 : 72-75; Acts 7 : 6, 7. Abraham and Hagar, Gen. 16—see Gal. 4 : 24. Father of many nations, Gen. 17 : 5—see Rom. 4 : 16, 17. Circumcision (ver. 10), Rom. 4 : 11, 12. Abraham and the angels, Gen. 18 (ver. 2-5)—see Heb. 13 : 2. Sarah calls him " lord " (ver. 12) —see 1 Pet. 3 : 6. Sodom and Gomorrah

—Lot, Gen. 19—see Matt. 10 : 15; 11 : 24; Mark 6 : 11; Luke 10 : 12; 17 : 28, 29; Rom. 9 : 29; 2 Pet. 2 : 6-8; Jude 7; cf. Rev. 11 : 8. Lot's wife (ver. 26)—see Luke 17 : 32. Birth of Isaac, Gen. 21—see Gal. 4 : 23, 28. Sarah's faith (ver. 2), Heb. 11 : 11. Issac's circumcision (ver. 4), Acts 7 : 8. Ishmael mocking (ver. 9), Gal. 4 : 29. Bondwoman cast out, Gal. 4 : 30. Offering up of Isaac, Gen. 22 : 10—see Heb. 11 : 17-19; Jas. 2 : 21-24. Promise " by oath " (ver. 17)—see Luke 1 : 72-75; Heb. 6 : 13, 14. " Thy seed " (ver. 18)—see Acts 3 : 25; Gal. 3 : 16, 17. Jacob and Esau, Rom. 9 : 7 ff. Esau and his birthright, Gen. 25 : 34—see Heb. 12 : 16. Esau's sorrow, Gen. 27 : 34—see Heb. 12 : 17. Isaac and " things to come " (vers. 34-40)—see Heb. 11 : 20. Jacob's dream, Gen. 28 :12—see John 1 : 51. Jacob's history, Gen. 37—see Acts 7 : 8 ff.; Heb. 11 : 9. Joseph and his brethren (ver. 28), Acts 7 : 9 ff. Jacob blessing Joseph's sons, Gen. 48 : 20—see Heb. 11 : 21. The " lion's whelp," Gen. 49 : 9—see Rev. 5 : 5. " The Royal tribe " (ver. 10)—see Heb. 7 : 14. Joseph's bones, Gen. 50 : 25—see Heb. 11 : 22.

(b) Exodus.—Israel in Egypt, Ex. 1—see Acts 7 : 15 ff. Story of Moses, Ex. 2 —see Acts 7 : 20 ff.; Heb. 11 : 23 ff. Burning bush, Ex. 3—see Luke 20 : 37; Acts 7 : 30. Magicians of Egypt—Moses, Ex. 7 : 11—see 2 Tim. 3 : 8. Pharaoh's obstinacy, Ex. 9 ff.—see Rom. 9 : 17. The Passover and the firstborn, Ex. 12— see Heb. 11 : 28. Putting away of leaven (ver. 15)—see 1 Cor. 5 : 7. The Exodus (vers. 37-51)—see Acts 7 : 36; 13 : 17; Jude 5. Pillar of cloud, Ex. 13 : 21—see 1 Cor. 10 : 1. Passage of the Red Sea, Ex. 14 : 22—see Acts 7 : 36; 1 Cor. 10 : 1, 2; Heb. 9 : 29. Song of Victory, Ex. 15—see Rev. 15 : 3. Manna in wilderness, Ex. 16 : 15—see John 6 : 31, 32; 1 Cor. 10 : 3. Gathering of manna— see 2 Cor. 8 : 15. Pot of manna (vers. 33, 34)—see Heb. 9 : 4. Smitten rock, Ex. 17—see 1 Cor. 10 : 4. Giving of law on Sinai, Ex. 19, 20—see Acts 7 : 38 ff.; Gal. 3 : 19; 4 : 24, 25; Heb. 12 : 18, 21. Mount not to be touched, Ex. 19 : 12— see Heb. 12 : 20. Sprinkling of the people, Ex. 24 : 8—see Heb. 9 : 18-20. Ark and mercy seat, Ex. 25 : 10-16—see Heb. 9 : 4, 5. Shewbread and candlestick (vers. 23, 31), Heb. 9 : 2. Tabernacle, Ex. 26 : 30—see Acts 7 : 44; Heb. 8 : 5; 9 : 2, 7. The veil (vers. 31-33)— see Matt. 27 : 51; Mark 15 : 38; Heb. 6 : 19; 9 : 3. Most Holy place (ver. 33) —see Heb. 9 : 7, 8; 10 : 19. Daily offering, Ex. 29 : 38—see Heb. 10 : 11. Golden altar, Ex. 30 ; 1-3—see Heb. 9 : 4 [see marg. R.V.]; Rev. 8 : 3, 4. Golden calf, Ex. 32 : 4-6—see Acts 7 : 40; 1 Cor. 10 : 7. Tables of stone (ver. 16)—see

2 Cor. 3 : 3; Heb. 9 : 4. Veil on Moses' face, Ex. 34 ; 33—see 2 Cor. 3 : 13.

(c) Leviticus. — Circumcision, Lev. 12 : 3 ff.—see John 7 : 22. Purification of women, Lev. 12 : 6—see Luke 2 : 22-24. Law of leprosy, Lev. 14 : 2—see Matt. 8 : 4; Luke 17 : 14. Day of Atonement, Lev. 16—see Heb. 6 : 19, 20; 9 : 7 ff.; 13 : 10-13. See Summary of Old Testament on Leviticus. Adulteress to be stoned, Lev. 20 : 10—see John 8 : 5. Shewbread for Priests, Lev. 24 : 5, 9—see Matt. 12 : 4.

(d) Numbers.—Oath of exclusion, Num. 14 : 23—see Heb. 3 : 11; " Breach of promise " (ver. 29)—see Heb. 3 : 16, 17; 4 : 1; Jude 5. The Forty years (ver. 33) —see Acts 7 : 36, 42; 13 : 18; Heb. 3 : 9. Rebellion of Korah, Num. 16 : 32, 33— see Jude 11. Aaron's rod, Num. 17 : 2, 4, 10—see Heb. 9 : 4. Fiery serpents, Num. 21 : 6—see 1 Cor. 10 : 9. Serpent of brass (ver. 8), see John 3 : 14. The story of Balaam, Num. 22—see Jude 11; 2 Pet. 2 : 16; Rev. 2 : 14. Rebellions of Israel, Num. 25 : 1-9—see 1 Cor. 10 : 1-10.

(e) Deuteronomy.—Expulsion of Canaanites, Deut. 7 : 1—see Acts 13 : 19. Prophet like Moses, Deut. 18 : 15, 18, 19 —see Acts 7 : 37. Law about oxen, Deut. 25 : 4. Divorce, Deut. 24 : 1—see Matt. 19 : 7; Mark 10 : 4, etc. Two witnesses, Deut. 19 : 15—see 2 Cor. 13 : 1. Body of Moses, Deut. 34 : 8—see Jude 9 [also Zech. 3].

(2) The Historical Books.

Joshua.—God's promise never to forsake Joshua, see Heb. 13 : 5. Rahab and spies, Josh. 2—see Heb. 11 : 31; Jas. 2 : 25. Walls of Jericho, Josh. 6 : 20—see Heb. 11 : 30. Tabernacle at Shiloh, Josh. 18 : 1—see Acts 7 : 45. Division of land (ver. 10)—see Acts 13 : 19. Removal of Joseph's bones, Josh. 24 : 32—see Heb. 11 : 22.

Judges.—Rule of the judges, Judg. 2 : 16—see Acts 13 : 20. Gideon, Judg. 6–8. Barak, Judg. 4. Samson, Judg. 14, 15. Jephthah, Judg. 11—see Heb. 11 : 32.

1 Samuel.—Samuel, 1 Sam. 3 : 20— see Acts 13 : 20; Heb. 11 : 32. People ask a king, 1 Sam. 8 : 5—see Acts 13 : 21. Saul, 1 Sam. 10 : 21—see Acts 13 : 21, 22. David, 1 Sam. 13 : 14—see Acts 7 : 46; 13 : 22. David and the shewbread, 1 Sam. 21 : 6—see Matt. 12 : 3, 4.

2 Samuel.—David's exploits, 2 Sam.— see Heb. 11 : 32. David's seed, 2 Sam. 5 : 4—see Acts 13 : 22. Successors of David, Matt. 1 : 6 ff.; Luke 3 : 23 ff. David and the Temple, 2 Sam. 7 : 2, 3— see Acts 7 : 46.

1 Kings.—Solomon, 1 Ki. 6—see Acts 7 : 4. Queen of Sheba, 1 Ki. 10 : 1—see Matt. 16 : 42; Luke 11 : 31. Jezebel, 1 Ki. 16 : 31-33—see Rev. 2 : 20. Elijah and the drought, 1 Ki. 17 : 1—see Luke

4 : 25; Jas. 5 : 17. Widow of Zarephath (ver. 9), Luke 4 : 26. Raising of the widow's son (ver. 23)—see Heb. 11 : 35. Elijah's intercession, 1 Ki. 19 : 14—see Rom. 11 : 3; Jas. 5 : 17, 18. Seven thousand faithful (ver. 18), see Rom. 11 : 4.

2 Kings.—The Shunammite's son, 2 Ki. 4 : 34—see Heb. 11 : 35. Naaman and Elisha, 2 Ki. 5—see Luke 4 : 27. Star worship, 2 Ki. 16 : 3; 17 : 16; 24 : 4, 5 —see Acts 7 : 42. Exile to Babylon, 2 Ki. 24 : 15—see Matt. 1 : 11; Acts 7 : 43.

1 Chronicles.—See the genealogies in Matt. 1 and Luke 3.

2 Chronicles.—The murder of Zechariah, 2 Chr. 24 : 20, 21—see Matt. 23 : 35; Luke 11 : 51.

Ezra.—See references in Matt. 1 : 12 and Luke 3 : 27 to Zorobabel and Salathiel (Shealtiel).

(3) Histories in Other Books.

Job.—Patience of Job, Job 1 : 22—see Jas. 5 : 11.

Daniel.—Daniel's three friends, Dan. 3 : 27—see Heb. 11 : 34. Daniel and lions, Dan. 6 : 22—see Heb. 11 : 33. Daniel the prophet, see Matt. 24 : 15; Mark 13 : 14.

Jonah.—Jonah in the fish, Jonah 1 : 17 —see Matt. 12 : 40; 16 : 4. Mission to Nineveh, Jonah 3 : 4—see Luke 11 : 30.

Refine, Isa. 48 : 10; Zech. 13 : 9.

Refiner, the, Mal. 3 : 2.

Reformation, Heb. 9 : 10, until the time of r.

Refrain, Gen. 45 : 1, Joseph could not r. himself.

Job 7 : 11, I will not r. my mouth.

Ps. 40 : 9, I have not r. my lips.

119 : 101, 1 r. my feet from every evil way.

Prov. 1 : 15, r. thy foot from their path.

10 : 19, he that r. his lips is wise.

Isa. 64 : 12, wilt thou r. thyself, O Lord ?

Acts 5 : 38, r. from these men.

1 Pet. 3 : 10, r. his tongue from evil.

Refresh, Ex. 31 : 17, on the seventh day Lord rested, and was r.

1 Ki. 13 : 7, come home, and r. thyself.

Job 32 : 20, I will speak that I may be r.

Acts 3 : 19, when times of r. shall come.

Rom. 15 : 32, I may with you be r.

Refuge, Deut. 33 : 27, the eternal God is thy r.

Josh. 20 : 3, r. from avenger of blood.

2 Sam. 22 : 3, my high tower and r.

Ps. 9 : 9, Lord will be a r. for the oppressed.

14 : 6, the Lord is his r.

59 : 16, my r. in the day of trouble.

71 : 7; 142 : 5, my strong r.

104 : 18, high hills a r. for wild goats.

Isa. 28 : 17, hail shall sweep away r. of lies.

Heb. 6 : 18, who have fled for r.

cities of. The six cities of refuge, three east and three west of Jordan, were (Josh. 20 : 7-9) Bĕ-zĕr, near the Arnon; Rä-mŏth Gilead, north of the Jabbok;

and Gō-lăn, east of the sea of Galilee; with Hĕ-brŏn, Shĕ-chĕm, and Kĕ-dĕsh Naphtali, in Upper Galilee.

Refuse, Ex. 16 : 28, how long r. ye to keep my commandments ?

Job 34 : 33, whether thou r. or choose.

Ps. 118 : 22, the stone which the builders r.

Prov. 1 : 24, I have called, and ye r.

8 : 33, be wise, and r. it not.

15 : 32, he that r. instruction despiseth his soul.

21 : 25, his hands r. to labour.

Isa. 7 : 15, 16, may know to r. the evil.

Jer. 8 : 5, they r. to return.

13 : 10, people r. to hear my words.

31 : 15, Rachel r. to be comforted.

38 : 21, if thou r. to go forth.

Hos. 11 : 5, because they r. to return.

Zech. 7 : 11, they r. to hearken.

Acts 7 : 35, this Moses whom they r.

25 : 11, I r. not to die.

1 Tim. 4 : 4, nothing to be r.

4 : 7, r. profane fables.

Heb. 12 : 25, see that ye r. not him that speaketh.

See Lam. 3 : 45; Amos 8 : 6.

Regard, Ex. 5 : 9, let them not r. vain words.

Deut. 10 : 17, that r. not persons.

28 : 50, not r. person of the old.

1 Ki. 18 : 29, nor any that r.

Job 3 : 4, let not God r. it from above.

4 : 20, they perish without any r. it.

34 : 19, nor r. rich more than poor.

35 : 13, nor will the Almighty r. it.

36 : 21, r. not iniquity.

Ps. 28 : 5; Isa. 5 : 12, they r. not works of the Lord.

31 : 6, that r. lying vanities.

66 : 18, if I r. iniquity in my heart.

Ps. 102 : 17, he will r. the prayer of the destitute.

Prov. 1 : 24, no man r.

5 : 2, thou mayest r. discretion.

6 : 35, he will not r. any ransom.

12 : 10, righteous r. life of his beast.

13 : 18; 15 : 5, he that r. reproof.

Lam. 4 : 16, the Lord will no more r. them.

Dan. 11 : 37, r. God of his fathers, nor any god.

Mal. 1 : 9, will he r. your persons ?

Matt. 22 : 16; Mark 12 : 14, thou r. not the person of men.

Luke 18 : 4, fear not God, nor r. man.

Rom. 14 : 6, he that r. the day, r. it to the Lord.

Phil. 2 : 30, not r. his life.

Heb. 8 : 9, I r. them not, saith Lord.

Regeneration, Matt. 19 : 28; John 1 : 13; 3 : 3; Titus 3 : 5.

Region, Matt. 3 : 5, all the r. round about.

4 : 16, the r. and shadow of death.

Register, Ezra 2 : 62; Neh. 7 : 5, 64.

Rehearse, Ex. 17 : 14, r. it in ears of Joshua.

Judg. 5 : 11, r. righteous acts of the Lord.

Acts 14 : 27, they r. all God had done.

Rehoboam (Engl. Rē-hŏ-bō-ăm—this form has come through the Vulgate; the Hebrew is quite different) [increase of people ?], king of Judah, 1 Ki. 11 : 43, etc.

Reign, Gen. 37 : 8, shalt thou indeed r. over us ?

Ex. 15 : 18; Ps. 146 : 10, the Lord shall r. for ever.

Lev. 26 : 17, they that hate you shall r. over you.

Deut. 15 : 6, thou shalt r. over many nations.

Judg. 9 : 8, trees said, r. thou over us.

1 Sam. 12 : 12, a king shall r. over us.

2 Sam. 3 : 21, thou mayest r. over all.

Job 34 : 30, that the hypocrite r. not.

Ps. 47 : 8, God r. over the heathen.

93 : 1; 96 : 10; 97 : 1; 99 : 1, the Lord r.

Prov. 8 : 15, by me kings r.

30 : 22, a servant when he r.

Eccl. 4 : 14, out of prison he cometh to r.

Isa. 24 : 23, Lord of hosts shall r. in Zion.

32 : 1, a king shall r. in righteousness.

52 : 7, saith unto Zion, thy God r.

Jer. 22 : 15, shalt thou r. because ?

23 : 5, a king shall r. and prosper.

Mic. 4 : 7, the Lord shall r. over them.

Luke 19 : 14, we will not have this man to r. over us.

Rom. 5 : 17, shall r. in life by Jesus Christ.

6 : 12, let not sin r. in your bodies.

1 Cor. 4 : 8, I would to God ye did r.

15 : 25, he must r. till.

2 Tim. 2 : 12, if we suffer, we shall also r. with him.

Rev. 5 : 10, we shall r. on the earth.

11 : 15, he shall r. for ever and ever.

19 : 6, the Lord God omnipotent r.

20 : 6, shall r. with him a thousand years.

22 : 5, they shall r. for ever and ever.

Reins, Job 16 : 13, he cleaveth my r. asunder.

19 : 27, though my r. be consumed.

Ps. 7 : 9, God trieth the hearts and r.

16 : 7, my r. instruct me in night.

26 : 2, examine me, try my r.

73 : 21, thus was I pricked in my r.

139 : 13, thou hast possessed my r.

Prov. 23 : 16, my r. shall rejoice.

Isa. 11 : 5, faithfulness shall be the girdle of his r.

Jer. 11 : 20, O Lord, that triest the r.

12 : 2, thou art far from their r.

20 : 12, seest the r.

Lam. 3 : 13, arrows to enter into my r.

Rev. 2 : 23, I am he who searcheth the r.

Reject, 1 Sam. 10 : 19, ye have this day r. God.

15 : 26, Lord hath r. thee from being king.

Isa. 53 : 3, he is r. of men.

Hos. 4 : 6, thou hast r. knowledge.

Matt. 21 : 42; Mark 12 : 10; Luke 20 : 17, stone which builders r.

Mark 7 : 9, ye r. the commandment of God.

8 : 31; Luke 9 : 22, he shall be r. of the elders.

Luke 17 : 25, be r. of this generation.

John 12 : 48, he that r. me, and receiveth not my words.

Heb. 12 : 17, have inherited blessing, he was r.

Rejoice, Deut. 12 : 7, shall r. in all ye put your hand to.

26 : 11, thou shalt r. in every good thing.

28 : 63; 30 : 9, the Lord will r. over you.

1 Sam. 2 : 1, I r. in thy salvation.

1 Chr. 16 : 10; Ps. 105 : 3, let the heart of them r. that seek the Lord.

2 Chr. 6 : 41, let thy saints r. in goodness.

20 : 27; Neh. 12 : 43, the Lord had made them to r.

Job 31 : 25, if I r. because my wealth was great.

39 : 21, the horse r. in his strength.

Ps. 2 : 11, r. with trembling.

5 : 11, let all that trust in thee r.

9 : 14, I will r. in thy salvation.

14 : 7, Jacob shall r.

19 : 5, r. as a strong man to run a race.

33 : 21, our heart shall r. in him.

35 : 19, let not mine enemies r. over me.

38 : 16, hear me, lest they should r. over me.

51 : 8, the bones which thou has broken may r.

63 : 7, in shadow of thy wings will I r.

68 : 3, let the righteous r.

85 : 6, that thy people may r. in thee.

89 : 16, in thy name shall they r. all the day.

96 : 11, let the heavens r.

97 : 1, let the earth r.

104 : 31, the Lord shall r. in his works.

107 : 42, righteous shall see it, and r.

119 : 162, I r. at thy word.

149 : 2, let Israel r. in him that made him.

Prov. 2 : 14, who r. to do evil.

5 : 18, r. with the wife of thy youth.

23 : 15, if thine heart be wise, my heart shall r.

24 : 17, r. not when thine enemy falleth.

29 : 2, when the righteous are in authority people r.

Eccl. 2 : 10, my heart r. in all my labour.

3 : 12, for a man to r. and do good.

3 : 22; 5 : 19, than that a man should r.

11 : 9, r., O young man, in thy youth.

Isa. 9 : 3, as men r. when they divide the spoil.

24 : 8, noise of them that r. endeth.

29 : 19, poor among men shall r.

35 : 1, the desert shall r.

62 : 5, as the bridegroom r. over the bride.

65 : 13, my servants shall r., but ye.

66 : 14, when ye see this, your heart shall r.

Jer. 32 : 41, I will r. over them to do them good.

Ezek. 7 : 12, let not the buyer r.

Hos. 9 : 1, r. not, O Israel, for joy.

Amos 6 : 13, r. in a thing of nought.

Mic. 7 : 8, r. not against me, O enemy.

Hab. 3 : 18, yet I will r. in the Lord.

Zeph. 3 : 17, the Lord will r. over thee.

Zech. 9 : 9, r. greatly, O daughter of Zion.

Matt. 18 : 13, he r. more of that sheep.

Luke 1 : 14, many shall r. at his birth.

6 : 23, r. ye in that day, and leap for joy.

10 : 20, in this r. not, but rather r. because.

15 : 6, 9, **r.** with me.
John 4 : 36, and he that reapeth may **r.**
 5 : 35, willing for a season to **r.**
 14 : 28, if ye loved me, ye would **r.**
 16 : 20, ye shall weep, but the world shall **r.**
Acts 2 : 26, therefore did my heart **r.**
Rom. 5 : 2, **r.** in hope of glory of God.
 12 : 15, **r.** with them that do **r.**
1 Cor. 7 : 30, they that **r.** as though they **r.** not.
 13 : 6, **r.** not in iniquity, but **r.** in the truth.
Phil. 1 : 18, I do **r.**, yea, and will **r.**
 2 : 17, I joy and **r.** with you all.
 3 : 1; 4 : 4, **r.** in the Lord.
1 Thess. 5 : 16, **r.** evermore.
Jas. 1 : 9, let brother of low degree **r.**
1 Pet. 1 : 8, ye **r.** with joy unspeakable.
Rejoicing, 1 Ki. 1 : 45, came up from thence **r.**
Job 8 : 21, till he fill thy lips with **r.**
Ps. 19 : 8, statutes right, **r.** the heart.
 107 : 22, declare his works with **r.**
 118 : 15, voice of **r.** is in tabernacles of righteous.
 126 : 6, shall doubtless come again with **r.**
Prov. 8 : 31, **r.** in habitable part of earth.
Isa. 65 : 18, I create Jerusalem a **r.**
Jer. 15 : 16, thy word was the **r.** of my heart.
Zeph. 2 : 15, this is the **r.** city.
Luke 15 : 5, layeth it on his shoulders **r.**
Acts 5 : 41, **r.** that they were counted worthy.
 8 : 39, went on his way **r.**
Rom. 12 : 12, **r.** in hope.
2 Cor. 6 : 10, as sorrowful, yet always **r.**
1 Thess. 2 : 19, what is our crown of **r.** ?
Heb. 3 : 6, **r.** of hope firm to the end.
Release, year of, Ex. 21 : 2; Deut. 15 : 1; 31 : 10; Jer. 34 : 14.
Mark 15 : 9, **r.** unto you the King of the Jews ?
John 19 : 12, Pilate sought to **r.** him.
Relieve, Lev. 25 : 35, if brother be poor, thou shalt **r.** him.
Ps. 146 : 9, he **r.** the fatherless.
Isa. 1 : 17, **r.** the oppressed.
Lam. 1 : 16, comforter that should **r.** my soul is far from me.
Religion, Acts 26 : 5, straitest sect of our **r.**
Gal. 1 : 14, profited in the Jews **r.**
Jas. 1 : 27, pure **r.** and undefiled before God.
Religious, Acts 13 : 43; Jas. 1 : 26.
Rely, 2 Chr. 13 : 18; 16 : 7, 8.
Remain, Gen. 8 : 22, while earth **r.**
Ex. 12 : 10, let nothing **r.** until the morning.
Deut. 21 : 23, his body shall not **r.** on tree.
Josh. 13 : 1, **r.** yet much land to be possessed.
1 Ki. 18 : 22, I, even I, only, **r.** a prophet.
1 Chr. 13 : 14, ark **r.** in the family of Obed-edom.
Job 21 : 32, yet shall he **r.** in the tomb.
Prov. 2 : 21, the perfect shall **r.** in the land.
Eccl. 2 : 9, my wisdom **r.** with me.

Matt. 11 : 23, it would have **r.** until this day.
John 6 : 12, gather up the fragments that **r.**
Acts 5 : 4, whiles it **r.**, was it not thine own ?
1 Thess. 4 : 15, we who **r.** unto coming of the Lord.
Heb. 4 : 9, there **r.** a rest to the people of God.
 10 : 26, there **r.** no more sacrifice for sins.
Rev. 3 : 2, strengthen things which **r.**
Remedy, 2 Chr. 36 : 16; Prov. 6 : 15; 29 : 1.
Remember, Gen. 41 : 9, I do **r.** my faults this day.
Ex. 20 : 8, **r.** the sabbath day to keep it holy.
Num. 15 : 39, **r.** all the commandments of the Lord.
Deut. 8 : 2, **r.** all the way the Lord led thee.
 8 : 18, thou shalt **r.** the Lord thy God.
 32 : 7, **r.** the days of old.
1 Chr. 16 : 12; Ps. 105 : 5, **r.** his marvellous works.
Job 10 : 9, **r.** thou hast made me as clay.
 24 : 20, the sinner shall be no more **r.**
Ps. 20 : 7, we will **r.** the name of Lord.
 25 : 6, **r.** thy mercies.
 63 : 6, when I **r.** thee upon my bed.
 79 : 8, **r.** not against us former iniquities.
 89 : 47, **r.** how short my time is.
 105 : 8, hath **r.** his covenant for ever.
 136 : 23, who **r.** us in our low estate.
Eccl. 12 : 1, **r.** now thy Creator.
Song of Sol. 1 : 4, we will **r.** thy love.
Isa. 43 : 18; 46 : 9, **r.** yet not the former things.
Jer. 31 : 20, I do earnestly **r.** him still.
Lam. 1 : 9, she **r.** not her last end.
Ezek. 16 : 61; 20 : 43; 36 : 31, then shalt thou **r.** thy ways.
Hab. 3 : 2, in wrath **r.** mercy.
Matt. 26 : 75, Peter **r.** word of Jesus.
Luke 1 : 72, to **r.** his holy covenant.
 16 : 25, **r.** that thou in thy lifetime.
 17 : 32, **r.** Lot's wife.
 23 : 42, Lord, **r.** me when thou comest into thy kingdom.
John 15 : 20, **r.** the word that I said unto you.
Acts 20 : 35, **r.** the words of the Lord Jesus.
Gal. 2 : 10, we should **r.** the poor.
Eph. 2 : 11, **r.** that being in time past Gentiles.
Col. 4 : 18, **r.** my bonds.
2 Tim. 2 : 8, **r.** that Jesus Christ was raised from the dead.
Heb. 8 : 12, their iniquities I will **r.** no more.
 13 : 7, **r.** them that have the rule over you.
Rev. 2 : 5, **r.** from whence thou art fallen.
 3 : 3, **r.** how thou hast received.
Remembrance, Num. 5 : 15, bringing iniquity to **r.**
Deut. 32 : 26, make the **r.** of them to cease.
2 Sam. 18 : 18, no son to keep my name in **r.**
1 Ki. 17 : 18, art thou come to call my sin to **r.** ?

Job 18 : 17, his **r.** shall perish from the earth.

Ps. 6 : 5, in death there is no **r.**

30 : 4; 97 : 12, give thanks at **r.** of his holiness.

112 : 6, the righteous shall be in everlasting **r.**

Eccl. 1 : 11, there is no **r.** of former things.

2 : 16, no **r.** of wise more than the fool.

Isa. 43 : 26, put me in **r.**

Lam. 3 : 20, my soul hath them in **r.**

Ezek. 23 : 19, calling to **r.** days of youth.

29 : 16, bringeth their iniquity to **r.**

Mal. 3 : 16, a brook of **r.** was written.

Luke 22 : 19; 1 Cor. 11 : 24, this do in **r.** of me.

John 14 : 26, bring all things to your **r.**

Acts 10 : 31, thine alms are had in **r.**

2 Tim. 1 : 3, I have **r.** of thee.

2 : 14, of these things put them in **r.**

Heb. 10 : 32, call to **r.** the former days.

2 Pet. 3 : 1, stir up your pure minds by way of **r.**

Remission, Matt. 26 : 28, blood shed for **r.** of sins.

Mark 1 : 4; Luke 3 : 3, baptism of repentance for **r.**

Luke 24 : 27, that **r.** should be preached.

Acts 10 : 43, whosoever believeth shall receive **r.**

Rom. 3 : 25, for **r.** of sins that are past.

Heb. 9 : 22, without shedding of blood no **r.**

See John 20 : 23.

Remit, John 20 : 23.

Remnant, Lev. 5 : 13, the **r.** shall be the priest's.

2 Ki. 19 : 4; Isa. 37 : 4, lift up thy prayer for the **r.**

Ezra 9 : 8, to leave us a **r.**

Isa. 1 : 9, except Lord had left a **r.**

16 : 14, the **r.** shall be very small.

Jer. 23 : 3, I will gather the **r.** of my flock.

Ezek. 6 : 8, yet will I leave a **r.**

Matt. 22 : 6, the **r.** took his servants.

Rom. 11 : 5, at present time there is a **r.**

One of the most outstanding Old Testament " proofs " of the divine control of Hebrew history is the belief—justified by an appeal to history—that even when the nation as a whole deserted the faith of their fathers, there remained a " remnant " whose faithfulness prevailed. The outstanding example of this is, of course, the " righteous remnant " who returned from the exile.

Remove, Deut. 19 : 14, not **r.** neighbour's landmark.

Ps. 36 : 11, let not the hand of the wicked **r.** me.

39 : 10, **r.** thy stroke away from me.

46 : 2, not fear, though the earth be **r.**

103 : 12, so far hath he **r.** our transgressions.

125 : 1, as Mount Zion, which cannot be **r.**

Prov. 4 : 27, **r.** thy foot from evil.

10 : 30, the righteous shall never be **r.**

Eccl. 11 : 10, **r.** sorrow from thy heart.

Isa. 13 : 13, earth shall **r.** out of her place.

24 : 20, earth shall be **r.** like a cottage.

29 : 13, have **r.** their heart far from me.

30 : 20, ye shall not teachers be **r.**

54 : 10, the hills shall be **r.**

Jer. 4 : 1, return, then shalt thou not **r.**

Lam. 3 : 17, thou hast **r.** my soul from peace.

Matt. 17 : 20, say **r.** hence, it shall **r.**

Luke 22 : 42, if willing, **r.** this cup from me.

1 Cor. 13 : 2, so that I could **r.** mountains.

Gal. 1 : 6, I marvel ye are so soon **r.**

Rev. 2 : 5, else I will **r.** thy candlestick.

Rend, Lev. 10 : 6, neither **r.** your clothes.

1 Ki. 11 : 11, I will **r.** the kingdom.

Eccl. 3 : 7, a time to **r.**

Isa. 64 : 1, that thou wouldest **r.** the heavens.

Hos. 13 : 8, I will **r.** the caul of their heart.

Joel 2 : 13, **r.** your heart.

Matt. 7 : 6, lest they turn and **r.** you.

John 19 : 24, not **r.** it, but cast lots.

Render, Deut. 32 : 41, I will **r.** vengeance.

1 Sam. 26 : 23, the Lord **r.** to every man his faithfulness.

Job 33 : 26, he will **r.** to man his righteousness.

34 : 11, the work of a man shall be **r.** to him.

Ps. 116 : 12, what shall I **r.** to the Lord ?

Prov. 24 : 12; Rom. 2 : 6, **r.** to every man according to his works.

Prov. 26 : 16, seven men who can **r.** a reason.

Hos. 14 : 2, so will we **r.** the calves of our lips.

Zech. 9 : 12, I will **r.** double.

Matt. 21 : 41, **r.** to him fruits in their seasons.

22 : 21; Mark 12 : 17; Luke 20 : 25, **r.** unto Cæsar.

Rom. 13 : 7, **r.** to all their dues.

1 Thess. 3 : 9, what thanks can we **r.** to God ?

5 : 15; 1 Pet. 3 : 9, not **r.** evil for evil.

Rending the clothes, Gen. 37 : 34; 2 Sam. 13 : 19; 2 Chr. 34 : 27; Ezra 9 : 5; Job 1 : 20; 2 : 12, Joel 2 : 13, by the high priest, Matt. 26 : 65; Mark 14 : 63.

Renew, Ps. 51 : 10, **r.** a right spirit within me.

103 : 5, thy youth is **r.** like the eagle's.

104 : 30, thou **r.** the face of the earth.

Isa. 40 : 31, they that wait on the Lord shall **r.** their strength.

Lam. 5 : 21, **r.** our days as of old.

2 Cor. 4 : 16, the inward man is **r.** day by day.

Eph. 4 : 23, be **r.** in the spirit of your mind.

Col. 3 : 10, new man, which is **r.** in knowledge.

Heb. 6 : 6, if they fall away, to **r.** them again.

Renounced, 2 Cor. 4 : 2, have **r.** hidden thing of dishonesty.

Renown, Gen. 6 : 4; Num. 16 : 2, men of **r.**

Isa. 14 : 20, seed of evil-doers shall never be **r.**

Ezek. 34 : 29, a plant of **r.**

Dan. 9 : 15, gotten the **r.** as at this day.

Rent, Gen. 37 : 33, Joseph is **r.** in pieces.

Josh. 9 : 4, bottles old and r.
1 Ki. 13 : 3, the altar shall be r.
Job 26 : 8, the cloud is not r. under them.
Matt. 9 : 16; Mark 2 : 21, the r. is made worse.
Matt. 27 : 51; Mark 15 : 38; Luke 23 : 45, veil of temple was r. in twain.
Repair, 2 Chr. 24 : 5, gather money to r. the house.
Isa. 61 : 4, they shall r. waste cities.
Repay, Deut. 7 : 10, he will r. him to his face.
Job 21 : 31, who shall r. him what he hath done ?
Isa. 59 : 18, to islands r. recompense.
Luke 10 : 35, when I come again, I will r. thee.
Rom. 12 : 19, vengeance is mine, I will r.
Philem. 19, I have written it, I will r. it.
Repent, Gen. 6 : 6, it r. the Lord.
Ex. 13 : 17, lest the people r.
32 : 14; 2 Sam. 24 : 16; 1 Chr. 21 : 15; Jer. 26 : 19, Lord r. of the evil he thought to do.
Num. 23 : 19, neither Son of man that he should r.
Deut. 32 : 36, the Lord shall r. for his servants.
1 Sam. 15 : 29, strength of Israel not r.
Job 42 : 6, I r. in dust and ashes.
Ps. 90 : 13, let it r. thee concerning thy servants.
110 : 4; Heb. 7 : 21, Lord hath sworn and will not r.
Jer. 18 : 8; 26 : 13, if nation turn, I will r.
Joel 2 : 14, if he will return and r.
Matt. 12 : 41; Luke 11 : 32, they r. at preaching of Jonas.
Matt. 21 : 29, afterward he r. and went.
27 : 3, Judas r. himself.
Mark 6 : 12, preached that men should r.
Luke 13 : 3, except ye r.
15 : 7, joy over one sinner that r.
17 : 3, if thy brother r., forgive him.
Acts 2 : 38, r. and be baptized.
3 : 19, r. ye therefore and be converted.
8 : 22, r. of this thy wickedness.
17 : 30, commandeth all men to r.
26 : 20, they should r., and turn to God.
Rev. 2 : 16, r., or else I will come quickly.
3 : 19, be zealous therefore and r.
Repentance, Hos. 13 : 14, r. shall be hid from mine eyes.
Matt. 3 : 8; Luke 3 : 8; Acts 26 : 20, fruits meet for r.
Matt. 9 : 13; Mark 2 : 17; Luke 5 : 32, to call sinners to r.
Rom. 2 : 4, goodness of God leadeth thee to r.
Rom. 11 : 29, gifts of God are without r.
2 Cor. 7 : 10, godly sorrow worketh r.
Heb. 6 : 1, not laying again the foundation of r.
6 : 6, impossible to renew them again to r.
12 : 17, he found no place of r.
2 Pet. 3 : 9, that all should come to r.
Repetitions, Matt. 6 : 7, use not vain r. as the heathen do.

Repliest, Rom. 9 : 20, who art thou that r. against God ?
Report, Gen. 37 : 2, their evil r.
Ex. 23 : 1, thou shalt not raise a false r.
Num. 13 : 32, an evil r. of the land.
Deut. 2 : 25, nations who shall hear r. of thee.
1 Sam. 2 : 24, it is no good r. I hear.
1 Ki. 10 : 6; 2 Chr. 9 : 5, it was a true r.
Prov. 15 : 30, a good r.
Isa. 53 : 1, who hath believed our r. ?
Acts 6 : 3, men of honest r.
10 : 22, of good r. among the Jews.
2 Cor. 6 : 8, by evil r. and good r.
Phil. 4 : 8, whatsoever things are of good r.
1 Tim. 3 : 7, a bishop must have a good r.
Heb. 11 : 39, these having obtained a good r.
Neh. 6 : 6, it is r. among the heathen.
Jer. 20 : 10, r., say they, and we will r. it.
Matt. 28 : 15, this saying is commonly r.
Acts 16 : 2, well r. of.
1 Cor. 14 : 25, he will r. that God is in you.
1 Tim. 5 : 10, well r. for good works.
Reproach, Gen. 34 : 14, that were a r. to us.
Num. 15 : 30, doeth presumptuously, r. the Lord.
1 Sam. 17 : 26, taketh away the r.
Neh. 2 : 17, that we be no more a r.
2 Ki. 19 : 22; Isa. 37 : 23, whom hast thou r. ?
Job 27 : 6, my heart shall not r. me.
Ps. 15 : 3, that taketh not up a r.
22 : 6, a r. of men.
42 : 10; 102 : 8, mine enemies r. me.
44 : 16, the voice of him that r.
69 : 7, I have borne r.
69 : 9; Rom. 15 : 3, the r. of them that r. thee.
74 : 22, how the foolish man r. thee.
78 : 66, he put them to a perpetual r.
119 : 22, remove from me r.
119 : 42; Prov. 27 : 11, to answer him that r. me.
Prov. 6 : 33, his r. shall not be wiped away.
14 : 31; 17 : 5, oppresseth poor r. his Maker.
14 : 34, sin is a r. to any people.
18 : 3, with ignominy cometh r.
Isa. 51 : 7, fear ye not the r. of men.
Jer. 23 : 40, I will bring an everlasting r.
31 : 19, I did bear the r. of my youth.
Lam. 3 : 30, he is filled full with r.
Luke 6 : 22, men shall r. you for my sake.
11 : 45, thou r. us also.
2 Cor. 11 : 21, I speak as concerning r.
12 : 10, take pleasure in r.
1 Tim. 4 : 10, we labour and suffer r.
Heb. 11 : 26, esteeming the r. of Christ greater riches.
13 : 13, without the camp bearing his r.
1 Pet. 4 : 14, if ye be r. for Christ's sake.
Reprobate, Rom. 1 : 28, God gave them to a r. mind.
2 Cor. 13 : 5, Christ is in you, except ye be r.
2 Tim. 3 : 8, r. concerning the faith.
Titus 1 : 16, to every good work r.
Reproof, necessary, Lev. 19 : 17; Isa. 58 : 1;

Ezek. 2 : 3; 33; 2 Thess. 3 : 15; 1 Tim.
5 : 20; 2 Tim. 4 : 2; Titus 1 : 13; 2 : 15.
benefits of, Ps. 141 : 5; Prov. 9 : 8; 15 : 5;
24 : 25.
not to be despised, Prov. 1 : 25; 5 : 12;
10 : 17; 12 : 1; 15 : 10; 29 : 1.
Job 26 : 11, they are astonished at r.
Prov. 1 : 23, turn you at my r.
15 : 5, he that regardeth r. is prudent.
2 Tim. 3 : 16, Scriptures profitable for r.
Reprove, Job 6 : 25, what doth your arguing r. ?
13 : 10, he will r. if ye accept persons.
22 : 4, will he r. thee for fear ?
40 : 2, he that r. God, let him answer it.
Ps. 50 : 8, I will not r. thee for burnt-
offerings.
50 : 21, I will r. thee and set in order.
141 : 5, let him r. me, it shall be excellent
oil.
Prov. 9 : 8, r. not a scorner lest he hate
thee.
19 : 25, r. one that hath understanding.
29 : 1, he that being often r.
30 : 6, lest he r. thee, and thou be found
a liar.
Isa. 11 : 4, r. with equity for meek of the
earth.
Jer. 2 : 19, thy backslidings shall r. thee.
John 3 : 20, lest his deeds should be r.
16 : 8, he will r. the world of sin.
2 Tim. 4 : 2, r., rebuke, exhort.
Reputation, Eccl. 10 : 1, him that is in r. for
wisdom.
Acts 5 : 34, had in r. among the people.
Gal. 2 : 2, privately to them of r.
Phil. 2 : 7, made himself of no r.
2 : 29, hold such in r.
See Dan. 4 : 35.
Request, Judg. 8 : 24, I would desire a r. of
you.
Ezra 7 : 6, the king granted all his r.
Neh. 2 : 4, for what dost thou make r. ?
Job 6 : 8, Oh that I might have my r. ?
Ps. 21 : 2, hast not withholden the r. of his
lips.
106 : 15, he gave them their r.
Phil. 1 : 4, in every prayer making r.
4 : 6, let your r. be made known to God.
See 1 Ki. 19 : 4.
Require, Gen. 9 : 5, blood of your lives will
I r.
31 : 39, of my hand didst thou r. it.
Deut. 10 : 12; Mic. 6 : 8, what doth the
Lord r. ?
Josh. 22 : 23; 1 Sam. 20 : 16, let the Lord
r. it.
1 Sam. 21 : 8, the king's business r. haste.
2 Sam. 3 : 13, one thing I r. of thee.
19 : 38, whatsoever thou shalt r. I will do.
2 Chr. 24 : 22, the Lord look upon it, and
r. it.
Neh. 5 : 12, we will restore, and r. nothing.
Ps. 10 : 13, he hath said, thou wilt not r.
it.
40 : 6, sin offering hast thou not r.
Prov. 30 : 7, two things have I r. of thee.
Eccl. 3 : 15, God r. that which is past.
Isa. 1 : 12, who hath r. this at your hand ?

Ezek. 3 : 18; 33 : 6, his blood will I r. at
thine hand.
Luke 11 : 50, be r. of this generation.
12 : 20, this night thy soul shall be r.
12 : 48, of him shall much be r.
19 : 23, I might have r. mine own with
usury.
23 : 24, gave sentence that it should be
as r.
1 Cor. 1 : 22, the Jews r. a sign.
4 : 2, it is r. in stewards that they be
faithful.
Requite, Deut. 32 : 6, do ye thus r. the
Lord ?
Judg. 1 : 7, as I have done, so God hath r.
me.
2 Sam. 2 : 6, I also will r. you this kindness.
16 : 12, it may be the Lord will r. good for
this.
1 Tim. 5 : 4, learn to r. their parents.
Rereward, Isa. 52 : 12, God of Israel will be
your r.
58 : 8, glory of Lord shall be thy r.
Resemble, Judg. 8 : 18, each r. children of
a king.
Luke 13 : 18, whereunto shall I r. kingdom
of God ?
Reserve, Gen. 27 : 36, hast thou not r. a
blessing ?
Job 21 : 30, wicked r. to day of destruction.
Jer. 3 : 5, will he r. his anger for ever ?
5 : 24, he r. the appointed weeks of harvest.
Nah. 1 : 2, the Lord r. wrath for his
enemies.
1 Pet. 1 : 4, an inheritance r. in heaven.
2 Pet. 2 : 17, mist of darkness r. for ever.
3 : 7, heavens and earth are r. unto fire.
Jude 13, to whom is r. the blackness of
darkness.
Residue, Isa. 38 : 10, I am deprived of the
r. of my years.
Mal. 2 : 15, the r. of the Spirit.
Acts 15 : 17, that the r. might seek the
Lord.
Resist, Zech. 3 : 1, Satan at his right hand
to r.
Matt. 5 : 39, I say, that ye r. not evil.
Luke 21 : 15, your adversaries shall not be
able to r.
Acts 7 : 51, ye do always r. the Holy Ghost.
Rom. 9 : 19, who hath r. his will ?
13 : 2, whosoever r. the power r. ordin-
ance of God.
Jas. 4 : 6; 1 Pet. 5 : 5, God r. the proud.
Jas. 4 : 7, r. the devil, and he will flee.
1 Pet. 5 : 9, whom r. stedfast in the faith.
Resort, Ps. 71 : 3, whereunto I may r.
Mark 10 : 1, the people r. to him.
John 18 : 2, Jesus ofttimes r. thither.
Acts 16 : 13, spake to women who r. thither.
Respect, Gen. 4 : 4, the Lord had r. to Abel.
Ex. 2 : 25, God had r. unto them.
Lev. 19 : 15, thou shalt not r. person of
poor.
26 : 9, I will have r. unto you.
Deut. 1 : 17, ye shall not r. persons in
judgment.
1 Ki. 8 : 28; 2 Chr. 6 : 19, have r. to the
prayer of thy servant.

2 Ki. 13 : 23, the Lord had r. to them.
2 Chr. 19 : 7; Rom. 2 : 11; Eph. 6 : 9;
Col. 3 : 25, no r. of persons with God.
Job 37 : 24, he r. not wise of heart.
Ps. 40 : 4, blessed is the man that r. not proud.
74 : 20, r. unto thy covenant.
119 : 117, I will have r. to thy statutes.
138 : 6, yet hath he r. unto the lowly.
Prov. 24 : 23; 28 : 21, not good to have r. of persons.
Isa. 17 : 7, his eyes shall have r. to the Holy One.
22 : 11, nor had r. to him that fashioned it.
2 Cor. 3 : 10, had no glory in this r.
Phil. 4 : 11, not that I speak in r. of want.
1 Pet. 1 : 17, who without r. of persons.
Rest, Gen. 2 : 2, he r. on seventh day.
Ex. 31 : 15; 35 : 2; Lev. 16 : 31; 23 : 3, 32; 25 : 4, the Sabbath of r.
Ex. 33 : 14, I will give thee r.
34 : 21, in harvest thou shalt r.
Lev. 25 : 5, a year of r. to the land.
Num. 11 : 25, the Spirit r. upon them.
Deut. 3 : 20; Josh. 1 : 13, Lord have given r.
Josh. 3 : 13, feet of priests shall r.
Judg. 3 : 30, the land had r. fourscore years.
Ruth 1 : 9, Lord grant you may find r.
2 Sam. 21 : 10, the birds to r. on them by day.
1 Chr. 22 : 9, a man of r., and I will give him r.
28 : 2, to build a house of r.
Neh. 9 : 28, after they had r. they did evil.
Job 3 : 17, there the weary be at r.
3 : 18, there the prisoners r. together.
11 : 18, thou shalt take thy r. in safety.
17 : 16, our r. together is in the dust.
Ps. 16 : 9; Acts 2 : 26, my flesh shall r. in hope.
Ps. 37 : 7, r. in the Lord.
55 : 6, then would I fly away and be at r.
94 : 13, thou mayest give him r.
116 : 7, return to thy r., O my soul.
132 : 8, arise, O Lord into thy r.
132 : 14, this is my r. for ever.
Prov. 6 : 35, nor will he r. content.
Eccl. 2 : 23, his heart taketh not r. in the night.
Isa. 11 : 2, Spirit of the Lord shall r. upon him.
11 : 10, his r. shall be glorious.
14 : 3, the Lord shall give thee r.
14 : 7; Zech. 1 : 11, the earth is at r.
Isa. 28 : 12, this is the r. wherewith.
30 : 15, in returning and r. shall ye be saved.
57 : 20, like the sea when it cannot r.
63 : 14, Spirit of the Lord caused him to r.
66 : 1; Acts 7 : 49, where is the place of my r. ?
Jer. 6 : 16, ye shall find r. for your souls.
Ezek. 38 : 11, I will go to them that are at r.
Dan. 12 : 13, thou shalt r., and stand in thy lot.

Mic. 2 : 10, depart, this is not your r.
Matt. 11 : 28, I will give you r.
12 : 43; Luke 11 : 24, seeking r., and finding none.
Matt. 26 : 45; Mark 14 : 41, take your r.
Mark 6 : 31, come, and r. awhile.
John 11 : 13, he had spoken of taking r. in sleep.
2 Cor. 12 : 9, power of Christ may r. on me.
Heb. 4 : 9, remaineth a r. to people of God.
Rev. 4 : 8, they r. not day and night.
14 : 13, that they may r. from their labours.
Restore, Gen. 42 : 25, to r. every man's money.
Ex. 22 : 4, he shall r. double.
Lev. 6 : 5, he shall r. it in the principal.
Deut. 22 : 2, things strayed thou shalt r. again.
Ps. 23 : 3, he r. my soul.
51 : 12, r. to me the joy of thy salvation.
Isa. 1 : 26, I will r. thy judges.
Jer. 30 : 17, I will r. health to thee.
Matt. 17 : 11; Mark 9 : 12, Elias shall r. all things.
Luke 19 : 8, I r. him fourfold.
Acts 1 : 6, wilt thou r. the kingdom ?
Gal. 6 : 1, r. such an one in meekness.
Restrain, Gen. 8 : 2, rain from heaven was r.
11 : 6, nothing will be r. from them.
Ex. 36 : 6, people were r. from bringing.
1 Sam. 3 : 13, he r. them not.
Job 15 : 4, thou r. prayer before God.
15 : 8, dost thou r. wisdom ?
Ps. 76 : 10, wrath shalt thou r.
Acts 14 : 18, scarce r. they the people.
Resurrection, belief in. The belief in a resurrection of the body is typical of later Jewish thought, and may be contrasted with the corresponding Greek conception of the immortality of the soul. The two lines of thought are, in a sense, combined in Paul's conception of a " spiritual body."

The earliest hints of a future life in the Old Testament have behind them the idea of the re-establishment of the Jewish nation rather than the persistence of individual personality after death. Indeed, the whole subject, as dealt with in the Old Testament, is bound up with two further questions—the growing belief in the value of the individual, and the search for a solution to the problem of suffering. Jewish thought on these questions prepared the way for a doctrine of a future life for the individual in which moral values would persist and the inequalities of this life would somehow be made good.

The Christian doctrine of resurrection is based on the belief in the resurrection of Christ, and from the first has held a central place in Christian thought and preaching. " If Christ be not risen, then is our preaching vain, and your faith is also vain " (1 Cor. 15 : 14).
of the body foretold, Job 19 : 26; Ps. 17 : 15; Isa. 26 : 19; Dan. 12 : 2.
typified, Ezek. 37.
proclaimed by Christ, Matt. 22 : 31; Luke 14 : 14; John 5 : 28; 11 : 23.

FISHERMEN ON SEA OF GALILEE

VIEW TOWARDS MOUNT HERMON

preached by the apostles, Acts 4 : 2; 17 : 18; 24 : 15; 26 : 8; Rom. 6 : 5; 8 : 11; 1 Cor. 15; 2 Cor. 4 : 17; Phil. 3 : 20; Col. 3 : 3; 1 Thess. 4 : 15; 5 : 23; Heb. 6 : 2; 2 Pet. 1 : 11; 1 John 3 : 2.

Matt. 22 : 23; Mark 12 : 18; Acts 23 : 8; 1 Cor. 15 : 12, Sadducees who say there is no r.

John 11 : 25, Jesus said, I am the r. and the life.

Acts 17 : 18, he preached Jesus and the r.

Rom. 6 : 5, in likeness of his r.

Phil. 3 : 10, know the power of his r.

Heb. 11 : 35, might obtain a better r.

Rev. 20 : 5, this is the first r.

Retain, Job 2 : 9, dost thou r. thine integrity ?

Prov. 4 : 4, let thine heart r. my words.

11 : 16, a gracious woman r. honour.

Eccl. 8 : 8, no man hath power to r., the spirit.

John 20 : 23, whosesoever sins ye r., they are r.

Rom. 1 : 28, did not like to r. God.

Return, Gen. 3 : 19, to dust shalt thou r.

1 Sam. 7 : 3; Isa. 19 : 22; 55 : 7; Hos. 6 : 1, r. to the Lord.

1 Ki. 8 : 48, r. to thee with all their heart.

2 Ki. 20 : 10, let the shadow r. backward.

Job 1 : 21, naked shall I r. thither.

7 : 10, he shall r. no more.

15 : 22, believeth not he shall r. out of darkness.

22 : 23, if thou r. to the Almighty.

33 : 25, shall r. to the days of his youth.

Ps. 35 : 13, my prayer r. into mine own bosom.

73 : 10, his people r. hither.

90 : 3, thou sayest, r., ye children of men

104 : 29, they die, and r. to the dust.

116 : 7, r. to thy rest, O my soul.

Prov. 2 : 19, none that go to her r. again.

26 : 11, as a dog r. to his vomit.

Eccl. 5 : 15, naked shall he r. to go as he came.

12 : 7, dust r. to earth, and spirit r. to God.

Isa. 21 : 12, if ye will enquire, enquire ye, r., come.

35 : 10; 51 : 11, the ransomed of the Lord shall r.

55 : 11, it shall not r. to me void.

Jer. 4 : 1, if thou wilt r., saith the Lord, r. unto me.

24 : 7, they shall r. with their whole heart.

Ezek. 18 : 23, that the wicked r., and live.

Hos. 5 : 15, I will r. to my place.

7 : 16, they r., but not to the Most High.

Joel 2 : 14, who knoweth if he will r. and repent ?

Mal. 3 : 7, r. to me, and I will r. to you.

3 : 18, then shall ye r. and discern.

Matt. 12 : 44; Luke 11 : 24, I will r. into my house.

Matt. 24 : 18, neither let him in field r. back.

Luke 8 : 39, r. to thine own house.

17 : 18, not found that r. to give glory to God.

Acts 13 : 34, now no more to r. to corruption.

Heb. 11 : 15, opportunity to have r.

1 Pet. 2 : 25, now r. to the Shepherd of your souls.

from captivity, Ezra 1; Neh. 2; Jer. 16 : 14; 23; 24; 30; 31; 32; 50 : 4, 17, 33; Amos 9 : 14; Hag. 1; Zech. 1.

Reuben [see, a son !], Gen. 29 : 32.

Reubenites, their number and possessions, Num. 1; 2; 26; 32; Deut. 3 : 12; Josh. 13 : 15; 1 Chr. 5 : 18.

dealings of Moses and Joshua with, Num. 32; Deut. 33; Josh. 1 : 12; 22.

carried into captivity, 1 Chr. 5 : 26; (Rev. 7 : 5).

Reveal, Deut. 29 : 29, things r. belong to us and our children.

1 Sam. 3 : 7, nor was the word of the Lord r. to him.

Job 20 : 27, the heaven shall r. his iniquity.

Prov. 1 : 13; 20 : 19, a talebearer r. secrets.

Isa. 22 : 14, it was r. in mine ears.

40 : 5, glory of the Lord shall be r.

53 : 1; John 12 : 38, to whom is the arm of the Lord r. ?

Jer. 33 : 6, I will r. abundance of peace.

Dan. 2 : 28, there is a God that r. secrets.

Amos 3 : 7, he r. his secret to the prophets.

Matt. 10 : 26; Luke 12 : 2, nothing covered that shall not be r.

Matt. 11 : 25; Luke 10 : 21, hast r. them unto babes.

Matt. 16 : 17, flesh and blood hath not r. it.

Luke 2 : 35, thoughts of many hearts may be r.

17 : 30, in day when Son of man is r.

Rom. 1 : 18, wrath of God is r. from heaven.

8 : 18, glory which shall be r. in us.

1 Cor. 2 : 10, God hath r. them by his Spirit.

3 : 13, it shall be r. by fire.

Gal. 1 : 16, to r. his Son in me.

3 : 23, faith which should be r.

2 Thess. 1 : 7, when the Lord Jesus shall be r.

2 : 3, that man of sin be r.

1 Pet. 1 : 5, ready to be r. in last time.

5 : 1, partaker of glory that shall be r.

Revelation (of God). Christian thought recognises God's revelation of Himself in many spheres of thought and life, but over against this " general " revelation it holds that there is a " special " revelation in the history of the Hebrew race which finds its consummation in the life of Jesus Christ. It recognises in the life, death, and resurrection of Jesus Christ a special and final revelation of God.

(from God) : of mercy, etc., Deut. 29 : 29; Job 33 : 16; Isa. 40 : 5; 53 : 1; Jer. 33 : 6; Dan. 2 : 22; Amos 3 : 7; Matt. 11 : 25; 16 : 17; 1 Cor. 2 : 10; 2 Cor. 12; Gal. 1 : 12; Eph. 3 : 9; Phil. 3 : 15; 1 Pet. 1 : 5; 4 : 13.

of wrath, Rom. 1 : 18; 2 : 5; 2 Thess. 1 : 7.

Rom. 2 : 5, r. of righteous judgment of God.
16 : 25, r. of the mystery.
1 Cor. 14 : 26, every one hath a r.
2 Cor. 12 : 7, through abundance of the r.
Rev. 1 : 1, r. of Jesus Christ which God gave.

Revelation, Book of.
Authorship and Date.—The weight of evidence is in favour of A.D. 96, at the close of the reign of Domitian, as the time of writing. John, the apostle, was imprisoned by the Emperor on Patmos and afterward returned to Ephesus. The Fathers are explicit in their testimony to the Johannine origin of Revelation.
Interpretations.—There are three traditional interpretations of the book—the Præterist, the Continuous, or Historical, and the Futurist. The Præterists consider that the prophecies refer to events now past, and especially the overthrow of Jerusalem and of heathen Rome. The second school interpret the book as a series of prophecies which are being continuously fulfilled in the course of history. For the Futurists the fulfilment of the whole series of prophecies is bound up with the second coming of Christ.
Summary.—The book of Revelation has a Prologue and an Epilogue, between which (1 : 19—22 : 5) the Revelation proper lies. This consists of seven visions, in which the symbolical numbers, three, four, seven and twelve are frequent. There are occasional interludes between the parts : (1) the vision of the throne of God and of the lamb (4 : 5); (2) the vision of the seven seals (6 : 1—8 : 1); (3) the vision of the seven trumpets (8 : 2—9 : 19); (4) the vision of the woman and her enemies (12 : 1—13 : 18); (5) the vision of the lamb and the angels of judgment (14); (6) the vision of the seven vials of wrath (15 : 1—16 : 21); (7) the vision of final triumph (17 : 1—22 : 5).
The book ends, as it began, with the certainty of Christ's coming, and of His perfect victory over His enemies.
Revellings, Gal. 5 : 21, works of the flesh are r.
1 Pet. 4 : 3, we walked in lusts, r.
Revenge, Jer. 20 : 10, we shall take our r. on him.
Nah. 1 : 2, the Lord r., and is furious.
2 Cor. 7 : 11, what r. it wrought in you !
10 : 6, readiness to r. all disobedience.
See Num. 35 : 19; Rom. 13 : 4.
Revenue, Ezra 4 : 13, thou shalt endamage the r.
Prov. 8 : 19, my r. is better than silver.
16 : 8, a little is better than great r.
Isa. 23 : 3, harvest of river is her r.
Jer. 12 : 13, shall be ashamed of your r.
Reverence, Ps. 89 : 7, to be had in r. of all.
Matt. 21 : 37; Mark 12 : 6; Luke 20 : 13, they will r. my son.

Heb. 12 : 9, we gave them r.
12 : 28, that we may serve God with r.
See Ps. 111 : 9.
Revile, Ex. 22 : 28, thou shalt not r. the gods.
Matt. 5 : 11, blessed wher. men shall r. you.
27 : 39, they that passed by r. him.
Mark 15 : 32, they that were crucified r. him.
1 Cor. 4 : 12, being r., we bless.
1 Pet. 2 : 23, when he was r., r. not again.
See Isa. 51 : 7; 1 Cor. 6 : 10.
Revive, Neh. 4 : 2, will they r. stones ?
Ps. 85 : 6, wilt thou not r. us again ?
138 : 7, thou wilt r. me.
Isa. 57 : 15, to r. the spirit of the humble.
Hos. 6 : 2, after two days will he r. us.
14 : 7, they shall r. as corn.
Hab. 3 : 2, r. thy work in midst of years.
Rom. 7 : 9, when the commandment came, sin r.
14 : 9, Christ both died, rose, and r.
Revolt, Isa. 1 : 5, ye will r. more and more.
31 : 6, children of Israel have deeply r.
59 : 13, speaking oppression and r.
Jer. 5 : 23, this people are r. and gone.
See Hos. 5 : 2.
Reward, Gen. 15 : 1, thy exceeding great r.
44 : 4, wherefore have ye r. evil ?
Deut. 10 : 17, God who taketh not r.
32 : 41, I will r. them that hate me.
Ruth 2 : 12, a full r. be given thee of the Lord.
1 Sam. 24 : 19, the Lord r. thee good.
2 Sam. 4 : 10, thought I would have given him a r.
1 Ki. 13 : 7, I will give thee a r.
2 Chr. 15 : 7, your work shall be r.
20 : 11, behold, how they r. us.
Job 6 : 22, did I say, give a r. ?
7 : 2, as an hireling looketh for r.
21 : 19, he r. him, and he shall know it.
Ps. 15 : 5, nor taketh r. against innocent.
19 : 11, in keeping them is great r.
31 : 23, plentifully r. the proud doer.
35 : 12; 109 : 5, they r. me evil for good.
58 : 11, there is a r. for the righteous.
70 : 3, let them be turned back for a r.
91 : 8, shalt see the r. of the wicked.
103 : 10, nor r. us according to our iniquities.
Prov. 11 : 18, a sure r.
13 : 13, feareth commandment be r.
17 : 13, whoso r. evil, evil shall not depart.
24 : 20, no r. to the evil man.
25 : 22, the Lord shall r. thee.
26 : 10, both r. the fool, and r. transgressors.
Eccl. 4 : 9, they have a good r. for labour.
9 : 5, neither have they any more a r.
Isa. 1 : 23, every one followeth after r.
5 : 23, justify the wicked for r.
40 : 10; 62 : 11, his r. is with him.
Jer. 31 : 16, thy work shall be r.
Dan. 5 : 17, give thy r. to another.
Hos. 9 : 1, thou hast loved a r.
Mic. 7 : 3, the judge asketh for a r.
Matt. 5 : 12; Luke 6 : 23, great is your r. in heaven.
Matt. 5 : 46, what r. have ye ?
6 : 2, 5, 16, they have their r.

6 : 4, 18, Father shall r. thee.
10 : 41, shall receive a prophet's r.
10 : 42; Mark 9 : 41, in no wise lose his r.
16 : 27, he shall r. every man according to his works.
Luke 6 : 35, your r. shall be great.
23 : 41, we receive due r. of our deeds.
Acts 1 : 18, purchased field with r. of iniquity.
Rom. 4 : 4, the r. is not reckoned of grace.
1 Cor. 3 : 8, every man shall receive his own r.
9 : 18, what is my r. ?
Col. 2 : 18, let no man beguile you of your r.
3 : 24, the r. of the inheritance.
1 Tim. 5 : 18, the labourer is worthy of his r.
2 Tim. 4 : 14, the Lord r. him.
Heb. 2 : 2; 10 : 35; 11 : 26, recompence of r.
2 Pet. 2 : 13, the r. of unrighteousness.
2 John 8, that we receive a full r.
Rev. 18 : 6, r. her even as she r. you.
22 : 12, I come quickly, my r. is with me.
See Heb. 11 : 6.
to the righteous, Gen. 15 : 1; Ps. 19 : 11; 58 : 11; Prov. 11 : 18; 25 : 22; Matt. 5 : 12; 6 : 1; 10 : 41; Luke 6 : 35; 1 Cor. 3 : 8; Col. 2 : 18; 3 : 24; Heb. 10 : 35; 11 : 6; Rev. 22 : 12.
threatened to the wicked, Deut. 32 : 41; 2 Sam. 3 : 39; Ps. 54 : 5; 91 : 8; 109; Obad. 15; 2 Pet. 2 : 13; Rev. 19 : 17; 20 : 15; 22 : 15.
Rewarder, Heb. 11 : 6, a r. of them that diligently seek him.
Rezin (rē-zĭn) [firm], king of Syria, 2 Ki. 15 : 37; 16 : 5, 9; Isa. 7 : 1.
Rhoda [a rose], Acts 12 : 13.

Rhodes.

Rhodes, an island of the Mediterranean, Acts 21 : 1.
Ribband, Num. 15 : 38, on fringe of borders a r. of blue.
Ribs, Gen. 2 : 21; Dan. 7 : 5.
Rich, Gen. 14 : 23, lest thou shouldest say, I have made Abraham r.

Ex. 30 : 15, the r. shall not give more.
Lev. 25 : 47, if a stranger wax r.
1 Sam. 2 : 7, the Lord maketh poor and maketh r.
2 Sam. 12 : 1, two men in city, one r., the other poor.
Job 15 : 29, he shall not be r.
Ps. 45 : 12, the r. shall entreat thy favour.
49 : 16, be not afraid when one is made r.
Prov. 10 : 4, hand of diligent maketh r.
10 : 22, the blessing of the Lord maketh r.
14 : 20, the r. hath many friends.
18 : 23, the r. answereth roughly.
21 : 17, he that loveth wine shall not be r.
22 : 2, the r. and poor meet together.
23 : 4, labour not be r.
28 : 11, the r. man is wise in his own conceit.
Eccl. 10 : 20, curse not the r. in thy bedchamber.
Isa. 53 : 9, with the r. in his death.
Jer. 9 : 23, let not the r. man glory.
Hos. 12 : 8, Ephraim said, I am r.
Zech. 11 : 5, blessed be the Lord, for I am r.
Mark 12 : 41, many that were r. cast in much.
Luke 1 : 53, the r. he hath sent empty away.
6 : 24, woe to you r., for.
12 : 21, that is not r. toward God.
14 : 12, call not thy r. neighbours.
18 : 23, sorrowful, for he was very r.
Rom. 10 : 12, the Lord is r. to all.
1 Cor. 4 : 8, now ye are full, now ye are r.
2 Cor. 6 : 10, poor, yet making many r.
8 : 9, r., yet for your sakes he became poor.
Eph. 2 : 4, God who is r. in mercy.
1 Tim. 6 : 18, he r. in good works.
Jas. 2 : 5, hath not God chosen the poor r. in faith ?
Rev. 3 : 17, because thou sayest, I am r.
Riches, given by God, 1 Sam. 2 : 7; Prov. 10 : 22; Eccl. 5 : 19.
earthly, Deut. 8 : 17; 1 Chr. 29 : 12; Ps. 49 : 6; Prov. 11 : 4; 15 : 16; 23 : 5; 27 : 24; Eccl. 4 : 8; 5 : 10; 6; Jer. 9 : 23; 48 : 36; Ezek. 7 : 19; Zeph. 1 : 18; Matt. 6 : 19; 13 : 22; 1 Tim. 6 : 17; Jas. 1 : 11; 5 : 2; 1 Pet. 1 : 18.
dangers of, Deut. 8 : 13; 32 : 15; Neh. 9 : 25; Prov. 15 : 17; 18 : 23; 28 : 11; 30 : 8; Eccl. 5 : 12; Hos. 12 : 8; Matt. 13 : 22; 19 : 23; Mark 10 : 22; Luke 12 : 15; 1 Tim. 6 : 10; Jas. 2 : 6; 5-1.
proper use of, 1 Chr. 29 : 3; Job 31 : 16, 24; Ps. 62 : 10; Jer. 9 : 23; Matt. 6 : 19; 19 : 21; Luke 16 : 9; 1 Tim. 6 : 17; Jas. 1 : 9; 1 John 3 : 17.
evil use of, Job 20 : 15; 31 : 24; Ps. 39 : 6; 49 : 6; 73 : 12; Prov. 11 : 28; 13 : 7, 11; 15 : 6; Eccl. 2 : 26; 5 : 10; Jas. 5 : 3.
the true, Luke 16 : 11; Eph. 3 : 8; Col. 2 : 3; Rev. 3 : 18.
end of the wicked rich, Job 20 : 16; 21 : 13; 27 : 16; Ps. 52 : 7; Prov. 11 : 4; 22-26; Eccl. 5 : 14; Jer. 17 : 11; Mic. 2 : 3; Hab. 2 : 6; Luke 6 : 24; 12 : 16; 16 : 29; Jas. 5 : 1.

Gen. 31 : 16, the r. God hath taken.
1 Sam. 17 : 25, enrich with great r.
1 Ki. 3 : 11; 2 Chr. 1 : 11, neither hast asked r.
1 Chr. 29 : 12, r. and honour come of thee.
Job 36 : 19, will he esteem thy r. ?
Ps. 39 : 6, he heapeth up r.
    49 : 6, boast themselves in their r.
    52 : 7, trusted in abundance of his r.
    62 : 10, if r. increase, set not your heart on them.
    73 : 12, the ungodly increase in r.
    104 : 24, O Lord, the earth is full of thy r.
    112 : 3, wealth and r. shall be in his house.
Prov. 8 : 18, r. and honour are with me.
    11 : 4, r. profit not in day of wrath.
    13 : 8, ransom of a man's life are his r.
    23 : 5, r. make themselves wings.
    27 : 24, r. are not for ever.
    30 : 8, give me neither poverty nor r.
Eccl. 4 : 8, nor his eye satisfied with r.
    5 : 13, r. kept for the owners.
Isa. 45 : 3, I wi'l give thee hidden r.
Jer. 17 : 11, he that getteth r., and not by right.
Matt. 13 : 22; Mark 4 : 19; Luke 8 : 14, deceitfulness of r.
Mark 10 : 23, how hardly shall they that have r. !
Rom. 2 : 4, despiseth thou the r. of his goodness ?
    9 : 23, make known the r. of his glory.
    11 : 33, O the r. of wisdom of God.
Eph. 1 : 7, redemption according to the r. of grace.
    2 : 7, the exceeding r. of his grace.
    3 : 8, the unsearchable r. of Christ.
Phil. 4 : 19, according to his r. in glory by Christ.
Col. 1 : 27, what the r. of the glory.
1 Tim. 6 : 17, nor trust in uncertain r.
Heb. 11 : 26, the reproach of Christ greater r.
Jas. 5 : 2, your r. are corrupted.
Rev. 5 : 12, worthy is the lamb to receive r.
    18 : 17, so great r. come to nought.
See Col. 3 : 16.
Richly, Col. 3 : 16; 1 Tim. 6 : 17.
Rid, Ex. 6 : 6; Ps. 82 : 4; 144 : 7, 11.
Riddance, Lev. 23 : 22; Zeph. 1 : 18.
Riddle, of Samson, Judg. 14 : 12.
Ride, Deut. 33 : 26, who r. upon the heaven.
Ps. 45 : 4, in majesty r. prosperously.
    66 : 12, hast caused men to r. over our heads.
    68 : 4, 33, extol him that r. on the heavens.
Isa. 19 : 1, the Lord r. on a swift cloud.
Zech. 9 : 9, thy king cometh unto thee r.
Ridges, Ps. 65 : 10, thou waterest the r. thereof.
Right, Gen. 18 : 25, shall not the Judge of all do r. ?
    24 : 48, Lord who led me in r. way.
Deut. 6 : 18; 12 : 25; 21 : 9, thou shalt do that is r.
    21 : 17, the r. of the first-born is his.
    32 : 4, God of truth, just and r. is he.
Ruth 4 : 6, redeem thou my r.

1 Sam. 12 : 23, I will teach you good and r. way.
2 Sam. 15 : 3, thy matters are good and r.
Neh. 9 : 33, thou hast done r.
Job 6 : 25, how forcible are r. words.
    34 : 6, should I lie against my r. ?
    34 : 23, he will not lay on man more than r.
    35 : 2, thinkest thou this to be r. ?
    36 : 6, he giveth r. to the poor.
Ps. 9 : 4, thou hast maintained my r.
    17 : 1, hear the r., O Lord.
    19 : 8, statutes of the Lord are r.
    45 : 6, sceptre of thy kingdom is a r. sceptre.
    51 : 10, renew a r. spirit within me.
    119 : 75, thy judgments are r.
    140 : 12, the Lord will maintain the r. of the poor.
Prov. 4 : 11, I have led thee in r. paths.
    8 : 6, opening of my lips shall be r. things.
    12 : 5, thoughts of righteous are r.
    14 : 12; 16 : 25, there is a way that seemeth r.
    16 : 13, they love him that speaketh r.
    21 : 2, every way of a man is r. in his own eyes.
Isa. 30 : 10, prophesy not r. things.
Jer. 17 : 11, that getteth riches, and not by r.
Ezek. 21 : 27, till he comes whose r. it is.
Hos. 14 : 9, ways of the Lord are r.
Amos 3 : 10, they know not to do r.
Matt. 20 : 4, whatsoever is r. I will give you.
Mark 5 : 15; Luke 8 : 35, in his r. mind.
Luke 12 : 57, why judge ye not what is r. ?
Eph. 6 : 1, obey your parents, this is r.
2 Pet. 2 : 15, forsaken the r. way.
Righteous, blessings and privileges of the, Job 36 : 7; Ps. 1; 5 : 12; 14 : 5; 15; 32 : 11; 34 : 15; 37; 52 : 6; 55 : 22; 58 : 10; 64 : 10; 89; 92 : 12; 97 : 11; 112; 125 : 3; 146 : 8; Prov. 2 : 7; 3 : 32; 12 : 26; 10–13; 28 : 1; Isa. 3 : 10; 26 : 2; 60 : 21; Ezek. 18; Matt. 13 : 43; Acts 10 : 35; Rom. 2 : 10; 1 Pet. 3 : 12; 1 John 3 : 7; Rev. 22 : 11.
Gen. 7 : 1, thee have I seen r. before me.
    18 : 23, wilt thou destroy r. with wicked ?
    20 : 4, wilt thou slay a r. nation ?
Num. 23 : 10, let me die the death of the r.
Deut. 25 : 1; 2 Chr. 6 : 23, they shall justify r.
Judg. 5 : 11; 1 Sam. 12 : 7, r. acts of the Lord.
1 Sam. 24 : 17, thou art more r. than I.
1 Ki. 2 : 32, two men more r. than he.
Job 4 : 7, where were the r. cut off ?
    9 : 15, though I were r., yet would I not answer.
    15 : 14, what is man, that he should be r. ?
Ps. 1 : 5, the congregation of the r.
    1 : 6, the Lord knoweth the way of r.
    5 : 12, thou wilt bless r. with favour.
    7 : 9, the r. God trieth the hearts.
    14 : 5, God is in generation of the r.
    34 : 17, the r. cry, and the Lord heareth them.
    37 : 16, a little that a r. man hath.

37 : 25, have not seen the r. forsaken.
37 : 30, the mouth of r. speaketh wisdom.
55 : 22, never suffer the r. to be moved.
58 : 11, there is a reward for the r.
64 : 10, the r. shall be glad in Lord.
92 : 12, the r. shall flourish like palm tree.
112 : 6, r. shall be in everlasting remembrance.
118 : 20, gate, into which r. shall enter.
125 : 3, rod of wicked shall not rest on lot of r.
141 : 5, let the r. smite me.
146 : 8, the Lord loveth the r.
Prov. 2 : 7, he layeth up wisdom for r.
10 : 3, the Lord will not suffer the r. to famish.
10 : 16, labour of r. tendeth to life.
10 : 25, the r. is an everlasting foundation.
10 : 30, the r. shall never be removed.
11 : 8, the r. is delivered out of trouble.
12 : 10, a r. man regardeth the life of his beast.
13 : 9, the light of the r. rejoiceth.
13 : 21, to the r. good shall be repaid.
14 : 9, among the r. there is favour.
14 : 32, the r. hath hope in his death.
15 : 6, in the house of the r. is much treasure.
15 : 29, he heareth the prayer of r.
18 : 10, the r. runneth into it, and is safe.
28 : 1, the r. are bold as a lion.
29 : 2, when the r. are in authority, people rejoice.
29 : 7, the r. considereth cause of the poor.
Eccl. 3 : 17, God shall judge r. and wicked.
7 : 16, be not r. over much.
9 : 1, the r. and the wise are in the hand of God.
9 : 2, one event, to r. and wicked.
Isa. 3 : 10, say to r., it shall be well.
24 : 16, songs, even glory to the r.
26 : 2, that r. nation may enter in.
53 : 11, shall my r. servant justify many.
57 : 1, r. perisheth, no man layeth it to heart.
60 : 21, thy people shall be all r.
Amos 2 : 6, they sold the r. for silver.
Mal. 3 : 18, discern between the r. and wicked.
Matt. 9 : 13; Mark 2 : 17; Luke 5 : 32, not come to call the r.
Matt. 13 : 43, then shall the r. shine forth.
23 : 28, outwardly appear r. to men.
25 : 46, the r. into life eternal.
Luke 1 : 6, they were both r. before God.
18 : 9, trusted they were r., and despised others.
23 : 47, certainly this was a r. man.
John 7 : 24, judge r. judgment.
17 : 25, O r. Father.
Rom. 3 : 10, there is none r., no, not one.
5 : 19, by obedience of one many be made r.
2 Tim. 4 : 8, the Lord, the r. Judge.
Heb. 11 : 4, obtained witness that he was r.
1 Pet. 3 : 12, eyes of the Lord are over the r.
4 : 18, if the r. scarcely be saved.

2 Pet. 2 : 8, Lot vexed his r. soul.
1 John 3 : 7, is r., even as he is r.
Rev. 16 : 7, true and r. are thy judgments.
22 : 11, he that is r., let him be r. still.
Righteously, Deut. 1 : 16; Prov. 31 : 9, judge r.
Ps. 67 : 4; 96 : 10, thou shalt judge the people r.
Isa. 33 : 15, he that walketh r. shall dwell on high.
Jer. 11 : 20, O Lord, that judgest r.
Titus 2 : 12, we should live soberly, r.
Righteousness, by faith, Gen. 15 : 6; Ps. 106 : 31; Rom. 4 : 3; Gal. 3 : 6; Jas. 2 : 23.
of Christ, imputed to the Church, Isa. 54 : 17; Jer. 23 : 6; 33 : 16; Hos. 2 : 19; Mal. 4 : 2; Rom. 1 : 17; 3 : 22; 10 : 3; 1 Cor. 1 : 30; 2 Cor. 5 : 21; Phil. 3 : 9; Titus 2 : 14; 2 Pet. 1 : 1.
of the law and faith, Rom. 10.
of man, Deut. 9 : 4; Isa. 64 : 6; Dan. 9 : 18; Phil. 3 : 9.
Gen. 30 : 33, so shall my r. answer for me.
Deut. 6 : 25, it shall be our r. if.
33 : 19, shall offer sacrifices of r.
1 Sam. 26 : 23, Lord render to every man his r.
Job 29 : 14, I put on r., and it clothed me.
35 : 2, thou saidst, my r. is more than God's.
36 : 3, I will ascribe r. to my Maker.
Ps. 4 : 5, offer the sacrifices of r.
9 : 8, he shall judge the world in r.
17 : 15, I will behold thy face in r.
23 : 3, leadeth me in paths of r.
24 : 5, r. from the God of his salvation.
40 : 9, I have preached r.
45 : 7; Heb. 1 : 9, thou lovest r.
Ps. 85 : 10, r. and peace have kissed each other.
94 : 15, judgment shall return unto r.
97 : 2, r. is the habitation of his throne.
118 : 19, open to me the gates of r.
132 : 9, let thy priests be clothed with r.
Prov. 8 : 18, riches and r. are with me.
10 : 2; 11 : 4, r. delivereth from death.
11 : 5, r. of the perfect shall direct his way.
11 : 19, r. tendeth to life.
12 : 28, in the way of r. is life.
14 : 34, r. exalteth a nation.
16 : 8, better is a little with r.
16 : 12, the throne is established by r.
16 : 31, crown of glory, if found in way of r.
Eccl. 7 : 15, a just man that perisheth in his r.
Isa. 11 : 5, r. shall be the girdle of his loins.
26 : 9, inhabitants of the world will learn r.
28 : 17, r. will I lay to the plummet.
32 : 1, a king shall reign in r.
32 : 17, work of r. shall be peace.
41 : 10, uphold thee with right hand of my r.
59 : 16, his r. sustained him.
64 : 6, our r. as filthy rags.
Jer. 23 : 6; 33 : 16, name, the Lord our r.
Ezek. 18 : 20, the r. of the righteous shall be upon him.

Dan. 4 : 27, break off thy sins by **r.**
9 : 7, O Lord, **r.** belongeth to thee.
9 : 24, to bring in everlasting **r.**
12 : 3, they that turn many to **r.**
Hos. 10 : 12, till he rain **r.** upon you.
Amos 5 : 24, let **r.** run down as a stream.
Mal. 4 : 2, sun of **r.** arise.
Matt. 3 : 15, to fulfil all **r.**
5 : 6, that hunger and thirst after **r.**
5 : 20, except your **r.** exceed the **r.** of scribes.
21 : 32, John came in the way of **r.**
Luke 1 : 75, in **r.** before him.
John 16 : 8, reprove the world of **r.**
Acts 10 : 35, he that worketh **r.** is accepted.
13 : 10, thou enemy of all **r.**
24 : 25, as he reasoned of **r.**
Rom. 1 : 17; 3 : 5; 10 : 3, the **r.** of God.
4 : 6, man to whom God imputeth **r.**
4 : 11, a seal of the **r.** of faith.
5 : 21, grace reign through **r.**
6 : 13, members as instruments of **r.**
8 : 10, the Spirit is life because of **r.**
9 : 30, the **r.** of faith.
10 : 4, Christ is the end of the law for **r.**
14 : 17, kingdom of God is **r.**, peace.
1 Cor. 1 : 30, Christ is made unto us **r.**
15 : 34, awake to **r.**
2 Cor. 5 : 21, made the **r.** of God in him.
6 : 7, the armour of **r.**
6 : 14, what fellowship hath **r.** with unrighteousness ?
Gal. 2 : 21, if **r.** come by the law.
Eph. 6 : 14, the breastplate of **r.**
Phil. 1 : 11, filled with the fruits of **r.**
3 : 6, touching the **r.** in the law blameless.
1 Tim. 6 : 11; 2 Tim. 2 : 22, follow **r.**
2 Tim. 4 : 8, a crown of **r.**
Titus 3 : 5, not by works of **r.**
Heb. 7 : 2, king of **r.**
12 : 11, the peaceable fruit of **r.**
Jas. 1 : 20, wrath of man worketh not the **r.** of God.
Jas. 3 : 18, fruit of **r.** is sown in peace.
1 Pet. 2 : 24, dead to sins, should live unto **r.**
2 Pet. 2 : 5, a preacher of **r.**
3 : 13, new earth wherein dwelleth **r.**
1 John 2 : 29, every one that doeth **r.**
Rightly, Gen. 27 : 36, is not he **r.** named Jacob ?
Luke 7 : 43, said, thou hast **r.** judged.
20 : 21, we know thou teachest **r.**
2 Tim. 2 : 15, **r.** dividing word of truth.
Rimmon [pomegranate], Josh. 15 : 32.
as the name of a god [in Assyrian, Rammanu = thunderer], 2 Ki. 5 : 18.
Ring. The ring was an important article of a Hebrew's attire in that it contained his signet. It was hence a symbol of authority (cf. Gen. 41, 42; Esther 3 : 10). Rings were also worn by women as jewellery (cf. Isa. 3 : 21).
Riot, Rom. 13 : 13, walk not in **r.** drunkenness.
Titus 1 : 6, children not accused of **r.**
1 Pet. 4 : 4, that you run not to **r.**
2 Pet. 2 : 13, count it pleasure to **r.**

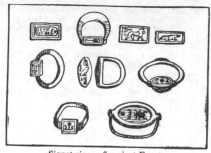

Signet rings of ancient Egypt.

See Prov. 28 : 7; Luke 15 : 13.
Ripe, Gen. 40 : 10, brought forth **r.** grapes.
Ex. 22 : 29, offer the first of thy **r.** fruits.
Num. 18 : 13, whatsoever is first **r.** shall be thine.
Joel 3 : 13, put in sickle, for harvest is **r.**
Rev. 14 : 15, harvest of earth is **r.**
Rise, Num. 24 : 17, a sceptre shall **r.** out of Israel.
32 : 14, ye are **r.** up in your fathers' stead.
Job 9 : 7, commandeth the sun, and it **r.** not.
14 : 12, man lieth down, and **r.** not.
31 : 14, what shall I do when God **r.** up ?
Ps. 27 : 3, though war should **r.** against me.
127 : 2, it is vain to **r.** up early.
Eccl. 12 : 4, he shall **r.** at the voice of the bird.
Isa. 24 : 20, earth shall fall, and not **r.**
33 : 10, now will I **r.**, saith the Lord.
60 : 1, the glory of the Lord is **r.** upon thee.
Jer. 7 : 13; 25 : 3; 35 : 14, I spake unto you, **r.** early.
11 : 7, **r.** early and protesting.
Lam. 3 : 63, sitting down and **r.** up.
Matt. 5 : 45, he maketh sun to **r.** on evil and good.
20 : 19; Mark 9 : 31; 10 : 34; Luke 18 : 33; 24 : 7, the third day he shall **r.** again.
Matt. 26 : 46, **r.**, let us be going.
Mark 10 : 49, **r.**, he calleth thee.
Luke 11 : 7, I cannot **r.** and give thee.
24 : 34, the Lord is **r.** indeed.
John 11 : 23, thy brother shall **r.** again.
Acts 10 : 13, **r.**, Peter, kill and eat.
26 : 23, the first that should **r.** from the dead.
Rom. 8 : 34, Christ that died, yea rather, that is **r.** again.
15 : 12, he that shall **r.** to reign.
1 Cor. 15 : 15, if the dead **r.** not.
Col. 3 : 1, if ye then be **r.** with Christ.
1 Thess. 4 : 16, the dead in Christ shall **r.** first.
Rites, Num. 9 : 3; Acts 6 : 14; Heb. 9 : 10.
River, Gen. 41 : 1, he stood by the **r.**
Ex. 7 : 19; 8 : 5, stretch out hand on **r.**
Josh. 13 : 9; 2 Sam. 24 : 5, the city in the midst of the **r.**

Judg. 5 : 21, **r.** Kishon that ancient **r.**
2 Sam. 17 : 13, draw it into the **r.**
Job 28 : 10, he cutteth out **r.** among rocks.
2 Ki. 5 : 12, are not **r.** of Damascus better ?
29 : 6, **r.** of oil.
40 : 23, he drinketh up a **r.**
Ps. 1 : 3, a tree planted by the **r.**
36 : 8, the **r.** of thy pleasure.
46 : 4, there is a **r.**, the streams whereof make glad.
65 : 9, enrichest it with **r.** of God.
72 : 8, have dominion from the **r.**
119 : 136, **r.** of waters run down mine eyes.
137 : 1, by **r.** of Babylon we wept.
Eccl. 1 : 7, all the **r.** run into the sea.
Isa. 32 : 2, as **r.** of water in a dry place.
43 : 19, I will make **r.** in the desert.
48 : 18, then had thy peace been as a **r.**
66 : 12, I will extend peace like a **r.**
Lam. 2 : 18, let tears run down like a **r.**
Mic. 6 : 7, be pleased with **r.** of oil ?
Zech. 9 : 10, his dominion from the **r.**
John 7 : 38, **r.** of living water.
Acts 16 : 13, on Sabbath we went by a **r.** side.
Rev. 22 : 1, a pure **r.** of water of life.
Rizpah (riz′păh) [hot stone], 2 Sam. 3 : 7. The same word is translated " a live coal " in the story of Isaiah's call, Isa. 6 : 6. cf. 2 Sam. 21 : 9-11.
Roar, 1 Chr. 16 : 32; Ps. 96 : 11; 98 : 7, let the sea **r.**
Ps. 46 : 3, not fear, though waters **r.**
104 : 21, young lions **r.** after their prey.
Prov. 19 : 12, king's wrath is as the **r.** of a lion.
Isa. 59 : 11, we **r.** all like bears.
Jer. 6 : 23, their voice **r.** like the sea.
25 : 30, the Lord shall **r.** from on high.
31 : 35, divideth sea, when waves **r.**
Hos. 11 : 10, he shall **r.** like a lion.
Joel 3 : 16; Amos 1 : 2, the Lord shall **r.** out of Zion.
Amos 3 : 4, will a lion **r.** if he hath no prey ?
Luke 21 : 25, the sea and waves **r.**
1 Pet. 5 : 8, the devil as a **r.** lion.
Rob, Prov. 22 : 22, **r.** not the poor.
Isa. 10 : 2, they may **r.** the fatherless.
42 : 22, this is a people **r.** and spoiled.
Mal. 3 : 8, will a man **r.** God?
2 Cor. 11 : 8, I **r.** other churches.
See Job 12 : 6; Jer. 7 : 11; John 10 : 1; 2 Cor. 11 : 26; Phil. 2 : 6.
Robbery forbidden, Lev. 19 : 13; Ps. 62 : 10; Prov. 21 : 7; 22 : 22; 28 : 24; Isa. 10 : 2; 61 : 8; Ezek. 22 : 29; Amos 3 : 10; 1 Cor. 6 : 8; 1 Thess. 4 : 6.
Robe, Job 29 : 14, my judgment was as a **r.**
Isa. 61 : 10, covered me with **r.** of righteousness.
Matt. 27 : 28, put on Jesus a scarlet **r.**
Luke 15 : 22, bring forth the best **r.**
20 : 46, scribes walk in long **r.**
Rev. 6 : 11, white **r.** were given them.
Rock, Ex. 17 : 6, I will stand before thee on the **r.**

33 : 22, I will put thee in a clift of the **r.**
Num. 20 : 8, speak to the **r.** before their eyes.
24 : 21, thou puttest thy nest in a **r.**
Deut. 8 : 15, who brought thee water out of the **r.**
32 : 4, he is the **R.**
32 : 15, lightly esteemed the **R.** of his salvation.
32 : 31, their **r.** is not as our **R.**
1 Sam. 2 : 2, neither is there any **r.** like our God.
2 Sam. 22 : 2; Ps. 18 : 2; 92 : 15, the Lord is my **r.**
2 Sam. 22 : 32; Ps. 18 : 31, who is a **r.** save our God ?
1 Ki. 19 : 11, strong wind brake in pieces the **r.**
Job 14 : 18, the **r.** is removed out of his place.
19 : 24, graven in the **r.** for ever.
Ps. 27 : 5; 40 : 2, he shall set me upon a **r.**
31 : 3; 71 : 3, thou art my **r.** and my fortress.
61 : 2, lead me to the **r.** that is higher than I.
89 : 26; 95 : 1, **r.** of salvation.
Prov. 30 : 26, their houses in the **r.**
Song of Sol. 2 : 14, that art in the clefts of the **r.**
Isa. 17 : 10, not mindful of the **r.** of thy strength.
32 : 2, as the shadow of a great **r.**
Jer. 23 : 29, hammer that breaketh the **r.** in pieces.
Matt. 7 : 25; Luke 6 : 48, it was founded upon a **r.**
Matt. 16 : 18, upon this **r.** I will build my church.
Luke 8 : 6, some fell upon a **r.**
Rom. 9 : 33; 1 Pet. 2 : 8, I lay in Zion a **r.** of offence.
1 Cor. 10 : 4, drank of that spiritual **r.**
Rev. 16 : 6, said to the **r.**, fall on us.
Rod, Ex. 4 : 4, it became a **r.** in his hand.
Job 21 : 9, neither is the **r.** of God upon them.
Ps. 2 : 9, break them with a **r.** of iron.
23 : 4, thy **r.** and staff comfort me.
110 : 2, the Lord shall send the **r.** of strength.
Prov. 10 : 13; 26 : 3, a **r.** for back of fools.
13 : 24, he that spareth the **r.**
29 : 15, **r.** and reproof give wisdom.
Isa. 11 : 1, shall come forth a **r.**
Ezek. 20 : 37, cause you to pass under the **r.**
Mic. 6 : 9, hear the **r.**, and who hath appointed it.
2 Cor. 11 : 25, thrice was I beaten with **r.**
Rev. 12 : 5, rule nations with a **r.** of iron.
Roe, Roebuck, the gazelle. This animal is mentioned among the beasts allowed for food (Deut. 14 : 5), but its beauty and gentleness seem to have made it an object of special fondness, and its name is frequently used as one expressing endearment. This is true to the present day in the East. 2 Sam. 2 : 18; Isa. 13 : 14.

Roll of prophecy, Isa. 8 : 1; Jer. 36 : 2; Ezek. 2 : 9; 3 : 1; Zech. 5 : 1.

Rolled, Isa. 34 : 4, the heavens shall be r. together.

Matt. 28 : 2, r. back the stone.

Rev. 6 : 14, as a scroll when it is r. together.

Romans, Epistle to the.

Author and Date.—The Epistle to the Romans stands in the second group of Paul's Epistles, along with those to the Corinthians and the Galatians. The authenticity of this group is undoubted, and when taken together they contain all the essentials of Pauline Christianity. Historically, they stand after the early Epistles to the Thessalonians, and before the Epistles of the captivity. The Epistle to the Romans was written in the spring of 58, from Corinth, during a stay of three months in Greece.

The Church at Rome.—The origin of the Church at Rome is unknown. There is no trustworthy historical evidence for the belief that it was founded by the Apostle Peter. Owing to its geographical position, the Roman Church was naturally of great strategic importance for the Christian cause, and it played an important part in the days of persecution by the Emperors. It appears to have been from the start a representative and cosmopolitan body, including a fair proportion of both Jewish and Gentile Christians. Both are addressed in the course of the Epistle, and of the persons mentioned by Paul, some are Jews, some Greeks, and two (Urban and Ampliatus) have Latin names.

Character and Contents of the Epistle.— The Epistle is worthy of the Church to which it is addressed. It is really an elaborate theological treatise in which the Apostle expounds his faith, dealing with the great fundamental questions of sin, salvation, faith, and righteousness. The main body of the Epistle may be divided into two sections, theoretical and practical, with the division taking place at the beginning of Chapter 12. There is a short introduction, and the last chapter contains many personal greetings.

Rome, strangers of, at Pentecost, Acts 2 : 10; Jews ordered to depart from, Acts 18 : 2; Paul preaches there, Acts 28.

Roof, Gen. 19 : 8, under the shadow of my r.

Deut. 22 : 8, make a battlement for thy r.

Job 29 : 10; Ps. 137 : 6; Ezek. 3 : 26, tongue cleaveth to r. of mouth.

Matt. 8 : 8; Luke 7 : 6, I am not worthy thou shouldest come under my r.

Mark 2 : 4, they uncovered the r.

Room, Gen. 24 : 23, is there r. for us ?

26 : 22, the Lord hath made r. for us.

Ps. 31 : 8, hast set my feet in a large r.

80 : 9, thou preparedst r. before it.

Prov. 18 : 16, a man's gift maketh r. for him.

Mal. 3 : 10, there shall not be r. enough.

Matt. 23 : 6; Mark 12 : 39; Luke 20 : 46, love the uppermost r.

Mark 2 : 2, there was no r. to receive them.

14 : 15; Luke 22 : 12, a large upper r.

Luke 2 : 7, no r. for them in the inn.

12 : 17, no r. to bestow my fruits.

14 : 7, how they chose out the chief r.

14 : 22, yet there is r.

1 Cor. 14 : 16, that occupieth the r. of the unlearned.

Root, Deut. 29 : 18, a r. that beareth gall.

1 Ki. 14 : 15, he shall r. up Israel.

2 Ki. 19 : 30, shall again take r. downward.

Job 5 : 3, I have seen the foolish taking r.

18 : 14, confidence shall be r. out.

19 : 28, the r. of the matter.

Ps. 52 : 5, r. thee out of the land of the living.

Prov. 12 : 12, the r. of righteous yieldeth fruit.

Isa. 5 : 24, their r. shall be rottenness.

11 : 1, a Branch shall grow out of his r.

11 : 10; Rom. 15 : 12, a r. of Jesse.

53 : 2, as a r. out of a dry ground.

Ezek. 31 : 7, his r. was by great waters.

Hos. 14 : 5, cast forth his r. as Lebanon.

Mal. 4 : 1, shall leave them neither r. nor branch.

Matt. 3 : 10; Luke 3 : 9, axe is laid to r. of trees.

13 : 6; Mark 4 : 6; Luke 8 : 13, because they had no r.

15 : 13, shall be r. up.

Rom. 11 : 16, if the r. be holy.

Eph. 3 : 17, being r. and grounded in love.

Col. 2 : 7, r. and built up in him.

1 Tim. 6 : 10, love of money is the r. of all evil.

Heb. 12 : 15, lest any r. of bitterness.

Jude 12, trees plucked up by the r.

Rev. 22 : 16, the r. and offspring of David.

Rose, Song of Sol. 2 : 1, I am the r. of Sharon; Isa. 35 : 1, desert shall blossom as the r. The Hebrew word occurs only these two times. It seems to indicate some bulbous plant, and may refer to the autumn crocus as suggested in the margin of the Revised Version. Some have suggested a mallow. The plant now called Rose of Sharon is a rock cistus.

Gen. 4 : 8, Cain r. up against Abel.

32 : 31, the sun r. upon him.

Josh. 3 : 16, waters r. up upon an heap.

Ps. 124 : 2, when men r. up against us.

Luke 16 : 31, not be persuaded, though one r. from the dead.

Rom. 14 : 9, Christ both died and r.

1 Cor. 10 : 7, people r. up to play.

15 : 4, he was buried, and r. again.

2 Cor. 5 : 15, him who died and r. again.

Rot, Prov. 10 : 7, name of wicked shall r.

Isa. 40 : 20, chooseth a tree that will not r.

See Prov. 14 : 30; Isa. 5 : 24.

Rough, Isa. 27 : 8, he stayeth his r. wind.

40 : 4, r. places be made plain.

Luke 3 : 5, r. ways be made smooth.

See Gen. 42 : 7; Prov. 18 : 23.

Royal, Gen. 49 : 20, yield r. dainties.

1 Sam. 27 : 5, why should I dwell in the r. city ?

Esther 1 : 7, r. wine.
5 : 1;   6 : 8;   8 : 15;   Acts 12 : 21, r. apparel.
Jas. 2 : 8, if ye fulfil the r. law.
1 Pet. 2 : 9, ye are a r. priesthood.
Rubies, Job 28 : 18;   Prov. 8 : 11, price of wisdom is above r. The Hebrew word means red coral, or, as some maintain, red pearls. It is doubtful if the true ruby was known in Biblical times.
Rudder, Acts 27 : 40, loose the r. bands. Greek and Roman sailing vessels were steered by means of two paddle-rudders, one of which was fixed to each side of the vessel. When at anchor these paddle-rudders were hoisted up and lashed. To " loose the rudder bands " was to undo this lashing, and replace the paddle-rudders in position to steer the ship.
Ruddy, 1 Sam. 16 : 12;   17 : 42, David was r.
Song of Sol. 5 : 10, my beloved is white and r.
Lam. 4 : 7, more r. than rubies.
Rudiments, Col. 2 : 8, 20, the r. of the world.
Rue, Luke 11 : 42, ye tithe mint and r. Rue is a plant of little value, although when dried it is used as medicine. A tithe of it was required by the Pharisees.
Rufus [red], Mark 15 : 21;   Rom. 16 : 13.
Ruhamah (rū-hä-măh)   [compassionate], Hos. 2 : 1.
Ruin, 2 Chr. 28 : 23, they were the r. of him.
Ps. 89 : 40, hast brought his strongholds to r.
Prov. 26 : 28 a flattering mouth worketh r.
Isa. 25 : 2, made of a defenced city a r.
Ezek. 18 : 30, iniquity shall not be your r.
Luke 6 : 49, the r. of that house was great.
Acts 15 : 16, build again the r. thereof.
Rule, Gen. 1 : 16, to r. the day.
3 : 16, thy husband shall r. over thee.
Judg. 8 : 23, I will not r. over you.
2 Sam. 23 : 3, he that r. over men must be just.
Esther 9 : 1, Jews had r. over them.
Ps. 66 : 7, he r. by his power for ever.
89 : 9, thou r. the raging of the sea.
103 : 19, his kingdom r. over all.
110 : 2, r. in midst of enemies.
Prov. 16 : 32, that r. his spirit.
17 : 2, a wise servant shall have r.
19 : 10, a servant to have r. over princes.
25 : 28, no r. over his own spirit.
Eccl. 8 : 9, one man r. over another.
Isa. 3 : 4, babes shall r. over them.
32 : 1, princes shall r. in judgment.
40 : 10, his arm shall r. for him.
63 : 19, thou never barest r. over them.
Ezek. 29 : 15, no more r. over nations.
Joel 2 : 17, heathen should r. over them.
Mark 10 : 42, who are accounted to r.
Rom. 12 : 8, he that r., with diligence.
1 Cor. 15 : 24, put down all r.
2 Cor. 10 : 13, measure of the r.
Gal. 6 : 16, as many as walk according to this r.
Phil. 3 : 16, let us walk by the same r.

Col. 3 : 15, let the peace of God r. in your hearts.
1 Tim. 3 : 5, how to r. his house.
5 : 17, elders that r. well.
Heb. 13 : 7, 17, that have the r. over you.
Ruler, Ex. 22 : 28, thou shalt not curse r. of people.
Num. 13 : 2, every one a r. among them.
Prov. 23 : 1, when thou sittest to eat with a r.
28 : 15, a wicked r. over the poor.
Isa. 3 : 6, be thou our r.
Mic. 5 : 2, out of thee shall come r.
Matt. 9 : 18, there came a certain r.
25 : 21, I will make thee r.
John 3 : 1, a r. of the Jews.
7 : 48, have any of the r. believed on him ?
Rom 13 : 3, r. are not a terror to good works.
Eph. 6 : 12, r. of the darkness of world.
Rumour, Jer. 49 : 14, heard a r. from the Lord.
Ezek. 7 : 26, r. shall be upon r.
Matt. 24 : 6;   Mark 13 : 7, wars and r. of wars.
Luke 7 : 17, this r. went forth.
Run, 2 Sam. 22 : 30;   Ps. 18 : 29, I have r. through a troop.
2 Chr. 16 : 9;   Zech. 4 : 10, the eyes of the Lord r. to and fro.
Ps. 19 : 5, as a strong man to r. a race.
23 : 5, my cup r. over.
119 : 32, I will r. the way of thy commandments.
147 : 15, his word r. very swiftly.
Prov. 1 : 16;   Isa. 59 : 7, their feet r. to evil.
Song of Sol. 1 : 4, we will r. after thee.
Isa. 40 : 31, they shall r., and not be weary.
55 : 5, nations shall r. to thee.
Jer. 12 : 5, if thou hast r. with the footmen.
51 : 31 one post shall r. to meet another.
Hab. 2 : 2, that he may r. that readeth.
Zech. 2 : 4, r., speak to this young man.
Rom. 9 : 16, nor of him that r.
1 Cor. 9 : 24, they which r. in a race, r. all.
Gal. 2 : 2, lest I should r., or had r. in vain.
5 : 7, ye did r. well.
Heb. 12 : 1, let us r. with patience.
1 Pet. 4 : 4, that ye r. not to the same excess.
Rush, Isa. 17 : 13, nations shall r. like r. of many waters.
Jer. 8 : 6, as horse r. into battle.
Acts 2 : 2, sound as of a r. mighty wind.
Rust, Matt. 6 : 19, 20, where moth and r. doth corrupt.
Jas. 5 : 3, the r. of them shall be a witness against you.
Ruth, Book of. The book of Ruth, considered from a purely literary point of view, ranks very high in Hebrew literature. It is a good example of the Hebrew tendency to subordinate strict historical accuracy to literary and religious values. The historical purpose of the book is apparently to establish the existence of a Moabitish ancestress for the house of David. But to the modern reader the

chief interest and charm of the book lies in the simplicity and beauty of the book itself.

The contents may be summarised as follows: (1) the sojourn of Elimelech and Naomi, with their sons, in Moab, and the death of the father and sons (1 : 1-5); (2) the return of Naomi and her daughter-in-law, Ruth, to Bethlehem (1 : 6-22); (3) Ruth's work in the fields of her kinsman, Boaz (2 : 1-23); (4) Boaz recognises her kinship and rights (3 : 1-18); (5) Ruth marries Boaz, from which marriage David is descended.

S

Sabachthani (să-băch-̓thă-nī) [thou hast forsaken me], Matt. 27 : 46; Mark 15 : 34. The word is part of the cry on the Cross which Mark quotes in the original Aramaic in which we may presume that our Lord spoke.

Sabaoth (să-bā-̓ŏth) [hosts], the Lord of, Rom. 9 : 29; Jas. 5 : 4.

Sabbath. The Sabbath is the only season of worship to which the decalogue makes any reference, and it stands first among the " feasts " in the catalogue contained in Lev. 23. Like the other festivals, it is called a " holy convocation." Its maintenance as a strict day of rest was insisted on even in the " earing time " and " harvest " (Ex. 34 : 21). In the later days of the exile, the prophets gave special prominence in their teaching to the sanctity of the Sabbath (Ezek. 22 : 26; cf. Jer. 17 : 19-27; Ezek. 44 : 24; Isa. 56 : 2; 58 : 13), enforcing the precepts that found legislative expression in stringent regulations (Ex. 31 : 14; 35 : 2, 3; Num. 15 : 32-35), and in the reforming zeal of Nehemiah (13 : 15-19).

What the precise form of Sabbath worship was, both before and after the exile, we cannot determine. Probably in earlier times it mainly consisted in sacrificial acts; probably also it was employed as a day for consulting the prophets in cases of difficulty, or the priests for responses with ephod or with Urim and Thummim (cf. 2 Ki. 4 : 23). During the Greek and Roman periods, when synagogue worship became established among all the Jewish settlements throughout Asia Minor, Egypt, and Europe, the reading of the Jewish Scriptures became the regular characteristic feature of Sabbath ritual.

The traditional Jewish Sabbath provided a basis for our distinctively Christian Sabbath, or " Lord's Day." The latter title is the more correct, as the early Christians made the first day of the week (the day following the Jewish Sabbath) their day of worship in memory of our Lord's Resurrection on that day. instituted, Gen. 2 : 2; (Heb. 4 : 4).

to be kept holy, Ex. 16 : 23; 20 : 8; 23 : 12; 31 : 13; 34 : 21; 35 : 2; Lev. 25 : 3; Num. 15 : 32; Deut. 5 : 12; Neh. 10 : 31; 13 : 15; Isa. 56; Jer. 17 : 21; Ezek. 20 : 12.

its offerings, Num. 28 : 9.

of the seventh year, Ex. 23 : 11; Lev. 25 : 1 ff.

Christ the Lord of, Luke 6 : 5.

the Jews' hypocrisy concerning, reproved, Matt. 12; Mark 2 : 23; 3; Luke 13 : 14 ff.; John 7 : 23.

first day of the week kept as, Acts 20 : 7; 1 Cor. 16 : 2; Rev. 1 : 10.

Ex. 31 : 14, 16, ye shall keep the s.

Lev. 16 : 31; 23 : 3, 32, s. of rest.

2 Ki. 4 : 23, it is neither new moon nor s.

Neh. 9 : 14, madest known thy holy s.

Isa. 58 : 13, call s. a delight.

Ezek. 46 : 1, on s. it shall be opened.

Amos 8 : 5, when will the s. be gone ?

Mark 2 : 27, the s. was made for man.

2 : 28; Luke 6 : 5, the Son of man is Lord of the s.

Luke 13 : 15, doth not each one of you on s. loose his ox ?

John 5 : 18, he not only had broken the s.

See Matt. 28 : 1; Mark 16 : 2, 9; John 20 : 1, 19, 26.

Sabeans (să-bē-̓ăns), people of Seba or Sheba, Job 1 : 15; Isa. 45 : 14.

Sack, Gen. 42 : 25; 43 : 21; Josh. 9 : 4.

Sackbut, Dan. 3 : 5; 7 :10, a musical instrument. See **Musical Instruments.**

Sackcloth.

Sackcloth, coarse cloth made of goat's hair (Isa. 50 : 3; Rev. 6 : 12). It was used in making sacks, but was also used for the rough garments worn by mourners.

2 Sam. 3 : 31; 1 Ki. 20 : 32; 21 : 27; 2 Ki. 6 : 30; Job 16 : 15; Isa. 32 : 11; Neh. 9 : 1; Esther 4 : 1; Ps. 30 : 11; Jonah 3 : 5.

Sacrifices, types of Christ, Heb. 9 : 11.
Gen. 31 : 54, Jacob offered s.
Ex. 5 : 17; 8 : 8, do s. to the Lord.
20 : 24, thou shalt s. burnt offerings.
Lev. 7 : 12; Ps. 116 : 17, offer s. of thanksgiving.
1 Sam. 2 : 29, wherefore kick ye at my s. ?
15 : 22, to obey is better than s.
Ezra 4 : 2, we seek your God, and do s. to him.
Neh. 4 : 2, will they s. ?
Ps. 4 : 5, offer s. of righteousness.
40 : 6; 51 : 16, s. thou didst not desire.
51 : 17, the s. of God are a broken spirit.
54 : 6, I will freely s. to thee.
118 : 27, bind the s. to horns of the altar.
141 : 2, lifting up of my hands as the evening s.
107 : 22, s. sacrifices of thanksgiving.
Prov. 15 : 8, s. of wicked an abomination.
17 : 1, a house full of s. with strife.
21 : 3, to do justice is more acceptable than s.
Eccl. 5 : 1, the s. of fools.
9 : 2, to him that s. and that s. not.
Isa. 1 : 11, to what purpose the multitude of your s. ?
Jer. 6 : 20, nor your s. sweet unto me.
33 : 11, that bring s. of praise.
Ezek. 39 : 17, gather to my s., a great s.
Dan. 8 : 11; 9 : 27; 11 : 31, daily s. taken away.
Hos. 6 : 6; Matt. 9 : 13; 12 : 7, I desired mercy, not s.
8 : 13, they s., but the Lord accepteth not.
Amos 5 : 25, have ye offered unto me s. ?
Hab. 1 : 16, they s. unto their net.
Zeph. 1 : 7, the Lord hath prepared a s.
Mark 9 : 49, every s. shall be salted.
12 : 33, to love the Lord is more than s.
Acts 7 : 42, have ye offered s. forty years ?
14 : 13, would have done s.
Rom. 12 : 1, present your bodies a living s.
1 Cor. 5 : 7, Christ our passover is s. for us.
8 : 4; 10 : 19, 28, offered in s. to idols.
10 : 20, things Gentiles s., they s. to devils.
Eph. 5 : 2, a s. to God for a sweet-smelling savour.
Phil. 2 : 17, offered on s. of your faith.
4 : 18, a s. acceptable, well-pleasing to God.
Heb. 9 : 26, put away sin by the s. of himself.
10 : 26, there remaineth no more s. for sin.
13 : 15, let us offer the s. of praise.
1 Pet. 2 : 5, to offer up spiritual s.
Rev. 2 : 14, 20, things s. to idols.
custom of. The custom of offering sacrifices, by which atonement was made for sin, formed an important element in early

Jewish religious rites and ceremonies. In patriarchal times the sacrificial rites were performed by the head of the family, but in later times these duties were performed by the official priesthood, who were drawn from the tribe of Levi.

The custom of sacrifice was one point at which the great prophets attacked the religion of their day. The prophets held that the moral obligations of the worship of Jehovah were being neglected in favour of the more outward and ceremonial obligations, of which the various sacrifices were a conspicuous example.

Sacrilege, Rom. 2 : 22.
Sad, 1 Sam. 1 : 18, countenance no more s.
1 Ki. 21 : 5, why is thy spirit so s. ?
Matt. 6 : 16, be not of a s. countenance.
Mark 10 : 22, he was s. at that saying.
Luke 24 : 17, as ye walk and are s.
Saddle, 2 Sam. 19 : 26; 1 Ki. 13 : 13, 27.
Sadducees, their controversies with Christ, Matt. 16 : 1; 22 : 23; Mark 12 : 18; Luke 20 : 27; with the apostles, Acts 4 : 1; with Paul, Acts 23 : 8; their doctrines, Matt. 22 : 23; Mark 12 : 18; Acts 23 : 8.

The Sadducees, or "righteous ones," were a Jewish sect or party, whose origin can be traced to the time of the Antiochian persecution in the second century before Christ. They were drawn largely from the priestly class, and through their religious position they became an extremely influential body.

Their doctrines centred in an extravagant reverence for the law, coupled with a contempt for all later traditions. This led them into conflict with the Pharisees, the other great Jewish sect, particularly on the subject of the future life. The Sadducees, inasmuch as they excluded all future rewards and punishments, were remarkably severe in their enforcing of the old Mosaic criminal code. Their only way to discourage crime was by enforcing the temporal terrors of the law.

Sadness, Eccl. 7 : 3.
Safe, 2 Sam. 18 : 29, is the young man s. ?
Job 21 : 9, houses are s. from fear.
Ps. 119 : 117, hold me up, and I shall be s.
Prov. 18 : 10, righteous runneth into it, and is s.
29 : 25, whoso trusteth in the Lord shall be s.
Luke 15 : 27, received him s.
Acts 27 : 44, they escaped all s. to land.
Phil. 3 : 1, for you it is s.
Safeguard, 1 Sam. 22 : 23.
Safety, Job 3 : 26, I was not in s.
5 : 4, his children are far from s.
11 : 18, thou shalt take thy rest in s.
Ps. 12 : 5, I will set him in s.
33 : 17, an horse is a vain thing for s.
Prov. 11 : 14; 24 : 6, in multitude of counsellors is s.
21 : 31, s. is of the Lord.
Isa. 14 : 30, needy shall lie down in s.
Acts 5 : 23, prison shut with all s.

1 Thess. 5 : 3, shall say, peace and s.

Saffron [Heb. karkom] is the dried and pressed petal-like stigmas of the flower of the crocus (Crocus sativus). Several species of this genus abound in Palestine, and from several of these is the saffron collected. It is used for seasoning food, having to some an agreeable flavour. The word is only once found in the Old Testament in Song of Sol. 4 : 14.

Sail, Isa. 33 : 23; Luke 8 : 23; Acts 20 : 3, 16; 27 : 1, 2, 6, 9.

Sailors, Rev. 18 : 17.

Saints, their blessings and privileges, Deut. 33 : 2; Ps. 145 : 10; 148 : 14; 149; Dan. 7 : 18; Zech. 14 : 5; Rom. 8 : 27; Col. 1 : 12; Rev. 5 : 8.

their duty, 2 Chr. 6 : 41; Ps. 30 : 4; 34 : 9; 132 : 9; Rom. 16 : 2, 15; 1 Cor. 6 : 2; 2 Cor. 8 : 4; Eph. 4 : 12; 6 : 18; Phil. 4 : 22; Heb. 6 : 10; 13 : 24.

Deut. 33 : 3, and all his s. are in thy hand.

1 Sam. 2 : 9, keep the feet of his s.

Job 15 : 15, he putteth no trust in his s.

Ps. 16 : 3, to the s. that are in the earth.

31 : 23, love the Lord, all ye his s.

37 : 28, the Lord forsaketh not his s.

50 : 5, gather my s. together.

89 : 7, God is to be feared in the assembly of s.

97 : 10, he preserveth souls of his s.

116 : 15, precious is the death of his s.

Prov. 2 : 8, preserveth way of his s.

Matt. 27 : 52, many bodies of s. arose.

Acts 9 : 13, evil he hath done to thy s.

26 : 10, many of the s. did I shut up.

Rom. 1 : 7; 1 Cor. 1 : 2, called to be s.

Rom. 8 : 27, maketh intercession for the s.

12 : 13, distributing to the necessity of s.

1 Cor. 6 : 2, s. shall judge the world.

16 : 15, the ministry of s.

Eph. 1 : 18, his inheritance in the s.

4 : 12, perfecting of the s.

Col. 1 : 12, the s. in light.

1 Thess. 3 : 13, coming of our Lord with his s.

2 Thess. 1 : 10, to be glorified in his s.

Jude 3, faith once delivered to the s.

Rev. 8 : 3, the prayers of s.

It is interesting to note that the word "saint" which in Catholic tradition has been reserved for a few outstanding examples of Christian living, was in the Early Church the common word applied to all believers in Christ (cf. Rom. 1 : 7; 1 Cor. 1 : 2, called to be s.).

Sake, Gen. 3 : 17, cursed is the ground for thy s.

Gen. 8 : 21, not curse the ground any more for man's s.

18 : 26, spare the place for their s.

Num. 11 : 29, enviest thou for my s. ?

2 Sam. 9 : 1, kindness for Jonathan's s.

18 : 5, deal gently for my s.

Neh. 9 : 31, for thy great mercies' s.

Ps. 6 : 4; 31 : 16, save me for thy mercies' s.

23 : 3, for his name's s.

44 : 22; Rom. 8 : 36, for thy s. are we killed.

143 : 11, quicken me for thy name's s.

Matt. 10 : 39; 16 : 25; Mark 8 : 35; Luke 9 : 24, he that loseth his life for my s.

Matt. 24 : 9; Mark 13 : 13; Luke 21 : 17, hated for my name's s.

Luke 6 : 22, cast out for Son of man's s.

John 11 : 15, I am glad for your s.

13 : 38, wilt thou lay down thy life for my s. ?

14 : 11, believe me for work's s.

Acts 26 : 7, for which hope's s. am accused.

1 Cor. 4 : 10, we are fools for Christ's s.

2 Cor. 4 : 5, your servants for Jesus' s.

Col. 1 : 24, for his body's s., which is the church.

1 Thess. 5 : 13, esteem them for their work's s.

2 Tim. 2 : 10, for the elect's s.

2 John 2, for the truth's s.

Sala, or Salah (sā-läh) [sprout], Gen. 10 : 24; Luke 3 : 35.

Salamis (săl-ă-mĭs), a city on the coast of Cyprus, Acts 13 : 5.

Salathiel (să-lā-thĭ-ĕl), 1 Chr. 3 : 17; Matt. 1 : 12.

Salcah, or Salchah (săl-chăh) [wandering], city of Bashan, Deut. 3 : 10; Josh. 12 : 5; 1 Chr. 5 : 11.

Salem (sā-lĕm) [peace], supposed to be the original name of Jerusalem, Gen. 14 : 18; Ps. 76 : 2; Heb. 7 : 1, 2.

Salim (sā-lĭm) [peaceful], John 3 : 23.

Sallai (săl-lā-ī) [basket-maker], Neh. 11 : 8; 12 : 20.

Sallu (săl-lû) [weighed], 1 Chr. 9 : 7; Neh. 12 : 7.

Salma, Salmah (săl-mă), or **Salmon** (săl-mŏn) [clad], Ruth 4 : 20, 21; 1 Chr. 2 : 11; Luke 3 : 32.

Salmone (săl-mō-nē), the eastern point of Crete, Acts 27 : 7.

Salome (să-lō-mē), Mark 15 : 40; 16 : 1.

Salt abounds under various conditions in Palestine, the Dead Sea being only one important source. Its essential usefulness to man has caused it to be frequently referred to in the Bible, both literally and figuratively, Gen. 19 : 26; Lev. 2 : 13; Matt. 5 : 13; Mark 9 : 49; Luke 14 : 34.

Lot's wife becomes a pillar of, Gen. 19 : 26.

of the earth, Matt. 5 : 13; Luke 14 : 34; (Col. 4 : 6).

Sea (Siddim), Gen. 14 : 3; Num. 34 : 3, 12; Deut. 3 : 17; Josh. 3 : 16; 12 : 3; 15 : 2.

Salutations. Oriental courtesies at meeting and parting are wont to be ceremonious. Spoken salutations among the Hebrew people were such as "The Lord bless thee" (Ruth 2 : 4); "We bless you in the name of the Lord" (Ps. 129 : 8). From the general use of the word "bless" in greetings, that term came to signify "salute," and is sometimes translated "salute" (1 Sam. 13 : 10). Parting salutations were mostly a benedictory prayer, such as, "Go in peace" (1 Sam. 1 : 17). This form was in use in the time of Christ (Mark 5 : 34). The salutation to be used by the disciples on entering a house was " Peace be to this house " (Luke 10 : 5). When the risen Lord met the disciples His salutation was " Peace be unto you " (John 20 : 19). The Eastern salaam (from the Arabic salam = peace, safety) consists in bowing very low with the open palm of the right hand placed on the forehead. In courtesies more deferential and cordial the hand is placed on the lips and on the heart also.

Salute, Matt. 5 : 47, if ye s. your brethren only.
10 : 12, when ye come into an house, s. it.
Mark 15 : 18, began to s. him.
Luke 10 : 4, s. no man by the way.
2 Cor. 13 : 13; Phil. 4 : 22, saints s. you.
Phil. 4 : 21, s. every saint in Christ Jesus.
See Mark 12 : 38; Luke 1 : 29; 1 Cor. 16 : 21.

Salvation, Gen. 49 : 18, I have waited for thy s.
Ex. 14 : 13; 2 Chr. 20 : 17, see the s. of the Lord.
Ex. 15 : 2, the Lord is become my s.
Deut. 32 : 15, lightly esteemed the Rock of his s.
1 Sam. 11 : 13; 19 : 5, Lord wrought s. in Israel.
2 Sam. 22 : 51, he is tower of s. for his king.
1 Chr. 16 : 23, show forth from day to day his s.
2 Chr. 6 : 41, let thy priests be clothed with s.
Ps. 3 : 8, s. belongeth to the Lord.
13 : 5, my heart shall rejoice in thy s.
25 : 5, the God of my s.
27 : 1; 62 : 6; Isa. 12 : 2, the Lord is my s.
Ps. 37 : 39, the s. of righteous is of the Lord.
50 : 23, to him will I show the s. of God.
51 : 12; 70 : 4, restore the joy of thy s.
68 : 20, he that is our God, is the God of s.
71 : 15, my mouth shall show forth thy s.
74 : 12, working s. in the midst of the earth.
78 : 22, they trusted not in his s.
85 : 9, his s. is nigh them that fear him.
91 : 16, will show him my s.
95 : 1, Rock of our s.
96 : 2, show forth his s. from day to day.
98 : 3, all ends of earth have seen the s. of God.
116 : 13, the cup of s.
118 : 14; Isa. 12 : 2, the Lord is become my s.
Ps. 119 : 155, s. is far from wicked.
144 : 10, that giveth s. unto kings.
149 : 4, he will beautify the meek with s.
Isa. 12 : 3, the wells of s.
26 : 1, s. will God appoint for walls.
33 : 2, be thou our s. in time of trouble.
45 : 17, saved with an everlasting s.
49 : 8, in a day of s. have I helped thee.

52 : 7, feet of him that publisheth s.
52 : 10, ends of earth shall see the s. of God.
59 : 16, his arm brought s.
59 : 17, an helmet of s. on his head.
60 : 18, call thy walls S.
61 : 10, the garments of s.
Jer. 3 : 23, in vain is s. hoped for.
Lam. 3 : 26, wait for the s. of Lord.
Jonah 2 : 9, s. is of the Lord.
Hab. 3 : 8, ride on thy chariots of s.
3 : 18, I will joy in the God of my s.
Zech. 9 : 9, thy King, just, and having s.
Luke 1 : 69, raised an horn of s. for us.
2 : 30, mine eyes have seen thy s.
3 : 6, all flesh shall see the s. of God.
19 : 9, this day is s. come to this house.
John 4 : 22, s. is of the Jews.
Acts 4 : 12, neither is there s. in any other.
16 : 17, show the way of s.
Rom. 1 : 16, the power of God unto s.
10 : 10, confession is made to s.
13 : 11, now is our s. nearer.
2 Cor. 6 : 2, now is the day of s.
7 : 10, sorrow worketh repentance to s.
Eph. 1 : 13, the gospel of your s.
6 : 17 ; 1 Thess. 5 : 8, the helmet of s.
Phil. 2 : 12, work out your s. with fear.
2 Tim. 3 : 15, scriptures able to make wise to s.
Titus 2 : 11, grace of God that bringeth s.
Heb. 1 : 14, them who shall be heirs of s.
2 : 3, if we neglect so great s.
2 : 10, the captain of their s.
5 : 9, the author of eternal s.
9 : 28, appear without sin unto s.
1 Pet. 1 : 9, end of faith, the s. of your souls.
2 Pet. 3 : 15, longsuffering of the Lord is s.
Jude 3, the common s.
Rev. 7 : 10, saying, s. to our God.
12 : 10, now is come s. and strength.

Samaria (să-mâr-ĭ-ă) [Heb. Shomeron = watch-tower], capital of the Northern Kingdom of Israel. The capture of Samaria, which signified the end of the Northern Kingdom, took place in 722 B.C., after a siege of three years. 1 Ki. 16 : 24; 20 : 1; 2 Ki. 6 : 24.

Samaritan, parable of, Luke 10 : 33.
miracle performed on, Luke 17 : 16.

Samaritans. The Samaritans were a mixed race, composed of imported colonists and the Israelites who remained when the bulk of the Ten Tribes were carried into captivity. They had a temple to Jehovah on Mount Gerizim, their sacred mountain, they accepted Moses as their lawgiver and the Pentateuch as their law, but they rejected the traditions and rules of the Pharisees. They observed the rite of circumcision, the requirements of the Sabbath, and the yearly Jewish festivals, but denied the Jewish priesthood, and refused to accept Jerusalem as the one place where the temple of Jehovah should stand.

After the return from captivity there was considerable bitterness between the Jews and the Samaritans. To pious

Jews the term " Samaritan " was a term of reproach.

Same, Ps. 102 : 27; Heb. 1 : 12, thou art the s.

Acts 1 : 11, this s. Jesus shall come.

Rom. 10 : 12, the s. Lord over all.

Heb. 13 : 8, the s. yesterday, to-day, and for ever.

Samson, Greek form of Shimshon [sun man], which was retained in the Latin Vulgate, and so passed into common use.

his deeds, etc., Judg. 13 : 16.

delivered up to Philistines, Judg. 16 : 21.

his death, Judg. 16 : 30.

Samuel [name of God], born and presented to the Lord, 1 Sam. 1 : 19, 26.

ministers to the Lord, 1 Sam. 3.

the Lord speaks to, 1 Sam. 3 : 11.

judges Israel, 1 Sam. 7; 8 : 1; Acts 13 : 20.

anoints Saul king, 1 Sam. 10 : 1.

rebukes Saul for disobedience, 1 Sam. 13 : 13; 15 : 16.

anoints David, etc., 1 Sam. 16; 19 : 18.

his death, 1 Sam. 25 : 1; 28 : 3.

his spirit consulted by Saul, 1 Sam. 28 : 12.

as a prophet, Ps. 99 : 6; Acts 3 : 24; Heb. 11 : 32.

Samuel, Book of.

Name.—In Hebrew MSS. the two books of Samuel are regarded as one; but in the Greek and Latin versions they are entitled the First and Second Books of Kings. The English version accepted the division into two books, and gave to them the name of Samuel, who is the most important character in the opening portion.

Author and Date.—The book belongs to an early date, probably shortly after the separation of the kingdoms of Judah and Israel (cf. 1 Sam. 27 : 6). In its present form, however, the work appears to have undergone considerable modification. This seems clear from the additions, omissions, double narratives, and discrepancies that can be traced in it. In 1 Chr. 29 : 29, " the book of Samuel the seer " is mentioned; and in 1 Sam. 10 : 25 mention is made of a work by Samuel which contained at least the law of the kingdom. In all probability these early sources were employed by the compiler of the books of Samuel.

Contents.—The books relate the histories of Samuel, Saul, and David, and may be divided into three parts: (1) 1 Sam. 1-12, the history of Samuel until he retires from his position as judge—Eli's history being narrated so far as connected with that of Samuel; (2) 1 Sam. 13— 2 Sam. 1, the history of Saul from his accession until his death; (3) 2 Sam. 2-24, the reign of David.

Sanballat (săn-băl-lăt), derivation uncertain, Neh. 2 : 10; 4 : 1, 7.

Sanctification, by Christ, John 17 : 19; 1 Cor. 1 : 2, 30; Eph. 5 : 26; Heb. 10 : 10; Jude 1.

by the Spirit, 2 Thess. 2 : 13; 1 Pet. 1 : 2.

Sanctified, the seventh day, Gen. 2 : 3.

the firstborn to be, Ex. 13 : 2.

the people, Ex. 19 : 10; Num. 11 : 18; Josh. 3 : 5.

the tabernacle, etc., Ex. 29 : 30; Lev. 8 : 10.

the priests, Lev. 8 : 30; 9; 2 Chr. 5 : 11.

Sanctify, Ex. 31 : 13, the Lord that doth s. you.

Lev. 11 : 44; 20 : 7; Josh. 7 : 13; 1 Sam. 16 : 5, s. yourselves.

Isa. 8 : 13, s. the Lord of hosts.

29 : 23, they shall s. the Holy One.

66 : 17, that s. themselves in gardens.

Jer. 1 : 5, I s. and ordained thee a prophet.

Ezek. 36 : 23, I will s. my great name.

Joel 1 : 14; 2 : 15, s. ye a fast.

John 10 ; 36, him whom the Father hath s.

17 : 17, s. them through thy truth.

Acts 20 : 32; 26 : 18, inheritance among them which are s.

Rom. 15 : 16, being s. by the Holy Ghost.

1 Cor. 6 : 11, but ye are s.

7 : 14, unbelieving husband is s. by the wife.

1 Thess. 5 : 23, the very God of peace s. you.

1 Tim. 4 : 5, it is s. by the word of God.

2 Tim. 2 : 21, a vessel is s. for the Master's use.

Heb. 2 : 11, he that s. and they who are s.

10 : 14, he perfected for ever them that are s.

13 : 12, that he might s. the people.

1 Pet. 3 : 15, s. the Lord God in your hearts.

Sanctuary, God, of his people, Isa. 8 : 14; Ezek. 11 : 16.

Ex. 15 : 17, plant them in the s.

25 : 8, let them make me a s.

Ps. 63 : 2, as I have seen thee in the s.

73 : 17, till I went into the s. of God.

Isa. 60 : 13, beautify the place of my s.

Heb. 9 : 1, first covenant had a worldly s.

See Ps. 20 : 2; 68 : 24; 77 : 13; 78 : 54; 96 : 6; 134; 150; Heb. 8 : 9.

Sand, Gen. 22 : 17; 32 : 12, multiply as the s.

Ps. 139 : 18, more in number than s.

Prov. 27 : 3, stone is heavy, s. weighty.

Matt. 7 : 26, man built his house on the s.

Rev. 20 : 8, number of whom is as the s.

See Hos. 1 : 10; Heb. 11 : 12.

Sandal. See Shoes.

Sang, 2 Chr. 29 : 28, 30; Ezra 3 : 11; Job 38 : 7; Acts 16 : 25.

Sanhedrin, The. The Sanhedrin, or Jewish Council, was an assembly of seventy persons, recruited principally from the ranks of the ruling oligarchy. Its action was authoritative in both the religious and the secular sphere; and it was presided over by the high priest. During the Roman period in Jewish history, however, its power was weakened, and in such cases as capital charges, it had to submit its decisions for the approval of the Roman procurator. The authority of the Sanhedrin was not confined to

Palestine, but extended to Jewish communities in other countries.

Sap, Ps. 104 : 16.

Sapphira (săpph-ĭ-răͅ) [beautiful], Acts 5 : 1.

Sapphire. The true sapphire does not appear to have been known in Old Testament times, but it is referred to in the New Testament as " jacinth." Ex. 24 : 10; 28 : 18; Ezek. 1 : 26; 10 : 1; 28 : 13; Rev. 21 : 19.

Sarah [princess], Gen. 17 : 15; Heb. 11 : 11; 1 Pet. 3 : 6. See **Abraham**.

Sarai [probably " contention "], Gen. 11 : 29.

Sardine, a precious stone, Rev. 4 : 3.

Sardis, church of, Rev. 1 : 11; 3 : 1. Sardis was the ancient capital of Lydia, and one of the seats of the Early Church.

Sardius, Ex. 28 : 17; 39 : 10; Ezek. 28 : 13; Rev. 21 : 20. The sard may be described as a variety of what we call carnelian, but it is of a deeper and somewhat brownish tinge. It has been extensively used, since early times, for signets and intaglios. The name is derived from Sardis in Lydia, one of the numerous localities where it is obtained.

Sardonyx, Rev. 21 : 20. Sardonyx is an onyx with the addition of a third layer of sard. There is no reference to it in the Old Testament.

Sarepta (să-rĕp-tă), Luke 4 : 26. See **Zarephath**.

Sargon (sär-gŏn) [Assyrian " sarrukin," he established the king], Isa. 20 : 1.

Sat, Ps. 26 : 4, I have not s. with vain persons.
Matt. 4 : 16, the people who s. in darkness.
Mark 16 : 19, he s. on the right hand of God.
Luke 7 : 15, he that was dead s. up.
10 : 39, Mary s. at Jesus' feet.
19 : 30, a colt whereon never man s.
John 4 : 6, Jesus s. on the well.
Acts 3 : 10, s. for alms at gate of the temple.

Satan [adversary], 1 Chr. 21 : 1, S. provoked David.
Job 1 : 12, S. went from presence of the Lord.
Ps. 109 : 6, let S. stand at his right hand.
Matt. 12 : 26; Mark 3 : 23; Luke 11 : 18, if S. cast out S.
Matt. 16 : 23; Mark 8 : 33; Luke 4 : 8, get thee behind me, S.
Luke 10 : 18, I beheld S. as lightning fall.
Acts 5 : 3, why hath S. filled thine heart ?
26 : 18, turn them from the power of S.
Rom. 16 : 20, God shall bruise S. under feet.
2 Cor. 2 : 11, lest S. get advantage of us.
12 : 7, messenger of S. to buffet me.
2 Thess. 2 : 9, after the working of S.
1 Tim. 1 : 20, whom I have delivered unto S.
1 Tim. 5 : 15, some have turned aside after S.
Rev. 2 : 13, seat where S. dwelleth.

Satiate, Jer. 31 : 14, s. soul of priests with fatness.
46 : 10, sword shall be s. with blood.

Satisfy, Job 38 : 27, to s. the desolate ground.

Ps. 17 : 15, I shall be s. with thy likeness.
22 : 26, the meek shall eat and be s.
37 : 19, in days of famine be s.
63 : 5, my soul shall be s.
90 : 14, O s. us early with thy mercy.
91 : 16, with long life will I s. him.
103 : 5, who s. thy mouth with good things.
105 : 40, he s. them with bread from heaven.
107 : 9, he s. the longing soul.
132 : 15, I will s. her poor with bread.
145 : 16, thou s. every living thing.
Prov. 6 : 30, if he steal to s. his soul.
12 : 11, he that tilleth his land shall be s.
14 : 14, a good man shall be s. from himself.
20 : 13, open thine eyes, and thou shalt be s.
30 : 15, three things are never s.
Eccl. 1 : 8, the eye is not s. with seeing.
5 : 10, shall not be s. with silver.
Isa. 9 : 20; Mic. 6 : 14, shall eat, and not be s.
53 : 11, see of travail of his soul and be s.
58 : 11, the Lord shall s. thy soul.
Jer. 31 : 14, people be s. with my goodness.
Hab. 2 : 5, he is as death, and cannot be s.
Mark 8 : 4, whence s. these with bread ?

Satyr, thought to be the dog-faced baboon (Cynocephalus), which was worshipped by the Egyptians, Isa. 13 : 21; 34 : 14.

Saul [asked for], king of Israel, his parentage, anointing by Samuel, prophesying, and acknowledgement as king, 1 Sam. 9 : 10.
his disobedience and rejection by God, 1 Sam. 15.
troubled by an evil spirit, 1 Sam. 16 : 14.
favours David, 1 Sam. 18 : 5; seeks to kill him, 1 Sam. 18 : 10; pursues him, 1 Sam. 20 : 23; 24 ; 26.
slays the priests at Nob, 1 Sam. 22 : 18, 19.
inquires of the witch at Endor, 1 Sam. 28 : 7.
his ruin foretold, 1 Sam. 28 : 15 ff.
his death, 1 Sam. 31; 1 Chr. 10.
his descendants, 1 Chr. 8 : 33.
of Tarsus. See **Paul**.

Save, Gen. 45 : 7, to s. your lives.
Deut. 20 : 4, the Lord goeth to s. you.
Judg. 6 : 15, wherewith shall I s. Israel ?
1 Sam. 14 : 6, no restraint to s. by many or by few.
Job 2 : 6, he is in thine hand, but s. his life.
22 : 29, he shall s. the humble.
Ps. 7 : 10, God, who s. the upright.
34 : 18, he s. such as he of contrite spirit.
44 : 3, neither did their own arms s. them.
60 : 5, s. with thy right hand.
69 : 35, God will s. Zion.
72 : 4, he shall s. the children of the needy.
86 : 2, s. thy servant.
109 : 31, to s. him from those that condemn.
118 : 25, s. now, I beseech thee.
138 : 7, thy right hand shall s. me.
145 : 19, hear their cry, and s. them.
Prov. 20 : 22, wait on the Lord, and he shall s. thee.

Isa. 35 : 4, your God, will come and s. you.
45 : 20, pray unto a God that cannot s.
45 : 22, look unto me, and be ye s.
59 : 1, Lord's hand is not shortened, that it cannot s.
63 : 1, mighty to s.
Jer. 2 : 28, let them arise, if they can s. thee.
8 : 20, summer is ended, and we are not s.
15 : 20; 30 : 11; 42 : 11, I am with thee to s. thee.
17 : 14, s. me and I shall be s.
Hos. 1 : 7, I will s. them by the Lord.
13 : 10, is there any other that may s. thee ?
Hab. 1 : 2, cry unto thee, and thou wilt not s.
Zeph. 3 : 17, he will s.
Matt. 1 : 21, s. his people from their sins.
16 : 25; Mark 8 : 35; Luke 9 : 24, whosoever will s. his life.
Matt. 18 : 11; Luke 19 : 10, to seek and to s. that which was lost.
Matt. 19 : 25; Mark 10 : 26; Luke 18 : 26, who then can be s. ?
Matt. 27 : 42; Mark 15 : 31, he s. others, himself he cannot s.
Mark 3 : 4; Luke 6 : 9, is it lawful to s. life ?
Luke 9 : 56, not to destroy but to s.
23 : 35, let him s. himself.
John 5 : 34, these things I say that ye might be s.
12 : 47, I came not to judge, but to s.
Acts 2 : 40, s. yourselves from this generation.
4 : 12, none other name whereby we must be s.
16 : 30, what must I do to be s.?
Rom. 8 : 24, we are s. by hope.
11 : 14; 1 Cor. 9 : 22, if I might s. some.
1 Cor. 1 : 21, by foolishness of preaching to s. some.
3 : 15, s. as by fire.
1 Tim. 1 : 15, Christ came to s. sinners.
4 : 16, thou shalt s. thyself and them.
Heb. 5 : 7, able to s. him from death.
7 : 25, able to s. to the uttermost.
Jas. 1 : 21, word which is able to s. your souls.
2 : 14, can faith s. him ?
4 : 12, able to s. and destroy.
5 : 15, prayer of faith shall s. the sick.
5 : 20, shall s. a soul from death.
1 Pet. 4 : 18, if the righteous scarcely be s.
Jude 23, others s. with fear.
Saving, Heb. 11 : 7, an ark to the s. of his house.
Saviour, God, Isa. 43 : 3; Jer. 14 : 8; Hos. 13 : 4; Luke 1 : 47.
Christ, Luke 2 : 11; Acts 5 : 31; 13 : 23; 2 Pet. 1 : 1; 3 : 2; 1 John 4 : 14.
2 Sam. 22 : 3, my refuge, my s.
2 Ki. 13 : 5, the Lord gave Israel a s.
Ps. 106 : 21, they forgat God their S.
Isa. 19 : 20, he shall send them a s.
43 : 11, I am the Lord, beside me there is no s.
45 : 15, hidest thyself, O God, the S.

45 : 21, a just God and a S.
60 : 16, shalt know I am thy S.
63 : 8, so he was their S.
John 4 : 42, this is Christ, the S. of the world.
Acts 13 : 23, God raised unto Israel a S.
Eph. 5 : 23, Christ is the s. of the body.
Phil. 3 : 20, whence we look for the S.
1 Tim. 4 : 10, God, who is the S. of all men.
Titus 2 : 10, adorn doctrine of God our S.
2 Pet. 2 : 20, knowledge of the Lord and S.
Jude 25, the only wise God our S.
See Christ.
Savour, a sweet (of the sacrifices), Gen. 8 : 21; Ex. 29 : 18.
type of Christ, 2 Cor. 2 : 14.
Ex. 5 : 21, made our s. to be abhorred.
Song of Sol. 1 : 3, s. of thy good ointments.
Matt. 5 : 13; Luke 14 : 34, if the salt have lost his s. ?
2 Cor. 2 : 16, s. of life unto life.
Eph. 5 : 2, a sacrifice to God for a sweet-smelling s.
See Gen. 27 : 4; Matt. 16 : 23; Mark 8 : 33.
Saw, Gen. 26 : 28, we s. the Lord was with thee.
Ex. 24 : 10, they s. the God of Israel.
2 Chr. 15 : 9, s. the Lord was with him.
25 : 21, they s. one another in the face.
Job 29 : 11, when the eye s. me, it gave witness.
Ps. 77 : 16, the waters s. thee.
114 : 3, sea s. it and fled.
Eccl. 2 : 24, this I s., that it was from the hand of God.
Song of Sol. 3 : 3, s. ye him whom my soul loveth ?
Matt. 17 : 8, they s. no man.
Mark 8 : 23, asked if he s. ought.
Luke 24 : 24, but him they s. not.
John 1 : 48, under fig tree I s. thee.
8 : 56, Abraham s. my day.
19 : 35, he that s. it bare record.
Say, Gen. 44 : 16, what shall we s. unto my lord ?
Ex. 3 : 13, what shall I s. to them ?
Num. 22 : 19, know what the Lord will s.
Ezra 9 : 10, what shall we s.?
Job 9 : 12; Eccl. 8 : 4, who will s. unto him, What doest thou ?
Matt. 3 : 9; Luke 3 : 8, think not to s. within yourselves.
7 : 22, many will s. in that day.
16 : 15; Mark 8 : 29; Luke 9 : 20, whom s. ye that I am ?
Matt. 23 : 3, they s., and do not.
Luke 7 : 40, have somewhat to s. to thee.
John 8 : 54, of whom ye s. that he is your God.
Heb. 11 : 32, what shall I more s. ?
Jas. 4 : 15, ye ought to s., If the Lord will.
Saying, Deut. 1 : 23, the s. pleased me well.
1 Ki. 2 : 38, the s. is good.
Ps. 49 : 4, my dark s. upon the harp.
78 : 2, utter dark s. of old.
Jonah 4 : 2, was not this my s. ?
Matt. 19 : 11, all men cannot receive this s.
28 : 15, this s. is commonly reported.

Luke 9 : 44, let these s. sink into your ears.
John 4 : 37, herein is that s. true.
  6 : 60, an hard s.
1 Cor. 15 : 54, he brought to pass the s.
1 Tim. 1 : 15, this is a faithful s.
Scab, Lev. 13 : 2; Deut. 28 : 27; Isa. 3 : 17.
Scabbard, Jer. 47 : 6.
Scaffold, 2 Chr. 6 : 13.
Scales, Lev. 11 : 10; Isa. 40 : 12; Acts 9 : 18.
Scall, Lev. 13 : 30; 14 : 54.
Scalp, Ps. 68 : 21.
Scant, Mic. 6 : 10.
Scapegoat, Lev. 16 : 20, 21; (Isa. 53 : 6).
Scarcely, Rom. 5 : 7, s. for righteous man will one die.
1 Pet. 4 : 18, if righteous s. be saved.
See Gen. 27 : 30; Deut. 8 : 9; Acts 14 : 18.
Scarest, Job 7 : 14.
Scarlet, Song of Sol. 4 : 3, like a thread of s.
  Isa. 1 : 18, sins be as s.
  Matt. 27 : 28, put on him a s. robe.
Scatter, Gen. 11 : 9, thence did the Lord s. them.
Lev. 26 : 33, I will s. you among the heathen.
Num. 10 : 35; Ps. 68 : 1, let thine enemies be s.
Job 37 : 11, he s. his bright cloud.
  38 : 24, which s. the east wind.
Ps. 68 : 30, s. the people that delight in war.
  92 : 9, workers of iniquity shall be s.
  106 : 27, lifted up hand to s. them.
  147 : 16, he s. the hoar frost.
Prov. 11 : 24, there is that s., and yet increaseth.
Jer. 23 : 1, woe to pastors that s. the sheep.
Zech. 13 : 7; Matt. 26 : 31; Mark 14 : 27, sheep shall be s.
Matt. 9 : 36, s. as sheep having no shepherd.
  12 : 30; Luke 11 : 23, he that gathereth not, s.
John 10 : 12, wolf s. the sheep.
Scent, Job 14 : 9; Hos. 14 : 7.
Sceptre, Gen. 49 : 10, the s. shall not depart from Judah.
Esther 4 : 11, hold out the golden s.
Ps. 45 : 6, s. of thy kingdom is a right s.
Sceva (scḗ-vă), derivation doubtful, Acts 19 : 14.
Schism, condemned, 1 Cor. 1; 3; 11 : 18; 12 : 25.
Scholar, 1 Chr. 25 : 8, the teacher as the s.
Mal. 2 : 12, Lord will cut off master and s.
School, Acts 19 : 9.
Schoolmaster, Gal. 3 : 24, 25.
Science, Dan. 1 : 4, understanding s.
1 Tim. 6 : 20, avoiding oppositions of s.
Scoff, Hab. 1 : 10, they shall s. at the kings.
2 Pet. 3 : 3, in the last days s.
Scorch, Matt. 13 : 6; Rev. 16 : 8, 9.
Scorner, Prov. 9 : 8, reprove not a s. lest he hate thee.
Prov. 13 : 1, a s. heareth not rebuke.
  15 : 12, a s. loveth not one that reproveth.
  19 : 25, smite a s.
  21 : 11, when s. is punished, the simple is made wise.

  24 : 9, the s. is abomination to men.
Isa. 29 : 20, the s. is consumed.
Hos. 7 : 5, he stretched his hand with s.
See Prov. 1 : 22; 3 : 34; 14 : 6; 21 : 24; Isa. 28 : 14.
Scornful, Ps. 1 : 1; Prov. 29 : 8.
Scorpions [Heb. akrabbim]. Several species of these venomous creatures are to be found in Palestine, some quite small and others nearly half a foot in length.

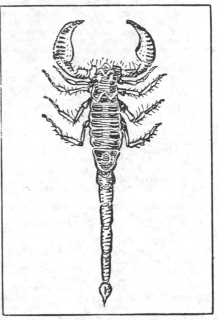

Scorpion.

Their claws are graspers of food, but the last joint of their bodies is slender and furnished with a sting, supplied by a poison gland. The sting inflicts the wound and the poison irritates it. Rehoboam threatened to lacerate and irritate the backs of his people by using scorpions instead of whips (1 Ki. 12 : 11 and 2 Chr. 10 : 14). Scorpions are common in desolate places, as mentioned in Deut. 8 : 15.
See Luke 11 : 12; Rev. 9 : 3, 5.
Scourge, Job 5 : 21, s. of the tongue.
Job 9 : 23, if the s. slay suddenly.
Isa. 10 : 26, the Lord shall stir up a s.
  28 : 15, the overflowing s.
John 2 : 15, a s. of small cords.
Matt. 20 : 19; Mark 10 : 34; Luke 18 : 33, shall s. him.
Acts 22 : 25, is it lawful to s. a Roman ?
Heb. 12 : 6, the Lord s. every son whom he receiveth.

Scourging, Lev. 19 : 20; Deut. 25 : 3; 2 Cor. 11 : 24. Scourging was a common practice in Roman times; and often, as in the case of our Lord, it preceded death by crucifixion.

of Christ, Matt. 27 : 26; Luke 23 : 16.

Scrabbled [ar.], scrawled, 1 Sam. 21 : 13.

Scrape, Lev. 14 : 41, 43.

Screech, Isa. 34 : 14.

Scribes. The primary work of the scribes was to study and interpret the Mosaic Law and the growing body of traditional law, and to promote among the people a spirit of reverence for them. They sought to interpret the law in terms of the every-day life of the people. In this work they became closely associated with the Pharisees.

the body of Jewish teachers of the law, 2 Sam. 8 : 17; 20 : 25; 1 Ki. 4 : 3; 2 Ki. 19 : 2; 22 : 8; Ezra 7 : 6; Jer. 36 : 26.

and Pharisees, censured by Christ, Matt. 15 : 1 ff.; 23 : 2; Mark 2 : 16; 3 : 22; Luke 11 : 53; 20 : 1.

conspire against Christ, Mark 11 : 18; Luke 20 : 19; 22 : 2; 23 : 10.

persecute Stephen, Acts 6 : 12.

1 Chr. 27 : 32, wise man and a s.

Isa. 33 : 18, where is the s. ?

Jer. 8 : 8, pen of the s. is in vain.

Matt. 5 : 20, exceed the righteousness of the s.

13 : 52, every s. instructed unto the king-dom.

Mark 12 : 38; Luke 20 : 46, beware of the s.

1 Cor. 1 : 20, where is the s. ?

Scrip, small bag or wallet, 1 Sam. 17 : 40, David put stones in s.

Matt. 10 : 10; Mark 6 : 8; Luke 9 : 3; 10 : 4, nor s. for your journey.

Luke 22 : 36, let him take his purse and s.

Scriptures, the Holy, given by inspiration of God through the Holy Ghost, Acts 1 : 16; Heb. 3 : 7; 2 Pet. 1 : 21.

to be kept unaltered, Deut. 4 : 2; Prov. 30 : 6; Rev. 22 : 18.

profitable for doctrine, instruction, etc., Ps. 19 : 7; 119 : 11; John 17 : 17; Acts 20 : 32; Rom. 15 : 4; 16 : 26.

referred to and expounded by Christ, Matt. 4 : 4; Luke 24 : 27; John 7 : 42.

testify of Christ, John 5 : 39; Acts 10 : 43; 18 : 28; 1 Cor. 15 : 3.

make wise unto salvation, John 20 : 31; Rom. 1 : 2; 2 Tim. 3 : 15; Jas. 1 : 21; 2 Pet. 1 : 19.

formerly given by God through the prophets, Luke 16 : 31; Rom. 3 : 2; 9 : 4; Heb. 1 : 1; in the last days through Jesus Christ, Heb. 1 : 2.

fulfilled by Christ, Matt. 5 : 17; John 19 : 24; Acts .13 : 29.

appealed to by the Apostles, Acts 2; 3; 17 : 2; 18 : 24; 28 : 23.

danger of rejecting, John 12 : 48; Heb. 2 : 3; 10 : 28; 12 : 25.

Dan. 10 : 21, what is noted in s.

Mark 12 : 10, have ye not read this s. ?

Acts 8 : 32, the place of the s. which he read.

2 Tim. 3 : 16, all s. is given by inspiration of God.

Jas. 4 : 5, do ye think that the s. saith in vain ?

1 Pet. 2 : 6, contained in the s.

2 Pet. 1 : 20, no prophecy of s. of private interpretation.

Scroll, Isa. 34 : 4; Rev. 6 : 14.

Scythian, inhabitant of Scythia, used as a type of the greatest barbarians, Col. 3 : 11.

Sea, God's power over, Ex. 14 : 16; 15; Neh. 9 : 11; Job 38 : 11; Ps. 65 : 7; 66 : 6; 89 : 9; 93 : 4; 107 : 23; 114 : 3, 5; Prov. 8 : 29; Isa. 51 : 10; Nah. 1 : 4.

calmed by Christ, Matt. 8 : 26; Mark 4 : 39.

the molten, 1 Ki. 7 : 23; 2 Chr. 4 : 2.

of glass, Rev. 4 : 6; 15 : 2.

no more, Rev. 21 : 1.

Seafaring, Ezek. 26 : 17.

Seah, a measure. See **Measures.**

Sealed, believers, 2 Cor. 1 : 22; Eph. 1 : 13; 4 : 30; Rev. 7.

book opened, Rev. 5 : 9.

utterances of the seven thunders, Rev. 10 : 4.

Seam, John 19 : 23.

Search, Num. 13 : 2, that they may s. the land.

1 Chr. 28 : 9, the Lord s. all hearts.

Job 13 : 9, is it good that he should s. you out ?

36 : 26, neither can the number of years be s. out.

Ps. 44 : 21, shall not God s. this out ?

139 : 23, s. me, O God.

Prov. 25 : 2, honour of kings to s. a matter.

Eccl. 1 : 13; 7 : 25, I gave my heart to s. wisdom.

Jer. 17 : 10, I the Lord s. the heart.

29 : 13, when ye s. for me with all your heart.

Lam. 3 : 40, let us s. our ways.

Ezek. 34 : 11, I will s. my sheep.

Zeph. 1 : 12, I will s. Jerusalem with candles.

John 5 : 39; Acts 17 : 11, s. the scriptures.

Rom. 8 : 27, he that s. hearts knoweth mind of the Spirit.

1 Cor. 2 : 10, the Spirit s. all things.

1 Pet. 1 : 10, prophets s. diligently.

Rev. 2 : 23, he which s. the reins.

See Ps. 64 : 6; 77 : 6; Jer. 2 : 34.

Searching, Job 11 : 7, canst thou by s. find out God ?

Isa. 40 : 28, there is no s. of his under-standing.

Seared, 1 Tim. 4 : 2.

Seasons, continuance of, promised, Gen. 8 : 22.

Gen. 1 : 14, for signs, and for s.

Deut. 28 : 12, give rain in his s.

Josh. 24 : 7, dwelt in wilderness a long s.

2 Chr. 15 : 3, for a long s. without the true God.

Job 5 : 26, as a shock of corn in his s.

Ps. 1 : 3, bringeth forth fruit in his **s.**
22 : 2, I cry in the night **s.**
Prov. 15 : 23, a word spoken in due **s.**
Eccl. 3 : 1, to every thing there is a **s.**
Isa. 50 : 4, know how to speak a word in **s.**
Jer. 5 : 24, former and latter rain in his **s.**
33 : 20, day and night in their **s.**
Dan. 2 : 21, changeth the times and **s.**
7 : 12, lives prolonged for a **s.**
Matt. 21 : 41, render fruits in their **s.**
Luke 13 : 1, were present at that **s.**
23 : 8, desirous to see Jesus of a long **s.**
John 5 : 4, angel went down at a certain **s.**
5 : 35, willing for a **s.** to rejoice.
Acts 1 : 7, not for you to know times or **s.**
13 : 11, not seeing the sun for a **s.**
24 : 25, a convenient **s.**
2 Tim. 4 : 2, be instant in **s.**, out of **s.**
Heb. 11 : 25, pleasures of sin for a **s.**
1 Pet. 1 : 6, though now for a **s.**
See Mark 9 : 50; Luke 14 : 34; Col. 4 : 6.
Seat, Job 23 : 3, that I might come even to his **s.**
Matt. 21 : 12; Mark 11 : 15, the **s.** of them that sold doves.
Matt. 23 : 6; Mark 12 : 39; chief **s.** in the synagogues.
Rev. 2 : 13, dwellest, even where Satan's **s.** is.
Sebat (sē-băt) or **Shebat** (shē-băt) [Assyrian "sabatu"], the month of February-March, Zech. 1 : 7. See **Months.**
Second coming, Christ's, Acts 1 : 11.
death, Rev. 20 : 14.
Secret, things, belong to God, Deut. 29 : 29; Job 15 : 8.
revealed by him, Amos 3 : 7; Matt. 11 : 25; 13 : 35; Rom. 16 : 25; 2 Cor. 3 : 14.
all known to him, Ps. 44 : 21, 90 . 8, Eccl. 12 : 14; Mark 4 : 22; Rom. 2 : 16.
secrets not to be revealed, Prov. 25 : 9; Matt. 18 : 15.
Gen. 49 : 6, come not into their **s.**
Job 29 : 4, the **s.** of God was upon my tabernacle.
Ps. 25 : 14, the **s.** of the Lord is with them that fear him.
27 : 5, in **s.** of his tabernacle hide me.
64 : 4, may shoot in **s.** at the perfect.
139 : 15, when I was made in **s.**
Prov. 3 : 32, his **s.** is with the righteous.
9 : 17, bread eaten in **s.**
21 : 14, a gift in **s.** pacifieth anger.
Isa. 45 : 19; 48 : 16, I have not spoken in **s.**
Matt. 6 : 4, thy Father who seeth in **s.**
John 18 : 20, in **s.** have I said nothing.
Judg. 3 : 19, I have a **s.** errand.
13 : 18, why askest my name, seeing it is **s.** ?
Ps. 19 : 12, cleanse thou me from **s.** faults.
90 : 8, **s.** sins in light of thy countenance.
91 : 1, **s.** place of the Most High.
Prov. 27 : 5, open rebuke better than **s.** love.
Matt. 24 : 26, he is in the **s.** chambers.
Luke 11 : 33, no man putteth candle in a **s.** place.
Secretly, Gen. 31 : 27, wherefore didst thou flee **s.** ?
1 Sam. 23 : 9, Saul **s.** practised mischief.

2 Sam. 12 : 12, thou didst it **s.**
Job 4 : 12, a thing was **s.** brought to me.
31 : 27, my heart hath been **s.** enticed.
Ps. 10 : 9, he lieth in wait **s.** as a lion.
31 : 20, keep them **s.** in a pavilion.
John 11 : 28, she called her sister **s.**
19 : 38, a disciple, but **s.** for fear of the Jews.
Sect, Acts 5 : 17, **s.** of Sadducees.
15 : 5, **s.** of Pharisees.
24 : 5, the **s.** of the Nazarenes.
26 : 5, the straitest **s.** of our religion.
Secure, Job 12 : 6, they that provoke God are **s.**
Prov. 3 : 29, seeing he dwelleth **s.**
Matt. 28 : 14, persuade him, and **s.** you.
Security, Acts 17 : 9, they had taken **s.**
Sedition, Luke 23 : 19; Acts 24 : 5; Gal. 5 : 20.
Seduce, Ezek. 13 : 10; Mark 13 : 22; 2 Tim. 3 : 13.
See, Gen. 11 : 5, Lord came down to **s.** the city.
Gen. 44 : 23, you shall **s.** my face no more.
Ex. 12 : 13, when I **s.** the blood.
33 : 20, there shall no man **s.** me and live.
Num. 24 : 17, I shall **s.** him, but not now.
Deut. 3 : 25, let me **s.** the good land.
2 Ki. 6 : 17, open his eyes, that he may **s.**
Job 7 : 7, mine eye shall no more **s.** good.
19 : 26, in my flesh shall I **s.** God.
Ps. 14 : 2; 53 : 2, God looked to **s.** if any did understand.
34 : 8, O taste and **s.** that the Lord is good.
40 : 3, many shall **s.** it, and trust in the Lord.
66 : 5, come and **s.** the works of God.
94 : 9, he that formed the eye, shall he not **s.** ?
Isa. 6 : 10, lest they **s.** with their eyes.
30 : 20, thine eyes shall **s.** thy teachers.
32 : 3, the eyes of them that **s.** shall not be dim.
33 : 17, thine eyes shall **s.** the King in his beauty.
52 : 8, they shall **s.** eye to eye.
53 : 2, when we shall **s.** him.
Matt. 5 : 8, pure in heart shall **s.** God.
11 : 4, show John the things ye **s.** and hear.
12 : 38, we would **s.** a sign.
13 : 14; Mark 4 : 12; Acts 28 : 26, **s.** ye shall **s.**
Matt. 27 : 4, **s.** thou to that.
28 : 6, come **s.** the place where the Lord lay.
Mark 8 : 18, having eyes, **s.** yet not ?
Luke 17 : 22, desire to **s.**, and ye shall not **s.**
John 1 : 39; 11 : 34; Rev. 6 : 1, come and **s.**
John 3 : 36, he shall not **s.** life.
9 : 25, I was blind, now I **s.**
9 : 39, that they who **s.** not, might **s.**
1 Cor. 13 : 12, we **s.** through a glass.
Heb. 2 : 8, we **s.** not yet all things put under him.
1 Pet. 1 : 8, though now ye **s.** him not.
1 John 3 : 2, we shall **s.** him as he is.

Rev. 1 : 7, every eye shall s. him.

Seed, of the woman, Gen. 3 : 15 ; Rev. 12.
  parables about, Matt. 13; Luke 8 : 5.
  Ex. 16 : 31, manna, like coriander s.
  Lev. 19 : 19, thou shalt not sow mingled s.
  26 : 16, ye shall sow your s. in vain.
  27 : 16, estimation shall be according to s.
  Num. 20 : 5, it is no place of s.
  Deut. 11 : 10, Egypt, where thou sowedst
    thy s.
  14 : 22, tithe all the increase of your s.
  28 : 38, thou shalt carry much s. out into
    the field.
  Ps. 126 : 6, bearing precious s.
  Eccl. 11 : 6, in the morning sow thy s.
  Isa. 17 : 11, make thy s. to flourish.
  55 : 10, may give s. to sower.
  Jer. 35 : 7, sow s., not plant vineyard.
  Joel 1 : 17, the s. is rotten under the clods.
  Amos 9 : 13, overtake him that soweth s.
  Hag. 2 : 19, is the s. yet in the barn ?
  Zech. 8 : 12, the s. shall be prosperous.
  Mal. 2 : 3, I will corrupt your s.
  2 : 15, might seek a godly s.
  Matt. 13 : 19, s. by the wayside.
  13 : 37, that soweth good s. is Son of man.
  Mark 4 : 26, a man should cast s. into
    ground.
  Luke 8 : 11, the s. is the word of God.
  1 Cor. 15 : 38, to every s. his own body.
  2 Cor. 9 : 10, ministereth s. to sower.
  1 Pet. 1 : 23, born again, not of corrup-
    tible s.
  1 John 3 : 9, his s. remaineth in him.

Seek, Gen. 43 : 18, that he may s. occasion.
  Deut. 4 : 29, if thou s. him with all thy
    heart.
  23 : 6; Ezra 9 : 12, thou shalt not s. their
    peace.
  1 Ki. 19 : 10, 14, they s. my life to take it.
  1 Chr. 28 : 9; 2 Chr. 15 : 2, if thou s. him
    he will be found.
  2 Chr. 19 : 3; 30 : 19, prepared heart to s.
    God.
  34 : 3, Josiah began to s. after God.
  Ezra 4 : 2, we s. your God, as ye do.
  Neh. 2 : 10, to s. the welfare of Israel.
  Job 5 : 8, I would s. unto God.
  7 : 21, shalt s. me in the morning.
  8 : 5, wouldest s. unto God betimes.
  20 : 10, children shall s. to please the poor.
  Ps. 9 : 10, hast not forsaken them that s.
    thee.
  10 : 15, s. out his wickedness.
  14 : 2; 53 : 2, if there were any that did
    s. God.
  24 : 6, generation of them that s. him.
  27 : 4, one thing have I desired, that will I
    s. after.
  27 : 8, s. ye my face; thy face, Lord,
    will I s.
  34 : 14; 1 Pet. 3 : 11, s. peace and pur-
    sue it.
  Ps. 63 : 1, early will I s. thee.
  69 : 32, your heart shall live that s. God.
  70 : 4, let those that s. thee rejoice.
  83 : 16, that they may s. thy name.
  104 : 21, young lions s. meat from God.
  119 : 2, s. him with the whole heart.

122 : 9, I will s. thy good.
  Prov. 1 : 28, they shall s. me, but not find
    me.
  8 : 17, those that s. me early shall find me.
  23 : 35, I will s. it yet again.
  Song of Sol. 3 : 2, I will s. him whom my
    soul loveth.
  Isa. 1 : 17, learn to do well; s. judgment.
  8 : 19, should not a people s. unto their
    God ?
  34 : 16, s. ye out of the book of the Lord.
  45 : 19, I said not, S. ye me in vain.
  Jer. 29 : 13, s. me, and find me.
  Lam. 3 : 25, Lord is good to the soul that
    s. him.
  Ezek. 7 : 25, they shall s. peace.
  34 : 16, s. that which was lost.
  Dan. 9 : 3, I set my face to s. by prayer.
  Amos 5 : 4, s. ye me.
  8 : 12, to s. the word of the Lord.
  Zeph. 2 : 3, s. ye the Lord, all ye meek.
  Mal. 2 : 7, they should s. the law.
  Matt. 6 : 32, after all these things do the
    Gentiles s.
  6 : 33; Luke 12 : 31, s. ye first the king-
    dom of God.
  Matt. 7 : 7; Luke 11 : 9, s., and ye shall
    find.
  Matt. 28 : 5; Mark 16 : 6, I know that ye
    s. Jesus.
  Mark 1 : 37, all men s. for thee.
  Luke 12 : 30, these things the nations s.
  13 : 24, many will s. to enter in.
  15 : 8, doth she not s. diligently ?
  17 : 33, whosoever shall s. to save his
    life.
  19 : 10, the Son of man is come to s. and
    to save.
  John 1 : 38, Jesus saith, What s. ye ?
  7 : 34, ye shall s. me, and shall not find
    me.
  Acts 10 : 19, three men s. thee.
  Rom. 2 : 7, to them who s. for glory.
  3 : 11, none that s. after God.
  1 Cor. 10 : 24, let no man s. his own.
  13 : 5, charity s. not her own.
  Phil. 2 : 21, all s. their own.
  Col. 3 : 1, s. those things which are above.
  Heb. 11 : 14, declare plainly that they s. a
    country.
  13 : 14, but we s. one to come.
  Rev. 9 : 6, in those days shall men s. death.

Seem, Gen. 27 : 12, I shall s. as a deceiver.
  Num. 16 : 9, s. it but a small thing ?
  Prov. 14 : 12, there is a way that s. right.
  Luke 8 : 18, taken that which he s. to have.
  1 Cor. 3 : 18, if any s. to be wise.
  Heb. 4 : 1, lest any s. to come short.
  12 : 11, no chastening s. to be joyous.
  Jas. 1 : 26, if any man s. to be religious.

Seen, Gen. 32 : 30, I have s. God face to
    face.
  Ex. 19 : 4, ye have s. what I did to Egyp-
    tians.
  20 : 22, ye have s. that I talked with you.
  Judg. 13 : 22, die, because we have s. God.
  2 Ki. 20 : 15, what have they s. ?
  Job 13 : 1, mine eye hath s. all this.
  Ps. 68 : 24, they have s. thy goings, O God.

Eccl. 6 : 5, he hath not s. the sun.
Isa. 6 : 5, mine eyes have s. the Lord.
64 : 4; 1 Cor. 2 : 9, neither hath eye s.
Isa. 66 : 8, who hath s. such things ?
Jer. 12 : 3, thou hast s. me, tried heart.
Matt. 6 : 1; 23 : 5, to be s. of men.
9 : 33, never so s. in Israel.
Mark 9 : 9, tell no man what they had s.
Luke 5 : 26, we have s. strange things.
24 : 23, they had s. a vision of angels.
John 1 : 18, no man hath s. God.
3 : 11, we testify that we have s.
8 : 57, hast thou s. Abraham ?
14 : 9, he that hath s. me, hath s. the Father.
20 : 29, because thou hast s., thou hast believed.
Acts 4 : 20, speak things we have s.
1 Cor. 9 : 1, have I not s. Jesus Christ ?
1 Tim. 6 : 16, whom no man hath s.
Heb. 11 : 1, evidence of the things not s.
1 Pet. 1 : 8, whom having not s., ye love.
1 John 4 : 20, can he love God whom he hath not s. ?
Seer, 1 Sam. 9 : 9; 2 Sam. 24 : 11.
Seethe, Ex. 16 : 23; 2 Ki. 4 : 38; Mic. 3 : 7.
Seir (sē-ĭr) Mount [the rugged], inheritance of Esau, Gen. 14 : 6; 32 : 3; 36 : 8, 20; Deut. 33 : 2; Josh. 24 : 4; Ezek. 25 : 8.
predictions about, Num. 24 : 18; Isa. 21 : 11; Ezek. 35 : 2.
Seize, Job 3 : 6; Ps. 55 : 15; Matt. 21 : 38.
Selah (sē-läh). This word is found periodically in the Psalms. It probably refers to the music rather than to the contents; and signifies an intensifying of the instrumentation. Ps. 3 : 2; 4 : 2, etc.
the capital of Edom, 2 Ki. 14 : 7.
Self, 1 Cor. 4 : 3, judge not mine own s.
Philem. 19, even thine own s.
1 Pet. 2 : 24, own s. bare our sins.
Self-denial, Prov. 23 : 2; Jer. 35; Luke 3 : 11; 14 : 33; Acts 2 : 45; Rom. 6 : 12; 14 : 20; 15 : 1; 1 Cor. 10 : 23; 13 : 5; Gal. 5 : 24; Phil. 2 : 4; Titus 2 : 12; 1 Pet. 2 : 11.
Christ an example of, Matt. 4 : 8; 8 : 20; Rom. 15 : 3; Phil. 2 : 6.
incumbent on his followers, Matt. 10 : 38; 16 : 24; Mark 8 : 34; Luke 9 : 23.
Self-examination, enjoined, Ps. 4 : 4; Lam. 3 : 40; 1 Cor. 11 : 28; 2 Cor. 13 : 5.
Selfishness, condemned, Isa. 56 : 11; 1 Cor. 10 : 24; 2 Cor. 5 : 15; Phil. 2 : 4, 21; 2 Tim. 3 : 2; Jas. 2 : 8.
Selfsame, Matt. 8 : 13; 1 Cor. 12 : 11; 2 Cor. 5 : 5; 7 : 11.
Selfwill, condemned, Ps. 75 : 5; Titus 1 : 7; 2 Pet. 2 : 10.
Sell, Gen. 25 : 31, s. me thy birthright.
Gen. 37 : 27, let us s. him to the Ishmaelites.
1 Ki. 21 : 25, Ahab did s. himself to work wickedness.
Neh. 5 : 8, will ye even s. your brethren ?
10 : 31, victuals on sabbath day to s.
Prov. 23 : 23, buy the truth, and s. it not.
Joel 3 : 8, I will s. your sons and daughters.
Amos 8 : 6, s. the refuse of the wheat.

Matt. 19 : 21; Mark 10 : 21; Luke 18 : 22, go and s. that thou hast.
Luke 22 : 36, let me s. his garment.
Jas. 4 : 13, we will buy and s.
See Isa. 24 : 2; Acts 16 : 14.
Selvage, Ex. 26 : 4.
Senate, Acts 5 : 21.
Senators, Ps. 105 : 22.
Send, Gen. 24 : 7, shall s. his angel.
24 : 12, s. me good speed.
45 : 5, God did s. me to preserve life.
Ex. 4 : 13, s. by hand of him whom thou wilt s.
Lev. 16 : 21, s. him away by a fit man.
Judg. 13 : 8, man of God thou didst s.
Ps. 43 : 3, s. out thy light and thy truth.
118 : 25, Lord, s. now prosperity.
Isa. 6 : 8, whom shall I s. ?
19 : 20, he shall s. them a saviour.
Matt. 9 : 38; Luke 10 : 2, s. labourers.
Matt. 15 : 23, s. her away.
Mark 3 : 14, that he might s. them to preach.
John 14 : 26, whom the Father will s. in my name.
17 : 8, believed that thou didst s. me.
Sennacherib (sĕn-năch-ĕr-ĭb) [Assyr., " Sin-akhe-eriba," Sin (the moon-god) has increased the brothers], king of Assyria, invades Judah, 2 Ki. 18 : 13.
his blasphemous letter, 2 Ki. 19 : 9.
his army destroyed, 2 Ki. 19 : 35.
slain by his sons, 2 Ki. 19 : 37.
See 2 Chr. 32; Isa. 36; 37. See Chronology, Old Testament.
Sense, Neh. 8 : 8.
Senses, Heb. 5 : 14.
Sensual, Jas. 3 : 15; Jude 19.
Sent, Gen. 45 : 7, God s. me before you.
Ex. 3 : 14, I AM hath s. me unto you.
Matt. 15 : 24, I am not s. but to lost sheep of Israel.
21 : 37; Mark 12 : 6, last of all he s. unto them his son.
John 4 : 34, the will of him that s. me.
9 : 4, work the works of him that s. me.
11 : 42, may believe that thou hast s. me.
17 : 3, eternal life to know him whom thou hast s.
Rom. 10 : 15, how shall they preach except they be s. ?
1 Pet. 1 : 12, the Holy Ghost s. from heaven.
1 John 4 : 9, God s. his only begotten Son.
Sentence, Ps. 17 : 2, let my s. come forth.
Prov. 16 : 10, a divine s. is in the lips of the king.
Eccl. 8 : 11, because s. is not executed speedily.
Dan. 8 : 23, a king understanding dark s.
Luke 23 : 24, Pilate gave s.
2 Cor. 1 : 9, we had the s. of death.
Separate, Deut. 19 : 2, thou shalt s. three cities.
Prov. 16 : 28; 17 : 9, s. friends.
19 : 4, the poor is s. from his neighbour.
Matt. 25 : 32, he shall s. them.
Rom. 8 : 35, who shall s. us from the love of Christ ?
2 Cor. 6 : 17, be ye s.

Heb. 7 : 26, **s.** from sinners.

Separation, Lev. 12; Num. 6 : 19.

Septuagint, or LXX. Version. See Versions.

Sepulchre, Abraham's, Gen. 23 : 6; 25 : 9; Acts 7 : 16.

of Moses, unknown, Deut. 34 : 6.

of Christ, Matt. 27 : 60; Mark 15 : 46; Luke 23 : 55; John 19 : 41.

See Matt. 23 : 27.

Seraphim (sĕr-ă-phīm), Isa. 6 : 2, 6.

Sermon on the Mount, Matt. 5–7; Luke 6 : 20 ff. These two passages give us the most famous collection of the sayings of Christ, commonly called The Sermon on the Mount. In this sermon we have the fullest and most convenient statement of the moral teaching of Jesus. By common consent, it sets forth an ideal which " carried morality to the sublimest point attained, or even attainable, by humanity."

In its present form, the sermon probably represents a collection of scattered sayings rather than a single coherent and complete address. The general order of thought, however, can be traced through the whole discourse, and the central theme throughout is the righteousness required of those who would enter the kingdom of Christ.

Notes.—(a) (Matt. 5 : 3; Luke 6 : 20). The form of the Beatitudes as given by the two Evangelists has occasioned some discussion. That adopted by St. Luke is terse, striking, even paradoxical—" Blessed be ye poor "; while that found in St. Matthew defines the poverty indicated as spiritual poverty. We know that among the characteristics of the teaching of Jesus was the use of brief, startling sayings, by which He arrested the attention of His hearers and set them thinking. These were not always to be taken literally, but to be interpreted by the general tenor of His instruction. In the Sermon on the Mount—"Resist not evil," " Be not anxious," are not meant to inculcate abject submission or want of prudence. Such were also the sayings—" Beware of the leaven of the Pharisees and Sadducees," and " Except ye eat the flesh of the Son of man, and drink his blood, ye have no life in you." It is noteworthy that in the parable of Dives and Lazarus, narrated only by St. Luke, nothing is said of the character of Lazarus, reference being made only to his extreme poverty. In Mark 10 : 23, 24, both forms of expression are attributed to Jesus—"They that have riches " being explained by " They that trust in riches," though the reading is not undisputed. We may conclude, therefore, regarding the Beatitudes, that either form may be original, while in either case the meaning is explicitly and accurately conveyed by St. Matthew.

(b) (Luke 6 : 24-26). The four Beatitudes of St. Luke are paralleled by four " Woes " to which we find nothing corresponding in the generally more extended report of the first Evangelist. The explanation of this omission is probably to be found in the change from the form of direct address (the second person) to that of general reflection or aphorism (the third person). To the latter form denunciation obviously does not lend itself; hence the omission of the " Woes " by St. Matthew.

(c) (Matt. 5 : 15). Read " lamp " for " candle," " the stand " for " a candlestick," and " the bushel " for " a bushel," as in the R.V.

(d) (Matt. 5 : 21, 27, etc.). For " by them of old time " read " to them of old time."

(e) (Matt. 5 : 22). " Judgment " is the subordinate tribunal referred to in ver. 21. " Council " is the Sanhedrin, the supreme court of the Jews. " Hell fire," extreme punishment, literally " fire of Gehenna." The three offences in this verse— " anger without cause," " saying Raca (an expression of contempt)," " saying Thou Fool (a still stronger expression, conveying malignant feeling)," form a climax.

(f) (Matt. 6 : 1). The word translated " alms " in the A.V. should in this case be rendered " righteousness "; it denotes that of which all the three cases that follow are examples, viz.: alms-giving, prayer, and fasting.

(g) (Matt. 6 : 31, 34). For " Take no thought " read " Be not anxious."

(h) (Matt. 7 : 24, 25). For " a rock " read " the rock." Note the additional particular in Luke 6 : 48, " digged and went deep " (R.V.). The difference between the two builders is not that one searched about until he found a rock on which to build—the houses may have stood side by side; but the wise builder dug through the gravel and clay till he came to the rocky foundation.

Serpent, cursed by God, Gen. 3 : 14; (2 Cor. 11 : 3; Rev. 12 : 9).

brazen one made, Num. 21 : 9.

brazen one destroyed, 2 Ki. 18 : 4.

Gen. 3 : 1, **s.** was more subtil.

49 : 17, Dan shall be a **s.** by the way.

Job 26 : 13, his hand formed the crooked **s.**

Ps. 58 : 4, like the poison of a **s.**

140 : 3, sharpened their tongues like a **s.**

Prov. 23 : 32, at last it biteth like a **s.**

Eccl. 10 : 8; Amos 5 : 19, a **s.** shall bite him.

Isa. 14 : 29, a fiery flying **s.**

27 : 1, the Lord shall punish the **s.**

65 : 25, dust shall be the **s.** meat.

Mic. 7 : 17, lick dust like a **s.**

Matt. 7 : 10; Luke 11 : 11, will he give him a **s.** ?

Matt. 10 : 16, be ye wise as a **s.**

Mark 16 : 18, shall take up **s.**

John 3 : 14, as Moses lifted up the **s.**

1 Cor. 10 : 9, destroyed of **s.**

Naja Haje, the rod serpent of Egypt.

Rev. 20 : 2, that old s., which is the Devil.
Servants, laws concerning, Ex. 20 : 10; 21; Deut. 5 : 14.
advice to, Mal. 1 : 6; Eph. 6 : 5; Col. 3 : 22; 1 Tim. 6 : 1; Titus 2 : 9; 1 Pet. 2 : 18.
Gen. 9 : 25, a s. of s. shall he be.
Ex. 21 : 5, if the s. plainly say.
Job 7 : 2, as a s. desireth the shadow.
Ps. 116 : 16; 119; 125; 143 : 12, I am thy s.
Prov. 22 : 7, the borrower is s. to the lender.
Isa. 24 : 2, as with the s., so with his master.
Jer. 2 : 14, is Israel a s. ?
Matt. 10 : 25, enough for s. to be as his Lord.
25 : 21, good and faithful s.
Mark 12 : 2, sent to husbandmen a s.
Luke 12 : 47, that s., which knew his lord's will.
17 : 9, doth he thank that s. ?
20 : 10, at the season he sent a s.
John 8 : 35, the s. abideth not in the house for ever.
13 : 16; 15 : 20, the s. is not greater than his lord.
Rom. 1 : 1, a s. of Jesus Christ.
1 Cor. 7 : 21, art thou called, being a s. ?
Phil. 2 : 7, took the form of a s.
Philem. 16, not as a s., but above a s.
Heb. 3 : 5, Moses was faithful as a s.
Serve, Gen. 15 : 14, nation they s. will I judge.
Gen. 25 : 23; Rom. 9 : 12, the elder shall s. the younger.
Ex. 20 : 5; Deut. 5 : 9, not bow down to them nor s. them.
Deut. 6 : 13; 10 : 12; 11 : 13; 13 : 4; Josh. 22 : 5; 24 : 14; 1 Sam. 7 : 3; 12 : 14, thou shalt fear the Lord, and s. him.
Josh. 24 : 15, choose you whom ye will s.
2 Sam. 22 : 44, people I knew not shall s. me.
1 Chr. 28 : 9, s. him with a perfect heart.

Job 21 : 15, what is the Almighty, that we should s. him ?
Ps. 22 : 30, a seed shall s. him.
72 : 11, all nations shall s. him.
97 : 7, confounded that s. graven images.
Isa. 43 : 24, made me to s. with thy sins.
56 : 6, join themselves to the Lord, to s. him.
Dan. 6 : 16, thy God whom thou s. will deliver.
Zeph. 3 : 9, to s. him with one consent.
Mal. 3 : 14, said, It is vain to s. God.
Matt. 6 : 24; Luke 16 : 13, no man can s. two masters.
Luke 10 : 40, left me to s. alone.
15 : 29, these many years do I s. thee.
22 : 26, he that is chief, as he that doth s.
John 12 : 26, if any man s. me, let him follow me.
Acts 6 : 2, leave word of God, and s. tables.
Rom. 7 : 6, should s. in newness of spirit.
Gal. 5 : 13, by love s. one another.
Col. 3 : 24, ye s. the Lord Christ.
1 Thess. 1 : 9, turned from idols to s. the living God.
Heb. 12 : 28, we may s. God acceptably.
Rev. 7 : 15, they s. him day and night.
Service, Ex. 12 : 26, what mean ye by this s. ?
1 Chr. 29 : 5, who is willing to consecrate his s. to the Lord ?
John 16 : 2, will think he doeth God s.
Rom. 12 : 1, which is your reasonable s.
Eph. 6 : 7, doing s. as to the Lord.
Heb. 9 : 1, ordinances of divine s.
Rev. 2 : 19, I know thy works and s.
Servile work forbidden on holy days, Lev. 23 : 7; Num. 28 : 18; 29 : 1.
Set, Gen. 9 : 13, I do s. my bow in the cloud.
Deut. 7 : 7, Lord did not s. his love on you.
11 : 26, I s. before you a blessing and a curse.
30 : 15, I s. before thee life and death.
Job 33 : 5, s. thy words in order before me.
Ps. 4 : 3, Lord hath s. apart him that is godly.
16 : 8, I s. the Lord always before me.
Ps. 20 : 5, we will s. up our banners.
40 : 2, s. my feet upon a rock.
91 : 14, he hath s. his love upon me.
118 : 5, s. me in a large place.
Eccl. 7 : 14, God hath s. one against the other.
Jer. 21 : 8, I s. before you the way of life.
Matt. 5 : 14, a city s. on a hill.
Luke 11 : 6, nothing to s. before thee.
23 : 11, Herod s. him at nought.
John 3 : 33, s. to his seal that God is true.
Acts 18 : 10, no man shall s. on thee.
Heb. 6 : 18, lay hold on hope s. before us.
Rev. 3 : 8, s. before thee an open door.
Seth [appointed], Gen. 5 : 3; Luke 3 : 38.
Settle, Ps. 65 : 10, thou s. the furrows thereof.
Luke 21 : 14, s. it in your hearts.
Col. 1 : 23, in faith grounded and s.
1 Pet. 5 : 10, God strengthen, s. you.
[ar.], seat or base, Ezek. 45 : 19.
Sevenfold, Ps. 79 : 12; Prov. 6 : 31; Isa. 30 : 26.

Seventy, elders, the, Ex. 18 : 25; 24; Num. 11 : 16.

year's captivity foretold, Jer. 25 : 11.

weeks, Daniel's prophecy concerning, Dan. 9 : 24.

disciples sent forth, Luke 10.

Sever, Ezek. 39 : 14; Matt. 13 : 49.

Severity, Rom. 11 : 22.

Sew, Gen. 3 : 7, they s. fig leaves together.

Eccl. 3 : 7, a time to rend, a time to s.

Ezek. 13 : 18, woe to the women that s. pillows.

Mark 2 : 21, no man s. new cloth on old garments.

Shaalbim (shā-ăl-´bĭm) [region of foxes], Judg. 1 : 35.

Shaaph (shā-´ăph), 1 Chr. 2 : 47, 49.

Shaaraim (shā-ă-rā-´ĭm) [two gates], 1 Sam. 17 : 52.

Shaashgaz (shā-ăsh-´găz), Esther 2 : 14.

Shabbethai (shăb-´bĕ-thāi) [born on the Sabbath], Ezra 10 : 15.

Shade, Ps. 121 : 5; Job 40 : 21, 22.

Shadow, of heavenly things, Heb. 8 : 5; 10 : 1.

Gen. 19 : 8, the s. of my roof.

2 Ki. 20 : 9, shall the s. go forward ?

Job 7 : 2, servant desireth the s.

14 : 2, he fleeth, as a s., and continueth not.

Ps. 17 : 8, hide me under the s. of thy wings.

91 : 1, abide under the s. of the Almighty.

102 : 11, my days are like a s.

109 : 23, I am gone like the s. when it declineth.

114 : 4; Eccl. 8 : 13, his days are as a s.

Eccl. 6 : 12, life he spendeth as a s.

Song of Sol. 2 : 3, I sat under his s. with great delight.

2 : 17; 4 : 6, till the s. flee away.

Isa. 4 : 6, for a s. in the daytime.

25 : 4, a s. from the heat.

32 : 2, as the s. of a great rock.

49 : 2; 51 : 16, in the s. of his hand.

Jer. 6 : 4, the s. of evening are stretched out.

Lam. 4 : 20, under his s. we shall live.

Hos. 4 : 13, the s. thereof is good.

14 : 7, they that dwell under his s. shall return.

Mark 4 : 32, fowls of air may lodge under s. of it.

Acts 5 : 15, the s. of Peter might over-shadow.

Col. 2 : 17, a s. of things to come.

Jas. 1 : 17, with whom is no s. of turning.

See 1 Chr. 29 : 15; Job 8 : 9; Ps. 36 : 7; 63 : 7.

Shadrach (shā-´drăch) [Assyr., " Sudur-Aku," command of Aku], Hananiah, the companion of Daniel, Dan. 1 : 7.

Shaft, Ex. 25 : 31; Isa. 49 : 2.

Shake, Judg. 16 : 20, I will s. myself.

Job 9 : 6, s. the earth out of her place.

Ps. 46 : 3, though the mountains s.

72 : 16, the fruit thereof shall s. like Lebanon.

Isa. 2 : 19, when he ariseth to s. the earth.

13 : 13; Hag. 2 : 6, 21, I will s. the heavens.

Isa. 24 : 18, foundations of earth do s.

52 : 2, s. thyself from the dust.

Hag. 2 : 7, I will s. all nations.

Matt. 10 : 14; Mark 6 : 11; Luke 9 : 5, s. dust off your feet.

Matt. 28 : 4, for fear the keepers did s.

Luke 6 : 38, good measure, s. together.

2 Thess. 2 : 2, be not soon s. in mind.

Heb. 12 : 26, I s. not the earth only.

Shalish, a musical instrument. See Musical Instruments.

Shallum (shăl-lŭm) [recompense], king of Israel, 2 Ki. 15 : 10.

son of Josiah, 1 Chr. 3 : 15; 7 :13; 9 : 17; Neh. 3 : 12; 15.

Shalmander, carries ten tribes captive, 2 Ki. 17; 18 : 9.

Shame, consequence of sin, Gen. 2 : 25; 3 : 10; Ex. 32 : 25.

of God's enemies, Ps. 40 : 14; 109 :29; Ezek. 7 : 18.

subdued by hope, Rom. 5 : 5.

Ps. 4 : 2, how long turn my glory to s. ?

83 : 17, let them be put to s.

132 : 18, enemies will I clothe with s.

Prov. 10 : 5; 17 : 2, a son that causeth s.

Isa. 61 : 7, for your s. ye shall have double.

Dan. 12 : 2, awake, some to s.

Luke 14 : 9, begin with s. to take the lowest room.

Acts 5 : 41, counted worthy to suffer s.

Phil. 3 : 19, whose glory is in their s.

Heb. 6 : 6, put him to an open s.

12 : 2, endured the cross, despising the s.

See Prov. 3 : 35; 11 : 2; 13 : 5; Ezek. 16 : 63; Rom. 6 : 21.

Shamed (shā-´mĕd), 1 Chr. 8 : 12.

Shamefacedness [ar.], modesty; R.V., " shamefastness," 1 Tim. 2 : 9.

Shamefully, Luke 20 : 11; 1 Thess. 2 : 2.

Shamgar (shăm-´găr), judges Israel, Judg. 3 : 31.

Shamhuth (shăm-´hŭth) and **Shammoth** (shăm-´mōth), 1 Chr. 11 : 27; probably " Shammah," 1 Chr. 27 : 8.

Shamir (shā-´mĭr) [thorn], Josh. 15 : 48.

Shammai (shăm-´mā-ĭ), 1 Chr. 2 : 28, 32.

Shammua (shăm-´mū-ă) [heard], Num. 13 : 4.

Shamsherai (shăm-´shĕ-rāi), 1 Chr. 8 : 26.

Shape, Luke 3 : 22, descended in bodily s.

John 5 : 37, nor seen his s.

Rev. 9 : 7, s. of the locusts were.

See Ps. 51 : 5.

Shaphan (shā-´phăn) [rock badger], appointed to repair the temple, 2 Ki. 22 : 3; 2 Chr. 34 : 8.

Shaphat (shā-´phăt) [judge], Num. 13 : 5; 1 Chr. 27 : 29.

Shapher (shā-´phĕr) [brightness], Num. 33 : 23, 24.

Sharai (shăr-ā-ĭ) [freeing], Ezra 10 : 40.

Sharaim (shă-rā-´ĭm) [two gates], Josh. 15 : 36.

Share, 1 Sam. 13 : 20.

Sharezer (shă-rē-´zĕr) or **Sarezer** [Assyr., " Sarasur," Asshur protect the king], 2 Ki. 19 : 37.

Hyrax Syriacus, or Shaphan.

Sharon (shâr-ọn) or **Saron** [plain], rose of, Song of Sol. 2 : 1. See **Rose.**
plain of, 1 Chr. 5 : 16; 27 : 29; Isa. 33 : 9; 35 : 2; 65 : 10; Acts 9 : 35. See **Palestine.**
Sharp, Josh. 5 : 2, make thee s. knives.
Ps. 45 : 5, arrows s. in the heart.
52 : 2, tongue like a s. razor.
57 : 4, their tongue a s. sword.
Prov. 25 : 18, man that beareth false witness in a s. arrow.
Acts 15 : 39, the contention was so s.
Heb. 4 : 12, word of God s. than any two-edged sword.
Sharpen, 1 Sam. 13 : 20, to s. every man his share.
Prov. 27 : 17, iron s. iron; so a man s. the countenance of his friend.
Sharply, Judg. 8 : 1; Titus 1 : 13.
Shaving, the head, Lev. 13 : 33; 14 : 8; Num. 6 : 9; 8 : 7.
the beard, Lev. 21 : 5.
See Job 1 : 20; Ezek. 44 : 20; Acts 21 : 24; 1 Cor. 11 : 5.
Shearers, Isa. 53 : 7; Acts 8 : 32.
Shearing, sheep, feast at, 1 Sam. 25 : 4; 2 Sam. 13 : 23.
Shear-jashub (shē-är-jäsh-üb) [a remnant shall return], Isa. 7 : 3. The name of Isaiah's son. The doctrine of the survival of a "righteous remnant" became one of the leading ideas of Hebrew prophecy.
Sheath, Ezek. 21 : 3, 4; John 18 : 11.
Sheaves, Joseph's dream concerning, Gen. 37 : 7.
of the firstfruits, Lev. 23 : 10.
to be left in the field, Deut. 24 : 19; Job 24 : 10.
typical, Ps. 126 : 6; Mic. 4 : 12; Matt. 13 : 30.
Sheba (shē-bä) [seven], Gen. 25 : 3; Job 6 : 19; Ps. 72 : 10; Jer. 6 : 20; Ezek. 27 : 22; 38 : 13.
queen of, 1 Ki. 10; 2 Chr. 9; Matt. 12 : 42.
Benjamite, revolts, 2 Sam. 20.
Shebna (shéb-nä), the scribe, 2 Ki. 18 : 18; 19 : 2; Isa. 22 : 15; 36 : 3; 37 : 2.
Shechem (shē-chěm) [shoulder, mountain ridge], the Hivite, Gen. 34 : 2.
Shechem, always celebrated for its fertility (Gen. 49 : 22), is still a town of 15,000 inhabitants, including some 140 Samari-

tans, with a large church, now a mosque, and a ruined hospice of St. John, now the home of the lepers. The ancient Samaritan MS. of the Pentateuch is kept in their synagogue here. Josh. 17 : 7; Ps. 60 : 6.
charge of Joshua at, Josh. 24.
its treachery and penalty, Judg. 9 : 1, 41.
Shed, Gen. 9 : 6, by man shall his blood be s.
Matt. 26 : 28, is s. for many for remission of sins.
Rom. 5 : 5, love of God is s. abroad in our hearts.
Titus 3 : 6, which he s. on us through Jesus Christ.
Heb. 9 : 22, without s. of blood is no remission.
Sheep. The sheep is the first animal mentioned by name in the Bible, and was among the Jews' most treasured possessions. The patriarchs counted their sheep by thousands, and they moved from place to place as pasture for these was needed. Not only was the flesh of the sheep used for food and sacrifice, but their skins were among the most primitive forms of clothing, and in progress of time their fleeces were spun and woven. Shepherds were an abomination to the Egyptians, and on account of this occupation the land of Goshen was given to the Israelites to live in.
for sacrifice, Lev. 1 : 10; 1 Ki. 8 : 63; 2 Chr. 30 : 24.
the church compared to, Ps. 74 : 1; 79 : 13; 100 : 3; Ezek. 34 : 6, 8; Mic. 2 : 12; Matt. 15 : 24; 25 : 32; 1 Pet. 2 : 25.
emblem of Christ, Isa. 53 : 7; Acts 8 : 32.
emblem of his people, Ps. 95 · 7
Gen. 4 : 2, Abel was a keeper of s.
Num. 27 : 17; 1 Ki. 22 : 17; 2 Chr. 18 : 16; Matt. 9 : 36; Mark 6 : 34, as s. which have no shepherd.
1 Sam. 15 : 14, what meaneth this bleating of s. ?
2 Ki. 5 : 26, is it a time to receive s. ?
Ps. 49 : 14, like s. they are laid in the grave.
Isa. 53 : 6, all we like s. have gone astray.
Jer. 12 : 3, like s. for the slaughter.
Matt. 7 : 15, false prophets in s. clothing.
10 : 6, go to lost s. of Israel.
12 : 12, how much is a man better than a s. ?
John 10 : 2, shepherd of s.
21 : 16, Feed my s.
Heb. 13 : 20, Lord Jesus, that great Shepherd of the s.
Sheepcote, 2 Sam. 7 : 8.
Sheepfold, Ps. 78 : 70; John 10 : 1.
Sheepskins, Heb. 11 : 37.
Sheet, Judg. 14 : 12; Acts 10 : 11; 11 : 5.
Shekel, a measure of weight and money, Gen. 23 : 15; Ex. 30 : 13; Josh. 7 : 21; 2 Sam. 14 : 26; 1 Ki. 10 : 16; Neh. 5 : 15; Jer. 32 : 9; Ezek. 4 : 10. See **Money,** also **Weights.**
Shelah (shē-läh) [short], son of Judah, Gen. 38 : 5; Num. 26 : 20.
Shelemiah (shěl-ē-mī-äh) [Jehovah is re-

compensel, 1 Chr. 26 : 14; Neh. 3 : 30.
Sheleph (shē-lĕph) [drawing out], Gen. 10 : 26.
Shelomi (shĕ-lō-mī) [peaceful], Num. 34 : 27.
Shelomith (shĕ-lō-mĭth) [peaceful], Lev. 24 : 11; 1 Chr. 26 : 25.
Shelter, Job 24 : 8; Ps. 61 : 3.
Shem [name, renown], Gen. 9 : 18; 10 : 21; 11 : 10; 1 Chr. 1 : 17.
Shemaiah (shĕm-â-ĭ-ăh) [Jehovah hears], prophet, 1 Ki. 12 : 22; 2 Chr. 11 : 2; 12 : 5.
denounced for opposing Jeremiah, Jer. 29 : 24.
Shemariah (shĕm-ă-rī-ăh) or **Shamariah** [Jehovah guards], 1 Chr. 12 : 5; 15 : 8; 24 : 6.
Shemer (shē-mĕr) [watch], 1 Ki. 16 : 24.
Shemida (shĕ-mī-dă) [name of knowledge], Num. 26 : 32; Josh. 17 : 2.
Sheminith (shĕm-ĭn-ĭth), technical term in music, " low bass," 1 Chr. 15 : 21.
Shemiramoth (shē-mĭ-ră-mŏth) [height of renown], 1 Chr. 15 : 18.
Shemuel (shĕ-mū-ĕl) [heard of God], Num. 34 : 20; 1 Chr. 6 : 33.
Shen [tooth], 1 Sam. 7 : 12.
Shenir (shē-nĭr) or **Senir,** Amorite name of " Hermon," Deut. 3 : 9.
Shephatiah (shĕph-ă-tī-ăh) [Jehovah judges], 2 Sam. 3 : 4.
Shepherd, of Israel, Ps. 80 : 1; Ezek. 34 : 12.
Christ the good, Zech. 11 : 16; John 10 : 14; Heb. 13 : 20; 1 Pet. 2 : 25.
Gen. 46 : 34, every s. is an abomination unto the Egyptians.
Ps. 23 : 1, the Lord is my s.
Isa. 40 : 11, he shall feed his flock like a s.
Jer. 50 : 6, their s. caused them to go astray.
Zech. 11 : 17, woe to the idol s.
13 : 7, awake, O sword, against my S.
John 10 : 16, one fold, one s.
1 Pet. 5 : 4, when the chief S. shall appear.
See Gen. 46 : 32; 47 : 3; Jer. 33 : 12; Ezek. 34 : 2; Luke 2 : 8.
Shephi (shē-phī), or **Shepho** [bareness], Gen. 36 : 23; 1 Chr. 1 : 40.
Sherebiah (shĕr-ē-bī-ăh) [glow of Jehovah], Ezra 8 : 18; Neh. 10 : 12.
Sheshach (shē-shăch), name of Babylon, Jer. 25 : 26.
Sheshai (shē-shâi) [whitish], Num. 13 : 22.
Sheshbazzar (shĕsh-băz-zär), Persian name of Zerubbabel [fire worshipper], Ezra 1 : 8.
Sheth [tumult], Num. 24 : 17.
Shethar (shē-thär) [a star], Esther 1 : 14.
Shethar-boznai (shē-thär-bŏz-nâi), and Tatnai oppose rebuilding of temple, Ezra 5 : 6.
Shewbread, Ex. 25 : 30; Lev. 24 : 5; Heb. 9 : 2.
given to David, 1 Sam. 21 : 6; (Matt. 12 : 4; Mark 2 : 26; Luke 6 : 4).
Shibboleth (shĭb-bŏ-lĕth) [ear of corn]. The Gileadites used this word as a test for detecting the Ephraimites. The latter were unable to pronounce the initial " sh "

and pronounced the word as if it were " sibboleth." Judg. 12 : 6.
Shield, God, of his people, Deut. 33 : 29; Ps. 33 : 20.
of faith, Eph. 6 : 16.
Goliath's, 1 Sam. 17 : 7.
Solomon's, 1 Ki. 10 : 17.
Gen. 15 : 1, I am thy s. and reward.
Ps. 5 : 12, compass him as with a s.
59 : 11; 84 : 9, the Lord is our s.
84 : 11, a sun and s.
91 : 4, his truth shall be thy s.
115 : 9, he is their help and s.
Prov. 30 : 5, a s. to them that trust him.
Isa. 21 : 5, anoint the s.
Shiggaion (shĭg-gâi-ŏn) [lively song], in the singular occurs in Ps. 7 (title), and its plural **Shigionoth** (shĭg-ĭ-ō-nŏth) in Hab. 3 : 1. It possibly means a spirited or dithyrambic song, but this explanation rests only on etymology, as if from a verb meaning " wander."
Shiloah (shĭlō-ăh) [sending forth, of waters], spelled Siloah (Neh. 3 : 15). The New Testament form is Siloam, John 9 : 7; Isa. 8 : 6.
Shiloh (shĭ-lōh) [place of rest], a city of Ephraim, surrounded by barren mountains,
prophecy concerning, Gen. 49 : 10.
site of tabernacle, Josh. 18 : 1; Judg. 21 : 19; 1 Sam. 1 : 3; 2 : 14; 3 : 21; Ps. 78 : 60; Jer. 7 : 12; 26 : 6.
Shimei (shĭm-ĕ-ī) [famous], curses David, 2 Sam. 16 : 5; 1 Ki. 1 : 8; 1 Chr. 27 : 27; Esther 2 : 5.
slain by Solomon, 1 Ki. 2 : 46.
Shine, Num. 6 : 25, Lord make his face s. upon thee.
Job 22 : 28, light shall s. upon thy ways.
29 : 3, when his candle s. upon my head.
Ps. 104 : 15, oil to make his face to s.
119 : 135, make thy face to s. upon thy servant.
139 : 12, the night s. as the day.
Prov. 4 : 18, as light that s. more and more.
Isa. 60 : 1, arise, s., for thy light is come.
Matt. 5 : 16, let your light so s. before men.
13 : 43, righteous s. as the sun.
17 : 2, his face did s. as the sun.
2 Cor. 4 : 6, God, who commanded the light to s.
2 Pet. 1 : 19, a light that s. in a dark place.
1 John 2 : 8, the true light now s.
Shining, of God's face, Ps. 31 : 16; 50 : 2; 67 : 1; 80 : 1; Dan. 9 : 17.
Skin of Moses' face, Ex. 34 : 29; 2 Cor. 3.
of Christ's countenance, Luke 9 : 29; Rev. 1 : 16.
of Christians, as lights of the world, Matt. 5 : 16; (John 5 : 35); Phil. 2 : 15; and in the kingdom of heaven, Dan. 12 : 3.
of the gospel, 2 Cor. 4 : 4; Isa. 9 : 2.
Shipmaster, Jonah 1 : 6; Rev. 18 : 17.
Shipmen, Acts 27 : 27, 30.
Ships, mentioned, Gen. 49 : 13; Num. 24 : 24.
a navy formed by Solomon, 1 Ki. 9 : 26; by Jehoshaphat, 1 Ki. 22 : 48.

Ship, from a painting at Pompeii.

of Tarshish, Ps. 48 : 7; Isa. 2 : 16; 23 : 1; 60 : 9; Ezek. 27 : 25.
See John 6 : 24.
Shipwreck, 2 Cor. 11 : 25; 1 Tim. 1 : 19.
Shishak (shī-shăk) [Egypt., "Sheshonk "], king of Egypt, invades Jerusalem and spoils the temple, 1 Ki. 14 : 25; 2 Chr. 12.
Shittah tree, or **Shittim wood.** These Hebrew words are left untranslated in the A.V., but in the R.V. are translated " acacia tree " and " acacia wood." It is pretty certain that the tree is the " acacia seyal." It is a spiny tree, adapted for an arid desert country; its timber is hard; it exudes a brownish gum arabic; its fruit is a legume or pod.
Shivers, Rev. 2 : 27.
Shock, Judg. 15 : 5; Job 5 : 26.
Shod, Mark 6 : 9; Eph. 6 : 15.
Shoes. The shoes or sandals consisted of a sole fastened to the foot by means of a strap or thong called the " shoe latchet " (Gen. 14 : 23). Various materials were used in making the soles, such as wood, leather, papyrus stalks, and palm leaves. In Egypt, the soles were turned up at the toes like skates, but the Hebrews preferred rounded or pointed forms. To " put off the shoes " was an act of reverence (Ex. 3 : 5; Josh. 5 : 15),

Ancient Sandals.

accordingly the priests were barefooted when officiating in the Temple.
Shook, 2 Sam. 22 : 8; Ps. 18 : 7, earth **s.** and trembled.
Acts 13 : 51, **s.** off the dust of their feet.
Heb. 12 : 26, voice then **s.** the earth.
Shoot, 2 Ki. 13 : 17; Ps. 22 : 7; Amos 7 : 1; Mark 4 : 32.
Shore, Gen. 22 : 17; John 21 : 4; Acts 21 : 5.
Short, Num. 11 : 23, is the Lord's hand waxed **s.** ?
Job 20 : 5, triumphing of wicked is **s.**
Ps. 89 : 47, remember how **s.** my time is.
Rom. 3 : 23, come **s.** of the glory of God.
9 : 28, a **s.** work will the Lord make on the earth.
1 Cor. 7 : 29, the time is **s.**
See Isa. 28 : 20; 59 : 1; Matt. 24 : 22; Mark 13 : 20.
Shoshannim (shō-shănn-ĭm) [set to], occurs in the titles of Ps. 45, 69, 80. The word means " lilies," and perhaps indicates the name of a tune.
Shoulder, in sacrifices, Ex. 29 : 22, 27; Lev. 7 : 34; 10 : 14; Num. 6 : 19.
Shout, Num. 23 : 21, **s.** of king among them.
Ezra 3 : 13, people **s.** with a loud **s.**
Ps. 32 : 11, **s.** for joy.
47 : 5, God is gone up with a **s.**
1 Thess. 4 : 16, Lord shall descend with a **s.**
Shouting, in war, Josh. 6 : 5; 1 Sam. 4 : 5; 2 Chr. 13 : 15.
in worship, 2 Sam. 6 : 15; Ezra 3 : 11; Ps. 47 : 1; Zeph. 3 : 14.
Shovel, Ex. 27 : 3; Isa. 30 : 24.
Show, Ps. 39 : 6, every man walketh in a vain **s.**
Luke 20 : 47, for a **s.** make long prayers.
Gal. 6 : 12, to make a fair **s.** in the flesh.
Col. 2 : 15, made a **s.** of them openly.
Ps. 4 : 6, who will **s.** us any good ?
16 : 11, thou wilt **s.** me the path of life.
Isa. 60 : 6, **s.** forth the praises of the Lord.
John 5 : 20, Father, **s.** the Son all things.
1 Cor. 11 : 26, ye do **s.** the Lord's death.
1 John 1 : 2, **s.** unto you eternal life.
Shower, Ps. 65 : 10, makest earth soft with **s.**
Ps. 72 : 6, like **s.** that water the earth.
Ezek. 34 : 26, cause **s.** to come in season.
Luke 12 : 54, ye say, there cometh **s.**
Shrines, Acts 19 : 24.
Shroud, Ezek. 31 : 3.
Shrubs, Gen. 21 : 15.
Shulamite (shū-lă-mīte), or **Shunammite** (inhabitant of Shunem), 1 Ki. 1 : 3; Song of Sol. 6 : 13.
Shun, Acts 20 : 27; 2 Tim. 2 : 16.
Shusan-eduth (shū-shăn-ē-dúth) [set to], is found in the title of Ps. 60. It means " lily of testimony," probably the name of a tune.
Shut, Gen. 7 : 16, Lord **s.** him in.
Ps. 77 : 9, hath he **s.** up tender mercies ?
Isa. 22 : 22, he shall open, and none shall **s.**
60 : 11, thy gates shall be **s.** day nor night.
Matt. 23 : 13, ye **s.** up the kingdom of heaven.

Luke 4 : 25, heaven was s. up three years.

Rev. 3 : 8, an open door, and no man can s. it.

Sick, Prov. 13 : 12, hope deferred maketh the heart s.

Prov. 23 : 35, stricken me, and I was not s.

Isa. 1 : 5, whole head is s.

33 : 24, inhabitant shall not say I am s.

Matt. 25 : 36, was s., and ye visited me.

Jas. 5 : 15, prayer of faith shall save the s.

See 1 Cor. 11 : 30.

Sickle, Deut. 16 : 9; 23 : 25.

typical, Joel 3 : 13; Mark 4 : 29; Rev. 14 : 14.

Sickness, behaviour under, Ps. 35 : 13; Isa. 38 : 12; Jas. 5 : 14.

of persons healed miraculously, Hezekiah, 2 Ki. 20 : 1; 2 Chr. 32 : 24; Peter's wife's mother, Matt. 8 : 14; Mark 1 : 30; Luke 4 : 38; Lazarus, John 11 : 1; Dorcas, Acts 9 : 37.

cured by Christ and his disciples, Matt. 8 : 16; 10 : 8; Mark 16 : 18; Luke 7 : 10.

Ps. 41 : 3, thou wilt make his bed in s.

Hos. 5 : 13, when Ephraim saw his s.

Matt. 8 : 17, himself bare our s.

9 : 35, Jesus went about healing s.

John 11 : 4, this s. is not unto death.

See Lev. 26 : 16; Deut. 28 : 27; 2 Sam. 12 : 15; 2 Chr. 21 : 15. See **Affliction**.

Siege, Isa. 29 : 3; Ezek. 4 : 7; 5 : 2.

Sieve, Isa. 30 : 28; Amos 9 : 9.

Sift, Isa. 30 : 28, s. the nations with the sieve of vanity.

Amos 9 : 9, will s. Israel as corn is s.

Luke 22 : 31, Satan hath desired to s. you.

Sigh, Isa. 24 : 7, merryhearted s.

Isa. 35 : 10, sorrow and s. shall flee away.

Mark 7 : 34, looking up to heaven he s.

Sight, Ex. 3 : 3, see this great s.

Eccl. 6 : 9, better is s. of eyes.

Matt. 11 : 5; Luke 7 : 21, blind receive their s.

Luke 4 : 18, recovering of s. to the blind.

18 : 42; Acts 22 : 13, receive thy s.

Luke 24 : 31, he vanished out of their s.

2 Cor. 5 : 7, we walk by faith, not by s.

1 Pet. 3 : 4, in s. of God of great price.

Signet, Gen. 38 : 18; Ex. 28 : 11; 39 : 6; Jer. 22 : 24; Dan. 6 : 17.

Signification, 1 Cor. 14 : 10.

Signify, John 12 : 33; Acts 11 : 28; Heb. 12 : 27; Rev. 1 : 1.

Signs, sun and moon, Gen. 1 : 14; rainbow, Gen. 9 : 13; circumcision, Gen. 17 : 10; sabbath, Ex. 31 : 13; Jonas, Matt. 12 : 39; false, Deut. 13 : 1; Matt. 24 : 24; 2 Thess. 2 : 9.

of the times, Matt. 16 : 3.

Pharisees ask for, Matt. 12 : 38; Mark 8 : 11.

Deut. 6 : 8; 11 : 18, bind for s. on hand.

Isa. 7 : 11, ask thee a s. of the Lord.

55 : 13, for an everlasting s.

Matt. 16 : 1; Luke 11 : 16, we would see a s.

Luke 2 : 34, for a s. which shall be spoken against.

John 4 : 48, except ye see s.

Acts 2 : 19, I will show s. in the earth.

2 : 22, approved of God by s.

1 Cor. 1 : 22, Jews require a s.

See 1 Ki. 13 : 3; Isa. 8 : 18; 20 : 3; Acts 2 : 43.

Sihon (sī-hŏn) [sweeping away ?], king of the Amorites, Num. 21 : 21; Deut. 1 : 4; 2 : 26; Ps. 135 : 11; 136 : 19.

Silas [wood], shortened form of " Silvanus," companion of Paul, Acts 15 : 22; 16 : 19; 17 : 4.

See 2 Cor. 1: 19; 1 Thess. 1 : 1; 1 Pet. 5 : 12.

Silence, Job 2 : 13; Ps. 39 : 2; Prov. 10 : 19; 11 : 12; 17 : 28.

women to keep, 1 Tim. 2 : 11.

in heaven, Rev. 8 : 1.

Silent, 1 Sam. 2 : 9, be s. in darkness.

Ps. 28 : 1, be not s. to me.

Zech. 2 : 13, be s., O all flesh, before the Lord.

See Ps. 94 : 17; 1 Tim. 2 : 12; 1 Pet. 2 : 15.

Silk, Prov. 31 : 22; Ezek. 16 : 10, 13; Rev. 18 : 12.

Silly, Job 5 : 2, envy slayeth the s. one.

Hos. 7 : 11, Ephraim is like a s. dove.

2 Tim. 3 : 6, lead captive s. women.

Siloam (sī-lō-ăm) [sent], pool near Jerusalem, John 9 : 7.

Silvanus (sĭl-vā-nŭs) [sylvan], 2 Thess. 1 : 1.

Silver. In Abraham's time commerce was carried on with silver by weight. In the age of Solomon it was abundant, and it was coined in the time of the Maccabees. Gen. 23 : 15.

used in the tabernacle, Ex. 26 : 19; Num. 7 : 13.

as money, Gen. 23 : 15; 44 : 2; Deut. 22 : 19; 2 Ki. 5 : 22.

Silversmith, Acts 19 : 24.

Simeon [hearing], son of Jacob, Gen. 29 : 33; 34 : 7, 25; 42 : 24.

probably concerning, Gen. 49 : 5.

his descendants, Gen. 46 : 10; Ex. 6 : 15; Num. 1 : 22; 26 : 12; 1 Chr. 4 : 24; 12 : 25.

allotment of, Josh. 19 : 1.

blesses Christ, Luke 2 : 25.

brother of James, Acts 15 : 14.

Similitude, Num. 12 : 8, the s. of the Lord.

Deut. 4 : 12, saw no s.

Ps. 144 : 12, after the s. of a palace.

Rom. 5 : 14, after the s. of Adam's transgression.

Heb. 7 : 15, after s. of Melchisedec.

Jas. 3 : 9, men made after s. of God.

Simon, brother of Christ, Matt. 13 : 55; Mark 6 : 3.

Zelotes, apostle, Matt. 10 : 4; Mark 3 : 18; Luke 6 : 15.

Pharisee, reproved, Luke 7 : 36.

leper, Matt. 26 : 6; Mark 14 : 3.

of Cyrene, bears the cross of Jesus, Matt. 27 : 32; Mark 15 : 21; Luke 23 : 26.

a tanner, Peter's vision in his house, Acts 9 : 43; 10 : 6.

a sorcerer, baptized, Acts 8 : 9; rebuked by Peter, Acts 8 : 18 ff.

Peter. See Peter.

Simple, Ps. 19 : 7, making wise the s.
Ps. 116 : 6, the Lord preserveth the s.
119 : 130, it giveth understanding to the s.

Prov. 1 : 22, how long, s. ones, will ye love simplicity ?
22 : 3; 27 : 12, the s. pass on, and are punished.

Simplicity, in Christ, Rom. 16 : 19; 12 : 8; 2 Cor. 1 : 12; 11 : 3.

Sin. The problem of the origin and universality of sin underlies the whole moral teaching of the Old Testament, just as the salvation from sin offered in Christ is fundamental to the message of the New Testament. The first is probably one of those problems which the human mind can never satisfactorily answer. We can, however, say that had there been no such thing as human sin, we could never have known God in all His fulness as a merciful God, one of whose characteristics is that of forgiving love, revealed unto mankind in Jesus Christ.

origin of, Gen. 3 : 6; Matt. 15 : 19; John 8 : 44; Rom. 5 : 12; 1 John 3 : 8.

characterised, Deut. 9 : 7; Josh. 1 : 18; Prov. 15 : 9; 24 : 9; Isa. 1 : 18; Eph. 5 : 11; Heb. 3 : 13; 6 : 1; 9 : 14; Jas. 1 : 15; 4 : 17; 1 John 3 : 4; 5 : 17.

all born in, and under, Gen. 5 : 3; Job 15 : 14; 25 : 4; Ps. 51 : 5; Rom. 3 : 9.

Christ alone without, 2 Cor. 5 : 21; Heb. 4 : 15; 7 : 26; 1 John 3 : 5.

Christ's blood redeems from, Eph. 1 : 7; 1 John 1 : 7; 3 : 5.

a fountain opened for, Zech. 13 . 1.

repented of and confessed, Job 33 : 27; Ps. 38 : 18; 97 : 10; Prov. 28 : 13; Jer. 3 : 21; 1 John 1 : 9.

striven against and mortified, Ps. 19 : 13; 51 : 2; 139 : 23; Matt. 6 : 13; Rom. 8 : 13; Col. 3 : 5; Heb. 12 : 4.

excludes from heaven, 1 Cor. 6 : 9; Gal. 5 : 19; Eph. 5 : 5; Rev. 21 : 27.

wages of, death, Rom. 6 : 23.

sting of death, 1 Cor. 15 : 56.

against the Holy Ghost, Mark 3 : 29; Luke 12 : 10.

wilderness of, Ex. 16 : 1; Num. 13 : 21; 27 : 14.

city called by the Greeks " Pelusium, clay city," Ezek. 30 : 15.

Gen. 4 : 7, s. lieth at the door.

Ex. 34 : 7, forgiving iniquity and s.

Deut. 24 : 16; 2 Ki. 14 : 6; 2 Chr. 25 : 4, put to death for his own s.

Job 10 : 6, thou searchest after my s.

Ps. 32 : 1, blessed is he whose s. is covered.
51 : 3, my s. is ever before me.
103 : 10, not dealt with us after our s.

Prov. 10 : 19, in multitude of words there wanteth not s.
14 : 34, s. is a reproach to any people.

Isa. 30 : 1, may add s. to s.
53 : 12, he bare the s. of many.

Mic. 6 : 7, fruit of body for s. of my soul.

Matt. 12 : 31, all manner of s. shall be forgiven.

John 1 : 29, taketh away the s. of the world.
16 : 8, Comforter will reprove the world of s.

Acts 7 : 60, lay not this s. to their charge.

Rom. 4 : 7, blessed whose s. are covered.
5 : 20, where s. abounded.
6 : 1, shall we continue in s. ?
7 : 9, commandment came, s. revived.
8 : 10, body dead, because of s.
14 : 23, whatsoever is not of faith is s.

Gal. 3 : 22, concluded all under s.

2 Thess. 2 : 3, that man of s.

Heb. 9 : 26, he appeared to put away s.

1 Pet. 2 : 24, his own self bare our s.

1 John 1 : 8, if we say we have no s.

Sin.
Ex. 9 : 27; Num. 22 : 34; Josh. 7 : 20; 1 Sam. 15 : 24; 26 : 21; 2 Sam. 12 : 13; Job 7 : 20; Ps. 41 : 4; Matt. 27 : 4;

Luke 15 : 18, I have s.

1 Ki. 8 : 46, no man that s. not.

Job 10 : 14, if I s., thou markest me.

Ps. 4 : 4, stand in awe, and s. not.
39 : 1, I s. not with my tongue.

Prov. 8 : 36, he that s. against me.

Isa. 43 : 27, thy first father hath s.

Ezek. 18 : 4, soul that s., it shall die.

Hos. 13 : 2, now they s. more and more.

Matt. 18 : 21, Lord, how oft shall my brother s.?

John 5 : 14; 8 : 11, s. no more.

Rom. 6 : 15, shall we s., because not under the law ?
1 Cor. 15 : 34, awake to righteousness, and s. not.

Eph. 4 : 26, be ye angry, and s. not.

Heb. 10 : 26, if we s. wilfully.

1 John 3 : 9, he cannot s., because he is born of God.

See Heb. 6 : 4; 1 John 5 : 16.

Sinai (sī´-nâī) [a bush], Ex. 16 : 1. The names Sinai and Horeb are applied both to particular mountains, and to the whole range of mountains in the Sinaitic peninsula. The actual mountain from which the law was given is placed in all ancient writings at the site now generally indicated, namely, Jebel Musa; and Mount Hor is placed near Petra where the isolated summit of Jebel Harum (" Aaron's mountain ") is shown. (Num. 20 : 22.)

Sincere, Phil. 1 : 10, may be s. till day of Christ.

1 Pet. 2 : 2, as babes desire s. milk of the word.

See Judg. 9 : 16, 19; Phil. 1 : 16.

Sincerity, exhortations to, Josh. 24 : 14; 1 Cor. 5 : 8; Eph. 6 : 24; Titus 2 : 7.

Sinew, Gen. 32 : 32; Isa. 48 : 4; Ezek. 37 : 6.

Sinful, Isa. 1 : 4; Luke 5 : 8; 24 : 7; Rom. 8 : 3.

Sing, Ex. 15 : 21; 1 Chr. 16 : 23; Ps. 30 : 4; 95 : 1; 98 : 1; 149 : 1; Isa. 12 : 5, s. to the Lord.

Ps. 66 : 2, s. forth the honour of his name.

Eph 5 : 19; Col. 3 : 16, s. in your hearts.
Rev. 15 : 3, they s. song of Moses.
Singers, 1 Ki. 10 : 12; Ps. 68 : 25; 87 : 7; Hab. 3 : 19.
Singing, Ps. 100 : 2, come before his presence with s.
Song of Sol. 2 : 12, time of the s. of birds. See Psalmody.
Single, Matt. 6 : 22; Luke 11 : 34, if thine eye be s.
Singleness, Acts 2 : 46; Eph. 6 : 5; Col. 3 : 22.
See Lev. 27 : 2.
Sink, Ps. 69 : 2; Matt. 14 : 30; Luke 9 : 44.
Sinner, Gen. 13 : 13, men of Sodom were s.
Ps. 1 : 1, standeth not in way of s.
26 : 9, gather not my soul with s.
51 : 13, s. shall be converted to thee.
Prov. 1 : 10, if s. entice thee.
13 : 21, evil pursueth s.
Eccl. 9 : 18, one s. destroyeth much good.
Matt. 9 : 13; Mark 2 : 17, came not to call righteous but s.
Matt. 11 : 19; Luke 7 : 34, a friend of s.
Luke 7 : 37, woman who was a s.
15 : 7, joy in heaven over one s.
18 : 13, be merciful to me a s.
John 9 : 16, how can a man that is a s. do such miracles ?
Rom. 5 : 8, while we were yet s.
Jas. 5 : 20, converteth s., shall save a soul.
Sion (sī-ǫn) [surrounded], see Zion.
Sisera (sĭs-ĕr-ă) [leader ?], Judg. 4 : 2, 22; 5 : 26; 1 Sam. 12 : 9; Ps. 83 : 9.
Sister, Job 17 : 14, said to worm, Thou art my s.
Matt. 12 : 50; Mark 3 : 35, same is my brother and s.
John 19 : 25, stood by cross his mother's s.
Sit, Judg. 5 : 10, ye that s. in judgment.
2 Ki. 7 : 3, why s. we here till we die ?
Ps. 26 : 5, will not s. with wicked.
69 : 12, they that s. in the gate.
110 : 1, s. thou at my right hand.
Isa. 30 : 7, their strength is to s. still.
Jer. 8 : 14, why do we s. still ?
Mic. 4 : 4, s. every man under his vine.
Matt. 20 : 23; Mark 10 : 37, to s. on my right hand.
Jas. 2 : 3, s. thou here in a good place.
Rev. 3 : 21, to s. with me in my throne.
Sith [since], Ezek. 35 : 6, s. thou hast not hated blood.
Situation, 2 Ki. 2 : 19, the s. of this city is pleasant.
Ps. 48 : 2, beautiful for s., joy of earth.
Sivan (sī-văn) [Assyr., " Sivanu "], month of June, Esther 8 : 9. See Months.
Skilful, 1 Chr. 28 : 21; 2 Chr. 2 : 14; Ps. 33 : 3; Dan. 1 : 4.
Skill, 1 Ki. 5 : 6; 2 Chr. 2 : 8, s. to hew timber.
2 Chr. 2 : 7, men that can s. to grave.
34 : 12, all that could s. of instruments of music.
Dan. 1 : 17, God gave them s. in wisdom.
Skin, Ex. 34 : 29, wist not that s. of his face shone.
Job 2 : 4, s. for s.

10 : 11, thou hast clothed me with s. and flesh.
19 : 20, escaped with s. of my teeth.
19 : 26, after my s. worms destroy this body.
Ps. 102 : 5, my bones cleave to my s.
Jer. 13 : 23, can the Ethiopian change his s. ?
Heb. 11 : 37, wandered in sheep-s.
Skip, Ps. 29 : 6, maketh them also to s.
Ps. 114 : 4, mountains s. like rams.
Song of Sol. 2 : 8, he cometh s. upon the hills.
Jer. 48 : 27, thou s. for joy.
Skirt, 1 Sam. 24 : 4; Ps. 133 : 2; Ezek. 5 : 3.
Skull, Mark 15 : 22; Judg. 9 : 53.
Sky, Isa. 45 : 8, let the s. pour down righteousness.
Jer. 51 : 9, is lifted up even to s.
Matt. 16 : 2, 3, for the s. is red.
Heb. 11 : 12, many as stars of s.
Slack, Deut. 7 : 10, he will not be s. to him that hateth.
Prov. 10 : 4, poor that dealeth with s. hand.
2 Pet. 3 : 9, Lord is not s. concerning his promise.
Slain, Gen. 4 : 23, I have s. a man.
Prov. 7 : 26, strong men have been s. by her.
22 : 13, the slothful man saith, I shall be s.
Isa. 26 : 21, the earth shall no more cover her s.
66 : 16, the s. of the Lord shall be many.
Ezek. 37 : 9, breathe upon these s.
Acts 2 : 23, by wicked hands have s.
Eph. 2 : 16, by cross, having s. enmity.
Rev. 5 : 6, a Lamb as it had been s.
6 : 9, souls of them that were s.
Slander, Ex. 23 : 1; Ps. 15 : 3; 31 : 13; 34 : 13; (1 Pet. 3 : 10); 50 : 20; 64 : 3; 101 : 5; Prov. 10 : 18; Jer. 6 : 28; 9 : 4; Rom. 3 : 8; Eph 4 : 31; 1 Tim 3 : 11; Titus 3 : 2.
effects of, Prov. 16 : 28; 17 : 9; 18 : 8; 26 : 20, 22; Jer. 38 : 4; Ezek. 22 : 9; Matt. 26 : 59; Acts 6 : 11; 17 : 7; 24 : 5.
behaviour under, Matt. 5 : 11; 1 Cor. 4 : 12.
Slaughter, Ps. 44 : 22; Rom. 8 : 36, as sheep for the s.
Isa. 53 : 7; Jer. 11 : 19, brought as a lamb to the s.
Jer. 7 : 32; 19 : 6, valley of s.
Acts 9 : 1, Saul, yet breathing out s.
Jas. 5 : 5, nourish your hearts as in a day of s.
Slaves [bodies], Rev. 18 : 13, s. and souls of men.
Slay, Gen. 18 : 25, far from thee to s. righteous.
Job 13 : 15, though he s. me, yet will I trust in him.
Luke 19 : 27, bring hither, and s. them.
Slaying unpremeditatedly, Num. 35 : 11; Deut. 4 : 42; 19 : 3; Josh. 20 : 3.
Sleep, of death, Ps. 13 : 3; Dan. 12 : 2; Mark 13 : 36; 1 Cor. 11 : 30; 15 : 20.
1 Sam. 26 : 12, a deep s. from God.
Job 33 : 15, when deep s. falleth upon men.
Ps. 127 : 2, he giveth his beloved s.
132 : 4, I will not give s. to mine eyes.

Prov. 3 : 24, thy **s.** shall be sweet.
6 : 10; 24 : 33, yet a little **s.**
Eccl. 5 : 12, the **s.** of a labouring man is sweet.
Luke 9 : 32, heavy with **s.**
John 11 : 13, taking of rest in **s.**
Rom. 13 : 11, time to awake out of **s.**
Sleep.
Ex. 22 : 27, where in shall he **s.** ?
1 Sam. 3 : 3, was laid down to **s.**
Job 7 : 21, now shall I **s.** in the dust.
Ps. 4 : 8, I will lay me down and **s.**
121 : 4, neither slumber nor **s.**
Prov. 4 : 16, they **s.** not, except they have done mischief.
6 : 10; 24 : 33, folding of hands to **s.**
10 : 5, he that **s.** in harvest.
Song of Sol. 5 : 2, I **s.**, but my heart waketh.
Dan. 12 : 2, many that **s.** in the dust.
Matt. 9 : 24; Mark 5 : 39; Luke 8 : 52, maid is not dead, but **s.**
Matt. 26 : 45; Mark 14 : 41, **s.** on now.
Luke 22 : 46, why **s.** ye ? rise and pray.
John 11 : 12, if he **s.**, he shall do well.
1 Cor. 15 : 51, we shall not all **s.**
Eph. 5 : 14, awake thou that **s.**
1 Thess. 4 : 14, them which **s.** in Jesus.
5 : 6, let us not **s.**, as do others.
See Gen. 2 : 21; 15 : 12; Job 4 : 13; Prov. 6 : 4-11; 19 : 15; 20 : 13; Jonah 1 : 6.
Sleight, Eph. 4 : 14.
Slew, Gen. 4 : 8; Ex. 2 : 12; 1 Sam. 29 : 5; Matt. 2 : 16; Acts 5 : 30; 1 John 3 : 12.
Slide, Deut. 32 : 35, foot shall **s.** in due time.
Ps. 26 : 1, I shall not **s.**
37 : 31, none of his steps shall **s.**
Hos. 4 : 16, Israel **s.** back.
Slightly, Jer. 6 : 14; 8 : 11.
Slime, Gen. 11 : 3; Ex. 2 : 3.
Slimepits, Gen. 14 : 10.
Sling, Goliath slain by, 1 Sam. 17 : 49.
figurative, 1 Sam. 25 : 29; Prov. 26 : 8.
See Judg. 20 : 16; 2 Ki. 3 : 25; 2 Chr. 26 : 14.
Slingstones, Job 41 : 28.
Slip, 2 Sam. 22 : 37; Ps. 18 : 36, my foot did not **s.**
Job 12 : 5, he that is ready to **s.**
Ps. 17 : 5, that my footsteps **s.** not.
73 : 2, my steps had well nigh **s.**
Heb. 2 : 1, lest we should let them **s.**
Slippery, Ps. 35 : 6; 73 : 18; Jer. 23 : 12.
Slothful, Judg. 18 : 9, be not **s.** to possess the land.
Prov. 18 : 9, the **s.** is brother to great waster.
21 : 25, the desire of the **s.** killeth him.
Matt. 25 : 26, wicked and **s.** servant.
Rom. 12 : 11, not **s.** in business.
Heb. 6 : 12, that ye be not **s.**
Slothfulness, Prov. 12 : 24, 27; 15 : 19; 19 : 15, 24; 22 : 13; 24 : 30; 26 : 13-16; Eccl. 10 : 18; Rom. 11 : 8.
condemned, Prov. 6 : 4; Rom. 13 : 11; 1 Thess. 5 : 6.
Slow, Ex. 4 : 10, I am **s.** of speech.
Neh. 9 : 17, a God **s.** to anger.
Prov. 14 : 29, that is **s.** to wrath.
Luke 24 : 25, **s.** of heart.
Jas. 1 : 19, **s.** to speak, **s.** to wrath.

See Acts 27 : 7.
Sluggard, Prov. 6 : 6; 10 : 26; 13 : 4; 20 : 4; 26 : 16.
Sluices, Isa. 19 : 10.
Slumber, Ps. 121 : 3, he that keepeth thee will not **s.**
Isa. 5 : 27, none shall **s.** nor sleep.
Nah. 3 : 18, thy shepherds **s.**
Matt. 25 : 5, while bridegroom tarried, they **s.**
Prov. 6 : 4, give not **s.** to thine eyelids.
Rom. 11 : 8, God hath given them the spirit of **s.**
Small, Ex. 16 : 14, **s.** round thing, **s.** as hoar frost.
Num. 16 : 13, is it a **s.** thing that thou hast brought us ?
2 Sam. 7 : 19; 1 Chr. 17 : 17, a **s.** thing in thy sight.
1 Ki. 19 : 12, after the fire a still **s.** voice.
Isa. 7 : 13, is it a **s.** thing to weary men ?
54 : 7, for a **s.** moment.
60 : 22, a **s.** one shall become a strong nation.
Zech. 4 : 10, the day of **s.** things.
Acts 15 : 2, no **s.** dissension.
Smart, Prov. 11 : 15.
Smell, Gen. 27 : 27, as **s.** of a field.
1 Cor. 12 : 17, where were the **s.** ?
Phil. 4 : 18, an odour of a sweet **s.**
Job 39 : 25, he **s.** the battle afar.
Ps. 45 : 8, thy garments **s.** of myrrh.
115 : 6, noses have they, but **s.** not.
Smite, Ex. 21 : 12, he that **s.** a man.
2 Ki. 6 : 21, shall I **s.** them ?
Ps. 121 : 6, the sun shall not **s.** thee by day.
Prov. 19 : 25, **s.** a scorner.
Isa. 49 : 10, neither shall heat **s.** thee.
Lam. 3 : 30, giveth his cheek to him that **s.** thee.
Nah. 2 : 10, knees **s.** together.
Zech. 13 : 7; Matt. 26 : 31; Mark 14 : 27, **s.** the Shepherd.
Mal. 4 : 6, lest I **s.** the earth with a curse.
Matt. 5 : 39, **s.** thee on right cheek.
24 : 49, begin to **s.** his fellow-servants.
John 18 : 23, why **s.** thou me ?
Smith, 1 Sam. 13 : 19; 2 Ki. 24 : 14; Jer. 24 : 1. See **Handicraft.**
Smitten, Deut. 28 : 25, Lord cause thee to be **s.** before enemies.
Job 16 : 10, they have **s.** me upon the cheek.
Ps. 102 : 4, my heart is **s.**
Isa. 53 : 4, **s.** of God.
Hos. 6 : 1, he hath **s.**, and he will bind.
Smoke, Gen. 19 : 28, as the **s.** of a furnace.
Deut. 29 : 20, the anger of the Lord shall **s.**
Ps. 37 : 20, wicked shall consume into **s.**
68 : 2, as **s.** is driven away.
102 : 3, my days are consumed like **s.**
104 : 32, he toucheth hills, and they **s.**
119 : 83, like a bottle in the **s.**
Prov. 10 : 26, as **s.** to the eyes.
Isa. 6 : 4, the house was filled with **s.**
51 : 6, heavens shall vanish like **s.**
Hos. 13 : 3, as **s.** out of the chimney.
Rev. 19 : 3, her **s.** rose up for ever.
See Isa. 42 : 3; Matt. 12 : 20.
Smooth, Gen. 27 : 11, I am a **s.** man.

1 Sam. 17 : 40, five s. stones.
Ps. 55 : 21, words were s. than butter.
Isa. 30 : 10, speak unto us s. things.
Luke 3 : 5, rough ways shall be made s.
Smote, Gen. 19 : 11, s. men with blindness.
Num. 20 : 11, Moses s. the rock.
Song of Sol. 5 : 7, the watchman s. me.
Isa. 60 : 10, in my wrath I s. thee.
Hag. 2 : 17, s. you with blasting.
Matt. 26 : 68; Luke 22 : 64, who is he that s. thee ?
Luke 18 : 13, publican s. upon his breast.
Acts 12 : 23, angel of the Lord s. him.
Snail, occurs once, in Ps. 58 : 8. The description rather refers to the slug, which is a snail with a minute internal shell, and which in great heat soon " melts away."
Snare, Ex. 10 : 7, how long shall this man be a s. unto us ?
Josh. 23 : 13, they shall be s. unto you.
1 Sam. 28 : 9, wherefore layest thou a s. for my life ?
2 Sam. 22 : 6; Ps. 18 : 5, the s. of death prevented me.
Ps. 11 : 6, upon the wicked he shall rain s.
69 : 22, let their table become a s.
91 : 3, deliver thee from s. of fowler.
124 : 7, the s. is broken.
142 : 3, they privily laid s. for me.
Prov. 7 : 23, as a bird hasteth to the s.
13 : 14; 14 : 27, the s. of death.
29 : 25, fear of man bringeth a s.
Eccl. 9 : 12, as birds caught in the s.
Isa. 24 : 17; Jer. 48 : 43, the s. are upon thee.
Lam. 3 : 47, fear and a s. is come upon us.
Hos. 9 : 8, the prophet is a s. of a fowler.
Amos 3 : 5, can a bird fall in a s. ?
Luke 21 : 35, as a s. shall it come.
1 Tim. 3 : 7, lest he fall into s. of devil.
6 : 9, they that will be rich fall into a s.
2 Tim. 2 : 26, recover out of s. of the devil.
Snatch, Isa. 9 : 20.
Sneezed, 2 Ki. 4 : 35.
Snout, Prov. 11 : 22.
Snow, Ex. 4 : 6; Num. 12 : 10; 2 Ki. 5 : 27, leprous as s.
2 Sam. 23 : 20, slew lion in time of s.
Job 6 : 16, wherein the s. is hid.
9 : 30, if I wash myself with s. water.
37 : 6, saith to s., Be thou on earth.
38 : 22, the treasures of the s.
Ps. 51 : 7, I shall be whiter than s.
147 : 16, he giveth s. like wool.
Prov. 25 : 13, as cold of s. in harvest.
26 : 1, as s. in summer.
31 : 21, she is not afraid of the s.
Isa. 1 : 18, your sins shall be white as s.
55 : 10, as s. from heaven returneth not.
Lam. 4 : 7, Nazarites purer than s.
Dan. 7 : 9, whose garment was white as s.
Matt. 28 : 3; Mark 9 : 3, raiment white as s.
Rev. 1 : 14, his hairs white as s.
Snuffed, Jer. 14 : 6, wild asses s. up the wind.
Mal. 1 : 13, ye have s. at it, saith the Lord.
Snuffers, Ex. 37 : 23; Jer. 52 : 18.
Soaked, Isa. 34 : 7.
Soap, Jer. 2 : 22; Mal. 3 : 2. Soap was made by mixing oil with a potash which was

obtained from certain plants which grew in salt marshes.
Sober, 2 Cor. 5 : 13, s. for your cause.
1 Thess. 5 : 6, let us watch and be s.
1 Tim. 3 : 2; Titus 1 : 8, a bishop must be s.
Titus 2 : 2, that aged men be s.
1 Pet. 4 : 7, be s., and watch unto prayer.
5 : 8, be s., be vigilant.
See Acts 26 : 25; Titus 2 : 12.
Sobriety, Rom. 12 : 3; 1 Thess. 5 : 6; 1 Tim. 2 : 9; 3 : 2; Titus 1 : 8; 1 Pet. 1 : 13; 4 : 7; 5 : 8.
Sod, Sodden (from seethe) [means boiled], Gen. 25 : 29.
Sodering, Isa. 41 : 7.
Sodom [surrounded ?], its wickedness and destruction, Gen. 13 : 13; 18 : 20; 19 : 4; Deut. 23 : 17; 1 Ki. 14 : 24.
Lot's deliverance from, Gen. 19.
a warning, Deut. 29 : 23; Isa. 1 : 9; 13 : 19; Lam. 4 : 6; Matt. 10 : 15; Luke 17 : 29; Jude 7; Rev. 11 : 8.
vine of. The words occur only in Deut. 32 : 32. From its being called " gephen " or " vine," it would appear to be a trailing plant with tendrils and with a bitter fruit. These would apply to the colocynth plant (Citrullus colocynthis), which grows in the neighbourhood of the Dead Sea.
Soft, Job 23 : 16, God maketh my heart s.
Job 41 : 3, will he speak s. words ?
Ps. 65 : 10, thou makest it s. with showers.
Prov. 15 : 1, a s. answer turneth away wrath.
25 : 15, a s. tongue breaketh the bone.
Matt. 11 : 8, a man clothed in s. raiment.
See Ps. 55 : 21; Isa. 38 : 15; Acts 27 : 13.
Soil, Ezek. 17 : 8.
Sojourn, Gen. 19 : 9, this fellow came in to s.
47 : 4, to s. in the land are we come.
2 Ki. 8 : 1, s. wheresoever thou canst s.
Ps. 120 : 5, woe is me, that I s.
Isa. 52 : 4, my people went to Egypt to s.
Acts 7 : 6, should s. in a strange land.
Heb. 11 : 9, by faith he s. in land of promise.
1 Pet. 1 : 17, pass the time of your s. in fear.
Sojourner, Lev. 25 : 23; 1 Chr. 29 : 15; Ps. 39 : 12.
Sold, Gen. 25 : 33, s. his birthright.
45 : 4, whom ye s. into Egypt.
Lev. 27 : 28, no devoted thing shall be s.
Deut. 32 : 30, except their Rock had s. them.
1 Ki. 21 : 20, thou hast s. thyself to work evil.
Isa. 52 : 3, ye have s. yourselves for nought.
Joel 3 : 3, they have s. a girl for wine.
Amos 2 : 6, they s. the righteous for silver.
Matt. 10 : 29, are not two sparrows s. for a farthing ?
13 : 46, went and s. all that he had.
18 : 25, his lord commanded him to be s.
21 : 12; Mark 11 : 15, cast out them that s.

Matt. 26 : 9; Mark 14 : 5; John 12 : 5, ointment might have been s.

Luke 17 : 28, they bought, they s.

Rom. 7 : 14, s. under sin.

1 Cor. 10 : 25, whatsoever is s. in the shambles.

Soldiers, admonition to, Luke 3 : 14.

at the crucifixion, John 19 : 2, 23, 32.

as guards, Matt. 27 : 66; 28 : 4, 12; Acts 12 : 4; 23 : 10; 27 : 42.

Ezra 8 : 22, ashamed to require s.

Matt. 8 : 9; Luke 7 : 8, having s. under me.

Luke 3 : 14, the s. demanded. And what shall we do ?

John 19 : 23, to every s. a part.

Acts 10 : 7, a devout s.

2 Tim. 2 : 3, endure hardness as a good s. of Christ.

Sole, Gen. 8 : 9, dove found no rest for s. of foot.

2 Sam. 14 : 25; Isa. 1 : 6, from s. of foot to crown.

Solemn, Num. 10 : 10, in your s. days.

Ps. 92 : 3, sing praise with a s. sound.

See Gen. 43 : 3; I Sam. 8 : 9; Isa. 30 : 29.

Solitary, Ps. 68 : 6, God setteth the s. in families.

107 : 4, wandered in a s. way.

Isa. 35 : 1, wilderness and s. place shall be glad.

Mark 1 : 35, Jesus departed to a s. place.

Solomon [peaceful], king of Israel, 2 Sam. 12 : 24; 1 Ki. 1; 2 : 25; 1 Chr. 28 : 9; 29.

asks of God wisdom, 1 Ki. 3 : 5; 4 : 29; 2 Chr. 1 : 7.

his wise judgment, 1 Ki. 3 : 16.

his league with Hiram, 1 Ki. 5; 2 Chr. 2.

builds the temple (2 Sam. 7 : 12; 1 Chr 17 : 11); 1 Ki. 6; 2 Chr. 3–5.

his prayer at the dedication, 1 Ki. 8; 2 Chr. 6.

God's covenant with, 1 Ki. 9; 2 Chr. 7 : 12.

visited by the queen of Sheba, 1 Ki. 10; 2 Chr. 9; (Matt. 6 : 29); Matt. 12 : 42.

David's prayer for, Ps. 72.

his idolatry, rebuke, and death, 1 Ki. 11 : 1, 9 : 41; 2 Chr. 9 : 29; Neh. 13 : 26.

his Proverbs and Song, Prov. 1 : 1; Eccl. 1 : 1; Song of Sol. 1 : 1.

Somebody, Luke 8 : 46, s. hath touched me.

Acts 5 : 36, boasting himself to be s.

Something, 1 Sam. 20 : 26, s. hath befallen him.

John 13 : 29, should give s. to the poor.

Acts 3 : 5, expecting to receive s.

Gal. 6 : 3, think himself to be s. when he is nothing.

Sometime, Eph. 2 : 13; 1 Pet. 3 : 20.

Somewhat, 1 Ki. 2 : 14; Acts 23 : 20; Rev. 2 : 4.

Son, of God. See **Christ.**

of man, Ezek. 2 : 1; Matt. 8 : 20; Acts 7 : 56.

sons of God, Job 1 : 6; 38 : 7; John 1 : 12; Rom. 8 : 14; 2 Cor. 6 : 18; Heb. 2 : 10; 12 : 5; Jas. 1 : 18; 1 John 3 : 1.

obligations of, Eph. 5 : 1; Phil. 2 : 15; 1 Pet. 1 : 13; 2 : 9.

Ps. 2 : 12, kiss the S., lest he be angry.

86 : 16, save s. of thine handmaid.

Prov. 10 : 1; 15 : 20, a wise s. maketh a glad father.

Isa. 9 : 6, unto us a s. is given.

14 : 12, s. of the morning.

Dan. 3 : 25; Luke 3 : 38; John 1 : 34; Acts 9 : 20, the S. of God.

Mal. 3 : 17, as a man spareth his own s.

Matt. 11 : 27, no man knoweth the S.

13 : 55, the carpenter's s.

17 : 5, this is my beloved S.

22 : 42, Christ ? whose s. is he ?

Mark 14 : 61, art thou the Christ, the S. of the Blessed ?

Luke 7 : 12, only s. of his mother.

12 : 53, father divided against the s.

John 1 : 18; 3 : 18, only begotten S.

5 : 23, men should honour the S.

8 : 36, if the S. shall make you free.

17 : 12; 2 Thess. 2 : 3, the s. of perdition.

Acts 4 : 36, the s. of consolation.

23 : 6, the s. of a Pharisee.

Rom. 8 : 3, God, sending his own S.

8 : 32, spared not his own S.

Gal. 4 : 7, if a s., then an heir.

Heb. 1 : 2, God hath spoken to us by his S.

5 : 8, though he were a S., yet learned he obedience.

12 : 6, scourgeth every s. whom he receiveth.

1 John 5 : 12, he that hath the S. hath life.

Song of Solomon (Song of Songs).

Author and Date.—The traditional view is that the author of this book is Solomon, but there is no decisive evidence on the question. It is conjectured from the language of the poem, and the writer's familiarity with the various places in Northern Palestine, that the author was a native of one of the northern tribes. From the way in which Tirzah is mentioned in Chap. 6 : 4, together with Jerusalem, it has been inferred that the former in the time of the author, was the capital of the northern kingdom, and that the Song was composed before Omri constituted Samaria the metropolis of his kingdom. If this conjecture be correct, the poem may be assigned to a date about 930 B.C.

Contents.—It is now generally admitted that the Song is a single poem, the production of one author. The structure of the book is dramatic, and by some supposed to have been designed for the stage. But that view is erroneous. Different parts of the poem are put in the mouths of various speakers. There are three principal characters in the poem, viz., Solomon, a beautiful Shulamite maiden, and her lover, a shepherd. The maiden is brought by the king to Jerusalem, and efforts made by the monarch and the ladies of his court to induce her to give up her home and lover, and enter the royal harem. The damsel, however, repels all the king's advances, and is finally permitted to return to her home, where, at the close of the poem, the lovers appear together, and express in glowing terms the superiority of pure and genuine affection over that which may be obtained by wealth and position. A noteworthy element throughout the poem is the chorus, which is composed of the daughters of Jerusalem. The poem is divided into twelve scenes, each commencing and ending with a sort of refrain, which separates one scene from the preceding and following.

Songs, of Moses, Ex. 15; Num. 21 : 17; Deut. 32; Rev. 15 : 3; of Deborah, Judg. 5; of Hannah, 1 Sam. 2; of David, 2 Sam. 22 (see **Psalms**); of Mary, Luke 1 : 46; of Zacharias, Luke 1 : 68; of the angels, Luke 2 : 13; of Simeon, Luke 2 : 29; of the redeemed, Rev. 5 : 9; 19.

of Degrees. See **Psalms.**
Job 30 : 9, now am I their s.
Ps. 33 : 3; Isa. 42 : 10, sing a new s.
Ps. 40 : 3, he hath put a new s. in my mouth.
42 : 8, his s. shall be with me.
69 : 12, s. of the drunkards.
118 : 14; Isa. 12 : 2, the Lord is my strength and s.
137 : 4, how shall we sing the Lord's s. ?
Song of Sol. 1 : 1, S. of s.
Isa. 24 : 16, we heard s.
35 : 10, come to Zion with s.
Ezek. 33 : 32, as a very lovely s.
Eph. 5 : 19; Col. 3 : 16, speaking in psalms and spiritual s.

Soothsayer, Josh. 13 : 22; Mic. 5 : 12.
Soothsaying, Acts 16 : 16.
Sop, John 13 : 26, 27, 30.
Sorcery, Isa. 47 : 9; 57 : 3; Acts 8 : 9; 13 : 6; Rev. 18 : 23; 21 : 8; 22 : 15. Sorcery, or witchcraft, was common in the ancient world, as it is still among primitive peoples. It has always held a place among the rites and practices of primitive religions.

Sore, Job 5 : 18, maketh s. and bindeth up.
Ps. 118 : 13, thou hast thrust s. at me.
Matt. 21 : 15, they were s. displeased.
Acts 20 : 37, wept s.
See Isa. 1 : 6; Heb. 10 : 29.

Sorrow, godly, 2 Cor. 7 : 10; earthly, Job 17 : 7; Ps. 13 : 2; Isa. 35 : 10; Rom. 9 : 2; consequences of sin, Gen. 3 : 16; Ps. 51.
Gen. 42 : 38, with s. to the grave.
Job 6 : 10, I would harden myself in s.
41 : 22, s. is turned into joy.
Ps. 90 : 10, their strength is labour and s.
116 : 3, I found trouble and s.
Prov. 10 : 22, it maketh rich, and he addeth no s.
23 : 29, who hath s. ?
Eccl. 1 : 18, increaseth knowledge increased s.
7 : 3, s. is better than laughter.
11 : 10, remove s. from thy heart.
Isa. 17 : 11, day of desperate s.
51 : 11, s. and sighing shall flee away.

53 : 3, a man of s.
Jer. 49 : 23, there is s. on the sea.
Lam. 1 : 12, any s. like unto my s.
Matt. 24 : 8; Mark 13 : 8, beginning of s.
Luke 25 : 45, sleeping for s.
John 16 : 6, s. hath filled your heart.
2 Cor. 2 : 7, overmuch s.
Rev. 21 : 4, be no more death, neither s.
1 Thess. 4 : 13, ye s. not as others.

Sorrowful, 1 Sam. 1 : 15, a woman of a s. spirit.
Ps. 69 : 29, I am poor and s.
Prov. 14 : 13, even in laughter the heart is s.
Matt. 19 : 22; Luke 18 : 23, went away s.
Matt. 26 : 37, he began to be s.
26 : 38; Mark 14 : 34, my soul is exceeding s.
John 16 : 20, ye shall be s.
2 Cor. 6 : 10, as s., yet alway rejoicing.
See Ps. 38 : 18; Isa. 51 : 19; Matt. 14 : 9; 17 : 23.

Sosthenes (sŏs⸗thĕn⸗ēs) [safe in strength], Acts 18 : 17.

Soul, man endowed with, Gen. 2 : 7.
atonement for, Lev. 17 : 11.
redemption of, Ps. 34 : 22; 49 : 15.
its inestimable value, Matt. 16 : 26; Mark 8 : 37.
Deut. 11 : 13, serve him with all your s.
13 : 3; Josh. 22 : 5, love the Lord with all your s.
1 Sam. 18 : 1, the s. of Jonathan was knit with s. of David.
1 Ki. 8 : 48, return with all their s.
1 Chr. 22 : 19, set your s. to seek the Lord.
Job 3 : 20, life unto the bitter in s.
12 : 10, in whose hand is the s. of every living thing.
16 : 4, if your s. were in my s. stead.
33 : 19, to deliver their s. from death.
49 : 8, redemption of their s. is precious.
63 : 1, my s. thirsteth for God.
103 : 1; 104 : 1, bless the Lord, O my s.
116 : 7, return unto thy rest, O my s.
Ps. 142 : 4, no man cared for my s.
Prov. 11 : 25, liberal s. shall be made fat.
19 : 2, that the s. be without knowledge, it is not good.
Isa. 55 : 3, hear, and your s. shall live.
58 : 10, if thou satisfy the afflicted s.
Jer. 31 : 12, their s. shall be as a garden.
38 : 16, Lord that made this s.
Ezek. 18 : 4, all s. are mine.
Hab. 2 : 10, sinned against thy s.
Matt. 10 : 28, to destroy both s. and body.
Mark 8 : 36, lose his own s.
Luke 21 : 19, in patience possess ye your s.
Acts 4 : 32, of one s.
Rom. 13 : 1, let every s. be subject unto higher powers.
1 Thess. 5 : 23, your s. and body be preserved.
Heb. 6 : 19, an anchor of the s.
10 : 39, believe to saving of s.
Jas. 5 : 20, shall save a s. from death.
1 Pet. 2 : 11, lusts which war against the s.
4 : 19, commit the keeping of their s. to him.

3 John 2, even as thy s. prospereth.
Rev. 16 : 3, every living s. died in the sea.
Sow, Job 4 : 8, they that s. wickedness, reap the same.
Ps. 126 : 5, that s. in tears shall reap in joy.
Eccl. 11 : 4, he that observeth the wind shall not s.
   11 : 6, in the morning s. thy seed.
Isa. 32 : 20, that s. beside all waters.
Jer. 4 : 3, s. not among thorns.
Hos. 10 : 12, s. in righteousness, reap in mercy.
Mic. 6 : 15, thou shalt s., but not reap.
Hag. 1 : 6, ye have s. much, and bring in little.
Matt. 6 : 26, they s. not.
   13 : 3; Mark 4 : 3; Luke 8 : 5, sower went forth to s.
Luke 19 : 21, reapest that thou didst not s.
John 4 : 36, he that s. and he that reapeth.
1 Cor. 15 : 36, that which thou s. is not quickened.
2 Cor. 9 : 6, he which s. sparingly.
Gal. 6 : 7, whatsoever a man s., that shall he also reap.
Sower, Isa. 55 : 10; Jer. 50 : 16; 2 Cor. 9 : 10.
parable of, Matt. 13 : 3; Mark 4 : 3; Luke 8 : 5.
Spake, Ps. 33 : 9, he s., and it was done.
Ps. 78 : 19, they s. against God.
Jer. 7 : 13, I s. unto you, rising up early.
Mal. 3 : 16, feared the Lord s. often one to another.
John 7 : 46, never man s. like this man.
   9 : 29, God s. to Moses.
Acts 7 : 6, God s. on this wise.
1 Cor. 13 : 11, I s. as a child.
Heb. 1 : 1, God, who s. in time past.
   12 : 25, refused him that s. on earth.
2 Pet. 1 : 21, men of God s. as they were moved.
Spare, Gen. 18 : 26, I will s. the place for their sakes.
Neh. 13 : 22, s. me according to thy mercy.
Ps. 39 : 13, s. me, that I may recover strength.
   72 : 13, he shall s. poor and needy.
Prov. 13 : 24, he that s. the rod.
   19 : 18, let not thy soul s. for his crying.
Isa. 58 : 1, s. not, lift up thy voice.
Jonah 4 : 11, should not I s. Nineveh ?
Mal. 3 : 17, I will s. them, as a man s. his own son.
Luke 15 : 17, have bread enough and to s.
Rom. 8 : 32, he that s. not his own Son.
   11 : 21, lest he also s. not thee.
2 Pet. 2 : 4, if God s. not angels.
See 2 Cor. 9 : 6.
Spark, Job 5 : 7, as s. fly upward.
   18 : 5, s. of his fire shall not shine.
Isa. 1 : 31, maker of it shall be as a s.
Sparrow. The Hebrew word occurs very often in the Bible. It would seem to apply to all manner of small perching birds, of which great numbers are to be found in Palestine. Lev. 14 : 4; Ps. 84 : 3; Matt. 10 : 29; Luke 12 : 6.

Speak, Gen. 18 : 27, taken upon me to s. unto the Lord.
   24 : 50, we cannot s. bad or good.
Ex. 4 : 14, he can s. well.
   33 : 11, as a man s. to his friend.
   34 : 34, went in to s., with the Lord.
1 Sam. 3 : 9, s., Lord, thy servant heareth.
Job 33 : 14, God s. once, yea twice.
   36 : 2, yet to s. on God's behalf.
Ps. 85 : 8, I will hear what the Lord will s.
   145 : 21, my mouth shall s. the praise of the Lord.
Prov. 23 : 9, s. not in the ears of a fool.
Eccl. 3 : 7, a time to s.
Isa. 50 : 4, to s. a word in season.
   63 : 1, I that s. in righteousness.
Hab. 2 : 3, at the end it shall s.
Zech. 8 : 16; Eph. 4 : 25, s. every man the truth.
Matt. 10 : 19; Mark 13 : 11, how ye shall s.
Matt. 12 : 36, every idle word that men shall s.
Luke 6 : 26, when all men s. well of you.
John 3 : 11, we s. that we do know.
Acts 4 : 20, we cannot but s.
   26 : 1, permitted to s. for thyself.
1 Cor. 1 : 10, that ye all s. the same thing.
2 Cor. 2 : 17, in sight of God s. we in Christ.
   4 : 13, we believe, and therefore s.
1 Thess. 2 : 4, we s. not as pleasing men.
Titus 3 : 2, to s. evil of no man.
Heb. 12 : 25, see that ye refuse not him that s.
Jas. 1 : 19, slow to s.
Spear, Josh. 8 : 18, stretch out the s.
1 Sam. 17 : 45, comest with a s.
Ps. 46 : 9, he cutteth the s. in sunder.
Isa. 2 : 4; Mic. 4 : 3, beat s. into pruning-hooks.
John 19 : 34, with s. pierced his side.
Speech, Gen. 11 : 1, whole earth was of one s.
Ex. 4 : 10, I am slow of s.
Deut. 32 : 2, my s. shall distil as dew.
1 Ki. 3 : 10, Solomon's s. pleased the Lord.
Ps. 19 : 2, day unto day uttereth s.
Prov. 17 : 7, excellent s. becometh not a fool.
Song of Sol. 4 : 3, thy s. is comely.
Isa. 29 : 4, thy s. shall be low out of the dust.
   33 : 19, of deeper s. than thou canst perceive.
Matt. 26 : 73, thy s. bewrayeth thee.
1 Cor. 2 : 1, not with excellency of s.
2 Cor. 10 : 10, his s. is contemptible.
Col. 4 : 6, let your s. be alway with grace.
Titus 2 : 8, sound s., that cannot be condemned.
Speed, Gen. 24 : 12, send me good s.
Isa. 5 : 26, they shall come with s.
2 John 10, neither bid him God s.
Speedily, Ps. 31 : 2, deliver me s.
   69 : 17; 143 : 7, hear me s.
   79 : 8, let thy mercies s. prevent us.
   102 : 2, when I call, answer me s.
Eccl. 8 : 11, because sentence is not executed s.

Isa. 58:8, thy health shall spring forth s.

Luke 18 : 8, he will avenge them s.

Spend, Job 21 : 13, they s. their days in wealth.

36 : 11, they shall s. their days in prosperity.

Ps. 90 : 9, we s. our years as a tale that is told.

Isa. 55 : 2, why s. money for that which is not bread?

2 Cor. 12 : 15, very gladly s. and be s. for you.

Spent, Gen. 21 : 15, the water was s.

47 : 18, our money is s.

Lev. 26 : 20, your strength be s. in vain.

Job 7 : 6, my days are s. without hope.

Ps. 31 : 10, my life is s. with grief.

Isa. 49 : 4, I have s. my strength for nought.

Mark 5 : 26; Luke 8 : 43, had s. all that she had.

Acts 17 : 21, s. their time to tell some new thing.

Rom. 13 : 12, the night is far s.

Spices, for religious rites, Ex. 25 : 6; 30 : 23, 34; 37 : 29; Ps. 45 : 8.

for embalming 2 Chr. 16 : 14; Mark 16 : 1; Luke 23 : 56; John 19 : 40.

Spies, sent into Canaan by Moses, Num. 13 : 3; 14 : 36; Deut. 1 : 22; Heb. 3 : 17.

sent to Jericho by Joshua, Josh. 2 : 1; 6 : 17, 23.

Spikenard [Heb., "nerd"], a product of a plant found in Nepal, which is a perennial herb, famous as a medicinal plant. The roots contain a highly odoriferous oil, which is used either in a liquid, oily form, or is rubbed up with fat into an ointment. Song of Sol. 4 : 13; Joyn 12 : 3. It was used in the anointing of Christ's feet by Mary. (John 12 : 3.)

Spin, Ex. 35 : 25, wisehearted did s.

Luke 12 : 27, they s. not.

Spirit, of God, the Holy Spirit, or Holy Ghost. See God.

of man, Eccl. 12 : 7; Zech. 12 : 1; 1 Cor. 2 : 11.

broken, Ps. 51 : 17; Prov. 15 : 13; 17: 22.

of Christ, Rom. 8 : 9; 1 Pet. 1 : 11.

of antichrist, 1 John 4 : 3.

born of, John 3 : 5; Gal. 4 : 29.

fruit of, Gal. 5 : 22.

of truth, John 14 : 17; 15 : 26; 16 : 13.

of bandage, Rom. 8 : 15.

of jealousy, Num. 5 : 14.

of divination, Acts 16 : 16.

of slumber, Rom. 11 : 8.

of fear, 2 Tim. 1 : 7.

Gen. 6 : 3, my s. shall not always strive.

Ex. 35 : 21, every one whom his s. made willing.

Num. 11 : 17, take of the s. which is upon thee.

14 : 24, he had another s. with him.

27 : 18, a man in whom is the s.

Josh. 5 : 1, nor was there any more s. in them.

2 Ki. 2 : 9, a double portion of thy s.

Neh. 9 : 20, thou gavest thy good s. to instruct.

Job 15 : 13, thou turnest thy s. against God.

26 : 4, whose s. came from thee?

32 : 8, there is a s. in man.

Ps. 31 : 5; Luke 23 : 46, into thine hand I commit my s.

Ps. 32 : 2, in whose s. there is no guile.

51 : 10, renew a right s. within me.

78 : 8, whose s. was not stedfast.

139 : 7, whither shall I go from thy S.?

143 : 10, thy s. is good.

Prov. 14 : 29, he that is hasty of s.

16 : 18, a haughty s. goeth before a fall.

16 : 32, he that ruleth his s.

20 : 27, s. of man is candle of the Lord.

Eccl. 3 : 21, who knoweth s. of man?

8 : 8, no man hath power over s. to retain s.

11 : 5, knowest not what is the way of the s.

Isa. 32 : 15, until the S. be poured upon us.

42 : 1, I have put my S. upon him.

61 : 1; Luke 4 : 18, the S. of the Lord is upon me.

Mic. 2 : 11, walking in the s. and falsehood.

Matt. 26 : 41; Mark 14 : 38, the s. is willing.

Mark 1 : 10; John 1 : 32, the S. descending on him.

Mark 8 : 12, he sighed deeply in his s.

Luke 1 : 80, waxed strong in s.

8 : 55, her s. came again.

9 : 55, ye know not what manner of s. ye are of.

24 : 39, a s. hath not flesh and bones.

John 3 : 34, God giveth not the S. by measure.

4 : 24, God is a S.

6 : 63, it is the S. that quickeneth.

Acts 2 : 4, began to speak, as the S. gave utterance.

6 : 10, not able to resist the wisdom and s.

17 : 16, his s. was stirred in him.

23 : 8, Sadducees say there is neither angel not s.

Rom. 8 : 1, walk not after flesh, but after the S.

8 : 26, S. maketh intercession.

1 Cor. 2 : 10, the S. searcheth all things.

6 : 17, he that is joined to the Lord is one s.

15 : 45, last Adam was made a quickening s.

2 Cor. 3 : 6, the letter killeth, but the s. giveth life.

3 : 17, where the S. of the Lord is, there is liberty.

Gal. 3 : 3, having begun in the S.

5 : 16, walk in the S. !

6 : 8, he that soweth to the S. shall of the S. reap.

Eph. 2 : 18, we have access by one S.

2 : 22, habitation of God through the S.

4 : , there is one body, and one S.

5 : 9, the fruit of the S.

5 : 18, be filled with the S.

6 : 17, take the sword of the S.

Phil. 2 : 1, if there be any fellowship of the S.

1 Thess. 5 : 19, quench not the S.

1 Tim. 3 : 16, justified in the S.

Heb. 1 : 14, ministering s.

  4 : 12, dividing asunder of soul and s.

  9 : 14, who through the eternal S. offered himself.

Jas. 2 : 26, the body without the s. is dead.

  4 : 5, the s. lusteth to envy.

1 Pet. 3 : 4, ornament of a meek and quiet s.

  4 : 6, live according to God in the s.

1 John 4 : 1, try the s. whether they are of God.

  5 : 6, it is the S. that beareth witness.

Rev. 1 : 10, I was in the S. on the Lord's day.

  22 : 17, the S. and the bride say, Come.

Spiritual, body, etc., 1 Cor. 12; 14; 15 : 44; Phil. 3 : 21; 1 John 3 : 2.

Hos. 9 : 7, the s. man is mad.

Rom. 1 : 11, impart some s. gift.

  7 : 14, the law is s.

  15 : 27, partakers of their s. things.

1 Cor. 2 : 13, comparing s. things with s.

  2 : 15, he that is s. judgeth all things.

  3 : 1, I could not speak unto you as unto s.

  9 : 11, have sown unto you s. things.

  10 : 3, did all eat the same s. meat.

  12 : 1; 14 : 1, s. gifts.

Gal. 6 : 1, ye which are s. restore such an one.

Eph. 1 : 3, blessed us with s. blessings.

  5 : 19; Col. 3 : 16, in psalms and hymns and s. songs.

Eph. 6 : 12, s. wickedness in high places.

1 Pet. 2 : 5, a s. house, to offer s. sacrifices.

Spiritually, Rom. 8 : 6; 1 Cor. 2 : 14; Rev. 11 : 8.

Spite, Ps. 10 : 14, thou beholdest mischief and s.

Spitefully, Matt. 22 : 6, they entreated them s.

Luke 18 : 32, he shall be s. entreated.

Spitting, Num. 12 : 14; Deut. 25 : 9; Job 30 : 10.

endured by Christ (Isa. 50 : 6); Matt. 26 : 67; 27 : 30; Mark 10 : 34; 14 : 65; 15 : 19.

Spoil, Gen. 49 : 27, at night he shall divide the s.

Judg. 5 : 30, necks of them that take s.

1 Sam. 14 : 32, the people flew upon the s.

2 Chr. 15 : 11, they offered to the Lord of the s.

Esther 3 : 13; 8 : 11, take the s. of them for a prey.

Ps. 68 : 12, that tarried at home divided the s.

  119 : 162, rejoice as one that findeth great s.

Prov. 16 : 19, than to divide the s. with the proud.

  31 : 11, have no need of s.

Isa. 42 : 24, who gave Jacob for a s. ?

  53 : 12, he shall divide the s. with the strong.

Nah. 2 : 9, s. of silver, s. of gold.

Spoil.

Ex. 3 : 22, ye shall s. the Egyptians.

Ps. 89 : 41, all that pass by the way s. him.

Song of Sol. 2 : 15, the little foxes, that s. the vines.

Isa. 33 : 1, woe to thee that s., and thou wast not s.

Jer. 4 : 30, when thou art s., what wilt thou do ?

Matt. 12 : 29; Mark 3 : 27, s. his goods.

Col. 2 : 8, beware lest any man s. you.

  2 : 15, having s. principalities.

Spot, Num. 28 : 3; 29 : 17, lambs without s.

Deut. 32 : 5, their s. is not the s. of his children.

Song of Sol. 4 : 7, there is no s. in thee.

Jer. 13 : 23, can the leopard change his s. ?

Eph. 5 : 27, a glorious church, not having s.

1 Tim. 6 : 14, keep commandment without s.

Heb. 9 : 14, offered himself without s.

1 Pet. 1 : 19, as a lamb without s.

2 Pet. 3 : 14, that ye may be found without s.

Jude 12, these are s. in your feasts.

Spouse, Song of Sol. 4 : 8, 9, 10, 11, 12.

Sprigs, Isa. 18 : 5; Ezek. 17 : 6.

Spring, Ps. 87 : 7, all my s. are in thee.

Ps. 104 : 10, he sendeth the s. into valleys.

  107 : 35, he turneth dry ground into water s.

Prov. 25 : 26, troubled fountain, and a corrupt s.

Num. 21 : 17, s. up, O well.

Job 5 : 6, neither doth trouble s. out of the ground.

Ps. 85 : 11, truth shall s. out of the earth.

Isa. 58 : 8, thine health shall s. forth.

Joel 2 : 22, the pastures do s.

Mark 4 : 27, seed should s., he knoweth not how.

John 4 : 14, well of water s. up.

Springs. See **Palestine Springs.**

Sprinkle, Isa. 52 : 15, so shall he s. many nations.

Ezek. 36 : 25, s. clean water upon you.

Heb. 10 : 22, hearts s. from an evil conscience.

Sprinkling, of blood, the passover, Ex. 12 : 22; Heb. 11 : 28.

the covenant of, Ex. 24 : 8; Heb 9 : 13.

cleansing the leper by, Lev. 14 : 7.

of oil, Lev. 14 : 16.

of the blood of Christ, Heb. 10 : 22; 12 : 24; 1 Pet. 1 : 2.

    The practice of sprinkling with blood is common in many primitive religions, and had a place in the rites of Jewish religion in Old Testament times.

Spun, Ex. 35 : 25, 26.

Spy, Num. 13 : 16, Moses sent to s. out the land.

Josh. 2 : 1, sent two men to s. secretly.

Gal. 2 : 4, who came in to s. out our liberty.

Stacks, Ex. 22 : 6.

Staff, Gen. 32 : 10, with my s. I passed over.

Ex. 12 : 11, eat it with s. in hand.

Judg. 6 : 21, the angel put forth end of his s.

2 Ki. 4 : 29, lay my s. upon face of the child.

2 Ki. 18 : 21; Isa. 36 : 6, thou trustest upon the s.

Ps. 23 : 4, thy rod and s. comfort me.

Isa. 3 : 1, Lord doth take away the stay and s.

9 : 4, thou hast broken the s. of his shoulder.

10 : 15, as if the s. should lift up itself.

14 : 5, Lord hath broken the s. of the wicked.

28 : 27, fitches are beaten out with a s.

30 : 32, where the grounded s. shall pass.

Jer. 48 : 17, how is the strong s. broken.

Zech. 11 : 10, took my s., even Beauty.

Mark 6 : 8, take nothing, save a s. only.

Heb. 11 : 21, leaning on the top of his s.

Stain, Isa. 23 : 9; 63 : 3; Job 3 : 5.

Stairs, 1 Ki. 6 : 8, went up with winding s.

Song of Sol. 2 : 14, in secret places of the s.

Acts 21 : 40, Paul stood on the s.

Stall, Amos 6 : 4, out of the midst of the s.

Hab. 3 : 17, be no herd in the s.

Mal. 4 : 2, grow up as calves of the s.

Luke 13 : 15, loose his ox from the s.

Stammerers, Isa. 32 : 4.

Stammering, Isa. 28 : 11, with s. lips and another tongue.

Isa. 33 : 19, not see a people of s. tongue.

Stand, Ex. 14 : 13; 2 Chr. 20 : 17, s. still, and see the salvation of the Lord.

Deut. 29 : 10, ye s. this day all of you before the Lord.

1 Ki. 17 : 1; 18 : 15; 2 Ki. 3 : 14; 5 : 16, the Lord, before whom I s.

2 Ki. 10 : 4, two kings s. not: how then shall we s. ?

Esther 8 : 11, to s. for their life.

Job 19 : 25, he shall s. at latter day upon the earth.

Ps. 1 : 5, the ungodly shall not s. in judgment.

4 : 4, s. in awe, and sin not.

24 : 3, who shall s. in his holy place ?

33 : 11, the counsel of the Lord s. for ever.

76 : 7, who may s. in thy sight ?

122 : 2, our feet shall s. within thy gates.

130 : 3, if thou shouldest mark iniquities who shall s. ?

Prov. 19 : 21, counsel of the Lord shall s.

22 : 29, a man diligent shall s. before kings.

27 : 4, who is able to s. before envy ?

Eccl. 8 : 3, s. not in an evil thing.

Isa. 40 : 8, word of our God shall s. for ever.

65 : 5, s. by thyself; I am holier than thou.

Jer. 6 : 16, s. in the ways, ask for the old paths.

Dan. 12 : 13, s. in thy lot at end of days.

Nah. 2 : 8, s., s., shall they cry.

Mal. 3 : 2, who shall s. when he appeareth ?

Matt. 12 : 25; Mark 3 : 25, house divided shall not s.

Matt. 20 : 6, why s. ye all the day idle ?

Acts 1 : 11, why s. ye gazing up into heaven ?

Rom. 5 : 2, this grace where in we s.

14 : 4, God is able to make him s.

1 Cor. 16 : 13, s. fast in the faith.

Gal. 5 : 1, s. fast in the liberty.

Phil. 1 : 27, s. fast in one spirit.

Eph. 6 : 13, having done all, to s.

Phil. 4 : 1; 1 Thess. 3 : 8, s. fast in the Lord.

2 Tim. 2 : 19, the foundation of God s. sure.

Jas. 5 : 9, the Judge s. before the door.

1 Pet. 5 : 12, true grace of God wherein ye s.

Rev. 3 : 20, I s. at the door and knock.

6 : 17, who shall be able to s. ?

20 : 12, the dead, small and great, s. before God.

Standards, of the twelve tribes, Num. 2.

Num. 1 : 52, every man by his own s.

Isa. 49 : 22, set up my s. to the people.

59 : 19, Lord shall lift up a s.

Stank, Ex. 7 : 21; 16 : 20; 2 Sam. 10 : 6.

Star, Balaam's prophecy concerning, Num. 24 : 17.

at Christ's birth, Matt. 2 : 2.

morning star, Christ. Rev. 22 : 16.

great star falls from heaven, Rev. 8 : 10.

stars, created, Gen. 1 : 16.

mentioned, Gen. 15 : 5; 37 : 9; Judg. 5 : 20; Heb. 11 : 12; Rev. 8 : 12; 12 : 1.

not to be worshipped, Deut. 4 : 19.

Num. 24 : 17, shall come a S. out of Jacob.

Job 38 : 7, the morning s. sang together.

Dan. 12 : 3, they shall shine as s. for ever.

Matt. 2 : 2, we have seen his s. in the east.

Acts 7 : 43, ye took up the s. of your god.

1 Cor. 15 : 41, one s. differeth from another s.

Jude 13, wandering s.

Rev. 9 : 1, I saw a s. fall from heaven to earth.

Stargazers, Isa. 47 : 13.

State, Ps. 39 : 5, man at his best s. is vanity.

Matt. 12 : 45; Luke 11 : 26, last s. worse than the first.

See Ezek. 23 : 41.

Stater, a coin. See **Money.**

Station, 1 Chr. 35 : 15; Isa. 22 : 19.

Stature, Num. 13 : 32, men of great s.

1 Sam. 16 : 7, look not on height of his s.

Song of Sol. 7 : 7, thy s. is like to a palm tree.

Isa. 10 : 33, high ones of s. shall be hewn down.

Matt. 6 : 27; Luke 12 : 25, not add to s.

Luke 2 : 52, Jesus increased in s.

19 : 3, little of s.

Eph. 4 : 13, measure of the s. of the fulness of Christ.

Statutes, of the Lord, 1 Chr. 29 : 19; Ps. 119 : 12, 16.

Ex. 15 : 25, he made a s. and an ordinance.

18 : 16, make them know the s. of God.

Lev. 3 : 17; 16 : 34; 24 : 9, a perpetual s.

Ps. 19 : 8, the s. of the Lord are right.

Ezek. 5 : 6, hath changed my s.

33 : 15, walk in the s. of life.

Staves, for the tabernacle, Ex. 25 : 13; 37 : 15; 40 : 20; Num. 4 : 6.

Steal, Gen. 31 : 27, wherefore didst thou s. away ?

44 : 8, how should we s. silver or gold ?

Prov. 6 : 30, if he s. to satisfy his soul.

30 : 9, lest I be poor, and s.

Jer. 23 : 30, prophets that s. my words.

Matt. 6 : 19, thieves break through and s.
John 10 : 10, thief cometh not, but for to s.
Eph. 4 : 28, let him that stole s. no more.
Stealing, Ex. 20 : 15; 21 : 16; Lev. 19 : 11;
    Deut. 5 : 19; 24 : 7; Ps. 50 : 18; Zech.
    5 : 4;   Matt.   19 : 18;   Rom.   13 : 9;
    1 Pet. 4 : 15.
    restitution to be made, Ex. 22 : 1; Lev. 6 : 4.
Stealth, 2 Sam. 19 : 3; Job 4 : 12.
Stedfast, Job 11 : 15, thou shalt be s.
    Ps. 78 : 8, spirit not s. with God.
Dan. 6 : 26, living God, and s. for ever.
Heb. 2 : 2, word spoken by angels was s.
    3 : 14, hold our confidence s. unto the
    end.
    6 : 19, hope as an anchor, sure and s.
1 Pet. 5 : 9, whom resist s. in the faith.
See Luke 9 : 51; Acts 7 : 55; 2 Cor. 3 : 13.
Stephen [Gr., " Stephanos," crown], deacon
    and first martyr, Acts 6 : 5; 7 : 59.
Steps, Ex. 20 : 26, neither go up by s.
1 Sam. 20 : 3, but a s. between me and
    death.
2 Sam. 22 : 37; Ps. 18 : 36, thou hast en-
    larged my s.
Job 14 : 16, thou numberest my s.
    31 : 4, doth not he count my s. ?
    31 : 7, if my s. hath turned out of the way.
Ps. 37 : 23, the s. of a good man are ordered
    by the Lord.
    44 : 18, nor have our s. declined.
    73 : 2, my s. had well nigh slipped.
    119 : 133, order my s. in thy word.
Prov. 4 : 12, thy s. shall not be straitened.
    16 : 9, the Lord directeth his s.
Jer. 10 : 23, not in man to direct his s.
Rom. 4 : 12, walk in s. of that faith.
2 Cor. 12 : 18, walked we not in the same s. ?
1 Pet. 2 : 21, that ye should follow his s.
Stern, Acts 27 : 29.
Steward, parable of, Luke 16 : 1.
    of God, a bishop is, Titus 1 : 7.
Gen. 15 : 2, the s. of my house.
1 Ki. 16 : 9, drunk in house of his s.
Luke 12 : 42, faithful and wise s.
    16 : 8, the Lord commended the unjust s.
1 Cor. 4 : 1, s. of the mysteries of God.
1 Pet. 4 : 10, as good s. of grace of God.
Stiff, Ex.   32 : 9;   34 : 9;   Deut.   9 : 13;
    10 : 16, a s.-necked people.
Ps. 75 : 5, speak not with a s. neck.
Ezek.   2 : 4,   impudent   children   and   s.-
    hearted.
Acts 7 : 51, ye s.-necked, ye always resist
    the Holy Ghost.
Still, Ex. 15 : 16, as s. as a stone.
2 Ki. 7 : 4, if we sit s. here, we die.
Ps. 23 : 2, beside the s. waters.
    46 : 10, be s., and know that I am God.
    83 : 1, be not s., O God.
    107 : 29, so that the waves thereof are s.
Isa. 30 : 7, their strength is to sit s.
    42 : 14, I have been s.
Jer. 8 : 14, why do we sit s. ?
Mark 4 : 39, said to sea, Peace, be s.
2 Sam. 14 : 32, good to have been there s.
Job 2 : 9, dost thou s. retain thine integrity ?
Rev. 22 : 11, he that is unjust, let him be
    unjust s.

Ps. 8 : 2, though mightiest s. the enemy.
Sting, Prov. 23 : 32, it s. like an adder.
1 Cor. 15 : 55, O death, where is thy s. ?
Rev. 9 : 10, there were s. in their tails.
Stocks, Jeremiah put in, Jer. 20 : 2; Paul
    and Silas, Acts 16 : 24.
    See Job 13 : 27; 33 : 11; Prov. 7 : 22.
Stoicks (stō-ĭcks), Acts 17 : 18. With the
    decline of the old pagan religions in the
    Roman world in the early days of the
    Empire, Stoicism became the accepted
    faith of a large section of the more
    educated classes of the Empire. It
    readily commended itself through its
    extreme moral earnestness, although it
    had a strong note of austerity, and was
    conspicuous for the lack of those gentler
    virtues which characterise Christian
    morality. Stoicism helped to prepare
    the way for the spread of Christianity,
    and lived to be one of its great rivals
    among the religions of the Empire.
Stole, 2 Sam. 15 : 6, Absalom s. the hearts
    of the men.
Matt. 28 : 13, s. him away while we slept.
Eph. 4 : 28, let him that s. steal no more.
Stolen, Gen. 31 : 19, Rachel had s. the
    images.
Josh. 7 : 11, they have s., and dissembled.
Obad. 5, would they not have s. till they
    had enough ?
Prov. 9 : 17, s. waters are sweet.
Stomach, 1 Tim. 5 : 23.
Stone, corner, Christ is (Isa. 28 : 16); Matt.
    21 : 42; Mark 12 : 10; 1 Pet. 2 : 6.
    stones, precious, in the high priest's breast-
    plate, Ex. 28 : 17. See Precious Stones.
    in the temple, 1 Chr. 29 : 2; 2 Chr. 3 : 6.
    in the new Jerusalem, Rev. 21 : 19.
Gen. 11 : 3, they had brick for s.
    28 : 22, this s., which I have set for a
    pillar.
Josh. 24 : 27, this s. shall be a witness.
Job 14 : 19, the waters wear the s.
    41 : 24, his heart is as firm as a s.
Ps. 91 : 12; Matt. 4 : 6; Luke 4 : 11, lest
    thou dash thy foot against a s.
Ps. 118 : 22, the s. which the builders
    refused.
Prov. 27 : 3, a s. is heavy.
Isa. 54 : 11, I will lay thy s. with fair
    colours.
    60 : 17, for s. I will bring iron.
Dan. 2 : 34, a s. was cut out without hands.
Hab. 2 : 19, that saith to the dumb s.,
    Arise.
Hag. 2 : 15, before s. was laid upon s.
Zech. 7 : 12, they made their hearts as s.
Matt. 7 : 9; Luke 11 : 11, will he give him
    a s. ?
    21 : 44; Luke 20 : 18, whosoever shall fall
    on this s.
Matt. 24 : 2; Mark 13 : 2; Luke 19 : 44;
    21 : 6, not be left one s. upon another.
Mark 16 : 4; Luke 24 : 2, found the s. rolled
    away.
Luke 4 : 3, command this s. that it be made
    bread.
John 1 : 42, Cephas, by interpretation, a s.

11 : 39, take ye away the s.

Acts 17 : 29, that the Godhead is like unto s.

2 Cor. 3 : 3, not in tables of s.

1 Pet. 2 : 5, ye, as lively s., are built up.

Stony, Ezek. 36 : 26; Matt. 13 : 5.

Stool, 2 Ki. 4 : 10.

Stoop, Prov. 12 : 25, heaviness maketh the heart s.

Isa. 46 : 2, they s., they bow down.

John 8 : 6, Jesus s. down, and wrote.

Store, Deut. 28 : 5, blessed be thy basket and s.

1 Chr. 29 : 16, all this s. cometh of thine hand.

Ps. 144 : 13, our garners affording all manner of s.

Nah. 2 : 9, none end of the s.

1 Cor. 16 : 2, let every one lay by him in s.

1 Tim. 6 : 19, laying up in s. a good foundation.

2 Pet. 3 : 7, by the same word are kept in s.

Storehouse, Mal. 3 : 10, bring ye all the tithes into the s.

Luke 12 : 24, neither have s. nor barn.

Stork. This bird is a regular migrant in Palestine. During April it covers the land, appearing in the south and moving northwards a few miles each day. It flies at a great height. Ps. 104 : 17; Jer. 8 : 7; Zech. 5 : 9.

Storm, Job 21 : 18, as chaff that the s. carrieth away.

Ps. 107 : 29, he maketh the s. a calm.

Isa. 4 : 6, a covert from s.

25 : 4, a refuge from the s.

28 : 2, as a destroying s.

Nah.1 : 3, the Lord hath his way in the s.

Mark 4 : 37, arose a great s.

See Ps. 107 : 25; 148 : 8.

Story, 2 Chr. 13 : 22; 24 : 27.

Stout, Isa. 10 : 12, punish fruit of s. heart.

Dan. 7 : 20, whose look was more s.

Mal. 3 : 13, your words have been s. against me.

See Ps. 76 : 5; Isa. 46 : 12.

Straight, Ps. 5 : 8, make thy way s.

Eccl. 1 : 15; 7 : 13, crooked cannot be made s.

Isa. 40 : 3, make s. in the desert a highway.

40 : 4; 42 : 16; 45 : 2; Luke 3 : 5, crooked shall be made s.

Jer. 31 : 9, cause them to walk in a s. way.

Matt. 3 : 3; Mark 1 : 3; Luke 3 : 4; John 1 : 23, make his paths s.

Acts 9 : 11, street which is called S.

Heb. 12 : 13, make s. paths for your feet.

See Mark 1 : 21; Luke 12 : 54; Jas. 1 : 24.

Strain, Matt. 23 : 24, s. at a gnat.

Strait, 2 Sam. 24 : 14, I am in a great s.

Job 20 : 22, he shall be in s.

Phil. 1 : 23, I am in a s. betwixt two.

2 Ki. 6 : 1, place where we dwell is too s.

Isa. 49 : 20, place is too s. for me.

Matt. 7 : 13; Luke 13 : 24, enter in at the s. gate.

See Mic. 2 : 7; Luke 12 : 50; Acts 26 : 5; 2 Cor. 6 : 12.

Straitness, Deut. 28 : 53; Job 36 : 16; Jer. 19 : 9.

Strangers, among the Israelites, not to be oppressed, Ex. 23 : 9; Lev. 19 : 33; Deut. 1 : 16; 10 : 18; 23 : 7; 24 : 14; Mal. 3 : 5.

regulations as to the passover, the priest's office, marriage, and the laws concerning them, Ex. 12 : 43; 34 : 16; Lev. 17 : 10; 22 : 10; 24 : 16; Num. 1 : 51; 18 : 7; 19 : 10; 35 : 15; Deut. 7 : 3; 17 : 15; 25 : 5; 31 : 12; Josh. 8 : 33; Ezra 10 : 2; Neh. 13 : 27; Ezek. 44 : 9.

and pilgrims, 1 Pet. 2 : 11.

Gen. 23 : 4; Ps. 39 : 12; 119 : 19, I am a s.

Ex. 22 : 21, thou shalt not oppress a s.

1 Chr. 29 : 15, we are s., as were all our fathers.

Job 31 : 32, the s. did not lodge in the street.

Ps. 109 : 11, let the s. spoil his labour.

146 : 9, the Lord preserveth the s.

Prov. 2 : 16, to deliver thee from s.

11 : 15, he that is surety for a s.

14 : 10, a s. doth not intermeddle.

27 : 2, let a s. praise thee.

Isa. 56 : 3, neither let son of the s. speak.

Jer. 14 : 8, why be as a s. in the land ?

Matt. 25 : 35, I was a s., and ye took me in.

Eph. 2 : 12, s. from the covenants.

2 : 19, ye are no more s.

Heb. 11 : 13, confessed they were s.

13 : 2, be not forgetful to entertain s.

Stream, Job 6 : 15, as the s. of brooks they pass away.

Ps. 124 : 4, the s. had gone over.

Isa. 35 : 6, s. in the desert.

Amos 5 : 24, righteousness as a mighty s.

Street, 2 Sam. 22 : 43; Mic. 7 : 10, as mire of the s.

Prov. 1 : 20, wisdom uttereth her voice in the s.

Eccl. 12 : 5, mourners go about the s.

Luke 14 : 21, go into s. and lanes of city.

Rev. 21 : 21, the s. of the city was pure gold.

Strength, of Israel, the Lord ,Ex. 15 : 2; Ps. 28 : 8; 29 : 11; 46 : 1; Isa. 26 : 4; Joel 3 : 16; Zech. 12 : 5.

of sin, the law, 1 Cor. 15 : 56; Rom. 7.

made perfect in weakness, 2 Cor. 12 : 9; Heb. 11 : 34.

1 Sam. 2 : 9, by s. shall no man prevail.

15 : 29, the S. of Israel will not lie.

Job 9 : 19, if I speak of s., lo, he is strong.

12 : 13, with him is wisdom and s.

12 : 21, he weakeneth s. of mighty.

Ps. 8 : 2, out of mouth of babes hast thou ordained s.

18 : 2; 28 : 7; 118 : 14; Isa. 12 : 2, the Lord is my s.

Ps. 18 : 32, girdeth me with s.

27 : 1, the Lord is the s. of my life.

33 : 16, mighty not delivered by much s.

46 : 1, God is our refuge and s.

68 : 35, God giveth s.

73 : 26, God is the s. of my heart.

Ps. 84 : 5, blessed is the man whose s. is in thee.
84 : 7, they go from s. to s.
93 : 1, the Lord is clothed with s.
96 : 6, s. and beauty are in his sanctuary.
138 : 3, strengthenedst me with s.
Prov. 10 : 29, the way of the Lord is s. to the upright.
Eccl. 9 : 16, wisdom is better than s.
Isa. 25 : 4, a s. to the poor, a s. to the needy.
40 : 29, he increaseth s.
51 : 9, awake, put on s.
Luke 1 : 51, he hath showed s. with his arm.
Rom. 5 : 6, when we were without s.
Rev. 3 : 8, thou hast a little s.
5 : 12, worthy is the Lamb to receive s.
12 : 10, now is come salvation and s.
Strengthen, Ps. 20 : 2, the Lord s. thee out of Zion.
41 : 3, Lord will s. him upon bed of languishing.
104 : 15, bread which s. man's heart.
Isa. 35 : 3, s. ye the weak hands.
Luke 22 : 32, when converted, s. thy brethren.
Eph. 3 : 16; Col. 1 : 11, s. with might.
Phil. 4 : 13, do all things through Christ which s. me.
Rev. 3 : 2, s. the things which remain.
Stretch, Ps. 68 : 31, soon s. out her hands unto God.
104 : 2, s. out the heavens like a curtain.
Prov. 31 : 20, she s. out her hands to the poor.
Isa. 28 : 20, bed shorter than that a man can s. himself.
Jer. 10 : 12; 51 : 15, he hath s. out the heavens.
Matt. 12 : 13, s. forth thine hand.
2 Cor. 10 : 14, we s. not beyond measure.
Stricken, Prov. 23 : 35; Isa. 53 : 4; Jer. 5 : 3; Luke 1 : 18.
Strife, its origin, Prov. 10 : 12; 13 : 10; 15 : 18; 16 : 28; 22 : 10; 23 : 29; 26 : 20; 28 : 25; 30 : 33; 1 Tim. 6 : 4; 2 Tim. 2 : 23; Jas. 4 : 1.
its results, Gal. 5 : 15; Jas. 3 : 16.
reproved, 1 Cor. 1 : 11; 6; 11 : 17.
See Prov. 17 : 14; 25 : 8; 26 : 17; Rom. 13 : 13; 1 Cor. 3 : 3; Gal. 5 : 20; Phil. 2 : 3; Titus 3 : 9; Jas. 3 : 14.
Strike, Job 17 : 3; Prov. 22 : 26, s. hands.
Ps. 110 : 5, he shall s. through kings.
Prov. 7 : 23, till a dart s. through.
Mark 14 : 65, did s. Jesus with their hands.
Stripes, Deut. 25 : 3; Acts 16 : 23; 2 Cor. 11 : 24.
Strive, Gen. 6 : 3, Spirit shall not always s.
Ps. 35 : 1, plead with them that s. with me.
Prov. 3 : 30, s. not without cause.
Matt. 12 : 19, he shall not s. nor cry.
Luke 13 : 24, s. to enter in at strait gate.
2 Tim. 2 : 24, the servant of the Lord must not s.
Strong, 1 Sam. 4 : 9; 2 Chr. 15 : 7; Isa. 35 : 4, be s.

Job 9 : 19, if I speak of strength, he is s.
Ps. 19 : 5, as a s. man to run a race.
24 : 8, the Lord s. and mighty.
31 : 2, be thou my s. rock.
71 : 7, thou art my s. refuge.
89 : 8, who is a s. Lord like unto thee ?
Prov. 18 : 10, name of the Lord is a s. tower.
Eccl. 9 : 11, the battle is not to the s.
Song of Sol. 8 : 6, love is s. as death.
Isa. 26 : 1, we have a s. city.
40 : 26, for that he is s. in power.
53 : 12, he shall divide the spoil with the s.
Jer. 50 : 34, their Redeemer is s.
Joel 3 : 10, let the weak say, I am s.
Luke 11 : 21, a s. man armed keepeth his palace.
Rom. 4 : 20, s. in faith.
15 : 1, we that are s. ought to bear infirmities of weak.
1 Cor. 4 : 10, we are weak, but ye are s.
Heb. 5 : 12, need of milk, and not of s. meat.
11 : 34, out of weakness were made s.
See Job 17 : 9; Jer. 20 : 7; 1 Cor. 1 : 25; 10 : 22.
Stubble, Ex. 15 : 7, wrath consumed them as s.
Job 21 : 18; Ps. 83 : 13, as s. before the wind.
Isa. 33 : 11, conceive chaff, bring forth s.
41 : 2, as driven s.
Jer. 13 : 24, I will scatter them as s.
1 Cor. 3 : 12, upon this foundation, hay, s.
Stubbornness, punishment of, Deut. 21 : 18; Prov. 1 : 24; 29 : 1.
forbidden, 2 Chr. 30 : 8; Ps. 32 : 9; 75 : 4.
of the Jews, 2 Ki. 17 : 14; Jer. 5 : 3; 7 : 28; 32 : 23.
Stuck, 1 Sam. 26 : 7; Ps. 119 : 31; Acts 27 : 41.
Stumble, Prov. 3 : 23, foot shall not s.
4 : 19, know not at what they s.
Isa. 5 : 27, none shall be weary nor s.
28 : 7, they s. in judgment.
59 : 10, we s. at noonday.
Jer. 46 : 6; Dan. 11 : 19, s. and fall.
Mal. 2 : 8, ye have caused many to s.
Rom. 9 : 32, they s. at that stumblingstone.
14 : 21, whereby thy brother s.
1 Pet. 2 : 8, which s. at the word.
Stumblingblock, not to be placed before the blind, Lev. 19 : 14; Deut. 27 : 18.
figurative of offence, Isa. 8 : 14; Rom. 14 : 21; 1 Cor. 1 : 23; 8 : 9; 1 Pet. 2 : 8.
Subdue, Ps. 47 : 3, he shall s. the people.
Mic. 7 : 19, he will s. our iniquities.
1 Cor. 15 : 28, when all things shall be s. unto him.
Phil. 3 : 21, able to s. all things.
Heb. 11 : 33, through faith s. kingdoms.
Submit, Gen. 16 : 9, s. thyself under her hands.
2 Sam. 22 : 45; Ps. 18 : 44, strangers shall s. themselves unto me.
Ps. 66 : 3, enemies shall s. themselves unto thee.
68 : 30, till every one s. himself.

Eph. 5 : 22; Col. 3 : 18, wives, s. yourselves unto husbands.

1 Pet. 2 : 13, s. yourselves to every ordinance.

Subscribe, Isa. 44 : 5, another shall s. unto the Lord.

Jer. 32 : 44, men shall s. evidences.

Substance, Gen. 15 : 14, shall they come with great s.

Deut. 33 : 11, bless, Lord, his s.

Job 15 : 29, nor shall his s. continue.

30 : 22, thou dissolvest my s.

Ps. 17 : 14, they leave their s. to babes.

139 : 15, my s. was not hid from thee.

Prov. 3 : 9, honour the Lord with thy s.

28 : 8, he that by usury increaseth his s.

Hos. 12 : 8, I have found me out s.

Mic. 4 : 13, I will consecrate their s.

Luke 8 : 3, ministered to him of their s.

15 : 13, wasted his s.

Heb. 10 : 34, in heaven a better s.

11 : 1, faith is the s. of things hoped for.

Subtil, Gen. 3 : 1, serpent was more s. than any beast.

2 Sam. 13 : 3, a s. man.

Prov. 7 : 10, s. of heart.

See Gen. 27 : 35; Matt. 26 : 4; Acts 13 : 10.

Subvert, Lam. 3 : 36, to s. a man in his cause.

Acts 15 : 24, s. souls.

Titus 1 : 11, who s. whole houses.

2 Tim. 2 : 14, to the s. of the hearers.

Success, Josh. 1 : 8; Ps. 111 : 10; Prov. 3 : 4.

Succoth (sŭc-cŏth) [booths], a city east of the Jordan, identified with Tell Darala, Gen. 33 : 17; Josh. 13 : 27; 1 Ki. 7 : 46; Ps. 60 : 6.

punished by Gideon, Judg. 8 : 5, 16.

in Egypt, Ex. 12 : 37; 13 : 20.

Succour, 2 Cor. 6 : 2; Heb. 2 : 18.

Suck, Deut. 32 : 13, s. honey out of rock.

33 : 19, s. of abundance of the seas.

Job 20 : 16, he shall s. the poison of asps.

Isa. 60 : 16, s. the milk of the Gentiles.

Matt. 24 : 19; Mark 13 : 17; Luke 21 : 23, woe to them that give s. in those days.

Sucklings, Ps. 8 : 2; Matt. 21 : 16.

Suffer, Ps. 55 : 22, never s. righteous to be moved.

89 : 33, nor s. my faithfulness to fail.

121 : 3, s. thy foot to be moved.

Prov. 10 : 3, Lord not s. righteous to famish.

19 : 15, an idle soul shall s. hunger.

Matt. 3 : 15, Jesus said, S. it to be so now.

8 : 21; Luke 9 : 59, s. me first to bury my father.

Matt. 16 : 21; 17 : 12; Mark 8 : 31; Luke 9 : 22, must s. many things.

Matt. 19 : 14; Mark 10 : 14; Luke 18 : 16, s. little children.

Luke 24 : 46, it behoved Christ to s.

Acts 3 : 18, that Christ should s.

Rom. 8 : 17, if we s. with him.

1 Cor. 3 : 15, he shall s. loss.

10 : 13, he will not s. you to be tempted.

2 Tim. 2 : 12, if we s., we shall also reign.

Heb. 11 : 25, choosing rather to s. affliction.

13 : 22, s. the word of exhortation.

1 Pet. 2 : 21, Christ s. for us, leaving us an example.

Sufficeth, John 14 : 8.

Sufficient, Isa. 40 : 16, not s. to burn.

Matt. 6 : 34, s. unto the day is the evil thereof.

2 Cor. 2 : 16, who is s. for these things ?

See 2 Cor. 3 : 5; 9 : 8.

Sun, created, Gen. 1 : 14; Ps. 74 : 16.

not to be worshipped, Deut. 4 : 19; Job 31 : 26; Ezek. 8 : 16.

stayed by Joshua, Josh. 10 : 12.

brought backward for Hezekiah, 2 Ki. 20 : 9.

darkened at crucifixion, Luke 23 : 45.

of righteousness, Mal. 4 : 2.

Job 9 : 7, commandeth s., and it riseth not.

Ps. 19 : 4, he set a tabernacle for the s.

84 : 11, Lord is a s. and shield.

121 : 6, the s. shall not smite thee by day.

Eccl. 1 : 9, no new thing under the s.

12 : 2, while the s. or stars be not darkened.

Song of Sol. 6 : 10, clear as the s.

Isa. 60 : 20, thy s. shall no more go down.

Mal. 4 : 2, the S. of righteousness arise.

Matt. 5 : 45, he maketh his s. to rise on evil and good.

13 : 43, then shall righteous shine as the s.

1 Cor. 15 : 41, there is one glory of the s.

Eph. 4 : 26, let not the s. go down upon your wrath.

Rev. 21 : 23; 22 : 5, city had no need of the s.

Sung, Isa. 26 : 1, shall this song be s.

Matt. 26 : 30, had s. an hymn.

Rev. 5 : 9, they s. a new song.

Sunrising, Num. 21 : 11; 34 : 15; Josh. 1 : 15.

Sup, Luke 17 : 8, make ready wherewith I may s.

1 Cor. 11 : 25, took the cup, when he had s.

Rev. 3 : 20, I will s. with him, and he with me.

Superstition, Acts 17 : 22; 25 : 19.

Supper, parable of, Luke 14 : 16.

marriage of the Lamb, Rev. 19 : 9.

Lord's. See **Communion.**

Supplant, Gen. 27 : 36; Jer. 9 : 4.

Supple, Ezek. 16 : 4.

Suppliants, Zeph. 3 : 10.

Supplication, 1 Ki. 9 : 3, I have heard thy s.

Job 9 : 15, I would make s. to my judge.

Ps. 6 : 9, the Lord hath heard my s.

Dan. 9 : 20, I was presenting s. before God.

Zech. 12 : 10, spirit of grace and of s.

Eph. 6 : 18, with all prayer and s.

Phil. 4 : 6, in every thing by s.

1 Tim. 2 : 1, that s. be made for all men.

Supply, Phil. 1 : 19, through prayer and the s. of the spirit.

4 : 19, shall s. all your need by Christ.

Support, Acts 20 : 35; 1 Thess. 5 : 14, ye ought to s. the weak.

Supposed, Matt. 20 : 10; Mark 6 : 49; Acts 25 : 18; Phil. 1 : 16; 1 Tim. 6 : 5.

Supreme, 1 Pet. 2 : 13.

Sure, Num. 32 : 23, be s. your sin will find you out.

2 Sam. 23 : 5, covenant ordered and s.

Job 24 : 22, no man is s. of life.

Ps. 111 : 7, his commandments are s.

Prov. 6 : 3, make s. thy friend.

Isa. 33 : 16, his waters shall be s.

55 : 3; Acts 13 : 34, the s. mercies of David.

2 Tim. 2 : 19, the foundation of God standeth s.

2 Pet. 1 : 10, your calling and election s.

1 : 19, a more s. word of prophecy.

Surety, Ps. 119 : 122, be s. for thy servant.

Prov. 6 : 1, be s. for thy friend.

22 : 26, not of them that are s.

Heb. 7 : 22, Jesus made a s. of a better testament.

Surmisings, 1 Tim. 6 : 4.

Surprised, Isa. 33 : 14; Jer. 48 : 41; 51 : 41.

Susanna [lily], Luke 8 : 3.

Sustain, Ps. 3 : 5, the Lord s. me.

55 : 22, Lord, he shall s. thee.

Prov. 18 : 14, the spirit of man will s. his infirmity.

Isa. 59 : 16, his righteousness s. him.

Sustenance, Judg. 6 : 4; Acts 7 : 11.

Swaddling, Luke 2 : 7, 12.

Swallow, Isa. 25 : 8, he will s. up death in victory.

Matt. 23 : 24, strain at a gnat, and s. a camel.

1 Cor. 15 : 54, death is s. up in victory.

2 Cor. 5 : 4, that mortality might be s. up of life.

bird. The word so translated occurs in Ps. 84 : 3 and Prov. 26 : 2, and refers to some species of the genus " Hirundo," of which our own common swallow and others frequent the Holy Land.

Swan, enumerated among the unclean birds in Lev. 11 : 18 and Deut. 14 : 16.

Swear, Lev. 19 : 12, ye shall not s. by my name falsely.

Ps. 15 : 4, that s. to his hurt.

Eccl. 9 : 2, he that s., as he that feareth an oath.

Isa. 45 : 23, unto me every tongue shall s.

65 : 16, shall s. by the God of truth.

Jer. 4 : 2, thou shalt s., The Lord liveth.

Zech. 5 : 3, every one that s. shall be cut off.

Matt. 5 : 34; Jas. 5 : 12, s. not.

Jer. 23 : 10, because of s. the land mourneth.

Hos. 4 : 2, by s., and lying, they break out.

Sweat, Gen. 3 : 19, in s. of face eat bread.

Luke 22 : 44, his s. was as drops of blood.

Sweep, Prov. 28 : 3; Isa. 28 : 17; Matt. 12 : 44; Luke 15 : 8.

Swelling, Jer. 12 : 5, how wilt thou do in s. of Jordan ?

2 Pet. 2 : 18, speak s. words of vanity.

Swift, Prov. 6 : 18, feet s. in running to mischief.

Eccl. 9 : 11, the race is not to the s.

Isa. 19 : 1, the Lord rideth upon a s. cloud.

Rom. 3 : 15, feet are s. to shed blood.

See Job 7 : 6; 9 : 25; Ps. 147 : 15.

Swim, 2 Ki. 6 : 6, the iron did s.

Isa. 25 : 11, spread forth hands to s.

Ezek. 47 : 5, waters to s. in.

Swine, unclean, Lev. 11 : 7; Deut. 14 : 8; Isa. 65 : 4.

devils sent into herd of, Matt. 8 : 32; Mark 5 : 13; Luke 8 : 33.

typical of unbelievers and apostates, Matt. 7 : 6; 2 Pet. 2 : 22.

Swollen, Acts 28 : 6.

Swoon, Lam. 2 : 11, children s. in the streets.

Sword, of the Lord, Deut. 32 : 41; Judg. 7 : 18; 1 Chr. 21 : 12; Ps. 45 : 3; Isa. 34 : 5; 66 : 16; Jer. 47 : 6; Ezek. 21 : 4; 30 : 24; 32 : 10; Zeph. 2 : 12.

Gen. 3 : 24, cherubim and a flaming s.

Deut. 33 : 29, the s. of thy excellency.

Judg. 7 : 20, s. of the Lord and of Gideon.

Ps. 57 : 4, their tongue is a sharp s.

Song of Sol. 3 : 8, every man hath his s. upon his thigh.

Isa. 2 : 4, nation shall not lift up s. against nation.

Jer. 12 : 12, the s. of the Lord shall devour.

15 : 2; 43 : 11, such as are for the s., to the s.

Zech. 11 : 17, the s. shall be upon his arm.

13 : 7, awake, O s., against my Shepherd.

Matt. 10 : 34, not to send peace, but a s.

Luke 2 : 35, a s. shall pierce through thy own soul.

Rom. 13 : 4, he beareth not the s. in vain.

Eph. 6 : 17, the s. of the Spirit.

Heb. 4 : 12, sharper than any two-edged s.

Rev. 1 : 16; 19 : 15, out of his mouth went a sharp s.

13 : 10, he that killeth with the s. must be killed with the s.

Sycamine tree is mentioned once in the New Testament (Luke 17 : 6). It is the black mulberry tree (Morus nigra), still known by this name in Greece.

Sycamore [Heb. shikmah pl. shikmim; Ficus sycamorus]. It has no relationship with the English sycamore, which is a maple (Acer pseudoplatanus). It grows to a considerable size, is evergreen, and bears large quantities of fruits, which grow from numerous small branches, separate from the leaf-bearing ones. The fruit is small, sweetish, but dry and without flavour. It abounded in Egypt, but also grew in some parts of Palestine. Probably the place, in Amos 7 : 14, where the prophet describes himself as a gatherer or scraper of figs, may refer to the practice of scraping or scoring the bark of the trees. In Luke 19 : 4, it is mentioned as the tree into which Zacchaeus climbed.

Synagogue, The. The Synagogue is the name of the place where Jews meet for worship. The Jewish religion centres in the Temple, at Jerusalem, but through force of circumstances, first in the Exile, and later among the scattered Jewish communities throughout the world, the local synagogues became for all practical purposes the centres of worship. The practice of worshipping in the local synagogue grew until in the time of Christ there were nearly five hundred synagogues in Jerusalem alone. The form of worship in the synagogue included prayer, the reading of Scripture, and the interpretation of Scripture in the language of the local congregation. In the form of worship, therefore, the synagogue provided an example which was followed by the Early Church, the essentials of which remain in our modern Christian Church services.

Christ teaches in, Matt. 12 : 9; Luke 4 : 16; John 6 : 59; 18 : 20.
Paul teaches in, Acts 13 : 5; 14 : 1; 18 : 4.
Matt. 13 : 54; Mark 6 : 2, taught in their s.
Luke 7 : 5, he hath built us a s.
John 12 : 42, lest they should be put out of the s.
16 : 2, put you out of the s.
Rev. 2 : 9; 3 : 9, the s. of Satan.
Syrians, subdued by David, 2 Sam. 8 : 10.
tributary to Solomon, 1 Ki. 10 : 29.
contend with Israel, 1 Ki. 11 : 25; 20; 22 : 34; 2 Ki. 6 : 24; 7; 8 : 13; 13 : 7; 16 : 6; 2 Chr. 18 : 33.
employed to punish Joash, 2 Chr. 24 : 23.
the gospel preached to, Matt. 4 : 24; Acts 15 : 23; 18 : 18; Gal. 1 : 21.
See Gen. 25 : 20; Deut. 26 : 5; 2 Chr. 28 . 23; Isa. 7 : 2; Ezek. 27 : 16; Hos. 12 : 12; Amos 1 : 5.
Syrophenician (sȳ-rō-phē-nĭc'-ĭ-ăn), a Phœnician of Syria, Mark 7 : 26.

T

Taanach (tā-'ă-năch), hamlet west of the Plain of Esdraelon, Josh. 12 : 21.
Taanath-shiloh (tā-'ă-năth-shī-lōh) [approach to Shiloh], Josh. 16 : 6.
Taberah (tăb-ĕ-räh) [burning], Num. 11 : 3.
Tabering [tapping, as on a drum], Nah. 2 : 7.
Tabernacle, The. The Tabernacle erected by Moses in the wilderness is described in Exodus 26 and 27. It was divided into three main portions: the Outer Court, the Sanctuary, and the Holy of Holies.

(1) The Outer Court—The Outer Court was surrounded by fine twined linen screens five cubits in height, hung by silver hooks, upon pillars of brass resting in sockets of brass. Of these pillars there were twenty on the southern side, twenty on the northern, and ten on the western. The eastern side had also ten pillars. On four of the six pillars in the centre was hung the screen of twenty cubits of "blue and purple and scarlet and fine twined linen," which served the purpose of an entrance gate. The six other pillars were placed three on either side, and from them were hung fixed screens as on the north, south, and west. The space thus enclosed was 100 cubits by 50, or in round numbers 150 feet by 75.

In the outer court, which was accessible to all the Israelites, stood the altar of burnt-offering, square in shape, five cubits in length and breadth, and three in height (Ex. 27 : 1-8).

Between the altar and the Tabernacle proper was the laver of brass, which is minutely described in Ex. 30 : 17-21. This outer court was a perfect square (50 cubits by 50), occupying exactly half of the space of the whole enclosure.

(2) The Tabernacle Proper, its Construction and Coverings.—Inside the enclosure fifty cubits from the entrance into the outer court, towards the western end, was the Tabernacle proper, "mishcan," covered by a large tent, " ohel," spread " over it," thus protecting it from sun and rain (Ex. 26 : 7; 36 : 14). The Tabernacle proper was thirty cubits long, ten broad, and ten high. It was externally a parallelogram, with an entrance on the eastern side; its innermost shrine, the Holy of Holies, was towards the west. The two longer sides, the northern and southern, were each composed of twenty boards of shittim or acacia wood, overlaid with gold, each board being ten cubits in height and one and a half in breadth. The western side was formed of eight such boards (Ex. 26 : 25), two of which formed the posts at the angles (Ex. 26 : 22-24). On the eastern side was the entrance, closed by the curtains of "blue, and purple, and scarlet, and fine twined linen, the work of the embroiderer."

The ceiling of the Tabernacle was formed of ten curtains; each curtain was twenty-eight cubits long by four broad. The covering composed of these curtains, when joined together (forty cubits long by twenty-eight wide), sufficed to cover the Tabernacle above, with its northern and southern sides, leaving only a small space uncovered near the ground on each side.

Such was the Mishcan, or Tabernacle proper. Over the whole of this splendid structure an outer tent was pitched. In order to give the fullest protection to the interior Tabernacle, the outer tent had three special coverings. The first and innermost was composed of curtains of goats' hair, the second was a curtain of rams' skins, and the third a covering composed of the skins of some species of porpoise or dolphin.

(3) The Holy Place and its Furniture.—The Sanctuary, or the Holy Place, was twenty cubits long by ten wide, and ten cubits in height. Its ceiling has already been described. Its walls on the northern and southern sides were composed of the boards covered with gold, also mentioned before. It was closed on the other two sides by curtains, that on the western end dividing it from the Holy of Holies. This outer chamber of the Tabernacle proper was accessible only to the priests.

In it stood the altar of incense, the seven-branched candlestick, and the table of shewbread.

(a) The Altar of Incense was also square, a cubit long by a cubit broad, and two cubits in height (Ex. 30 : 1-10). It was formed of acacia wood, overlaid with pure gold, with horns of gold, and a crown or rim of gold round its sides, with golden rings on two sides, and staves overlaid with gold by which it could be carried.

(b) The Candlestick was of pure gold of beaten work. It had seven arms, the centre one being the shaft, formed on each side of three cups of almond blossoms, their knops and flowers (Ex. 25 : 31-40). The height of the candlestick is not mentioned. Its lamps were lighted and trimmed daily by the priests, and kept constantly burning (Ex. 27 : 20, 21).

(c) The Table of Shewbread was also of acacia wood, overlaid with pure gold —two cubits in length, one in breadth, and one and a half in height. It also had a crown, or rim of gold round it, staves overlaid with gold to carry it with, which were placed in four golden rings (Ex. 25 : 23-30). On this table were every week placed twelve loaves of bread to represent the twelve tribes, arranged in two rows of six loaves each. The loaves which were removed were eaten by the priests in the Holy Place.

(4) The Holy of Holies and the Ark of the Covenant.—The Holy of Holies, or Most Holy Place, was in the Mosaic Tabernacle completely dark. It was ten cubits long by ten in width, and ten in height, being a perfect cube. Three of its sides were formed of the acacia boards covered with gold noticed before, its fourth side being formed by the curtain or veil, suspended from four pillars, which veil screened off the Most Holy from the Holy Place. Into the Holy of Holies no one was permitted to enter except the high priest on the annual Day of Atonement, described in Lev. 16.

The sole furniture of the Holy of Holies consisted of the Ark of the Covenant. The latter was an oblong chest made of acacia wood, overlaid within and without with gold. Its dimensions were two and a half cubits long by one and a half in breadth and depth. Its lid, termed " the Mercy Seat," was also overlaid with gold, with a golden rim or crown round it; out of the same piece of beaten gold were formed two cherubim, one cherub at the one end and one cherub at the other end of the lid. These cherubim spread out their wings on high, covering the mercy seat with them, their faces being towards one another, but their countenances directed as if looking down upon the mercy seat (Ex. 37 : 1-9). Above these cherubim the glory of God appeared, hence the Lord is often represented as throned between the cherubim.

On the sides of the ark were placed four golden rings, through which staves of acacia wood, overlaid with gold, were placed, so that the ark could be carried thereby. In the journeys of the children of Israel, the ark was borne by the sons of Kohath. Inside the ark were the two tables of stone, termed " the testimony," on which were the ten commandments, written with the finger of God. It is expressly stated that when the ark was brought into the Temple

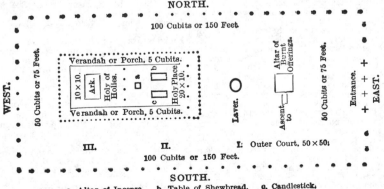

Ground Plan of Tabernacle.

With Outer Enclosure, showing Open Verandah or Porch formed by the Ohel or Tent overshadowing the Mishcan or Tabernacle proper.

NORTH.

100 Cubits or 150 Feet.

WEST.   50 Cubits or 75 Feet.

Verandah or Porch, 5 Cubits.

10 × 10.   Ark.   Holy of Holies.   Holy Place. 20 × 10.

Verandah or Porch, 5 Cubits.

Laver.   Ascent to   Altar of Burnt Offerings.   50 Cubits or 75 Feet.   Entrance.   EAST.

III.   II.   I: Outer Court, 50 × 50.

100 Cubits or 150 Feet.

SOUTH.

a. Altar of Incense.   b. Table of Shewbread.   c. Candlestick.

of Solomon, it contained nothing else (1 Ki. 8 : 9). The pot of manna (Ex. 16 : 35) and Aaron's rod that budded (Num. 17 : 10) were laid up " before the testimony," but were not placed inside the ark.

its construction, Ex. 25–27; 36–38; 40.

covered by the cloud, Ex. 40 : 34; Num. 9 : 15.

consecrated by Moses, Lev. 8 : 10.

directions concerning its custody and removal, Num. 1 : 50, 53; 3; 4; 9 : 18; 1 Chr. 6 : 48.

set up at Shiloh, Josh. 18 : 1; at Gibeon, 1 Chr. 21 : 29; 2 Chr. 1 : 3.

David's love for, Ps. 27; 42; 43; 84; 132.

typical, Heb. 8 : 2; 9 : 2.

of witness, Num. 17 : 7; 18 : 2; 2 Chr. 24 : 6; Acts 7 : 44.

of testimony, Ex. 38 : 21.

in heaven, Rev. 15 : 5.

the human body compared to, 2 Cor. 5 : 1; 2 Pet. 1 : 13.

Job 5 : 24, thy t. shall be in peace.

Ps. 15 : 1, who shall abide in thy t. ?

27 : 5, in secret of his t. shall he hide me.

84 : 1, how amiable are thy t.

118 : 15, salvation is in the t. of the righteous.

Isa. 33 : 20, a t. that shall not be taken down.

Ezek. 37 : 27, my t. shall be with them.

2 Cor. 5 : 4, we that are in this t. do groan.

Tabernacles, Feast of. This great Jewish feast lasted one week, and was held annually, beginning on the fifteenth day of the seventh month. The object of the feast was to commemorate the forty years spent in the wilderness. Booths were erected, in which the people lived during the feast. The first and last days of the feast were days of holy convocation or public worship, and the intervening days were devoted to the free enjoyment of the festal season. Throughout the week an elaborate scheme of sacrificial offerings was carried through.

Tabitha [gazelle], see **Dorcas**, Acts 9 : 36.

Table. Tables for serving food were in the form of three sides of a square. The guests reclined on cushioned benches on the outside, the inside being occupied by attendants. The place of the host or head of the company was at the centre of the cross-table. On his right hand reclined the most honoured guest. The posture at table was reclining on the left side with the legs bent so as to allow the feet to extend outwards and behind. " The chief rooms " (Luke 14 : 7) mean the chief places at table. " The highest room " means the place next the host; other places of honour were the centre seats of the tables in front of that where the host reclined.

of the Lord, in the tabernacle, Ex. 25 : 23; 31 : 8; 37 : 10; 40 : 4; Ezek. 41 : 22.

profanation of, condemned, Mal. 1 : 7, 12.

shewbread placed thereon, Ex. 25 : 30; Lev. 24 : 6; Num. 4 : 7.

tablet for writing with pencil, Luke 1 : 63.

Ps. 23 : 5, thou preparest a t. before me.

69 : 22, let their t. become a snare.

128 : 3, like olive plants about thy t.

Prov. 3 : 3; 7 : 3, write on t. of heart.

9 : 2, wisdom hath furnished her t.

Isa. 21 : 5, prepare the t.

Jer. 17 : 1, graven on t. of heart.

Matt. 15 : 27; Mark 7 : 28, crumbs from their master's t.

1 Cor. 10 : 21, partakers of Lord's t. and t. of devils.

2 Cor. 3 : 3, flesh t. of the heart.

Tables of stone, containing the law, Ex. 24 : 12; 31 : 18.

broken by Moses, Ex. 32 : 19; Deut. 9 : 17.

renewed, Ex. 34; Deut. 10.

See 2 Cor. 3 : 3.

Tablet [an armlet or locket], Ex. 35 : 22, rings and t.

Tabor (tā-bŏr) [lofty], mountain in Palestine, 1800 feet above the sea, with a dome-shaped summit, Judg. 4 : 14.

See Judg. 8 : 18; 1 Sam. 10 : 3; Ps. 89 : 12; Jer. 46 : 18; Hos. 5 : 1.

Mount Tabor.

Tabret, musical instrument, Gen. 31 : 27; 1 Sam. 18 : 6; Isa. 5 : 12. See **Musical Instruments.**

Taches [clasps, fastenings], Ex. 26 : 6; 39 : 33.

Tackling, Isa. 33 : 23; Acts 27 : 19.

Tadmor (tăd-môr) [palm tree], a city built by Solomon, 1 Ki. 9 : 18; 2 Chr. 8 : 4.

Take, Ex. 6 : 7, I will t. you for a people.

Ex. 20 : 7; Deut. 5 : 11, not t. the name of Lord in vain.

Ex. 34 : 9, t. us for thine inheritance.

Job 23 : 10, he knoweth the way that I t.

Ps. 27 : 10, then the Lord will t. me up.

51 : 11, t. not thy Holy Spirit from me.

116 : 13, I will t. the cup of salvation.

Hos. 14 : 2, t. with you words.

Matt. 18 : 16, t. with thee one or two more.

20 : 14, t. that thine is, and go thy way.

26 : 26; Mark 14 : 22; 1 Cor. 11 : 24, t., eat.

Luke 12 : 19, soul, t. thine ease.

John 16 : 15, he shall t. of mine.
1 Cor. 6 : 7, why not rather t. wrong ?
1 Pet. 2 : 20, if ye t. it patiently.
Rev. 3 : 11, that no man t. thy crown.
   22 : 19, if any man t. away from this prophecy.
Tale, Ps. 90 : 9, we spend our years as a t.
Ezek. 22 : 9, that carry t. to shed blood.
Luke 24 : 11, their words seemed as t.
[ar], number, Ex. 5 : 18; 1 Chr. 9 : 28.
Talebearers, Lev. 19 : 16; Prov. 11 : 13; 18 : 8; 26 : 20; 1 Tim. 5 : 13; 1 Pet. 4 : 15.
Talent, a measure of weight, 2 Sam. 12 : 30; Rev. 16 : 21. See Weights.
of gold, Ex. 25 : 39; 2 Ki. 23 : 33. See Money.
of silver, 1 Ki. 20 : 39; 2 Ki. 5 : 22. See Money.
of lead, Zech. 5 : 7. See Weights.
Talents, parables of, Matt. 18 : 24; 25 : 14.
Talitha cumi (tăl-ĭ-thă cū-mĭ) [damsel, arise], Mark 5 : 41. This is one of several Aramaic phrases which Mark has preserved. Aramaic is the language in which we may presume that our Lord spoke.
Talk, Deut. 5 : 24, God doth t. with man.
   6 : 7, t. of them when thou sittest.
Job 13 : 7, will ye t. deceitfully for him ?
Ps. 71 : 24, t. of thy righteousness.
   77 : 12, I will t. of thy doings.
   145 : 11, t. of thy power.
Prov. 6 : 22, it shall t. with thee.
Jer. 12 : 1, let me t. with thee of thy judgments.
Luke 24 : 32, while he t. with us by the way.
John 9 · 37, it is he that t. with thee.
   14 : 39, I will not t. much with you.
Job 11 : 2, a man full of t.
Matt. 22 : 15, might entangle him in his t.
Eph. 5 : 4, nor foolish t.
Talking, vain, censured, 1 Sam. 2 : 3; Prov. 13 : 3; 24 : 2; Eccl. 10 : 14; Ezek. 33 : 30; 36 : 3; Titus 1 · 10
See Slander.
Tall, Deut. 1 : 28; 2 : 10; Isa. 37 : 24.
Talmud [doctrine]. The Talmud is a collection of writings bearing on the Jewish Law. It had its origin in the oral teaching of the Rabbis, handed on from mouth to mouth for centuries, and was only by degrees committed to writing.
Tame, Mark 5 : 4, neither could any man t. him.
Jas. 3 : 8, tongue can no man t.
Tammuz (tăm-mŭz) [son of life], a Syro-Phœnician god, Adonis of the Greeks, Ezek. 8 : 14. See Jephthah.
month of June-July.
Tanner, Acts 9 : 43; 10 : 6.
Tapestry, Prov. 7 : 16; 31 : 22.
Tares. A weed which, until it is fully grown, closely resembles wheat. It is poisonous, and if its fruit or flower be eaten, death often results. Matt. 13 : 25.
Target, 1 Sam. 17 : 6; 2 Chr. 14 : 8.
Targums. See Versions, Old Testament.

Tarry, Gen. 19 : 2, t. all night.
Judg. 5 : 28, why t. the wheels of his chariots ?
2 Ki. 7 : 9, if we t. till morning light.
Ps. 68 : 12, she that t. at home.
   101 : 7, he that telleth lies shall not t. in my sight.
Prov. 23 : 30, they that t. long at the wine.
Isa. 46 : 13, my salvation shall not t.
Hab. 2 : 3, though it t., wait for it.
Matt. 25 : 6, the bridegroom t.
   26 : 38; Mark 14 : 34, t. ye here, and watch.
Luke 24 : 29, he went in to t. with them.
John 21 : 22, if I will that he t.
Acts 22 : 16, why t. thou ? arise and be baptized.
1 Cor. 11 : 33, t. one for another.
Heb. 10 : 37, will come, and will not t.
See Ps. 40 : 17; 70 : 5.
Task, Ex. 5 : 13, 14, 19.
Taskmasters, Ex. 1 : 11; 5 : 6.
Taste, Ex. 16 : 31, t. of manna like wafers.
Num. 11 : 8, the t. of it as t. of fresh oil.
Job 6 : 6, is there any t. in the white of an egg ?
Ps. 119 : 103, how sweet are thy words to my t.
Song of Sol. 2 : 3, fruit was sweet to my t.
Jer. 48 : 11, his t. remained in him.
Taste.
Job 12 : 11, doth not mouth t. meat ?
Ps. 34 : 8, O t. and see that the Lord is good.
Matt. 16 : 28; Mark 9 : 1; Luke 9 : 27, some which shall not t. of death.
Luke 14 : 24, none bidden shall t. of my supper.
John 8 : 52, keep my saving, he shall never t. of death.
Col. 2 : 21, touch not, t. not.
Heb. 2 : 9, should t. death for every man.
   6 : 4, have t. of the heavenly gift.
1 Pet. 2 : 3, have t. that the Lord is gracious.
Tatnai (tăt-nâi), [present], and Shethar-boznai, hinder the rebuilding of the temple, Ezra 5 : 3; 6 : 13.
Taught, 2 Chr. 6 : 27, thou hast t. them the good way.
Eccl. 12 : 9, he t. the people knowledge.
Isa. 29 : 13, their fear is t. by precept of men.
   54 : 13, thy children shall be t. of the Lord.
Jer. 32 : 33, though I t. them, rising up early.
Matt. 7 : 29; Mark 1 : 22, he t. as one having authority.
Luke 13 : 26, thou hast t. in our streets.
John 6 : 45, they shall be all t. of God.
Gal. 6 : 6, him t. in the word.
Eph. 4 : 21, if ye have been t. by him.
1 John 2 : 27, as anointing hath t. you.
Taunt, Ezek. 5 : 15; Hab. 2 : 6.
Taverns, the three. Acts 28 : 15.
Taxation, of all the world, under Cæsar Augustus, Luke 2 : 1.
See 2 Ki. 23 : 35; Acts 5 : 37.
   Taxation, in the Roman Empire, does not imply the paying of taxes, but corre-

sponds rather to the modern custom of taking a census.

Teach, Ex. 4 : 15, I will t. you.
Deut. 4 : 10, that they may t. their children.
33 : 10, they shall t. Jacob thy judgments.
1 Sam. 12 : 23, I will t. you the good way.
2 Chr. 17 : 7, to t. in cities of Judah.
Job 6 : 24, t. me, and I will hold my tongue.
21 : 22, shall any t. God knowledge ?
37 : 19, t. us what we shall say.
Ps. 25 : 4, t. me thy paths.
25 : 8, he will t. sinners.
34 : 11, I will t. you the fear of the Lord.
51 : 13, then will I t. transgressors thy ways.
90 : 12, so t. us to number our days.
94 : 10, he that t. man knowledge.
Isa. 2 : 3; Mic. 4 : 2, he will t. us of his ways.
Isa. 28 : 9, whom shall he t. knowledge ?
Mic. 3 : 11, priests t. for hire.
Matt. 28 : 19, t. all nations.
Luke 11 : 1, t. us to pray.
John 9 : 34, dost thou t. us ?
John 14 : 26, Holy Ghost shall t. you all things.
Acts 5 : 42, they ceased not to t. and preach.
1 Cor. 11 : 14, doth not even nature t. you ?
Col. 1 : 28, t. every man in all wisdom.
3 : 16, t. and admonishing one another.
1 Tim. 2 : 12, I suffer not a woman to t.
3 : 2; 2 Tim. 2 : 24, apt to t.
1 Tim. 4 : 11, these things command and t.
2 Tim. 2 : 2, faithful men, able to t. others.
Titus 2 : 12, t. us that, denying ungodliness.
Heb. 5 : 12, ye have need that one t. you.
8 : 11, t. no more every man his neighbour.
Teachers, Ezra 7 : 10; Acts 13 : 1; Rom. 12 : 7; 1 Cor. 12 : 28; 1 Tim. 3.
false, foretold and described, Jer. 5 : 13; 6 : 13; Ezek. 14 : 9; 22 : 25; Hos. 9 : 7; Mic. 2 : 11; 3 : 11; Zeph. 3 : 4; Matt. 24 : 4; Acts 13 : 6; 20 : 29; 2 Cor. 11 : 13; 1 Tim. 1 : 6; 4 : 1; 6 : 3; 2 Tim. 3 : 8; Titus 1 : 11; Jude 4; Rev. 2 : 14, 20.
not to be listened to, Deut. 13 : 1; 1 Tim. 1 : 4; Heb. 13 : 9; 2 John 10.
their condemnation, Deut. 18 : 20; Isa. 8 : 20; 9 : 15; Jer. 28 : 15; Ezek. 13 : 8; 14 : 10; Gal. 1 : 8; 2 Tim. 3 : 9; Jude 10, 15.
to be tried and avoided, 1 John 4 : 1; Rom. 16 : 17.
1 Chr. 25 : 8, as well the t. as the scholar.
Ps. 119 : 99, I have more understanding than all my t.
Isa. 30 : 20, thine eyes shall see thy t.
Hab. 2 : 18, a t. of lies.
John 3 : 2, a t. come from God.
Rom. 2 : 20, a t. of babes.
1 Cor. 12 : 29, are all t. ?
Eph. 4 : 11, pastors and t.
1 Tim. 1 : 7, desiring to be t. of the law.
2 Pet. 2 : 1, shall be false t.
Tears, Job 16 : 20, mine eye poureth out t.
Ps. 6 : 6, I water my couch with t.
42 : 3, my t. have been my meat.
56 : 8, put my t. into bottle.
80 : 5, the bread of t.

126 : 5, they that sow in t.
Isa. 16 : 9, I will water thee with my t.
25 : 8, Lord will wipe away t.
Jer. 9 : 1, oh that mine eyes were a fountain of t.
31 : 16, refrain thine eyes from t.
Lam. 2 : 11, mine eyes do fail with t.
Ezek. 24 : 16, neither shall thy t. run down.
Mal. 2 : 13, covering altar of Lord with t.
Luke 7 : 38, to wash his feet with t.
Acts 20 : 31, ceased not to warn with t.
Heb. 5 : 7, offered up supplications with t.
12 : 17, he sought it carefully with t.
Rev. 7 : 17; 21 : 4, God shall wipe away t.
Tebet, or **Tebeth** (tĕ-ʹbĕth) [Assyr., " Tebetum "], month of December-January, tenth Jewish month, Esther 2 : 16.
Teeth, Gen. 49 : 12, his t. shall be white with milk.
Job 19 : 20, escaped with skin of my t.
Prov. 10 : 26, as vinegar to the t.
Song of Sol. 4 : 2; 6 : 6, thy t. are like a flock.
Isa. 41 : 15, an instrument having t.
Jer. 31 : 29; Ezek. 18 : 2, children's t. are set on edge.
Amos 4 : 6, cleanness of t.
Matt. 27 : 44, cast the same in his t.
Tekel (tĕ-ʹkĕl) [weighed], Dan. 5 : 25, 27.
Tekoa, Tekoah (tĕ-kō-ʹä) [blast of the trumpet], son of Ashur, 1 Chr. 2 : 24; 4 : 5.
a city of Judah, 2 Chr. 11 : 6; Amos 1 : 1.
widow of, 2 Sam. 14.
Temper, Ex. 30 : 35; Ezek. 46 : 14; 1 Cor. 12 : 24.
Temperance, exhortations to, 1 Cor. 9 : 25; Eph. 5 : 18; Titus 1 : 8; 2 : 2.
Acts 24 : 25, as he reasoned of t.
Gal. 5 : 23, meekness, t.
2 Pet. 1 : 6, add to knowledge t.; and to t. patience.
The word " temperance " does not appear in the Old Testament, but the virtue of self-control is fully recognised there as well as in the New Testament writings. It appears particularly in the book of Proverbs.
Tempest, Job 9 : 17, he breaketh me with a t.
Ps. 11 : 6, on wicked he shall rain a t.
55 : 8, I hasten from storm and t.
Isa. 28 : 2, as a t. of hail.
32 : 2, covert from the t.
Heb. 12 : 18, not come to darkness and t.
2 Pet. 2 : 17, clouds carried with a t.
Temple, the. The Temple, in Jerusalem, was the centre of Jewish religious life. The first Temple was built under Solomon, and was destroyed some four hundred years later by the Babylonians, in B.C. 587. More than fifty years later, on the return of the Jews from captivity, the rebuilding of the Temple was started under Zerubbabel. The site, and general structure of the Temple were the same as in Solomon's time. In the Roman period this second Temple was rebuilt, under Herod, on a more magnificent scale, and stood till A.D. 70, when

it was destroyed by the Romans, under Titus.

(1) The Solomonic Temple, described in 1 Ki. 6 and 2 Chr. 3, 4, was for the most part only an enlarged edition of the Mosaic Tabernacle with the modifications necessitated by the requirements of such a splendid edifice. The plan of the Solomonic Temple was, according to the Chronicler, handed over by David to Solomon. That plan David was " made to understand in writing from the hand of the Lord " (1 Chr. 28 : 19; see also vers. 11, 12 ff.). That statement is not, however, at variance with the facts afterwards recorded, that ornamental details and subsidiary constructions were added by Solomon and the Tyrian artificers who assisted him in the building.

Avoiding, as impossible here to be discussed, all architectural details, it should be noticed that a brazen altar of very different dimensions from that of the Tabernacle was erected by Solomon (2 Chr. 4 : 1): that in place of the single laver in the outer court of the Tabernacle, Solomon placed ten lavers in the Temple —five on the right and five on the left— to wash the holy vessels in (2 Chr. 4 : 6), while he provided a much larger one, the brazen sea, described in 2 Chr. 4 : 2-6, for the priests to wash in. In place of the single seven-armed candlestick, Solomon made ten of a similar pattern to that in the Tabernacle, which were arranged in two rows of five each (2 Chr. 4 : 7). In the Holy of Holies, which is termed " the oracle," he erected as a canopy overshadowing the Ark, two gigantic cherubim of olive wood overlaid with gold, whose wings extended twenty cubits, and under their shadow the Ark with its mercy-seat and cherubim was placed. There were also in the Temple carved cherubim on the walls of the innermost shrine, which was still left in total darkness, so that the carved figures, which were in no wise resemblances of the Deity, were not seen by the people, and could be no incentives to image worship. Chains of gold were drawn before the oracle, and two doors of olive wood were provided for it; but inside these there was still the mysterious secret hiding veil (2 Chr. 3 : 14). In the Holy Place, also, there were ten extra tables (2 Chr. 4 : 8), but the Table of Shewbread was not interfered with. We need do no more here than allude to the pillars Jachin and Boaz mentioned in 2 Chr. 3 : 17.

(2) The Temple of Zerubbabel.—This Temple is roughly described in the decree of Cyrus (Ezra 6 : 3). It was to be sixty cubits in height, only half as high as the Solomonic, but much broader, being sixty in place of the forty, which was the width of the Solominic. It seems to have been increased in later times. When originally erected it was far inferior to that of Solomon, and the signs of the inferiority were no doubt visible from the very beginning. For it is doubtful whether the Exiles were able to attempt the erection of so large a building as that originally contemplated in Cyrus' decree. Hence the account in Ezra 3 : 12, 13 is quite credible.

It is, however, important to note that in this second Temple the high-priestly breastplate, with its Urim and Thummim, was no longer in existence (Neh. 7 : 65). The Ark of the Covenant, too, was no longer with Israel.

In the Temple of Zerubbabel there appears to have been only one seven-branched candlestick in the Holy Place. Though similar in form to that in the Tabernacle of Moses, it cannot have been identical in ornamentation, for the griffins on its pedestal, which appear on the Triumphal Arch of Titus, are suggestive of a foreign origin. In all other particulars the furniture of the Holy Place appears to have been like that in the Tabernacle.

(3) Herod's Temple.—The magnificence of this Temple is spoken of in the New Testament, and also the forty-six years spent in the building of it, but no details are there given of its dimensions or of its chambers. Information from other sources, however, shows that it maintained the essential features of Zerubbabel's Temple. The Holy Place was duly furnished, as in the former Temple, and the Holy of Holies was separated from it by the veil, and was empty.

(4) To these accounts of the three Temples must be added a reference to Ezekiel's vision of the Temple (Ezek. 40-48). The interpretation of this passage is difficult. It may be wrong to describe the whole as " nothing but a gigantic allegory," for in that case it would be requisite to point out the symbolical significance of at least the majority of the details, which cannot be done. But it is equally clear that the vision of the Temple was not intended to be taken literally. It was an ideal representation, in which the Prophet, who " looked for redemption in Israel," and the nation to whom he belonged, were taught through well-known symbols to look forward to something grander and nobler than even that displayed to the eye, in those " visions of God."

David desires to build, 2 Sam. 7 : 3; 1 Chr. 17 : 2; 28 : 2; forbidden to build, 2 Sam. 7 : 5; 1 Chr. 17 : 4; 28 : 3.

Solomon to build, 2 Sam. 7 : 12; 1 Chr. 17 : 11; 28 : 5; builds, 1 Ki. 6; 2 Chr. 3; 4.

its solemn dedication, 1 Ki. 8; 9; 2 Chr. 6; 7.

plundered by Shishak, king of Egypt, 1 Ki. 14 : 25; 2 Chr. 12 : 9.

restored by Joash, 2 Ki. 12 : 5, 12.

cleansed by Hezekiah, 2 Chr. 29 : 5.
polluted by Manasseh, 2 Chr. 33 : 7.
repaired by Josiah, 2 Chr. 34.
spoiled by the Chaldeans, 2 Ki. 25 : 9.
decrees of Cyrus and Darius for rebuilding,
Ezra 6 : 3, 13.
finished and dedicated, Ezra 6 : 15, 16.
Christ drives out buyers and sellers, Matt.
21 : 12; Mark 11 : 15; Luke 19 : 45;
John 2 : 14.
Christ foretells its destruction, Matt. 24 : 2;
Mark 13 : 2; Luke 21 : 6.
house of God, Ps. 65 : 4; Eccl. 5 : 1; Heb.
10 : 21; 1 Pet. 4 : 17.
symbolical of the body of Christ. John
2 : 19-21.
of God and Holy Ghost, Christians are,
2 Cor. 6 : 16.
2 Sam. 22 : 7; Ps. 18 : 6, he did hear my
voice out of his t.
Ps. 27 : 4, to enquire in his t.
29 : 9, in his t. doth every one speak of
his glory.
Isa. 6 : 1, his train filled the t.
Mal. 3 : 1, the Lord shall suddenly come to
his t.
Matt. 12 : 6, one greater than the t.
John 2 : 19, destroy this t.
Acts 7 : 48; 17 : 24, t. made with hands.
1 Cor. 3 : 16, ye are the t. of God.
6 : 19, body is t. of Holy Ghost.
Rev. 7 : 15, serve day and night in his t.
21 : 22, no t. therein.
See Ps. 84 : 1, 10; 100 : 4; 122; Isa. 2 : 3;
Rev. 3 : 12; 15 : 8.
Temporal, 2 Cor. 4 : 18.
Tempt, Gen. 22 : 1, God did t. Abraham.
Ex. 17 : 2, wherefore do ye t. the Lord ?
Deut. 6 : 16; Matt. 4 : 7; Luke 4 : 12, shall
not t. the Lord.
Isa. 7 : 12, I will not ask, neither will I t.
the Lord.
Mal. 3 : 15, they that t. God are even
delivered.
Matt. 22 : 18; Mark 12 : 15; Luke 20 : 23,
why t. ye me ?
Acts 5 : 9, agreed together to t. the Spirit.
15 : 10, why t. ye God ?
1 Cor. 10 : 13, will not suffer you to be t.
Gal. 6 : 1, lest thou also be t.
1 Thess. 3 : 5, lest the tempter t. you.
Heb. 2 : 18, hath suffered, being t.
4 : 15, in all points t. like as we are.
Jas. 1 : 13, God cannot be t., neither t. he
any man.
Temptation, trial of faith, Gen. 22; Dan.
12 : 10; Luke 12 : 31, 40; Heb. 11 : 17;
1 Pet. 1 : 7; 4 : 12.
of Christ, by the devil, Matt. 4; Mark
1 : 13; Luke 4.
Ps. 95 : 8; Heb. 3 : 8, as in the day of t.
in wilderness.
Matt. 6 : 13; Luke 11 : 4, lead us not into t.
Matt. 26 : 41; Mark 14 : 38; Luke 22 : 46,
lest ye enter into t.
Luke 8 : 13, in time of t. fall away.
1 Cor. 10 : 13, there hath no t. taken you.
1 Tim. 6 : 9, they that will be rich fall into
t.

Jas. 1 : 12, blessed is that man that en-
dureth t.
2 Pet. 2 : 9, how to deliver out of t.
Rev. 3 : 10, keep thee from hour of t.
Tempter, Matt. 4 : 3; 1 Thess. 3 : 5.
Tender, 2 Ki. 22 : 19; 2 Chr. 34 : 27, thine
heart was t.
Job 38 : 27, cause the t. herb to spring.
Isa. 47 : 1, no more be called t.
53 : 2, grow up as a t. plant.
Luke 1 : 78, through the t. mercy of our
God.
Jas. 5 : 11, Lord is pitiful and of t. mercy.
Tenderhearted, 2 Chr. 13 : 7; Eph. 4 : 32.
Tenor, Gen. 43 : 7; Ex. 34 : 27.
Tenth, Gen. 28 : 22, give the t. unto thee.
Lev. 27 : 32, t. shall be holy unto the Lord.
Tents, Num. 24 : 5, how goodly are thy t.
1 Ki. 12 : 16, to your t., O Israel.
Ps. 84 : 10, than to dwell in t. of wickedness.
See Gen. 12 : 8; 25 : 27; Acts 18 : 3.
Terah (tēr-räh) [loiterer], Gen. 11 : 24; Josh.
24 : 2.
Teraphim. The Hebrew Teraphim were
images which appear to have been regarded very much as the Romans regarded their household gods (cf. the early
story of Rachel stealing her father's
" images," Gen. 31). It appears also
that their use was bound up with various
magical practices. In particular they
were associated with the common ancient
practice of the giving and receiving of
oracles (Ezek. 21 : 21; Zech. 10 : 2).
Judg. 17 : 5; 18 : 14; 1 Sam. 19 : 13.
Termed, Isa. 62 : 4, thou shalt no more be
t. forsaken.
Terraces, 2 Chr. 9 : 11.
Terrestrial, 1 Cor. 15 : 40.
Terror, Gen. 35 : 5, the t. of God.
Deut. 32 : 25, the sword without and t.
within.
Job 18 : 11, t. shall make him afraid.
24 : 17, in the t. of the shadow of death.
31 : 23, destruction was a t. to me.
Ps. 55 : 4, the t. of death are fallen upon
me.
91 : 5, not afraid for t. by night.
Isa. 33 : 18, thine heart shall meditate t.
54 : 14, thou shalt be far from t.
Jer. 17 : 17, be not a t. unto me.
20 : 4; Ezek. 26 : 21, I will make thee
a t.
Ezek. 27 : 36; 28 : 19, thou shalt be a t.
Rom. 13 : 3, rulers are not a t. to good
works.
2 Cor. 5 : 11, knowing t. of the Lord.
1 Pet. 3 : 14, be not afraid of their t.
Testament, the new, of Christ's blood, Matt.
26 : 28; Luke 22 : 20; 2 Cor. 3 : 6.
superior to the old, Heb. 8 : 6, 7; 9; 10;
12 : 24.
Mark 14 : 24, this is my blood of the new t.
1 Cor. 11 : 25, cup is the new t.
Heb. 7 : 22, surety of a better t.
9 : 16, where a t. is, there must be the
death of the testator.
Testify, Num. 35 : 30, one witness shall
not t.

Neh. 9 : 34, wherewith thou didst t. against them.

Job 15 : 6, thine own lips t. against thee.

Isa. 59 : 12, sins t. against us.

Hos. 5 : 5; 7 : 10, pride of Israel doth t.

Mic. 6 : 3, t. against me.

John 2 : 25, any should t. of man.

3 : 11, we t. that we have seen.

5 : 39, scriptures t. of me.

15 : 26, he shall t. of me.

21 : 24, disciple which t. of these things.

Acts 20 : 24, to t. gospel of grace of God.

Eph. 4 : 17, this I say, and t. in the Lord.

1 Tim. 2 : 6, gave himself to be t. in due time.

Heb. 2 : 6, one in a certain place t.

1 Pet. 1 : 11, t. beforehand the sufferings.

1 John 4 : 14, we have seen, and do t.

Testimony, of the apostles, Acts 22 : 18; 2 Thess. 1 : 10; 2 Tim. 1 : 8; Rev. 11 : 7; 12 : 17.

testimonies, of God, Ps. 119 : 2.

2 Ki. 11 : 12; 2 Chr. 23 : 11, gave him the t.

Ps. 78 : 5, he established a t. in Jacob.

93 : 5, thy t. are very sure.

119 : 24, thy t. are my delight.

119 : 59, I turned my feet to thy t.

119 : 129, thy t. are wonderful.

Isa. 8 : 16, bind up the t.

8 : 20, to the law and to the t.

Matt. 10 : 18; Mark 13 : 9, for a t. against them.

John 3 : 32, no man receiveth his t.

21 : 24, we know that his t. is true.

Acts 14 : 3, gave t. to the word of his grace.

1 Cor. 2 : 1, declaring the t. of God.

2 Cor. 1 : 12, the t. of our conscience.

Heb. 11 : 5, Enoch had this t.

Rev. 1 : 2; 19 : 10, the t. of Jesus.

See Ex. 25 : 16, 21.

Tetrarch (tē-trärch) [governor of a fourth part of the country], Luke 3 : 1; 3 : 19; 9 : 7.

Thaddæus (thăd-dǣ-ŭs), one of the twelve apostles, Matt. 10 : 3; Mark 3 : 18.

Thank, 1 Chr. 29 : 13, our God, we t. thee.

Matt. 11 : 25; Luke 10 : 21; John 11 : 41, I t. thee, O Father.

Rom. 6 : 17, God be t., ye were.

1 Cor. 1 : 4, I t. God on your behalf.

2 Thess. 1 : 3, we are bound to t. God.

Thankful, Ps. 100 : 4, be t. unto him.

Rom. 1 : 21, neither were t.

Col. 3 : 15, and be ye t.

See Acts 24 : 3.

Thanks, Dan. 6 : 10, he prayed, and gave t.

Matt. 26 : 27; Luke 22 : 17, he took the cup, and gave t.

Rom. 14 : 6, he giveth God t.

1 Cor. 15 : 57, t. be to God, who giveth us the victory.

2 Cor. 9 : 15, t. be to God for his unspeakable gift.

Eph. 5 : 20, giving t. always for all things.

1 Thess. 3 : 9, what t. can we render ?

Thanksgiving, exhortations to, Ps. 34 : 3; 95 : 2; 100 : 4; 107 : 22; 136; 2 Cor. 9 : 12; Col. 2 : 7.

at the Lord's Supper, Matt. 26 : 27; Mark 14 : 23; Luke 22 : 17; 1 Cor. 11 : 24.

at meals, Mark 8 : 6; John 6 : 11; Acts 27 : 35; Rom. 14 : 6; Eph. 5 : 20.

Neh. 11 : 17, principal to begin the t.

Ps. 26 : 7, publish with voice of t.

50 : 14, offer unto God t.

100 : 4, enter into his gates with t.

Isa. 51 : 3, t. and melody shall be found therein.

Amos 4 : 5, offer a sacrifice of t.

Phil. 4 : 6, with t. let your requests be made known.

Col. 4 : 2, watch in the same with t.

1 Tim. 4 : 3, to be received with t.

Rev. 7 : 12, t. and honour be to our God.

Theophilus (thē-ŏph-ĭ-lŭs) [friend of God]. Theophilus was one of the first Christians, and apparently a friend of Luke, the author of the Third Gospel, and of the book of Acts. Both books are dedicated to him. Luke 1 : 3.

Thessalonians (thĕss-ă-lō-nĭ-ăns), Acts 20 : 4; 1 Thess. 1 : 1.

Thessalonians, Epistles to.

Date.—These two Epistles form the earliest group among the letters of St. Paul; and the first of them is probably the earliest Christian document that has come down to us. The first Epistle in particular bears strong marks of an early date, for it was obviously written at a time when it was expected that most Christians would live to see Christ's return and when it was feared that those who died before he came might lose some of the blessings of his coming. The first Epistle was written from Corinth, late in 52 or early in 53, and the second Epistle probably about a year later.

The Church.—Thessalonica was a prosperous city on the Thermaic Gulf, the capital of Macedonia Secunda, and seat of a Roman proconsul. Many Jews had settled there for the sake of its commercial advantages. St. Paul founded the Church there on his second missionary journey, in company with Silas, about A.D. 52. He preached in the synagogue and converted some Jews and many proselytes.

Latterly, however, he met with considerable hostility from the Jewish community, and was forced to leave the city. The Epistles show us a young church which had embraced the faith with enthusiasm, but is not yet free from heathen vices.

Contents.—First Epistle—This is the least dogmatic of St. Paul's Epistles; yet it clearly teaches the following important doctrines: that Christ is one with the Father (1 : 1; 3 : 11); is our Redeemer and Saviour (1 : 11; 5 : 9, 10); is the Lord (2 : 15; 4 : 16), and our Lord (2 : 19; 5 : 23), who is coming again from heaven (4 : 14-18). After the Salutations and Thanksgiving (1) we have two main divisions; Declarations of

Affection and Satisfaction (2 : 1–3 : 13); Advice and Comfort (4 : 1–5 : 22). In the Conclusion (5 : 23-28), the direction that the Epistle is to be read to all the brethren, and not retained by a select few, is quite in place in the first letter written by the Apostle to a Christian Church.

Second Epistle.—The main divisions of this Epistle are marked by the chapters, as follows: Salutation and thanksgiving (1); warning about the date of Christ's coming (2); exhortation to prayer and work (3 : 1-15); benediction (3 : 16); and autograph conclusion (3 : 17-18).

Thief, punishment of, Ex. 22 : 2; Deut. 24 : 7; Zech. 5 : 4; 1 Cor. 6 : 10.

his conduct described, Job 24 : 14; Jer. 49 : 9; Luke 10 : 30.

Christ's second coming typified by Luke 12 : 39; 1 Thess. 5 : 2; Rev. 3 : 3; 16 : 15.

Ps. 50 : 18, when thou sawest a t.

Jer. 2 : 26, as the t. is ashamed.

Hos. 1 : 7, the t. cometh in.

Joel 2 : 9, enter at windows like a t.

Matt. 24 : 43, what watch the t. would come.

26 : 55; Mark 14 : 48; Luke 22 : 52, are ye come as against a t. ?

Luke 12 : 33, where no t. approach.

John 10 : 1, the same is a t. and a robber.

1 Pet. 3 : 10, day of the Lord cometh as a t. See Matt. 6 : 19; John 10 : 8.

Thieves, at crucifixion, Matt. 27 : 38; Mark 15 : 27; Luke 23 : 39.

Think, Gen. 40 : 14, t. on me when it shall be well.

Neh. 5 : 19, t. upon me, my God, for good.

Ps. 40 : 17, the Lord t. upon me.

Prov. 23 : 7, as he t. in his heart.

Jonah 1 : 6, if God will t. upon us.

Matt. 3 : 9, t. not to say within yourselves.

5 : 17, t. not I am come to destroy.

6 : 7, t. they shall be heard.

9 : 4, why t. ye evil in your hearts ?

17 : 25; 22 : 17, what t. thou ?

22 : 42, what t. ye of Christ ?

John 16 : 2, will t. that he doeth God service.

Rom. 12 : 3, not to t. more highly than he ought to t.

1 Cor. 10 : 12, let him that t. he standeth.

2 Cor. 3 : 5, to t. any thing as of ourselves.

Gal. 6 : 3, if a man t. himself to be something.

Eph. 3 : 20, able to do above all we ask or t.

Phil. 4 : 8, t. on these things.

Jas. 1 : 7, let not that man t. he shall receive.

4 : 5, do ye t. that the scripture saith in vain ?

Thirst, Ex. 17 : 3, to kill us with t.

Deut. 29 : 19, to add drunkenness to t.

Judg. 15 : 18, now I shall die for t.

Ps. 69 : 21, in my t. they gave me vinegar.

104 : 11, wild asses quench their t.

Isa. 41 : 17, when their tongue faileth for t.

Amos 8 : 11, nor a t. for water, but hearing words of the Lord.

2 Cor. 11 : 27, in hunger and t.

Ps. 42 : 2; 63 : 1; 143 : 6, my soul t. for God.

Isa. 49 : 10; Rev. 7 : 16, shall not hunger nor t.

Isa. 55 : 1, every one that t.

Matt. 5 : 6, hunger and t. after righteousness.

John 4 : 14; 6 : 35, shall never t.

7 : 37, if any man t., let him come unto me.

19 : 28, Jesus saith, I t.

Rom. 12 : 20, if enemy t., give him drink.

Thirsty, Judg. 4 : 19, give me a little water; for I am t.

Ps. 63 : 1; 143 : 6, a t. land.

107 : 5, hungry and t., their soul fainted.

Prov. 25 : 25, as cold water to a t. soul.

Isa. 21 : 14, water to him that was t.

29 : 8, as when a t. man dreameth.

35 : 7, t. land becomes springs of water.

44 : 3, pour water on him that is t.

65 : 13, servants drink, but ye shall be t.

Matt. 25 : 35, I was t., and ye gave me drink.

Thomas [twin], (Gr. form of Heb. " Tāām "), one of twelve apostles, Matt. 10 : 3; Mark 3 : 18; Luke 6 : 15; Acts 1 : 13.

his zeal, John 11 : 16.

his unbelief and confession, John 20 : 24 ff.

Thorns, crown of, placed on Christ, Mark 15 : 17; John 19 : 2.

Num. 33 : 35; Judg. 2 : 3, t. in your sides.

Ps. 118 : 12, quenched as the fire of t.

Prov. 15 : 19, way of slothful as hedge of t.

22 : 5, t. are in the way of the froward.

24 : 31, it was grown over with t.

26 : 9, as t. goeth into hand.

Eccl. 7 : 6, as crackling of t. under a pot.

Song of Sol. 2 : 2, as the lily among t.

Isa. 33 : 12, as t. cut up shall they be burned.

34 : 13, t. shall come up in her palaces.

55 : 13, instead of the t. shall come up the fir tree.

Jer. 4 : 3, sow not among t.

12 : 13, sown wheat, but shall reap t.

Hos. 2 : 6, I will hedge up way with t.

9 : 6, t. shall be in their tabernacles.

10 : 8, the t. shall come up on their altars.

Mic. 7 : 4, the most upright is sharper than t. hedge.

Matt. 7 : 16, do men gather grapes of t. ?

13 : 7; Mark 4 : 7, some fell among t.

Matt. 27 : 29, platted a crown of t.

2 Cor. 12 : 7, a t. in the flesh.

Thought, Gen. 6 : 5, t. of his heart only evil.

1 Chr. 28 : 9, the Lord understandeth the t.

Job 4 : 13, in t. from the visions of the night.

42 : 2, no t. can be withholden from thee.

Ps. 10 : 4, God is not in all his t.

40 : 5, thy t. cannot be reckoned.

92 : 5, thy t. are very deep.

94 : 11, the Lord knoweth the t. of man.

139 : 17, how precious are thy t. to me.

139 : 23, try me, and know my t.

Prov. 12 : 5, the t. of the righteous are right.

15 : 26, the t. of the wicked are abomination.

16 : 3, thy t. shall be established.

Isa. 55 : 7, let the unrighteous forsake his t.

55 : 8, my t. are not your t.

Mic. 4 : 12, they know not the t. of the Lord.

Matt. 9 : 4; 12 : 25; Luke 5 : 22; 6 : 8; 11 : 17, Jesus knowing their t.

Matt. 15 : 19; Mark 7 : 21, out of the heart proceed evil t.

Luke 9 : 47, Jesus, perceiving the t. of their heart.

24 : 38, why do t. arise in your hearts ?

1 Cor. 3 : 20, the Lord knoweth the t. of the wise.

2 Cor. 10 : 5, bringing into captivity every t.

Heb. 4 : 12, the word of God is a discerner of the t.

Jas. 2 : 4, are become judges of evil t.

Gen. 50 : 20, yet t. evil against me.

2 Ki. 5 : 11, I t. He will surely come out.

Ps. 48 : 9, we have t. of thy lovingkindness.

50 : 21, thou t. I was such an one as thyself.

73 : 16, when I t. to know this.

119 : 59, I t. on my ways.

Jer. 18 : 8, I will repent of the evil I t. to do.

Zech. 8 : 15, I t. to do well.

Mal. 3 : 16, for them that t. upon his name.

Mark 14 : 72, when he t. thereon, he wept.

Luke 12 : 17, he t. within himself, What shall I do ?

19 : 11, they t. the kingdom of God should appear.

John 11 : 13, they t. he had spoken of taking of rest.

Acts 15 : 38. t. not good to take him.

26 : 8, why should it be t. a thing incredible ?

1 Cor. 13 : 11, I t. as a child.

Phil. 2 : 6, t. it not robbery to be equal with God.

Threaten, Acts 4 : 17, let us straitly t. them.

1 Pet. 2 : 23, when he suffered, he t. not.

See Acts 9 : 1; Eph. 6 : 9.

Thresh, Isa. 41 : 15, thou shalt t. the mountains.

Jer. 51 : 33, it is time to t. her.

Mic. 4 : 13, arise and t.

Hab. 3 : 12, thou didst t. the heathen.

1 Cor. 9 : 10, he that t. in hope.

See Lev. 26 : 5; 1 Cor. 21 : 20; Isa. 21 : 10; 28 : 28.

Threshingfloor, Ruth 3 : 2; 1 Chr. 21 : 15, 21, 22.

Threshold, 1 Sam. 5 : 5; Ezek. 46 : 2; Zeph. 2 : 14.

Threw, 2 Sam. 16 : 13, t. stones at him.

2 Chr. 31 : 1, t. down the high places.

Acts 22 : 23, t. dust into air.

See Mic. 5 : 11; Mal. 1 : 4; Luke 4 : 35; Rev. 18 : 21.

Throat, Ps. 5 : 9; Rom. 3 : 13, their t. is an open sepulchre.

Ps. 115 : 7, neither speak they through their t.

Prov. 23 : 2, put a knife to thy t.

Matt. 18 : 28, took him by the t.

Throne, Gen. 41 : 40, in the t. will I be greater.

Ps. 11 : 4, the Lord's t. is in heaven.

47 : 8, God sitteth upon t. of his holiness.

89 : 14, justice and judgment are habitation of thy t.

94 : 20, shall t. of iniquity have fellowship with thee ?

Prov. 20 : 28, his t. is upholden by mercy.

25 : 5, his t. shall be established in righteousness.

Isa. 66 : 1; Acts 7 : 49, heaven is my t.

Jer. 17 : 12, a glorious high t.

Lam. 5 : 19, thy t. from generation to generation.

Dan. 7 : 9, his t. was like the fiery flame.

Matt. 19 : 28; 25 : 31, the Son of man shall sit in the t.

Heb. 4 : 16, the t. of grace.

Rev. 3 : 21, to him will I grant to sit on my t.

20 : 11, a great white t.

Throng, Mark 3 : 9, lest they should t. him.

5 : 24; Luke 8 : 42, much people t. him.

Luke 8 : 45, the multitude t. thee.

Thummim, on high priest's breastplate, Ex. 28 : 30; Lev. 8 : 8; Deut. 33 : 8; Ezra 2 : 63; Neh. 7 : 65.

Thunder, Ex. 9 : 23; 1 Sam. 7 : 10; 12 : 18; Ps. 78 : 48.

thunders, seven, Rev. 10 : 3, 4.

See Ex. 19 : 16; Rev. 4 : 5; 16 : 18.

Thyatira (thȳ-ȧ-tī′-rȧ), a city of Asia Minor, north-west of Sardis, now called Ak Hissar. It was one of the seats of the Early Church, and is mentioned in Acts as the city of Lydia, an early convert. Acts 16 : 14; Rev. 1 : 11; 2 : 18.

Thyine, wood, sandarac tree.

Tiberias (tī-bē′-rī-ȧs), a town on the shore of the Sea of Galilee. The name, which is Roman, was applied to the sea itself. Later the town became the seat of the Sanhedrin, and the tombs of many famous Rabbis are there. John 6 : 1, 23.

Tiberius (tī-bē′-rī-ŭs), the Roman emperor, Luke 3 : 1.

Tidal (tī-dăl), LXX., " Thargal," Gen. 14 : 1.

Tidings, 2 Sam. 18 : 31, said T., my lord the king.

Ps. 112 : 7, not be afraid of evil t.

Dan. 11 : 44, t. out of the east.

Luke 8 : 1, showing glad t. of kingdom of God.

Rom. 10 : 15, glad t. of good things.

Tie, Prov. 6 : 21; Matt. 21 : 2; Mark 11 : 2.

Tiglath-pileser (tĭg-lăth-pī-lē′-sĕr), 2 Ki. 15 : 29; 16 : 7; 1 Chr. 5 : 6, 26; 2 Chr. 28 : 20.

Tile, Ezek. 4 : 1; Luke 5 : 19.

Till, Gen. 2 : 5; 3 : 23, to t. the ground.

Prov. 12 : 11; 28 : 19, he that t. his hand.

Ezek. 36 : 34, desolate land shall be t.

Timber, 1 Ki. 5 : 18, they prepared t. and

stones to build. See also 2 Chr. 2 : 9;
2 Ki. 22 : 6; Neh. 2 : 8.

Timbrel, Judg. 11 : 34, his daughter came
out to meet him with t. See also 2 Sam.
6 : 5; Job 21 : 12; Ps. 68 : 25; 81 : 2;
150 : 4. The timbrel was a kind of tam-
bourine, used on joyful occasions, chiefly
by women.

Time, redemption of, Ps. 39 : 4; 90 : 12;
Eccl. 12 : 1; Isa. 55 : 6; Matt. 5 : 25;
Luke 19 : 42; John 9 : 4; 12 : 35;
2 Cor. 6 : 2; Gal. 6 : 9; Eph. 5 : 16.

for all things, Eccl. 3.

the end of, Rev. 10 : 6.

times, the last, signs of, Matt. 16 : 3; Acts
3 : 21; 1 Thess. 5 : 1; 2 Thess. 2; 1 Tim.
4 : 1; 2 Tim. 3 : 1.

Ps. 32 : 6, in a t. when thou mayest be
found.

37 : 19, not be ashamed in the evil t.

41 : 1, deliver him in t. of trouble.

56 : 3, what t. I am afraid.

69 : 13; Isa. 49 : 8, in an acceptable t.

89 : 47, remember how short my t. is.

Eccl. 3 : 1, there is a t. to every purpose.

9 : 11, t. and chance happeneth to all.

Isa. 60 : 22, I will hasten it in his t.

Ezek. 16 : 8, thy t. was the t. of love.

Dan. 7 : 25, a t. and t. and the dividing of t.

Hos. 10 : 12, it is t. to seek the Lord.

Hag. 1 : 4, is it t. to dwell in houses ?

Mal. 3 : 11, neither shall vine cast fruit
before the t.

Mark 4 : 17, endure but for a t.

6 : 35, now the t. is far passed.

Luke 19 : 44, knewest not the t. of thy
visitation.

John 7 : 6, my t. is not yet come.

Acts 17 : 21, spent their t. in nothing else.

Rom. 13 : 11, high t. to awake.

1 Cor. 7 : 29, the t. is short.

Col. 4 : 5, redeeming the t.

2 Tim. 4 : 6, the t. of my departure is at
hand.

Heb. 4 : 16, grace to help in t. of need.

Jas. 4 : 14, that appeareth for a little t.

1 Pet. 1 : 17, pass the t. of sojourning in
fear.

Timotheus (Timothy), accompanies Paul,
Acts 16 : 3; 17 : 14, 15; Rom. 16 : 21;
2 Cor. 1 : 1, 19.

commended, 1 Cor. 16 : 10; Phil. 2 : 19.

Timothy, Epistles to.

Author and Date.—The date of these
Epistles can only be approximately fixed
as shortly before Paul's martyrdom in
67 or 68, with the first Epistle to Timothy
probably about a couple of years earlier
than the other two.

First Epistle to Timothy.—The Apostle
writes to instruct Timothy about a variety
of matters, and thus there is little definite
arrangement in the letter. The subjects
are taken just as they occur to the writer,
in an easy manner, which is perfectly
natural in a genuine letter, but which a
forger, writing to promote his own views,
could not readily have assumed. We
have the eminently Pauline Salutation

(1 : 1, 2) and Thanksgiving (1 : 12-17) at
the outset. Then the subjects of Public
Worship (2), Officers of the Church (3),
False Teachers and Asceticism (4),
Widows and Elders (5), Slaves, False
Teachers, and Covetousness (6 : 1-19)
are discussed; and the letter closes with
a Charge and a Benediction (6 : 20, 21).

Second Epistle to Timothy.—There is no
letter in any of the groups more manifestly Pauline in character than the
Second Epistle to Timothy. It contains
his last instructions to his disciple and
delegate, and to all future ministers in
the Church; and it was written in the
conviction that the end is near at hand.
Dark days are coming, and even love is
waxing cold: hence the urgent appeals all
through the letter to be firm and coura-
geous (1 : 6-14; 2 : 1-13; 3 : 14; 4 : 1-5).
The conduct of Timothy occupies about
one-third of the Epistle, the second main
subject being the present and future
condition of the Church (2 : 14–3 : 17).
Towards the close the Apostle speaks
of himself (4 : 6-21). The immediate
motive of the letter is the desire to see
Timothy, a desire so urgent that it is
expressed four times (1 : 4; 4 : 9, 11,
21). But the writer takes the opportunity
of expressing a great deal more than this
personal wish. Like the First Epistle,
the letter has the thoroughly Pauline
Salutation (1 : 1, 2), Thanksgiving (1 : 3-5)
and Benediction (4 : 22); which last contains the last recorded words of the
Apostle of the Gentiles. Of Timothy we
read again in Heb. 13 : 23.

Tin [Heb., " bedil "]. The chief use of tin
in early times was most probably as a
constituent of the alloy, with copper,
known as bronze. (See **Brass.**) It was
brought to Tyre and other marts by the
Phœnician traders from Spain, to which
country it came from Britain. Num.
31 : 22; Isa. 1 : 25; Ezek. 27 : 12.

Tishri, or **Ethanim,** month of September-
October. See **Months.**

Tithe, or tenth, is the proportion of property
given, under the Jewish law, for religious
purposes. The custom is found too in
the older stories of Abraham (Gen.
14 : 20), giving a " tithe " to Melchizedek,
and of Jacob's vow at Bethel (Gen. 28 : 22).

due to God, Gen. 28 : 22; Lev. 27 : 30;
Prov. 3 : 9; Mal. 3 : 8.

granted to the Levites, Num. 18 : 21; 2
Chr. 31 : 5; Neh. 10 : 37; Heb. 7 : 5.

for the feasts, and poor, Deut. 14 : 23, 28.

Title, 2 Ki. 23 : 17, what t. is that that I see ?
John 19 : 19, Pilate wrote a t.

Tittle [a point], Matt. 5 : 18; Luke 16 : 17,
one t. shall not pass from the law.

Titus (tī-tŭs) [honourable], a Greek, Gal.
2 : 3.

Paul's love for, 2 Cor. 2 : 13; 7 : 6, 13.

See Titus, 1; 2; 3.

Titus, Epistle to.

Date.—This Epistle ranks with the Epistles

to Timothy as the latest of all the Pauline Epistles. The date can only be approximately fixed as shortly before Paul's martyrdom in 67 or 68.

Contents.—Titus was one of Paul's most trusted disciples; and the main object of the letter is to instruct him how to carry on the work which Paul had left so incomplete. Particular attention is paid to the combating of false teachers and to the organising of a regular ministry. Great stress is also laid on sobriety in conduct, and on the maintenance of "piety." As in the letters to Timothy, there is little systematic thought or arrangement. The rather long and solemn salutation (1 : 1-4) is followed by a discussion of the needs of the Church (1 : 5-3 : 11); after which we have personal details followed by the Conclusion (3 : 12-15).

Tobiah (tō-bī-ăh) [Jehovah is good], Ezra 2 : 60.

the Ammonite, vexes the Jews, Neh. 4 : 3; 6 : 1, 12; 13 : 4.

Toil, Gen. 5 : 29, t. of our hands.
Matt. 6 : 28, they t. not, neither.
Mark 6 : 48, them t. in rowing.
Luke 5 : 5, have t. all the night.

Token, Ps. 65 : 8, they are afraid at thy t.
86 : 17, show me a t. for good.
Phil. 1 : 28, an evident t. of perdition.
2 Thess. 1 : 5, a t. of righteous judgment of God.

Tomb, Matt. 27 : 60, in his own new t.
Mark 5 : 3, dwelling among the t.
See Matt. 23 : 29; Luke 8 : 27.

Tongs, Num. 4 : 9; Isa. 6 : 6; 44 : 12.

Tongue, unruly, Jas. 3.
to be bridled, Ps. 39 : 1; Prov. 4 : 24; 10 : 19; 14 : 23; 17 : 20; 18 : 6; Eccl. 3 : 7; 10 : 12; Matt. 5 : 22; 12 : 36; Eph. 4 : 29; 5 : 4; Col. 3 : 8; 4 : 6; Titus 1 : 10; 2 : 8; 3 : 2; 1 Pet. 3 : 10; Jude 16.

tongues, confusion of, Gen. 11.
gift of, Acts 2 : 3; 10 : 46; 19 : 6; 1 Cor. 12 : 10; 13 : 1; 14 : 2.
Job 5 : 21, hid from scourge of t.
20 : 12, hide wickedness under his t.
29 : 10, t. cleaved to roof of mouth.
Ps. 5 : 9, they flatter with their t.
34 : 13; 1 Pet. 3 : 10, keep thy t. from evil.
Prov. 10 : 20, t. of the just as choice silver.
12 : 18, t. of the wise is health.
12 : 19, a lying t. is but for a moment.
15 : 4, a wholesome t. is a tree of life.
18 : 21, death and life are in the power of the t.
21 : 23, whoso keepeth his t. keepeth his soul.
25 : 15, a soft t. breaketh the bone.
Isa. 30 : 27, his t. as a devouring fire.
50 : 4, given me the t. of the learned.
Jer. 9 : 5, taught their t. to speak lies.
18 : 18, let us smite him with the t.
Jas. 1 : 26, and bridleth not his t.
3 : 5, the t. is a little member.

3 : 8, the t. can no man tame.
1 John 3 : 18, let not us love in t.

Tooth, Ex. 21 : 24; Deut. 19 : 21; Matt. 5 : 38, t. for a t.
Prov. 25 : 19, like a broken t.

Topaz. It is doubtful whether the true topaz is referred to in the Old Testament, though crysolite is. In Rev. 21 : 20, both are mentioned together. The Oriental topaz, a variety of corundum, from Ceylon, has long been held in high esteem. Ex. 28 : 17; Job 28 : 19.

Torches, Nah. 2 : 3, 4; Zech. 12 : 6; John 18 : 3.

Torment, Matt. 8 : 29, art thou come to t. us ?
Luke 16 : 23, being in t.
1 John 4 : 18, fear hath t.
Rev. 14 : 11, the smoke of their t.

Tortoise, occurs in the A.V. in Lev. 11 : 29; but is given in the R.V. as "great lizard."

Toss, Ps. 109 : 23, I am t. up and down.
Isa. 22 : 18, he will t. thee like a ball.
54 : 11, t. with tempest.
Eph. 4 : 14, children t. to and fro.
Jas. 1 : 6, he that wavereth is like a wave t.

Touch, Gen. 3 : 3, nor shall ye t. it, lest ye die.
1 Chr. 16 : 22; Ps. 105 : 15, t. not mine anointed.
Job 5 : 19, there shall no evil t. thee.
Isa. 6 : 7, lo, this hath t. thy lips.
52 : 11; 2 Cor. 6 : 17, t. no unclean thing.
Jer. 1 : 9, the Lord t. my mouth.
Zech. 2 : 8, he that t. you t. the apple of his eye.
Matt. 9 : 21; Mark 5 : 28, if I may but t. his garment.
Mark 10 : 13; Luke 18 : 15, children, that he should t. them.
Luke 11 : 46, ye yourselves t. not the burdens.
John 20 : 17, t. me not.
Col. 2 : 21, t. not, taste not.
1 John 5 : 18, wicked one t. him not.

Tower, of Babel, Gen. 11.
of Penuel, Judg. 8 : 17.
of Shechem, Judg. 9 : 46.
of Siloam, Luke 13 : 4.
Gen. 11 : 4, let us build us a city, and a t.
2 Sam. 22 : 3; Ps. 18 : 2; 144 : 2, God is my high t.
Ps. 61 : 3, a strong t. from the enemy.
Prov. 18 : 10, name of the Lord is a strong t.
Isa. 5 : 2; Matt. 21 : 33; Mark 12 : 1, built a t.

Town, 1 Sam. 16 : 4; Matt. 10 : 11; Luke 9 : 6.

Train, Prov. 22 : 6, t. a child in way he should go.
Isa. 6 : 1, his t. filled the temple.

Traitor, Luke 6 : 16, Judas Iscariot, which also was the t.
2 Tim. 3 : 4, in last days shall men be t.

Trample, Ps. 91 : 13, dragon t. under feet.
Isa. 63 : 3, I will t. them in my fury.
Matt. 7 : 6, lest they t. them under foot.

Tranquillity, Dan. 4 : 27.

Transfiguration, of Christ, Matt. 17; Mark 9 : 2; Luke 9 : 29; John 1 : 14; 2 Pet. 1 : 16.

Transformed, Rom. 12 : 2, be ye t. by renewing of your mind.

2 Cor. 11 : 14, Satan is t. into an angel of light.

Transgress, Num. 14 : 41; 2 Chr. 24 : 20, wherefore do ye t. commandments of Lord ?

1 Sam. 2 : 24, ye make the Lord's people to t.

Neh. 1 : 8, if ye t., I will scatter you.

Ps. 17 : 3, my mouth shall not t.

35 : 3, ashamed which t. without cause.

Prov. 28 : 21, for a piece of bread that man will t.

Amos 4 : 4, come to Bethel and t.

Hab. 2 : 5, he t. by wine.

1 John 3 : 4, whosoever committeth sin t. the law.

Transgression, Ex. 34 : 7; Num. 14 : 18, forgiving t.

1 Sam. 24 : 11, there is no t. in my hand.

1 Chr. 10 : 13, Saul died for his t.

Ezra 10 : 6, he mourned because of their t.

Job 7 : 21, why dost thou not pardon my t. ?

13 : 23, make me to know my t.

Ps. 19 : 13, innocent from the great t.

32 : 1, blessed is he whose t. is forgiven.

65 : 3, as for our t., thou shalt purge them away.

89 : 32, I will visit their t.

107 : 17, fools because of their t. are afflicted.

Prov. 17 : 9, he that covereth t.

Isa. 44 : 22, blotted out thy t.

53 : 8, for the t. of my people was he stricken.

58 : 1, show my people their t.

Ezek. 33 : 12, not deliver in day of his t.

Mic. 1 : 5, what is the t. of Jacob ?

7 : 18, that passeth by t. of remnant.

Rom. 4 : 15, where no law is, is not t.

5 : 14, after similitude of Adam's t.

Transgressor, Ps. 51 : 13, then will I teach t. thy ways.

Prov. 13 : 15, way of t. is hard.

21 : 18, the t. shall be ransom for the upright.

Isa. 48 : 8, thou wast called a t. from the womb.

53 : 12; Mark 15 : 28; Luke 22 : 37, he was numbered with the t.

Jas. 2 : 11, thou art become a t. of the law.

Translated, Col. 1 : 13, t. us into kingdom of his dear Son.

Heb. 11 : 5, Enoch was t. that he should not see death.

Translation, of Enoch, Gen. 5 : 24; Heb. 11 : 5.

of Elijah, 2 Ki. 2.

Travail, Job 15 : 20, wicked man t. with pain.

Ps. 7 : 14, he t. with iniquity.

Rom. 8 : 22, whole creation t. in pain.

Gal. 4 : 19, my children, of whom t.

Isa. 53 : 11, the t. of his soul.

1 Thess. 5 : 3, destruction cometh as t.

Treacherously, Isa. 21 : 2; 24 : 16, treacherous dealer dealeth t.

33 : 1, dealest t.

Jer. 12 : 1, why are they happy that dealt t. ?

Lam. 1 : 2, her friends have dealt t.

Hos. 5 : 7, they dealt t. against the Lord.

Mal. 2 : 10, why do we deal t. ?

Treachery, instances of, Gen. 34 : 13; Judg. 9; 1 Sam. 21 : 7; 22 : 9; 2 Sam. 3 : 27; 11 : 14; 16; 20 : 9; 1 Ki. 21 : 5; 2 Ki. 10 : 18; Esther 3; Matt. 26 : 47; Mark 14 : 43; Luke 22 : 47; John 18 : 3.

Tread, Deut. 11 : 24, whereon your feet t.

25 : 4; 1 Cor. 9 : 9; 1 Tim. 5 : 18, not muzzle ox when he t. corn.

Job 40 : 12, t. down wicked in their place.

Ps. 7 : 5, let him t. down my life.

44 : 5, through thy name will we t. them under.

60 : 12; 108 : 13, shall t. down our enemies.

91 : 13, thou shalt t. upon lion and adder.

Isa. 1 : 12, to t. my courts.

10 : 6, to t. them down like mire.

16 : 10, treaders shall t. out no wine.

63 : 3, I will t. them in mine anger.

Jer. 25 : 30, as they that t. grapes.

48 : 33, none shall t. with shouting.

Hos. 10 : 11, loveth to t. out corn.

Luke 10 : 19, power to t. on scorpions.

Rev. 11 : 2, city shall they t. under foot.

19 : 15, he t. wine-press of wrath.

Treason, instances of, 2 Sam. 15-18; 1 Ki. 1; 16 : 10; 2 Ki. 11; 15 : 10; 2 Chr. 22 : 10; Esther 2 : 21.

Treasure, Gen. 42 : 43, God hath given you t.

Ex. 19 : 5; Ps. 135 : 4, a peculiar t. to me.

Deut. 28 : 12, Lord shall open his good t.

Job 3 : 21, dig for it more than for hid t.

38 : 22, t. of the snow, t. of hail.

Prov. 2 : 4, searchest as for hid t.

10 : 2, t. of wickedness profit nothing.

15 : 16, than great t., and trouble therewith.

21 : 20, there is a t. to be desired.

Isa. 33 : 6, the fear of the Lord is his t.

Matt. 6 : 21; Luke 12 : 34, where your t. is.

Matt. 12 : 35; Luke 6 : 45, out of good t. of his heart.

Matt. 13 : 44, t. hid in a field.

13 : 52, bringeth out of his t. things new and old.

19 : 21; Mark 10 : 21; Luke 18 : 22, t. in heaven.

Luke 12 : 21, that layeth up t. for himself.

2 Cor. 4 : 7, we have this t. in earthen vessels.

Col. 2 : 3, in whom are hid t. of wisdom.

Heb. 11 : 26, greater riches than the t. in Egypt.

Jas. 5 : 3, ye have heaped t. together.

See Isa. 23 : 18; Rom. 2 : 5.

From time immemorial it has been a custom in the East for wealthy persons to convert part of their wealth into " treasure " in t he form of jewels, which, in case of danger, could readily be hid in the earth. In the case of the death of the owner, it often happened that the hiding place of the treasure was unknown, until by accident some one was lucky enough to discover it. (cf. Matt. 13 : 44.)

Treasury. This name is applied in Luke 21 : 1, to the thirteen brazed trumpet-shaped chests in the great central hall of the Temple, for receiving the offerings of the people. Of these treasure-chests, nine were for receiving the sacrifice-offerings or their equivalent in money, and four were for freewill offerings. The smallest coin allowed to be put into the treasure was the copper mite, two of which were given by the widow whom Jesus commended.

Matt. 27 : 6, not lawful to put into t.

Mark 12 : 41; Luke 21 : 1, Jesus beheld them casting money into t.

Tree, of life, Gen. 2 : 9; 3 : 22; Prov. 3 : 18; 11 : 30; Ezek. 47 : 7, 12; Rev. 22 : 2, 14.

of knowledge of good and evil, Gen. 2 : 17; 3.

Nebuchadnezzar's vision of, Dan. 4 : 10.

trees, laws concerning, Lev. 19 : 23; 27 : 30; Deut. 20 : 19.

Jotham's parable of the, Judg. 9 : 8.

figuratively mentioned, Num. 24 : 6; 1 Chr. 16 : 33; Ps. 1 : 3; (Jer. 17 : 8); 92 : 12; Song of Sol. 2 : 3; Isa. 41 : 19; Ezek. 17 : 24; 31 : 5; Matt. 3 : 10; 12 : 33; Luke 3 : 9; 21 : 29; Jude 12.

Gen. 1 : 29, given you every t.

Deut. 20 : 19, the t. of field is man's life.

Job 14 : 7, there is hope of a t., if cut down.

24 : 20, wickedness shall be broken as a t.

Ps. 1 : 3; Jer. 17 : 8, like a t. planted by rivers.

Ps. 104 : 16, the t. of the Lord are full of sap.

Prov. 13 : 12; 15 : 4, a t. of life.

Eccl. 11 : 3, where the t. falleth.

Isa. 56 : 3, I am a dry t.

61 : 3, called t. of righteousness.

Ezek. 15 : 2, what is the vine t. more than any t. ?

Matt. 7 : 17; Luke 6 : 43, good t. bringeth forth good fruit.

1 Pet. 2 : 24, bare our sins in his own body on the t.

Rev. 2 : 7, I will give to eat of t. of life.

Trespass, offerings, laws concerning, Lev. 5 : 6; Num. 5.

Gen. 50 : 17, forgive the t. of thy servants.

Ezra 9 : 6, our t. is grown unto the heavens.

Ps. 68 : 21, goeth on still in his t.

Matt. 6 : 14, if ye forgive men their t.

18 : 35, if ye forgive not every one his brother their t.

2 Cor. 5 : 19, not imputing their t.

Eph. 2 : 1, dead in t. and sins.

Luke 17 : 3, 4, if thy brother t. against thee.

Col. 2 : 13, having forgiven you all t.

Trial, of the heart, God's prerogative, Ps. 26 : 2; 66 : 10; Prov. 17 : 3; Jer. 11 : 20; 1 Thess. 2 : 4.

of faith, Job 23 : 10; Zech. 13 : 9; Heb.

11 :17; Jas. 1 : 3; 1 Pet. 4 : 12; Rev. 3 : 10. See **Temptation.**

Job 9 : 23, the t. of the innocent.

2 Cor. 8 : 2, a great t. of affliction.

1 Pet. 1 : 7, the t. of your faith.

Tribes, of Israel, blessed, Gen. 49; Num. 23 : 20; 24; Deut. 33.

their ordering and numbering, Num. 1; 2; 10 : 14; 26; 2 Sam. 24; 1 Chr. 21.

number of those sealed, Rev. 7 : 4.

Ps. 105 : 37, not one feeble among their t.

122 : 4, whither the t. go up.

Isa. 63 : 17, for the t. of thine inheritance.

Hab. 3 : 9, according to oaths of the t.

Matt. 24 : 30, then shall all t. of the earth mourn.

Tribulation, connected with the gospel. Matt. 13 : 21; John 16 : 33; 1 Thess. 3 : 4; Rev. 7 : 14.

Deut. 4 : 30, when thou art in t.

Judg. 10 : 14, let them deliver you in t.

1 Sam. 26 : 24, deliver me out of all t.

Matt. 24 : 21, then shall be great t.

Acts 14 : 22, we must through much t. enter.

Rom. 5 : 3, t. worketh patience.

8 : 35, shall t. separate us from love of Christ ?

12 : 12, patient in t.

2 Cor. 7 : 4, exceeding joyful in t.

Rev. 7 : 14, they which come out of great t.

Tribute. Among the Jews there were two kinds: (1) the temple tax, or half-shekel, which was the coin Peter took from the fish's mouth (Matt. 17 : 24); (2) the civil tribute exacted by the Roman authorities. The Roman tribute was paid in Roman currency, which bore Cæsar's image and superscription (Matt. 22 : 19).

Gen. 49 : 15, a servant to t.

Num. 31 : 28, levy a t. to the Lord.

Deut. 16 : 10, a t. of a freewill offering.

Ezra 4 : 20, and custom was paid to them.

7 : 24, not lawful to impose t.

Prov. 12 : 24, the slothful shall be under t.

Matt. 22 : 17; Mark 12 : 14; Luke 20 : 22. Is it lawful to give t. unto Cæsar ?

Rom. 13 : 7, render t. to whom t. is due.

Triumph, Ex. 15 : 1, hath t. gloriously.

Ps. 25 : 2, let not mine enemies t. over me.

92 : 4, I will t. in works of thy hands.

94 : 3, how long shall the wicked t. ?

106 : 47, give thanks, and t. in thy praise.

2 Cor. 2 : 14, causeth us to t. in Christ.

Col. 2 : 15, a show of them openly t. over them.

Troas (trō-ăs), visited by Paul, Acts 16 : 8; 20 : 5; 2 Cor. 2 : 12; 2 Tim. 4 : 13.

Trodden, Judg. 5 : 21, hast t. down strength.

Job 22 : 15, old way which wicked men have t.

Ps. 119 : 118, thou hast t. down all that err.

Isa. 63 : 3, I have t. the winepress alone.

Mic. 7 : 10, now shall she be t. as mire.

Matt. 5 : 13, salt to be t. under foot.

Luke 8 : 5, fell by wayside, and was t.

21 : 24, Jerusalem shall be t. of Gentiles.

Heb. 10 : 29, hath t. under foot the Son of God.

Trophimus   (trŏph-ĭ-mŭs),   accompanied

Paul to Jerusalem, Acts 20 : 4; 21 : 29; 2 Tim. 4 : 20.

Trouble, 2 Chr. 15 : 4; Neh. 9 : 27, in t. sought the Lord.

Job 5 : 6, neither doth t. spring out of the ground.

14 : 1, man is of few days and full of t.

Ps. 9 : 9, Lord will be a refuge in times of t.

22 : 11, for t. is near.

27 : 5, in time of t. he shall hide me.

46 : 1, a very present help in t.

60 : 11, give us help from t.

73 : 5, they are not in t. as other men.

91 : 15, I will be with him in t.

119 : 143, t. and anguish have taken hold on me.

143 : 11, bring my soul out of t.

Prov. 11 : 8, righteous delivered out of t.

Isa. 17 : 14, at eveningtide t.

26 : 16, in t. they visited thee.

33 : 2, our salvation in time of t.

Jer. 8 : 15, we looked for health, and behold t.

1 Cor. 7 : 28, such shall have t. in the flesh.

2 Cor. 1 : 4, able to comfort them in t.

Trouble.

Josh. 7 : 25, Lord shall t. thee this day.

1 Ki. 18 : 17, art thou he that t. Israel ?

Ps. 3 : 1, how are they increased that t. me.

46 : 3, though waters roar and be t.

Prov. 25 : 26, is as a t. fountain.

Isa. 57 : 20, wicked are like the t. sea.

Dan. 5 : 10, let not thy thoughts t. thee.

Matt. 24 : 6; Mark 13 : 7, be not t.

Matt. 26 : 10; Mark 14 : 6, why t. ye the woman ?

Luke 7 : 6, Lord, t. not thyself.

11 : 7, t. me not: door is shut.

John 11 : 33; 12 : 27; 13 : 21, Jesus was t.

14 : 1, 27, let not your heart be t.

2 Cor. 4 : 8; 7 : 5, we are t. on every side.

Gal. 6 : 17, let no man t. me.

Heb. 12 : 15, lest any bitterness t. you.

See Job 3 : 17; John 5 : 4.

Trough, Gen. 24 : 20; 30 : 38; Ex. 2 : 16.

Truce, 2 Tim. 3 : 3, in last days men shall be t.-breakers.

True, Gen. 42 : 11, we are t. men.

1 Ki. 22 : 16, tell me nothing but that which is t.

2 Chr. 15 : 3, Israel hath been without the t. God.

Neh. 9 : 13, thou gavest them t. laws.

Ps. 19 : 9, judgments of the Lord are t.

119 : 160, thy word is t. from the beginning.

Jer. 10 : 10, the Lord is the t. God.

42 : 5, the Lord be a t. witness.

Matt. 22 : 16; Mark 12 : 14, we know that thou art t.

Luke 16 : 11, the t. riches.

John 1 : 9, that was the t. light.

4 : 37, herein is that saying t.

5 : 31, if I bear witness of myself, my witness is not t.

6 : 32, the t. bread.

10 : 41, all things that John spake were t.

15 : 1, the t. vine.

17 : 3, 1 John 5 : 20, to know thee the only t. God.

John 19 : 35; 21 : 24, his record is t.

2 Cor. 1 : 18, as God is t.

6 : 8, as deceivers, and yet t.

Phil. 4 : 8, whatsoever things are t.

Heb. 10 : 22, draw near with a t. heart.

Rev. 15 : 3, just and t. are thy ways.

19 : 11, he that sat upon him was called Faithful and T.

Trump, 1 Cor. 15 : 52, at last t. the dead shall be raised.

1 Thess. 4 : 16, the Lord shall descend with t.

Trumpet, giving uncertain sound, 1 Cor. 14 : 8.

trumpets, their use, Num. 10; Josh. 6 : 4; Ps. 81 : 3; Ezek. 7 : 14; 33 : 3; Joel 2 : 1.

employed in worship, 1 Chr. 13 : 8; 15 : 24; 2 Chr. 5 : 12; 29 : 27; Ps. 98 : 6.

the seven, Rev. 8; 9; 11.

Isa. 58 : 1, lift up thy voice like a t.

Matt. 6 : 2, do not sound a t. before thee.

Rev. 1 : 10; 4 : 1, I heard voice as of a t.

Trumpets, Feast of. The feast of Trumpets, called in Lev. 23 : 24, a " blowing commemoration " by trumpets, marked the commencement of the first month of the " civil " year, and was thus a " new year " festival. It was held as a solemn rest-day or Sabbath, on which no work was done.

Trust, in God, Ps. 4 : 5; 34; 40 : 3; 64 : 10; 84 : 12; 115 : 9; Prov. 3 : 5; 16 : 20; Isa. 51 : 5; Jer. 17 : 7.

exemplified, 1 Sam. 17 : 45; 30 : 6; 2 Ki. 18 : 5; 2 Chr. 20 : 12; Dan. 3 : 28; 2 Tim. 1 : 12; 4 : 18.

blessings resulting from, Ps. 5 : 11; 26 : 1; 32 : 10; 33 : 21; 34 : 8, 22; 37 : 5, 40; 56 : 11; 112 : 7; 125; Prov. 16 : 20; 28 : 25; 29 : 25; Isa. 26 : 3; 57 : 13; Heb. 13 : 6.

in man, riches, etc., vain, Job 31 : 24; Ps. 20 : 7; 33 : 16; 44 : 6; 49 : 6; 52 : 7; 62 : 10; 118 : 8; 146 : 3; Prov. 11 : 28; 28 : 26; Isa. 30 : 3; Jer. 7 : 4; 17 : 5; 46 : 25; 49 : 4; Ezek. 33 : 13; 1 Tim. 6 : 17.

Job 15 : 15, he putteth no t. in his saints.

Ps. 40 : 4, maketh the Lord his t.

141 : 8, in thee is my t.

2 Sam. 22 : 3; Ps. 18 : 2; 91 : 2, in him will I t.

Job 13 : 15, though he slay me, yet will I t. in him.

Ps. 25 : 2; 55 : 23; 56 : 3; 143 : 8, I t. in thee.

37 : 3; 62 : 8; Isa. 26 : 4, t. in the Lord.

Ps. 118 : 8, it is better to t. in the Lord.

Isa. 12 : 2, I will t., and not be afraid.

50 : 10, let him t. in the name of the Lord.

Jer. 9 : 4, t. not in any brother.

49 : 11, let thy widows t. in me.

Mic. 7 : 5, t. ye not in a friend.

Nah. 1 : 7, the Lord knoweth them that t. in him.

Matt. 12 : 21; Rom. 15 : 12, in his name shall Gentiles t.

Mark 10 : 24, them that t. in riches.

Luke 18 : 9, certain which t. in themselves.
2 Cor. 1 : 9, should not t. in ourselves.
1 Tim. 4 : 10, we t. in the living God.
Truth, of God, Num. 23 : 19; Ps. 19 : 9;
33 : 4; 57 : 10; 85 : 10; 86 : 15; 89 : 14;
96 : 13; 100 : 5; 146 : 6; Isa. 25 : 1;
65 : 16; Mic. 7 : 20; John 17 : 17;
2 Cor. 1 : 20; Rev. 15 : 3; 16 : 7.
word of, Ps. 119 : 43; 2 Cor. 6 : 7; Eph.
1 : 13; Col. 1 : 5; Jas. 1 : 18.
gospel is, John 1 : 17; 4 : 24; 5 : 33;
17 : 17; 18 : 37; Rom. 2 : 8; 1 Cor.
13 : 6; 2 Cor. 4 : 2; Gal. 3 : 1; Eph.
6 : 14; 2 Thess. 2 : 10; 1 Tim. 2 : 7;
4 : 3; 6 : 5; 2 Tim. 3 : 8; 4 : 4; Titus
1 : 1; 1 Pet. 1 : 22.
Ex. 34 : 6, abundant in goodness and t.
Deut. 32 : 4, a God of t.
Ps. 15 : 2, speaketh t. in his heart.
25 : 10, the paths of the Lord are mercy
and t.
51 : 6, thou desirest t. in the inward parts.
91 : 4, his t. shall be thy shield.
117 : 2, t. of the Lord endureth for ever.
119 : 142, thy law is t.
Prov. 12 : 19, the lip of t. shall be established.
23 : 23, buy the t.
Isa. 26 : 2, nation which keepeth t.
59 : 14, t. is fallen in the street.
Jer. 9 : 3, they are not valiant for the t.
Dan. 4 : 37, all whose works are t.
Mal. 2 : 6, law of t. was in his mouth.
Mark 12 : 32, Master, thou hast said the t.
John 1 : 14, full of grace and t.
8 : 32, know the t., and the t. shall make
you free.
14 : 6, I am the way, the t., and the life.
16 : 13, Spirit of t will guide you into all
t.
18 : 38, what is t. ?
Rom. 1 : 18, who hold the t. in unrighteousness.
2 : 2, judgment of God is according to t.
1 Cor. 5 : 8, unleavened bread of t.
2 Cor. 13 : 8, can do nothing against the t.
Gal. 5 : 7, that ye should not obey the t.
Eph. 4 : 15, speaking the t. in love.
1 Tim. 3 : 15, pillar and ground of the t.
2 Tim. 2 : 15, rightly dividing the word of t.
3 : 7, to come to the knowledge of the t.
Jas. 3 : 14, lie not against the t.
Jas. 5 : 19, if any err from the t.
1 John 5 : 6, the Spirit is t.
Truthfulness, Prov. 12 : 17; Zech. 8 : 16;
Eph. 4 : 25.
Tubal-cain (tū-băl-cain) [hammer blow of
the smith], Gen. 4 : 22.
Tumults, under David, 2 Sam. 20 : 1;
Rehoboam, 1 Ki. 12 : 16.
against Christ, Matt. 27 : 24; Paul, Acts
14 : 5; 17 : 5; 18 : 12; 19 : 24 ff.;
21 : 27.
Turn, Job 23 : 13, who can t. him ?
Ps. 7 : 12, if he t. not, he will whet his
sword.
Prov. 1 : 23, t. you at my reproof.
Jer. 31 : 18, t. thou me, and I shall be t.
Lam. 5 : 21, t. us unto thee, O Lord.

Ezek. 14 : 6; 18 : 32; 33 : 9; Hos. 12 : 6;
Joel 2 : 12, repent, and t.
Dan. 12 : 3, that t. many to righteousness.
Zech. 9 : 12, t. you to the strong hold.
Mal. 4 : 6, he shall t. heart of fathers.
Matt. 5 : 39, t. the other also.
Acts 26 : 20, they should repent and t. to
God.
Jas. 1 : 17, with whom is no shadow of t.
Turtle, Song of Sol. 2 : 12; Jer. 8 : 7; Luke
2 : 24.
Turtle dove. This bird is distinguished
from the dove or pigeon. It is a migrant
bird, and though allowed to be offered
in sacrifice could not be obtained during
the winter, when the dove or young wild
pigeon could be had.
used for offerings, Gen. 15 : 9; Lev. 1 : 14;
12 : 6; Num. 6 : 10; Luke 2 : 24.
Tutors, Gal. 4 : 2.
Twain, Isa. 6 : 2, with t. he covered his face.
Matt. 5 : 41, to go a mile, go with him t.
19 : 6; Mark 10 : 8, they are no more t.
Matt. 27 : 51; Mark 15 : 38, veil of temple
was rent in t.
Eph. 2 : 15, to make in himself of t. one
new man.
Twilight, 2 Ki. 7 : 7, arose and fled in the t.
Job 3 : 9, stars of the t. thereof.
Prov. 7 : 9, in the t. in the evening.
Twinkling, 1 Cor. 15 : 52.
Two-edged, Ps. 149 : 6; Heb. 4 : 12; Rev.
1 : 16.
Twofold, Matt. 23 : 15.
Tychicus (tўch-ĭ-cŭs), companion of Paul,
Acts 20 : 4; 2 Tim. 4 : 12; Titus 3 : 12.
commended, Eph. 6 : 21; Col. 4 : 7.
Tyre (tÿre) or **Tyrus** (tÿ-rŭs) [Heb. " tzōr,"
rock], its fall and wealth, Ez. 26 : 7; 27.
Christ visits the coasts of, Matt. 15 : 21.
Paul lands at, Acts 21 : 3.

U

Ucal (ū-căl), Prov. 30 : 1. This is probably
not a proper name.
Ulai (ū-lāi), river at Susa, Persia, Dan. 8 : 2.
Ulam (ū-lăm) [porch], 1 Chr. 7 : 16.
Ulla (ŭl-lă) [yoke], 1 Chr. 7 : 39.
Ummah (ŭm-măh) [conjunction], Josh.
19 : 30.
Unawares, Ps. 35 : 8, destruction come upon
him at u.
Luke 21 : 34, that day come upon you u.
Heb. 13 : 2, entertained angels u.
Jude 4, certain men crept in u.
Unbelief, sin, John 16 : 9; Titus 1 : 15;
1 John 5 : 10.
its source, Mark 16 : 14; Luke 8 : 12;
24 : 25; John 8 : 45; 10 : 26; 12 : 39;
2 Cor. 4 : 4; Eph. 2 : 2.
the world condemned for, John 3 : 18.
its effects, 1 Ki. 17 : 18; Ps. 78 : 19;
106 : 24; Isa. 53 : 1; John 12 : 37;
16 : 19; Acts 14 : 2; 19 : 9.
instances of, Gen. 3 : 4; Num. 13; 14;
20 : 12; Deut. 9 : 23; 2 Ki. 7 : 2; Ps.
17; 78 : 106; Matt. 13 : 57; Luke 1 : 20;

22 : 67; John 5 : 38; 7 : 5; 12 : 37; 20 : 25; Acts 17 : 5; Heb. 3 : 19.

denounced, Matt. 17 : 17; John 20 : 27, 29.

Matt. 13 : 58, because of their **u.**

Mark 9 : 24, help thou mine **u.**

Rom. 3 : 3, shall **u.** make faith without effect ?

11 : 20, because of **u.** they were broken.

11 : 32, God hath concluded them all in **u.**

Heb. 3 : 12, an evil heart of **u.**

4 : 11, fall after same example of **u.**

See Luke 12 : 46.

Unbelievers, Rom. 16 : 17; 2 Cor. 6 : 14; Phil. 3 : 2; 1 Tim. 6 : 5.

fate of, Mark 16 : 16; John 3 : 18; 8 : 24; Eph. 5 : 6; 2 Thess. 2 : 12; Heb. 11 : 6; Jas. 5; 2 Pet. 2; 3; Jude 5; Rev. 21 : 8.

Unchangeable, Heb. 7 : 24.

Uncircumcised, Ex. 6 : 12, who am of **u.** lips.

Ezek. 44 : 7, **u.** in heart, and **u.** in flesh.

Acts 7 : 51, ye stiffnecked and **u.**

1 Cor. 7 : 18, let him not become **u.**

Unclean, animals, Lev. 11; 20 : 25; Deut. 14 : 3.

spirits, Matt. 10 : 1; 12 : 43, 45; Acts 5 : 16; Rev. 16 : 13.

Lev. 10 : 10; 11 : 47, difference between **u.** and clean.

Isa. 6 : 5, I am a man of **u.** lips.

Acts 10 : 28, not call any man **u.**

Rom. 14 : 14, nothing is **u.** of itself.

2 Cor. 6 : 17, touch not the **u.** thing.

Uncleanness, Lev. 5; 7; 11; 12; 15; 22; Num. 5; 19; Deut. 23 : 10; 24 : 1.

typical of sin, Zech. 13 : 1; Matt. 23 : 27.

Uncondemned, Acts 16 : 37; 22 : 25.

Uncorruptible, Rom. 1 : 23.

Unction, 1 John 2 : 20, ye have an **u.** from the Holy One.

Undefiled, Ps. 119 : 1, blessed are **u.** in the way.

Heb. 7 : 26, holy, harmless, **u.**

Jas. 1 : 27, pure religion and **u.**

1 Pet. 1 : 4, an inheritance incorruptible, **u.**

Undergirding, Acts 27 : 17.

Understanding, Ex. 31 : 3; Deut. 4 : 6, wisdom and **u.**

1 Ki. 3 : 11, hast asked **u.**

4 : 29, God gave Solomon wisdom and **u.**

7 : 14, filled with wisdom and **u.**

1 Chr. 12 : 32, men that had **u.** of the times.

2 Chr. 26 : 5, had **u.** in visions.

Job 12 : 13, he hath counsel and **u.**

17 : 4, thou hast hid their heart from **u.**

28 : 12, where is the place of **u.** ?

28 : 28, to depart from evil is **u.**

32 : 8, the Almighty giveth them **u.**

38 : 36, who hath given **u.** to the heart ?

39 : 17, neither imparted to her **u.**

Ps. 47 : 7, sing ye praises with **u.**

49 : 3, meditation of my heart shall be of **u.**

119 : 34, give me **u.**

119 : 99, I have more **u.** than my teachers.

147 : 5, his **u.** is infinite.

Prov. 2 : 2, apply thine heart to **u.**

2 : 11, **u.** shall keep thee.

3 : 5, lean not to thine own **u.**

3 : 13, happy is the man that getteth **u.**

3 : 19, by **u.** hath he established the heavens.

4 : 5, 7, get wisdom, get **u.**

8 : 1, doth not **u.** put forth her voice ?

9 : 6, go in the way of **u.**

9 : 10, the knowledge of the holy is **u.**

14 : 29, he that is slow to wrath is of great **u.**

16 : 22, **u.** is a wellspring of life.

19 : 8, he that keepeth **u.** shall find good.

21 : 30, there is no **u.** against the Lord.

23 : 23, by instruction and **u.**

24 : 3, by **u.** an house is established.

28 : 16, prince that wanteth **u.**

30 : 2, have not the **u.** of a man.

Eccl. 9 : 11, nor riches to men of **u.**

Isa. 11 : 2, the spirit of **u.** shall rest on him.

11 : 3, make him of quick **u.**

27 : 11, a people of no **u.**

29 : 14, the **u.** of prudent men shall be hid.

40 : 28, there is no searching of his **u.**

Jer. 51 : 15, he stretched out the heaven by **u.**

Dan. 4 : 34, mine **u.** returned unto me.

Matt. 15 : 16; Mark 7 : 18, are ye without **u.** ?

Mark 12 : 33, to love him with all the **u.**

Luke 2 : 47, astonished at his **u.**

24 : 45, then opened he their **u.**

Rom. 1 : 31, without **u.**

1 Cor. 1 : 19, bring to nothing **u.** of prudent.

14 : 15, pray with the **u.** also.

14 : 20, in **u.** be men.

Eph. 1 : 18, eyes of **u.** being enlightened.

4 : 18, having the **u.** darkened.

Phil. 4 : 7, peace of God, which passeth all **u.**

Col. 1 : 9, filled with all spiritual **u.**

2 : 2, riches of full assurance of **u.**

1 John 5 : 20, God hath given us an **u.**

Unfruitful, Matt. 13 : 22; Mark 4 : 19, becometh **u.**

1 Cor. 14 : 14, my understanding is **u.**

Eph. 5 : 11, no fellowship with **u.** works of darkness.

2 Pet. 1 : 8, neither barren nor **u.**

Ungirded, Gen. 24 : 32.

Ungodly, 2 Sam. 22 : 5; Ps. 18 : 4, **u.** men made me afraid.

2 Chr. 19 : 2, shouldest thou help the **u.** ?

Job 16 : 11, God hath delivered me to the **u.**

34 : 18, is it fit to say, Ye are **u.** ?

Ps. 1 : 1, the counsel of the **u.**

1 : 6, the way of the **u.** shall perish.

43 : 1, plead my cause against an **u.** nation.

73 : 12, these **u.** who prosper.

Prov. 16 : 27, an **u.** man diggeth up evil.

19 : 28, an **u.** witness scorneth judgment.

Rom. 5 : 6, Christ died for the **u.**

1 Pet. 4 : 18, where shall the **u.** appear ?

2 Pet. 2 : 6, ensample unto those that live **u.**

3 : 7, perdition of **u.** men.

Jude 4, **u.** men, turning grace of God into lasciviousness.

See Rom. 1 : 18; 2 Tim. 2 : 16; Titus 2 : 12.

Unholy, Lev. 10 : 10, difference between holy and **u.**

1 Tim. 1 : 9, law is made for the **u.**

2 Tim. 3 : 2, men shall be **u.**

Heb. 10 : 29, counted blood of covenant an **u.** thing.

Unicorn. The word so translated in the A.V. without doubt applies to the great " wild ass," and is so rendered in the R.V. The animal is no longer found in Palestine. Deut. 33 : 17; Job 39 : 9-12; Ps. 92 : 10.

Union, in worship and prayer, Ps. 34 : 3; 55 : 14; 122; Rom. 15 : 30; 2 Cor. 1 : 11; Eph. 6 : 18; Col. 1 : 3; 3 : 15; Heb. 10 : 25.

Unity, of the church, John 10 : 16; Rom. 12 : 5; 1 Cor. 10 : 17; 12 : 13; Gal. 3 : 28; Eph. 1 : 10; 2 : 19; 4 : 4; 5 : 23, 30.

of brethren, Ps. 133 : 1; John 17 : 21; Acts 2 : 42.

enjoined, Rom. 12 : 16; 15 : 5; 1 Cor. 1 : 10; 2 Cor. 13 : 11; Phil. 1 : 27; 2 : 2; 1 Pet. 3 : 8.

Ps. 133 : 1, for brethren to dwell together in **u.**

Eph. 4 : 3, endeavouring to keep **u.** of the Spirit.

4 : 13, till we come in **u.** of the faith.

See Gen. 49 : 6; Ps. 86 : 11.

Unjust, Ps. 43 : 1, deliver me from **u.** man.

Prov. 11 : 7, hope of **u.** man perisheth.

28 : 8, he that **u.** gain.

29 : 27, an **u.** man is an abomination.

Zeph. 3 : 5, the **u.** knoweth no shame.

Matt. 5 : 45, he sendeth rain on just an **u.**

Luke 16 : 10, he that is **u.** in least is **u.** in much.

18 : 6, hear what the **u.** judge saith.

18 : 11, not as other men, **u.**

Acts 24 : 15, resurrection of just and **u.**

1 Cor. 6 : 1, go to law before the **u.**

1 Pet. 3 : 18, Christ suffered, the just for the **u.**

2 Pet. 2 : 9, reserve **u.** to day of judgment.

Rev. 22 : 11, he that is **u.** let him be **u,** still.

Unknown, Acts 17 : 23, to the **u.** God.

1 Cor. 14 : 2, speaketh in **u.** tongue.

2 Cor. 6 : 9, as **u.** and yet well known.

Unlawful, Acts 10 : 28, an **u.** thing for a Jew

2 Pet. 2 : 8, vexed his soul with their **u.** deeds.

Unleavened bread, Ex. 12 : 39; 13 : 7; Lev. 2 : 4; 7 : 12; 8 : 26; Num. 6 : 19.

typical, 1 Cor. 5 : 7

fast of, Lev. 23 : 6. The eating of unleavened bread was a prominent feature of the Jewish Passover feast.

Unloose, Mark 1 : 7; Luke 3 : 16.

Unmarried, Paul's exhortation to, 1 Cor. 7 : 8, 11, 25, 32.

Unmerciful, Rom. 1 : 31, without natural affection, **u.**

Unmindful, Deut. 32 : 18, of Rock thou art **u.**

Unmoveable, Acts 27 : 41, fore part stuck fast, and remained **u.**

1 Cor. 15 : 58, be stedfast, **u.**

Unoccupied, Judg. 5 : 6.

Unperfect, Ps. 139 : 16

Unprepared, 2 Cor. 9 : 4.

Unprofitable, Job 15 : 3, reason with **u.** talk.

Matt. 25 : 30, cast **u.** servant into darkness.

Luke 17 : 10, say, We are **u.** servants.

Rom. 3 : 12, together become **u.**

Philem. 11, in time past **u.**

Heb. 13 : 17, not with grief: for that is **u.** See Heb. 7 : 18.

Unrighteous, Ex. 23 : 1, an **u.** witness.

Ps. 71 : 4, deliver me out of hand of **u.**

Isa. 10 : 1, decree **u.** decrees.

55 : 7, let **u.** man forsake his thoughts.

Luke 16 : 11, not faithful in **u.** mammon.

Rom. 3 : 5, is God **u.** who taketh vengeance?

1 Cor. 6 : 9, **u.** shall not inherit the kingdom.

Heb. 6 : 10, God not **u.** to forget.

Unrighteousness, Lev. 19 : 15, do no **u.** in judgment.

Ps. 92 : 15, there is no **u.** in him.

Luke 16 : 9, mammon of **u.**

John 7 : 18, true, and no **u.** in him.

Rom. 1 : 18, hold the truth in **u.**

2 : 8, them that obey **u.**

3 : 5, if our **u.** commend righteousness.

6 : 13, instruments of **u.**

9 : 14, is there **u.** with God?

2 Cor. 6 : 14, what fellowship with **u.?**

2 Thess. 2 : 12, pleasure in **u.**

Heb. 8 : 12, be merciful to their **u.**

2 Pet. 2 : 13, receive the reward of **u.**

1 John 1 : 9, to cleanse us from all **u.**

5 : 17, all **u.** is sin.

Unripe, Job 15 : 33.

Unruly, 1 Thess. 5 . 14, warn them that are **u.**

Titus 1 : 6, not accused of riot, or **u.**

Jas. 3 : 8, the tongue is an **u.** evil.

Unsearchable, Job 5 : 9, God doeth great things and **u.**

Ps. 145 : 3, his greatness is **u.**

Rom. 11 . 33, how **u.** are his judgments.

Eph. 3 : 8, preach **u.** riches of Christ.

Unseemly, Rom. 1 : 27, working that which is **u.**

1 Cor. 13 : 5, doth not behave **u.**

Unshod, Jer. 2 : 25.

Unspeakable, 2 Cor. 9 : 15, thanks to God for his **u.** gift.

2 Cor. 12 : 4, caught up, and heard **u.** words.

1 Pet. 1 : 8, rejoice with joy **u.**

Unspotted, Jas. 1 : 27.

Unstable, Gen. 49 : 4, **u.** as water.

Jas. 1 : 8, a double-minded man is **u.**

2 Pet. 2 : 14, beguiling **u.** souls.

3 : 16, unlearned and **u.** wrest.

Untimely, Job, 3 : 16; Ps. 58 : 8; Eccl. 6 : 3; Rev. 6 : 13.

Untoward, Acts 2 : 40.

Unwise, Deut. 32 : 6, do ye thus requite the Lord **u.** people.

Hos. 13 : 13, an **u.** son.

Rom. 1 : 14, debtor to wise and **u.**

Eph. 5 : 17, be not **u.,** but understanding.

Unworthy, Acts 13 : 46, ye judge your-selves **u.**

1 Cor. 6 : 2, are ye **u.** to judge ?

11 : 27, drink cup of Lord **u.**

Upbraid, Matt. 11 : 20, then began he to **u.** cities.

Mark 16 : 14, he **u.** them with their un-belief.

Jas. 1 : 5, that giveth liberally, and **u.** not.

Uphold, Ps. 51 : 12, **u.** me with thy free spirit.

Ps. 54 : 4, Lord is with them that **u.** my soul.

119 : 116, **u.** me according to thy word.

145 : 14, the Lord **u.** all that fall.

Prov. 29 : 23, honour shall **u.** humble.

Isa. 41 : 10, I will **u.** thee with the right hand.

42 : 1, my servant, whom I **u.**

63 : 5, wondered that there was none to **u.**

Heb. 1 : 3, **u.** all things by word of his power.

Uppermost, Gen. 40 : 17, **u.** basket.

Isa. 17 : 6, top of the **u.** bough.

Luke 11 : 43, love the **u.** seats.

Upright, 2 Sam. 22 : 26; Ps. 18 : 25, with **u.** show thyself **u.**

Job 12 : 4, the **u.** man is laughed to scorn.

17 : 8, **u.** men shall be astonied.

Ps. 25 : 8; 92 : 15, good and **u.** is the Lord.

37 : 37, mark the perfect man, and behold the **u.**

49 : 14, the **u.** shall have dominion.

111 : 1, the assembly of the **u.**

112 : 4, to the **u.** ariseth light.

125 : 4, that are **u.** in their hearts.

140 : 13, the **u.** shall dwell in thy presence.

Prov. 2 : 21, the **u.** shall dwell in the land.

10 : 29, way of Lord is strength to the **u.**

11 : 3, the integrity of the **u.**

11 : 20, **u.** in their way are his delight.

14 : 11, tabernacle of **u.** shall flourish.

15 : 8, the prayer of the **u.** is his delight.

28 : 10, the **u.** shall have good things.

Eccl. 7 : 29, God hath made man **u.**

Hab. 2 : 4, his soul is not **u.** in him.

Uprightly, Ps. 15 : 2, that walketh **u.** shall abide.

58 : 1; 75 : 2, judge **u.**

84 : 11, withhold no good from them that walk **u.**

Prov. 2 : 7, a buckler to them that walk **u.**

10 : 9; 15 : 21; 28 : 18; Mic. 2 : 7, that walketh **u.**

Isa. 33 : 15; Amos 5 : 10, that speaketh **u.**

Uprightness, 1 Ki. 3 : 6, walked in **u.** of heart.

1 Chr. 29 : 17, thou hast pleasure in **u.**

Job 4 : 6, the **u.** of thy ways.

33 : 23, to show unto man his **u.**

Ps. 25 : 21, let **u.** preserve me.

111 : 8, stand fast and are done in **u.**

143 : 10, lead me into the land of **u.**

Prov. 2 : 13 who leave paths of **u.**

28 : 6, better is poor that walketh in **u.**

Isa. 26 : 7, way of the just is **u.**

Dan. 11 : 17, set his face to enter, and **u.** with him.

Ur [light], a town of Mesopotamia, referred to as the original home of Abraham's family, Gen. 11 : 28; 1 Chr. 11 : 35; Neh. 9 : 7.

Urfah, supposed Ur of the Chaldees.

Uriah (ūr-ĭ-ăh), or **Urijah** (ūr-ĭ-jăh) [Jeho-vah is my light], the Hittite, 2 Sam. 11; 1 Ki. 15 : 5; Matt. 1 : 6.

the priest, 2 Ki. 16 : 10, 16.

the prophet, Jer. 26 : 20.

Use, Eph. 4 : 29, good to **u.** of edifying.

2 Tim. 2 : 21, meet for master's **u.**

Titus 3 : 14, works for necessary **u.**

Matt. 6 : 7, **u.** not vain repetitions.

1 Cor. 7 : 31, that **u.** this world, as not abusing it.

Gal. 5 : 13, **u.** not liberty for an occasion to the flesh.

1 Tim. 1 : 8, if a man **u.** it lawfully.

1 Pet. 2 : 16, not **u.** liberty for a cloak.

Usurer, Ex. 22 : 25.

Usurp, 1 Tim. 2 : 12, I suffer not a woman to **u.** authority.

Usury, Deut. 23 : 20, thou mayest lend upon **u.**

Ps. 15 : 5, putteth not his money to **u.**

Prov. 28 : 8, by **u.** increaseth substance.

Isa. 24 : 2, as with taker of **u.**, so with giver of **u.**

Matt. 25 : 27; Luke 19 : 23, received mine own with **u.**

See Ex. 22 : 25; Lev. 25 : 36; Deut. 23 : 19; Neh. 5; Ezek. 18 : 8, 13, 17; 22 : 12.

Utter, Job 33 : 3, my lips shall **u.** knowledge.

Ps. 19 : 2, day unto day **u.** speech.

78 : 2, I will **u.** dark sayings.

106 : 2, who can **u.** the mighty acts of the Lord ?

145 : 7, shall **u.** memory of goodness.

Prov. 1 : 20, wisdom **u.** her voice.

14 : 5, false witness will **u.** lies.

23 : 33, thine heart shall **u.** perverse things.

29 : 11, a fool **u.** all his mind.

Eccl. 5 : 2, let not thine heart be hasty to **u.** before God.

Joel 2 : 11, Lord shall **u.** his voice.

Rom. 8 : 26, groanings that cannot be **u.**

2 Cor. 12 : 4, not lawful for a man to **u.**

Heb. 5 : 11, things hard to be **u.**

Utterance, Acts 2 : 4, speak as the Spirit gave them **u.**

1 Cor. 1 : 5, ye are enriched in all **u.**

Col. 4 : 3, God would open a door of u.
Uttermost, Ps. 2 : 8, give u. parts of earth for possession.
Matt. 5 : 26, till thou hast paid the u. farthing.
12 : 42, came from u. parts to hear.
1 Thess. 2 : 16, wrath is come to the u.
Heb. 7 : 25, save them to the u. that come.
Uz [council], Gen. 10 : 23; 36 : 28; Job 1 : 1.
Uzza (ŭz-'ză) or Uzzah [strength], 2 Sam. 6 : 3; 1 Chr. 13 : 7.
Uzzen-sherah (ŭz-'zĕn-shē-'räh) [summit of Sherah], 1 Chr. 7 : 24.
Uzzi (ŭz-'zĭ) [Jehovah is strength], 1 Chr. 6 : 5.
Uzziah (ŭz-zĭ-'äh) [Jehovah is my strength], 2 Ki. 15 : 13; Isa. 6 : 1.
Uzziel (ŭz-zĭ-'ĕl) [God is my strength], Ex. 6 : 18; Lev. 10 : 4; 1 Chr. 4 : 42; 6 : 2.

V

Vagabond, Gen. 4 : 14, a fugitive and a v.
Acts 19 : 13, certain of the v. Jews.
Vain, Ex. 5 : 9, not regard v. words.
20 : 7; Deut. 5 : 11, not take the name of the Lord in v.
Deut. 32 : 47, it is not a v. thing for you.
1 Sam. 12 : 21, turn not after v. things.
2 Ki. 18 : 20; Isa. 36 : 5, they are but v. words.
Job 11 : 12, v. man would be wise.
16 : 3, shall v. words have an end ?
Ps. 2 : 1; Acts 4 : 25, the people imagine a v. thing.
Ps. 26 : 4, not sat with v. persons.
33 : 17, horse is a v. thing for safety.
39 : 6, every man walketh in a v. show.
60 : 11; 108 : 12, v. is the help of man.
89 : 47, wherefore hast thou made all men in v. ?
127 : 2, it is v. for you to rise early.
Prov. 12 : 11; 28 : 19, followeth v. persons.
31 : 30, beauty is v.
Eccl. 6 : 12, all the days of his v. life.
Isa. 1 : 13, bring no more v. oblations.
45 : 19, I said not, Seek ye me in v.
49 : 4, laboured in v., spent strength in v.
Jer. 3 : 23, in v. is salvation hoped for.
4 : 14, how long shall thy v. thoughts lodge ?
46 : 11, in v. shalt thou use medicines.
Mal. 3 : 14, ye have said, It is v. to serve God.
Matt. 6 : 7, v. repetitions.
15 : 9; Mark 7 : 7, in v. do they worship me.
Rom. 1 : 21, became v. in their imaginations.
13 : 4, he beareth not the sword in v.
1 Cor. 15 : 58, your labour is not in v.
2 Cor. 6 : 1, receive not the grace of God in v.
Gal. 2 : 2, lest I should run in v.
Col. 2 : 8, philosophy and v. deceit.
1 Tim. 6 : 20; 2 Tim. 2 : 16, v. babblings.
Jas. 1 : 26, this man's religion is v.

1 Pet. 1 : 18, redeemed from v. conversation.
Vainglory, Phil. 2 : 3; Gal. 5 : 26.
Valiant, 1 Sam. 18 : 17, be v. for me.
26 : 15; 1 Ki. 1 : 42, a v. man.
Isa. 10 : 13, put down inhabitants like a v man.
33 : 7, their v. ones shall cry.
Jer. 9 : 3, they are not v. for the truth.
Heb. 11 : 34, waxed v. in fight.
See 1 Chr. 19 : 13; Ps. 60 : 12; 118 : 15.
Valley, Ps. 23 : 4, v. of the shadow of death.
84 : 6, through v. of Baca.
Jer. 21 : 13, inhabitant of the v.
Luke 3 : 5, every v. shall be filled.
valley of Achor, Josh. 7 : 24.
Ajalon, Josh. 10 : 12.
Baca, Ps. 84 : 6.
Decision, Joel 3 : 14.
Giants, Josh. 15 : 8.
Gibeon, Isa. 28 : 21.
Hebron, Gen. 37 : 14.
Hinnom, Josh. 15 : 8.
Jehoshaphat, Joel 3 : 2.
Jezreel, Josh. 17 : 16.
Megiddo, 2 Chr. 35 : 22.
Mizpeh, Josh. 11 : 8.
Salt, 2 Sam. 8 : 13.
Slaughter, Jer. 7 : 32.
Succoth, Ps. 60 : 6.
the King, 2 Sam. 18 : 18.
the Passengers, Ezek. 39 : 11.
Vision, Isa. 22 : 1.
Valour, Josh. 1 : 14; 10 : 7.
Value, Job 13 : 4, physicians of no v.
Matt. 10 : 31; Luke 12 : 7, ye are of more v. than many sparrows.
Matt. 27 : 9, whom they of Israel did v.
Vanish, Isa. 51 : 6, heavens shall v. away.
Luke 24 : 31, he v. out of their sight.
1 Cor. 13 : 8, knowledge, it shall v.
Heb. 8 : 13, waxeth old, ready to v.
Jas. 4 : 14, life is a vapour that v.
Vanity, of worldly things, Ps. 39 : 11; 49 : 10; Eccl. 1.
of Idolatry, Deut. 32 : 21; Jer. 10 : 8; 14 : 22; 18 : 15; Acts 14 : 15.
2 Ki. 17 : 15, they followed v.
Job 7 : 3, to possess months of v.
35 : 13, God will not hear v.
Ps. 4 : 2, how long will ye love v. ?
12 : 2, they speak v. every one.
39 : 5, man at his best state is v.
62 : 9, are v. and lighter than v.
119 : 37, turn eyes from beholding v.
144 : 4, man is like to v.
Prov. 13 : 11, wealth gotten by v.
22 : 8, that soweth iniquity shall reap v.
30 : 8, remove from me v.
Eccl. 3 : 19; 11 : 8; 12 : 8, v. of v., all is v.
11 : 10, childhood and youth are v.
Isa. 5 : 18, draw iniquity with cords of v.
30 : 28, sift with sieve of v.
40 : 17, nations are counted v.
Hab. 2 : 13, people weary themselves for v.
Rom. 8 : 20, the creature was made subject to v.
Eph. 4 : 17, walk in v. of mind.

2 Pet. 2 : 18, swelling words of v.

Vapours, Job 36 : 27; Ps. 135 : 7; 148 : 8; Jer. 10 : 13.

Variableness, Jas. 1 : 17, with whom is no v.

Variance, Matt. 10 : 35, set a man at v. against his father.

Gal. 5 : 20, works of flesh are hatred, v.

Vashti (văsh-tĭ) [the best], queen, Esther 1.

Vaunt, Judg. 7 : 2, lest Israel v. against me.

1 Cor. 13 : 4, charity v. not itself.

Vehement, Song of Sol. 8 : 6, love that hath a v. flame.

Jonah 4 : 8, a v. wind.

Mark 14 : 31, Peter spake more v.

Luke 6 : 48, stream beat v. on house.

2 Cor. 7 : 11, what v. desire.

Veil, of women, Gen. 24 : 65; Ruth 3 : 15; 1 Cor. 11 : 10.

of Moses, Ex. 34 : 33; 2 Cor. 3 : 13.

of the tabernacle and temple, Ex. 26 : 31; 36 : 35; 2 Cor. 3 : 14.

of temple, rent at the crucifixion, Mark 15 : 38; Luke 23 : 45.

Matt, 27 : 51, v. of temple was rent.

2 Cor. 3 : 14, which v. is done away in Christ.

Heb. 6 : 19, entereth within the v.

9 : 3, after the second v.

10 : 20, consecrated for us, through the v.

Vein, Job 28 : 1.

Vengeance, belongs to God, Deut. 32 : 35; Ps. 99 : 8; Isa. 34 : 8; Jer. 50 : 15; Ezek. 24 : 25; Nah. 1 : 2; 2 Thess. 1 : 8.

Ps. 58 : 10, rejoice when he seeth v.

94 : 1; Heb. 10 : 30, to me belongeth v.

Prov. 6 : 34; Isa. 34 : 8; 61 : 2; Jer. 51 : 6, the day of v.

Isa. 35 : 4, your God will come with v.

59 : 17, garments of v. for clothing.

Luke 21: 22, for these be days of v.

Acts 28 : 4, whom v. suffereth not to live.

Rom. 12 : 19, v. is mine, saith the Lord.

Jude 7, the v. of eternal fire.

Venison, Gen. 25 : 28; 27 : 3.

Venom, Deut. 32 : 33.

Verity, Ps. 111 : 7, works of his hands are v.

1 Tim. 2 : 7, a teacher in faith and v.

Vermilion, Jer. 22 : 14; Ezek. 23 : 14.

Versions of the Bible.

I.—Ancient Versions.—(1) With the spread of the Greek language, Hebrew ceased to be a spoken language among the Jews and became the language of the learned. This led inevitably to the production of a Greek version of the Jewish Scriptures. This version known as the Septuagint, or LXX, was used in early Christian times, and all the New Testament quotations from the Old Testament are from the Septuagint version.

(2) A further consequence of the loss of the Hebrew language was the common synagogue practice whereby the passage read was explained in the local dialect. The writing down of these explanations gave rise to the Targums, written in Aramaic. They are of great value in that they give us the traditional exegesis of the Jews in the early Christian centuries.

(3) The Syriac Version, or Peshitto, was compiled to meet the needs of the Syrian Christians, both Jew and Gentile, probably early in the second century.

(4) The Old Latin Version, written in a rude, provincial dialect, originated in Africa in the second century, and was used by the early Latin Fathers. It is a rendering of the Septuagint, not of the Hebrew. This version was in use till the end of the fourth century, when Jerome made his famous translation, known as the Vulgate, from the original Hebrew.

II.—English Versions.—The whole Bible was never translated into Anglo-Saxon, only portions by Cædmon, Bede, Alfred the Great, and others. The earliest translation of any book of Scripture into English prose was the Psalms about 1327 followed in 1382-3 by Wycliff's Bible, a translation of the Vulgate; it's influence may be traced in every later version.

The direct history of the English Bible begins with William Tyndale. The publication of Tyndale's New Testament was begun in Cologne, and finished at Worms in 1525. In 1534 he published, at Antwerp, a revised edition, with a translation of extracts from the Old Testament. In 1530 his translation of the Pentateuch appeared, and in 1531 the book of Jonah. A Bible, published a year after his martyrdom, contains translation of all the books from Genesis to 2 Chronicles. For five centuries his version has shaped the diction, phraseology, and the style of every other. Its spirit pervades all its successors. The simple, sublime, and pure language of the Authorised Version is due to it. Its influence may be said to have informed and consecrated the English language itself.

The next thirty years saw several versions appear, notably Miles Coverdale's Great Bible (so called because of its size), the Geneva Bible (the first English Bible divided into verses), and the Bishop's Bible. The latter remained the standard version till the appearance of the Authorised Version in 1611.

The Authorised Version was the work of forty-seven scholars appointed by James I. Seven years were spent on the work. The scholars, divided into six companies, were each assigned a particular portion of the work. The renderings of the six companies were then reviewed by the entire body. Directly or indirectly, every prior version influenced their translation whether in diction, style, or interpretation. So skilfully did they interweave with their own original rendering what was truest, and fittest, and worthiest, in other versions, and so aptly did they conform their English to the sense of the original Hebrew and Greek, that the very idioms of these sacred tongues enter readily into the thought and emotion of ordinary readers.

The Revised Version (New Testament 1881; Old Testament 1885) was the result of a movement, both in Britain and America, to bring the Authorised Version into accord with the existing standard of Biblical knowledge. By substituting modern terms for obsolete and archaic ones, great gain in clearness has been effected.

The American Standard Version, published in 1901, embodies the proposed changes which were rejected by the English revisers. The Revised Standard Version is a revision by American scholars of the American Standard Version and was published in 1952 (New Testament 1946). The International Council of Religious Education was granted the copyright of the American Standard Version in 1928 and authorised the new revision in 1937.

The New English Bible is a completely new translation of the original Hebrew and Greek into Modern English. The New Testament was published in 1961 followed by the Old Testament in 1970. The work of translation has been divided between three panels of translators (one for the New Testament, one for the Old Testament and one for the Apocrypha) under the general directorship of Dr. C. H. Dodd.

During this century several New Testament translations have appeared, notably those by Weymouth, Goodspeed and Phillips; and the translation of the whole Bible by Moffatt.

The Good News Bible—Today's English Version—published October 1976 (New Testament 1966) is a new translation which tries to state clearly the meaning of the original text in words and forms that are acceptable to people who use modern English for communication. The translation does not follow the traditional vocabulary and style found in historic versions but attempts to present the Bible content and message in easily understood language.

Vessels, of the temple, 1 Ki. 7 : 40; carried to Babylon, 2 Ki. 25 : 14; profaned, Dan. 5; restored, Ezra, 1 : 7.
Ps. 2 : 9, in pieces like a potter's v.
31 : 12, I am like a broken v.
Jer. 22 : 28; Hos. 8 : 8, v. wherein is no pleasure.
Matt. 25 : 4, the wise took oil in their v.
Acts 9 : 15, he is a chosen v. unto me.
Rom. 9 : 22, 23, v. of wrath, v. of mercy
1 Thess. 4 : 4, to possess his v. in sanctification.
2 Tim. 2 : 21, he shall be a v. unto honour.
1 Pet. 3 : 7, honour unto wife, as unto the weaker v.
Vestment, 2 Ki. 10 : 22.
Vestry, 2 Ki. 10 : 22, said to him over the v.
Vesture, Ps. 22 : 18; Matt. 27 : 35; John 19 : 24, they cast lots upon my v.
Ps. 102 : 26, as a v. shalt thou change them.
Heb. 1 : 12, as a v. shalt thou fold them.

Rev. 19 : 13, clothed with v. dipped in blood.
Vex, Ex. 22 : 21; Lev. 19 : 33, thou shalt not v. a stranger.
2 Sam. 12 : 18, how will he v. himself?
Job 19 : 2, how long will ye v. my soul?
Ps. 2 : 5, shall v. them in his displeasure.
Isa. 11 : 13, Judah shall not v. Ephraim.
63 : 10, they rebelled, and v. his Holy Spirit.
2 Pet. 2 : 8, v. his righteous soul.
Vexation, Eccl. 1 : 14; 2 : 11; 4 : 4; 6 : 9, vanity and v. of spirit.
See Eccl. 2: 22; Isa. 28: 19; 65: 14.
Vials, full of odours, Rev. 5 : 8.
the seven, Rev. 15 : 7; 16 : 1.
Victory, over death, Isa. 25 : 8; by faith, 1 John 5: 4.
1 Chr. 29 : 11, thine O Lord is the v.
Ps. 98 : 1, arm hath gotten him v.
1 Cor. 15 : 54, he will swallow up death in v.
Matt. 12 : 20, send forth judgement unto v.
Victuals, Neh. 10 : 31; Jer. 44 : 17; Matt. 14 : 15; Luke 9 : 12.
Vigilant, 1 Tim. 3 : 2, a bishop must be v.
1 Pet. 5 : 8, be v.; because your adversary walketh about.
Vile, Deut. 25 : 3, thy brother should seem v.
1 Sam. 3 : 13, sons made themselves v.
Job 18 : 3, wherefore are we reputed v.?
40 : 4, I am v.; what shall I answer thee?
Ps. 15 : 4; Isa. 32 : 5; Dan. 11 : 21, a v. person.
Jer. 15:19, take forth the precious from the v.
Rom. 1 : 26, God gave them up to v. affections.
Phil. 3 : 21, who shall change our v. body.
Jas. 2 : 2, a poor man in v. raiment.
Village, Ex. 8 : 13; Matt. 21 : 2; Acts 8 : 25.
Villany, Isa. 32 : 6; Jer. 29 : 23.
Vine, Its culture was well understood by the Israelites, and there are numerous references, both in reality and in parable to the vine, its clusters of fruit, the pressing of the wine, and its manufacture. There can be no doubt, from the descriptions given, that the wine was made by the fermentation of the juice of the grape. The grapes were also dried in the sun as raisins.
Deut. 32 : 32, their v. is of the v. of Sodom.
Judg. 9 : 12, trees said unto the v., Come, reign over us.
13 : 14, not eat of any thing that cometh of the v.
1 Ki. 4 : 25, dwelt every man under his v.
2 Ki. 18 : 31; Isa. 36 : 16, eat every man of his own v.
Ps. 80 : 8, a v. out of Egypt.
128: 3, thy wife as a fruitful v.
Isa. 24 : 7, the v. languisheth.
Jer. 2 : 21, I planted thee a noble v.
Hos. 10 : 1, Israel is an empty v.
14 : 7, they shall grow as the v.
Mic. 4 : 4, sit every man under his v.
Matt. 26 : 29; Mark 14 : 25; Luke 22 : 18, fruit of the v.
John 15 : 1, I am the true v.
Vinegar, offered to Christ on the cross; Matt. 27 : 34, 48; Mark 15 : 36; Luke 23 : 36; John 19 : 29.

See Ps. 69 : 21; Prov. 10 : 26; 25 : 20.

Vineyard, Noah's, Gen. 9 : 20.

Naboth's, 1 Ki. 21.

parables of, Matt. 20 : 1; 21 : 33; Mark 12 : 1; Luke 20 : 9.

laws concerning, Ex. 22 : 5; 23 : 11; Lev. 19 : 10; 25 : 3; Deut. 20 : 6; 22 : 9; 23 : 24; 24 : 21.

Vintage, Job 24 : 6; Isa. 32 : 10; Jer. 48 : 32.

Viol, Isa. 5 : 12; Amos 6 : 5.

Violence, Gen. 6 : 11, earth was filled with v.

Ps. 11 : 5, him that loveth v.

72 : 14, redeem their soul from v.

73 : 6, v. covereth them as a garment.

Prov. 4 : 17, they drink the wine of v.

Isa. 53 : 9, because he had done no v.

60 : 18, v. shall no more be heard.

Ezek. 8 : 17; 28 : 16, they have filled the land with v.

Hab. 1 : 2, cry to thee of v.

Mal. 2 : 16, covereth v. with garment.

Matt. 11 : 12, kingdom of heaven suffereth v.

Luke 3 : 14, do v. to no man.

Heb. 11 : 34, quenched v. of fire.

Viper. This word is several times used to denote a small venomous snake. The viper that fastened on St. Paul's hand was probably the Mediterranean viper (Acts 28 : 3).

Virgin, Christ born of, Matt. 1 : 18; Luke 1 : 27.

virgins, parable of ten, Matt. 25 : 1-13.

Isa. 7 : 14; Matt. 1 : 23, a v. shall conceive.

Matt. 25 : 1, kingdom of heaven is likened unto ten v.

2 Cor. 11 : 2, present you as a chaste v. to Christ.

Virtue, Mark 5 : 30; Luke 6 : 19; 8 : 46, v. had gone out of him.

Phil. 4 : 8, if there be any v.

2 Pet. 1 : 5, add to your faith v.; and to v. knowledge.

Virtuous, Prov. 12 : 4; 31 : 10, 29.

Visage, Isa. 52 : 14, his v. was so marred.

Dan. 3 : 19, form of v. was changed.

Visions, sent by God, Gen. 12 : 7; Num. 24 : 4; Job 7 : 14; Isa. 1 : 1; Acts 2 : 17; 2 Cor. 12 : 1.

of Abram, Gen. 15 : 12; Jacob, Gen. 28 : 10; Pharaoh, Gen. 41; Isaiah, Isa. 6; Ezekiel, Ezek. 1; 10; 11; 37; 40; Nebuchadnezzar, Dan. 4; Daniel, Dan. 7; Zechariah, Zech. 1; Peter, Acts 10 : 9; John, Rev. 1 : 4.

1 Sam. 3 : 1, there was no open v.

Job 20 : 8, as a v. of the night.

Ps. 89 : 19, spakest in v. to Holy One.

Prov. 29 : 18, where there is no v., the people perish.

Isa. 28 : 7, they err in v.

Hos. 12 : 10, I have multiplied v.

Joel 2 : 28; Acts 2 : 17, young men shall see v.

Hab. 2 : 3, the v. is for appointed time.

Matt. 17 : 9, tell the v. to no man.

Luke 1 : 22, perceived he had seen a v.

24 : 23, they had seen a v. of angels.

Acts 26 : 19, not disobedient to heavenly v.

Visit, Gen. 50 : 24; Ex. 13 : 19, God will v. you.

Ex. 20 : 5; 34 : 7; Num. 14 : 18; Deut. 5 : 9, v. iniquity of fathers.

Ex. 32 : 34, when I v. I will v. their sin upon them.

Job 7 : 18, that thou shouldest v. him.

Ps. 8 : 4; Heb. 2 : 6, the son of man, that thou v. him.

Ps. 80 : 14, look down, and v. this vine.

106 : 4, v. me with thy salvation.

Jer. 5 : 9; 9 : 9, shall I not v. for these things ?

Matt. 25 : 36, I was sick, and ye v. me.

Luke 1 : 68, God hath v. and redeemed his people.

Acts 7 : 23, to v. his brethren.

15 : 14, God did v. Gentiles.

Jas. 1 : 27, to v. fatherless and widows.

Visitation, Num. 16 : 29, visited after v. of all men.

Job 10 : 12, thy v. preserved my spirit.

Isa. 10 : 3, what will ye do in the day of v. ?

Jer. 8 : 12; 10 : 15; 46 : 21; Luke 19 : 44, time of v.

1 Pet. 2 : 12, glorify God in day of v.

Vocation, Eph. 4 : 1, walk worthy of the v.

Voice, of God, proclaims the law, Ex. 19 : 19; 20 : 1.

its majesty and power, Job 37 : 4; Ps. 18 : 13; 46 : 6; 68 : 33; Joel 2 : 11.

heard by Elijah, 1 Ki. 19 : 12; by Ezekiel, Ezek. 1 : 24; 10 : 5; by Christ at his baptism, etc., Matt. 3 : 17; John 12 : 28; by disciples at the transfiguration, Matt. 17 : 5; Mark 9 : 7; Luke 9 : 35; 2 Pet. 1 : 18; by Paul, Acts 9 : 4; by John, Rev. 1 : 10.

Gen. 4 : 10, the v. of thy brother's blood.

27 : 22, the v. is Jacob's v.

Ex. 23 : 21, beware of him, and obey his v.

24 : 3, all the people answered with one v.

Deut. 4 : 33, did ever people hear v. of God, and live ?

1 Ki. 19 : 12, after the fire a still small v.

2 Ki. 4 : 31, there was neither v. nor hearing.

Job 30 : 31, the v. of them that weep.

40 : 9, canst thou thunder with a v. like him ?

Ps. 31 : 22; 86 : 6, the v. of my supplications.

42 : 4, with the v. of joy.

93 : 3, the floods have lifted up their v.

95 : 7; Heb. 3 : 7, 15, to-day if ye will hear his v.

Ps. 103 : 20, hearkening to v. of his word.

Prov. 8 : 4, my v. is to sons of man.

Eccl. 12 : 4, rise up at the v. of the bird.

Song of Sol. 2 : 12, the v. of the turtle is heard.

Isa. 30 : 19, gracious at v. of thy cry.

40 : 3, the v. of him that crieth.

48 : 20, a v. of singing.

52 : 8, with the v. together shall they sing.

65 : 19, the v. of weeping shall be no more heard.

Jer. 30 : 19, the **v.** of them that make merry.
Ezek. 23 : 42, a **v.** of a multitude at ease.
  33 : 32, one that hath a pleasant **v.**
  43 : 2; Rev. 1 : 15, **v.** like a noise of many waters.
Jonah 2 : 9, with **v.** of thanksgiving.
Matt. 3 : 3; Mark 1 : 3; Luke 3 : 4; John 1 : 23, the **v.** of one crying in the wilderness.
Matt. 12 : 19, neither shall any man eahr his **v.**
Mark 1 : 11; Luke 3 : 22, a **v.** from heaven.
John 5 : 25, the dead shall hear the **v.** of the Son of God.
  10 : 4, the sheep know his **v.**
  12 : 30, this **v.** came not because of me.
  18 : 37, every one that is of the truth heareth my **v.**
Acts 24 : 21, except it be for this one **v.**
  26 : 10, I gave my **v.** against them.
1 Cor. 14 : 19, by my **v.** I might teach others.
Gal. 4 : 20, I desire to change my **v.**
1 Thess. 4 : 16, descend with **v.** of archangel.
Rev. 3 : 20, any man hear my **v.**
Void, Gen. 1 : 2; Jer. 4 : 23, earth without form and **v.**
Deut. 32 : 28, a nation **v.** of counsel.
Ps. 89 : 39, made **v.** the covenant.
  119 : 126, thcy have made **v.** thy law.
Prov. 11 : 12, he that is **v.** of wisdom.
Isa. 55 : 11, word shall not return unto me **v.**
Acts 24 : 16, a conscience **v.** of offence.
Rom. 3 : 31, do we make **v.** the law ?
  4 : 14, faith is made **v.**
Voluntary, Lev. 1 : 3; Ezek. 46 : 12; Col. 2 : 18.
Vows, laws concerning, Lev. 27; Num. 6 : 2; 30; Deut. 23 : 21.
Gen. 28 : 20; 31 : 13, Jacob vowed a **v.**
Judg. 11 : 30, Jephthah vowed a **v.**
Job 22 : 27, thou shalt pay thy **v.**
Ps. 22 : 25; 66 : 13; 116 : 14, I will pay my **v.** unto the Lord.
  50 : 14, pay thy **v.** unto the Most High.
  61 : 8, that I may daily perform my **v.**
  65 : 1, unto thee shall the **v.** be performed.
Prov. 31 : 2, the son of my **v.**
Eccl. 5 : 4, when thou **v.** a **v.**
Isa. 19 : 21, they shall **v.** a **v.** unto the Lord.
Jonah 1 : 16, feared the Lord, and made **v.**
Acts 21 : 23, which have a **v.** on them.
Deut. 23 : 22, if thou forbear to **v.**
Ps. 76 : 11, **v.** and pay to the Lord.
  132 : 2, **v.** to the mighty God.
Jonah 2 : 9, I will pay that I have **v.**
See Ps. 116 : 18; Mal. 1 : 14.
Vulture. One of the " unclean " birds, mentioned in Lev. 11 : 14. It may have been one of the smaller birds of prey, like the kite. Isa. 34 : 15.

W

Wafers, used as offerings, Ex. 29 : 2, 23; Lev. 2 : 4; 8 : 26; Num. 6 : 15.
Wages, to be duly paid, Lev. 19 : 13; Deut. 24 : 15; Jas. 5 : 4.
Gen. 29 : 15, what shall thy **w.** be ?
Ex. 2 : 9, nurse this child, and I will give **w.**
Jer. 22 : 13, useth service without **w.**
Hag. 1 : 6, earneth **w.** to put into bag with holes.
Mal. 3 : 5, oppress hireling in **w.**
Luke 3 : 14, content with your **w.**
John 4 : 36, he that reapeth receiveth **w.**
Rom. 6 : 23, the **w.** of sin is death.
2 Pet. 2 : 15, the **w.** of unrighteousness.
Wail, Mic. 1 : 8, I will **w.** and howl.
Mark 5 : 38, them that **w.** greatly.
Rev. 1 : 7, kindreds of earth shall **w.**
Matt. 13 : 42, **w.** and gnashing of teeth.
Rev. 18 : 15, merchants shall stand afar off, **w.**

Jews' Wailing Place.

Wait, 2 Ki. 6 : 33, should I **w.** for the Lord any longer ?
Job 14 : 14, I will **w.** till my change come.
  17 : 13, if I **w.**, the grave is my house.
  29 : 23, they **w.** for me as for rain.
Ps. 25 : 3; 69 : 6, let none that **w.** be ashamed.
  27 : 14; 37 : 34; Prov. 20 : 22, **w.** on the Lord.
Ps. 33 : 20, our soul **w.** for the Lord.
  40 : 1, I **w.** patiently for the Lord.
  62 : 1; 130 : 6, my soul **w.** upon God.
  65 : 1, praise **w.** for thee, O God, in Zion.
  104 : 27; 145 : 15, these **w.** upon thee.
  123 : 2, our eyes **w.** upon the Lord.
Prov. 27 : 18, he that **w.** on his master.
Isa. 25 : 9, our God, we **w.** for him.
  30 : 18, the Lord **w.** to be gracious.
  40 : 31, they that **w.** upon the Lord shall renew strength.
  42 : 4, the isles shall **w.** for his law.
  59 : 9, we **w.** for light.

Lam. 3 : 26, good that a man hope and quietly w.

Hos. 12 : 6, w. on thy God continually.

Mic. 7 : 7, I will w. for the God of my salvation.

Hab. 2 : 3, though the vision tarry, w. for it.

Mark 15 : 43, who w. for the kingdom of God.

Luke 2 : 25, w. for the consolation of Israel.

12 : 36, like men that w. for their lord.

Acts 1 : 4, w. for promise of the Father.

Rom. 8 : 25, then do we with patience w. for it.

12 : 7, let us w. on our ministering.

Gal. 5 : 5, we w. for the hope of righteousness.

1 Thess. 1 : 10, to w. for his Son from heaven.

Wake, Song of Sol. 5 : 2, I sleep, but my heart w.

Isa. 50 : 4, w. mine ear to hear.

Jer. 51 : 39, sleep a perpetual sleep, and not w.

Joel 3 : 9, w. up the mighty men.

Zech. 4 : 1, angel came, and w. me.

1 Thess. 5 : 10, whether we w. or sleep.

Walk, Gen. 17 : 1, w. before me, and be perfect.

Gen. 24 : 40, the Lord, before whom I w.

Ex. 16 : 4, whether they will w. in my law.

Lev. 26 : 12, I will w. among you.

Deut. 29 : 19, though I w. in imagination of heart.

Job 22 : 14, he w. in the circuit of heaven.

Ps. 23 : 4, though I w. through valley of shadow of death.

26 : 11, I will w. in mine integrity.

48 : 12, w. about Zion.

Ps. 55 : 14, we w. to house of God in company.

56 : 13, that I may w. before God in light of living.

84 : 11, from them that w. uprightly.

89 : 15, shall w. in light of thy countenance.

91 : 6, the pestilence that w. in darkness.

115 : 7, feet have they, but w. not.

116 : 9, I will w. before the Lord.

119 : 45, I will w. at liberty.

138 : 7, though I w. in midst of trouble.

143 : 8, cause me to know wherein I should w.

Prov. 2 : 20, mayest w. in way of good men.

10 : 9; 28 : 18, he that w. uprightly.

13 : 20, he that w. with wise men shall be wise.

19 : 1; 28 : 6, the poor that w. in integrity.

Isa. 2 : 5, let us w. in the light of the Lord.

9 : 2, the people that w. in darkness.

30 : 21, this is the way, w. in it.

35 : 9, the redeemed shall w. there.

40 : 31, shall w. and not faint.

Jer. 6 : 16, the good way, and w. therein.

10 : 23, it is not in man that w. to direct his steps.

Dan. 4 : 37, those that w. in pride.

Hos. 14 : 9, the just shall w. in them.

Amos 3 : 3, can two w. together, except they be agreed ?

Mic. 6 : 8, to w. humbly with thy God.

Zech. 10 : 12, they shall w. up and down.

Mark 16 : 12, Jesus appeared to two of them, as they w.

Luke 13 : 33, I must w. to-day and to-morrow.

John 8 : 12, shall not w. in darkness.

11 : 9, if any man w. in the day.

Rom. 6 : 4, w. in newness of life.

8 : 1, who w. not after the flesh, but after the Spirit.

2 Cor. 5 : 7, we w. by faith.

Gal. 6 : 16, as many as w. according to this rule.

Eph. 2 : 10, ordained that we should w. in them.

4 : 1, w. worthy of the vocation.

5 : 15, see that ye w. circumspectly.

Phil. 3 : 18, many w., of whom I told you.

Col. 1 : 10; 1 Thess. 2 : 12, that ye might w. worthy of the Lord.

1 Thess. 4 : 1, how ye ought to w.

2 Thess. 3 : 6, brother that w. disorderly.

1 Pet. 5 : 8, w. about seeking whom he may devour.

1 John 1 : 7, if we w. in the light.

2 : 6, ought so to w. as he w.

Walking, with God, Deut. 5 : 33; 28 : 9; Josh. 22 : 5; 1 Ki. 8 : 36; Ps. 1; 112; Prov. 2 : 7; Isa. 2 : 3; Jer. 7 : 23; Ezek. 37 : 24; of Enoch, Gen. 5 : 24; of Noah, Gen. 6 : 9.

in faith, love, etc., Rom. 6 : 4; 8 : 1; 13 : 13; 2 Cor. 5 : 7; Gal. 5 : 16; Eph. 5 : 2; Phil. 3 : 16; Col. 1 : 10; 2 : 6; 1 John 1 : 6; Rev. 3 : 4; 21 : 24.

Deut. 2 : 7, the Lord knoweth thy w.

Job 1 : 7; 2 : 2, from w. up and down.

31 : 26, the moon w. in brightness.

Dan. 3 : 25, four men w. in the fire.

Mic. 2 : 11, if a man w. in the spirit.

Matt. 14 : 25, Jesus went w. on sea.

Mark 8 : 24, I see men as trees w.

Luke 1 : 6, w. in all commandments of the Lord.

Acts 9 : 31, w. in the fear of the Lord.

2 Cor. 4 : 2, not w. in craftiness.

Wall, Gen. 49 : 22, whose branches run over the w.

Ex. 14 : 22, the waters were a w. to them.

Num. 22 : 24, a w. being on this side and a w. on that.

1 Sam. 25 : 16, a w. by night and day.

2 Sam. 22 : 30; Ps. 18 : 29, I have leaped over a w.

1 Ki. 4 : 33, hyssop that springeth out of w.

2 Ki. 20 : 2; Isa. 38 : 2, turned his face to the w.

Neh. 4 : 6, so built we the w.

Ps. 62 : 3, as a bowing w. shall ye be.

122 : 7, peace be within thy w.

Prov. 18 : 11, as high w. in his own conceit.

24 : 31, stone w. was broken down.

25 : 28, like a city without w.

Isa. 25 : 4, as a storm against the w.

26 : 1, salvation will God appoint for w.

59 : 10, we grope for the w.

60 : 18, thou shalt call thy w. Salvation.
Jer. 15 : 20, will make thee fenced w.
Ezek. 8 : 7, a hole in the w.
Dan. 5 : 5, fingers wrote upon the w.
Joel 2 : 7, they shall climb the w.
Amos 5 : 19, leaned hand on w. and serpent bit him.
Hab. 2 : 11, the stone shall cry out of the w.
Acts 23 : 3, thou whited w.
Eph. 2 : 14, the middle w. of partition.
Rev. 21 : 14, the w. of the city had twelve foundations.

Wander, Gen. 20 : 13, God caused me to w.
Num. 14 : 33; Ps. 107 : 49, w. in wilderness.
Deut. 27 : 18, cursed be he that maketh blind to w.
Job 12 : 24, he causeth them to w.
15 : 23, he w. abroad for bread.
38 : 41, ravens w. for lack of meat.
Ps. 55 : 7, then would I w. far off.
59 : 15, let them w. up and down.
Prov. 27 : 8, as a bird that w. from nest.
Isa. 47 : 15, shall w. every one to his quarter.
Jer. 14 : 10, they loved to w.
Amos 8 : 12, shall w. from sea to sea.
Heb. 11 : 37, they w. about in sheepskins.

Want, Deut. 28 : 48, serve thine enemies in w.
Judg. 18 : 10, a place where there is no w.
19 : 20, let all thy w. lie on me.
Job 31 : 19, if I have seen any perish for w.
Ps. 34 : 9, there is no w. to them that fear him.
Prov. 6 : 11; 24 : 34, w. as an armed man.
Amos 4 : 6, I have given w. of bread.
Mark 12 : 44, she of her w. cast in all.
Luke 15 : 14, he began to be in w.
Phil. 4 : 11, not that I speak of w.
Ps. 23 : 1, I shall not w.
34 : 10, that seek the Lord shall not w. any good thing.
Prov. 9 : 4, him that w. understanding.
13 : 25, the wicked shall w.
Isa. 34 : 16, none shall w. her mate.
Ezek. 4 : 17, that they may w. bread and water.
John 2 : 3, when they w. wine.
2 Cor. 11 : 9, when I w., I was chargeable to no man.
Jas. 1 : 4, perfect and entire, w. nothing.

Wanton, 1 Tim. 5 : 11, to wax w. against Christ.
Jas. 5 : 5, ye have lived and been w.

Wantonness, censured, Isa. 3 : 16; Rom. 13 : 13; 2 Pet. 2 : 18.

War, laws of, Deut. 20; 23 : 9; 24 : 5.
Ex. 32 : 17, a noise of w. in the camp.
Num. 21 : 14, in book of w. of the Lord.
Josh. 11 : 23; 14 : 15, land rested from w.
2 Ki. 18 : 20, strength for w.
1 Chr. 5 : 22, the w. was of God.
Job 10 : 17, changes and w. are against me.
38 : 23, reserved against the day of w.
Ps. 27 : 3, though w. should rise against me.
46 : 9, he maketh w. to cease.

68 : 30, scatter the people that delight in w.
120 : 7, I am for peace: they are for w.
Prov. 20 : 18, with good advice made w.
Eccl. 3 : 8, a time of w.
8 : 8, there is no discharge in that w.
Isa. 2 : 4; Mic. 4 : 3, nor learn w. any more.
Mic. 2 : 8, as men averse from w.
Matt. 24 : 6; Mark 13 : 7; Luke 21 : 9, w. and rumours of w.
Luke 14 : 31, what king going to make w. ?
Jas. 4 : 1, from whence come w. ?
Rev. 12 : 7, there was w. in heaven.
13 : 7, to make w. with saints.

War.
2 Sam. 22 : 35; Ps. 18 : 34; 144 : 1, Lord teacheth my hands to w.
Isa. 41 : 12, they that w. against thee be as nothing.
2 Cor. 10 : 3, we do not w. after the flesh.
1 Tim. 1 : 18, mightest w. a good warfare.
2 Tim. 2 : 4, no man that w. entangleth himself.
Jas. 4 : 2, ye fight and w., yet ye have not.
1 Pet. 2 : 11, lusts which w. against the soul.

Warfare, Isa. 40 : 2, her w. is accomplished.
1 Cor. 9 : 7, who goeth a w. at his own charges ?
2 Cor. 10 : 4, weapons of our w. are not carnal.

Warn, Ps. 19 : 11, by them is thy servant w.
Ezek. 3 : 18; 33 : 8, to w. the wicked.
Matt. 3 : 7, who hath w. you ?
Acts 20 : 31, I ceased not to w. every one.
1 Thess. 5 : 14, w. them that are unruly.
Heb. 11 : 7, Noah, being w. of God.

Warning, 2 Chr. 19 : 10; Ezek. 3 : 17; 33 : 3.
Paul's example, 1 Cor. 4 : 14; Col. 1 : 28.

Warp, Lev. 13 : 48-49, " the w. or woof of it."

Wash, 2 Ki. 5 : 10, go, w. in Jordan.
Job 9 : 30, if I w. myself with snow water.
14 : 19, thou w. away things which grow.
29 : 6, when I w. my steps with butter.
Ps. 26 : 6, I will w. my hands in innocency.
51 : 2, w. me throughly from mine iniquity.
51 : 7, w. me, and I shall be whiter than snow.
Isa. 1 : 16, w. you, make you clean.
Jer. 2 : 22, though thou w. thee with nitre.
4 : 14, w. thy heart from wickedness.
Ezek. 16 : 4, nor wast w. in water.
Matt. 6 : 17, when thou fastest, w. thy face.
Mark 7 : 4, except they w., they eat not.
Luke 7 : 38, began to w. his feet with tears.
John 9 : 7, go, w. in the pool of Siloam.
13 : 5, Jesus began to w. disciples' feet.
Acts 22 : 16, w. away thy sins.
Heb. 10 : 22, having our bodies w. with pure water.
Rev. 1 : 5, w. us from our sins.
7 : 14, have w. their robes.

Washing. The custom of washing the hands and feet has great significance in the East, and among the Jews the custom has, from the earliest times, had a particular religious significance. Frequent purification of the person is taken as symbolic of spiritual cleansing under the Mosaic Law. To offer facilities for the washing of hands and feet is one of the recognised rites of Eastern hospitality.

enjoined by the law, Ex. 29 : 4; Lev. 6 : 27; 13 : 54; 14 : 8; Deut. 21 : 6; 2 Chr. 4 : 6.

of the feet, Gen. 18 : 4; 24 : 32; 43 : 24; 1 Sam. 25 : 41; I Tim. 5 : 10.

of the hands, Deut. 21 : 6; Matt. 27 : 24.

Christ washes disciples' feet, John 13.

traditional, censured, Mark 7 : 3; Luke 11 : 38.

figuratively mentioned, Isa. 4 : 4; Eph. 5 : 26; Titus 3 : 5.

through the blood of Christ, 1 Cor. 6 : 11.

Watch, Ps. 90 : 4, as a w. in the night.

141 : 3, set a w. before my mouth.

Jer. 51 : 12, make the w. strong.

Hab. 2 : 1, I will stand upon my w.

Matt. 27 : 66, sealing the stone, and setting a w.

Watch.

Gen. 31 : 49, the Lord w. between me and thee.

Job 14 : 16, dost thou not w. over my sin?

Ps. 102 : 7, I w., and am as a sparrow.

130 : 6, more than they that w. for morning.

Isa. 21 : 5, w. in the w.-tower.

29 : 20, all that w. for iniquity are cut off.

Jer. 44 : 27, I will w. over them for evil.

Matt. 24 : 42; Luke 21 : 36; Acts 20 : 31, w. therefore.

Matt. 26 : 41; Mark 13 : 33; 14 : 38, w. and pray.

1 Cor. 16 : 13, w. ye, stand fast in the faith.

1 Thess. 5 : 6; 1 Pet. 4 : 7, let us w. and be sober.

Heb. 13 : 17, they w. for your souls.

Rev. 16 : 15, blessed is he that w.

See Luke 12 : 37; 2 Cor. 11 : 27.

Watchfulness, enjoined, Matt. 25 : 13; Mark 13 : 35; Luke 12 : 35; 1 Cor. 10 : 12; Eph. 6 : 18; Col. 4 : 2; 2 Tim. 4 : 5; 1 Pet. 4 : 7; 5 : 8; Rev. 3 : 2.

Watchmen, their duty, 2 Sam. 18 : 25; 2 Ki. 9 : 17; Ps. 127 : 1; Song of Sol. 3 : 3; 5 : 7; Isa. 21 : 5, 11; 52 : 8; Jer. 6 : 17; 31 : 6; Ezek. 3: 17; 33.

evil, described, Isa. 56 : 10.

Water, miraculously supplied, Gen. 21 : 19; Ex. 15 : 23; 17 : 6; Num. 20 : 7; 2 Ki. 3 : 20.

used in the trial of jealousy, Num. 5 : 17.

of affliction, 1 Ki. 22 : 27.

used in baptism, Matt. 3 : 11; Acts 8 : 36.

Christ walks on, Matt. 14 : 25; Mark 6 : 48; John 6 : 19.

changed into wine, John 2 : 3.

figuratively mentioned, Isa. 41 : 17; Ezek. 47; Zech. 13 : 1; John 4 : 10; 7 : 38; Rev. 21 : 6; 22.

waters, of creation, Gen. 1 : 2, 6, 9.

the flood, Gen. 6 : 17; 7 : 6.

fountain of living, Jer. 2 : 13; 17 : 13.

living fountains of, Rev. 7 : 17.

Gen. 49 : 4, unstable as w.

Deut. 11 : 11, the land drinketh w. of rain of heaven.

Josh, 7 : 5, their hearts melted, and became as w.

1 Sam. 26 : 11, take the cruse of w.

2 Sam. 14 : 14, as w. spilt on the ground.

2 Chr. 18 : 26. bread and w. of affliction.

Job 8 : 11, can the flag grow without w.?

15 : 16, who drinketh iniquity like w.

22 : 7, thou hast not given w. to the weary.

38 : 30, the w. are hid as with a stone.

Ps. 22 : 14, I am poured out like w.

23 : 2, beside the still w.

46 : 3, though the w. roar and be troubled.

63 : 1, a dry and thirsty land, where no w. is.

65 : 9. river of God that is full of w.

77 : 16, the w. saw thee.

79 : 3, blood have they shed like w.

124 : 4, then w. had overwhelmed us.

Prov. 5 : 15, drink w. out of thine own cistern.

20 : 5, counsel is like deep w.

25 : 25, as cold w. to a thirsty soul.

27 : 19, as in w. face answereth to face.

30 : 4, who hath bound the w. in a garment.

Eccl. 11 : 1, cast thy bread upon the w.

Song of Sol. 4 : 15; John 4 : 14, a well of w.

Isa. 1 : 22, thy wine is mixed with w.

3 : 1, Lord doth take away stay of w.

11 : 9; Hab. 2 : 14, as the w. cover the sea.

Isa. 32 : 20, blessed are ye that sow beside all w.

33 : 16, his w. shall be sure.

35 : 6, in wilderness shall w. break out.

43 : 2, when thou passest through the w.

44 : 3, pour w. on him that is thirsty.

55 : 1, come ye to the w.

Jer. 9 : 1, O that my head were w.

Ezek. 7 : 17; 21 : 7, knees be weak as w.

36 : 25, then will I sprinkle clean w. upon you.

Amos 8 : 11, not a famine of bread, nor a thirst for w.

Matt. 10 : 42; Mark 9 : 41, whoso giveth a cup of cold w.

Matt. 27 : 24, Pilate took w. and washed.

Mark 1 : 8; Luke 3 : 16; John 1 : 26, I baptize you with w.

Luke 8 : 23, ship was filled with w.

16 : 24, dip the tip of his finger in w.

John 3 : 5, except a man be born of w.

4 : 15, give me this w.

5 : 3, waiting for moving of the w.

19 : 34, came thereout blood and w.

Acts 10 : 47, can any forbid w.?

Eph. 5 : 26, cleanse it with washing of w.

1 Pet. 3 : 20, eight souls were saved by w.

2 Pet. 2 : 17, wells without w.

1 John 5 : 6, this is he that came by w.

Jude 12, clouds they are without w.

Rev. 22 : 17, let him take the w. of life freely.

Gen. 2 : 10, river to w. the garden.

13 : 10, the plain was well w.

Deut. 11 : 10, **w.** it with thy foot, as a garden.

Ps. 6 : 6, I **w.** my couch with tears.

72 : 6, as showers that **w.** the earth.

104 : 13, he **w.** the hills from his chambers.

Prov. 11 : 25, he that **w.**, shall be **w.**

Isa. 27 : 3, I will **w.** it every moment.

55 : 10, returneth not, but **w.** the earth.

58 : 11; Jer. 31 : 12, thou shalt be like a **w.** garden.

1 Cor. 3 : 6, I have planted, Apollos **w.**

waters of Merom Lake, ten miles north of the sea of Chinnereth, through which the Jordan flows, Josh. 11 : 5, 7.

waters of strife, Ezek. 47 : 19; 48 : 28. See **Meribah.**

Waterpot, John 2 : 6, 7; 4 : 28.

Waterspouts, Ps. 42 : 7.

Watersprings, Ps. 107 : 33, 35.

Wavering, exhortations against, Heb. 10 : 23; Jas. 1 : 6.

Waves, Ps. 42 : 7, all thy **w.** are gone over me.

65 : 7; 89 : 9; 107 : 29, stilleth the **w.**

93 : 4, Lord is mightier than mighty **w.**

Isa. 48 : 18, thy righteousness as **w.** of the sea.

Matt. 8 : 24, ship was covered with **w.**

14 : 24; Mark 4 : 37, tossed with **w.**

Jude 13, raging **w.** of the sea.

Wax, Ps. 22 : 14, my heart is like **w.**

68 : 2, as **w.** melteth, wicked perish.

97 : 5, hills melted like **w.** at presence of Lord.

Mic. 1 : 4, cleft as **w.** before the fire.

Ex. 22 : 24; 32 : 10, my wrath shall **w.** hot.

Num. 11 : 23, is the Lord's hand **w.** short ?

Deut. 8 : 4; 29 : 5; Neh. 9 : 21, raiment **w.** not old.

Deut. 32 : 15, **w.** fat and kicked.

1 Sam. 3 : 2, eyes began to **w.** dim.

Ps. 102 : 26; Isa. 50 : 9; 51 : 6; Heb. 1 : 11, shall **w.** old as a garment.

Matt. 13 : 15; Acts 28 : 27, people's heart **w.** gross.

Matt. 24 : 12, love of many shall **w.** cold.

Luke 12 : 33, bags which **w.** not old.

Way, Gen. 24 : 42, if thou prosper my **w.**

Ex. 13 : 21, pillar of cloud to lead the **w.**

Josh. 23 : 14; 1 Ki. 2 : 2, the **w.** of all the earth.

1 Sam. 12 : 23, I will teach you the good and right **w.**

2 Sam. 22 : 31; Ps. 18 : 30, as for God, his **w.** is perfect.

2 Chr. 6 : 27, when thou hast taught them the good **w.**

Ezra 8 : 21, seek of him a right **w.**

Job 3 : 23, to a man whose **w.** is hid.

12 : 24; Ps. 107 : 40, to wander where there is no **w.**

Job 16 : 22, I go the **w.** whence I shall not return.

22 : 15, hast thou marked the old **w.** ?

23 : 10, he knoweth the **w.** that I take.

38 : 19, where is the **w.** where light dwelleth ?

Ps. 1 : 6, the Lord knoweth the **w.** of the righteous.

2 : 12, lest ye perish from the **w.**

25 : 9, the meek will he teach his **w.**

37 : 5, commit thy **w.** unto the Lord.

39 : 1, I will take heed to my **w.**

49 : 13, this their **w.** is their folly.

67 : 2, that thy **w.** may be known.

78 : 50, he made a **w.** to his anger.

101 : 2, behave wisely in a perfect **w.**

Ps. 119 : 32, I will run the **w.** of thy commandments.

139 : 24, lead me in the **w.** everlasting.

Prov. 2 : 8, Lord preserveth the **w.** of his saints.

3 : 6, in all thy **w.** acknowledge him.

3 : 17, her **w.** are **w.** of pleasantness.

6 : 6, consider her **w.** and be wise.

6 : 23; 15 : 24; Jer. 21 : 8, the **w.** of life.

10 : 29, the **w.** of the Lord is strength.

22 : 6, train up a child in the **w.** he should go.

Eccl. 11 : 5, the **w.** of the spirit.

Isa. 30 : 21, this is the **w.**, walk ye in it.

35 : 8, a **w.**, called The **w.** of holiness.

40 : 3; Luke 3 : 4, prepare the **w.** of the Lord.

Isa. 40 : 27, my **w.** is hid from the Lord.

55 : 8, neither are your **w.** my **w.**

59 : 8; Rom. 3 : 17, the **w.** of peace they know not.

Jer. 6 : 16, where is the good **w.** ?

10 : 23, the **w.** of man is not in himself.

32 : 39, I will give them one heart and one **w.**

50 : 5, they shall ask the **w.** to Zion.

Ezek. 18 : 29, are not my **w.** equal.

Amos 2 : 7, turn aside **w.** of the meek.

Nah. 1 : 3, the Lord hath his **w.** in the whirlwind.

Hag. 1 : 5, consider your **w.**

Mal. 3 : 1, he shall prepare the **w.** before me.

Matt. 7 : 13, broad is the **w.** that leadeth to destruction.

22 : 16; Mark 12 : 14; Luke 20 : 21, teachest the **w.** of God in truth.

Luke 15 : 20, when he was a great **w.** off.

John 10 : 1, but climbeth up some other **w.**

14 : 4, the **w.** ye know.

14 : 6, I am the **w.**, the truth, and the life.

Acts 16 : 17, show unto us the **w.** of salvation.

18 : 26, expounded the **w.** of God more perfectly.

24 : 14, after the **w.** which they call heresy.

Rom. 3 : 12, they are all gone out of the **w.**

11 : 33, his **w.** are past finding out.

1 Cor. 10 : 13, make a **w.** to escape.

12 : 31, a more excellent **w.**

Col. 2 : 14, took handwriting out of **w.**

Heb. 5 : 2, compassion on them out of the **w.**

9 : 8, the **w.** into the holiest.

10 : 20, by a new and living **w.**

2 Pet. 2 : 2, the **w.** of truth be evil spoken of.

2 : 15, have forsaken the right **w.**

Jude 11, they have gone in the **w.** of Cain.

Rev. 15 : 3, just and true are thy **w.**

Weak, in the faith, Rom. 14 : 15; 1 Cor. 8; 1 Thess. 5 : 14; Heb. 12 : 12.

Paul's example, 1 Cor. 9 : 22.

2 Chr. 15 : 7, let not your hands be w.
Job 4 : 3, thou hast strengthened the w. hands.
Ps. 6 : 2, I am w.
Isa. 35 : 3, strengthen ye the w. hands.
Ezek. 7 : 17; 21 : 7, knees w. as water.
Joel 3 : 10, let the w. say, I am strong.
Matt. 26 : 41; Mark 14 : 38, the flesh is w.
Acts 20 : 35, ye ought to support the w.
Rom. 4 : 19, being not w. in faith.
8 : 3, the law was w. through the flesh.
14 : 1, that is w. in the faith.
1 Cor. 1 : 27, w. things to confound the mighty.
11 : 30, for this cause many are w.
2 Cor. 10 : 10, his bodily presence is w.
12 : 10, when I am w. then am I strong.
Gal. 4 : 9, how turn ye to the w. elements ?
See 2 Sam. 3 : 1; Job 12 : 21; Ps. 102 : 23; 1 Pet. 3 : 7.
Weakness, 1 Cor. 1 : 25, the w. of God is stronger than men.
15 : 43, it is sown in w., raised in power.
2 Cor. 12 : 9, strength is made perfect in w.
13 : 4, though he was crucified through w.
Heb. 11 : 34, out of w. were made strong.
Wealth, Deut. 8 : 18, Lord giveth power to get w.
2 Chr. 1 : 11, thou hast not asked w.
Job 21 : 13, they spend their days in w.
31 : 25, if I rejoiced because my w. was great.
Ps. 49 : 6, they that trust in w.
49 : 10, leave w. to others.
112 : 3, w. and riches shall be in his house.
Prov. 10 : 15; 18 : 11, the rich man's w. is his strong city.
13 : 11, w. gotten by vanity.
19 : 4, w. maketh many friends.
Acts 19 : 25, by this craft we have our w. (=welfare), 1 Cor. 10 : 24, seek every man another's w.
Wealthy, Ps. 66 : 12; Jer. 49 : 31.
Weaned, Ps. 131 : 2, as child w. of mother.
Isa. 11 : 8, the w. child put his hand.
28 : 9, them that are w. from milk.
Weapon, Job 20 : 24, he shall flee from iron w.
Isa. 13 : 5; Jer. 50 : 25, the w. of his indignation.
Isa. 54 : 17, no w. formed against thee shall prosper.
Ezek. 9 : 1, with destroying w. in his hand.
2 Cor. 10 : 4, w. of our warfare.
Wearied, Isa. 43 : 24, thou hast w. me with thine iniquities.
47 : 13, w. in multitude of counsels.
57 : 10, art w. in greatness of way.
Jer. 12 : 5, run with footmen, and they w. thee.
Ezek. 24 : 12, she hath w. herself with lies.
Mic. 6 : 3, wherein have I w. thee ?
Mal. 2 : 17, wherein have we w. the Lord ?
John 4 : 6, Jesus, being w., sat on the well.
Heb. 12 : 3, lest ye be w. and faint.
Weariness, Eccl. 12 : 12, much study is a w.
2 Cor. 11 : 27, w. and painfulness.

See Job 7 : 3.
Weary, Gen. 27 : 46, I am w. of my life.
Job 3 : 17, there the w. be at rest.
10 : 1, my soul is w. of life.
22 : 7, not given water to the w. to drink.
Ps. 6 : 6, I am w. with groaning.
Prov. 3 : 11, be not w. of Lord's correction.
25 : 17, lest he be w. of thee.
Isa. 5 : 27, none shall be w. among them.
28 : 12, cause the w. to rest.
32 : 2, as shadow of a great rock in a w. land.
40 : 28, God fainteth not, neither is w.
40 : 31, they shall run, and not be w.
50 : 4, a word in season to him that is w.
Jer. 15 : 6, I am w. of repenting.
20 : 9, I was w. of forbearing.
31 : 25, I have satiated the w. soul.
Gal. 6 : 9; 2 Thess. 3 : 13, let us not be w. in welldoing.
Isa. 7 : 13, will ye w. God also ?
Jer. 9 : 5, they w. themselves to commit iniquity.
Luke 18 : 5, lest by continual coming she w. me.
Weave, Judg. 16 : 13, thou w. the seven locks.
Isa. 19 : 9, they that w. networks.
59 : 5, w. the spider's web.
Weaver, Ex. 35 : 35; Job 7 : 6; Isa. 38 : 12.
Web, Job 8 : 14, trust shall be a spider's w.
Isa. 59 : 5, weave the spider's w.
Wedding, Matt. 22 : 3, them that were bidden to the w.
22 : 11, man had not on a w. garment.
Luke 12 : 36, when he will return from the w.
14 : 8, when thou art bidden to a w.
Wedge, Josh. 7 : 21, a w. of gold.
Isa. 13 : 12, more precious than golden w. of Ophir.
Wedlock, Ezek. 16 : 38.
Weep, Gen. 43 : 30, he sought where to w.
1 Sam. 11 : 5, what aileth the people that they w. ?
30 : 4, no more power to w.
2 Sam. 12 : 21, thou didst w. for the child.
Neh. 8 : 9, mourn not, nor w.
Job 27 : 15, his widows shall not w.
30 : 25, did not I w. for him ?
Eccl. 3 : 4, a time to w.
Isa. 22 : 4, I will w. bitterly.
30 : 19, thou shalt w. no more.
Jer. 9 : 1, that I might w. day and night.
22 : 10, w. not for the dead.
Joel 1 : 5, awake, ye drunkards, and w.
Mic. 1 : 10, declare it not, w. not.
Mark 5 : 39, why make ye this ado, and w. ?
Luke 6 : 21, blessed are ye that w. now.
7 : 13; 8 : 52; Rev. 5 : 5, w. not.
John 11 : 31, she goeth to the grave to w. there.
16 : 20, ye shall w., but the world shall rejoice.
Acts 21 : 13, what mean ye to w. ?
Rom. 12 : 15, w. with them that w.
Jas. 4 : 9, be afflicted, mourn, and w.
Weeping, for the dead, etc., Gen. 23 : 2; 2 Sam. 1 : 24; Eccl. 3 : 4; Jer. 9 : 17;

Ezek. 24 : 16; Amos 5 : 16; John 11 : 35; 20 : 13; 1 Thess. 4 : 13.

none in heaven, Rev. 21 : 4.

2 Sam. 15 : 30, w. as they went.

Ezra 3 : 13, could not discern noise of joy from w.

Job 16 : 16, my face is foul with w.

Ps. 30 : 5, w. may endure for a night.

Isa. 65 : 19, voice of w. be no more heard.

Jer. 31 : 16, refrain thy voice from w. 48 : 5, continual w. shall go up.

Joel 2 : 12, turn with fasting and w.

Matt. 24 : 51; 25 : 30; Luke 13 : 28, there shall be w.

Luke 7 : 38, stood at his feet behind him w.

John 20 : 11, Mary stood at sepulchre w.

Acts 9 : 39, widows stood by w.

Phil. 3 : 18, now tell you even w.

See Ps. 6 : 8; Matt. 8 : 12; 22 : 13; Luke 7 : 38; 1 Cor. 7 : 30.

Weigh, Job 6 : 2, oh, that my grief were throughly w. 31 : 6, let me be w. in an even balance.

Prov. 16 : 2, the Lord w. the spirits.

Isa. 26 : 7, thou dost w. the path of the just. 40 : 12, who hath w. the mountains ?

Dan. 5 : 27, thou art w. in the balances.

Zech. 11 : 12, they w. the thirty pieces of silver.

Weights, table of. The following table shows the modern equivalent for the more important of the ancient Jewish weights:—

| | Troy Weight | | |
	lbs.	oz.	dwts.	grs.
1 Gerah	0	0	0	12.65
1 Bekah (10 gerahs)	0	0	5	6.5
1 Shekel (2 bekahs)	0	0	10	13
1 Maneh or mina (60 shekels)	2	7	12	12
1 Talent [kikkar] (60 manehs), i.e., weight-talent " of the king "	158	1	10	0

Weights, just, commanded, Lev. 19 : 35; Deut. 25 : 13; Prov. 11 : 1; 20 : 10, 23; Ezek. 45 : 10; Mic. 6 : 10.

Deut. 25 : 15, thou shalt have just w.

Job 28 : 25, to make the w. for the winds.

Prov. 16 : 11, a just w. and balance are the Lord's.

Ezek. 4 : 16, they shall eat bread by w.

2 Cor. 4 : 17, a more exceeding w. of glory.

Heb. 12 : 1, let us lay aside every w.

Well, of Bethlehem, 1 Chr. 11 : 17.

wells, of Abraham, Gen. 26 : 15; Isaac, Gen. 26 : 25; Uzziah, 2 Chr. 26 : 10; Jacob, John 4 : 6.

Num. 21 : 17, spring up, O w.

2 Sam. 23 : 15; 1 Chr. 11 : 17, water of w. of Bethlehem.

Ps. 84 : 6, passing through valley of Baca make it a w.

Prov. 5 : 15, waters of thine own w. 10 : 11, mouth of righteous man is a w. of life.

Song of Sol. 4 : 15; John 4 : 14, w. of living water.

Isa. 12 : 3, the w. of salvation.

2 Pet. 2 : 17, w. without water.

Gen. 4 : 7, if thou doest w. 29 : 6, is he w. ?

Ex. 4 : 14, I know he can speak w.

Deut. 4 : 40; 5 : 16; 6 : 3; 12 : 25; 19 : 13; 22 : 7; Ruth 3 : 1; Eph. 6 : 3, that it may go w. with thee.

Ps. 49 : 18, when thou doest w. to thyself.

Eccl. 8 : 12, it shall be w. with them that fear God.

Isa. 3 : 10, say to the righteous that it shall be w. with him.

Jonah 4 : 4, doest thou w. to be angry ?

Matt. 25 : 21; Luke 19 : 17, w. done, good servant.

Luke 6 : 26, when all men speak w. of you. 20 : 39; John 4 : 17, thou hast w. said.

1 Tim. 5 : 17, elders that rule w.

Wellbeloved, Isa. 5 : 1; Mark 12 : 6.

Wellpleasing, Phil. 4 : 18, w. to God.

Heb. 13 : 21, w. in his sight.

Wellspring, Prov. 16 : 22; 18 : 4.

Wench, maidservant, 2 Sam. 17 : 17.

Wept, Ezra 10 : 1; Neh. 8 : 9, the people w. very sore.

Neh. 1 : 4, I w. before God.

Ps. 137 : 1, by rivers of Babylon we w.

Luke 7 : 32, we mourned, ye have not w. 19 : 41, he beheld the city, and w. over it.

John 11 : 35, Jesus w.

1 Cor. 7 : 30, they that weep, as though they w. not.

Wet, Job 24 : 8; Dan. 4 : 15.

Whale [Heb., " tannin "], mentioned, Gen. 1 : 21; Job 7 : 12; Ezek. 32 : 2.

Jonah swallowed by one, Jonah 1 : 17; Matt. 12 : 40. (R.V., marg., " sea-monster,")

Whatsoever, Matt. 7 : 12, w. ye would that men.

Matt. 20 : 4, w. is right I will give.

John 14 : 13, w. ye shall ask.

1 Cor. 10 : 31, w. ye do, do all.

Phil. 4 : 8, w. things are true.

Wheat, parable concerning, Matt. 13 : 25.

Judg. 15 : 1; Ruth 2 : 23; 1 Sam. 12 : 17, w. harvest.

Ezra 7 : 22; Luke 16 : 7, an hundred measures of w.

Job 31 : 40, let thistles grow instead of w.

Ps. 81 : 16; 147 : 14, the finest of the w.

Jer. 12 : 13, they have sown w., but reap thorns. 23 : 28, what is the chaff to the w. ?

Joel 2 : 24, floors shall be full of w.

Amos 8 : 6, sell refuse of w.

Matt. 3 : 12; Luke 3 : 17, gather his w.

Matt. 13 : 25, enemy sowed tares among the w.

Luke 22 : 31, sift you as w.

John 12 : 24, except corn of w. fall into ground.

1 Cor. 15 : 37, may chance of w.

Rev. 6 : 6, measure of w. for a penny.

See Ex. 29 : 2; 1 Ki. 5 : 11; Ezek. 27 : 17.

Wheels, vision of, Ezek. 1 : 15; 3 : 13; 10 : 9.

Ex. 14 : 25, took off their chariot w.

Judg. 5 : 28, why tarry the **w.** of his chariots ?

Ps. 83 : 13, make them like a **w.**

Prov. 20 : 26, king bringeth the **w.** over them.

Eccl. 12 : 6, or the **w.** broken at the cistern.

Isa. 28 : 28, nor break it with the **w.** of his cart.

Jer. 47 : 3, at the rumbling of his **w.**

Nah. 3 : 2, noise of rattling of the **w.**

Whelps, lions', parable of, Ezek. 19 : 1-9; Nah. 2 : 12.

Whip, 1 Ki. 12 : 11, chastised you with **w.**

Prov. 26 : 3, a **w.** for the horse.

Nah. 3 : 2, noise of a **w.**

Whirlwinds, 2 Ki. 2 : 1; Job 37 : 9; 38 : 1; Isa. 66 : 15; Jer. 23 : 19; Ezek. 1 : 4; Nah. 1 : 3; Zech. 9 : 14.

Whisper, 2 Sam. 12 : 19, David saw servants **w.**

Ps. 41 : 7, all that hate me **w.**

Isa. 29 : 4, thy speech **w.** out of dust.

Whispering, Prov. 16 : 28; 26 : 20; Rom. 1 : 29; 2 Cor. 12 : 20.

White, horse, Rev. 6 : 2; 19 : 11.

cloud, Rev. 14 : 14.

throne, Rev. 20 : 11.

raiment, of Christ at the transfiguration, Matt. 17 : 2; Mark 9 : 3; Luke 9 : 29; of angels, Matt. 28 : 3; Mark 16 : 5; of the redeemed, Rev. 3 : 5; 4 : 4; 7 : 9; 19 : 8, 14.

Gen. 49 : 12, his teeth be **w.** with milk.

Job 6 : 6, is there any taste in the **w.** of an egg ?

Eccl. 9 : 8, let thy garments be always **w.**

Song of Sol. 5 : 10, my beloved is **w.** and ruddy.

Isa. 1 : 18, sins shall be **w.** as snow.

Dan. 12 : 10, many shall be purified and made **w.**

Matt. 5 : 36, canst not make one hair **w.** or black.

John 4 : 35, fields are **w.** to harvest.

Rev. 2 : 17, a **w.** stone.

3 : 4, shall walk with me in **w.**

Whited, Matt. 23 : 27; Acts 23 : 3.

Whiter, Ps. 51 : 7; Lam. 4 : 7.

Whole, made, Matt. 12 : 13; Mark 3 : 5; Luke 6 : 10. See **Miracles.**

2 Sam. 1 : 9, my life is yet **w.** in me.

Matt. 9 : 12, the **w.** need not a physician.

Mark 2 : 17; Luke 5 : 31, **w.** have no need of physician.

Mark 5 : 34; Luke 8 : 48; 17 : 19, faith hath made thee **w.**

John 5 : 6, wilt thou be made **w.** ?

Acts 9 : 34, Jesus Christ maketh thee **w.**

1 Cor. 12 : 17, if the **w.** body were an eye.

Whomsoever, Luke 4 : 6; 12 : 48; John 13 : 20; Acts 8 : 19.

Whore, vision of the great, Rev. 17.

Whoredom, condemned, Lev. 19 : 20; Deut. 22 : 21; 23 : 17.

spiritual, Ezek. 16 : 23; Jer. 3; Hos. 1; 2.

Whoremongers, condemned, Eph. 5 : 5; 1 Tim. 1 : 10; Heb. 13 : 4; Rev. 21 : 8; 22 : 15.

Whosoever, Lev. 22 : 21, **w.** offereth a sacrifice of peace.

24 : 15, **w.** curseth his God shall bear his.

Deut. 18 : 19, **w.** will not hearken unto my words.

Josh. 1 : 18, **w.** doth rebel against thy commandments.

Ezra 6 : 11, **w.** shall alter this word, let him.

Dan. 5 : 7, **w.** shall read this writing.

Matt. 5 : 22, **w.** is angry with his brother.

5 : 28, **w.** looketh on a woman to lust.

5 : 39, **w.** shall smite thee on the right.

5 : 41, **w.** shall compel thee to go a mile.

10 : 33, **w.** deny me before men.

12 : 50, **w.** shall do the will of my Father.

18 : 4, **w.** therefore shall humble himself.

Mark 8 : 34, **w.** will come after me, let him.

Luke 9 : 5, **w.** will not receive you, when ye.

12 : 8, **w.** shall confess me before men.

14 : 14, **w.** exalteth himself shall be abased.

14 : 27, **w.** doth not bear his cross.

John 4 : 13, **w.** drinketh of this water shall thirst.

11 : 26, **w.** liveth and believeth in me.

Acts 2 : 21, **w.** shall call on the name of the.

Rom. 2 : 1, thou art inexcusable **w.** thou art.

10 : 11, **w.** believeth on him shall not be.

10 : 13, **w.** shall call upon his name.

1 John 5 : 1, **w.** believeth that Jesus is the Christ.

5 : 18, **w.** is born of God sinneth not.

Rev. 20 : 15, **w.** was not found written in the book of life.

22 : 15, and **w.** loveth and maketh a lie.

Wicked, their character and punishment, Deut. 32 : 5; Job 5; 15; 18; 20 : 21; 24; 27 : 13; 30; 36 : 12; Eccl. 8 : 10; Isa. 1 : 22; 28; 29; 37 : 21; 44 : 9; 45 : 9; 47; 57–59; 66; Jer. 2; Ezek. 5; 16; Hos. to Mal.; Matt. 5–7; 13 : 37; 15; 16; 21 : 33; 25; John 5 : 29; 10; Rom. 1 : 21; 3 : 10; 1 Cor. 5 : 11; Gal. 5 : 19; Eph. 4 : 17; 5 : 5; Phil. 3 : 18; Col. 3 : 6; 2 Thess. 2; 1 Tim. 1 : 9; 4; 6 : 9; 2 Tim. 3 : 13; Titus 1 : 10; Heb. 6 : 4; Jas. 4 : 5; 1 Pet. 4; 2 Pet. 2 : 3; 1 John 2 : 18; 4; Jude; Rev. 9 : 20; 14 : 18; 18; 20 : 13; 22 : 15.

their prosperity not to be envied, Ps. 37 : 1; 73; Prov. 3 : 31; 23 : 17; 24 : 1, 19; Jer. 12.

friendship with, forbidden, Gen. 28 : 1; Ex. 23 : 32; 34 : 12; Num. 16 : 26; Deut. 7 : 2; 13 : 6; Josh. 23 : 7; Judg. 2 : 2; 2 Chr. 19 : 2; Ezra 9 : 12; 10 : 10; Prov. 1 : 10; 4 : 14; 12 : 11; 14 : 7; Jer. 2 : 25; 51 : 6; Rom. 16 : 17; 1 Cor. 5 : 9; 15 : 33; 2 Cor. 6 : 14; Eph. 5 : 7, 11; Phil. 2 : 15; 2 Thess. 3 : 6; 1 Tim. 6 : 5; 2 Tim. 3 : 5; 2 Pet. 3 : 17; Rev. 18 : 4.

Gen. 18 : 23, destroy righteous with **w.**

Ex. 23 : 7, I will not justify the **w.**

Deut. 15 : 9, a thought in thy **w.** heart.

1 Sam. 2 : 9, the **w.** shall be silent in darkness.

Job 3 : 17, there the **w.** cease from troubling.

8 : 22, dwelling place of the **w.** shall come to nought.

21 : 7, wherefore do the **w.** live ?

34 : 18, is it fit to say to a king, Thou art **w.** ?

Ps. 7 : 11, God is angry with the **w.**

9 : 17, the **w.** shall be turned into hell.

10 : 4, the **w.** will not seek God.

11 : 6, upon the **w.** he shall rain snares.

34 : 21, evil shall slay the **w.**

37 : 35, I have seen the **w.** in great power.

58 : 3, the **w.** are estranged from the womb.

94 : 3, how long shall the **w.** triumph ?

119 : 155, salvation is far from the **w.**

139 : 24, see if there be any **w.** way in me.

145 : 20, all the **w.** will he destroy.

Prov. 11 : 5, **w.** shall fall by his own wickedness.

11 : 21, the **w.** shall not be unpunished.

15 : 29, the Lord is far from the **w.**

28 : 1, the **w.** flee when no man pursueth.

Eccl. 7 : 17, be not over much **w.**

Isa. 53 : 9, he made his grave with the **w.**

55 : 7, let the **w.** forsake his way.

57 : 20, the **w.** are like the troubled sea.

Jer. 17 : 9, the heart is desperately **w.**

Ezek. 3 : 18; 33 : 8, to warn the **w.**

18 : 23, have I any pleasure that the **w.** should die ?

Dan. 12 : 10, the **w.** shall do wickedly.

Nah. 1 : 3, the Lord will not acquit the **w.**

Matt. 13 : 49, sever the **w.** from the just.

Acts 2 : 23, by **w.** hands have slain him.

Eph. 6 : 16, the fiery darts of the **w.**

Col. 1 : 21, enemies by **w.** works.

2 Thess. 2 : 8, then shall that **W.** be revealed.

Wickedly, Job 13 : 7, will you speak **w.** for God ?

34 : 12, surely God will not do **w.**

Ps. 73 : 8; 139 : 20, they speak **w.**

74 : 3, the enemy hath done **w.**

Mal. 4 : 1, all that do **w.**

Wickedness, Gen. 6 : 5, God saw **w.** was great.

39 : 9, this great **w.**

1 Sam. 24 : 13, **w.** proceedeth from the wicked.

Job 4 : 8, they that sow **w.** reap the same.

20 : 12, though **w.** be sweet.

22 : 5, is not thy **w.** great ?

Ps. 55 : 15, **w.** is in their dwellings.

84 : 10, than to dwell in tents of **w.**

Prov. 4 : 17, they eat the bread of **w.**

8 : 7, **w.** is abomination to my lips.

10 : 2, treasures of **w.** profit nothing.

13 : 6, **w.** overthroweth the sinner.

Eccl. 7 : 25, the **w.** of folly.

8 : 8, neither shall **w.** deliver.

Isa. 9 : 18, **w.** burneth as the fire.

58 : 6, to loose the bands of **w.**

Jer. 2 : 19, thine own **w.** shall correct thee.

8 : 6, no man repented of his **w.**

14 : 20, we acknowledge our **w.**

Ezek. 3 : 19, if he turn not from his **w.**

33 : 12, in the day that he turneth from his **w.**

Hos. 9 : 15, for the **w.** of their doings.

10 : 13, ye have plowed **w.**

Mic. 6 : 10, treasures of **w.** in house of wicked.

Mark 7 : 22, out of the heart proceed **w.**

Luke 11 : 39, inward part is full of **w.**

Acts 8 : 22, repent of this thy **w.**

Rom. 1 : 29, being filled with all **w.**

1 Cor. 5 : 8, the leaven of **w.**

Eph. 6 : 12, spiritual **w.** in high places.

1 John 5 : 19, whole world lieth in **w.**

Widow, Elijah sustained by, 1 Ki. 17.

parable of the importunate, Luke 18 : 3.

the widow's mite, Mark 12 : 42; Luke 21 : 2.

figurative, Isa. 47 : 9; 54 : 4; Lam. 1 : 1.

widows, to be honoured, and relieved, Ex. 22 : 22; Deut. 14 : 29; 24 : 17; Job 29 : 13; Isa. 1 : 17; Jer. 7 : 6; Acts 6 : 1; 9 : 39; 1 Tim. 5 : 3; Jas. 1 : 27.

especially under God's protection, Deut. 10 : 18; Ps. 68 : 5; 146 : 9; Prov. 15 : 25; Jer. 49 : 11.

injurers of, condemned, Deut. 27 : 19; Ps. 94 : 6; Isa. 1 : 23; 10 : 2; Ezek. 22 : 7; Mal. 3 : 5; Matt. 23 : 14; Mark 12 : 40; Luke 20 : 47.

laws relating to their marriages, Lev. 21 : 14; Deut. 25 : 5; Ezek. 44 : 22; Mark 12 : 19.

See 1 Cor. 7 : 8.

Wife, a type of the church, Eph. 5 : 23; Rev. 19 : 7; 21 : 9.

wives, their duties to husbands, Gen. 3 : 16; Ex. 20 : 14; Rom. 7 : 2; 1 Cor. 7 : 3; 14 : 34; Eph. 5 : 22, 33; Titus 2 : 4; 1 Pet. 3 : 1.

good, characterised, Prov. 12 : 4; 18 : 22; 19 : 14; 31 : 10.

Levitical laws concerning, Ex. 21 : 3, 22; 22 : 16; Num. 5 : 12; 30; Deut. 21 : 10, 15; 24 : 1; Jer. 3 : 1; Matt. 19 : 3.

Prov. 5 : 18; Eccl. 9 : 9, the **w.** of thy youth.

Prov. 18 : 22, whoso findeth a **w.** findeth a good thing.

19 : 14, a prudent **w.** is from the Lord.

Hos. 12 : 12, Israel served for a **w.**

Luke 17 : 32, remember Lot's **w.**

1 Cor. 7 : 14, the unbelieving **w.** is sanctified.

Eph. 5 : 23, the husband is the head of the **w.**

1 Pet. 3 : 7, giving honour unto the **w.**

Rev. 21 : 9, the bride, the Lamb's **w.**

Wilderness, the Israelites' journeys in, Ex. 14; Num. 10 : 12; 13 : 3; 20; 33; Deut. 1 : 19; 8 : 2; 32 : 10; Neh. 9 : 19; Ps. 29 : 8; 78 : 40; 107 : 4.

Hagar's flight into, Gen. 16 : 7.

Elijah's flight into, 1 Ki. 19 : 4.

John the Baptist preaches in the wilderness of Judæa, Matt. 3.

Ps. 95 : 8, day of temptation in the **w.**

Isa. 35 : 1 the **w.** shall be glad.

Matt. 3 : 3; Mark 1 : 3; Luke 3 : 4; John 1 : 23, voice of one crying in the w.

Wiles, Num. 25 : 18, they vex you with w.

Eph. 6 : 11, able to stand against w. of devil.

Wilfully, Heb. 10 : 26.

Will, of God, irresistible, Dan. 4 : 17, 35; Rom. 9 : 19; Eph. 1 : 5; Jas. 1 : 18.

fulfilled by Christ, Mark 14 : 36; John 5 : 30; Heb. 10 : 7.

how performed, John 7 : 17; Eph. 6 : 6; Col. 4 : 12; 1 Thess. 5 : 18; Heb. 13 : 21; 1 Pet. 2 : 15; 4 : 2; 1 John 2 : 17; 3 : 23.

to be submitted to, Jas. 4 : 15.

of man, Rom. 9 : 16; Eph. 2 : 3; 1 Pet. 4 : 3.

Deut. 33 : 16, the good w. of him that dwelt in the bush.

Ps. 40 : 8, I delight to do thy w., O God.

Matt. 6 : 10; Luke 11 : 2, thy w. be done in earth, as in heaven.

Matt. 7 : 21; 12 : 50, doth the w. of my Father.

18 : 14, it is not the w. of your Father.

26 : 42, thy w. be done.

Luke 2 : 14, good w. toward men.

John 1 : 13, born not of the w. of the flesh.

4 : 34, to do the w. of him that sent me.

6 : 39, this is the Father's w.

Acts 21 : 14, the w. of the Lord be done.

Eph. 5 : 17, what the w. of the Lord is.

6 : 7, good w. doing service.

Rom. 7 : 18, to w. is present with me.

Phil. 2 : 13, both to w. and to do.

Rev. 22 : 17, whosoever w., let him take.

See Rom. 1 : 10; 15 : 32.

Willing, Ex. 35 : 5, whosoever is of a w. heart.

1 Chr. 28 : 9, serve God with a w. mind.

Ps. 110 : 3, people shall be w. in day of thy power.

Matt. 26 : 41, the spirit is w.

Luke 22 : 42, if thou be w., remove this cup.

John 5 : 35, ye were w. for a season to rejoice.

Rom. 9 : 22, if God, w. to show wrath.

2 Cor. 5 : 8, w. rather to be absent.

8 : 12, if there be first a w. mind.

1 Tim. 6 : 18, w. to communicate.

2 Pet. 3 : 9, not w. that any should perish.

Willingly, Judg. 5 : 2, 9, people w. offered themselves.

Lam. 3 : 33, Lord doth not afflict w.

Rom. 8 : 20, creature was made subject to vanity, not w.

Philem. 14; 1 Pet. 5 : 2, not as of necessity, but w.

2 Pet. 3 : 5, they w. are ignorant.

Willow, occurs only in Ezek. 17 : 5.

Win, 2 Chr. 32 : 1, he thought to w. them.

Prov. 11 : 30, he that w. souls is wise.

Phil. 3 : 8, that I may w. Christ.

Wind, miraculous effects of, Gen. 8 : 1; Ex. 15 : 10; Num. 11 : 31; Jonah 1 : 4.

rebuked by Christ, Matt. 8 : 26.

figuratively mentioned, Job 7 : 7; 8 : 2; John 3 : 8; Jas. 3 : 4.

Job 6 : 26, speeches which are as w.

Ps. 147 : 18, he causeth his w. to blow.

Prov. 11 : 29, he shall inherit w.

25 : 23, north w. driveth away rain.

30 : 4, who hath gathered the w. in his fists ?

Eccl. 11 : 4, he that observeth the w.

Isa. 7 : 2, as trees are moved with w.

26 : 18, as it were brought forth w.

27 : 8, he stayeth his rough w.

32 : 2, a hiding place from the w.

Jer. 10 : 13; 51 : 16, bringeth w. out of his treasures.

Ezek. 37 : 7, prophesy to the w.

Hos. 8 : 7, they have sown w.

12 : 1, feedeth on w.

Amos 4 : 13, he that createth the w.

Matt. 11 : 7; Luke 7 : 24, a reed shaken with the w.

Eph. 4 : 14, carried about with every w. of doctrine.

Jas. 1 : 6, like wave driven with the w.

Windows, Gen. 7 : 11, w. of heaven were opened.

2 Ki. 7 : 2, 19, if the Lord make w. in heaven.

Eccl. 12 : 3, they that look out of w. be darkened.

Isa. 60 : 8, fly as doves to their w.

Jer. 9 : 21, death is come into our w.

Mal. 3 : 10, if I will not open w. of heaven.

Wine, made by Noah, Gen. 9 : 20.

used by Abram and Melchizedek, Gen. 14 : 18.

employed in offerings, Ex. 29 : 40; Lev. 23 : 13; Num. 15 : 5.

in the Lord's Supper, Matt. 26 : 29.

forbidden to the Nazarites, Num. 6 : 3; Judg. 13 : 14.

Rechabites abstain from, Jer. 35.

water changed to, by Christ, John 2.

love of, Prov. 21 : 17; 23 : 20, 30; Hos. 4 : 11.

its lawful use, Judg. 9 : 13; 19 : 19; Prov. 31 : 6; Eccl. 10 : 19.

Ps. 104 : 15, w. that maketh glad the heart.

Prov. 20 : 1, w. is a mocker.

23 : 31, look not on w. when it is red.

Isa. 5 : 11, till w. inflame them.

25 : 6, w. on the lees well refined.

28 : 7, they have erred through w.

55 : 1, buy w. and milk.

Hos. 3 : 1, love flagons of w.

Hab. 2 : 5, he transgresseth by w.

Eph. 5 : 18, be not drunk with w.

1 Tim. 3 : 3; Titus 1 : 7; 2 : 3, not given to w.

5 : 23, use w. for stomach's sake.

1 Pet. 4 : 3, walked in excess of w.

    While the Biblical references to the use of wine are, on the whole, contradictory, it is certainly true to say that its abuse is condemned universally both in the Old and New Testaments.

Winebibber, Prov. 23 : 20; Matt. 11 : 19.

Winefat, Isa. 63 : 2; Mark 12 : 1.

Winepress, of the wrath of God, Rev. 14 : 19; 19 : 15.

See Isa. 5 : 2; 62 : 3; Lam. 1 : 15; Matt. 21 : 33.

Wings, Ex. 19 : 4, bare you on eagles' w.

396

Ps. 17 : 8; 36 : 7; 57 : 1; 61 : 4; 91 : 4, the shadow of thy **w.**
18 : 10; 104 : 3, **w.** of the wind.
55 : 6, oh that I had **w.** like a dove.
139 : 9, **w.** of the morning.
Prov. 23 : 5, riches make themselves **w.**
Isa. 40 : 31, mount with **w.** as eagles.
Mal. 4 : 2, with healing in his **w.**
Matt. 23 : 37; Luke 13 : 34, as a hen gathereth chickens under **w.**
Winnow, Ruth 3 : 2; Isa. 30 : 24.
Winter, Gen. 8 : 22, **w.** shall not cease.
Ps. 74 : 17, hast made summer and **w.**
Song of Sol. 2 : 11, lo, the **w.** is past.
Matt. 24 : 20; Mark 13 : 18, pray that your flight be not in **w.**
1 Cor. 16 : 6, I will **w.** with you.
Wisdom, given by God, Ex. 31 : 3; 1 Ki. 3 : 12; 4 : 29; 1 Chr. 22 : 12; 2 Chr. 1 : 10; Ezra 7 : 25; Prov. 2 : 6; Eccl. 2 : 26; Dan. 2 : 20; Acts 6 : 10; 7 : 10; 2 Pet. 3 : 15.
 characterised, Ps. 111 : 10; Prov. 1 : 2; 9; 14 : 8; 24 : 7; 28 : 7; Eccl. 2 : 13; 7 : 19; 9 : 13; Matt. 7 : 24; Jas. 3 : 13.
 acquisition of, Rom. 16 : 19; Eph. 5 : 15.
 blessings attending, Prov. 3 : 13; 8 : 11; 24 : 3, 14; Eccl. 7 : 11; 9 : 13; 12 : 11; Matt. 25 : 1.
 obtained in answer to prayer by Solomon, etc., 1 Ki. 3 : 9; 10 : 6; Prov. 2 : 3; Dan. 2 : 21.
 personified, Prov. 1 : 20; 8; 9.
 danger of despising, Prov. 1 : 24; 2 : 12; 3 : 21; 5 : 12; 8 : 36; 10 : 21; 11 : 12.
 apparent in the works of God, Ps. 104 : 1, 24; 136 : 5; Prov. 3 : 19; 6 : 6; Jer. 10 : 12; Rom. 1 . 20; 11 : 33.
 of Joseph, Gen. 41 : 33; 47 : 13; Solomon, 1 Ki. 4 : 29; Daniel, Ezek. 28 : 3; Dan. 1 : 17; 5 : 14.
 worldly, vanity of, Isa. 5 : 21; Zech. 9 : 2; Matt. 11 : 25; 1 Cor. 2 : 4; 2 Cor. 1 : 12; Jas. 3 : 15.
Deut. 4 . 6, this is your **w.**
Job 4 : 21, they die without **w.**
28 : 12, where shall **w.** be found ?
Ps. 90 : 12, apply our hearts to **w.**
Prov. 4 : 5, get **w.**, get understanding.
4 : 7, is the principal thing.
16 : 16, better to get **w.** than gold.
19 : 8. he that getteth **w.** loveth his own soul.
23 : 4, cease from thine own **w.**
Eccl. 1 : 18, in much **w.** is much grief.
9 : 10, there is no **w.** in the grave.
Isa. 10 : 13, by my **w.** I have done it.
29 : 14, the **w.** of their wise men shall perish.
33 : 6, **w.** shall be the stability of thy times.
Jer. 51 : 15, established the world by **w.**
Matt. 11 : 19, **w.** is justified of her children.
13 : 54, whence hath this man **w.** ?
Luke 2 : 52, Jesus increased in **w.** and stature.
1 Cor. 1 : 17, not with **w.** of words.
1 : 21, world by **w.** knew not God.
1 : 24, Christ, the **w.** of God.

3 : 19, the **w.** of this world is foolishness with God.
Eph. 3 : 10, the manifold **w.** of God.
Col. 1 : 9, that ye might be filled with all **w.**
4 : 5, walk in **w.** toward them that are without.
Jas. 1 : 5, if any lack **w.**
3 : 17, **w.** from above is pure.
Rev. 5 : 12, worthy is the Lamb to receive **w.**
13 : 18, here is **w.**
Wise, Gen. 3 : 6, a tree to make one **w.**
Ex. 23 : 8; Deut. 16 : 19, the gift blindeth the **w.**
Deut. 32 : 29, oh that they were **w.**
Job 5 : 13, taketh the **w.** in their own craftiness.
11 : 12, vain man would be **w.**
32 : 9, great men are not always **w.**
37 : 24, he respecteth not any **w.** of heart.
Ps. 2 : 10, be **w.** now, O kings.
19 : 7, making **w.** the simple.
94 : 8, ye fools, when will ye be **w.** ?
107 : 43, whoso is **w.**, and will observe.
Prov. 1 : 5, a **w.** man shall attain **w.** counsels.
3 : 7, be not **w.** in thine own eyes.
3 : 35, the **w.** shall inherit glory.
9 : 12, thou shalt be **w.** for thyself.
11 : 30, he that winneth souls is **w.**
13 : 20, he that walketh with **w.** men shall be **w.**
20 : 1, whosoever is deceived thereby is not **w.**
26 : 12, a man **w.** in his own conceit.
Eccl. 6 : 8, what hath the **w.** more than the fool ?
7 : 4, heart of **w.** is in house of mourning.
9 : 1, the **w.** are in the hand of God.
12 : 11, the words of the **w.** are as goads.
Isa. 5 : 21, woe unto them that are **w.** in their own eyes.
Jer. 4 : 22, they are **w.** to do evil.
Dan. 12 : 3, they that be **w.** shall shine.
Matt. 10 : 16, be ye **w.** as serpents.
11 : 25, thou hast hid these things from the **w.**
Rom. 1 : 22, professing themselves to be **w.**
12 : 16, be not **w.** in your own conceits.
1 Cor. 1 : 20, where is the **w.** ?
3 : 20, Lord knoweth thoughts of the **w.**
4 : 10, ye are **w.** in Christ.
2 Tim. 3 : 15, to make **w.** unto salvation.
Wise men, Matt. 2 : 1, 2.
Wisely, Ps. 58 : 5, charmers, charming never so **w.**
101 : 2, I will behave myself **w.**
Prov. 16 : 20, handleth a matter **w.**
Eccl. 7 : 10, thou dost not enquire **w.**
Luke 16 : 8, because he had done **w.**
Wiser, 1 Ki. 4 : 31, Solomon was **w.** than all men.
Prov. 9 : 9. he will be yet **w.**
Luke 16 : 8, in their generation **w.** than children of light.
1 Cor. 1 : 25, foolishness of God is **w.** than men.
Wish, Ps. 73 : 7, more than heart could **w.**
Rom. 9 : 3, could **w.** myself accursed.
2 Cor. 13 : 9, we **w.** even your perfection.
3 John 2 : 1, I **w.** that thou mayest prosper.

Wist [knew], Judg. 16 : 20; Mark 9 : 6; Luke 2 : 49.

Witch, of Endor, 1 Sam. 28.

Witchcraft, forbidden, Ex. 22 : 18; Lev. 19 : 26, 31; 20 : 6, 27; Deut. 18 : 10; Mic. 5 : 12; Mal. 3 : 5; Gal. 5 : 20; Rev. 21 : 8; 22 : 15.

abolished by Josiah, 2 Ki. 23 : 24.

practised by Saul, 1 Sam. 28; Manasseh, 2 Ki. 21 : 6; 2 Chr. 33 : 6; Israelites, 2 Ki. 17 : 17; Simon of Samaria, Acts 8 : 9; Philippians, Acts 16 : 16; Ephesians, Acts 19 : 19.

Withdraw, Job 9 : 13, if God will not w. his anger.

Job 33 : 17, that he may w. man from his purpose.

Isa. 60 : 20, neither shall thy moon w. itself.

2 Thess. 3 : 6, w. from brother that walketh disorderly.

Wither, Ps. 1 : 3, his leaf shall not w.

37 : 2, they shall w. as the green herb.

90 : 6, it is cut down, and w.

Isa. 40 : 7; 1 Pet. 1 : 24, the grass w.

Matt. 13 : 6; Mark 4 : 6, having no root w.

Matt. 21 : 19; Mark 11 : 21, the fig tree w. away.

John 15 : 6, cast forth as a branch, and is w.

Jude 12, trees whose fruit w.

Withered hand, of Jeroboam healed, 1 Ki. 13.

healed by Christ, Matt. 12 : 10; Mark 3; Luke 6 : 6.

Withhold, Ps. 40 : 11, w. not thy mercies.

84 : 11, no good thing will he w.

Prov. 3 : 27, w. not good from them to whom it is due.

23 : 13, w. not correction from the child.

Eccl. 11 : 6, w. not thy hand.

Withstand, 2 Chr. 20 : 6, none able to w. thee.

Eccl. 4 : 12, two shall w. him.

Acts 11 : 17, what was I, that I could w. God ?

Eph. 6 : 13, able to w. in the evil day.

Witness, God invoked as, Gen. 31 : 50; Judg. 11 : 10; 1 Sam. 12 : 5; Mic. 1 : 2; Rom. 1 : 9; 1 Thess. 2 : 5.

borne to Christ, by the Father, Matt. 3 : 16; Luke 3 : 22; John 12 : 28; Heb. 2 : 4; 1 John 5 : 7.

by the Holy Ghost, Matt. 3 : 16; Luke 3 : 22; John 1 : 33; 15 : 26; Acts 5 : 32; 20 : 23; Heb. 10 : 15; 1 John 5 : 7.

by the apostles, Acts 1 : 8; 2 : 32; 4 : 33; 5 : 32, 10 : 41; 22 : 15; 26 : 16; 1 Pet. 5 : 1; Rev. 20 : 4.

by the prophets, Acts 10 : 43; 1 Pet. 1 : 10.

Christ the faithful and true, Rev. 1 : 5; 3 : 14.

false, Ex. 20 : 16; 23 : 1; Lev. 19 : 11; Deut. 5 : 20; 19 : 16; Prov. 6 : 16, 19; 12 : 17; 19 : 5, 9, 28; 21 : 28; 25 : 18; Jer. 7 : 9; Zech. 5 : 4; Luke 3 : 14.

against Christ, Matt. 26 : 60; Mark 14 : 56.

witnesses, two or three required, Num. 35 : 30; Deut. 17 : 6; 19 : 15; Matt. 18 : 16; 2 Cor. 13 : 1; 1 Tim. 5 : 19.

the two, vision of, Rev. 11.

Gen. 31 : 44, covenant be a w. between us.

31 : 50, God is w. betwixt me and thee.

Josh. 24 : 27, this stone shall be a w.

Job 16 : 19, my w. is in heaven.

Ps. 89 : 37, a faithful w. in heaven.

Prov. 14 : 5, a faithful w. will not lie.

14 : 25, a true w. delivereth souls.

24 : 18, be not w. against thy neighbour without cause.

Isa. 55 : 4, I have given him for a w. to the people.

Jer. 42 : 5, the Lord be a faithful w. between us.

Mal. 3 : 5, a swift w. against the sorcerers.

Matt. 24 : 14, for a w. to all nations.

Mark 14 : 55, sought w. against Jesus.

John 1 : 7, the same came for a w.

3 : 11, ye receive not our w.

5 : 37, the Father hath borne w. of me.

Acts 14 : 17, he left not himself without w.

Rom. 2 : 15; 9 : 1, conscience bearing w.

Heb. 12 : 1, compassed with cloud of w.

1 John 5 : 9, we receive w. of men.

5 : 10, hath the w. in himself.

Rev. 1 : 5, Jesus Christ the faithful w.

Witness.

Deut. 4 : 26, I call heaven and earth to w.

1 Sam. 12 : 3, w. against me.

Isa. 3 : 9, their countenance doth w. against them.

Matt. 26 : 62; Mark 14 : 60, what is it which these w. against thee ?

Acts 20 : 23, Holy Ghost w. in every city.

26 : 22, w. both to small and great.

Rom. 3 : 21, being w. by the Law and the Prophets.

1 Tim. 6 : 31, before Pilate w. a good confession.

Heb. 7 : 8, of whom it is w. that he liveth.

Woes, pronounced against wickedness, etc., Isa. 5 : 8; 10 : 1; 29 : 15; 31 : 1; 45 : 9; Jer. 22 : 13; Amos 6 : 1; Mic. 2 : 1; Hab. 2 : 6; Zeph. 3 : 1; Zech. 11 : 17; Matt. 26 : 24; Luke 6 : 24; Jude 11; Rev. 8 : 13; 9 : 12; 11 : 14; against unbelief, Matt. 11 : 21; 23 : 13; Luke 10 : 13; 11 : 42.

Wolf. The wolf is frequently mentioned in the Bible. Its habit of hunting for its prey by night is alluded to in Jer. 5 : 6, etc.

wolves, unjust judges and false teachers so called, Zeph. 3 : 3; Matt. 10 : 16; Luke 10 : 3.

Isa. 11 : 6, the w. shall dwell with the lamb.

65 : 25, the w. and the lamb shall feed together.

Matt. 7 : 15, inwardly they are w.

John 10 : 12, hireling seeth the w. coming.

Acts 20 : 29, w. shall enter among you.

Woman, creation of, Gen. 2 : 22.

fall of, Gen. 3.

Christ the seed of (Gen. 3 : 15); Gal. 4 : 4.

women, duty of the aged, Titus 2 : 3; of the young, 1 Tim. 5 : 14; Titus 2 : 4; 1 Pet. 3. See Wife.

Gen. 3 : 15, enmity between thee and the w.

Judg. 5 : 24, blessed above w.

2 Sam. 1 : 26, passing of the love of w.

Ps. 45 : 9, among thy honourable **w.**
48 : 6; Isa. 13 : 8; 21 : 3; 26 : 17; Jer. 4 : 31; 6 : 24; 13 : 21; 30 : 6; 31 : 8; 48 : 41; 49 : 22; 50 : 43, pain as of a **w.** in travail.
Prov. 9 : 13, a foolish **w.** is clamorous.
12 : 4; 31 : 10, a virtuous **w.**
14 : 1, every wise **w.** buildeth her house.
21 : 9, with a brawling **w.** in a wide house.
31 : 3, give not thy strength to **w.**
Eccl. 7 : 28, a **w.** among all those have I not found.
Isa. 3 : 12, **w.** rule over them.
32 : 9, ye **w.** that are at ease.
49 : 15, can a **w.** forget her suckling child ?
54 : 6, as a **w.** forsaken.
Jer. 31 : 22, a **w.** shall compass a man.
Matt. 5 : 28, whoso looketh on a **w.**
11 : 11; Luke 7 : 28, among them born of **w.**
Matt. 15 : 28, O **w.**, great is thy faith.
24 : 41; Luke 17 : 35, two **w.** grinding at the mill.
26 : 10, why trouble ye the **w.** ?
26 : 13, this, that this **w.** hath done, be told.
Luke 1 : 28, blessed art thou among **w.**
John 2 : 4, **W.**, what have I to do with thee ?
8 : 3, a **w.** taken in adultery.
19 : 26, **w.**, behold thy son.
Rom. 1 : 27, the natural use of the **w.**
1 Cor. 7 : 1, good not to touch a **w.**
11 : 7, the **w.** is the glory of the man.
14 : 34, let your **w.** keep silence.
1 Tim. 2 : 9, that **w.** adorn themselves in modest apparel.
2 : 12, I suffer not a **w.** to teach.
2 : 14, the **w.** being deceived was in the transgression.
2 Tim. 3 : 6, lead captive silly **w.**
Heb. 11 : 35, **w.** received their dead.
1 Pet. 3 : 5, holy **w.** adorned themselves.
Womb, Gen. 49 : 25, blessings of the **w.**
1 Sam. 1 : 5, the Lord had shut up her **w.**
Ps. 22 : 9, he that took me out of the **w.**
22 : 10, I was cast upon thee from the **w.**
110 : 3, from the **w.** of the morning.
127 : 3, the fruit of the **w.** is his reward.
139 : 13, thou hast covered me in my mother's **w.**
Eccl. 11 : 5, how bones grow in the **w.**
Isa. 44 : 2; 49 : 5, the Lord formed thee from the **w.**
48 : 8, a transgressor from the **w.**
66 : 9, to bring forth, and shut the **w.** ?
Hos. 9 : 14, give them a miscarrying **w.**
Luke 1 : 42, blessed is the fruit of thy **w.**
11 : 27, blessed is the **w.** that bare thee.
23 : 29, blessed are the **w.** that never bare.
Wonder, Deut. 13 : 1; 28 : 46, a sign and **w.**
Ps. 71 : 7, I am as a **w.** unto many.
77 : 14, thou art the God that doest **w.**
88 : 10, wilt thou show **w.** to the dead ?
96 : 3, declare his **w.** among all people.
136 : 4, who alone doeth great **w.**
Isa. 20 : 3, walked barefoot for a sign and a **w.**
29 : 14, I will do a marvellous work and a **w.**

Dan. 12 : 6, how long to the end of these **w.** ?
Joel 2 : 30; Acts 2 : 19, I will show **w.**
Acts 3 : 10, they were filled with **w.**
Isa. 29 : 9, stay yourselves, and **w.**
59 : 16, he **w.** that there was no intercessor.
Hab. 1 : 5, regard, and **w.** marvellously.
Luke 4 : 22, they **w.** at the gracious words.
Rev. 17 : 8, that dwell on the earth shall **w.**
See Ex. 3 : 20; Deut. 6 : 22; Ps. 89 : 5.
Wonderful, 2 Sam. 1 : 26, thy love was **w.**
Job 42 : 3, things too **w.** for me.
Ps. 119 : 129, thy testimonies are **w.**
139 : 6, such knowledge is too **w.** for me.
Isa. 9 : 6, his name shall be called **W.**
25 : 1, thou hast done **w.** things.
28 : 29, Lord, which is **w.** in counsel.
Matt. 21 : 15, when they saw the **w.** things that he did.
Wondrous, 1 Chr. 16 : 9; Ps. 26 : 7; 105 : 2; 119 : 27; 145 : 5, talk of his **w.** works.
Job 37 : 16, dost thou know the **w.** works of him ?
Ps. 72 : 18; 86 : 10, God doeth **w.** things.
119 : 18, **w.** things out of thy law.
See Joel 2 : 26.
Wont, Matt. 27 : 15, the governor was **w.** to release.
Ex. 21 : 29, if the ox were **w.** to push with his horns.
Mark 10 : 1, as he was **w.** he taught.
Luke 22 : 39, he went, as he was **w.**, to the mount.
Acts 16 : 13, where prayer was **w.** to be made.
Wood, Gen. 22 : 7, behold the fire and the **w.**
Josh. 9 : 21; Jer. 46 : 22, hewers of **w.**
Ps. 80 : 13, boar out of the **w.** doth waste it.
141 : 7, as one cleaveth **w.**
Prov. 26 : 20, where no **w.** is, the fire goeth out.
Isa. 60 : 17, for **w.** I will bring brass.
1 Cor. 3 : 13, upon this foundation **w.**, hay.
Woof, Lev. 13 : 48, 58, 59.
Wool, Ps. 147 : 16, he giveth snow like **w.**
Prov. 31 : 13, she seeketh **w.** and flax.
Isa. 1 : 18, your sins shall be as **w.**
Ezek. 27 : 18, merchant in **w.**
Dan. 7 : 9; Rev. 1 : 14, hair like **w.**
Word, men to be judged for words, Eccl. 5 : 2; Ezek. 35 : 13; Mal. 2 : 17; 3 : 13; Matt. 12 : 37.
Deut. 4 : 2, not add unto the **w.** which I command you.
8 : 3; Matt. 4 : 4, every **w.** of God.
Deut. 30 : 14; Rom. 10 : 8, the **w.** is nigh.
Job 12 : 11, doth not the ear try **w.**
38 : 2, darkeneth counsel by **w.**
Ps. 19 : 14, let the **w.** of my mouth be acceptable.
68 : 11, the Lord gave the **w.**
139 : 4, there is not a **w.**, but thou knowest it.
Prov. 15 : 23, a **w.** spoken in due season.
25 : 11, a **w.** fitly spoken.
Isa. 29 : 21, make a man an offender for a **w.**

30 : 21, thine ears shall hear a w. behind thee.

45 : 23, the w. is gone out of my mouth.

50 : 4, to speak a w. in season.

Jer. 5 : 13, the w. is not in them.

18 : 18, nor shall the w. perish.

44 : 16, the w. thou hast spoken.

Dan. 7 : 25, speak great w. against the Most high.

Hos. 14 : 2, take with you w.

Matt. 8 : 8, speak the w. only.

12 : 36, every idle w. that men shall speak.

24 : 35, my w. shall not pass away.

Mark 4 : 14, the sower soweth the w.

Luke 4 : 36, what a w. is this!

24 : 19, a prophet mighty in deed and w.

John 1 : 1, in the beginning was the W.

1 : 14, the W. was made flesh.

6 : 68, thou hast the w. of eternal life.

14 : 24, w. ye hear is not mine.

15 : 3, ye are clean through the w. I have spoken.

17 : 8, I have given them the w. thou gavest me.

Acts 13 : 15, any w. of exhortation.

13 : 26, to you is w. of salvation sent.

17 : 11, received the w. with readiness.

20 : 32, the w. of his grace.

26 : 25, the w. of truth and soberness.

1 Cor. 4 : 20, kingdom of God is not in w., but in power.

2 Cor. 1 : 18, our w. was not yea and nay.

5 : 19, the w. of reconciliation.

Gal. 5 : 14, all the law is fulfilled in one w.

6 : 6, him that is taught in the w.

Phil. 2 : 16, holding forth the w. of life.

Col. 3 : 17, whatsoever ye do in w. or deed.

1 Thess. 1 : 5, our gospel came not in w. only.

4 : 18, comfort one another with these w.

1 Tim. 5 : 17, labour in the w. and doctrine.

2 Tim. 4 : 2, preach the w.

Titus 1 : 9, holding fast the faithful w.

Heb. 2 : 2, if the w. spoken by angels was stedfast.

4 : 2, the w. preached did not profit.

4 : 12, the w. of God is quick and powerful.

5 : 13, is unskilful in the w. of righteousness.

6 : 5, have tasted the good w. of God.

13 : 22, suffer the w. of exhortation.

Jas. 1 : 21, receive the engrafted w.

1 : 22, be ye doers of the w.

3 : 2, if any offend not in w.

1 Pet. 2 : 2, the sincere milk of the w.

3 : 1, if any obey not the w.

2 Pet. 1 : 19, a more sure w. of prophecy.

3 : 5, by the w. of God the heavens were of old.

1 John 3 : 18, not love in w. but in deed.

Rev. 3 : 10, hast kept the w. of my patience.

Word of God, a name of Christ, John 1 : 14; 1 John 1 : 1; 5 : 7; Rev. 19 : 13.

the Scriptures, Luke 5 : 1; Acts 4 : 31; 8 : 14; 13 : 7; 16 : 6.

Works, of God, Job 9; 37–41; Ps. 8; 19; 89; 104; 111; 145; 147; 148; Eccl. 8 : 17; Jer. 10 : 12.

of the law, insufficiency of, Rom. 3 : 20, 4 : 2; Gal. 3.

good, the evidence of faith, Acts 26 : 20.

exhortations to, Matt. 5 : 16; (Acts 9 : 36); 2 Cor. 9; 8; Eph. 2 : 10; Heb. 10 : 24; 1 Pet. 2 : 12.

Gen. 2 : 3, God rested from his w.

Ex. 20 : 9; 23 : 12; Deut. 5 : 13, six days do all thy w.

Deut. 4 : 28; 2 Ki. 19 : 18; 2 Chr. 32 : 17; Ps. 115 : 4; 135 : 15, the w. of men's hands.

Deut. 33 : 11, accept the w. of his hands.

1 Chr. 29 : 1; Neh. 4 : 19, the w. is great.

2 Chr. 34 : 12, the men did the w. faithfully.

Ezra 6 : 7, let the w. of the house of God alone.

Neh. 6 : 16, they perceived this w. was of God.

Job 1 : 10, thou hast blessed the w. of his hands.

10 : 3, despise the w. of thine hands.

14 : 15, have desire to w. of thine hands.

34 : 11, the w. of a man shall he render unto him.

Ps. 8 : 3, the w. of thy fingers.

33 : 4, all his w. are done in truth.

90 : 17, establish thou the w. of our hands.

101 : 3, I hate the w. of them that turn aside.

111 : 2, the w. of the Lord are great.

143 : 5, muse on w. of thy hands.

Prov. 20 : 11, whether his w. be pure.

24 : 12; Matt. 16 : 27; 2 Tim. 4 : 14, render to every man according to his w.

Eccl. 3 : 17, there is a time for every w.

5 : 6, why should God destroy w. of thine hands?

8 : 9, I applied my heart to every w.

9 : 10, there is no w. in the grave.

12 : 14, God shall bring every w. into judgment.

Isa. 5 : 19, let him hasten his w.

10 : 12, when the Lord hath performed his whole w.

28 : 21, do his w., his strange w.

49 : 4, my w. is with God.

64 : 8, we are the w. of thy hand.

Jer. 32 : 19, great in counsel, and mighty in w.

Hab. 1 : 5, I will w. a w. in your days.

3 : 2, revive thy w. in the years.

Matt. 23 : 5, all their w. they do to be seen of men.

Mark 6 : 5, he could there do no mighty w.

John 6 : 29, this is the w. of God, that ye believe.

7 : 21, I have done one w., and ye all marvel.

9 : 3, that the w. of God should be made manifest.

10 : 32, for which of those w. do ye stone me?

14 : 12, the w. that I do shall he do also; and greater w.

17 : 4, I have finished the w. which thou gavest me.

Acts 5 : 38, if this w. be of men.

14 : 26, the w. which they fulfilled.

15 : 38, went not with them to the w.

Rom. 2 : 15, show w. of law written.
3 : 27, by what law ? of w. ?
9 : 28, a short w. will the Lord make upon the earth.
11 : 6, otherwise w. is no more w.
13 : 12; Eph. 5 : 11, the w. of darkness.
1 Cor. 3 : 13, every man's w. shall be made manifest.
9 : 1, are not ye my w. in the Lord ?
Gal. 2 : 16, by w. of the law shall no flesh be justified.
6 : 4, let every man prove his own w.
Eph 2 : 9, not of w., lest any man should boast.
4 : 12, the w. of the ministry.
Col. 1 : 21, enemies in your mind by wicked w.
1 Thess. 5 : 13, esteem them in love for their w. sake.
2 Thess. 1 : 11, God fulfil w. of faith.
2 : 17, stablish you in every good word and w.
2 Tim. 1 : 9, saved us, not according to our w.
4 : 5, do the w. of an evangelist.
Titus 1 : 16, in w. they deny him.
Heb. 6 : 1; 9 : 14, from dead w.
Jas. 1 : 4, let patience have her perfect w.
2 : 14, if he have not w., can faith save him ?
2 : 17, faith, if it hath not w., is dead.
2 : 22, and by w. was faith made perfect.
2 Pet. 3 : 10, earth and w. therein shall be burned up.
1 John 3 : 8, might destroy the w. of the devil.
Rev. 2 : 26, he that keepeth my w. to the end.
3 . 2, I have not found thy w. perfect.
9 : 20, repented not of w.
14 : 13, their w. do follow them.
22 : 12, to give every man as his w. shall be.
Works.
Ex. 34 : 21, six days thou shalt w.
1 Sam. 14 : 6, may be the Lord will w. for us.
1 Ki. 21 : 20, sold thyself to w. evil.
Neh. 4 : 6, the people had a mind to w.
Job 23 : 9, on the left hand, where he doth w.
33 : 29, all these things w. God with man.
Ps. 58 : 2, in heart ye w. wickedness.
101 : 7, he that w. deceit.
119 : 126, it is time for thee, Lord, to w.
Prov. 26 : 28, a flattering mouth w. ruin.
31 : 13, she w. with her hands.
Isa. 43 : 13, I will w., and who shall let it ?
44 : 12, the smith w. in the coals.
Dan. 6 : 27, he w. signs and wonders.
Mic. 2 : 1, woe to them that w. evil.
Hag. 2 : 4, w. for I am with you.
Mal. 3 : 15, they that w. wickedness are set up.
Matt. 21 : 28, go w. in my vineyard.
John 5 : 17, my Father w. hitherto, and I w.
6 : 28, that we might w. the works of God.
6 : 30, what dost thou w. ?
9 : 4, the night cometh, when no man can w.

Acts 10 : 35, he that w. righteousness.
Rom. 5 : 3, tribulation w. patience.
8 : 28, all things w. together for good.
1 Cor. 12 : 6, it is the same God that w. all in all.
2 Cor. 4 : 12, death w. in us.
4 : 17, w. for us a far more exceeding weight of glory.
Gal. 5 : 6, faith which w. by love.
Eph. 1 : 11, who w. all things after counsel of his will.
2 : 2, the spirit that w. in children of disobedience.
3 : 20, according to power that w. in us.
4 : 28, w. thing that is good.
Phil. 2 : 12, w. out your own salvation.
1 Thess. 4 : 11, w. with your own hands.
2 Thess. 2 : 7, the mystery of iniquity doth w.
3 : 10, if any would not w., neither should he eat.
Heb. 13 : 21, w. that which is pleasing.
Jas. 1 : 20, wrath of man w. not righteousness of God.
Workers, Ps. 5 : 5; Job 31 : 3; Prov. 10 : 29; 1 Cor. 12 : 29; 2 Cor. 6 : 1; Phil. 3 : 2.
Workman, Isa. 40 : 19, the w. melteth a graven image.
Matt. 10 : 10, the w. is worthy of his meat.
2 Tim. 2 : 15, a w. that needeth not to be ashamed.
See Eph. 2 : 10.
World, created, Gen. 1 : 2; John 1 : 10; Col. 1 : 16; Heb. 1 : 2.
its corruption by the fall, Rom. 5 : 12, 8 : 22.
exhortations against conformity to, Rom. 12 : 2; Gal. 6 : 14; Jas. 1 : 27.
1 Sam. 2 : 8, he set the w. upon them.
1 Chr. 16 : 30, the w. shall be stable.
Job 18 : 18, chased out of the w.
34 : 13, who hath disposed the whole w.
37 : 12, upon the face of the w.
Ps. 17 : 14, from men of the w.
24 : 1; 98 : 7; Nah. 1 : 5, the w. and they that dwell therein.
Ps. 50 : 12, the w. is mine.
73 : 12, the ungodly, who prosper in the w.
93 : 1; 96 : 10, w. is established.
Eccl. 3 : 11, he hath set the w. in their heart.
Isa. 14 : 21, nor fill the face of the w. with cities.
24 : 4, the w. languisheth.
34 : 1, let the w. hear.
45 : 17, not confounded, w. without end.
Matt. 4 : 8; Luke 4 : 5, all the kingdoms of the w.
Matt. 5 : 14, the light of the w.
13 : 22; Mark 4 : 19, the cares of this w.
Matt. 13 : 38, the field is the w.
13 : 40, in the end of this w.
16 : 26; Mark 8 : 36; Luke 9 : 25, gain the whole w.
Matt. 18 : 7, woe to the w. because of offences.
24 : 14; Mark 14 : 9, shall be preached in all the w.

Mark 10 : 30; Luke 18 : 30, in the w. to come eternal life.

Luke 1 : 70; Acts 3 : 21, since the w. began.

Luke 20 : 35, worthy to obtain that w.

John 1 : 29, taketh away the sin of the w.

3 : 16, God so loved the w.

4 : 42; 1 John 4 : 14, the Saviour of the w.

John 6 : 33, bread of God giveth life to the w.

8 : 12; 9 : 5, Jesus said, I am the light of the w.

12 : 47, I came not to judge the w., but to save the w.

14 : 27, not as the w. giveth, give I unto you.

14 : 30, the prince of this w. cometh.

John 15 : 18; 1 John 3 : 13, if the w. hate you.

John 16 : 28, I leave the w., and go to the Father.

17 : 9, I pray not for the w.

17 : 21, 23, that the w. may believe thou hast sent me.

21 : 25, the w. could not contain the books.

Acts 17 : 6, turned the w. upside down.

Rom. 3 : 19, that all the w. may become guilty.

12 : 2, and be not conformed to this w.

1 Cor. 1 : 21, the w. by wisdom knew not God.

7 : 31, they that use this w., as not abusing it.

2 Cor. 4 : 4, the god of this w. hath blinded.

Gal. 1 : 4, deliver us from this present evil w.

Eph. 2 : 12, without God in the w.

1 Tim. 6 : 7, we brought nothing into this w.

Heb. 11 : 38, of whom the w. was not worthy.

Jas. 3 : 6, the tongue is a w. of iniquity.

4 : 4, the friendship of the w.

1 John 2 : 15, love not the w.

3 : 1, the w. knoweth us not.

5 : 19, the whole w. lieth in wickedness.

Worldly, Titus 2 : 12; Heb. 9 : 1.

Worm, Ex. 16 : 24, neither was there any w. therein.

Job 7 : 5, my flesh is clothed with w. and dust.

17 : 14, said to the w., Thou art my mother.

19 : 26, though w. destroy this body.

24 : 20, the w. shall feed sweetly on him.

25 : 6, man, that is a w.

Ps. 22 : 6, I am a w., and no man.

Isa. 14 : 11, the w. is spread under thee.

41 : 14, fear not, thou w. Jacob.

66 : 24; Mark 9 : 44, 46, 48, their w. shall not die.

Acts 12 : 23, eaten of w.

Wormwood. Several species grow in Palestine. It is chiefly noted for its bitterness when used as a drink dissolved in spirit or wine.

figurative, Deut. 29 : 18; Prov. 5 : 4; Lam. 3 : 15.

Jer. 9 : 15; 23 : 15, feed them with w.

Amos 5 : 7, who turn judgment to w.

Rev. 8 : 11, name of star is called W.

Worse, Gen. 19 : 9, now will we deal w. with thee than.

2 Sam. 19 : 7, that will be w. unto thee than all the.

2 Ki. 14 : 12, Judah was put to the w. before Israel.

Ezek. 7 : 24, wherefore I will bring the w. of the.

Matt. 9 : 16, from the garment and the rent is made w.

12 : 45, the last state of that man is w.

John 2 : 10, then that which is w.

1 Cor. 11 : 17, together not for the better but for the w.

See also Mark 2 : 21; 5 : 26; Luke 11 : 26; John 5 : 14; 2 Tim. 3 : 13; 2 Pet. 2 : 20.

Worship, to be rendered to God alone, Ex. 20 : 1; Deut. 5 : 7; 6 : 13; Matt. 4 : 10; Luke 4 : 8; Acts 10 : 26; 14 : 15; Col. 2 : 18; Rev. 19 : 10; 22 : 8.

how to be performed, Lev. 10 : 3; Eccl. 5; Joel 2 : 16; John 4 : 24; 1 Cor. 11; 14.

exhortations to, 2 Ki. 17 : 36; 1 Chr. 16 : 29; Ps. 29; 95 : 6; 99 : 5; 100.

1 Chr. 16 : 29; Ps. 29 : 2; 96 : 9, w. the Lord in beauty of holiness.

Ps. 81 : 9, neither w. any strange god.

95 : 6, let us w. and bow down.

97 : 7, w. him, all ye gods.

99 : 5, w. at his footstool.

Isa. 27 : 13, shall w. the Lord in holy mount.

Zeph. 1 : 5, w. the host of heaven.

Matt. 4 : 9; Luke 4 : 7, if thou wilt w. me.

Matt. 15 : 9, in vain they do w. me.

John 4 : 20, the place where men ought to w.

4 : 22, ye w. ye know not what.

4 : 24, that w. him must w. in spirit and truth.

Acts 17 : 23, whom ye ignorantly w.

24 : 14, so w. I the God of my fathers.

Rom. 1 : 25, w. the creature more than the Creator.

1 Cor. 14 : 25, falling down, he will w. God.

Heb. 1 : 6, let angels of God w. him.

Rev. 4 : 10, w. him that liveth for ever.

Worth, Job 24 : 25, make speech nothing w.

Prov. 10 : 20, heart of wicked little w.

Ezek. 30 : 2, woe w. the day !

Worthy, Gen. 32 : 10, I am not w. of thy mercies.

1 Ki. 1 : 52, show himself a w. man.

Matt. 3 : 11, whose shoes I am not w. to bear.

8 : 8; Luke 7 : 6, I am not w. thou shouldest come under my roof.

Matt. 10 : 10, the workman is w. of his meat.

10 : 37, that loveth father more than me is not w. of me.

22 : 8, they which were bidden were not w.

Mark 1 : 7; Luke 3 : 16; John 1 : 27, I am not w. unloose.

Luke 3 : 8, fruits w. of repentance.

7 : 7, neither thought I myself w.

10 : 7; 1 Tim. 5 : 18, the labourer is w. of his hire.

Luke 15 : 19, no more w. to be called thy son.
20 : 35, accounted w. to obtain that world.
Acts 24 : 2, very w. deeds are done by thee.
Rom. 8 : 18, not w. to be compared with the glory.
Eph. 4 : 1; Col. 1 : 10; 1 Thess. 2 : 12, walk w.
1 Tim. 1 : 15; 4 : 9, w. of all acceptation.
Heb. 10 : 29, of how much sorer punishment shall he be thought w.
11 : 38, of whom the world was not w.
Jas. 2 : 7, that w. name.
Rev. 3 : 4, they are w.
4 : 11; 5 : 12, thou art w. to receive glory.
Wound, Ex. 21 : 25, give w. for w.
Job 34 : 6, my w. is incurable.
Ps. 147 : 3, he bindeth up their w.
Prov. 20 : 30, blueness of a w. cleanseth.
27 : 6, faithful are the w. of a friend.
Isa. 1 : 6, no soundness, but w. and bruises.
Jer. 15 : 18, why is my w. incurable ?
30 : 12; Nah. 3 : 19, thy w. is grievous.
Zech. 13 : 6, what are these w. in thy hands ?
Luke 10 : 34, bound up his w.
Rev. 13 : 3, his w. was healed.
Wound.
Deut. 32 : 39, I w., and I heal.
Job 5 : 18, he w., and his hands make whole.
Ps. 68 : 21, God shall w. his enemies.
109 : 22, my heart is w. within me.
Prov. 18 : 14, a w. spirit who can bear ?
Isa. 53 : 5, he was w. for our transgressions.
Hab. 3 : 13, thou w. head of wicked.
Wrap, Isa. 28 : 20, covering narrower than he can w. himself in it.
Mic. 7 : 3, so they w. it up.
Matt. 27 : 59; Mark 15 : 46; Luke 23 : 53, w. the body.
Wrath, Gen. 49 : 7, cursed be their w.
Num. 16 : 46, there is w. gone out from the Lord.
Deut. 32 : 27, were it not I feared the w. of the enemy.
Job 5 : 2, w. killeth the foolish man,
21 : 20, drink of w. of the Almighty.
36 : 18, because there is w., beware.
Ps. 76 : 10, the w. of man shall praise thee.
90 : 7, by thy w. are we troubled.
95 : 11, to whom I sware in my w.
Prov. 15 : 1, soft answer turneth away w.
16 : 14, w. of a king is as messengers of death.
27 : 4, w. is cruel, and anger outrageous.
Eccl. 5 : 17, much w. with his sickness.
Isa. 54 : 8, in a little w. I hid my face.
Hab. 3 : 2, in w. remember mercy.
Matt. 3 : 7; Luke 3 : 7, from the w. to come.
Rom. 2 : 5, treasurest up w. against the day of w.
12 : 19, rather give place to w.
Eph. 4 : 26, let not the sun go down on your w.
6 : 4, father, provoke not your children to w.
Col. 3 : 8, put off these, w., malice.
1 Thess. 1 : 10, delivered us from w. to come.
5 : 9, God hath not appointed us to w.

1 Tim. 2 : 8, lifting up holy hands without w.
Jas. 1 : 19, slow to speak, slow to w.
Rev. 6 : 16, hide us from w. of the Lamb.
Wrathful, Ps. 69 : 24, let thy w. anger take hold on them.
Prov. 15 : 18, a w. man stirreth up strife.
Wrestle, Gen. 32 : 24, there w. a man with him.
32 : 25, thigh was out of joint as he w. with.
Eph. 6 : 12, for we w. not against flesh and blood.
Wretched, Rom. 7 : 24, O w. man that I am !
Rev. 3 : 17, knowest not thou art w.
Wrinkle, Job 16 : 8, thou hast filled me with w.
Eph. 5 : 27, not having spot or w.
Write, Deut. 6 : 9; 11 : 20, w. them on posts of thy house.
Prov. 3 : 3; 7 : 3, w. them upon the table of thine heart.
Isa. 10 : 19, a child may w. them.
Jer. 22 : 30, w. ye this man childless.
31 : 33; Heb. 8 : 10, I will w. law in their hearts.
Hab. 2 : 2, w. the vision on tables.
John 19 : 21, w. not, The King of the Jews.
Rev. 3 : 12, I will w. on him my new name.
Writer, Judg. 5 : 14, handle the pen of the w.
Ps. 45 : 1, the pen of a ready w.
Ezek. 9 : 2, the w. inkhorn.
Written, Ex. 31 : 18, w. with the finger of God.
Job 19 : 23, O that my words were w.
Ps. 69 : 28, let them not be w. with the righteous.
102 : 18, w. for the generation to come.
Prov. 22 : 20, have I not w. to thee excellent things ?
Eccl. 12 : 10, that which was w. was upright.
Ezek. 2 : 10, roll w. within and without.
Dan. 5 : 24, the writing was w.
Matt. 27 : 37, set up his accusation w.
John 19 : 22, what I have w. I have w.
1 Cor. 10 : 11, w. for our admonition.
2 Cor. 3 : 2, ye are our epistle w. in our hearts.
1 Pet. 1 : 16, is it w., Be ye holy.
Wrong, Ex. 2 : 13, to him that did the w.
Deut. 19 : 16, to testify what is w.
1 Chr. 12 : 17, there is no w. in mine hands.
16 : 21; Ps. 105 : 14, he suffered no man to do them w.
Job 19 : 7, I cry out of w., but am not heard.
Jer. 22 : 3, do no w., do no violence.
Matt. 20 : 13, friend, I do thee no w.
Acts 18 : 14, a matter of w.
1 Cor. 6 : 7, why do ye not take w. ?
Col. 3 : 25, he that doeth w. shall receive for the w.
Wronged, 2 Cor. 7 : 2, we have w. no man.
Philem. 18, if he hath w. thee.
See Prov. 8 : 36.
Wrongfully, Job 21 : 27, devices ye w. imagine.
Ps. 69 : 4, being mine enemies w.
1 Pet. 2 : 19, suffering w.

Wroth, Gen. 4 : 6, Lord said, Why art thou w. ?

Deut. 1 : 34; Ps. 78 : 21, Lord heard your words, and was w.

Deut. 3 : 26, Lord was w. with me for your sakes.

2 Sam. 22 : 8, foundations of heaven because he was w.

2 Ki. 5 : 11, Naaman was w.

13 : 19, man of God was w. with him.

Ps. 89 : 38, thou hast been w. with thine anointed.

Isa. 47 : 6, I was w. with my people.

54 : 9, I have sworn that I would not be w.

57 : 16, neither will I be always w.

64 : 9, be not w. very sore, O Lord.

Lam. 5 : 22, thou art very w. against us.

Matt. 18 : 34, his lord was w.

22 : 7, the king was w.

Wrought, Num. 23 : 23, what hath God w.

1 Sam. 6 : 6, God hath w. wonderfully.

11 : 13; 19 : 5, Lord w. salvation in Israel.

Neh. 4 : 17, every one w. in the work.

6 : 16, this work was w. of God.

Job 12 : 9, the hand of the Lord hath w. this.

36 : 23, who can say, Thou hast w. iniquity ?

Ps. 31 : 19, hast w. for them that trust in thee.

68 : 28, strengthen that which thou hast w. for us.

139 : 15, curiously w. in lowest parts of the earth.

Eccl. 2 : 17, work w. under the sun.

Isa. 26 : 12, thou hast w. all our works in us.

41 : 4, who hath w. and done it ?

Ezek. 20 : 9, I w. for my name's sake.

Dan. 4 : 2, the wonders God hath w. toward me.

Jonah 1 : 11, the sea w., and was tempestuous.

Matt. 20 : 12, these last have w. but one hour.

26 : 10; Mark 14 : 6, she hath w. a good work on me.

John 3 : 21, manifest, that they are w. in God.

Acts 15 : 12, what wonders God had w.

18 : 3, he abode with them, and w.

Rom. 15 : 18, things which Christ hath not w. by me.

2 Cor. 5 : 5, he that hath w. us for the selfsame thing is God.

Gal. 2 : 8, he that w. effectually.

Eph. 1 : 20, which he w. in Christ.

Heb. 11 : 33, through faith w. righteousness.

Jas. 2 : 22, how faith w. with his works.

1 Pet. 4 : 3, to have w. the will of the Gentiles.

2 John 8, lose not those things which we have w.

Wrung, Lev. 1 : 15; 5 : 9, blood shall be w. out.

Ps. 73 : 10, waters of full cup w. out to them.

Isa. 51 : 17, hast w. out dregs of cup.

Y

Yea, Matt. 5 : 37; Jas. 5 : 12, let your communication be Y., y.

2 Cor. 1 : 17, there should be y. y., and nay nay.

1 : 20, promises of God in him are y.

Year, beginning of, changed, Ex. 12 : 1; Lev. 23 : 5.

Gen. 1 : 14, for seasons, and for days, and y.

47 : 9, few and evil have the y. of my life been.

Ex. 13 : 10, keep this ordinance from y. to y.

Lev. 16 : 34, make atonement once a y.

25 : 5, a y. of rest.

Deut. 14 : 22, thou shalt tithe the increase y. by y.

32 : 7, consider the y. of many generations.

1 Sam. 7 : 16, went from y. to y. in circuit.

Job 10 : 5, are thy y. as man's days ?

16 : 22, when a few y. are come.

32 : 7, multitude of y. should teach wisdom.

36 : 26, neither can the number of his y. be searched out.

Ps. 31 : 10, my y. are spent with sighing.

61 : 6, prolong his y. as many generations.

65 : 11, thou crownest the y. with thy goodness.

77 : 10, the y. of the right hand of the Most High.

78 : 33, their y. did he consume in trouble.

90 : 4; 2 Pet. 3 : 8, a thousand y. in thy sight.

90 : 9, we spend our y. as a tale that is told.

90 : 10, the days of our y. are threescore y. and ten.

102 : 24, thy y. are throughout all generations.

102 : 27, thy y. shall have no end.

Prov. 4 : 10, the y. of thy life shall be many.

10 : 27, the y. of the wicked shall be shortened.

Eccl. 12 : 1, nor the y. draw nigh.

Isa. 21 : 16, according to the y. of an hireling.

29 : 1, add ye y. to y.

61 : 2; Luke 4 : 19, the acceptable y. of the Lord.

Isa. 63 : 4, the y. of my redeemed is come.

Jer. 11 : 23; 23 : 12; 48 : 44, the y. of their visitation.

17 : 8, not be careful in y. of drought.

28 : 16, this y. thou shalt die.

Ezek. 22 : 4, thou art come unto thy y.

46 : 17, it shall be his to the y. of liberty.

Joel 2 : 2, the y. of many generations.

Hab. 3 : 2, revive thy work in midst of the y.

Luke 13 : 8, let it alone this y.

Gal. 4 : 10, ye observe months and y.

Heb. 1 : 12, thy y. shall not fail.

Jas. 4 : 13, continue there a y., and buy.

Yearly, Judg. 11 : 40; 1 Sam. 1 : 3; 20 : 6; Neh. 10 : 32.

Yearn, Gen. 43 : 30; 1 Ki. 3 : 26.
Yell, Jer. 2 : 15; 51 : 38.
Yellow, Lev. 13 : 30-36; Ps. 68 : 13.
Yes, Matt. 17 : 25; Mark 7 : 28; Rom. 3 : 29; 10 : 18.
Yesterday, Job 8 : 9 we are of y., and know nothing.
  Heb. 13 : 8, Christ the same y., and to day, and for ever.
Yield, Gen. 4 : 12, ground not y. her strength.
  Lev. 19 : 25, that it may y. the increase.
  26 : 4; Ps. 67 : 6; 85 : 12, the land shall y. her increase.
  2 Chr. 30 : 8, y. ourselves unto the Lord.
  Ps. 107 : 37, vineyards, which may y. fruits.
  Hos. 8 : 7, the bud shall y. no meal.
  Joel 2 : 22, fig tree and vine y. their strength.
  Hab. 3 : 17, though fields shall y. no meat.
  Matt. 27 : 50, Jesus y. up the ghost.
  Acts 23 : 21, do not thou y. unto them.
  Rom. 6 : 13, y. yourselves unto God.
  6 : 19, y. your members servants to righteousness.
  Heb. 12 : 11, it y. the peaceable fruit of righteousness.
  Jas. 3 : 12, no fountain can y. salt water and fresh.
Yoke, of Christ, easy, Matt. 11 : 30; 1 John 5 : 3.
  typical, Jer. 27.
  Gen. 27 : 40; Jer. 30 : 8, break his y.
  Num. 19 : 2; 1 Sam. 6 : 7, on which never came y.
  Deut. 28 : 48, he shall put a y. on thy neck.
  1 Ki. 12 : 4, thy father made our y. grievous.
  Isa. 9 : 4, thou hast broken the y. of his burden.
  58 : 6, that ye break every y.
  Jer. 2 : 20, of old time I have broken thy y.
  31 : 18, as a bullock unaccustomed to the y.
  Lam. 3 : 27, it is good to bear the y. in youth.
  Hos. 11 : 4, as they that take off the y.
  Matt. 11 : 29, take my y. upon you.
  Luke 14 : 19, I have bought five y. of oxen.
  Acts 15 : 10, to put a y. upon the neck of the disciples.
  Gal. 5 : 1, be not entangled with the y. of bondage.
  Phil. 4 : 3, I entreat thee, true y.-fellow.
  1 Tim. 6 : 1, as many as are under the y.
  See 2 Cor. 6 : 14.
Yonder, Gen. 22 : 5, I and the lad will go y.
  Num. 23 : 15 while I meet the Lord y.
  Matt. 17 : 20, say, Remove to y. place.
Young, exhortations to, Lev. 19 : 32; Prov. 1 : 8; Eccl. 12 : 1.
  Christ's example, Luke 2 : 46, 51.
  Deut. 28 : 50, not show favour to the y.
  32 : 11, as an eagle fluttereth over her y.
  Job 38 : 41, when his y. ones cry to God.
  Ps. 37 : 25, I have been y., and now am old.
  84 : 3, a nest where she may lay her y.
  147 : 9, he giveth food to the y. ravens.
  Isa. 11 : 7, their y. ones shall lie down together.
  40 : 11, gently lead those that are with y.

John 21 : 18, when y., thou girdedst thyself.
Titus 2 : 4, teach y. women to be sober.
Younger, Gen. 25 : 23, the elder shall serve the y.
  Job 30 : 1, they that are y. have me in derision.
  Luke 22 : 26, he that is greatest, let him be as the y.
  1 Tim. 5 : 1, entreat the y. men as brethren.
  1 Pet. 5 : 5, ye y. submit yourselves to the elder.
  See Gen. 44 : 2, 12, 23; 1 Sam. 17 : 14.
Yours, 2 Chr. 20 : 15, the battle is not y., but God's.
  Luke 6 : 20, for y. is the kingdom of God.
  1 Cor. 3 : 21, all things are y.
Youth, Gen. 8 : 21, imagination evil from his y.
  1 Sam. 17 : 33, a man of war from his y.
  2 Sam. 19 : 7, all the evil that befell thee from thy y.
  1 Ki. 18 : 12, I fear the Lord from my y.
  Job 13 : 26, to possess the iniquities of my y.
  29 : 4, as I was in days of my y.
  30 : 12, on my right hand rise the y.
  33 : 25, he shall return to the days of his y.
  36 : 14, hypocrites die in y.
  Ps. 25 : 7, remember not the sins of my y.
  71 : 5, thou art my trust from my y.
  71 : 17, thou hast taught me from my y.
  89 : 45, days of his y. hast thou shortened.
  103 : 5, thy y. is renewed like the eagle's.
  110 : 3, thou hast the dew of thy y.
  129 : 1, they have afflicted me from my y.
  144 : 12, as plants grow up in y.
  Prov. 2 : 17, forsaketh the guide of her y.
  5 : 18, rejoice with the wife of thy y.
  Eccl. 11 : 9, rejoice, young man, in thy y.
  11 : 10, childhood and y. are vanity.
  12 : 1, remember thy Creator in days of thy y.
  Isa. 40 : 30, even the y. shall faint.
  Jer. 2 : 2, the kindness of thy y.
  3 : 4, thou art the guide of my y.
  48 : 11, been at ease from his y.
  Hos. 2 : 15, sing as in days of her y.
  Matt. 19 : 20; Mark 10 : 20; Luke 18 : 21, these have I kept from my y.
  1 Tim. 4 : 12, let no man despise thy y.
  See 2 Tim. 2 : 22.
You-ward, 2 Cor. 1 : 12; 13 : 3; Eph. 3 : 2.

Z

Zaanan (zā-ă-năn) [rich in flocks], Mic. 1 : 11.
Zaanannim (ză-ă-năn-nĭm) [wandering], Josh. 19 : 33.
Zaavan (zā-ă-văn) [unquiet], Gen. 36 : 27.
Zabad (zā-băd) [bestowed], 1 Chr. 2 : 36, 37.
Zabdi (zăb-dĭ) [my portion], Josh. 7 : 1.
Zaccai (zăc-cā-ī) [pure], New Testament form is Zaccheus, Ezra 2 : 9; Neh. 7 : 14.
Zacchæus (zăc-chāē-ŭs), Luke 19 : 2, 5, 8.
Zachariah (zăch-ă-rī-ăh) [Jehovah remembers], king of Israel, 2 Ki. 14 : 29; 2 Chr. 29 : 1.

smitten by Shallum, 2 Ki. 15 : 10.

Zacharias (zăch-ă-rī-ăs), father of John the Baptist, commended as blameless before God, Luke 1 : 6.

is promised a son, Luke 1 : 13.

stricken with dumbness for his unbelief, Luke 1 : 18, 22.

his recovery and song, Luke 1 : 64, 68.

Zadok (zā-dŏk) [just], priest, 2 Sam. 8 : 17; 15 : 24; 20 : 25.

anoints Solomon king, 1 Ki. 1 : 39.

Zair (zā-ĭr) [little], 2 Ki. 8 : 21.

Zalmon (zăl-mŏn) [shady], Judg. 9 : 48.

Zalmonah (zăl-mō-năh) [shady place], Num. 33 : 41.

Zalmunna (zăl-mŭn-nă) [the shade is refused], Judg. 8 : 5.

Zamzummims (zăm-zŭm-mĭms) [humming crowd ?], giant race, Deut. 2 : 20, 21.

Zanoah (ză-nō-ăh) [morass ?], Josh. 15 : 34.

Zaphnath-paaneah (zăph-năth-pā-ă-nē-ăh) [supporter of life], Gen. 41, 45.

Zaphon (zā-phŏn) [north], Josh. 13 : 27.

Zarah (zâ-răh) or Zerah (zē-răh) [sunrising], Gen. 38 : 30; Josh. 7 : 1; 2 Chr. 14 : 7.

Zared (zâr-ĕd) [luxuriant growth], Num. 21 : 12.

Zarephath (zăr-ē-phăth) [smelting place], a city of the Sidonians, 1 Ki. 17 : 9; 9 : 10. New Testament form is Sarepta. See Luke 4 : 26.

Zeal, of Phinehas, Num. 25 : 7, 11; Ps. 106 : 30.

of Jehu, 2 Ki. 10 : 16.

of the Jews for the law, Acts 21 : 20; Rom. 10 : 2.

of Paul for the Jewish religion, Acts 22 : 3; Gal. 1 : 14; Phil. 3 : 6.

Christ an example of, Ps. 69 : 9; John 2 : 17.

in good works, etc., Gal. 4 : 18; Titus 2 : 14; Rev. 3 : 19.

2 Ki. 10 : 16, see my z. for the Lord.

19 : 31; Isa. 37 : 32, the z. of the Lord shall do this.

Ps. 69 : 9; John 2 : 17, the z. of thine house.

Ps. 119 : 139, my z. hath consumed me.

Isa. 9 : 7, the z. of the Lord will perform this.

59 : 17, clad with z. as a cloak.

63 : 15, where is thy z. ?

Ezek. 5 : 13, I the Lord have spoken it in my z.

Rom. 10 : 2, have a z. of God.

2 Cor. 7 : 11, yea, what z.

9 : 2, your z. hath provoked very many.

Phil. 3 : 6, concerning z., persecuting the church.

Col. 4 : 13, that he hath a great z. for you.

Zealots. The Zealots were a Jewish party who held strong nationalistic views. They flourished during the Roman period, when they strongly opposed all recognition of the Imperial power. Simon, one of the twelve disciples, was a Zealot; and one tradition holds that Judas also shared their nationalistic views.

Zealous, Num. 25 : 11, he was z. for my sake.

Acts 21 : 20, they are all z. of the law.

22 : 3, z. toward God.

1 Cor. 14 : 12, as ye are z. of spiritual works.

Titus 2 : 14, people z. of good works.

Rev. 3 : 19, be z. therefore and repent.

Zealously, Gal. 4 : 17, they z. affect you, but not well.

4 : 18, good to be z. affected always in a good thing.

Zebedee (zĕb-ē-dĕē), the New Testament form of Zebediah, the father of James and John, Matt. 4 : 21; Mark 1 : 19; Luke 5 : 10; John 21 : 2.

Zebulun (zĕ-bū-lŭn) [intercourse], son of Jacob, Gen. 30 : 20; 35 : 23.

blessed by Jacob, Gen. 49 : 13.

his descendants, Num. 1 : 30; 26 : 26; Deut. 33 : 18; Josh. 19 : 10; Judg. 4 : 6; 5 : 14, 18; 6 : 35; 2 Chr. 30 : 11, 18; Ps. 68 : 27; Ezek. 48 26, Rev. 7 : 8.

Christ preaches in the land of (Isa. 9 : 1); Matt. 4 : 13.

Zechariah (zĕch-ă-rī-ăh), son of Jehoiada, stoned in the court of the Lord's house, 2 Chr. 24 : 20 21.

referred to, Matt. 23 : 35; Luke 11 : 51.

the prophet, his exhortations to repentance, his visions and predictions, Zech. 1–14.

Zechariah, Book of.

Author and Date.—Zechariah was the son of Berechiah, and grandson of Iddo, one of the priests who returned with Zerubbabel (Neh. 12 : 4, 16). He prophesied in the second and fourth years of Darius Hystaspis (520 and 518 B.C.) and was associated with the prophet Haggai.

Contents.—(1) God reasons with his people, stating that his dealings with them have been as he had foretold and that he is still jealous for Jerusalem. (2) Zion is bidden to rejoice, for the Lord will dwell in the midst of her. (3) The prophecy of the Branch. (4) "Not by might nor by power." (5) Vision of the ephah. (6) The Branch shall bear the glory, shall rule and be a priest upon his throne. (7) Because the hearts of Israel were as adamant, the people were scattered among the nations. (8) "Fear not, but let your hands be strong." (9) Triumphal Entry foretold. (10) Gathering out of all countries foretold. (11) Thirty pieces of silver, the price of betrayal and of the potter's field. (12) "They shall look upon me whom they have pierced." (13) The fountain opened for sin and for uncleanness. God will say, ' It is my people: and they shall say, The Lord is my God." (14) The day of the Lord. The Mount of Olives cloven by the feet of Him who stands upon it. The new earth. The river of water of life. The Lord King over all the earth.

Zedekiah (zĕd-ē-kī-ăh) [Jehovah is righteousness], a false prophet, 1 Ki. 22 : 11; 2 Chr. 18 : 10, 23.

Mattaniah, king of Judah, his evil reign, 2 Ki. 24 : 17; 2 Chr. 36 : 10.

his dealings with Jeremiah, Jer. 37 : 6, 16; 38.

carried captive to Babylon, 2 Ki. 25; 2 Chr. 36 : 17; Jer. 39 : 7.

Zeeb (zéeb) [wolf], Judg. 7 : 25; 8 : 3; Ps. 83 : 11. See Oreb.

Zelah (zē-lăh) [slope], 2 Sam. 21 : 14.

Zelek (zē-lĕk) [cleft], 1 Chr. 11 : 39.

Zelophehad (zē-lŏph-ĕ-hăd). Num. 26 : 33.

Zelotes (zē-lō-tĕs) [zealot], Luke 6 : 15; Acts 1 : 13.

Zelzah (zĕl-zăh) [shade from the sun], 1 Sam. 10 : 2.

Zephaniah, Book of.

Author and Date.—Zephaniah was a great-grandson of Hezekiah. He prophesied in the reign of Josiah, probably before the Reformation in 621 B.C.

Contents.—The prophecy falls into three parts—(1) In Chap. 1 the prophet graphically describes the great day of wrath coming upon the nations of the earth, and especially upon Judah and Jerusalem. (2) In Chap. 2 : 1–3 : 8, the prophet exhorts the people to repent, and thus escape the doom that threatens the Philistines, Moab, Ammon, Ethiopia, and even Nineveh itself, the capital of Assyria. (3) in Chap. 3 : 8-20, the prophet promises the Messianic blessings to the remnant of Israel, and announces that these blessings will also extend to all the nations of the earth. Zephaniah predicts the destruction of Nineveh, but not the agents who were to accomplish it. Some have supposed that the descriptions in Zephaniah refer to the inroad of Scythian hordes into Judah, which coincided with the early years of the reign of Josiah. This is not probable, although the news of the approach of these formidable hosts may have coloured the prophet's language, especially in his description of the day of the Lord.

Zephath (zē-phăth) [watch-tower], Judg. 1 : 17.

Zepho (zē-phō) [watch], Gen. 36 : 11.

Zereda (zĕr-ĕ-dă), 1 Ki. 11 : 26.

Zeresh (zē-rĕsh) [gold], Esther 5 : 10, 14; 6 : 13.

Zeror (zē-rôr) [bundle] 1] Sam. 9 : 1.

Zeruah (zē-rū-ăh) [leprous], 1 Ki. 11 : 26.

Zerubbabel (zĕ-rŭb-bă-bĕl) [scattered in Babylon], prince of Judah, Ezra 2 : 2.

restores the worship of God, Ezra 3 : 1; Neh. 12 : 47; Hag. 1 : 1, 14; 2 : 1; Zech. 4 : 6. See Matt. 1 : 12, 13.

Zeruiah (zĕr-ū-ī-ăh) [guarded], 2 Sam. 2 : 18.

Zetham (zē-thăm) [rich in olives], 1 Chr. 23 : 8; 26 : 22.

Zethan (zē-thăn), a Benjamite, 1 Chr. 7 : 10.

Zethar (zē-thär), Esther 1 : 10.

Ziba (zī-bă) [pillar ?], 2 Sam. 9 : 2.

Zibeon (zīb-ĕ-ŏn) [coloured], Gen. 36 : 2.

Zibia, Zibiah (zī-bī-ă) [gazelle], 1 Chr. 8 : 9; 2 Ki. 12 : 1.

Zichri (zĭch-rī) [famous], Ex. 6 : 21; 1 Chr. 26 : 25.

Zidon (zī-dŏn) [fishing], Gen. 49 : 13; Josh. 11 : 8; Judg. 10 : 6; 18 : 7; 1 Ki. 11 : 1; Ezra 3 : 7; Luke 4 : 26; Acts 12 : 20.

prophecies concerning, Isa. 23; Jer. 25 : 22; 27 : 3; 47 : 4; Ezek. 27 : 8; 28 : 21; 32 : 30; Joel 3 : 4; Zech. 9 : 2.

Zif [splendour], the month of April-May, 1 Ki. 6 : 37. See Months.

Ziklag [wilderness of ruin ?], a town in the south country of Judah, Josh. 15 : 31; 1 Sam. 27 : 6; 30 : 1 ff.; 2 Sam. 1 : 1; 1 Chr. 12 : 1.

Zillah [shadow], Gen. 4 : 19.

Zilpah [dripping of balsam], Gen. 29 : 24.

Zimmah [mischief], 1 Chr. 6 : 20.

Zimran [renowned], Gen. 25 : 2.

Zimri, Zimran, 1 Ki. 16 : 9; 2 Ki. 9 : 31.

Zin [rock wall ?], wilderness, part of the desert of Paran, Num. 13 : 21; Josh. 15 : 1.

Zion [dry place], a hill on the south-west side of Jerusalem. In the poetic writings Zion is often used to represent the city itself. 2 Sam. 5 : 7; 1 Ki. 8 : 1; Rom. 11 : 26; Heb. 12 : 22; Rev. 14 : 1.

Zior (zī-ôr) [littleness], Josh. 15 : 54.

Ziph [battlement of wall ?], Josh. 15 : 24, 55.

Ziphion (zīph-ī-ŏn) or Zephon [longing ?], Gen. 46 : 16.

Zippor (zĭp-pôr) [bird], Num. 22 : 2.

Zipporah (zĭp-pôr-ăh), wife of Moses, Ex. 2 : 21; 4 : 20.

Zithri (zīth-rī) [protection of Jehovah], Ex. 6 : 22.

Ziz (zīz) [flower], 2 Chr. 20 : 16.

Zoan (zō-ăn) [migration], Num. 13 : 22; Ps. 78 : 12; Isa. 19 : 11, 13; Ezek. 30 : 14.

Zoar (zō-är) or Bela [littleness], Gen. 14 : 2; 19 : 22; (Isa. 15 : 5); Deut. 34 : 3; Jer. 48 : 34.

Zobah (zō-băh) [an army], kings of, subdued, 1 Sam. 14 : 47; 2 Sam. 8 : 3; 2 Ki. 11 : 23.

Zohar (zō-här) [brightness], Gen. 23 : 8.

Zoheleth (zō-hĕ-lĕth) [serpent], 1 Ki. 1 : 9.

Zophar (zō-phär), Job 2 : 11; 11; 20; 42 : 9.

Zorah (zôr-ăh) [hornet], a city of Samson, Josh. 19 : 41; Judg. 13 : 2, 25; 16 : 31.

Zorobabel (zō-rŏb-ă-bĕl), New Testament form of "Zerubbabel," Matt. 1 : 12; Luke 3 : 27.

Zuar (zū-är) [smallness], Num. 1 : 8.

Zuph [honey cell], 1 Sam. 1 : 1.

Zur [stone], Num. 25 : 15.

Zurishaddai (zū-rī-shăd-dâi) [the Almighty is my rock], Num. 1 : 6.

Zuzims (zū-zĭms), Gen. 14 : 5.

BIBLICAL GAZETTEER

AND

INDEX TO SCRIPTURE ATLAS

BIBLICAL GAZETTEER

AND

INDEX TO SCRIPTURE ATLAS

This concise Gazetteer and Index is intended to assist the Biblical student in determining the geographical position of the various places, and to give a practical knowledge of the incidents connected with each place mentioned in the Bible.

It is impossible, however, to minutely describe all the places of minor importance, but an explanation of certain of the terms and contractions used may be found of service. Thus:—

AIN or EN	before a place means	*fountain of.*		KEFR	before a place means	*a small village.*
BEIT	,,	,,	*house of.*	KH. or KHAN	,,	,,	*a caravansary.*
BIR	,,	,,	*well of.*	KHIRBET	,,	,,	*ruin of.*
BIRKET	,,	,,	*lake of.*	N. or NAHR	,,	,,	*a river.*
DEIR	,,	,,	*convent of.*	TELL	,,	,,	*a mound or hill.*
J., JEB, or JEBEL	,,	,,	*a mountain.*	W. or WADY	,,	,,	*a valley and brook.*

The references to the Maps immediately follow the names within parentheses, the figures and letters indicating the situation of the places on the respective Maps; thus, ABANA (7 C b) appears on Map 7, in the square C b.

ABANA (7 C b), a river of Damascus, 2 Ki. 5. 12.

ABARIM (5 C e), a range of high hills north-east of Salt Sea. Num. 27. 12 : 33. 47. 48 : Deut. 32. 49.

ABDON (5 B b), a town of Asher, now called *Abdeh*, Josh. 21. 30 ; 1 Chr. 6. 74.

ABEL-BETH-MAACHAH (5 C b ; 7 B bf; 9 A b), a city of the tribe of Naphtali, at foot of Mount Hermon, now called *Abl*. 2 Sam. 20. 14, 15 ; 1 Ki. 15. 20 : 2 Ki. 15. 29.

ABEL-MEHOLAH (7 B c), a city west of the Jordan ; birth-place of Elisha, 1 Ki. 4. 12 ; 19. 16.

ABEL-SHITTIM (5 C e), a city east of the Jordan, Num. 33. 49 ; Josh. 2. 1.

ABILA (7 B c ; 10 C c), a town on the borders of Bashan and Gilead, now called *Abil*.

ABILENE (10 C b), a small canton in Syria, Lk. 3. 1.

ACCAD (1 F b ; 2 E c), a city in Shinar, built by Nimrod, Gen. 10. 8. 10.

ACCHO or **AKKA** (5 B c ; 7 B c ; 9 A b), a seaport town of Canaan, now called *Acre*, Jud. 1. 31.

ACHAIA (14 C b ; 15 D c), Roman province, of which Corinth was the capital. See Acts 18. 12.

ACHZIB (5 B b ; 9 A b), a city of the tribe of Asher, on the shore of the Mediterranean Sea, Josh. 19. 29 ; Mic. 1. 14.

ACRE, BAY OF (11 B c).

ADANA (3 D b ; 14 F b), a town near Tarsus.

ADLUN (11 B b), a village, famous for its caves and tombs.

ADRAMYTTIUM (14 D b), a town on coast of Mysia, Acts 27. 2.

ADRIA (14 B b), sea between Italy and Greece. See Acts 27. 27.

ADULLAM (7 A d), an ancient city of Judah ; in a cave near it David hid from Saul, 1 Sam. 22. 1.

AEOLIAN ISLETS (14 A b), off coast of Sicily.

AI (5 B e ; 6 C d), a city near Bethel ; scene of Joshua's defeat and signal victory, Josh. 8. 1-29.

AIN SHEMS (11 A e), the modern name for *Beth-Shemesh*.

AJALON (5 B e), a city of the tribe of Dan, Jud. 1. 35 ; in vicinity was valley memorable for Joshua's miracle, Josh. 10. 12. 13.

AJLAN (11 A e), the ancient *Eglon*.

AKIR (11 A e), the modern name for *Ekron*.

ALEXANDRIA (3 B c ; 14 D c ; 15 E c), a celebrated city of Egypt, Acts 18. 24-28.

ALUSH (4 C b), a place in neighbourhood of Red Sea, Num. 33. 13.

AMALEKITES (6 B d), a powerful people residing in desert of Paran, Ex. 17. 8 ; 1 Sam. 14. 48 ; 15. 7.

AMASIA (14 F a), a town in Pontus.

AMASTRIS (14 E a ; 15 E b), a town in Bithynia.

AMATHUS (10 C d), a city east of the Jordan, now called *Amateh*.

AMMAN (3 D c ; 11 C e ; 12 C c), the modern name for *Rabbath Ammon*.

AMORITES (1 E b ; 2 D c), a tribe of idolatrous Canaanites, Gen. 10. 16 ; Deut. 20. 17 ; Jud. 1. 34.

AMPHIPOLIS (14 C a), a city of Macedonia, Acts 17. 1.

AMWAS (11 A e), thought by some to be Emmaus, but most improbable.

ANAB (5 A f), a town of Judah, Josh. 15. 50.

ANATA (11 B e), the ancient *Anathoth*.

ANATHOTH (5 B e ; 7 B d), a city of Benjamin, birth-place of Jeremiah, Jer. 1. 1.

ANCYRA (14 E b), a town in Galatia.

ANTIOCH (14 F b ; 15 E c), the capital of Syria, Acts 11. 26.

ANTIOCH (14 E b), of Pisidia, a city of Asia Minor, Acts 13. 14.

ANTIPATRIS (10 A d), a town near Joppa, Acts 23, 31.

APHEK (5 C c), a royal city of the Canaanites, 1 Sam. 4. 1 ; 29. 1 1 Ki. 20. 26.

APOLLONIA (14 C a), a city of Macedonia, Acts 17. 1.

APOLLONIA (10 A d), a seaport town of Samaria.

APPII FORUM (14 A a), or market-place of Appius, where Paul, on his way a prisoner to Rome, met company of Christians, Acts 28. 15.

AR MOAB (5 C f ; 7 B d), the capital of Moab, Num. 21. 28.

ARABIA (14 F c ; 15 E c), an extensive country of Asia, comprising three divisions.

ARAD (4 D a ; 5 B f ; 7 B d), a royal city of the Canaanites. Num. 21. 1.

ARAIR (11 C f), the modern name for Aroer on the Arnon.

ARAM (1 E b ; 5 D a), country north-east of Palestine, usually called *Syria*, Num. 23. 7.

ARARAH (11 A f), modern name for *Aroer*.

ARARAT (3 E b), mountainous region in Armenia, resting-place of the ark, Gen. 8. 4.

ARAXES or **GIHON** (3 F b), a river in Armenia, Gen. 8. 4.

ARBELA (13 B b), a town in Assyria.

ARCHELAIS (13 G a ; 14 E b), a city in Asia Minor, east of Antioch.

ARIMATHEA [(10 B d), home of Joseph, who buried Jesus in his own tomb, Matt. 27. 57-60.

ARNON (5 C f ; 7 B d ; 11 C f ; 12 C c), a river which formed the north boundary of Moab, Num. 21. 13 ; 22. 36.

AROER (5 C f ; 4 D a), a city situated on river Arnon, Jos. 13. 16 ; Jud. 11. 26.

AROER (5 A f), a city of Simeon. See 1 Sam. 30. 28.

ARPAD (8 B b), a city of Syria.

ARRABE or **ARRABY** (11 B d), a village in mountains of Nablus.

ARSUF (11 A d), possibly Apollonia.

ARVAD (9 A a), a city of Phœnicia, situated on a small island, Gen. 10. 18 ; Ezek. 27. 8.

ASCALON or **ASKALAN** (10 A e ; 11 A e), a Philistine town, formerly called *Askelon*.

ASHDOD (11 A e), a fortified town in plain of Philistia, I Sam. 5. 1.

ASHER (5 B c), allotment of, Josh. 19. 24.

ASHKENAZ (1 F b), territory of Ashkenaz, son of Gomer, Gen. 10. 3.

ASHKENAZ SEA (1 F b), inland sea, called the *Black Sea*.

ASHTORETH KARNAIM (6 D c), a ruined mound, now called *Tell Ashtara*. See Gen. 14. 5.

ASIA (14 D b ; 15 E c), Roman province, within which the seven churches were situated, Rev. 1. 4.

ASSHUR (2 E b ; 8 C b), ancient city of *Assyria*.

ASSOS (14 D b), a seaport town of Mysia, Acts 20. 13, 14.

ASSYRIA (1 F b ; 2 E b), an ancient kingdom, so named from Asshur, Gen. 2. 14 : 2 Ki. 15. 29 ; Is. 11. 11.

ATHENS (3 A b ; 14 C b ; 15 D c), the capital of Attica in Greece, visited by Paul, Acts 17. 16-22.

ATHLIT (11 A c), Phœnician ruins at.

ATTALIA (14 E b), a town on coast of Pamphylia, Acts 14. 25.

AZOTUS (10 A e), a city on the borders of the Mediterranean, Acts 8. 40, identical with Ashdod.

AZZAH (6 B d), another form for *Gaza.*

BAAL HAZOR (5 B e), a city near Bethel, now called *Tell Asur*, 2 Sam. 13. 23.

BAAL-MEON [(5 C e), a town of the Reubenites, Num. 32. 38.

BABYLON (1 F b; 2 E c; 8 C b), the capital of Chaldea, built by Nimrod, Gen. 10. 10; Dan. 1. 1.

BABYLONIA (2 E c), called the land of Shinar, Gen. 10. 10.

BAGHDAD (3 E c), an important town on river Tigris.

BASHAN (7 C c), a large fertile region east of the Jordan, Num. 21. 33.

BASRA (3 F c), a city on the Tigris.

BEEROTH (5 B e), a city near Bethel, now called *Bireh*, Josh. 9. 17.

BEERSHEBA (4 D a; 5 A f; 6 B d; 7 A d; 12 B c), city and site of a well in the south of Canaan, Gen. 21. 33; 1 Ki. 19. 3; now called *Bir-es-Seba.*

BEIRUT (3 D c), seaport on the Mediterranean.

BEISAN (11 B d), identical with Bethshan.

BEIT JIBRIN (11 A e), site of the ancient *Eleutheropolis.*

BEIT RIMA (11 B d), the ancient *Beth Rimmon.*

BELA (6 C a), a town of Reuben, Gen. 14. 8.

BENJAMIN (5 B e), allotment of, Josh. 18. 11.

BEREA (13 F d; 14 C a), a town of Macedonia, Acts 17. 10.

BETHABARA (10 C c), one of the principal fords of the Jordan; place where John baptised, John 1. 28.

BETHANY (10 C e; 13 F e; 13 H a), a village near Jerusalem; the home of Lazarus and his sisters, Matt. 21. 17.

BETH DAGON (5 A d), a city of Judah, now called *Beit Dejan*, Josh. 15. 41.

BETHEL (5 B e; 6 C a; 7 B d; 9 A c; 10 B e; 12 C c), a city twelve miles north of Jerusalem, Gen. 28. 19; 1 Sam. 7. 16; Ki. 12. 29-33.

BETH HORON (7 B d), two towns of Ephraim, upper and nether.

BETH JESHIMOTH (5 C e), a city of the Reubenites, Josh. 13. 20.

BETHLEHEM (4 D a; 5 B c; 5 B e; 6 C a; 7 B d; 9 A c; 10 B e; 11 B e; 12 C c; 13 F e), birth-place of our Lord, as foretold, Mic. 5. 2; Matt. 2. 1. 6.

BETHSAIDA (10 C c; 13 C a), a city of Galilee, birth-place of Andrew, Peter, and Philip, John 1. 44.

BETHSHAN (5 B d; 7 B c; 9 A b), a city west of the Jordan, Josh. 17. 11; 1 Sam. 13. 10.

EBTH SHEMESH (5 A e), a city of Judah, Josh. 15. 10; 21. 16.

BETH-ZUR (5 B e; 7 B d), a city of Judah, now called *Beit Sur*, Josh. 15. 58.

BITHYNIA (14 E a; 15 E b), a province of Asia Minor, to the

Christians of which Peter addressed his first epistle, 1 Pet. 1. 1.

BLACK SEA or EUXINE (2 C a; 3 C a; 14 E a; 15 E b), an inland sea, forming part of the south boundary of Europe.

BOZRAH (4 D a), a city of Moab Jer. 48. 24.

BRUNDUSIUM (14 B a), a seaport town of Italy.

BYZANTIUM (14 D a; 15 D b), the modern Constantinople.

CABUL (5 B c; 7 B c), one of the cities that Solomon gave to Hiram, king of Tyre, 1 Ki. 9. 13.

CÆSAREA (10 A d; 11 A d; 12 B b; 14 E c; 15 Bc), the capital of Palestine, Acts 8. 40.

CÆSAREA PHILIPPI (10 C b; 14 F b; 15 E c), a city now called *Banias*, Mk. 8. 27.

CALAH (1 F b), one of the most ancient cities of Assyria, Gen. 10. 11. 12.

CALNEH (8 B b), a city of Assyria, built by Nimrod, Gen. 10. 10.

CANA (10 B c ; 13 A b), a town of Galilee, where our Lord performed His first miracle, John 2. 1-11.

CANAAN (1 E b; 4 D a; 6 B d), the country so named from Canaan, the son of Ham, Gen. 10. 15.

CAPERNAUM (10 C c; 13 C a), a city on west shore of Sea of Galilee, the scene of many of our Lord's miracles, Matt. 8. 5-15; Mk. 2. 1-12; John 4. 46-53.

CAPHTOR or RAHAB (1 D b; 8 A b), in Upper Egypt, Amos 9. 7.

CAPITOLIAS (10 C c), a small town of Decapolis, now called *Beit er Ras.*

CAPPADOCIA (14 E b; 15 E c), a province of Asia Minor, Acts 2. 9.

CARCHEMISH (2 D b; 8 B b), a city on the Euphrates, 2 Chr. 35. 20.

CARIA (14 D b), a maritime province of Asia.

CARMEL (5 A c; 6 B c; 7 B c; 9 A b; 10 A c; 11 B c; 12 C b), a famous mountain in Palestine, 1 Ki. 18. 19; Is. 33. 9; 35. 2; Jer. 50. 19; Amos 1. 2.

CARMEL (5 B f; 7 B d), a city of Judah, now called *El Kurmul*, 1 Sam. 15. 12; 25. 5.

CARPATHOS (14 D b), an island south-west of Rhodes.

CASPIAN SEA (2 G a; 3 G a; 8 C a), an inland sea of Western Asia.

CAUCASUS MOUNT (3 F a), an extensive and lofty range of mountains between the Euxine and Caspian Seas.

CENCHREA (14 C b), a seaport of Corinth, Acts 18. 18.

CEPHALLENIA (14 C b), the largest of the Ionian Islands.

CHELIDONIÆ ISLETS (14 E b), off the coast of Lycia.

CHINNERETH SEA (6 C c ; 7 B c; 9 A b; 15 C c), now called *Sea of Galilee*, or *Lake of Tiberias.*

CHIOS (14 D b), an island off Smyrna, Acts 20. 15.

CHORAZIN (10 C c; 13 C a), a city on shore of Sea of Galilee, near to Capernaum, Matt. 11. 21; Lk. 10. 13.

CILICIA (14 E b), a maritime Roman province in south-east of Asia Minor, its capital being

Tarsus, the birth-place of Paul, Acts 22. 3.

CLAUDA (14 C c), a small island south-west of Crete, Acts. 27. 16.

CNIDUS (14 D b), a city standing on a promontory in Caria, Acts 27. 7.

COLOSSÆ (14 D b), a city of Phrygia in Asia Minor, Col. 1. 2.

COOS or COS (14 D b), a small island off the coast of Caria, Acts 21. 1.

CORCYRA (14 D b), an island in the Adriatic Sea.

CORINTH (14 C b; 15 B c) the capital of Achaia, Acts 18. 1.

CRETE (3 A b; 14 C b; 15 D c), a large island in the Mediterranean, Acts 27. 12. 13; Tit. 1. 5.

CUSH (1 D c), generally called *Ethiopia*, an extensive country of Africa, Gen. 10. 6. 7.

CYPRUS (3 C b; 14 E b; 15 E c), a large island in the Mediterranean, situated between Cilicia and Syria.

CYRENE (15 D c), a town in Libya, Matt. 27. 32; Acts 2. 10; 11. 20; 13. 11.

DABSHEH (11 B c), a city of Zebulon, Josh. 19. 11.

DABERATH (5 B c; 13 B b), a town near the foot of Mount Tabor, Josh. 19. 12; 1 Chr. 6. 72.

DAMASCUS (2 D c; 5 D a; 6 D b; 7 C b; 8 B b; 9 B b; 10 D a; 11 D a; 12 D a; 15 E c), an ancient and celebrated city of Syria, Gen. 14. 15; Acts 9. 2.

DAN (5 A e; 7 B b; 9 A b; 11 C b), allotment of, Josh. 19. 40.

DAN or LAISH (5 C b; 6 C b; 7 B b), a city east of the Jordan, Gen. 14. 14; Jud. 18. 29.

DANUBE (15 C b; 15 D b), second river of Europe.

DEAD SEA (3 D c; 7 B a; 10 B e; 11 B e; 12 C c; 13 H c; 14 F c), called also *Salt Sea, Sea of the Plain*, a lake of South Palestine.

DEBIR (5 A f), a city of the tribe of Judah, Josh. 11. 21; 21. 15.

DECAPOLIS (10 C c; 13 C c), "ten cities," Eastern Palestine, Matt. 4. 25; Mark 5. 20; 7. 31.

DEDAN (1 E c), the modern *Aden*, a seaport of Arabia, Ezek. 27. 15.

DERBE (14 E b), a city of Lycaonia, Acts 14. 6.

DIBON, or DHIBAN, or **DIBAN** (4 D a; 5 C e; 6 C a; 7 B d; 11 C e), a town of Moab assigned to Reuben, Josh. 13. 9. 17.

DIBBIN (11 C d), a city east of the Jordan.

DION (10 D c), a town of Decapolis.

DOPHKAH (4 C b), an encampment of the Israelites, Num. 33. 12.

DOR (5 A c; 7 A c; 9 A b; 10 A c), a city on shore of the Mediterranean, Jud. 1. 27; 1 Ki. 4. 11.

DOTHAN (5 B d; 6 C c; 7 B c), a town in the plain north of Samaria, memorable as the place where Joseph was sold by his brethren, Gen. 37. 17.

DUMAH (8 B b), country so named from a son of Ishmael, Is. 21. 11.

DURA (11 B e), a city south-west of Hebron, the ancient *Adoraim.*

DYRRACHIUM (14 B a; 15 c b),

a town on coast of Illyricum.

EBAL (5 B d ; 6 C c ; 7 B c ; 10 B d), a hill near Shechem, from which curses were to be pronounced, Deut. 11. 29 : 27. 13.

EDOM (4 D a ; 7 B e), land inhabited by descendants of Edom, Gen. 32. 3 : 36. 8.

EDREI (5 D c), the capital of kingdom of Bashan, now called *Ed Derdah*, Num. 21. 33.

EGLON (5 A e), a city of Judah, Josh. 15. 39.

EGYPT (1 D c ; 3 B d ; 4 B a ; 14 D c), a country in north-east of Africa, frequently mentioned in Scripture.

EGYPT, RIVER OF (4 C a ; 6 A d ; 9 A c), to be distinguished from the Nile.

EIDUN (11 C d). Identical with *Dion*.

EKRON (5 A e ; 7 A d ; 9 A c), a principal city of the Philistines, 1 Sam. 5. 10 ; 2 Ki. 1. 2.

ELAM (1 F b ; 2 F c ; 8 C b), a country of Persia, Dan. 8. 2.

ELATH (4 D b ; 8 B c ; 9 A d), a town at the head of the Arabian Gulf, on the route of the Israelites, Deut. 2. 8.

ELEALEH (5 C e), a city near Heshbon, Num. 32. 37 : Is. 15. 4.

ELIM (4 C b), encampment of the Israelites after crossing the Red Sea, Ex. 15. 27.

ELIS (14 C b), a town of Achaia.

EL MEJDEL (11 A e), a village near Askalan.

EMMAUS (10 A e ; 13 E d), a village near Jerusalem, memorable for Christ's interview with two disciples on their way thither, Lk. 24. 13.

ENDOR (5 B c ; 9 A b ; 11 B c ; 13 B c), a city south of Mount Tabor, memorable for the account given of the witch of, 1 Sam. 28. 7.

ENGANNIM (5 B d), a town in vicinity of Mount Gilboa, Josh. 15. 34 : 19. 21 : 21. 29.

EN-GEDI (7 B d), a town in wilderness of Judah, Josh. 15. 62.

EPHESUS (14 D b ; 15 D c), a celebrated city of Asia Minor, scene of Paul's labours for three years, Acts 19. 20. See Rev. 2. 1.

EPHRAIM (5 B d), allotment of, Josh. 16. 5.

EPHRAIM (5 B d), a mountain, Josh. 17. 15 ; Jud. 2. 9 : 7. 24.

EPHRAIM (10 B e ; 13 F d), a city eight miles from Jerusalem, John 11. 54.

EPHRATH (6 C d), the ancient name of *Bethlehem*, Gen. 35. 16-19.

EPIRUS (14 C b), Grecian territory lying between Macedonia and Achaia.

ERECH (1 F b ; 8 C b), a city in Shinar, founded by Nimrod, Gen. 10. 10.

ESDRAELON, PLAIN OF (10 B c ; 11 B c ; 12 C b), an extensive valley in which many battles were fought.

ES SAFI, TELL (11 A e), the site of an ancient city, probably *Gath*.

ES SALT (11 C d), a city north-east of the Dead Sea.

ETAM (5 B c), a city of Judah, 2 Chr. 11. 6. See Jud. 15. 8.

ET TELL (11 C c), probably the site of the ancient *Bethsaida*.

EUBOEA (14 C b), an island of Greece.

EUPHRATES (2 E c ; 3 F c ; 9 C a ; 14 F b ; 15 F c), the largest and most important river of Western Asia, Gen. 2. 14 ; Deut. 11. 24 ; Rev. 9. 14.

EZION-GEBER (4 D b ; 9 A d), site of Israelite encampment, Num. 33. 35 ; here, too, Solomon equipped his fleet, 1 Ki. 9. 26.

FAIR HAVENS (14 D c), a harbour on south coast of Crete, near Lasea, Acts 27. 8.

GAD (5 C d), allotment of, Josh. 13. 24.

GADARA (10 G c ; 13 D c), a celebrated city east of the Sea of Galilee, Mk. 5. 1-20 ; Lk. 8. 26-27.

GALATIA (14 E b), Roman province of Asia Minor, scene of Paul's labours during his second and third missionary tours, Acts 16. 6 : 18. 23.

GALILEE (7 B c ; 9 A b ; 10 B c), scene of the greater part of our Lord's life and labours, Matt. 2. 22 : 4. 23 : 28. 7.

GALILEE, SEA OF (10 C c ; 11 C c ; 12 C b ; 13 C b), called also the *Sea of Chinnereth*, Num. 34. 11, the *Sea of Tiberais*, John 6. 1, and the *Sea of Gennesaret*, Lk. 5. 1.

GATH (5 A e ; 9 A c), a celebrated city of the Philistines, 1 Sam. 5. 8 ; 2 Chr. 26. 6.

GAULUS (14 A b), a small island beside Melita.

GAZA (1 E b ; 4 D a ; 5 A e ; 6 B d ; 7 A d ; 9 A c ; 10 A f ; 11 A e ; 12 B c), a border city of the Philistines, Jud. 16.

GEBA (7 B d), a town of Benjamin assigned to the priests, Josh. 18. 24 : 21. 17.

GEBAL (6 C a ; 8 B b ; 9 A a), a city of the Giblites on coast of Phoenicia, famous for its masonry and shipbuilding, 1 Ki. 5. 18 ; Ezek. 27. 9.

GEDOR (5 B e), a town in mountains of Judah, now called *Jedur*, Josh. 15. 58.

GENNESARET, LAKE OF. See *Galilee, Sea of.*

GERAR (4 D a ; 5 A f ; 6 B d ; 7 A d), a royal city of the Philistines, Gen. 10. 10 : 20. 1 ; 26. 6 ; now called *Kh. Umm Jerrar.*

GERASA (10 C d), a Syrian city, now called *Jerash.*

GERGESENES (10 C c ; 13 C b), the inhabitants of Gadara.

GERIZIM (5 B d ; 6 C c ; 7 B c ; 10 B d ; 12 C b), a mountain of Samaria, near Shechem, from which the blessings were to be pronounced, Deut. 27. 12 ; Josh. 8. 33.

GESHURITES (5 C b), people dwelling east of the Jordan, 2 Sam. 3. 3 : 13. 37. 38.

GEZER (9 A c), a city of Ephraim, Josh. 10. 33 ; 1 Ki. 9. 16.

GIBEON (5 B e ; 7 B d ; 9 A c), a city north of Jerusalem, now called *El Jib*, Josh. 9. 3-27 : 10. 1-14.

GIBLITES (9 A a), inhabitants of Gebal, Josh. 13. 5.

GIHON or **ARAXES** (3 F b), a river in Armenia, Gen. 2. 13.

GILBOA (5 B d ; 6 C c ; 7 B c), a mountain west of the Jordan, noted for the slaughter of Saul and his three sons by the Philistines, 1 Sam. 31. 1-6 ; 2 Sam. 1. 21.

GILEAD (5 C d ; 11 C d), a range of mountains in the vicinity of river Jabbok, which abounded

with trees producing a valuable gum called the "balm of Gilead," Gen. 37. 25 ; Jer. 8. 22.

GILGAL (5 B e ; 7 A c), site of first Israelite encampment after crossing the river Jordan, Josh. 4. 19.

GOLAN (5 C c ; 7 B c ; 10 C c), a city of Manasseh, appointed to be a city of refuge, Deut. 4. 43 ; Josh. 21. 27.

GOMER (1 E a), a district of Asia Minor inhabited by descendants of Gomer, the eldest son of Japheth, Gen. 10. 2 ; Ezek. 38. 6.

GOSHEN (4 B a), a province in Egypt, which Joseph procured for his father and brethren to settle in, Gen. 45. 10 : 47. 1-6.

GOZAN (8 C b), a river of Assyria, 2 Ki. 17. 6 ; 1 Chr. 5. 26 ; Is. 37. 12.

GREAT SEA (1 C b ; 2 B c ; 4 A a ; 5 A c ; 6 B c ; 7 A b ; 8 A b ; 9 A a ; 10 B c ; 14 B c), the Mediterranean, Num. 34. 6 ; Josh. 1. 4 : 15. 12 ; Ezek. 47. 10 ; Dan. 7. 2.

HALHUL (5 B e), a town in mountains of Judah, Josh. 15. 58.

HAM (6 C c ; 6 C d), descendants and land of.

HAMATH (2 D b ; 6 D a ; 8 B d ; 9 B a), a city and province of Syria, in valley of the Orontes, Num. 13. 21 ; Jud. 3. 3 ; Ezek. 4. 81.

HAMMATH (5 B c ; 13 C b), a fenced city of Naphtali, now called *Hammam*, Josh. 19. 35.

HANNATH (b B c), a city of Naphtali, now called *Kefr Anan.*

HARAN (2 D b ; 8 B b), a town of Padanaram, Gen. 11. 31.

HASBEIYA (11 C b), a town on river Hasbany.

HAVILAH (1 F d), land inhabited by descendants of Havilah, son of Cush, Gen. 2. 11 : 10. 7 : 25. 18 ; 1 Sam. 15. 7.

HAZARMAVETH (1 F d), land occupied by descendants of Hazarmaveth, son of Joktan, 1 Chr. 1. 20.

HAZEROTH (4 D b), a place where the Israelites encamped in the wilderness, Num. 11. 35 ; 12. 16.

HAZEZON TAMAR (6 C d), ancient name of Engedi, on the west of the Salt Sea, Gen. 14. 7 ; 2 Chr. 20. 2.

HAZOR (5 C b ; 6 C b ; 7 B b), principal royal Canaanite city, near Lake Merom, Josh. 11. 10.

HEBRON (5 B e ; 6 B d ; 7 B d ; 9 A c ; 10 B e ; 11 B e ; 12 C c), one of the oldest cities in the world, Gen. 13. 18 ; Jud. 1. 10.

HELBON (7 C b), a city of Syria, famed for its excellent wine, Ezek. 27. 18.

HERMON (5 C b ; 7 B b ; 10 C b ; 11 C b ; 12 C a ; 14 F c, 17 D b), a mountain in the north-eastern boundary of Palestine, Deut. 3. 8 ; Josh. 12. 5 ; Ps. 89. 12 : 133. 3.

HESHBON (5 C e ; 6 C d ; 7 B d ; 9 A c ; 10 C e ; 12 C c), a city of the Reubenites, Num. 32. 37 ; Josh. 13. 17.

HIERAPOLIS (14 D b ; 15 D c), a city of Phrygia, Col. 4. 13.

HIPPOS (10 C c ; 13 C b), a village south-east of Sea of Galilee.

HITTITES (2 C b ; 6 C d), descendants of Heth, 2 Ki. 7. 6.

HIVITES (1 F b), a tribe of the Canaanites, Gen. 10. 17.

HOBATH (6 D b), a town near Damascus, Gen. 14. 15.

HOR (9 A c), a mountain on the borders of Edom, where Aaron died and was buried, Num. 20. 22-29.

HOREB (4 C b), a mountain in Arabia, near Mount Sinai, where the angel of the Lord appeared to Moses, Ex. 3. 1. 2.

ICONIUM (14 E b), the capital of Lycaonia, where Paul and Barnabas preached, Acts 14. 1.

IJON (7 B b), an ancient city now in ruins, situated in a plain, 1 Ki. 15. 20; 2 Ki. 15. 29; 2 Chr. 16. 4.

ILLYRICUM (14 B a), Roman province on the shore of the Adriatic, scene of Paul's labours, Rom. 15. 19.

ISRAEL (7 B c; 9 A b), kingdom of the ten tribes, 1 Ki. 11. 38.

ISSACHAR (5 B c), allotment of, Josh. 19. 17.

ISSUS (14 F b), a seaport on the Gulf of Issus in Cilicia.

ITUREA (10 C b), a province of Syria, Lk. 3. 1.

JABBOK (5 C d; 6 C c; 7 B c; 11 C d; 12 C b), a rivulet on the east side of the Jordan, Gen. 32. 22; Deut. 2. 37.

JABESH-GILEAD (5 C d; 7 B c; 9 A b), a city of the half tribe of Manasseh, Jud. 21. 8; 1 Sam. 31. 11.

JABNEH (5 A e; 7 A d), a city of the tribe of Dan, 2 Chr. 26. 6.

JACOB'S WELL (5 B d; 10 B d), a fountain near Shechem, John 4. 6.

JAMNIA (10 A e), the modern town called *Yebna*.

JAPHIA (5 B c; 13 A b), city of Zebulon, Josh. 19. 12.

JAPHO (5 A d), a seaport town, now *Joppa*, Josh. 19. 46.

JARMUTH (5 A e; 7 A d), a city of Judah, now called *Yarmuk*, Josh. 10. 5; 21. 29.

JATTIR (5 B f), a city of Judah, now called *Kh. Attir*, Josh. 15. 48.

JAVAN (1 D b), i.e., *Greece*, Gen. 10. 2; Is. 66. 19.

JAZER (5 C e), a city of Gad, Josh. 21. 39; Is. 16. 8. 9.

JEBA (11 B d), a village in Nablus.

JEBEL JERMUK (11 B c), name of a mountain.

JEDUR (11 B e), the modern name for *Iturea*.

JENIN (11 B d), same as *En-gannim*.

JERICHO (4 D a; 5 B e; 7 B d; 10 B e; 11 B e; 12 C c; 13 G d), a royal city of great antiquity Deut. 32. 49; Josh. 6. 1; 1 Ki. 16. 34; Lk. 19. 1.

JERUSALEM (2 D c; 3 D c; 5 B e; 6 C d; 7 B d; 8 B d; 9 A c; 10 B e; 11 B e; 12 C c; 13 F e; 14 F c; 15 E c), the metropolis of Palestine from the time of David, 2 Sam. 5. 6.

JEZREEL (5 B c; 7 B c; 9 A b), a celebrated city west of the Jordan, Josh. 19. 18; 1 Ki. 21. 1; 2 Ki. 9. 30-37.

JEZREEL, VALLEY OF (5 B c).

JILJILIA (11 B d), probably the site of the ancient *Gilgal*.

JIMZU (11 A e), same as *Gimso*.

JISH (11 B b), a village in Beirut, destroyed by an earthquake.

JOKNEAM (5 B c; 7 B c), a city of Zebulon, now called *Tell Keimun*, Josh. 12. 22.

JOKTAN (1 F d), land occupied by the descendants of Joktan, son of Eber, Gen. 10. 25; 1 Chr. 1. 19.

JOPPA (7 A c; 9 A b; 10 A d; 12 B b; 14 E c; 15 E c), a seaport town on the Mediterranean, 2 Chr. 2. 16; Jon. 1. 3; Acts 9. 36; 10. 5.

JORDAN (5 C b; 5 C a; 6 C c; 7 B c; 9 A b; 10 C b; 10 C d; 11 C b; 11 C d; 12 C b; 13 C b; 13 H d), a celebrated river of Palestine, which falls into the Dead Sea, Josh. 3. 1; 2 Ki. 2. 7; Matt. 3. 6.

JORDAN, PLAIN OF (3 D c).

JUDAH (5 A e; 7 A d; 9 A c), allotment of, Josh. 15. 1.

JUDAH, WILDERNESS OF (5 B f).

JUDAEA (10 A e; 14 E c), southern division of Palestine.

JUTTAH or **YUTTA** (5 B f; 10 B f), a city of Judah, Josh. 15. 55.

KABUL (11 B c). See *Cabul*.

KADES (11 C b). See *Kadesh*.

KADESH (2 D c; 9 B a), a city on the borders of the Promised Land, Num. 13. 26; 32. 8.

KANAH, BROOK (5 A d; 12 B b). See Josh. 16. 8; 17. 9.

KEDESH (5 C b; 7 B b; 9 A b), a town belonging to the tribe of Naphtali, Josh. 19. 37; 20. 7.

KEFR ANAN (11 B c). See *Hannathon*.

KEFR KENNA (11 B c), thought by some to be Cana of Galilee.

KENATH (7 C c; 9 B b), a town of Manasseh, Num. 32. 42.

KERAZEH (11 B c), a village north of the Sea of Galilee.

KERIOTH (5 B f), a city of Judah, now called *Kh. Kureitein*, Josh. 15. 25.

KERIOTH (7 C c), a city of Moab, Jer. 48. 24.

KERSA or **GERSA** (11 C c), a town on east shore of Sea of Galilee; the ancient *Gergesa*, Matt. 8. 28.

KIRIATHAIM (6 C d), a city of the Reubenites, Num. 32. 37; Jer. 48. 1. 23.

KIRJATH-ARBA (4 D a; 6 C d), the ancient name of *Hebron*, Gen. 23. 2; Josh. 14. 15.

KIR MOAB (5 C f; 7 B d), one of the two chief strongholds of Moab.

KISHON (5 B c; 6 C c; 9 A b; 10 B c; 12 C b), a rivulet which rises in Mount Tabor and falls in to the Mediterranean, Jud. 4. 7; 5. 21; Ps. 83. 9.

KITTIM (1 E b; 8 B b; 9 A a), land occupied by descendants of Kittim, son of Javan, Gen. 10. 4: probably *Cyprus*.

KUNEITRA (11 C b), the site of an ancient ruin.

KURN (11 B b), a river entering the Mediterranean near Zib.

KUTHA (2 D c; 8 E c), a city near Babylon.

LACHISH (5 A e; 7 A d), a city of Judah, now called *Tell el Hesy*, Josh. 10. 31. 32; 2 Chr. 11. 9.

LAISH (5 C b; 6 C b; 7 B b), original name of the city of Dan, Jud. 18. 29.

LAODICEA (14 D b), a city of Phrygia, near Colossæ, Col. 2. 1 : 4. 13; Rev. 3. 14.

LAODICEA (14 F b), a city of Syria, near Antioch.

LEBANON (3 D c; 5 B b; 6 C b; 7 B b; 9 A b; 10 B b; 11 B b), an extensive range of mountains on the north of Canaan, Deut. 3. 25; Jud. 3. 3; 1 Ki. 7. 2.

LEBANON, VALLEY OF (7 C b).

LEBONAH (7 B c), a village near Shiloh, Jud. 21. 19.

LEHABIM (1 D b), country occupied by descendants of Cush, 1 Chr. 1. 11.

LEONTES (5 B b; 6 C b; 10 B b; 11 B b; 12 C a), a river of Phœnicia.

LIBNAH (7 A d), a town of Judah, assigned to the priests, Josh. 21. 13.

LOD (7 A d), a Benjamite town, 1 Chr. 8. 12, identical with *Ludd*.

LUBBAN (11 B d), the modern name for *Lebonah*.

LUDD or **LYDDA** (10 A e; 11 A e; 14 E c; 15 E c), a village near Joppa, Acts 9. 32.

LUZ (6 C d), the ancient name of *Bethel*, Gen. 28. 19.

LYCAONIA (14 E b), a province of Asia Minor: chief scene of Paul's labours during his first missionary tour, Acts 14. 6.

LYCIA (14 D b), a province of Asia Minor, Acts 27. 5.

LYDDA (10 A e; 11 A e; 14 E c; 15 E c), " nigh to Joppa," Acts 9. 32; 35. 38.

LYDIA (14 D b), country of Asia, Ezek. 30. 5.

LYSTRA (14 E b; 15 E c), city of Lycaonia, Acts 14. 8.

MACEDONIA (14 C a; 15 D b), a large country lying between the Adriatic and Aegean Seas, Acts 16. 9; Rom. 15. 26.

MAGDALA (10 B e; 13 C b), a town on the shore of the Sea of Galilee, Matt. 15. 39; Lk. 8. 2.

MAGOG (1 F a), land occupied by descendants of a son of Japheth, Gen. 10. 2.

MAHANAIM (5 C d; 6 C c; 7 B c), a city east of the Jordan, Gen. 32. 2; Josh. 21. 38; 2 Sam. 2. 8.

MANASSEH (5 B d; 5 C d), allotment of, Josh. 13. 29 : 17. 1.

MAON (5 B f; 7 B d), a city of Judah, now called *Kh. Main*, Josh. 15. 55; 1 Sam. 23. 24: 25. 2.

MARAH (4 C b), site of Israelite encampment, where bitter waters were made sweet, Ex. 15. 23.

MARESHAH (5 A e; 7 A d), a city of Judah, now called *Kh. Merash*, Josh. 15. 44.

MASADA (10 B f), a famous crag with a castle built on it.

MEDEBA (5 C e; 6 C d; 7 B d), a city of Moab, Num. 21. 30; Josh. 13. 16; Is. 15. 2.

MEDITERRANEAN SEA (3 B c; 11 A c; 12 A b; 14 C c; 15 B c), a large gulf of the Atlantic Ocean, dividing Europe from Africa.

MEGIDDO (5 B c; 6 C c; 7 B c), a city of the tribe of Manasseh, Josh. 17. 11; Jud. 5. 19; 2 Ki. 23. 29. 30.

MELITA (14 A b; 15 C c), now called *Malta*, an island south of Sicily, Acts 28. 1.

MEROM, WATERS OF (5 C b; 6 C b; 7 B b), a lake supplied by the Jordan, Josh. 11. 5.

MESHECH (1 E b), land occupied by the descendants of Meshech, son of Japheth, Gen. 10. 2.

MESOPOTAMIA (3 E c), a province situated between the Euphrates and Tigris, Gen. 11. 31.

4

MICHMASH (5 B e; 13 F d), a city of Benjamin, 1 Sam. 13. 5; Neh. 11. 31.

MILIAN (4 D b), land of the Midianites, Ex. 2. 15.

MILETUS (14 D b), a seaport city south of Ephesus, Acts 20. 15. 17.

MITYLENE (3 B b; 14 D b), capital of the island of Lesbos, Acts 20. 14.

MIZRAIM (1 E c; 2 C d), the old name for *Egypt*.

MOAB (4 D a; 5 C f; 7 B d; 9 A c), an ancient kingdom east of the Dead Sea.

MOLADAH (7 B d), a city of Judah, Josh. 15. 26 : 19. 2.

MOSUL (3 E b), a city on the right bank of the Tigris, opposite Nineveh.

MYRA (14 E b; 15 E c), a city of Lycia, Acts 27. 5.

MYSIA (14 D b), a province of Asia Minor, Acts 16. 7. 8.

NABLUS (11 B d), the ancient *Shechem*.

NAIN (10 B c; 13 B c), a city of Galilee, memorable as the place where Christ restored to life the widow's son, Lk. 7. 11-15.

NAPHTALI (5 B c), allotment of, Josh. 19. 32.

NAZARETH (10 B c; 11 B c; 12 C b; 13 Ab), a town of Galilee, where Christ spent His early years, and where He afterwards preached.

NEAPOLIS (14 C a), a city of Macedonia, Acts 16. 11.

NEBO MOUNT (4 D a; 5 C e; 7 B d; 11 C e; 12 C c), in the land of Moab, where Moses died, Deut. 32. 49.

NICÆA (14 D a; 15 D b), a city in Bithynia.

NICOPOLIS (13 E e; 14 C b; 15 D c), a town in Thrace, near the borders of Macedonia. Tit. 3. 12.

NILE (2 C d; 3 C d; 4 B b; 15 E d), a celebrated river of Egypt, Gen. 41.

NINEVEH (1 F b; 2 E b; 8 C b), one of the oldest and largest cities of the world, situated on the left bank of the Tigris, Jon. 1. 2 : 3; Nah. 1. 2 : 3.

OLIVES, MOUNT OF (5 B e; 10 B e; 13 F e), situated east of Jerusalem, scene of several impressive events in our Lord's history.

ONO (5 A d), a city of Benjamin, now called *Kefr Ana*, 1 Chr. 8. 12.

OPHIR (1 F d), a country celebrated for its gold and precious stones, 1 Ki. 9. 28 : 22. 48; 2 Chr. 8. 18; Job 22. 24; Is. 13. 12.

OPHRA (7 B d), a city of Benjamin, Josh. 18. 23; Jud. 6. 11.

ORONTES (9 B a; 14 F b), a river of North Syria.

PAMPHYLIA (14 E b), a province of Asia Minor, Acts 13. 13 : 14. 24 : 27. 5.

PAPHLAGONIA (14 E a), a district of Asia Minor.

PAPHOS (14 E c; 15 E c), a city of Cyprus, Acts 13. 6.

PARAN (4 C b), the site of the Israelite encampment.

PARAN, DESERT OF (4 C b; 9 A c), in Arabia Petræa, the scene of the wanderings of the Israelites, Num. 10. 12 : 12. 16; 13. 3.

PATARA (14 D b), a seaport town of Lycia, Acts 21. 1.

PATMOS (14 D b), an island in the Aegean Sea to which John was banished, and where he wrote the book of Revelation, Rev. 1. 9.

PELLA (10 C d), a town of Decapolis.

PELLA (14 C a), the ancient capital of Macedonia.

PENUEL (6 C c; 7 B c), a place on the east of Jordan, where Jacob wrestled with God, Gen. 32. 24-30.

PERÆA (10 C d), a division of Palestine.

PERGA (14 E b), a city of Pamphylia, Acts 13. 14 : 14. 25.

PERGAMOS (14 D b), a city of Mysia, seat of one of the seven churches of Asia, Rev. 1. 11: 2. 12.

PERIZZITES (6 B c), a tribe of the ancient Canaanites, Gen. 13. 7 : 15. 20; Jud. 1. 4.

PERSIA (3 F c; 8 D c), an ancient kingdom of Asia.

PERSIAN GULF (2 F d; 3 F d), an arm of the Indian Ocean, extending between Persia and Arabia.

PHARPAR (5 D b; 7 C b; 11 D b), a river of Damascus, 2 Ki. 5. 12.

PHILADELPHIA (14 D b), a city of Lydia, seat of one of the seven churches of Asia, Rev. 1. 11: 3. 7.

PHILADELPHIA (10 C e), a city of Decapolis.

PHILIPPI (14 C a), a chief city of Macedonia, Acts 16. 12.

PHILISTINES (9 A c), the inhabitants of Philistia.

PHŒNICE (14 C b), a city of Crete.

PHŒNICIA (7 B b; 10 B a; 14 F c), a country bounded on the west by the Mediterranean, and on the east and north by Syria.

PHRYGIA (14 D b; 15 E c), a district of Asia Minor, Acts 16. 6.

PISIDIA (14 E b), a province of Asia Minor, Acts 13. 14 : 14. 24.

PONTUS (14 F a; 15 E b), a province of Asia Minor, Acts 2. 9; 1 Pet. 1. 1.

PONTUS EUXINUS (14 E a), i.e., the *Black Sea*.

PROPONTIS (14 D a), a sea in Asia Minor, now called the *Sea of Marmora*.

PTOLEMAIS (10 B c; 14 F c), same as *Accho*.

PUTEOLI (14 A a; 15 C b), a seaport town of Italy, Acts 28. 13.

RAAMAH (1 F d), land occupied by the descendants of Ham. Gen. 10. 7.

RABBA or RABBAH (11 C f), the chief city of the Ammonites. 2 Sam. 11. 1 : 12. 26.

RABBATH-AMMON (5 C e; 7 B d; 9 A c), the metropolis, and very strong fortress of the Ammonites, Deut. 3. 11.

RABBATH MOAB (9 A c), the capital of Moab, also called *Ar*.

RACHEL'S TOMB (5 B e; 6 C d), near Bethlehem, Gen. 48. 7.

RAGABA (10 C d), a city east of the Jordan, now called *Ragib*.

RAMAH (5 B e; 7 B d; 13 F d), a city of Benjamin, now called *er Ram*, Josh. 18. 25; 1 Sam. 1. 19; Jer. 31. 15 : 40. 1.

RAMLA (7 B c), a city of Galilee.

RAMLA (11 B b), a city of Beirut.

RAMLE (11 A e), a village famous for its noble tower.

RAMOTH GILEAD (5 D c;

7 B c), a town of Gad. appointed as a city of refuge, Josh. 20. 8.

RAS EN NAKURAH (11 B b), a promontory on the Mediterranean.

RED SEA (2 C d; 3 C d; 4 D c), an arm of the Indian Ocean between Arabia and Africa, miraculously crossed by the Israelites, Ex. 14.

REIMUN (11 C d), the modern name for *Ramoth Gilead*.

REMTHEH (11 D c), a place east of the Jordan.

REPHAIMS (6 C c), a tribe of Canaanites, Gen. 14. 5.

REPHIDIM (4 C b), a place where the Israelites encamped, Ex. 17. 1.

REUBEN (5 C e), allotment of, Num. 32; Josh. 13. 15.

RHEGIUM (14 B b), a maritime city of Italy, Acts 28. 13.

RHODES (3 B b; 14 D b), an island of the Mediterranean, Acts 21. 1.

RIBLAH (9 B a), a city of Syria, 2 Ki. 23. 33 : 25. 6; Jer. 39. 5.

RIMMON (5 B e), a steep rock which served as a fortress to the Benjamites four months, Jud. 20. 45. 47.

RIMMON (5 B c), a city of Zebulon.

RIPHATH (1 E a), the territory of the descendants of Riphath, son of Gomer, Gen. 10. 3.

ROME (14 A b; 15 C b), the chief city of Italy, and long the mistress of the world.

RUAD (9 A a), same as *Arvad*.

RUMMANEH (11 B c), the modern name for *Rimmon* of Zebulon.

SALAMIS (13 B a; 14 E b; 15 E c), a city in the island of Cyprus, Acts 13. 5.

SALCAH (7 C c; 9 B b), limit of Bashan and of Gad, Deut. 3. 10; Josh. 12. 5 : 13. 11; 1 Chr. 5. 11.

SALEM (4 D a; 6 C d), supposed to be the original name of *Jerusalem*, in the days of Melchizedek, Gen. 14. 18.

SALMONE, CAPE (14 D b), a promontory of Crete, Acts 27. 7.

SALT SEA (5 B e; 6 C d; 9 A c), i.e., the *Dead Sea*.

SAMARIA (7 B c; 10 B d; 14 F c; 15 E c), the capital city of the Ephraimites, about forty miles north from Jerusalem, 1 Ki. 16. 24.

SAMARIA (10 B d), the district between Judea and Galilee.

SAMOS (14 D b), an island in the Mediterranean, off the coast of Asia Minor, Acts 20. 15.

SAMOTHRACIA (14 D a), a small island on the coast of Thracia, Acts 16. 11.

SANGARIUS (14 E a), a river flowing through Bithynia, into the Black Sea.

SARDIS (14 D b; 15 D c), the ancient capital of Lydia, and site of one of the seven churches of Asia, Rev. 1. 11: 3. 1.

SAREPTA (10 B b), a city of the Sidonians, situated between Tyre and Sidon, Lk. 4. 26, identical with *Zarephath*.

SCYROS (14 C b), an island east of Eubœa.

SCYTHOPOLIS (10 B d), i.e., *Bethshan*.

SEBA or SHEBA (1 E d), the principal city of the Sabæans, 1 Ki. 10. 1; Jer. 6. 20; Ezek. 27. 22.

SEBBEH (11 B f), probably *Masada*.

SEILUN (11 B d), the modern name for *Shiloh*.

SEIR, MOUNT (4 D a ; 9 A c), a range of mountains south-east of the Dead Sea, inhabited by the Horites, Gen. 14. 6.

SELAH (9 A c), the capital of Edom, 2 Ki. 14. 7.

SELEUCIA (10 C b), a city on the Tigris.

SELEUCIA (14 F b), once the seaport of Antioch, Acts 13. 4.

SELEUCIA (14 E b), a city of Cilicia.

SEMAKH (11 C c), a village on the Sea of Galilee, probably the ancient *Hippos*.

SEPPHORIS (13⟨A b), the capital of Lower Galilee in the time of Christ.

SHALEM (9 A b), a city near Shechem, Gen. 33. 18.

SHARON, PLAIN OF (5 A d ; 7 A c ; 10 A d ; 11 A d), celebrated for its beauty and fertility, Song 2. 1 ; Is. 35. 2.

SHECHEM (2 D c ; 5 B d ; 6 C c ; 7 B c ; 9 A b ; 10 B d), an ancient city north of Jerusalem, Gen. 33. 19 ; Josh. 24. 1.

SHILOH (5 B d ; 7 B c ; 9 A b), a city of Ephraim, where the ark of God remained for about 300 years, Josh. 18. 1 ; Jud. 18. 31 ; 1 Sam. 1. 3.

SHINAR (1 F b), a province of Babylonia, where the tower of Babel stood, Gen. 10. 10.

SHUNEM (5 B c ; 7 B c), a city of Issachar, where Elisha brought to life the Shunammite's son, 2 Ki. 4. 8-37.

SHUSHAN or **SUSA** (8 C b), the capital and usual residence of the kings of Persia, Neh. 1. 1 ; Est. 2. 8 ; Dan. 8. 2.

SHUWEIKEH (11 A e), the modern name for *Socoh*.

SICILY (15 C c), the largest island in the Mediterranean.

SIDON (1 E b ; 2 D c ; 5 B a ; 6 C b ; 7 B b ; 9 A b ; 10 B a ; 12 C a ; 14 F c ; 15 E c), the capital of Phœnicia, situated on the shore of the Mediterranean, Gen. 10. 19 ; Matt. 15. 21 ; Acts 27. 3.

SIDONIANS (6 C b ; 9 A b), the people living in Sidon, Deut. 3. 9.

SIMEON (5 A f), allotment of, Josh. 19. 1.

SIN (4 C a), a city of Egypt, Ezek. 30. 15.

SIN, WILDERNESS OF (4 C b), place reached by the Israelites, Ex. 16. 1.

SINAI (4 C b), a mountain in the wilderness of Horeb, Ex. 19. 20.

SMYRNA (14 D b ; 15 D c), a large city of Asia Minor, site of one of the seven churches, Rev. 1. 11 ; 2. 8.

SOCOH (5 A f), a city of Judah, Josh. 15. 48.

SOLI (14 E b), a city of Cilicia.

SUCCOTH (5 C d ; 6 C c), a city east of the Jordan, allotted to Gad, Josh. 13. 27.

SUCCOTH (4 C a), a place in Egypt, Ex. 12. 37.

SUEZ, GULF OF (3 C d), the north-western arm of the Red Sea.

SUNAMEIN (11 D b), a city in El Hauran.

SURAFEND (11 B b), probably the ancient *Zarephath*.

SURAH (11 A e), the modern name for *Zorah*.

SYCHAR (10 B d), the capital of Samaria, John 4. 5.

SYRACUSE (14 B b ; 15 C c), a city of the island of Sicily, Acts 28. 12.

SYRIA (3 D b ; 7 C b ; 9 B b ; 11 D b ; 14 F b ; 15 E c), an ancient kingdom, bounded on the west by the Mediterranean, and on the east by the Euphrates 2 Sam. 8. 6 ; 2 Chr. 28. 5 ; Matt. 4. 24.

SYRIAN DESERT (3 D c ; 12 D b), an extensive desert lying between Damascus and Babylon.

TAANACH (6 C c ; 7 B c), a city of the Manassites, Josh. 17. 11.

TABOR, MOUNT (5 B c ; 6 C c ; 7 B c ; 12 C b ; 13 B b), a celebrated mountain in Palestine, Jud. 4. 14 ; Ps. 89. 12 ; Jer. 46. 18.

TADMOR or **PALMYRA** (9 C a), a city built by Solomon, 1 Ki. 9. 18 ; 2 Chr. 8. 4.

TANNAK (11 B c), the modern name for *Taanach*.

TANTURAH (11 A c), the modern name for *Dor*.

TARSUS (14 E b ; 15 E c), the capital of Cilicia, Acts 21. 39 ; the place to which Solomon sent fleets, 1 Ki. 10 .22 ; 2 Chr. 9. 21.

TARTESSUS (1 B b), a town in Spain.

TAURUS (3 C b), a mountain in Cilicia.

TAVIUM (14 E b), a town in the province of Galatia.

TEKOA (5 B e), a city of Judah, 2 Sam. 14. 2 ; 2 Chr. 11. 6.

TELL HUM (11 C c), a place containing the ruins of a large town.

TELL NIMRIN (11 C e), the ancient *Beth Nimrah*.

TELL RAMEH (11 C e), the ancient *Beth Horon (Upper)*.

THASOS (14 C a), an island in the Aegean Sea.

THEBEZ (5 B d), a city of Ephraim, where Abimelech was slain, now called *Tubas*, Jud. 9. 50-54.

THESSALONICA (14 C a ; 15 D b), the capital of Macedonia ; site of Christian Church, to the people of which Paul sent two epistles, Acts 17. 1 ; 1 Thes. 1. 1 ; 2 Thes. 1. 1.

THRACIA (14 C a), a province of Asia Minor.

THYATIRA (14 D b), a city of Lydia, Acts 16. 14 ; Rev. 2. 18.

TIBERIAS (10 C c ; 11 C c ; 12 C b ; 13 C b), a town on the western shore of the Sea of Galilee, now called *Tubariya*.

TIBERIAS, SEA OF, or **BAHRTUBARIYA** (13 C b), i.e., the *Sea of Galilee*.

TIBNAH (11 A e), probably the ancient *Timnath*.

TIGRIS or **HIDDEKEL** (2 E c ; 3 F c ; 15 F c), a celebrated river of Babylonia, Dan. 10. 4.

TIMNATH (6 B d), a city of Judah, Jud. 14. 1.

TIPHSAH or **THAPSACUS** (8 B b ; 9 C a), a city on the Euphrates, 1 Ki. 4. 24.

TIRZAH (5 B d ; 7 B c ; 9 A b), a city of the Ephraimites,

residence of the kings of Israel from the time of Jeroboam to that of Omri, 1 Ki. 14. 17 ; 2 Ki. 15. 16 ; now called *Teiasir*.

TOGARMAH (1 F b), land occupied by descendants of Gomer, Gen. 10. 3 ; Ezek. 27. 14.

TOPHEL (4 D a ; 9 A c), a place supposed to be in the country of Moab, Deut. 1. 1.

TRIPOLIS (14 F c), a coast town of Phœnicia.

TROAS (14 D b ; 15 D c), a seaport of Mysia, Acts 16. 8 ; Cor. 2. 12.

TROGYLLIUM (14 D b), a town on a promontory, about five miles from Samos, Acts 20. 15.

TUBAL (1 E b), land occupied by descendants of Japheth, Gen. 10. 2.

TYRE (2 D c ; 5 B b ; 6 C b ; 7 B b ; 8 B b ; 9 A b ; 10 B b ; 11 B b ; 12 C a ; 14 F c ; 15 E c), an ancient city of Phœnicia, Josh. 19. 29 ; 1 Ki. 7. 13 ; Is. 23. 1 ; Ezek. 27. 1 ; Zech. 9. 3.

UMM KEISS (11 C c), the ancient Gadara.

UMM LAKIS (11 A e), a place deriving its name from its vicinity to the ancient Lachish.

UR or **URFA** (2 F c), an ancient city of Mesopotamia or Chaldea, Gen. 11. 28 ; Neh. 9. 7.

VAN (3 E b), a lake between Armenia and Kurdistan.

WELLS OF MOSES (4 C b).

WILDERNESS OF SINAI (4 C b), south of Mount Sinai.

WILDERNESS OF SHUR (4 C a). See Ex. 15. 22.

WILDERNESS OF ZIN (4 D a ; 7 A e). See Num. 20. 1 ; 27. 14 ; Deut. 32. 51.

YARMUK (11 C c ; 12 c b ; 13 C c), a river running east of the Jordan.

YERKA (11 B c), a village occupying the site of some ancient town.

ZAGROS MOUNTAINS (3 G c), a range in Media.

ZAREPHATH (5 B b), a city of the Sidonians, 1 Ki. 17. 9.

ZERED (4 D a ; 11 C f ; 12 C c), a brook from the mountains of Moab, falling into the Salt Sea, Num. 21. 12 ; Deut. 2. 14.

ZERIN (11 B c), the modern name for *Jezreel*.

ZIFTEH (11 B b), a village containing rock tomb and ruins of an ancient city.

ZIPH (5 B f), a city of Judah, where David fled from Saul, now called *Tell es Zif*, Josh. 15. 55 ; 1 Sam. 23. 14.

ZOAN (4 B a), an ancient city of Egypt, Num. 13. 22.

ZOAR or **BELA** (6 C d), one of the cities of the plain, spared at the intercession of Lot, Gen. 14. 2 : 19. 22.

ZORAH (5 A e ; 7 A d), a city of the tribe of Dan, the birth-place of Samson, Jud. 13. 2.

ZUZIM or **ZAMZUMMIN** (6 D c), a race of giants inhabiting the territory east of the Jordan, Gen. 14. 5 ; Deut. 2. 20.

6

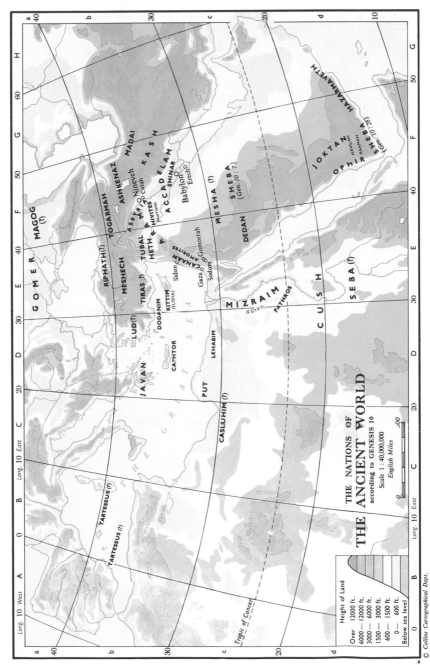

THE NATIONS OF
THE ANCIENT WORLD
according to GENESIS 10
Scale 1:40,000,000

0   English Miles   500

Height of Land

Over 12000 ft.
6000 — 12000 ft.
3000 — 6000 ft.
1500 — 3000 ft.
600 — 1500 ft.
0 — 600 ft.
Below sea level

Long. 10 West
Long. 10 East
Long. 10 East
Tropic of Cancer

GOMER
MAGOG (?)
RIPHATH(?)
MESHECH
TOGARMAH
ASHKENAZ
MADAI
KASH
TUBAL
TIRAS ?)
HETH
HIVITES
(Hurrians)
ASSYR.
Nineveh
Calah
ELAM
ACCAD
SHINAR
Babylon
Erech
MESHA (?)
SHEBA
(Gen. 10:7)
DEDAN
CANAAN
AMORITES
Sidon
Gaza
Gomorrah
Sodom
JAVAN
LUD(?)
DODANIM
KITTIM
(ELISHA)
CAPHTOR
PUT
LEHABIM
CASLUHIM (?)
MIZRAIM
(EGYPT)
PATHROS
CUSH
SEBA (?)
JOKTAN
OPHIR
SHEBA
HAVILAH
RAAMAH
(Gen. 10:28)
HAZARMAVETH
THE GREAT SEA
TARTESSUS (?)
TARTESSUS (?)

© Collins Cartographical Dept.

1

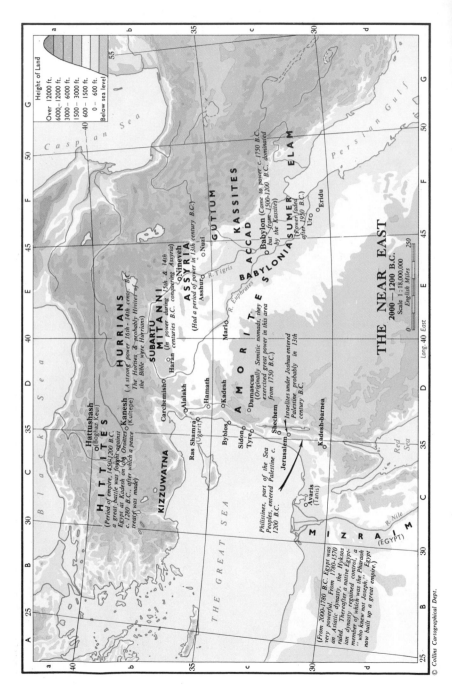

THE NEAR EAST
2000 – 1200 B.C.

Scale 1 : 18,000,000

English Miles
0 ___ 50 ___ 100 ___ 150 ___ 200 ___ 250

Height of Land

	Over 12000 ft.
	6000 – 12000 ft.
	3000 – 6000 ft.
	1500 – 3000 ft.
	600 – 1500 ft.
	0 – 600 ft.
	Below sea level

Caspian Sea

Black Sea

THE GREAT SEA

Red Sea

Persian Gulf

R. Tigris
R. Euphrates
R. Nile

Long. 40 East

HITTITES
(Period of empire, 1450-1200 B.C.
a great battle was fought against
Egypt at Kadesh on the Orontes
c. 1280 B.C., after which a peace
treaty was made)

Hattushash
(Boghaz Keui)

Kanesh
(Kultepe)

KIZZUWATNA

HURRIANS
(A strong power 16th – 14th centy. B.C.
The Horites, & probably Hivites of
the Bible were Hurrians)

SUBARTU

MITANNI
(In power during 15th & 14th
centuries B.C. conquering Assyria)

Harran

ASSYRIA
(Had a period of power in 13th century B.C.)

Nineveh
Asshur
Nuzi

Carchemish

Alalakh
Hamath
Kadesh

Ras Shamra
Ugarit

Byblos
Sidon
Tyre

Damascus

AMORITES
(Originally Semitic nomads, they
exercised great power in this area
from 1750 B.C.)

Mari

Shechem

Israelites under Joshua entered
Palestine probably in 13th
century B.C.

Jerusalem

Kadesh-barnea

Philistines, part of the Sea
Peoples, entered Palestine c.
1200 B.C.

Avaris
(Tanis)

M I Z R A I M
(EGYPT)

GUTIUM

KASSITES
(Came to power c. 1750 B.C.
but from 1500-1200 B.C. dominated
by the Kassites)

ACCAD

BABYLONIA

SUMER
(Power faded
after 1950 B.C.)

Babylon

ELAM

Ur
Eridu

(From 2000-1780 B.C. Egypt was
very powerful. From 1780-1570
an Asiatic dynasty, the Hyksos
ruled. Thereafter a native Egyptian dynasty regained control, a
member of which was the Pharaoh
"who knew not Joseph." Egypt
now built up a great empire.)

© Collins Cartographical Dept.

2

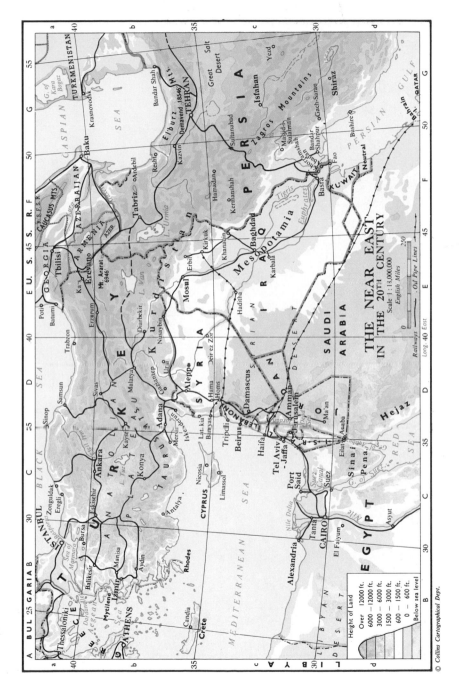

THE NEAR EAST
IN THE 20TH CENTURY

Scale 1 : 13,000,000

Height of Land

Over 12000 ft.	
6000 – 12000 ft.	
3000 – 6000 ft.	
1500 – 3000 ft.	
600 – 1500 ft.	
0 – 600 ft.	
Below sea level	

© Collins Cartographical Dept.

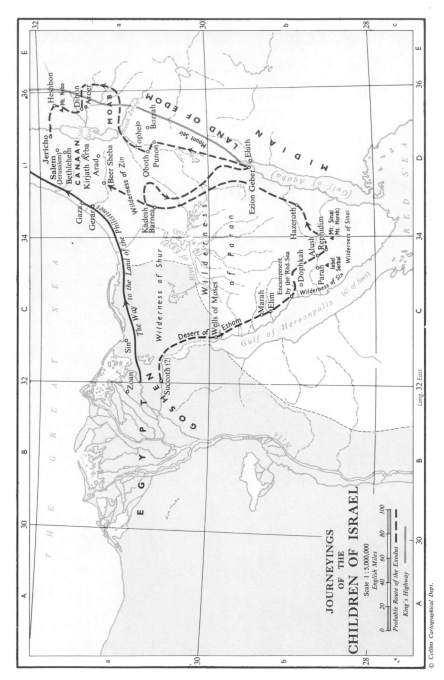

JOURNEYINGS
OF THE
CHILDREN OF ISRAEL

Scale 1 : 5,000,000
English Miles
0   20   40   60   80   100

Probable Route of the Exodus
King's Highway

© Collins Cartographical Dept.

4

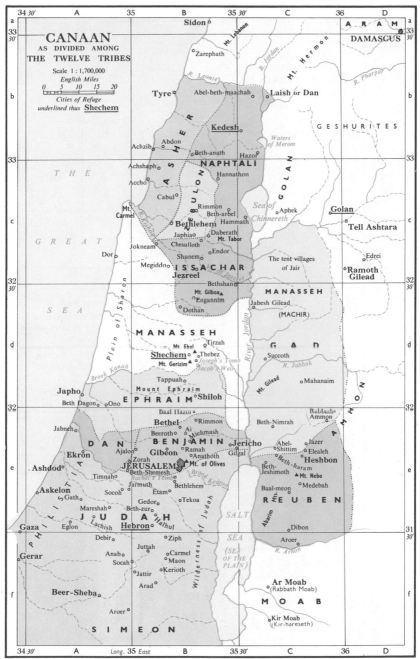

CANAAN
AS DIVIDED AMONG
THE TWELVE TRIBES

Scale 1 : 1,700,000
English Miles
0   5   10   15   20
Cities of Refuge
underlined thus **Shechem**

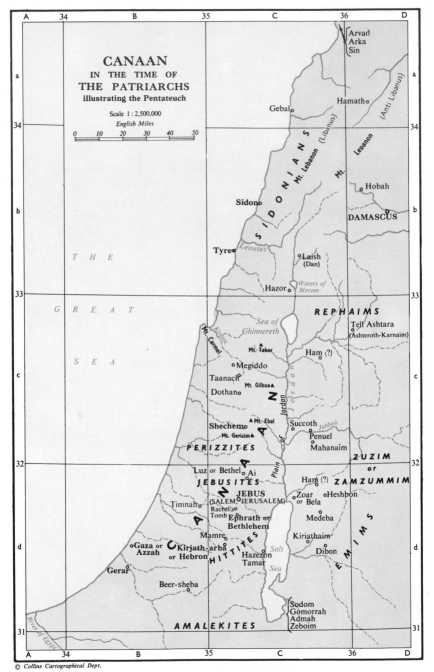

CANAAN

IN THE TIME OF
THE PATRIARCHS
illustrating the Pentateuch

Scale 1 : 2,500,000
English Miles

0   10   20   30   40   50

Arvad
Arka
Sin

Hamath○

(Anti Libanus)

Gebal○

S I D O N I A N S

Mt. Lebanon (Libanus)

Mt. Lebanon

○Hobah

Sidon○

DAMASCUS○

Leontes

Tyre○

○Laish
(Dan)

Hazor○   *Waters of
Merom*

T H E

*Sea of
Chinnereth*

R E P H A I M S

G R E A T

Tell Ashtara
(Ashteroth-Karnaim)

Mt. Carmel   *Kishon*

▲Mt. Tabor

Ham (?)

S E A

○Megiddo

Taanach○

Mt. Gilboa▲

Dothan○

Plain of Jordan

C

▲Mt. Ebal

Shechem○   Succoth   *Jabbok*
Mt. Gerizim▲   Penuel○
Mahanaim○

A

N

A

A

N

P E R I Z Z I T E S

Z U Z I M
or
Z A M Z U M M I M

Luz or Bethel○   ○Ai

J E B U S I T E S

Ham (?)

Timnah○   JEBUS
(SALEM, JERUSALEM)   Zoar○   ○Heshbon
or Bela

Rachel's
Tomb○   Ephrath or
Bethlehem   Medeba○

Mamre○   Kiriathaim○

E M I M S

○Gaza or
Azzah   ○Kirjath-arba
or Hebron   H I T T I T E S   Hazezon
Tamar○   *Salt
Sea*   Dibon○

Gerar○

Beer-sheba○

A M A L E K I T E S   Sodom
Gomorrah
Admah
Zeboim

River of Egypt

6

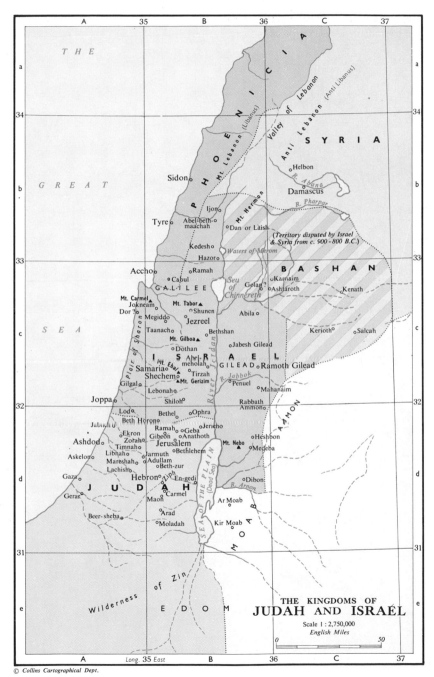

THE KINGDOMS OF
JUDAH AND ISRAEL
Scale 1 : 2,750,000
English Miles
0   50

7

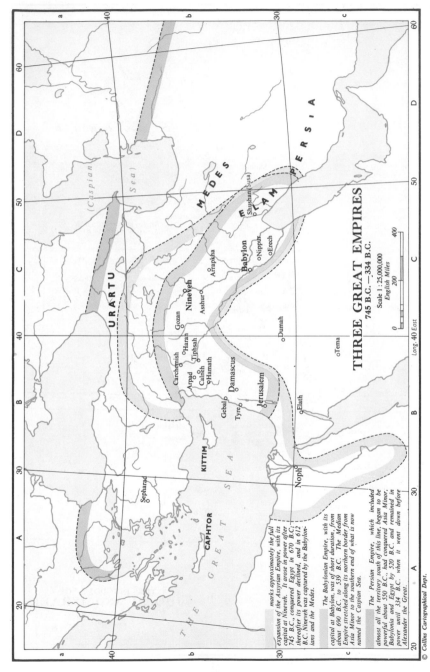

THREE GREAT EMPIRES
745 B.C. – 334 B.C.

Scale 1 : 25,000,000
English Miles
0   200   400

marks approximately the full
expansion of the Assyrian Empire, with its
capital at Nineveh. It arose in power after
745 B.C., conquered Egypt in 670 B.C.,
thereafter its power declined, and in 612
B.C. Nineveh was captured by the Babylonians and the Medes.

The Babylonian Empire, with its
capital at Babylon, was of short duration, from
about 690 B.C. to 539 B.C. The Median
Empire stretched along its northern border from
Asia Minor to the southern end of what is now
named the Caspian Sea.

The Persian Empire, which included
almost all the territory south of this line, began to be
powerful about 550 B.C., had conquered Asia Minor,
Babylonia and Egypt by 520 B.C. and remained in
power until 334 B.C. when it went down before
Alexander the Great.

MEDES

URARTU

PERSIA

ELAM

CAPHTOR

KITTIM

THE GREAT SEA

(Caspian Sea)

Sepharad

Noph

Gebal
Tyre
Jerusalem
Elath
Damascus
Hamath
Calneh
Arpad
Carchemish
Tiphsah
Haran
Gozan
Nineveh
Asshur
Arrapkha
Babylon
Nippur
Erech
Shushan (Susa)
Dumah
Tema

Long. 40 East

© Collins Cartographical Dept.

8

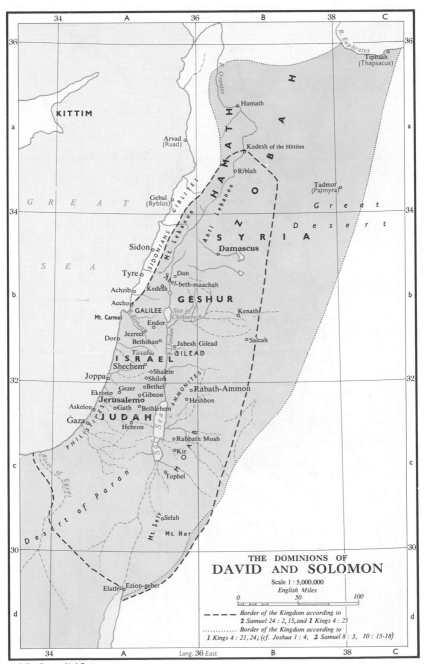

THE DOMINIONS OF
DAVID AND SOLOMON

Scale 1 : 5,000.000
English Miles

0   50   100

– – –   *Border of the Kingdom according to*
     2 *Samuel 24 : 2,15, and* **1** *Kings 4 : 25*
· · · · · ·   *Border of the Kingdom according to*
     1 *Kings 4 : 21, 24; (cf. Joshua 1 : 4,* **2** *Samuel 8 : 3, 10 : 15-18)*

© *Collins Cartographical Dept.*

9

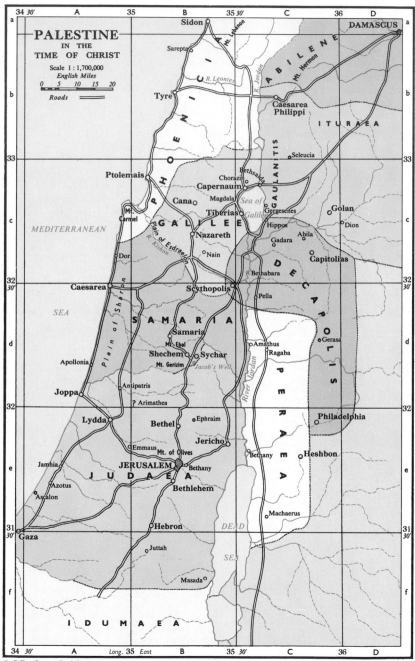

PALESTINE
IN THE
TIME OF CHRIST

Scale 1 : 1,700,000
English Miles

0   5   10   15   20

Roads ══════

DAMASCUS

a

Sidon

Sarepta

Mt. Lebanon

A B I L E N E

R. Leontes

R. Jordan

Mt. Hermon

b

Tyre

Caesarea Philippi

I T U R A E A

P
H
O
E
N
I
C
I
A

33

Seleucia

Ptolemais

Bethsaida

Chorazin

Capernaum

G A U L A N I T I S

Cana ○

Magdala

Sea of Galilee

Gergesenes

Golan

Tiberias

Hippos

Dion

c

Mt. Carmel

G A L I L E E

Nazareth

Abila

MEDITERRANEAN

Plain of Esdraelon

Gadara

R. Kishon

○ Nain

Capitolias

Dor ○

Bethabara

D E C A P O L I S

32 30'

Caesarea

Scythopolis

Pella

SEA

S A M A R I A

Samaria

d

Mt. Ebal

○ Amathus

Gerasa ○

Apollonia ○

Shechem

Sychar

Ragaba

Mt. Gerizim

Jacob's Well

River Jordan

Antipatris

P
E
R
A
E
A

Joppa ○

? Arimathea

32

Lydda

Bethel

○ Ephraim

Philadelphia ○

Jericho

Emmaus

Mt. of Olives

Heshbon

Jamnia ○

JERUSALEM

Bethany ○

Bethany

e

Azotus ○

J U D A E A

Ascalon ○

Bethlehem

31 30'

Hebron

Machaerus ○

DEAD

Gaza

Juttah ○

SEA

Masada ○

f

I D U M A E A

Long. 35 East

© *Collins Cartographical Dept.*

10

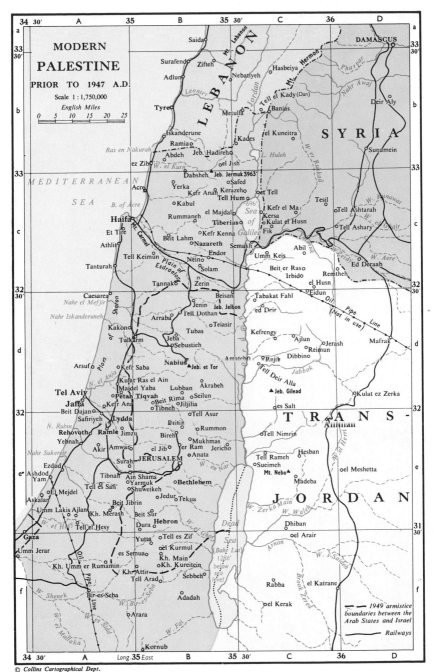

© Collins Cartographical Dept.

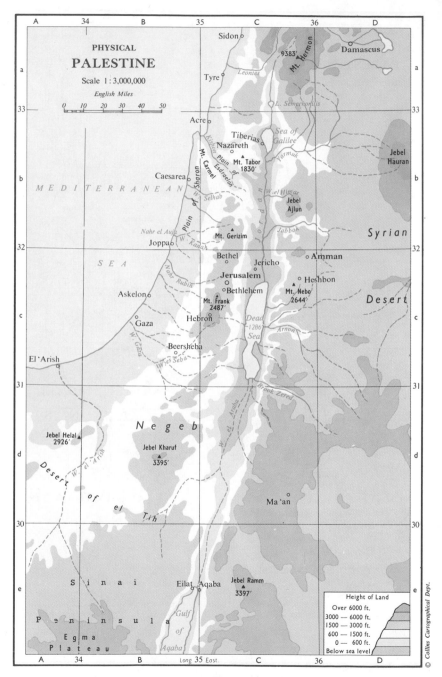

PHYSICAL
PALESTINE
Scale 1 : 3,000,000
English Miles
0 10 20 30 40 50

A 34 B 35 C 36 D

Sidon
Mt. Hermon
9383'
Damascus
Tyre
Leontes
L. Semechonitis
Acre
Sea of Galilee
Tiberias
Nazareth
Mt. Tabor
1830'
Jebel Hauran
Caesarea
Mt. Carmel
Plain of Esdraelon
W. Selhab
Yarmuk
W. el Hima
Jebel Ajlun
Plain of Sharon
Jabbok
M E D I T E R R A N E A N
Nahr el Auja
W. Kanah
Mt. Gerizim
Joppa
S E A
Bethel
Jericho
Amman
JERUSALEM
Heshbon
Nahr Rubin
Bethlehem
Askelon
Mt. Frank
2487'
Mt. Nebo
2644'
D e s e r t
Gaza
Hebron
Dead
-1286'
Sea
W. Gaza
Beersheba
Arnon
El 'Arish
W'ses Seba
Brook Zered
N e g e b
Jebel Helal
2926'
W. el 'Arish
Jebel Kharuf
3395'
W. el Araba
Desert
of
el
Tih
Ma'an
S i n a i
Eilat Aqaba
Jebel Ramm
3397'
P e n i n s u l a
Gulf
of
E g m a
Aqaba
P l a t e a u

S y r i a n

Long 35 East.

Height of Land
Over 6000 ft.
3000 — 6000 ft.
1500 — 3000 ft.
600 — 1500 ft.
0 — 600 ft.
Below sea level

© Collins Cartographical Dept.

12

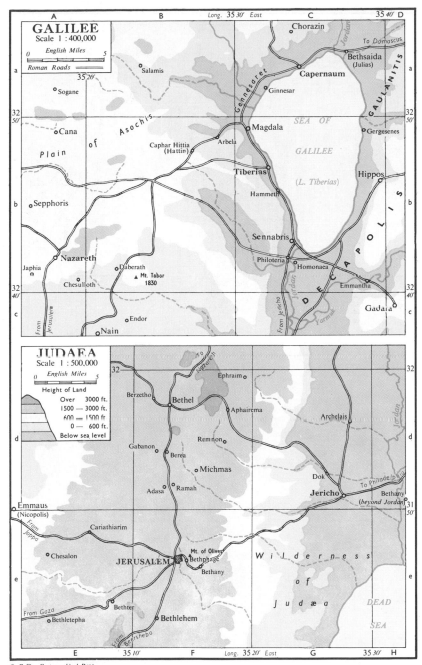

GALILEE
Scale 1 : 400,000

English Miles

Roman Roads

Long. 35 30' *East*

A   B   C   35 40' D

Chorazin

To Damascus

Bethsaida
(Julias)

Salamis

Capernaum

Sogane

Ginnesar

Cana

Asochis

Magdala

SEA OF

Gergesenes

Caphar Hittia
(Hattin)

Arbela

GALILEE

Plain   of

Tiberias

(L. Tiberias)

Hippos

Sepphoris

Hammeth

Sennabris

Nazareth

Philoteria

Homonaea

Japhia

Daberath

▲ Mt. Tabor
1830

Emmantha

Chesulloth

Gadara

Endor

Nain

JUDAEA
Scale 1 : 500,000

English Miles

Height of Land

Over	3000 ft.
1500 — 3000 ft.	
600 — 1500 ft	
0 — 600 ft.	
Below sea level	

To Neapolis

Ephraim

Berzetho

Bethel

Aphairema

Archelais

Gabanon

Remnon

Berea

Michmas

Dok

To Philadelphia

Adasa

Ramah

Jericho

Bethany
(beyond Jordan)

Emmaus
(Nicopolis)

From Joppa

Cariathiarim

Mt. of Olives

Chesalon

JERUSALEM

Bethphage

W I L D E R N E S S

Bethany

o f

From Gaza

Bethther

J u d æ a

DEAD
SEA

Bethletepha

Bethlehem

From Beersheba

E   35 10'   F   *Long.* 35 20' *East* G   35 30' H

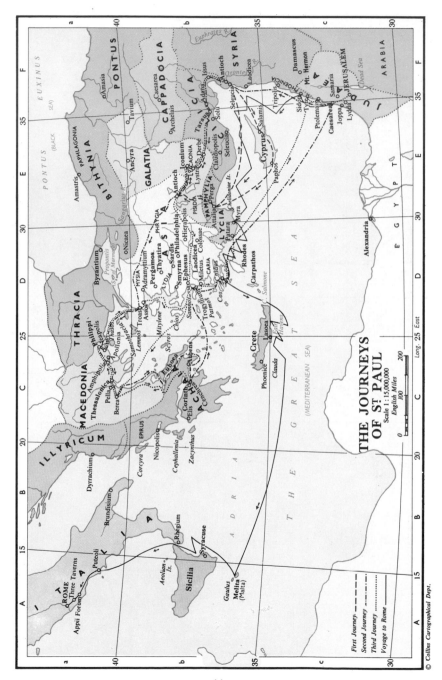

THE JOURNEYS
OF ST PAUL

Scale 1:15,000,000

English Miles

First Journey
Second Journey
Third Journey
Voyage to Rome

© Collins Cartographical Dept.

14

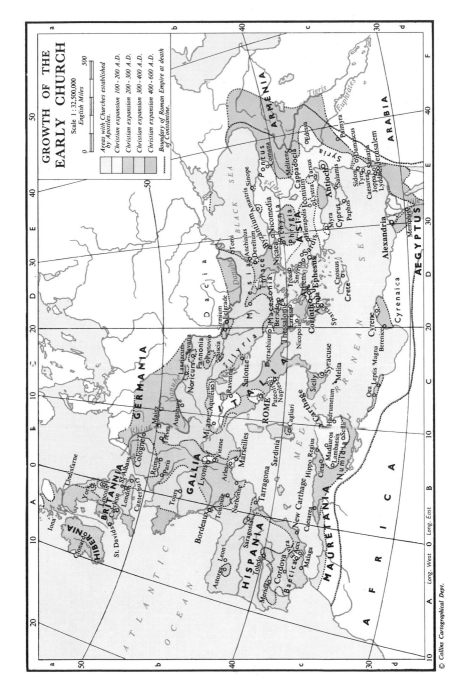

GROWTH OF THE
EARLY CHURCH

Scale 1:32,500,000

English Miles
0   500

Areas with Churches established
by Apostles.
Christian expansion 100 - 200 A.D.
Christian expansion 200 - 300 A.D.
Christian expansion 300 - 400 A.D.
Christian expansion 400 - 600 A.D.
Boundary of Roman Empire at death
of Constantine.

© Collins Cartographical Dept.

15

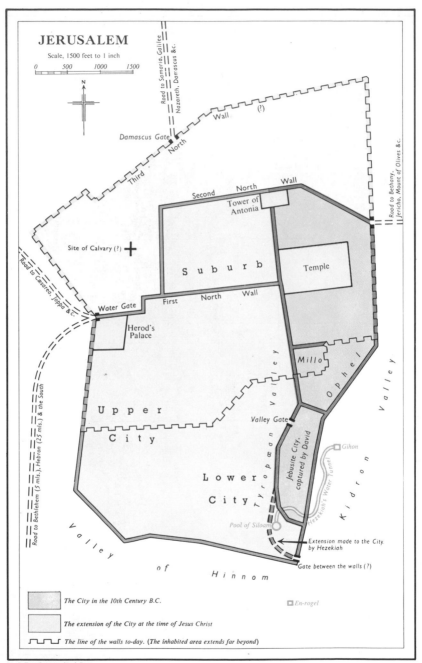

JERUSALEM

Scale, 1500 feet to 1 inch

0   500   1000   1500

N

Road to Samaria, Galilee
Nazareth, Damascus &c.

Damascus Gate

North

Third

Wall   (?)

Road to Bethany,
Jericho, Mount of Olives &c.

Second   North   Wall

Tower of
Antonia

Site of Calvary (?)

S u b u r b

Temple

Road to Cæsarea, Joppa &c.

First   North   Wall

Water Gate

Herod's
Palace

Millo

O p h e l

K i d r o n   V a l l e y

U p p e r

C i t y

Valley Gate

Road to Bethlehem (5 mls.), Hebron (25 mls.) & the South

L o w e r

C i t y

Jebusite City,
captured by David

Gihon

Hezekiah's Water Tunnel

Pool of Siloam

Extension made to the City
by Hezekiah

V a l l e y

o f   H i n n o m

Gate between the walls (?)

The City in the 10th Century B.C.

En-rogel

The extension of the City at the time of Jesus Christ

The line of the walls to-day. (The inhabited area extends far beyond)